NX 7
for Engineers & Designers

CADCIM Technologies
525 St. Andrews Drive
Schererville, IN 46375, USA
(www.cadcim.com)

Contributing Authors

Sham Tickoo
Professor
Department of Mechanical Engineering Technology
Purdue University Calumet
Hammond, Indiana
USA

Sandeep Prem Dass
Sr. CAD Engineer
CADSoft Technologies

Published by:
dreamtech PRESS

ISBN: 978-93-5004-054-6

Reprint: 2012

Printed at: Himal Impressions, New Delhi.

DEDICATION

To teachers, who make it possible to disseminate knowledge to enlighten the young and curious minds of our future generations

To students, who are dedicated to learning new technologies and making the world a better place to live in

THANKS

To the faculty and students of the MET department of Purdue University Calumet for their cooperation

To Anju Jethwani and Sudam C. Mishra for copy editing this manuscript

Online Training Program Offered by CADCIM Technologies

CADCIM Technologies provides effective and affordable virtual online training on various software packages including Computer Aided Design and Manufacturing (CAD/CAM), computer programming languages, animation, architecture, and GIS. The training is delivered 'live' via Internet at any time, any place, and at any pace to individuals, students of colleges, universities, and CAD/CAM training centers. The main features of this program are:

Training for Students and Companies in a Class Room Setting

Highly experienced instructors and qualified Engineers at CADCIM Technologies conduct the classes under the guidance of Prof. Sham Tickoo of Purdue University Calumet, USA. This team has authored several textbooks that are rated "one of the best" in their categories and are used in various colleges, universities, and training centers in North America, Europe, and in other parts of the world.

Training for Individuals

The cost effective and time saving initiative of CADCIM Technologies strives to deliver the training in the comfort of your home or work place, thereby relieving you from the hassles of traveling to training centers.

Training Offered on Software Packages

We provide basic and advanced training on the following software packages:

***CAD/CAM/CAE**: CATIA, Pro/ENGINEER Wildfire, SolidWorks, Autodesk Inventor, Solid Edge, NX, AutoCAD, AutoCAD LT, Customizing AutoCAD, EdgeCAM, and ANSYS*

***Computer Programming**: C++, VB.NET, Oracle, AJAX, and Java*

***Animation and Styling**: Autodesk 3ds Max, 3ds Max Design, Maya, and Autodesk Alias*

***Architecture and GIS**: Autodesk Revit Building, Autodesk Revit Structures, AutoCAD Civil 3D, and Autodesk Map 3D*

For more information, please visit the following link:

http://www.cadcim.com

Note

The free teaching and learning resources, mentioned in the cover page of this textbook, are available only for those who buy the textbook from our web site *www.cadcim.com* or the university/college bookstores. We need proof of purchase when you request the technical support from us.

Table of Contents

Chapter 3: Adding Geometric and Dimensional Constraints to Sketches

Chapter 4: Editing, Extruding, and Revolving Sketches

Chapter 5: Working with Datum Planes, Coordinate Systems, and Datum Axes

Chapter 6: Advanced Modeling Tools-I

Chapter 7: Advanced Modeling Tools-II

Chapter 8: Editing Features and Advanced Modeling Tools-III

Chapter 9: Assembly Modeling-I

Chapter 10: Assembly Modeling-II

Chapter 11: Surface Modeling

Chapter 12: Advanced Surface Modeling

Chapter 13: Generating, Editing, and Dimensioning the Drawing Views

Chapter 14: Synchronous Modeling

Preface

NX 7

NX7, a product of SIEMENS Corp., is one of the world's leading CAD/CAM/CAE packages. Being a solid modeling tool, it not only unites 3D parametric features with 2D tools, but also addresses every design-through-manufacturing process. Besides providing an insight into the design content, the package promotes collaboration between companies and provides them an edge over their competitors.

In addition to creating solid models and assemblies, the 2D drawing views can also be generated easily in the **Drafting** environment of NX. The drawing views that can be generated include orthographic, section, auxiliary, isometric, and detail views. The model dimensions and reference dimensions in the drawing views can also be generated. The bidirectionally associative nature of this software ensures that the modifications made in the model are reflected in the drawing views and vice-versa.

The **NX 7 for Designers** textbook has been written with the intention of helping the readers effectively use the solid modeling tools in NX. The mechanical engineering industry examples and tutorials used in this book ensure that the users can relate the knowledge of this book with the actual mechanical industry designs. The main features of this textbook are as follows:

- **Tutorial Approach**
  The author has adopted the tutorial point-of-view and the learn-by-doing theme throughout the textbook. This approach guides the users through the process of creating the models in the tutorials.

- **Real-World Projects as Tutorials**
  The author has used about 50 real-world mechanical engineering projects as tutorials in this book. This enables the readers to relate the tutorials to the models in the mechanical engineering industry. In addition, there are about 30 exercises that are also based on the real-world mechanical engineering projects.

- **Tips and Notes**
  The additional information related to various topics is provided to the users in the form of tips and notes.

- **Learning Objectives**
  The first page of every chapter summarizes the topics that are covered in that chapter.

- **Self-Evaluation Test, Review Questions, and Exercises**
  Every chapter ends with a Self-Evaluation Test so that the users can assess their knowledge of the chapter. The answers to the Self-Evaluation test are given at the end of the chapter. Also, the Review Questions and Exercises are given at the end of each chapter and can be used by the Instructors as test questions and exercises.

- **Heavily Illustrated Text**
  The text in this book is heavily illustrated with about 1100 line diagrams and screen capture images.

Free Companion Website

It has been our constant endeavor to provide you the best textbooks and services at affordable price. In this endeavor, we have come out with a Free companion website that will facilitate the process of teaching and learning of NX 7. If you purchase this textbook from our website (*www.cadcimtech.com*), you will get access to the companion website.

To access the files, you need to register by visiting the **Resources** section at ***www.cadcim.com***. The following resources are available for the faculty and students in this website:

Faculty Resources

- **Technical Support**
  The faculty can get online technical support by contacting *techsupport@cadcim.com*.

- **Instructor's Guide**
  Solutions to all review questions and exercises in the textbook are provided in this link to help faculty members test the skills of the students.

- **PowerPoint Presentations**
  The contents of the book are arranged in customizable powerpoint slides that can be used by the faculty for their lectures.

- **Part Files**
  The part files used in illustrations, tutorials, and exercises are available for free download.

If you are a faculty member, please contact the publisher at *sales@cadcim.com* or the author at *stickoo@calumet.purdue.edu* to access the Website that contains the teaching resources.

Student Resources

- **Technical Support**
  The students can get online technical support by contacting *techsupport@cadcim.com*.

- **Part Files**
  The part files used in illustrations and tutorials are available for free download.

- **Additional Student Projects**
  Various projects are provided for the students to practice.

If you face any problem in accessing these files, please contact the publisher at ***sales@cadcim.com*** or the author at ***stickoo@calumet.purdue.edu*** or ***tickoo525@gmail.com***.

Symbols Used in the Text

Note

The author has provided additional information related to various topics in the form of notes.

Tip

The author has provided a lot of useful information to the users about the topic being discussed in the form of tips.

New

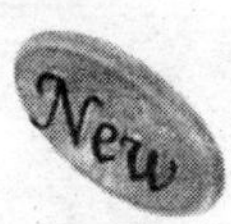

This icon indicates the new command or tool introduced in NX 7.

Enhanced

This icon indicates the existing command and tool that has been enhanced in NX 7.

Chapter 1

Introduction

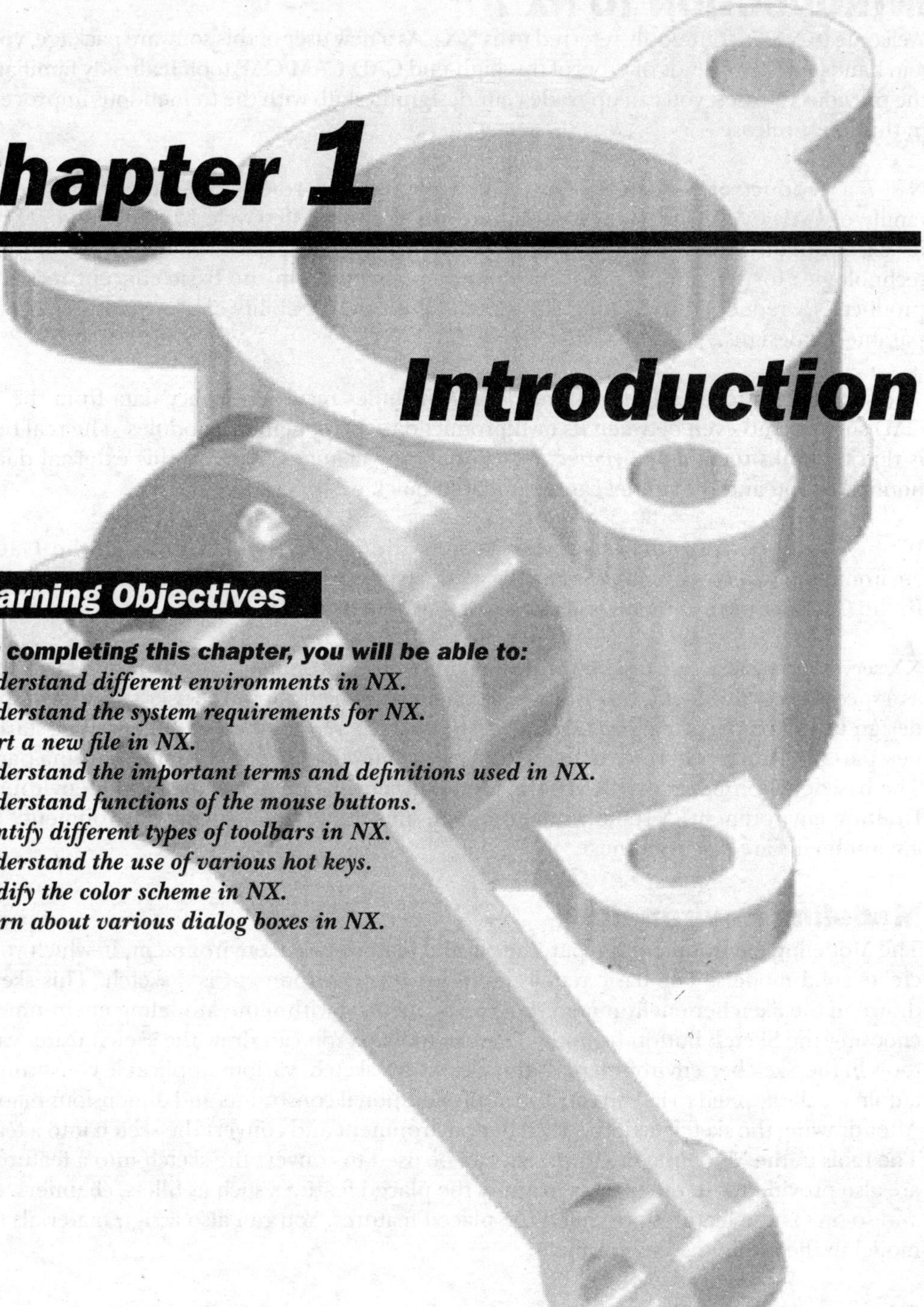

Learning Objectives

After completing this chapter, you will be able to:

- *Understand different environments in NX.*
- *Understand the system requirements for NX.*
- *Start a new file in NX.*
- *Understand the important terms and definitions used in NX.*
- *Understand functions of the mouse buttons.*
- *Identify different types of toolbars in NX.*
- *Understand the use of various hot keys.*
- *Modify the color scheme in NX.*
- *Learn about various dialog boxes in NX.*

INTRODUCTION TO NX 7

Welcome to NX 7 (commonly referred to as NX). As a new user of this software package, you will join hands with thousands of users of this high-end CAD/CAM/CAE tool. If already familiar with the previous releases, you can upgrade your designing skills with the tremendous improvement in this latest release.

NX 7 a product of SIEMENS Corp., is a completely re-engineered, next-generation family of CAD/CAM/CAE software solutions for Product Life Cycle Management. Through its exceptionally easy-to-use and state-of-the-art user interface, NX delivers innovative technologies for maximum productivity and creativity, from the basic concept to the final product. NX reduces the learning curve, as it allows the flexibility of using feature-based and parametric designs.

The subject of interpretability offered by NX includes receiving legacy data from the other CAD systems and even between its own product data management modules. The real benefit is that the links remain associative. As a result, any changes made to this external data are notified to you and the model can be updated quickly.

When you open an old file or start a new file in NX, you will enter the Gateway environment. It allows you to examine the geometry and drawing views that have been created. In the **Gateway** environment, you can invoke any environment of NX.

NX serves the basic design tasks by providing different environments. An environment is defined as a specified environment, consisting of a set of tools, which allows the user to perform specific design tasks in a particular area. You need to start the required environment after starting a new part file. As a result, you can invoke any environment of NX in the same working part file. The basic environments in NX are the Modeling environment, Shape Studio environment, Drafting environment, Assembly environment, and the Manufacturing environment. These environments are discussed next.

Modeling Environment

The Modeling environment is a parametric and feature-based environment, in which you can create solid models. The basic requirement for this environment is a sketch. This sketch is drawn in the Sketcher environment that can be invoked within the Modeling environment by choosing the **Sketch** button from the **Feature** toolbar. You can draw the sketch using various tools in the Sketcher environment. While drawing a sketch, various applicable constraints are automatically applied to it. You can also apply additional constraints and dimensions manually. After drawing the sketch, exit the Sketcher environment and convert the sketch into a feature. The tools in the Modeling environment can be used to convert the sketch into a feature. You are also provided with other tools to apply the placed features such as fillets, chamfers, taper, and so on. These features are called the placed features. You can also assign materials to the model in the Modeling environment.

Shape Studio Environment

The Shape Studio environment is also a parametric and feature-based environment, in which you can create surface models. The tools in this environment are similar to those in the

Modeling environment. The only difference is that the tools in this environment are used to create basic and advanced surfaces. You are also provided with the surface editing tools, which are used to manipulate the surfaces to obtain the required shape. This environment is useful for conceptual and industrial design.

Assembly Environment

The Assembly environment is used to assemble the components using the assembly constraints available in this environment. There are two types of assembly design approaches in NX, Bottom-up and Top-down.

In the bottom-up approach of the assembly, the previously created components are assembled together to maintain their design intent. In the top-down approach, components are created in the assembly in the Assembly environment.

You can also assemble an existing assembly with the current assembly. The Check Clearance analysis provides the facility to check the interference between the components in an assembly.

Drafting Environment

The Drafting environment is used for the documentation of the parts or assemblies created earlier in the form of drawing views and their detailing. There are two types of drafting techniques, Generative drafting and Interactive drafting.

The generative drafting technique is used to automatically generate the drawing views of the parts and assemblies. The parametric dimensions added to the component in the Modeling environment during its creation can also be generated and displayed automatically in the drawing views. The generative drafting is bidirectionally associative in nature. If you modify the dimensions in the Drafting environment, the model will automatically update in the Modeling environment and vice-versa. You can also generate the Bill of Material (BOM) and balloons in the drawing views.

In interactive drafting, you need to create the drawing views by sketching them using the normal sketching tools and then adding the dimensions.

SYSTEM REQUIREMENTS

The following are the system requirements to ensure the smooth running of NX:

- **Operating System**: Windows XP Home Edition, Windows XP Professional, Windows Vista, Windows Vista X 64 bit (Professional, Ultimate, and Enterprise Editions), or UNIX.
- **Memory**: 256 MB of RAM is the minimum requirement for all applications and 512 MB of RAM is recommended for DMU applications.
- **Disk drive**: 4 GB Disk Drive space (Minimum recommended size)
- **Internal/External drives**: A CD-ROM drive is required for the program installation.
- **Display**: A graphic color display compatible with the selected platform-specific graphic adapter is required. The minimum recommended monitor size is 17 inches.
- **Graphics adapter**: A graphics adapter with a 3D OpenGL accelerator is required with a

minimum resolution of 1024x768 for Microsoft Windows workstations and 1280x1024 for UNIX workstations.

GETTING STARTED WITH NX

Install NX on your system and then start it by double-clicking on the shortcut icon of NX 7.0 on the desktop of your computer. Alternatively, you can choose **Start > All Programs > UGS NX 7 .0 > NX 7.0** from the taskbar menu to start NX, as shown in Figure 1-1.

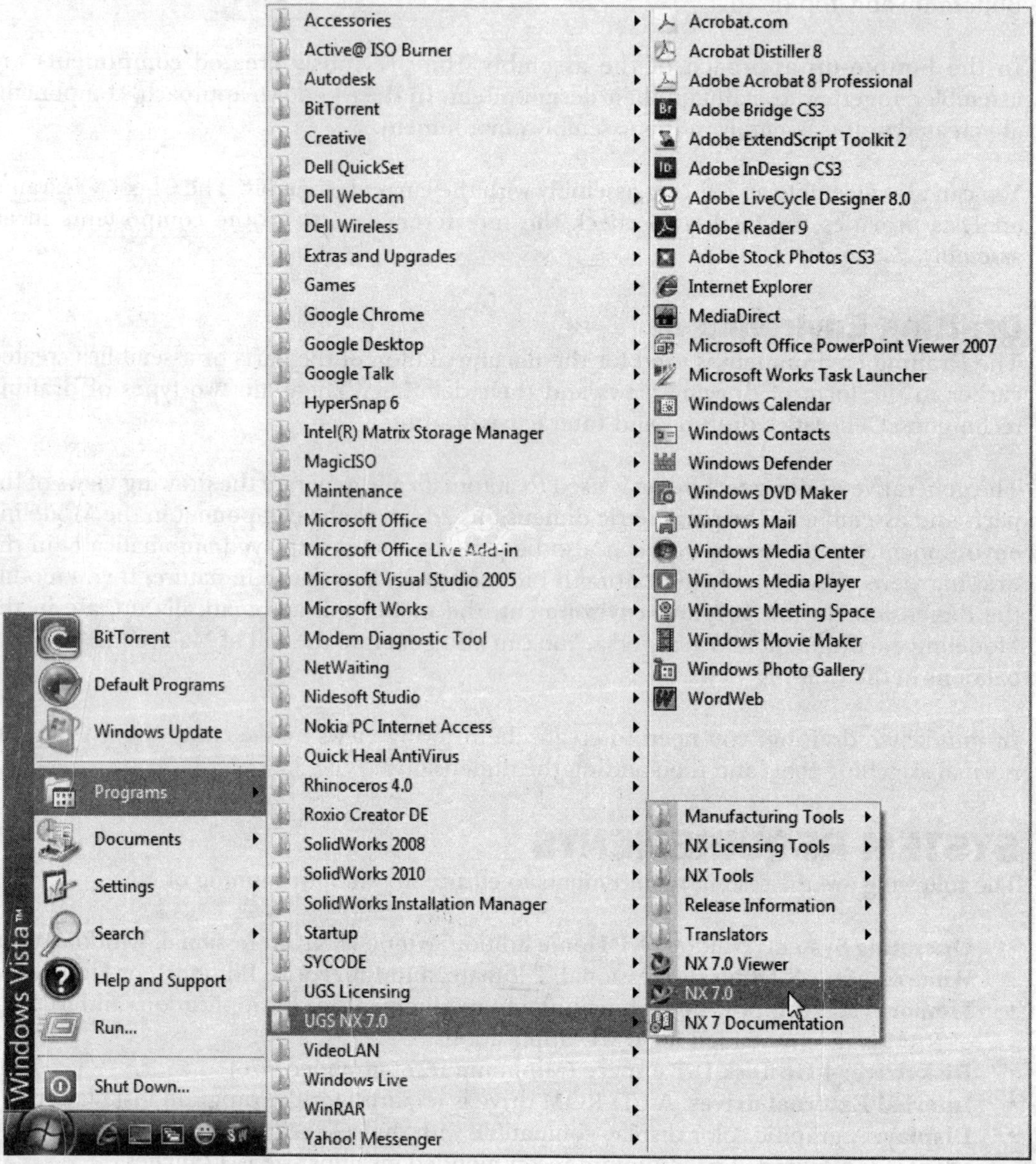

***Figure 1-1** Starting NX 7 using the taskbar menu*

After the system has loaded all the required files to start NX, the **Welcome to NX** window will be displayed on your screen, as shown in Figure 1-2.

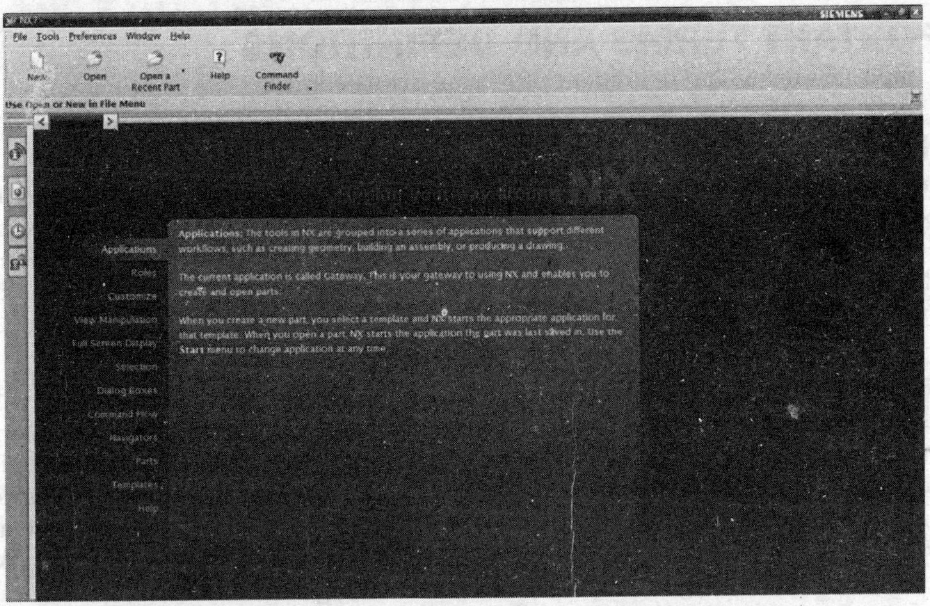

__Figure 1-2__ The initial screen that appears after starting NX 7

Choose **File > New** from the menu bar; the **File** dialog box will be displayed. Enter the name of the file in the **Name** edit box and choose the **OK** button; the Modeling environment will be displayed on the screen, refer to Figure 1-3.

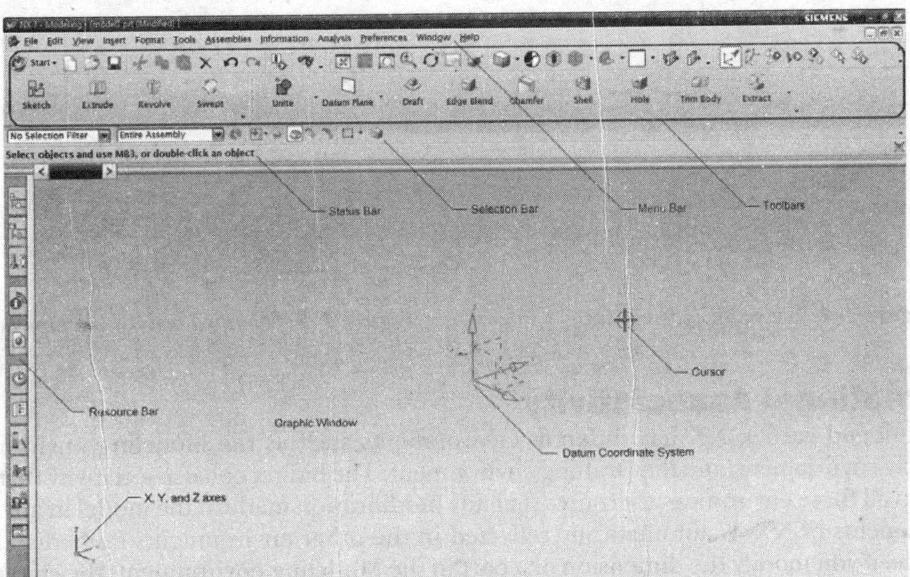

__Figure 1-3__ The Modeling environment displayed on screen

In this text book, the Model template is used to create a new file. The procedure for starting a new file using the Model template is discussed in the next chapter.

IMPORTANT TERMS AND DEFINITIONS

Some important terms and definitions of NX are discussed next.

Feature-based Modeling

A feature is defined as the smallest building block that can be modified individually. A model created in NX is a combination of a number of individual features and each feature is related to the other directly or indirectly. If a proper design intent is maintained while creating the model, then these features automatically adjust their values to any change in their surroundings. This provides a great flexibility to the design.

Parametric Modeling

The parametric nature of a software package is defined as its ability to use the standard properties or parameters in defining the shape and size of a geometry. The main function of this property is to derive the selected geometry to a new size or shape without considering its original dimensions. You can change or modify the shape and size of any feature at any stage of the designing process. This property makes the designing process an easy task. For example, consider the design of the body of a pipe housing, as shown in Figure 1-4.

To change the design by modifying the diameter of the holes and their number on the front, top, and bottom face, you need to select the feature and change the diameter and the number of instances in the pattern. The modified design is shown in Figure 1-5.

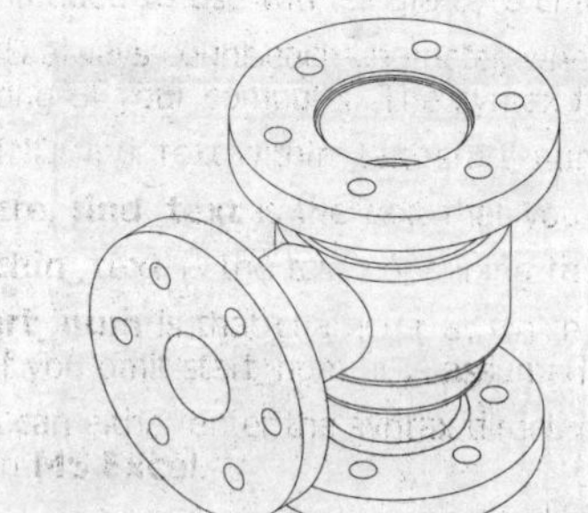

Figure 1-4 Body of a pipe housing

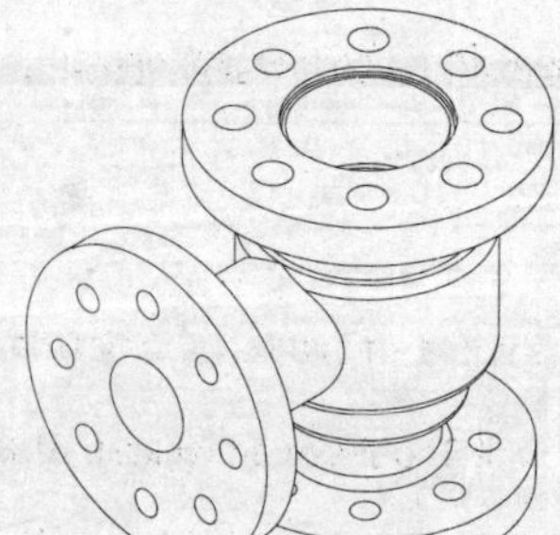

Figure 1-5 Modified body of the pipe housing

Bidirectional Associativity

As mentioned earlier, NX has different environments such as the Modeling environment, Assembly environment, and the Drafting environment. The bidirectional associativity that exists between all these environments ensures that any modification made in the model in any of the environments of NX, is automatically reflected in the other environments immediately. For example, if you modify the dimension of a part in the Modeling environment, the change will be reflected in the Assembly and the Drawing environments as well. Similarly, if you modify the dimensions of a part in the drawing views generated in the Drafting environment, the changes will be reflected in the Modeling and Assembly environments. Consider the drawing views of the pipe housing shown in Figure 1-6. When you modify the model in the Modeling environment, the changes will be reflected in the Drafting environment automatically. Figure 1-7 shows the drawing views of the pipe housing after increasing the diameter and the number of holes.

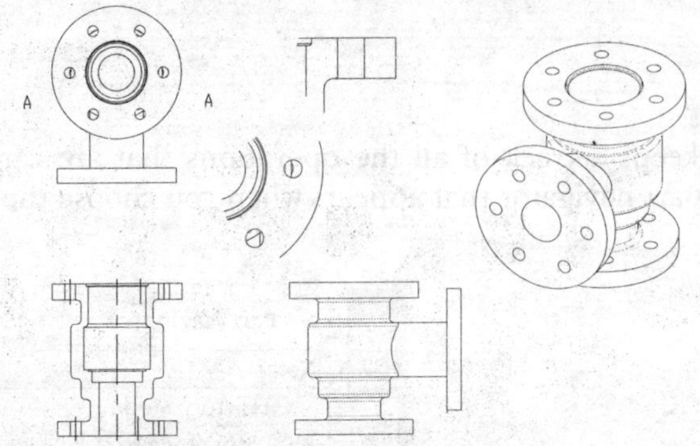

***Figure 1-6** The drawing views of the body part before making the modifications*

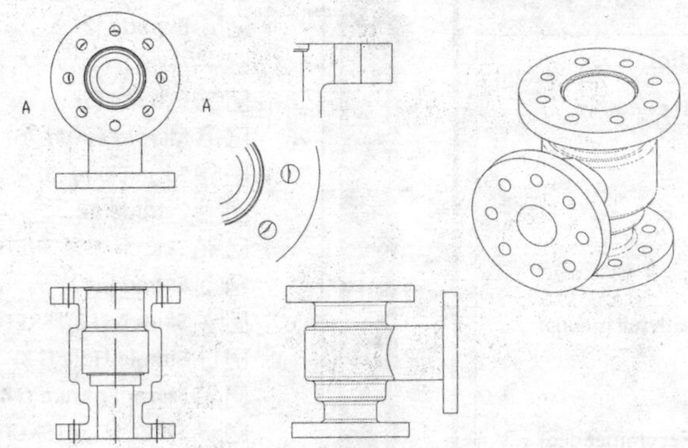

***Figure 1-7** The drawing views after making the modifications*

*.prt

*.prt is a file extension associated with all the files that are created in the Sketcher, Modeling, Shape Studio, Assembly, and Drafting environments of NX.

Resource Bar

The **Resource Bar** combines all navigator windows, a history palette, an integrated web browser, and a parts template in one common place for a better user interface. By default, the **Resource Bar** is located on the left side of the NX window.

Roles

Roles are a set of system customized tools and toolbars used for different applications. In NX, you have different roles for different industrial applications. The **Roles** tab in the **Resource Bar** is used to activate the required role. In this book, the **Essentials with full menus** role has been used, as it contains all the required tools. To activate this role, choose the **Roles** tab from the **Resource Bar** and click on the **System Defaults** option, if it is not expanded already; a flyout will be displayed. Click on the **Essentials with full menus** icon to activate that role. Figure 1-8 shows the **Roles** navigator that appears when you choose the **Roles** tab in the **Resource Bar**.

Part Navigator

The **Part Navigator** keeps a track of all the operations that are carried out on the part. Figure 1-9 shows the part navigator that appears when you choose the **Part Navigator** tab in the **Resource Bar**.

*Figure 1-8 The **Roles** navigator*

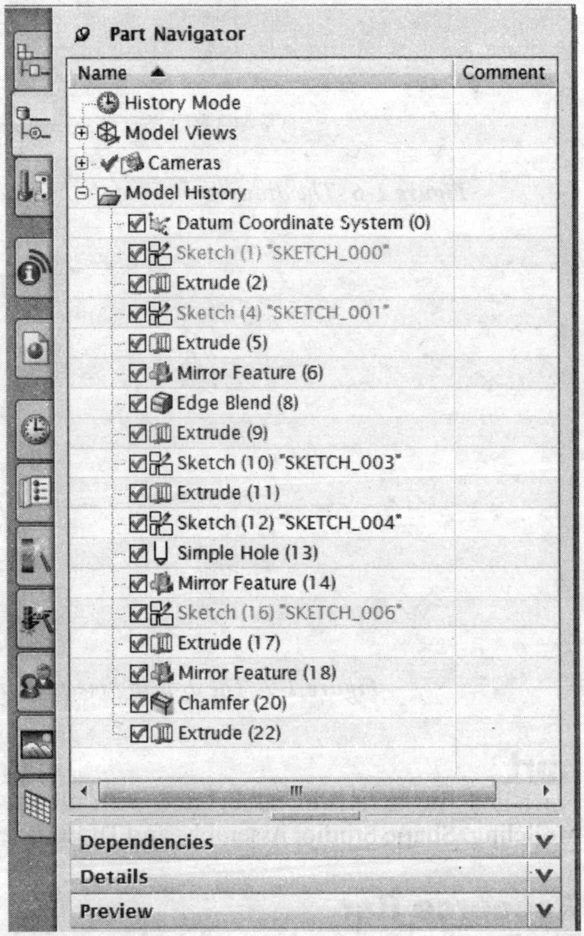

*Figure 1-9 The **Part Navigator***

Constraints

Constraints are the logical operations that are performed on the selected element to define its size and location with respect to the other elements or reference geometries. There are three types of constraints in NX: Geometric, Dimensional, and Assembly constraints. The constraints in the Sketcher environment are called geometric and dimensional constraints and these are used to precisely define the size and position of the sketched elements with respect to the surroundings. The assembly constraints are available in the Assembly environment and are used to define the precise position of the components in the assembly. These constraints are discussed next.

Geometric Constraints

These are the logical operations performed on the sketched elements to define their size and position with respect to the other elements. Geometric constraints are applied using two methods, automatic constraining and manual constraining. While drawing the sketch, some constraints are automatically applied to it.

Dimensional Constraints

After creating the sketch, you need to apply different types of dimensional constraints to it. Various types of dimensions in NX are:

1. Horizontal Dimensions
2. Vertical Dimensions
3. Parallel Dimensions
4. Perpendicular Dimensions
5. Angular Dimensions
6. Diameter Dimensions
7. Radius Dimensions
8. Perimeter Dimensions

NX is a parametric software and therefore, you can modify the dimensions created at any time by entering the Sketcher environment.

Assembly Constraints

The constraints in the Assembly environment are the logical operations performed to restrict the degrees of freedom of the component and to define its precise location and position with respect to the other components of the assembly.

Solid Body

The solid body contains all the features such as extrude, pad, pocket, hole, and so on.

Sheet Body or Surfaces

Surfaces are geometric features that have no thickness. They are used to create complex shapes that are difficult to be created using the solid features. After creating the surface, you can assign a thickness to it in order to convert it into a solid body. Surfaces are created in the Modeling environment. No separate environment is required to create the surfaces.

Features

A feature is defined as the basic building block of a solid model. The combination of various features results in a solid body. In the Modeling environment of NX, the features are of the following two types:

1. Sketch-based features
2. Placed-features

The sketch-based features are the ones that require a sketch for their creation. The placed-features do not require a sketch to create them.

WCS (Work Coordinate System)

The WCS is a local coordinate system and can be repositioned to a convenient location while making a model. The XC-YC plane of the WCS is used to perform many operations. When you create a new file, by default, the WCS is positioned at the Datum Coordinate System origin, which is (0,0,0). By default, the display of WCS is turned off. To turn on the display of WCS, choose the **Display WCS** button from the **Utility** toolbar; the WCS will be displayed at the origin of the drawing window.

UNDERSTANDING THE FUNCTIONS OF THE MOUSE BUTTONS

To work in the NX environments, it is necessary that you understand the functions of the mouse buttons. The efficient use of these three buttons, along with the CTRL key, can reduce the time required to complete the design task. The different combinations of the CTRL key and the mouse buttons are listed below:

1. The left mouse button is to make a selection by simply selecting a face, surface, sketch, or an object from the geometry area or from the **Part Navigator**. For multiple selections, select the entities using the left mouse button.

2. The right mouse button is used to invoke the shortcut menu, which has different options such as **Zoom**, **Fit**, **Rotate**, **Pan**, and so on.

3. Press and hold the middle and the right mouse buttons to invoke the **Pan** tool. Next, drag the mouse to pan the model. You can also invoke the **Pan** tool by first pressing and holding the SHIFT key and then the middle mouse button. Figure 1-10 shows the use of a three button mouse in performing the pan functions.

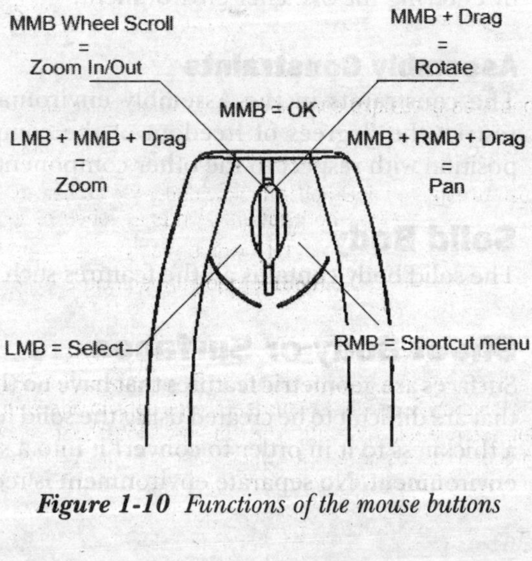

***Figure 1-10** Functions of the mouse buttons*

4. Press and hold the middle mouse button to invoke the **Rotate** tool. Next, drag the mouse to dynamically rotate the view of the model in the geometry area and view it from different directions. Figure 1-10 shows the use of the three button mouse in performing the rotate operation.

5. Press and hold the CTRL key and then the middle mouse button to invoke the **Zoom** tool. Alternatively, press and hold the left mouse button and then the middle mouse button to invoke the **Zoom** tool. Next, drag the mouse dynamically to zoom in or out the model in the geometry area. Figure 1-10 shows the use of the three mouse buttons in performing the zoom functions.

TOOLBARS

NX offers a user-friendly design environment by providing specific toolbars for each environment. Therefore, it is important that you get acquainted with various standard toolbars and buttons that appear in different environments of NX. These toolbars are discussed next.

Application Toolbar

This toolbar is common to all environments of NX. Figure 1-11 shows the **Application** toolbar. You can invoke any other environment from the currently invoked environment. For example, you can invoke the Assembly and Drafting environments from the Modeling environment using this toolbar to complete the design.

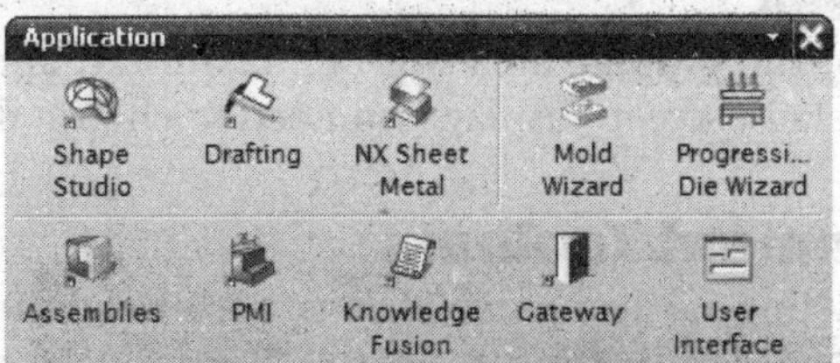

*Figure 1-11 The **Application** toolbar*

Standard Toolbar

This toolbar is common to all environments of NX. Figure 1-12 shows the **Standard** toolbar. The buttons in this toolbar are used to start a new file, open an existing file, save a file, and print the current document. These buttons are also used to cut and place the selection on a temporary clipboard, copy a selection, paste the content from the clipboard to a selected location, undo, redo, and invoke the help topics. The **Start** button in this toolbar is used to invoke different NX environments.

*Figure 1-12 The **Standard** toolbar*

Status Bar

The status bar that appears at the top of the drawing window comprises of two areas, as shown in Figure 1-13. These areas are discussed next.

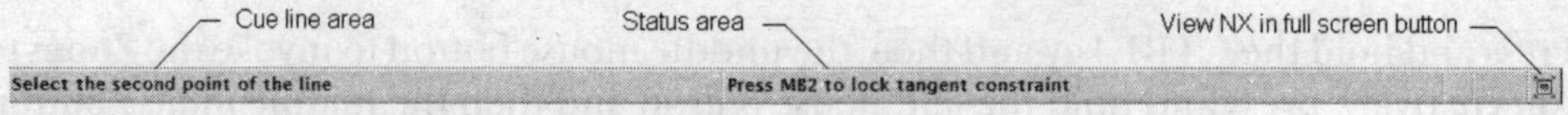

Figure 1-13 *The* ***Status*** *bar*

Cue Line Area

The cue line area is the prompt area. In this area, you will be prompted to select the entities for completing the tool task.

Tip: *By default, some of the toolbars are available in their respective environments. You can add more toolbars that are not available by default. To do so, right-click on any toolbar; a shortcut menu will be displayed. You will observe that the tools that are not available in the graphics window are unselected. Select any unselected toolbar; it will become available in the graphics window.*

Status Area

It gives information about the operations that can be carried out.

View NX in Full Screen

If you choose this button, the graphic area will be maximized and it gives you full screen display. For getting the default screen display, you need to choose this button again.

Modeling Environment Toolbars

You can invoke the Modeling environment, if it is not already invoked, by choosing the **Modeling** button from the **Application** toolbar. Alternatively, you can choose **Start > Modeling** from the **Standard** toolbar. The toolbars in the Modeling environment are discussed next.

View Toolbar

The tools in the **View** toolbar, as shown in Figure 1-14, are used for manipulating the views of the model. The **View** toolbar is available in all the environments. Some of the buttons in the **View** toolbar are not available in the **Drafting** environment.

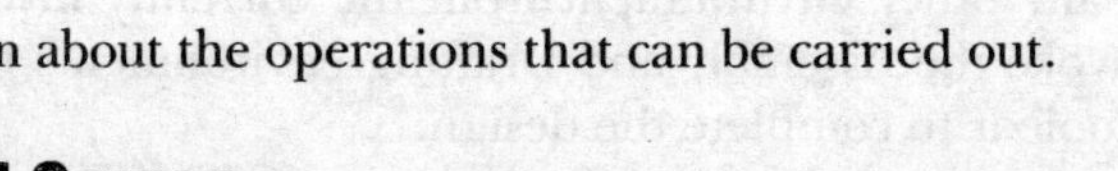

Figure 1-14 *The* ***View*** *toolbar*

Feature Toolbar

The tools in this toolbar, as shown in Figure 1-15, are used to convert a sketch drawn in the Sketcher environment into a feature. This toolbar contains sketch-based feature tools and placed feature tools. You can create the datum plane, axis, and points using the tools in this toolbar.

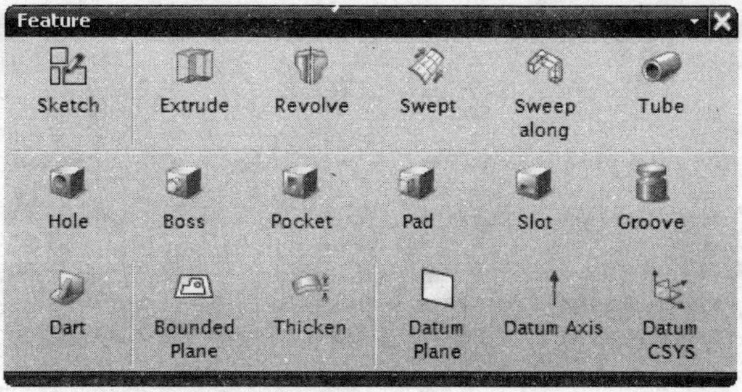

*Figure 1-15 The **Feature** toolbar*

Sketcher Environment Toolbar

The **Sketch** button in the **Feature** toolbar is used to invoke the Sketcher environment, where you can create a sketch. After choosing the **Sketch** button, select a plane or a planar face to invoke the Sketcher environment. The toolbars in the Sketcher environment are discussed next.

Sketcher Toolbar

The **Finish Sketch** button in the **Sketcher** toolbar is used to switch back to the **Modeling** environment, where you can convert the sketch into a feature. Figure 1-16 shows the buttons that are available in the **Sketcher** toolbar.

*Figure 1-16 The **Sketcher** toolbar*

Sketch Tools Toolbar

It is one of the most important toolbars in the Sketcher environment. The tools in the **Sketch Tools** toolbar are used to draw the sketches as well as edit the drawn sketches. Additionally, you can apply constrains to the geometric entities and assign dimension to a sketch using the tools in this toolbar. You can make a sketch fully defined using these tools. Figure 1-17 shows the buttons that are available in the **Sketch Tools** toolbar.

Once the basic sketch is complete, you need to convert it into a feature. Choose the **Finish Sketch** button from the **Sketcher** toolbar and switch back to the Modeling environment. The remaining toolbars in the Modeling environment are discussed next.

Feature Operation Toolbar

The tools in the **Feature Operation** toolbar are used to apply the placed features such as taper, fillet, hole, shell, and so on. Figure 1-18 shows the buttons in the **Feature Operation** toolbar.

Surface Design Toolbars

You can create the surface design in the same Modeling environment. A separate environment is not required to create the surface design. The tools used to create the solid bodies are also used to create the surface bodies. Some of the toolbars used to create the surface design are discussed next.

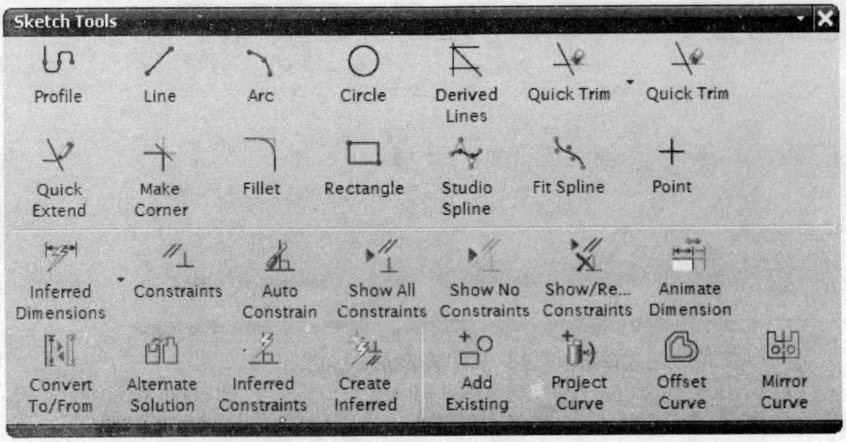

*Figure 1-17 The **Sketch Tools** toolbar*

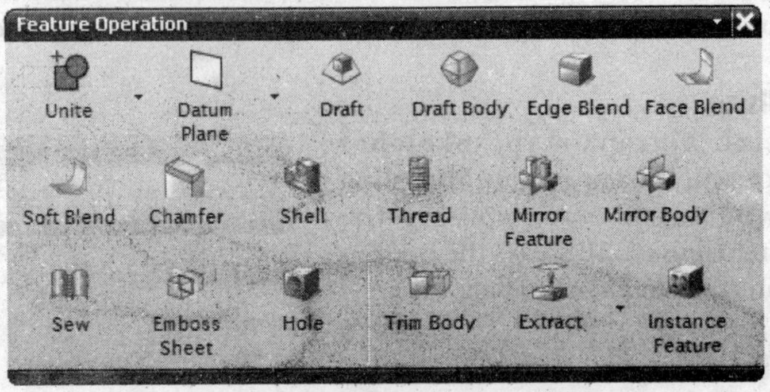

*Figure 1-18 The **Feature Operation** toolbar*

Surface Toolbar

The tools in the **Surface** toolbar are used to create complicated surfaces. Figure 1-19 shows the **Surface** toolbar.

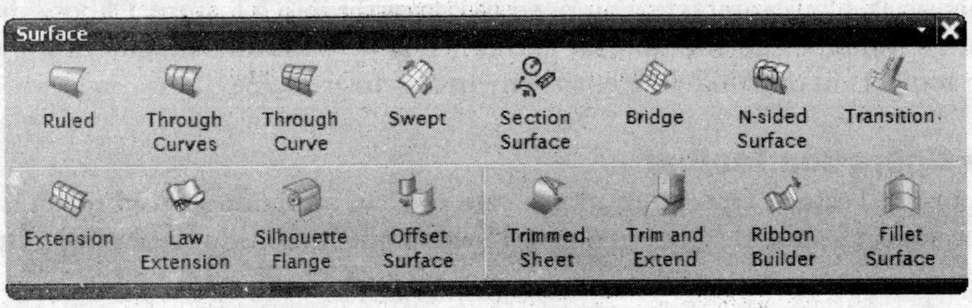

*Figure 1-19 The **Surface** toolbar*

Freeform Shape Toolbar

The tools in the **Freeform Shape** toolbar are used to create advanced surfaces. Figure 1-20 shows the **Freeform Shape** toolbar.

*Figure 1-20 The **Freeform Shape** toolbar*

Tip. *You can add tools in any toolbar as per the requirement. To do so, click on the down arrow in the title bar of a toolbar; a cascading menu will be displayed. Move the cursor over the **Add or Remove Buttons** option in the cascading menu; another cascading menu will be displayed. Now, move the cursor over the name of the required toolbar; another cascading menu will be displayed containing all the tools related to that toolbar. You will observe that the tools which are not available in the toolbar are unselected. If you select any unselected tool, it will become available in the toolbar.*

Assembly Environment Toolbars

You can create the assembly in the same Modeling environment. The toolbars that are used to create the assembly can be invoked by choosing **Start > Assemblies** from the **Standard** toolbar. Alternatively, choose the **Assemblies** button from the **Application** toolbar. The toolbars used in the assembly design are discussed next.

Assemblies Toolbar

The tools in the **Assemblies** toolbar are used to insert an existing part or assembly in the current assembly file. You can also create a new component in the assembly file using the tools in this toolbar. Figure 1-21 shows the buttons in the **Assemblies** toolbar.

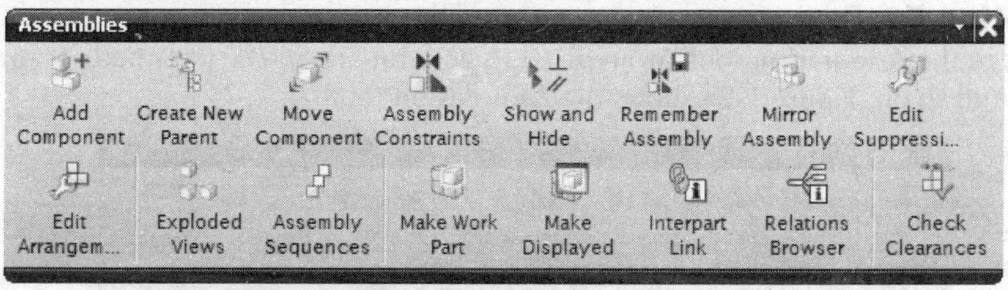

*Figure 1-21 The **Assemblies** toolbar*

Drafting Environment Toolbars

To invoke the Drafting environment, choose the **Drafting** button from the **Application** toolbar. Alternatively, this environment can be invoked by choosing **Start > Drafting** from the **Standard** toolbar. The toolbars in the Drafting environment are discussed next.

Drawing Toolbar

The tools in the **Drawing** toolbar are used to insert a new sheet, create a new view, generate an orthographic view, section view, and detail views for a solid part or an assembly. Figure 1-22 shows the **Drawing** toolbar.

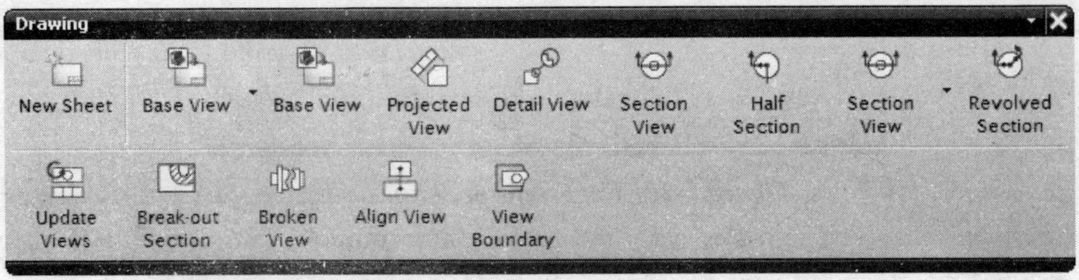

*Figure 1-22 The **Drawing** toolbar*

Dimension Toolbar

The tools in the **Dimension** toolbar are used to generate various dimensions in the drawing views. Figure 1-23 shows the **Dimension** toolbar.

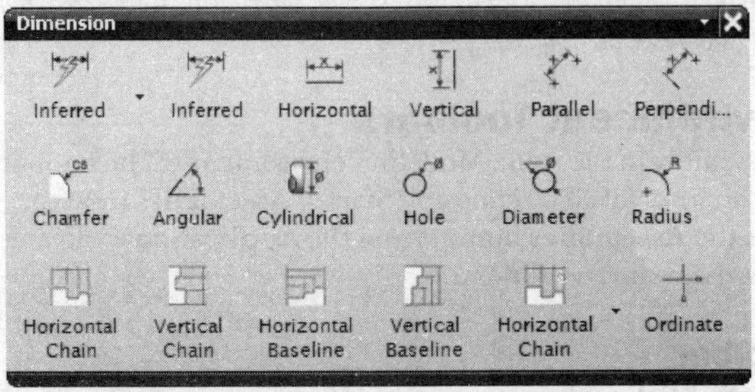

*Figure 1-23 The **Dimension** toolbar*

Annotation Toolbar

The tools in the **Annotation** toolbar are used to generate the GDT parameters, annotations, symbols, and so on. Figure 1-24 shows the **Annotation** toolbar.

*Figure 1-24 The **Annotation** toolbar*

Synchronous Modeling Toolbar

The Synchronous Modeling Technology is one of the latest enhancements in NX. The tools available in this toolbar are used to modify and improve an existing design in the shortest period of time. Figure 1-25 shows the **Synchronous Modeling** toolbar.

HOT KEYS

NX is more popularly known for its icon driven structure. However, you can still use the keys on the keyboard to invoke some tools. These keys are called hot keys. The hot keys, along with their functions, are listed in the table given next.

Hot Keys	Function
CTRL+Z	Invokes the **Undo** tool
CTRL+Y	Invokes the **Repeat** tool
CTRL+S	Saves the current document
F5	Refreshes the **Drawing** window
F1	Invokes the NX **Help** tool
F6	Invokes the **Zoom** tool
F7	Invokes the **Rotate** tool
CTRL+M	Invokes the Modeling environment
CTRL+SHIFT+D	Invokes the Drafting environment

*Figure 1-25 The **Synchronous Modeling** toolbar*

COLOR SCHEME

NX allows you to use various color schemes as the background screen color and also for displaying the solid bodies on the screen. To change the background color scheme, choose **Preferences > Background** from the menu bar; the **Edit Background** dialog box will be displayed.

Select the **Plane** radio button from the **Shaded Views** and **Wireframe Views** areas. Next, choose the color swatch available on the right side of the **Plain Color** option; the **Color** dialog box will be displayed. Select the **White** color swatch from the **Color** dialog box and choose the **OK** button twice to apply the new color scheme to the NX environment.

Note

For the purpose of printing, this book will follow the white background of the NX environment. However, for a better understanding and also for a clear visualization at various places, this book will follow other color schemes also.

DIALOG BOXES IN NX

To create any feature, you need to follow certain steps in a particular order. These steps are placed in a top-down order in the corresponding dialog boxes. This layout of dialog boxes will help you throughout the feature creation operation, refer to Figure 1-26.

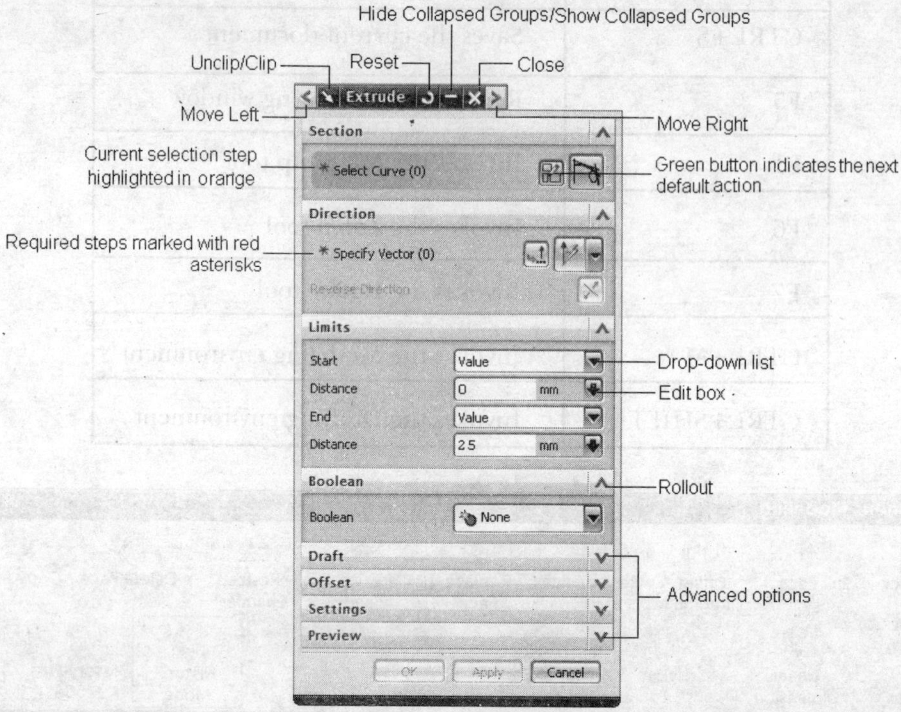

*Figure 1-26 The **Extrude** dialog box attached with the Dialog Rail*

The current selection step will be highlighted in orange. The required steps are marked with red asterisks, and the completed steps are marked with green check marks. The advanced options are collapsed and hidden in the rollouts. The button highlighted in green indicates the next default action.

The **Reset** button is used to reset the dialog box to its initial settings. The **Hide Collapsed Groups** button is used to hide all collapsed rollouts to simplify the dialog box. To view all the collapsed rollouts, choose the **Show Collapsed Groups** button, which will be available only after choosing the **Hide Collapsed Groups** button. The **Close** button is used to exit the dialog box.

Dialog Rail

By default, all the dialog boxes are attached to the Dialog Rail, refer to Figure 1-26. However, you can detach the dialog boxes from the Dialog Rail by choosing the **Unclip** button, refer to Figure 1-27. Use the **Clip** button to attach a dialog box to the Dialog Rail. You can move a dialog box to the extreme right or extreme left of the rail using the **Move Right** or **Move Left** button, respectively. To hide a dialog box, click on the name of the dialog box displayed on the Dialog Rail. Similarly, to display the hidden dialog box, click again on its name in the Dialog Rail.

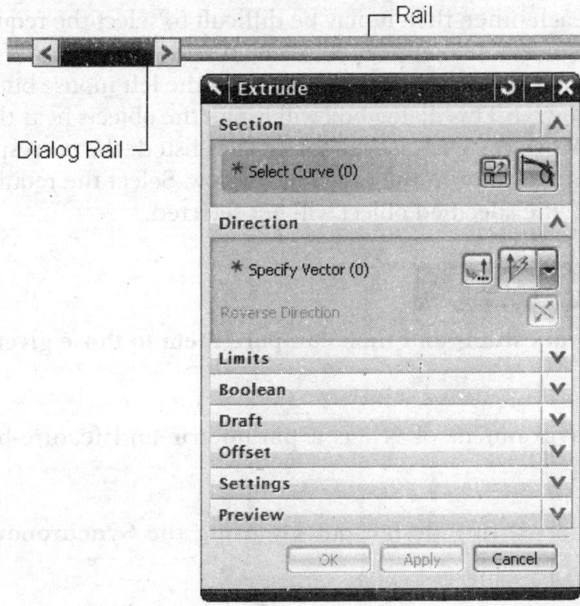

Figure 1-27 The ***Extrude*** *dialog box detached from the Dialog Rail*

Note

To move the attached dialog box, press and hold the left mouse button on the Dialog Rail and drag the mouse. In all the further chapters, the dialog boxes are displayed after detaching them from the Dialog Rail.

SELECTING OBJECTS

When no tool is invoked in the current environment, the select mode will be activated. You can ensure that the select mode is active by pressing the ESC key. In this mode, you can select a wide range of objects from different environments such as individual features, part bodies, surface bodies, planar and non-planar faces, sketched entities, sketcher and assembly constraints, and so on by clicking on them. Alternatively, press and hold the left mouse button and drag a box around the objects; all objects that lie completely inside the box are selected.

DESELECTING OBJECTS

By default, the selected objects are displayed in orange color. If you want to deselect any specific object from the selection, press and hold the SHIFT key and click on it; the object will be deselected. If you want to deselect all the selected entities, press the ESC key. Alternatively, press and hold the SHIFT key and drag a box around the entities; all entities that lie completely inside the box are deselected. Also, you can choose the **Deselect All** button from the **Selection** bar to deselect all the selected entities.

SELECTING OBJECTS USING THE QUICKPICK DIALOG BOX

If objects are close to each other, then it may be difficult to select the required object. In such cases, move the cursor over the object to be selected and wait for three seconds; the cursor will be changed to '+' sign with three dots. Next, press the left mouse button; the **QuickPick** dialog box will be displayed. This dialog box will list all the objects near the selected object in the drawing window. Move the cursor over the objects listed; the corresponding objects will be highlighted in magenta color in the drawing window. Select the required object from the **QuickPick** dialog box; the specified object will get selected.

Self-Evaluation Test

Answer the following questions and then compare them to those given at the end of this chapter:

1. The Modeling environment of NX is a parametric and feature-based environment. (T/F)

2. You can modify an existing design quickly using the **Synchronous Modeling** tools. (T/F)

3. The generative drafting technique is used to automatically generate the drawing views of the parts and assemblies. (T/F)

4. By default, the **Resource Bar** is located on the left side of the NX window. (T/F)

5. The __________ analysis provides the interference check between the components in an assembly.

6. The __________ is a file extension associated with all the files that are created in different environments of NX.

7. The __________ keeps a track of all the operations that are carried out on the part.

8. The __________ constraint is used to fix a selected entity in terms of its position with respect to the coordinate system of the current sketch.

9. Press and hold the middle mouse button to invoke the __________ tool.

10. The __________ toolbar is used to generate the GDT parameters, annotations, and symbols.

Answers to Self-Evaluation Test

1. T, **2.** T, **3.** T, **4.** T, **5.** Check Clearance, **6.** *.prt, **7. Part Navigator**, **8.** fixed, **9. Rotate**, **10. Annotation**

Chapter 2

Drawing Sketches for Solid Models

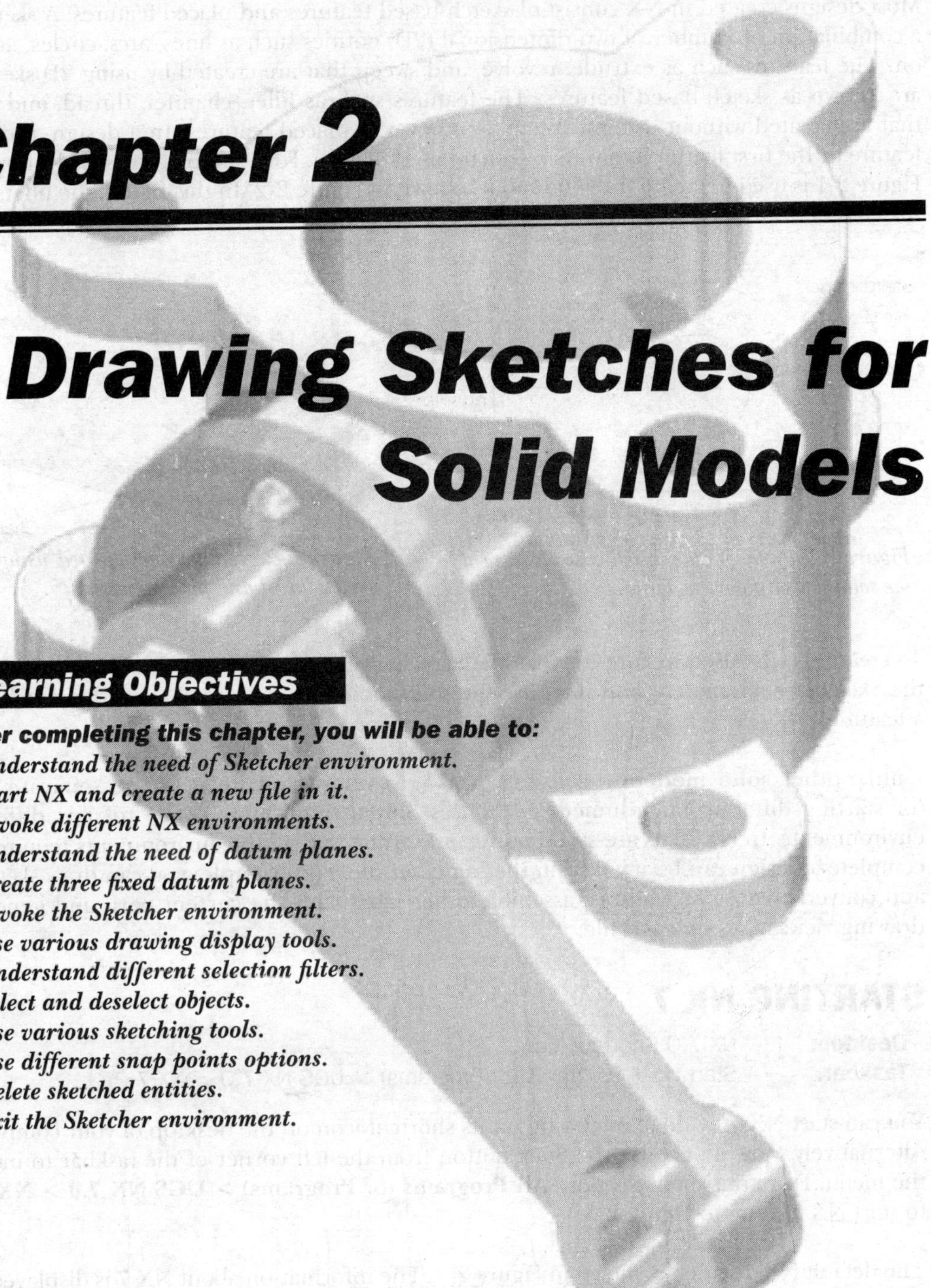

Learning Objectives

After completing this chapter, you will be able to:

- *Understand the need of Sketcher environment.*
- *Start NX and create a new file in it.*
- *Invoke different NX environments.*
- *Understand the need of datum planes.*
- *Create three fixed datum planes.*
- *Invoke the Sketcher environment.*
- *Use various drawing display tools.*
- *Understand different selection filters.*
- *Select and deselect objects.*
- *Use various sketching tools.*
- *Use different snap points options.*
- *Delete sketched entities.*
- *Exit the Sketcher environment.*

THE SKETCHER ENVIRONMENT

Most designs created in NX consist of sketch-based features and placed features. A sketch is a combination of number of two-dimensional (2D) entities such as lines, arcs, circles, and so on. The features such as extrude, revolve, and sweep that are created by using 2D sketches are known as sketch-based features. The features such as fillet, chamfer, thread, and shell that are created without using a sketch are known as placed features. In a design, the base feature or the first feature is always a sketch-based feature. For example, the sketch shown in Figure 2-1 is used to create the solid model shown in Figure 2-2. In this figure, the fillets and the chamfers are the placed features.

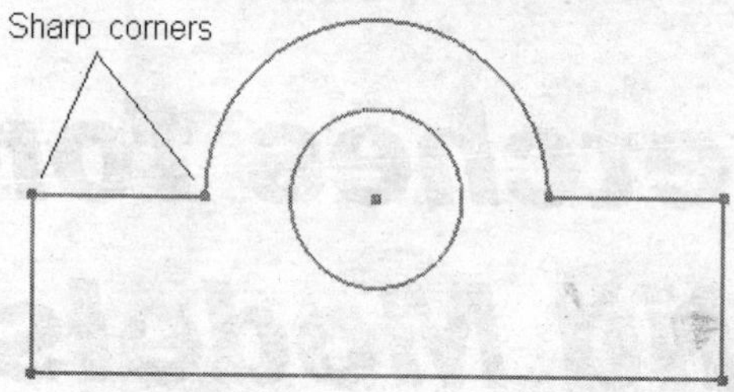

Figure 2-1 Profile for the sketch-based feature of the solid model shown in Figure 2-2

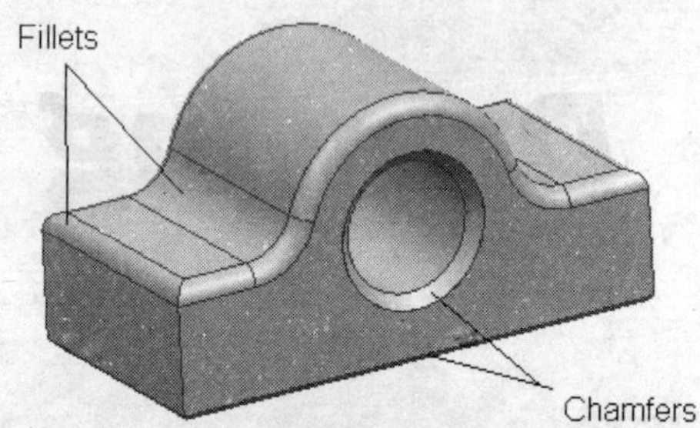

Figure 2-2 Solid model created using the sketch-based and placed features

To create sketch-based features, invoke the Sketcher environment and draw the sketch. Exit the Sketcher environment and then use the solid modeling tools to convert the sketch into a feature.

Unlike other solid modeling software packages where you need to use separate files for starting different environments, NX uses only a single type of file to start different environments. In NX, files are saved in the *.prt* format and all the environments required to complete a design can be invoked in the same *.prt* file. For example, you can draw sketches and convert them into features, assemble other parts with the current part, and generate drawing views in a single *.prt* file.

STARTING NX 7

Desktop:	NX 7.0 Shortcut Icon
Taskbar:	Start > All Programs (or Programs) > UGS NX 7.0 > NX 7.0

You can start NX 7 by double-clicking on its shortcut icon on the desktop of your computer. Alternatively, you can choose the **Start** button from the left corner of the taskbar to invoke the menu. From this menu, choose **All Programs** (or **Programs**) **> UGS NX 7.0 > NX 7.0** to start NX 7, refer to Figure 2-3.

The default NX 7 screen is shown in Figure 2-4. The information about NX 7 is displayed on this screen, which helps you learn more about NX 7. You can also view other information by moving the cursor over the topics displayed on the left of the NX 7 screen.

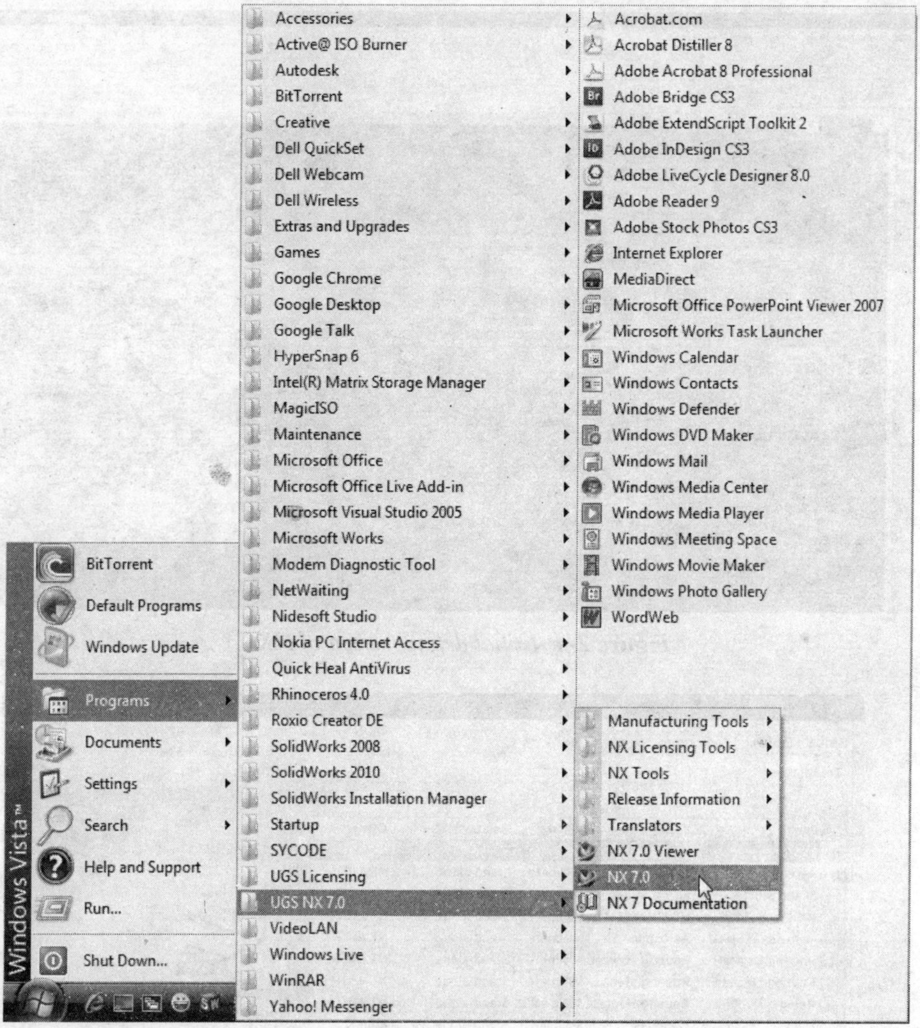

Figure 2-3 Starting NX 7 from the taskbar

Tip: *It is advised to read the information on the default initial screen of NX whenever you start a new session. This information will help you learn additional things about NX.*

STARTING A NEW DOCUMENT IN NX 7

Menu:	File > New
Toolbar:	Standard > New

To start a new file, choose the **New** button from the **Standard** toolbar or choose **File > New** from the menu bar; the **New** dialog box will be displayed, as shown in Figure 2-5.

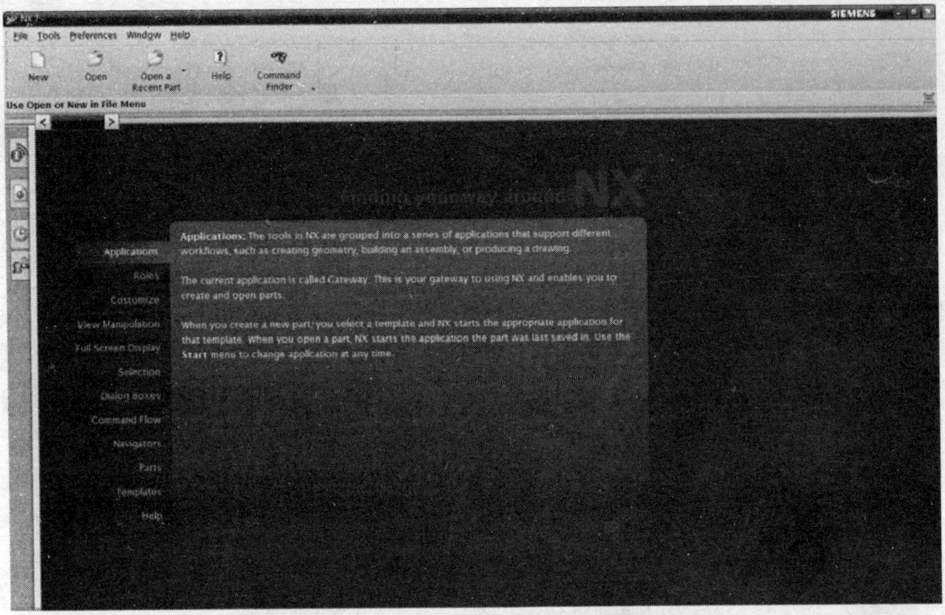

Figure 2-4 *Initial default screen of NX 7*

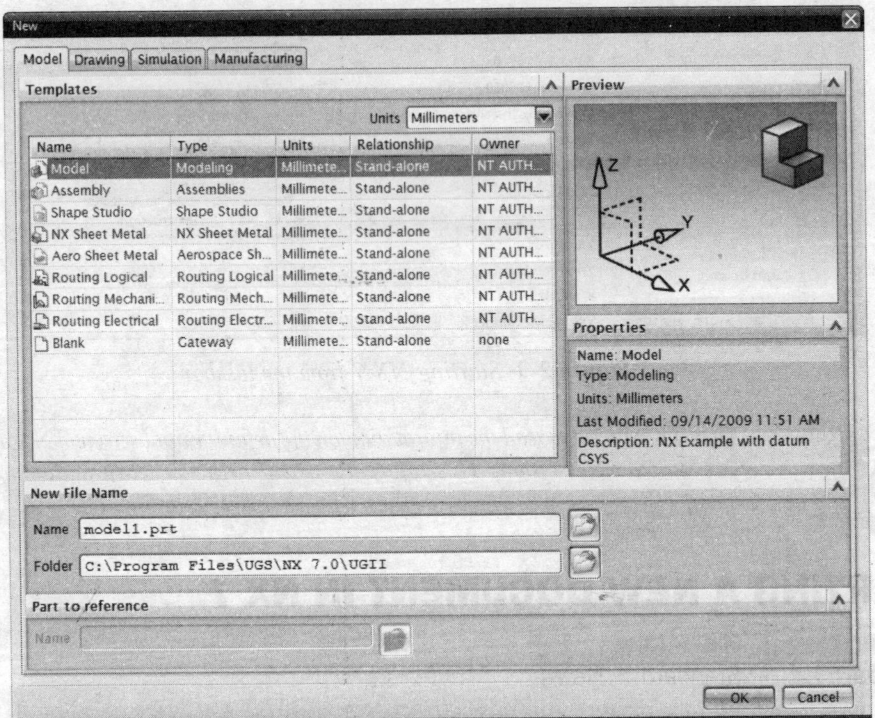

Figure 2-5 *The **New** dialog box*

The various tabs and options in this dialog box are discussed next.

Templates Rollout

In the **New** dialog box, templates are grouped together under various environment types such as Modeling, Drawing, Simulation, and Manufacturing. The template files related to these environments are available in their respective tabs. These files are used whenever you start a new file. These template files provide a predefined set of tools with specified environment. This saves a lot of time in setting environment and displaying tools according to your requirements.

Model Tab

By default, this tab will be chosen and the modeling templates are displayed in the **Templates** rollout. Some of the important modeling templates are discussed next.

Model

By default, the **Model** template will be selected. This template is used to start a new part file in the Modeling environment for creating solid and surface models.

Assembly

The **Assembly** template is used to start a new assembly file in the Assembly environment for assembling various parts of the assembly.

Shape Studio

The **Shape Studio** template is used to start a new part file in the Shape Studio environment for creating advanced surface models.

Blank

The **Blank** template is used to start a new file in the Gateway environment. The Gateway environment allows you to examine the geometry and drawing views created. You cannot modify a model in the Gateway environment. However, you can invoke any environment of NX from it.

Drawing Tab

Choose the **Drawing** tab; the drawing templates are displayed in the **Templates** rollout. These templates are used to start a new drawing file in the Drafting environment for generating the drawing views. These templates are arranged according to the sheet size (A0, A1, A2, A3, and A4) in the **Drawing** tab. There are two types of templates for each sheet size, views and no views. If you select the views template, then the drawing views are automatically generated in the drawing sheet. If you select the no views template, then a blank drawing sheet will be opened and you have to create the drawing views manually.

Units

The **Units** drop-down list is used to filter the templates as per the unit. The options in this drop-down list are discussed next.

Millimeters
If you select the **Millimeters** option, the templates only with the millimeters unit will be displayed in the **Templates** area.

Inches
If you select the **Inches** option, the templates only with the inches units will be displayed in the **Templates** area.

All
Select this option to display all the templates (with both millimeters and inches units).

New File Name Rollout
This rollout is used to specify the name and location to save the file. The options in this rollout are discussed next.

Name
Enter the name of the new file in the **Name** text box. Alternatively, choose the button on the right side of the **Name** text box; the **Choose New File Name** dialog box will be displayed. Enter the name in the **File name** edit box. Also, to specify the location to save the new file, browse to the folder where you need to save the file and choose the **OK** button. However, there is a separate option to specify the location, which is discussed next.

Folder
Specify the location to save the new file in the **Folder** text box. Alternatively, choose the button to the right side of the **Folder** text box; the **Choose Directory** dialog box will be displayed. Next, browse to the folder where you want to save the file and choose the **OK** button.

Note

It is recommended that you create a folder with the name NX 7 in the primary drive of your computer and then create individual folder for each chapter within the NX 7 folder. Now, you can save the part files of all chapters in their respective folders. This will ensure a better organization of the part files that you create.

*In this textbook, the **Model** template has been used for starting a new file for illustrations.*

After specifying all required options in the **New** dialog box, choose the **OK** button; the new file will start in the specified environment. Figure 2-6 shows the default initial screen of a new file invoked by using the **Model** template.

INVOKING DIFFERENT NX ENVIRONMENTS
You can invoke any NX environment in the same part file at any time. To invoke different environments, choose the **Start** button from the **Standard** toolbar; a flyout will be displayed, as shown in Figure 2-7. Choose the environment that you want to invoke from this flyout.

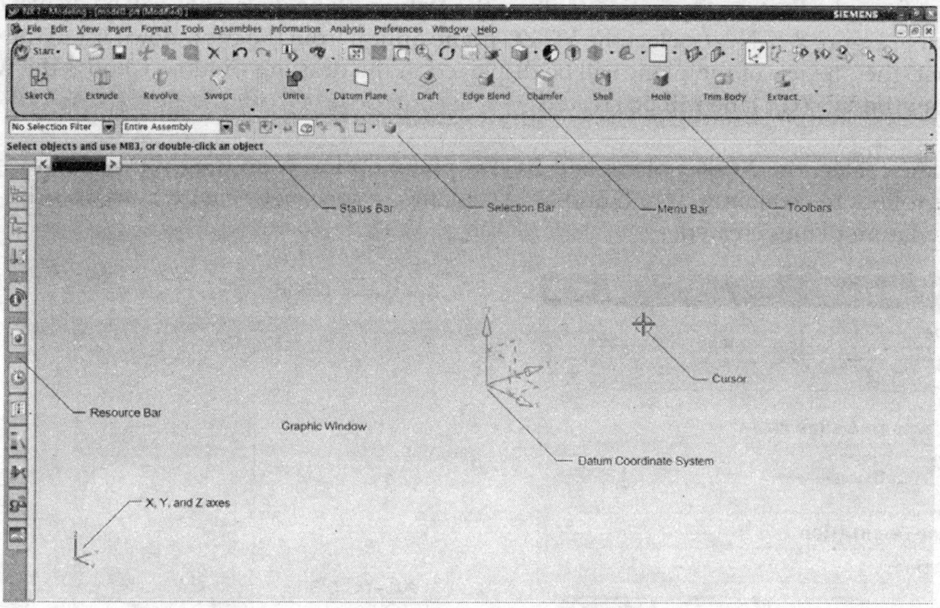

Figure 2-6 Default Initial screen of a new part file

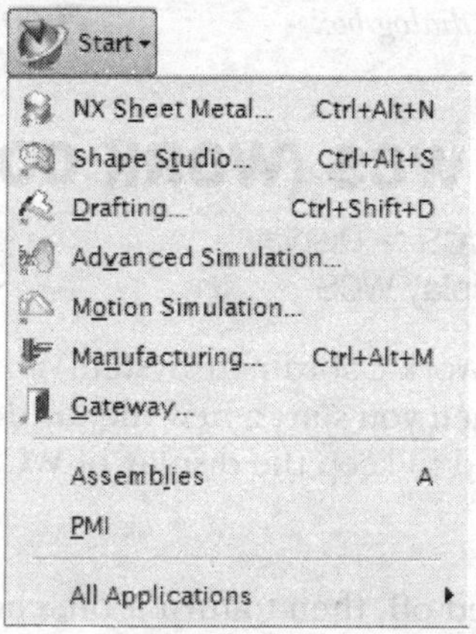

Figure 2-7 Different environments of NX

CREATING THREE FIXED DATUM PLANES (XC-YC, YC-ZC, XC-ZC)

Menu: Insert > Datum/Point > Datum Plane
Toolbar: Feature Operation > Datum Plane

You can select the datum coordinate system plane (XC-YC, YC-ZC, or XC-ZC) from the drawing window to create the base feature. You also create three fixed datum planes (YC-ZC, XC-ZC, and XC-YC) first and then use one of them to start the Sketcher environment. To create three fixed datum planes, choose **Insert > Datum/Point > Datum Plane** from the menu bar. Alternatively, choose the **Datum Plane**

button from the **Feature Operation** toolbar; the **Datum Plane** dialog box will be displayed, as shown in Figure 2-8. Next, select the **YC-ZC plane** option from the drop-down list in the **Type** rollout; the preview of the plane will be displayed in the drawing window. Choose the **Apply** button; the YC-ZC plane will be created.

Similarly, select the **XC-ZC plane** and **XC-YC plane** option from the drop-down list in the **Type** rollout to create the XC-ZC and XC-YC planes, respectively. Figure 2-9 shows the three fixed datum planes created.

*Figure 2-8 The **Datum Plane** dialog box*

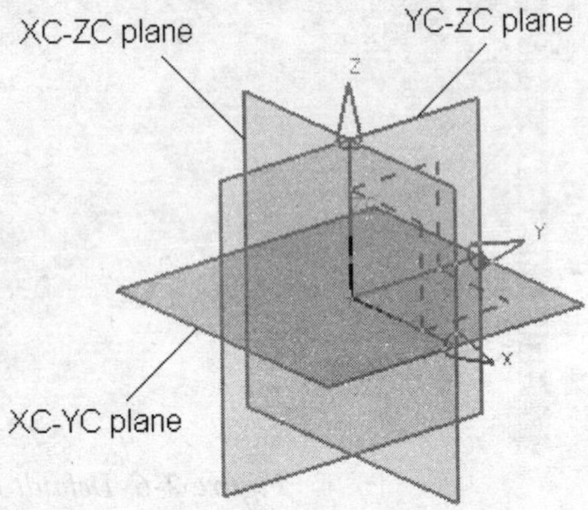

Figure 2-9 Three fixed datum planes

DISPLAYING THE WCS (WORK COORDINATE SYSTEM)

Menu: Format > WCS > Display
Toolbar: Utility > Display WCS

The display of WCS (Work Coordinate System) is important in selecting the planes for drawing sketches. When you start a new file, by default, the display of WCS is turned on. It is recommended to keep the display of WCS turned on while drawing sketches and creating features.

If the display of WCS is turned off, then to turn it on, choose the **Display WCS** button from the **Utility** toolbar; the WCS will be displayed at the origin of the drawing window. Figure 2-10 shows the WCS with the datum coordinate system hidden for better visualization. The **Display WCS** button is the toggle button. Choose this button again to turn off the display of WCS.

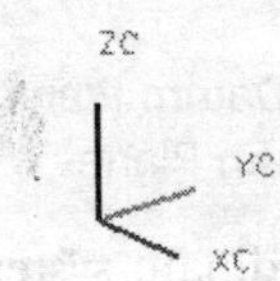

Figure 2-10 The WCS (Work Coordinate System)

INVOKING THE SKETCHER ENVIRONMENT

As mentioned earlier, the base feature or the first feature in a design is always a sketch-based feature. The profiles of the sketch-based features are defined by using a sketch. Therefore, to create the base feature, first you need to invoke the Sketcher environment.

In NX, you can invoke the Sketcher environment by using the datum coordinate system plane (XC-YC, YC-ZC, or XC-ZC), any reference plane, or the existing face of the model.

To invoke the Sketcher environment, choose the **Sketch** button from the **Feature** toolbar. Alternatively, choose **Insert > Sketch** from the menu bar; the **Create Sketch** dialog box will be displayed, as shown in Figure 2-11. Also, the Sketcher environment will be invoked, but no tool will be activated. Enter the name for the sketch in the **Sketch Name** drop-down list of the **Sketcher** toolbar and press the ENTER key. If you do not specify the name, NX will automatically name the sketches as SKETCH_000, SKETCH_001, SKETCH_002, and so on. In this textbook, you will accept the default sketch name given by NX. The **Sketch Name** drop-down list is also used to edit the sketches created earlier; this is discussed later in this textbook.

***Figure 2-11** The **Create Sketch** dialog box*

You will be prompted to select an object for the sketch plane or to select a sketch axis to orient in the prompt area above the drawing window. The options in the various rollouts of the **Create Sketch** dialog box are discussed next.

Type Rollout

The options in this rollout are used to specify whether you want to draw the sketch on existing plane or on a temporary plane defined on the path.

On Plane

By default, this option will be selected from the drop-down list. It is used to specify the existing plane, face, or datum coordinate system plane as a sketching plane.

On Path

Select this option from the drop-down list to specify the sketch plane on the existing path. The temporary sketch plane will be created perpendicular to the path selected.

Depending on the option selected from the drop-down list, the **Create Sketch** dialog box will be modified. The various rollouts in the modified dialog box for both the options are discussed next.

On Plane Options

By default, the rollouts related to the **On Plane** option will be displayed in the **Create Sketch** dialog box, refer to Figure 2-11. The rollouts in this dialog box are discussed next.

Sketch Plane Rollout

The options in this rollout are used to specify the sketch plane by different methods. The options in this rollout are as follows:

Plane Option

This drop down list provides various options to select the sketch plane. Some of these options are discussed below.

Existing Plane

By default, this option will be selected from the **Plane Option** drop-down list and it allows you to select the existing plane or face as the sketch plane.

Create Plane

Select this option to create a new datum plane and use it as the current sketch plane. As you select this option, the **Specify Plane** area is displayed in the **Sketch Plane** rollout. The options in the **Specify Plane** area are used to create a datum plane. The options to create a datum plane are discussed in later chapter.

Create Datum CSYS

Select this option to create a new datum coordinate system.

Reverse Direction

The **Reverse Direction** button in the **Sketch Plane** rollout is used to reverse the direction of the sketching plane.

Sketch Orientation Rollout

The options in this rollout are used to specify the horizontal or vertical reference for the sketch. The sketching plane gets orientated according to the specified references. The options in this rollout are discussed next.

Reference

Select the required option (**Horizontal** or **Vertical**) from the **Reference** drop-down list to specify the reference for the sketch.

Select Reference

This button is used to specify the horizontal or vertical reference by selecting the existing planar face, edge, datum axis, or datum plane. The sketching plane gets oriented according to the specified reference. The horizontal and vertical constraints will be added to the sketch with respect to the specified reference direction.

Reverse Direction

The **Reverse Direction** button in the **Sketch Orientation** rollout is used to reverse the direction of reference specified (horizontal or vertical).

On Path Options

Select this option from the drop-down list in the **Type** rollout to create a sketching plane on a selected path; the rollouts related to the **On Path** option will be displayed in the **Create Sketch** dialog box, as shown in Figure 2-12. The options in these rollouts are discussed next.

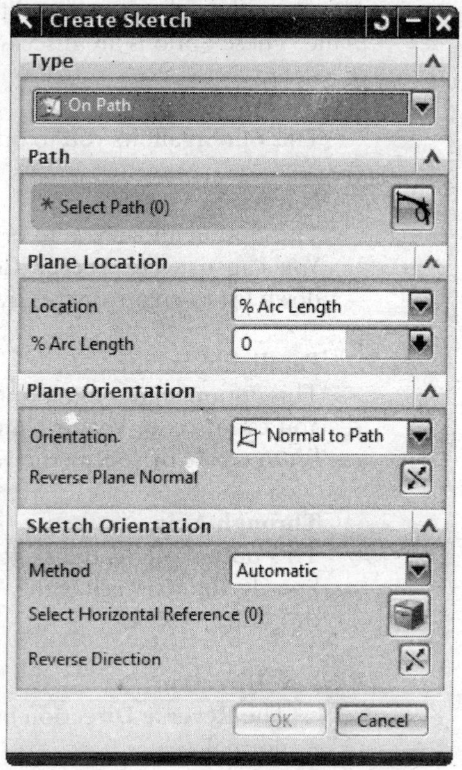

***Figure 2-12** The rollouts related to the **On Path** option*

Path Rollout

The **Curve** button in this rollout is used to select the path. The path may be a curve or the edge of an existing solid body.

Plane Location Rollout

The options in this rollout are used to specify the location of the sketch plane along the path in terms of arc length or point. These options are discussed next.

Location

This drop-down list contains different options to specify the location of the sketch plane along the path. These options are as follows:

Arc Length

This option allows you to specify the sketch plane distance from the start point of path. Enter the distance in the **Arc Length** edit box.

Note

The nearest endpoint of the selected path will be considered as the start point of the path.

% Arc Length

This option allows you to specify the distance of the sketch plane in terms of the percentage of arc length from the start point of path. Enter the % value in the **% Arc Length** edit box.

Through Point

This option allows you to specify the sketch plane by picking a point on the path. You can use **Point Constructor** button or **Inferred Point** drop-down list to create or locate a point.

Plane Orientation Rollout

The options in this rollout are used to specify the direction of the sketch plane with respect to the selected path. These options are discussed below:

Orientation

This drop-down list contains different options to specify the direction of the sketch plane. These options are discussed next.

Normal to Path

This option allows you to orient the sketch plane normal to the selected path.

Normal to Vector

This option allows you to orient the sketch plane normal to the specified vector. You can use the **Vector Constructor** button or the **Inferred Vector** drop-down list to create or specify the vector.

Parallel to Vector

This option allows you to specify the sketch plane parallel to the specified vector. You can use the **Vector Constructor** button or the **Inferred Vector** drop-down list to create or specify the vector.

Through Axis

This option aligns the sketch plane so that it passes though the specified axis. Specify the axis using the **Vector Constructor** button or the **Inferred Vector** drop-down list.

Reverse Direction

The **Reverse Direction** button is used to reverse the direction of sketch plane normal.

Sketch Orientation Rollout

The options in this rollout are used to specify the reference for a sketch. The sketching plane will be orientated according to the specified reference. The options in this rollout are discussed next.

Method

The options in this drop-down list are used to specify references for the orientation of a sketch. These options are discussed next.

Automatic

The **Automatic** option is selected by default in this drop-down list. This option allows you to select the horizontal reference by using the **Select Horizontal Reference** button. Specify the horizontal reference for the sketch; the sketching plane will be oriented based on the specified reference.

Note

*In the **Automatic** option, if you select an existing curve as a path, the sketch will be oriented* *using the curve parameters and if you select an existing edge as a path, the sketch will be oriented relative to face.*

Relative to Face

This option allows you to orient a sketch with respect to a selected face.

Use Curve Parameters

This option allows you to orient a sketch by using curve parameters.

Reverse Direction

The **Reverse Direction** button in this rollout is used to reverse the direction of the specified reference.

All the options in the **Create Sketch** dialog box have already been discussed. Now, for illustration purpose, select the **On Plane** option from the drop-down list. By default, the XC-YC plane will be selected. Next, choose the **OK** button from the **Create Sketch** dialog box; the plane will be oriented parallel to the screen and the Sketcher environment will be invoked. By default, the **Profile** tool will be invoked. Figure 2-13 shows the default screen display of the Sketcher environment of NX.

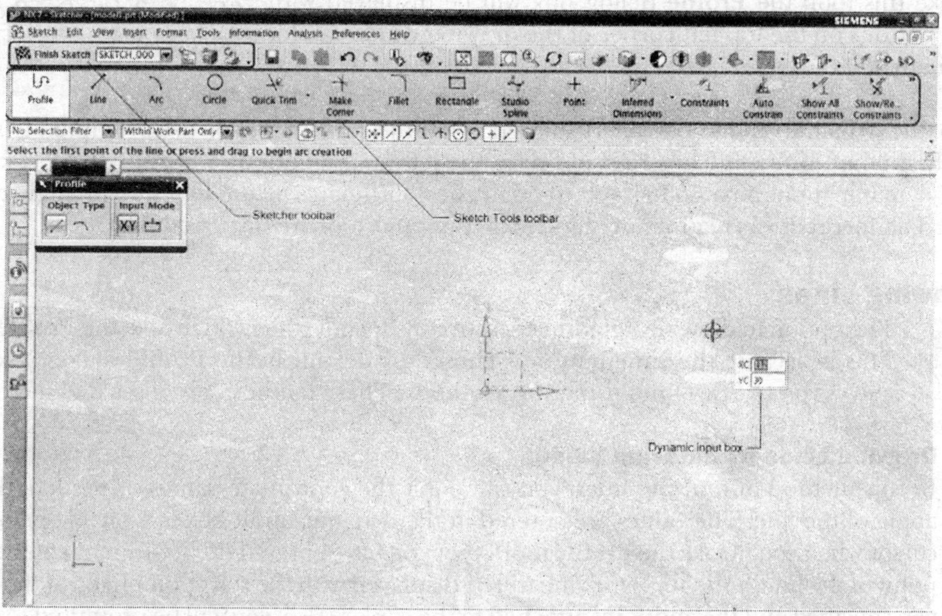

Figure 2-13 The default screen display of the Sketcher environment of NX

Tip: *If the toolbar icons appear large, you can reduce their size. To do so, right-click on any toolbar to display the shortcut menu and then choose the* ***Customize*** *option at the bottom; the* ***Customize*** *dialog box will be displayed. Choose the* ***Options*** *tab and then select the* ***Extra Small (16)*** *radio button from the* ***Toolbar Icon Size*** *area.*

SKETCHING TOOLS

Most of the tools required to draw a sketch in the Sketcher environment of NX are available in the **Sketch Tools** toolbar located on top of the drawing window. These tools are discussed next.

By default, some of the tools are not available in the toolbars. However, you can customize the toolbars to add these tools. You will learn more about customizing the toolbars later in this chapter.

Drawing Sketches Using the Profile Tool

Menu:	Insert > Curve > Profile
Toolbar:	Sketch Tools > Profile

By default, the **Profile** tool is invoked in the **Sketch Tools** toolbar, when you invoke the Sketcher environment. The **Profile** tool is the most commonly used tool to draw sketches in NX. This tool allows you to draw continuous lines and tangent/normal arcs. When you invoke this tool, the **Profile** dialog box will be displayed with four buttons on the top left corner of the drawing window, refer to Figure 2-14.

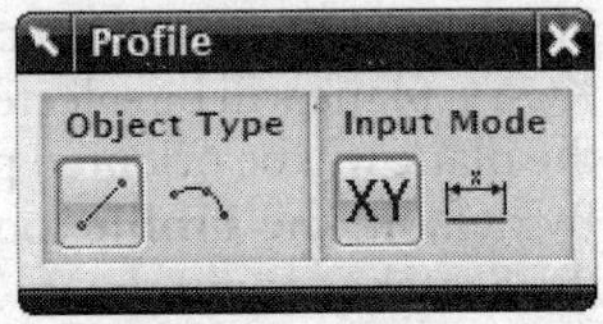

*Figure 2-14 The **Profile** dialog box*

Also, the dynamic input boxes are displayed below the cursor and you are prompted to select the first point of the line or press and drag the left mouse button to begin the arc creation. The dynamic input boxes allow you to enter the coordinates or the length and angle of the line. The methods of creating lines and arcs using this tool are discussed next.

Drawing Lines

The option to draw straight lines is active by default when you invoke the **Profile** tool. This is because the **Line** button is chosen by default in the **Profile** dialog box. NX allows you to draw lines using two methods. These methods are discussed next.

Drawing Lines by Entering Values

In this method of drawing lines, you can enter the coordinate values or the length and angle of the line. The values are entered in the dynamic input boxes available below the cursor when you invoke the **Profile** tool. After you have entered the coordinates of the start point of the line, a rubber-band line will be displayed with the start point fixed at the point you specified and the endpoint attached to the cursor. Also, you will be prompted to select the second point of the line. On specifying the start point of the line, the dynamic input boxes will change into the length and angle modes, as shown in Figure 2-15.

This happens because the **Parameter Mode** button is automatically chosen in the **Profile** dialog box. As you move the cursor in the drawing window, the length and angle of the line is modified, based on the relative position of the cursor with respect to the point specified earlier in the dynamic input boxes. You can draw a line by specifying its length and angle in these boxes.

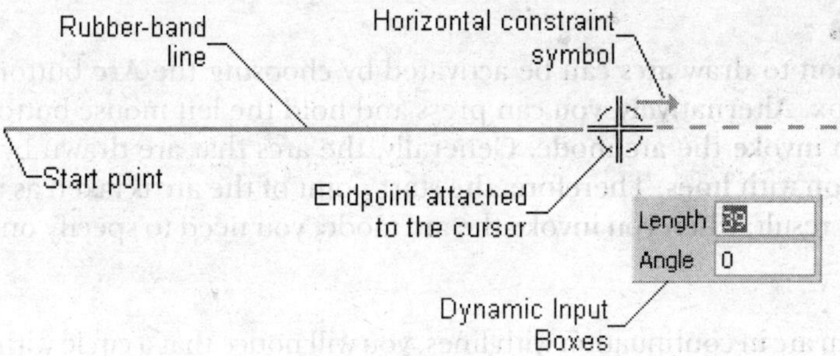

Figure 2-15 Drawing a horizontal line

Note

*After specifying the start point of the line, if you choose the **Coordinate Mode** button from the **Profile** dialog box, the coordinate mode option for specifying the endpoint of the line will be restored.*

The line drawing process does not end after you specify the second point of the line. Instead, another rubber-band line starts with its start point at the endpoint of the last line and the endpoint attached to the cursor. You can repeat the above-mentioned process to draw a chain of continuous lines.

Tip: *You can toggle between the two dynamic input boxes by pressing the TAB key. Note that once you specify a value in one of the boxes and press the TAB key; the second dynamic input box will be activated. Specify the value in the second box and then press the ENTER key or the TAB key to register the values and draw the line using these values.*

Drawing Lines by Picking Points in the Drawing Window

This is the most convenient method of drawing lines and is extensively used in sketching. The parametric nature of NX ensures that irrespective of the length of the line that is drawn, you can modify it to the required values using dimensions. To draw lines using this method, invoke the **Profile** tool and pick a point in the drawing window; a rubber-band line appears. Specify the endpoint of the line by picking a point in the drawing window; another rubber-band line will appear with the start point as the endpoint of the last line and the endpoint attached to the cursor. You can continue specifying the endpoints of the lines to draw a chain of continuous lines.

While drawing a line, you will notice that some symbols are displayed on the right of the cursor. For example, after specifying the start point of the line, if you move the cursor in the horizontal direction, an arrow pointing toward the right will be displayed, refer to Figure 2-15. This arrow is the symbol of the **Horizontal** constraint that is applied to the line. This constraint will ensure that the line you draw is horizontal. These constraints are automatically applied to the sketch while drawing. You will learn more about the constraints in the later chapters.

Note

While drawing lines, you can disable the constraints temporarily by pressing the ALT key.

Drawing Arcs

The option to draw arcs can be activated by choosing the **Arc** button in the **Profile** dialog box. Alternatively, you can press and hold the left mouse button and drag the cursor to invoke the arc mode. Generally, the arcs that are drawn by using this tool are in continuation with lines. Therefore, the start point of the arc is taken as the endpoint of the last line. As a result, when you invoke the arc mode, you need to specify only the endpoint of the arc.

When you draw an arc in continuation with lines, you will notice that a circle with four quadrants will be displayed at the start point of the arc, as shown in Figure 2-16. This symbol is called the quadrant symbol and it helps you in defining whether you need to draw a tangent arc or a normal arc. This symbol also helps you in specifying the direction of the arc.

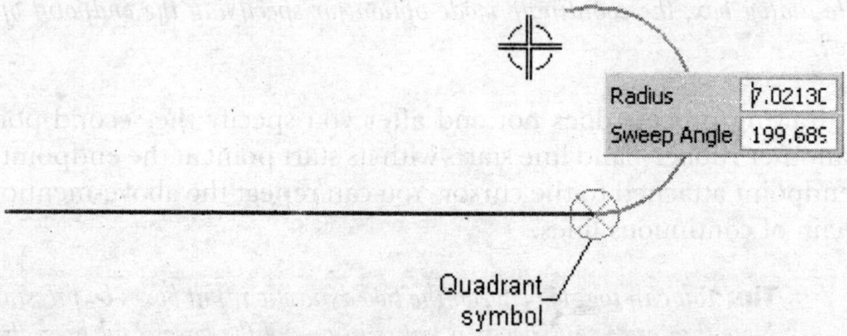

***Figure 2-16** Quadrant symbol displayed while drawing an arc using the **Profile** tool*

As evident from Figure 2-16, there are four quadrants in the quadrant symbol. The movement of the cursor in these quadrants will determine whether the arc will be tangent to the line or normal to the line. To draw a tangent arc, move the cursor to the start point of the arc and then move it in the quadrants along the line through a small distance; the tangent arc appears. Now, move the cursor to size the arc, as shown in Figure 2-16.

To draw a normal arc, move the cursor through a small distance in the quadrant normal to the line; the normal arc appears. Move the cursor to size the arc, as shown in Figure 2-17. As you invoke the arc mode, the current dynamic input boxes change into the **Radius** and **Sweep Angle** input boxes. These boxes allow you to specify the radius and the sweep angle to draw the arc.

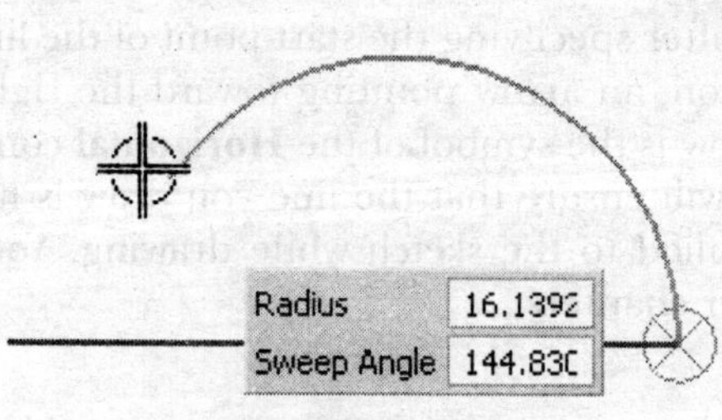

***Figure 2-17** Drawing the normal arc*

Tip: *To restart drawing lines using the **Profile** tool or to break the sequence of continuous lines, press the ESC key once.*

*Press the ESC key twice to exit the tool. Alternatively, right-click on the drawing area and choose the **OK** option from the shortcut menu.*

Note

*If you are not drawing the arc in continuation with a line or an arc, this tool will work similar to the **Arc by 3 Points** tool, which is discussed later in this chapter.*

Using Help Lines to Locate Points

You will notice that when a sketching tool is active while drawing sketches, some dotted lines are displayed from the keypoints of the existing entities. The keypoints include endpoints, midpoints, center points, and so on. These dotted lines are called the help lines. If the help lines are not displayed automatically, move the cursor to the keypoints and then move the cursor away; the help lines will be displayed. The help lines are used to locate the points with reference to the keypoints of the existing entities. Figure 2-18 shows the use of the help lines to locate the start point of a new line. You can temporarily disable the help lines by pressing the ALT key.

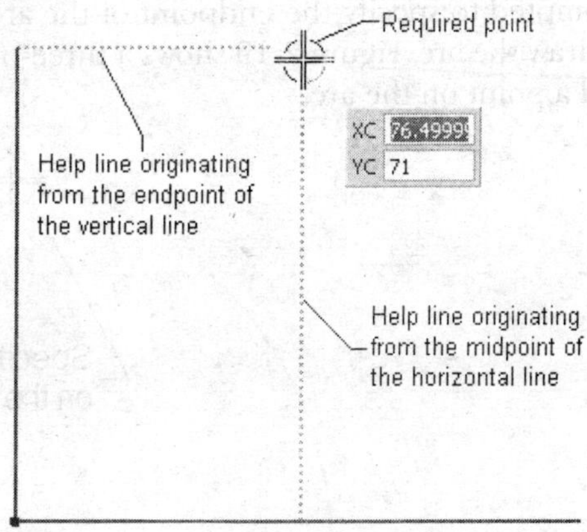

***Figure 2-18** Using the help lines to locate a point*

Drawing Individual Lines

Menu:	Insert > Curve > Line
Toolbar:	Sketch Tools > Line

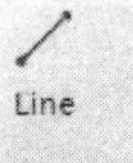

NX also allows you to draw individual lines. This can be done using the **Line** tool. The working of this tool is similar to the working of the line mode of the **Profile** tool. The only difference is that this tool allows you to draw only one line. As a result, after you specify the endpoint of the line, no rubber-band line is displayed. Instead, you are prompted to specify the first point of the line. You can specify the first point and the second point of the lines by picking points on the screen or by entering values in the dynamic input boxes. You can use this tool to draw as many individual lines as required.

Drawing Arcs

Menu:	Insert > Curve > Arc
Toolbar:	Sketch Tools > Arc

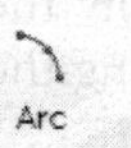

NX allows you to draw arcs using two methods. These methods can be activated by choosing their respective buttons from the **Arc** dialog box that will be displayed when you invoke the **Arc** tool. These methods of drawing arcs are discussed next.

Drawing Arcs Using Three Points

This method is used to draw an arc by specifying its start point, endpoint, and a point on the arc. When you invoke the **Arc** tool, this method is activated by default and you will be prompted to specify the start point of the arc. You can specify the start point by clicking in the drawing window or by entering the coordinates in the dynamic input boxes. After specifying the start point of the arc, you will be prompted to specify the endpoint. You can also specify the radius of the arc by entering its value in the dynamic input box.

Note that the next prompt will depend on how you specify the endpoint. If you specify the endpoint of the arc by clicking a point in the drawing window, you will be prompted to select a point on the arc and the **Radius** dynamic input box will be displayed. However, if you specify the radius of the arc in the dynamic input box after specifying the start point, then you will be prompted to specify the endpoint of the arc. You can click anywhere in the drawing window to draw the arc. Figure 2-19 shows a three-point arc being drawn by specifying two endpoints and a point on the arc.

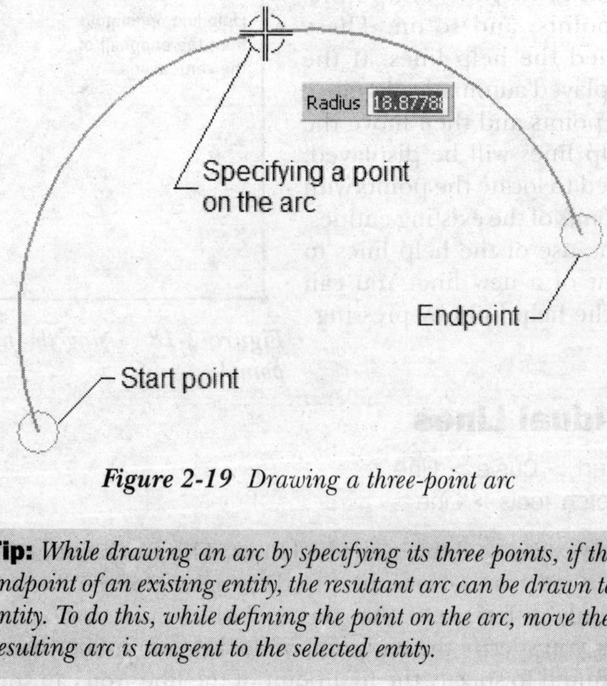

Figure 2-19 Drawing a three-point arc

Tip: *While drawing an arc by specifying its three points, if the start point is at the endpoint of an existing entity, the resultant arc can be drawn tangent to the selected entity. To do this, while defining the point on the arc, move the cursor such that the resulting arc is tangent to the selected entity.*

Drawing an Arc by Specifying its Center Point and Endpoints

This method is used to draw an arc by specifying its center point, start point, and endpoint. To invoke this method, choose the **Arc by Center and Endpoints** button from the **Arc** dialog box; you will be prompted to specify the center point of the arc. Specify the center point of the arc by clicking in the drawing area or by entering coordinates in the dynamic input boxes. On doing so, you will be prompted to specify the start point of the arc. After specifying the start point of the arc, you will be prompted to specify the endpoint of the arc. Note that when you specify the start point of the arc after specifying the center point, the radius of the arc will automatically be defined. Therefore, the endpoint is used only to define the arc length. Figure 2-20 shows an arc being drawn using this method.

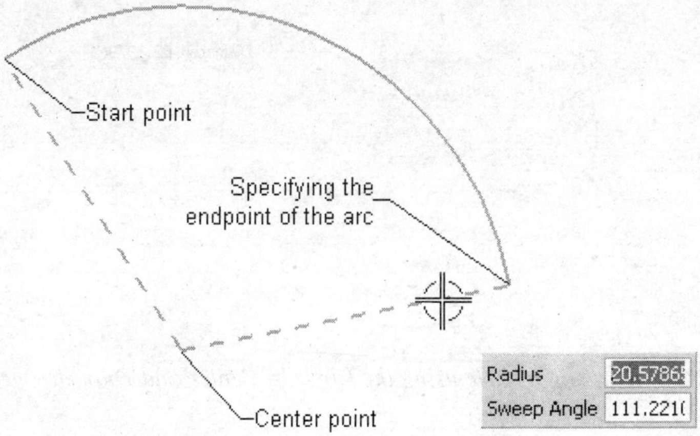

***Figure 2-20** Drawing an arc by specifying its center, start, and end points*

Tip: *After specifying the center point of the arc, you can also specify its radius and the sweep angle in the dynamic input boxes. In this case, you will be prompted to specify the start point and then the endpoint of the arc. The endpoint will define the direction of the arc.*

Drawing Circles

Menu:	Insert > Curve > Circle
Toolbar:	Sketch Tools > Circle

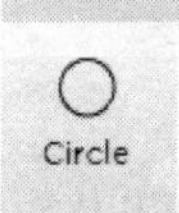

In NX, you can draw circles using two methods. These methods can be activated by choosing their respective buttons from the **Circle** dialog box that are displayed when you invoke the **Circle** tool. These methods of drawing circles are discussed next.

Drawing a Circle by Specifying the Center Point and Diameter

This method is active by default when you invoke the **Circle** tool and is the most widely used method of drawing circles. In this method, you need to specify the center point of a circle and a point on the circumference of the circle. The point on the circumference of the circle defines the radius or the diameter of the circle. To draw a circle using this method, choose the **Circle by Center and Diameter** button from the **Circle** dialog box; you will be prompted to specify the center point of the circle. Specify the center point of the circle in the drawing window. Next, you will be prompted to specify a point. Specify a point to define the radius. Alternatively, you can enter the value of the diameter in the dynamic input box. Figure 2-21 shows a circle being drawn by using this method.

Tip: *After specifying the center point of the circle, if you specify the value of diameter in the dynamic input box, the circle of the specified diameter will be created. Also, the preview of the circle of the same diameter will be attached to the cursor. Now, you can place multiple copies of the circle by specifying the center point.*

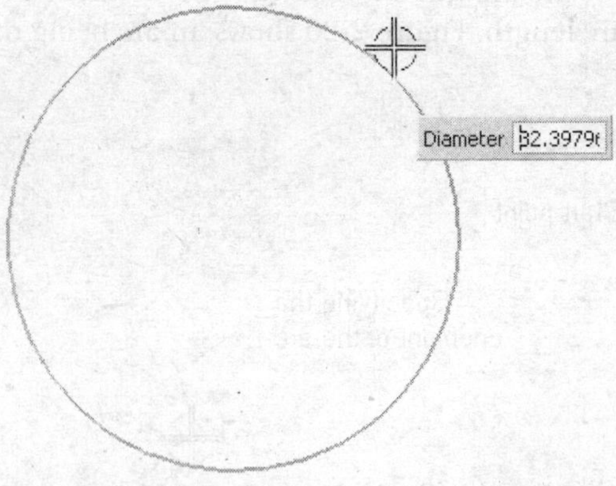

Figure 2-21 Drawing a circle using the Circle by Center and Diameter method

Drawing a Circle by Specifying Three Points

This method is used to draw a circle by specifying three points on circumference. To invoke this method, choose the **Circle by 3 Points** button from the **Circle** dialog box; you will be prompted to specify the first point of the circle. This point is actually the first point on the circumference of the circle. After specifying the first point, you will be prompted to specify the second point of the circle. On specifying these two points, small reference circles will be displayed on these two points, as shown in Figure 2-22. Now, specify the third point, which is a point on the circle. You can also enter its diameter value in the **Diameter** input box. This completes the creation of the circle.

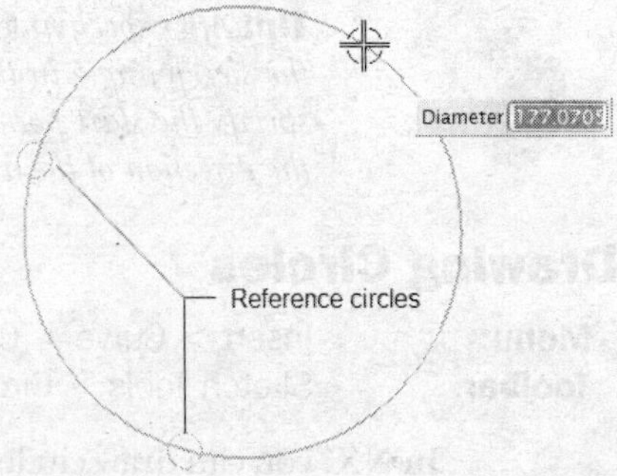

Figure 2-22 Drawing a circle using the Circle by 3 Points method

Drawing Rectangles

Menu: Insert > Curve > Rectangle
Toolbar: Sketch Tools > Rectangle

In NX, you can draw rectangles using three methods. These methods can be used by choosing their respective buttons from the **Rectangle** dialog box. To invoke this dialog box, choose the **Rectangle** button from the **Sketch Tools** toolbar. Alternatively, choose **Insert > Curve > Rectangle** from the menu bar to display the **Rectangle** dialog box. The three methods of drawing rectangles are discussed next.

Drawing Rectangles by Specifying Corners

The By 2 Points method is used to draw a rectangle by specifying the diagonally opposite corners of rectangle. When you invoke the **Rectangle** tool, the **By 2 Points** button will be chosen by default in the **Rectangle Method** area of the **Rectangle** dialog box. Also, you will be prompted to specify the first point of the rectangle. This point will work as one of the corners of the rectangle. After specifying the first point, you will be prompted to specify the point to create the rectangle. This point will be diagonally opposite to the point that you have specified earlier. You can click anywhere on the screen to specify the second corner or enter the width and height of the rectangle in the dynamic input boxes. Figure 2-23 shows a rectangle being drawn by using the By 2 Points method.

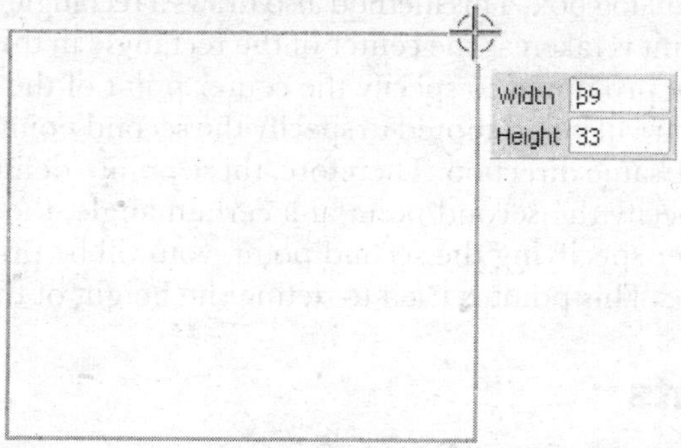

Figure 2-23 Rectangle being drawn by using the By 2 Points method

Tip: *If you specify the width and height of a rectangle in the dynamic input boxes after specifying the first point, the preview of the rectangle with the specified width and height will be attached to the cursor. Now, you need to specify a point to define the direction of rectangle.*

Drawing Three Points Rectangles

You can draw a three points rectangle by choosing the **By 3 Points** button from the **Rectangle** dialog box. This method draws a rectangle using three points. The first two points are used to define the length and angle of one of the sides of the rectangle and the third point is used to define the height of the rectangle. When you invoke this method, you will be prompted to specify the first point of the rectangle. Once you specify the first point, you will be prompted to specify the second point of the rectangle. Both these corners are along the same direction. Therefore, these points define the length and orientation of the rectangle. Note that if you specify the second point at a certain angle, the resulting rectangle will also be at an angle. After specifying the second point, you will be prompted to specify a point to create the rectangle. This point is used to define the height of the rectangle. After specifying the first point, you can also specify the height, width, and the angle of the rectangle in the dynamic input boxes. Figure 2-24 shows an inclined rectangle drawn by using the By 3 Points method.

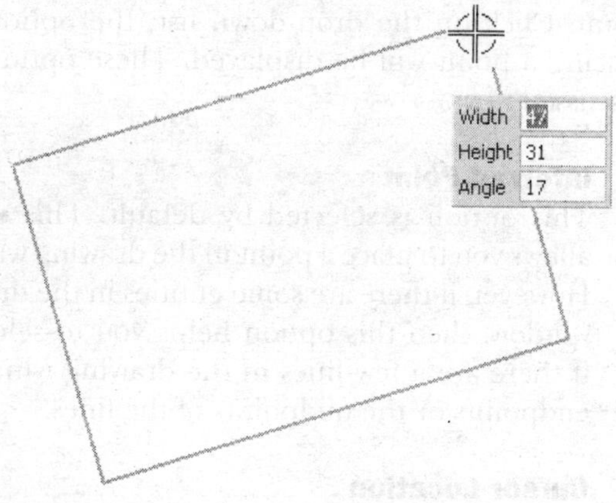

Figure 2-24 Inclined rectangle drawn by using the By 3 Points method

Tip: *After specifying the first point of a rectangle, you can toggle between the **By 2 Points** and **By 3 Points** buttons by dragging the left mouse button.*

Drawing Centerpoint Rectangles

You can draw a centerpoint rectangle by choosing the **From Center** button in the **Rectangle** dialog box. This method also draws a rectangle using three points. However, the first point is taken as the center of the rectangle in this case. When you invoke this method, you will be prompted to specify the center point of the rectangle. Once you specify the center point, you will be prompted to specify the second point of the rectangle. Both these points are along the same direction. Therefore, these points define the width of the rectangle. Note that if you specify the second point at a certain angle, the resulting rectangle will also be at an angle. After specifying the second point, you will be prompted to specify a point to create the rectangle. This point is used to define the height of the rectangle.

Placing Points

Menu:	Insert > Datum/Point > Point
Toolbar:	Sketch Tools > Point

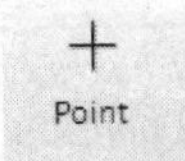

In NX, points are placed by using the **Point** dialog box. To invoke this dialog box, choose the **Point** button from the **Sketch Tools** toolbar; the **Point** dialog box will be displayed, refer to Figure 2-25 and you will be prompted to select the object to infer point. This dialog box contains four main rollouts, **Type**, **Point Location**, **Coordinates**, and **Offset**. The options in these rollouts are discussed next.

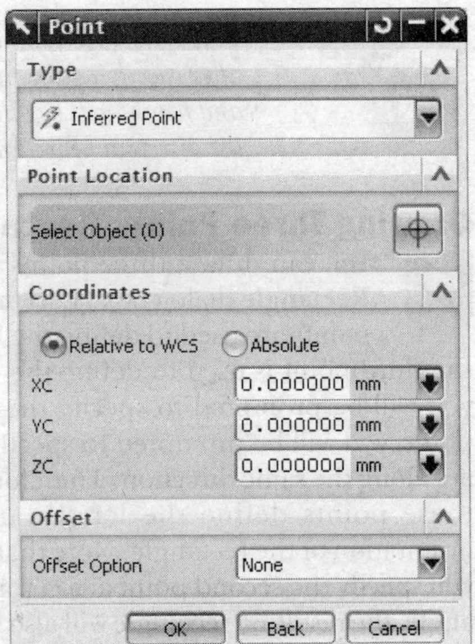

***Figure 2-25** The **Point** dialog box*

Type Rollout

This rollout has a drop-down list from which you can select a method to specify the location for the resulting point. Click on the drop-down list; the options for placing a point will be displayed. These options are discussed next.

Inferred Point

This option is selected by default. This option allows you to place a point in the drawing window. However, if there are some entities in the drawing window, then this option helps you to select the keypoints of the entity. For example, if there are a few lines in the drawing window, then this option helps you to select the endpoints or the midpoints of the lines.

Cursor Location

This option allows you to place a point at a location where you will click the cursor in the drawing window. If the **Cursor Location** option is selected, then the other entities in the drawing window will not be considered.

Existing Point

This option allows you to select the points that are already placed in the drawing window. As a result, you can place new point on top of the existing point.

End Point

This option allows you to place the point at the endpoint of the existing lines, arcs, or splines.

Control Point

This option allows you to place the point at the control point of the existing sketched entities. The control points include the endpoints and midpoints of lines or arcs, center points of circles, ellipses, control points of splines, and so on.

Intersection Point

This option allows you to place the point at the intersection point of the two existing sketched entities. To do so, select the **Intersection Point** option from the drop-down list in the **Type** rollout; you will be prompted to select the first and second intersecting entities. Specify the two intersecting entities in the drawing area; a point will be placed at the intersection point of the two existing entities.

Arc/Ellipse/Sphere Center

This option allows you to place the point at the center of an existing arc, circle, ellipse, or sphere.

Angle on Arc/Ellipse

This option allows you to place the point on the circumference of the selected arc, circle, or ellipse such that the resulting point is at the specified angle with respect to X-axis. When you choose this option, the **Point** dialog box will be modified and you will be prompted to select an arc or ellipse. Select the arc or ellipse in the drawing; the point will be placed on the circumference of the selected entity. Next, enter the angle value for the point in the **Angle** edit box of the **Angle on Curve** rollout.

Quadrant Point

This option allows you to place the point at the quadrant of a circle, arc, or an ellipse. The point will be placed at the quadrant that is closest to the current location of the cursor.

Point on Curve/Edge

This option allows you to place the point on the selected curve or edge. The location of the point is defined in terms of its curve parameter percentage from the start point of the curve. When you select the **Point on Curve/Edge** option, the **Point** dialog box will be modified and you will be prompted to select the curve to specify the point location. Click anywhere on the curve or the edge; you will be prompted to specify the curve parameter percentage. Next, enter the distance of the point, in terms of curve parameter percentage (0 to 1), from the start point of the curve in the **U Parameter** edit box of the **Location on Curve** rollout.

Point on Face
This option allows you to place the point on the selected face. The location of the point is defined by specifying values in the **U Parameter** and **V Parameter** edit boxes. The **U Parameter** edit box is used to specify the horizontal position of the point, where as the **V Parameter** is used to specify the vertical position of the point. The values of these edit boxes must be between 0.0 and 1.0. As value of the **U Parameter** edit box increases, the position of the point shifts from right to left; and if the value of the **V Parameter** edit box increases, the position of the point shifts from bottom to top.

Between Two Points
This option allows you to create a point between two existing points or between two keypoints of an entity. When you select this option from the **Type** drop-down list, the **Point** dialog box will be modified and you will be prompted to select object to infer point. Select the first point from the drawing window; you will be prompted again to select object to infer point. Select the second point; a point will be created between the two selected points. You can change the location of this point by entering the percentage value in the **%Location** edit box of the **Location Between Points** rollout.

By Expression
This option allows you to specify a point expression by using the X, Y, and Z coordinates. When you select this option from the **Type** drop-down list, the **Point** dialog box will be modified with new rollouts such as **Choose Expression**, **Coordinates**, and **Offset**. The **Choose Expression** rollout is used to display the point expression created already in the part. To create a new expression, choose the **Create Expression** button; the **Expressions** dialog box will be displayed. Enter the name of the point expression in the **Name** edit box, and then edit the point formula as per your requirement in the **Formula** edit box. Once you have edited the values of the X, Y, and Z coordinates in the **Formula** edit box, the **Accept Edit** button will be available. Choose the **Accept Edit** button and then choose the **OK** button from this dialog box; the **Point** dialog box will be displayed. The newly created point expression will be listed in the **Expression** list area of the **Choose Expression** rollout. Select the point expression from the list and then choose the **OK** button from the **Point** dialog box; a point will be created with the specified coordinates in the expression.

Point Location Rollout
This rollout is used to select a point and will not be available for the **Intersection Point**, **Angle on Arc/Ellipse**, **Point on Curve/Edge**, and **Point on Face** options.

Coordinates Rollout
This rollout is used to enter the X, Y, and Z coordinates to specify the location of the point. Also, you can specify or determine the 3D location of the points using this rollout. You can specify the point relative to the Work Coordinate System (WCS) or Absolute Coordinate System by selecting their respective radio buttons.

Offset Rollout
This rollout is used to create a point at a specified distance from a pre-selected point. You can select an option to specify the distance of the required point from the **Offset Option** drop-down list in this rollout. The options in this drop-down list are discussed next.

Rectangular
This option allows you to create a point by specifying its X, Y, Z coordinates with respect to the pre-selected point in the **Delta XC**, **Delta YC**, and **Delta ZC** edit boxes, respectively.

Cylindrical
This option allows you to create a point according to the cylindrical coordinate system with respect to the pre-selected point by specifying the radius, angle, and Z direction in the **Radius**, **Angle**, and **Delta Z** edit boxes, respectively.

Spherical
This option allows you to create a point according to the spherical coordinate system with respect to the pre-selected point by specifying the **Radius**, **Angle 1**, and **Angle 2** in their respective edit boxes.

Along Vector
This option allows you to create a point along the specified vector direction at a distance specified in the **Distance** edit box.

Along Curve
This option allows you to create a point on the specified curve. The distance of the point on arc can be specified by entering the **Arc Length** or **Percentage** value in the respective edit box.

Tip: *By default, some of the tools are not available in the toolbars. However, you can customize the toolbars to add these tools. To customize the toolbars, choose the black arrow at the bottom of the vertical toolbar or on the right of the horizontal toolbar. When you choose this arrow; a cascading menu will be displayed. Select **Add or Remove Buttons** from the cascading menu; another cascading menu will be displayed with the names of a few toolbars. Move-the cursor over the name of the toolbar in which you need to add more tools; another cascading menu will be displayed with all the tools that can be added to the selected toolbar. Note that all the tools that are currently available in the toolbar will have a check mark on their left. Select the name of the tools which you want to add to the toolbar; the selected tools will be added at the end of the toolbar.*

Drawing Ellipses or Elliptical Arcs

Menu:	Insert > Curve > Ellipse
Toolbar:	Sketch Tools > Conic > Ellipse *(Customize to add)*

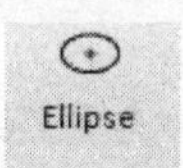

In NX, you can draw ellipses or elliptical arcs by using the **Ellipse** tool. To invoke this tool, choose **Insert > Curve > Ellipse** option from the menu bar; the **Ellipse** dialog box will be displayed, as shown in Figure 2-26. Also, you will be prompted to select the object to infer a point. Select the **Point Constructor** button from the **Center** rollout; the **Point** dialog box will be displayed, refer to Figure 2-25. Using the **Point** dialog box, you can define the center point of ellipse. Alternatively, you can define the center point of the ellipse by selecting the required option from the drop-down list available on the right of the **Point Constructor** button. After defining the center point by using the **Point** dialog box, choose the **OK** button from it; the **Ellipse** dialog box will be displayed again. Also, the preview of the ellipse will be displayed. Next, specify the major and the minor radii of the ellipse in the **Major Radius** and **Minor Radius** edit boxes in the **Ellipse** dialog box, respectively. If you want to draw an elliptical arc, clear the **Closed** check box in the **Limits** rollout; the **Ellipse** dialog box will be modified and the **Start Angle** and **End Angle** edit boxes for the arc will appear in it. You can specify the start and end angles in their respective edit boxes. Figure 2-27 shows the parameters related to an ellipse and Figure 2-28 shows the parameters related to an elliptical arc. If you want to retain the complement of the elliptical arc, choose the **Complement** button below the **End Angle** edit box in the **Limits** rollout; the preview of the complement of the elliptical arc will be displayed. Figure 2-29 shows an elliptical arc and Figure 2-30 shows the complement of the elliptical arc. Note that Figure 2-27 shows an inclined ellipse. To create an inclined ellipse, you need to enter rotation angle in the **Angle** edit box of the **Rotation** rollout. The specified angle value will be measured with respect to X-axis in counterclockwise direction.

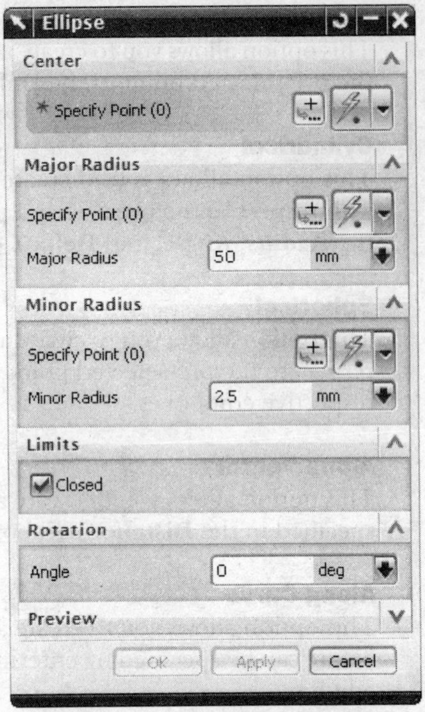

***Figure 2-26** The **Ellipse** dialog box*

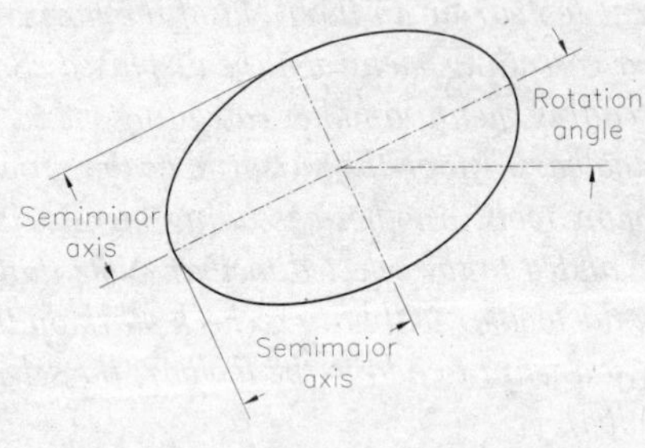

***Figure 2-27** Parameters related to an ellipse*

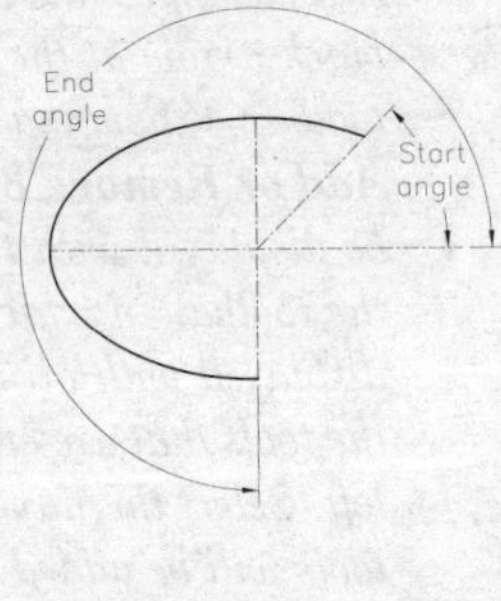

***Figure 2-28** Parameters related to an elliptical arc*

***Figure 2-29** An elliptical arc*

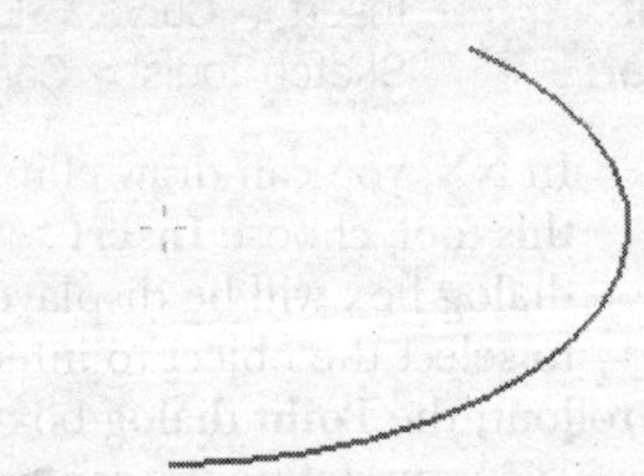

***Figure 2-30** Complement of the elliptical arc shown in Figure 2-29*

Tip: *Sometimes while placing points or drawing an ellipse, some red cross marks are displayed on the screen. To remove them, refresh the screen by pressing the F5 key.*

Drawing Conics

Menu: Insert > Curve > Conic
Toolbar: Sketch Tools > Conic *(Customize to add)*

The **Conic** tool allows you to create a conic section in the Sketcher environment using three points. The first two points define the endpoints of the conic and the third point defines the apex of the conic. Also, you need to specify the projective discriminant value, termed as rho value. To invoke the **Conic** tool, choose **Insert > Curve > Conic** from the menu bar; the **Conic** dialog box will be displayed, as shown in Figure 2-31. In this dialog box, you can specify the start point and endpoint of the conic using the options in the **Limits** rollout. After specifying the start point and the endpoint of the conic, you need to specify the apex of the conic as the third point. Specify the apex of the conic by using the options in the **Specify Control Point** area of the **Control Point** rollout. Next, enter the Rho value in the **Value** edit box. This rho value will define the exact shape of conics.

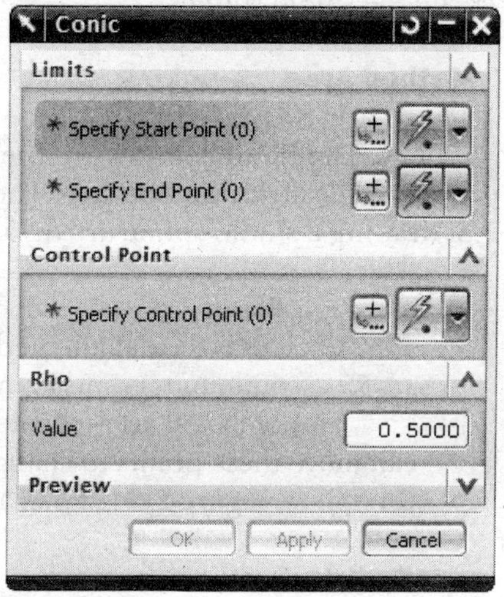

Figure 2-31 *The **Conic** dialog box*

If $0 < \text{Rho} < 0.5$, then conics of elliptical shape will be created.
If $\text{Rho} = 0.5$, then conics of parabolic shape will be created.
If $0.5 < \text{Rho} < 1$, then conics of hyperbolic shape will be created.

Figure 2-32 shows conics with different rho values.

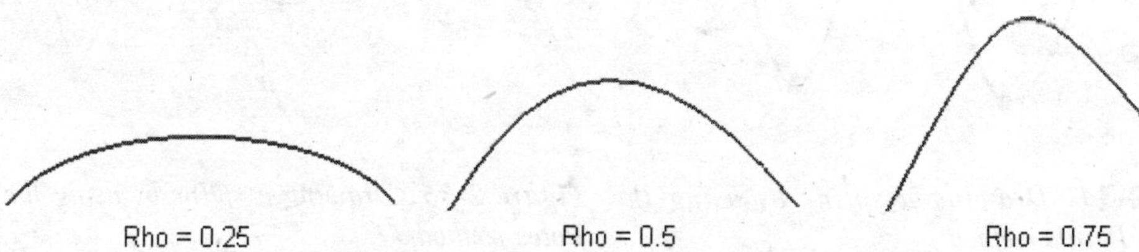

Figure 2-32 *Conics with different rho values*

Drawing Studio Splines

Menu: Insert > Curve > Studio Spline
Toolbar: Sketch Tools > Studio Spline

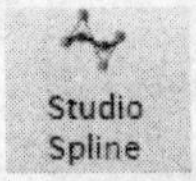

This tool allows you to create studio splines for creating free form features. When you invoke this tool, the **Studio Spline** dialog box will be displayed, as shown in Figure 2-33. The various rollouts in this dialog box are discussed next.

***Figure 2-33** The **Studio Spline** dialog box*

Spline Setting Rollout

This rollout contains different methods and options to create the studio splines.

Method Area

There are two methods of drawing studio splines. The buttons to invoke these methods are available in the **Method** area. These methods of drawing a studio spline are discussed next.

Through Points

This is the default method of drawing splines. In this method, you can specify continuous points in the drawing area by clicking the left mouse button. These points will act as the defining points of the spline. While drawing a spline, you can move these points to change the shape of the spline, and then continue drawing the spline. Figure 2-34 shows a spline being drawn by using this method.

By Poles

If you use this method, the points that you specify in the drawing window act as the poles of the spline. Figure 2-35 shows a spline being drawn by using this method. Remember that the display of poles is automatically removed when you finish drawing the spline.

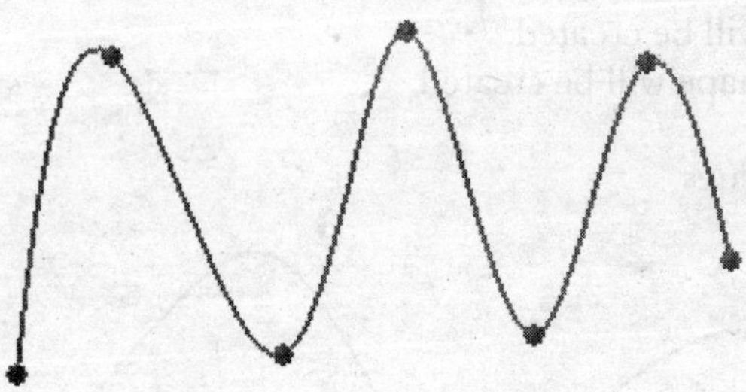

***Figure 2-34** Drawing a spline by using the **Through Points** method*

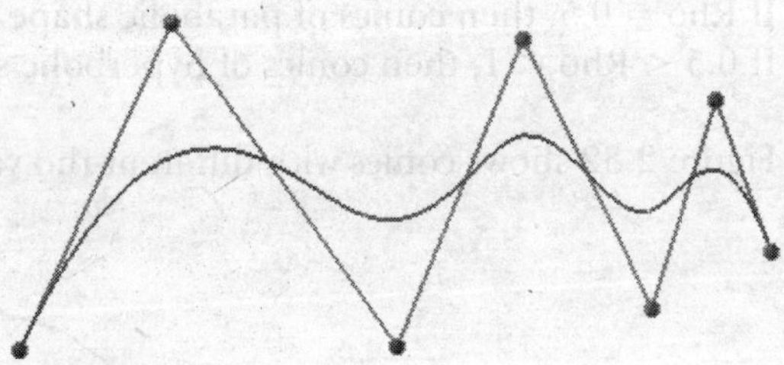

***Figure 2-35** Drawing a spline by using the **By Poles** method*

Degree Spinner

The **Degree** spinner is used to specify the degree of a spline. Figures 2-36 and 2-37 show splines of various degrees. Note that the degree of a spline cannot be more than the number of poles used to draw it.

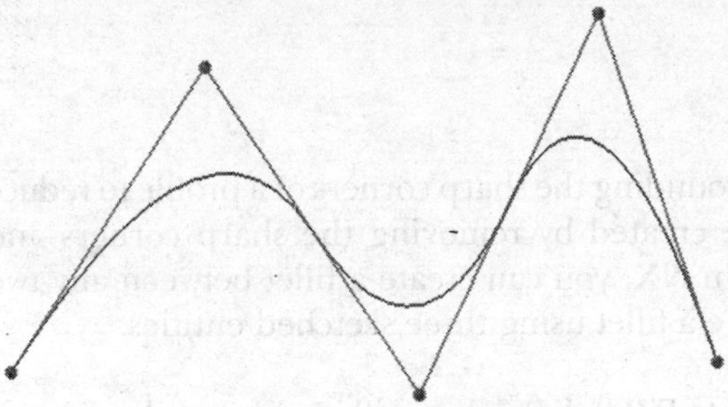

Figure 2-36 Spline of degree 2

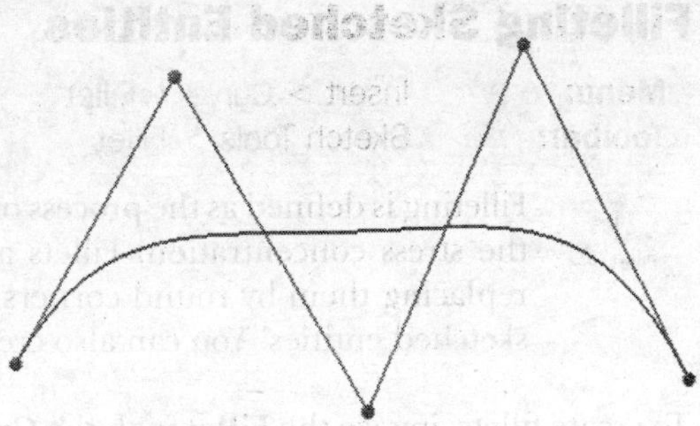

Figure 2-37 Spline of degree 4

Single Segment
This check box is available only with the **By Poles** method and is used to create a single segment spline. However, you can specify as many numbers of poles as you require. If you select this check box, the **Degree** spinner will not be available.

Matched Knot Position
This check box is available only with the **Through Points** method and is used to create a spline by matching the position of the defining points with the knots. In this case, the knots are placed only at the places where the defining points are specified. If you select this check box, the **Closed** check box will not be available.

Closed
This check box is available for both the methods and is used to create closed splines. Figure 2-38 shows a closed spline.

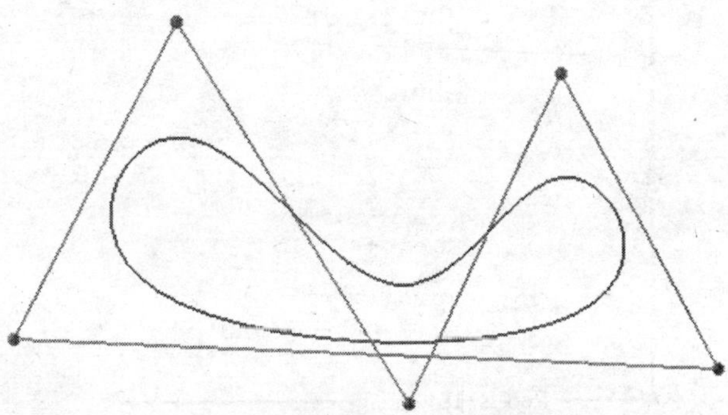

Figure 2-38 A closed spline

Associative
The **Associative** check box is used to make the spline associative to its parent feature. This means that if you modify the parent feature, the spline will also be modified. By default, this check box is cleared, which means there is no associativity of the spline with its parent feature.

Filleting Sketched Entities

Menu:	Insert > Curve > Fillet
Toolbar:	Sketch Tools > Fillet

Filleting is defined as the process of rounding the sharp corners of a profile to reduce the stress concentration. Fillets are created by removing the sharp corners and replacing them by round corners. In NX, you can create a fillet between any two sketched entities. You can also create a fillet using three sketched entities.

To create fillets, invoke the **Fillet** tool; the **Create Fillet** dialog box will be displayed, as shown in Figure 2-39. Also, you will be prompted to select or drag the cursor over curves to create a fillet.

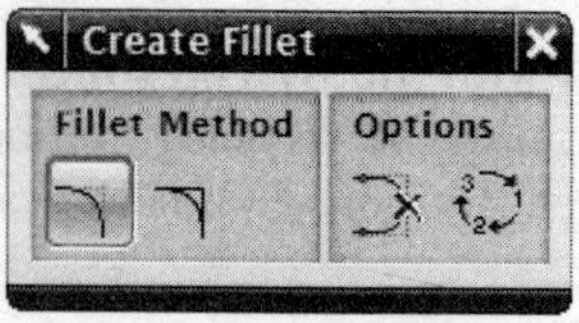

***Figure 2-39** The **Create Fillet** dialog box*

The **Radius** dynamic input box will be displayed below the cursor. You do not need to necessarily specify the fillet radius in advance. Instead, you can select the two entities to fillet and then move the cursor to define the radius of the fillet. Figure 2-40 shows the preview of a fillet being created between two lines. In this case, the radius value is not defined in advance. As a result, as you move the cursor, the fillet radius is modified dynamically. The **Create Fillet** dialog box is divided into two areas, **Fillet Method** and **Options**.

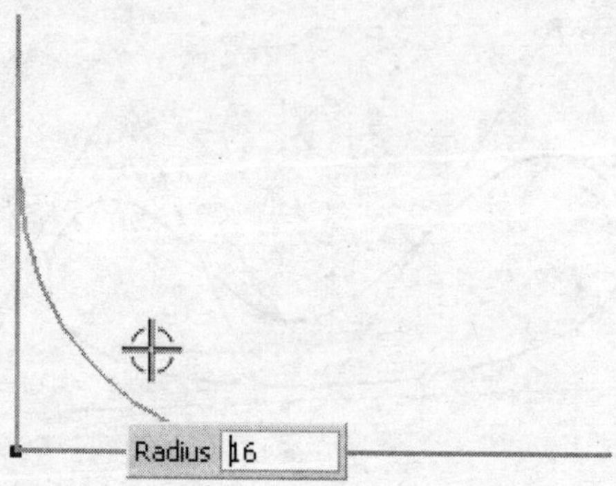

***Figure 2-40** Preview of a fillet being created between two lines*

Fillet Method

The first button in this area is the **Trim** button and is chosen by default. As a result, the sharp corner will automatically be trimmed after filleting, as shown in Figure 2-41. If you choose the **Untrim** button, the sharp corner will not be trimmed after filleting, as shown in Figure 2-42.

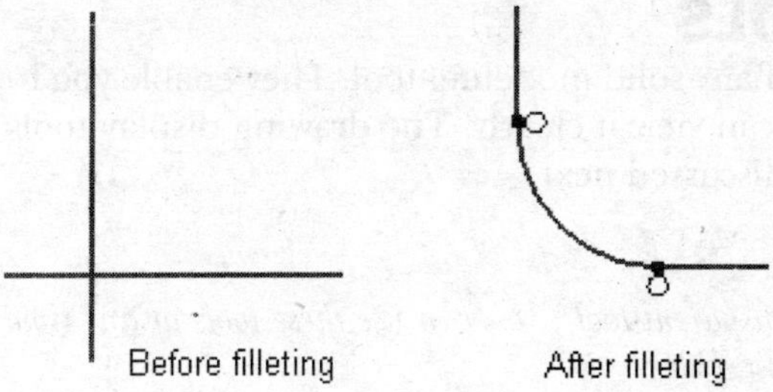

*Figure 2-41 Sharp corner before and after filleting using the **Trim** button*

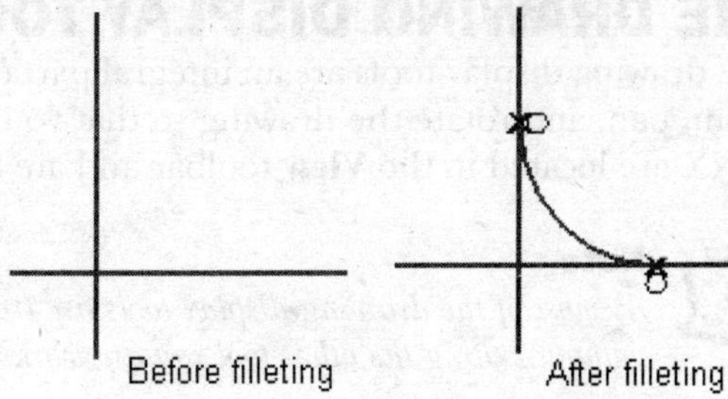

*Figure 2-42 Sharp corner before and after filleting using the **Untrim** button*

Tip: *Ideally, the profiles created with the fillet may not give the desired result when used to create features. Therefore, they should be avoided in the **Sketcher** environment.*

Options Area

The **Delete Third Curve** button in this area is useful if you are creating a fillet by using three entities. While using this option, the middle entity should be selected last. This button ensures that if the fillet is tangent to the middle entity then the middle entity is automatically deleted, as shown in Figure 2-43. If this button is deactivated, the middle entity will not be deleted, as shown Figure 2-44. The **Create Alternate Fillet** button in this area will show all alternative solutions for the fillet. It is recommended that this button should be turned off.

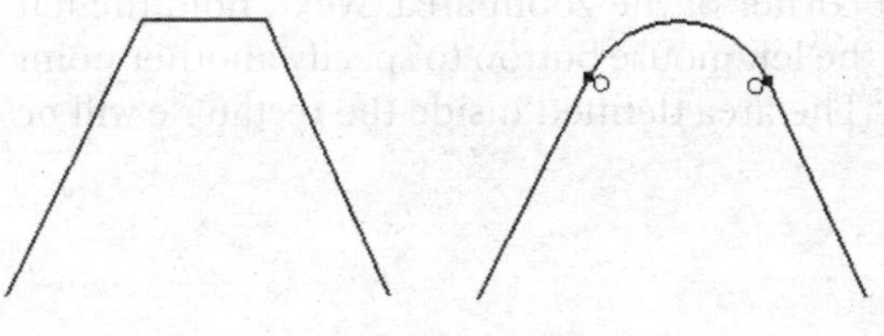

Figure 2-43 Before and after filleting with the third curve deleted

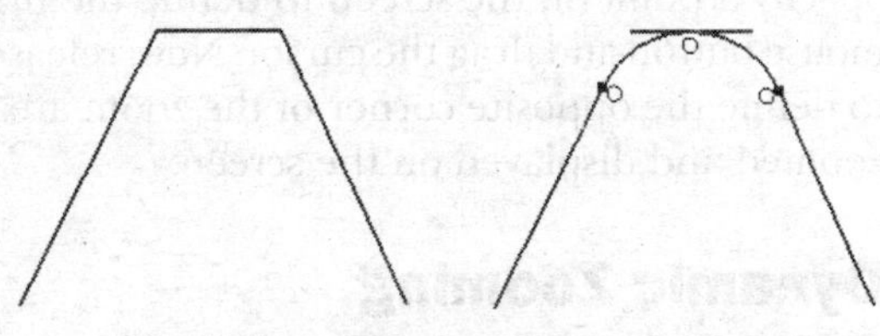

Figure 2-44 Before and after filleting with the third curve retained

Tip: *In NX, you can create fillets by simply dragging the cursor across the entities that you need to fillet. For example, if you need to fillet two lines, invoke the **Fillet** tool and drag the cursor across them; the corner of these two lines will be filleted. The radius of the fillet will depend on how far you dragged the mouse from the corner.*

When you fillet two entities, and there are more than one solution for fillet. The best solution is displayed by default. If you want to view the alternate solution, press the PAGE UP key.

THE DRAWING DISPLAY TOOLS

The drawing display tools are an integral part of any solid modeling tool. They enable you to zoom, pan, and rotate the drawing so that you can view it clearly. The drawing display tools in NX are located in the **View** toolbar and are discussed next.

Note

As most of the drawing display tools are transparent tools, you can use these tools at any time without exiting the other tool you are working with.

Fitting Entities in the Current Display

Menu:	View > Operation > Fit
Toolbar:	View > Fit

The **Fit** tool enables you to modify the drawing display area such that all entities in the drawing fit in the current display. You can also use the CTRL+F keys to fit the entities in the current display.

Zooming to an Area

Menu:	View > Operation > Zoom
Toolbar:	View > Zoom

The **Zoom** tool allows you to zoom in to a particular area by defining a box around it. When you choose this tool, the default cursor is replaced by the magnifying glass cursor and you will be prompted to drag the cursor to indicate the zoom rectangle. Specify a point on the screen to define the first corner of the zoom area. Next, hold the left mouse button and drag the cursor. Now, release the left mouse button to specify another point to define the opposite corner of the zoom area. The area defined inside the rectangle will be zoomed and displayed on the screen.

Dynamic Zooming

Toolbar:	View > Zoom In/Out

The **Zoom In/Out** tool enables you to dynamically zoom in or out of the drawing. When you invoke this tool, the default cursor is changed into a magnifying glass cursor with a '+' and a '-' sign at the center of the cursor. To zoom in, press and hold the left mouse button in the drawing window and then drag the cursor down. Similarly, to zoom out, press and hold the left mouse button and drag the cursor upward.

Tip: *NX allows you to restore the view, before it was modified using the* ***Zoom*** *or the* ***Zoom In/Out*** *tool. This can be done by choosing* ***View > Operation > Unzoom*** *from the menu bar.*

Panning Drawings

Toolbar: View > Pan

The **Pan** tool allows you to dynamically pan drawings in the drawing window. When you invoke this tool, the cursor is replaced by a hand cursor and you are prompted to drag the cursor to pan the view. Press and hold the left mouse button in the drawing window and then drag the mouse to pan the drawing.

*Tip: In NX, you can also display the Selection MiniBar and the View shortcut menu by right-clicking in the drawing area. The Selection MiniBar is the compact version of the **Selection bar**.*

Fitting View to Selection

Toolbar: View > Fit View to Selection

This tool zooms the display such that the selected entity fits in the current display area. This tool is available only when an entity is selected in the drawing window.

Restoring the Original Orientation of the Sketching Plane

Menu: View > Orient View to Sketch
Toolbar: Sketcher > Orient View to Sketch

Sometimes while using the drawing display tools, you may change the orientation of the sketching plane. The **Orient View to Sketch** tool restores the original orientation that was active when you invoked the Sketcher environment. This tool is available only in the Sketcher environment.

SETTING SELECTION FILTERS IN THE SKETCHER ENVIRONMENT

NX provides you with various object selection filters in the Sketcher environment. These filters allow you to define the type of entities you want to select. All these filters are available in the **Selection Bar** on the upper left corner of the drawing window. Some of these filters are discussed next.

Type Filter

The **Type Filter** drop-down list is used to specify the type of entity to be selected. By default, the **No Selection Filter** option is selected, refer to Figure 2-45. This option allows you to select any entity from the drawing window. These entities include curves, points, dimensions, symbols, sketch constraints, and so on. Select the required entity from the **Type Filter** drop-down list. Now, you can select only the specified entity from the drawing window.

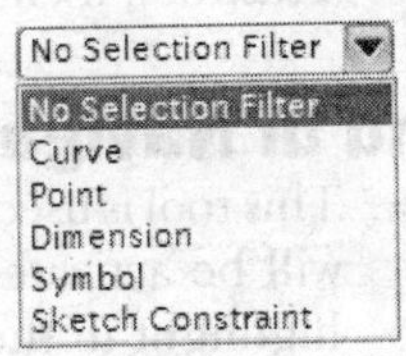

***Figure 2-45** The **Type Filter** drop-down list*

Selection Scope

This drop-down list allows you to filter the selection from the entire assembly, workpart only, or from the active sketch only. Select the required option from the **Selection Scope** drop-down list.

General Selection Filters

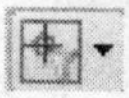

This tool is used to provide the detailed filter options. When you choose this tool, the **General Selection Filters** flyout will be displayed, as shown in Figure 2-46. The options in this flyout are discussed next.

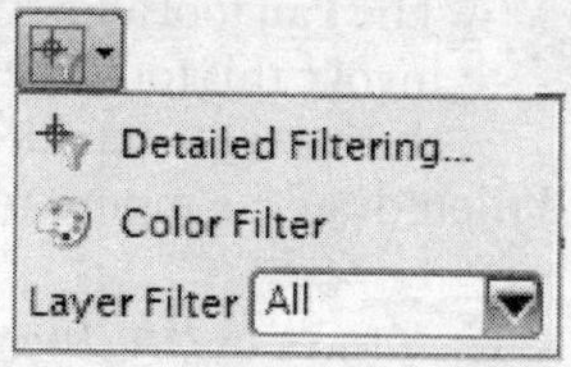

*Figure 2-46 The **General Selection Filters** flyout*

Detailed Filtering

This option is used to filter the selection using layers, types of entity, display attributes, and detailed types of entity. Select the **Detailed Filtering** option in the **General Selection Filter** flyout; the **Detailed Filtering** dialog box will be displayed. In this dialog box, you can specify layers, types of entity, detailed types of entity, and display attributes to be filtered.

Color Filter

This option allows you to filter the selection using a specific color. Only the entities in the specified color will be selected.

Layer Filter

This drop-down list allows you to filter the selection using a specific layer. You need to select the layer from the **Layer Filter** drop-down list and the entities in this layer can only be selected. By default, the **All** option is selected, which allows to select the entities from all the layers.

Reset Filters

This tool is used to reset all filtering options defined in the **General Selection Filters** flyout and the **Type Filter** drop-down list to their default states.

Allow Selection of Hidden Wireframe

This tool allows you to select the hidden wireframe geometries such as curves and edges.

Deselect All

This tool, if chosen, deselects all currently selected entities.

Find in Navigator

This tool is used to highlight the selected entities in the **Part** or **Assembly Navigator** and will be activated only when you select an entity. Select the entities that you want to highlight in the **Part** or **Assembly Navigator** and choose the **Find in Navigator** tool in the **Selection Bar**. Next, choose the **Part Navigator** tab from the **Resource Bar** to view the highlighted entities.

SELECTING OBJECTS

After setting the selection filters, you can select objects in the Sketcher environment of NX. When there is no tool active in the Sketcher environment, the select mode will be invoked. In this mode, you can select individual sketched entities from the drawing window by clicking on them. To select multiple entities, you can use the following two methods:

Rectangle

If you choose this tool from the **Selection Bar** and drag the cursor in the drawing window, temporary rectangle will be created according to the movement of the cursor. Also, all entities lying completely within the temporary rectangle will get selected.

Lasso

If you choose this tool from the **Selection Bar** and drag the cursor in the drawing window, a temporary free form curve will be created according to the movement of the cursor. Also, all entities lying completely within the free form curve will get selected.

DESELECTING OBJECTS

By default, the selected objects are displayed in orange color. If you want to deselect the individual objects from the selection, press and hold the SHIFT key and click on it; the entity will be deselected. If you want to deselect all the selected entities, press the ESC key. Alternatively, press and hold the SHIFT key and drag a box around the entities; all entities that lie completely inside the box will get deselected. Also, you can choose the **Deselect All** tool from the **Selection Bar** to deselect all the selected entities.

USING SNAP POINTS OPTIONS WHILE SKETCHING

While drawing in the Sketcher environment, you will notice that the cursor automatically snaps to some keypoints of the sketched entities. For example, if you are specifying the center point of a circle and you move the cursor close to the endpoint of an existing line, the cursor snaps to the endpoint of the line and changes its shape to the snap cursor. Also, the endpoint snap symbol is displayed below the cursor. This suggests that the endpoint of the line has been snapped and if you click now, the center point of the circle will coincide with the endpoint of the line.

NX allows you to control these snap settings using the snap points option tools in the **Selection Bar**, as shown in Figure 2-47. In this bar, some tools are chosen, by default. You can choose more tools to turn on the respective snapping option.

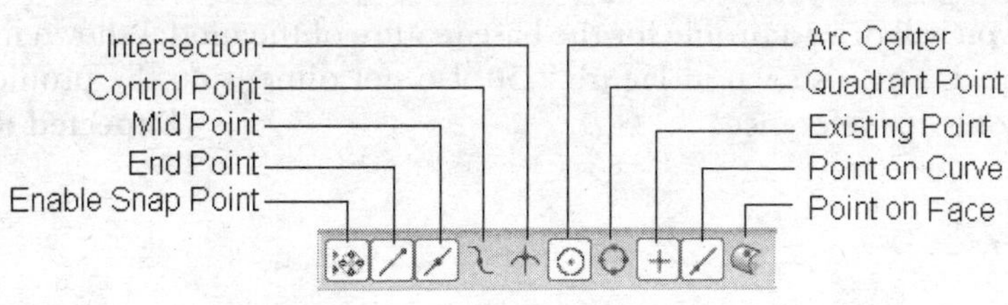

***Figure 2-47** Buttons used for snap settings*

Note

The tools to control these snap settings are available only in the Sketcher environment.

DELETING SKETCHED ENTITIES

Menu: Edit > Delete
Toolbar: Standard > Delete *(Customize to add)*

You can delete the sketched entities by selecting them and pressing the DELETE key. You can also choose the **Delete** button from the **Standard** toolbar to delete the sketched entities. If you select the entities and then choose the **Delete** button, the selected entities will be deleted. However, if you choose this button without selecting any sketched entity, the **Sketcher Delete** dialog box will be displayed, as shown in Figure 2-48. You can now select the entities to be deleted and then choose the **OK** button in this dialog box. To close the dialog box, choose the **Back** or **Cancel** button.

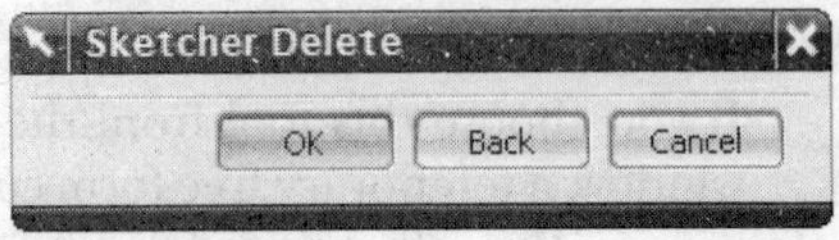

*Figure 2-48 The **Sketcher Delete** dialog box*

EXITING THE SKETCHER ENVIRONMENT

Menu: Sketch > Finish Sketch
Toolbar: Sketcher > Finish Sketch

After drawing the sketch, you need to exit the Sketcher environment to convert the sketch into a feature. To exit the Sketcher environment, choose the **Finish Sketch** button from the **Sketcher** toolbar. Alternatively, right-click in the drawing area and select the **Finish Sketch** option from the shortcut menu. When you exit the Sketcher environment, the **Modeling** environment is invoked and the current view is changed to the Trimetric view.

TUTORIALS

As mentioned in the introduction, NX is parametric in nature. Therefore, you can draw a sketch of any dimensions and then modify its size by changing the values of dimensions. However, in this chapter, you will use the dynamic input boxes to draw the sketch of exact dimensions. This will help you in improving your sketching skills.

Tutorial 1

In this tutorial, you will draw a profile for the base feature of the model shown in Figure 2-49. The profile to be drawn is shown in Figure 2-50. Do not dimension the profile because the dimensions are only for reference. **(Expected time: 30 min)**

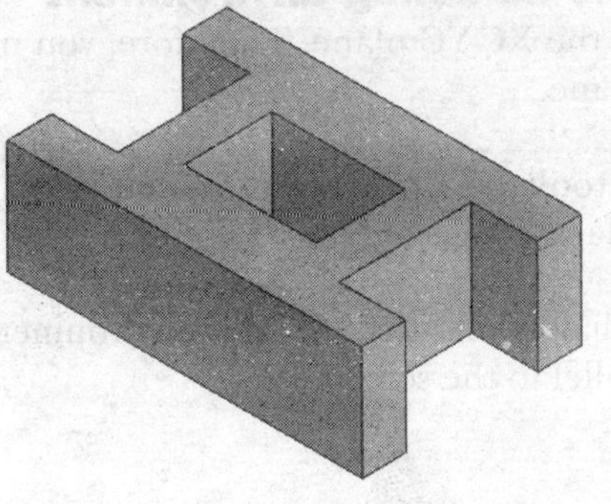

Figure 2-49 Model for Tutorial 1

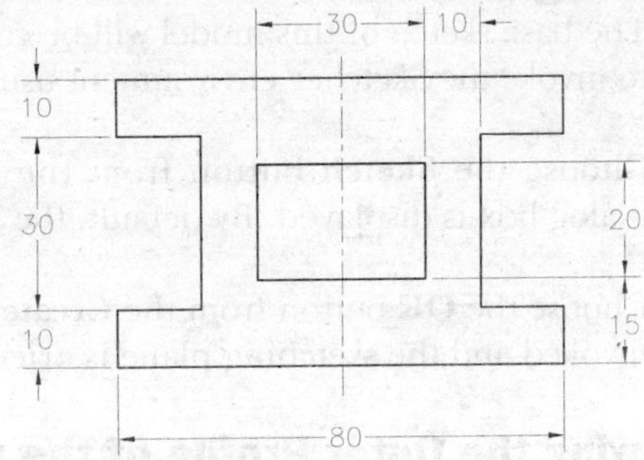

Figure 2-50 Sketch for Tutorial 1

The following steps are required to complete this tutorial:

a. Start a new file.
b. Select the XC-YC plane as the sketching plane and invoke the Sketcher environment.
c. Draw the sketch of the model by using the **Profile** and **Rectangle** tools.
d. Finish the sketch and save the file.

Starting NX 7 and Starting a New File

First, you need to start NX 7 and then start a new file.

1. Choose the **Start** button at the lower left corner of the screen to display a menu with additional options. Next, choose **All Programs (or Programs) > UGS NX 7.0 > NX 7.0** to start NX 7. Alternatively, double-click on NX 7.0 shortcut icon on the desktop of your computer.

2. To start a new file, choose the **New** button from the **Standard** toolbar or choose **File > New** from the menu bar; the **New** dialog box is displayed.

3. Select the **Model** template from the **Templates** rollout.

4. Enter ***c02tut1*** as the name of the document in the **Name** text box of the dialog box.

5. Choose the button on the right of the **Folder** text box; the **Choose Directory** dialog box is displayed.

It is recommended that you create a folder with the name NX 7 in the hard drive of your computer and then create separate folders for each chapter inside it for saving the tutorial files of this textbook.

6. In this dialog box, browse to *NX 7/c02* folder and then choose the **OK** button twice; the new file is started in the Modeling environment.

Invoking the Sketcher Environment in the Modeling Environment

The base sketch of this model will be created on the XC-YC plane. Therefore, you need to invoke the Sketcher environment using this plane.

1. Choose the **Sketch** button from the **Feature** toolbar; the **Create Sketch** dialog box is displayed. By default, the XC-YC plane is selected.

2. Choose the **OK** button from the **Create Sketch** dialog box; the Sketcher environment is invoked and the sketching plane is oriented parallel to the screen.

Drawing the Outer Profile of the Sketch

The outer profile of the sketch consists of lines and can be drawn by using the **Profile** tool.

1. By default, the **Profile** tool is invoked and the **Profile** dialog box is displayed. The **Line** button is active, by default in this dialog box. Also, the dynamic input boxes are displayed below the line cursor.

2. Move the cursor close to the origin; the coordinates of the point are displayed as 0,0 in the dynamic input boxes. Click to specify the start point of the line at this point.

   As you move the cursor on the screen, the line stretches and its length and angle values are modified dynamically in the dynamic input boxes.

3. Enter **80** in the **Length** dynamic input box and press the TAB key. Next, enter **0** in the **Angle** dynamic input box and press the ENTER key.

4. Choose the **Fit** button from the **View** toolbar to fit the sketch into the drawing window.

5. Enter **10** as the length and **90** as the angle in the **Length** and **Angle** dynamic input boxes, respectively. Press the ENTER key.

6. Enter **15** as the length and **180** as the angle in the **Length** and **Angle** dynamic input boxes, respectively. Press the ENTER key.

7. Enter **30** as the length and **90** as the angle in the **Length** and **Angle** dynamic input boxes, respectively. Press the ENTER key.

8. Enter **15** as the length and **0** as the angle in the **Length** and **Angle** dynamic input boxes, respectively. Press the ENTER key.

9. Enter **10** as the length and **90** as the angle in the **Length** and **Angle** dynamic input boxes, respectively. Press the ENTER key.

10. Enter **80** as the length and **180** as the angle in the **Length** and **Angle** dynamic input boxes, respectively. Press the ENTER key.

11. Enter **10** as the length and **-90** as the angle in the **Length** and **Angle** dynamic input boxes, respectively. Press the ENTER key.

12. Enter **15** as the length and **0** as the angle in the **Length** and **Angle** dynamic input boxes, respectively. Press the ENTER key.

13. Enter **30** as the length and **-90** as the angle in the **Length** and **Angle** dynamic input boxes, respectively. Press the ENTER key.

14. Enter **15** as the length and **180** as the angle in the **Length** and **Angle** dynamic input boxes, respectively. Press the ENTER key.

15. Move the cursor to the start point of the first line and click when the cursor snaps to the start point of the line.

16. Press the ESC key twice to exit the **Profile** tool. The outer profile of the sketch is shown in Figure 2-51.

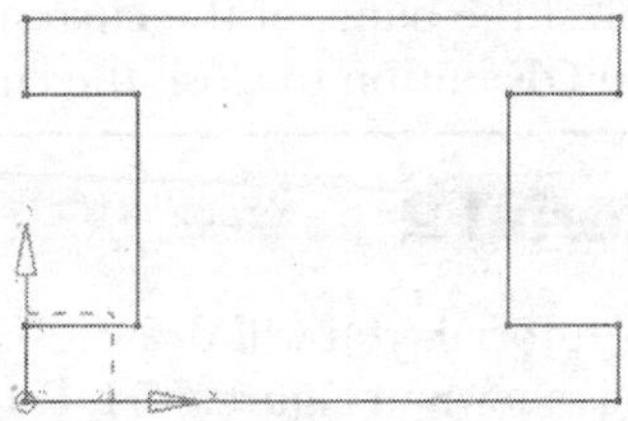

Figure 2-51 *Outer profile of the sketch*

Drawing the Rectangle

Next, you need to draw the inner profile, which is a rectangle. You can use the **By 2 Points** option of the **Rectangle** tool to draw the rectangle.

1. Choose the **Rectangle** button from the **Sketch Tools** toolbar; the **Rectangle** dialog box is displayed and the **By 2 Points** button is chosen by default in this dialog box.

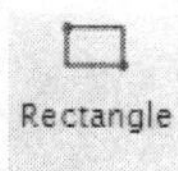

2. Enter **25** and **15** as the coordinates of the first point of the rectangle in the **XC** and **YC** dynamic input boxes, respectively. Next, press the ENTER key.

3. Enter **30** and **20** as the width and height of the rectangle in the **Width** and **Height** dynamic input boxes, respectively. Next, press the ENTER key. The preview of the rectangle is displayed, but it is not actually drawn yet. As you move the cursor in the drawing window, the rectangle also moves.

4. Move the cursor close to the top left corner of the drawing window and then click to draw the rectangle.

5. Press the ESC key to exit the tool. The final sketch for Tutorial 1 is shown in Figure 2-52.

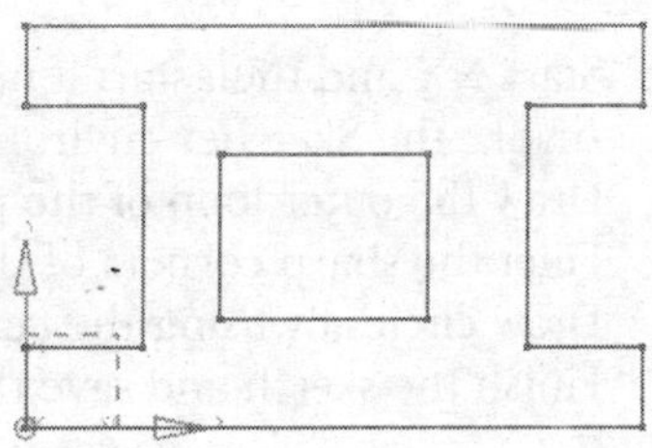

Figure 2-52 *Final sketch for Tutorial 1*

Finishing the Sketch and Saving the File

NX allows you to save the sketch file in the Sketcher environment.

1. Choose the **Save** button from the **Standard** toolbar to save the sketch.

2. Choose the **Finish Sketch** button from the **Sketcher** toolbar; the Modeling environment is invoked.

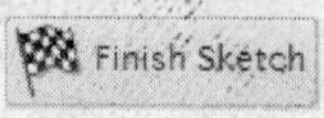

3. Choose **File > Close > Selected Parts** from the menu bar; the **Close Part** dialog box is displayed.

4. Select the name of the current file from the list area in the **Part** rollout and then choose the **OK** button to close the current file.

Tutorial 2

In this tutorial, you will draw a sketch for the model shown in Figure 2-53. The sketch to be drawn is shown in Figure 2-54. Do not dimension the sketch because the dimensions are given only for reference. **(Expected time: 30 min)**

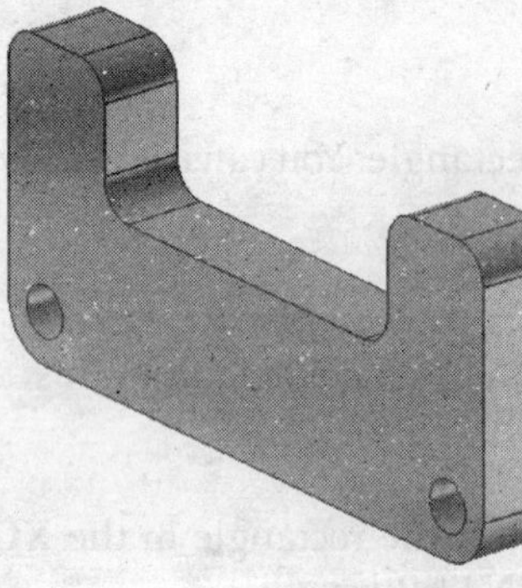

Figure 2-53 *Model for Tutorial 2*

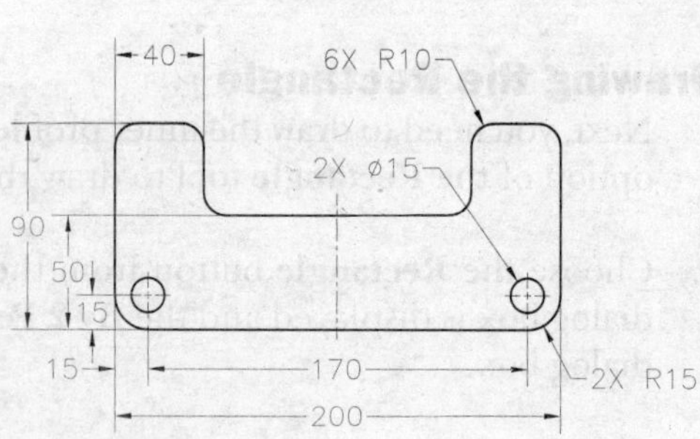

Figure 2-54 *Sketch for Tutorial 2*

The following steps are required to complete this tutorial:

a. Start NX and then start a new file.
b. Invoke the Sketcher environment by using the XC-ZC plane as the sketching plane.
c. Draw the outer loop of the profile by using the **Profile** tool.
d. Fillet the sharp corners of the outer loop using the **Fillet** tool.
e. Draw circles by using the centers of fillets to complete the profile.
f. Finish the sketch and save the file.

Starting NX 7 and Starting a New File

First, you need to start NX 7 and then start a new file.

1. Choose the **Start** button at the lower left corner of the screen to display a menu. Next, choose **All Programs** (or **Programs**) **> UGS NX 7.0 > NX 7.0** to start NX 7. Alternatively, double-click on **NX 7.0** shortcut icon on the desktop of your computer.

2. To start a new file, choose the **New** button from the **Standard** toolbar or choose **File > New** from the menu bar; the **New** dialog box is displayed.

3. Select the **Model** template from the **Templates** rollout.

4. Enter ***c02tut2*** as the name of the document in the **Name** text box of the dialog box.

5. Choose the button on the right side of the **Folder** text box; the **Choose Directory** dialog box is displayed.

6. In this dialog box, browse to *NX 7/c02* folder and then choose the **OK** button twice; the new file is started in the Modeling environment.

Invoking the Sketcher Environment in the Modeling Environment

The base sketch of this model will be created on the XC-ZC plane. Therefore, you need to invoke the Sketcher environment using this plane.

1. Choose the **Sketch** button from the **Feature** toolbar; the **Create Sketch** dialog box is displayed.

2. Select the XC-ZC plane from the drawing window.

3. Choose the **OK** button from the **Create Sketch** dialog box; the Sketcher environment is invoked and the sketching plane is oriented parallel to the screen.

Drawing Lines of the Outer Loop

You will draw the lines of the outer loop by using the line mode of the **Profile** tool. The line will start from the origin, which is the point where the XC-YC, YC-ZC, and ZC-XC planes intersect. The coordinates of the origin are 0,0,0. In the current view, the origin is the intersection point of the two planes displayed as the horizontal and vertical lines.

By default, the **Profile** tool is invoked and the **Profile** dialog box is displayed. The **Line** button is chosen by default in the dialog box. Also, the dynamic input boxes are displayed below the line cursor.

1. Move the cursor close to the origin; the coordinates of the point are displayed as 0,0 in the dynamic input boxes. Next, click to specify the start point of the line.

The point you specified is selected as the start point of the line and the endpoint is attached to the cursor. As you move the cursor on the screen, the line stretches and its length and angle values are modified dynamically in the dynamic input boxes. Next, you need to specify the endpoint of this line and the points to define the remaining lines. This will be done by using the **Length** and **Angle** dynamic input boxes.

2. Enter **200** in the **Length** dynamic input box and press the TAB key. Next, enter **0** in the **Angle** dynamic input box and press the ENTER key.

   You will notice that the line is drawn, but it is not completely displayed in the current display. To include it into the current display, you need to modify the drawing display area by using the **Fit** tool.

3. Choose the **Fit** button from the **View** toolbar; the current drawing display area is modified and the line is displayed completely in the current view. Also, the **Line** tool is still active and you are prompted to specify the second point of the line.

4. Enter **90** in the **Length** dynamic input box and press the TAB key. Next, enter **90** in the **Angle** dynamic input box and press the ENTER key; a vertical line of 90 mm is drawn.

5. Choose the **Fit** button again to fit the drawing into the current display.

6. Move the cursor away from the end point of the last line and then enter **40** in the **Length** dynamic input box and press the TAB key. Next, enter **-180** in the **Angle** dynamic input box and press the ENTER key; a horizontal line of 40 mm is drawn.

7. Move the cursor away from the end point of the last line and then enter **40** in the **Length** dynamic input box and press the TAB key. Next, enter **-90** in the **Angle** dynamic input box and press the ENTER key; a vertical line of 40 mm is drawn downward.

8. Move the cursor away from the end point of the last line and then enter **120** in the **Length** dynamic input box and press the TAB key. Next, enter **180** in the **Angle** dynamic input box and press the ENTER key; a horizontal line of 120 mm is drawn.

9. Move the cursor vertically upward; a rubber-band line is displayed with its starting point at the endpoint of the previous line and the endpoint attached to the cursor.

10. Move the cursor once toward the vertical line of 40 mm drawn earlier and then move it back to the vertical direction from the start point of this line. When the line is vertical, the vertical constraint symbol is displayed.

11. Move the cursor vertically upward until the horizontal help line is displayed from the top endpoint of the vertical line of 40 length. Note that at this point, the value of the length in the **Length** dynamic input box is **40** and the value of the angle is **90**. Click to specify the endpoint of this line.

12. Move the cursor horizontally toward the left and make sure that the horizontal constraint symbol is displayed. Click to specify the endpoint of the line when the vertical help line is

displayed from the vertical plane. If the help line is not displayed, move the cursor once on the vertical plane and then move it back.

13. Move the cursor vertically downward to the origin. If the first line is not highlighted in yellow, move the cursor over it once and then move it back to the origin; the cursor snaps to the endpoint of the first line.

14. Click to specify the endpoint of the line when the vertical constraint symbol is displayed. Choose the **Fit** button to fit the sketch into the drawing window.

15. Press the ESC key twice to exit the **Profile** tool. The sketch after drawing the lines is shown in Figure 2-55.

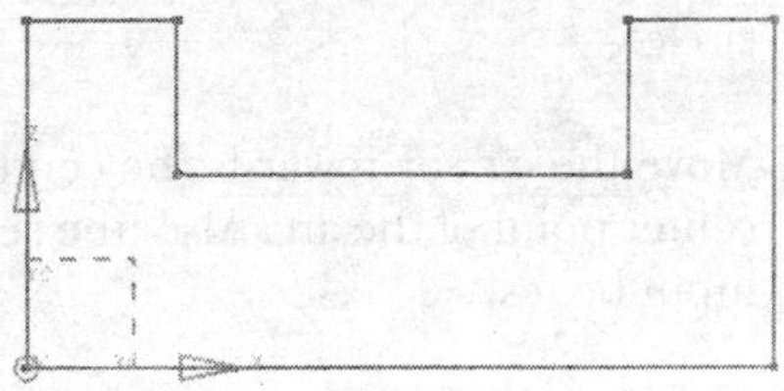

***Figure 2-55** Sketch after drawing the lines*

Filleting Sharp Corners

Next, you need to fillet sharp corners so that no sharp edges are in the final model by using the **Fillet** tool.

1. Choose the **Fillet** button from the **Sketch Tools** toolbar; the **Create Fillet** dialog box is displayed.

In this tutorial, the lower left and lower right corners are filleted with a radius of 15 mm and the remaining corners are filleted with a radius of 10 mm.

2. Enter **15** in the **Radius** dynamic input box and press the ENTER key.

3. Move the cursor over the lower left corner of the sketch; the two lines comprising this corner are highlighted in yellow. Click to select this corner; a fillet is created at the lower left corner.

4. Similarly, move the cursor over the lower right corner and click to select it when the two lines that form this corner are highlighted in yellow.

Next, you need to modify the fillet radius value and fillet the remaining corners.

5. Enter **10** in the **Radius** dynamic input box and press the ENTER key.

6. Select the remaining corners of the sketch one by one and fillet them with a radius of 10.

7. Right-click, and then select the **OK** option from the shortcut menu to exit the **Fillet** tool. The fillets are created, refer to Figure 2-56.

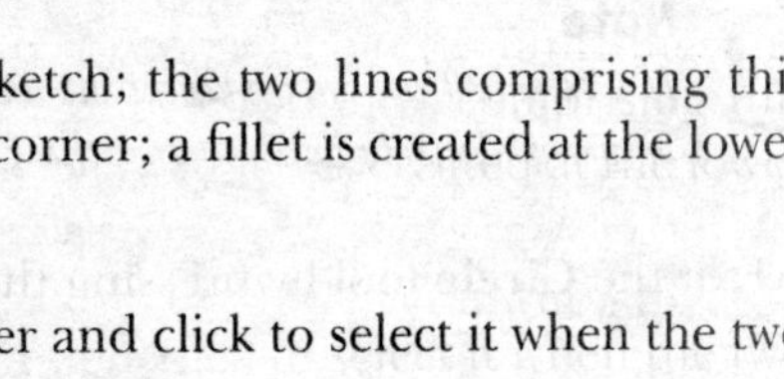

***Figure 2-56** Sketch after creating fillets*

Drawing Circles

Finally, you need to draw circles to complete the sketch. The circles will be drawn by using the **Circle** tool. Use the center points of the fillets as the center points of the circles.

1. Choose the **Circle** button from the **Sketch Tools** toolbar; the **Circle** dialog box is displayed. By default, the **Circle by Center and Diameter** button is chosen in this dialog box. Also, you are prompted to select the center of the circle.

2. Move the cursor towards the center point of the lower left fillet; the cursor snaps to the center point of the arc. Also, the center point snap symbol is displayed above the dynamic input boxes.

3. Click when the cursor snaps to the center point of the fillet to specify the center point of the circle.

4. Enter **15** in the **Diameter** dynamic input box and press the ENTER key; a circle of the specified diameter is drawn at the specified center point. Also, another circle of 15 diameter is attached to the cursor.

5. Move the cursor towards the center point of the lower right fillet; the cursor snaps to the center point of the arc and the center point snap symbol is displayed above the dynamic input box.

6. Click when the cursor snaps to the center point of the arc; the circle is drawn at the specified location.

Note

*If you select an incorrect point as the center point of the circle by mistake, you can remove the unwanted circle by choosing the **Undo** button from the **Standard** toolbar.*

7. Exit the **Circle** tool by pressing the ESC key twice.

This completes the sketch of the model for Tutorial 2. The final sketch for Tutorial 2 is shown in Figure 2-57.

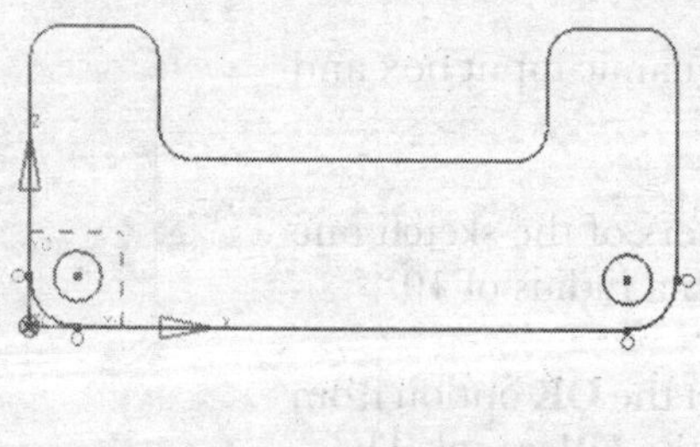

Figure 2-57 *Final sketch for Tutorial 2*

Finishing the Sketch and Saving the File

NX allows you to save the sketch file in the Sketcher environment.

1. Choose the **Fit** button to fit the sketch into the drawing window.

2. Choose the **Save** button from thc **Standard** toolbar to save the sketch.

3. Choose the **Finish Sketch** button from the **Sketcher** toolbar; the Modeling environment is invoked.
4. Choose **File > Close > Selected Parts** from the menu bar; the **Close Part** dialog box is displayed.
5. Select the name of the current file from the list area in the **Part** rollout and then choose the **OK** button to close the current file.

Note

For better visualization, the background color of graphics in this textbook is set to white. To change the background color, choose ***Preferences > Background*** *from the menu bar; the* ***Edit Background*** *dialog box is displayed. Select the* ***Plain*** *radio button from both the* ***Shaded Views*** *and* ***Wireframe Views*** *areas. Next, choose the* ***Plain Color*** *swatch; the* ***Color*** *dialog box is displayed. In this dialog box, select the white color and choose the* ***OK*** *button twice to exit the* ***Edit Background*** *dialog box.*

Tutorial 3

In this tutorial, you will draw the profile of the model shown in Figure 2-58. The profile to be drawn is shown in Figure 2-59. Do not dimension the profile because the dimensions are given only for reference. **(Expected time: 30 min)**

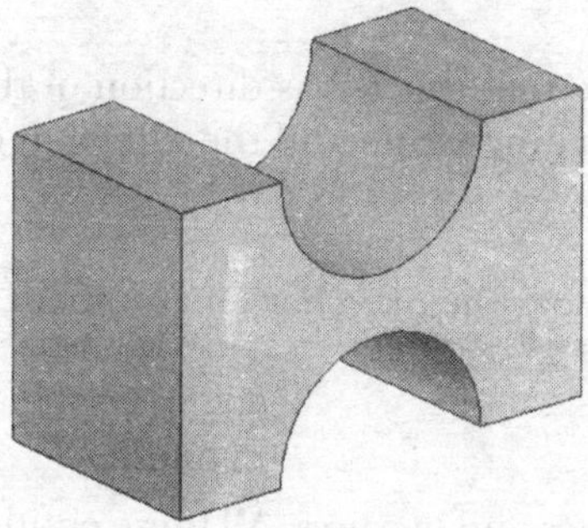

Figure 2-58 *Model for Tutorial 3*

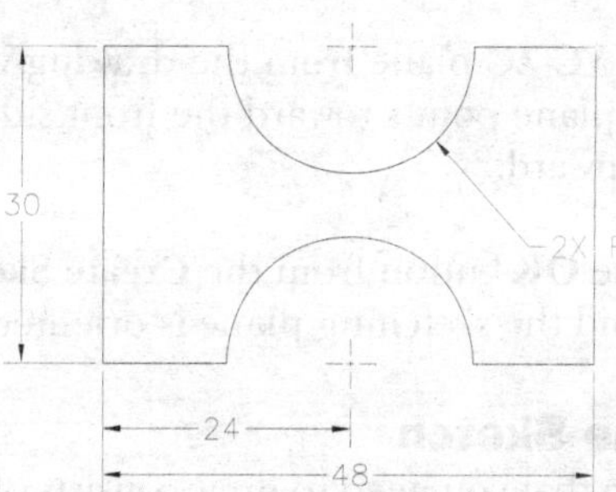

Figure 2-59 *Sketch for Tutorial 3*

The following steps are required to complete this tutorial:

a. Start a new file.
b. Select the YC-XC plane as the sketching plane and invoke the Sketcher environment.
c. Draw the sketch of the model by using the **Profile** tool.
d. Finish the sketch and save the file.

Starting a New File

If you continue working after completing Tutorial 2, you do not need to open a new session of NX. You can start a new part file by selecting the **Model** template from the **New** dialog box.

1. To start a new file, choose the **New** button from the **Standard** toolbar or choose **File > New** from the menu bar; the **New** dialog box is displayed.

2. Select the **Model** template from the **Templates** rollout.

3. Choose the button on the right of the **Name** text box; the **Choose New File Name** dialog box is displayed.

4. In this dialog box, browse to *NX 7/c02* folder and then enter *c02tut3* in the **File name** edit box. Next, choose the **OK** button twice; the new file is started in the Modeling environment.

Invoking the Sketcher Environment in the Modeling Environment

The base sketch of this model will be created on the YC-ZC plane. Therefore, you need to invoke the Sketcher environment using this plane.

1. Choose the **Sketch** button from the **Feature** toolbar; the **Create Sketch** dialog box is displayed.

2. Select the YC-ZC plane from the drawing window. Note that the Z-axis direction of the sketching plane points toward the front side of the sketching plane and the direction of Y-axis is upward.

3. Choose the **OK** button from the **Create Sketch** dialog box; the Sketcher environment is invoked and the sketching plane is oriented parallel to the screen.

Drawing the Sketch

The sketch that you need to draw consists of multiple lines and two arcs. All these entities can be drawn by using the **Line** and **Arc** options of the **Profile** tool.

1. By default, the **Profile** tool is invoked and the **Profile** dialog box is displayed. The **Line** button is activated, by default, in this dialog box. Also, the dynamic input boxes are displayed below the line cursor.

2. Move the cursor close to the origin; the coordinates of the point are displayed as 0,0 in the dynamic input boxes. Click to specify the start point of the line at this point.

   The point you specified is selected as the start point of the line and the endpoint is attached to the cursor. As you move the cursor on the screen, the line stretches and its length and angle values are modified dynamically in the dynamic input boxes.

   Next, you need to specify the endpoint of this line and the points to define the remaining lines. This will be done by using the **Length** and **Angle** dynamic input boxes.

3. Enter **12** in the **Length** dynamic input box and press the TAB key. Next, enter **0** in the **Angle** dynamic input box and press the ENTER key. The first line is drawn and the rubber-band line is displayed with the start point at the endpoint of the previous line and the endpoint attached to the cursor. Now, you need to invoke the arc mode because the next entity to be drawn is an arc.

4. Choose the **Arc** button from the **Object Type** area of the **Profile** dialog box to invoke the arc mode.

   A rubber-band arc is displayed with the start point fixed at the endpoint of the last line and the endpoint attached to the cursor. Also, the quadrant symbol is displayed at the start point of the arc.

5. Move the cursor to the start point of the arc and then move it vertically upward through a small distance. Next, move the cursor toward the right; you will notice that a normal arc starts from the endpoint of the last line.

6. Enter **12** in the **Radius** dynamic input box and press TAB key. Next, enter **180** in the **Sweep Angle** dynamic input box and press the ENTER key.

   The preview of the resulting arc is displayed, but the arc is still not drawn. To draw the arc, you need to specify a point on the screen with the values mentioned in the dynamic input boxes.

7. Move the cursor horizontally toward the right and click when the preview of the required arc is displayed. The arc is drawn and the line mode is invoked again.

8. Enter **12** as the length and **0** as the angle in the **Length** and **Angle** dynamic input boxes, respectively, and then press ENTER key. Choose the **Fit** button from the **View** toolbar to fit the sketch into the drawing window.

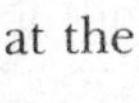

9. Enter **30** as the length and **90** as the angle in the **Length** and **Angle** dynamic input boxes, respectively, and then press ENTER key.

10. Move the cursor horizontally toward the left. Make sure that the horizontal constraint symbol is displayed. Click to specify the endpoint of the line when the vertical help line is displayed from the endpoint of the arc.

Next, you need to draw the arc by invoke the arc mode.

11. Choose the **Arc** button from the **Profile** dialog box to invoke the arc mode; a rubber-band arc is displayed with its start point fixed at the endpoint of the last line.

12. Move the cursor to the start point of the arc and then move it vertically downward through a small distance. When the normal arc appears, move the cursor toward the left.

13. Move the cursor over the lower arc once and then move it toward the left, in line with the upper right horizontal line from where this arc starts, refer to the Figure 2-60.

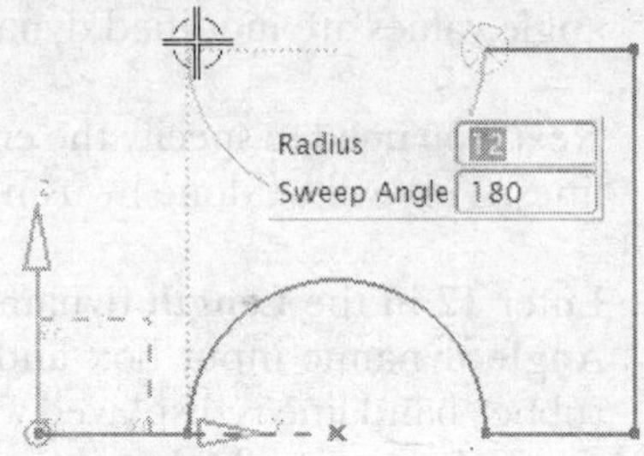

Figure 2-60 *Horizontal and vertical help lines displayed to define the endpoint of the arc*

A horizontal help line is displayed originating from the center of the arc being drawn. At the point where the cursor is vertically in line with the start point of the lower arc, the vertical help line appears from the start point of the lower arc, refer to the Figure 2-60.

14. Click to define the endpoint of the arc when the horizontal and vertical help lines are displayed. The arc is drawn and the line mode is invoked again.

15. Enter **12** as the length and **180** as the angle in the **Length** and **Angle** dynamic input boxes, respectively, and then press ENTER key.

16. Move the cursor to the first line and then move it to the start point of this line; the cursor snaps to the start point of the line.

17. Click to define the endpoint of this line when the cursor snaps to the start point of the first line.

18. Press the ESC key twice to exit the **Profile** tool. The final sketch of the model is shown in Figure 2-61.

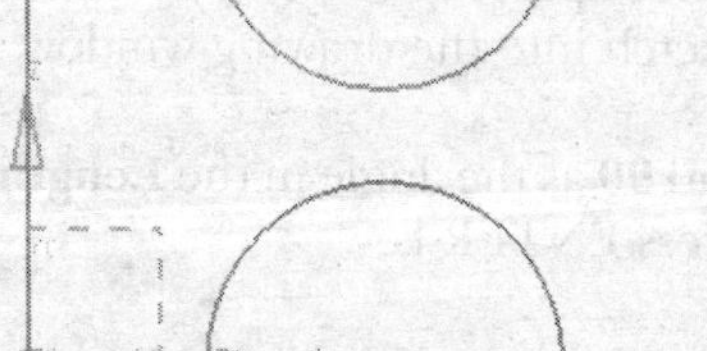

Figure 2-61 *Final sketch for Tutorial 3*

Finishing the Sketch and Saving the File

NX allows you to save the sketch file in the Sketcher environment.

1. Choose the **Save** button from the **Standard** toolbar to save the sketch.

2. Choose the **Finish Sketch** button from the **Sketcher** toolbar; the Modeling environment is invoked.
3. Choose **File > Close > Selected Parts** from the menu bar; the **Close Part** dialog box is displayed.
4. Select the name of the current file from the list area in the **Part** rollout and then choose the **OK** button to close the current file.

Self-Evaluation Test

Answer the following questions and then compare them to those given at the end of this chapter:

1. Most of the designs created in NX consist of sketch-based features and placed features. (T/F)
2. When you invoke the Sketcher environment, the **Profile** tool is invoked by default. (T/F)
3. You can use the dynamic input boxes to specify the exact values of sketched entities. (T/F)
4. The **Sketch** button is chosen to invoke the Sketcher environment. (T/F)
5. You can restore the original orientation of the sketching plane by using the __________ tool in the **Sketcher** toolbar.
6. You can invoke the arc mode within the **Profile** tool by choosing the __________ button from the **Profile** dialog box.
7. You can fillet corners in a sketch by using the __________ tool.
8. You can draw an elliptical arc by using the __________ tool.
9. If you choose the __________ button from the **Rectangle** dialog box, it will enable you to draw a centerpoint rectangle.
10. You can exit the Sketcher environment by choosing the __________ button from the **Sketcher** toolbar.

Review Questions

Answer the following questions:

1. Which one of the following dialog boxes is displayed when you choose the **New** button from the **Standard** toolbar to start a new file?

   (a) **New Part File** (b) **New**
   (c) **File New** (d) **Part File**

2. Which of the following tools in NX is used to create conics?

   (a) **General Conic** (b) **Conic**
   (c) **Round** (d) None

3. Which mode is automatically invoked from the **Profile** dialog box when you specify the start point of a line?

   (a) **Coordinate Mode** (b) **Angle Mode**
   (c) **Parameter Mode** (d) None

4. In NX, how many methods are used to start a new file?

   (a) 1 (b) 2
   (c) 3 (d) 5

5. Which of the following methods is available in the **Studio Spline** dialog box along with the **By Poles** method to draw splines?

   (a) **No Poles** (b) **From Poles**
   (c) **From Points** (d) **Through Points**

6. The files in NX are saved with *.prt* extension. (T/F)

7. You can select entities by dragging a box around them. (T/F)

8. You can set the selection mode to select only the sketched entities. (T/F)

9. In NX, you can create fillets by simply dragging the cursor across the entities that you want to fillet. (T/F)

10. In NX, you cannot draw a rectangle from its center. (T/F)

Exercises

Exercise 1

Draw a sketch for the base feature of the model shown in Figure 2-62. The sketch to be drawn is shown in Figure 2-63. Do not dimension the profile because the dimensions are given only for reference. **(Expected time: 30 min)**

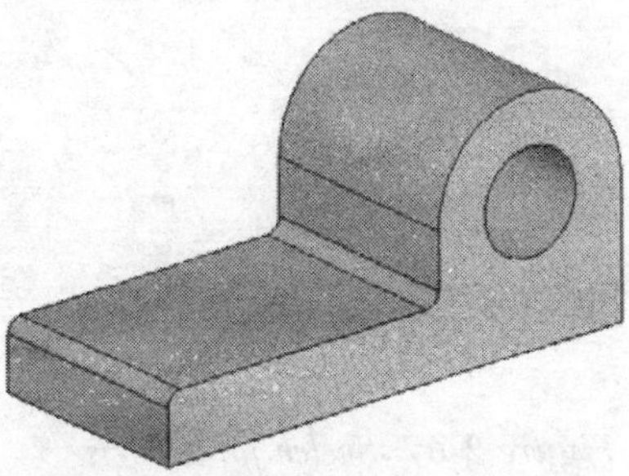

Figure 2-62 *Model for Exercise 1*

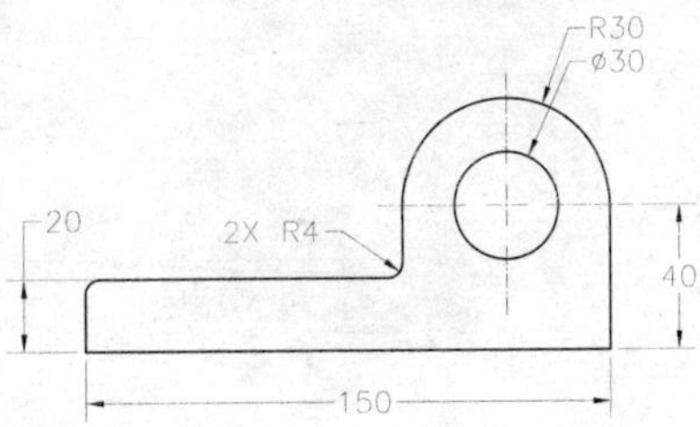

Figure 2-63 *Sketch for Exercise 1*

Exercise 2

Draw a sketch for the base feature of the model shown in Figure 2-64. The sketch to be drawn is shown in Figure 2-65. Do not dimension the profile because the dimensions are given only for reference. **(Expected time: 30 min)**

Figure 2-64 *Model for Exercise 2*

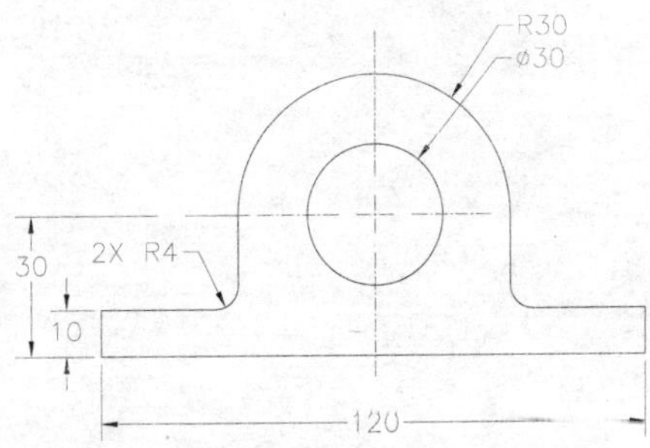

Figure 2-65 *Sketch for Exercise 2*

Exercise 3

Draw a sketch for the base feature of the model shown in Figure 2-66. The sketch to be drawn is shown in Figure 2-67. Do not dimension the profile because the dimensions are given only for reference. **(Expected time: 30 min)**

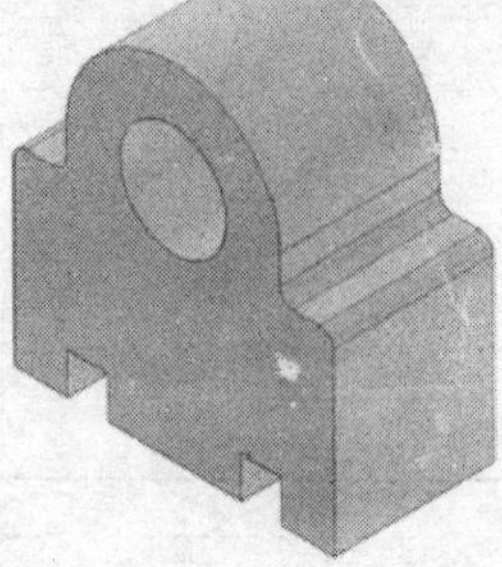

Figure 2-66 Model for Exercise 3

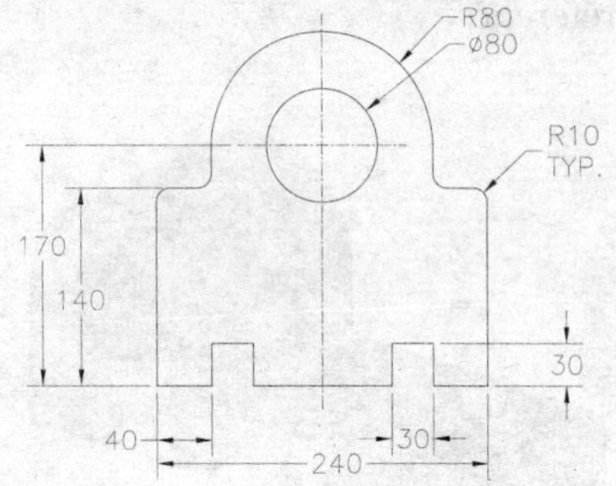

Figure 2-67 Sketch for Exercise 3

Answers to Self-Evaluation Test

1. T, **2.** T, **3.** T, **4.** T, **5. Orient View to Sketch**, **6. Arc**, **7. Fillet**, **8. Ellipse**, **9. From Center**, **10. Finish Sketch**

Chapter 3

Adding Geometric and Dimensional Constraints to Sketches

Learning Objectives

After completing this chapter, you will be able to:

- *Understand the concept of under-constrained, fully-constrained, and over-constrained sketches.*
- *Understand different types of geometric constraints.*
- *Configure settings for applying constraints automatically while sketching.*
- *Force additional geometric constraints to sketches.*
- *View and delete geometric constraints from sketches.*
- *Animate a fully-constrained sketch.*
- *Understand different types of dimensional constraints.*
- *Measure the distance value between objects in a sketch.*
- *Measure the angle between entities.*

CONSTRAINING SKETCHES

In the previous chapter, you learned to draw sketches in the Sketcher environment of NX. In this chapter, you will constrain the sketches to restrict their degrees of freedom to make them stable. The stability ensures that the size, shape, and location of the sketches do not change unexpectedly with respect to the surrounding. Therefore, it is always recommended to constrain the sketches. The first step is to apply the geometrical constraints to the sketch; some of them are automatically applied while drawing. After applying the geometrical constraints, you need to add dimensional constraints using the tools in the **Sketch Tools** toolbar.

CONCEPT OF CONSTRAINED SKETCHES

After drawing and applying the constraints, the sketch can attain any one of the following three stages:

1. Under-Constrain
2. Fully-Constrain
3. Over-Constrain

These stages are described next.

Under-Constrain

An under-constrained sketch is the one in which all degrees of freedom of each entity are not completely defined using the geometric and dimensional constraints. The elements of the sketch that are displayed in maroon color are under-constrained. You need to apply additional constraints to them in order to constraint their degree of freedom. The under-constrained sketches tend to change their position, size, or shape unexpectedly. Therefore, it is necessary to fully define the sketched elements. Figure 3-1 shows an under-constrained sketch.

Fully-Constrain

The fully-constrained sketch is the one in which all degrees of freedom of each element are defined using the geometric and dimensional constraints. As a result, the sketch cannot change its position, shape, or size unexpectedly. These dimensions can change only if they are modified deliberately by the user. The elements of a fully-constrained sketch are displayed in dark green color. Figure 3-2 shows a fully-constrained sketch.

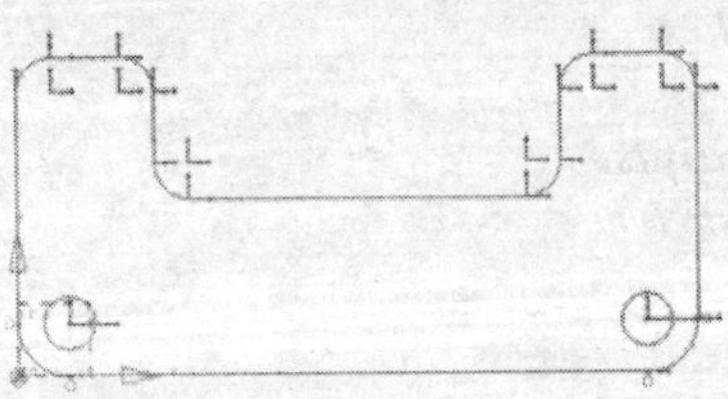

Figure 3-1 An under-constrained sketch

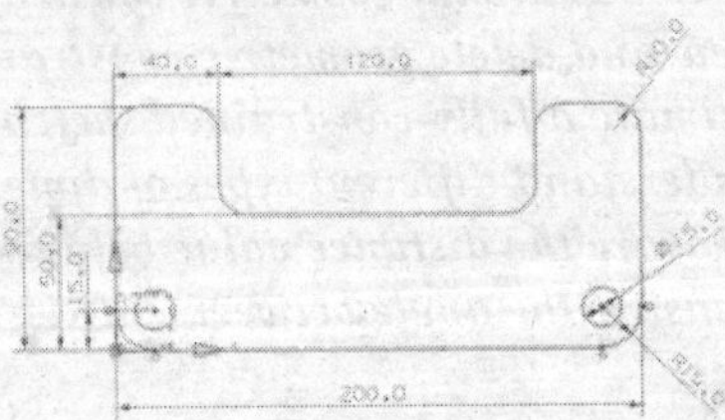

Figure 3-2 A fully-constrained sketch

Over-Constrain

An over-constrained sketch is the one in which some additional constraints are applied. The over-constrained entities are displayed in red color. The entities that are affected due to over-constraining are displayed in magenta color. It is always recommended to delete additional constraints and make the sketch fully-constrained before exiting the Sketcher environment. Figure 3-3 shows an over-constrained sketch.

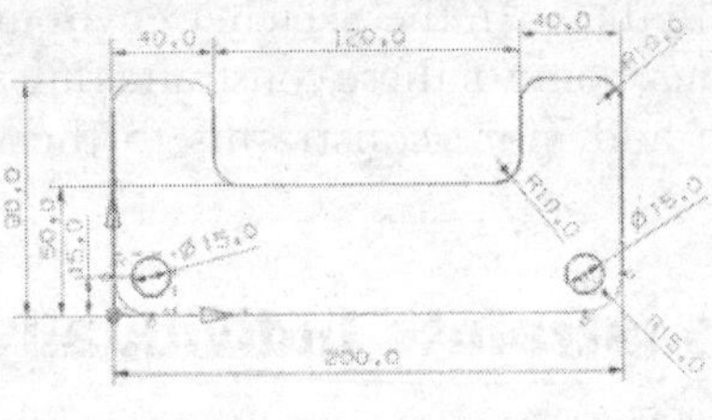

Figure 3-3 An over-constrained sketch

While applying the geometric and dimensional constraints, the status area of the **Status Bar** displays the number of constraints needed to fully constrain the sketch. After fully constraining the sketch, you will be informed in the status area of the **Status Bar** that the sketch is fully constrained.

Also, if the sketch is over-constrained, you will be informed that the sketch contains over constrained geometry. In this case, you needed to remove one or more constraints applied.

DEGREE OF FREEDOM ARROWS

The degree of freedom arrows displayed on the points that are free to move (under-constrain), refer to Figure 3-4. Note that the degree of freedom arrows will be displayed only when you choose any constraint tool (geometrical or dimensional). These tools are discussed later in this chapter.

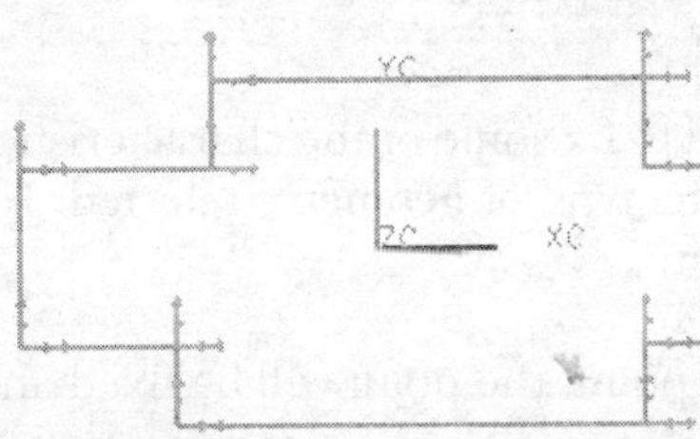

Figure 3-4 The degree of freedom arrows displayed on points

The direction of arrow at a particular point indicates that you need to constrain the movement along that direction. When you constrain a point, NX will remove the degree of freedom arrows. The sketch will be fully-constrained only when all the arrows disappear. The horizontal and vertical arrows indicate that the point is free to move in the X and Y directions, respectively.

Various geometric and dimensional constraint tools used to fully-constrain the sketch are discussed next.

GEOMETRIC CONSTRAINTS

Geometric constraints are the logical operations that are performed on the sketched entities to relate them to the other sketched entities using the standard properties such as collinearity, concentricity, tangency, and so on. These constraints reduce the degrees of freedom of the sketched entities and make the sketch more stable so that it does not change its shape and location unpredictably at any stage of the design. All geometric constraints have separate symbols associated with them. These symbols can be seen on the sketched entities when the constraints are applied to them. In the Sketcher environment of NX, you can add eleven types of geometric constraints. Some of these constraints are added automatically while sketching. Additionally, you can add more constraints to the sketch manually. This is discussed next.

Applying Additional Constraints Individually

Menu:	Insert > Constraints
Toolbar:	Sketch Tools > Constraints

In NX, you can apply additional constraints manually by using the **Constraints** tool in the **Sketch Tools** toolbar. To apply constraints, invoke the **Constraints** tool and then select the entities to which you want to add constraints; the constraints that can be applied to the selected sketched entities will be displayed in the **Constraints** dialog box, as shown in Figure 3-5.

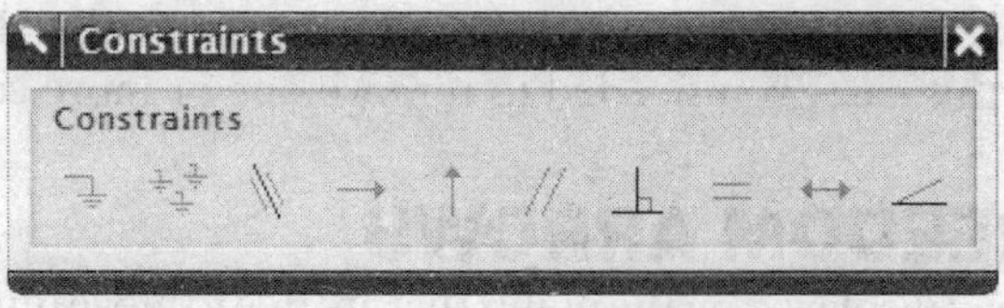

Figure 3-5 The ***Constraints*** *dialog box*

Various constraints that can be applied to the sketched entities in NX are discussed next.

Fixed Constraint

The **Fixed** constraint is used to fix some of the characteristics of the geometry. These characteristics depend on the type of geometry selected. Following are some of the examples of Fixed constraint:

1. If you apply this constraint to a point, the point will be fixed and cannot be moved.

2. If you apply this constraint to a line, its angle will be fixed; however, you can move and stretch the line.

3. If you apply this constraint to the circumference of a circular arc or an elliptical arc, the radius of the arc and the location of the center point will be fixed. However, you can change the arc-length.

To apply this constraint, select the entity and choose the **Fixed** button from the **Constraints** dialog box; the selected entity will be fixed.

Fully Fixed Constraint

This constraint is same as the **Fixed** constraint with the only difference being that this constraint fixes all characteristics of a geometry. For example, if you apply this constraint to a line, the line will be fully-constrained and it cannot be moved or stretched. To apply this constraint, select the entity and choose the **Fully Fixed** button from the **Constraints** dialog box; the selected entity will be fully fixed.

Horizontal Constraint

The **Horizontal** constraint forces the selected line segment to become horizontal irrespective of its original orientation. To apply this constraint, select the entity and then choose the **Horizontal** button from the **Constraints** dialog box; the selected line segment will be forced to become horizontal.

Vertical Constraint

The **Vertical** constraint is similar to the **Horizontal** constraint with the only difference being that this constraint will force the selected line to become vertical.

Coincident Constraint

The **Coincident** constraint forces two or more keypoints to share the same location. The keypoints that can be used to apply this constraint include the endpoints, center points, control points of splines, and so on. To apply this constraint, invoke the **Constraints** tool and then select the keypoints of the sketched entities. Next, choose the **Coincident** button from the **Constraints** dialog box. Note that if you select the sketched entities other than the keypoints, this constraint will not be available in the **Constraints** dialog box. Figure 3-6 shows the endpoints of the two lines selected to be made coincident and Figure 3-7 shows the lines after applying constraint.

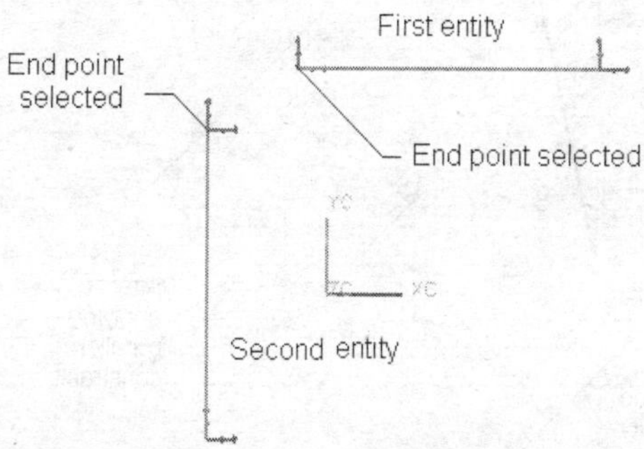

Figure 3-6 The endpoints of the first and second entities selected

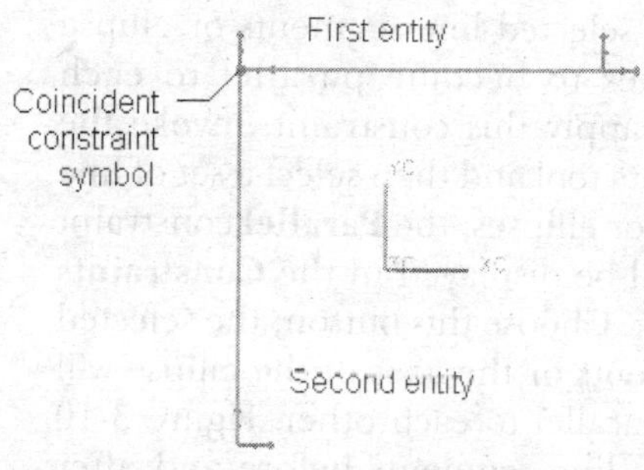

*Figure 3-7 The resulting sketch after applying the **Coincident** constraint*

Point On Curve Constraint

The **Point On Curve** constraint is used to place a selected keypoint on a selected curve or line. As a result, the selected point always lies on the selected curve. To apply this constraint, invoke the **Constraints** tool and select a keypoint, such as the endpoint or the center point. Next, select a curve; the **Point On Curve** constraint button will be displayed in the **Constraints** dialog box. Choose this button; the point will be placed on the curve. Figure 3-8 shows a sketch before applying this constraint and Figure 3-9 shows a sketch after applying this constraint.

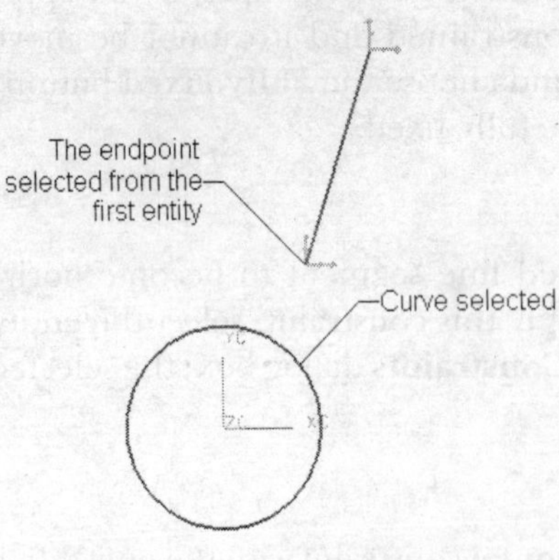

*Figure 3-8 The reference elements selected from the entity to apply the **Point On Curve** constraint*

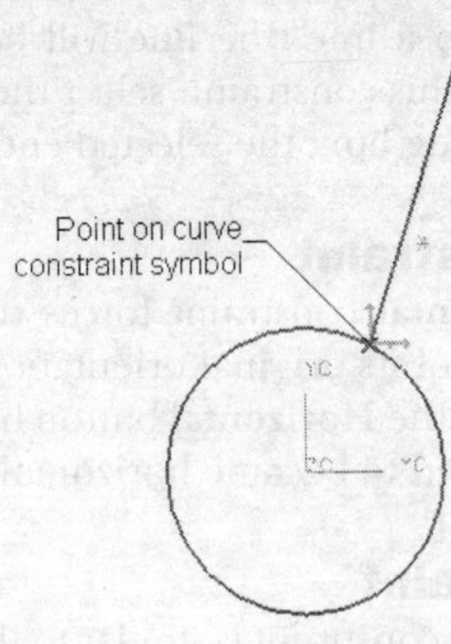

*Figure 3-9 The resulting sketch after applying the **Point On Curve** constraint*

Midpoint Constraint

NX provides you with an extension of the **Point on Curve** constraint, which is the **Midpoint** constraint. This constraint forces the selected point to be placed in line with the midpoint of the selected curve. Note that this constraint is available only when the selected curve is an open entity such as a line segment or an arc. Also, it is important to note that you need to select the curve anywhere other than at its endpoints.

Parallel Constraint

The **Parallel** constraint forces a set of selected line segments or ellipse axes to become parallel to each other. To apply this constraint, invoke the **Constraints** tool and then select a set of line segments or ellipses; the **Parallel** constraint button will be displayed in the **Constraints** dialog box. Choose this button; the selected line segments or the axes of the ellipse will become parallel to each other. Figure 3-10 shows two line segments before and after applying this constraint.

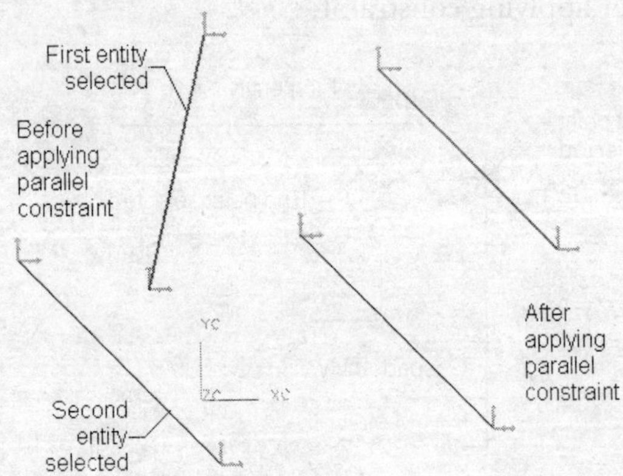

*Figure 3-10 Applying the **Parallel** constraint*

Perpendicular Constraint

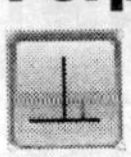

The **Perpendicular** constraint forces a set of selected line segments or ellipsc axes to become normal to each other. Figure 3-11 shows two line segments before and after applying this constraint.

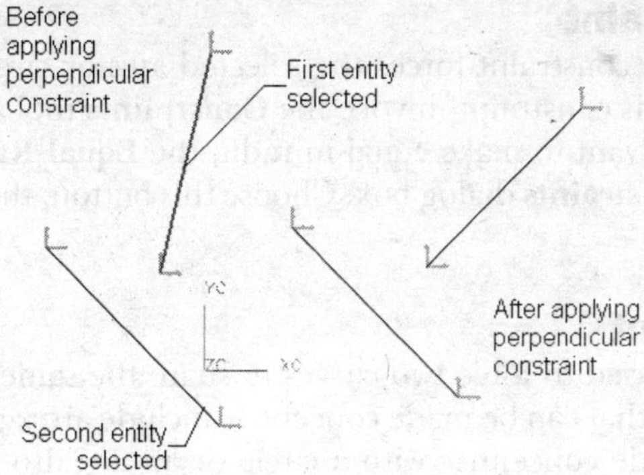

*Figure 3-11 Sketch before and after applying the **Perpendicular** constraint*

Tangent Constraint

The **Tangent** constraint forces the selected line segment or curve to become tangent to another curve. To apply this constraint, invoke the **Constraints** tool and then select a line and a curve or select two curves; the **Tangent** constraint button will be displayed in the **Constraints** dialog box. Choose this button; the selected sketched line or curve will become tangent to the other curve. Figures 3-12 and 3-13 show the use of the **Tangent** constraint.

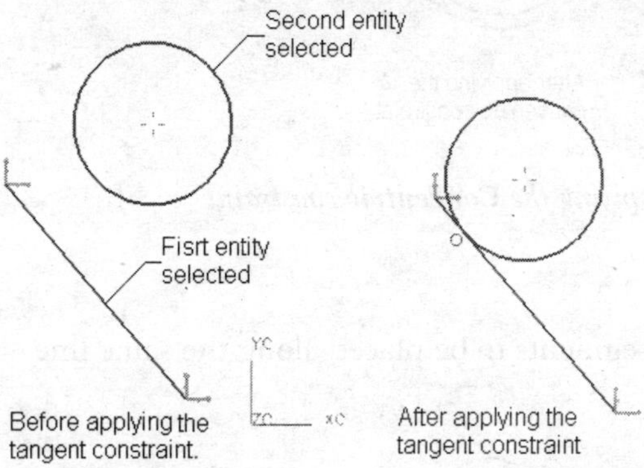

*Figure 3-12 Sketch before and after applying the **Tangent** constraint*

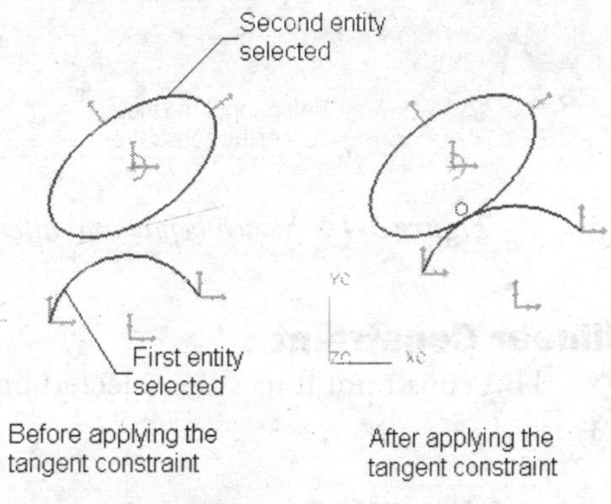

*Figure 3-13 Sketch before and after applying the **Tangent** constraint*

Note

*By default, symbols of all constraints are not displayed in the sketch. You can turn on the display of constraints using the **Show All Constraints** tool, which is discussed later in this chapter.*

Equal Length Constraint

The **Equal Length** constraint forces the length of the selected line segments to become equal. To apply this constraint, invoke the **Constraints** tool and then select the line segments that you want to make equal in length; the **Equal Length** constraint button will be displayed in the **Constraints** dialog box. Choose this button; the selected line segments will become equal in length.

Equal Radius Constraint

The **Equal Radius** constraint forces the selected arcs or circles to become equal in radius. To apply this constraint, invoke the **Constraints** tool and then select the arcs or circles that you want to make equal in radii; the **Equal Radius** constraint button will be displayed in the **Constraints** dialog box. Choose this button; the selected arcs or circles will be equal in radii.

Concentric Constraint

This constraint is used to force two curves to share the same location of the center points. The curves that can be made concentric include arcs, circles, and ellipses. The ellipses can be made concentric with a circle or an arc also. Figure 3-14 shows two circles before and after adding this constraint.

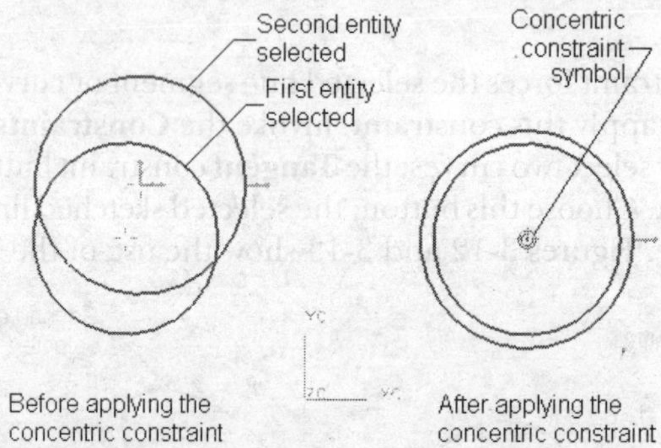

*Figure 3-14 Sketch before and after applying the **Concentric** constraint*

Collinear Constraint

This constraint forces the selected line segments to be placed along the same line.

Constant Length Constraint

The **Constant Length** constraint makes the length of the selected line segments constant. As a result, you will not be able to modify the length of the line by using the dimension constraints or by dragging.

Constant Angle Constraint

The **Constant Angle** constraint makes the angle between the selected line segments constant. As a result, you will not be able to modify the angle between the lines by using the dimension constraints or by dragging.

Slope of Curve Constraint

The **Slope of Curve** constraint button is available only when you select a control point of a spline along with a line, an arc, or a spline segment. This constraint will force the slope of the spline at the selected control point to be equal to the slope of the selected line, arc, or spline segment.

Uniform Scale Constraint

The **Uniform Scale** constraint button is displayed only when you select a spline. This constraint ensures that if you modify the distance between the endpoints of the splines, the entire spline will be scaled uniformly.

Non-Uniform Scale Constraint

The **Non-Uniform Scale** constraint button is displayed only when you select a spline. This constraint ensures that if you modify the distance between the endpoints of splines, it will be scaled non-uniformly and appears to stretch.

Applying Automatic Constraints to a Sketch

Menu:	Tools > Constraints > Auto Constrain
Toolbar:	Sketch Tools > Auto Constrain

The **Auto Constrain** tool allows you to apply the possible constraints automatically to the entire sketch. This tool is mainly used when you import geometry from another CAD system. To apply automatic constraints, choose the **Auto Constrain** button from the **Sketch Tools** toolbar; the **Auto Constrain** dialog box will be displayed, as shown in Figure 3-15. The options in this dialog box are discussed next.

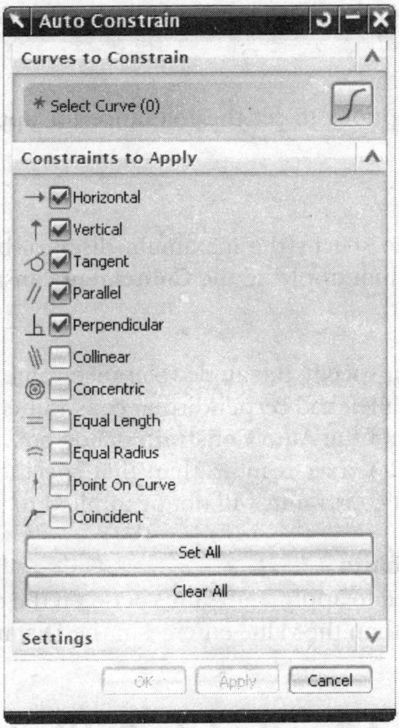

*Figure 3-15 The **Auto Constrain** dialog box*

Curves to Constrain Rollout

This rollout is used to select a line, a circle, or a curve to which constraints will be applied. Select the sketched entities to which the constraints are to be applied. As you select the sketched entities, the **Apply** and **OK** buttons of this dialog box will be enabled.

Constraints to Apply Rollout

This rollout consists of various check boxes for major geometric constraints in NX. You can select the check boxes of the constraints that should be applied to the sketch. After selecting all the required check boxes of the constraints, choose the **Apply** button and then exit from the dialog box by choosing the **Cancel** button. After you exit the **Auto Constrain** dialog box, all possible constraints from the selected constraints will be applied to the sketch. Also, this rollout contains the options to set and clear all the geometric constraint check boxes. These options are discussed next.

Set All

If you choose this button, the check boxes of all constraints will be selected. As a result, all the possible constraints will be automatically applied to the sketch after you exit this dialog box.

Clear All

If you choose this button, the check boxes of all constraints will be cleared.

Settings Rollout

This rollout provides the options to set the tolerance for applying the constraints. These options are discussed next.

Distance Tolerance

In this edit box, you can specify the maximum distance between the endpoints of two entities to be considered for applying the **Coincident** constraint.

Angle Tolerance

In this edit box, you can specify the angle tolerance value that will control whether the Horizontal, Vertical, Parallel, and Perpendicular constraints should be applied to the lines in the sketch after you exit the **Auto Constrain** dialog box. For example, if the deviation of lines from the X and Y axes is more than that specified value in this edit box, the **Horizontal** and **Vertical** constraints will not be applied to them.

Apply Remote Constraints

This check box is selected to apply constraints between the objects that are separated by a distance or angle more than the value entered in the **Distance Tolerance** and the **Angle Tolerance** edit boxes.

Controlling Inferred Constraints Settings

Menu: Tools > Constraints > Inferred Constraints
Toolbar: Sketch Tools > Inferred Constraints

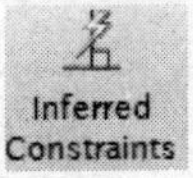

As mentioned earlier, some of the constraints are automatically applied to the sketched entities while they are being sketched. These settings are controlled by the **Inferred Constraints** tool. When you invoke this tool, the **Inferred Constraints** dialog box will be displayed, as shown in Figure 3-16.

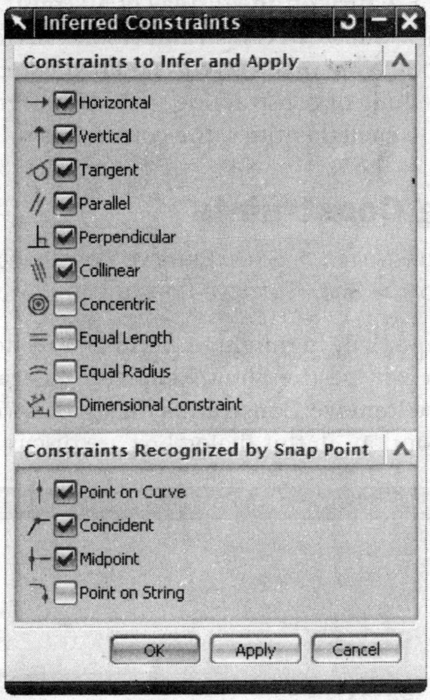

*Figure 3-16 The **Inferred Constraints** dialog box*

This dialog box provides you the check boxes of the main constraints that are available in NX. You can select the check boxes of the constraints that should be applied to the sketch while sketching.

If you select the **Dimensional Constraint** check box, then the dimensions of the entities created by entering the values inside the input boxes will be displayed.

Showing All Constraints in a Sketch

Menu:	Tools > Constraints > Show All Constraints
Toolbar:	Sketch Tools > Show All Constraints

By default, all the constraints that are applied to the sketch are not displayed automatically. For example, constraints such as Concentric, Coincident, and so on are displayed by default. However, constraints such as Parallel, Perpendicular, and so on are not displayed by default. You can turn on the display of these constraints using the **Show All Constraints** button. This is a toggle button and when you turn it on, it remains on until you turn it off. With this tool turned on, you can continue working with the other sketching tools.

Turning off the Display of All Constraints in a Sketch

Menu:	Tools > Constraints > Show No Constraints
Toolbar:	Sketch Tools > Show No Constraints *(Customize to Add)*

NX also allows you to turn off the display of all constraints in the sketch. This can be done by using the **Show No Constraints** tool. This tool is a toggle with the **Show All Constraints** tool. Note that with this tool turned on, you can continue working with the other sketching or constraining tools. However, if this tool is turned on and you apply constraints to the sketched entities, the constraints will not be displayed.

Showing/Removing Constraints

Menu:	Tools > Constraints > Show/Remove Constraints
Toolbar:	Sketch Tools > Show/Remove Constraints

If you want to temporarily highlight or permanently delete the constraints applied to the sketch, you can use the **Show/Remove Constraints** tool. When you invoke this tool, the **Show/Remove Constraints** dialog box will be displayed, as shown in Figure 3-17. The options in this dialog box are discussed next.

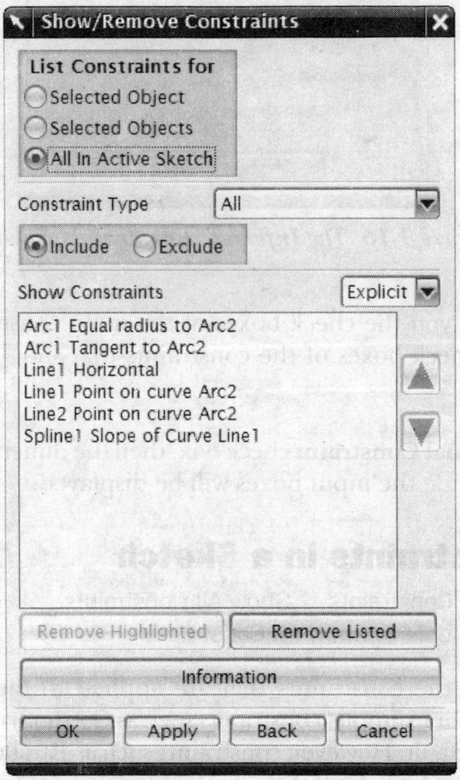

***Figure 3-17** The **Show/Remove Constraints** dialog box*

List Constraints for Area

This area provides three radio buttons, which are discussed next.

Selected Object

Selecting this radio button ensures that the constraints applied only to the currently selected entity are listed in the list box in the **Show Constraints** area. For example, when you select a sketched entity from the drawing window, the constraints applied to that entity are listed in the list box in the **Show Constraints** area. If you select another sketched entity, the constraints applied to the previously selected entity are removed and the constraints applied to the entity selected now are listed.

Selected Objects

This radio button is used to list the constraints applied to more than one entity. You can select any number of entities by picking them from the graphics window or by creating a temporary rectangle around them by dragging the cursor. The constraints applied to all selected entities will be listed in the list box in the **Show Constraints** area. You can select a constraint from this list box to highlight it in the drawing window.

All In Active Sketch

This radio button is selected to list the constraints applied to all the sketched entities in the current sketch.

Constraint Type Drop-down List

The **Constraint Type** drop-down list is used to select the type of constraints that are to be listed. By default, the **All** option is selected from this drop-down list. As a result, all constraints that are applied to the sketch are listed. However, you can select a particular type of constraint from this drop-down list. By doing so, you can ensure that only the specified type of constraint applied to the selected entity is highlighted. Below this drop-down list, there are two radio buttons and they are discussed next.

Include

This radio button ensures that the specified types of constraints selected from the **Constraint Type** drop-down list are included for listing in the dialog box.

Exclude

This radio button ensures that the specified type of constraints selected from the **Constraint Type** drop-down list are excluded for listing in the dialog box.

Show Constraints Area

The options in this area are discussed next.

Drop-down List

The drop-down list in the **Show Constraints** area allows you to specify whether you want to display the explicit constraints, the inferred coincident constraints, or both. Explicit constraints such as horizontal, vertical, midpoint, and so on are those constraints that are applied by the user while drawing the sketch, whereas, the Inferred coincident constraints such as coincident are those constraints that are applied automatically. For displaying the explicit constraints, you need to select the **Explicit** option, whereas for the inferred constraints, you need to select the **Inferred** option. If you select the **Both** option from the drop-down list, both types of constraints will be listed in the dialog box.

List Box

The constraints applied to the sketch are listed in this list box based on the specified selections. If you select a constraint from this list box, the sketched entities related to the constraints are highlighted in the graphics window. You can scroll the selection intent upward or downward over the constraints listed by choosing the **Step Up The List** or the **Step Down The List** buttons, respectively.

Remove Highlighted

When you choose this button, the selected constraints in the list box are deleted.

Remove Listed

Choosing this button deletes only the constraints that are listed in the list box. For example, if you have listed only the inferred constraints, they will be deleted and the explicit constraints will be retained. You can view them by listing the explicit constraints.

Information

This button is used to open a new window, which provides the information about the constraints listed in the **Show/Remove Constraints** dialog box.

Tip: *To select multiple constraints from the list box, press the CTRL key and select the constraints one by one.*

Tip: *Move the cursor over a constraint; all entities to which that particular constraint is applied will be highlighted. You can also highlight the constraints that are applied to the active sketched entities. To do so, select the **Sketch Constraint** option from the **Type Filter** drop-down list and then press CTRL+A keys; all constraints applied will be selected.*

*In order to select the sketched entities, make sure the selection filter is set to **No Selection Filter**.*

Converting a Sketch Entity into a Reference Entity

Menu:	Tools > Constraints > Convert To/From Reference
Toolbar:	Sketch Tools > Convert To/From Reference

The **Convert To/From Reference** tool in the **Sketch Tools** toolbar is used to covert or retain the reference property of a sketched entity. Generally, reference elements are created for assigning the axis of revolution or for applying dimensions with reference to an entity. To convert any of these sketched entities into a reference element, choose the **Convert To/From Reference** button from the **Sketch Tools** toolbar; the **Convert To/From Reference** dialog box will be displayed, as shown in Figure 3-18.

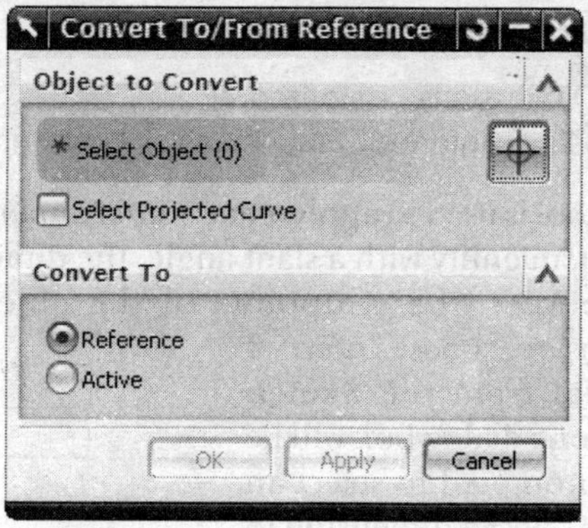

***Figure 3-18** The **Convert To/From Reference** dialog box*

By default, the **Reference** radio button is selected and you are prompted to select the reference entities. Select one or more objects, choose the **OK** button from the same dialog box to convert the selected objects into reference elements.

To convert the reference element into an active sketch, choose the **Active** radio button from the dialog box and select one or more reference elements. Choose the **OK** button.

Note

You can also convert dimension constraints into reference elements. When dimension constraints are converted into reference element, they are displayed in gray.

*You can also convert geometric entities into reference entities and vice-versa, without opening the **Convert To/From Reference** dialog box. Select the entities to be converted from the drawing window and then choose the **Convert To/From Reference** button from the **Sketch Tools** toolbar; the selected geometric entities will be converted into reference entities and vice-versa.*

DIMENSIONAL CONSTRAINTS

After creating the sketch, you need to apply different types of dimensions (dimensional constraints) to it. Various types of dimensions in NX are:

1. Horizontal Dimensions
2. Vertical Dimensions
3. Parallel Dimensions
4. Perpendicular Dimensions
5. Angular Dimensions
6. Diameter Dimensions
7. Radius Dimensions
8. Perimeter Dimensions

You can apply the dimensions listed above by using their respective tools or by using the **Inferred Dimensions** tool from the **Sketch Tools** toolbar. NX is a parametric software and so you can modify the dimension created at any time by entering the Sketcher environment. The methods for applying these dimensions are discussed next.

Applying Horizontal Dimensions

Menu: Insert > Dimensions > Horizontal
Toolbar: Sketch Tools > Inferred Dimensions > Horizontal

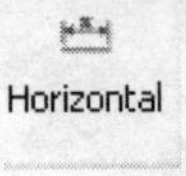

The **Horizontal** tool is used to apply a horizontal dimension between any two points. Even if you select an entity with a slant angle, the dimension will always be applied horizontally between the endpoints of the object selected. To apply the horizontal dimension, choose **Inferred Dimensions > Horizontal** from the **Sketch Tools** toolbar; the **Dimensions** dialog box will be displayed and you will be prompted to select an object to be dimensioned or select a dimension to be edited. Select the object to be dimensioned; the horizontal dimension of the selected object will be attached to the cursor. Next, you need to place it at the required location. Place the dimension above or below the selected object by pressing the left mouse button inside the drawing window; an edit box will be displayed. Enter the required value in this edit box, and then press ENTER. Figure 3-19 shows the horizontal dimensioning of lines.

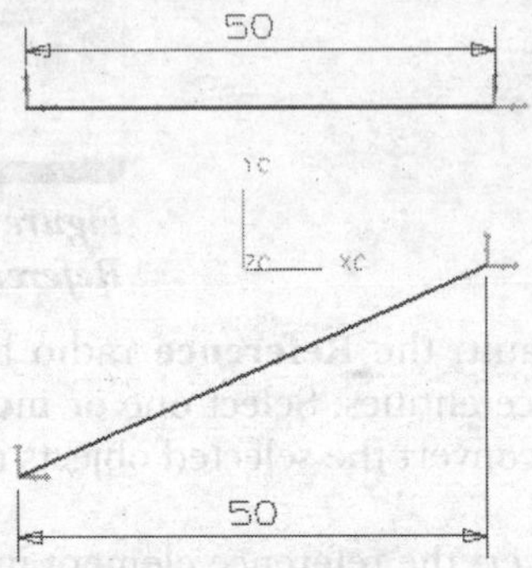

Figure 3-19 The horizontal dimension created for a horizontal line and an inclined line

Applying Vertical Dimensions

Menu: Insert > Dimensions > Vertical
Toolbar: Sketch Tools > Inferred Dimensions > Vertical

The **Vertical** tool is used to apply a vertical dimension between any two points. Even if you a select linear object with a slant angle, the dimension will always be applied vertically between the endpoints of the selected object. To apply the vertical dimension to an object, choose **Inferred Dimensions > Vertical** from the **Sketch Tools** toolbar; the **Dimensions** dialog box will be displayed and you will be prompted to select an object to be dimensioned or select a dimension to be edited. Select an object; the vertical dimension of the selected object will be attached to the cursor. Place the dimension left or right the selected object by pressing the left mouse button in the drawing window; an edit box will be displayed. Enter the required value in this edit box, and then press ENTER. Figure 3-20 shows the vertical dimensioning of lines.

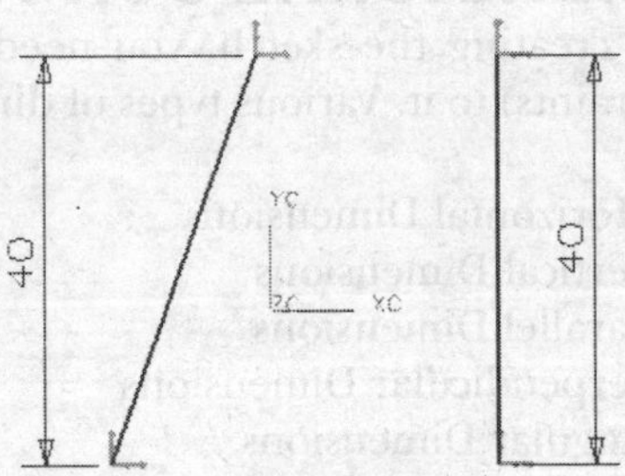

Figure 3-20 The vertical dimension created for a vertical line and an inclined line

Note

*In the figures, some of the dimension properties such as decimal places and label have been modified for better display of dimensions. To modify the dimension label, choose **Sketch > Sketch Style** from the menu bar; the **Sketch Style** dialog box will be displayed. In this dialog box, select the **Value** option from the **Dimension Label** drop-down list. Next, choose the **OK** button; the dimensions will be modified. Alternatively, choose **Preferences > Sketch** from the menu bar; the **Sketch Preferences** dialog box will be displayed. In this dialog box, choose the **Sketch Style** tab; the **Sketch Preferences** message box will be displayed. Choose **OK**. Next, in the **Dimension Label** drop-down list of the **Sketch Preferences** dialog box, select the **Value** option, and then choose the **OK** button; the dimensions will be modified.*

Applying Parallel Dimensions

Menu:	Insert > Dimensions > Parallel
Toolbar:	Sketch Tools > Inferred Dimensions > Parallel

The **Parallel** tool is used to measure the actual distance of a line (straight or inclined). You can apply dimension either by selecting a line or by selecting points, endpoints, or center points. To apply the parallel dimension, choose **Inferred Dimensions > Parallel** from the **Sketch Tools** toolbar; the **Dimensions** dialog box will be displayed and you will be prompted to select an object to be dimensioned or select a dimension to be edited. Select the objects between which the dimension has to be applied; the dimension will be attached to the cursor. Place the dimension at the desired location by clicking the left mouse button; an edit box will be displayed. Enter the required value in this edit box, and then press ENTER. Figures 3-21 and 3-22 show the parallel dimension applied to the sketches.

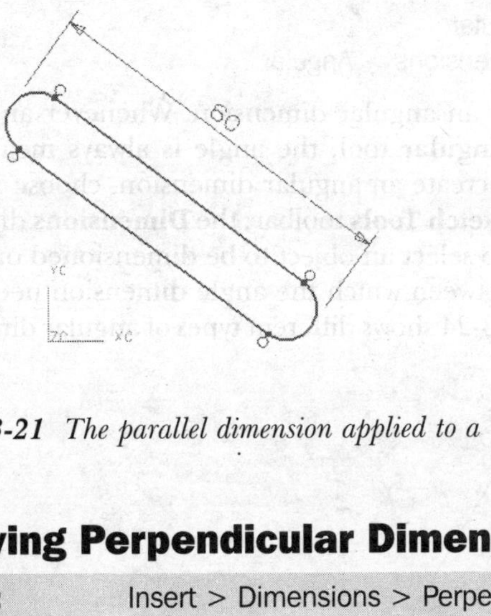

Figure 3-21 *The parallel dimension applied to a sketch*

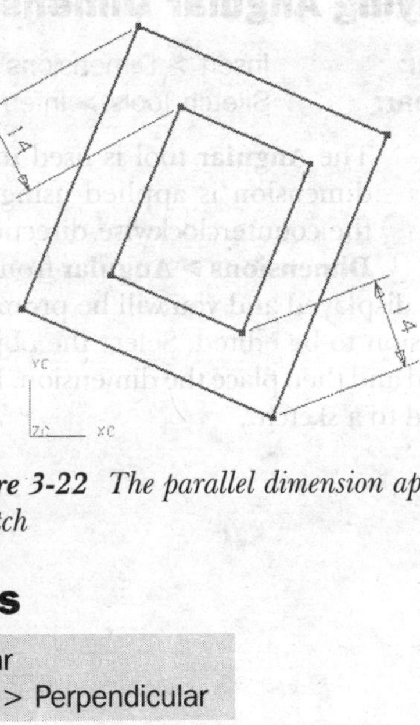

Figure 3-22 *The parallel dimension applied to a sketch*

Applying Perpendicular Dimensions

Menu:	Insert > Dimensions > Perpendicular
Toolbar:	Sketch Tools > Inferred Dimensions > Perpendicular

The **Perpendicular** tool is used to create the perpendicular dimension between a linear object and a point. It is mandatory that any one of the objects selected must be a linear object. To create the perpendicular dimension, choose **Inferred Dimensions > Perpendicular** from the **Sketch Tools** toolbar; the **Dimensions** dialog box will be displayed and you will be prompted to select an object to be dimensioned or select a dimension to be edited. Select the objects between which the dimension needs to be applied and then place the dimension. As soon as you place the dimension; an edit box will be displayed. Enter the required value in this edit box, and then press ENTER. Figure 3-23 shows the perpendicular dimension applied to a sketch.

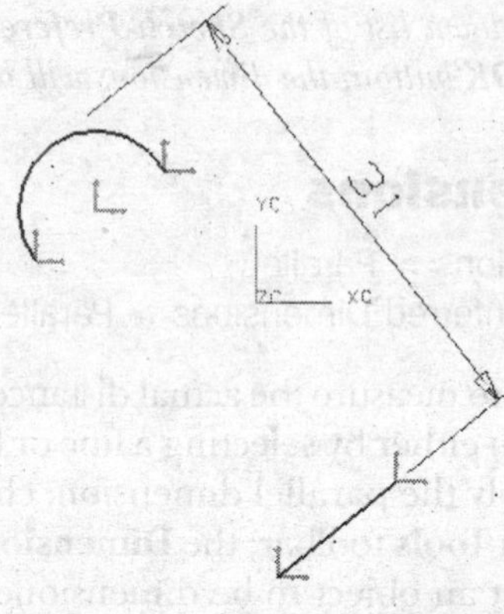

***Figure 3-23** The perpendicular dimension applied between the objects*

Applying Angular Dimensions

Menu:	Insert > Dimensions > Angular
Toolbar:	Sketch Tools > Inferred Dimensions > Angular

The **Angular** tool is used to apply an angular dimension. Whenever an angular dimension is applied using the **Angular** tool, the angle is always measured in the counterclockwise direction. To create an angular dimension, choose **Inferred Dimensions > Angular** from the **Sketch Tools** toolbar; the **Dimensions** dialog box will be displayed and you will be prompted to select an object to be dimensioned or select a dimension to be edited. Select the objects between which the angle dimension needs to be applied and then place the dimension. Figure 3-24 shows different types of angular dimensions applied to a sketch.

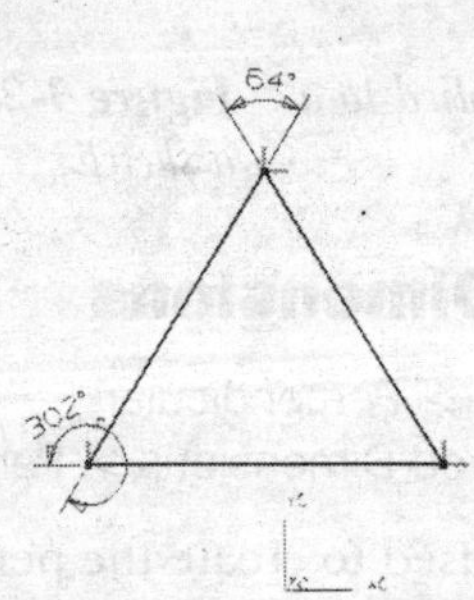

***Figure 3-24** Angular dimensions applied between the objects*

Applying Diameter Dimensions

Menu:	Insert > Dimensions > Diameter
Toolbar:	Sketch Tools > Inferred Dimensions > Diameter

The **Diameter** tool is used to apply the diameter dimension to an arc or a circle. Generally, diameter dimensions are applied to circles. To apply the diameter dimension, choose **Inferred Dimensions > Diameter** from the **Sketch Tools** toolbar; the **Dimensions** dialog box will be displayed and you will be prompted to select an arc to be dimensioned or a dimension to be edited. Select the object to be dimensioned and then place the dimension. As soon as you place the dimension, an edit box will be displayed. Enter the required value in this edit box, and then press ENTER. Figure 3-25 shows the diameter dimension applied to a circle and Figure 3-26 shows the diameter dimension applied to an arc.

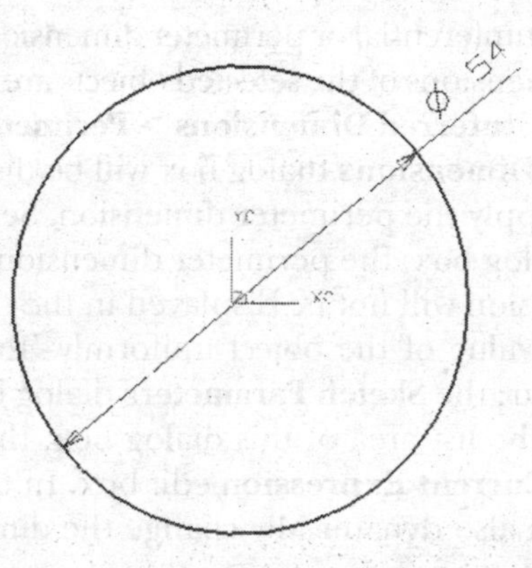

Figure 3-25 *The diameter dimension applied to a circle*

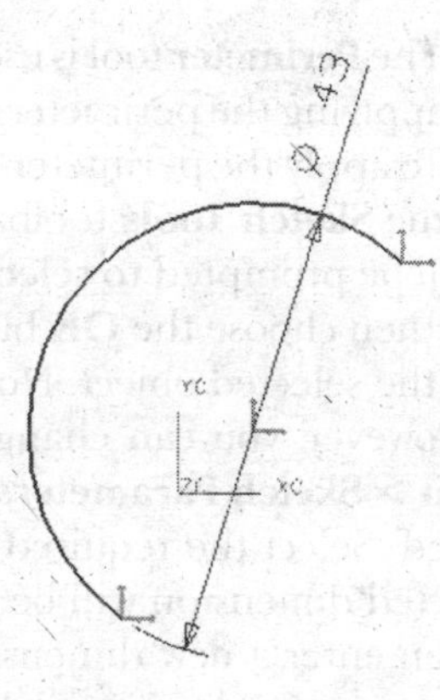

Figure 3-26 *The diameter dimension applied to an arc*

Applying Radius Dimensions

Menu:	Insert > Dimensions > Radius
Toolbar:	Sketch Tools > Inferred Dimensions > Radius

The **Radius** tool is used to apply the radius dimension to an arc or a circle. Generally, radius dimensions are applied to arcs. To apply radius dimension, choose **Inferred Dimensions > Radius** from the **Sketch Tools** toolbar; the **Dimensions** dialog box will be displayed and you will be prompted to select an arc to be dimensioned or a dimension to be edited. Select the object to be dimensioned and then place the dimension. As soon as you place the dimension, an edit box will be displayed. Enter the required value in this edit box, and then press ENTER. Figure 3-27 shows the radius dimension applied to a circle and Figure 3-28 shows the radius dimension applied to an arc.

Applying Perimeter Dimensions

Menu:	Insert > Dimensions > Perimeter
Toolbar:	Sketch Tools > Inferred Dimensions > Perimeter

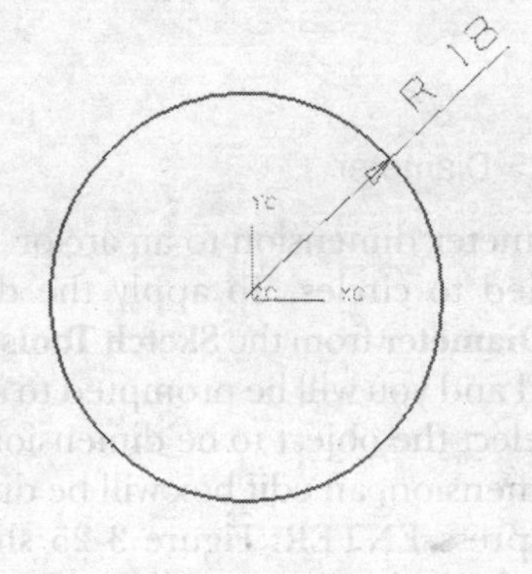

Figure 3-27 The radius dimension applied to a circle

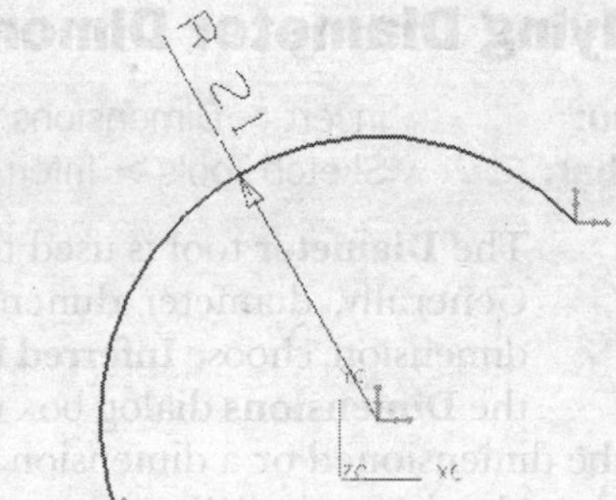

Figure 3-28 The radius dimension applied to an arc

The **Perimeter** tool is used to apply the circumferential or perimeter dimension. After applying the perimeter dimension, all dimensions of the selected objects are locked. To apply the perimeter dimension, choose **Inferred Dimensions > Perimeter** from the **Sketch Tools** toolbar; the **Perimeter Dimensions** dialog box will be displayed and you will be prompted to select lines or arcs to apply the perimeter dimension. Select the object and then choose the **OK** button from this dialog box; the perimeter dimension will be applied to the selected object. Note that this dimension will not be displayed in the drawing window. However, you can change the dimension value of the object uniformly. To do so, choose **Edit > Sketch Parameters** from the menu bar; the **Sketch Parameters** dialog box will be displayed. Select the required dimension from the list area of this dialog box; the value of the selected dimension will be displayed in the **Current Expression** edit box. In this edit box, you can enter a new dimension value. You can also dynamically change the dimension value by moving the slider available below this edit box.

You can also apply the perimeter dimension to a closed sketch. To do so, invoke the **Perimeter Dimensions** dialog box and then select all entities of the closed sketch one by one. Next, choose the **OK** button from the **Perimeter Dimensions** dialog box; the dimension will be applied to the sketch. Now, if you modify the dimension of any one of the entities, the dimension of other entities will also be modified such that the total perimeter of the sketch remains the same.

Applying Dimensions by Using the Inferred Dimensions

Menu: Insert > Dimensions > Inferred Dimensions
Toolbar: Sketch Tools > Inferred Dimensions

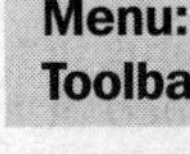

The **Inferred Dimensions** tool is used to apply all the dimension types discussed above. A dimension is applied based on the object selected and the location of the cursor. For example, if you select an arc, the radial dimension will be applied. Similarly, if you select a circle, the diameter dimension will be applied. Select an inclined line and move the cursor parallel to that line; a parallel dimension will be applied. If you move the cursor vertically upward or downward, a horizontal dimension will be applied. Similarly, if you move the cursor in the horizontal direction (right or left), a vertical dimension will be applied.

It is recommended that you use this tool to apply dimensions as it saves the time required for selecting various dimensioning tools. To apply inferred dimensions, choose the **Inferred Dimensions** button from the **Sketch Tools** toolbar; the **Dimensions** dialog box will be displayed and you will be prompted to select the object to be dimensioned or a dimension to be edited. According to the selection procedure adopted while selecting objects, the dimensions will be applied. Figure 3-29 shows the radial and linear dimensions created.

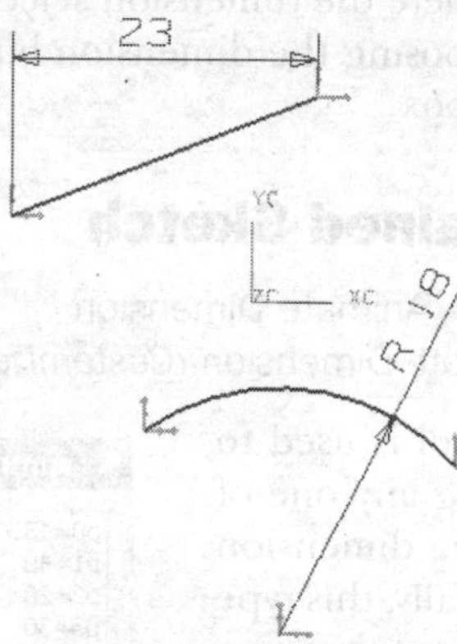

***Figure 3-29** The radial and linear dimensions created by using the **Inferred Dimensions** tool*

Editing the Dimension Value and Other Parameters

To edit a dimension that has already been placed, double-click on it; an edit box will be displayed. Enter value in this edit box and press ENTER.

You can also edit a dimension that has already been placed by using the **Dimensions** dialog box. To do so, invoke the **Dimensions** dialog box by choosing the **Inferred Dimensions** button from the **Sketch Tools** toolbar. Next, choose the **Sketch Dimensions Dialog** button from the **Dimensions** dialog box; the **Dimensions** dialog box will be modified, as shown in Figure 3-30. From the list box of this dialog box, select the dimension that you want to modify; the **Current Expression** area will be enabled. Note that the edit box on the right of this area displays the dimension value of the selected dimension. You can enter a new dimension value in the edit box and press the ENTER key.

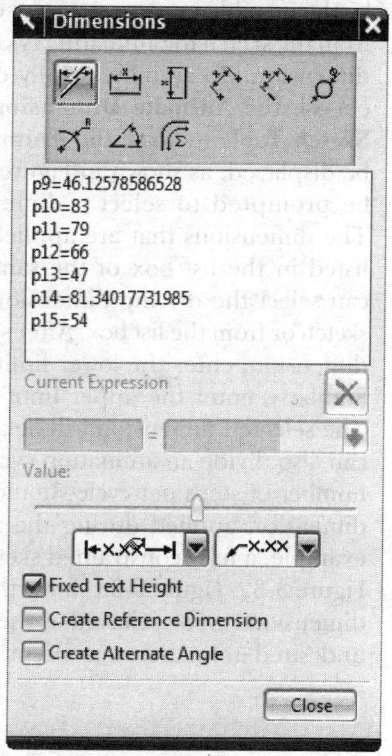

***Figure 3-30** The modified **Dimensions** dialog box*

You can also modify the value of the dimension dynamically by using the **Value** sliding bar in the **Current Expression** area. The first drop-down list below the **Value** sliding bar provides the options for placing the arrows with respect to the dimension line. The second drop-down list provides the options for placing the leader on the left or the right. The **Fixed Text Height** check box allows you to maintain the dimension text at a constant size when you zoom in or out a sketch. If you clear this check box, NX scales the dimension text as well as the sketch geometry. The **Create Reference Dimension** check box is used to create the reference (non-driving) dimensions. The **Create Alternate Angle** check box is used to calculate the maximum dimension between the sketch curves. Next, choose the **Close** button to reflect the changes. You can choose the **Remove Highlighted** button to delete the dimension selected from the list box. You can also apply a dimension by choosing the dimension buttons available above the list box in the **Dimensions** dialog box.

Animating a Fully-Constrained Sketch

Menu:	Tools > Constraints > Animate Dimension
Toolbar:	Sketch Tools > Animate Dimension *(Customize to Add)*

The **Animate Dimension** tool is used to animate a sketch by selecting any one of the dimensions as the driving dimension from the same sketch. Generally, this type of animation is used while creating basic mechanisms and links. When a dimension from a fully constrained sketch is animated, the whole sketch gets mechanized by the possible movements. The dimension selected from the sketch for animating is known as the driving dimension. To animate a fully constrained sketch, choose the **Animate Dimension** button from the **Sketch Tools** toolbar; the **Animate** dialog box will be displayed, as shown in Figure 3-31, and you will be prompted to select a dimension to animate. The dimensions that are applied to the sketch are listed in the list box of the same dialog box. You can select the driving dimension directly from the sketch or from the list box. After selecting the driving dimension, enter the lower limit value for the dimension inside the **Lower Limit** edit box. Similarly, enter the upper limit value for the dimension inside the **Upper Limit** edit box. The selected dimension will be animated between the lower and upper limits specified. You can also divide an animation cycle into a number of steps and then animate the design. The number of steps per cycle should be entered inside the **Steps/Cycle** edit box. To display the dimension applied during the animation, select the **Display Dimensions** check box. For example, a fully constrained sketch from which the driving dimension is selected is shown in Figure 3-32. Figure 3-33 shows the sketch while animating. Note that at an instance, only one dimension can be selected as the driving dimension. If the sketch is not fully constrained, an undesired animation may occur.

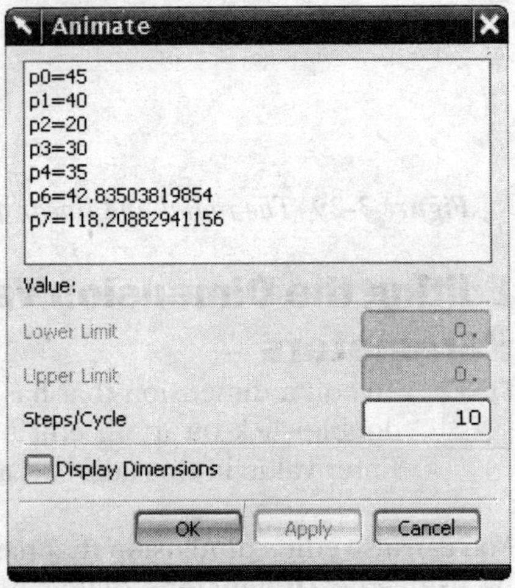

***Figure 3-31** The **Animate** dialog box*

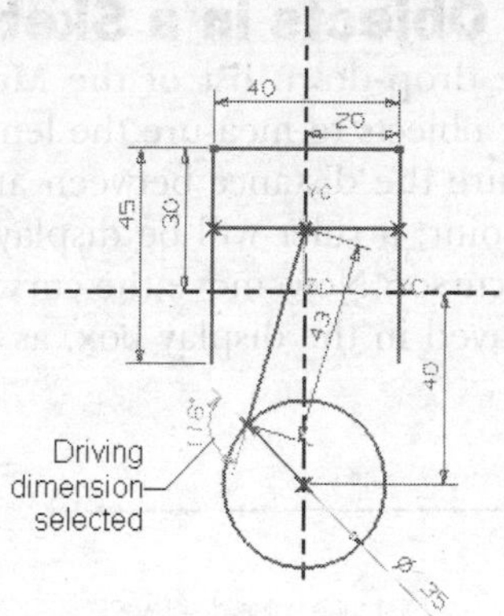

Figure 3-32 Driving dimension selected from the sketch

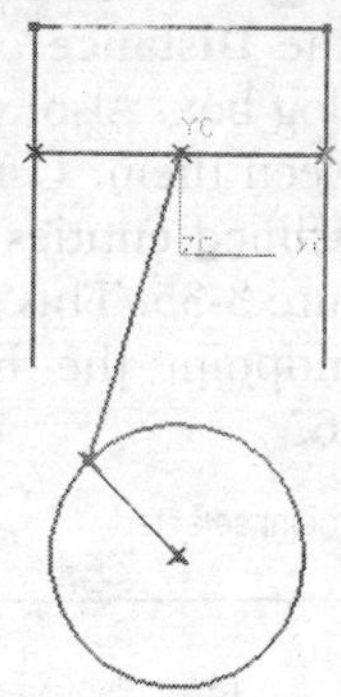

Figure 3-33 The sketch being animated

MEASURING THE DISTANCE VALUE BETWEEN OBJECTS IN A SKETCH

Menu:	Analysis > Measure Distance
Toolbar:	Utility > Measure Distance

While sketching, you may need to measure the dimension of various sketched entities. To do so, choose the **Measure Distance** button from the **Utility** toolbar; the **Measure Distance** dialog box will be displayed, as shown in Figure 3-34. Using this dialog box, you can measure the distance value between sketched entities through a number of methods. The methods for measuring the dimension of various sketched entities are discussed next.

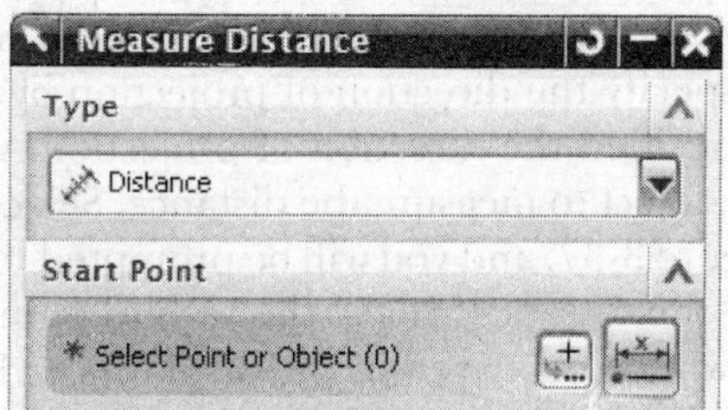

Figure 3-34 The ***Measure Distance*** *dialog box*

Measuring the Distance between Two Objects in a Sketch

By default, the **Distance** option is selected in the **Type** drop-down list of the **Measure Distance** dialog box. Also, you are prompted to select the objects to measure the length or distance between them. Using this option, you can measure the distance between any two linear and inclined entities of a sketch. Select the start point; a ruler will be displayed, as shown in Figure 3-35. This ruler stretches along with the cursor. Now, move the cursor and specify the endpoint; the distance measured will be displayed in the display box, as shown in Figure 3-36.

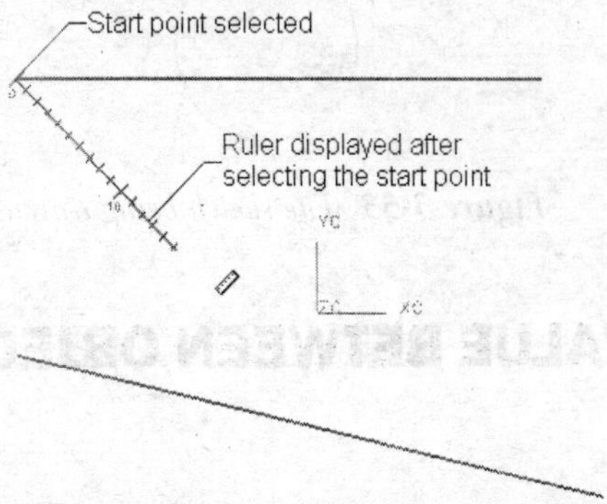

Figure 3-35 The ruler displayed after selecting the start point

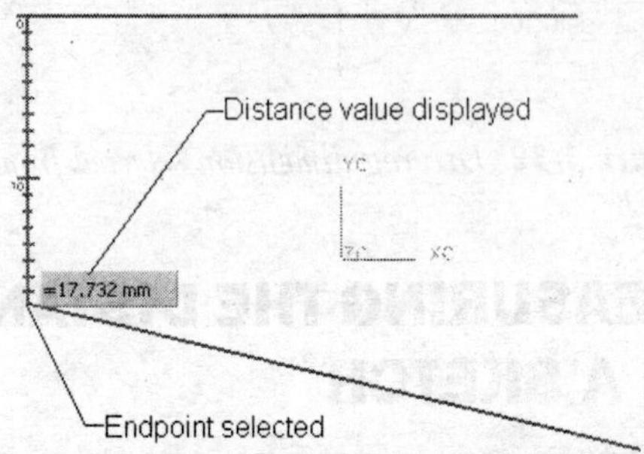

Figure 3-36 The distance value displayed in the display box

Measuring the Projected Distance between Two Objects

To measure the distance between two objects along a predefined projected direction, select the **Projected Distance** option from the **Type** drop-down list in the **Measure Distance** dialog box; the dialog box will be modified and you will be prompted to select the objects to infer vector. Select the object or use the **Inferred Vector** drop-down list to specify the direction of projection. You can also specify the direction of projection by using the **Vector Constructor** button. Once you have specified the direction of projection, you will be prompted to select the start point or the first object to measure the distance. Select the start point; a ruler will be displayed, as shown in Figure 3-37, and you will be prompted to select the second point or the second object to measure the distance. Select the second point to measure the distance; the measured distance value will be displayed in the display box. Figure 3-38 shows the distance value displayed in the display box.

Measuring the Screen Distance between Two Objects

The screen distance is the distance between any two objects in a particular orientation on the screen. To measure the screen distance between two objects, select the **Screen Distance** option from the **Type** drop-down list in the **Measure Distance** dialog box; you will be prompted to select the start point or the first object to measure the distance. Select the first object; a ruler will be displayed, as shown in Figure 3-39, and you will be prompted to select the second point or the second object to measure the distance. Select the second object; the distance value between the two objects selected for the particular view or orientation will be displayed in the display box, as shown in Figure 3-40. Note that if you measure the distance between two same objects by changing the orientation, the distance value will also be changed.

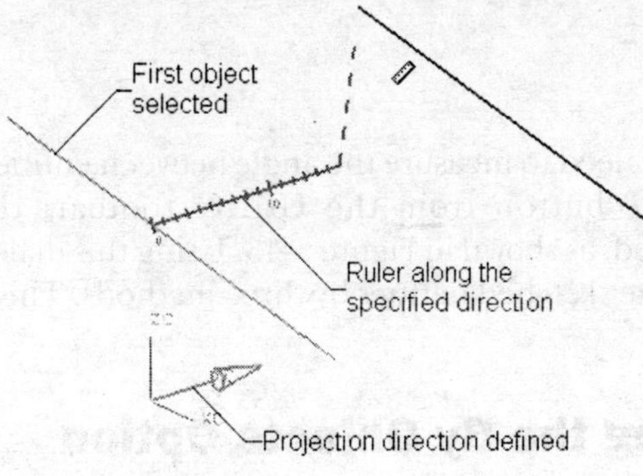

Figure 3-37 The ruler locked to the specified projection direction

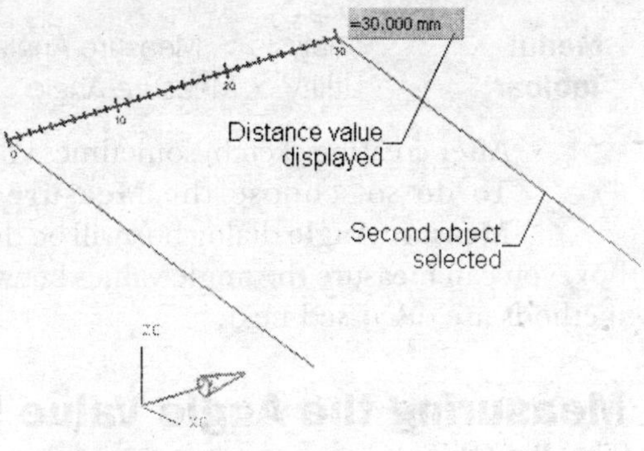

Figure 3-38 The distance value displayed in the display box

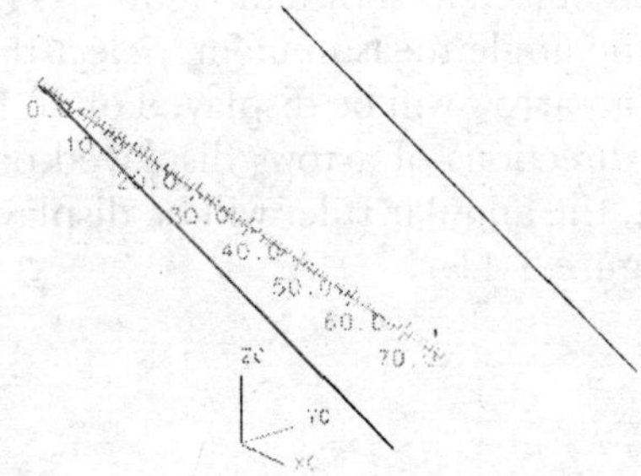

Figure 3-39 The ruler displayed after selecting the first object

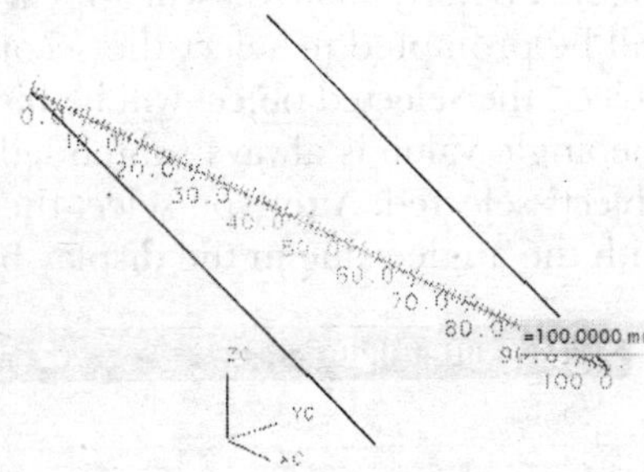

Figure 3-40 The distance value displayed on the display box

Measuring the Length of an Arc or a Line

To measure the length of an arc or a line, select the **Length** option from the **Type** drop-down list in the **Measure Distance** dialog box; you will be prompted to select the curve or the edge. Select an object (an arc or a line); the length of the selected object will be displayed instantly in the display box, as shown in Figures 3-41 and 3-42. Note that if you continue selecting the entities, the total arc length displayed will be the sum of the arc lengths of all the selected entities.

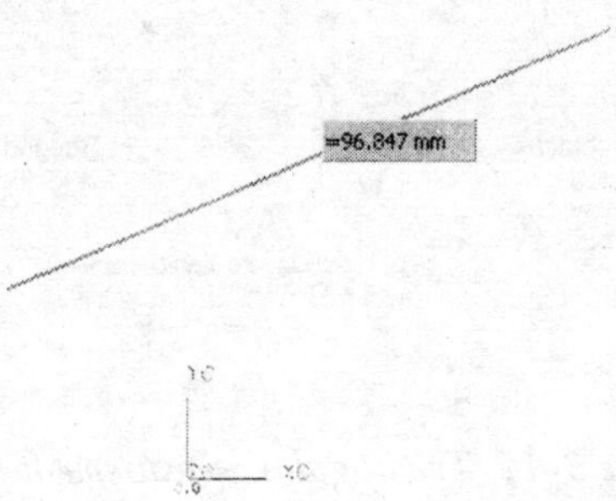

Figure 3-41 The length measurement displayed for a line

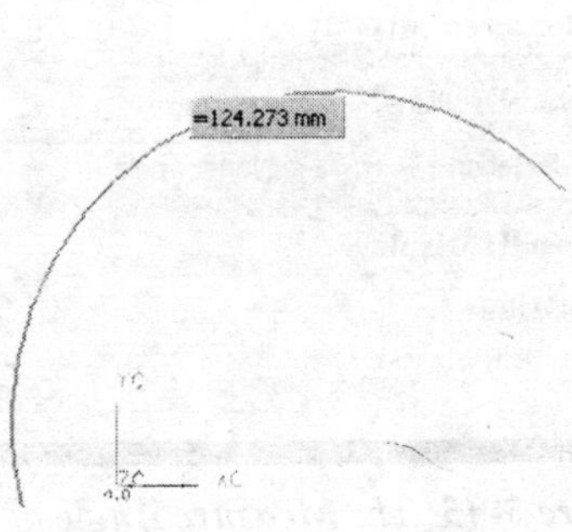

Figure 3-42 The arc length measurement displayed for an arc

MEASURING THE ANGLE BETWEEN ENTITIES

Menu:	Analysis > Measure Angle
Toolbar:	Utility > Measure Angle

After creating sketch, sometimes you may need to measure the angle between entities. To do so, choose the **Measure Angle** button from the **Utility** toolbar; the **Measure Angle** dialog box will be displayed, as shown in Figure 3-43. Using this dialog box, you can measure the angle values between the sketched entities by three methods. These methods are discussed next.

Measuring the Angle Value Using the By Objects Option

The **By Objects** option is used to measure the angle value subtended between any two selected objects. By default, this option is selected in the **Type** drop-down list of the **Measure Angle** dialog box and you are prompted to select the first object for the angle measurement. Select the first object; an arrow will appear on the selected object, as shown in Figure 3-44, and you will be prompted to select the second object for the angle measurement. Select the second object; the selected object will be highlighted and an arrow will be displayed on it. Note that the angle value is always subtended between the directions of arrows displayed on the two objects selected. After you select the second object, the angular ruler will be displayed along with the angle value in the display box, refer to Figure 3-44.

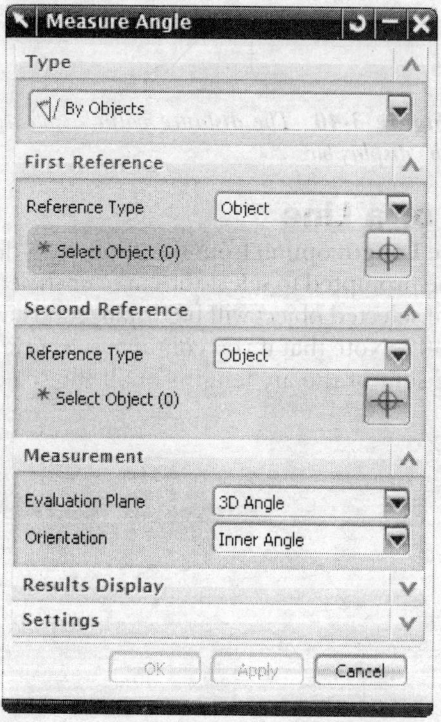

*Figure 3-43 The **Measure Angle** dialog box*

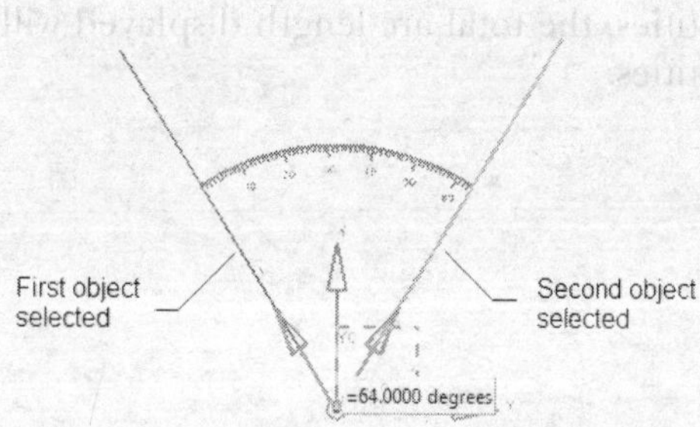

*Figure 3-44 The angular measurement displayed using the **By Objects** option*

Measuring the Angle Value Using the By 3 Points Option

The **By 3 Points** option is used to measure the angle value subtended between three selected points. To measure the angle value by using this option, select the **By 3 Points** option from the **Type** drop-down list in the **Measure Angle** dialog box; you will be prompted to select the start point for the angle measurement. Select the start point; you will be prompted to select the second point for the angle base line. Select the second point; you will be prompted again to select the third point to measure the angle. On selecting the third point, the angle value along with the angular ruler will be displayed in the display box, refer to Figure 3-45.

Measuring the Angle Value Using the By Screen Points Option

The **By Screen Points** option is used to measure the angle value between the three selected points for a particular orientation on the screen. The angle displayed between the selected objects is always subtended with respect to the view point (the point from which you are viewing the objects). To measure the angle value using this method, select the **By Screen Points** option from the **Type** drop-down list. You will be prompted to select the start point for the angle measurement. Select the start point; you will be prompted to select the second point for the angle base line. Select the second point; you will be prompted to select the third point to measure the angle. Select the third point; the angle value enclosed between the three points will be displayed in a display box along with the angular ruler. Figure 3-46 shows a sketch that was used to measure the angle using this method. However, in this figure, the view of the sketch is modified. As a result, the angle measurement has been modified on the basis of the current orientation of the view.

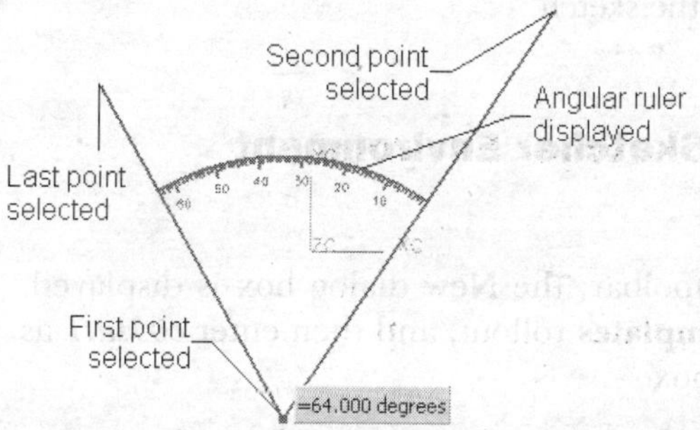

*Figure 3-45 The angle measured using the **By 3 Points** option*

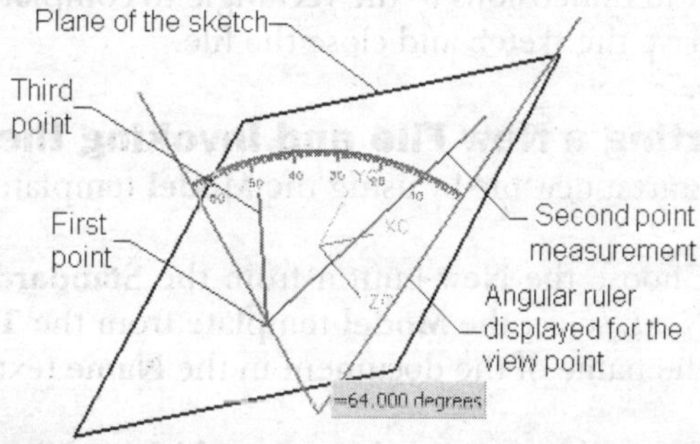

*Figure 3-46 The angular measurement displayed using the **By Screen Points** option*

TUTORIALS

From this chapter onward, you will use sketcher constraints and parametric dimensions to complete model.

Tutorial 1

In this tutorial, you will draw the profile of the model shown in Figure 3-47. The profile is shown in Figure 3-48. The profile should be symmetric about the origin. Also, you will use the parametric dimensions to complete the sketch. **(Expected time: 30 min)**

Figure 3-47 Model for Tutorial 1

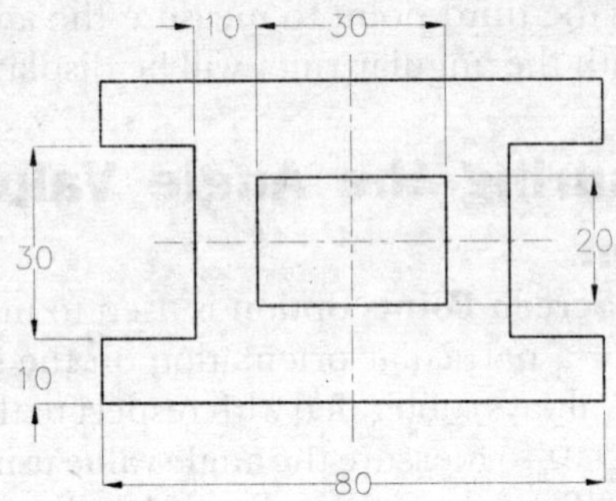

Figure 3-48 Sketch for Tutorial 1

The following steps are required to complete this tutorial:

a. Start a new file, and invoke the sketcher environment.
b. Draw the outer profile of the sketch using the **Profile** tool.
c. Add the geometric and dimensional constraints to the outer loop.
d. Draw a rectangle inside the outer loop using the **Rectangle** tool.
e. Add dimensions to the rectangle to complete the sketch.
f. Save the sketch and close the file.

Starting a New File and Invoking the Sketcher Environment

Start a new file by using the **Model** template.

1. Choose the **New** button from the **Standard** toolbar; the **New** dialog box is displayed. Next, select the **Model** template from the **Templates** rollout, and then enter ***c03tut1*** as the name of the document in the **Name** text box.

2. Choose the button on the right of the **Folder** text box; the **Choose Directory** dialog box is displayed. Next, browse to the *C:\NX 7\c03* folder, and then choose the **OK** button twice; the new file is started in the Modeling environment.

3. Turn on the display of WCS by choosing the **Display WCS** button from the **Utility** toolbar.

4. Invoke the Sketcher environment by using the XC-ZC plane as the sketching plane.

Drawing the Outer Loop and Adding Sketcher Constraints

If the sketch consists of more than one closed loop, it is recommended that you draw the outer loop first and then add all the required sketcher constraints and dimensions to it. This makes it easier to draw and dimension the inner loops. Next, you need to draw the inner loop.

1. By default, the **Profile** tool from the **Sketch Tools** toolbar is chosen and you are prompted to select the first point of the line or press and drag the left mouse button to begin with the arc creation.

2. Draw the sketch around the origin following the sequence shown in Figure 3-49. The sketch is non-symmetric at this stage. But, after adding the sketcher constraints and the required dimensions, it will become symmetric. You can use the help lines to draw the sketch. For your reference, the sequence in which the lines to be drawn in the sketch is indicated by numbers.

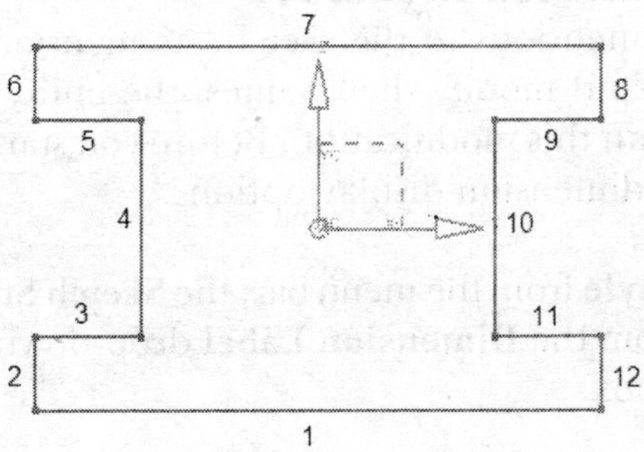

Figure 3-49 The outer loop of the profile and the sequence in which lines to be drawn

Next, you need to apply the geometric and dimensional constraints to the sketch members. But before you do that, it is recommended that you turn on the display of constraints, if it is not already on.

3. Choose the **Show All Constraints** button from the **Sketch Tools** toolbar to view the constraints applied to the sketch.

4. Next, choose the **Constraints** button from the **Sketch Tools** toolbar; you are prompted to select curves to create constraints.

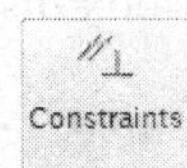

5. Select lines 1 and 7; the **Constraints** dialog box is displayed with all possible constraints that can be applied to the selected entities. Next, choose the **Equal Length** button from the **Constraints** dialog box. The symbol for the equal length constraint is displayed on both sketch members, indicating that this constraint is applied between the two selected entities.

6. Similarly, apply the equal length constraint between lines 8 and 6, 6 and 2, 2 and 12, 12 and 8, 3 and 11, 9 and 5, and 10 and 4. The sketch after applying the equal constraint to all these line entities is shown in Figure 3-50.

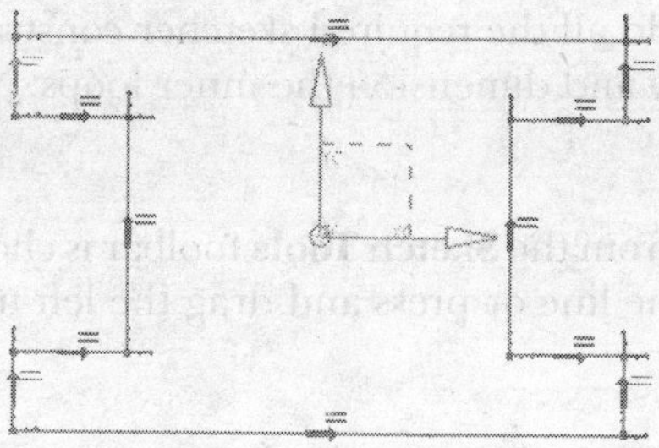

Figure 3-50 The outer profile after adding the ***Equal Length*** *constraint*

Adding Dimensions to Sketch Members

Next, you need to add dimensions to the sketch. As mentioned earlier, when you add dimensions to the sketch and modify their values, the entity is forced by the specified dimension value to maintain this modification. Before you start dimensioning the sketch, you need to modify some dimension display options.

1. Choose **Sketch > Sketch Style** from the menu bar; the **Sketch Style** dialog box is displayed. Select the **Value** option from the **Dimension Label** drop-down list. Next, choose the **OK** button to exit this dialog box.

2. Choose the **Inferred Dimensions** button from the **Sketch Tools** toolbar; you are prompted to select an object to dimension or the dimension to edit.

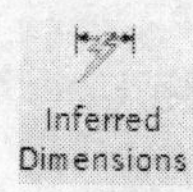

3. Select the line 1; the current dimension of the line 1 is attached to the cursor. Now, you need to place the dimension at the required location. Click the left mouse button below the line 1 to place the dimension, refer to Figure 3-51. As you place the dimension; an edit box is displayed. Enter **80** in the edit box and press ENTER. Next, choose the **Fit** button from the **View** toolbar.

4. Select the line 2 and place the dimensions on the left of the sketch. Enter **10** in the edit box displayed and press ENTER.

5. Select the line 4 and place the dimension on the left of the sketch. Next, modify the dimension value to **30** and press ENTER.

6. Select the line 5 and place the dimension below the line. Next, modify the dimension value to **15** and press ENTER.

   To make the sketch symmetric, you need to apply the dimension between line 7 and the horizontal datum axis and between line 10 and the vertical datum axis.

7. Select the line 7 and the horizontal axis and place the dimension on the right of the sketch. Next, modify the dimension value to **25** and press ENTER.

8. Select the line 10 and the vertical axis and place the dimension below the sketch. Next, modify the dimension value to **25** and press ENTER.

   When you place the dimensions, they generally scatter all around the sketch. It is a good practice to arrange them properly.

9. Exit the **Inferred Dimensions** tool by pressing the ESC key twice and then drag the dimensions to place them properly around the sketch, refer to Figure 3-51.

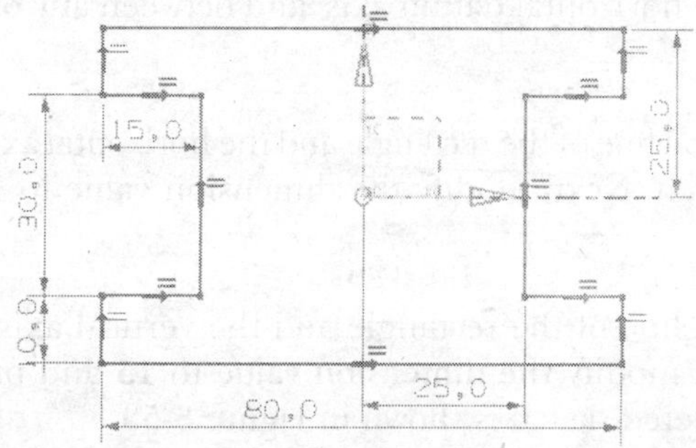

***Figure 3-51** The outer profile after adding the required dimensions*

Drawing the Inner Loop and Adding the Constraints and Dimensions

Next, you need to draw the rectangular profile inside the outer loop.

1. Choose the **Rectangle** button from the **Sketch Tools** toolbar; the **Rectangle** dialog box is displayed and you are prompted to select the first point of the rectangle.

2. Draw the rectangle inside the outer profile by specifying its first point and a point to create the rectangle, refer to Figure 3-52.

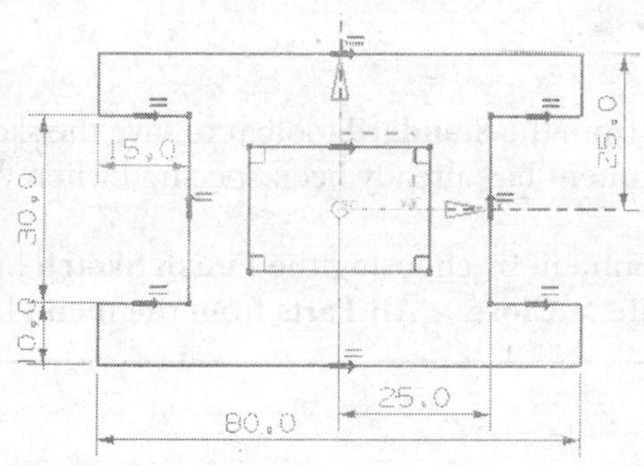

***Figure 3-52** The sketch after drawing the inner loop and turning on the display of constraints*

Next, you need to add dimensions to the inner profile.

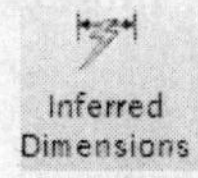

3. Choose the **Inferred Dimensions** button from the **Sketch Tools** toolbar and select the upper horizontal line of the rectangle. Place the dimension above the sketch. Next, modify the value to **30** and press ENTER.

4. Select the right vertical line of the rectangle and place the dimension on the right of the sketch. Next, modify the value to **20** and press ENTER, refer to Figure 3-53.

To make the rectangle symmetric, you need to apply the dimension between any of the horizontal lines and the horizontal datum axis, and between any of the vertical lines and the vertical datum axis.

5. Select the lower horizontal line of the rectangle and the horizontal axis. Place the dimension on the right of the sketch. Next, modify the dimension value to **10** and press ENTER, refer to Figure 3-53.

6. Select the right vertical line of the rectangle and the vertical axis. Place the dimension above the sketch. Next, modify the dimension value to **15** and press ENTER, refer to Figure 3-53. The completed sketch is shown in Figure 3-53.

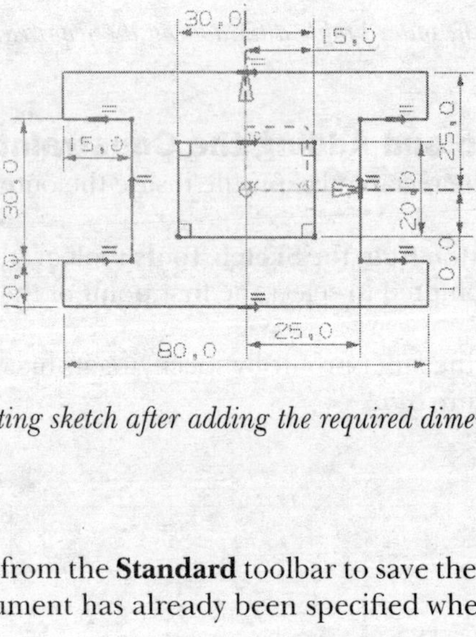

Figure 3-53 The resulting sketch after adding the required dimensions and constraints

Saving the File

1. Choose the **Save** button from the **Standard** toolbar to save the sketch. Note that the name and location of the document has already been specified when you started the new file.

2. Exit the Sketcher environment by choosing the **Finish Sketch** button from the **Sketcher** toolbar. Next, choose **File > Close > All Parts** from the menu bar to close the file.

Tutorial 2

In this tutorial, you will create the profile for the model shown in Figure 3-54. The profile is shown in Figure 3-55. You will use the geometric and dimensional constraints to complete this sketch. **(Expected time: 30 min)**

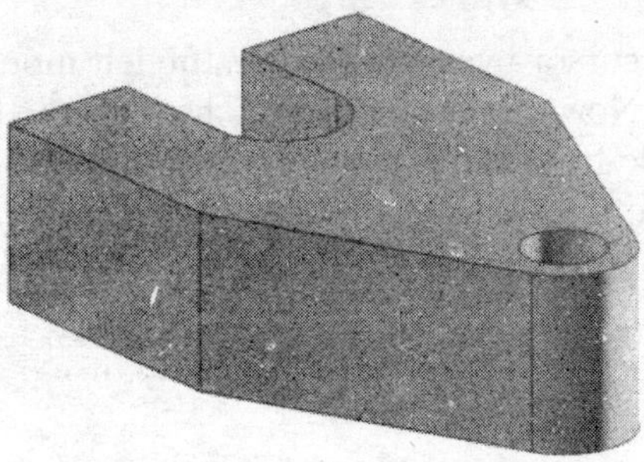

Figure 3-54 *Model for Tutorial 2*

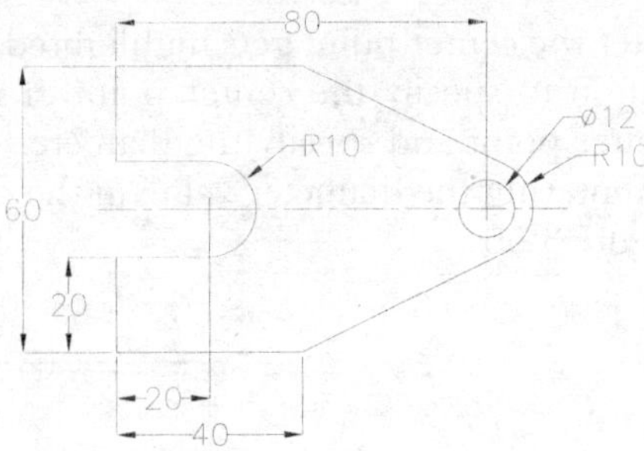

Figure 3-55 *Sketch for Tutorial 2*

The following steps are required to complete this tutorial:

a. Start a new file in NX and invoke the sketcher environment.
b. Draw the sketch using the **Profile** tool.
c. Add the geometric and dimensional constraints to the sketch.
d. Save the sketch and close the file.

Starting a New File in NX and Invoking the Sketcher Environment

1. Start a new file with the name *c03tut2.prt* using the **Model** template and specify its location as *C:\NX 7\c03*.

2. Turn on the display of WCS by choosing the **Display WCS** button from the **Utility** toolbar.

3. Invoke the Sketcher environment by using the XC-ZC plane as the sketching plane.

Drawing the Sketch

1. By default, the **Profile** button is chosen in the **Sketch Tools** toolbar. Draw the outer profile of the sketch, refer to Figure 3-56. You can draw the first line with exact dimensions and then draw the remaining sketched entities with dimension values close to the required dimension values. Note that the start point of the line 1 is at the origin.

   Note that after drawing the first line, you may need to modify the drawing display area by using the **Fit** button from the **View** toolbar.

2. Next, choose the **Circle** button from the **Sketch Tools** toolbar. Move the cursor over the arc that is numbered 3 in Figure 3-56; the center point of the arc is highlighted.

Note

*If the center point of the arc is not highlighted, choose the **Arc Center** button from the **Selection Bar**.*

3. After the center point gets highlighted, move the cursor over it and press the left mouse button to specify the center point of the circle. Now, move the cursor away from the center point and specify the diameter of the circle by clicking the left mouse button or by entering the diameter value in the diameter input box. The circle is created, refer to Figure 3-56.

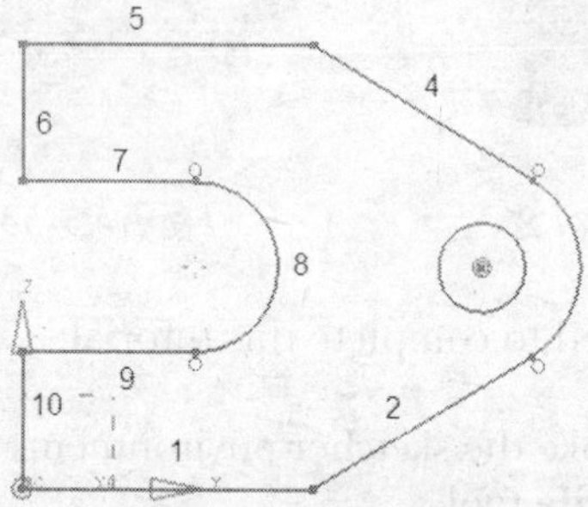

***Figure 3-56** The sequence to be followed for drawing the sketch*

Adding Constraints to the Sketch

1. Choose the **Constraints** button from the **Sketch Tools** toolbar.

2. Select the line 1 and apply the horizontal constraint by choosing the **Horizontal** button from the **Constraints** dialog box, if this constraint has not already been applied. Similarly, apply the horizontal constraints to lines 5, 7, and 9.

3. Similarly, apply the **Vertical** constraints to lines 6 and 10, if this constraint has not already been applied.

4. Next, select the circle and the arc 3 to apply the concentric constraint; the **Constraints** dialog box is displayed. Choose the **Concentric** button from it.

5. Select lines 1 and 5 and then choose the **Equal Length** button from the **Constraints** dialog box to apply the equal length constraint.

6. Similarly, apply the equal length constraint between lines 2 and 4, 6 and 10, and 7 and 9.

The sketch after applying all constraints is shown in Figure 3-57.

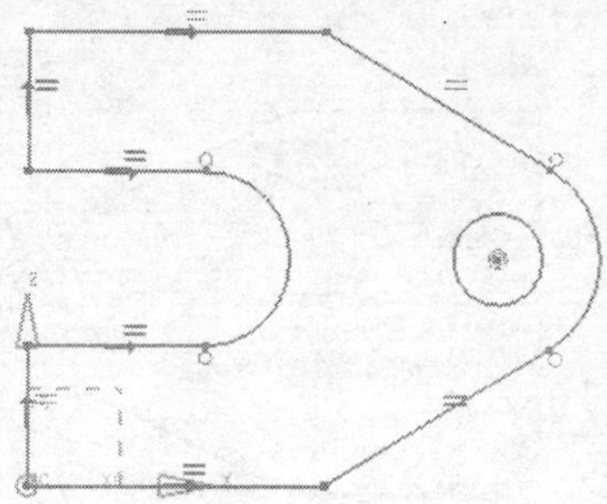

Figure 3-57 The sketch displayed after adding the required constraints

Adding Dimensions to the Sketch

Next, you need to add the dimensions to the sketch.

1. Choose the **Inferred Dimensions** button from the **Sketch Tools** toolbar.

2. Select the line 5 and place the dimension above the line. Modify the dimension value to **40** and press ENTER, refer to Figure 3-58.

3. Select the line 6 and the center point of the circle. Place the dimension above the previous dimension and modify the dimension value to **80**. Press the ENTER key.

4. Select the line 9 and place the dimension, refer to Figure 3-58. Next, modify the dimension value to **20** and press ENTER.

5. Select the line 10 and place the dimension on the left of the sketch. Next, modify the dimension value to **20** and press ENTER.

6. Select the arc 8 and place the dimension, refer to Figure 3-58. Next, modify the dimension value to **10** and press ENTER.

7. Select the arc 3 and place the dimension, refer to Figure 3-58. Next, modify the dimension value to **10** and press ENTER

8. Select the circle and place the dimension, refer to Figure 3-58. Next, modify the dimension value to **12** and press ENTER.

9. Choose the **Fit** button from the **View** toolbar.

The final sketch after adding the required dimensions is shown in Figure 3-58.

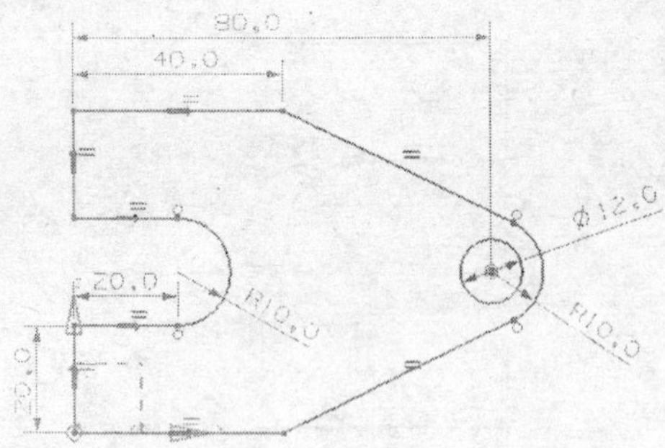

Figure 3-58 The final sketch after adding the required dimensions and constraints

Saving the File

1. Choose the **Save** button from the **Standard** toolbar to save the sketch. Note that the name and the location of the document has already been specified when you started the new file.

2. Exit the Sketcher environment and choose **File > Close > All Parts** from the menu bar to close the file.

Tutorial 3

In this tutorial, you will create the profile for the revolved model shown in Figure 3-59. The profile is shown in Figure 3-60. You will use the geometric and dimensional constraints to complete this sketch. **(Expected time: 30 min)**

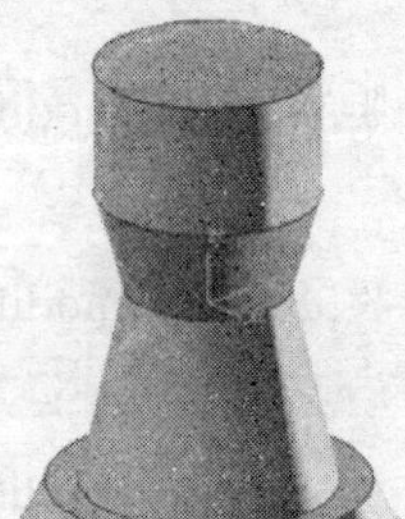

Figure 3-59 Model for Tutorial 3

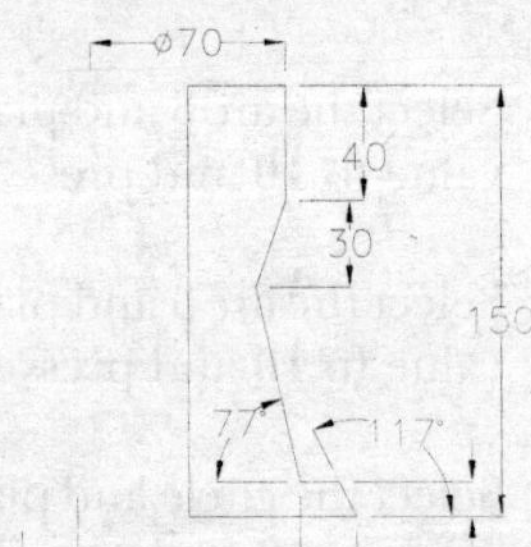

Figure 3-60 Sketch for Tutorial 3

The following steps are required to complete this tutorial:

a. Start a new file in NX and invoke the sketcher environment.
b. Draw the required profile of the sketch using the **Profile** tool.
c. Add the geometric and dimensional constraints to the sketch.
d. Save the sketch and close the file.

Starting a New File in NX and Invoking the Sketcher Environment

1. Start a new file with the name *c03tut3.prt* using the **Model** template and specify its location as *C:\NX 7\c03*.

2. Turn on the display of WCS by choosing the **Display WCS** button from the **Utility** toolbar.

3. Invoke the Sketcher environment using the XC-ZC plane as the sketching plane.

Drawing the Sketch

It is recommended that you create the first sketch member with the exact measurement by entering the value in the edit box displayed. After creating the first sketch member, you can create the other sketch members by taking the first entity as the reference. After creating the entire sketch, you can modify the values by using the dimensions tool.

1. By default, the **Profile** button is chosen in the **Sketch Tools** toolbar and you are prompted to specify the first point of the line. Specify the start point of the line at the origin. Next, move the cursor horizontally toward the right and enter **60** in the **Length** edit box and **0** in the **Angle** edit box. Next, press the ENTER key.

2. Follow the sequence given in Figure 3-61 for drawing the sketch. Draw the other entities of the sketch. For better understanding, the sketch has been numbered.

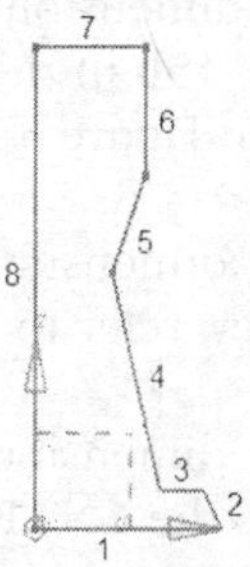

***Figure 3-61** The sequence for drawing the profile*

Adding Geometric Constraints to the Sketch

After completing the sketch, you need to apply constraints to it.

1. Choose the **Constraints** button from the **Sketch Tools** toolbar and select the line 8; the **Constraints** dialog box is displayed. Choose the **Vertical** button from this dialog box to apply the vertical dimension, if it is not applied automatically, while drawing the sketch.

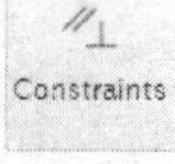

2. Similarly, apply the horizontal constraint to lines 1, 3, and 7, if this constraint is not applied automatically.

3. Apply the vertical constraint to line 6, if it is not applied automatically.

4. After applying the constraints, choose the **Show All Constraints** button from the **Sketch Constraints** toolbar. The resulting sketch is shown in Figure 3-62.

Show All Constraints

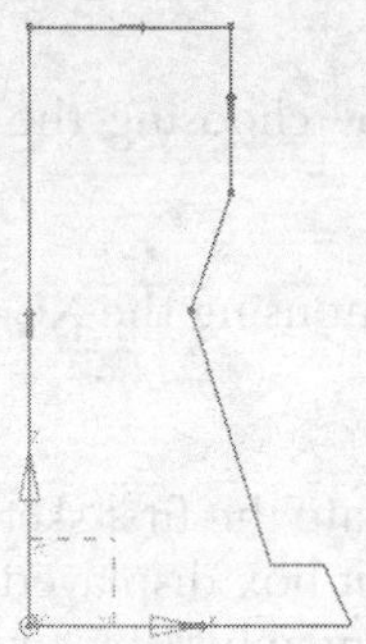

Figure 3-62 The resulting sketch displayed after adding the constraints

Adding Dimensions to the Sketch

Next, you need to apply dimensions to the sketch.

Inferred Dimensions

1. Choose the **Inferred Dimensions** button from the **Sketch Tools** toolbar; the **Dimensions** dialog box is displayed.

2. Select the line 8 and then place the dimension on the left of the sketch; an edit box with the default value is displayed. Enter **150** in this edit box and press the ENTER key; the dimension value is modified, refer to Figure 3-63.

3. Select the line 1 and then place the dimension below the sketch. Modify the dimension value to **60** and press the ENTER key, refer to Figure 3-63.

4. Select the line 5 and then place the dimension on the right of the sketch. Next, modify the dimension value to **30** and press the ENTER key, refer to Figure 3-63.

5. Select the line 6 and then place the dimension on the right of the sketch. Next, modify the dimension value to **40** and press the ENTER key, refer to Figure 3-63.

6. Select the line 7 and place the dimension above the sketch. Next, modify the dimension value to **35** and press the ENTER key, refer to Figure 3-63.

7. Select the line 2 and then the line 1; an angular dimension is attached to the cursor. Move the cursor outside the sketch toward the right and click the left mouse button to place the dimension. Next, modify the dimension value to **117** and press the ENTER key, refer to Figure 3-63.

8. Select lines 3 and 4; an angular dimension is attached to the cursor. Move the cursor inside the sketch and place the dimension. Next, modify the dimension value to **77** and press the ENTER key, refer to Figure 3-63.

9. Select the lower endpoint of the line 4 and then select the line 8; the dimension value is attached to the cursor. Place the dimension value below the sketch and then modify this value to **40**. Next, press ENTER.

10. Select the line 2 and place the dimension on the right of the line. Next, modify the dimension value to **12** and press ENTER, refer to Figure 3-63. Press the ESC key twice.

11. Choose the **Fit** button from the **View** toolbar. The resulting sketch after adding all dimensions is shown in Figure 3-63.

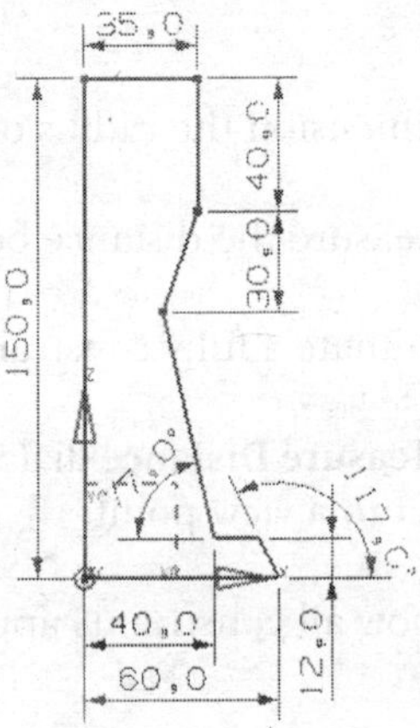

Figure 3-63 *The completed sketch displayed after adding the required constraints and dimensions*

Note

In Figure 3-63, the display of constraints is turned off to get a better display of dimensions. You can turn off the display of constraints by choosing the ***Show All Constraints*** *button. Note that it is a toggle button.*

Saving the File

1. Choose the **Save** button from the **Standard** toolbar to save the sketch. Note that the name and location of the document has already been specified when you started the new file.

2. Exit the Sketcher environment and choose **File > Close > All Parts** from the menu bar to close the file.

Self-Evaluation Test

Answer the following questions and then compare them to those given at the end of this chapter:

1. In NX, you can add all types of geometric constraints by using the **Constraints** tool in the **Sketch Tools** toolbar. (T/F)

2. The **Auto Constrain** tool allows you to apply all possible geometric constraints automatically to the entire sketch. (T/F)

3. The **Inferred Dimensions** tool in the **Sketch Tools** toolbar is used to add all possible dimension types. (T/F)

4. In NX, the diameter dimension is used to add the diameter dimension to the sketch members. (T/F)

5. The ________ constraint is used to force two curves to share the same location of the center points.

6. The ________ tool is used to dimension the radius of an arc.

7. The ________ tool is used to measure the distance between two objects.

8. The ________ tool is used to animate a fully constrained sketch.

9. The __________ option in the **Measure Distance** dialog box is used to measure the distance between the objects with respect to a view point.

10. The ________ tool is used to show all constraints applied to a sketch.

Review Questions

Answer the following questions:

1. Which one of the following tools is used to apply geometric constraints to a sketch?

   (a) **Constraints** (b) **Automatic Constraints**
   (c) **Inferred Dimensions** (d) None of these

2. Which one of the following tools is used to add a radial dimension to a sketch?

   (a) **Radius** (b) **Automatic Constraints**
   (c) **Inferred Dimensions** (d) None of these

3. Which one of the following tools is used to make the endpoints of selected objects coincident?

   (a) **Coincident** (b) **Concentric**
   (c) **Horizontal** (d) None of these

4. Which one of the following tools is used to apply the constant length constraint between sketch members?

   (a) **Equal Length** (b) **Automatic Constraints**
   (c) **Vertical** (d) None of these

5. Which one of the following tools is used to apply a parallel dimension to a sketch member?

(a) **Parallel** (b) **Automatic Constraints**
(c) **Inferred Dimensions** (d) None of these

6. Which one of the following tools is used to convert a sketch member into a reference element?

(a) **Convert To/From Reference** (b) **Automatic Constraints**
(c) **Constraints** (d) None of these

7. While measuring an angular dimension, you can display a major or minor dimension. (T/F)

8. The **Sketch Tools** toolbar contains all tools required to draw a sketch. (T/F)

9. The **Sketch** tool in the **Feature** toolbar is used to enter in the Sketcher environment. (T/F)

10. The **Finish Sketch** tool in the **Sketcher** toolbar is used to exit the Sketcher environment. (T/F)

Exercises

Exercise 1

Draw the base sketch of the model shown in Figure 3-64. The sketch to be drawn is shown in Figure 3-65. Use the geometric and dimensional constraints to complete this sketch.

(Expected time: 15 min)

Figure 3-64 Model for Exercise 1

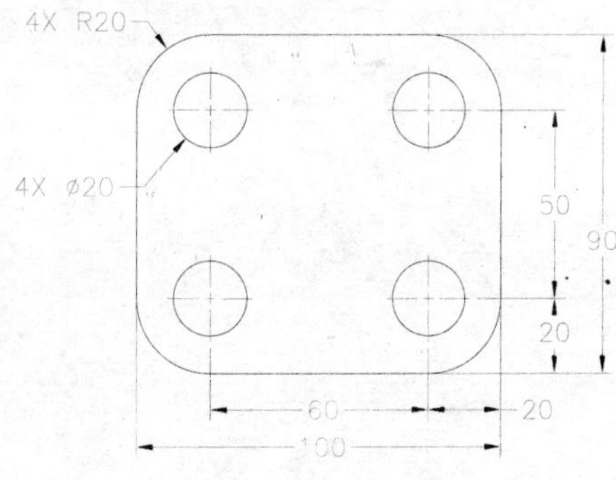

Figure 3-65 Sketch for Exercise 1

Exercise 2

Draw the base sketch of the model shown in Figure 3-66. The sketch to be drawn is shown in Figure 3-67. Use the geometric and dimensional constraints to complete this sketch.

(Expected time: 15 min)

Figure 3-66 *Model for Exercise 2*

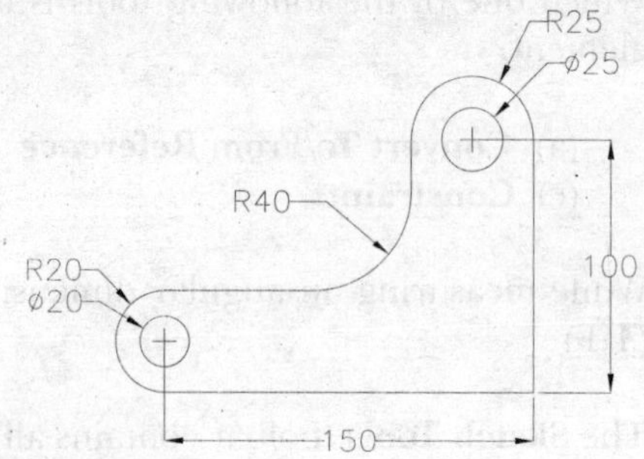

Figure 3-67 *Sketch for Exercise 2*

Answers to Self-Evaluation Test

1. T, **2.** T, **3.** T, **4.** T, **5. Concentric, 6. Radius, 7. Measure Distance, 8. Animate Dimension, 9. Screen Distance, 10. Show All Constraints**

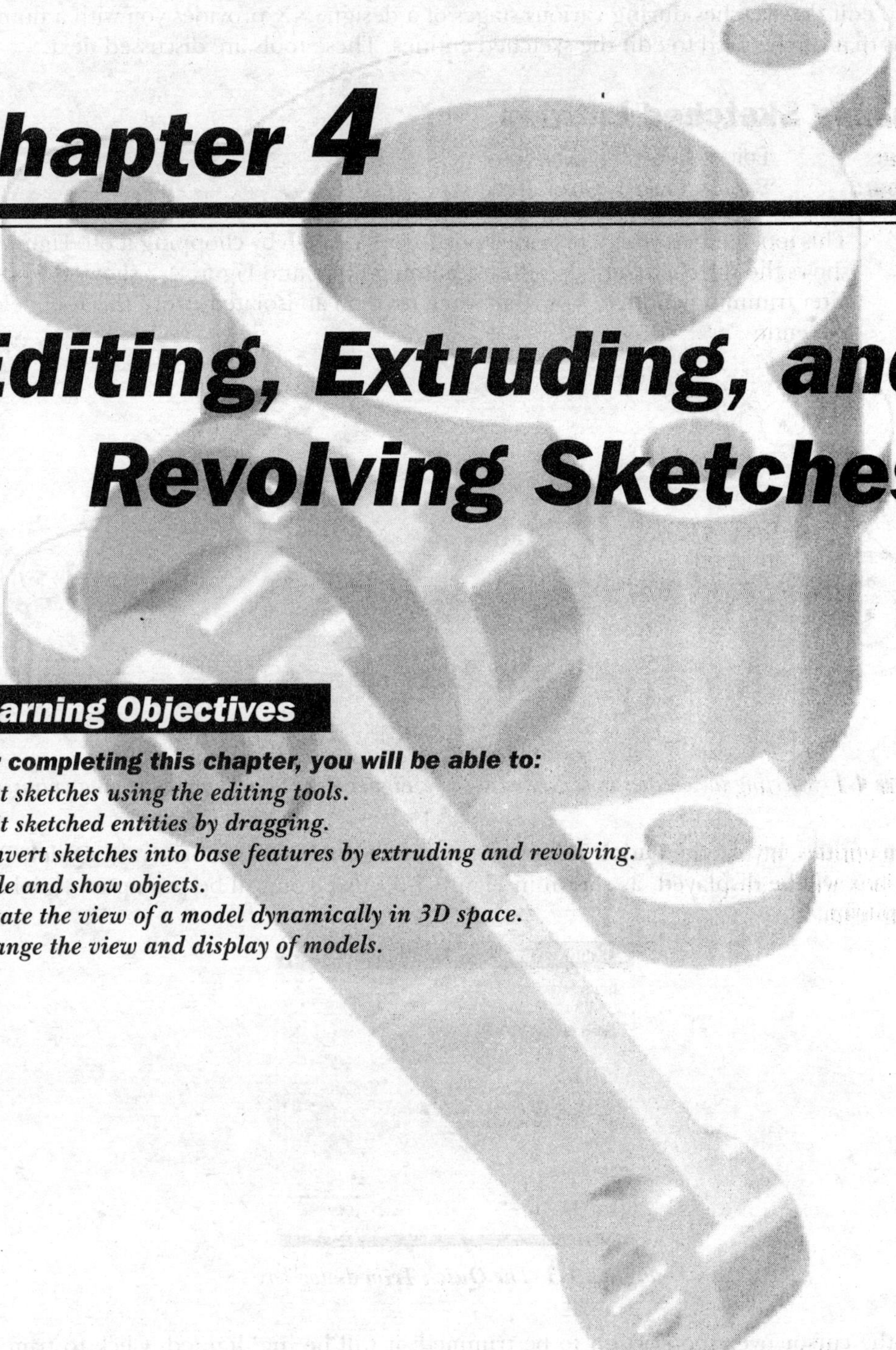

Chapter 4

Editing, Extruding, and Revolving Sketches

Learning Objectives

After completing this chapter, you will be able to:

- *Edit sketches using the editing tools.*
- *Edit sketched entities by dragging.*
- *Convert sketches into base features by extruding and revolving.*
- *Hide and show objects.*
- *Rotate the view of a model dynamically in 3D space.*
- *Change the view and display of models.*

EDITING SKETCHES

Editing is a very important part of sketching in any design or manufacturing program. You need to edit the sketches during various stages of a design. NX provides you with a number of tools that can be used to edit the sketched entities. These tools are discussed next.

Trimming Sketched Entities

Menu:	Edit > Curve > Quick Trim
Toolbar:	Sketch Tools > Quick Trim

This tool enables you to remove a portion of a sketch by chopping it off. Figure 4-1 shows the sketched entities before trimming them and Figure 4-2 shows the sketch after trimming entities. Note that when used on an isolated entity, this tool deletes the entity.

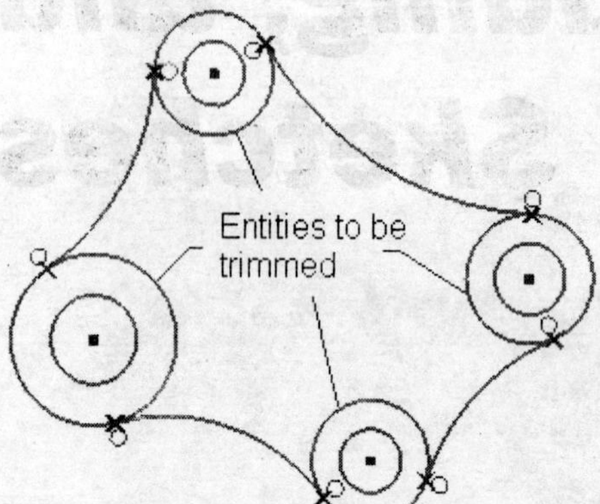

Figure 4-1 Selecting the entities to be trimmed

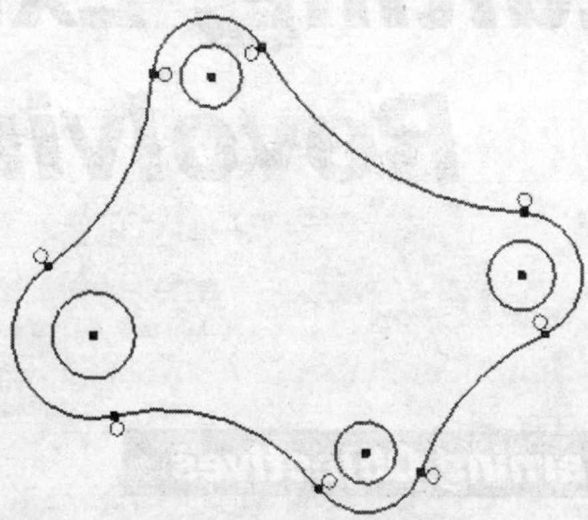

Figure 4-2 Sketch after trimming entities

To trim entities, invoke the **Quick Trim** tool from the **Sketch Tools** toolbar; the **Quick Trim** dialog box will be displayed, as shown in Figure 4-3. Also, you will be prompted to select a curve to trim.

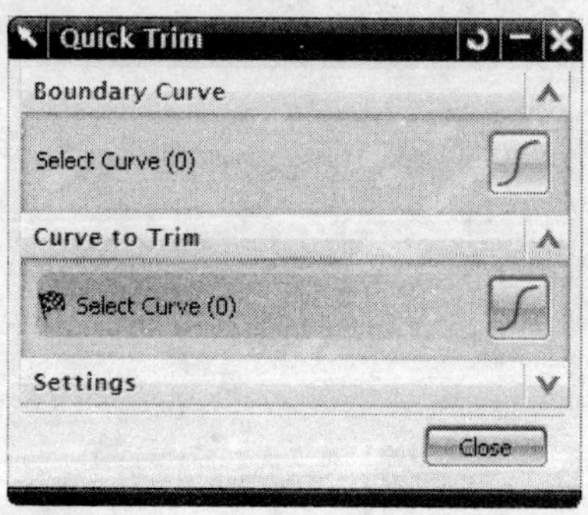

*Figure 4-3 The **Quick Trim** dialog box*

Move the cursor over the portion to be trimmed; it will be highlighted. Click to trim the highlighted portion. You will again be prompted to select the entity to be trimmed. After trimming all entities, press ESC to exit this tool.

To trim multiple entities, press and hold the left mouse button and drag the cursor over the entities to be trimmed. As you move the cursor over them, all the selected entities will be trimmed. Figure 4-4 shows multiple entities being trimmed by dragging the cursor over them and Figure 4-5 shows the resulting sketch.

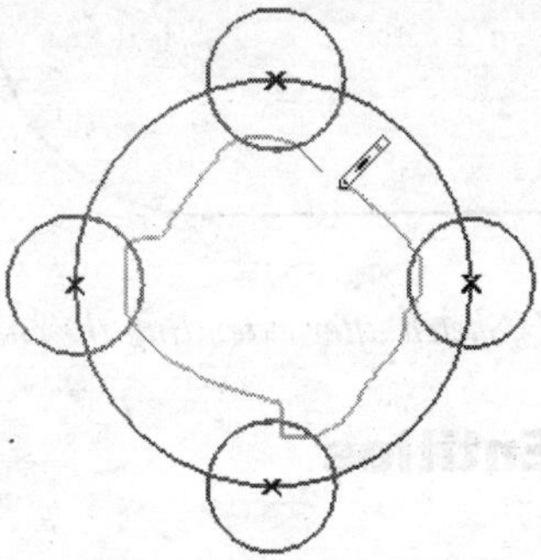

Figure 4-4 Dragging the cursor to trim multiple entities

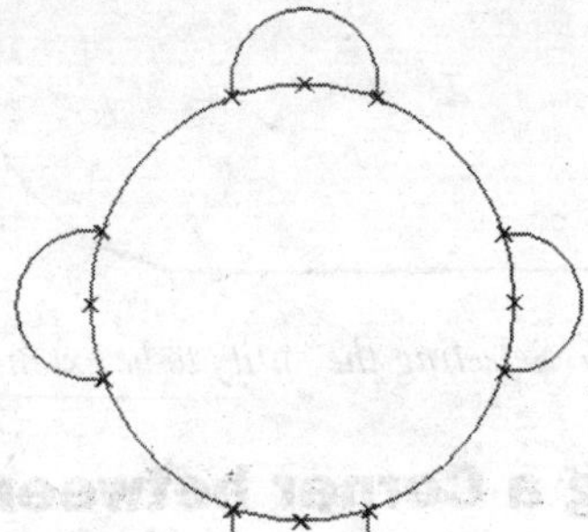

Figure 4-5 The resulting sketch

NX also allows you to select a sketched entity as a knife edge and then trim the other entities using this cutting edge. To trim entities using the cutting edge, choose the **Boundary Curve** button from the **Boundary Curve** rollout in the **Quick Trim** dialog box; you will be prompted to select the boundary curve. Select the curve from the drawing window; the curve becomes a knife edge. Next, choose the **Curve to Trim** button from the **Curve to Trim** rollout in the **Quick Trim** dialog box; you will be prompted to select the curve to be trimmed. Select the curve to be trimmed from the drawing area; the selected curve will be trimmed with respect to the knife edge specified. Similarly, select other curves that intersect the boundary curve; the selected curves will be trimmed. If the **Trim to Extension** check box is selected in the **Settings** rollout and the curve to be trimmed intersects the virtual boundary, then the curve will be trimmed on either side of the virtual boundary.

Extending Sketched Entities

Menu:	Edit > Curve > Quick Extend
Toolbar:	Sketch Tools > Quick Extend

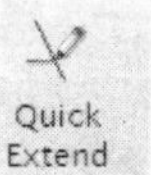

The **Quick Extend** tool enables you to extend or lengthen an open sketched entity up to the next entity that it intersects. Figure 4-6 shows the sketched entity before extending and Figure 4-7 shows the sketch after extending the entity. Note that this tool will not work on an entity that does not intersect with any existing sketched entity when extended.

You can also extend multiple entities by pressing and holding the left mouse button and dragging the cursor over them. All the other options of this tool are same as in the **Quick Trim** tool.

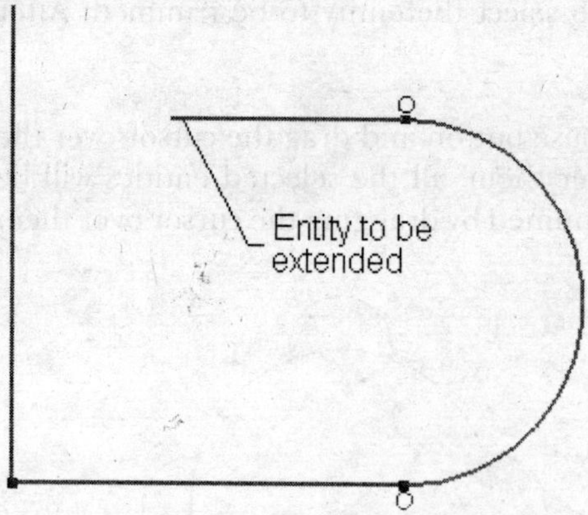

Figure 4-6 Selecting the entity to be extended

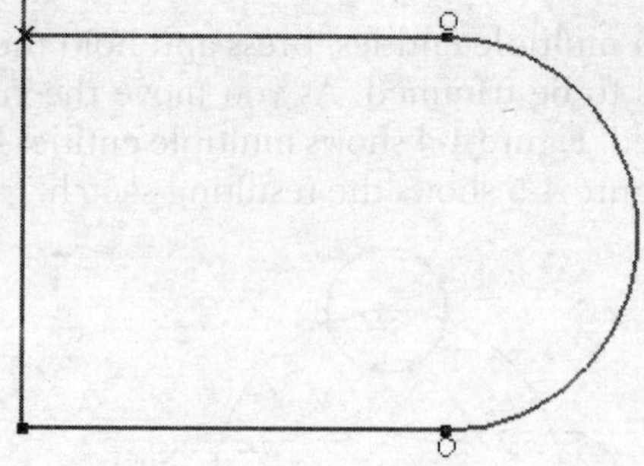

Figure 4-7 Sketch after extending the entity

Creating a Corner between Sketched Entities

Menu:	Edit > Curve > Make Corner
Toolbar:	Sketch Tools > Make Corner

You can create a corner between two existing sketch entities by using the **Make Corner** tool. To do so, invoke the **Make Corner** tool from the **Sketch Tools** toolbar; the **Make Corner** dialog box will be displayed, as shown in Figure 4-8. In this dialog box, the **Curve** button in the **Curve** rollout is chosen by default. Select the first curve, refer to Figure 4-9; you will be prompted to select the second curve. Select the second curve, refer to Figure 4-9; a corner will be created between the two sketched entities, refer to Figure 4-10. Next, exit from the dialog box by choosing the **Close** button from it.

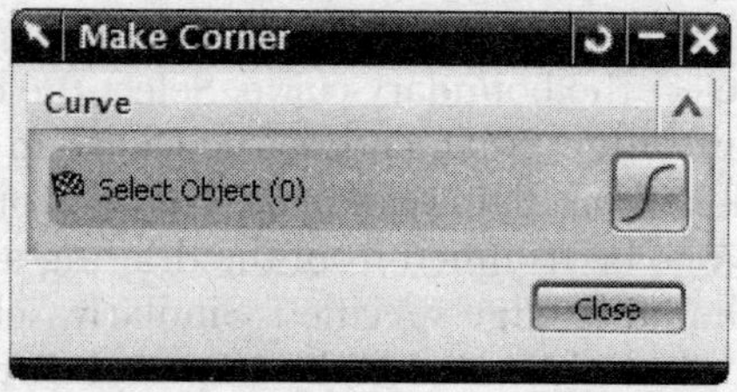

*Figure 4-8 The **Make Corner** dialog box*

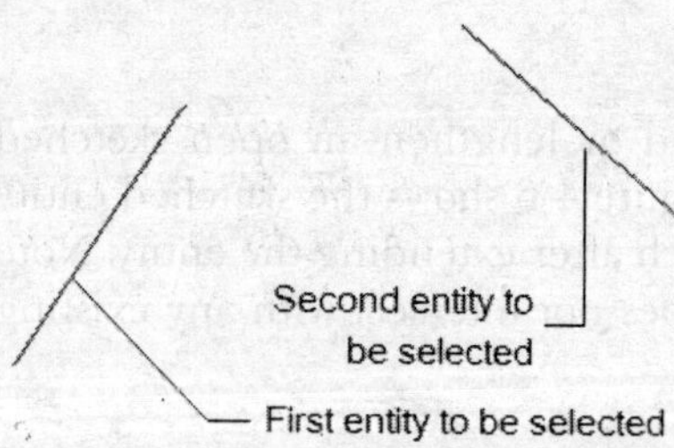

Figure 4-9 Two entities selected for creating a corner

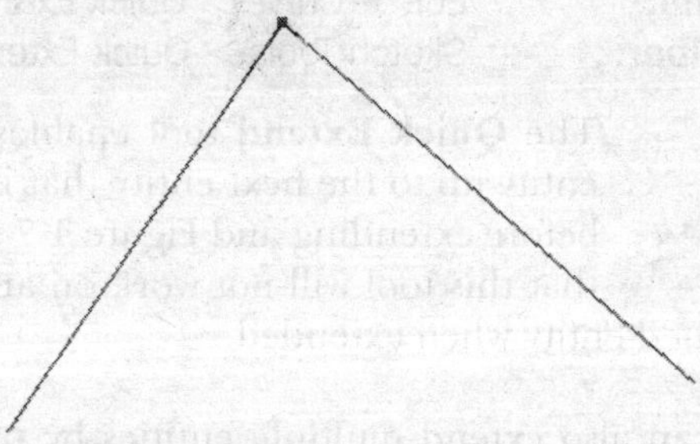

Figure 4-10 Corner created using the selected entities

Mirroring Sketched Entities

Menu: Insert > Curve from Curves > Mirror Curve
Toolbar: Sketch Tools > Mirror Curve

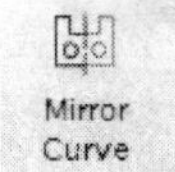

This tool enables you to create mirrored copies of the selected sketched entities. Before invoking this tool, you need to draw a line that will be the mirror line. This line will be converted into a reference line after the mirroring operation is completed.

To mirror sketched entities, choose the **Mirror Curve** button from the **Sketch Tools** toolbar; the **Mirror Curve** dialog box will be displayed, as shown in Figure 4-11. The **Mirror Centerline** button is chosen by default in the **Mirror Centerline** rollout of this dialog box. Also, you will be prompted to select a linear object or a plane for the centerline. Select the mirror centerline. As you select the mirror centerline, the **Curve to Mirror** button will be chosen in the **Curve to Mirror** rollout and you will be prompted to select the curves to mirror. Select the curves to be mirrored and choose the **OK** button; the selected entities will be mirrored and the mirror centerline will be converted into the reference line. Figure 4-12 shows the mirror line and entities to be mirrored and Figure 4-13 shows the sketch after mirroring the selected entities. Note that the mirror line is automatically converted into a reference line after mirroring.

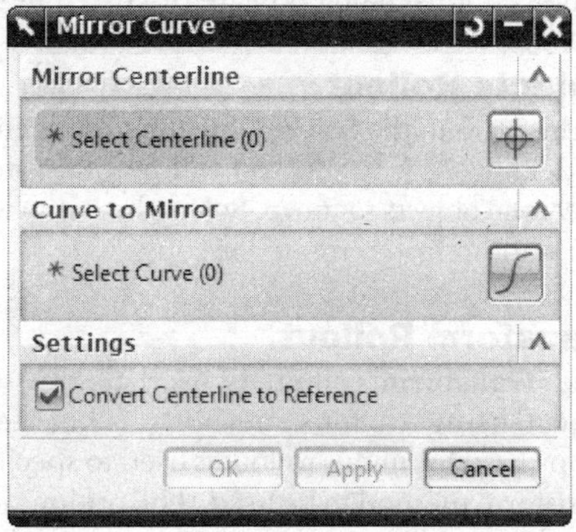

Figure 4-11 *The* ***Mirror Curve*** *dialog box*

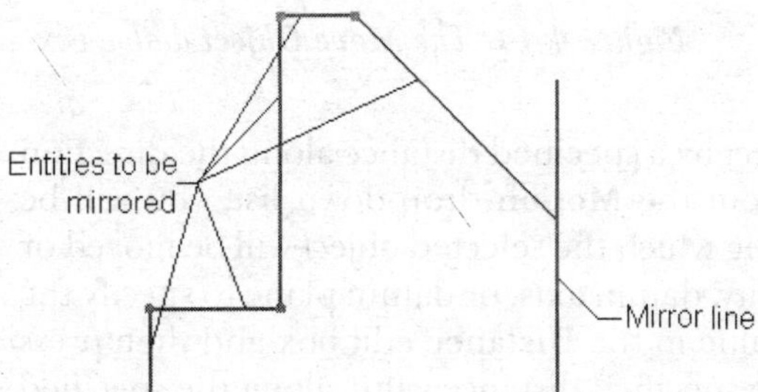

Figure 4-12 *Mirror line and entities selected to be mirrored*

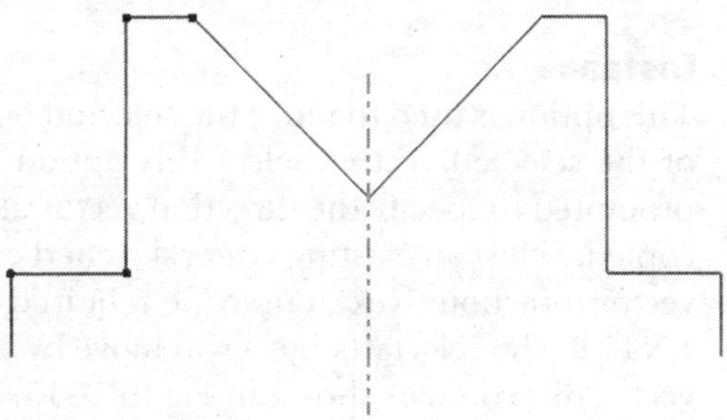

Figure 4-13 *Sketch after mirroring entities*

Tip: *After mirroring, if you select and drag any entity from its original portion, the same change will also be reflected dynamically in its mirrored portion. However, this relationship will end if you delete the mirror centerline.*

By default, the ***Convert Centerline to Reference*** *check box is selected in the* ***Settings*** *rollout of the* ***Mirror Curve*** *dialog box. As a result, the mirror line automatically converts into a reference line. However, if you clear this check box, then the mirror line will not convert into a reference line.*

Copying, Moving, and Rotating Sketched Entities

Menu:	Edit > Move Object
Toolbar:	Standard > Move Object

In NX, you can dynamically move, rotate, or copy solid objects as well as sketched entities by using the **Move Object** tool. To invoke this tool, choose **Edit > Move Object** from the menu bar; the **Move Object** dialog box will be displayed, as shown in Figure 4-14. The options in this dialog box are discussed next.

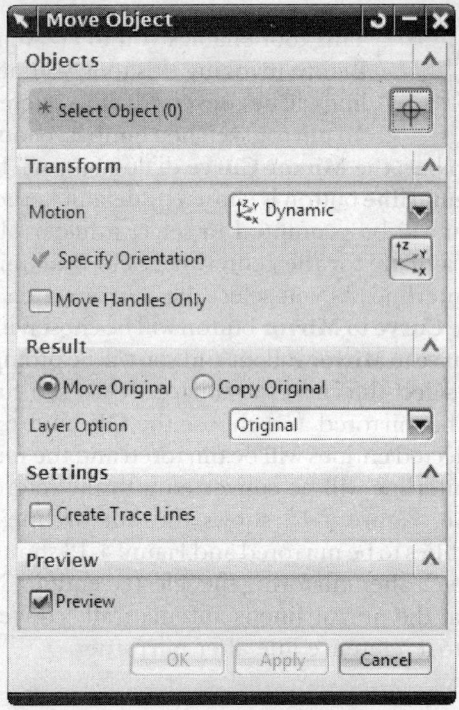

*Figure 4-14 The **Move Object** dialog box*

Objects Rollout

In this rollout, the **Select Object** button is chosen by default. As a result, you will be prompted to select the objects to move. Select the entity which you want to move, rotate, or copy.

Transform Rollout

The **Transform** rollout is used to transform object using various methods. The **Motion** drop-down list in this rollout is used to specify the transform method to be used. The options in the **Transform** rollout keep on changing according to the options selected from the **Motion** drop-down list. These options are discussed next.

Distance

This option is used to move the selected object by a specified distance along the direction of the selected vector. Select this option from the **Motion** drop-down list; you will be prompted to specify the direction vector along which the selected object will be moved or copied. Select an existing edge, sketched entity, datum axis, or datum plane to specify the vector direction. Next, enter the required value in the **Distance** edit box and then press ENTER; the selected object will move by the specified distance value along the specified vector direction, as shown in Figure 4-15. You can also flip the direction of the vector by choosing the **Reverse Direction** button or by double-clicking on the green arrowhead displayed in the graphics area. Next, choose the **OK** button.

Angle

The **Angle** option in the **Motion** drop-down list is used to rotate the selected entity with respect to the specified point. Select this option from the **Motion** drop-down list; you will be prompted to select the object to infer point. Select the point about which you want change the orientation of the object; you will be prompted to select the objects to move. Select the required entity to orient. Next, enter the angle value in the **Angle** edit box and press ENTER; the selected object will be oriented by the specified angle with respect to the specified point, as shown in Figure 4-16. Next, choose the **OK** button.

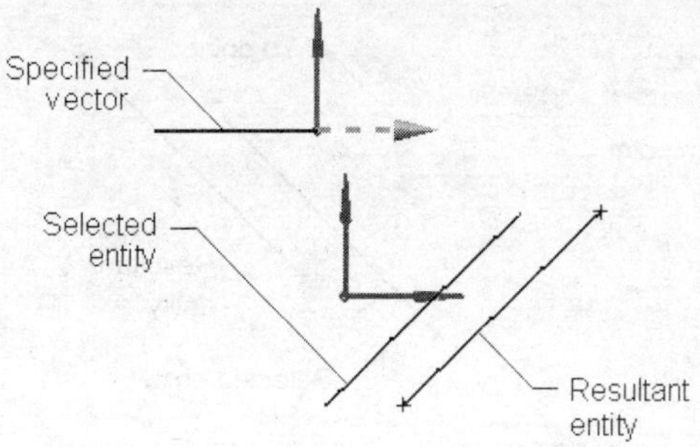

Figure 4-15 Entity transformed by using the ***Distance*** *option*

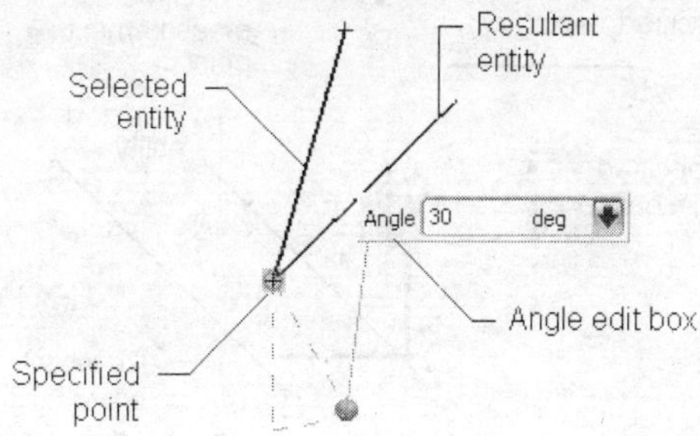

Figure 4-16 Entity transformed by using the ***Angle*** *option*

Distance between Points

This option is used to move an entity from one specified point to another specified point along a specified vector. Select this option from the **Motion** drop-down list; you will be prompted to select the object to infer point. Also, the **Specify Origin Point** area will be highlighted in the **Transform** rollout. Select a point to define the origin; the **Specify Measurement Point** area will be highlighted in the **Transform** rollout. Specify the measurement point by selecting another point; the **Specify Vector** area will be highlighted in the **Transform** rollout. Also, a triad of vector will be displayed in the drawing window. Select an existing edge, a sketched entity, or a datum axis to specify the vector direction; you will be prompted to select the object. Also, the **Distance** input edit box will be displayed attached to the specified measurement point. Select the object that you want to move. Next, enter the distance value in **Distance** input edit box to define the driven distance of the selected object along the specified vector. You can also enter the distance value in the **Distance** edit box of the dialog box. Note that the selected object will move by the difference between the origin point and the measurement point, along the direction of the vector specified. For example, if the distance between the origin point and the measurement point along the direction vector is 100 mm and you want to move the object to a distance of 50 mm, in this case, you need to enter the distance value of 150 mm in the **Distance** edit box. As you enter the distance value, the preview of the selected entity will be displayed in the graphics window, refer to Figure 4-17. You can flip the direction of the vector by choosing the **Reverse Direction** button or by double-clicking on the green arrowhead displayed in the graphics area. You can also dynamically move the selected object by dragging the arrowhead displayed in the graphics area.

Point to Point

This option is used to move the selected entity from one position to another with respect to one specified point to another. Select this option from the **Motion** drop-down list; you will be prompted to select the object to infer point. Also, the **Specify From Point** option will be highlighted in the **Transform** rollout. Specify the start point of the moving entity; you will be prompted to select the object to infer point. Also, the **Specify To Point** option will be highlighted in the **Transform** rollout. Next, specify the point upto which you want to move the entity; you will be prompted to select the object to move. Select the entity that you want to move; the selected entity will be moved as specified and the preview of the entity will be displayed in the graphics window, as shown in Figure 4-18.

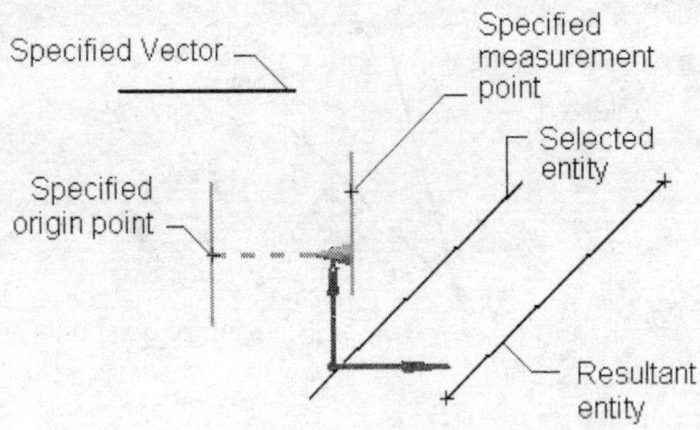

*Figure 4-17 Entity transformed by using the **Distance between Points** option*

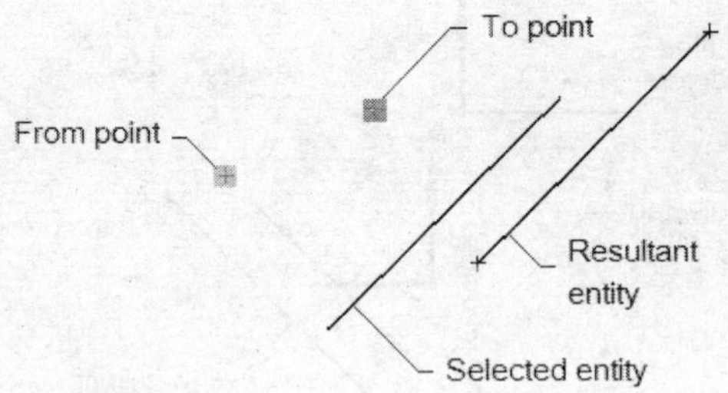

*Figure 4-18 Entity transformed by using the **Point to Point** option*

Rotate by Three Points

This option is used to rotate an entity by using three points. Select this option from the **Motion** drop-down list; you will be prompted to select the object to infer point, Also, the **Specify Pivot Point** option will be highlighted in the **Transform** rollout. Next, specify the pivot point relative to which the entity will change its orientation; the **Specify Start Point** area will be highlighted in the **Transform** rollout. As a result, you will be prompted to select the object to infer point. Specify the start point from where the orientation will start; you will be prompted to select the object to infer point and also the **Specify End Point** option will be highlighted in the **Transform** rollout. Specify the end point; you will be prompted to select the object to rotate. Select the entity to be rotated; the preview of the resultant entity will be displayed in the graphics window, as shown in Figure 4-19.

Align Axis to Vector

This option is used to rotate an object from one specified vector to another specified vector about the specified pivot point. Select this option from the **Motion** drop-down list; you will be prompted to select the object to infer vector. Specify the reference vector from which the rotation angle will be measured. After specifying the reference vector for the rotation angle; you will be prompted to select the object to infer a vector. Specify the reference vector for the rotation angle. Next, choose the **Inferred Point** button from the **Specify Pivot Point** area to choose the pivot point. Else, NX will take the pivot point automatically. Specify the pivot point in the graphics window; you will be prompted to select the object to move. Select the object to be moved; the preview of the resultant entity will be displayed in the graphics window, as shown in Figure 4-20.

Dynamic

This option is used to move or rotate an object dynamically. Select this option from the **Motion** drop-down list; a dynamic triad will be displayed at the origin, refer to Figure 4-21. Choose the **Object** button from the **Objects** rollout and select the object to move or rotate; the triad will be placed at the center of the selected object. You can use this triad to move or rotate the selected entity dynamically by using its handles or angular handles. If you drag the handles, the object will move linearly. If you drag the angular handles, the object will move angularly. Also, you can place the selected object from one point to another by selecting the center of the triad and then clicking at the point where you want to place the object. Note that instead of dragging the handles, you can also specify the values in their respective edit boxes, refer to Figure 4-22. You can select **Move Handles Only** check box in the **Transform** rollout to move the dynamic triad only.

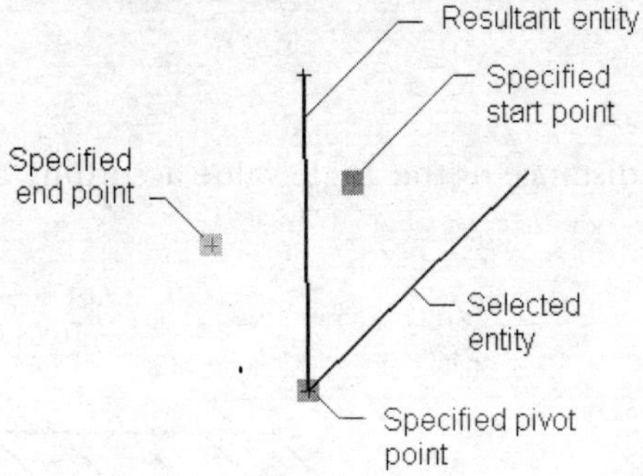

*Figure 4-19 Entity transformed by using the **Rotate by Three Points** option*

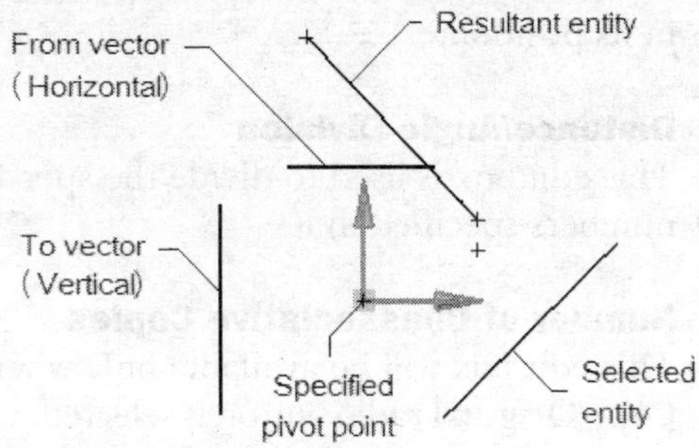

*Figure 4-20 Entity transformed by using the **Align Axis to Vector** option*

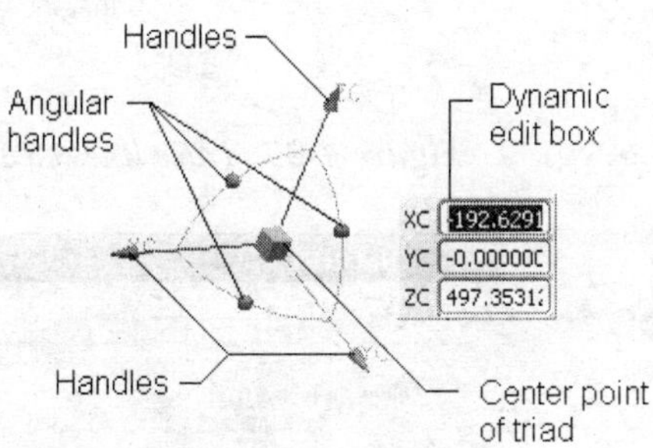

Figure 4-21 Dynamic triad

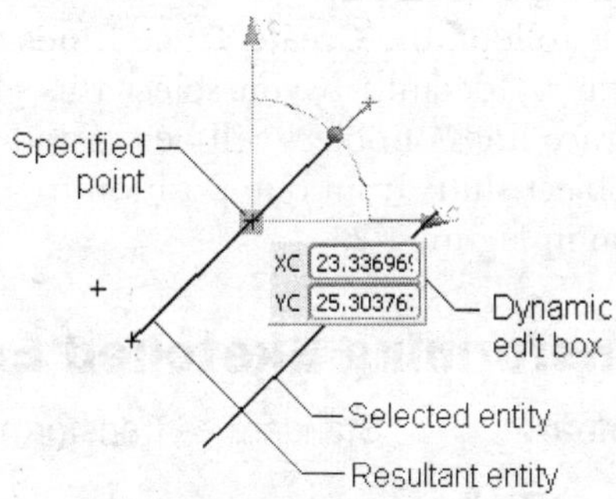

*Figure 4-22 Entity transformed by using the **Dynamic** option*

Delta XYZ

This option is used to move a selected entity from one position to another position with respect to the X, Y, and Z coordinates. Select the **Delta XYZ** option from the **Motion** drop-down list; you will be prompted to select the object to be moved. Select the object to be moved. Next, enter the required coordinate values in **XC**, **YC**, and **ZC** edit boxes in the **Transform** rollout of the dialog box, and then press ENTER; the preview of the resultant entity will be displayed in the graphics window. Note that the specified coordinate values are relative to the reference coordinate system that can be the Absolute Coordinate System or the World Coordinate System. You can select the required reference coordinate system from the **Reference** drop-down list in the **Transform** rollout of the dialog box.

Result Rollout

The options in this rollout are discussed next.

Move Original

This radio button is selected by default. As a result, the original entity itself will be transformed.

Copy Original

This radio button toggles with the **Move Original** radio button. Select the radio button, if you want to create multiple copies of the entity such that the original entity is retained in its position.

Distance/Angle Division

This edit box is used to divide the specified distance or the angle value according to the numbers specified in it.

Number of Unassociative Copies

This edit box will be available only when the **Copy Original** radio button is selected. In this edit box you can specify a number of instances to be created, excluding the original one.

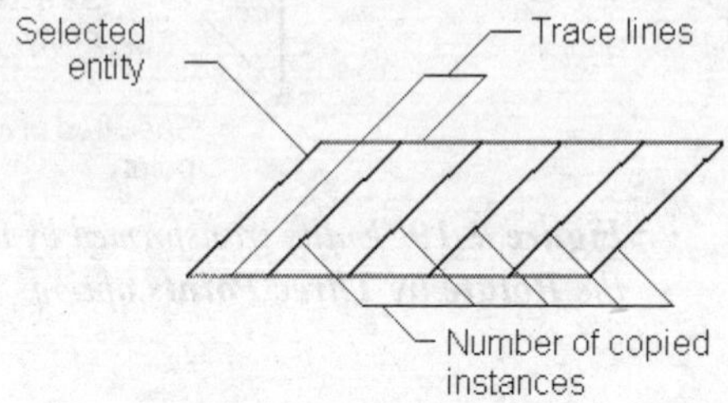

Figure 4-23 Trace lines created

Settings Rollout

In this rollout, the **Create Trace Lines** check box is clear by default. If you select this check box, the trace lines of object will be created whenever the object shifts from one position to another, as shown in Figure 4-23.

Transforming Sketched Entities

Toolbar:	Standard > Transform

NX allows you to perform editing operations on sketches using the **Transform** tool. To invoke this tool, choose the **Transform** button from the **Standard** toolbar; the **Transform** dialog box will be displayed, as shown in Figure 4-24 and you will be prompted to select objects to transform.

The **Transform** dialog box is used to select objects to perform a particular operation. Various rollouts in this dialog box are discussed next.

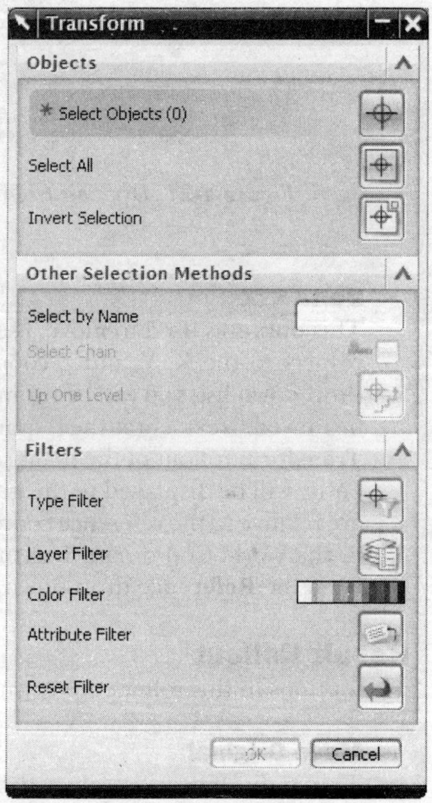

*Figure 4-24 The **Transform** dialog box*

Objects Rollout

The options in this rollout are used to define the selection methods, which are discussed next.

Select Objects

This button is used to select the objects one by one.

Select All

This button is used to select all objects in the

drawing window such as sketching entities, datum coordinate systems, work planes, and so on.

Invert Selection

This button is used to invert the selection.

Other Selection Methods Rollout

This rollout provides some additional selection methods.

Select by Name

Enter the name of the sketch that you need to select in this text box and press the ENTER key; the specified sketch will be selected.

Select Chain

This button is used to select the curves in chain. You need to select the first and the last curve from the sketch; all the sketched entities of the sketch (lines, arcs, and fillets) between these two specified curves will be selected.

Filters Rollout

This rollout is used to filter out the selection procedure. The options in this rollout have already been discussed in Chapter 2. Select the entities to be transformed and choose the **OK** button; the **Transformations** dialog box will be displayed, as shown in Figure 4-25.

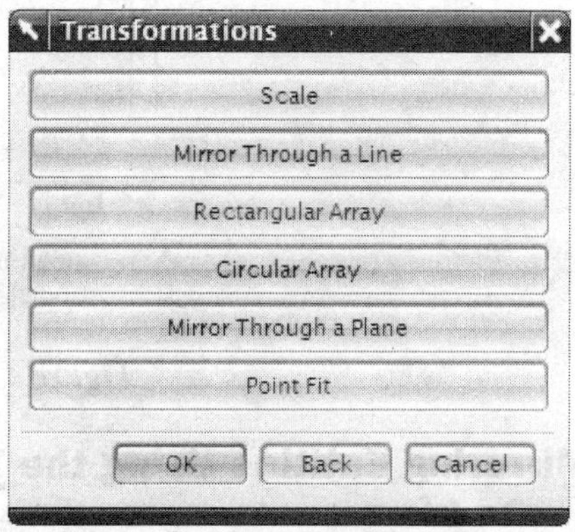

***Figure 4-25** The **Transformations** dialog box*

Some of the transformation tools in this dialog box are discussed next and the rest will be discussed in the later chapters.

Scaling the Copied Entities Using the Transformations Dialog Box

The **Scale** option allows you to create scaled copies of the selected objects. If required, you can also scale the objects nonuniformly in the X, Y, and Z directions.

The steps required to scale the sketched entities using the **Transformations** dialog box are discussed next.

1. Choose the **Transform** button from the **Standard** toolbar and then select entities using the **Transform** dialog box. Choose the **OK** button in this dialog box; the **Transformations** dialog box will be displayed.

2. Choose the **Scale** button in the **Transformations** dialog box; the **Point** dialog box will be displayed and you will be prompted to select the object to infer point.

3. Select a base point for scaling. You can select any point on the screen or any inferred point

from the sketch. On selecting a base point, the modified **Transformations** dialog box will be displayed.

4. Enter the scale factor in the **Scale** edit box. If you need to scale the sketched entities nonuniformly, choose the **Non-uniform Scale** button; the dialog box will modify and the edit boxes to specify different values of scale factor in the X, Y, and Z directions will be displayed.

5. After entering the required values, choose **OK**; the **Transformations** dialog box will expand. Choose the **Copy** button; the scaled copy of the selected entities will be displayed. Next, choose the **Cancel** button to exit from the dialog box. Figure 4-26 shows a uniformly scaled copy of the original sketch. The scale factor in this case is 1.5.

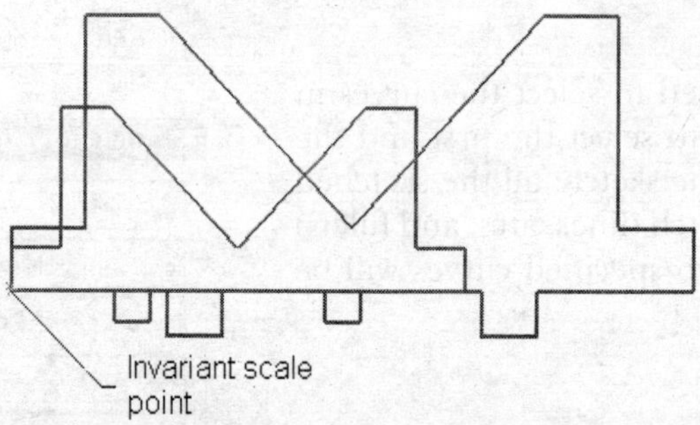

Figure 4-26 Uniformly scaled entities

Mirroring Entities Using the Transformations Dialog Box

The **Transformations** dialog box allows you to mirror the sketched entities using three methods. These methods are discussed next.

Mirroring Using Two Points

Invoke the **Transform** dialog box by choosing the **Transform** button from the **Standard** toolbar. Next, select the entity to be transformed and then choose the **OK** button in this dialog box; the **Transformations** dialog box will be displayed. Choose the **Mirror Through a Line** button from this dialog box; the **Transformations** dialog box will get modified. In the modified dialog box, choose the **Two Points** button; the **Point** dialog box will be displayed. Specify two points on the screen to define an imaginary line about which the sketch will be mirrored and then choose **OK**. Next, choose the **Move** button in the **Transformations** dialog box, if you need to delete the original sketch after mirroring it. Choose the **Copy** button, if you need to retain the original sketch along with the mirrored copy. Next, exit from the dialog box.

Mirroring Using an Existing Line

Invoke the **Transformations** dialog box and choose the **Mirror Through a Line** button; the **Transformations** dialog box will be modified. In the modified dialog box, choose the **Existing Line** button; the **Transformations** dialog box will be modified again and you will be prompted to select the line to mirror about. Select the line about which the sketch will be mirrored and choose the **Move** or **Copy** button. Next, exit from the dialog box.

Mirroring Using a Point and a Vector

Invoke the **Transformations** dialog box and choose the **Mirror Through a Line** button; the **Transformations** dialog box will be modified. In the modified dialog box, choose the **Point and Vector** button; the **Point** dialog box will be displayed and you will be prompted to select the object to infer point. Select a point on the screen or an inferred point from the sketch; the **Vector** dialog box will be displayed. Select the required option from the **Type** drop-down list in the dialog box. To mirror about the X-axis, choose the **XC Axis** option from the **Type** drop-down list. Similarly, to mirror about the Y-axis, choose the **YC Axis** button and then choose the **Move** or **Copy** button. Next, exit from the dialog box.

Editing Sketched Entities by Dragging

You can also edit the sketched entities by dragging them. Depending upon the type of entity selected and the point of selection, the object will be moved or stretched. For example, if you select a line at any point other than the endpoints and drag the mouse, the line will be moved. However, if you select a line at its endpoint, it will be stretched to a new size. Similarly, if you select an arc at its circumference or its endpoints, it will be stretched. But if you select the arc at its center point, it will be moved. Therefore, editing the sketched entities by dragging depends entirely upon their selection points. The following table gives the details of the operation that will be performed when you drag various entities. Note that while editing the sketched entities using the keypoints, all the related entities will also be moved or stretched.

Entity	Selection point	Operation
Circle	On circumference	Stretch
	Center point	Move
Arc	On circumference/endpoints	Stretch
	Center point	Move
Isolated line or multiple lines selected together	Anywhere other than the endpoints	Move
	Endpoints	Stretch
Curve	Any point other than the keypoints	Move
	Keypoints	Stretch
Rectangle	All lines selected together	Move
	Any one line or any endpoint	Stretch
Ellipse	Anywhere on the circumference or center point	Move

EXITING THE SKETCHER ENVIRONMENT

After drawing and dimensioning the sketch, you need to exit the Sketcher environment and invoke the **Modeling** environment to convert the sketch into a feature. To exit the Sketcher environment, choose the **Finish Sketch** button from the **Sketcher** toolbar. On exiting the Sketcher environment and entering the **Modeling** environment, you will notice that the **Sketch Tools** toolbar is replaced by the **Feature** and **Feature Operation** toolbars. Also, the dimensions of the sketch are hidden. Note that the current view will change to the trimetric view.

As mentioned in the earlier chapters, most designs are a combination of various sketched, placed, and reference features. The first feature, generally, is a sketched feature. Already you have learned to draw sketches for these base features and add constraints and dimensions to them. After drawing and dimensioning a sketch, you need to convert it into the base feature. NX provides you with a number of tools such as **Extrude**, **Revolve**, and so on to convert these base sketches into base features. In this chapter, you will learn to use the **Extrude** and **Revolve** tools. The remaining tools will be discussed in the later chapters. The base features are created in the Modeling environment.

CHANGING THE VIEW OF THE SKETCH

Sometimes you need to change the view of the sketch for better visualization. To change the view, choose the down arrow on the right of the **Trimetric** button in the **View** toolbar; a flyout will be displayed with various view options. Select the required view from this flyout; the current view will be changed to the selected view.

CREATING BASE FEATURES BY EXTRUDING

Menu:	Insert > Design Feature > Extrude
Toolbar:	Feature > Extrude

Extrude is defined as the process of creating a feature from a sketch by adding the material along the direction normal to the sketch or any other specified direction. Figure 4-27 shows the isometric view of a closed sketch and Figure 4-28 shows the extruded feature created using this sketch.

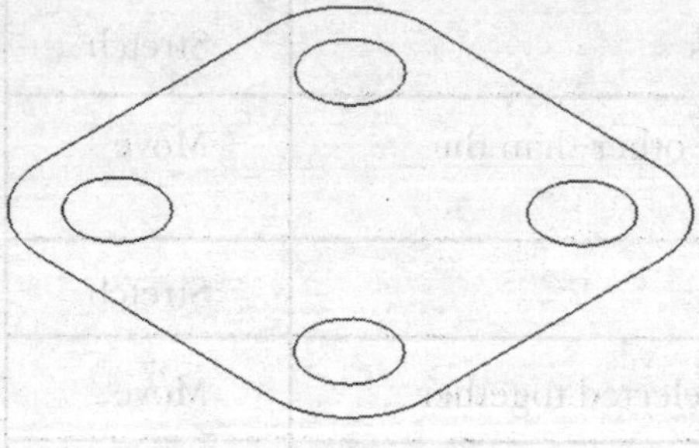

***Figure 4-27** Sketch for the extrude feature*

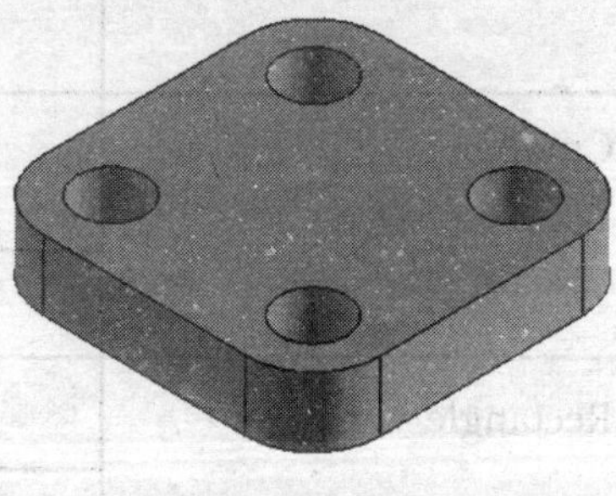

***Figure 4-28** Resulting extruded feature*

When you choose the **Extrude** button from the **Feature** toolbar, the **Extrude** dialog box will be displayed, as shown in Figure 4-29. Also, you will be prompted to select the planar face to sketch or the section geometry to be extruded. If you select the sketch at this stage, the preview of the extruded feature created using the default values will be displayed on the screen. If you select the sketch plane, the Sketcher environment will be invoked. Draw the sketch and exit the Sketcher environment; the preview of the extruded feature will be displayed in the Modeling environment.

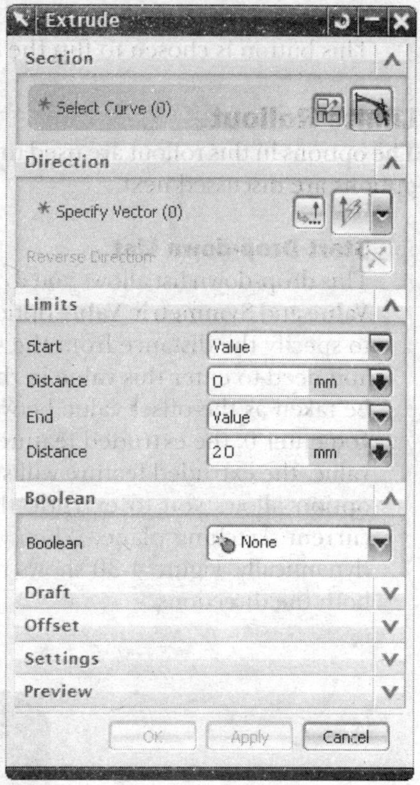

*Figure 4-29 The **Extrude** dialog box*

Extrude Dialog Box Options

The options in this dialog box are discussed next.

Section Rollout

The options in this rollout are used to sketch the section or select the section. By default, both the **Sketch Section** and **Curve** buttons will be chosen in this rollout and you will be prompted to select the planar face to sketch or the section geometry to be extruded. These options are discussed next.

Sketch Section

This button is used to draw the sketch for extrusion. By default, this button is chosen in the **Section** rollout and it is used to select the planar face to sketch. When you choose this button, the **Create Sketch** dialog box will be displayed and you will be prompted to select the object for the sketch plane. You can select a datum plane or the face of a solid body as the sketching plane.

Curve

By default, this button is also chosen from the **Section** rollout and it is used to select the already drawn section sketch.

Direction Rollout

By default, the direction of extrusion will be normal to the selected section. The options in this rollout are used to define the direction of extrusion. These options are discussed next.

Vector Constructor

If you choose this button, the **Vector** dialog box will be displayed. You can specify the extrude direction using this dialog box.

Inferred Vector Drop-down List

This drop-down list is used to specify the direction of extrusion. The default direction is normal to the selected section.

Reverse Direction

This button is chosen to flip the current extrusion direction.

Limits Rollout

The options in this rollout are used to specify the start and termination of the extrusion. These options are discussed next.

Start Drop-down List

This drop-down list allows you to specify the start point of the extrusion. You can select the **Value** and **Symmetric Value** options from this drop-down list. The **Value** option allows you to specify the distance from the sketching plane at which the extruded feature will start. You need to enter this value in the **Distance** edit box. If you enter a positive value, it will be taken as the offset value between the sketch and the start of the extrusion feature. If you enter 0, the extruded feature will start from the sketch plane. If you enter a negative value, the extruded feature will start from below the sketch plane. The **Symmetric Value** option allows you to extrude the sketch symmetrically in both the directions of the current sketching plane. When you select this option, the preview will also be modified dynamically. Figure 4-30 shows the preview of a sketch being extruded symmetrically in both the directions.

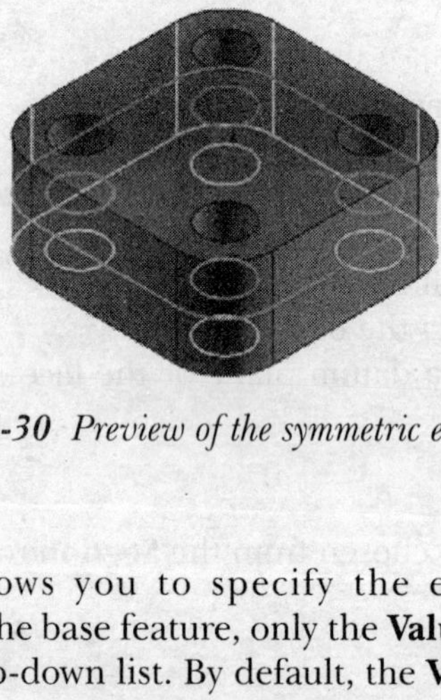

Figure 4-30 Preview of the symmetric extrusion

End Drop-down List

This drop-down list allows you to specify the extrusion termination in the direction of extrusion. For the base feature, only the **Value** and **Symmetric Value** options will be available in this drop-down list. By default, the **Value** option will be selected, and the value entered last will be displayed in the **Distance** edit box. As a result, the sketch will be extruded only in the specified direction.

Figure 4-31 shows the preview of the extrusion in only one direction and Figure 4-32 shows the preview of the extrusion with different values in both directions. In this figure, the extrusion value in the upward direction is 10 and in the downward direction is -5.

Note

The other extrusion termination options are discussed in the next chapter.

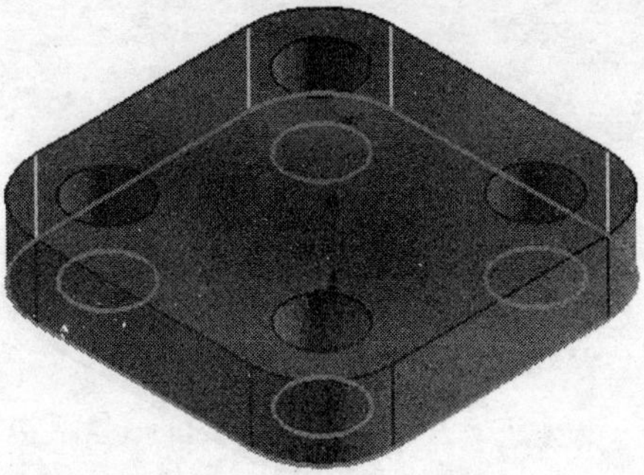

Figure 4-31 *Preview of the extrusion in only one direction*

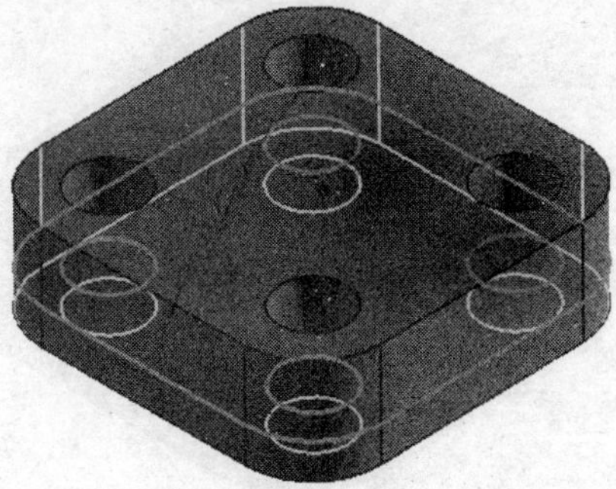

Figure 4-32 *Preview of the extrusion in two opposite directions with different values*

Tip. *You can also use the start and end drag handles in the preview of the extruded feature to modify the extrusion values in the start and end directions.*

Boolean Rollout

The options in this rollout allow you to select the boolean operation that you need to perform. These options are discussed in the next chapter.

Draft Rollout

The options in this rollout are used to specify a draft angle to the extrusion feature. The options in this area will be available only when you select the section to extrude. Various draft options in this rollout are discussed next.

Angle

This edit box allows you to specify the draft angle.

Draft

This drop-down list allows you to specify the type of draft to be applied to the feature. The options in this drop-down list are discussed next.

From Start Limit

This option adds the draft from the start section to the end section of the extruded feature. As a result, the dimension of the feature at the start section is the same as that of the original sketch and it tapers toward the end section. Figure 4-33 shows the preview of the extruded feature drafted using this option. It is evident from this figure that the bottom section of the extruded feature is the same as that of the original sketch and the feature tapers as it goes toward the top section.

From Section

This option is used to taper the extruded surface in such a way that the cross-section of the extruded feature remains the same at the sketching plane, as shown in Figure 4-34.

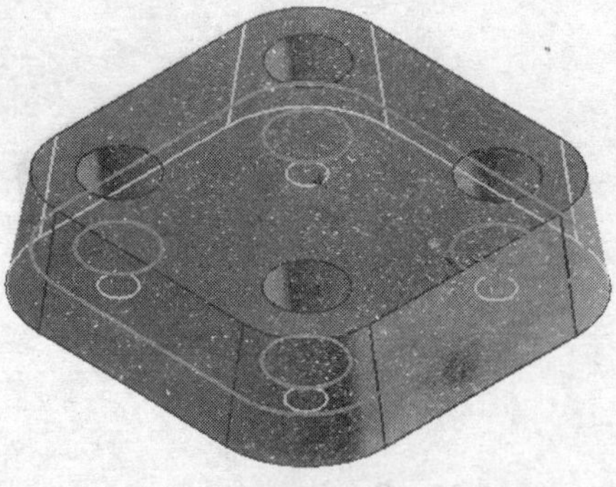

*Figure 4-33 Preview of the extrusion tapered using the **From Start Limit** option*

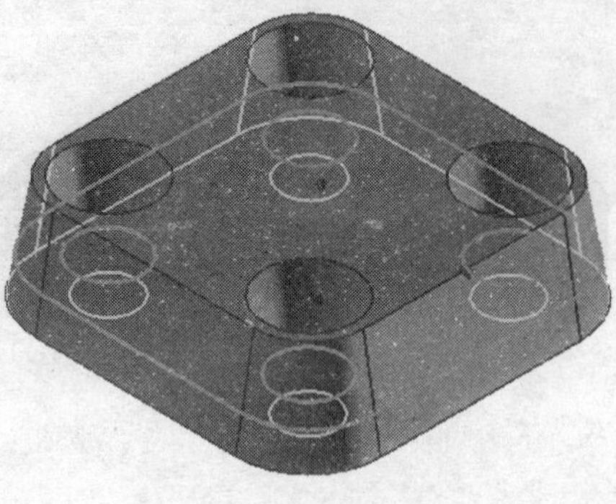

*Figure 4-34 Preview of the extrusion tapered using the **From Section** option*

From Section - Symmetric Angle
This option is available only when you select the **Symmetric Value** option from the **Limits** rollout or specify the values in both the start and the end directions. This option adds a symmetric taper in both directions of the sketch, as shown in Figure 4-35. In this draft type, if the distance value in one of the directions is more than the other, the section in that direction will also be smaller in size.

From Section - Matched Ends
This option is also available only when you select the **Symmetric Value** option from the **Limits** rollout or specify the values in both the start and the end directions. This option tapers the model such that the end sections in both the directions are of similar size, irrespective of the distance values in both directions, as shown in Figure 4-36.

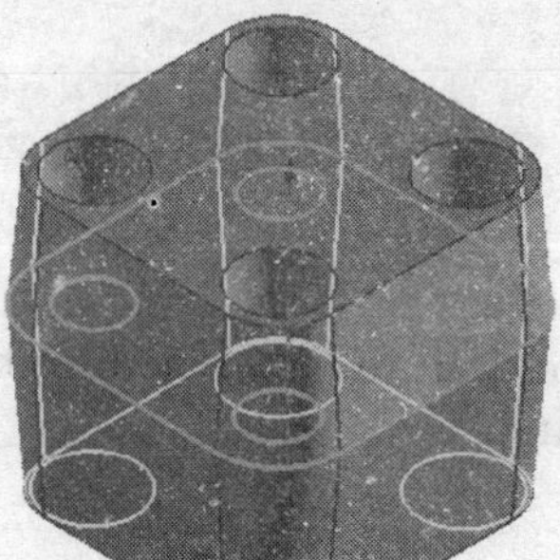

*Figure 4-35 Preview of the extrusion tapered using the **From Section - Symmetric Angle** option*

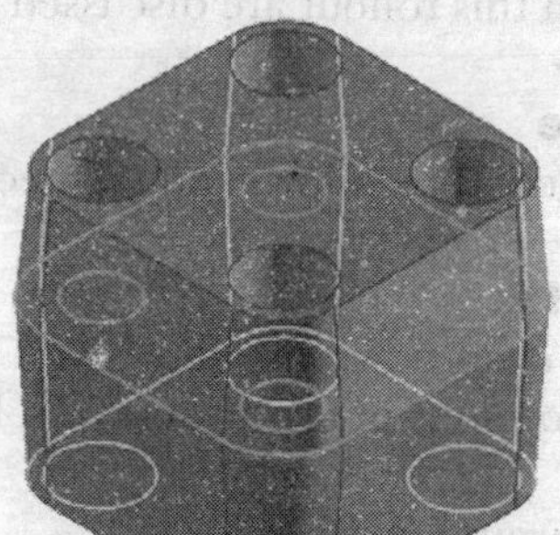

*Figure 4-36 Preview of the extrusion tapered using the **From Section - Matched Ends** option*

From Section - Asymmetric Angle
This option is also available only when you select the **Symmetric Value** option from the **Limits** rollout or specify the values in both the start and the end directions. This option adds different tapers in both directions of the sketch, as shown in Figure 4-37. When you select this option, the **Front Angle** and **Back Angle** edit boxes will be available in the **Draft** rollout. The front and back angle values will be applied at the front and back sides of the sketching plane.

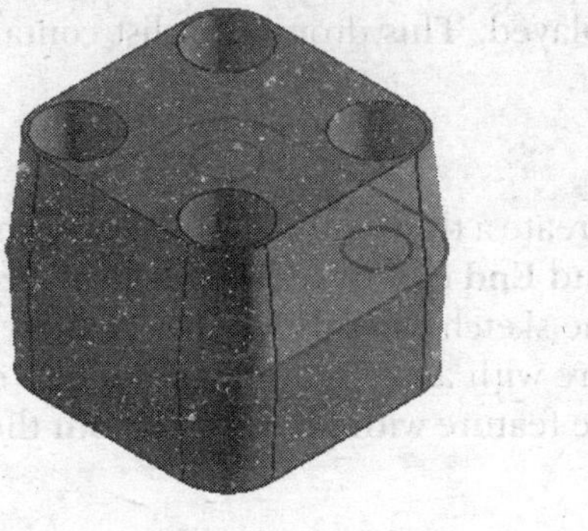

Figure 4-37 *Preview of the extrusion tapered using the* ***From Section - Asymmetric Angle*** *option*

Offset Rollout

NX also allows you to create thin base features by extruding open or closed sketches. For example, refer to the closed sketch shown in Figure 4-38. A thin feature created using this sketch is shown in Figure 4-39. Similarly, Figure 4-40 shows an open sketch and Figure 4-41 shows the resulting thin feature.

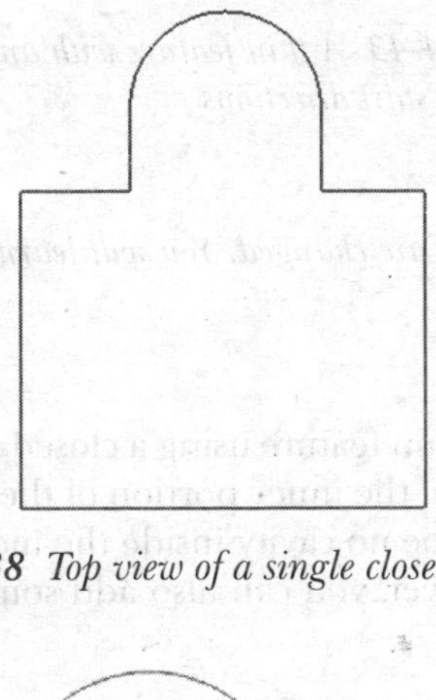

Figure 4-38 *Top view of a single closed sketch*

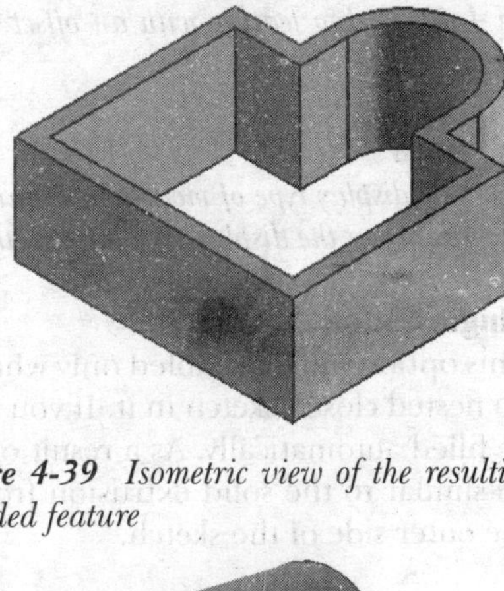

Figure 4-39 *Isometric view of the resulting thin extruded feature*

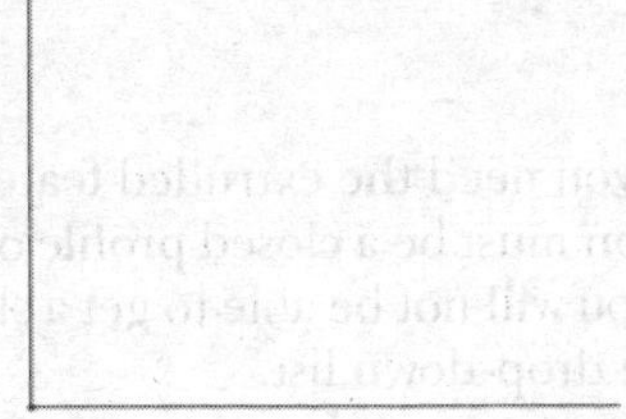

Figure 4-40 *Front view of an open sketch*

Figure 4-41 *Isometric view of the resulting thin extruded feature*

To create thin features, expand the **Offset** rollout in the **Extrude** dialog box; the **Offset** drop-down list will be displayed. This drop-down list contains three offset methods. These methods are discussed next.

Two-Sided

This option is used to create a thin feature by offsetting the sketch in two directions. Select this option; the **Start** and **End** edit boxes will be displayed. If you enter the positive value in the **End** edit box, the sketch will offset outward and vice-versa. Figure 4-42 shows the preview of a thin feature with an offset only in the end direction and Figure 4-43 shows the preview of the same feature with an offset in both the directions.

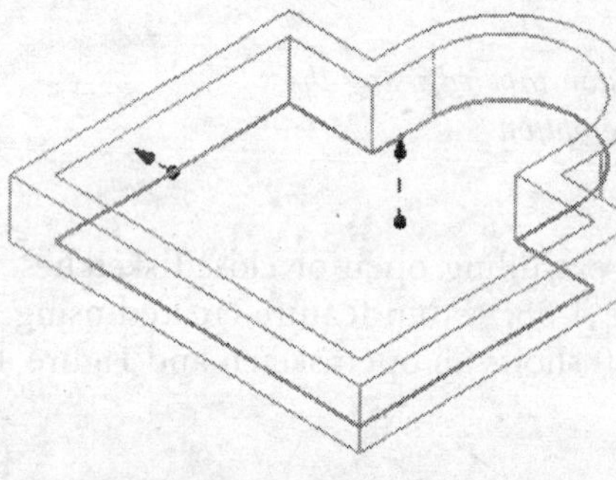

Figure 4-42 A thin feature with an offset only in the end direction

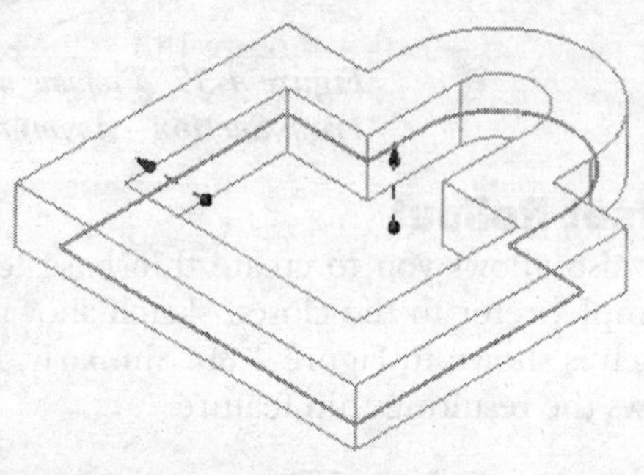

Figure 4-43 A thin feature with an offset in the end and start directions

Note

The display type of models in Figures 4-42 and 4-43 are changed. You will learn more about changing the display type later in this chapter.

Single-Sided

This option will be enabled only when you create a thin feature using a closed sketch with no nested closed sketch in it. If you select this option, the inner portion of the sketch will be filled automatically. As a result of this, there will be no cavity inside the model. It will be similar to the solid extrusion from inside. However, you can also add some offset to the outer side of the sketch.

Symmetric

This option is used to offset the material symmetrically on both sides of the sketch to create the thin feature.

Settings Rollout

The options in this rollout are used to specify whether you need the extruded feature to be a sheet body or a solid body. To get a solid body, the section must be a closed profile or an open profile with an offset. If you use a **Single-Sided** offset, you will not be able to get a sheet body. You can select the required option from the **Body Type** drop-down list.

Preview Rollout

This rollout is used to preview the model dynamically while modifying the values in the

Extrude dialog box. If you select the **Preview** check box, it will allow you to dynamically preview the changes in the model as you modify the values of the extrusion. The **Show Result** button is used to view the final model. The **Undo Result** button is used to go back to the preview mode.

After setting the values in the **Extrude** dialog box, choose **OK** to create the extruded feature and exit the dialog box. If you need to extrude more than one sketches, choose the **Apply** button; the selected sketch will be extruded and the dialog box will be retained. Also, you will be prompted to select the section geometry. Select the other sketch to extrude and choose the **OK** button.

You can also set and modify the values of extrusion using the drag handles that will be displayed in the preview of the extrusion feature, refer to Figure 4-44. The start drag handle will be a filled circle and the end drag handle will be an arrow. To modify the start limit, end limit, or draft angle values, click on their respective drag handles, and then press and hold the left mouse button and drag the mouse. You can also enter the new values in the edit boxes that will be displayed after clicking on the respective handles. To modify the type of limits or taper, right-click on their respective drag handles and select the type from the shortcut menu.

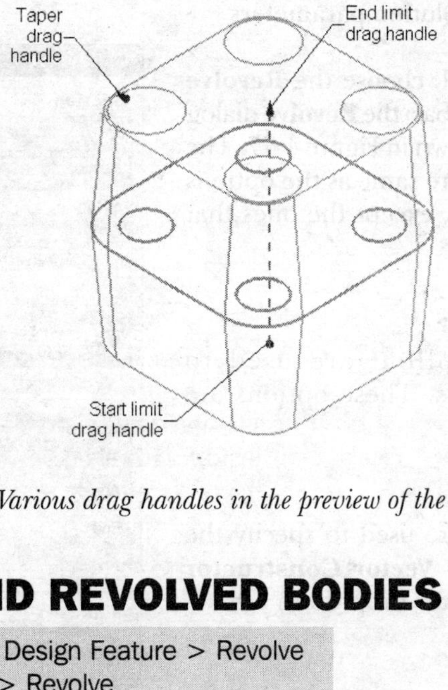

***Figure 4-44** Various drag handles in the preview of the extrusion feature*

CREATING SOLID REVOLVED BODIES

Menu:	Insert > Design Feature > Revolve
Toolbar:	Feature > Revolve

The **Revolve** tool allows you to create a solid body by revolving a sketch around the revolution axis, which could be a sketched line or an edge of an existing feature. Figure 4-45 shows a sketch for creating a revolved feature and Figure 4-46 shows the isometric view of the resulting feature revolved through an angle of 270 degrees.

To convert a sketch into a revolved body, you need to invoke the **Revolve** tool. This tool works in the following three steps:

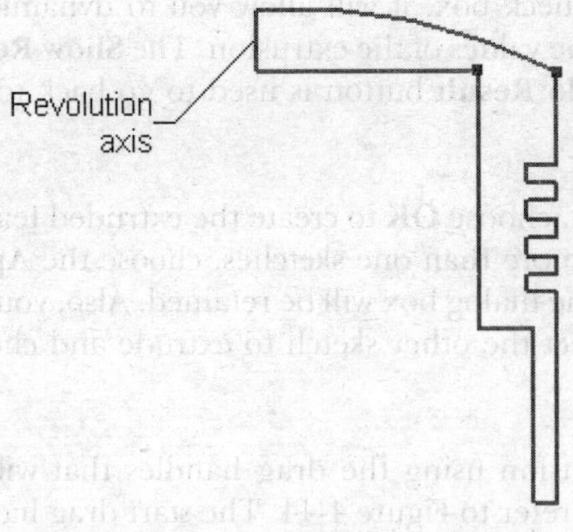

Figure 4-45 Sketch for creating the revolved feature and the revolution axis

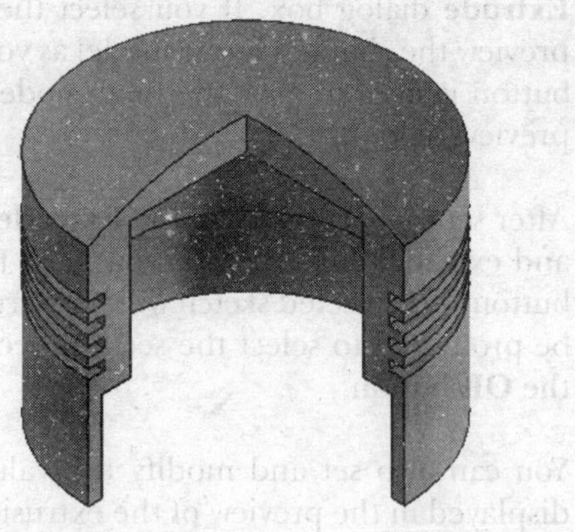

Figure 4-46 Isometric view of the resulting feature revolved through an angle of 270 degrees

Step 1: Select the sketch to be revolved
Step 2: Select the revolution axis
Step 3: Specify the revolution parameters

To invoke the **Revolve** tool, choose the **Revolve** button from the **Feature** toolbar; the **Revolve** dialog box will be displayed, as shown in Figure 4-47. The options in this dialog box are same as the options in the **Extrude** dialog box, except the ones that are explained next.

*Figure 4-47 The **Revolve** dialog box*

Axis Rollout

The options in this rollout are used to specify the revolution axis. These options are discussed next.

Specify Vector

The options in this area are used to specify the revolution axis using the **Vector Constructor** button or the **Inferred Vector** drop-down list.

Vector Constructor

When you choose this button, the **Vector** dialog box will be displayed. You can specify the revolution axis by using this dialog box.

Inferred Vector

The options in this drop-down list are used to specify the revolution axis. By default, the **Inferred Vector** option is selected in this drop-down list. As a result, you will be prompted to select the object to infer vector. You can select a sketched line, an axis, or an edge of an existing feature as the revolution axis.

Reverse Direction

You can choose this button to flip the direction of revolution.

Specify Point

The options in this area are used only when you use the vector method to specify the revolution axis.

Point Constructor

When you choose this button, the **Point** dialog box will be displayed. You can specify the point to define the revolution axis using this dialog box.

Inferred Point

This drop-down list contains the snap point options that are used to automatically snap the keypoints of the previously sketched entities or features.

Limits Rollout

The options in this rollout are used to specify the start and termination angles of revolution. These options are discussed next.

Start Drop-down List

This drop-down list allows you to specify the start angle of the revolution feature. You can select the **Value** and **Until Selected** options from this drop-down list. The **Value** option allows you to enter the value of the start angle in the **Angle** edit box. You need to enter a positive value of the angle. This value will be taken as the offset value between the sketch and the start of the revolved feature. The **Until Selected** option allows you to start the revolve feature from the selected plane, face, or body. When you select this option, the **Face, Body, Datum Plane** button will be chosen and you will be prompted to select the face, body, or datum plane to start the revolved feature.

End Drop-down List

This drop-down list allows you to specify the termination angle of the revolution feature. You can select the **Value** and **Until Selected** options from this drop-down list. The **Value** option allows you to enter the value of the end angle in the **Angle** edit box. You need to enter a positive value of the angle. This value will be taken as the offset value between the sketch and the end of the revolved feature. The **Until Selected** option allows you to terminate the revolve feature using the selected plane, face, or body. When you select this option, the **Face, Body, Datum Plane** button will be chosen and you will be prompted to select the face, body, or datum plane to start the revolved feature.

The default value of the end angle is the one that you have used to create the last revolved feature. Figure 4-48 shows a revolved feature with the start angle as 30 degrees and the end angle as 180 degrees. The sketch used to create this feature is also displayed.

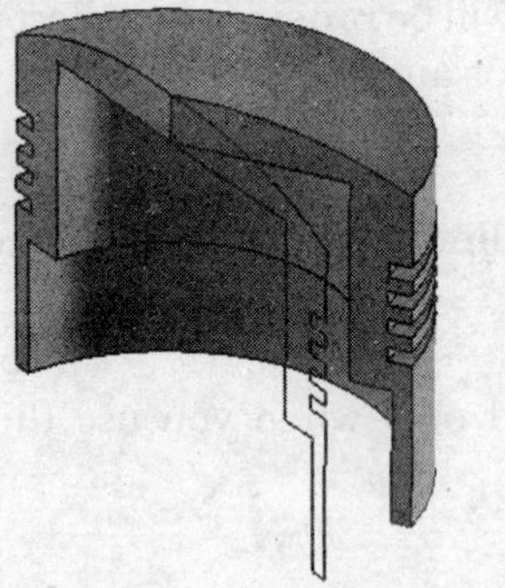

Figure 4-48 *Sketch revolved with start angle as 30 degrees and end angle as 180 degrees*

Note that NX uses the right-hand thumb rule to determine the direction of revolution. This rule states that if the thumb of your right hand points in the direction of the axis of revolution, then the direction of the curled fingers will define the direction of revolution, refer to Figure 4-49. Figure 4-50 shows the sketch and an arrow pointing in the direction of the axis of revolution and Figure 4-51 shows the resulting feature revolved through an angle of 180 degrees.

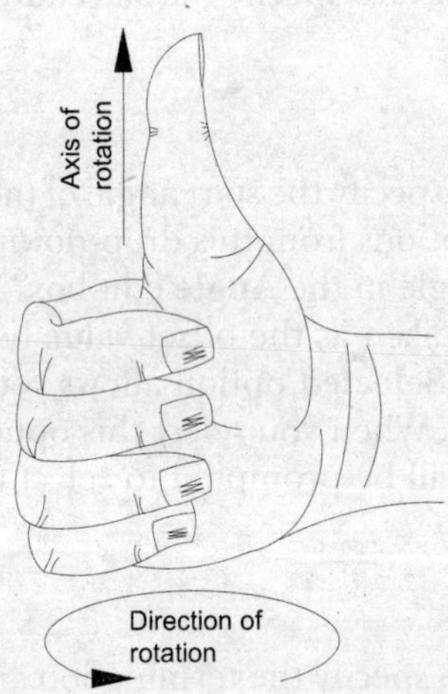

Figure 4-49 *The right-hand thumb rule*

Figure 4-52 shows the sketch and an arrow pointing in the direction of the axis of revolution and Figure 4-53 shows the resulting feature revolved through an angle of 180 degrees.

Offset Rollout

NX also allows you to create thin revolved bodies using the open and closed sketches. This process is similar to that of creating thin solid extruded features. Click on the **Offset** rollout in the **Revolve** dialog box; the rollout will expand and display the **Offset** drop-down list. There is only one option, **Two-Sided**, available in this drop-down list. Select this option; the **Start** and the **End** edit boxes will be available. Enter the start and end offset values in the

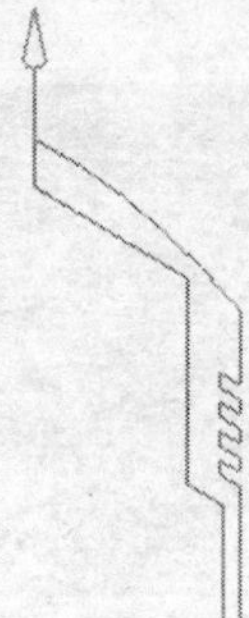

Figure 4-50 *Sketch for creating the revolved feature and the direction of the revolution axis*

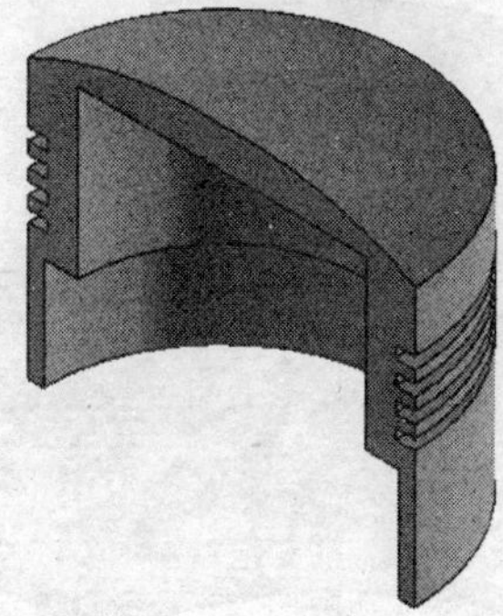

Figure 4-51 *Isometric view of the resulting feature revolved through an angle of 180 degrees*

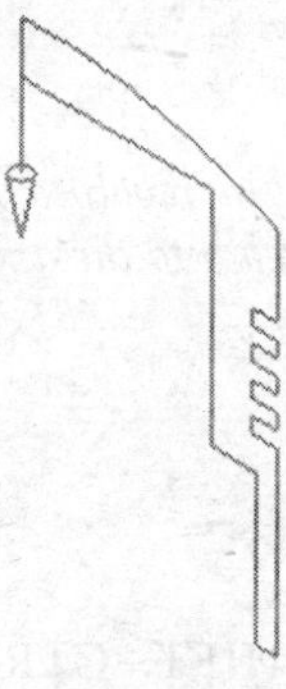

Figure 4-52 *Sketch for creating the revolved feature and the direction of the revolution axis*

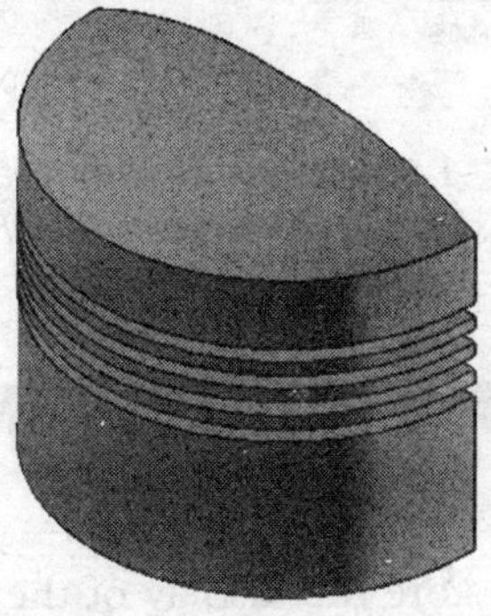

Figure 4-53 *Isometric view of the resulting feature revolved through an angle of 180 degrees*

respective edit boxes. Figure 4-54 shows a thin revolved model with the open sketch and the revolution axis used to create it. In this model, the start angle is 30 degrees, the end angle is 180 degrees, and the start offset value is 2.

Figure 4-55 shows a thin revolved model with the closed sketch and the revolution axis used to create it. In this model, the start angle is 45 degrees, the end angle is 270 degrees, and the start offset value is 2.

HIDING ENTITIES

Toolbar: Utility > Hide

Whenever you create a sketch-based feature, the sketch used to create it is retained on the screen, even after the feature is created. NX allows you to hide the sketches or any other entity on the screen using the **Hide** tool. To invoke this tool, press the CTRL+B keys; the **Class Selection** dialog box will be displayed. Alternatively, you can invoke the **Hide** tool from the **Utility** toolbar. Select the sketch or any other entity from the screen using this dialog box and choose the **OK** button; the selected entities will be hidden.

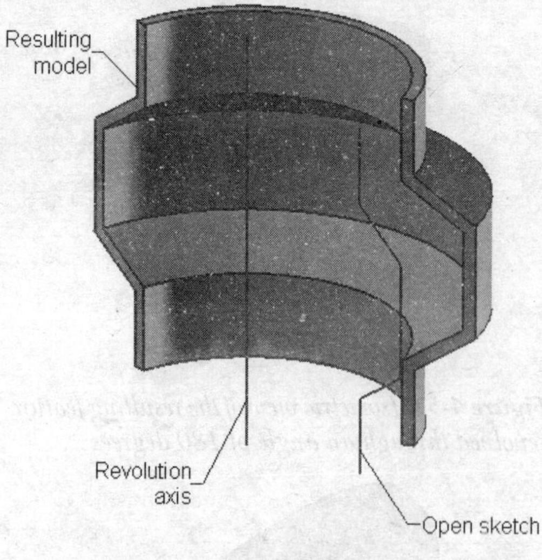

Figure 4-54 *A thin revolved feature with the original open sketch and the axis of revolution*

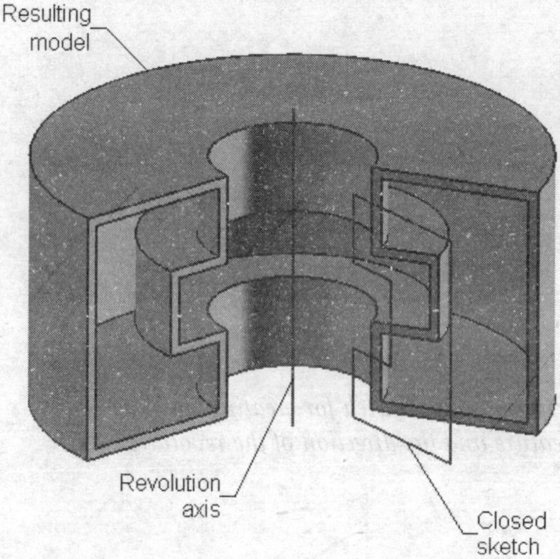

Figure 4-55 *A thin revolved feature with the original closed sketch and the axis of revolution*

SHOWING HIDDEN ENTITIES

Toolbar: Utility > Show

To restore the display of the hidden entities, press the SHIFT+CTRL+K keys; the **Class Selection** dialog box and the hidden entities will be displayed. Also, you will be prompted to select the objects to be displayed. Select the entities to be displayed and then choose the **OK** button.

Note

*The **Show** tool from the **Utility** toolbar can also be used to restore the display of the hidden entities.*

HIDING ALL ENTITIES USING A SINGLE TOOL

Toolbar: Utility > Show and Hide

NX allows you to hide or show all entities (all datum planes, coordinate systems, sketches, faceted bodies, solid bodies, and so on) from the drawing window using a single tool. To do so, choose the **Show and Hide** button from the **Utility** toolbar; the **Show and Hide** dialog box will be displayed, as shown in Figure 4-56.

All entities are divided into three categories, Bodies, Sketches, and Datums. Select the minus sign (-) from the respective rows; the corresponding entities will be hidden. For example, if you need to hide all the sketches in the drawing window, select the minus sign (-) from the **Sketches** row; all the sketches will be hidden.

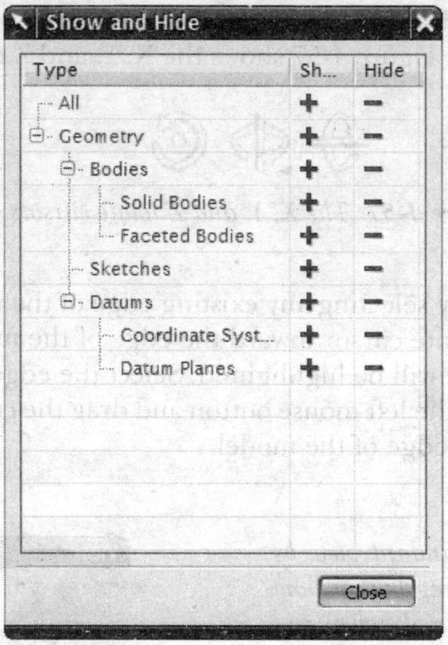

*Figure 4-56 The **Show and Hide** dialog box*

Similarly, to show hidden entities, select the plus sign (+) from the respective row; all entities under that category will be redisplayed in the drawing window.

Note

*The **Show and Hide** tool is very useful while working with complicated models and assemblies, where datum planes, coordinate systems, and sketches are in large numbers.*

You can also invoke this tool by pressing the CTRL+W keys.

ROTATING THE VIEW OF A MODEL IN 3D SPACE

Toolbar: View > Rotate

NX provides you with an option of rotating the view of a solid model freely in the 3-dimensional (3D) space. This enables you to visually maneuver around the solid model and view it from any direction. To do so, choose the **Rotate** button from the **View** toolbar; the cursor changes to the rotate view cursor and you will be prompted to drag the cursor to rotate the model. Next, press and hold the left mouse button and drag the cursor; the view of the model will be rotated and you can visually maneuver around it.

You can also rotate the view around the X, Y, or Z axis of the current view. To rotate the view around the X-axis of the current view, invoke the **Rotate** tool and move the cursor close to the left or right edge of the drawing window; the cursor changes to the X-rotate cursor. Press and hold the left mouse button and drag the cursor; the view will be rotated around the X-axis of the current view. Move the cursor close to the bottom edge of the drawing window and drag the cursor to rotate the view around the Y-axis of the current view. Similarly, move the cursor close to the top edge of the drawing window and drag the cursor to rotate the view around the Z-axis of the current view. Figure 4-57 shows the X, Y, and Z rotate cursors.

Figure 4-57 The X, Y, and Z rotate cursors

You can also rotate the view by selecting any existing edge of the model. To do so, invoke the **Rotate** tool and move the rotate cursor toward the edge of the model about which you want to rotate the model; the edge will be highlighted. Select the edge by clicking the left mouse button. Next, press and hold the left mouse button and drag the cursor; the view of the model will rotate about the selected edge of the model.

Note

*You can restore any standard view by choosing its corresponding button from the flyout that is displayed, when you choose the down arrow on the right of the **Trimetric** button in the **View** toolbar.*

SETTING DISPLAY MODES

You can set the display modes for the solid models using the buttons in the **View** toolbar. Figure 4-58 shows the partial display of the **View** toolbar with various buttons and flyout options that you can use to set the display modes of the model.

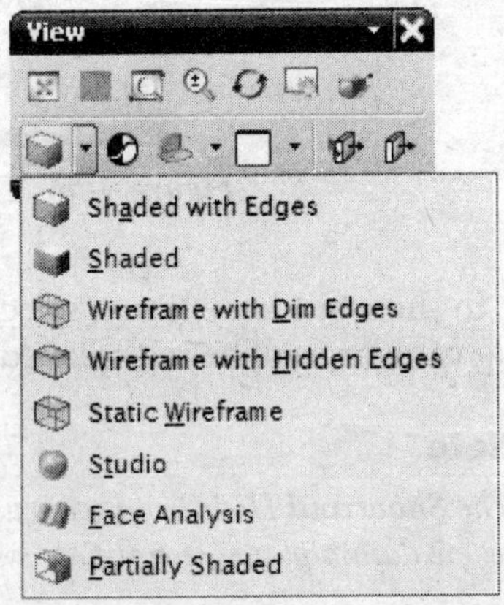

*Figure 4-58 Partial view of the **View** toolbar to display various options to set the display modes*

TUTORIALS

Tutorial 1

In this tutorial, you will create the model shown in Figure 4-59. The dimensions of the model are shown in Figure 4-60. The depth of extrusion of the model is 45.

(Expected time: 30 min)

The following steps are required to complete this tutorial:

a. Start a new part file using the **Model** template and then draw the profile of the outer loop. Add the required constraints.
b. Draw the inner loops and add the required dimensions to them.
c. Exit the Sketcher environment and invoke the **Extrude** tool. Define the depth of extrusion to create the final model.
d. Rotate the view in 3D space.
e. Save the file and close it.

Figure 4-59 Model for Tutorial 1

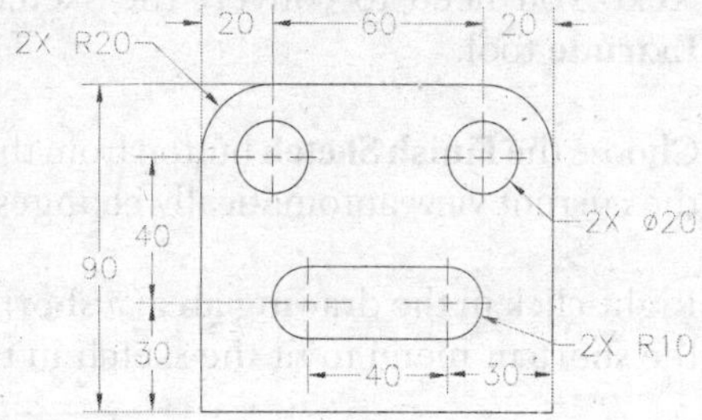

Figure 4-60 Dimensions of the model

Drawing the Sketch of the Model

The sketch of this model will be created on the XC-ZC plane. As mentioned earlier, when you extrude the sketch with nested closed loops, the inner loops are automatically subtracted from the outer sketch.

1. Start a new file with the name *c04tut1.prt* using the **Model** template and specify its location as *C:\NX 7\c04*.

2. Choose the **Display WCS** button from the **Utility** toolbar to turn on the display of WCS, if it is not displayed already.

3. Invoke the Sketcher environment using the XC-ZC plane as the sketching plane.

4. Draw the sketch of the outer loop and add the required geometric and dimensional constraints to it, as shown in Figure 4-61.

5. Draw the inner loops and then add the required geometric and dimensional constraints to them, as shown in Figure 4-62.

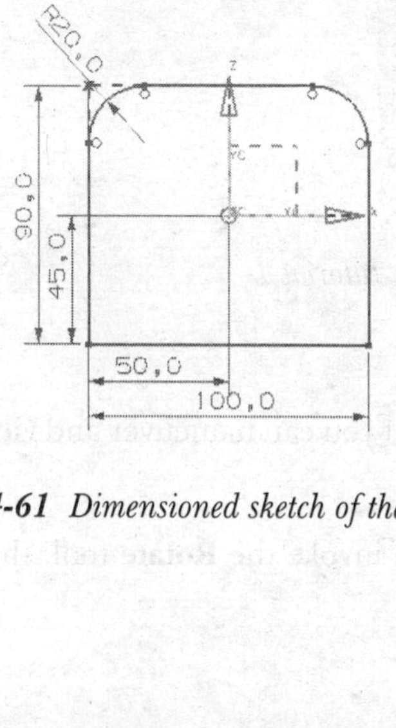

Figure 4-61 Dimensioned sketch of the outer loop

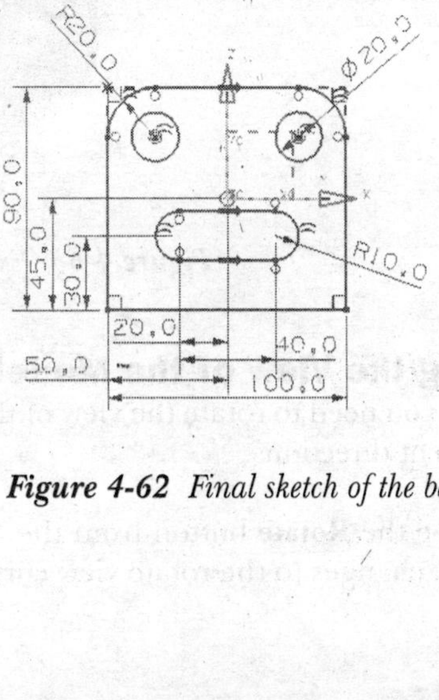

Figure 4-62 Final sketch of the base feature

Converting the Sketch into the Base Feature

Next, you need to convert the sketch into the base feature. This is done using the **Extrude** tool.

1. Choose the **Finish Sketch** button from the **Sketcher** toolbar to exit the Sketcher environment; the current view automatically changes to the Trimetric view.

2. Right-click in the drawing area; a shortcut menu is displayed. Choose the **Fit** option from the shortcut menu to fit the sketch in the screen.

3. Invoke the **Extrude** tool from the **Feature** toolbar; the **Extrude** dialog box is displayed and you are prompted to select the planar face to sketch or select the section geometry.

4. Select the sketch from the drawing window; the preview of the extruded feature is displayed. Also, the **End** dynamic input box is displayed in the drawing window.

5. Enter **45** in the **End** dynamic input box and press the ENTER key; the preview is modified accordingly.

6. Choose the **OK** button in the **Extrude** dialog box; the extrude feature is created and displayed in the drawing window.

7. Press the CTRL+B keys; the **Class Selection** dialog box is displayed. Select the sketch of the extruded feature to hide it. Next, choose the **OK** button from the dialog box. Figure 4-63 shows the extruded feature after hiding its sketch.

Figure 4-63 *Extruded model for Tutorial 1*

Rotating the View of the Model

Next, you need to rotate the view of the model so that you can maneuver and view it from different directions.

1. Choose the **Rotate** button from the **View** toolbar to invoke the **Rotate** tool; the cursor changes to the rotate view cursor.

2. Press and hold the left mouse button and drag the cursor in the drawing window to rotate the view of the model.

3. Exit from the **Rotate** tool by pressing the ESC key.

4. Choose the **Isometric** button from the **View** toolbar to restore the Isometric view. If this is not the button chosen by default, then click on the down arrow on the right of the button and choose the **Isometric** button from the flyout.

5. Right-click in the drawing window and choose **Fit** from the shortcut menu; the model fits in the drawing window.

Saving and Closing the File

1. Choose **File > Close > Save and Close** from the menu bar to save and close the file.

Tutorial 2

In this tutorial, you will create the model shown in Figure 4-64. Its dimensions are given in the drawing views shown in Figure 4-65. **(Expected time: 30 min)**

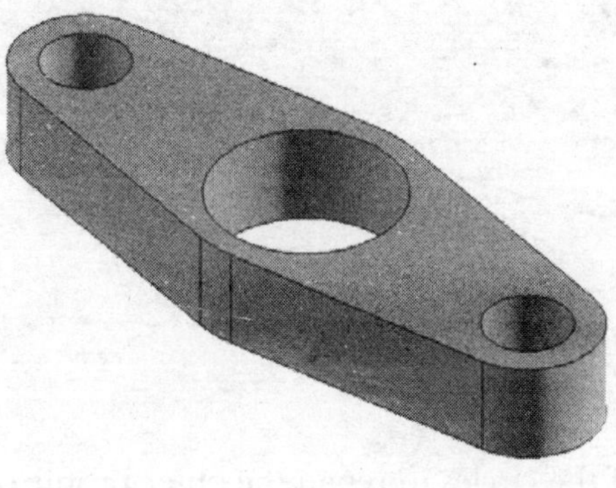

Figure 4-64 *Model for Tutorial 2*

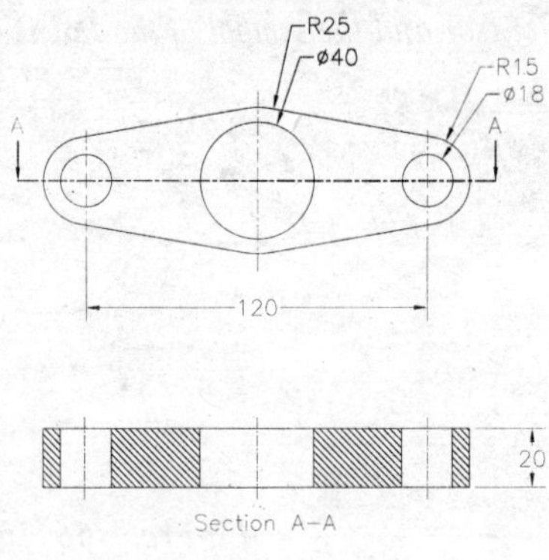

Figure 4-65 *Top and sectioned front views showing the dimensions of the model*

The following steps are required to complete this tutorial:

a. Start a new part file using the **Model** template and then draw the profile of the outer loop.
b. Add the required dimensions and constraints to the profile.
c. Draw the inner circles and add the required dimensions to them.
d. Exit the Sketcher environment and invoke the **Extrude** tool. Define the depth of extrusion to create the final model.
e. Rotate the view in 3D space, save the file, and close it.

Drawing the Sketch of the Model

The sketch of this model can be created using the **Sketch** tool. The inner circles will be automatically subtracted from the outer profile on extruding.

1. Start NX 7 and then start a new file with the name *c04tut2.prt* using the **Model** template and specify its location as *C:\NX 7\c04.*

2. Choose the **Display WCS** button from the **Utility** toolbar to turn on the display of WCS.

3. Invoke the Sketcher environment using the XC-YC plane as the sketching plane.

4. Draw the sketch using the **Circle** tool and the **Line** tool, as shown in Figure 4-66. Make sure that the **Tangent** and **Point On Curve** constraints are applied between the lines and the circles at all points where the lines intersect the circles. The **Tangent** constraint is represented by a small circle and the **Point On Curve** constraint is represented by a cross, as shown in Figure 4-66.

Note

To make sure that both the ***Tangent*** *and* ***Point on Curve*** *constraints are applied, specify the endpoint of the line only when the symbol of the* ***Tangent*** *constraint is displayed on the left of the cursor and the symbol of the* ***Point on Curve*** *constraint is displayed on the right of the cursor.*

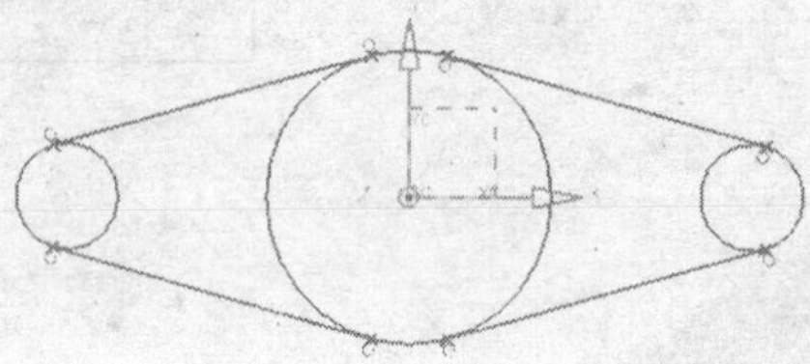

Figure 4-66 *Initial sketch for the base feature*

Next, you need to trim the unwanted portion of the circles to retain the outer profile of the model. The sketch is trimmed using the **Quick Trim** tool.

5. Choose the **Quick Trim** button from the **Sketch Tools** toolbar; the **Quick Trim** dialog box is displayed. Also, you are prompted to select the curve to be trimmed.

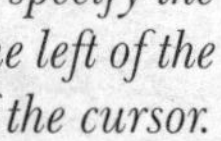

6. Press and hold the left mouse button inside the right circle and drag it horizontally toward the left, close to the center of the left circle.

7. Release the left mouse button to trim the unwanted portions of the circles, refer to Figure 4-67. Next, choose the **Close** button from the **Quick Trim** dialog box.

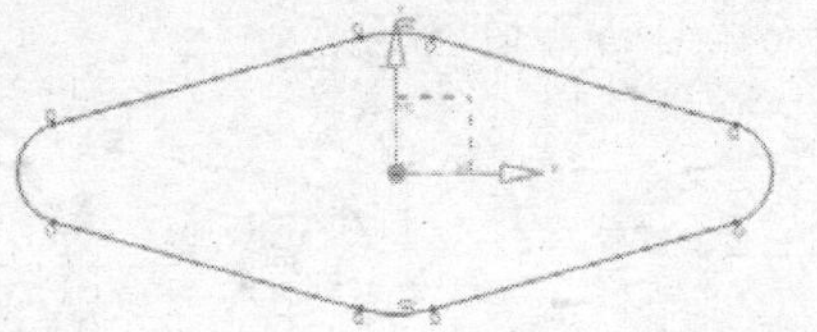

Figure 4-67 Sketch after trimming the unwanted portion of circles

Note

*If the **Point On Curve** and **Tangent** constraints are not applied automatically while drawing the sketch then you need to manually add these constraints to the circles and the lines of the sketch.*

Next, you need to add constraints to the sketch.

8. Choose the **Constraints** button from the **Sketch Tools** toolbar and make the radius of the left arc equal to that of the right arc. Similarly, make all lines equal using the **Equal Length** constraint. Note that you also need to add the **Point On Curve** constraint between the center of the left arc and the XC axis. Similarly, you need to apply the **Point On Curve** constraint between the right arc and the XC axis.

Note

*You can choose the **Show All Constraints** button from the **Sketch Tools** toolbar to view all the constraints that are applied to the sketch.*

Next, you need to add dimensions to the sketch.

9. Add dimensions to the sketch using the **Inferred Dimensions** tool, refer to Figure 4-68.

Note

*In this tutorial, the dimension style of the dimensions has been changed for clarity. To change the dimension style, choose **Sketch > Sketch Style** from the menu bar. On doing so, the **Sketch Style** dialog box is displayed. Select the **Value** option from the **Dimension Label** drop-down list. Next, choose the **OK** button from the dialog box.*

Next, you need to draw the inner circles. You can use the center points of the arcs to draw them.

10. Next, draw three circles using the center points of the arcs, refer to Figure 4-69.

11. Add the **Equal Radius** constraint to the left and right circles. Now, add the required dimensions to the circles to complete the sketch. The final sketch of the model is shown in Figure 4-69.

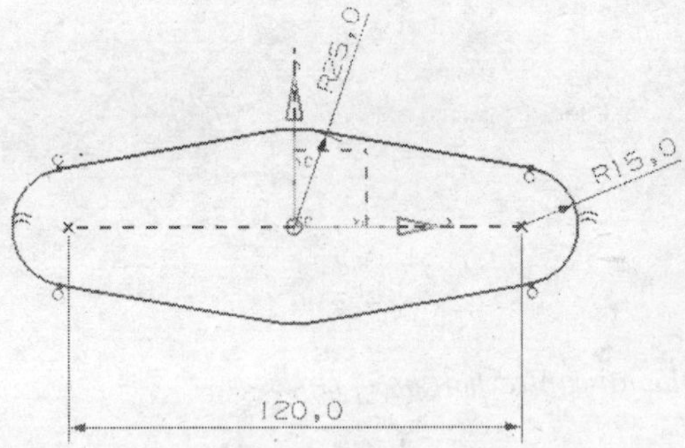

Figure 4-68 *Sketch after adding relationships and dimensions*

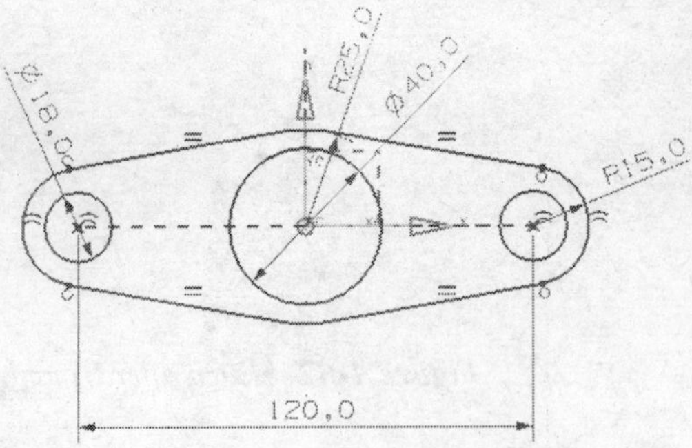

Figure 4-69 *Final sketch for Tutorial 2*

Converting the Sketch into the Base Feature

Next, you need to convert the sketch into the base feature. This is done using the **Extrude** tool.

1. Choose the **Finish Sketch** button from the **Sketcher** toolbar to exit the Sketcher environment; the current view automatically changes to the Trimetric view.

2. Invoke the **Extrude** tool from the **Feature** toolbar; the **Extrude** dialog box is displayed and you are prompted to select the planar face to sketch or select the section geometry to extrude.

3. Select the sketch from the drawing window; the preview of the extruded feature is displayed. Also, the **End** dynamic input box is displayed.

4. Enter **20** in the **End** dynamic input box and press the ENTER key; the preview is modified accordingly.

5. Choose the **OK** button in the **Extrude** dialog box; the extruded feature is created and displayed in the drawing window, as shown in Figure **4-70.**

   Notice that the datum plane, sketch, and datum axes are still displayed in the sketch. For a better visualization of the model, you can turn off the display of these entities.

6. Press the CTRL+B keys; the **Class Selection** dialog box is displayed. Select all the unwanted entities and then choose **OK**.

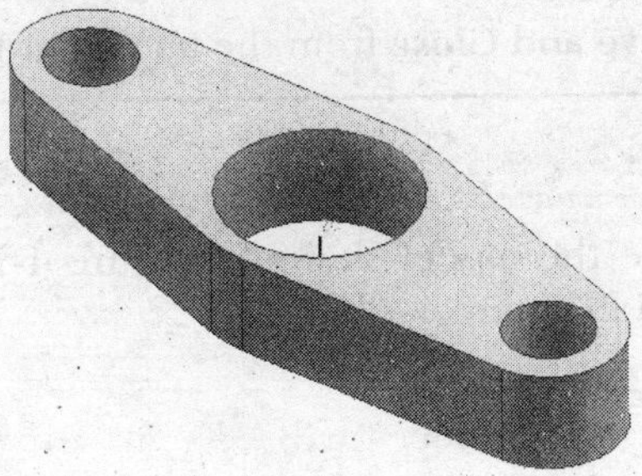

Figure 4-70 Model after extruding the sketch

Rotating the View of the Model

Next, you need to rotate the model to maneuver and view it from different directions.

1. Choose the **Rotate** button from the **View** toolbar; the cursor changes to the rotate view cursor.

2. Press and hold the left mouse button and drag the cursor in the drawing window. Figure 4-71 shows a model being rotated using the **Rotate** tool.

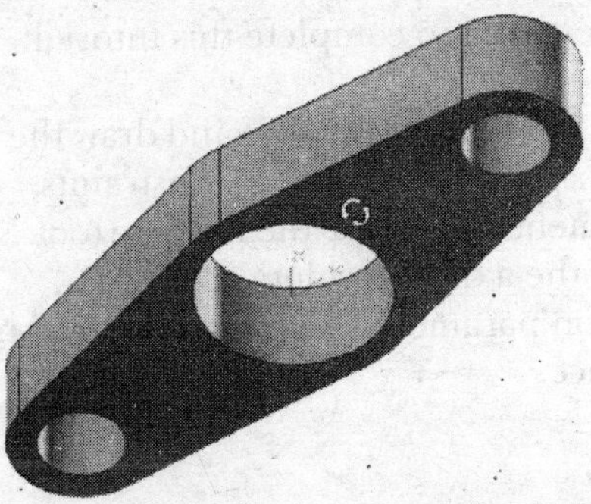

Figure 4-71 Rotating the model in 3D space

3. Choose the **Rotate** button again to finish rotating the model.

   Next, you need to restore the Isometric view of the model, which has been changed by the **Rotate** tool.

4. Choose the **Isometric** button in the **View** toolbar to restore the Isometric view. If this is not the button chosen by default, then click on the down arrow on the right of the button and choose the **Isometric** button from the flyout.

5. Now, right-click in the drawing window and choose **Fit** from the shortcut menu; the model fits in the drawing window.

Saving and Closing the File

1. Choose **File > Close > Save and Close** from the menu bar to save and close the file.

Tutorial 3

In this tutorial, you will create the model shown in Figure 4-72. This is a revolved body created using the sketch shown in Figure 4-73. **(Expected time: 30 min)**

Figure 4-72 Model for Tutorial 3

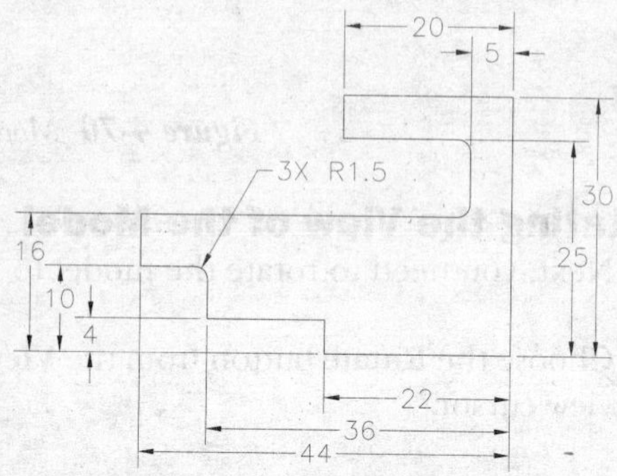

Figure 4-73 Dimensions of the model

The following steps are required to complete this tutorial:

a. Start a new part file using the **Model** template and draw the sketch of the revolved model. Add the required geometric and dimensional constraints.
b. Exit the Sketcher environment and invoke the **Revolve** tool. Select the sketch to be revolved and then the direction of the axis of revolution.
c. Define the other revolution parameters to create the final model.
d. Rotate the view in 3D space.
e. Save and close the file.

Drawing the Sketch of the Model

The sketch of the revolved model will be created on the YC-ZC plane.

1. Start a new file with the name *c04tut3.prt* using the **Model** template and specify its location as *C:\NX 7\c04*.

2. Invoke the Sketcher environment using the YC-ZC plane as the sketching plane.

3. Draw the sketch of the revolved feature and add the required geometric and dimensional constraints to it, as shown in Figure 4-74.

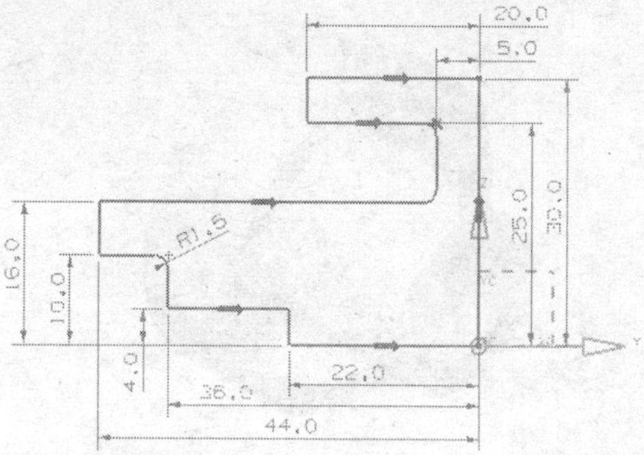

Figure 4-74 Dimensioned sketch of the revolved feature

Converting the Sketch into the Revolved Feature

Next, you need to convert the sketch into a revolved feature. This is done using the **Revolve** tool.

1. Choose the **Finish Sketch** button from the **Sketcher** toolbar to exit the Sketcher environment; the current view automatically changes to the Trimetric view.

2. Right-click in the drawing window; a shortcut menu is displayed. Choose the **Fit** option from the shortcut menu to fit the sketch in the screen.

3. Invoke the **Revolve** tool from the **Feature** toolbar; the **Revolve** dialog box is displayed and you are prompted to select the planar face to sketch or select the section geometry.

4. Select the sketch drawn and choose the **Inferred Vector** button from the **Axis** rollout of the dialog box; you are prompted to select the objects to infer vector.

5. Select the bottom horizontal line as the axis of revolution; the preview of the revolved body is displayed.

6. Accept the default options in the **Revolve** dialog box and choose the **OK** button; the revolved feature is created. Make sure that the angle of revolution of the model is 360 degrees.

7. Choose the **Show and Hide** button from the **Utility** toolbar; the **Show and Hide** dialog box is displayed. Click on the minus sign (-) in the **Datums** and **Sketches** rows to hide the sketch, the axes, and the sketching plane, and then close the dialog box. Next, fit the model in the screen. The revolved model after hiding the sketch, the axes, and the sketching plane is shown in Figure 4-75.

Rotating the View of the Model

Next, you need to rotate the model to maneuver and view it from different directions.

Figure 4-75 Revolved model of Tutorial 3

1. Choose the **Rotate** button from the **View** toolbar; the cursor changes to the rotate view cursor.

2. Press and hold the left mouse button and drag the cursor in the drawing window to rotate the view of the model. Next, exit from the **Rotate** tool by pressing the ESC key.

3. Choose the **Isometric** button in the **View** toolbar to restore the Isometric view. If this is not the button chosen by default, then click on the down arrow on the right of the button; a flyout is displayed. Now, choose the **Isometric** button from this flyout.

Saving and Closing the File

1. Choose **File > Close > Save and Close** from the menu bar to save and close the file.

Self-Evaluation Test

Answer the following questions and then compare them to those given at the end of this chapter:

1. The **Quick Trim** tool is used to remove a portion of the sketch by chopping it off. (T/F)

2. In NX, while extruding a sketch, you can add a draft to it. (T/F)

3. The **Quick Extend** tool is used to extend or lengthen an open sketched entity up to infinity. (T/F)

4. You can set the display modes for solid models using the buttons in the **Standard** toolbar. (T/F)

5. After invoking the **Quick Trim** tool, you can drag the cursor to trim __________ entities.

6. The __________ option is used to extrude the sketch symmetrically on both sides of the plane, on which the sketch is created.

7. The __________ option is used to add the draft that is aligned with the profile.

8. NX uses the __________ rule to determine the direction of revolution.

9. You can create thin features using the __________ or __________ sketches.

10. You can restore standard views by choosing various buttons from the __________ toolbar.

Review Questions

Answer the following questions:

1. Which of the following tools in NX 7 allows you to dynamically move, rotate, or copy the solid objects and the sketched entities?

   (a) **Transform** (b) **Modify**
   (c) **Move Object** (d) None

2. Which one of the following views is the default view in NX?

   (a) Trimetric (b) Isometric
   (c) Top (d) None

3. Which rollout is used to create a thin extruded feature by offsetting in two directions?

   (a) **Offset** (b) **Symmetric**
   (c) **Two Sided** (d) None

4. Which one of the following paths is used to invoke the **Move Object** tool?

   (a) **Edit > Move Object** (b) **Insert > Move Object**
   (c) **Preference > Move Object** (d) **Tool > Move Object**

5. Which one of the following rules is used to determine the direction of revolution?

   (a) Right-hand rule (b) Right-hand thumb rule
   (c) Left-hand rule (d) Left-hand thumb rule

6. In which of the following toolbars can you set the display modes for solid models?

   (a) **Standard** (b) **Sketch**
   (c) **Visible** (d) **View**

7. On choosing **Finish Sketch** from the **Sketcher** toolbar to exit the Sketcher environment, the Modeling environment will be invoked. (T/F)

8. When you mirror entities using the **Mirror Curve** tool, by default a mirrored copy of the selected entities is created and the original entities are deleted. (T/F)

9. In the **Results** rollout of the **Move Object** dialog box, you can specify whether you want to move the original entity or its copy by using the **Move Original** or **Copy Original** radio button. (T/F)

10. You can rotate a model in 3D space using the **Rotate** tool. (T/F)

Exercises

Exercise 1

Open the sketch drawn in Tutorial 3 of Chapter 3 and convert it into a full revolved body. After creating the model, use the **Rotate** tool to rotate its view. Save the file with a different name in the folder of this chapter. **(Expected time: 15 min)**

Exercise 2

Create the model shown in Figure 4-76. The dimensions of the model are shown in Figure 4-77. The depth of extrusion is 30. After creating the model, use the **Rotate** tool to rotate its view. Before closing the file, restore the Isometric view of the model. **(Expected time: 30 min)**

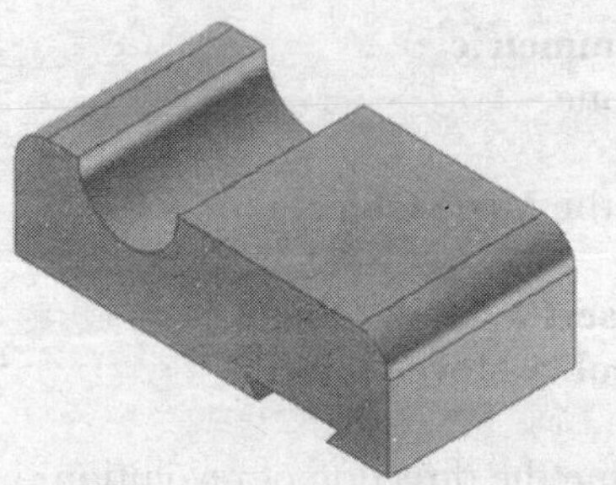

Figure 4-76 *Model for Exercise 2*

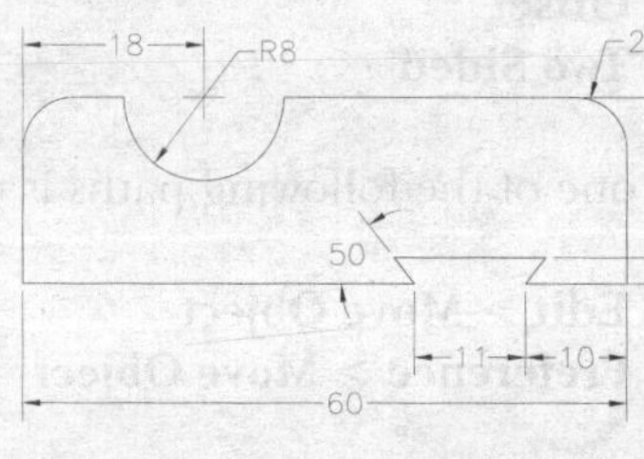

Figure 4-77 *Dimensions of the model*

Answers to Self-Evaluation Test

1. T, **2.** T, **3.** F, **4.** F, **5.** multiple, **6. Symmetric Value**, **7. From Section**, **8.** Right-hand thumb rule, **9.** open, close, **10. View**

Chapter 5

Working with Datum Planes, Coordinate Systems, and Datum Axes

Learning Objectives

After completing this chapter, you will be able to:

- *Understand the usage of reference geometries in NX.*
- *Understand different types of datum planes in NX.*
- *Create fixed and relative datum planes.*
- *Understand the usage of CSYS (coordinate system).*
- *Create coordinate systems using various methods.*
- *Understand the usage of datum axis.*
- *Create datum axis using various methods.*
- *Use additional extrude and revolve options.*
- *Project existing elements on the current sketching plane.*

ADDITIONAL SKETCHING AND REFERENCE PLANES

In the previous chapters, you learned to create basic models, which had features placed on one of the three datum planes of the Datum Coordinate System (YC-ZC, XC-ZC, or XC-YC). All these models were created by selecting any of the three datum planes of the Datum Coordinate System. Most real world models consist of multiple sketched features, reference geometries, and placed features. In NX, features can be added to base features by using the boolean operations such as subtract, unite, and intersect. These boolean operations are available in all tools. When you enter the Sketcher environment by choosing the **Sketch** button from the **Feature** toolbar, the **Create Sketch** dialog box will be displayed and you will be prompted to select a sketching plane. You can select any one of the three datum planes of the Datum Coordinate System as the sketching plane. You can also create a new datum plane by using the **Datum Plane** dialog box. On the basis of design requirement, you can select any plane as the sketching plane for the base feature. Also, you can create additional planes by taking reference of existing planes, faces, surfaces, sketches, or a combination of these objects. Figure 5-1 shows a model with multiple features.

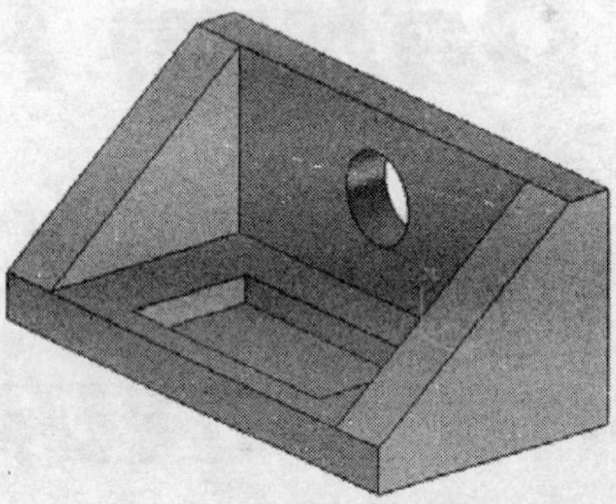

Figure 5-1 *Model with multiple features*

The base feature for this model is shown in Figure 5-2. The sketch for the base feature is drawn on the XC-YC datum plane of the Datum Coordinate System. As mentioned earlier, after creating the base feature, you need to create the other sketched features, placed features, and reference features, refer to Figure 5-3. The extrude features shown in Figure 5-3 require additional sketching planes on which the sketch for the other features will be created.

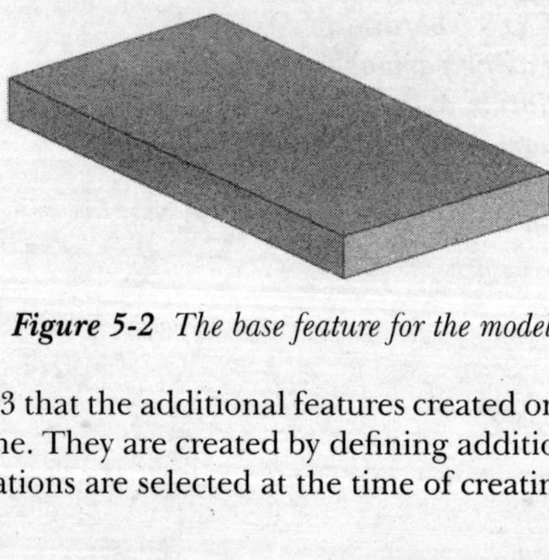

Figure 5-2 *The base feature for the model*

It is evident from Figure 5-3 that the additional features created on the base feature do not lie on the same sketching plane. They are created by defining additional sketching planes. Also, appropriate boolean operations are selected at the time of creating these features.

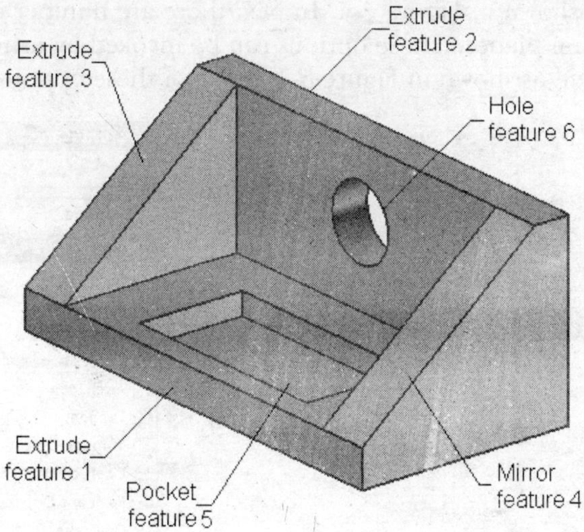

Figure 5-3 *Various features in the model*

As mentioned earlier, if you invoke a new part file by using the **Model** template, the Datum Coordinate System containing three datum planes, three datum axes, and a point will be displayed in the drawing window. You can select any of these datum planes as the sketching plane or you can create new datum planes by using the **Datum Plane** dialog box.

TYPES OF DATUM PLANES

There are three types of datum planes in NX: datum planes of the Datum Coordinate System, fixed datum planes, and relative datum planes. Fixed datum planes are the ones that pass through the origin. Relative datum planes are created in addition to fixed datum planes by taking the reference of objects such as curves, sketches, edges, faces, surfaces, and points. The methods of creating these datum planes are discussed next.

Creating Three Fixed (Principle) Datum Planes

In NX, the principle datum planes are called fixed datum planes. The detailed procedure for creating the fixed datum planes is discussed in Chapter 2.

Creating Relative Datum Planes

Menu:	Insert > Datum/Point > Datum Plane
Toolbar:	Feature Operation > Datum Plane

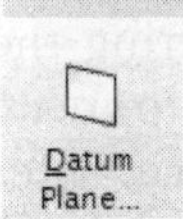

As mentioned earlier, relative datum planes are the additional planes that are created to assist you in completing a design. You can select objects such as curves, sketches, edges, faces, surfaces, datum planes of the Datum Coordinate System, and points as reference to create relative datum planes. To create relative datum planes, choose the **Datum Plane** button from the **Feature Operation** toolbar; the **Datum Plane** dialog box will be displayed, as shown in Figure 5-4. In NX, there are number of options available for creating relative datum planes. These options can be invoked by using the **Type** drop-down list in the **Type** rollout, as shown in Figure 5-5. Some of these options are discussed next.

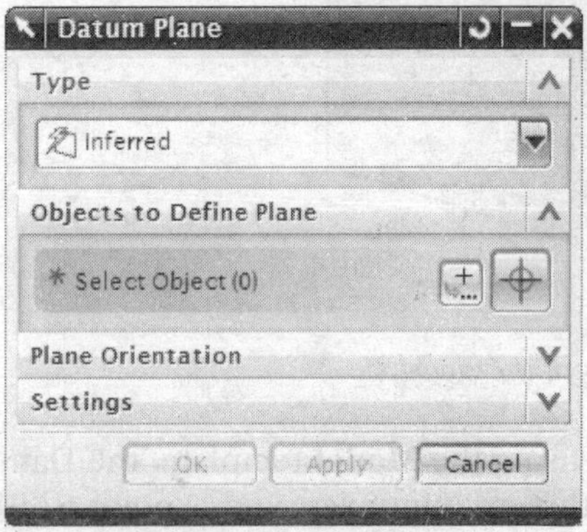

Figure 5-4 The ***Datum Plane*** *dialog box*

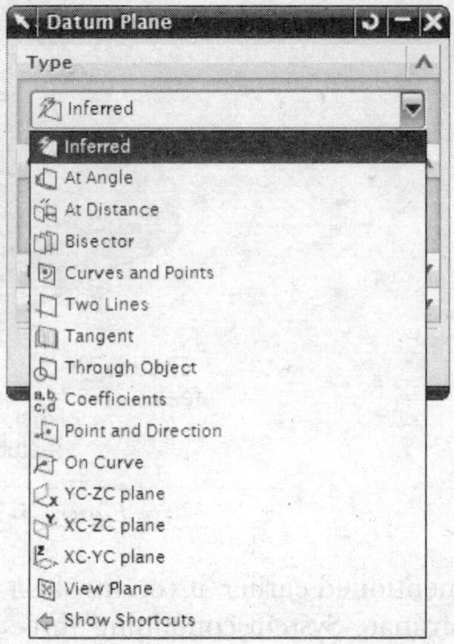

Figure 5-5 The ***Type*** *drop-down list of the* ***Datum Plane*** *dialog box*

At Distance

The **At Distance** option is used to create a plane offset to an existing planar face, a surface, or an existing datum plane.

To create an offset plane, you need to follow two steps. First, select the **At Distance** option from the drop-down list in the **Type** rollout. Next, select a planar face, a surface, or a datum plane to which the new plane will be parallel. After selecting the reference object, the preview of the plane will be displayed in green, as shown in Figure 5-6. Also, an arrow will be displayed from the center of the newly created plane, along with the **Distance** edit box.

The second step is to specify the offset distance. To do so, enter the offset distance in the **Distance** edit box and press ENTER; the preview of the plane will be modified accordingly. The arrow displayed from the center of the plane indicates the positive direction of the offset. If you need to offset the plane in the opposite direction, enter a negative distance value. Also, you can double-click on this arrow or choose the **Reverse Direction** button from the **Offset** rollout of the **Datum Plane** dialog box to change the offset direction. After entering the appropriate offset distance, choose the **OK** button from the **Datum Plane** dialog box to create a plane, as shown in Figure 5-7. To create multiple offset planes at specified distance, enter the number of planes in the **Number of Planes** edit box of the **Offset** rollout.

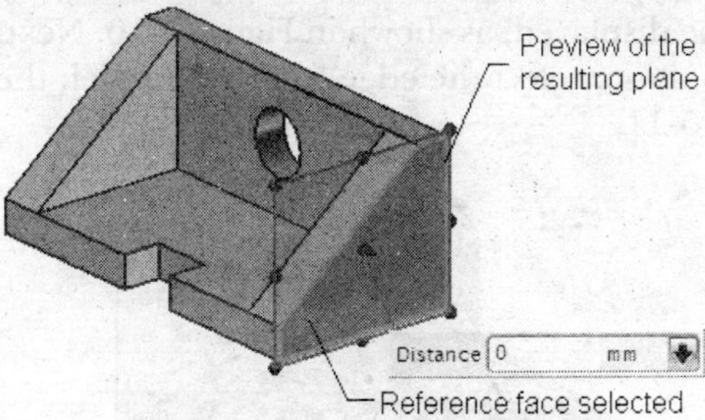

Figure 5-6 The preview of the plane

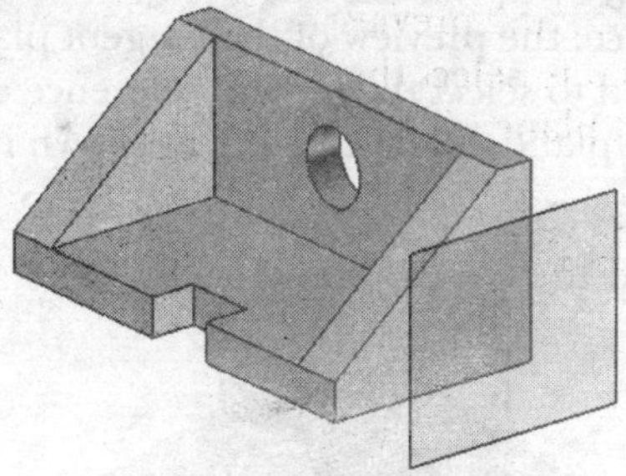

Figure 5-7 The resulting parallel plane

Note

While creating parallel planes, you can select only a planar face or surface as the reference object, not a non-planar face or surface.

At Angle

The **At Angle** option is used to create a plane at an angle to another plane passing through an edge, a linear sketched segment, or an axis. To create an angular plane, select the **At Angle** option from the drop-down list in the **Type** rollout. Next, select a planar face or a datum plane to which the resulting plane will be at angle. Next, you need to select an edge or a linear sketch through which the resulting plane will pass. On selecting both the references, the preview of the plane will be displayed in the graphic window. Also, the **Angle** edit box will be displayed along with an angular handle, as shown in Figure 5-8. You need to enter the required value in the **Angle** edit box. Figure 5-9 shows the datum plane created at an angle of 65 degrees.

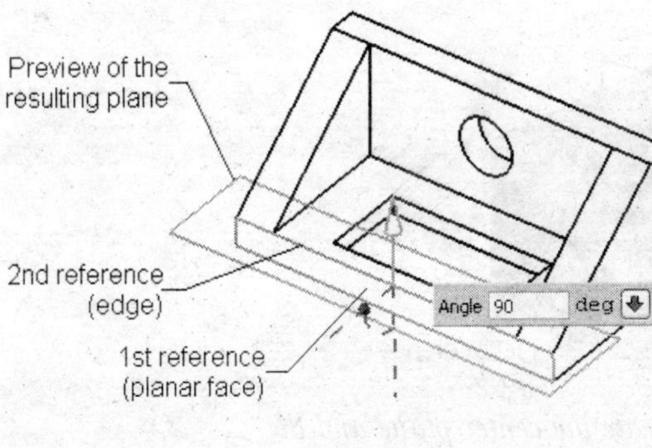

*Figure 5-8 The preview of the angular plane displayed along with the **Angle** edit box*

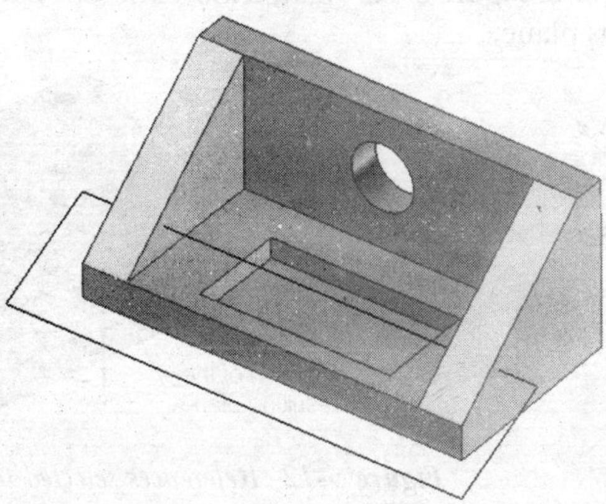

Figure 5-9 The plane created at an angle of 65 degrees

Tangent

The **Tangent** option is used to create a tangential plane. To do so, you need to select a cylindrical face and the second reference entity. The second reference entity can be a point, linear edge, line, datum axis, second cylindrical face, or a datum plane. To create a tangential plane, select the **Tangent** option from the drop-down list in the **Type** rollout. Next, select a cylindrical face or surface; the preview of the tangent plane will be displayed, as shown in Figure 5-10. Next, you need to select the second reference entity. To do so, select the edge from the model; the tangent plane will be created, as shown in Figure 5-11.

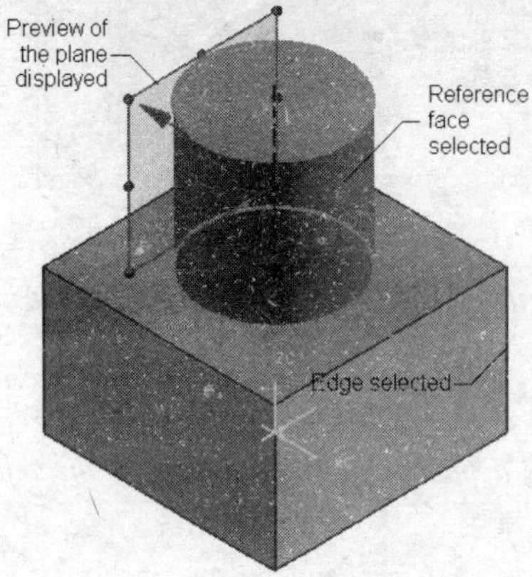

Figure 5-10 *The preview of the tangent plane*

Figure 5-11 *The tangent plane created after specifying the edge*

Bisector

The **Bisector** option is used to create a relative plane that is in the center of two specified planes or planar faces. To create a bisector plane, select the **Bisector** option from the drop-down list in the **Type** rollout. Then, one by one, select two planes or planar faces; the preview of the resulting plane placed at the center of the two selected planes or planar faces will be displayed, refer to Figure 5-12. Next, choose the **OK** button from the **Datum Plane** dialog box to create this plane.

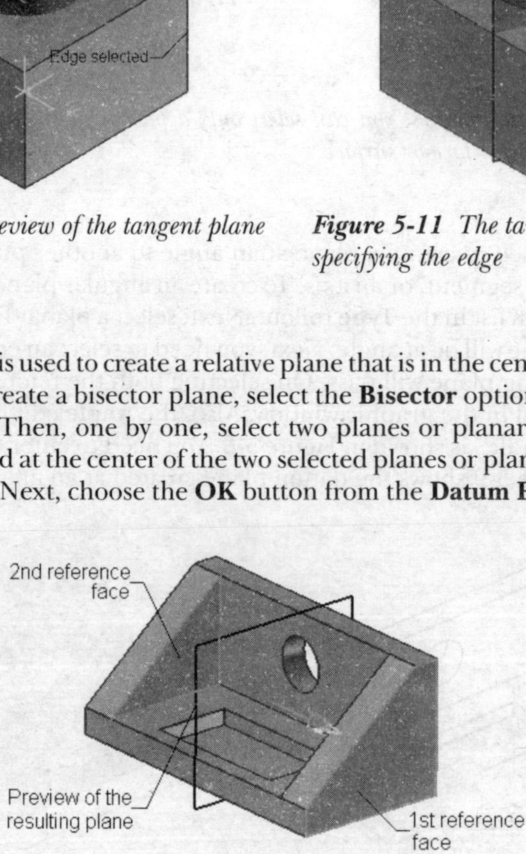

Figure 5-12 *References selected to create the center plane and the resulting plane*

Inferred

The **Inferred** option is used to create various types of planes, depending on the reference objects selected and the sequence, in which they are selected. To create planes using this tool, select the **Inferred** option from the drop-down list in the **Type** rollout. Depending on the reference objects selected and the sequence in which you select them, appropriate planes will be created. For example, if you select two parallel planes, then the plane will be created at the center of two selected planes. However, if you select a cylindrical surface and an edge, then the plane created will be tangent to the cylinder and it will pass through the selected edge.

Point and Direction

The **Point and Direction** option is used to create a plane at a specified point and oriented normal to the selected direction. You need to specify a fix point and define the normal direction to create the plane. The direction can be defined using an edge, linear sketch, or datum plane. If you select an edge or a linear sketch to define the direction, the plane will be created normal to it and it will pass through the specified point. However, if you select a datum plane or a planar face, the plane will be created parallel to it and will pass through the specified point.

To create this type of plane, select the **Point and Direction** option from the drop-down list in the **Type** rollout; you will be prompted to select the object to infer point. Specify the point at which the plane is to be created. Use the **Selection Bar** for an easy selection of the point. After specifying the point, the preview of the plane will be displayed.

Next, you need to define the direction of the plane by selecting a linear edge, sketch, planar face, or surface. You can also select a cylindrical face to define the direction. If you select a cylindrical face as the reference for defining the direction, the plane will be placed perpendicular to the axis of the cylindrical face selected. Figure 5-13 shows the reference selected to create this type of plane and Figure 5-14 shows the resulting plane.

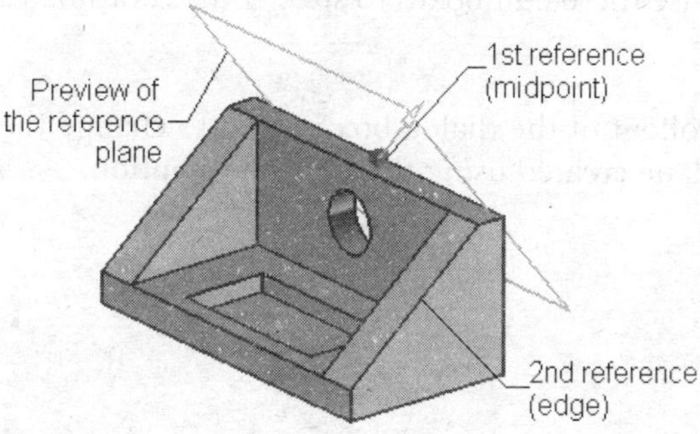

Figure 5-13 *The preview of the plane created using the* ***Point and Direction*** *option*

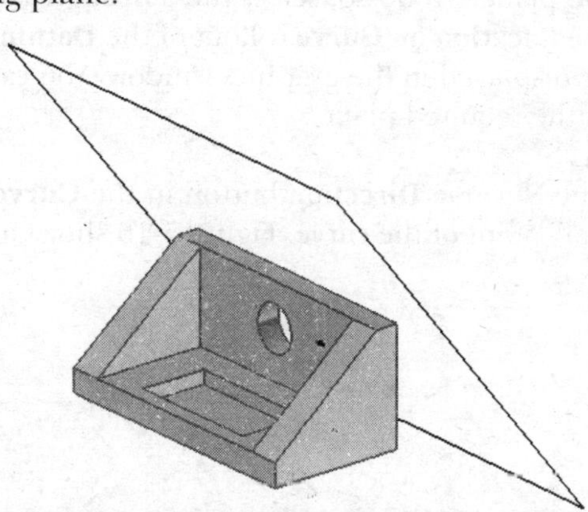

Figure 5-14 *The plane created using the* ***Point and Direction*** *option*

Note

After selecting the ***Point and Direction*** *option, the* ***Inferred Point*** *and* ***Inferred Vector*** *drop-down lists will be available in the* ***Datum Plane*** *dialog box. These drop-down lists contain the options for defining the point and direction to create the plane. By default, the* ***Inferred*** *option is selected in both these drop-down lists. To define a point or direction by constructing a new point and vector, choose the* ***Point Constructor*** *and* ***Vector Constructor*** *buttons, respectively.*

On Curve

The **On Curve** option is used to create a plane passing through a selected curve and located at a specified distance. To create a plane using this option, select the **On Curve** option from the drop-down list in the **Type** rollout. Next, select a curve or an edge to create the plane; the preview of the plane along with the **Arc Length** or **% Arc Length** edit box will be displayed, refer to Figure 5-15. The current positional value of the plane will be displayed in the **Arc Length** or **% Arc Length** edit box. The **Arc Length** or **% Arc Length** edit box will be displayed depending upon the option selected from the **Location** drop-down list.

Next, you need to specify the location of the resulting plane on the selected curve. Select the **Arc Length** option from the **Location** drop-down list in the **Location on Curve** rollout; the **Arc Length** edit box will be displayed. Now, you can locate the plane on the curve by entering the arc length value in the **Arc Length** edit box. This value will be taken from the start point of the curve. By default, the nearest point where you select the curve will be defined as the start point. You can also locate the plane by percentage of arc length. To do so, select the **% Arc Length** option from the **Location** drop-down list in the **Location on Curve** rollout; the **Arc Length** edit box will change to the **% Arc length** edit box. Enter the percent of arc length between 0 and 100 in the **% Arc Length** edit box and press the ENTER key; the plane will move to a new location. Note that you can also drag the cube in the preview of the plane to modify its location on the curve.

You can also specify the location of the plane on the curve by specifying the coordinates of the plane. To do so, select the **Through Point** option from the **Location** drop-down list in the **Location on Curve** rollout of the **Datum Plane** dialog box; the coordinate edit boxes will be displayed in the graphics window. You can use these edit boxes to specify the coordinates of the required plane.

The **Reverse Direction** button in the **Curve** rollout of the dialog box is used to change the start point of the curve. Figure 5-16 shows a plane created using the **On Curve** option.

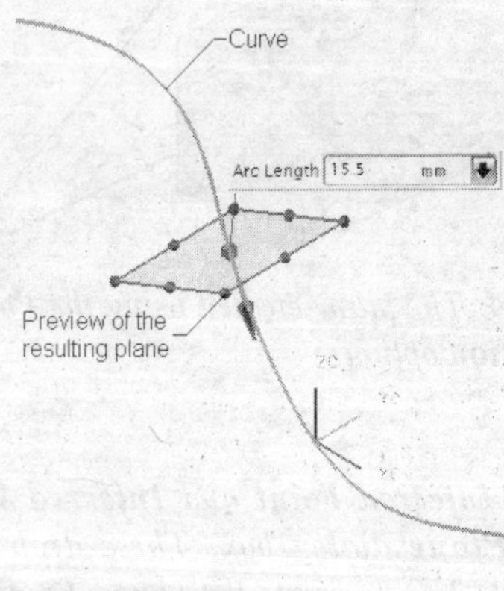

*Figure 5-15 The preview of the plane created using the **On Curve** option*

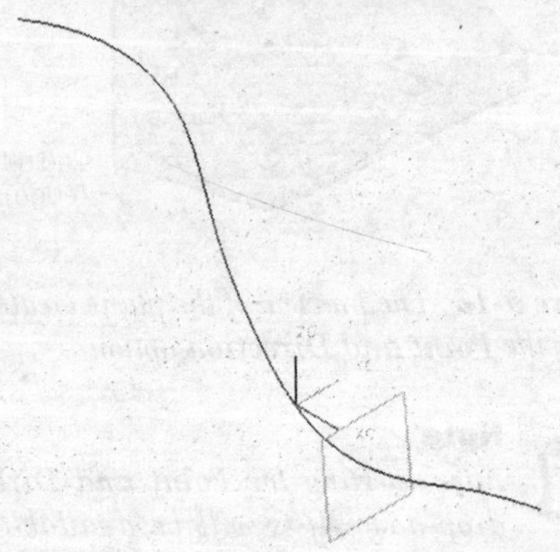

*Figure 5-16 The plane created using the **On Curve** option*

Other Options in the Datum Plane Dialog Box

The other rollouts in this dialog box are discussed next.

Plane Orientation Rollout

This rollout is used to define the orientation of the plane. The options in this rollout are discussed next.

Alternate Solution

This button allows you to preview all the possible orientations of a plane, based on its selected entities. Alternatively, you can use the Page Down and Page Up keys to preview all the possible orientations of the plane.

Reverse Direction

This button is used to change the direction of the plane normal by 180 degrees.

Settings Rollout

If you select the **Associative** check box in this rollout, the datum plane created will be associative with its parent features.

Note

For an associative datum plane, the name will be displayed as ***Datum Plane*** *in the* ***Part Navigator****. For a non-associative datum plane, the name will be displayed as* ***Fixed Datum Plane*** *in the* ***Part Navigator****.*

CREATING DATUM COORDINATE SYSTEMS

Menu: Insert > Datum/Point > Datum CSYS
Toolbar: Feature Operation > Datum Plane > Datum CSYS

As discussed earlier, on starting a new file using the **Model** template, you will only have the datum coordinate system at the origin. The handles of this coordinate system represent the X, Y, and Z directions in 3D space and form the basics for creating both the fixed and the relative datum planes. You can also create new coordinate systems for the separate features in a model. A part may contain any number of coordinate systems. The coordinate system can be used as a reference for creating features, sketches, and curves. Also, it can be used for assembling the parts in the assembly. The coordinate system is also treated as a feature and is displayed in the **Model History** section of the **Part Navigator**. The coordinate system is always associative with the object members or feature operation to which it is related.

To create the datum coordinate system, choose the **Datum CSYS** button from the **Feature Operation** toolbar. If this is not the default button in this toolbar, then choose the down arrow on the right of the **Datum Plane** button; a flyout will be displayed. Choose the **Datum CSYS** button from the flyout; the **Datum CSYS** dialog box will be displayed, as shown in Figure 5-17. By default, the **Dynamic** option is selected in the drop-down list in the **Type** rollout. As a result, you will be prompted to drag or select a handle for direct entry. There are different methods by which you can create an datum coordinate system. These methods are discussed next.

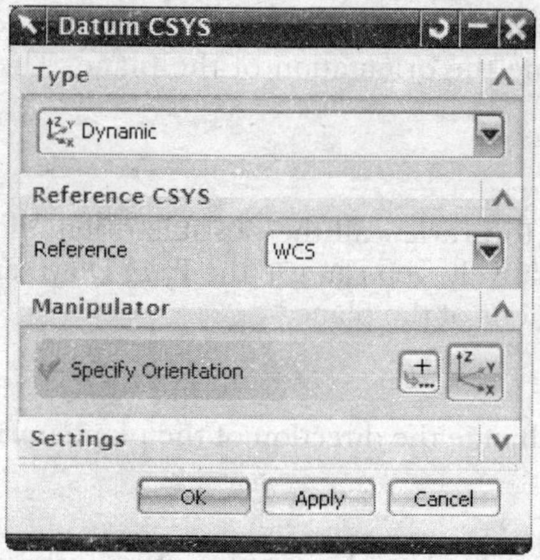

*Figure 5-17 The **Datum CSYS** dialog box*

Dynamic

This option is used to create the datum coordinate system by dragging it or entering the X, Y, and Z coordinates values. When you invoke the **Datum CSYS tool**, this option will be selected by default and you will be prompted to drag or select a handle for direct entry. Also, the preview of the datum coordinate system will be displayed at the origin in the drawing window, refer to Figure 5-18.

Select the cube displayed at the center of new datum coordinate system, and then press and hold the left mouse button. Next, drag the mouse to position the new datum coordinate system. Alternatively, enter the X, Y, and Z coordinates values in the respective edit boxes to position the datum coordinate system.

Also, you can move the new datum coordinate system in a particular direction (X, Y, or Z). To do so, click on the respective arrow handle; the **Distance** and **Snap** edit boxes will be displayed, as shown in Figure 5-19. Enter the required distance value in the **Distance** edit box and press ENTER; the datum coordinate system will move in the specified direction to the specified distance.

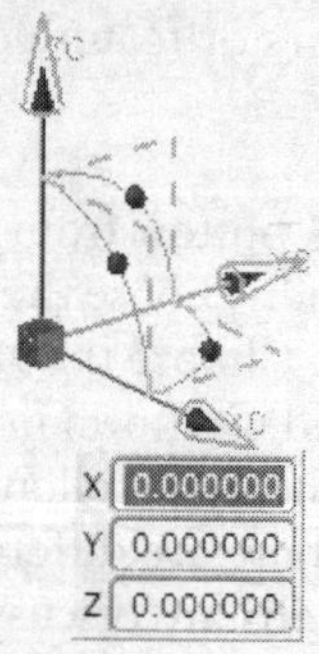

Figure 5-18 The preview of the datum coordinate system

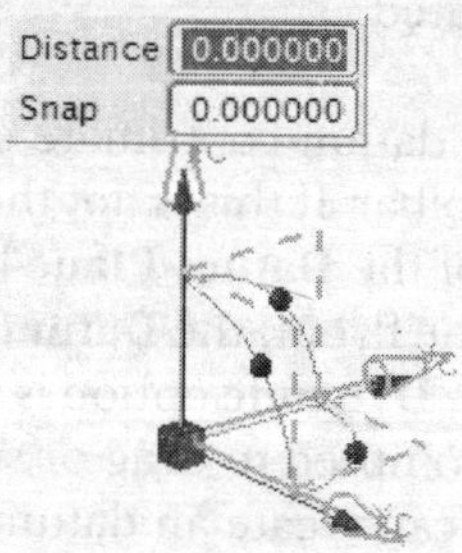

*Figure 5-19 The **Distance** and **Snap** edit boxes*

Similarly, you can rotate the new datum coordinate system along a particular axis (X, Y, or Z). To do so, click on the respective angular handle; the **Angle** and **Snap** edit boxes will be displayed. Enter the required angle value in the **Angle** edit box and press ENTER; the datum coordinate system will rotate along the specified axis as per the specified angle value.

Note

You can also move and rotate the new datum coordinate system dynamically. To do so, press and hold the left mouse button on the respective handle of the new datum coordinate system and then drag it.

Origin, X-Point, Y-Point

To create a datum coordinate system by using this option, select the **Origin, X-Point, Y-Point** option from the drop-down list in the **Type** rollout; you will be prompted to select the object to infer point. Next, you need to specify the origin point. Select the point on which you need to fix the origin of the datum coordinate system. While specifying the origin point, turn on the required snap button in the **Selection Bar** to select points easily. Next, you need to specify the points along the X and Y directions. Specify the X and Y points. Note that the X point is used to specify the X-axis direction of the datum coordinate system and the Y point is used to define the orientation of the XY plane.

After specifying the origin, X point, and Y point, the preview of the datum coordinate system will be displayed, as shown in Figure 5-20. Choose the **OK** button from the **Datum CSYS** dialog box to accept the datum coordinate system. Figure 5-21 shows the resulting datum coordinate system.

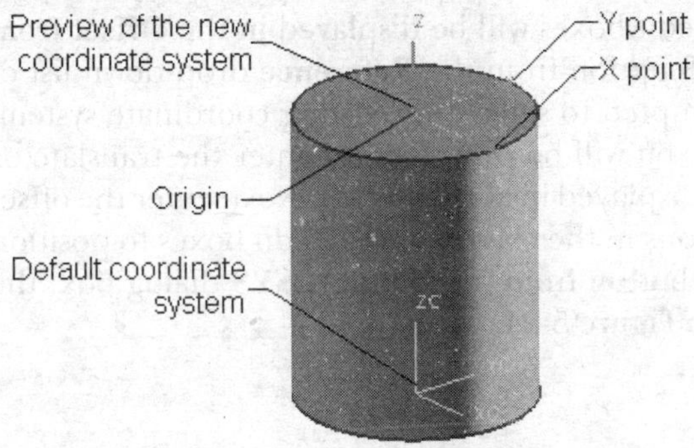

Figure 5-20 The preview of the CSYS created by using the ***Origin, X-point, Y-point*** *option*

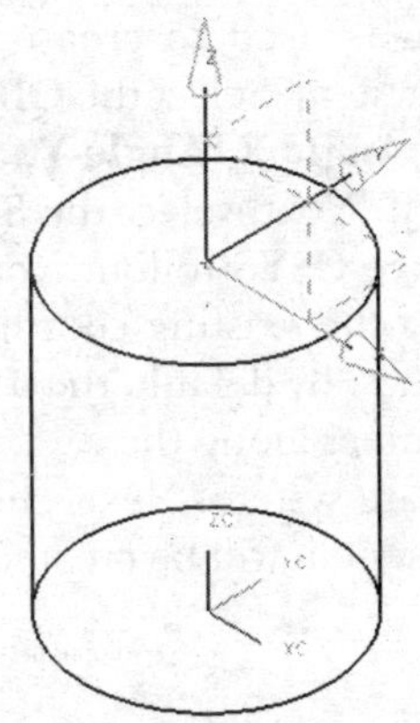

Figure 5-21 The CSYS created by using the ***Origin, X-point, Y-point*** *option*

Three Planes

To create a coordinate system by using this option, you need to select three reference objects that are mutually perpendicular to each other. You can only select faces or planes as reference objects.

Select the **Three Planes** option from the drop-down list in the **Type** rollout; you will be prompted to select a planar object (normal defines X-axis). Select the type of reference object from the **Type Filter** drop-down list in the **Selection Bar**. This allows you to customize the process of selecting a particular type of reference object. Next, select three reference objects. If the selected reference objects are not mutually perpendicular, then the **CSYS Message** window will be displayed, informing that the parallel planes are selected. After selecting the three reference objects, the preview of the datum coordinate system will be displayed, refer to Figure 5-22. Choose the **OK** button from the **Datum CSYS** dialog box to accept the datum coordinate system. The resulting datum coordinate system is shown in Figure 5-23.

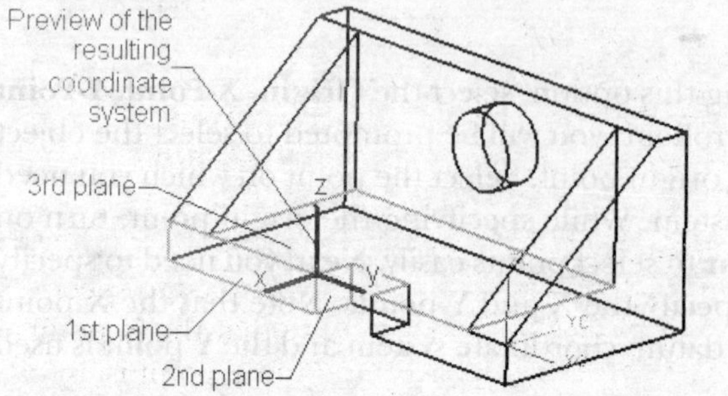

*Figure 5-22 The preview of the CSYS created by using the **Three Planes** option*

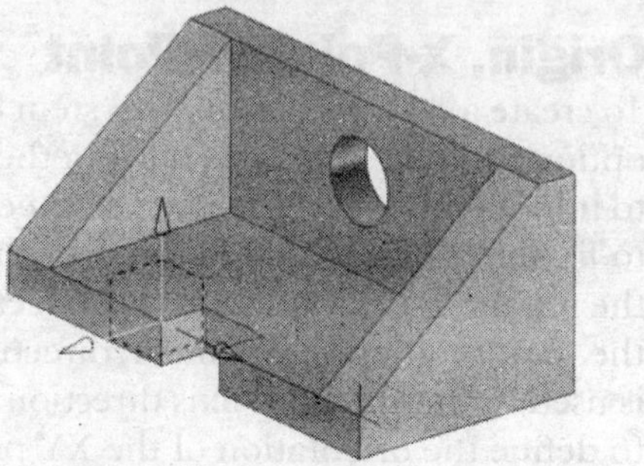

*Figure 5-23 The resulting CSYS created by using the **Three Planes** option*

Offset CSYS

This option is used to create a datum coordinate system offset to an existing datum coordinate system. Select the **Offset CSYS** option from the drop-down list in the **Type** rollout; the **X**, **Y**, **Z**, **Angle X**, **Angle Y**, and **Angle Z** edit boxes will be displayed in the **Offset from CSYS** rollout. Next, select the **Selected CSYS** option from the **Reference** drop-down list of the **Reference CSYS** rollout; you will be prompted to select the existing coordinate system. On selecting the existing coordinate system, you will be prompted to enter the translate or rotation values. By default, the **0** value will be displayed in all edit boxes. Next, enter the offset and angle values along the X, Y, and Z directions in the corresponding edit boxes to position the coordinate system. Next, choose the **OK** button from the **Datum CSYS** dialog box; the coordinate system will be created, as shown in Figure 5-24.

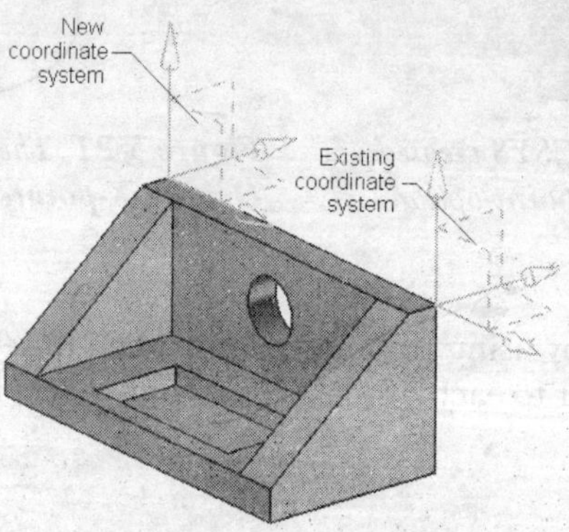

*Figure 5-24 The coordinate system created by using the **Offset CSYS** option*

Note

*After creating the coordinate system, you can modify its location by double-clicking on it. On doing so, the **Datum CSYS** dialog box will be displayed. Now, change the values entered in the edit boxes and choose the **OK** button; the modifications made in the coordinate system will be reflected in the drawing window.*

CSYS of Current View

The **CSYS of Current View** option can be used to create a datum coordinate system such that the Z-axis is normal to the current view on the screen. To create a datum coordinate system using this tool, orient the model to the required position and then select the **CSYS of Current View** option from the drop-down list in the **Type** rollout. Choose the **OK** button; the coordinate system for the modified orientation will be created.

Inferred

You can use the **Inferred** option to create different types of datum coordinate systems. The resulting datum coordinate system will depend on the reference objects selected and the sequence of their selection.

Other Options in the Datum CSYS Dialog Box

To display the other options in the **Datum CSYS** dialog box, expand the **Settings** rollout. The options in this rollout are discussed next.

Scale Factor

This edit box is used to change the size of the datum coordinate system, while creating it. You can use the scale factor value to change the size. By default, this value is 2. If you enter **1** as the scale factor value, the size of the datum coordinate system created will be half of the normal size (default size).

Associative

If you select this check box, the datum coordinate system created will be associative with its parent features.

CREATING FIXED AND RELATIVE DATUM AXES

Menu: Insert > Datum/Point > Datum Axis
Toolbar: Feature Operation > Datum Plane > Datum Axis

The datum axis can be used as a reference object while creating a sketch-based feature such as a revolved feature or while creating the feature-based operations such as the draft feature. There are two types of datum axes in NX: fixed datum axis and relative datum axis. A fixed datum axis can be created without specifying any reference object. When you start a new file by using the **Model** template, by default, three fixed datum axes will be present in that file, as shown in Figure 5-25.

However, for creating a relative datum axis, you need to select the reference object. To create the relative datum axis, choose **Datum Plane > Datum Axis** from the **Feature Operation** toolbar; the **Datum Axis** dialog box will be displayed, as shown in Figure 5-26. The drop-down list in the **Type** rollout of this dialog box contains the options to create the relative datum axes. These options are discussed next.

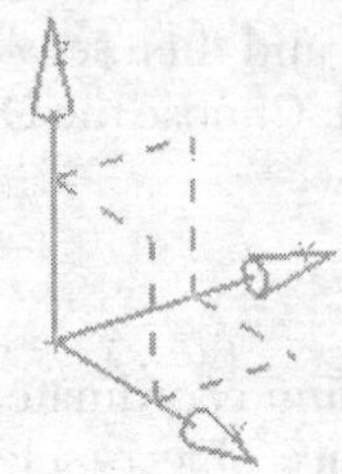

Figure 5-25 Fixed datum axes

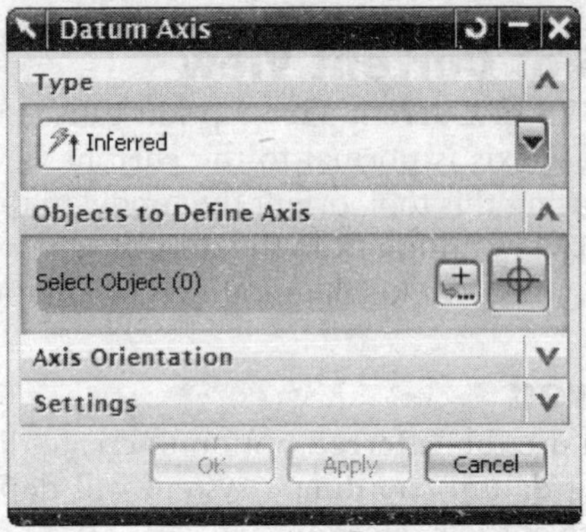

Figure 5-26 *The* ***Datum Axis*** *dialog box*

Point and Direction

The **Point and Direction** option is used to create a datum axis on a point along the defined direction. Select this option from the drop-down list in the **Type** rollout; you will be prompted to select an object to infer point. Select the fixed point, refer to Figure 5-27. You can choose the required buttons from the **Selection Bar** to enable an easy selection of the points. After specifying the fixed point, you will be prompted to select objects to infer vector. Next, you need to define the direction along which the datum axis will point. To define the direction, you can use the **Vector Constructor** button or the **Inferred Vector** drop-down list in the **Direction** rollout. Also, you can select an edge or a face for defining the direction. If you select an edge as the reference, the axis will be created coincident or parallel to the selected edge. If you select a face as the reference, the axis will be created perpendicular to it. Figure 5-27 shows the preview of the datum axis after selecting an edge as the reference vector. The resulting datum axis is shown in Figure 5-28.

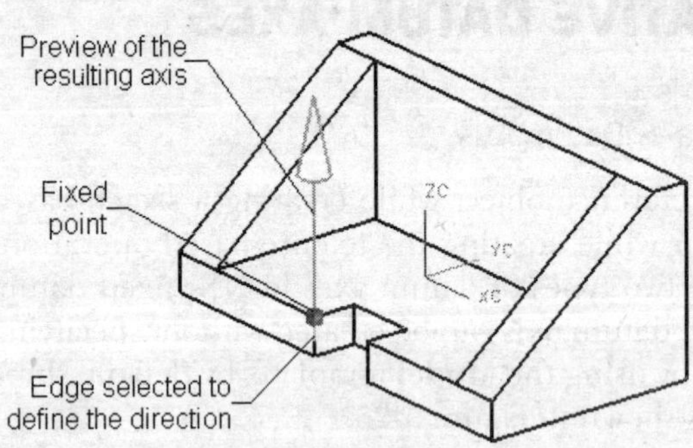

Figure 5-27 The preview of the relative datum axis

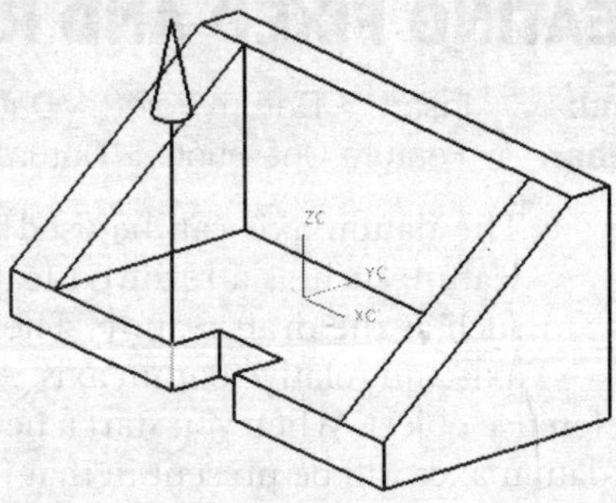

Figure 5-28 The resulting relative datum axis

By default, the **Parallel to Vector** option is selected from the **Orientation** drop-down list in the **Direction** rollout. As a result, the resulting axis will be created parallel to the reference vector. If you select the **Perpendicular to Vector** option, then the resulting axis will be created normal to the reference vector.

Note

You can also select an existing axis, linear curve, or a linear sketch member as a reference object for defining the direction of the datum axis.

Two Points

The **Two Points** option is used to create a datum axis between two selected points. Select the **Two Points** option from the drop-down list in the **Type** rollout; you will be prompted to select an object to infer point. Specify the first point. Next, you need to specify the endpoint toward which the axis will point. After you specify the second point, the preview of the datum axis will be displayed, as shown in Figure 5-29. Choose **Apply** and then the **OK** button from the **Datum Axis** dialog box to accept the axis created. The datum axis will be created, as shown in Figure 5-30.

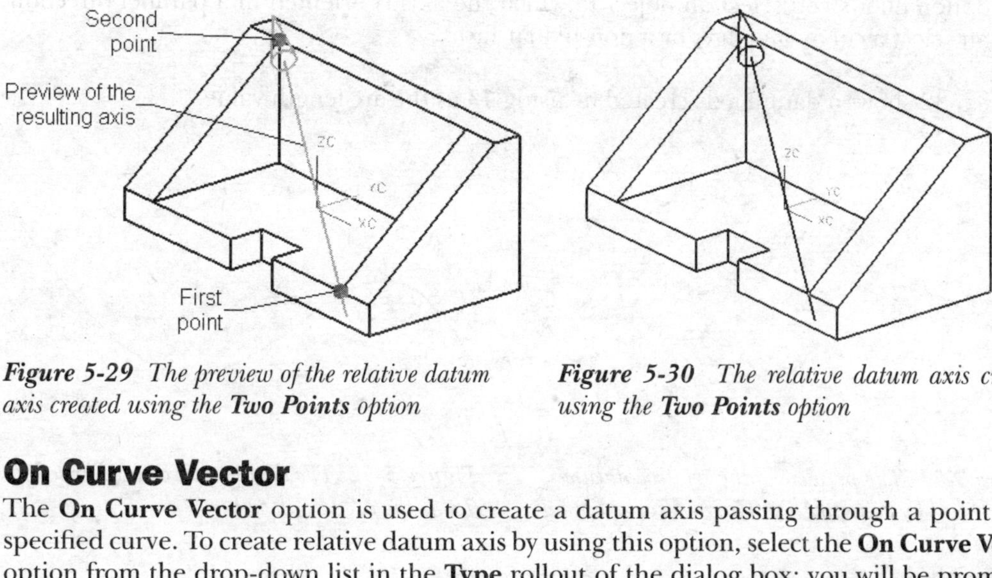

***Figure 5-29** The preview of the relative datum axis created using the **Two Points** option*

***Figure 5-30** The relative datum axis created using the **Two Points** option*

On Curve Vector

The **On Curve Vector** option is used to create a datum axis passing through a point on a specified curve. To create relative datum axis by using this option, select the **On Curve Vector** option from the drop-down list in the **Type** rollout of the dialog box; you will be prompted to select a point on the curve or the edge. On selecting the point on the curve or edge, the preview of the datum axis along with the **Arc Length** edit box will be displayed, as shown in Figure 5-31. Next, you need to locate the datum axis on the selected curve by entering a value in the **Arc Length** edit box or by dragging the cube in the preview. You can also locate the datum axis by percentage of arc length. To do so, select the **% Arc Length** option from the **Location** drop-down list in the **Location on Curve** rollout; the **Arc Length** edit box will change to the **% Arc Length** edit box. Enter the percent of arc length between 0 to 100 in the **% Arc Length** edit box and press the ENTER key; the datum axis will move to a new location. Figure 5-32 shows the datum axis created.

The options from the **Orientation** drop-down list in the **Orientation on Curve** rollout are used to orient the datum axis. These options are discussed next.

Tangent
Select this option to create the datum axis tangent to the selected curve or edge.

Normal
Select this option to create the datum axis normal to the selected curve or edge.

Bi-Normal
Select this option to create the datum axis bi-normal to the selected curve or edge.

Perpendicular to Object
This option allows you select an object to which the axis is oriented perpendicularly. You can select a curve, edge, planar face, or a datum plane.

Parallel to Object
This option allows you select an object to which the axis is oriented in a parallel direction. You can select a curve, an edge, or a non-planar face.

Figure 5-32 shows a datum axis created by using **73** as the arc length value.

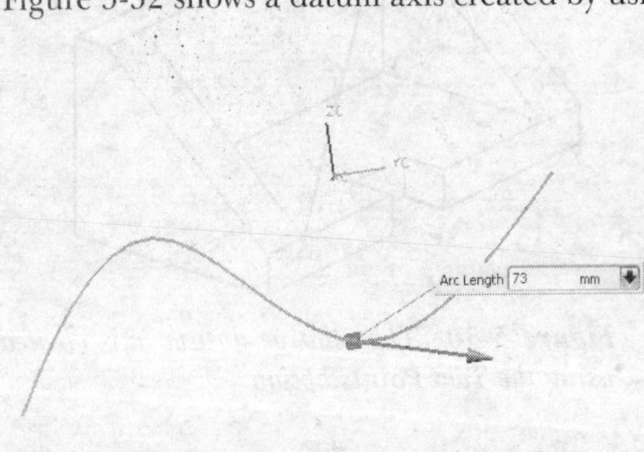

Figure 5-31 The preview of the relative datum axis created by using the ***On Curve Vector*** *option*

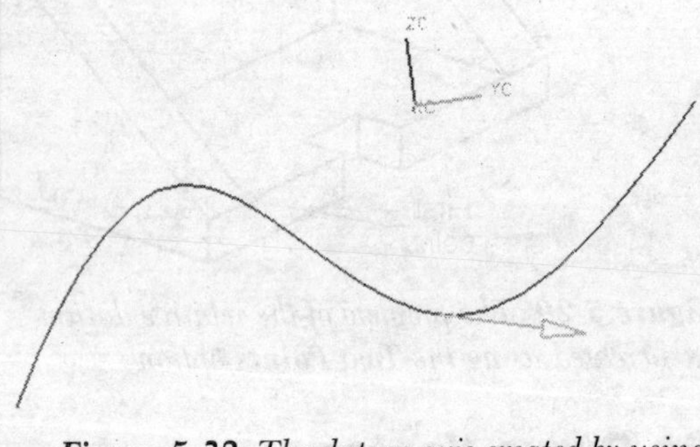

Figure 5-32 The datum axis created by using ***73*** *as the arc length value*

Inferred
You can also use the **Inferred** option from the drop-down list in the **Type** rollout to create the datum axes. The resulting datum axis will depend on the reference objects selected and the sequence of their selection.

Other Options in the Datum Axis Dialog box
To display the other options in the **Datum Axis** dialog box, expand the **Axis Orientation** and **Settings** rollouts. The options in these rollouts are discussed next.

Axis Orientation Rollout
The **Reverse Direction** button in this rollout is used to reverse the direction of the axis.

Settings Rollout

If you select the **Associative** check box in this rollout, the datum axis created will be associative with its parent features.

OTHER EXTRUSION OPTIONS

In the previous chapter, you learned about the basic extrude options. In this chapter, you will learn about the additional extrude options available in the **Extrude** dialog box.

Specifying the Boolean Operation

After creating the base feature, you can create additional features by using four types of boolean operations. These operations are available in the **Boolean** drop-down list, as shown in Figure 5-33. These boolean operations are discussed next.

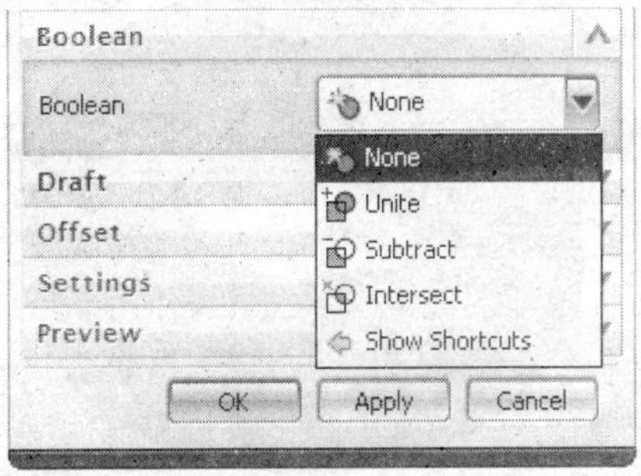

Figure 5-33 Various boolean operations

None

This option allows you to create a new body, which is independent of the existing feature. Draw the sketch for the additional feature. Next, invoke the **Extrude** dialog box; the **None** boolean type is selected by default.

Unite

The **Unite** boolean operation allows you to join the new feature with an existing feature. In this case, no additional solid body is created. Figure 5-34 shows the base feature and the sketch for the additional feature. Note that this sketch is created at a reference plane that is at some offset from the top face of the base feature. Figure 5-35 shows an additional feature created using the **Unite** boolean operation.

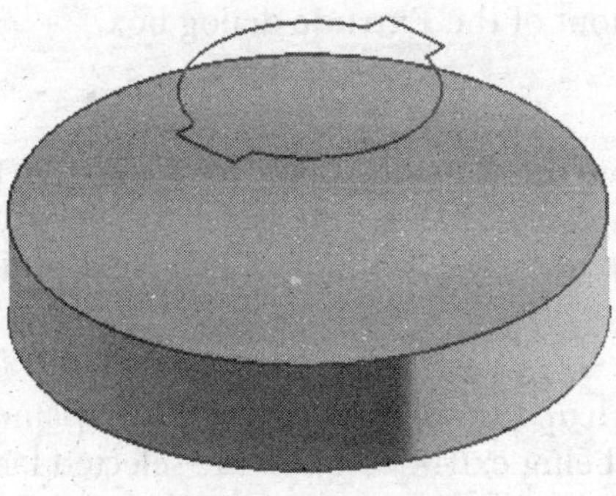

Figure 5-34 Base feature and sketch for the additional feature

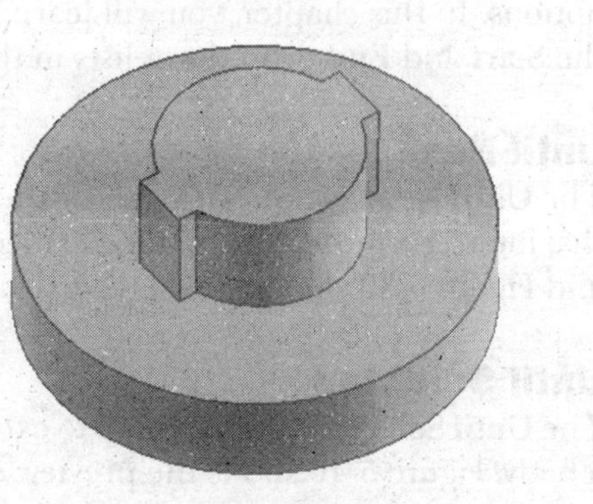

*Figure 5-35 3D view of the feature created using the **Unite** boolean operation*

Subtract

The **Subtract** boolean operation is used to create an extruded feature by removing material from the existing feature. The material to be removed will be defined by the sketch you have drawn. Figure 5-36 shows an extruded cut feature created using the **Subtract** boolean operation.

Intersect

The **Intersect** boolean operation is used to create an extruded feature by retaining the material common to the existing feature and the sketch, see Figure 5-37. In this case, the material of the base feature that lies outside the boundary of the sketch is removed.

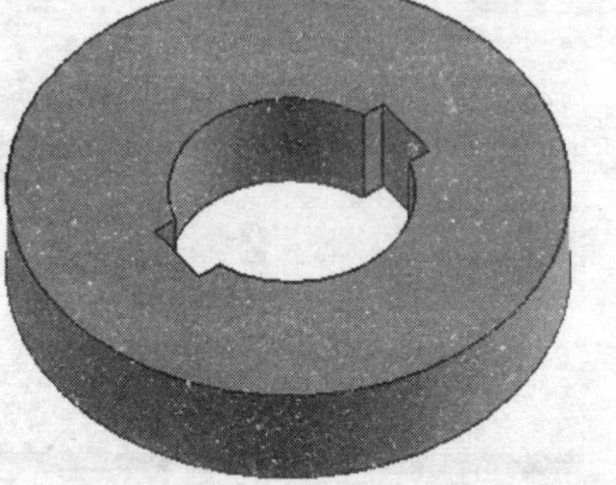

*Figure 5-36 Extruded cut feature created using the **Subtract** boolean operation*

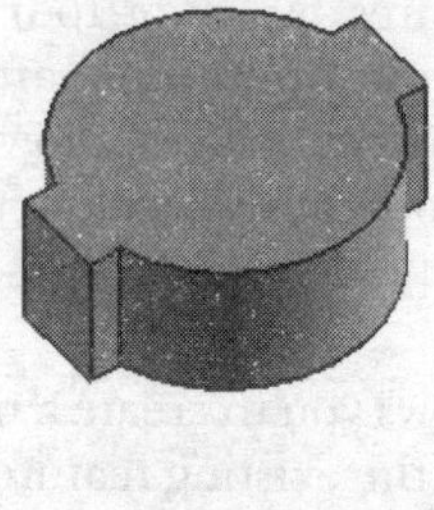

*Figure 5-37 Extruded cut feature created using the **Intersect** boolean operation*

Note

The models shown in Figures 5-36 and 5-37 have been created using the sketch shown in Figure 5-34.

Specifying Other Extrusion Termination Options

In the previous chapter, you learned about the **Value** and **Symmetric Value** termination options. In this chapter, you will learn about the remaining termination options available in the **Start** and **End** drop-down lists in the **Limits** rollout of the **Extrude** dialog box.

Until Next

The **Until Next** option is used to extrude a sketch from the sketching plane to the next surface that intersects the feature in the specified direction. Figure 5-38 shows the sketch to be extruded and Figure 5-39 shows the sketch extruded up to the next face using the **Until Next** option.

Until Selected

The **Until Selected** option is used to extrude the sketch up to a specified face, a datum plane, or a body. Figure 5-40 shows the preview of the sketch being extruded up to the selected face.

Until Extended

The **Until Extended** option is used to extrude the sketch up to a specified face, which does not intersect the sketch in its current size and shape. However, when extended, this face will intersect the extruded sketch. Figure 5-41 shows the preview of the sketch being extruded using this option.

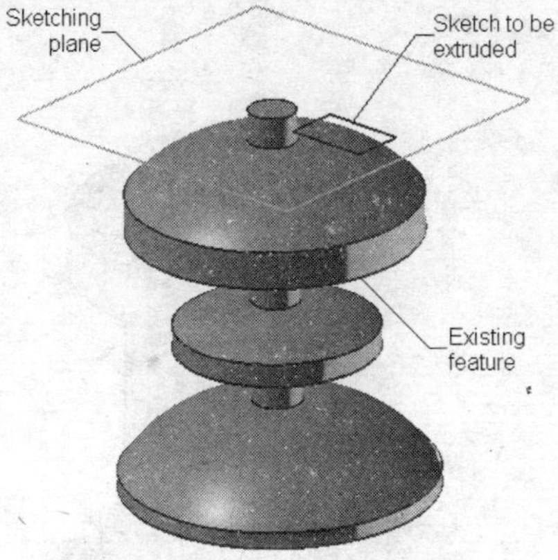

Figure 5-38 The existing feature and the sketch to be extruded

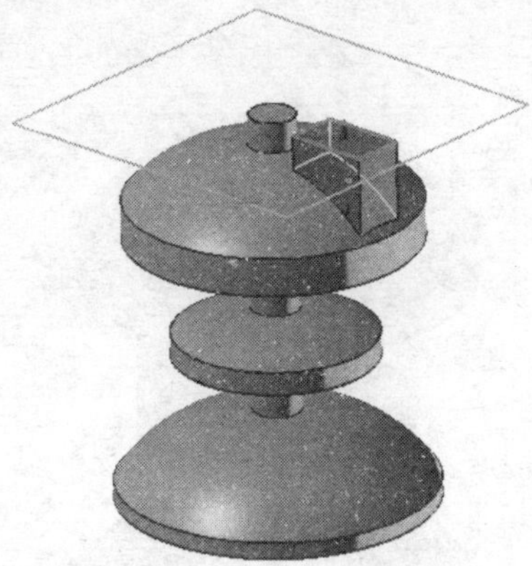

Figure 5-39 Preview of the sketch being extruded up to the next surface using the ***Until Next*** *option*

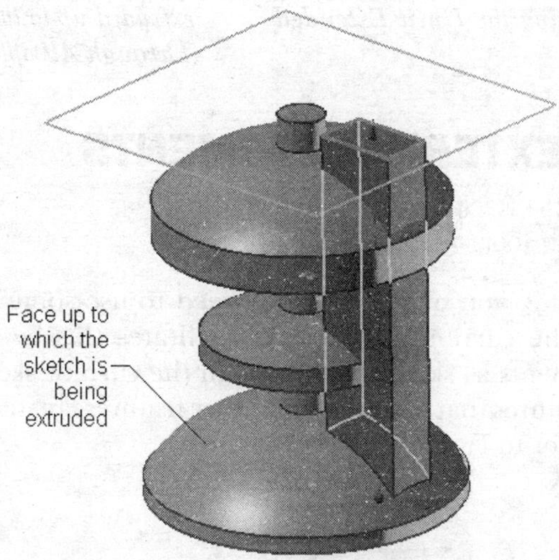

Figure 5-40 Preview of the sketch being extruded up to the selected surface using the ***Until Selected*** *option*

Through All

The **Through All** option is used to extrude the sketch through all the features and bodies that are in the path of the sketch. Figure 5-42 shows the preview of the feature extruded using this method.

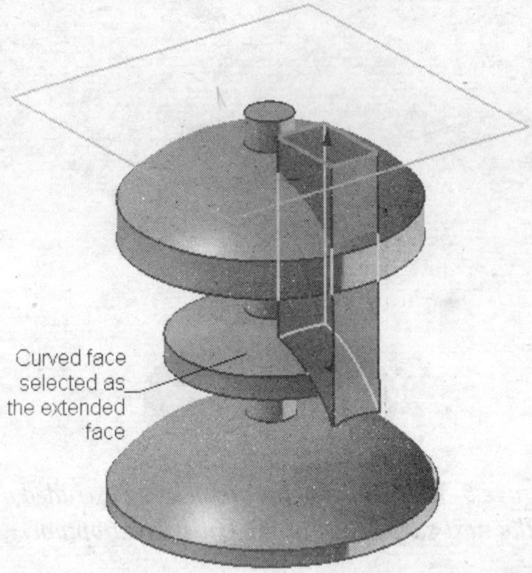

*Figure 5-41 Preview of the sketch being extruded up to the extended surface using the **Until Extended** option*

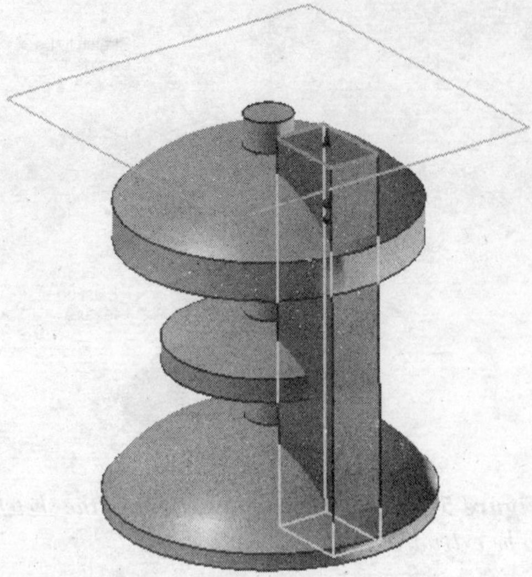

*Figure 5-42 Preview of the sketch being extruded up to the last surface using the **Through All** option*

PROJECTING EXTERNAL ELEMENTS

Menu:	Insert > Recipe Curve > Project Curve
Toolbar:	Sketch Tools > Project Curve

While sketching, you may sometimes need to use some elements of the existing features in the current sketch. NX facilitates this by allowing you to project external elements as sketched entities on the current sketching plane. This helps you create features that are similar to other features created on a different sketching plane. For example, refer to Figure 5-43.

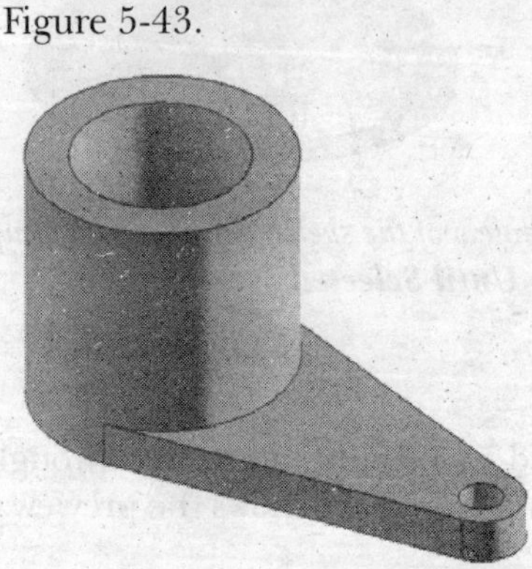

Figure 5-43 Model with two features

The model shown in this figure has a cylindrical base feature and another feature created at the bottom face of the base feature. Now, if you want to create the same feature on the top face of the cylindrical feature, you can simply define a new sketching plane on the top face of the base feature and then project the top face of the second feature. On doing so, the entities will be automatically placed on the current sketching plane, as shown in Figure 5-44.

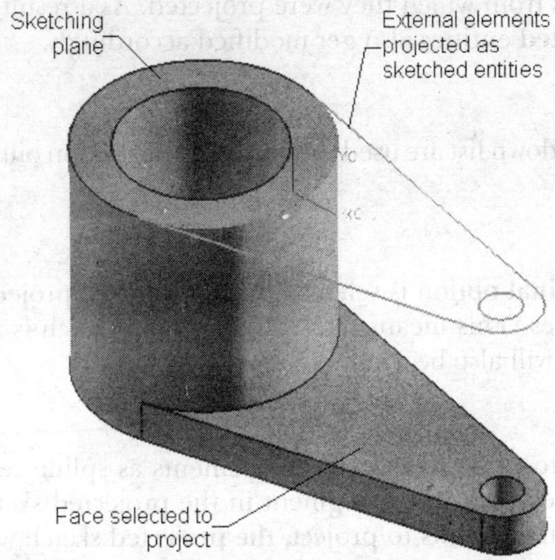

Figure 5-44 Face selected to be projected and the resulting sketch

To project external elements, invoke the Sketcher environment and then choose **Insert > Recipe Curve > Project Curve** from the menu bar; the **Project Curve** dialog box will be displayed, as shown in Figure 5-45.

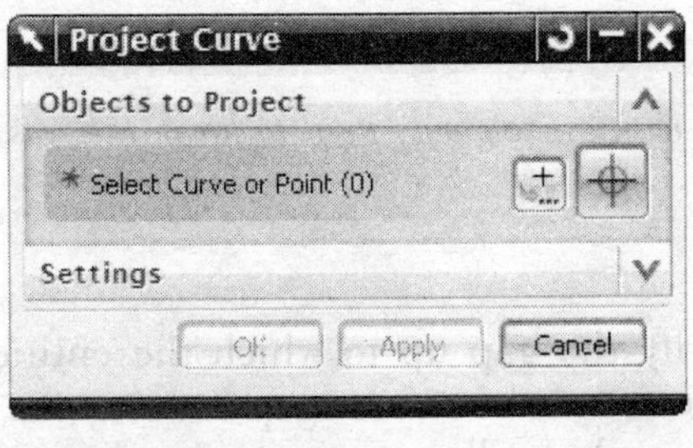

*Figure 5-45 The **Project Curve** dialog box*

The options in various rollouts of the **Project Curve** dialog box are discussed next.

Objects to Project Rollout

This rollout is used to the select the objects to be projected. By default, the **Curve** button is chosen in this rollout. As a result, you will be prompted to select curve or point to project. This button allows you to select the entities to project. You can select the curves, points, or edges of a model.

Settings Rollout

The options in the **Settings** rollout are discussed next.

Associative

If you select this check box, the projected sketched entities will be forced to be associative with the original entities from which they were projected. As a result, if the original entities are modified, the projected entities also get modified accordingly.

Output Curve Type

The options in this drop-down list are used to specify the projection output type. These options are discussed next.

Original

By default, the **Original** option is selected. As a result, the projected entities are similar to the original entities. This means that if the original sketch is a combination of lines, the projected sketch will also be a combination of lines only.

Spline Segment

This option is used to project the external elements as spline segments. Each external element is represented by a spline segment in the projected sketch. This means that if you select six original elements to project, the projected sketch will also comprise of six spline segments.

Single Spline

This option is used to project the external elements as a single continuous spline. As a result, irrespective of the number of entities you select to project, the projected sketch will have a single continuous spline.

Note

For editing the projected entities, you may need to break their associativity with the original elements.

Tolerance

This edit box is used to specify the gap up to which the entities will be considered as continuous entities in the projected sketch. If the gap between the original entities is more than that specified in this edit box, they will appear as noncontinuous entities in the projected sketch.

After specifying options in various rollouts, select the elements to be projected. You can select curves, points, or edges of the model. Next, choose the **OK** button from the **Project Curve** dialog box; the selected elements will be projected.

TUTORIALS

Tutorial 1

In this tutorial, you will create the model shown in Figure 5-46. The dimensions of the model are shown in Figure 5-47. **(Expected time: 30 min)**

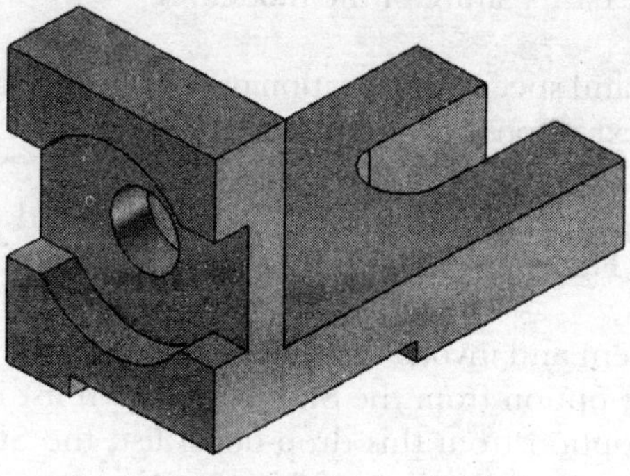

Figure 5-46 Model for Tutorial 1

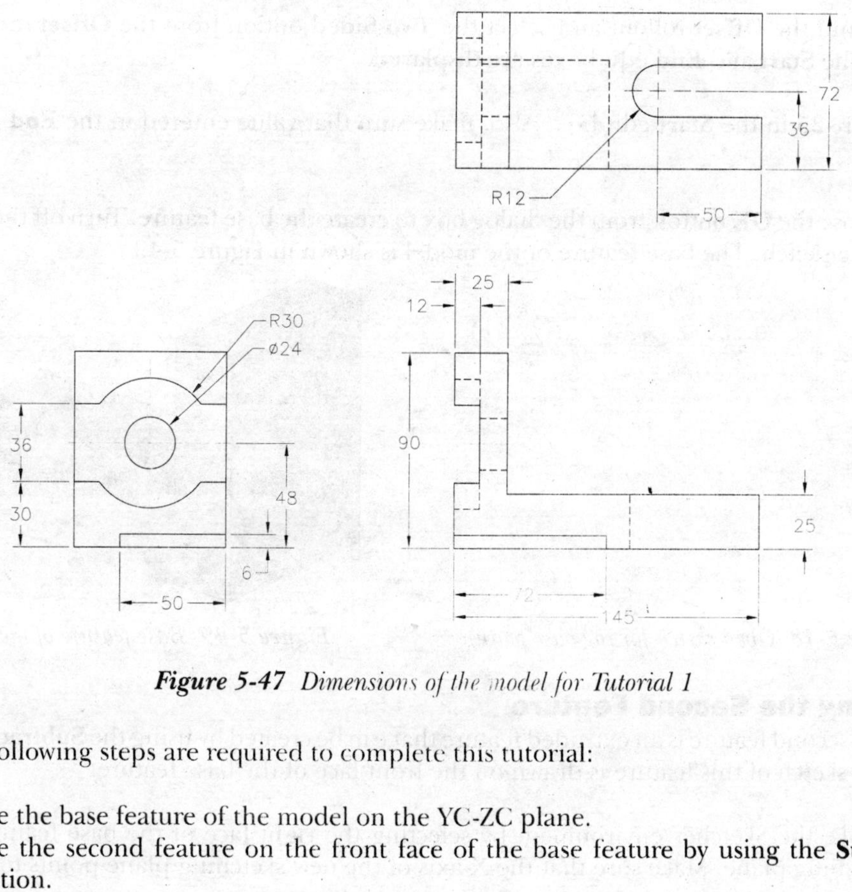

Figure 5-47 Dimensions of the model for Tutorial 1

The following steps are required to complete this tutorial:

a. Create the base feature of the model on the YC-ZC plane.
b. Create the second feature on the front face of the base feature by using the **Subtract** operation.
c. Create the third feature on the upper horizontal face of the base feature by using the **Subtract** operation.
d. Create the fourth and fifth features.

Creating the Base Feature

First, you need to create the base feature of the model.

1. Invoke the **New** dialog box and specify the location of the document as *C:\NX 7\c05 folder* and name as *c05tut1.prt*. Next, choose the **OK** button from it.

2. Invoke the Sketcher environment by using the YC-ZC plane and draw an open sketch similar to the one shown in Figure 5-48.

3. Exit the Sketcher environment and invoke the **Extrude** dialog box. Select the sketch and select the **Symmetric Value** option from the **Start** drop-down list in the **Limits** rollout. As soon as you select this option from this drop-down list, the **Start** drop-down list is converted into the **End** drop-down list. Enter **36** in the **Distance** edit box located below the **End** drop-down list and then press ENTER.

4. Expand the **Offset** rollout and select the **Two-Sided** option from the **Offset** drop-down list; the **Start** and **End** edit boxes are displayed.

5 Enter **-25** in the **Start** edit box. Also, make sure that value entered in the **End** edit box is **0**.

6. Choose the **OK** button from the dialog box to create the base feature. Turn off the display of the sketch. The base feature of the model is shown in Figure 5-49.

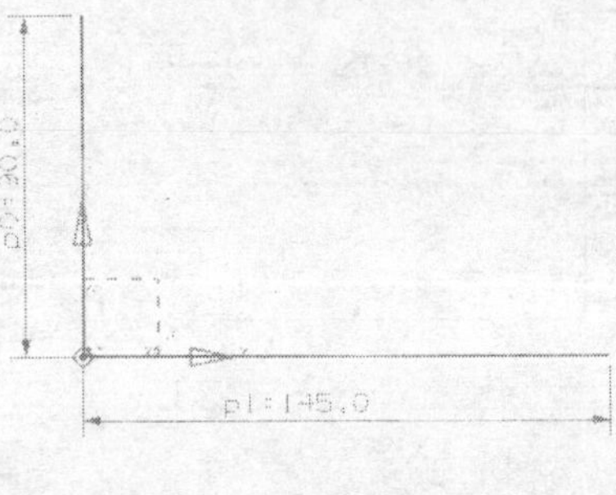

Figure 5-48 *Open sketch for the base feature*

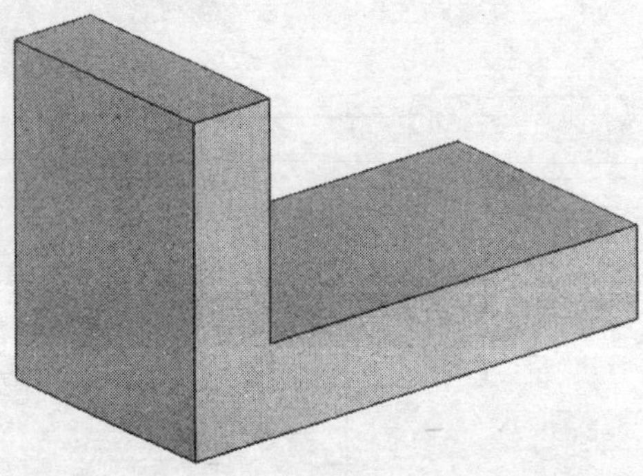

Figure 5-49 *Base feature of the model*

Creating the Second Feature

The second feature is an extruded feature that can be created by using the **Subtract** option. The sketch of this feature is drawn on the front face of the base feature.

1. Invoke the Sketcher environment by selecting the right face of the base feature as the sketching plane. Make sure that the X-axis of the new sketching plane points toward the edge which measures 145 mm.

2. Draw the rectangular sketch of the cut feature. Make the bottom line and the left line of the rectangle collinear with the edges of the base feature. Add the required dimensions to the sketch, as shown in Figure 5-50.

3. Exit the Sketcher environment and then invoke the **Extrude** dialog box. Now, select the sketch; the preview of the feature is displayed in the graphics window.

4. Select the **Subtract** option from the **Boolean** drop-down list and reverse the direction of extrusion by choosing the **Reverse Direction** button from the **Direction** rollout of the dialog box, if required. Enter **50** in the **Distance** edit box, which is available below the **End** drop-down list of the **Limits** rollout, and then choose the **OK** button from the **Extrude** dialog box.

5. Press CTRL+B; the **Class Selection** dialog box is displayed. Select the sketch of the second feature from the graphics window and choose the **OK** button from this dialog box; the selected sketch is hidden. The model with the cut feature created is shown in Figure 5-51.

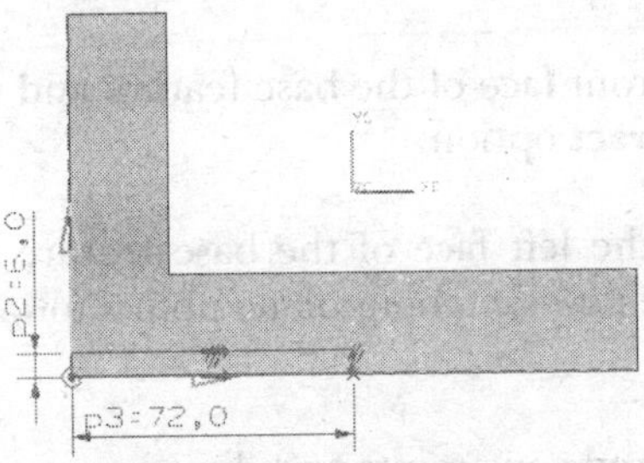

Figure 5-50 *Sketch created for the second feature*

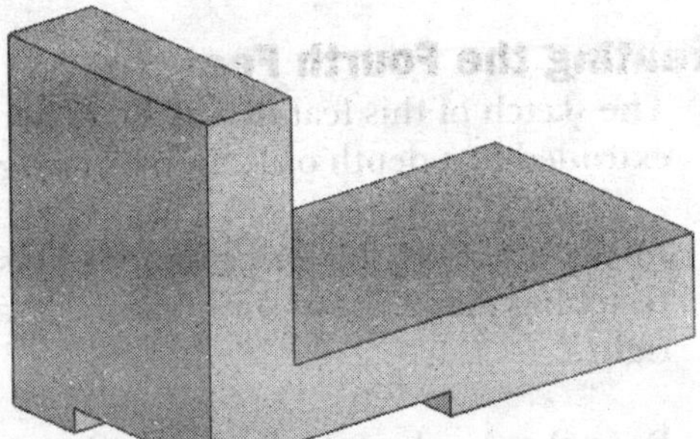

Figure 5-51 *Model with the cut feature*

Creating the Third Feature

The third feature is also an extruded feature, which will be created by using the **Subtract** option. The sketch of this feature will be drawn on the top lower face of the base feature.

1. Invoke the Sketcher environment by selecting the top lower face of the base feature. Make sure that the X-axis of the new sketching plane points toward the edge which measures 145 mm.

2. Draw the sketch of the feature and add the required constraints and dimensions to it, as shown in Figure 5-52.

3. Exit the Sketcher environment and then invoke the **Extrude** dialog box. Select the sketch; the preview of the feature is displayed in the drawing window.

4. Select the **Subtract** option from the **Boolean** drop-down list and reverse the direction of extrusion.

5. Select the **Through All** option from the **End** drop-down list and choose **OK** from the dialog box.

6. Hide the sketch. The model with the cut feature is shown in Figure 5-53.

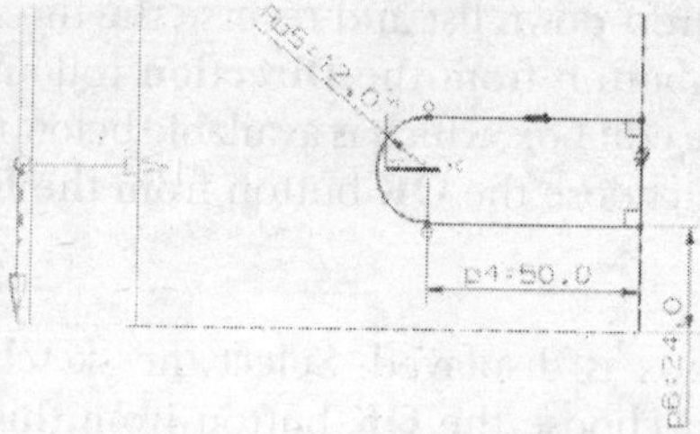

Figure 5-52 *Sketch created for the third feature*

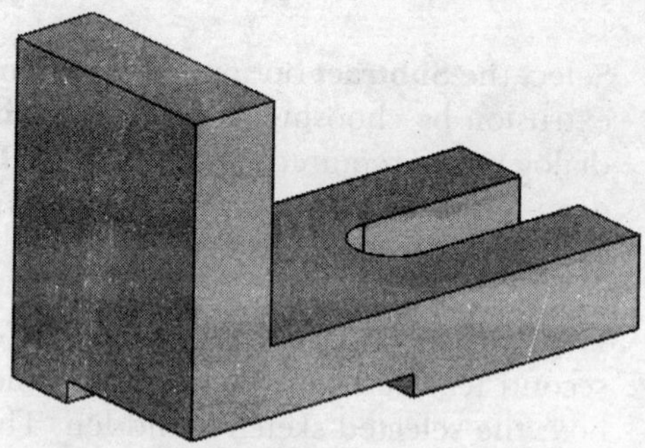

Figure 5-53 *Model with the cut feature*

Creating the Fourth Feature

The sketch of this feature will be drawn on the front face of the base feature and will be extruded to a depth of 12 mm by using the **Subtract** option.

1. Invoke the Sketcher environment by selecting the left face of the base feature as the sketching plane. Make sure that the X-axis of the new sketching plane points toward the right.

2. Draw the sketch of the feature and add the required constraints and dimensions to it, as shown in Figure 5-54.

3. Exit the Sketcher environment and then invoke the **Extrude** dialog box. Select the sketch.

4. Select the **Subtract** option from the **Boolean** drop-down list and reverse the direction of extrusion.

5. Enter **12** in the **Distance** edit box that is available below the **End** drop-down list, and then choose the **OK** button from the dialog box.

6. Hide the sketch. The model with the cut feature is shown in Figure 5-55.

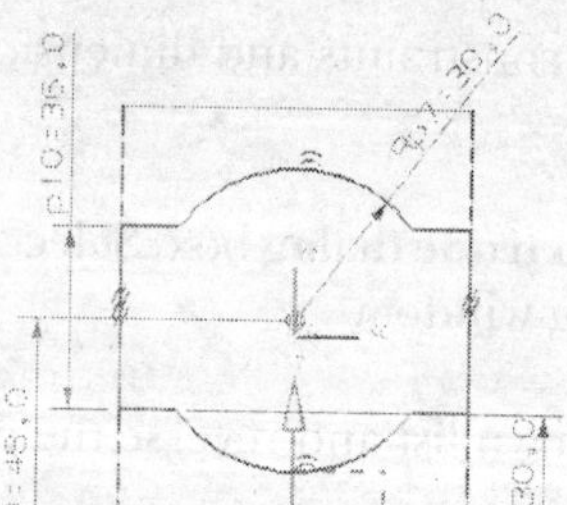

Figure 5-54 *Sketch created for the fourth feature*

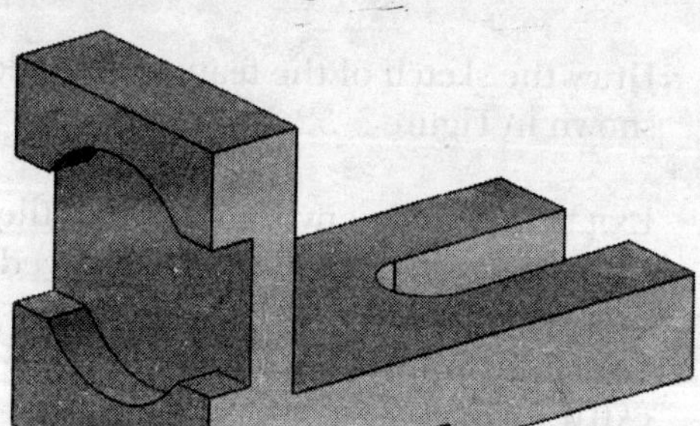

Figure 5-55 *Model with the fourth feature*

Creating the Fifth Feature

1. Similarly, draw a circle on the new face that is exposed because of the last cut feature and then extrude the circle by using the **Subtract** option and the **Through All** termination option. The final model for Tutorial 1 is shown in Figure 5-56.

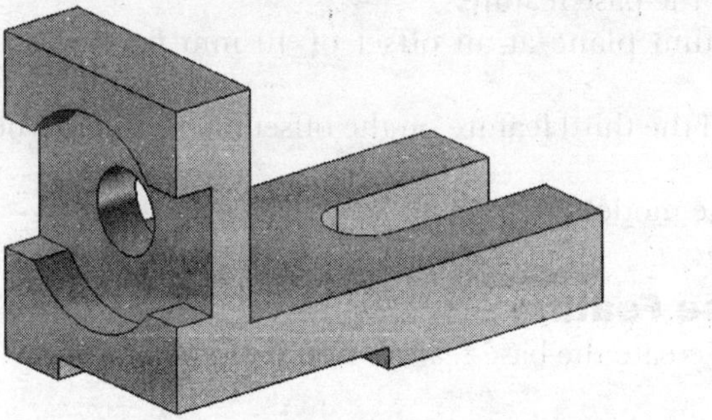

Figure 5-56 Final model for Tutorial 1

Saving and Closing the File

1. Choose **File > Close > Save and Close** from the menu bar to save and close the file.

Tutorial 2

In this tutorial, you will draw the model shown in Figure 5-57. The dimensions of the model are also shown in the same figure. **(Expected time: 30 min)**

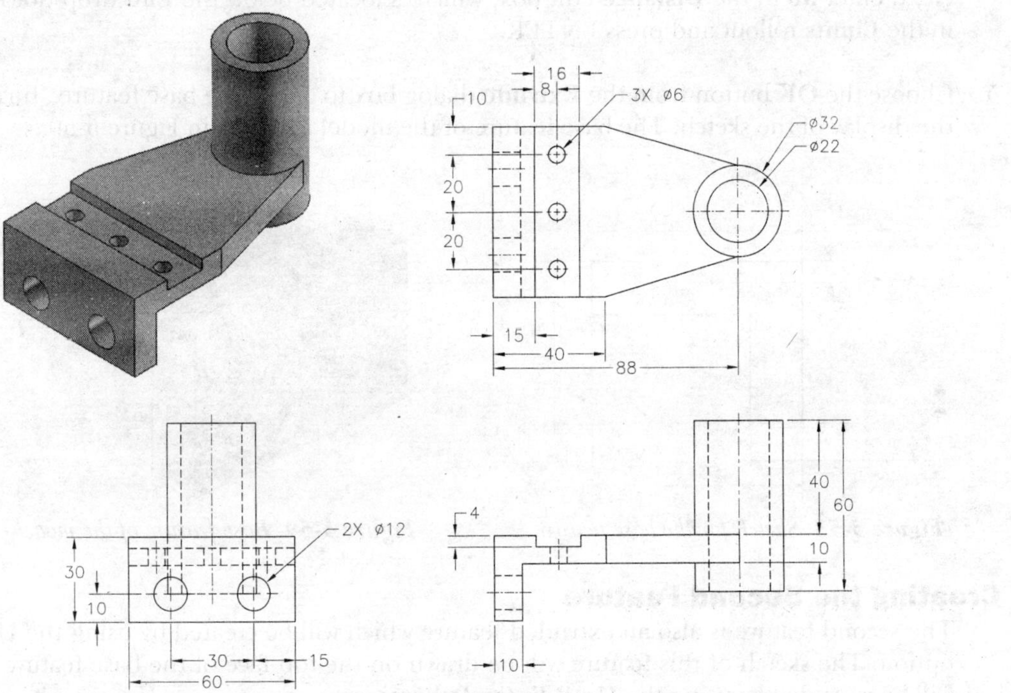

Figure 5-57 Model and its dimensions for Tutorial 2

The following steps are required to complete this tutorial:

a. Create the base feature of the model on the YC-ZC plane.
b. Create the second feature using the **Unite** option. The sketch of this feature will be drawn on the top face of the base feature.
c. Create a new datum plane at an offset of 40 mm from the top face of the second feature.
d. Draw the sketch of the third feature on the offset plane and extrude it by using the **Unite** option.
e. Create holes in the model.

Creating the Base Feature

First, you need to create the base feature of the model.

1. Start a new file with the name *c05tut2.prt* using the **Model** template and specify its location as *C:\NX 7\c05*.

2. Invoke the Sketcher environment by using the YC-ZC plane as the sketching plane and draw a sketch similar to the one shown in Figure 5-58.

3. Exit the Sketcher environment and invoke the **Extrude** dialog box. Select the sketch; the preview of the feature is displayed in the drawing window with the default value.

4. Select the **Symmetric Value** option from the **Start** drop-down list in the **Limits** rollout. Next, enter **30** in the **Distance** edit box, which is located below the **End** drop-down list in the **Limits** rollout and press ENTER.

5. Choose the **OK** button from the **Extrude** dialog box to create the base feature. Turn off the display of the sketch. The base feature of the model is shown in Figure 5-59.

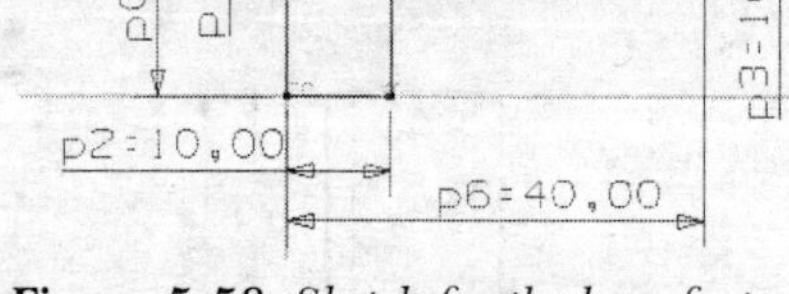

Figure 5-58 *Sketch for the base feature*

Figure 5-59 *Base feature of the model*

Creating the Second Feature

The second feature is also an extruded feature which will be created by using the **Unite** option. The sketch of this feature will be drawn on the top face of the base feature and will be extruded by using the **Until Extended** option.

1. Invoke the Sketcher environment by selecting the top face of the base feature as the sketching plane. Make sure that the X-axis of the new sketching plane points toward the right of the drawing window.

2. Draw the sketch of the feature and add the required constraints and dimensions to it, as shown in Figure 5-60.

3. Exit the Sketcher environment and then invoke the **Extrude** dialog box. Next, select the sketch; the preview of the extruded feature is displayed in the drawing window.

4. Select the **Unite** option from the **Boolean** drop-down list in the **Boolean** rollout of the dialog box.

5. Select the **Until Extended** option from the **End** drop-down list in the **Limits** rollout of the dialog box. Hold the middle mouse button and then rotate the view of the model such that its lower faces are visible. Next, select the bottom horizontal face shown in Figure 5-61 to define the termination of the second feature.

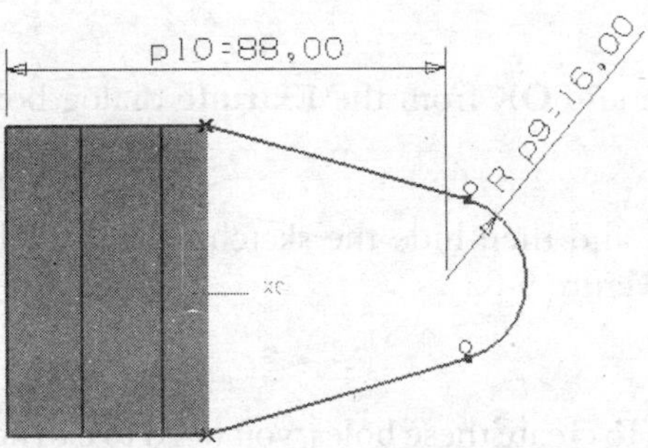

Figure 5-60 Sketch created for the second feature

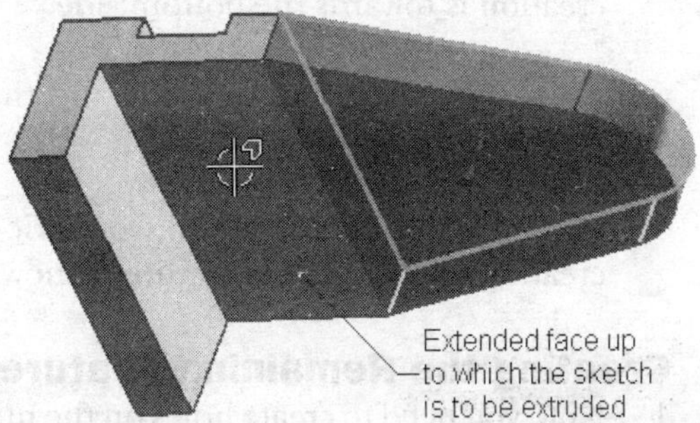

Figure 5-61 Face to be selected to terminate the second feature

6. Choose **OK** from the **Extrude** dialog box; the feature is created.

7. Change the current view to the isometric view and hide the sketch.

Creating the Third Feature

You need to create the third feature on a datum plane created at an offset of 40 mm from the top face of the second feature.

1. Choose the **Datum Plane** button from the **Feature Operation** toolbar; the **Datum Plane** dialog box is displayed.

2. Select the **At Distance** option from the drop-down list in the **Type** rollout, and then select the top face of the second feature.

3. Enter **40** in the **Distance** edit box and make sure that the value entered in the **Number of Planes** edit box is 1. Next, choose **OK** from the **Datum Plane** dialog box; a new plane is created.

4. Invoke the Sketcher environment by using the new datum plane. You can define the orientation of the X-axis of the sketching plane by using any one of the straight edges of the model.

5. Draw a circle for the third feature. Next, make the circle concentric with the curve in the second feature, and then make the curve and the circle of equal radius by using the **Equal Radius** tool. Now, as radii of both the curve and the circle are equal, you do not need to apply any dimensions to the sketch.

6. Exit the Sketcher environment, and then invoke the **Extrude** dialog box. Select the sketch; the preview of the feature is displayed in the drawing window.

7. Select the **Unite** option from the **Boolean** drop-down list in the **Extrude** dialog box. Next, choose the **Reverse Direction** button, if required. Note that the direction of feature creation is towards the bottom side.

8. Enter **-60** in the **End** edit box and then choose **OK** from the **Extrude** dialog box; the feature is created.

9. Change the current view to isometric view, and then hide the sketch. The model after creating the cylindrical feature is shown in Figure 5-62.

Creating the Remaining Features

1. Now, you need to create holes on the model. To create these holes, you need to extrude the sketches by using the **Subtract** option, refer to Figure 5-57. The final model for Tutorial 2 is shown in Figure 5-63.

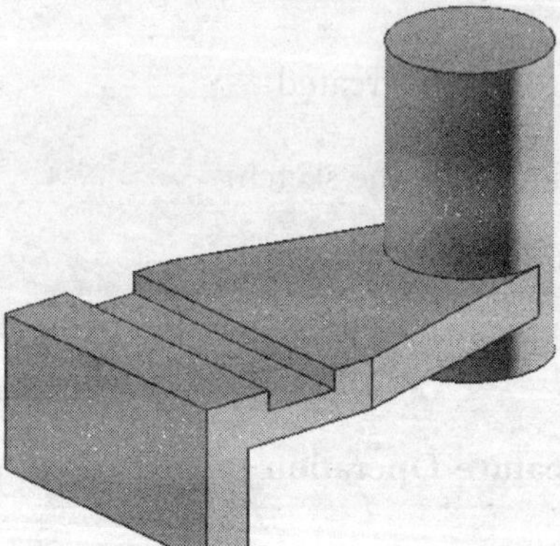

Figure 5-62 *Model after creating the cylindrical feature*

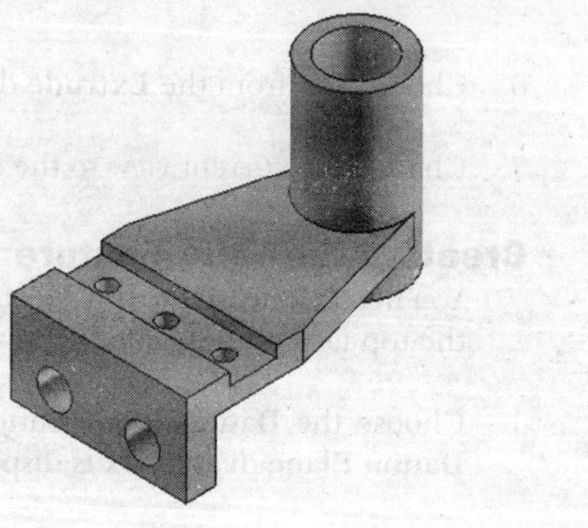

Figure 5-63 *Final model for Tutorial 2*

Saving and Closing the File

1. Choose **File > Close > Save and Close** from the menu bar to save and close the file.

Tutorial 3

In this tutorial, you will create the model shown in Figure 5-64. The dimensions of the model are given in Figure 5-65. **(Expected time: 30 min)**

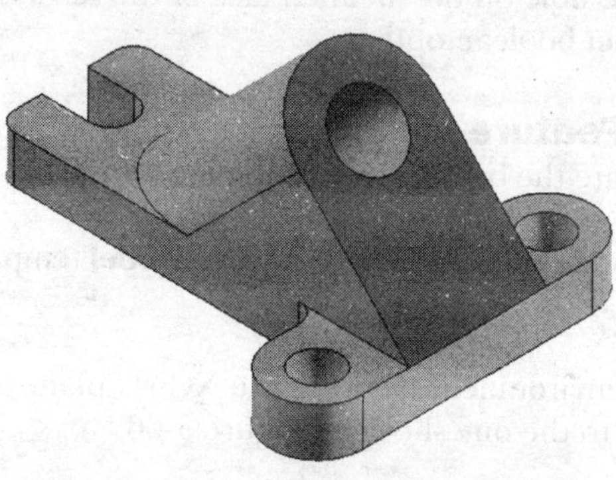

Figure 5-64 *Model for Tutorial 3*

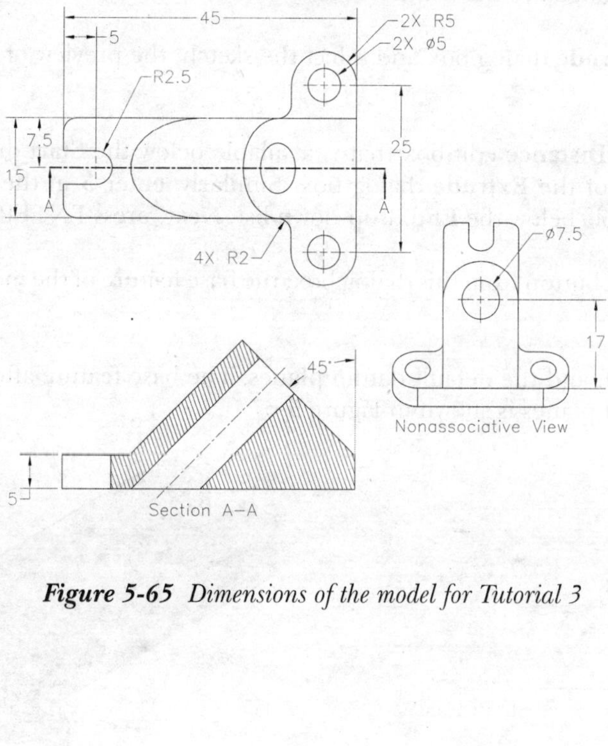

Figure 5-65 *Dimensions of the model for Tutorial 3*

The following steps are required to complete this tutorial:

a. Create the base feature of the model on the XC-YC plane.
b. Create a new datum plane at an angle of 45 degrees from the right face of the base feature.
c. Draw the sketch of the next extrude feature by using the new datum plane and extrude it by using the **Unite** boolean option.
d. Draw the sketch of the hole on the inclined face of the second feature and then extrude it by using the **Subtract** boolean option.

Creating the Base Feature

First, you need to create the base feature of the model.

1. Start a new file with the name *c05tut3.prt* using the **Model** template and specify its location as *C:\NX 7\c05*.

2. Invoke the Sketcher environment by using the XC-YC plane as the sketching plane and draw a sketch similar to the one shown in Figure 5-66.

3. Exit from the Sketcher environment by choosing the **Finish Sketch** button; the view of the sketch is changed to the trimetric view.

4. Invoke the **Extrude** dialog box and select the sketch; the preview of the extrude feature is displayed.

5. Enter **0** in the **Distance** edit box that is available below the **Start** drop-down list in the **Limits** rollout of the **Extrude** dialog box. Similarly, enter **5** in the **Distance** edit box, which is available below the **End** drop-down list. Next, press ENTER.

6. Choose the **OK** button from this dialog box; the base feature of the model is created, refer to Figure 5-67.

7. Hide the sketch and the default datum planes. The base feature after hiding the sketch and the default planes is shown in Figure 5-67.

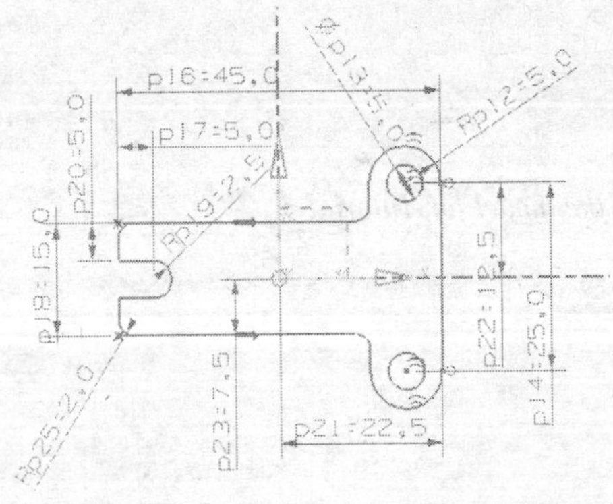

Figure 5-66 Sketch created for the base feature

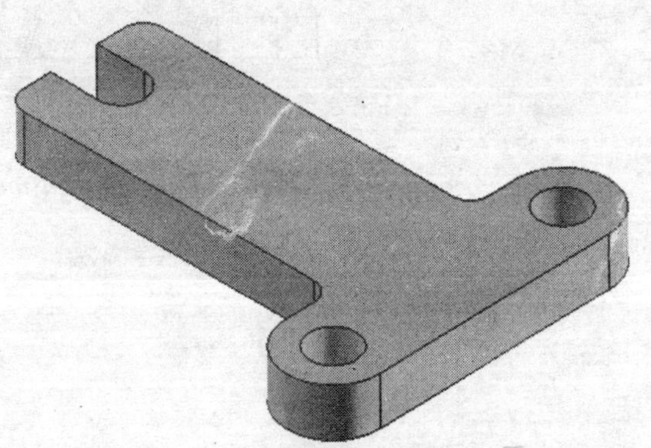

Figure 5-67 Base feature of the model

Creating the Second Feature

The second feature is also an extruded feature. However, to create the sketch of this feature, first you need to create a new datum plane at an angle of 45 degrees from the right face of the base feature.

1. Choose the **Datum Plane** button from the **Feature Operation** toolbar; the **Datum Plane** dialog box is displayed.

2. Select the **At Angle** option from the drop-down list in the **Type** rollout of this dialog box.

3. First select the right face of the base feature and then the edge to define the new datum plane, refer to Figure 5-68. On doing so, the **Angle** edit box is displayed.

4. Enter **45** in the **Angle** edit box, as shown in Figure 5-68, and then choose the **OK** button from the **Datum Plane** dialog box.

5. Draw the sketch of the second feature on the newly created datum plane, as shown in Figure 5-69. You need to apply collinear constraints between the lines in the sketch and the edges of the base feature to place the sketch at the desired location.

6. Exit the Sketcher environment and then invoke the **Extrude** dialog box.

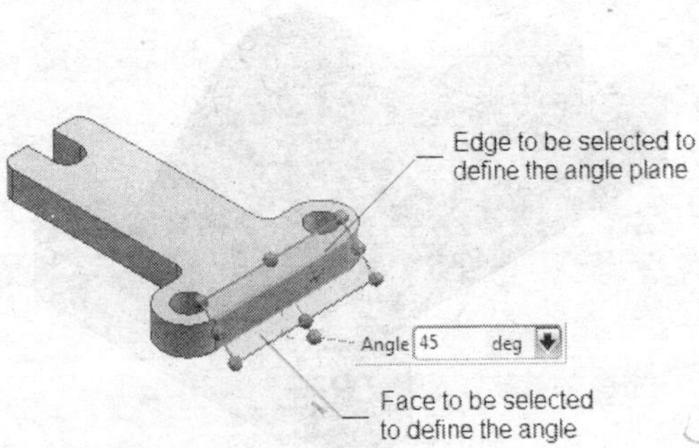

Figure 5-68 Defining a new datum plane

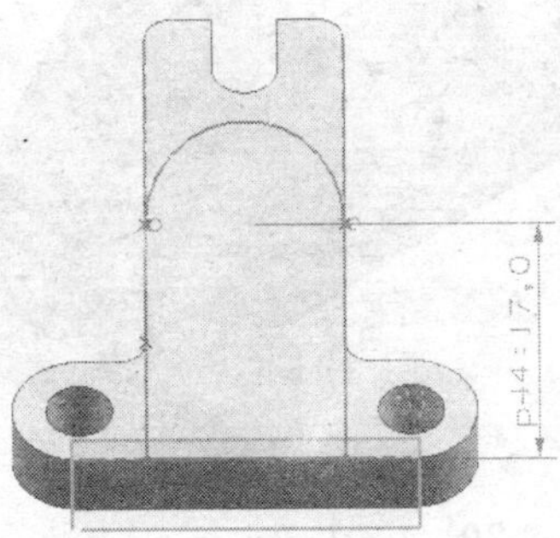

Figure 5-69 Sketch created for the second feature

7. Select the sketch and then select **Unite** from the **Boolean** drop-down list in the dialog box.

8. Select the **Until Next** option from the **Start** drop-down list in the **Limits** rollout, and then enter **0** in the **Distance** edit box, which is available below the **End** drop-down list in the **Limit** rollout of the dialog box.

9. Choose the **OK** button from the dialog box; the feature is created.

10. Hide the sketch and the datum plane. Figure 5-70 shows the model after creating the second feature.

Creating the Third Feature

The third feature is an extruded feature and will be created by using the **Subtract** boolean option. The sketch of this feature will be created on the inclined face of the second feature.

1. Invoke the Sketcher environment by selecting the inclined face of the second feature as the sketching plane and then draw the circle for the hole. Add the required dimensions and constraints to the circle, refer to Figure 5-65.
2. Exit the Sketcher environment and then invoke the **Extrude** dialog box.
3. Select the circle and then select the **Subtract** option from the **Boolean** drop-down list in the **Extrude** dialog box. The preview of the feature is displayed in the drawing window.
4. Choose the **Reverse Direction** button to reverse the direction of feature creation. Next, select **Through All** from the **Start** drop-down list in the **Limits** rollout.
5. Choose **OK**; the feature is created. Hide the sketch of the circle and then choose the **Fit** button to fit the model into the screen. The final model for this tutorial is shown in Figure 5-71.

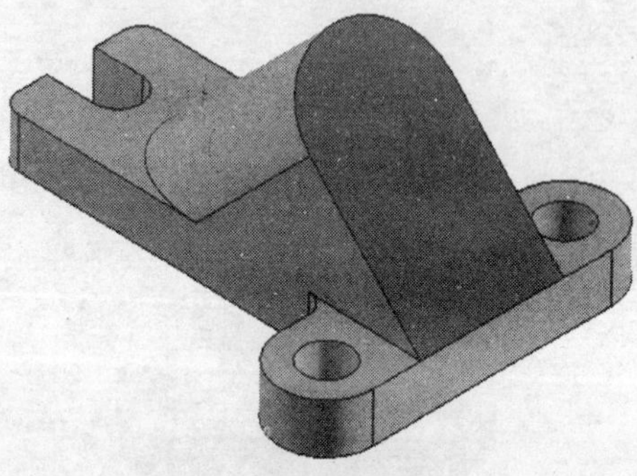

Figure 5-70 *Model after creating the second feature on the inclined datum plane*

Figure 5-71 *Final model for Tutorial 3*

Saving and Closing the File

1. Choose **File > Close > Save and Close** from the menu bar to save and close the file.

Self-Evaluation Test

Answer the following questions and then compare them to those given at the end of this chapter:

1. In mechanical designs, all features are created on a single plane. (T/F)

2. When you start a new part file, the fixed datum planes are provided by default. (T/F)

3. You can turn off the display of additional datum planes. (T/F)

4. In NX, you can extrude a sketch to perform only the **Unite** operation. (T/F)

5. Fixed datum planes are also termed as __________ datum planes.

6. The __________ boolean operation is used to create an extruded feature by removing material from an existing feature.

7. The __________ option is used to create a revolved feature that terminates at a specified face.

8. The __________ option is used to extrude a sketch up to a specified face, datum plane, or body.

9. The __________ option is used to create a plane at an angle to another plane passing through an edge, linear sketched segment, or axis.

10. The __________ boolean operation is used to create an extruded feature by retaining the material common to the existing feature and sketch.

Review Questions

Answer the following questions:

1. Which one of the following tools allows you to create additional datum planes?

(a) **Plane** (b) **Datum Plane**
(c) **Reference Plane** (d) None of these

2. Which of the following options in the **Insert** menu allows you to project existing entities on the current sketching plane?

(a) **Project Curve** (b) **Project Edges**
(c) **Divert** (d) None of these

3. Which one of the following operations allows you to join a new feature with an existing feature?

(a) **Join** (b) **Unite**
(c) **Combine** (d) None of these

4. Which one of the following options allows to you to extrude a sketch from the sketching plane to the next surface that intersects a feature in the specified direction?

   (a) **Until Selected** (b) **Until Next**
   (c) **Value** (d) None of these

5. Which of the following projection output types, projects external elements as a single continuous spline?

   (a) **Spline** (b) **Spline Segment**
   (c) **Single Spline** (d) None of these

6. If you create an associative datum plane, its name will be displayed as **Fixed Datum Plane** in the **Part Navigator**. (T/F)

7. While creating parallel planes, you can select only a planar face or a surface as reference object. (T/F)

8. After creating a coordinate system, you cannot modify its location. (T/F)

9. The **Until Selected** option is used to extrude a sketch up to a specified face, a datum plane, or a body. (T/F)

10. NX allows you to make the projected sketched entities associative with the original entities from which they were projected. (T/F)

Exercises

Exercise 1

Create the model shown in Figure 5-72. The dimensions of the model are also shown in the same figure. **(Expected time: 30 min)**

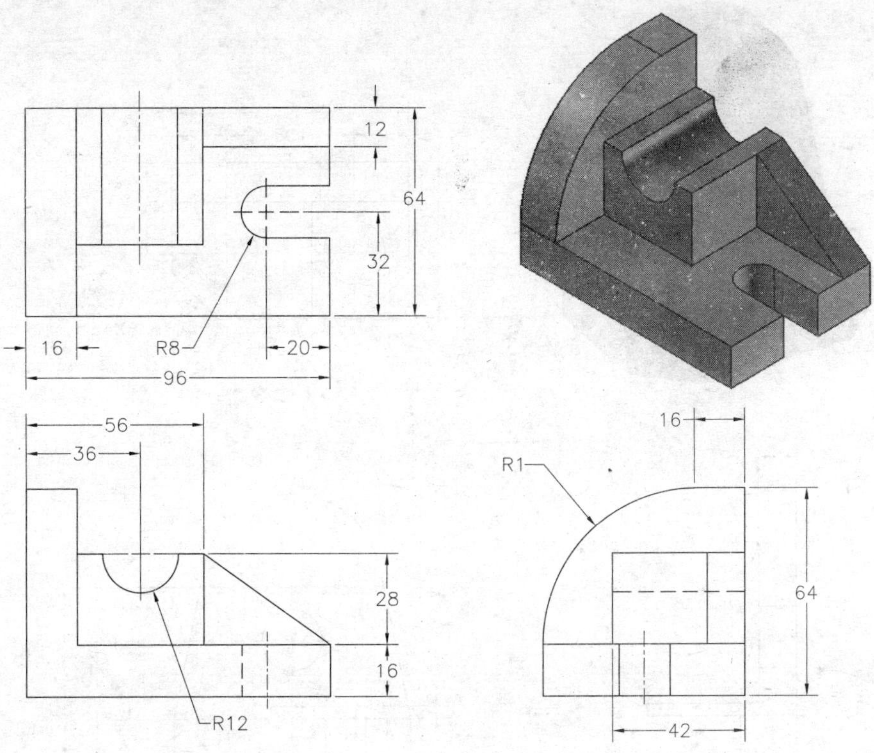

Figure 5-72 Model and its dimensions for Exercise 1

Exercise 2

Create the model shown in Figure 5-73. The dimensions of the model are also shown in the same figure. **(Expected time: 30 min)**

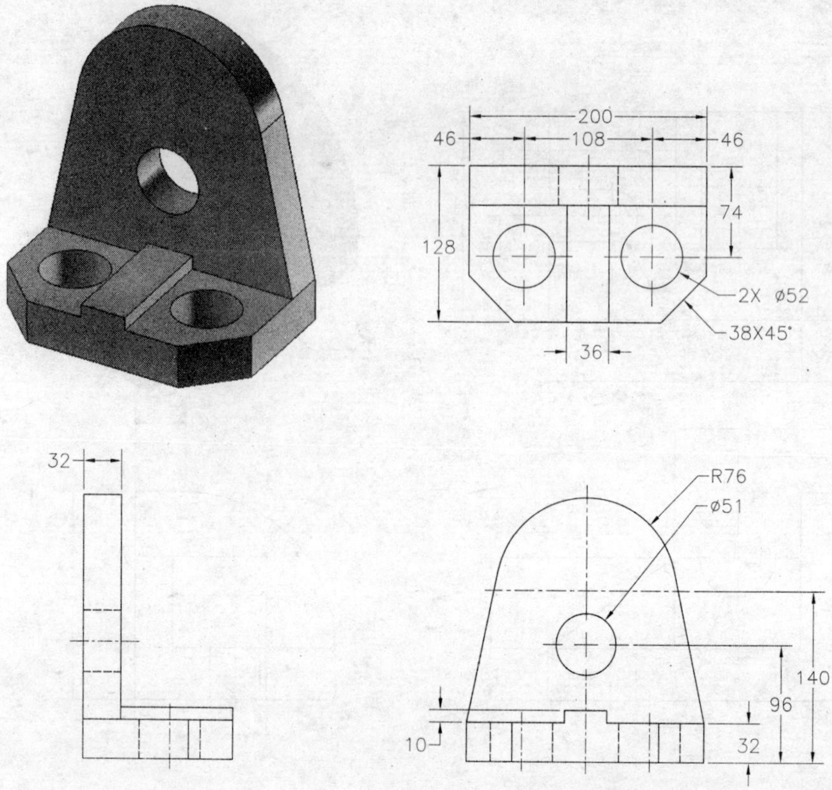

Figure 5-73 Model and its dimensions for Exercise 2

Answers to Self-Evaluation Test

1. F, 2. F, 3. T, 4. F, 5. principle, 6. **Subtract**, 7. **Until Selected**, 8. **Until Extended**, 9. **At Angle**, 10. **Intersect**

Chapter 6

Advanced Modeling Tools-I

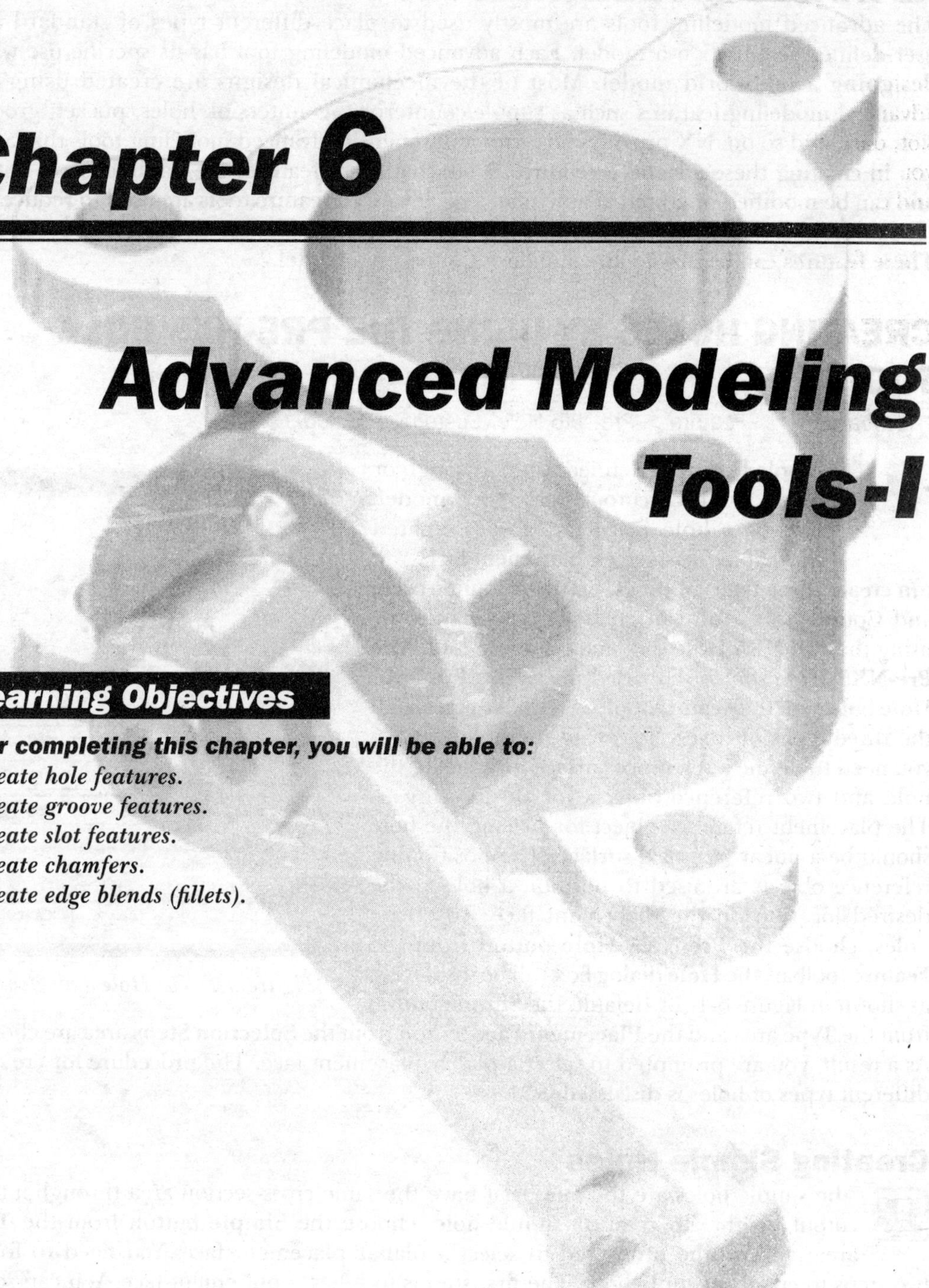

Learning Objectives

After completing this chapter, you will be able to:

- *Create hole features.*
- *Create groove features.*
- *Create slot features.*
- *Create chamfers.*
- *Create edge blends (fillets).*

ADVANCED MODELING TOOLS

The advanced modeling tools are mostly used to place different types of standard and user-defined features on a model. Each advanced modeling tool has its specific use while designing a real-world model. Most of the mechanical designs are created using the advanced modeling features such as simple/counterbore/countersink holes, pocket, groove, slot, dart, and so on. NX provides you with a number of advanced modeling tools that assist you in creating these advanced features. Note that these features are parametric in nature and can be modified or edited at any time. The advanced feature tools are used to reduce the time taken in creating the design. Also, you can create and save user-defined features in NX. These features can be placed any number of times on a model.

CREATING HOLES BY USING THE PRE-NX5 HOLE TOOL

Toolbar: Feature > Pre-NX5 Hole *(Customize to Add)*

A hole feature is defined as the through or blind cylindrical cutout created in a model. In NX, a hole feature is always created normal to the selected placement face. You can create three types of holes, Simple, Counterbore, and Countersink. You can create a hole feature by using the **Pre-NX5 Hole** tool and the **Hole** tool. The **Pre-NX5 Hole** tool is discussed next. The **Pre-NX5 Hole** button in the **Feature** toolbar is used to create all the three types of holes. To create the hole feature, you need to define a reference surface for placing the hole and two reference objects for positioning it. The placement reference object for placing the hole should be a linear face or a surface. The positioning reference objects are used to position a hole at the desired location on the placement face. To create holes, choose the **Pre-NX5 Hole** button from the **Feature** toolbar; the **Hole** dialog box will be displayed, as shown in Figure 6-1. By default, the **Simple** button from the **Type** area and the **Placement Face** button from the **Selection Steps** area are chosen. As a result, you are prompted to select a planar placement face. The procedure for creating different types of holes is discussed next.

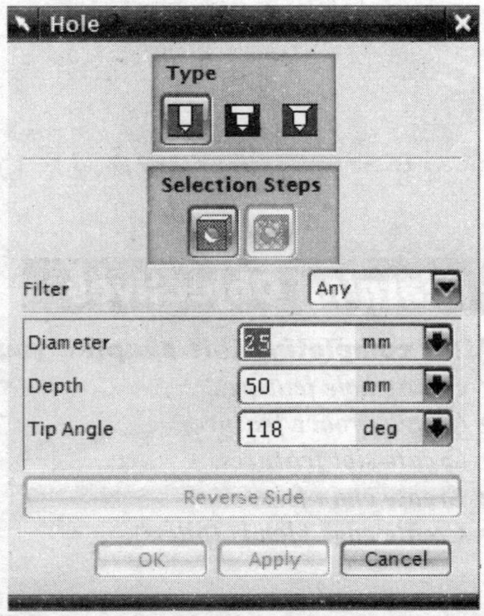

***Figure 6-1** The **Hole** dialog box*

Creating Simple Holes

The simple holes are the ones that have the same cross-section area throughout the cutout height. To create a simple hole, choose the **Simple** button from the **Type** area; you will be prompted to select a planar placement face. You need to follow two steps to create a simple hole. The first step is to select a placement face. You can select a face or a datum plane to start the hole feature. The options in the **Filter** drop-down list are used to customize the selection procedure while selecting the placement face and the through face for the hole. After selecting the placement face, the preview of the hole will be displayed with the default dimension values in the drawing window, refer to Figure 6-2. Note that as soon as you select the placement face, the **Thru Face** button will be chosen automatically in the **Selection Steps** area of the **Hole** dialog box to specify the hole termination.

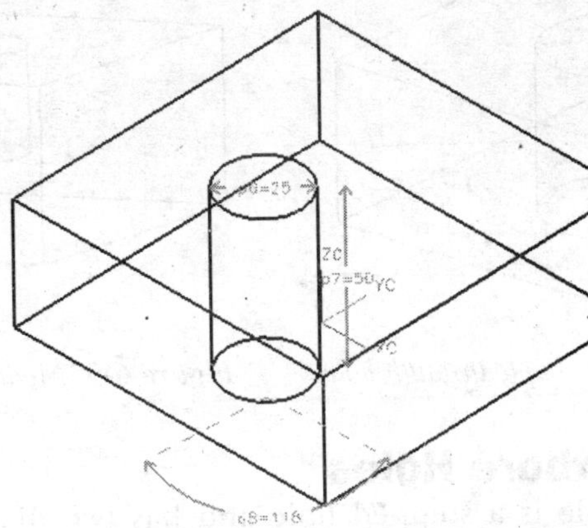

Figure 6-2 The preview of the hole

The second step is to specify the diameter and depth of the hole. To create a blind hole, enter the diameter of the hole to be created in the **Diameter** edit box and the depth of the hole in the **Depth** edit box of the dialog box. However, to create a through hole in the part, you do not need to specify the depth of the hole, you can select a face up to which the hole is to be created. NX also allows you to create an angular tip for the hole. By default, **118** is displayed as the value in the **Tip Angle** edit box, which is an ISO standard tip angle value. You can enter a different angle value in the **Tip Angle** edit box to create an angular tip.

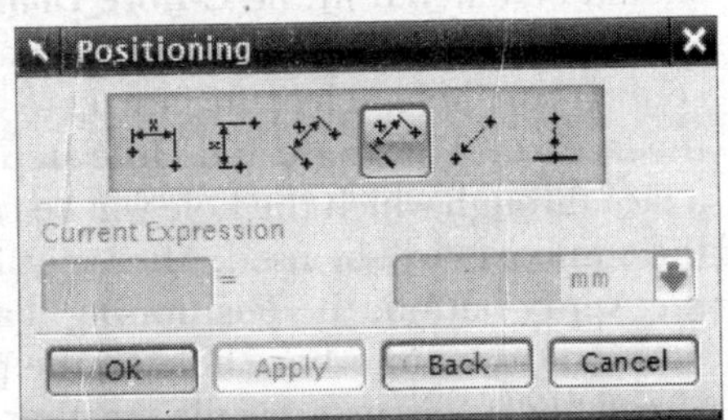

***Figure 6-3** The **Positioning** dialog box*

After entering the required data for the hole in the respective edit boxes, choose the **Apply** button; the **Positioning** dialog box will be displayed, as shown in Figure 6-3. You can use the buttons available in this dialog box to position the hole on the placement face. By default, the **Perpendicular** button is chosen in this dialog box. As a result, you can select two linear edges to position the hole. To do so, select the first linear edge; the edit box in the **Current Expression** area of the dialog box will be enabled with the current distance value. Enter the required distance value in this edit box. Next, select the second linear edge and enter the required distance value in the edit box. Note that perpendicular dimensions will be applied from the selected linear edges to the center of the hole. The other buttons in this dialog box can also be used to create dimensions between different types of reference objects and the hole for positioning it. For example, the **Horizontal** or **Vertical** button can be used to apply a horizontal or a vertical dimension between the center of the hole and the edge. In this case, first you need to define the horizontal reference by using a linear edge or an axis. After positioning the hole, choose the **OK** button from the dialog box. Figures 6-4 and 6-5 show the models with the through and blind holes, respectively. The tip angle value for holes in these figures is 0.

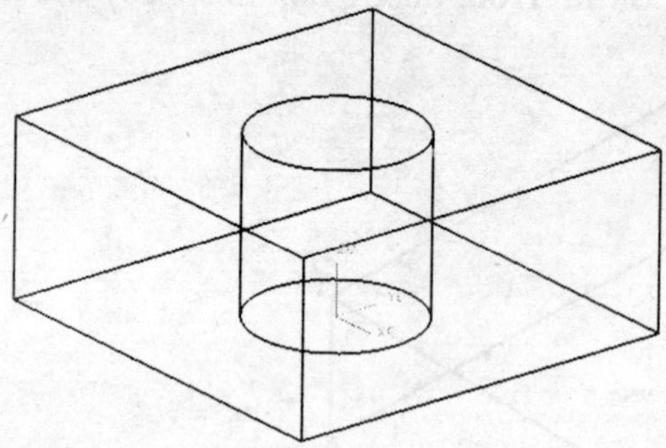

Figure 6-4 Model with a simple through hole

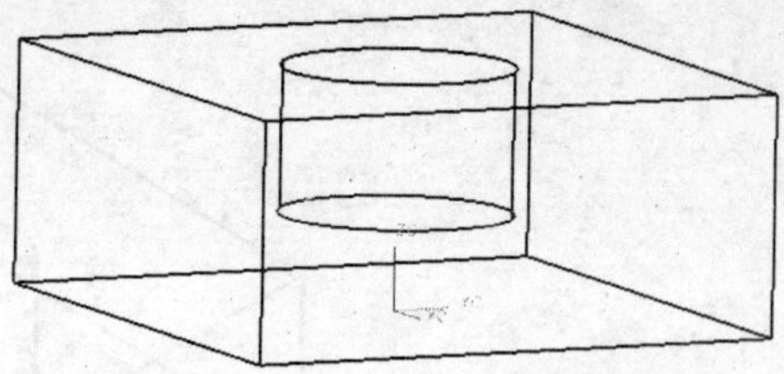

Figure 6-5 Model with a simple blind hole

Creating Counterbore Holes

A counterbore hole is a stepped hole and has two diameters, the counterbore diameter and the hole diameter. You need to define two diameters to create counterbore holes. The counterbore diameter must be greater than the hole diameter.

To create a counterbore hole, choose the **Counterbore** button from the **Type** area of the **Hole** dialog box; you will be prompted to select a planar placement face. Select a planar face as the placement face; the preview of the counterbore hole along with its parameters will be displayed, refer to Figure 6-6.

The parameters for defining the counterbore hole are displayed in the area below the **Filter** drop-down list in the dialog box. The diameter and the depth value of the counterbore hole should be entered in the **C-Bore Diameter** and **C-Bore Depth** edit boxes, respectively. The remaining parameters are the same as discussed for the simple hole. To create a through counterbore hole, select the face up to which the hole is to be created. Note that after selecting the face, the **Tip Angle** and **Hole Depth** edit boxes will not be available. If you do not select a face through which the hole will be created, the hole depth and tip angle values entered in the edit boxes will be used. After specifying the parameters for the counterbore hole, choose the **Apply** button; the **Positioning** dialog box will be displayed. This dialog box is used to position the counterbore hole on the placement face. The functions of this dialog box have already been discussed while creating simple holes. After positioning the hole, choose the **Apply** button in the **Positioning** dialog box to create the hole. Figure 6-7 shows the front view of a counterbore hole. The tip angle value for the hole in this figure is 118 degrees.

Note

*The **Reverse Side** button in the **Hole** dialog box is used to reverse the direction of the hole.*

Creating Countersink Holes

A countersink hole has two diameters, but the transition between the major diameter to the minor diameter is angular. The depth of the countersink depends upon the countersink angle value. In mechanical designs, countersink holes are used to insert screws.

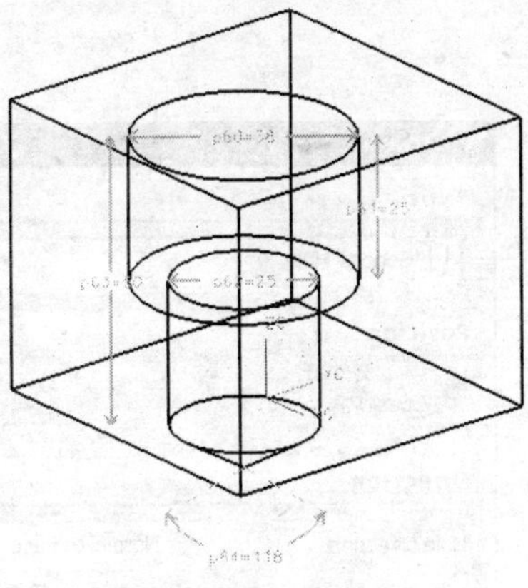

Figure 6-6 The preview of the counterbore hole

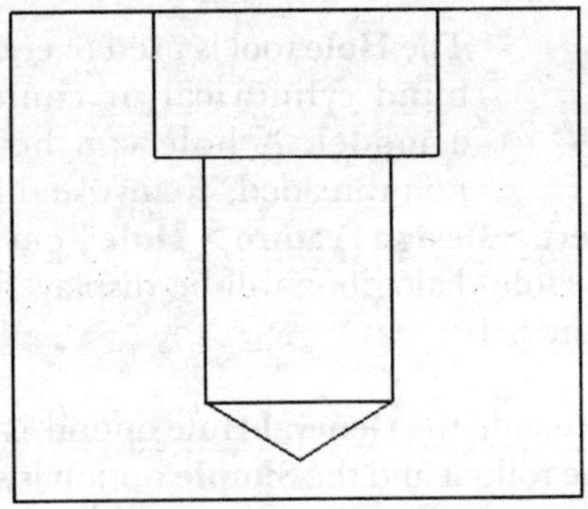

Figure 6-7 The front view of a counterbore hole

To create a countersink hole, choose the **Countersink** button from the **Type** area of the **Hole** dialog box; the countersink hole options will be displayed and you will be prompted to select a planar placement face. Specify the planar placement face; the preview of the countersink hole along with the parameters will be displayed, refer to Figure 6-8. The parameters for defining the countersink hole are displayed in the area below the **Filter** drop-down list. You can specify the diameter value of the countersink hole in the **C-Sink Diameter** edit box and the countersink angle value in the **C-Sink Angle** edit box. The remaining parameters are the same as discussed for the simple hole. To create a through countersink hole, select the face up to which the hole is to be created. Note that in this case, the **Hole Depth** and **Tip Angle** edit boxes will not be available. After specifying all parameters of the countersink hole, choose the **Apply** button; the **Positioning** dialog box will be displayed. Position the hole by using the buttons in this dialog box. Figure 6-9 shows the Front view of the countersink hole.

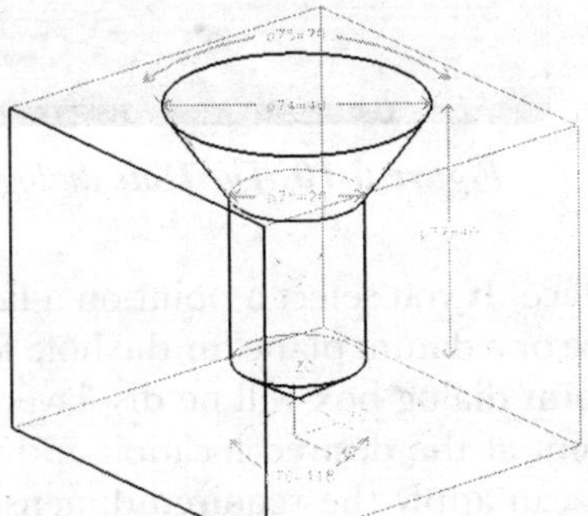

Figure 6-8 The preview of a countersink hole along with the parameters

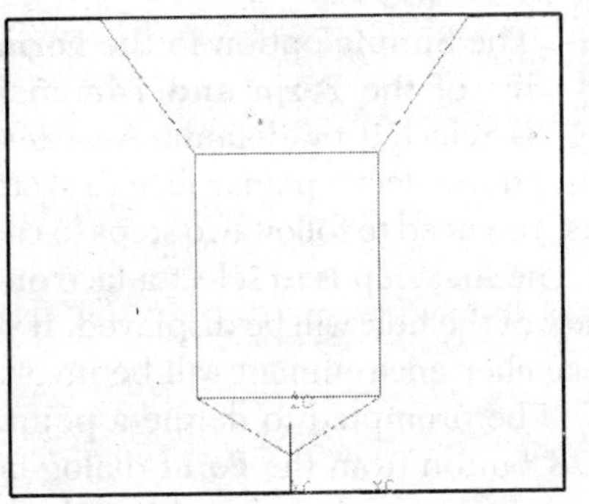

Figure 6-9 The front view of the resulting countersink hole

CREATING HOLES BY USING THE HOLE TOOL

Menu:	Insert > Design Feature > Hole
Toolbar:	Feature > Hole

The **Hole** tool is used to create a through, blind cylindrical or conical cutout in a model. A hole can be threaded or non-threaded. To invoke this tool, choose **Insert > Design Feature > Hole** from the menu bar; the **Hole** dialog box will be displayed, as shown in Figure 6-10.

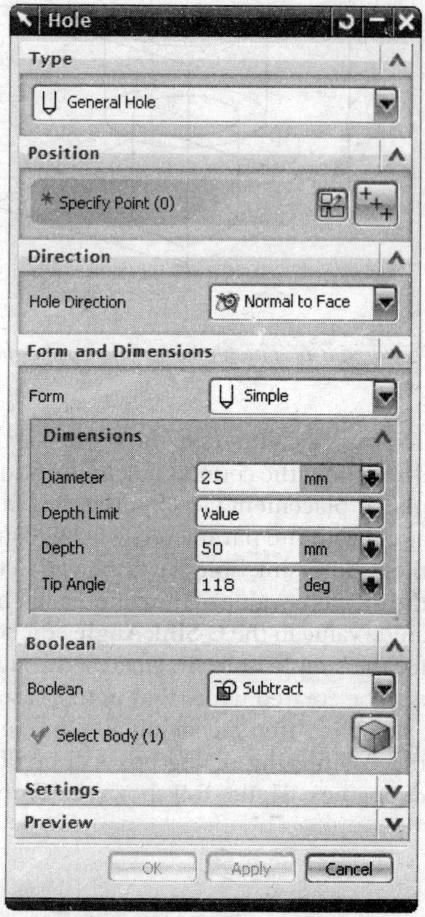

Figure 6-10 The ***Hole*** *dialog box*

By default, the **General Hole** option is chosen in the **Type** rollout and the **Simple** option is selected in the **Form** drop-down list. As a result, you are prompted to select a planar face to sketch or specify points. You can create different types of holes. The different types of holes and the methods to create them are discussed next.

Creating General Holes

The **General Hole** option in the **Type** drop-down list is chosen by default. By using this option, you can create simple, counterbore, countersunk, or tapered hole features.

The methods of creating different types of general holes are discussed next.

Simple Holes

The **Simple** option in the **Form** drop-down list of the **Form and Dimensions** rollout is selected by default. As a result, you are prompted to select a planar face to sketch or specify points. You need to follow two steps to create a simple hole. The first step is to select a face or a point on a face. If you select a point on a face, the preview of the hole will be displayed. If you select a face or a datum plane for the hole feature, the Sketcher environment will be invoked and the **Point** dialog box will be displayed. Also, you will be prompted to define a point. Specify a point at the desired location and choose the **OK** button from the **Point** dialog box. Next, you can apply the required dimensions to the specified point by using the tools available in the Sketcher environment. After applying the dimensions to the specified point, exit from the Sketcher environment; the preview of the hole feature will be displayed at the specified point. You can also define multiple points using the **Point** dialog box to create multiple simple holes at a time. To do so, after defining the required point, choose the **Apply** button instead of the **OK** button from the **Point** dialog box. Now, you can define one more point using the **Point** dialog box. Similarly, you can define multiple points to create multiple holes.

The second step is to specify the dimensions and parameters of the hole. To do so, enter the diameter of the hole to be created in the **Diameter** edit box of the **Form and Dimensions** rollout. The **Value** option in the **Depth Limit** drop-down list is selected by default. Now, you need to specify the depth and tip angle of the hole in their respective edit boxes. NX allows you to create an angular tip of the hole. By default, **118** is accepted as an ISO tip angle value in the **Tip Angle** edit box. You can enter a different tip angle value in the **Tip Angle** edit box to create an angular tip. To create a through hole in the component, select the **Through Body** option from the **Depth Limit** drop-down list. You can also use the **Until Next** or **Until Selected** option from the **Depth Limit** drop-down list to create a hole as explained in the previous chapter.

In the **Direction** rollout of the dialog box, you can specify the direction of the hole. By default, the **Normal to Face** option is selected in the **Hole Direction** drop-down list. As a result, the hole will be created normal to the selected face. To change the hole direction, select the **Along Vector** option in the **Hole Direction** drop-down list; the **Specify Vector** area will be displayed in the **Direction** rollout. Use this area to specify the hole direction.

After specifying the hole parameters, choose the **Apply** button; the hole will be created based on the specified parameters. Next, choose the **Cancel** button to exit from the dialog box.

Counterbore Holes

To create a counterbore hole, invoke the **Hole** dialog box by choosing the **Hole** tool from the **Feature** toolbar. Select the **Counterbore** option from the **Form** drop-down list in the **Hole** dialog box and follow the first step as explained earlier; the preview of the counterbore hole will be displayed. Also, its parameters will be displayed below the **Form** drop-down list. These options are similar to the options discussed earlier in this chapter.

Countersink Holes

To create a countersink hole, invoke the **Hole** dialog box by choosing the **Hole** tool from the **Feature** toolbar. Select the **Countersink** option from the **Form** drop-down list and follow the first step as explained earlier; the preview of the countersink hole will be displayed. Also, its parameters will be displayed below the **Form** drop-down list. These options are similar to those discussed earlier in this chapter.

Tapered Holes

To create a tapered hole, select the **Tapered** option from the **Form** drop-down list in the **Hole** dialog box and follow the first step as explained earlier; the preview of the tapered hole will be displayed. Also, its parameters will be displayed below the **Form** drop-down list. You can specify the tapering angle in the **Taper Angle** edit box.

Creating Drill Size Hole

The **Drill Size Hole** option of the **Type** drop-down list in the **Type** rollout is used to create a simple drill size hole feature using the ANSI or ISO standard by specifying its respective parameters. To create a drill size hole, choose this option from the **Type** drop-down list of the **Type** rollout and specify the placement point of the hole as discussed in the first step of creating the general holes. Note that as soon as you choose the **Drill Size Hole** option, the **Form and Dimensions** rollout will be modified. The options in this rollout are discussed next. Figure 6-11 shows various parameters associated with the drill size hole.

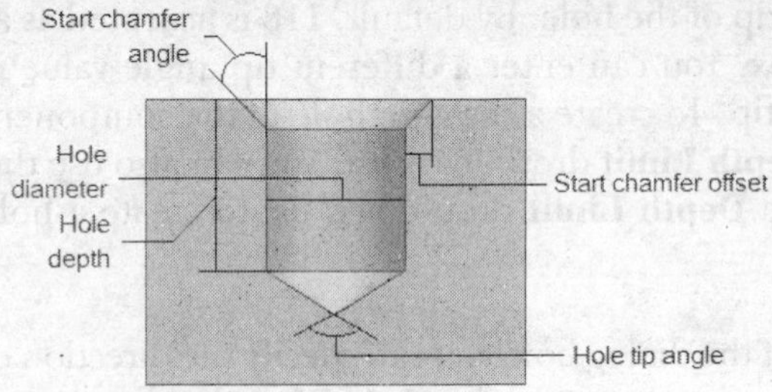

Figure 6-11 Various parameters of the drill size hole

Form and Dimensions Rollout

You can select a standard diameter for the drill size hole in the **Size** drop-down list of this rollout. The specified dimension in this drop-down list will apply only if the **Exact** option is selected in the **Fit** drop-down list, which is available below the **Size** drop-down list of this rollout. In this rollout, three more sub-rollouts **Dimensions**, **Start Chamfer**, and **End Chamfer** are available. These sub-rollouts are discussed next.

Dimensions

The **Diameter** edit box of this sub-rollout will be activated only if the **Custom** option is selected in the **Fit** drop-down list. This edit box is used to specify the diameter of the hole. You can also specify the depth and tip angle of the hole by using their respective edit boxes in this sub-rollout.

Start Chamfer

The options of this sub-rollout will be available only when the **Custom** option is selected in the **Fit** drop-down list. If you clear the **Enable** check box in this sub-rollout, all options in this rollout will be deactivated and a sharp edge will be generated at the starting plane of the resultant hole. In the **Offset** edit box, you can specify the chamfer depth. In the **Angle** edit box, you can specify the chamfer angle of the resultant hole at the starting plane of the hole.

End Chamfer

The options in this sub-rollout are similar to options of the **Start Chamfer** sub-rollout with the only difference that the options in this sub-rollout are used to specify chamfer settings at the end of the hole.

After specifying all required parameters for the drill size hole, choose the **OK** button in the **Hole** dialog box; the hole will be created.

Creating Screw Clearance Hole

On selecting the **Screw Clearance Hole** option from the **Type** drop-down list, you can create simple, counterbore, or countersunk screw clearance hole features according to the standard specified in the **Standard** drop-down list of the **Settings** rollout. If you choose this option from the **Type** rollout, the **Form and Dimensions** rollout will be modified. Most of the options in this rollout are the same as those discussed earlier in this chapter. You can select the required screw type option from the **Screw Type** drop-down list in the **Form and Dimensions** rollout. The options in the **Screw Type** drop-down list are displayed based on the option selected in the **Form** drop-down list. In the **Fit** drop-down list, you can specify the required fit for the hole such as interference (press) fit, transition fit, or loose fit by selecting the **Close**, **Normal**, or **Loose** option, respectively. You can specify the neck chamfer for the counterbore hole and relief depth for the Countersunk hole in the **Neck Chamfer** and **Relief** sub-rollouts, respectively.

Creating Threaded Hole

The **Threaded Hole** option in the **Type** drop-down list is used to create a threaded hole. The standard of a threaded hole depends upon the option selected in the **Standard** drop-down list of the **Settings** rollout. You can specify the required size of the standard threaded hole by selecting the options from the **Size** drop-down list. In the **Radial Engage** drop-down list available below the **Size** drop-down list, you can specify the percentage of radial engagement, which is used to calculate the tap drill diameter, refer to Figures 6-12 and 6-13. The **Tap Drill Diameter** edit box will be activated only when the **Custom** option is selected from the **Radial Engage** drop-down list. In this edit box, you can specify the customized value of the tap drill diameter. Similarly, you can specify the standard thread depth by selecting the required option from the **Length** drop-down list. To enter the customized thread depth value, select the **Custom** option from the **Length** drop-down list; the **Thread Depth** edit box will be displayed below the **Length** drop-down list. In this edit box, you can specify the thread depth value of the hole. In the **Rotation** area of the **Form and Dimensions** rollout, you can specify the right hand thread or the left hand thread by selecting the **Right** or **Left** radio button, respectively.

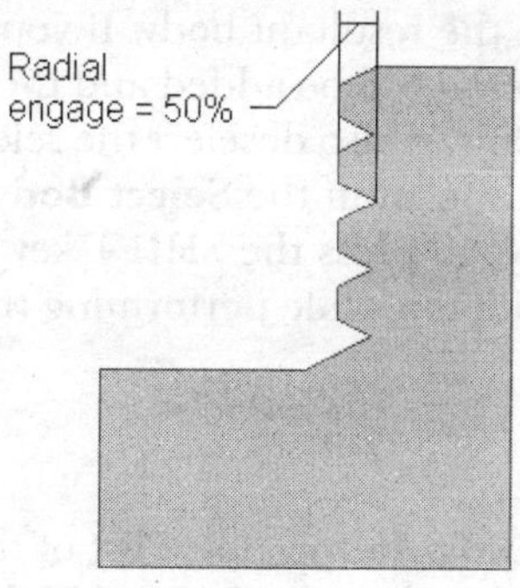

Figure 6-12 *Radial engage = 50%*

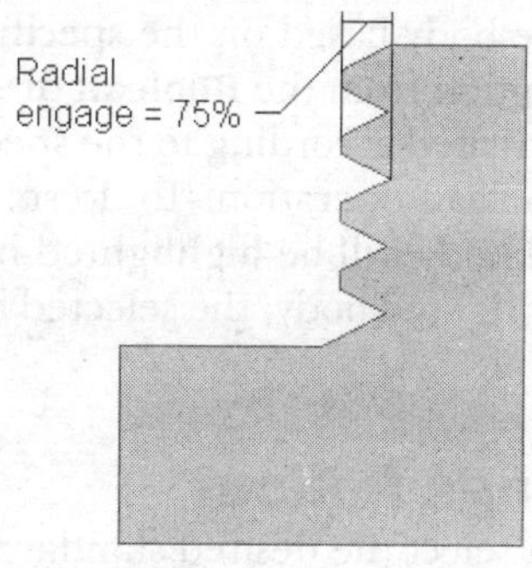

Figure 6-13 *Radial engage = 75%*

Note

*If the threaded holes are created by using the **Threaded Hole** option then the threads are represented in dotted lines. These threads are known as symbolic threads. Figures 6-12 and*

6-13 are for you reference only. To view these symbolic threads, change the display of the model to Static Wireframe.

Creating Hole Series

You can use the **Hole Series** option to create an aligned series of holes in multiple bodies, refer to Figure 6-14. If you select this option from the **Type** rollout, the **Specification** rollout will be displayed with three tabs. These tabs are discussed next.

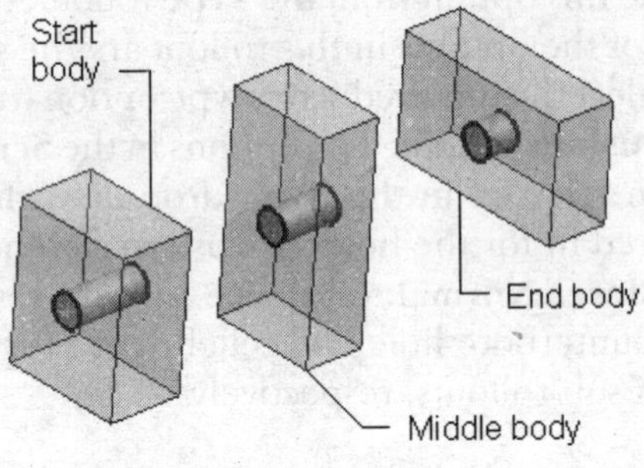

***Figure 6-14** Aligned series of holes*

The Start Tab

This tab is used to specify the parameters of a hole in the first body. The options in this tab are similar to those discussed earlier in this chapter.

The Middle Tab

This tab is used to specify the parameters of a hole in the middle body. The middle body hole is defined as the hole that lies in the middle body. By default, the **Match Dimensions of Start Hole** check box is selected in this tab. As a result, all dimensions of the hole match to the hole in the first body. To create a user-defined hole, clear this check box and select the **Custom** option from the **Fit** drop-down list; all parameters in this tab will be activated.

The End Tab

This tab is used to specify the parameters of the hole on the last body.

Boolean Rollout

This rollout is used to specify the boolean operations on a body. By default, the **Subtract** option is selected in the **Boolean** drop-down list of this rollout. As a result, the material is removed from the body based on the specification of the hole in the resultant body. If you select the **None** option from the **Boolean** drop-down list, the material will be added and the new body will be created according to the specified dimensions. You can also deselect the selected body for a boolean operation. To do so, choose the **Body** button from the **Select Body** area; the selected body will be highlighted in the graphic area. Next, press the SHIFT key and select the highlighted body; the selected body will not be considered while performing the boolean operation.

Settings Rollout

You can select the desired standard option from the **Standard** drop-down list of this rollout. The **Standard** drop-down list is available for all options other than the **General Hole** option of the **Type** drop-down list. Also, you can specify the predefined tolerance value in the **Tolerance** edit box in this rollout.

CREATING GROOVES

Toolbar: Feature > Groove *(Customize to Add)*

Grooves are the channels that are created on the outer surface of a cylinder or a conical feature. The groove operation can only be performed on the features that have their own center axis. To create grooves, choose the **Groove** button from the **Feature** toolbar; the **Groove** dialog box will be displayed, as shown in Figure 6-15. You will be prompted to choose the required groove type. In NX, you can create three types of grooves. The procedure for creating these grooves is discussed next.

*Figure 6-15 The **Groove** dialog box*

Creating Rectangular Grooves

To create a rectangular groove, choose the **Rectangular** button from the **Groove** dialog box; the **Rectangular Groove** dialog box will be displayed, as shown in Figure 6-16, and you will be prompted to select the placement face.

You can only select a conical or cylindrical face as the placement face. Select the placement face; the **Rectangular Groove** dialog box will be modified, refer to Figure 6-17. Next, you need to specify the groove diameter. The diameter value entered in the **Groove Diameter** edit box is always maintained from the central axis of the model. The remaining portion, which is left out from the placement face, will be removed from the channel. Also, you need to enter the width value for the channel in the **Width** edit box of the dialog box.

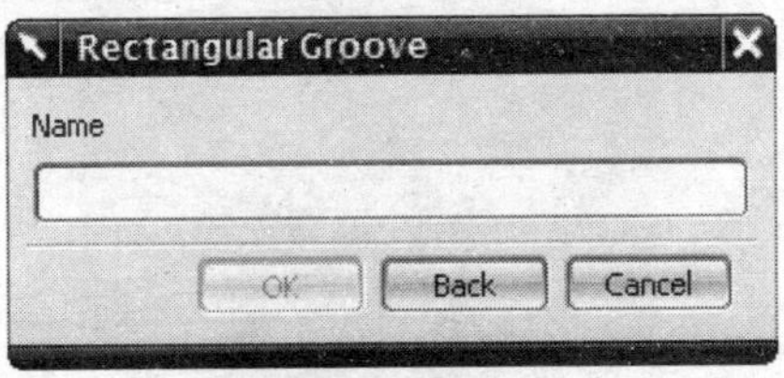

*Figure 6-16 The **Rectangular Groove** dialog box*

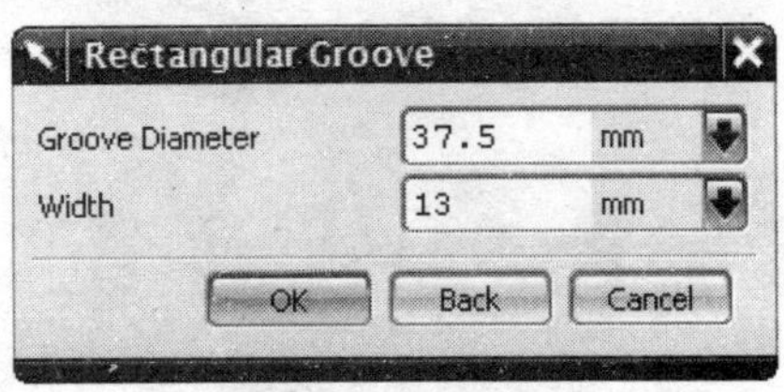

*Figure 6-17 The modified **Rectangular Groove** dialog box*

After specifying the width and diameter for the groove, choose the **OK** button from the **Rectangular Groove** dialog box; the **Position Groove** dialog box along with the preview of the groove feature will be displayed. Also, you will be prompted to select the target edge or choose the OK button to accept the initial position. Now, you can choose the **OK** button from the dialog box to create the groove at the current position. You can also position the groove at the required location. To do so, select an edge from the model, refer to Figure 6-18. On doing so, you will be prompted to select the tool edge. Select the edge from the tool (groove), refer to Figure 6-18. On selecting the tool edge, the **Create Expression** dialog box will be displayed. Enter the distance value in the edit box and choose the **OK** button; the groove feature will be created. The value specified in the **Create Expression** dialog box is the distance between the target edge and the tool edge. Once the feature is created, close the dialog box.

Figure 6-19 shows a rectangular groove feature created using the selections made in Figure 6-18. Figure 6-20 shows the groove feature created by specifying 0 mm as the distance between the target edge and the tool edge.

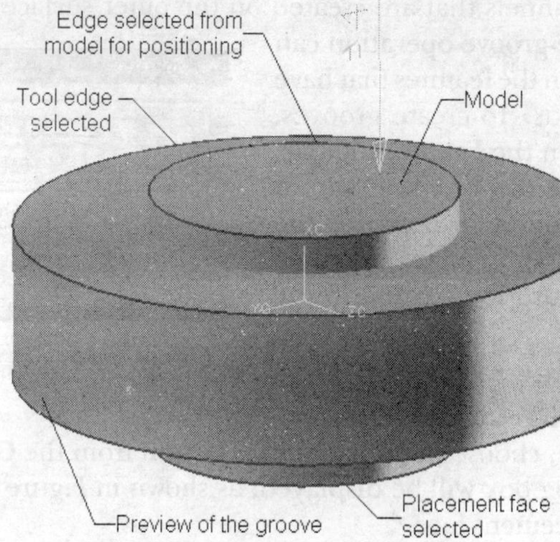

***Figure 6-18** The preview of the groove feature with the edges and model to be selected*

***Figure 6-19** The rectangular groove feature*

***Figure 6-20** The rectangular groove feature created with the distance between the target edge and the tool edge as 0*

Note

*If you enter 0 mm value in the **Groove Diameter** edit box, the **Message** window will be displayed and you will be informed that you have entered an invalid rectangular groove diameter. Similarly, if you enter a value larger than the diameter of the model in the **Groove Diameter** edit box, again the **Message** window will be displayed and you will be informed that the feature cannot be trimmed.*

*You can modify the parameters defined for the groove even after creating it. To edit the groove parameters, double-click on the groove feature; the **Edit Parameters** dialog box will be displayed. Choose the **Feature Dialog** button to edit the parameters.*

Creating Ball End Grooves

To create a ball end groove, invoke the **Groove** dialog box and choose the **Ball End** button from it; the **Ball End Groove** dialog box will be displayed and you will be prompted to select the placement face. You can select only a conical or a cylindrical face as the placement face. Planar faces cannot be selected for this feature. Select the placement face; the modified **Ball End Groove** dialog box will be displayed, as shown in Figure 6-21, and you will be prompted to enter the groove parameters.

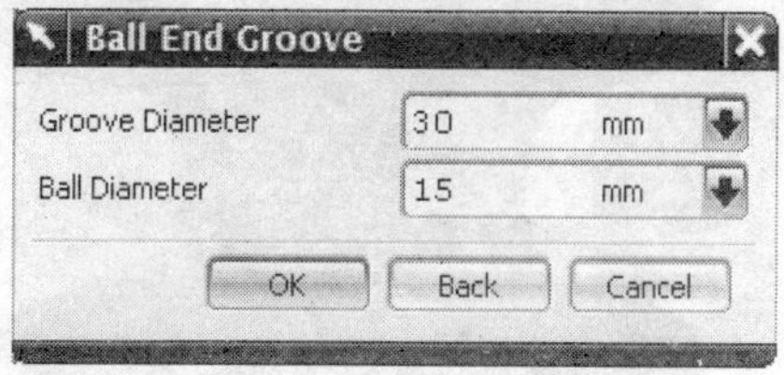

***Figure 6-21** The modified **Ball End Groove** dialog box*

In this dialog box, you need to specify the groove and ball diameters. The value entered in the **Groove Diameter** edit box is always maintained from the central axis of the model. The remaining portion of the selected placement face is removed from the channel. Enter the ball end diameter in the **Ball Diameter** edit box and choose the **OK** button; the **Position Groove** dialog box along with the preview of the groove feature will be displayed. Also, you will be prompted to select the target edge. Figure 6-22 shows the preview of the groove feature.

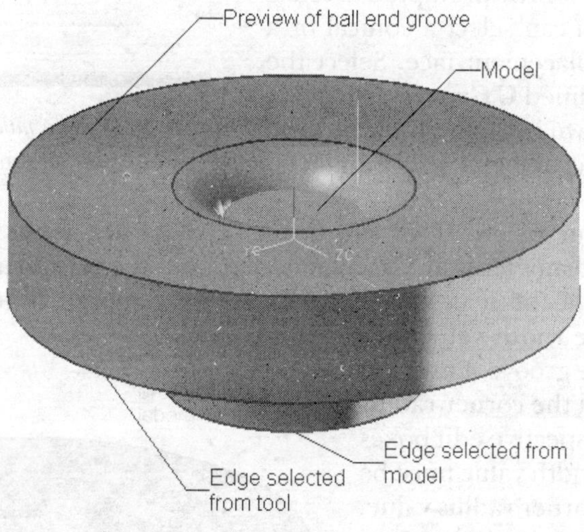

***Figure 6-22** The preview of the ball end groove feature with the edges and model to be selected*

To position the groove, select an edge from the model, refer to Figure 6-22; you will be prompted to select tool edge (groove). Select an edge from the tool, refer to Figure 6-22; the **Create Expression** dialog box will be displayed. Enter the distance value in its respective edit box and choose the **OK** button to create the groove feature. Once the feature is created, close the dialog box. Figure 6-23 shows a ball end groove feature created using the selections made in Figure 6-22. Figure 6-24 shows the groove feature created by specifying the distance between the target edge and the tool edge as 0 mm.

***Figure 6-23** The ball end groove feature created*

***Figure 6-24** The ball end groove feature created with the distance between the target and tool edge as 0*

Creating U Grooves

To create a U groove, choose the **U Groove** button in the **Groove** dialog box; the **U Groove** dialog box will be displayed and you will be prompted to select the placement face. You can select a conical or a cylindrical face as the placement face. Select the placement face; the modified **U Groove** dialog box will be displayed, as shown in Figure 6-25 and you will be prompted to enter the groove parameters.

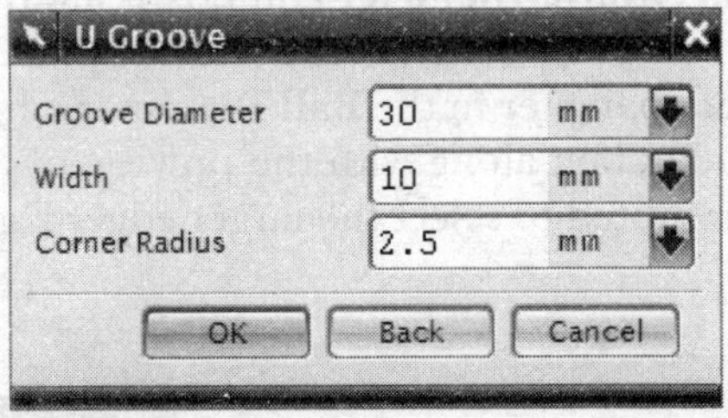

***Figure 6-25** The modified **U Groove** dialog box displaying the groove parameters*

Enter the diameter value of the U groove in the **Groove Diameter** edit box. The value entered for the groove diameter is always maintained from the central axis of the model and the remaining portion of the selected placement face is removed from the channel. Next, you need to specify the width value and the corner radius for the groove. Enter the values for the width and the corner radius of the groove in their respective edit boxes in the dialog box. The width value must be greater than twice the corner radius value. The edges formed between the normal faces due to the formation of this groove will automatically be filleted. The value entered in the **Corner Radius** edit box will be used as the fillet radius. After you specify the groove parameters, choose the **OK** button; the **Position Groove** dialog box will be displayed. The preview of the groove feature will displayed in the graphic window, refer to Figure 6-26. Also, you will be prompted to select the target edge from the model.

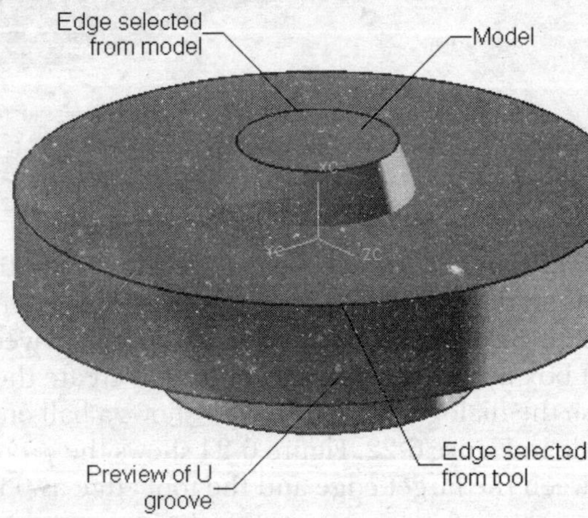

***Figure 6-26** The preview of the U groove feature*

To position the groove, select an edge from the model, refer to Figure 6-26; you will be prompted to select tool edge (groove). Select the edge from the tool, refer to Figure 6-26; the **Create Expression** dialog box will be displayed. Enter the distance value in its respective edit box and choose the **OK** button to create the groove feature, refer to Figure 6-27. Once the feature is created, close the dialog box. Figure 6-28 shows the groove feature created by specifying the distance between the target edge and the tool edge as 0 mm.

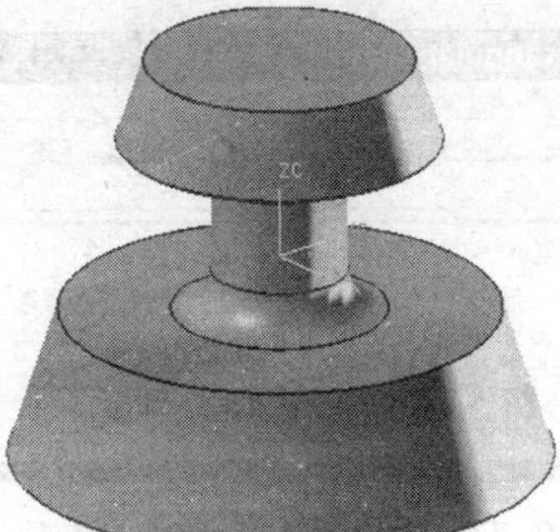

Figure 6-27 *The resulting U groove feature*

Figure 6-28 *The U groove feature created with the distance between the target edge and the tool edge as 0*

CREATING SLOTS

Toolbar: Feature > Slot *(Customize to add)*

Slots are the cutout features created on a planar surface of a model, which can be used as a guide way for another component to slide over it. To create a slot, choose the **Slot** button from the **Feature** toolbar; the **Slot** dialog box will be displayed, as shown in Figure 6-29. By default, the **Rectangular** radio button will be selected in this dialog box. In NX, you can create five different types of slots. The procedure to create these different type of slots is discussed next.

Creating Rectangular Slots

Rectangular slots are the ones that have a rectangular cross-section. To create a rectangular slot, invoke the **Slot** dialog box. By default, the **Rectangular** radio button is selected in this dialog box. Choose the **OK** button from the dialog box; the **Rectangular Slot** dialog box will be displayed, as shown in Figure 6-30, and you will be prompted to select a planar placement face.

You can specify a datum plane or a planar face as the placement face for the slot. To specify a datum plane as the placement face, choose the **Datum Plane** button in this dialog box and select a datum plane. Otherwise, choose the **Solid Face** button from in dialog box and select a planar face.

After specifying the placement face, the **Horizontal Reference** dialog box will be displayed, as shown in Figure 6-31. Next, you need to define the reference object, which will determine the orientation of the slot. You can use various options in this dialog box to select a particular reference object for defining the orientation of the slot. The slot is always oriented parallel to the direction of the selected reference object. Specify the reference object for the slot; the **Rectangular Slot** dialog box will be displayed, as shown in Figure 6-32. The default parameters for the slot will be displayed in the **Rectangular Slot** dialog box. Enter the required slot parameter values such as the length, width, and depth in their respective edit boxes in the dialog box.

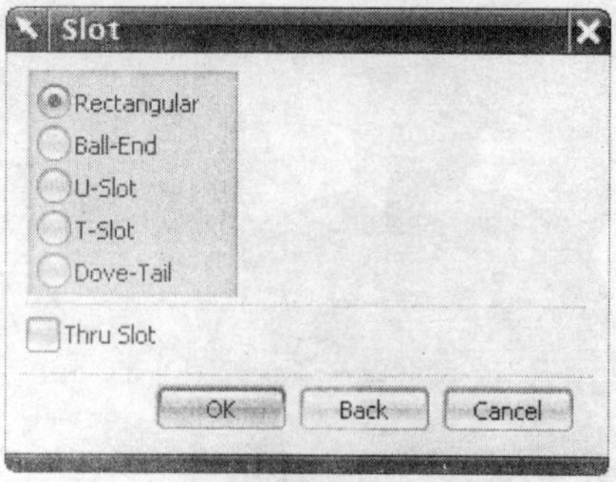

*Figure 6-29 The **Slot** dialog box*

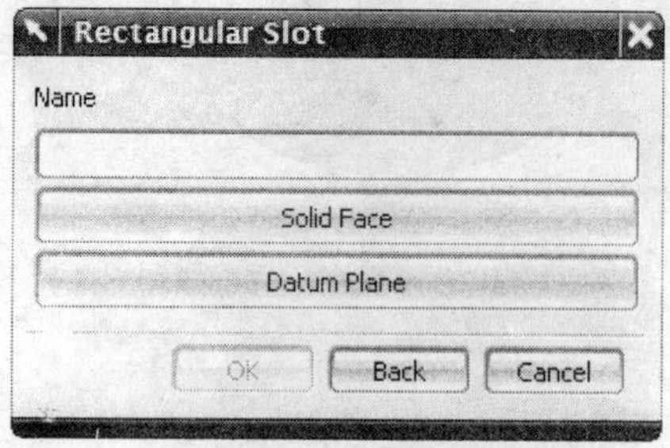

*Figure 6-30 The **Rectangular Slot** dialog box*

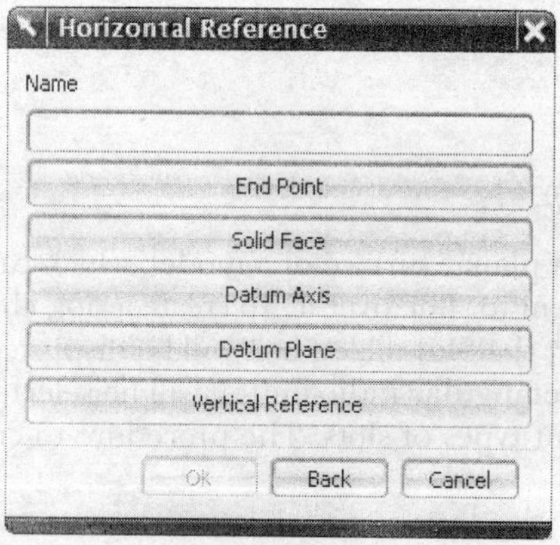

*Figure 6-31 The **Horizontal Reference** dialog box*

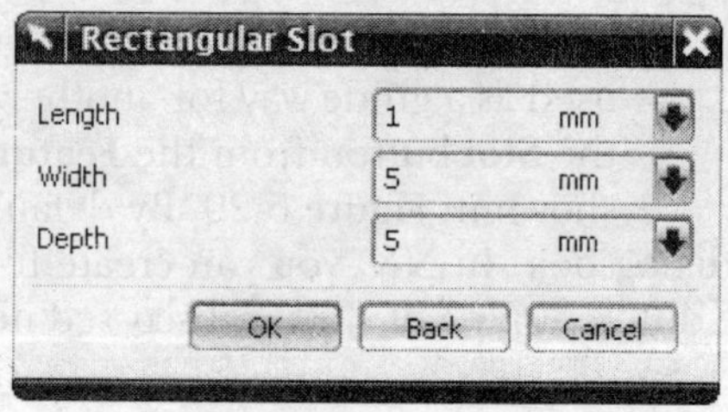

*Figure 6-32 The modified **Rectangular Slot** dialog box*

Note

*To create a through slot in the length aspect, you need to select the **Thru Slot** check box from the **Slot** dialog box. As a result, you need to define the start and end faces for defining the length value. The faces selected to define the through width should always be normal to the placement face. Select two faces that are parallel to each other and perpendicular to the placement face. Next, choose the **OK** button; the **Rectangular Slot** dialog box will be displayed. Specify the slot parameters in the respective edit boxes. In this case, the **Length** edit box will not be available. Figure 6-33 shows the faces selected to define the length of the through slot. Figure 6-34 shows the through slot created on a model.*

After specifying the slot parameters, choose the **OK** button from this dialog box; the preview of the slot will be displayed, refer to Figure 6-35. Also, the **Positioning** dialog box will be displayed. Next, position the slot using the **Positioning** dialog box and then choose the **OK** button from the same dialog box; the slot will be created, refer to Figure 6-36. Next, exit from the **Rectangular Slot** dialog box by choosing the **Cancel** button.

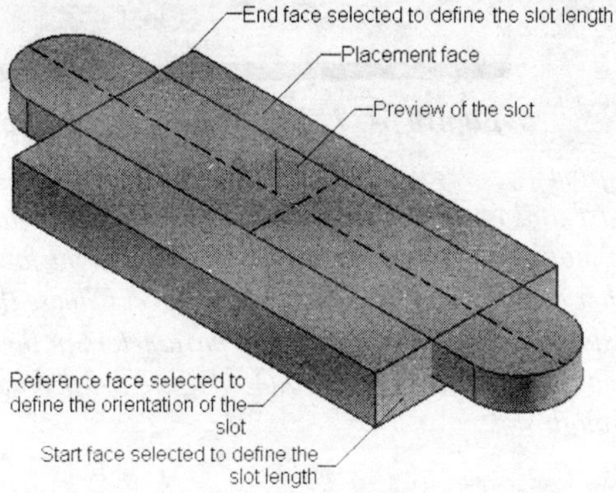

Figure 6-33 The preview of the through slot

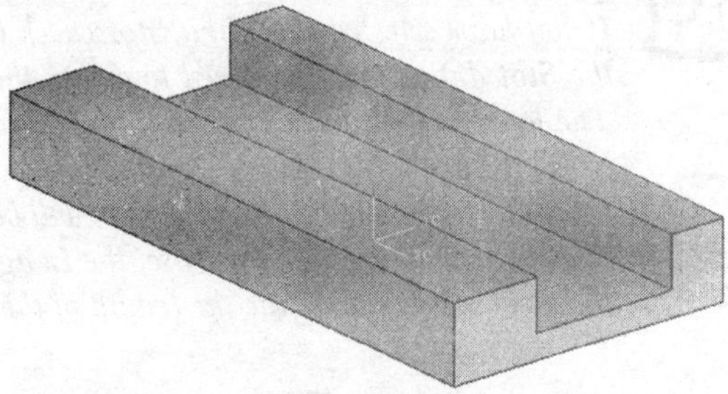

Figure 6-34 Model with a through slot feature

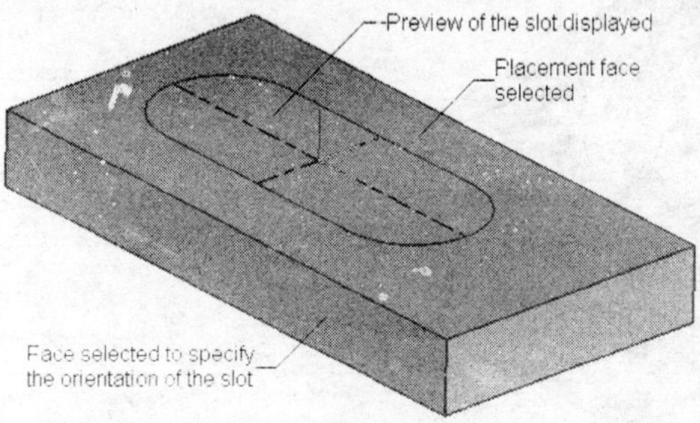

Figure 6-35 The preview of the slot feature

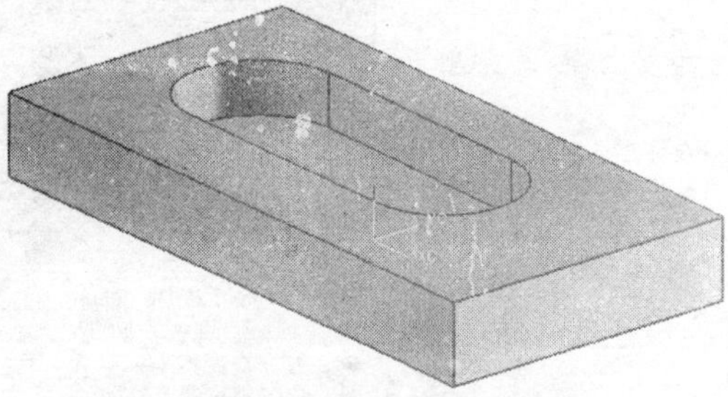

Figure 6-36 Model with a slot feature

Creating Ball-End Slots

The ball-end slots are the ones that have the rectangular cross-section with the filleted base and filleted side edges. The fillet radius will be half the width of the slot. To create this type of slot, select the **Ball-End** radio button from the **Slot** dialog box; the **Ball Slot** dialog box will be displayed and you will be prompted to select a planar placement face. You can specify a datum plane or a planar face as the placement face for the slot. To specify a datum plane as the placement face, choose the **Datum Plane** button from this dialog box and select a datum plane. Otherwise, choose the **Solid Face** button from this dialog box and select a planar face. As soon as you specify the placement face; the **Horizontal Reference** dialog box will be displayed. You need to define the reference object that will determine the orientation of the slot. You can use the options in this dialog box to select a particular reference object for defining the orientation of the slot. The slot is always oriented parallel to the direction of the reference object selected. Specify the orientation for the slot; the **Ball Slot** dialog box will be displayed with the default slot parameters, as shown in Figure 6-37.

Enter the slot parameter values such as the ball diameter, length, and depth in their respective edit boxes in the **Ball Slot** dialog box.

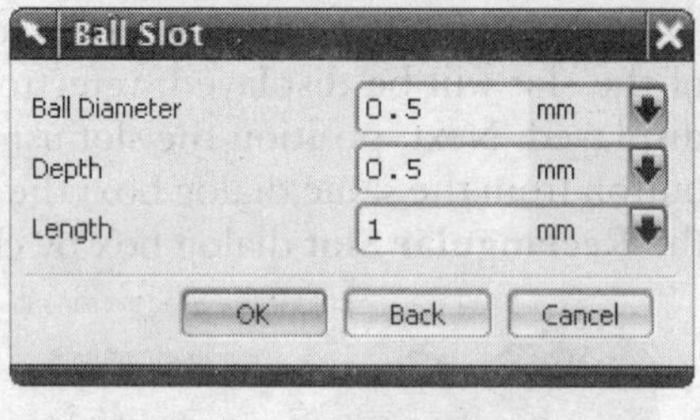

*Figure 6-37 The **Ball Slot** dialog box*

Note

*If you have selected the **Thru Slot** check box from the **Slot** dialog box, you need to define the start and end faces for defining the length value. The faces selected to define the through width should always be normal to the placement face. Select the two faces that are parallel to each other and normal to the placement face. Choose the **OK** button; the **Ball Slot** dialog box will be displayed. Next, specify the slot parameters in their respective edit boxes. In this case, the **Length** edit box will not be available. Figure 6-38 shows the faces selected to define the length of the through slot.*

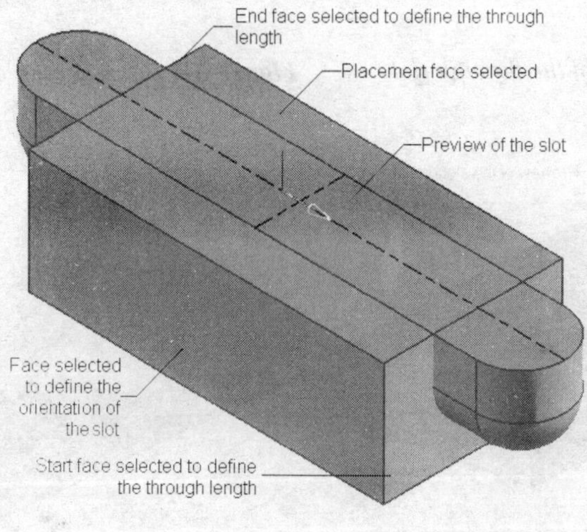

Figure 6-38 Objects selected to create a through slot feature

After specifying the slot parameters, choose the **OK** button from this dialog box; the preview of the slot will be displayed, as shown in Figure 6-39, and the **Positioning** dialog box will be displayed. The tools in this dialog box are used to position the slot.

After positioning the slot, choose the **OK** button in the dialog box to create the slot. Figure 6-40 shows the ball-end slot. Figure 6-41 shows the through ball-end slot created on the model.

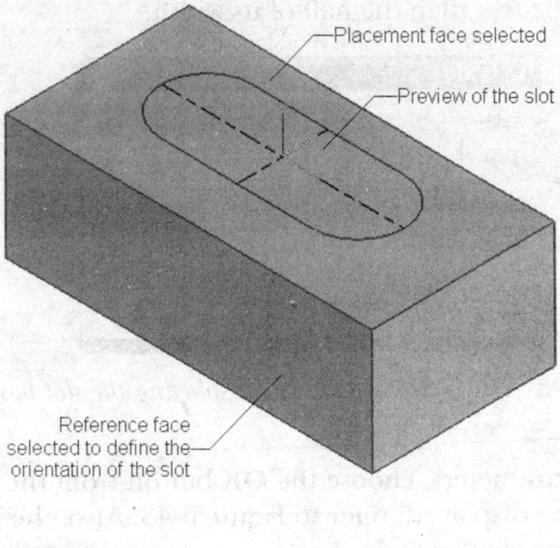

Figure 6-39 The preview of the ball-end slot feature

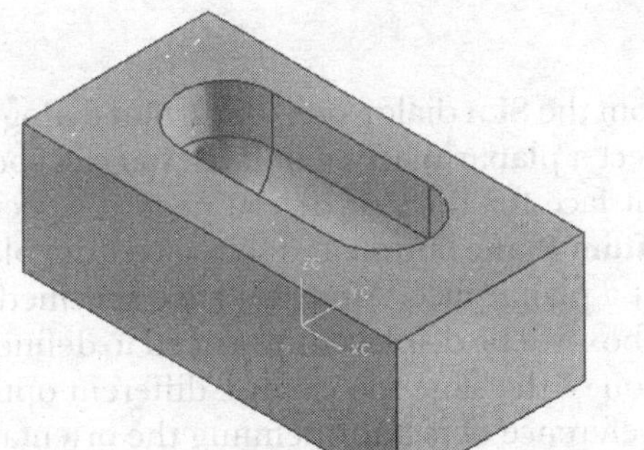

Figure 6-40 The ball-end slot feature

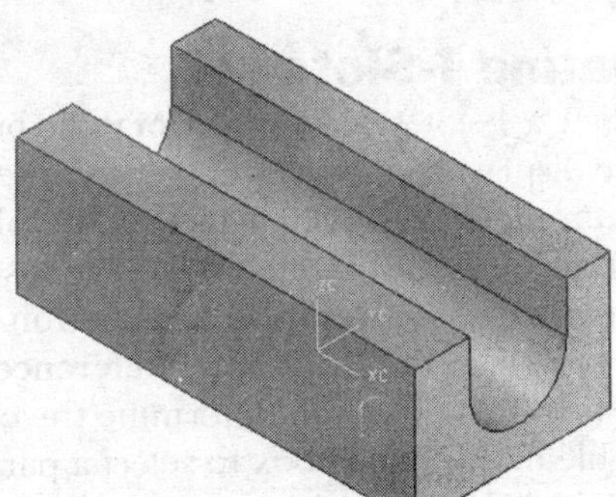

Figure 6-41 The through ball-end slot feature

Creating U-Slots

To create a U-slot, select the **U-Slot** radio button in the **Slot** dialog box; the **U Slot** dialog box will be displayed and you will be prompted to select a planar placement face. You can specify a datum plane or a planar face as the placement face for the slot. If you need to specify a datum plane as the placement face, choose the **Datum Plane** button and select a datum plane. Otherwise, choose the **Solid Face** button and select a planar face. After you have specified the placement face, the **Horizontal Reference** dialog box will be displayed. You need to define the reference object that will determine the orientation of the slot. You can use the options listed in this dialog box to select a particular reference object for defining the orientation of the slot. The U-slot is always oriented parallel to the direction of the reference object selected. Specify the orientation for the slot; the **U Slot** dialog box will be displayed with the default slot parameters, refer to Figure 6-42. Enter the slot parameter values such as corner radius, length, width, and depth in their respective edit boxes in this dialog box. Note that the corner radius of the U-slot must be less than the half of its width.

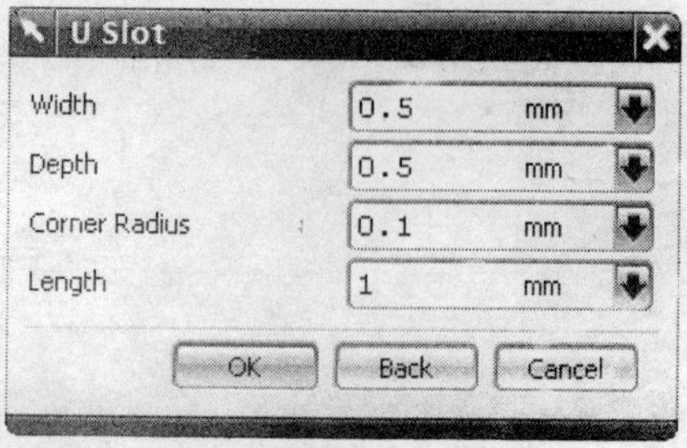

***Figure 6-42** The **U Slot** dialog box displaying the slot parameters*

After specifying the slot parameters, choose the **OK** button from the **U Slot** dialog box; the preview of the U-slot will be displayed, refer to Figure 6-43. Also, the **Positioning** dialog box will be displayed. The options in this dialog box are used to position the slot. After positioning the slot, choose the **OK** button to create the slot. Figure 6-44 shows the preview of the through U-slot with the faces selected to define the length of the slot. Figures 6-45 and 6-46 show the U-slot and through U-slot features, respectively.

Creating T-Slots

To create a T-slot, select the **T-Slot** radio button from the **Slot** dialog box; the **T Slot** dialog box will be displayed and you will be prompted to select a planar placement face. You can specify a datum plane or a planar face as the placement face for the slot. If you need to specify a datum plane as the placement face, choose the **Datum Plane** button and select a datum plane. Otherwise, choose the **Solid Face** button to select a planar face. After you have specified the placement face, the **Horizontal Reference** dialog box will be displayed. You need to define the reference object that will determine the orientation of the slot. You can use different options available in this dialog box to select a particular reference object for defining the orientation of the slot. The slot is always oriented parallel to the direction of the reference object selected. On specifying the orientation of the slot, the slot parameters will be displayed in the **T Slot** dialog box, as shown in Figure 6-47. Enter the slot parameter values such as the top width, top depth, bottom width, bottom depth, and length in their respective edit boxes.

Note

*If you enter the bottom width value less than or equal to the top width value, the **Message** window will be displayed and you will be informed about the same. To fix this error, choose the **OK** button from the same window; the **T Slot** dialog box will be displayed. Now, again enter the bottom width value, which is larger than the top width value.*

After specifying the slot parameters, choose the **OK** button in this dialog box; the preview of the slot will be displayed, refer to Figure 6-48. Also, the **Positioning** dialog box will be displayed. The tools in this dialog box are used to position the slot. After positioning the slot, choose the **OK** button to create the T-slot, refer to Figure 6-49. Figure 6-50 shows the faces selected to define the length of the through T-slot. Figure 6-51 shows the through T-slot created in the model.

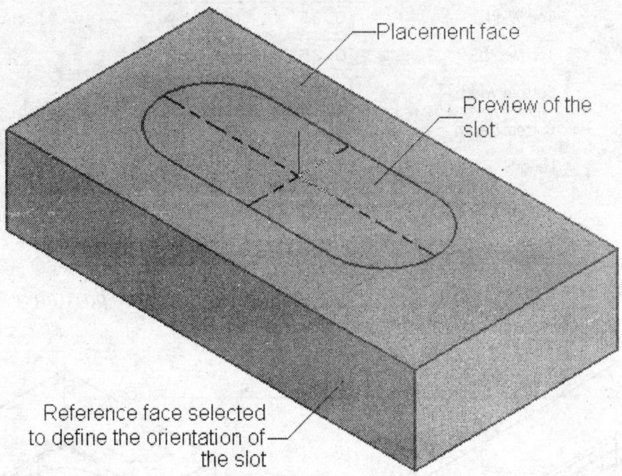

Figure 6-43 The preview of the U-slot feature

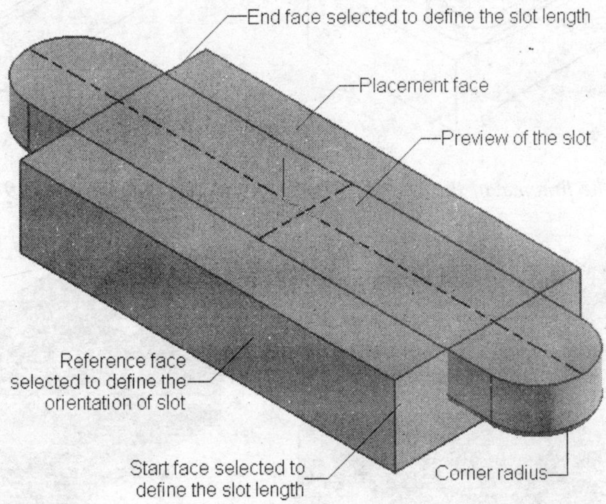

Figure 6-44 The preview of the through U-slot feature

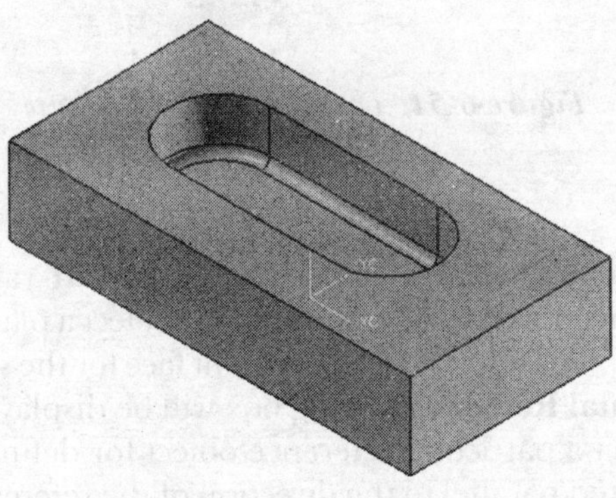

Figure 6-45 The U-slot feature

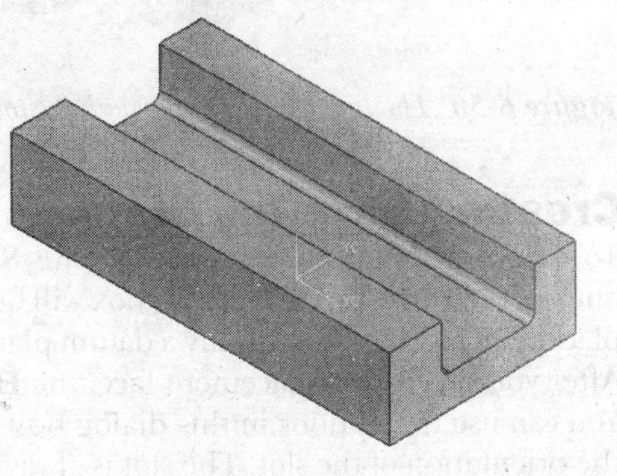

Figure 6-46 The through U-slot feature

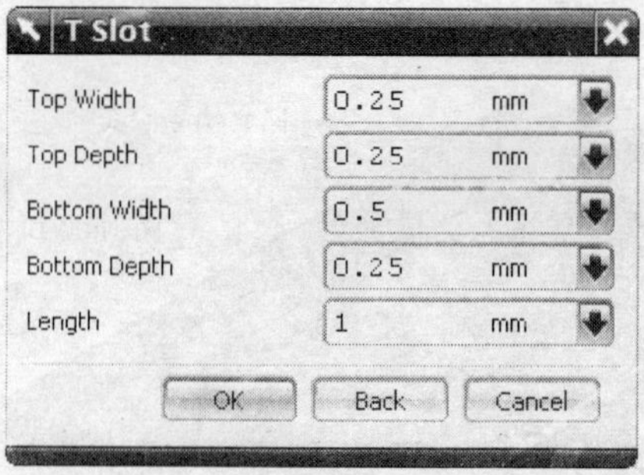

***Figure 6-47** The **T Slot** dialog box displaying the slot parameters*

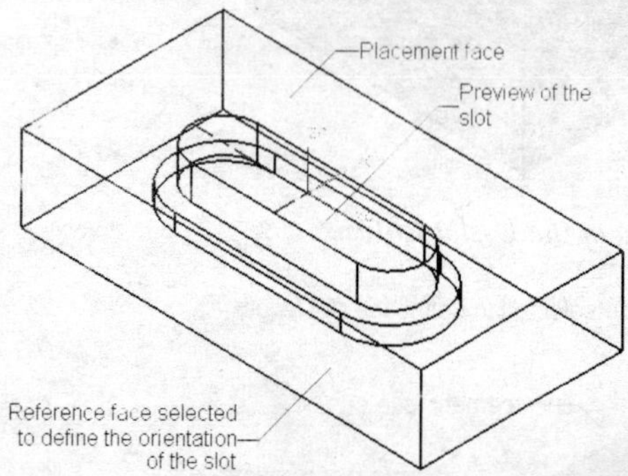

***Figure 6-48** The preview of the T-slot feature*

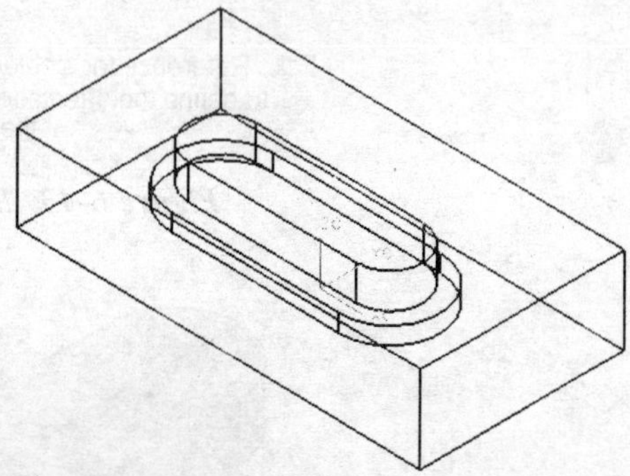

***Figure 6-49** The T-slot feature*

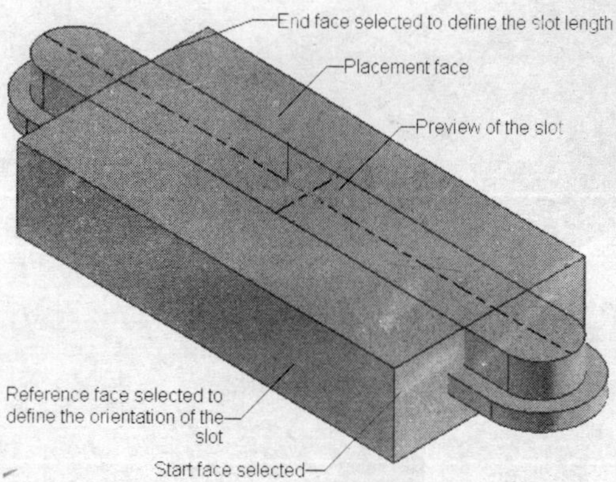

***Figure 6-50** The preview of the through T-slot*

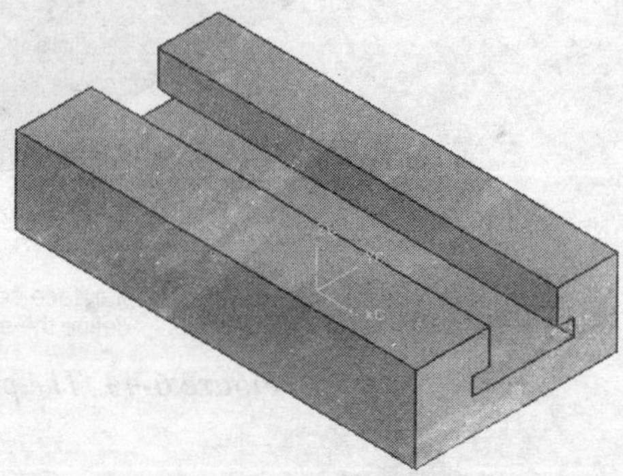

***Figure 6-51** The through T-slot feature*

Creating Dove-Tail Slots

To create a dove-tail slot, invoke the **Slot** dialog box and select the **Dove-Tail** radio button; the **Dove Tail Slot** dialog box will be displayed. You will be prompted to select a planar placement face. You can specify a datum plane or a planar face as the placement face for the slot. After you specify the placement face, the **Horizontal Reference** dialog box will be displayed. You can use the options in this dialog box to select a particular reference object for defining the orientation of the slot. The slot is always oriented parallel to the direction of the reference object selected. On specifying the orientation of the slot, the default slot parameters will be displayed in the **Dove Tail Slot** dialog box, as shown in Figure 6-52. Enter the slot parameter values such as the width, depth, angle, and length in their respective edit boxes.

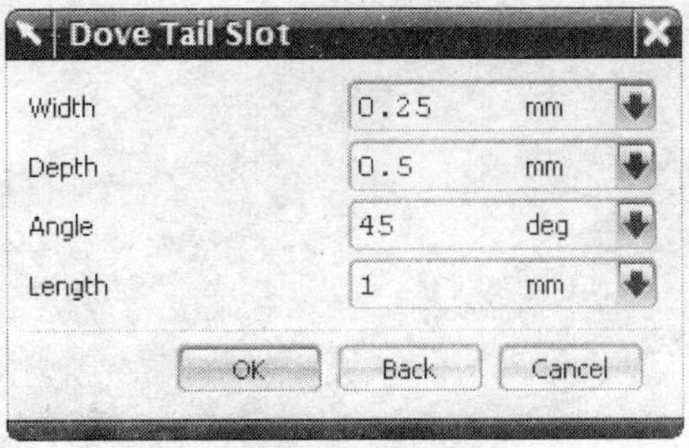

***Figure 6-52** The **Dove Tail Slot** dialog box displaying the slot parameters*

Note

*If you enter an angle value that is greater than or equal to 90, the **Message** window will be displayed and you will be informed that the dove-tail slot angle is invalid. To fix this error, choose the **OK** button from the same window; the **Dove Tail Slot** dialog box will be displayed. Next, enter the angle value that is less than or equal to 89.*

After specifying the slot parameters, choose the **OK** button; the preview of the dove-tail slot feature will be displayed, as shown in Figure 6-53. Also, the **Positioning** dialog box will be displayed. The tools in this dialog box are used to position the slot. After positioning the slot, choose the **OK** button to create the dove-tail slot, as shown in Figure 6-54. Figure 6-55 shows the objects to be selected to create the through dove-tail slot feature and its preview. Figure 6-56 shows the through slots created in the model. Once the slot is created, exit from the dialog box.

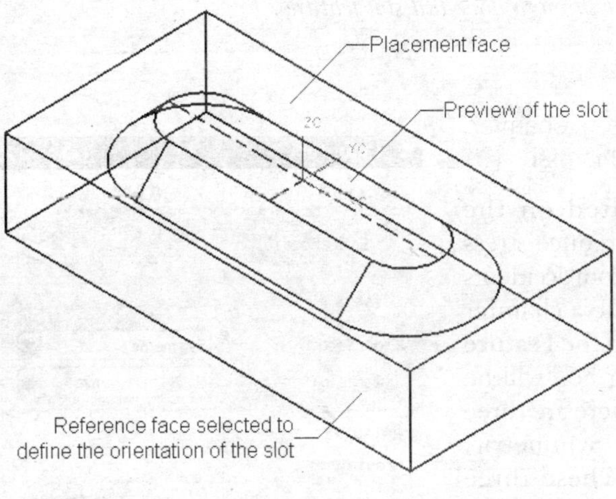

***Figure 6-53** The preview of the dove tail slot feature*

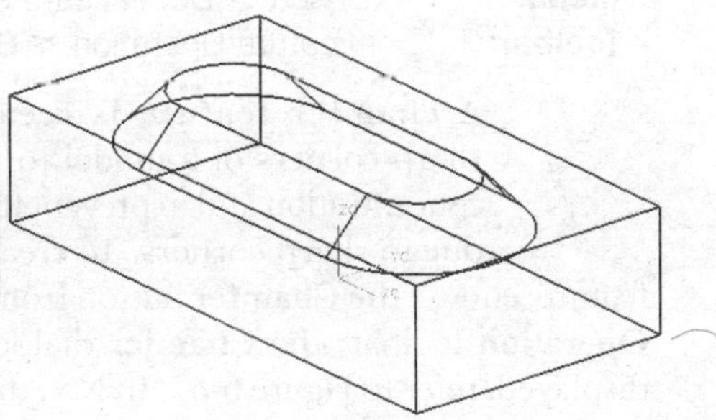

***Figure 6-54** The dove-tail slot feature*

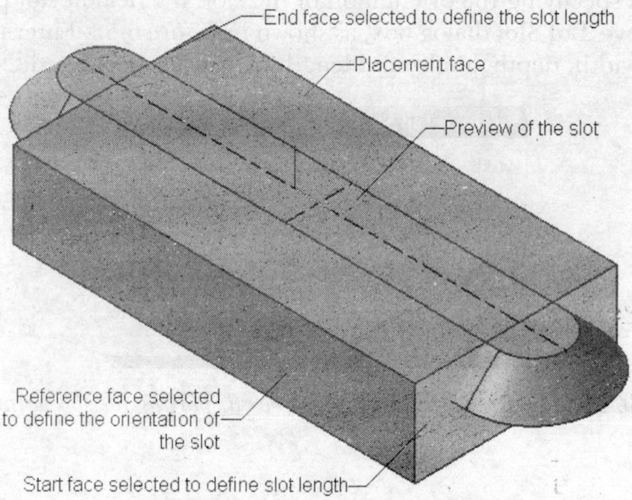

Figure 6-55 The preview of the through dove-tail slot feature

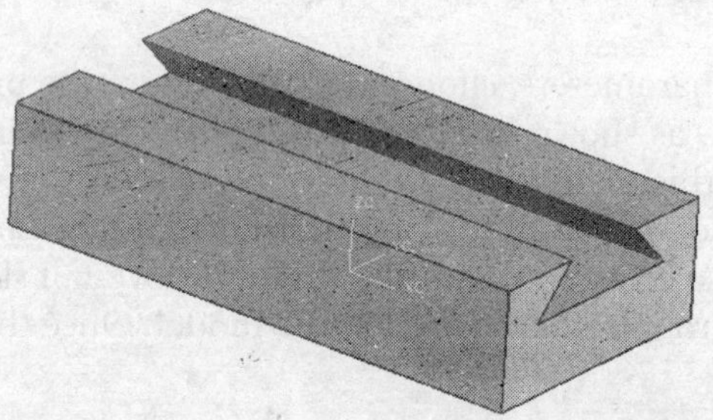

Figure 6-56 The through dove-tail slot feature

CREATING CHAMFERS

Menu: Insert > Detail Feature > Chamfer
Toolbar: Feature Operation > Chamfer

A chamfer feature is created on the sharp corners of a model to reduce stress concentration and to prevent from accidents due to sharp corners. To create a chamfer feature, choose the **Chamfer** button from the **Feature Operation** toolbar; the **Chamfer** dialog box will be displayed, refer to Figure 6-57. In NX, there are three methods to create a chamfer feature, Symmetric, Asymmetric, and Offset and Angle. These three methods are discussed next.

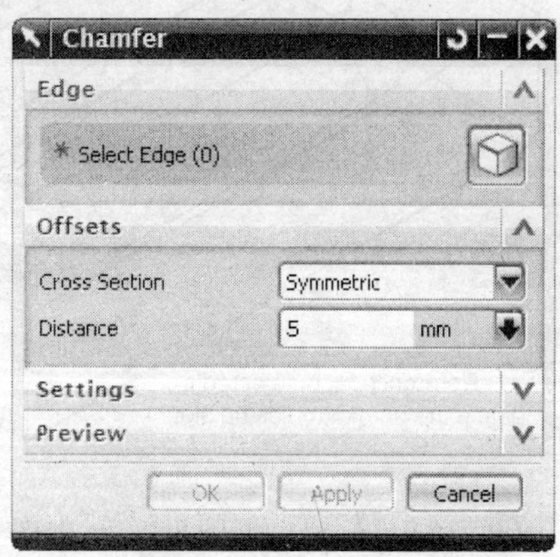

*Figure 6-57 The **Chamfer** dialog box*

Creating a Chamfer Feature Using the Symmetric Method

This method is used to create such chamfers whose distance from the selected edge is equal along both the faces. You need to specify a single positive value for both distances. To create the chamfer feature using the symmetric method, invoke the **Chamfer** dialog box. By default, the **Symmetric** option is selected in the **Cross Section** drop-down list of the **Offset** rollout in the dialog box. Also, you will be prompted to select the edges to chamfer. Select any number of edges to create the chamfer feature. Next, enter the distance value in the **Distance** edit box, which is available below the **Cross Section** drop-down list of the dialog box. This value is taken as the distance value on both sides of the edges. Other rollouts in the **Chamfer** dialog box are discussed next.

Settings Rollout

Expand the **Settings** rollout to define the offset methods. These methods determine how the offset will be used to create the chamfer. The options in this rollout are discussed next.

Offset Edges along Faces

This method is used to create chamfers for simple shapes. The offset values are measured along the faces from the edge being chamfered, refer to Figure 6-58. In this figure, a chamfer is created using the **Offset Edges along Faces** option with the **Distance** value taken as 10mm.

Offset Faces and Trim

This method is used to create chamfers for complex shapes. A chamfer is created by offsetting two surfaces virtually by the specified chamfer distance and dropping normal from the intersection point of the offset surface on the original surface. The chamfer will result between the two points where the normal will intersect with the original surface, refer to Figure 6-59. In this figure, the chamfer is created using the **Offset Faces and Trim** option and with the **Distance** value taken as 10mm.

Chamfer All Instances

This check box allows you to chamfer all instances in the instance set.

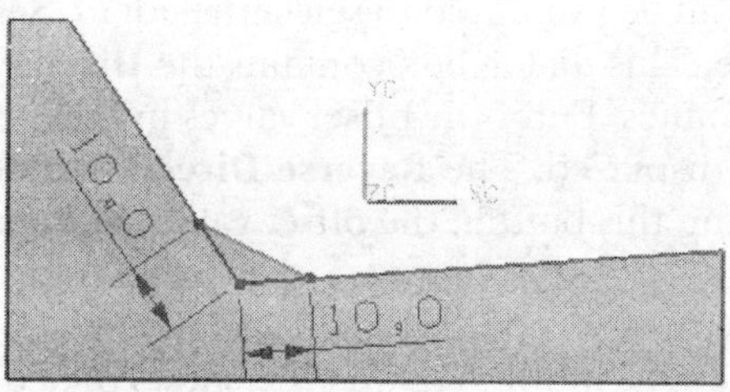

*Figure 6-58 Chamfer created using the **Offset Edges along Faces** option*

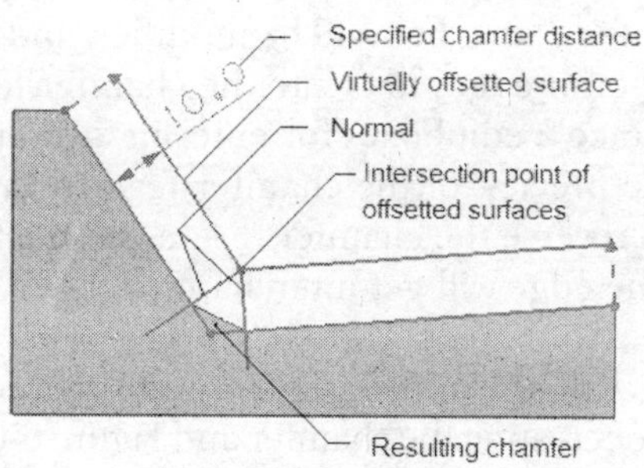

*Figure 6-59 Chamfer created using the **Offset Faces and Trim** option*

Preview Rollout

The options in this rollout are used to preview the chamfer feature.

Preview

This check box is used to preview the chamfer in wireframe.

Show Result / Undo Result

The **Show Result** button is used to preview the chamfer when you create it. After choosing this button, it will change to the **Undo Result** button that can be used to undo the chamfer.

After selecting the appropriate options, choose the **OK** button. Figure 6-60 shows the edges selected for creating the chamfer feature and Figure 6-61 shows the resulting chamfer feature created on the edges of the model.

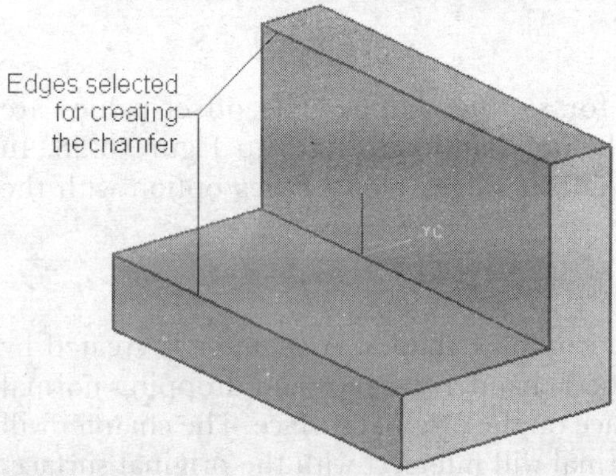

Figure 6-60 *The edges selected for creating the chamfer feature*

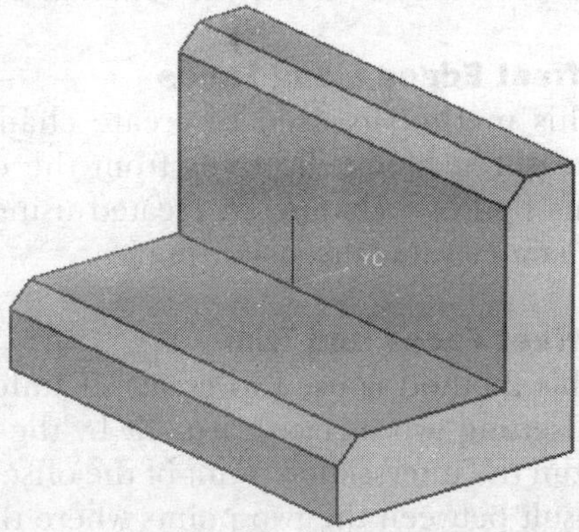

Figure 6-61 *The resulting chamfer feature created at the edges of the model*

Creating a Chamfer Feature Using the Asymmetric Method

This method is used to create the chamfer feature by specifying two different offset values along either side of the edge. To create the chamfer feature using the **Asymmetric** method, select the **Asymmetric** option from the **Cross Section** drop-down list in the **Chamfer** dialog box; the **Chamfer** dialog box will be modified and you will be prompted to select the edges. Select any number of edges to create the chamfer feature. This dialog box contains the **Distance 1** and **Distance 2** edit boxes for entering two offset values. Enter the offset values in these edit boxes; the preview of the chamfer feature will be displayed. The **Reverse Direction** button is used to reverse the chamfer distance. On choosing this button, the offset values of the two sides of the edge will get interchanged.

After selecting the appropriate options, choose the **OK** button. Figure 6-62 shows the edges selected for creating the chamfer and Figure 6-63 shows the resulting chamfer feature created on the edges of the model with two different offset values.

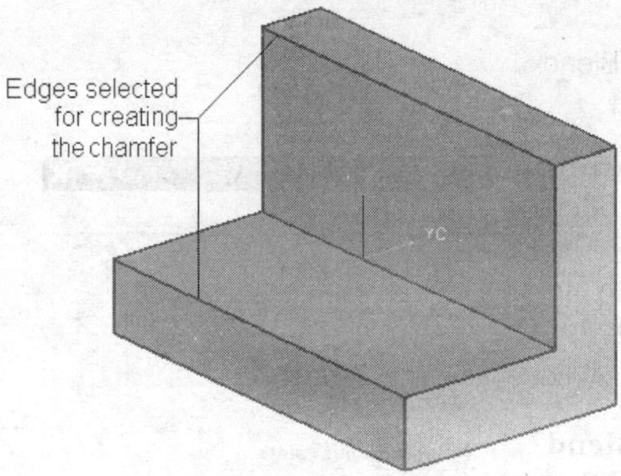

Figure 6-62 The edges selected for creating the chamfer feature

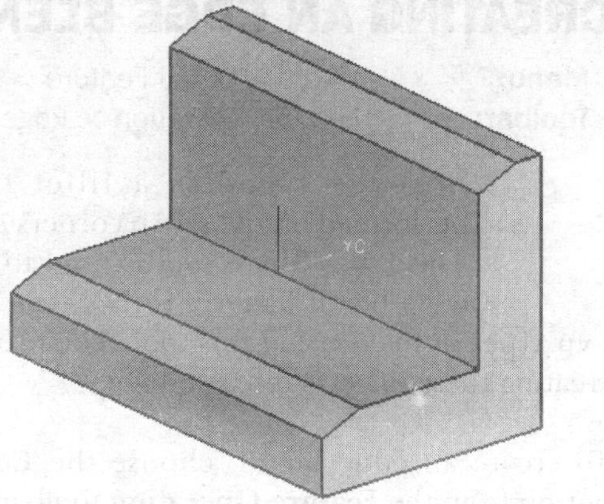

Figure 6-63 The resulting chamfer feature created on the edges with two different offset values

Creating a Chamfer Feature Using the Offset and Angle Method

This method is used to create a chamfer feature by defining an offset value and an angle value. The angle value is used to calculate the second offset value. To create the chamfer feature using the **Offset and Angle** method, select the **Offset and Angle** option from the **Cross Section** drop-down list; you will be prompted to select the edges. Also, the **Distance** and **Angle** edit boxes are displayed in the **Offsets** rollout. You can select any number of edges to create the chamfer feature. After selecting the edges, enter the values in the **Distance** and **Angle** edit boxes and choose the **OK** button. Figure 6-64 shows the edges selected for creating the chamfer feature and Figure 6-65 shows the resulting chamfer feature with an offset and an angle value.

Note

*To reverse the chamfer, choose the **Reverse Direction** button; the offset and angle values get changed from one side of the edge to the other.*

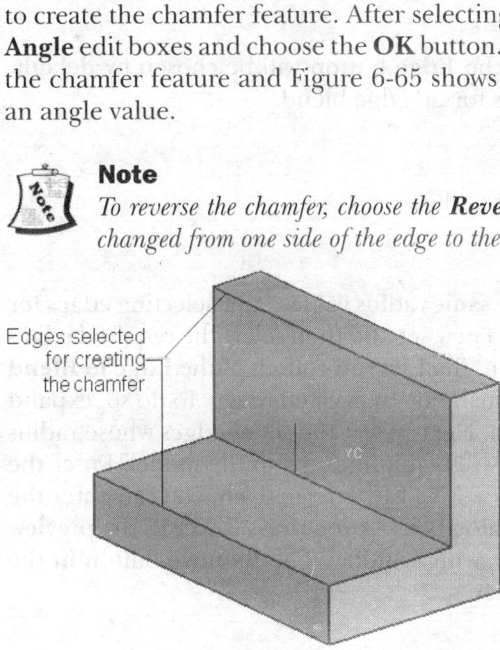

Figure 6-64 The edges selected for creating the chamfer feature

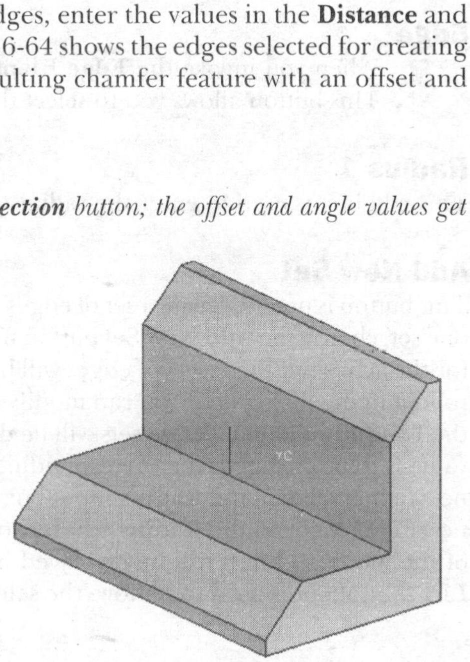

*Figure 6-65 The resulting chamfer feature created using the **Offset and Angle** method*

CREATING AN EDGE BLEND

Menu:	Insert > Detail Feature > Edge Blend
Toolbar:	Feature Operation > Edge Blend

An edge blend is a fillet operation performed on the sharp corners of a model. The **Edge Blend** tool is used to create the edge blend feature. In NX, you can create four types of fillets using this tool. The procedure for creating these fillets is discussed next.

To create an edge blend, choose the **Edge Blend** button from the **Feature Operation** toolbar; the **Edge Blend** dialog box will be displayed, refer to Figure 6-66. Also, you will be prompted to select the edges for the new set. Various rollouts in this dialog box are discussed next.

*Figure 6-66 The **Edge Blend** dialog box*

Edge to Blend Rollout

This rollout allows you to select the edges for an edge blend. Also, you can assign the radius value for edge blend in this rollout. The options in this rollout are as follows:

Edge

When you invoke the **Edge Blend** tool, the **Edge** button will be chosen by default. This button allows you to select the edges for an edge blend.

Radius 1

This edit box is used to enter the radius value for a fillet.

Add New Set

This button is used to create a set of edges with the same radius value. After selecting edges for one set, choose the **Add New Set** button to create a new set and then select the required edges for the active set; these sets of edges will be listed in the **List** sub-rollout of the **Edge to Blend** rollout in the dialog box. You can modify the radius value of each edge set. To do so, expand the **List** sub-rollout; all edge sets will be displayed. Next, select the set of edges whose radius value is to be changed; the corresponding edges will be highlighted in the model. Enter the new radius value in the **Radius** input box and press ENTER. Alternatively, you can enter the new radius value in the **Radius** edit box of the dialog box. As you press ENTER, the preview of the modified fillets will be displayed in the drawing window. The **Remove** button in the **List** sub-rollout is used to remove the selected edge set.

Note

You can complete an edge set by pressing the middle mouse button. The edge sets can be identified by a spherical handle in the drawing window.

Figure 6-67 shows the edges selected for creating the edge blend and Figure 6-68 shows the resulting edge blend feature.

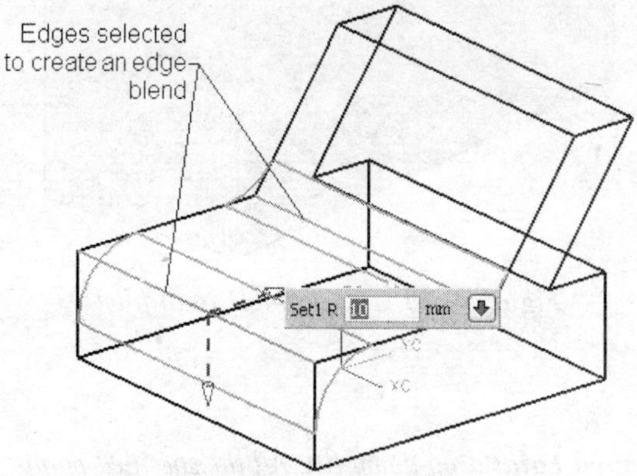

Figure 6-67 *Edges selected for edge blend*

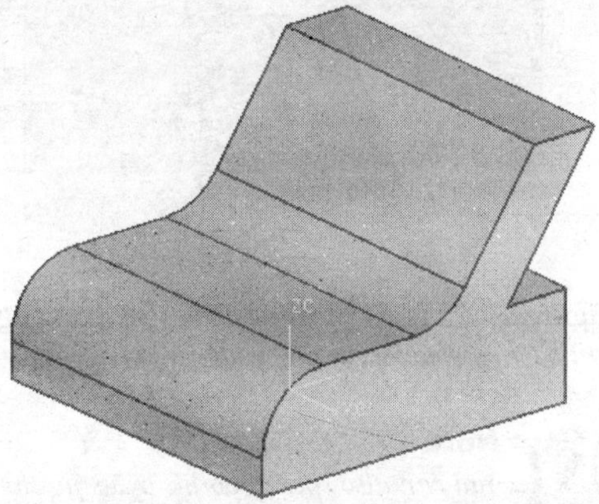

Figure 6-68 *The resulting edge blend feature*

Variable Radius Points Rollout

This rollout allows you to create the fillet with variable radii specified at different keypoints on an edge. To create the variable radius fillets, you need to follow three steps. The first step is to select the placement edge, second is to specify the keypoints for defining the multiple radii, and the third is to specify the radius value at each keypoint. Follow the steps given below to create the variable radii fillet:

1. Select the edge to create the variable radii edge blend and expand the **Variable Radius Points** rollout. This rollout has different options for specifying the keypoints.

2 Choose the **Point Constructor** button; the **Point** dialog box will be displayed and you will be prompted to select the object to infer a point.

3. Select a point on the edge and choose the **OK** button; the **Variable Radius Points** rollout will be modified. Also, the **V Radius 1** and **% Arc length** input edit boxes will be displayed on the model, refer to Figure 6-69.

4. You can locate the point using the options in the **Location** drop-down list. These options have already been discussed earlier.

5. Enter the radius value for this point in the **V Radius 1** edit box.

6. Similarly, specify multiple points and then radius value at each point. Figure 6-70 shows the variable radii fillet created on the edge.

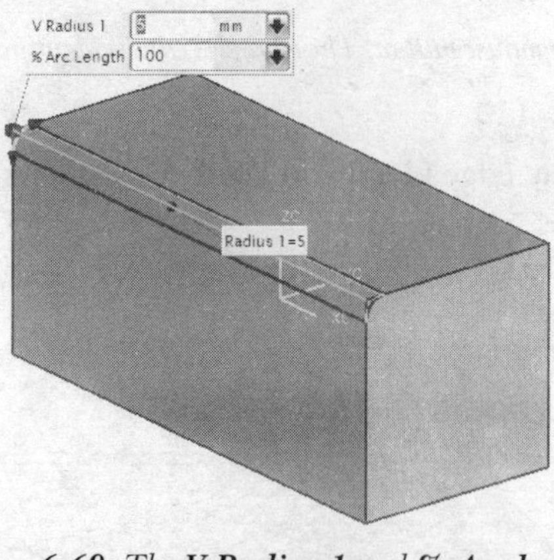

*Figure 6-69 The **V Radius 1** and **% Arc length** edit boxes displayed on the model*

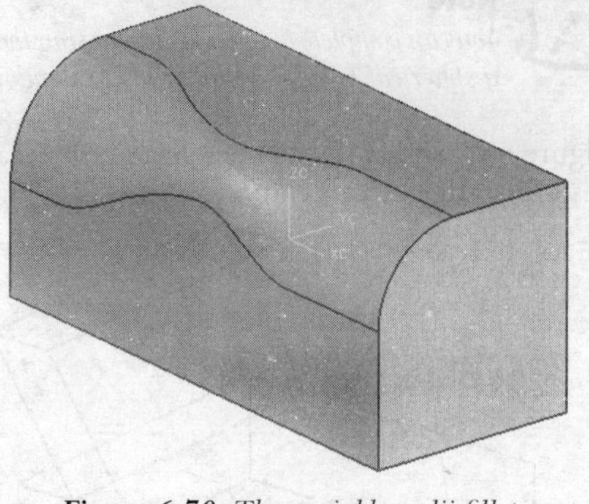

Figure 6-70 The variable radii fillet

Note

*You can also specify points by using the **Inferred Point** drop-down list. All the specified points will be listed in the **List** sub-rollout. You can modify the radius value at each point. To do so, expand the **List** rollout; all the specified points will be displayed. Next, select the point at which the radius value is to be changed and enter a new radius value in the respective edit box. The **Remove** button in the **List** rollout is used to remove the specified points.*

Corner Setback Rollout

The **Corner Setback** rollout is used to create a corner blend by smoothening the corner. Note that to create this type of corner blend, you need to select three or more edges that meet at a corner and then expand the **Corner Setback** rollout. Next, choose the **Point** button from the **Corner Setback** rollout; you will be prompted to select the vertex point to specify the setback distance. Select the corner point by using the left mouse button; the drag handles will be displayed along with the input edit boxes, refer to Figure 6-71. These drag handles are used to smoothen corners. By default, all handles are equally spaced and placed. You can modify this distance by dynamically dragging the handles or by entering the setback values in the respective edit boxes. To accept the corner edge blend, choose the **OK** button in the **Edge Blend** dialog box; the resulting corner edge blend will be displayed, as shown in Figure 6-72.

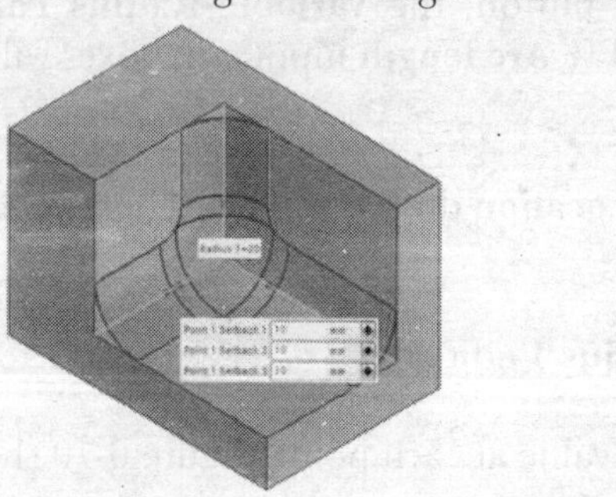

Figure 6-71 The preview of the corner edge blend

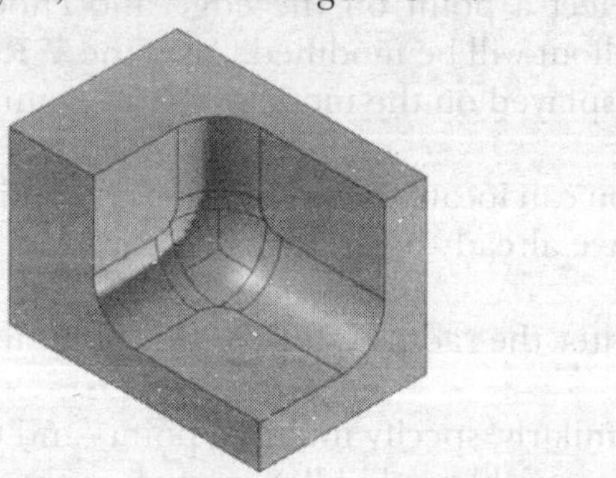

Figure 6-72 The resulting corner edge blend

Note

To specify the same offset value for all the three drag handles, select the corner point; the three input edit boxes will be displayed. Enter the same offset value in all the three edit boxes and press the ENTER key.

Stop Short of Corner Rollout

This rollout is used to create the fillet that can be limited to a desired distance on the selected edge. The specified length will be ignored and will not be filleted. Remember that the length can be ignored only from the endpoints of the selected edge and not at any intermediate portion.

Select an edge to create the stop short fillet and expand the **Stop Short of Corner** rollout. Next, choose the **Point** button; you will be prompted to select the vertex for specifying stop-short. You need to specify the point from where you need to limit the fillet. Note that only the **End Point** button will be available in the **Selection Bar**. This is because you can select only the endpoints from the edge. On selecting one of the endpoints, the **Arc Length** edit box will be displayed. Also, a stop short handle will be displayed on the selected endpoint. Enter the distance value in the **Arc Length** edit box. You can specify the distance value dynamically by dragging the stop short handle to a point on the selected edge. Note that you can specify the stop-short distance from both the ends of the selected edge. After entering the stop short value, press the ENTER key; the preview of the stop short fillet will be dynamically modified. To accept the stop short fillet, choose the **OK** button from the **Edge Blend** dialog box. The resulting stop short fillet is shown in Figure 6-73.

Figure 6-73 *The resulting stop short fillet*

Note

If there are two separate bodies and you are creating a fillet at one edge of a body, then the resulting fillet will be convex shaped, as shown in Figure 6-74. If you are creating a fillet at the common edge of two features of a solid body, then the resulting fillet will be concave shaped, as shown in Figure 6-75.

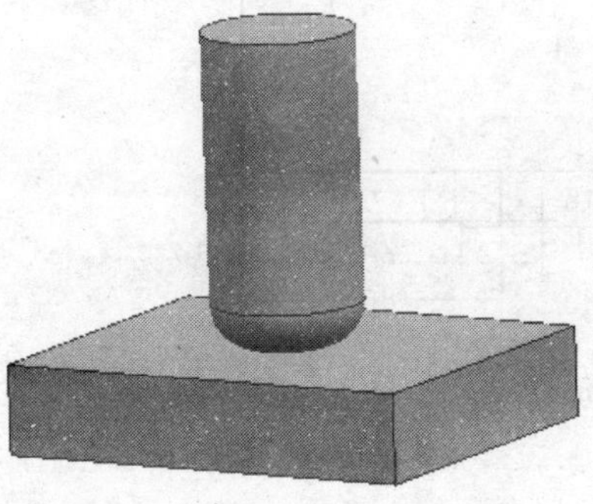

Figure 6-74 *Resulting fillet between two separate part bodies*

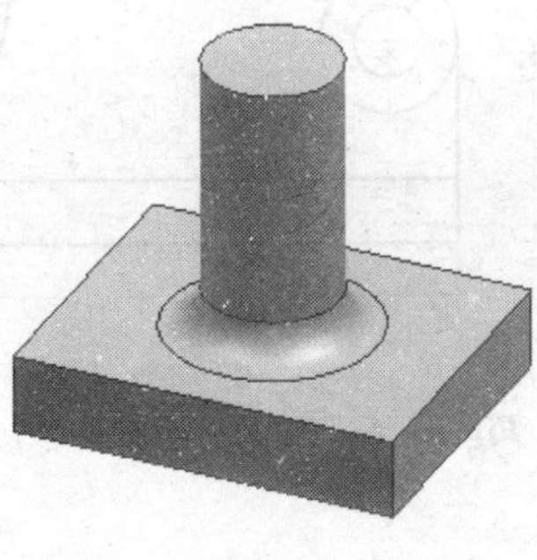

Figure 6-75 *Resulting fillet between the united part body*

TUTORIALS

Tutorial 1

In this tutorial, you will create the model shown in Figure 6-76. The dimensions of the model are shown in Figure 6-78. After creating the model, save it with the name *c06tut1.prt* at the location *\NX 7\c06.*

(Expected time: 30 min)

Figure 6-76 Solid model for Tutorial 1

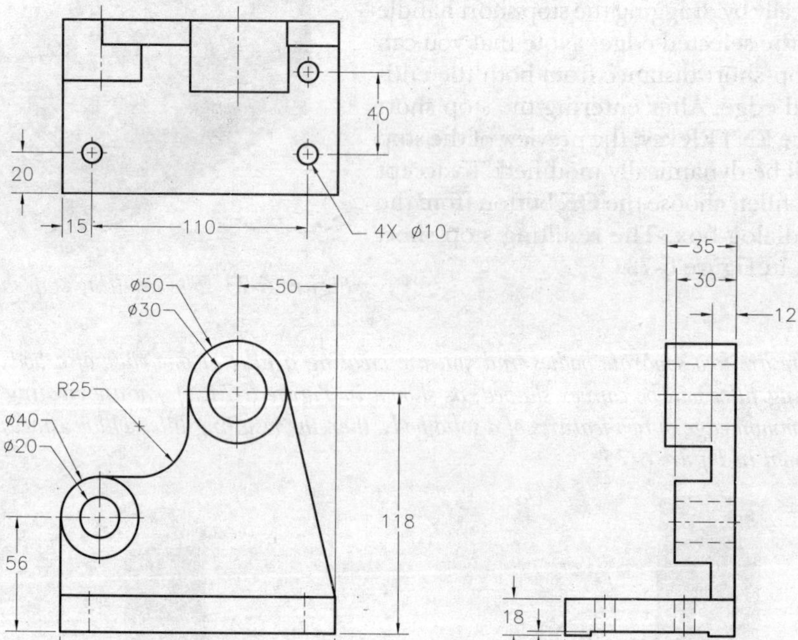

Figure 6-77 The drawing views and dimensions of the model for Tutorial 1

The following steps are required to complete this tutorial:

a. Draw the sketch for the base feature and extrude it.
b. Draw the sketch for the second feature and extrude it.
c. Draw the sketch for the third feature and extrude it.
d. Draw the sketch for the fourth feature and extrude it.
e. Create two holes on the side face of the model using the **Hole** tool.
f. Create four holes on the top face of the base feature using the **Hole** tool.
g. Save and close the file.

Creating the Base Feature of the Model

The base feature will be created using the profile of the right face of the model.

1. Start a new file with the name *c06tut1.prt* using the **Model** template and specify its location as *C:\NX 7\c06.*

2. Invoke the Sketcher environment by using the YC-ZC plane and draw the sketch, as shown in Figure 6-78.

3. Choose the **Finish Sketch** button from the **Sketcher** toolbar to exit from the Sketcher environment.

4. Choose the **Extrude** button from the **Feature** toolbar; the **Extrude** dialog box is displayed and you are prompted to select the planar face to sketch or select the section geometry. Select the sketch created for the base feature from the drawing window.

5. Select the **Symmetric Value** option from the **Start** drop-down list and enter **70** in the **Distance** edit box.

6. Choose the **Apply** button and then close the dialog box by choosing the **Cancel** button. The resulting base feature is shown in Figure 6-79.

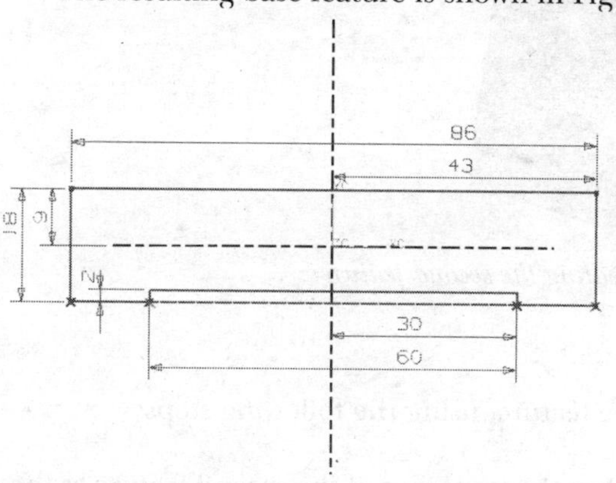

***Figure 6-78** Sketch for the base feature*

***Figure 6-79** The resulting base feature*

Creating the Second Feature

Follow the steps discussed next to create the second feature.

1. Invoke the **Create Sketch** dialog box by choosing the **Sketch** button from the **Feature** toolbar and selecting the back face of the base feature as the sketching plane.

2. Draw the sketch for the second feature, as shown in Figure 6-80.

3. Choose the **Finish Sketch** button from the **Sketcher** toolbar to exit the Sketcher environment.

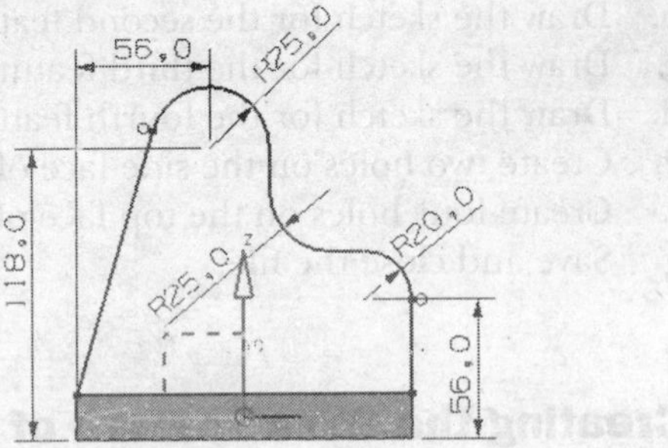

Figure 6-80 *Sketch for the second feature*

4. Choose the **Extrude** button from the **Feature** toolbar; you are prompted to select the planar face to sketch or select the section geometry.

5. Select the sketch created for the second feature. Next, enter **0** and **12** in the **Distance** edit boxes available below the **Start** and **End** drop-down lists, respectively, in the **Limits** rollout of the dialog box. Make sure the sketch is being extruded in the front direction.

6. Select the **Unite** option from the **Boolean** drop-down list in the **Boolean** rollout of the dialog box.

7. Choose the **Apply** button and then close the dialog box by choosing the **Cancel** button. The resulting model after creating the second feature is shown in Figure 6-81.

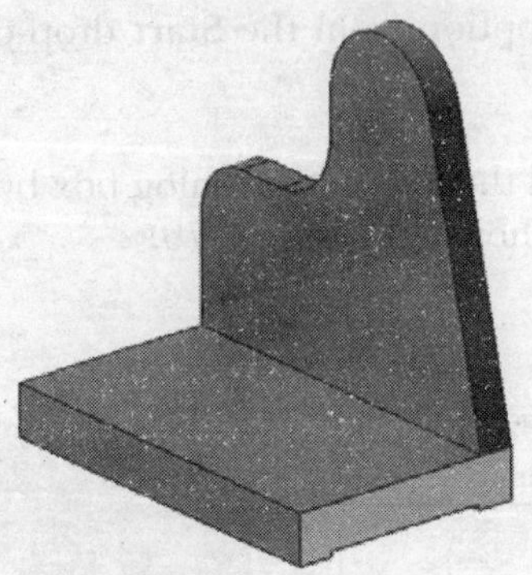

Figure 6-81 *Model after creating the second feature*

Creating the Third Feature

Create the third feature, which is an extrude feature, using the following steps:

1. Invoke the **Create Sketch** dialog box and select the front face of the second feature as the sketching plane; the Sketcher environment is invoked.

2. Draw the sketch for the third feature, which is a circle of 50 mm diameter, as shown in Figure 6-82.

3. Choose the **Finish Sketch** button from the **Sketcher** toolbar to exit the Sketcher environment.

4. Choose the **Extrude** button from the **Feature** toolbar; the **Extrude** dialog box is displayed and you are prompted to select the planar face to sketch or select the section geometry.

5. Select the sketch created for the third feature and enter **23** in the **Distance** edit box below the **End** drop-down list in the **Limits** rollout of the dialog box. Make sure the sketch is being extruded toward the screen.

6. Select the **Unite** option from the **Boolean** drop-down list in the **Boolean** rollout of the dialog box.

7. Choose the **OK** button from the dialog box. The model after creating the third feature is shown in Figure 6-83.

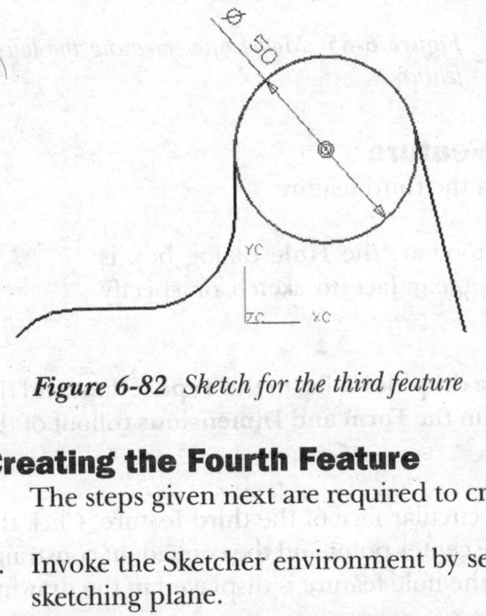

Figure 6-82 Sketch for the third feature

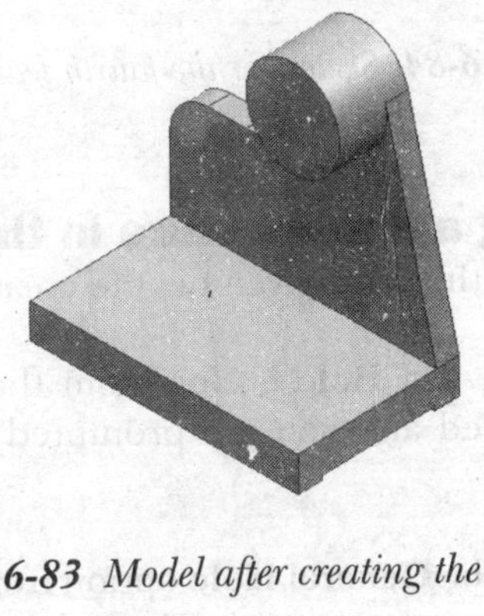

Figure 6-83 Model after creating the third feature

Creating the Fourth Feature

The steps given next are required to create the fourth feature.

1. Invoke the Sketcher environment by selecting the front face of the second feature as the sketching plane.

2. Draw the sketch for the fourth feature, which is a circle of 40 mm diameter, as shown in Figure 6-84.

3. Choose the **Finish Sketch** button from the **Sketcher** toolbar to exit the Sketcher environment.

4. Choose the **Extrude** button from the **Feature** toolbar; the **Extrude** dialog box is displayed and you are prompted to select the planar face to sketch or select the section geometry.

5. Select the sketch created for the fourth feature and enter **18** in the **Distance** edit box available below the **End** drop-down list. Make sure the sketch is being extruded toward the front.

6. Select the **Unite** option from the **Boolean** drop-down list in the **Boolean** rollout of the dialog box.

7. Choose the **OK** button from the dialog box. The resulting model after creating the fourth feature is shown in Figure 6-85.

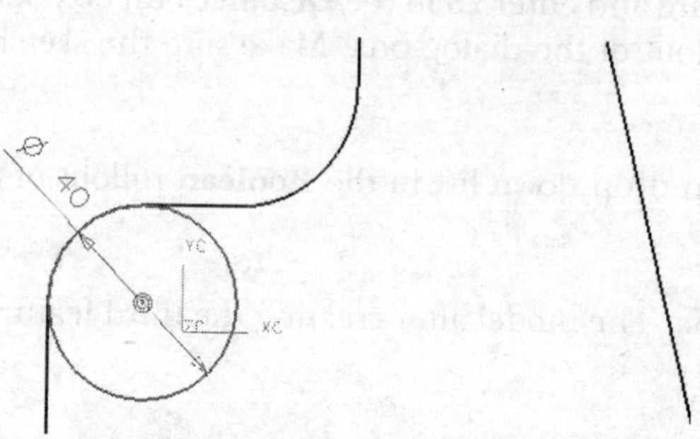

Figure 6-84 Sketch for the fourth feature

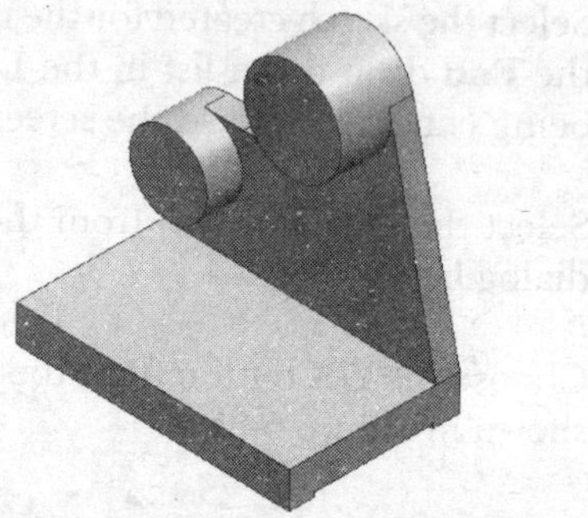

Figure 6-85 Model after creating the fourth feature

Creating a Hole Feature in the Third Feature

Follow the steps given next to create a hole in the third feature.

1. Choose the **Hole** button from the **Feature** toolbar; the **Hole** dialog box is displayed and you are prompted to select planar face to sketch or specify points.

2. Select the **General Hole** option from the **Type** drop-down list in the **Type** rollout and the **Simple** option from the **Form** drop-down list in the **Form and Dimensions** rollout of the dialog box, if they are not selected by default.

3. Move the cursor over the center point of the circular face of the third feature. Click the left mouse button when the cursor snaps to the center point and the coincident constraint is displayed below the cursor. The preview of the hole feature is displayed in the drawing window.

4. Enter **30** in the **Diameter** edit box of the **Dimensions** sub-rollout.

5. Select the **Through Body** option from the **Depth Limit** drop-down list in the **Dimensions** sub-rollout. Next, select the **Subtract** option from the **Boolean** drop-down list.

6. Accept the other default settings and choose the **OK** button from the dialog box; a hole is created in the third feature, as shown in Figure 6-86.

Creating a Hole Feature in the Fourth Feature

Create a hole in the fourth feature using the following steps:

1. Choose the **Hole** button from the **Feature** toolbar; the **Hole** dialog box is displayed and you are prompted to select a planar face to sketch or specify points.

2. Move the cursor over the center point of the circular face of the fourth feature; the center point is highlighted. Now, select it; the preview of the hole is displayed in the drawing window.

3. Enter **20** in the **Diameter** edit box in the **Dimensions** sub-rollout.

4. Select the **Through Body** option from the **Depth Limit** drop-down list in the **Dimensions** sub-rollout of the dialog box.

5. Accept the other default settings and choose the **OK** button from the **Hole** dialog box; a hole is created in the fourth feature, as shown in Figure 6-87.

Figure 6-86 Model after creating the hole in the third feature

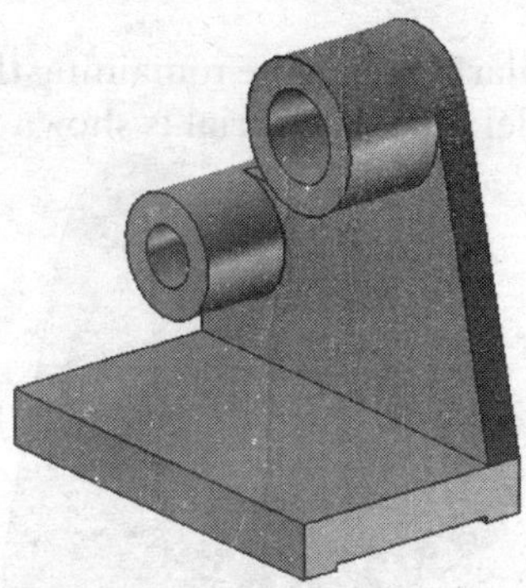

Figure 6-87 Model after creating the hole in the fourth feature

Creating Four Holes in the Base Feature

To complete the model, you need to create four holes in the base feature by using the steps discussed next.

1. Choose the **Hole** button from the **Feature** toolbar; the **Hole** dialog box is displayed and you are prompted to select a planar face to sketch or specify points.

2. Select the top face of the base feature as the planar placement plane; the **Point** dialog box is displayed and you are prompted to define a point. Also, the Sketcher environment is invoked

3. Specify a point anywhere on the face and then choose the **OK** button from the **Point** dialog box. Now, apply the dimension to the point, as shown in Figure 6-88.

4. Choose the **Finish Sketch** button from the **Sketcher** toolbar to exit from the Sketcher environment. As you exit from the Sketcher environment, the **Hole** dialog box is displayed again. Also, the preview of the hole is displayed. Note that the center of the hole is at the point that you have specified using the **Point** dialog box.

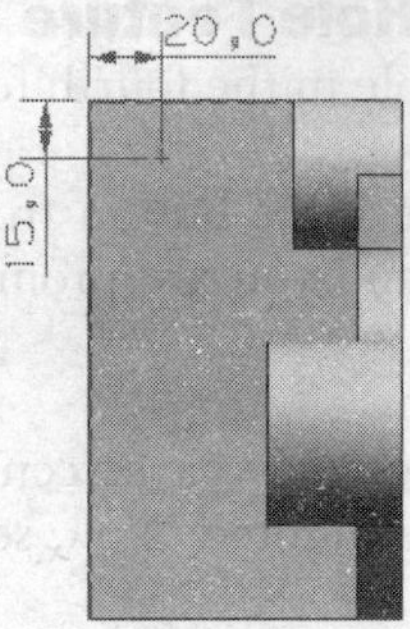

Figure 6-88 Point after applying the dimension

5. Enter **10** as the diameter of the hole in the **Diameter** edit box of the **Dimensions** sub-rollout in the **Hole** dialog box.

6. Select the **Through Body** option from the **Depth Limit** drop-down list in the **Dimensions** sub-rollout of the dialog box.

7. Accept the other default settings and choose the **OK** button from the dialog box; a hole is created in the base feature, as shown in Figure 6-89.

8. Similarly, create the remaining three holes. Refer to Figure 6-77 for dimensions. The final model for this tutorial is shown in Figure 6-90.

Figure 6-89 Model after creating the first hole in the base feature

Figure 6-90 Final model after creating all the four holes in the base feature

Saving and Closing the File

1. Choose **File > Close > Save and Close** from the menu bar to save and close the file.

Tutorial 2

In this tutorial, you will create the model shown in Figure 6-91. The drawing views and the dimensions are shown in Figure 6-92. After creating the model, save it with the name *c06tut2.prt* at the location *\NX 7\c06.* **(Expected time: 30 min)**

Figure 6-91 Model for Tutorial 2

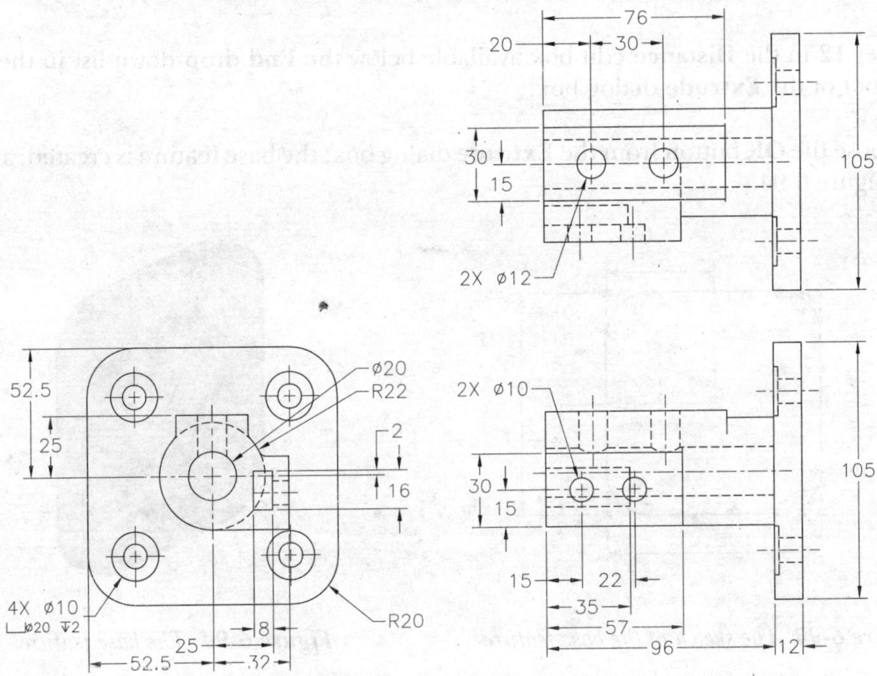

Figure 6-92 The drawing views and the dimensions of the model for Tutorial 2

The following steps are required to complete this tutorial:

a. Draw the sketch of the base feature of the model and extrude it.
b. Draw the sketch of the second feature, which is a circle, and extrude it.
c. Draw the sketch of the third and fourth features and extrude them.
d. Create the simple hole on the left face of the model using the **Hole** tool.
e. Create the rectangular cut extrude feature.
f. Create holes on the top and front faces of the model using the **Hole** tool.
g. Create four counterbore holes in the base feature using the **Hole** tool.
h. Save and close the file.

Creating the Base Feature of the Model

After starting a new file, you need to create the sketch of the base feature of the model by following the steps given next.

1. Start a new file with the name *c06tut2.prt* using the **Model** template and specify its location as *C:\NX 7\c06*.

2. Invoke the Sketcher environment by using the XC-ZC plane as the sketching plane and draw the sketch of the base feature, as shown in Figure 6-93. Next, exit the Sketcher environment.

3. Choose the **Extrude** button from the **Feature** toolbar; the **Extrude** dialog box is displayed and you are prompted to select the sketch to be extruded. Select the sketch created for the base feature.

4. Enter **12** in the **Distance** edit box available below the **End** drop-down list in the **Limits** rollout of the **Extrude** dialog box.

5. Choose the **OK** button from the **Extrude** dialog box; the base feature is created, as shown in Figure 6-94.

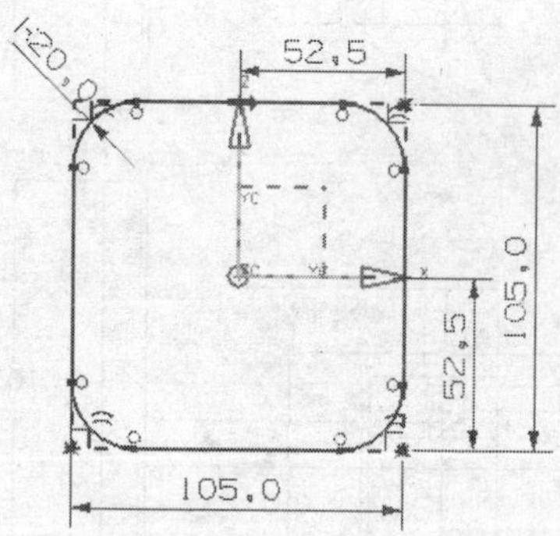

Figure 6-93 *The sketch of the base feature*

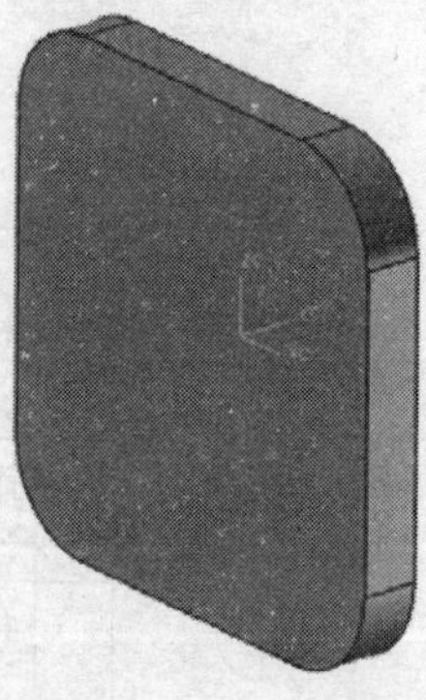

Figure 6-94 *The base feature*

Creating the Second Feature

The second feature of the model is a cylindrical extrude feature. The following steps explain the procedure to create this feature:

1. Invoke the Sketcher environment by selecting the front face of the base feature as the sketching plane.

2. Draw the sketch for the second feature, which is a circle of 44 diameter, refer to Figure 6-95. Next, choose the **Finish Sketch** button from the **Sketcher** toolbar to exit from the Sketcher environment.

3. Choose the **Extrude** button from the **Feature** toolbar; the **Extrude** dialog box is displayed and you are prompted to select a sketch.

4. Select the sketch created for the second feature and enter **96** in the **Distance** edit box available below the **End** drop-down list in the **Limits** rollout of the **Extrude** dialog box.

5. Select the **Unite** option from the **Boolean** drop-down list in the **Boolean** rollout.

6. Choose the **OK** button from the dialog box; the cylindrical extrude feature is created. The model after creating the second feature is shown in Figure 6-96.

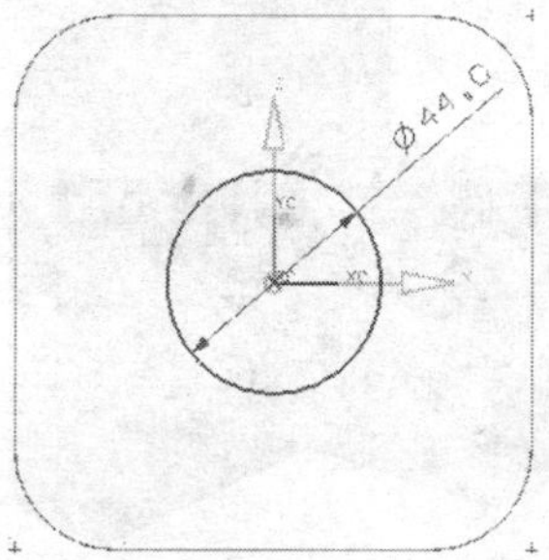

Figure 6-95 *The sketch for the second feature*

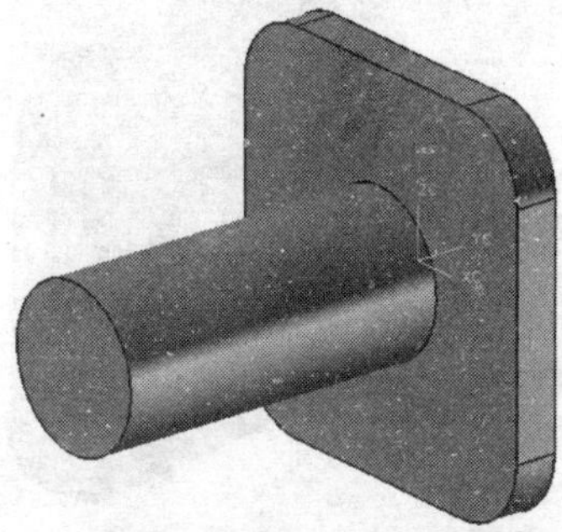

Figure 6-96 *Model after creating the second feature*

Creating the Third and Fourth Features

Create the third and fourth features, which are extrude features, by using the following steps:

1. Invoke the Sketcher environment by selecting the front face of the second feature as a sketching plane.

2. Draw the rectangular sketch for the third feature by using the dimensions given in Figure 6-92.

3. Choose the **Finish Sketch** button from the **Sketcher** toolbar to exit from the Sketcher environment.

4. Choose the **Extrude** button from the **Feature** toolbar; the **Extrude** dialog box is displayed. Select the sketch created for the third feature; the preview of the feature is displayed in the drawing window.

5. Reverse the direction of extrusion by choosing the **Reverse Direction** button from the **Direction** rollout of the dialog box.

6. Enter **76** as the depth value in the **Distance** edit box available below the **End** drop-down

list of the **Limits** rollout in the dialog box. Also, select the **Unite** option from the **Boolean** drop-down list in the **Boolean** rollout. Make sure the value in the **Distance** edit box available below the **Start** drop-down list is 0.

7. Choose the **OK** button from the dialog box; the extruded feature is created. The resulting model after creating the third feature is shown in Figure 6-97.

8. Similarly, create the fourth extruded feature by using the dimensions given in Figure 6-92. The model after creating the fourth feature is shown in Figure 6-98.

Figure 6-97 The resulting model after creating the third feature

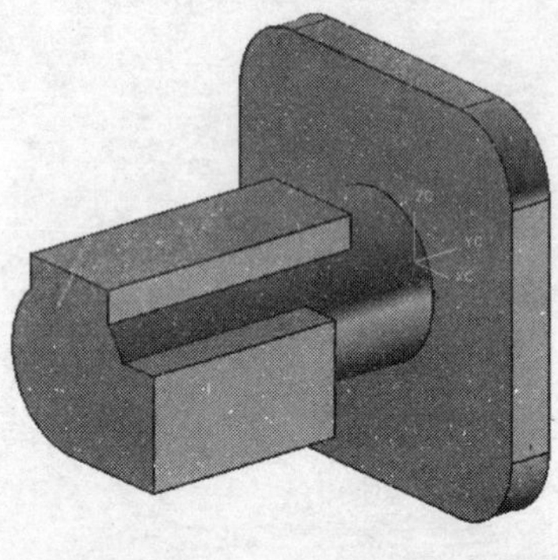

Figure 6-98 The model after creating the fourth feature

Creating the Hole Feature in the Model

Create a hole in the second feature by using the following steps:

1. Choose the **Hole** button from the **Feature** toolbar; the **Hole** dialog box is displayed and you are prompted to specify a point.

2. Select the center point of the front circular face of the second feature as the placement point; the preview of the hole feature is displayed in the drawing window. Make sure the **General Hole** and **Simple** options are selected in the **Type** and the **Form** drop-down lists, respectively, in their rollouts.

3. Enter **20** in the **Diameter** edit box. Next, select the **Value** option from the **Depth Limit** drop-down list and enter **96** in the **Depth** edit box. Also, enter **0** in the **Tip Angle** edit box in the **Dimensions** sub-rollout of the **Hole** dialog box.

4. Accept the other default settings and choose the **OK** button from the dialog box; a hole is created, as shown in Figure 6-99.

Creating the Rectangular Cut Extrude Feature

Create the rectangular cut extrude feature by using the following steps:

1. Invoke the Sketcher environment by selecting the front face of the fourth feature, which is merged with the front face of the second feature, as the sketching plane.

2. Draw the sketch of this feature by using the dimensions given in Figure 6-92. Choose the **Finish Sketch** button from the **Sketcher** toolbar to exit the Sketcher environment.

3. Choose the **Extrude** button from the **Feature** toolbar and select the sketch created for the feature; the preview of the feature is displayed in the drawing window. Reverse the direction of feature creation by using the **Reverse Direction** button, if required.

4. Enter the depth value **50** in the **Distance** edit box available below the **End** drop-down list. Make sure the value in the **Distance** edit box available below the **Start** drop-down list is 0. Next, select the **Subtract** option from the **Boolean** drop-down list in the **Boolean** rollout.

5. Choose the **OK** button from the dialog box; the cut extrude feature is created. The resulting model after creating this feature is shown in Figure 6-100.

Figure 6-99 Model after creating the hole feature

Figure 6-100 Model after creating the rectangular cut feature

Creating Holes in the Third and Fourth Features

Create holes in the third and fourth features by using the steps given next.

1. Choose the **Hole** button from the **Feature** toolbar; the **Hole** dialog box is displayed and you are prompted to select a planar face to sketch or specify a point. Make sure the **General Hole** and **Simple** options are selected in the **Type** and **Form** drop-down lists, respectively, in their rollouts.

2. Select the top planar face of the third feature as a placement face; the **Point** dialog box is displayed. Also, the Sketcher environment is invoked. Now, place the point anywhere on the face and then exit from the **Point** dialog box.

3. Apply dimensions to the point, refer to Figure 6-101. Next, exit from the Sketcher environment; the **Hole** dialog box is displayed. Also, the preview of the hole is displayed in the drawing window.

4. Enter **12** as the hole diameter in the **Diameter** edit box in the **Diameters** sub-rollout of the dialog box.

5. Select the **Until Selected** option from the **Depth Limit** drop-down list in the **Diameters** sub-rollout of the dialog box; you are prompted to select a face or a datum plane up to which the hole is to be created.

6. Select the cylindrical face of the hole created on the second feature as the face up to which the hole is to be created.

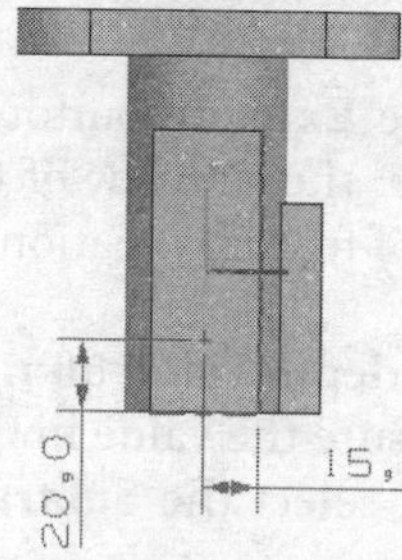

***Figure 6-101** Point after applying the dimensions*

7. Accept the other default settings and choose the **OK** button from the dialog box; a hole is created, as shown in Figure 6-102.

8. Similarly, create the second hole on the third feature of the model using the **Hole** dialog box. The model after creating the second hole is shown in Figure 6-103.

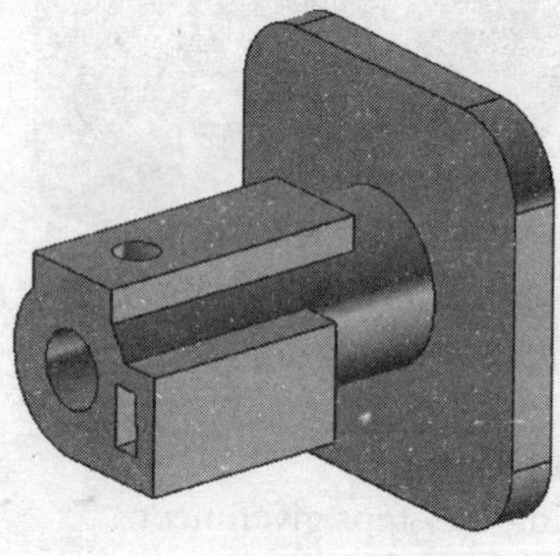

***Figure 6-102** Model after creating the first hole*

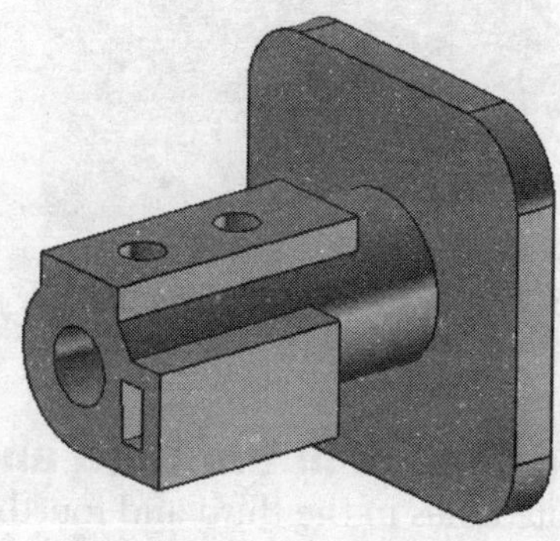

***Figure 6-103** Model after creating both holes*

After creating holes on the third feature, create holes on the fourth feature of the model by using the **Hole** dialog box. These holes will be created on the right face of the fourth feature. For dimensions of the holes, refer to Figure 6-92. The model after creating the holes in the fourth feature is shown in Figure 6-104.

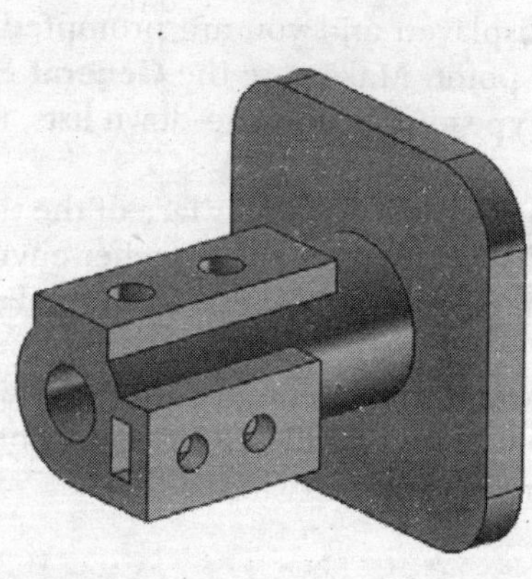

***Figure 6-104** Model after creating holes in the fourth feature*

Creating Counterbore Holes in the Model

Next, create four counterbore holes in the base feature by using the following steps:

1. Choose the **Hole** button from the **Feature** toolbar; the **Hole** dialog box is displayed and you are prompted to select the planar placement face.

2. Select the front face of the base feature as a placement face; the **Point** dialog box is displayed. Also, the Sketcher environment is invoked.

3. Move the cursor over the lower right round edge of the base feature and specify a point when the cursor snaps to its center point. Next, choose the **Ok** button from the **Point** dialog box and then exit from the Sketcher environment.

4. Select the **Counterbored** option from the **Form** drop-down list in the **Form and Dimensions** rollout of the dialog box. Make sure **General Hole** is selected in the **Type** drop-down list of the **Type** rollout in the dialog box.

5. Enter **20** in the **C-Bore Diameter** edit box, **2** in the **C-Bore Depth** edit box, and **10** in the **Diameter** edit box of the **Dimensions** sub-rollout of the **Form and Dimensions** rollout.

6. Select the **Until Selected** option from the **Depth Limit** drop-down list of the **Dimensions** sub-rollout in the dialog box and select the back face of the base feature to define the through face.

7. Choose the **OK** button from the dialog box; the counterbore hole is created, as shown in Figure 6-105.

8. Similarly, create the other three counterbore holes in the base feature of the model. The model after creating all the counterbore holes is shown in Figure 6-106.

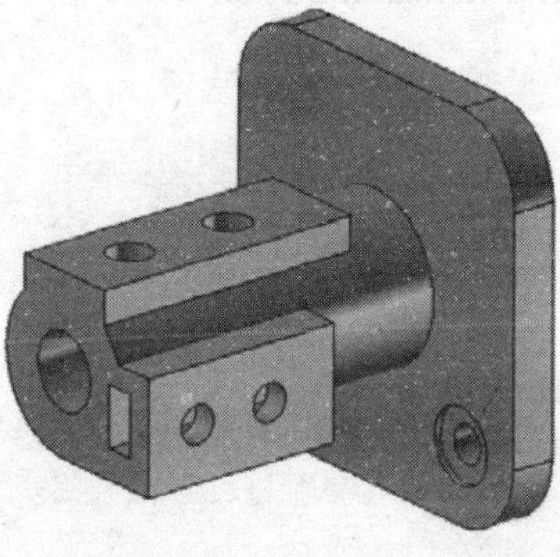

Figure 6-105 *The model after creating one counterbore hole*

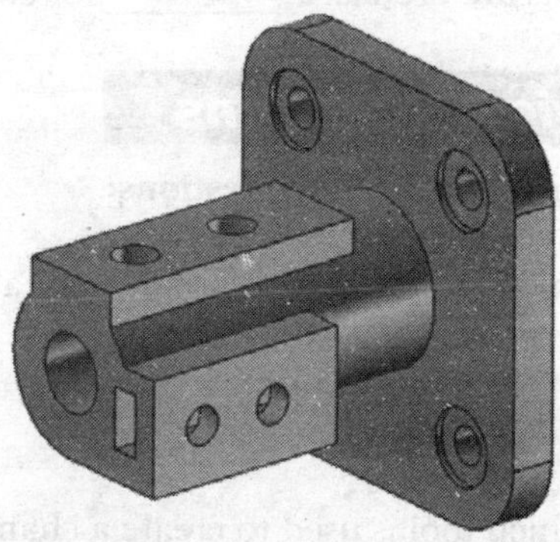

Figure 6-106 *The model after creating all counterbore holes*

Saving and Closing the File

1. Choose **File > Close > Save and Close** from the menu bar to save and close the current file.

Self-Evaluation Test

Answer the following questions and then compare them to those given at the end of this chapter:

1. You can invoke the **Hole** tool by choosing **Insert > Design Feature > Hole** from the menu bar. (T/F)
2. In NX, you can create an aligned series of holes in multiple bodies. (T/F)
3. The placement face selected for holes cannot be a nonuniform surface. (T/F)
4. In NX, you can create a number of holes at a time using the **Hole** tool. (T/F)
5. While creating counterbore holes, the counterbore diameter must be greater than the hole diameter. (T/F)
6. Grooves can be created on both _________ and _________ faces.
7. In NX, you can create _________ types of grooves.
8. Slots are _________ features.
9. Slot features cannot be placed on a _________ face.
10. Slots are used as a _________ for sliding a member in practical models.

Review Questions

Answer the following questions:

1. Which one of the following is not a hole type in NX?

   (a) **Counterbore** (b) **Countersink**
   (c) **Simple** (d) **Sectional**

2. Which tool is used to create a chamfer feature?

   (a) **Chamfer** (b) **Edge Blend**
   (c) **Datum Plane** (d) None of these

3. Which tool is used to create a blend (fillet) feature?

(a) **Edge Chamfer** (b) **Edge Blend**
(c) **Datum Plane** (d) None of these

4. Which rollout in the **Edge Blend** dialog box is used to create the variable radii blend feature?

(a) **Variable Radius Points** (b) **Variable Radius**
(c) **Variable Radius Blend** (d) None of these

5. Which rollout in the **Edge Blend** dialog box is used to create a corner blend feature?

(a) **Corner Blend** (b) **Blend Setback**
(c) **Corner Setback** (d) None of these

6. In T-slots, the bottom width value must be greater than the top width value. (T/F)

7. The **Stop Short of Corner** rollout from the **Edge Blend** dialog box is used to restrict the distance of the blend in the selected edge. (T/F)

8. You can chamfer circular edges. (T/F)

9. A counterbore hole has a uniform diameter throughout its length. (T/F)

10. Hole features can be placed on surfaces (sheet bodies). (T/F)

Exercises

Exercise 1

Create the model shown in Figure 6-107. The drawing views and dimensions of the model are given in Figure 6-108. After creating the model, save it with the name *c06exr1.prt* at the location *\NX 7\c06.* **(Expected time: 30 min)**

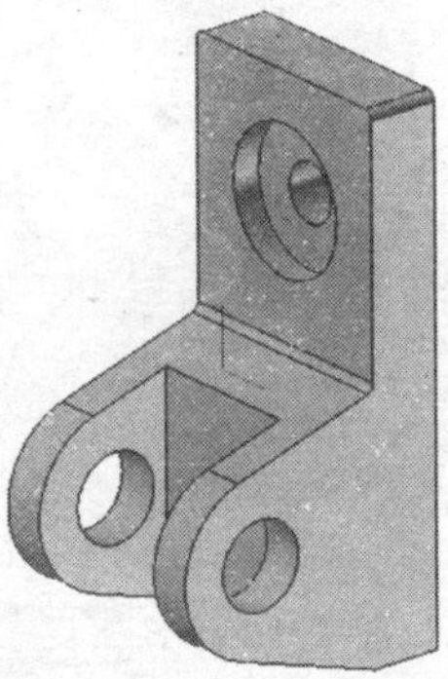

Figure 6-107 *Model for Exercise 1*

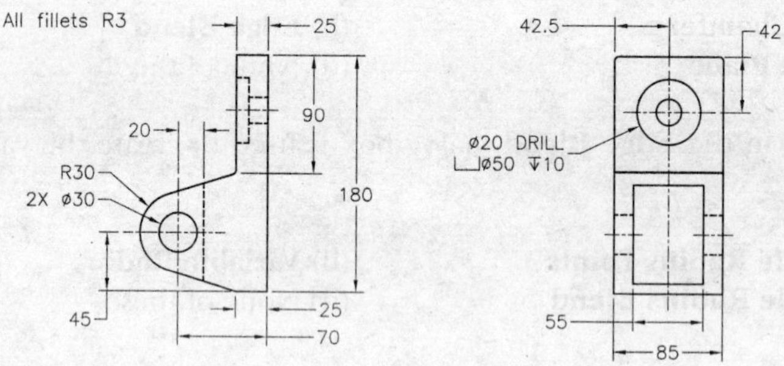

Figure 6-108 Dimensions and drawing views of the model for Exercise 1

Exercise 2

Create the model shown in Figure 6-109. The drawing views and dimensions of the model are given in Figure 6-110. After creating the model, save it with the name *c06exr2.prt* at the location *|NX 7|c06.* **(Expected time: 30 min)**

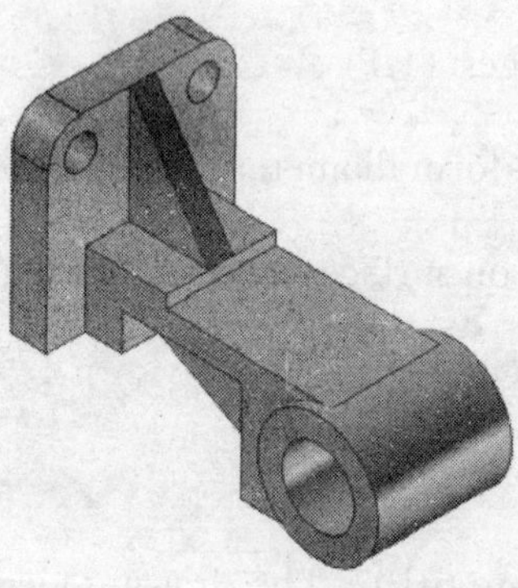

Figure 6-109 Model for Exercise 2

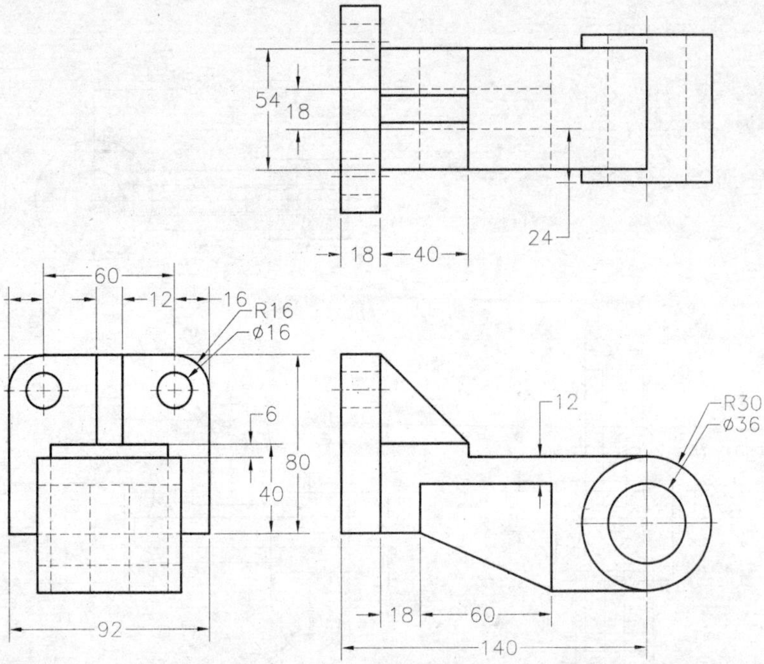

Figure 6-110 Drawing views and dimensions of the model for Exercise 2

Exercise 3

Create the model shown in Figure 6-111. The drawing views and dimensions of the model are given in Figure 6-112. After creating the model, save it with the name *c06exr3.prt* at the location *\NX 7\c06.* **(Expected time: 30 min)**

Figure 6-111 Model for Exercise 3

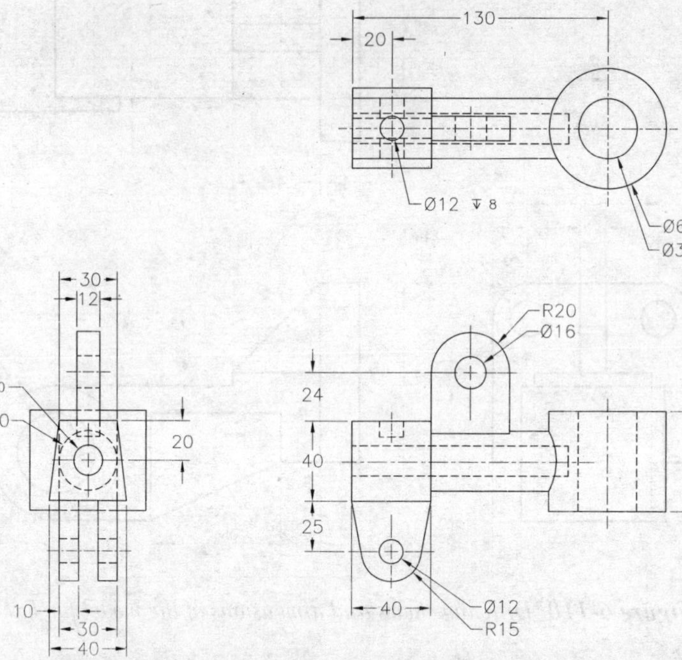

Figure 6-112 Drawing views and dimensions of the model for Exercise 3

Answers to Self-Evaluation Test

1. T, **2.** T, **3.** T, **4.** T, **5.** T, **6.** cylindrical, conical, **7.** three, **8.** placed, **9.** conical, **10.** guide way

Chapter 7

Advanced Modeling Tools-II

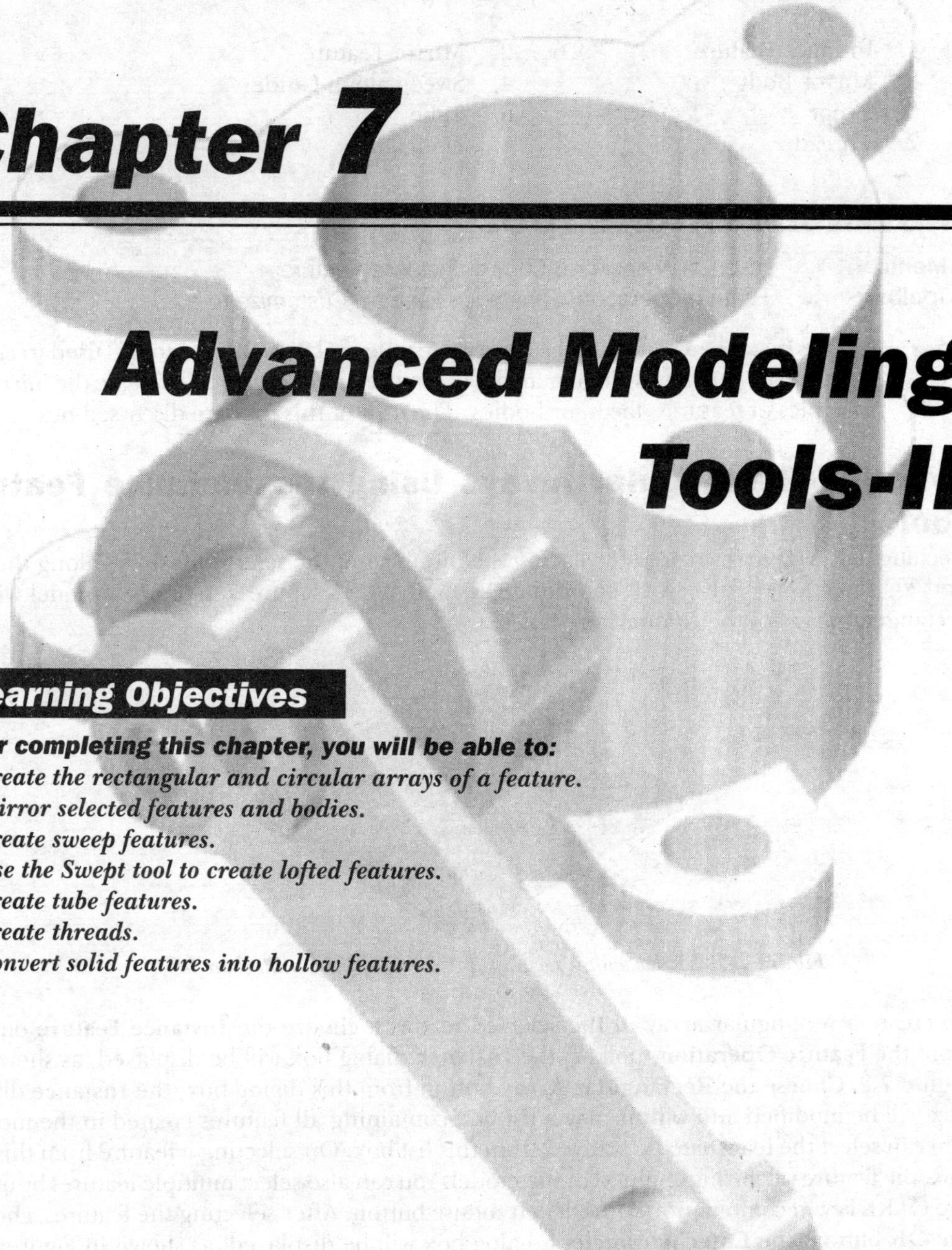

Learning Objectives

After completing this chapter, you will be able to:

- *Create the rectangular and circular arrays of a feature.*
- *Mirror selected features and bodies.*
- *Create sweep features.*
- *Use the Swept tool to create lofted features.*
- *Create tube features.*
- *Create threads.*
- *Convert solid features into hollow features.*

ADVANCED MODELING TOOLS

In this chapter, you will learn about the following advanced modeling tools:

1. Instance Feature
2. Mirror Feature
3. Mirror Body
4. Sweep along Guide
5. Swept
6. Tube
7. Thread
8. Shell

INSTANCE FEATURE TOOL

Menu: Insert > Associative Copy > Instance Feature
Toolbar: Feature Operation > Instance Feature *(Customize to add)*

The **Instance Feature** tool is a very versatile tool in NX. This tool is used to create the rectangular and circular arrays of features. Also, it is used to create the mirrored copies of features, faces, or bodies. The uses of this tool are discussed next.

Creating Rectangular Arrays Using the Instance Feature Tool

Rectangular arrays are created by placing the instances of the selected features along the XC and YC directions of the work coordinate system (WCS). Figure 7-1 shows a model with a rectangular array of the counterbore holes.

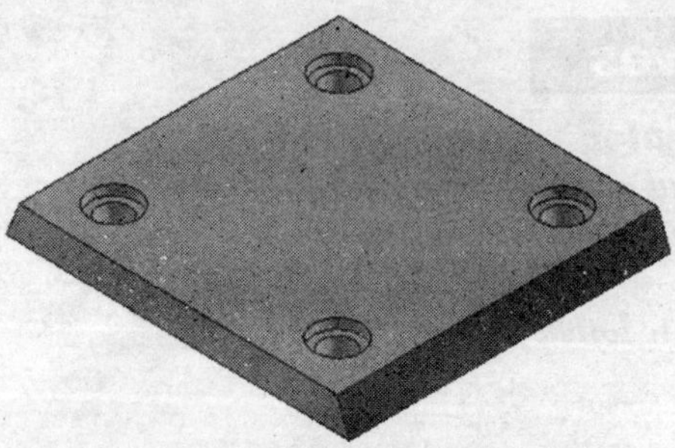

Figure 7-1 *Model with a rectangular array of the counterbore holes*

To create a rectangular array of the selected features, choose the **Instance Feature** button from the **Feature Operation** toolbar; the **Instance** dialog box will be displayed, as shown in Figure 7-2. Choose the **Rectangular Array** button from this dialog box; the **Instance** dialog box will be modified and will display a list box containing all features created in the model. You can select the feature to be arrayed from this list box. On selecting a feature from this list box, the feature will be highlighted in the model. You can also select multiple features by using the CTRL key in combination with the left mouse button. After selecting the features, choose the **OK** button; the **Enter parameters** dialog box will be displayed, as shown in Figure 7-3. Some of the options used for creating a rectangular array are discussed next. The remaining options in this dialog box will be discussed in the next section.

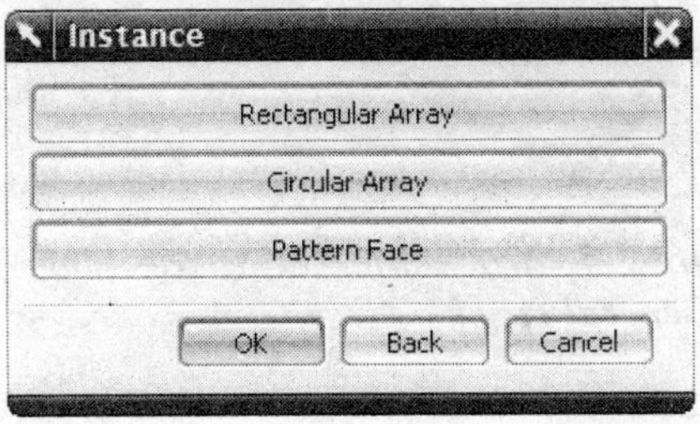

*Figure 7-2 The **Instance** dialog box*

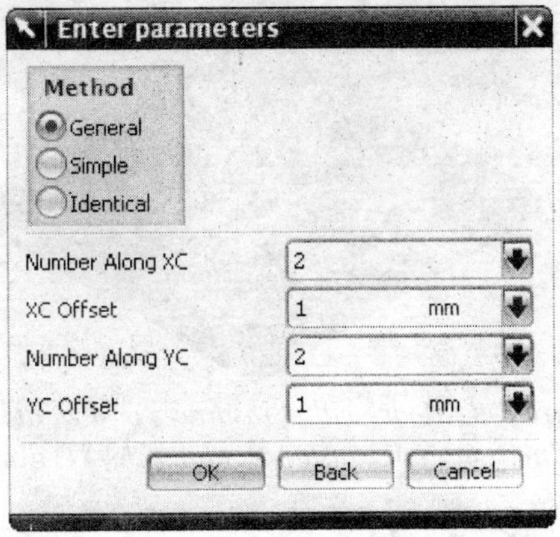

*Figure 7-3 The **Enter parameters** dialog box*

Number Along XC

This edit box is used to specify the number of instances along the XC direction of the work coordinate system.

XC Offset

This edit box is used to specify the spacing between two consecutive instances along the XC direction.

Number Along YC

This edit box is used to specify the number of instances along the YC direction of the work coordinate system.

YC Offset

This edit box is used to specify the spacing between two consecutive instances along the YC direction.

Figure 7-4 shows a rectangular pattern with 4 instances along the XC direction and 3 instances along the YC direction. There are three different methods to create an array. These are specified by selecting appropriate radio button from the **Method** area and they are discussed next.

General

The **General** method is used when the array instances are to be created across multiple faces. All features of the model are validated before creating the array instance. You can use this method when the feature crosses an edge of the face, as shown in Figure 7-5.

Simple

The **Simple** method is similar to the **General** method with the only difference that in the **Simple** method, only the required entities are validated and the feature cannot cross any edge of the face, as shown in Figure 7-6. This method reduces the time required to create an array.

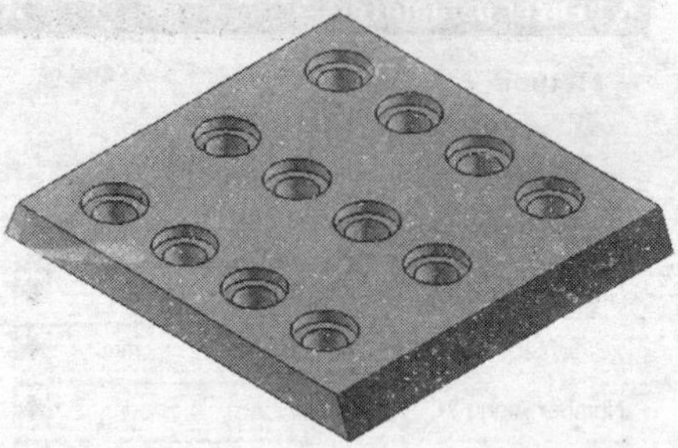

Figure 7-4 Model with 4 instances created along the XC direction and 3 instances along the YC direction

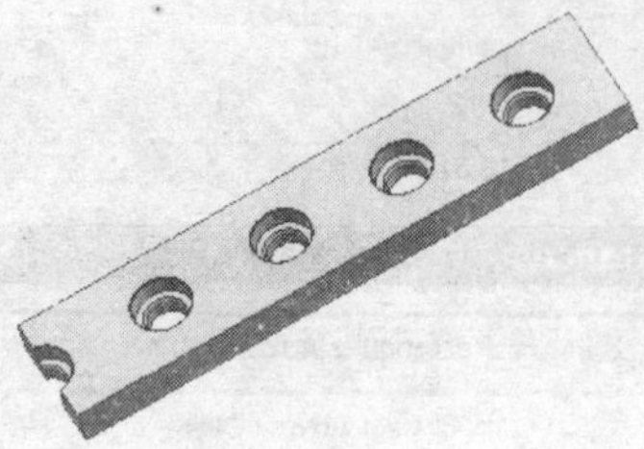

*Figure 7-5 Array instances created using the **General** option*

Identical

The **Identical** method is used to create an array in which instances are exactly identical to the original feature, as shown in Figure 7-7. In this figure, the original instance is created by extruding the sketch up to the curved surface. As a result, the shape of the arrayed instances is similar to that of the original instance.

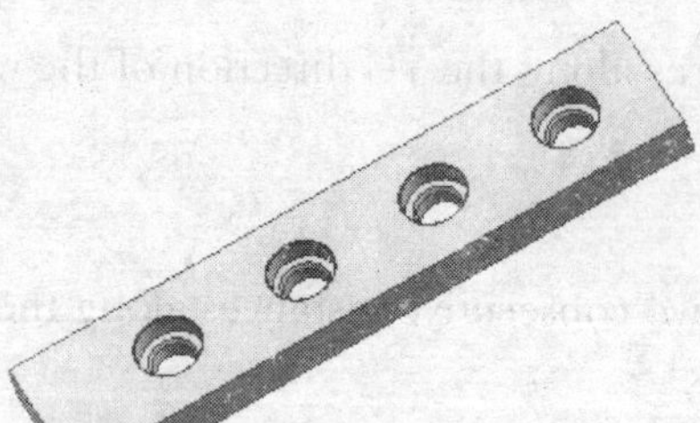

*Figure 7-6 Array instances created using the **Simple** option*

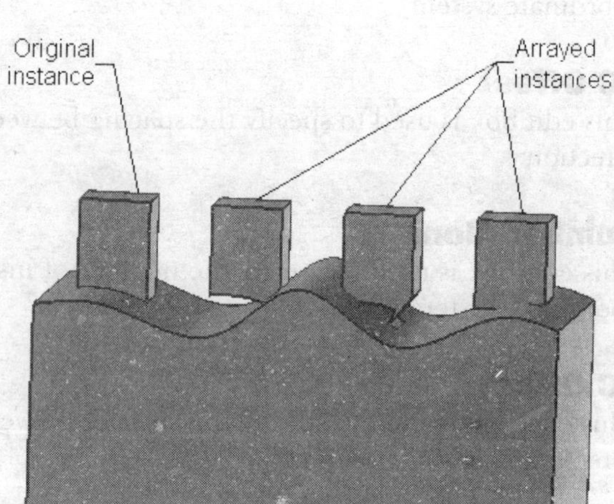

*Figure 7-7 Array instances created using the **Identical** option*

Tip: *To create instances of rectangular array, the required feature must be created by using the **Unite** or **Subtract** option so that it is a part of the target body.*

Creating Circular Arrays Using the Instance Feature Tool

Circular arrays are created by placing the instances of the selected features along the circumference of an imaginary circle. Figure 7-8 shows a model with a circular array of the counterbore hole.

To create a circular array of the selected features, invoke the **Instance Feature** tool; the **Instance** dialog box will be displayed. Choose the **Circular Array** button from the dialog box; the **Instance** dialog box will be modified and it shows a list box that lists all the features created in the model. You can select the features to be arrayed from this list box or directly from the drawing window. The feature that you select in the list box will be highlighted in the model also. Next, choose **OK** from this dialog box; the **Instance** dialog box will show the circular array options, as shown in Figure 7-9.

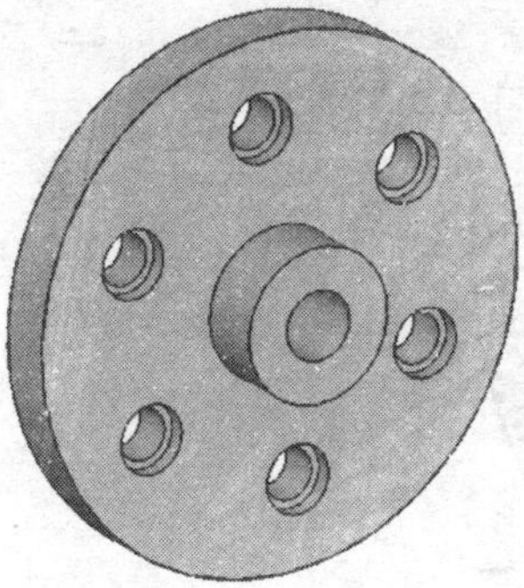

Figure 7-8 Circular array of counterbore holes

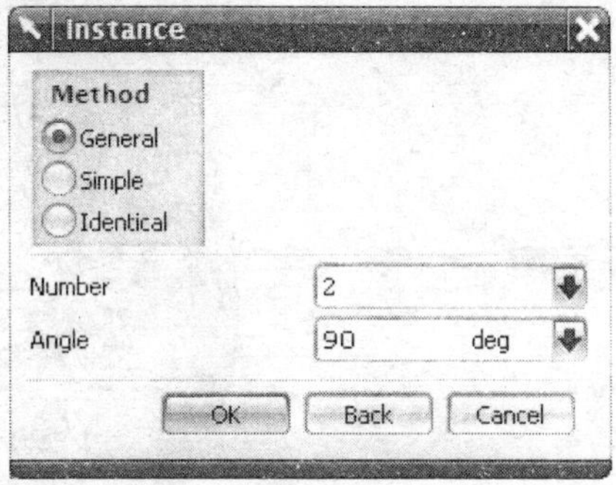

*Figure 7-9 The **Instance** dialog box*

The radio buttons in the **Method** area of this dialog box are similar to those discussed in the rectangular array. The remaining options are discussed next.

Number

This edit box is used to specify the number of instances in the circular array.

Angle

This edit box is used to specify the angle between the two instances of the circular array.

After you specify the parameters in the **Instance** dialog box, choose **OK**; the **Instance** dialog box will be modified and will display two options for creating the rotation axis of array, as shown in Figure 7-10. These options are discussed next.

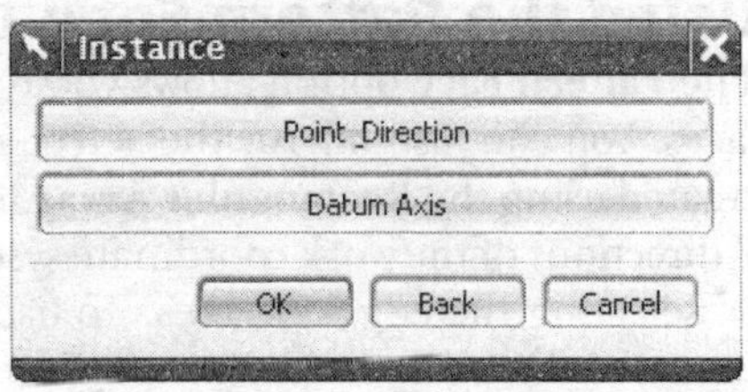

*Figure 7-10 The **Instance** dialog box*

Point _Direction

You can choose this button when you need to specify the center point of the circular array and the direction of axis around which the circular array will be created. When you choose this button, the **Vector** dialog box will be displayed and you will be prompted to select the circular array rotation axis. You can select a circular edge to select its center point as the center of the array. On doing so, an axis will be displayed at the center point of the circular edge. You can reverse the direction of the axis by choosing the **Reverse Direction** button in the dialog box. Note that the right-hand thumb rule is used to determine the direction of the circular array. After specifying these parameters, choose the **OK** button from the **Vector** dialog box;

the **Point** dialog box will be displayed and you will be prompted to specify the circular array reference point. You need to be careful while specifying the reference point of the circular array because this point will be taken as the center point of the array. Figure 7-11 shows the direction of the circular array rotation axis and the resulting circular array. In this case, the array has 6 instances and the angle between the consecutive instances is 30 degrees.

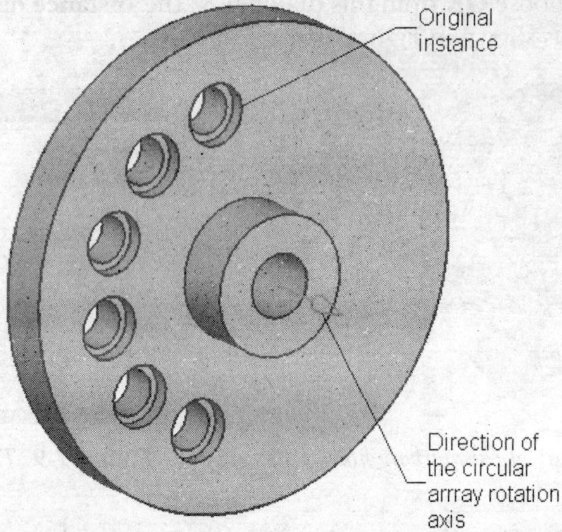

Figure 7-11 Circular array and the direction of the array axis

Datum Axis

You can choose this button when you need to select the datum axis as the rotation axis of the array. In this option, you will not be prompted to select the point.

Using the Pattern Face Option of the Instance Feature Tool

The **Pattern Face** option allows you to create a rectangular or circular pattern of the selected faces. You can also mirror the selected faces using this option. Unlike the rectangular array created using the **Rectangular Array** tool, where the instances are placed only along the X and Y directions of the work coordinate system, this tool allows you to define the X and Y directions by selecting the edges or axes. To use this option, choose the **Pattern Face** button from the **Instance** dialog box; the **Pattern Face** dialog box will be displayed, refer to Figure 7-12.

The **Type** rollout of this dialog box provides options to specify whether to create a rectangular pattern, a circular pattern, or mirrored images (reflections). The options displayed in the **Pattern Face** dialog box depend on the option selected in the drop-down list available in the **Type** rollout of this dialog box. For example, if you select the **Circular Pattern** option from the drop-down list of the **Type** rollout, the options related to circular pattern will be activated. By default, the **Rectangular Pattern** option will be selected and you will be prompted to select the faces to copy. Select the boundary faces that you want to pattern. From the **X Direction** rollout, you can specify the first direction to create patterns. To do so, click on the **Specify Vector** area in this rollout; you will be prompted to select an object to infer vector. You can select any edge or line to specify the first direction. Similarly, you can specify the second direction from the **Y Direction** rollout. Next, you can specify the distance value between two instances and number of instances along the x and y directions by using the respective edit boxes in the **Pattern Properties** rollout, refer to Figures 7-12 and 7-13.

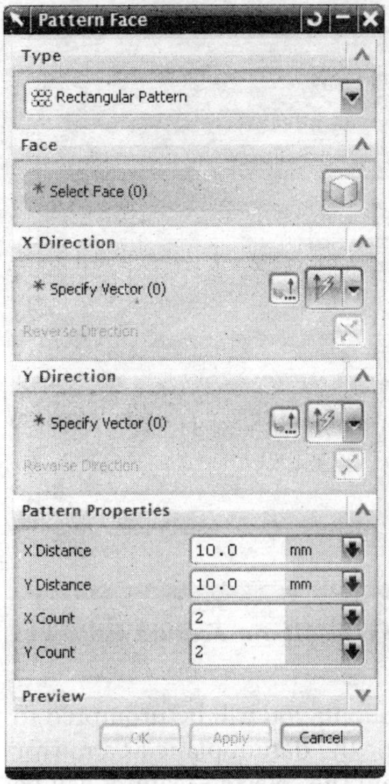

*Figure 7-12 The **Pattern Face** dialog box*

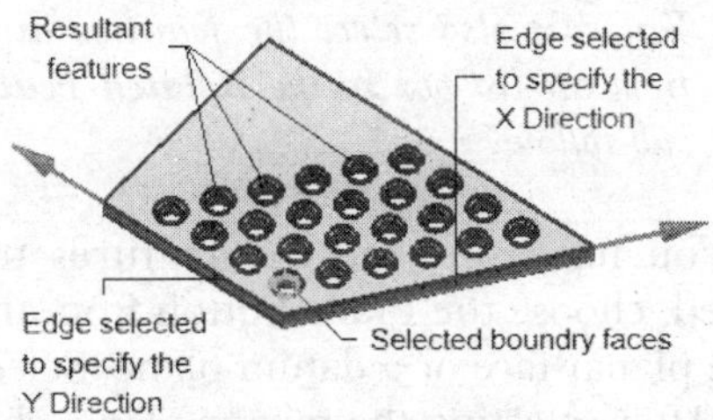

*Figure 7-13 Creating a rectangular pattern using the **Pattern Face** option*

Note

*On selecting the **Circular Pattern** option, you need to specify the axis of the circular pattern and the center point of the circular pattern by using the **Axis** rollout. In case of the **Mirror** option, you need to specify the mirror plane from the **Mirror Plane** rollout.*

MIRROR FEATURE TOOL

Menu:	Insert > Associative Copy > Mirror Feature
Toolbar:	Feature Operation > Mirror Feature *(Customize to add)*

The **Mirror Feature** tool is used to mirror selected features from a model. You can mirror features about a selected datum plane or a planar face. To do so, choose the **Mirror Feature** button from the **Feature Operation** toolbar; the **Mirror Feature** dialog box will be displayed, refer to Figure 7-14. All features available in the model will be listed in the list box of the **Related Features** sub-rollout in the dialog box.

By default, the **Feature** button is chosen in the **Feature** rollout of this dialog box and you are prompted to select the features to be mirrored. Select the features to be mirrored from the drawing window. Alternatively, you can select the features to be mirrored from the list box available in the **Related Features** sub-rollout. Expand the **Related Features** sub-rollout, if it is not expanded by default. The options in this sub-rollout are discussed next.

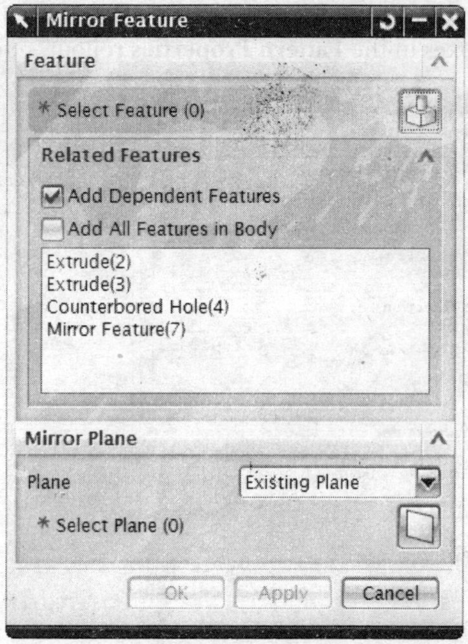

***Figure 7-14** The **Mirror Feature** dialog box*

Add Dependent Features

If this check box is selected, all features that are dependent on the selected feature will be taken for the mirror operation.

Add All Features in Body

If this check box is selected, all features in a body will be added on selecting any one of them.

Note

*You can also select the features directly from the list box in the **Related Features** sub-rollout.*

After you have selected the features to be mirrored, choose the **Plane** button from the **Mirror Plane** rollout; you will be prompted to select a planar face or a datum plane. Select the planar face or the datum plane as a mirror plane. After selecting the mirror plane, choose the **OK** button; the selected features will be mirrored.

Note

*The **Plane** drop-down list is used to select an existing datum plane or create a new datum plane as mirror plane.*

Figure 7-15 shows the features selected to be mirrored and the datum plane selected as the mirror plane. Figure 7-16 shows the resulting mirrored feature, after turning off the display of the mirror plane. In this case, the mirror plane is passing through the center of the semicircular base feature.

MIRROR BODY TOOL

Menu:	Insert > Associative Copy > Mirror Body
Toolbar:	Feature Operation > Mirror Body *(Customize to add)*

Mirror Body

The **Mirror Body** tool is used to mirror an entire body, thus creating a new body in the current file. However, you can mirror bodies only by using datum planes. You cannot use planar faces to mirror bodies. To mirror bodies, choose the **Mirror Body** button from the **Feature Operation** toolbar; the **Mirror Body** dialog box will be displayed. Also, you will be prompted to select the body to mirror. Select the body and then choose the **Plane** button; you will be prompted to select the plane to mirror. Select the datum plane and then choose the **OK** button from this dialog box; the selected body will be mirrored. Figure 7-17 shows the original body, the mirror plane, and the mirrored body.

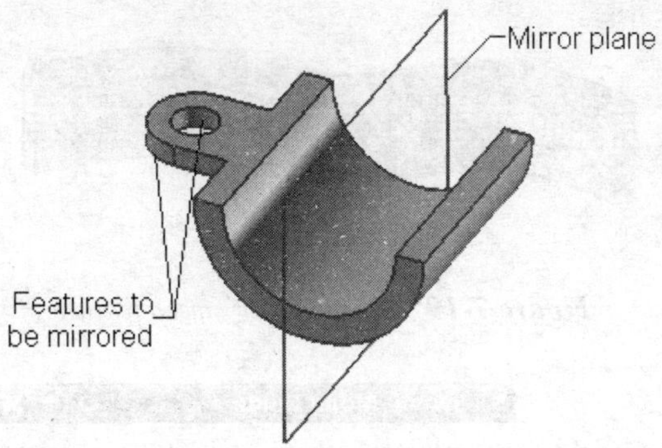

Figure 7-15 The mirror plane and the features to be mirrored

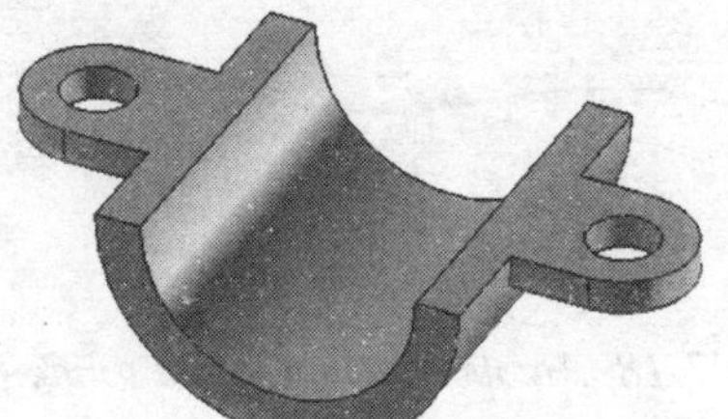

Figure 7-16 The resulting mirrored feature

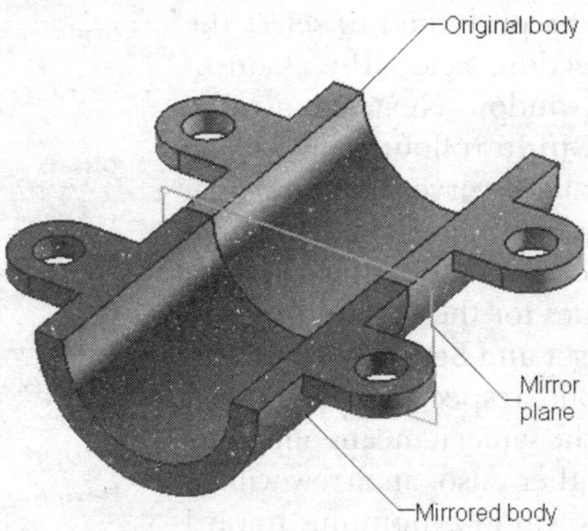

Figure 7-17 New body created by mirroring the existing body

Note

A group of features united together is called a body.

*After selecting the bodies to mirror, you can click the middle mouse button to activate the next option in the **Mirror Body** dialog box.*

SWEEPING SKETCHES ALONG THE GUIDE CURVES

Menu: Insert > Sweep > Sweep along Guide
Toolbar: Feature > Sweep along Guide *(Customize to add)*

The **Sweep along Guide** tool is used to create sweep features by sweeping an open or a closed section about a guide string. Figure 7-18 shows an open section and the guide string and Figure 7-19 shows the resulting sweep feature.

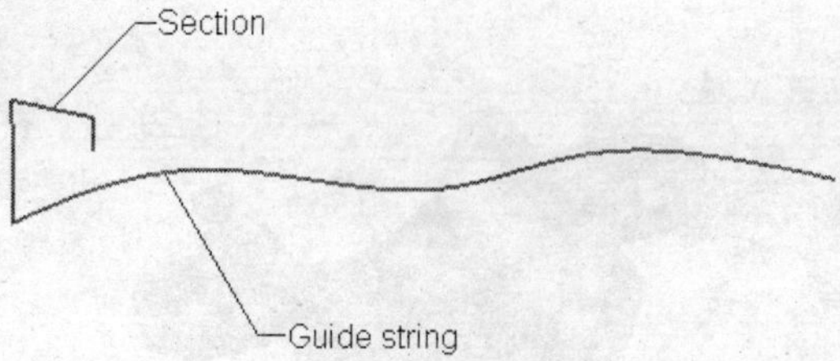

Figure 7-18 An open section and a guide string to create a sweep feature

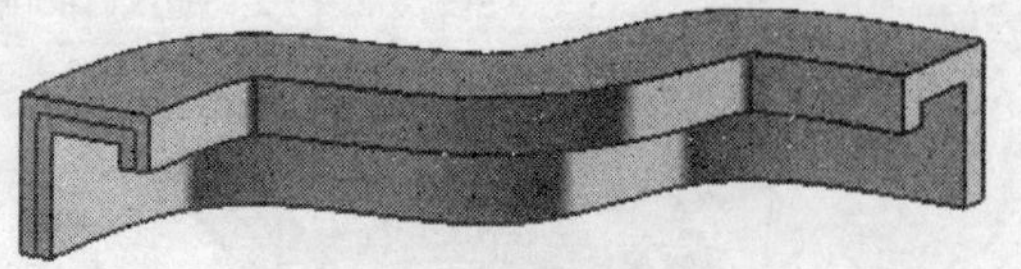

Figure 7-19 The resulting sweep feature

To invoke this tool, choose the **Sweep along Guide** button from the **Feature** toolbar; the **Sweep Along Guide** dialog box will be displayed, as shown in Figure 7-20, and you will be prompted to select the chain of curves for the section. Select the chain of curves from the drawing window. Next, choose the **Curve** button from the **Guide** rollout; you will be prompted to select the chain of curves for the guide. Note that if the guide has multiple strings, they all should be end-connected to each other. After selecting the guide curve, enter values for the first and second directions in the **First Offset** and **Second Offset** edit boxes of the **Offsets** rollout, respectively. Note that these values should not be the same; it means one value must be greater than the other. Also, an arrow will be displayed in the graphics window, pointing toward the second offset direction. You can use this arrow to dynamically increase or decrease the values of the first and second offset directions.

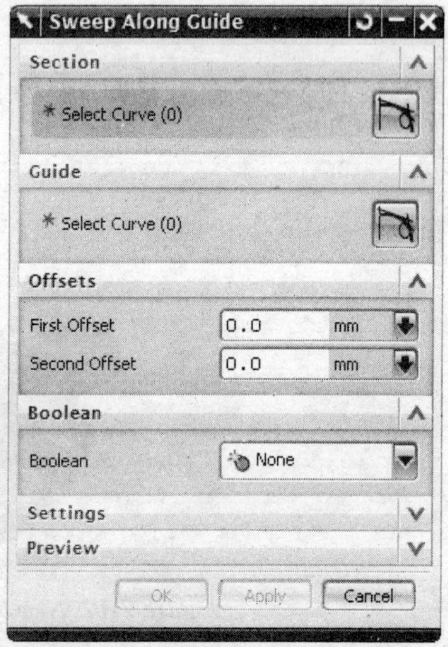

***Figure 7-20** The **Sweep Along Guide** dialog box*

Note

If the section for the sweep feature consists of nested closed loops, the guide string should only be drawn by using lines and arcs.

Select the required boolean operation from the **Boolean** drop-down list in the dialog box. Note that if the sweep feature is the base feature in the model, then only the **None** option will be available in the **Boolean** drop-down list. Next, choose the **OK** button from the **Sweep Along Guide** dialog box; the sweep feature will be created.

Tip: *To create features that are swept along a guide curve, first draw the guide curve and then define a datum plane at one of the ends of the guide curve. Next, use this datum plane to draw the sketch of the section.*

CREATING SWEPT FEATURES

Menu: Insert > Sweep > Swept
Toolbar: Feature > Swept

Swept features are created by sweeping one or more sections along one or more guide curves such that all sections are blended together. Figure 7-21 shows three section strings (ellipse, circle, and ellipse) and the two guide strings (splines), and Figure 7-22 shows the resulting swept feature.

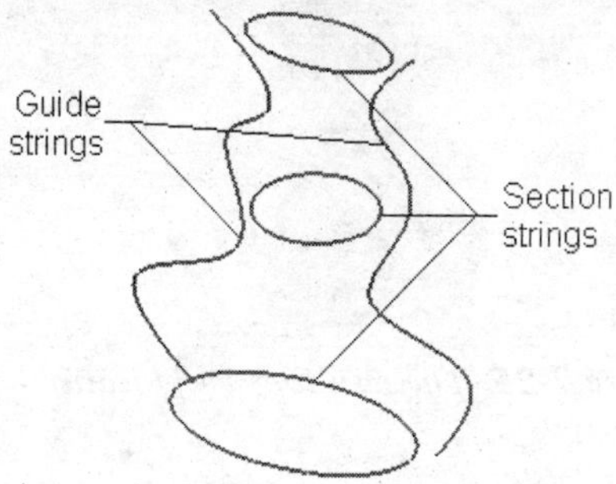

Figure 7-21 *Section strings and guide strings to create a sweep feature*

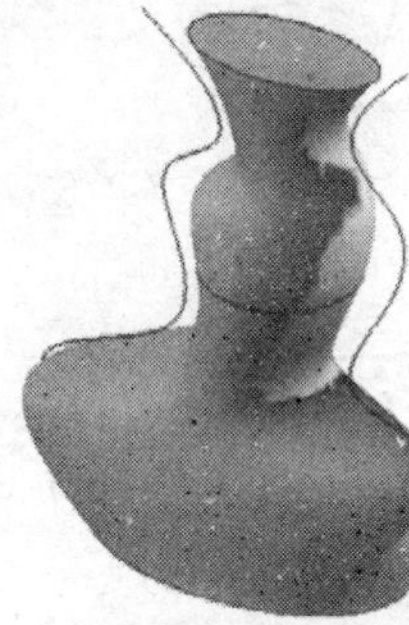

Figure 7-22 *The resulting swept feature*

To create swept features, invoke the **Swept** tool from the **Feature** toolbar; the **Swept** dialog box will be displayed and you will be prompted to select the section curves. On selecting the section curve, an arrow will be displayed on it. Press the middle mouse button to accept the curve. Similarly, select all the remaining section curves one by one. Note that while selecting the section curves, you need to be careful about the point from where you select them. It is recommended that multiple sections should be selected from the same quadrant. For example, if you need to select circles or ellipses, it is recommended that you select them from the same quadrant. Otherwise, a twist will be introduced in the swept model. Figure 7-23 shows the arrows displayed on the three sections that are selected to be swept. Notice that all arrows point in the same direction, thereby avoiding any twist in the model. However, you can change the direction of any arrow by double-clicking on it.

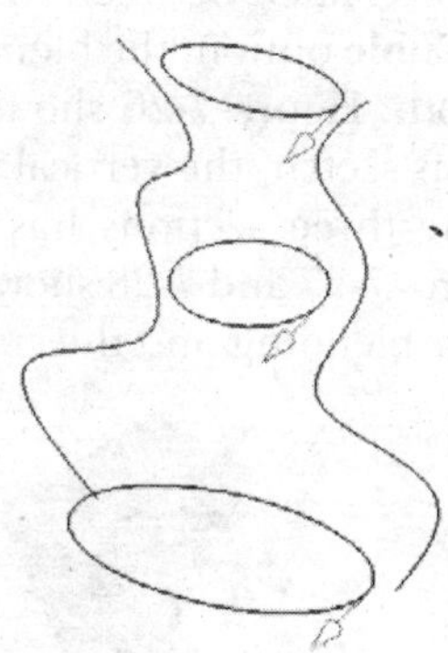

Figure 7-23 *Arrows displayed on the sections to be swept*

Note

After selecting each section curve, you need to press the middle mouse button to accept it. You can select any number of section curves.

After selecting the section curves, choose the **Guide** button from the **Guides** rollout; you will be prompted to select the guide curves. Select the guide curve; an arrow will be displayed at the end of the guide curve. Press the middle mouse button to accept the guide curve. Similarly, select the remaining guide curves one by one. You can select maximum of three guide curves.

Note that all arrows should point in the same direction. After selecting all guide curves, choose the **OK** button from the **Swept** dialog box; the swept feature will be created.

Figure 7-24 shows the sections, in which the arrows point in different directions and Figure 7-25 shows the resulting swept feature.

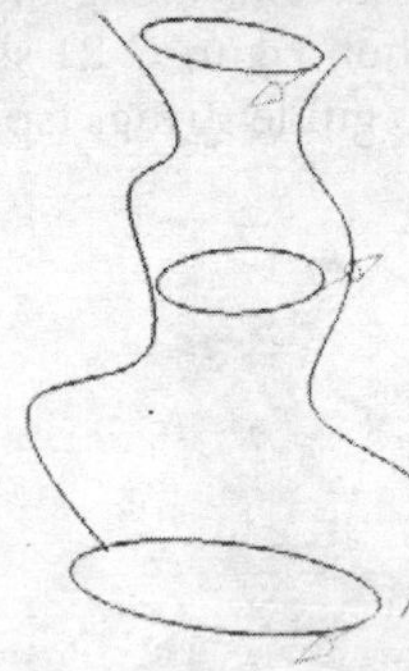

Figure 7-24 *Arrows on the section strings pointing in different directions*

Figure 7-25 *The resulting swept feature*

After selecting all the section and guide curves, you can use the **Interpolation** drop-down list in the **Section Options** rollout to specify the type of blending between the sections. There are two options in this drop-down list, **Linear** and **Cubic**. If you select the **Linear** option, a linear blending will be created between the sections. However, if you select the **Cubic** option, the blending between the sections will be smooth. Figure 7-26 shows the sketch for a swept feature. In this sketch, the vertical line passing through the centers of the three sections has been used as the guide curve. Figures 7-27 and 7-28 show the features created by using the linear blending and the cubic blending, respectively.

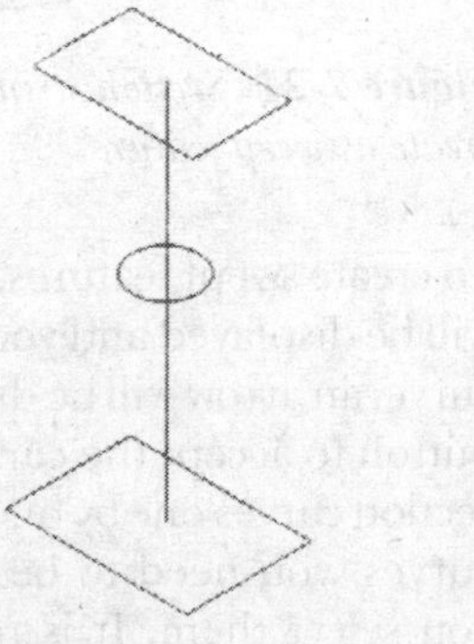

Figure 7-26 *Section and guide strings for the swept feature*

Figure 7-27 *Linear blending between the three sections*

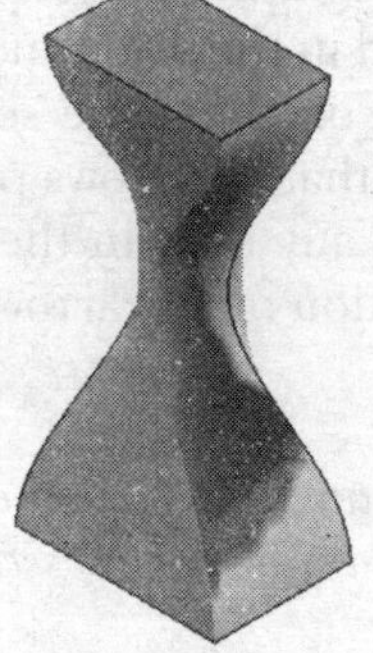

Figure 7-28 *Cubic blending between the three sections*

CREATING TUBES OR CABLES

Menu:	Insert > Sweep > Tube
Toolbar:	Feature > Tube *(Customize to add)*

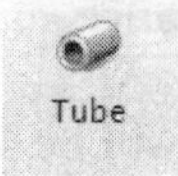

NX allows you to create tubes or cables using the **Tube** tool. To do so, you need to specify the guide curve about which the tube or cable will be created. To define the tube or cable section, enter its inner and outer diameter. To create a tube or a cable, first draw the sketch of the guide curve. Note that if the guide curve is a combination of multiple entities, all of them should be end-connected. Also, remember that there should be no sharp vertices in the guide curve. All sharp vertices should be filleted using the **Fillet** tool, or the curve should be created using some other tool.

After drawing the sketch for the guide curve, invoke the **Tube** tool; the **Tube** dialog box will be displayed, as shown in Figure 7-29, and you will be prompted to select curves for tube centerline path. Select the sketch drawn for the guide curve. The different rollouts in the **Tube** dialog box are discussed next.

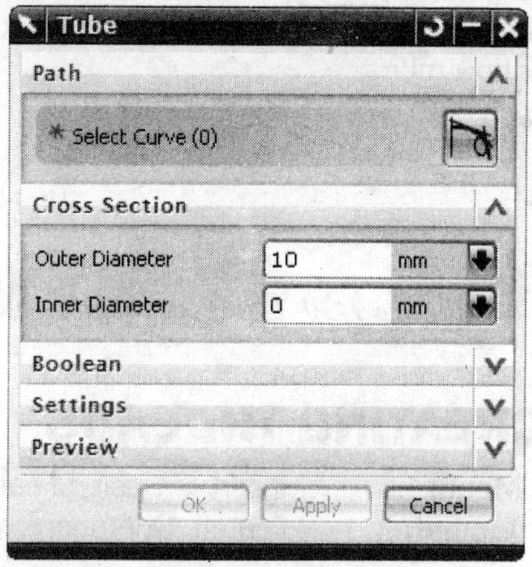

Figure 7-29 The ***Tube*** *dialog box*

Cross Section Rollout

The options in this rollout are used to define the cross-section of the tube.

Outer Diameter

This edit box is used to specify the outer diameter of the tube.

Inner Diameter

This edit box is used to specify the inner diameter of the tube. By specifying a value in this edit box, you can ensure that the tube is hollow. If you enter **0** in this edit box, the resulting tube will be solid filled.

Boolean Rollout

This rollout is used to specify the boolean operation to be performed.

Settings Rollout

This rollout is used to specify the output type and tolerance. The options in this rollout are discussed next.

Output

The options in this drop-down list are used to specify the output type for the tube feature. Select the **Multiple Segments** option, if you need the tube to have multiple lateral faces.

However, if you select the **Single Segment** option, the tube will have only one lateral face (if it is solid filled) or two lateral faces (if it is hollow).

Tolerance

The value in the **Tolerance** edit box is used to create a feature with the specified tolerance.

After setting the parameters in the **Tube** dialog box, choose the **OK** button; the tube will be created. Figure 7-30 shows the guide curve for the tube and Figure 7-31 shows the resulting hollow tube.

Figure 7-30 Guide curve for the tube

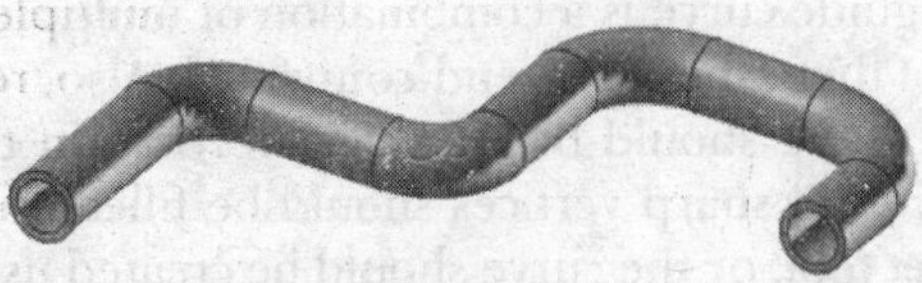

Figure 7-31 The resulting hollow tube

CREATING THREADS

Menu:	Insert > Design Feature > Thread
Toolbar:	Feature Operation > Thread *(Customize to add)*

Thread

NX allows you to create internal or external threads on a cylindrical model. Internal threads are those that are created on the internal faces of a model, similar to a hole in a model. External threads are those that are created on the outer face of a model. Figure 7-32 shows the external threading on a bolt and Figure 7-33 shows the internal threading in a nut.

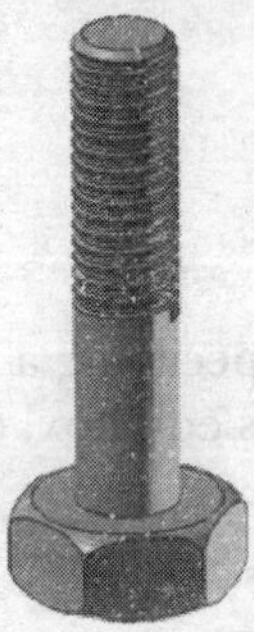

Figure 7-32 External threading on a bolt

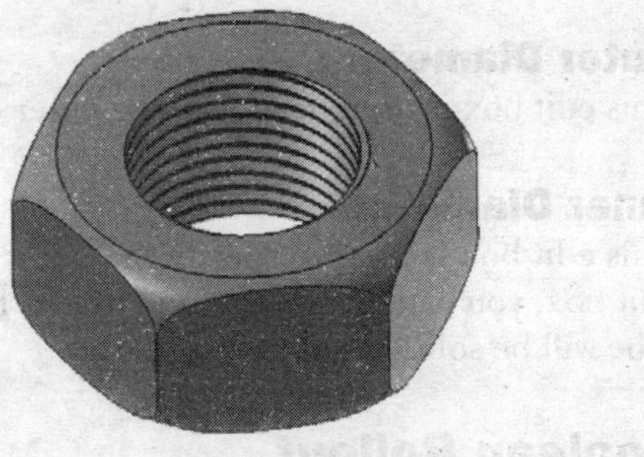

Figure 7-33 Internal threading in a nut

In NX, you can create detailed or symbolic threads. The detailed threads appear like actual threads, refer to Figures 7-32 and 7-33. However, symbolic threads just display the thread convention in the form of dashed lines, as shown in Figure 7-34.

Creating Symbolic Threads

To create symbolic threads, invoke the **Thread** tool; the **Thread** dialog box will be displayed. Select the **Symbolic** radio button, if it is not selected by default, to display the options to create symbolic threads, refer to Figure 7-35.

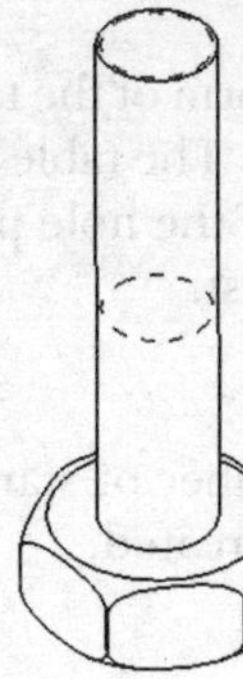

Figure 7-34 Symbolic thread on a bolt

There are two methods of creating symbolic threads. In the first method, the system automatically defines the thread specifications for the selected face using a thread table. In the other method, some thread specifications are calculated and displayed in the edit box, but you can also modify these values individually. Both these methods are discussed next.

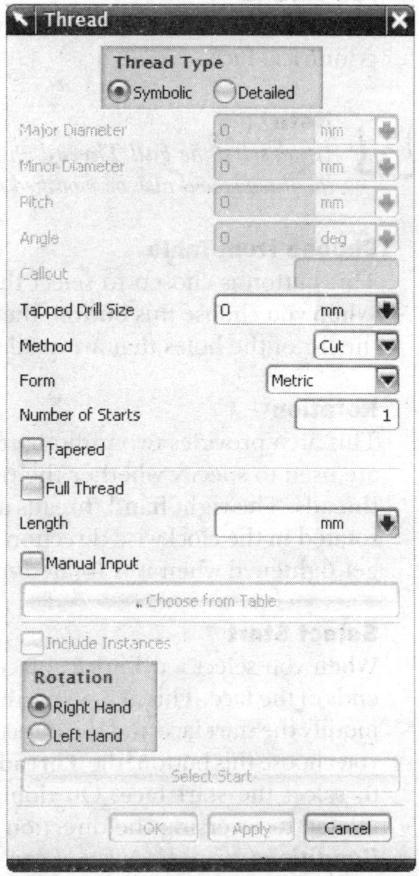

*Figure 7-35 The **Thread** dialog box*

Creating Symbolic Threads Using Table

To create a symbolic thread using table, invoke the **Thread** dialog box and clear the **Manual Input** check box if it is already selected; the options to specify the parameters of the thread will be disabled. Next, select the cylindrical face on which you need to create the threads; the face will be highlighted and an arrow will be displayed at one of the ends of the face. The options that will be available in the dialog box at this stage are discussed next.

Shaft Size / Tapped Drill Size

If you select an outer face to create threads, the **Shaft Size** edit box will be available. In this edit box, you can specify the size of the shaft. But if you select an interior face to create the thread, the **Tapped Drill Size** edit box will be available. Depending upon the face selected and the specifications from the table, a default value will be displayed in this edit box. You can accept the default value or enter a new value.

Method

This drop-down list is used to select the method that will be used to create threads. You can select the **Cut**, **Rolled**, **Ground**, or **Milled** option from this drop-down list.

Form
This drop-down list is used to select the form of the table, thus defining the type of table to be used to specify the thread parameters. The table that is used to create threads is called the lookup table. Note that the values of the hole parameters will be modified based on the form selected from this drop-down list.

Number of Starts
This edit box is used to specify the number of starts of the thread. If you specify more than one start, multiple threads will be created.

Tapered
This check box is selected to create tapered threads.

Full Thread
This check box is selected to create threads throughout the length of the selected cylindrical face.

Note

*If you select the **Full Thread** option and modify the length of the cylindrical face, the length of the threads will also be modified accordingly.*

Choose from Table
This button is chosen to select the thread type from the lookup table to create threads. When you choose this button, the **Thread** dialog box will be compressed and will display the list of the holes that are available in the current lookup table.

Rotation
This area provides two radio buttons, **Right Hand** and **Left Hand**. These radio buttons are used to specify whether the resulting threads will be right hand threads or left hand threads. The right hand threads are those that allow the screw to get tightened when it is rotated in the clockwise direction. The left hand threads are those that allow the screw to get tightened when it is rotated in the counterclockwise direction.

Select Start
When you select a cylindrical face to create threads, an arrow is displayed at one of the ends of the face. This arrow specifies the start face and the direction of the threads. You can modify the start face and the direction of threads by choosing the **Select Start** button. When you choose this button, the **Thread** dialog box will be compressed and you will be prompted to select the start face. On doing so, the **Thread** dialog box will display the options related to reversing the direction of the thread axis and start conditions. From the **Start Conditions** drop-down list, if you select the **Extend Thru Start** option, a complete thread will be created even in front of the plane that you select as the start plane. However, on selecting the **Do Not Extend** option, the threads will start from the plane that you select as the start plane of the thread. After specifying these options, choose the **OK** button to return to the options to create the threads.

Creating Symbolic Threads Using Manual Inputs

To create a symbolic thread using the manual inputs, invoke the **Thread** dialog box and choose the **Manual Input** check box; the options to specify the parameters of the thread will be enabled. Next, select the cylindrical face on which you need to create the threads; some default values will be displayed in the edit boxes to define the parameters of the threads. The options that are enabled to create threads with manual inputs are discussed next.

Major Diameter

This edit box is used to specify the major diameter of threads. Note that the major diameter should be more than the diameter of the cylindrical face selected to create threads.

Minor Diameter

This edit box is used to specify the minor diameter of threads. Note that the minor diameter should be less than the diameter of the cylindrical face selected to create threads.

Pitch

This edit box is used to specify the pitch of threads.

Angle

This edit box is used to specify the angle of threads.

Creating Detailed Threads

To create the detailed thread, invoke the **Thread** tool; the **Thread** dialog box will be displayed. Select the **Detailed** radio button to display the options to create detailed threads; the dialog box will be compressed and you will be prompted to select a cylindrical face. Select the face on which you need to create threads; the options in the dialog box will be enabled, as shown in Figure 7-36. Most of the options in this dialog box are similar to those discussed while creating symbolic threads. The only option, which is not yet discussed, is discussed next.

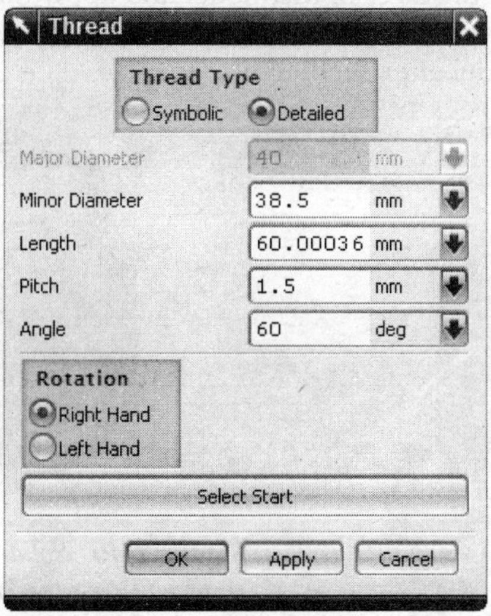

*Figure 7-36 The **Thread** dialog box*

Length

This edit box is used to specify the depth up to which the threads will be created. The default value that appears in this edit box is equal to the length of the cylindrical face that is selected to create threads. You can enter any other value in this edit box. Figure 7-37 shows a bolt with threads created throughout its length and Figure 7-38 shows a bolt with threads created up to a specified length.

Figure 7-37 *Threads created throughout the length of the bolt*

Figure 7-38 *Threads created up to a specified length*

CREATING SHELL FEATURES

Menu:	Insert > Offset/Scale > Shell
Toolbar:	Feature Operation > Shell

The **Shell** tool allows you to scoop out the material from a model and make it hollow from inside. The resulting model will be a structure of walls with a cavity inside. You can remove some of the faces of the model and apply different wall thicknesses to some of the faces. Figure 7-39 shows a solid model before scooping out material and Figure 7-40 shows the model after shelling it.

Figure 7-39 *Solid model before scooping out material*

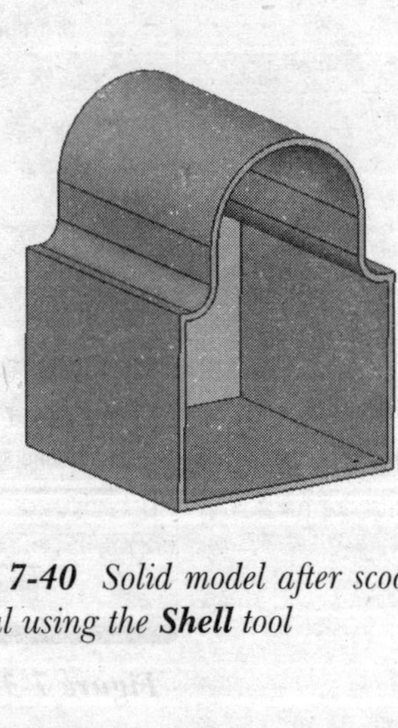

Figure 7-40 *Solid model after scooping out material using the **Shell** tool*

When you invoke this tool, the **Shell** dialog box will be displayed, refer to Figure 7-41. This dialog box allows you to hollow the models using various rollouts. These rollouts are discussed next.

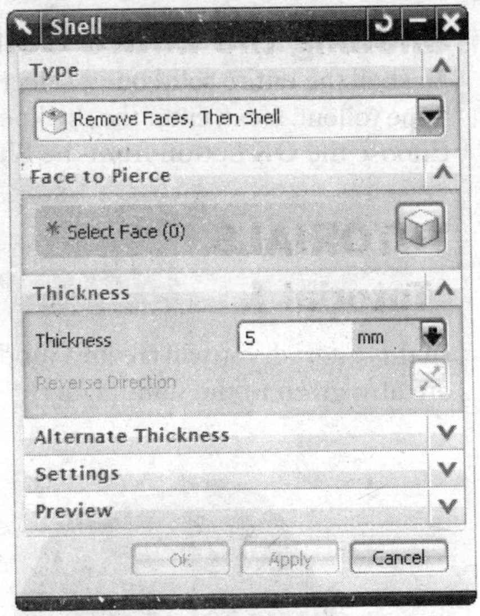

*Figure 7-41 The **Shell** dialog box*

Type Rollout

The drop-down list in this rollout is used to specify the type of shell that you need to create. The options in this rollout are discussed next.

Remove Faces, Then Shell

If you select this option, then the faces selected to shell the model will be removed.

Shell All Faces

If you select this option, then all faces of the model will be shelled and no faces will be removed.

Face to Pierce and Body to Shell Rollouts

Depending upon the option selected from the drop-down list in the **Type** rollout, the above mentioned rollouts will be available. For example, if you select the **Remove Faces, Then Shell** option, the **Face to Pierce** rollout will be available. The button in this rollout is used to select the faces to be removed from the shelled body. However, if you select the **Shell All Faces** option, the **Body to Shell** rollout will be available. The **Body to Shell** button in this rollout is used to select the body for shelling.

Thickness Rollout

The options in this rollout are discussed next.

Thickness

This edit box is used to specify the thickness of the shelled walls. Alternatively, you can drag the thickness handle from the drawing area to specify the thickness.

Reverse Direction

This button is used to flip the direction of offset.

Alternate Thickness Rollout

This rollout is used to assign unique wall thicknesses to selected face-sets in a shell feature. The **Shell Set** button in this rollout is used to create a set of faces to assign unique thickness. The set may contain one or more faces. Select faces and enter the thickness value in the **Thickness** edit box, which is below the **Shell Set** button in this rollout. After completing one set, choose the **Add New Set** button to create another set. These sets are displayed in the **List** sub-rollout. You can modify the thickness value of a particular set by selecting it and entering a different value in the **Thickness** edit box.

Shelling the Entire Solid Body

To shell the entire solid body, select the **Shell All Faces** option from the drop-down list in the **Type** rollout. Next, enter the thickness value in the **Thickness** edit box and select the solid body. Choose the **OK** button from the **Shell** dialog box; the entire solid body will be shelled.

TUTORIALS

Tutorial 1

In this tutorial, you will create a model of the Fixture Base shown in Figure 7-42. Its dimensions are also given in the same figure. **(Expected time: 30 min)**

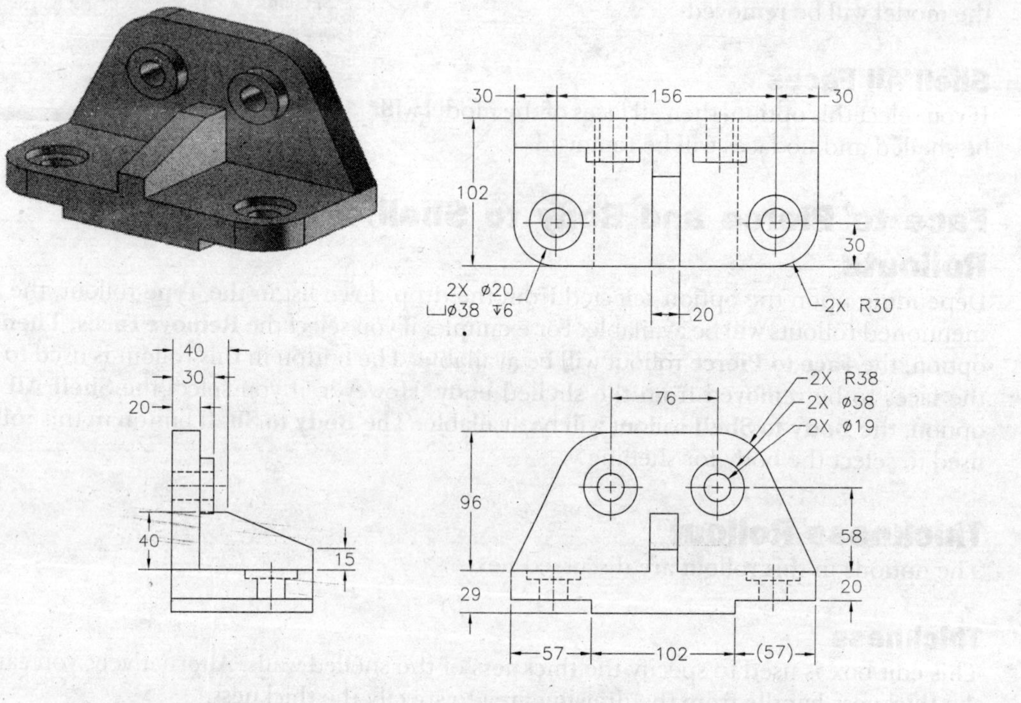

Figure 7-42 Model and its dimensions for Tutorial 1

The following steps are required to complete this tutorial:

a. Create the base feature of the model on the XC-ZC plane.
b. Create the second feature on the back face of the base feature.
c. Create the edge blend feature to fillet the two vertical edges of the base feature.
d. Create a counterbore hole on the right of the base feature by using the center point of the edge blend on the right.

e. Create the extruded join feature on the front face of the second feature and then create a hole on it.
f. Mirror the two holes by using the YC-ZC plane.
g. Create the central rib feature by drawing its sketch on the YC-ZC plane and extruding the sketch symmetrically in both directions.

Creating the Base Feature

1. Start a new file with the name *c07tut1.prt* using the **Model** template and specify its location as *C:\NX 7\c07*.

2. Create the sketch for the base feature on the XC-ZC plane. For dimensions, refer to Figure 7-42. Make sure that the sketch is symmetric about the YC-ZC plane because it will be used as the mirror plane at a later stage. Extrude the sketch symmetrically on both sides of the sketching plane through a symmetric distance of 51. The base feature of the model along with the YC-ZC plane is shown in Figure 7-43.

Creating the Second Feature

1. Create the second feature, which is an extruded join feature, by using the back face of the base feature as sketching plane, refer to Figure 7-44. For dimensions, refer to Figure 7-42.

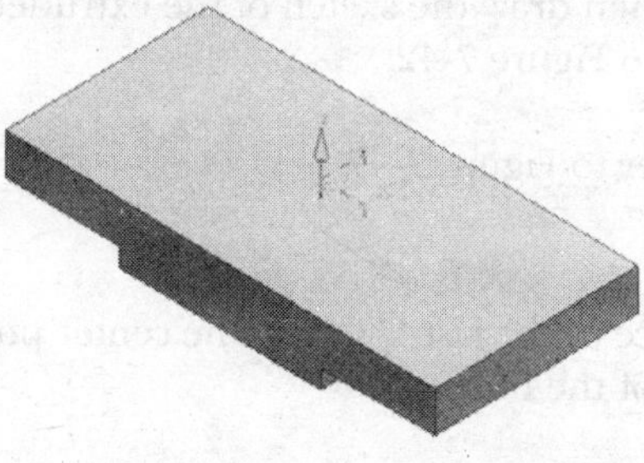

Figure 7-43 *Base feature of the model*

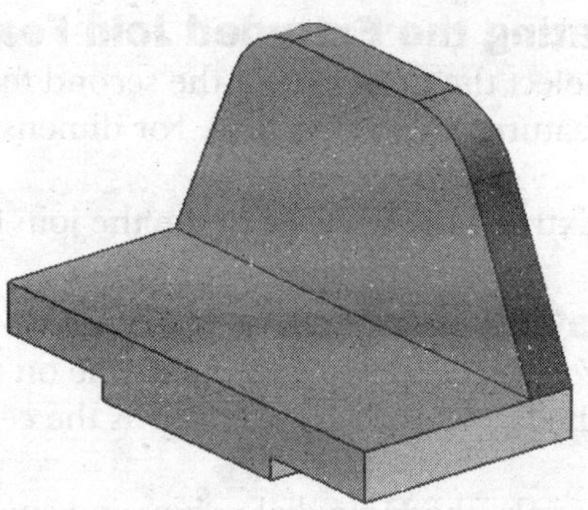

Figure 7-44 *Model after creating the second feature*

Creating the Edge Blend Feature

Next, you need to create the edge blend feature on the front vertical edges of the base feature. The center point of the right edge blend will be used to create the counterbore hole on the base feature.

1. Create the edge blend feature on the front vertical edges of the base feature, refer to Figure 7-45. For dimensions, refer to Figure 7-42.

Creating the Counterbore Hole

You need to create the counterbore hole on the right of the base feature and then mirror it to the other side. The center point of the edge blend on the right will be taken as the center point of the hole.

1. Invoke the **Hole** dialog box by choosing the **Hole** button from the **Feature Operation** toolbar and specify the parameters of the counterbore hole in it. Refer to Figure 7-42 for parameters.

2. Use the center point of the edge blend feature to place the counterbore hole. The model after creating the counterbore hole is shown in Figure 7-46.

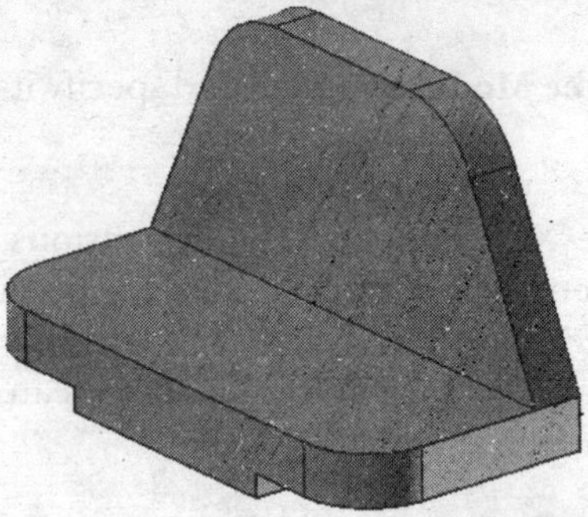

Figure 7-45 Model after creating the edge blend feature

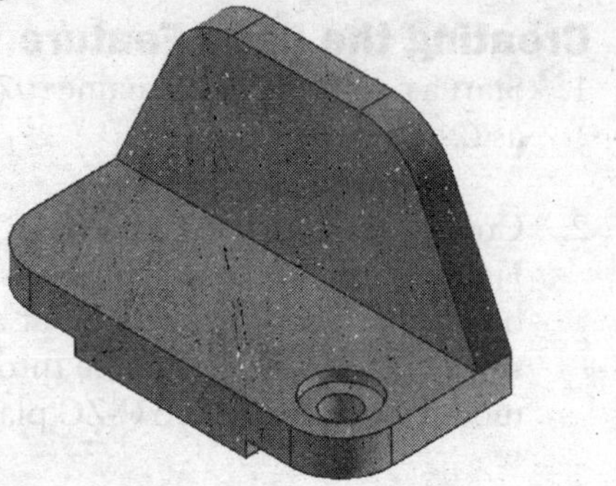

Figure 7-46 Model after creating the counterbore hole

Creating the Extruded Join Feature on the Second Feature

1. Select the front face of the second feature and then draw the sketch of the extruded join feature, which is a circle. For dimensions, refer to Figure 7-42.

2. Extrude the circle to create the join feature, refer to Figure 7-47.

Creating the Simple Hole

You need to create a simple hole on the front face of the last feature. The center point of the last feature will be used as the center point of the hole.

1. Invoke the **Hole** dialog box and specify the parameters of the simple hole in it, refer to Figure 7-42 for parameters.

2. Use the center point of the last feature to place the hole. The model after creating the simple hole is shown in Figure 7-48.

Mirroring Features

The sketch of the base feature was created symmetric about the YC-ZC plane, therefore, it will be used to mirror selected features.

1. Choose **Insert > Associative Copy > Mirror Feature** from the menu bar to invoke the **Mirror Feature** dialog box.

2. Select the counterbore hole, the extruded feature on the second feature, and the simple hole from the model; these features get highlighted in the model.

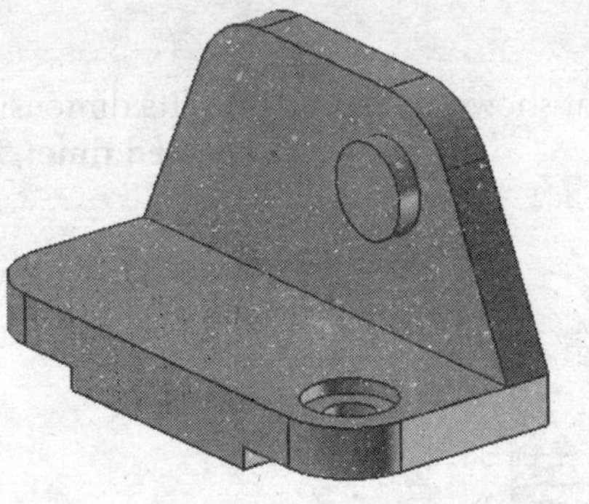

Figure 7-47 Model after creating the extruded join feature on the front face of the second feature

Figure 7-48 Model after creating the simple hole on the extruded join feature

3. Choose the **Plane** button from the **Mirror Plane** rollout of the **Mirror Feature** dialog box and then select the YC-ZC plane. To select this plane as a mirror plane, you may need to zoom out the model by using the **Zoom In/Out** tool.

4. Choose the **OK** button from this dialog box; the features are mirrored. The model after mirroring the features is shown in Figure 7-49.

Creating the Last Feature

1. Create the last feature, which is also an extruded join feature. The sketch of this feature will be drawn on the YC-ZC plane and will be extruded symmetrically. For dimensions, refer to Figure 7-42. The final model after creating this feature is shown in Figure 7-50.

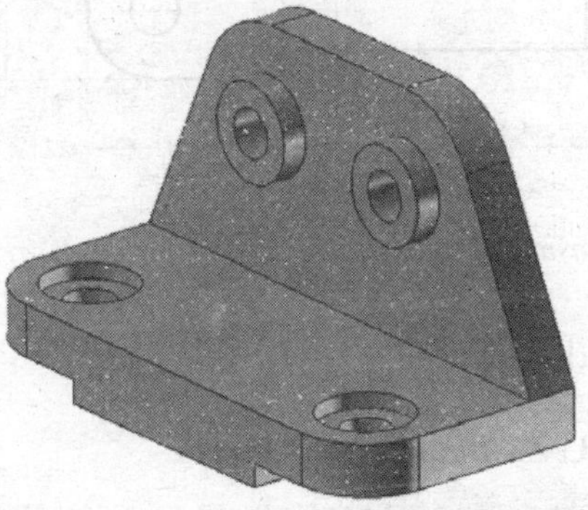

Figure 7-49 Model after mirroring the features and turning off the display of the datum plane

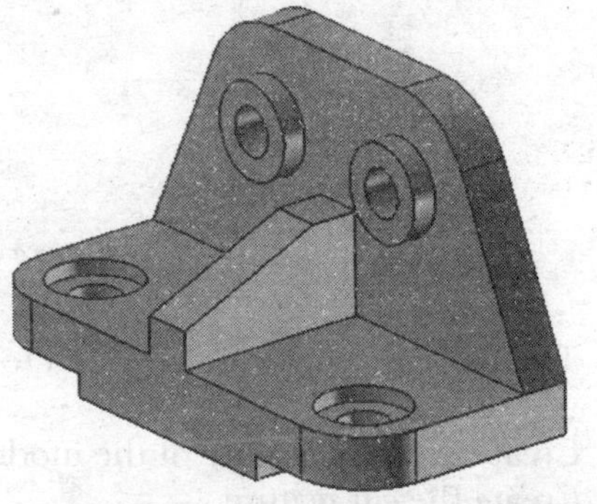

Figure 7-50 Final model for Tutorial 1

Saving and Closing the File

1. Choose **File > Close > Save and Close** from the menu bar to save and close the file.

Tutorial 2

In this tutorial, you will create a model of the Joint shown in Figure 7-51. Its dimensions are shown in Figure 7-52. **(Expected time: 30 min)**

Figure 7-51 Model of the Joint for Tutorial 2

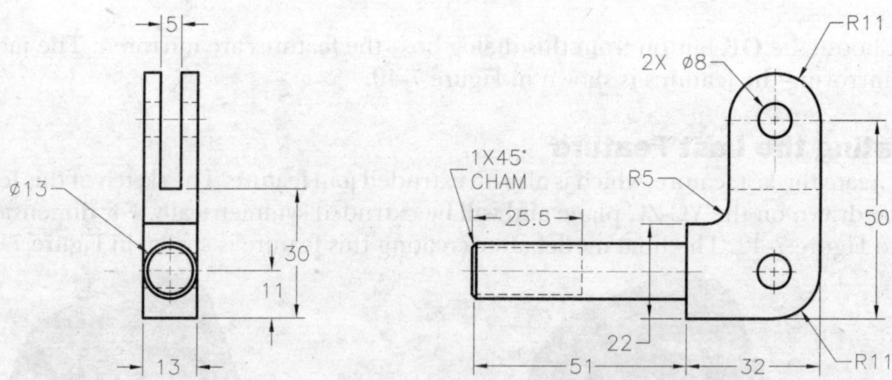

Figure 7-52 Dimension of the Joint

The following steps are required to complete this tutorial:

a. Create the base feature of the model on the YC-ZC plane.
b. Create the cut feature.
c. Create the extruded join feature on the left face and then create the chamfer feature.
d. Create holes on the base feature.
e. Finally, create threads on the cylindrical join feature by using the **Thread** tool.

Creating the Base Feature

1. Start a new file with the name *c07tut2.prt* using the **Model** template and specify its location as *C:\NX 7\c07*.

2. Create the base feature of the model on the YC-ZC plane, as shown in Figure 7-53. For dimensions, refer to Figure 7-52.

Creating the Cut Feature

1. Use the **Subtract** boolean option from the **Extrude** dialog box to create the cut feature in the base feature, refer to Figure 7-54. For dimensions of this cut feature, refer to Figure 7-52.

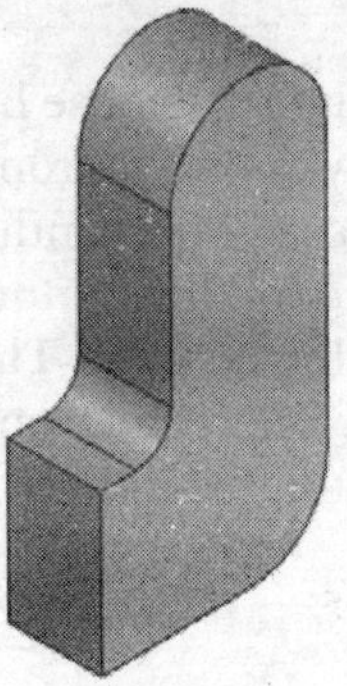

Figure 7-53 Base feature of the model

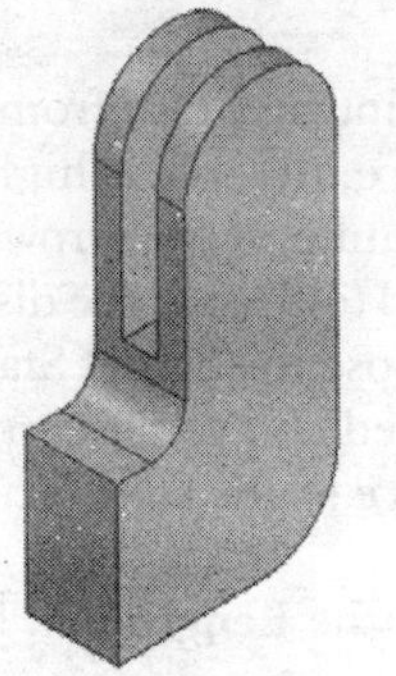

Figure 7-54 Model after creating the cut feature

Creating the Extruded Join Feature, Chamfer, and Holes

1. Use the **Unite** option of the **Extrude** dialog box to create the cylindrical feature on the front face of the base feature, refer to Figure 7-55. For dimensions of this extruded feature, refer to Figure 7-52.

2. Chamfer the front end of the cylindrical feature, refer to Figure 7-55. For its dimensions, refer to Figure 7-52.

3. Create two holes on the base feature, refer to Figure 7-56. For dimensions of the hole features, refer to Figure 7-52.

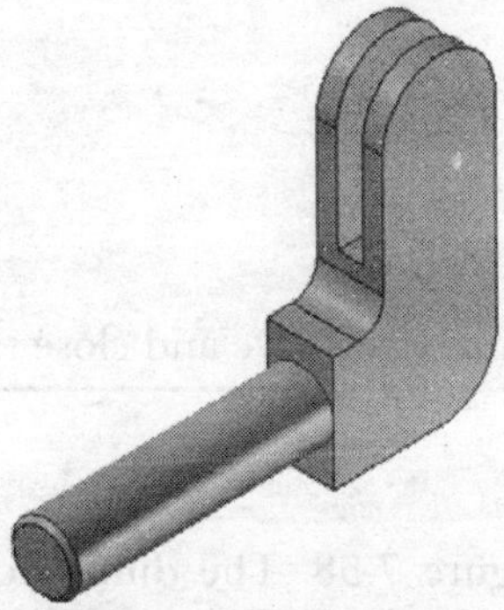

Figure 7-55 Model after creating and chamfering the cylindrical join feature

Figure 7-56 Model after creating holes

Creating Threads

Next, you need to create detailed threads on the cylindrical feature created on the front face of the base feature by using the **Thread** tool. When you invoke the **Thread** tool and select the cylindrical face, the thread parameters will automatically be defined in the edit boxes. You need to accept the default values for creating threads.

1. Choose **Insert > Design Feature > Thread** from the menu bar; the **Thread** dialog box is displayed.

2. In this dialog box, select the **Detailed** radio button; the thread options are modified and you are prompted to select a cylindrical face.

3. Select the cylindrical face from the drawing area by clicking the left mouse button closer to its front face; the face is highlighted and an arrow is displayed on the front face of the cylindrical feature. If the arrow is not displayed on the front face of the cylindrical feature, then you need to change the display of the arrow to the front face of the cylindrical feature. To do so, choose the **Select Start** button from the **Thread** dialog box; the **Thread** dialog box is modified and you are prompted to select the start face. Select the front face of the cylindrical face as the start face, and then choose the **OK** button from this dialog box.

4. Enter **25.5** in the **Length** edit box of the **Thread** dialog box.

5. Accept the other default values of thread parameters, which are displayed in various edit boxes of the **Thread** dialog box, and then choose **OK**; threads are created and the dialog box is closed. The final model of the Joint is shown in Figure 7-57.

***Figure 7-57** Final model of the Joint*

Saving and Closing the File

1. Choose **File > Close > Save and Close** from the menu bar to save and close the file.

Tutorial 3

In this tutorial, you will create the model shown in Figure 7-58. The dimensions of the model are shown in the same figure. **(Expected time: 30 min)**

The following steps are required to complete this tutorial:

a. Draw the sketch of the guide curve on the YC-ZC plane for the base feature.
b. Create a new datum plane at the start point of the guide curve and then draw the sketch of the section on this plane.
c. Create the sweep feature by using the **Sweep along Guide** tool.

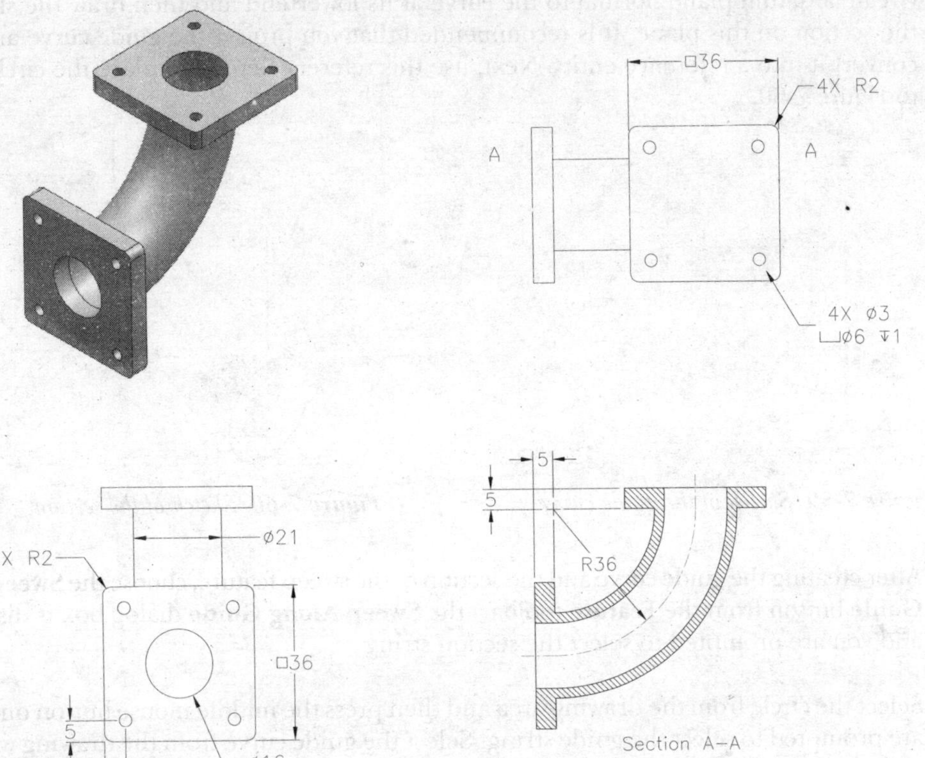

***Figure 7-58** Model and its dimensions for Tutorial 3*

d. Hollow the sweep feature.
e. Create extruded join features on the end faces of the sweep feature and then create holes on them.
f. Create the counterbore hole on one of the extruded features and then create the rectangular array of holes.
g. Similarly, create the counterbore hole on the other extruded feature and then create the array of holes.

Creating the Base Feature

The base feature of this model is a sweep feature. First you will draw the guide curve of the sweep feature and then create a datum plane at the lower end of the guide curve. Using this datum plane as sketching plane, you will sketch the section of the sweep feature.

1. Start a new file with the name *c07tut3.prt* using the **Model** template and specify its location as *C:\NX 7\c07*.

2. Draw the sketch of the guide curve on the YC-ZC plane, refer to Figure 7-59.

3. Create a datum plane normal to the curve at its lower end and then draw the sketch of the section on this plane. It is recommended that you project the guide curve and then convert it into a reference entity. Next, use this reference entity to place the circle, refer to Figure 7-60.

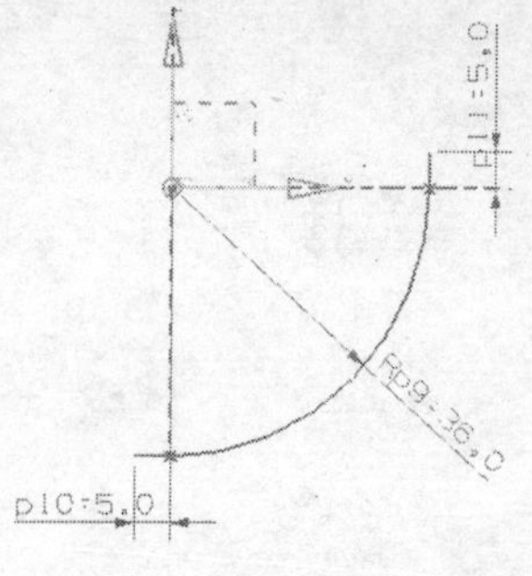

Figure 7-59 Sketch of the guide curve

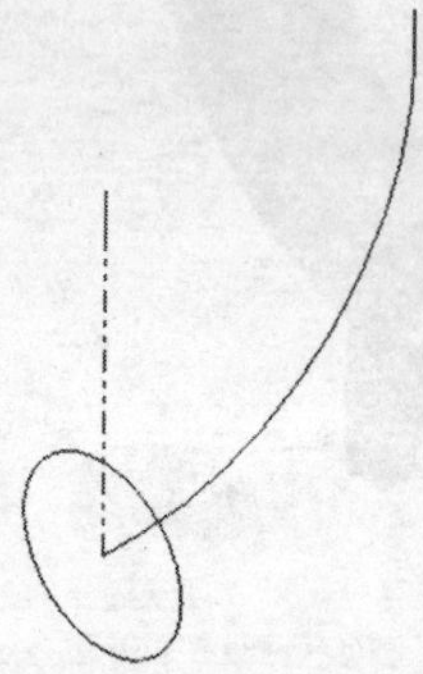

Figure 7-60 Sketch of the section

4. After creating the guide curve and the section of the sweep feature, choose the **Sweep along Guide** button from the **Feature** toolbar; the **Sweep Along Guide** dialog box is displayed and you are prompted to select the section string.

5. Select the circle from the drawing area and then press the middle mouse button once; you are prompted to select the guide string. Select the guide curve from the drawing window; the preview of the feature is displayed in the drawing window. Make sure the value **0** is entered in the **First Offset** and **Second Offset** edit boxes of the **Offset** rollout in the dialog box.

6. Choose the **OK** button from this dialog box; the sweep feature is created, as shown in Figure 7-61.

Hollowing the Base Feature

Next, you need to hollow the base feature by using the **Shell** tool.

1. Invoke the **Shell** tool; the **Shell** dialog box is displayed and you are prompted to select the faces to remove.

2. Enter **2.5** in the **Thickness** edit box and select the two end faces of the sweep feature.

3. Choose the **Apply** button and then choose **Cancel** to exit the dialog box. The model after hollowing the base feature is shown in Figure 7-62.

Note

*For hollowing the base feature, you can also enter -2.5 in the **First Offset** edit box of the **Offset** rollout in the **Sweep Along Guide** dialog box while creating it.*

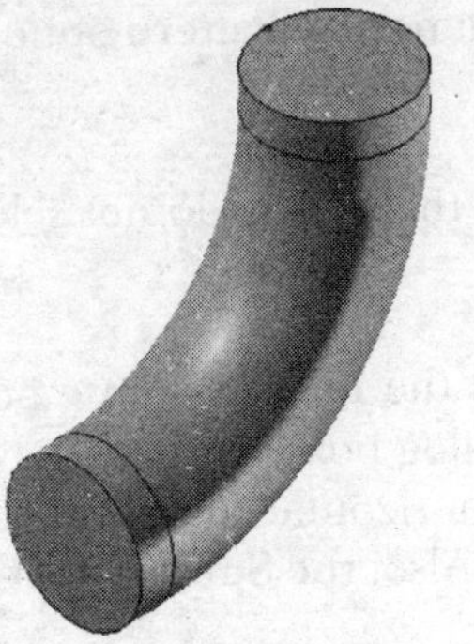

Figure 7-61 Base feature of the model

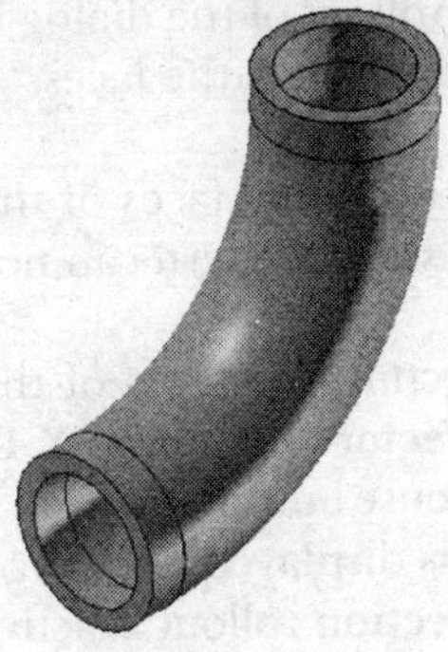

Figure 7-62 Model after hollowing the base feature

Creating Extruded Join Features on the End Faces of the Base Feature

1. Create the extruded join feature one by one on the two end faces of the base feature, as shown in Figure 7-63. Note that you need to reverse the direction of the feature creation. For dimensions, refer to Figure 7-58.

2. Create simple holes in the center of the extruded join features. Note that the holes need to be created only up to the back faces of the extruded features. For diameters of the holes, refer to Figure 7-58. Figure 7-64 shows the model after the holes have been created.

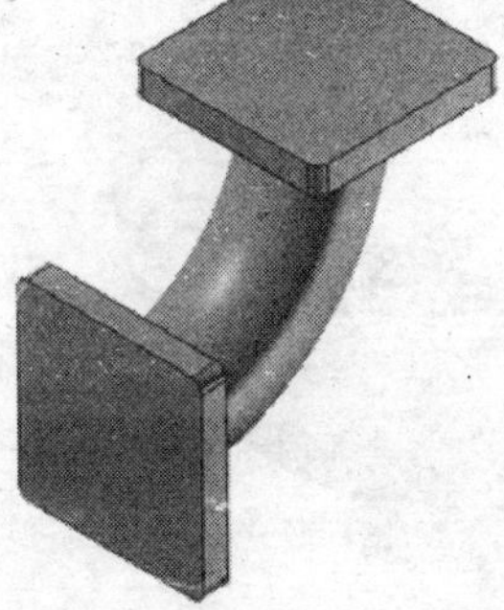

Figure 7-63 Extruded join features created on the two end faces of the base feature

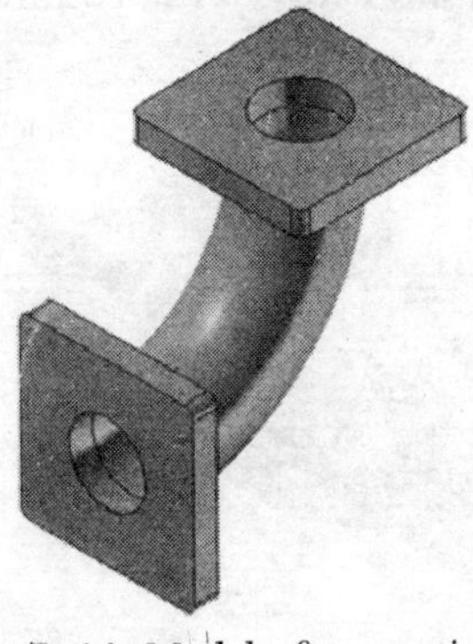

Figure 7-64 Model after creating holes

Creating Counterbore Holes

1. Create the counterbore hole on the lower right of the back face of the front extruded feature of the model. The rotated view of the model after creating the hole is shown in Figure 7-65. For dimensions of the counterbore hole, refer to Figure 7-58.

2. After creating the counterbore hole, choose **Insert > Associative Copy > Instance Feature** from the menu bar to invoke the **Instance** dialog box.

3. Choose the **Pattern Face** button from the **Instance** dialog box; the **Pattern Face** dialog box is displayed. Select the **Rectangular Pattern** option from the **Type** drop-down list in

the **Type** rollout of the dialog box. As you select the **Rectangular Pattern** option, you are prompted to select the faces.

4. Select all the three faces of the counterbore hole. Note that if you do not select all the three faces, the pattern can not be created.

5. After selecting the faces of the counterbore hole, press the middle mouse button; the **Specify Vector** area in the **X Direction** rollout of the dialog box is activated. Next, click the left mouse button near the left endpoint of the lower horizontal edge of the front face; an arrow is displayed pointing toward the left direction. Also, the **Specify Vector** area in the **Y Direction** rollout is activated.

6. Click the left mouse button near the top endpoint of the right vertical edge of the front face; an arrow is displayed pointing toward the upward direction.

7. Enter **2** in the **X Count** and **Y Count** edit boxes in the **Pattern Properties** rollout of the dialog box.

8. Enter **26** in both the **X Distance** and **Y Distance** edit boxes of the **Pattern Properties** rollout. Next, choose the **OK** button from the **Pattern Face** dialog box; the **Instance** dialog box is displayed. Choose the **Cancel** button from the **Instance** dialog box; a rectangular array of counterbore holes is created. The rotated view of the model after creating the rectangular array of the counterbore holes is shown in Figure 7-66.

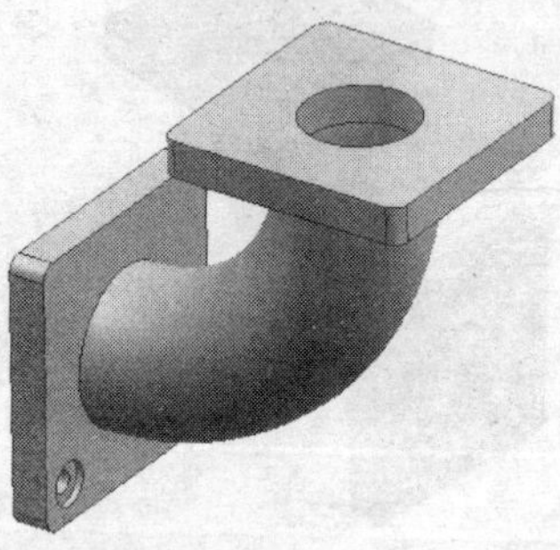

Figure 7-65 One of the counterbore holes created on the front face of the model

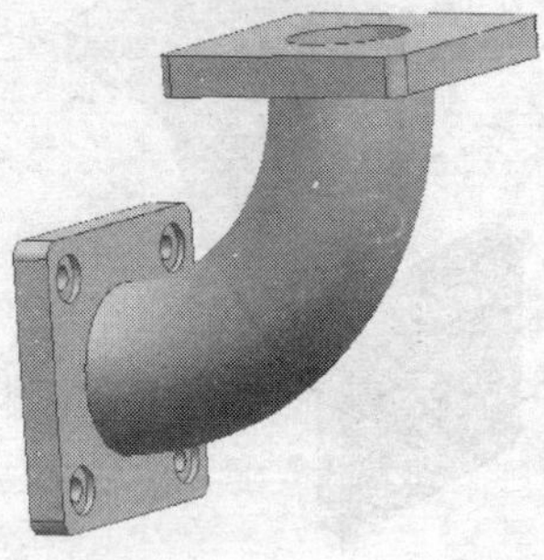

Figure 7-66 Model after creating the rectangular array of counterbore holes

Note

*If the direction arrows point in the directions opposite from what is required, then choose the **Reverse Direction** button.*

9. Similarly, create the counterbore hole on the bottom face of the top extruded feature and then create a rectangular array of counterbore holes on the bottom face of the top extruded feature. The final model for this tutorial is shown in Figure 7-67.

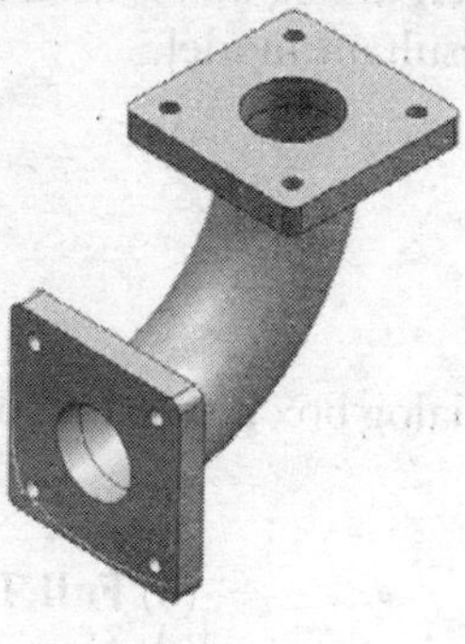

Figure 7-67 Final model for Tutorial 3

Saving and Closing the File

1. Choose **File > Close > Save and Close** from the menu bar to save and close the file.

Self-Evaluation Test

Answer the following questions and then compare them to those given at the end of this chapter:

1. In NX, you can sweep an open section along a guide curve. (T/F)

2. You can use the **Rectangular Array** button from the **Instance** dialog box to create a rectangular array of features, only along the X and Y directions of the work coordinate system. (T/F)

3. In NX, you can create only realistic threads. (T/F)

4. The **Tube** tool is used to create a tube of rectangular cross-section. (T/F)

5. The __________ tool is used to scoop out material from a model and make it hollow from inside.

6. The __________ features are created by sweeping one or more sections along one or more guide curves such that all sections are blended together.

7. The __________ radio button is selected from the **Thread** dialog box to create realistic threads.

8. The __________ arrays are created by placing the instances of the selected features along the circumference of an imaginary circle.

9. The __________ tool is used to select the X and Y directions of the rectangular pattern.

10. The __________ rollout in the **Shell** dialog box is used to specify the faces of a model that should not be displayed in the resultant model.

Review Questions

Answer the following questions:

1. Which check box in the **Thread** dialog box is selected to create threads through the length of a selected face?

   (a) **Full** (b) **Full Thread**
   (c) **Complete** (d) None of these

2. Which option is used to create an array in which instances are exactly identical to original feature?

   (a) **Similar** (b) **Equal**
   (c) **Identical** (d) None of these

3. Which of the following types of thread displays thread convention in the form of dashed lines?

   (a) Symbolic (b) Detailed
   (c) Convention (d) Improper

4. In the **Shell** dialog box, which of the following rollouts is used to select a face of a model to specify a different wall thickness?

   (a) **Alternate Thickness** (b) **Thickness**
   (c) **Settings** (d) **Offset face**

5. Which of the following tools does not need a section to create a feature?

   (a) **Sweep along Guide** (b) **Swept**
   (c) **Tube** (d) None of these

6. Which of the following threads allows the screw to get tightened when rotated in the clockwise direction?

   (a) Right hand (b) Left hand
   (c) Downward (d) Upward

7. The **Shell** dialog box allows you to hollow models by using three methods. (T/F)

8. The **Thread** dialog box does not allow you to select the start and the end of threads. (T/F)

9. The rectangular arrays can only be created by placing the instances of the selected features along the XC and YC directions of the work coordinate system (WCS). (T/F)

10. If you enter **0** in the **Inner Diameter** edit box, the resulting tube feature will be solid filled. (T/F)

Exercises

Exercise 1

Create the model shown in Figure 7-68. The dimensions of the model are given in Figure 7-69. Save the file with the name *c07exr1.prt* at the location */NX 7/c07.*

(Expected time: 30 min)

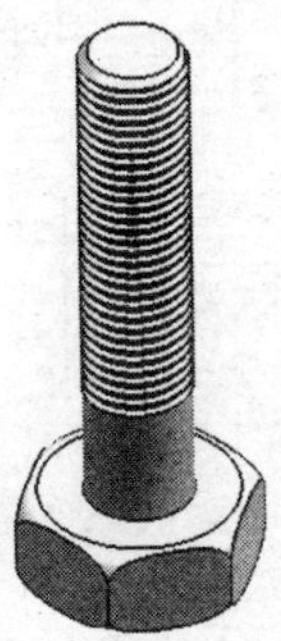

Figure 7-68 Model for Exercise 1

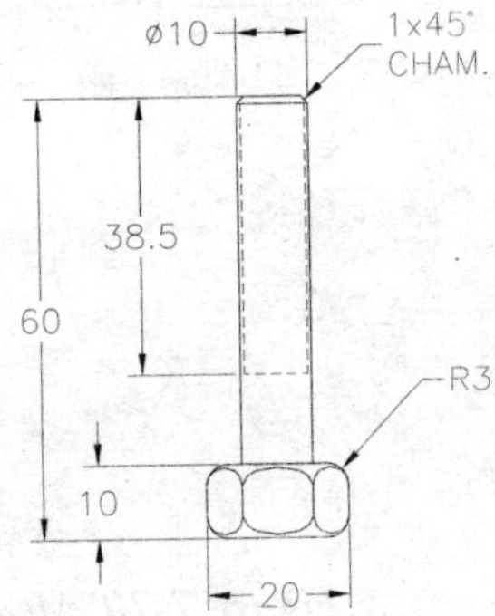

Figure 7-69 Dimensions for Exercise 1

Exercise 2

Create the model, as shown in Figure 7-70. The dimensions of the model are also given in the same figure. Save the file with the name *c07exr2.prt* at the location */NX 7/c07.*

(Expected time: 30 min)

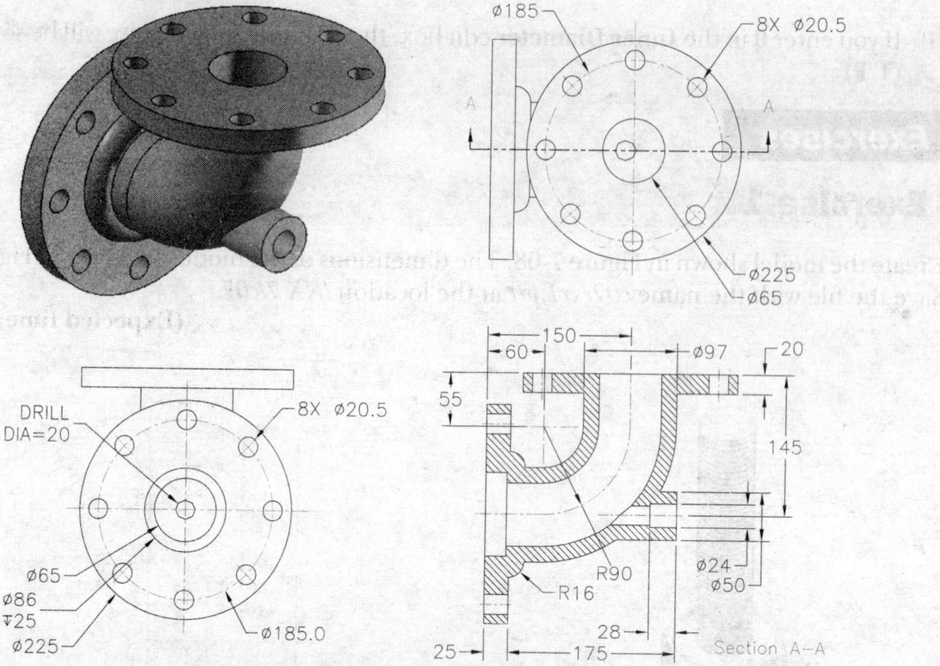

Figure 7-70 Model and its dimensions for Exercise 2

Answers to Self-Evaluation Test

1. T, **2.** T, **3.** F, **4.** F, **5. Shell**, **6.** swept, **7. Detailed**, **8.** circular, **9. Pattern Face**, **10. Face to Pierce**

Chapter 8

Editing Features and Advanced Modeling Tools-III

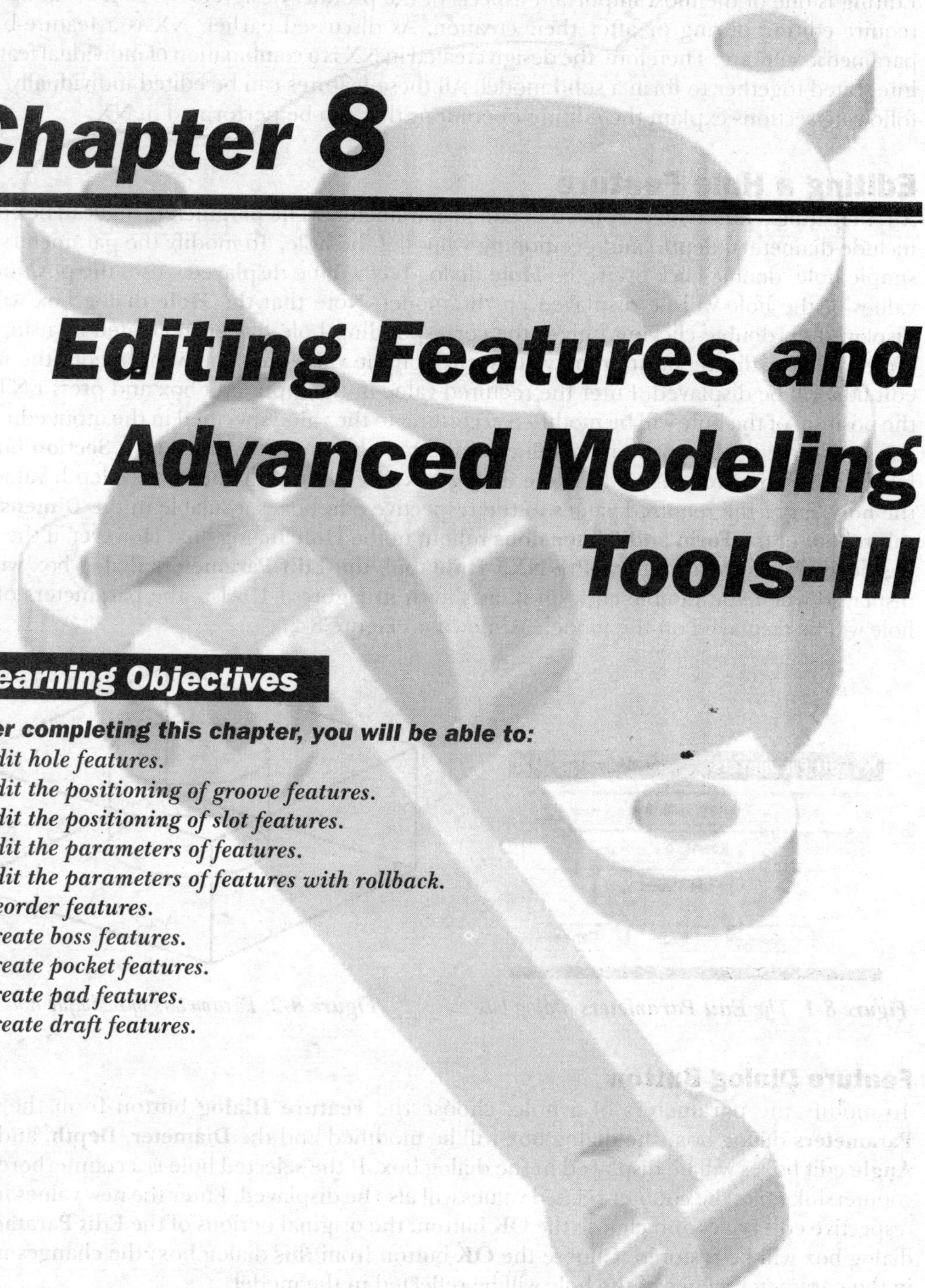

Learning Objectives

After completing this chapter, you will be able to:

- *Edit hole features.*
- *Edit the positioning of groove features.*
- *Edit the positioning of slot features.*
- *Edit the parameters of features.*
- *Edit the parameters of features with rollback.*
- *Reorder features.*
- *Create boss features.*
- *Create pocket features.*
- *Create pad features.*
- *Create draft features.*

EDITING FEATURES

Editing is one of the most important aspects of the product design cycle. Almost all designs require editing during or after their creation. As discussed earlier, NX is a feature-based parametric software. Therefore, the design created in NX is a combination of individual features integrated together to form a solid model. All these features can be edited individually. The following sections explain the editing operations that can be performed in NX:

Editing a Hole Feature

After creating a hole, you may need to edit its parameters. The parameters that can be edited include diameters, depth, and positioning values of the hole. To modify the parameters of a simple hole, double-click on it; the **Hole** dialog box will be displayed. Also, the positioning values of the hole will be displayed on the model. Note that the **Hole** dialog box will be displayed on double-clicking only if the corresponding hole has been created by using the **Hole** tool. To edit the positioning values, click on the value that you want to edit; the input edit box will be displayed. Enter the required value in the input edit box and press ENTER; the position of the hole will be modified according to the value specified in the input edit box. You can also edit the positioning values of the hole by choosing the **Sketch Section** button from the **Position** rollout of the **Hole** dialog box. To edit the diameter and depth values of the hole, enter the required values in the respective edit boxes available in the **Dimensions** sub-rollout of the **Form and Dimensions** rollout in the **Hole** dialog box. However, if the hole has been created by using the **Pre-NX5 Hole** tool, the **Edit Parameters** dialog box will be displayed when you double-click on it, as shown in Figure 8-1. Also, the parameters of the hole will be displayed on the model, as shown in Figure 8-2.

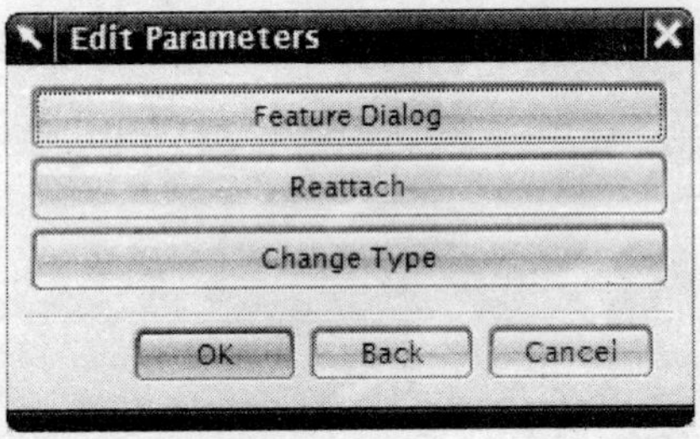

Figure 8-1 *The* ***Edit Parameters*** *dialog box*

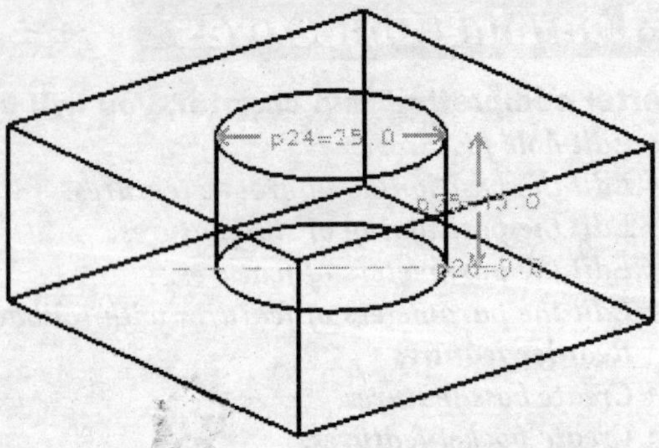

Figure 8-2 *Parameters of a simple hole*

Feature Dialog Button

To modify the parameters of a hole, choose the **Feature Dialog** button from the **Edit Parameters** dialog box; the dialog box will be modified and the **Diameter**, **Depth**, and **Tip Angle** edit boxes will be displayed in the dialog box. If the selected hole is a counterbore or a countersink hole, the counter related values will also be displayed. Enter the new values in the respective edit boxes and choose the **OK** button; the original options of the **Edit Parameters** dialog box will be restored. Choose the **OK** button from this dialog box; the changes made in the parameter values of the hole will be reflected in the model.

Reattach Button

To change the placement face of a hole, choose the **Reattach** button from the **Edit Parameters** dialog box; the **Reattach** dialog box will be displayed, as shown in Figure 8-3. By default, the **Specify Target Placement Face** button is chosen in the **Selection Steps** area, and you will be prompted to select the target face. Select a new placement face to reattach the hole. On doing so, the **Redefine Positioning Dimensions** button will be automatically chosen from the **Selection Steps** area of the **Reattach** dialog box. To retain the same positional reference for the hole on the new placement face and create it, choose the **OK** button.

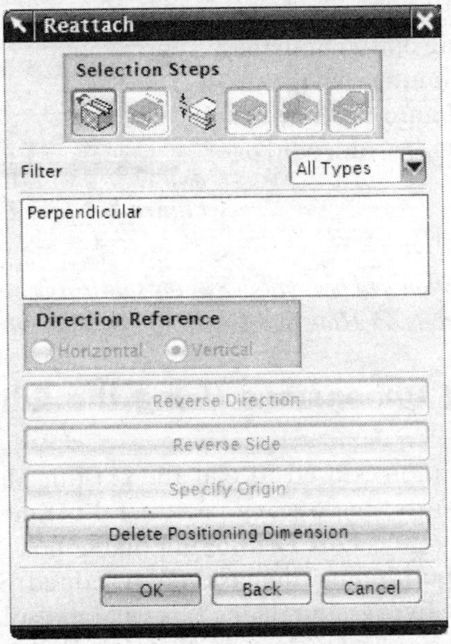

Figure 8-3 The **Reattach** dialog box

To specify a new positional reference for the hole, select the dimension from the graphics window; a dialog box will be displayed, which will be named based on the type of dimension used to place the hole. Also, you will be prompted to select the target object. Select an edge or a datum to define the new reference for the dimension in the new placement face; you will be prompted to select the reference from the tool (hole). Select the bottom circular edge from the hole; the **Select Arc Position** dialog box will be displayed. To define the positional between the selected edge/datum and the center point of the hole, choose the **Arc Center** button from the **Select Arc Position** dialog box. To define the positional value between the selected edge/datum and any of the quadrant points of the hole, choose the **End Point** button. To define the positional reference between the selected edge/datum and the tangent point on the bottom edge of the hole, choose the **Tangent Point** button. After specifying the new positional reference, choose the **OK** button from the **Reattach** dialog box. Next, choose the **OK** button from the **Edit Parameters** dialog box; the changes will be reflected in the model.

Note

*If the hole is a through hole, you can specify the new positional references for the hole only by choosing the **Identify Solid Face** button from the dialog box. On choosing this button, you will be prompted to select the cylindrical face. Select the cylindrical face of the hole to specify the reference from the hole.*

*You can also delete the hole dimensions using the **Reattach** dialog box. To do so, choose the **Delete Positioning Dimension** button from the **Reattach** dialog box and then select the dimension to be deleted.*

Editing the Positioning of a Hole Feature

NX allows you to edit the positioning of hole features. To do so, choose the **Part Navigator** tab from the **Resource Bar**; the **Part Navigator** will be displayed. Right-click on the hole feature, and then choose the **Edit Positioning** option from the shortcut menu; the **Edit Positioning** dialog box will be displayed, as shown in Figure 8-4. You can use the options in this dialog box to add, edit, or delete a dimension.

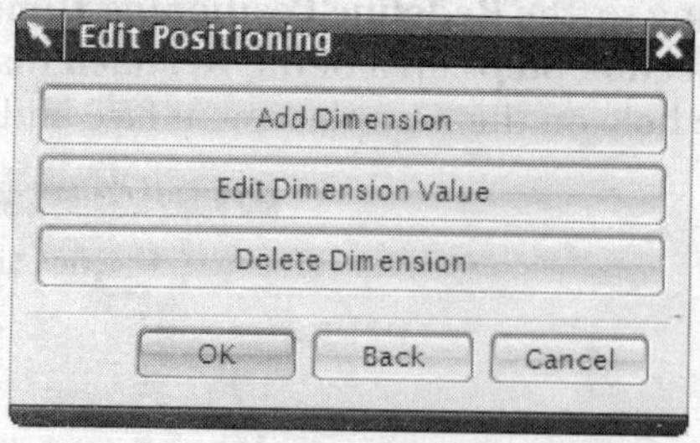

Figure 8-4 *The **Edit Positioning** dialog box*

Note

*The **Edit Positioning** option will be available in the shortcut menu only when the selected hole is created by using the **Pre-NX5 Hole** tool.*

Editing the Positioning Dimensions Using the Edit Dimension Value Button

The **Edit Dimension Value** button is used to edit the existing dimension values that are defined to position the hole feature. To do so, choose the **Edit Dimension Value** button from the **Edit Positioning** dialog box; the **Edit Positioning** dialog box will be modified and you will be prompted to select the positioning dimension to be edited. Select the dimension that needs to be modified; the **Edit Expression** dialog box will be displayed. Enter the required value in the edit box and choose the **OK** button; the **Edit Positioning** dialog box will be displayed again and you will be prompted to select the next positioning dimension be edited. Select another dimension that needs to be modified. Enter the required value in the edit box, and then choose the **OK** button from the **Edit Expression** dialog box. Next, choose the **OK** button twice; the position of the hole feature will be modified.

Adding the Positioning Dimensions Using the Add Dimension Button

The **Add Dimension** button is used to add a positioning dimensions to an already positioned feature. To add the new positioning dimensions, choose the **Add Dimension** button; the **Positioning** dialog box will be displayed. The tools in this dialog box can be used to create a new positioning dimensions, as discussed in the previous chapter.

Deleting the Positioning Dimensions Using the Delete Dimension Button

The **Delete Dimension** button is used to delete the positioning dimensions. To delete the positioning dimensions, choose the **Delete Dimension** button; the **Remove Positioning** dialog box will be displayed, and you will be prompted to select the positioning dimension to be deleted. Select the positioning dimensions to be deleted and choose the **OK** button; the selected dimensions will be deleted.

Editing the Positioning of a Groove Feature

As mentioned earlier, you can edit the positioning of a groove feature. To do so, choose the **Part Navigator** tab from the **Resource Bar**; the **Part Navigator** will be invoked. Right-click on the groove feature displayed in the **Part Navigator**; a shortcut menu will be displayed. Choose the **Edit Positioning** option from the shortcut menu; the **Edit Positioning** dialog box will be displayed. Also, the edges selected for applying the positioning dimension will be displayed in dashed line format. Next, choose the **Edit Dimension Value** button from the dialog box; the **Edit Expression** dialog box will be displayed. Enter the new positioning value in the edit box and choose the **OK** button; the **Edit Positioning** dialog box will be displayed again. Choose the **OK** button from this dialog box to reflect the changes made in the positioning value.

Editing the Positioning of a Slot Feature

To edit the positioning of a slot feature, invoke the **Part Navigator** by choosing the **Part Navigator** tab from the **Resource Bar**. Next, right-click on the slot feature displayed on the tree to display a shortcut menu. Next, choose the **Edit Positioning** option from the shortcut menu; the **Edit Positioning** dialog box will be displayed. Choose the **Edit Dimension Value** button from this dialog box; the **Edit Expression** dialog box will be displayed. Enter the new positioning value in the edit box and choose the **OK** button; the **Edit Positioning** dialog box will be displayed again. Choose the **OK** button from this dialog box to reflect the changes made in the positioning value.

Note

If a feature is created by specifying its two positioning dimension values, then on choosing the ***Edit Dimension Value*** *button from the* ***Edit Positioning*** *dialog box, the* ***Edit Positioning*** *dialog box will be modified and you will be prompted to select the positioning dimension value to be edited.*

Editing the Parameters of Features

Similar to editing the parameters of holes, NX also allows you to edit the parameters of other features such as extruded features, revolved features, and so on. To edit the parameters of these features, right-click on the name of the feature in the **Part Navigator**, and then choose the **Edit Parameters** from the shortcut menu displayed. Depending on the feature selected, the corresponding dialog box will be displayed. You can select the required options from this dialog box to modify the parameters of the selected feature.

Editing the Parameters of Features with Rollback

In NX, you can edit parameters of features such as extrude features, edge blend features, face blend features, and so on with rollback. This editing operation is similar to the editing parameters, except that this option temporarily suppresses all features created after the feature to be edited. To do so, right-click on the required feature, and then choose the **Edit with Rollback** option from the shortcut menu displayed; a dialog box corresponding to the selected feature will be displayed, in which you can modify parameters. Also, the features created after the selected feature will be temporarily suppressed from the model. Once the editing is completed, the suppressed features will be automatically restored.

Editing Sketches of the Sketch-based Features

NX also allows you to edit the sketches of the sketch-based features. To do so, right-click on the sketch in the **Part Navigator** and choose **Edit** from the shortcut menu displayed; the Sketcher environment will be invoked and the model will be oriented such that the selected sketch will be normal to the view. Also, all dimensions of the sketch will be displayed. You can modify the dimensions of the sketch or remove the existing entities and add new entities to the sketch. However, you need to make sure that the sketch is closed after adding or removing the sketched entities.

Note

*If the sketch of a feature is created by invoking the Sketcher environment using the corresponding feature creation tool, then the sketch will not be displayed in the tree of the **Part Navigator**. In this case, right-click on the feature whose sketch is to be edited; a shortcut menu will be displayed. Choose the **Edit Sketch** option from the shortcut menu; the Sketcher environment will be invoked. Now, you can edit the sketch.*

Reordering Features

This option allows you to change the order of the features, in which they are created. The feature can be reordered before or after the specified reference feature. To reorder a feature, right-click on the feature name in the **Part Navigator** and choose **Reorder Before** or **Reorder After** from the shortcut menu; the cascading menu containing the names of the reference features will be displayed. Select the feature after or before which you need to reorder a selected feature.

ADVANCED MODELING TOOLS

As discussed in the previous chapter, the advanced modeling tools are mostly used to place different types of standard and user-defined features on the model. Each advanced modeling tool has its specific use in designing a real-world component. These advanced feature tools reduce the time taken in creating a design.

Creating Boss Features

Toolbar: Feature > Boss *(Customize to add)*

The **Boss** tool is used to add the material to the model in a circular cross-section that has been defined by the user. The boss feature can be placed on a planar surface or a datum plane. Note that the boss feature cannot be the first feature of the model. This is because you need to associate it to an existing target body.

The boss feature is a placed feature, and therefore, it does not require a sketch. You need to specify its diameter, height, and taper angle. To create a boss feature, choose the **Boss** button from the **Feature** toolbar; the **Boss** dialog box will be displayed, as shown in Figure 8-5, and you will be prompted to select the planar placement face.

*Figure 8-5 The **Boss** dialog box*

Select the planar face or the datum plane; the preview of the boss will be displayed. Next, enter the values of the diameter, height, and taper in the respective edit boxes, and then choose the **OK** button; the **Positioning** dialog box will be displayed, as shown in Figure 8-6. Also, you will be prompted to select the positioning method. Using the buttons in this dialog box, you can position the boss about the placement face. Figure 8-7 shows a boss feature of diameter 50, height 30, and taper angle 2 degrees.

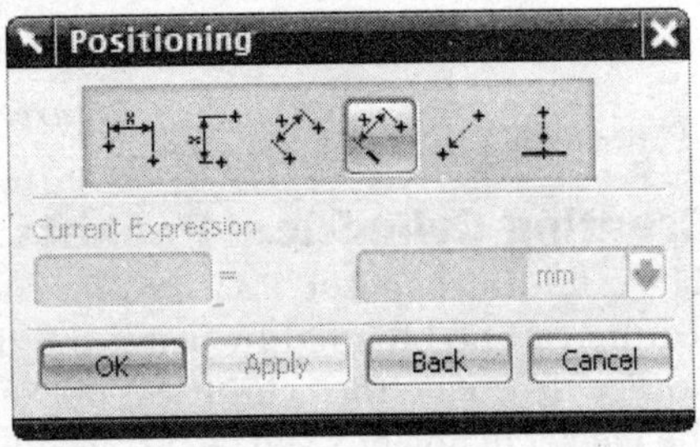

*Figure 8-6 The **Positioning** dialog box*

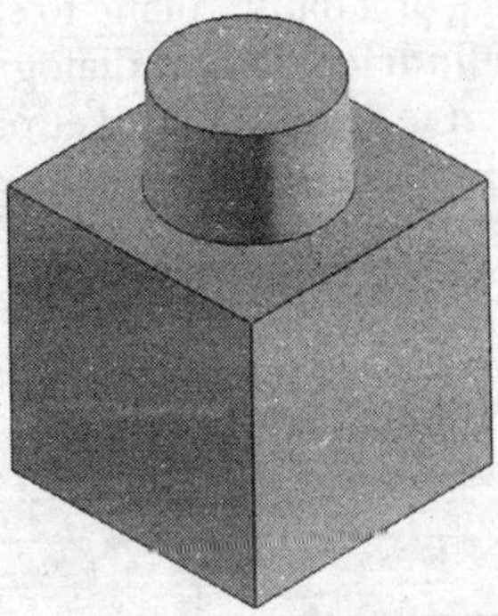

Figure 8-7 The resulting boss feature

Note

If you try to create the boss feature as the first feature, then after selecting the placement plane, you will be prompted to select a target body.

Creating Pocket Features

Toolbar: Feature > Pocket *(Customize to add)*

The **Pocket** tool is used to remove material from a model in the cylindrical or rectangular cross-section. To create a pocket, choose the **Pocket** button from the **Feature** toolbar; the **Pocket** dialog box will be displayed, as shown in Figure 8-8. In NX, you can create three types of pockets: cylindrical, rectangular, and general. The procedure to create different types of pockets is discussed next.

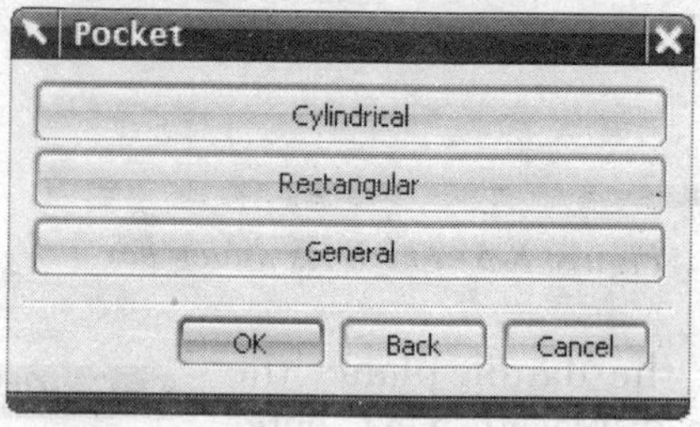

*Figure 8-8 The **Pocket** dialog box*

Creating Cylindrical Pockets

The cylindrical pocket has a circular cutout of a specific depth. The bottom edge of the pocket feature can be blended by using the floor radius. You can also define a taper angle for the pocket. To create the cylindrical pocket, choose the **Pocket** button from the **Feature** toolbar; the **Pocket** dialog box will be displayed. Choose the **Cylindrical** button from the **Pocket** dialog box; the **Cylindrical Pocket** dialog box will be displayed and you will be prompted to select a planar placement face. Select a face or a datum plane to specify the placement plane of the pocket feature. On doing so, the **Cylindrical Pocket** dialog box will be modified, as shown in Figure 8-9, and you will be prompted to enter the pocket parameters.

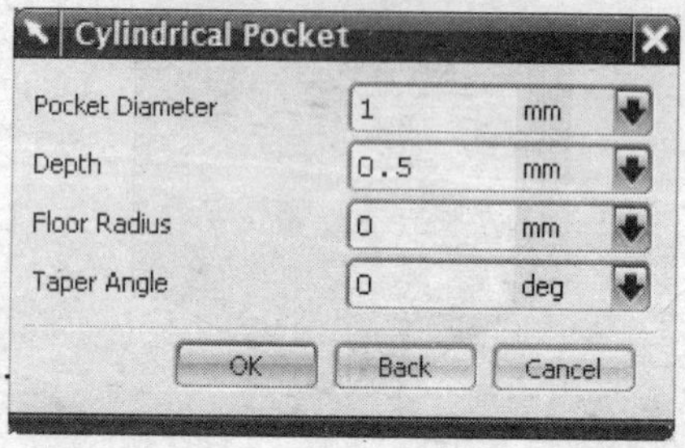

*Figure 8-9 The **Cylindrical Pocket** dialog box*

Enter the values of the diameter, depth, floor radius, and taper angle in the **Cylindrical Pocket** dialog box and choose the **OK** button; the **Positioning** dialog box will be displayed, along with the preview of the pocket. You can position the cylindrical pocket on the placement face using the options in this dialog box. Figure 8-10 shows a cylindrical pocket feature of diameter 40, depth 40, floor radius 10, and taper angle 5 degrees.

Creating Rectangular Pockets

This pocket type has a rectangular cutout of a specific depth, length, width, with or without radii in the corners and on the floors, and with or without straight or tapered sides. To create a rectangular pocket, choose the **Pocket** button from the **Feature** toolbar; the **Pocket** dialog box will be displayed. Choose the **Rectangular** button from the **Pocket** dialog box; the **Rectangular Pocket** dialog box will be displayed, as shown in Figure 8-11, and you will be prompted to select a planar placement face.

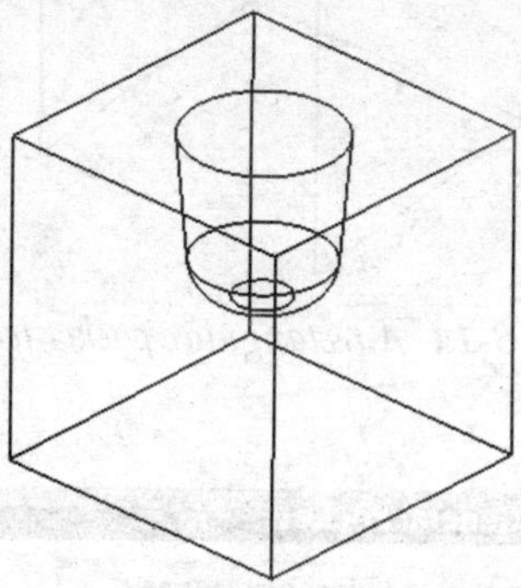

Figure 8-10 *A cylindrical pocket feature*

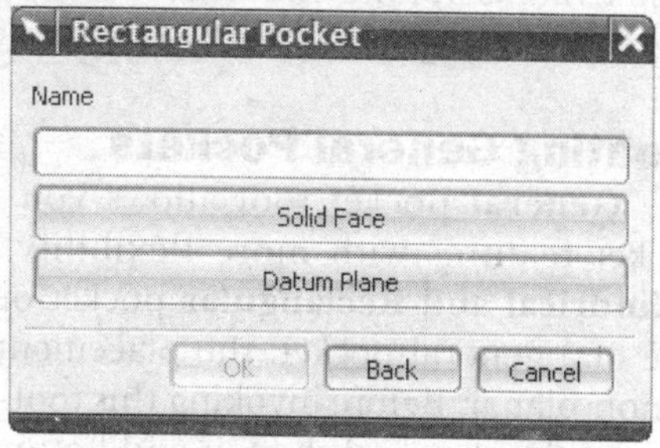

Figure 8-11 ***The Rectangular Pocket*** *dialog box*

Select a face or a datum plane to create the pocket feature; the **Horizontal Reference** dialog box will be displayed, as shown in Figure 8-12, and you will be prompted to select a horizontal reference. The length of the pocket will be parallel to the horizontal reference. You can select a linear edge to specify the horizontal reference. Alternatively, you can use the options in the **Horizontal Reference** dialog box to select the horizontal reference. On selecting the horizontal reference, the **Rectangular Pocket** dialog box will be displayed, as shown in Figure 8-13, and you will be prompted to enter the pocket parameters. Enter the values of the length, width, depth, corner radius, floor radius, and taper angle in their respective edit boxes of the **Rectangular Pocket** dialog box. Note that the corner radius must be greater or equal to the floor radius.

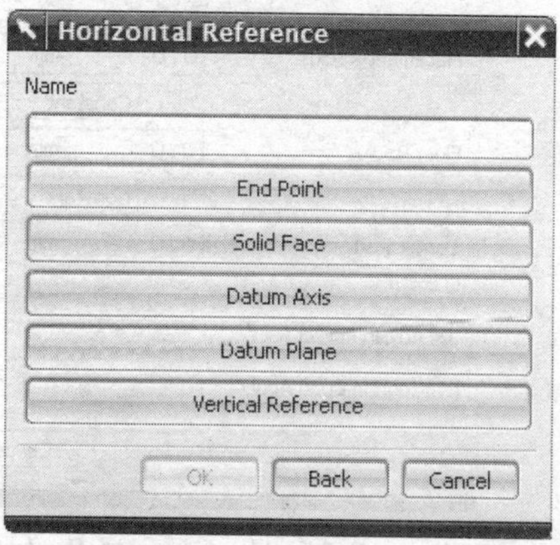

Figure 8-12 ***The Horizontal Reference*** *dialog box*

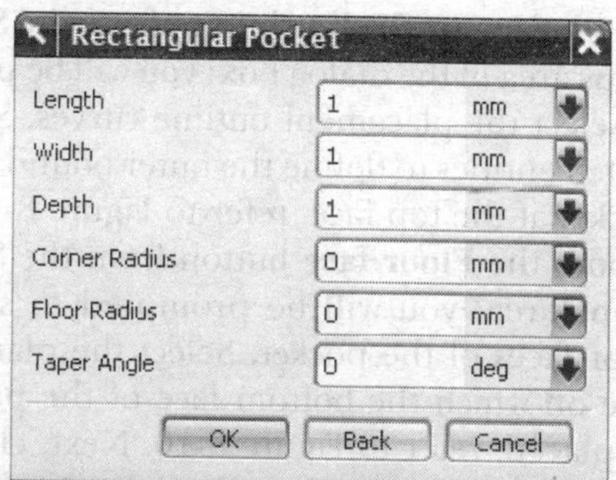

Figure 8-13 ***The Rectangular Pocket*** *dialog box*

After entering the values in the edit boxes, choose the **OK** button; the **Positioning** dialog box will be displayed, along with the preview of the pocket. Using the buttons in this dialog box, you can position the rectangular pocket about the placement face. Figure 8-14 shows a rectangular pocket feature of length 50, width 30, depth 35, corner radius 5, floor radius 3, and taper angle 2 degrees.

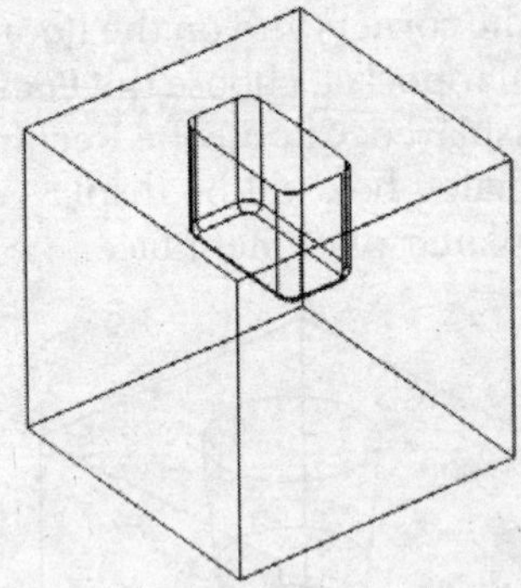

Figure 8-14 A rectangular pocket feature

Creating General Pockets

The **General** pocket tool allows you to create pocket features with more flexibility than the **Cylindrical** and **Rectangular** pocket options. In case of a general pocket, the placement face can be non-planar. Before invoking this tool, you need to draw the sketch of the top and bottom faces of the pocket feature. You do not need to draw the sketches on the faces where you want to place the feature. You can draw both the sketches on the same plane also. To create a general pocket, choose the **Pocket** button from the **Feature** toolbar; the **Pocket** dialog box will be displayed. Choose the **General** button from the **Pocket** dialog box; the **General Pocket** dialog box will be displayed, as shown in Figure 8-15.

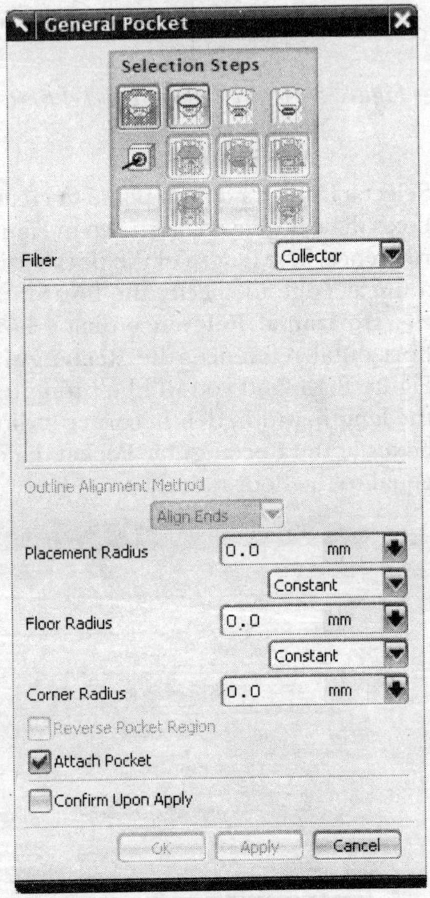

*Figure 8-15 The **General Pocket** dialog box*

By default, the **Placement Face** button is chosen in the **Selection Steps** area of this dialog box and you will be prompted to select the placement faces of the pocket. Select the top face of the model as the placement face, refer to Figure 8-16. Next, choose the **Placement Outline** button from the **Selection Steps** area of the dialog box; you will be prompted to select the placement outline curves. Select the sketch entities to define the outer boundary of the pocket at the top face, refer to Figure 8-16. Next, choose the **Floor face** button from the **Selection Steps** area; you will be prompted to select the floor faces of the pocket. Select the plane or the face on which the bottom face of the pocket will be placed, refer to Figure 8-16. Next, choose the **Floor outline** button from the **Selection Steps** area of the dialog box; you will be prompted to select the floor outline curves. Select the sketch entities to define the bottom face of the pocket, refer to Figure 8-16. Next, choose the **Target body** button from the **Selection Steps** area; you will be prompted to select the optional target body. Select the solid body to create the pocket feature, refer to Figure 8-16. Enter the values of the placement radius, floor radius, and corner radius in the respective edit boxes. The placement radius is the radius between the placement face and the sides of the pocket. The floor radius is the radius between the floor face and the sides of the pocket. The corner radius is the radius placed on the corners. Choose the **Apply** button and then the **Cancel** button from the **General Pocket** dialog box. Figure 8-17 shows a general pocket feature created by using the selections made in Figure 8-16.

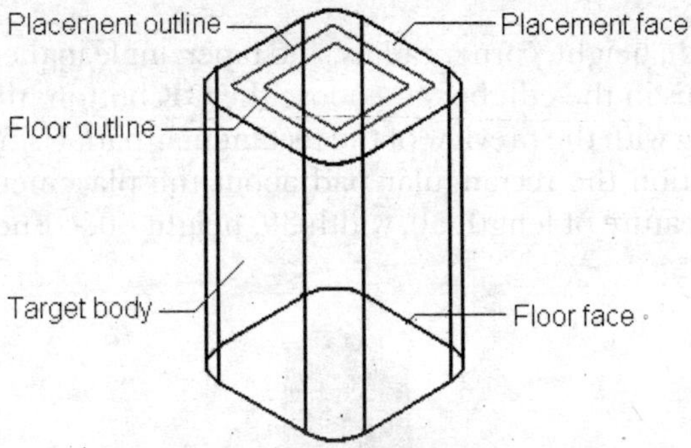

Figure 8-16 Objects to be selected

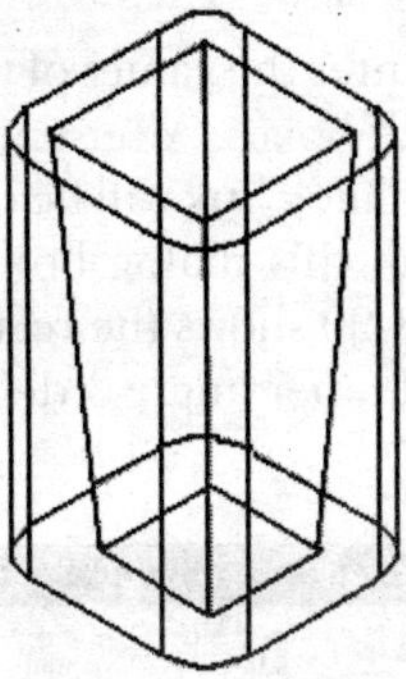

Figure 8-17 The general pocket feature

Creating Pad Features

Toolbar:	Feature > Pad *(Customize to add)*

The **Pad** tool is used to add material to a model in the rectangular or user-defined cross-sections. To create pad features, choose the **Pad** button from the **Feature** toolbar; the **Pad** dialog box will be displayed, as shown in Figure 8-18.

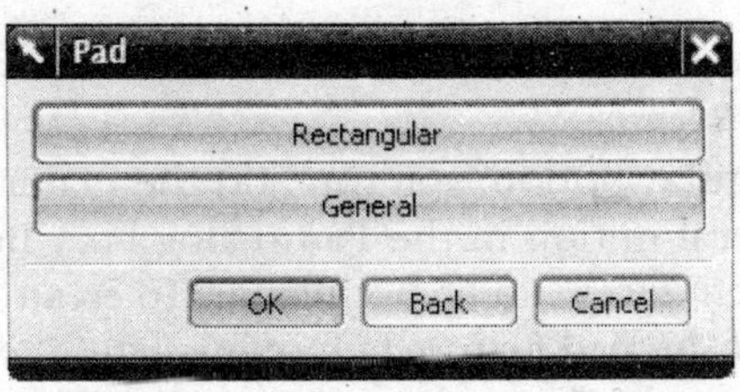

*Figure 8-18 The **Pad** dialog box*

In NX, you can create two types of pad features, rectangular and general. The procedure to create different types of pads is the same as for the pocket features and is discussed next.

Creating Rectangular Pads

This type of pad has a rectangular cross-section of a specific length, width, and height. You can also specify the corner radius and the taper angle for the pad feature. To create a rectangular pad, choose the **Pad** button from the **Feature** toolbar; the **Pad** dialog box will be displayed. Next, choose the **Rectangular** button from the dialog box; the **Rectangular Pad** dialog box will be displayed and you will be prompted to select a planar placement face. You can select the datum plane or planar face as the placement plane. Select the face or datum plane to start the pad feature; the **Horizontal Reference** dialog box will be displayed and you will be prompted to select the horizontal reference. The length of the pad will be parallel to the horizontal reference. The options in the **Horizontal Reference** dialog box can be used to select the horizontal reference. You can also directly select an edge of the model to define the horizontal reference. On doing so, the **Rectangular Pad** dialog box will be displayed, as shown in Figure 8-19, and you will be prompted to enter the pad parameters.

You need to enter the values of the length, width, height, corner radius, and taper angle in their respective edit boxes. After entering the values in the edit boxes, choose the **OK** button; the **Positioning** dialog box will be displayed, along with the preview of the rectangular pad. Using the options in this dialog box, you can position the rectangular pad about the placement face. Figure 8-20 shows the rectangular pad feature of length 50, width 30, height 60, corner radius 5, and taper angle 3 degree.

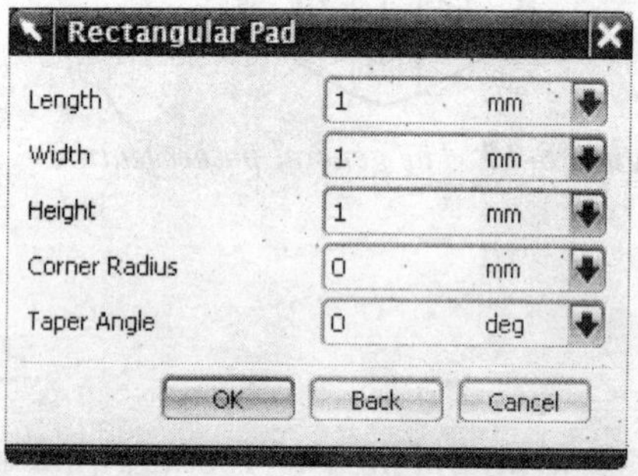

Figure 8-19 The **Rectangular Pad** *dialog box*

Figure 8-20 The resulting rectangular pad feature

Creating General Pads

As compared to the **Rectangular** option, you can add the material to a model with greater flexibility by using the **General** option in the **Pad** dialog box. But, in the case of using the **General** option, the placement faces can be nonplanar. To create a general pad feature, first you need to draw sketches of the pad feature before invoking the **Pad** dialog box. Note that sketches need not be drawn on the faces where you want to place the feature. You can draw both the sketches on the same plane. After drawing the sketches for the pad feature, choose the **Pad** button from the **Feature** toolbar; the **Pad** dialog box will be displayed. Choose the **General** button from the **Pad** dialog box; the **General Pad** dialog box will be displayed, as shown in Figure 8-21. By default, the **Placement Face** button will be chosen in the **Selection Steps** area of the dialog box and you will be prompted to select the placement face of the pad. Select a face of the model as the placement face, refer to Figure 8-22. Choose the **Placement Outline** button from the **Selection Steps** area; you will be prompted to select the placement outline curves. Select the sketch or curves that define the shape of the general pad at the top face, refer to Figure 8-22. Choose the **Top face** button from the **Selection Steps** area; you will be prompted to select the top faces. Select the top face of the model, refer to Figure 8-22. Choose the **Top Outline** button from the **Selection Steps** area; you will be prompted to select the top outline curves. Select the sketch or curves that will define the shape of the pad feature at the bottom, refer to Figure 8-22. Choose the **Target body** button from the **Selection Steps** area; you will be prompted to select the optional target body. Select the model as the target body to create the pad feature. Next, choose the **Placement Outline Projection Vector** button from the **Selection Steps** area, and then select the **Normal to Plane of Curves** option from the drop-down list that is available below the **Filter** drop-down list in the dialog box. Next, choose the **Top Outline Projection Vector** button from the **Selection Steps** area, and then select the **Normal to Plane of Curves** option from the drop-down list that is available below the **Filter** drop-down list in the dialog box. You can select the required option from this drop-down list to specify the direction vector. Next, choose **Apply** and then choose the **Cancel** button from the **General Pad** dialog box. The resultant general pad feature is shown in Figure 8-23.

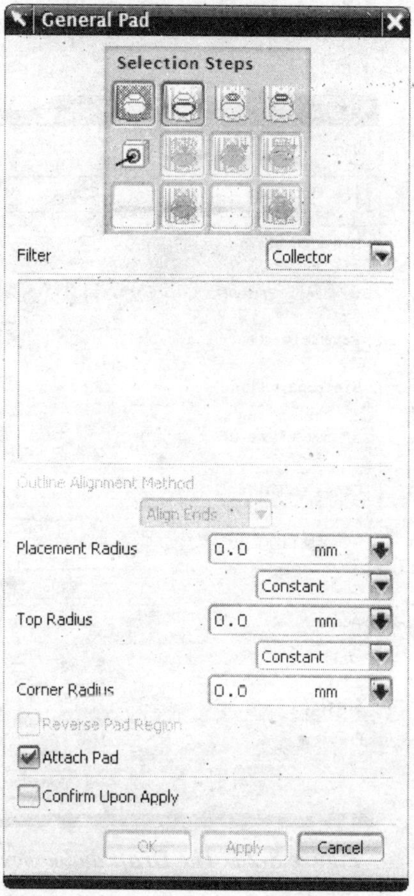

*Figure 8-21 The **General Pad** dialog box*

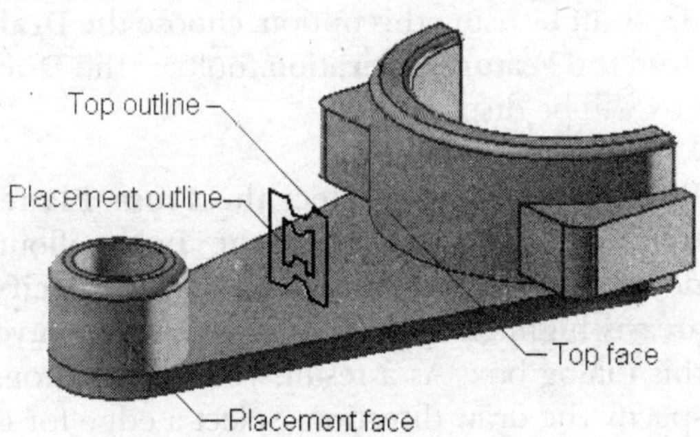

Figure 8-22 Objects to be selected

Note
The outline curves drawn should intersect the placement and top faces.

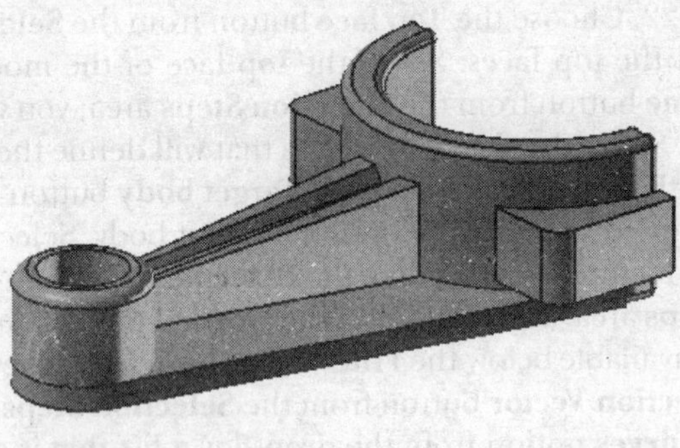

Figure 8-23 The resultant general pad feature

Creating Drafts

Menu:	Insert > Detail Feature > Draft
Toolbar:	Feature Operation > Draft

This tool is used to create a draft on an existing model. To create the draft, choose the **Draft** button from the **Feature Operation** toolbar; the **Draft** dialog box will be displayed, refer to Figure 8-24. In NX, you can create four types of drafts: draft from plane, draft from edges, draft tangent to faces, and draft to parting edges. The drop-down list in the **Type** rollout contains all four options to create the draft. The procedure for creating different types of drafts is discussed next.

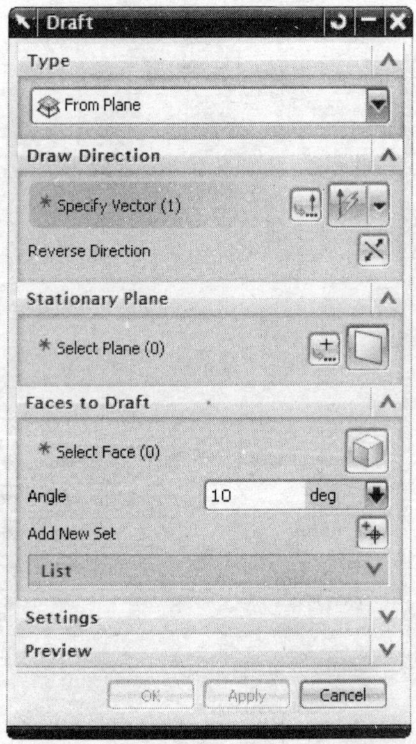

*Figure 8-24 The **Draft** dialog box*

Creating the Draft Using the From Plane Option

This type of draft is used to create a draft by selecting the stationary plane and faces of the model. To create the draft by using this option, choose the **Draft** button from the **Feature Operation** toolbar; the **Draft** dialog box will be displayed.

In this dialog box, select the **From Plane** option from the drop-down list in the **Type** rollout, if it is not selected by default. Note that the **Specify Vector** area is highlighted in the **Draw Direction** rollout of this dialog box. As a result, you will be prompted to specify the draw direction. Select a edge for the draw direction, refer to Figure 8-25. Alternatively, select the draw direction by using the **Inferred Vector** drop-down list. You can flip the draw direction by choosing the **Reverse Direction** button from the **Draw Direction** rollout. On doing so, you will be prompted to select the planar face. Select a face of the model as the stationary plane, refer to Figure 8-25. Next, you will be prompted to select the faces to draft. Select the faces, refer to Figure 8-25. Enter the angle value in the **Angle1** edit box of the **Faces to Draft** rollout, and then choose the **OK** button from this dialog box; the draft will be created. The model after creating the draft feature is shown in Figure 8-26.

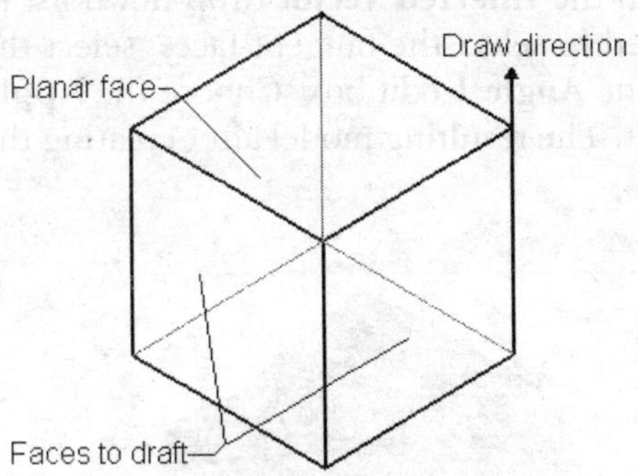

***Figure 8-25** Objects to be selected*

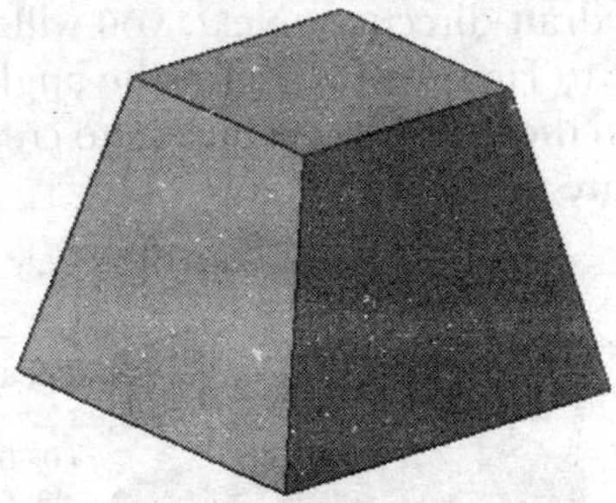

***Figure 8-26** The model after creating the draft feature*

You can create a set of faces to assign the unique angle value. The set may contain one or more faces to draft. To create a set of faces, select the faces to draft and enter the angle value in the **Angle1** edit box of the **Faces to Draft** rollout. After completing one set, choose the **Add New Set** button to create another set and follow the same procedure. The list of sets created will be displayed in the **List** sub-rollout of the **Faces to Draft** rollout. You can also modify the angle value of a particular set by selecting it and then entering a new angle value in the respective edit box.

Creating the Draft Using the From Edges Option

This option is used to create a draft by selecting the edges of a model. In such cases, you need to specify variable points and angles. This option is useful when the edges of the faces to be tapered are non linear. To create this type of draft, select the **From Edges** option from the drop-down list in the **Type** rollout; you will be prompted to specify the draw direction. Select the edge of the model to specify the draw direction, refer to Figure 8-27. Alternatively, you can use the options in the **Inferred Vector** drop-down list to specify the draw direction. You can flip the draw direction by choosing the **Reverse Direction** button from the **Draw Direction** rollout. Next, you will be prompted to select the stationary edges; select the edges, refer to Figure 8-27.

Now, you need to select the points on the stationary edges to specify different draft angles. You can enter different angles for different selected points. To do so, expand the **Variable Draft Points** rollout and choose the **Inferred Point** button; you will be prompted to select the points. You can select any number of points on the edges to specify different angle values. Next, select the variable angle points, refer to Figure 8-27. Enter different angle values in the **Pt A** edit boxes, displayed after selecting the points. Next, choose the **OK** button to create the draft. The model after creating the draft feature is shown in Figure 8-28.

Creating the Draft Using the Tangent to Faces Option

This option is used to create a draft that is tangent to the selected faces. In such cases, you need to specify the draw direction and the tangent face. To create this type of draft, select the **Tangent to Faces** option from the drop-down list in the **Type** rollout; you will be prompted to specify the draw direction. Select the edge of the model as the draft direction, refer to Figure 8-29. Alternatively, you can use the options in the **Inferred Vector** drop-down list to select the draft direction. Next, you will be prompted to select the tangent faces; select the face, refer to Figure 8-29. Enter the angle value in the **Angle 1** edit box. Choose the **Apply** button and then the **Cancel** button to create the draft. The resulting model after creating the draft feature is shown in Figure 8-30.

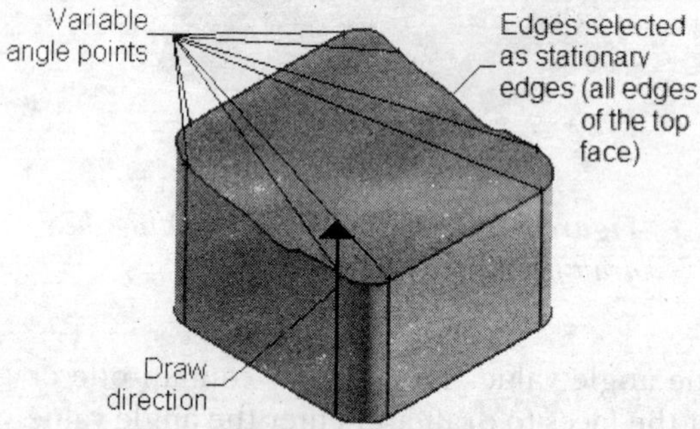

Figure 8-27 Objects to be selected

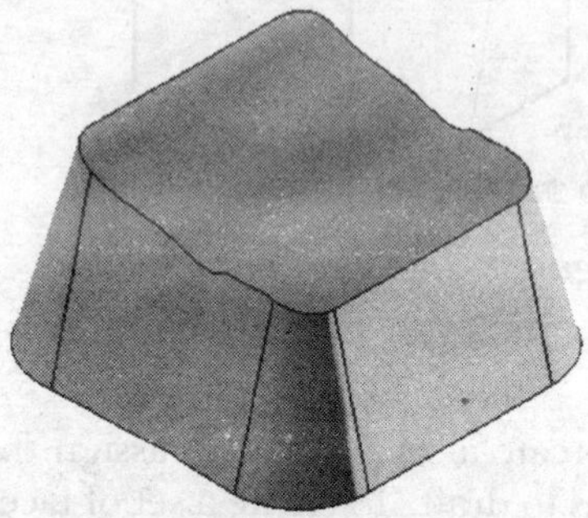

Figure 8-28 The draft created using the stationary edges

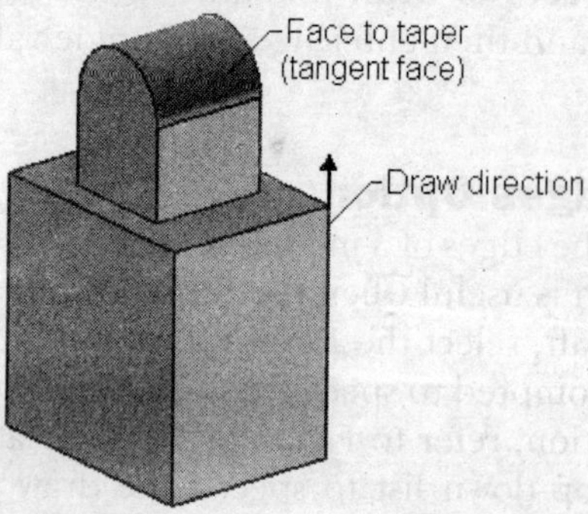

Figure 8-29 Objects to be selected

Figure 8-30 The draft created using the tangent faces

Creating the Draft Using the To Parting Edges Option

This draft type is used to create a draft along the selected set of edges by specifying the angle, draw direction, stationary plane, and parting edges. To create this type of draft, select the **To Parting Edges** option from the drop-down list in the **Type** rollout; you will be prompted to specify the draw direction. Select an edge as the draw direction, refer to Figure 8-31. You can also use the options in the **Inferred Vector** drop-down list to specify the draw direction. After specifying the draw direction, you will be prompted to select a planar face. Select a planar face, refer to Figure 8-31; you will be prompted to select parting edges. Select the parting edges, refer to Figure 8-31, and then enter the angle value in the **Angle 1** edit box. Next, choose **Apply** button, and then the **Cancel** button to create the draft. The resulting model after creating the draft feature is shown in Figure 8-32.

Note
*The **Draft All Instances** check box in the **Settings** rollout allows you to specify whether to draft only the specified instance or all the instances in the array.*

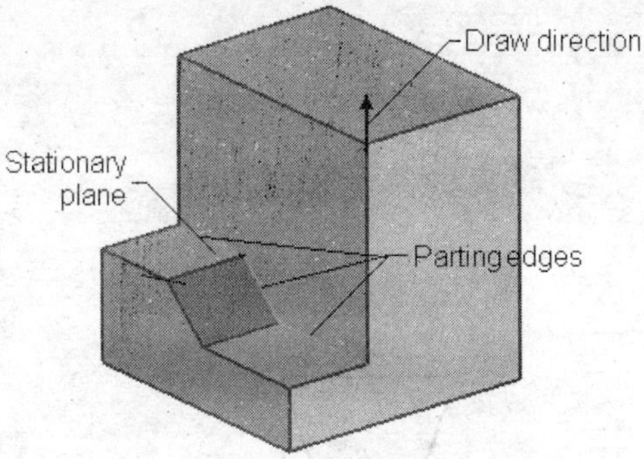

Figure 8-31 *Objects to be selected*

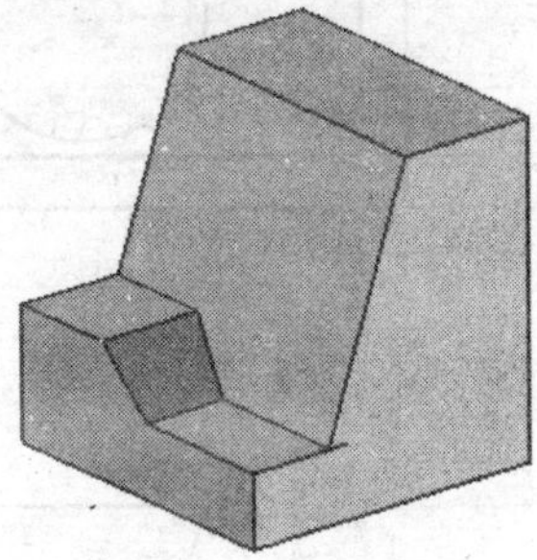

Figure 8-32 *The resulting draft feature created using the parting edges*

TUTORIALS

Tutorial 1

In this tutorial, you will create the model shown in Figure 8-33. The dimensions of this model are given in Figure 8-34. After creating the solid model, save it with the name *c08tut1.prt* at the location *\NX 7\c08.* **(Expected time: 30 min)**

Figure 8-33 *A rectangular pocket feature*

The following steps are required to complete this tutorial:

a. Draw the sketch for the base feature and extrude it.
b. Create the rectangular pad by using the **Pad** tool.
c. Create the boss feature by using the **Boss** tool.
d. Create the draft on the boss feature.

e. Create the edge blend on the rectangular pad and the boss features.
f. Save the file.

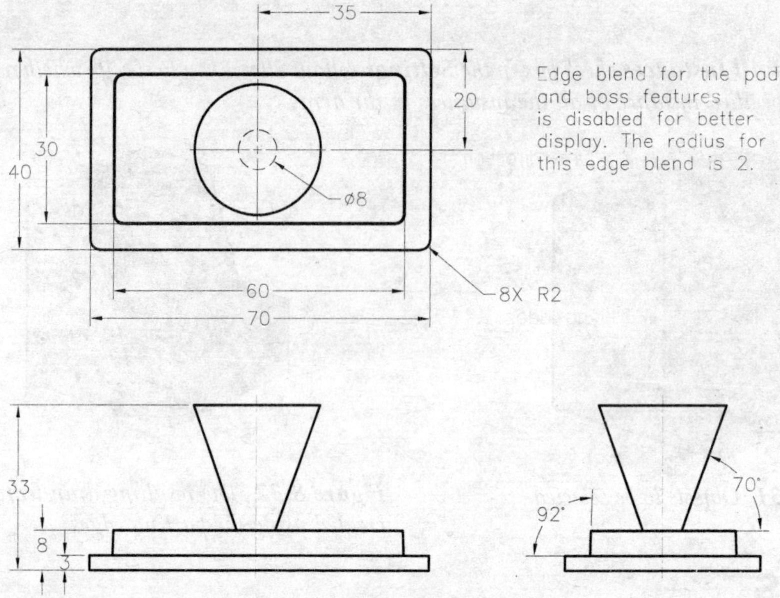

Figure 8-34 Views and dimensions for Tutorial 1

Creating the Base Feature of the Model

1. Start a new file with the name *c08tut1.prt* using the **Model** template and specify its location as *C:\NX 7\c08*.

2. Invoke the Sketcher environment by selecting the XC-YC plane as the sketching plane, and then create the sketch for the base feature, as shown in Figure 8-35.

3. Exit the Sketcher environment and invoke the **Extrude** dialog box. Select the sketch from the drawing area to create an extrude feature. Enter **0** in the **Distance** edit box available below the **Start** drop-down list and then enter **3** in the **Distance** edit box available below the **End** drop-down list in the **Limits** rollout of the dialog box. Next, choose the **OK** button from the dialog box; the extruded feature is created. Turn off the display of the sketch and the datum planes. The resulting base feature is shown in Figure 8-36.

Creating the Rectangular Pad Feature

1. Choose the **Pad** tool from the **Feature** toolbar; the **Pad** dialog box is displayed and you are prompted to select the pad type.

2. Choose the **Rectangular** button from this dialog box; the **Rectangular Pad** dialog box is displayed and you are prompted to select the planar placement face.

3. Select the top face of the base feature as the placement face; the **Horizontal Reference** dialog box is displayed and you are prompted to select the horizontal reference.

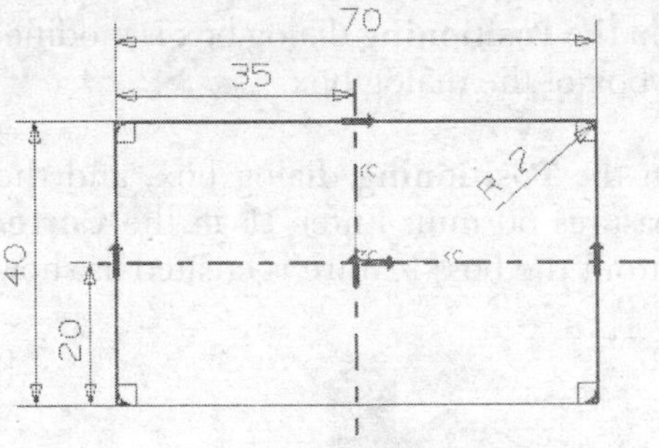

Figure 8-35 *Sketch for the base feature*

Figure 8-36 *Base feature of the model*

4. Select the edge of the base feature that measures 70 mm; the **Rectangular Pad** dialog box is displayed. Enter **60**, **30**, **5**, **2**, and **2** in the **Length**, **Width**, **Height**, **Corner Radius**, and **Taper Angle** edit boxes, respectively.

5. Choose the **OK** button from the dialog box; the **Positioning** dialog box along with the preview of the pad is displayed. Next, you need to position the pad on the base feature.

6. Choose the **Perpendicular** button from the **Positioning** dialog box. Next, select the edge of the base feature that measures 40 mm, and then select the edge of the pad that measures 30 mm; the **Create Expression** dialog box is displayed. Enter **5** in the edit box of this dialog box.

7. Choose the **OK** button from the dialog box; the **Positioning** dialog box is displayed. Choose the **Perpendicular** button from the **Positioning** dialog box. Next, select the edge of the base feature that measures 70 mm, and then select the edge of the pad that measures 60 mm; the **Create Expression** dialog box is displayed. Enter **5** in the edit box of this dialog box.

8. Choose the **OK** button twice, and then the **Cancel** button once. The resulting rectangular pad feature is shown in Figure 8-37.

Creating the Boss Feature

The third feature is a boss feature, and will be created by using the following steps:

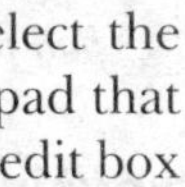

1. Choose the **Boss** tool from the **Feature** toolbar; the **Boss** dialog box is displayed and you are prompted to select the planar placement face.

2. Select the top face of the second feature as the placement face; the preview of the boss feature is displayed. Enter **8**, **25**, and **0** in the **Diameter**, **Height**, and **Taper Angle** edit boxes, respectively.

3. Choose the **OK** button from the **Boss** dialog box; the **Positioning** dialog box is displayed. Next, you need to position the boss on the second feature.

4. Choose the **Perpendicular** button from the **Positioning** dialog box, and then select the edge of the second feature that measures 30 mm; the **Positioning** dialog box is modified. Next, enter **30** in the **Current Expression** edit box of the dialog box.

5. Choose the **Perpendicular** button again from the **Positioning** dialog box, and then select the edge of the second feature that measures 60 mm. Enter **15** in the **Current Expression** edit box. Next, choose the **OK** button; the boss feature is created as shown in Figure 8-38.

Figure 8-37 *Model after creating the pad feature*

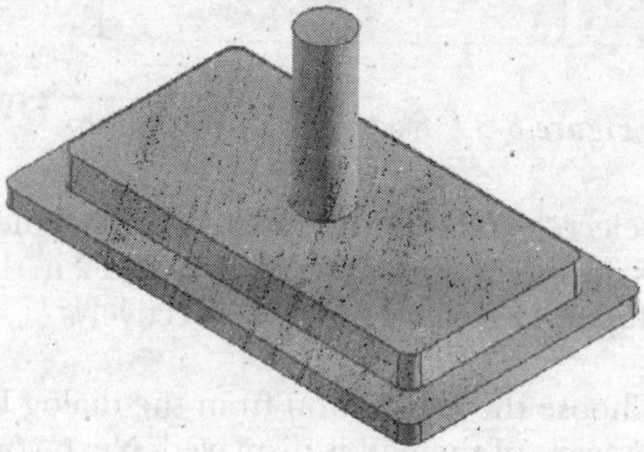

Figure 8-38 *Model after creating the boss feature*

Creating the Draft Feature

Next, you need to create a draft on the boss feature. Use the following steps to create the draft feature.

1. Choose the **Draft** tool from the **Feature Operation** toolbar; the **Draft** dialog box is displayed. In this dialog box, select the **From Plane** option from the drop-down list in the **Type** rollout; you are prompted to specify the draw direction.

2. Select the **- ZC Axis** option from the **Inferred Vector** drop-down list in the **Draw Direction** rollout of the dialog box to specify the draw direction; you are prompted to select the planar face. Select the top face of the rectangular pad feature; you are prompted to select faces for drafting.

3. Select the cylindrical face of the boss feature.

4. Enter **20** in the **Angle1** edit box and choose the **OK** button. The draft feature is created, as shown in Figure 8-39.

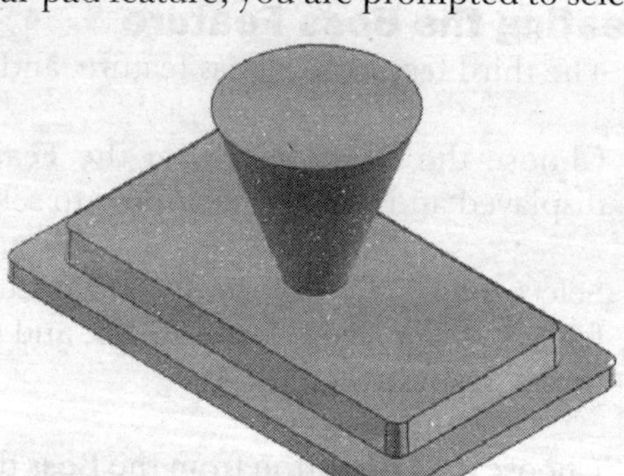

Figure 8-39 *The model after creating the draft feature*

Creating the Edge Blend Feature

You need to create the edge blend feature by using the following steps:

1. Choose the **Edge Blend** button from the **Feature Operation** toolbar; the **Edge Blend** dialog box is displayed.

2. Select the edges of the model, refer to Figure 8-40, and enter **2** in the **Radius 1** edit box. Next, choose the **OK** button from the **Edge Blend** dialog box; the final model for Tutorial 1 is created, as shown in Figure 8-41.

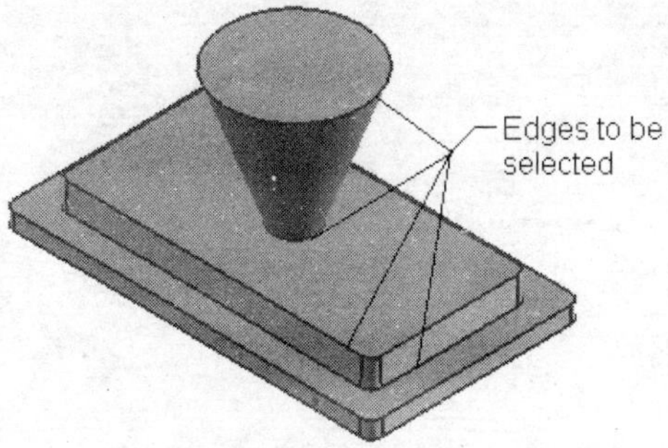

Figure 8-40 *Edges to be selected*

Figure 8-41 *The final model*

3. Choose **File > Close > Save and Close** from the menu bar to save and close the part file.

Tutorial 2

In this tutorial, you will create the model shown in Figure 8-42. The dimensions of this model are given in Figure 8-43. After creating the solid model, save it with the name *c08tut2.prt* at the location *\NX 7\c08*. **(Expected time: 30 min)**

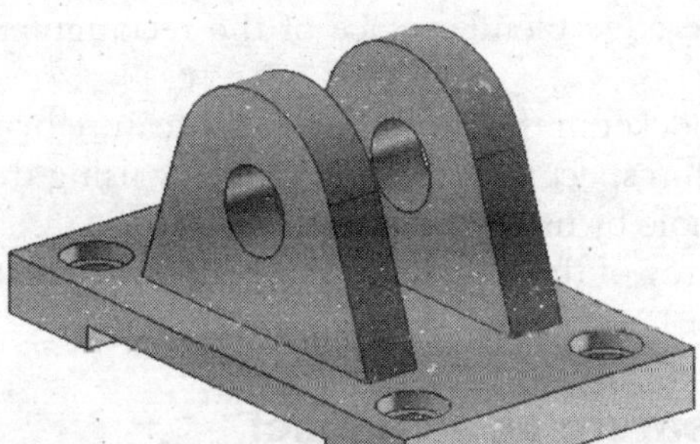

Figure 8-42 *The solid model for Tutorial 2*

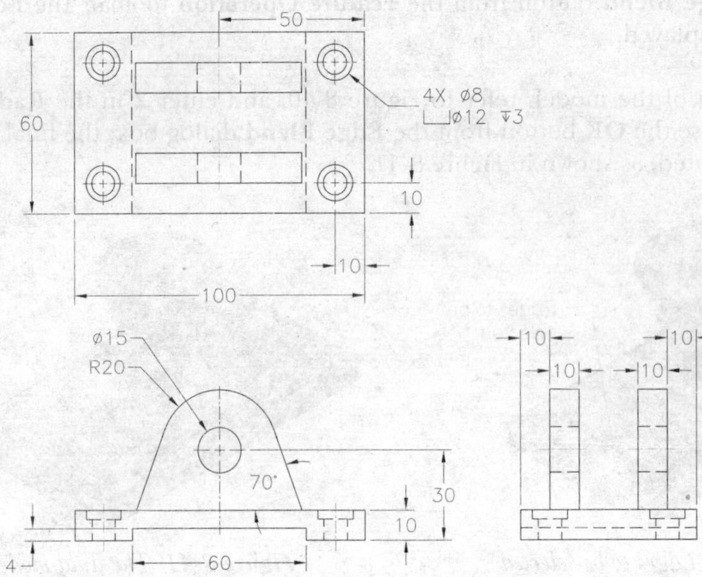

Figure 8-43 Views and dimensions for Tutorial 2

The following steps are required to complete this tutorial:

a. Draw the sketch for the base feature and extrude it.
b. Create the rectangular pocket by using the **Pocket** tool.
c. Create the rectangular pad by using the **Pad** tool.
d. Create the edge blend on the pad feature by using the **Edge Blend** tool.
e. Create the draft on the edge blend surface of the rectangular pad by using the **Draft** tool.
f. Create the cylindrical pocket in the rectangular pad feature by using the **Pocket** tool.
g. Mirror the features with respect to the datum plane by using the **Mirror Feature** tool.
h. Create a counterbore hole by using the **Hole** tool.
i. Create a rectangular array of the hole feature by using the **Instance Feature** tool.
j. Save the file.

Creating the Base Feature of the Model

1. Start a new file with the name *c08tut2.prt* using the **Model** template and specify its location as *C:\NX 7\c08*.

2. Select the XC-YC plane as the sketching plane and then create the sketch for the base feature, as shown in Figure 8-44.

3. Exit the Sketcher environment and extrude the sketch to a depth of 10 mm.

4. Turn off the display of all entities except the base feature. The resulting model is shown in Figure 8-45.

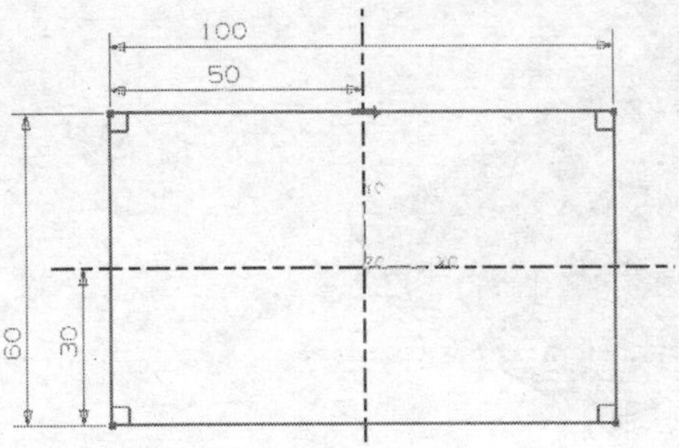

Figure 8-44 Sketch for the base feature

Figure 8-45 Base feature of the model

Creating the Rectangular Pocket Feature

Next, you need to create a rectangular pocket feature by using the following steps:

1. Choose the **Pocket** tool from the **Feature** toolbar; the **Pocket** dialog box is displayed and you are prompted to select the pocket type.

2. Choose the **Rectangular** button from this dialog box; the **Rectangular Pocket** dialog box is displayed and you are prompted to select the planar placement face.

3. Select the front face of the base feature; the **Horizontal Reference** dialog box is displayed and you are prompted to select the horizontal reference.

4. Select the top edge of the same face as the horizontal reference; the **Rectangular Pocket** dialog box is displayed. Enter **60**, **4**, and **60** in the **Length**, **Width**, and **Depth** edit boxes, respectively. Make sure that the **Corner Radius**, **Floor Radius**, and **Taper Angle** edit boxes of the dialog box are set to the value 0.

5. Choose the **OK** button; the **Positioning** dialog box, along with the preview of the pocket is displayed. Next, you need to position the pocket on the placement face.

6. Choose the **Perpendicular** button from the **Positioning** dialog box; the **Perpendicular** dialog box is displayed. Next, select the edge of the base feature that measures 10 mm and the vertical center line of the pocket; the **Create Expression** dialog box is displayed. Enter **50** in the edit box of this dialog box, and then choose the **OK** button from it; the **Positioning** dialog box is displayed again.

7. Choose the **Perpendicular** button from the **Positioning** dialog box, and then select the bottom edge of the base feature and the horizontal center line of the pocket; the **Create Expression** dialog box is displayed. Enter **2** in the edit box of this dialog box.

8. Choose the **OK** button twice and then the **Cancel** button once. The rectangular pocket feature is created, as shown in Figure 8-46.

Figure 8-46 The model after creating the rectangular pocket feature

Creating the Rectangular Pad Feature

The next feature is a rectangular pad feature, and will be created by using the following steps:

1. Choose the **Pad** button from the **Feature** toolbar; the **Pad** dialog box is displayed and you are prompted to select the pad type.

2. Choose the **Rectangular** button from this dialog box; the **Rectangular Pad** dialog box is displayed and you are prompted to select the planar placement face.

3. Select the top face of the base feature as the placement face; the **Horizontal Reference** dialog box is displayed and you are prompted to select the horizontal reference.

4. Select the edge of the base feature that measures 100 mm as the horizontal reference; the **Rectangular Pad** dialog box is displayed. Enter **40**, **10**, and **40** in the **Length**, **Width**, and **Height** edit boxes, respectively. Make sure that the value in the **Corner Radius** and **Taper Angle** edit boxes of the dialog box is set to 0.

5. Choose the **OK** button from the dialog box; the **Positioning** dialog box along with the preview of the pad is displayed. Next, you need to position the pad on the base feature.

6. Choose the **Perpendicular** button from the **Positioning** dialog box. Select the edge of the base feature that measures 60 mm, and then select the edge of the pad that measures 10 mm; the **Create Expression** dialog box is displayed. Enter **30** in the edit box of this dialog box. Next, choose the **OK** button; the **Positioning** dialog box is displayed again.

7. Choose the **Perpendicular** button from the **Positioning** dialog box; the **Perpendicular** dialog box is displayed. Select the top edge of the front face of the base feature and the bottom edge of the front face of the new pad feature that measures 40 mm; the **Create Expression** dialog box is displayed. Enter **40** in the edit box of this dialog box.

8. Choose the **OK** button from the **Create Expression** dialog box; the **Positioning** dialog box is displayed again.

9. Choose the **OK** button from the **Positioning** dialog box, and then the **Cancel** button from the **Rectangular Pad** dialog box. The rectangular pad feature is created, as shown in Figure 8-47.

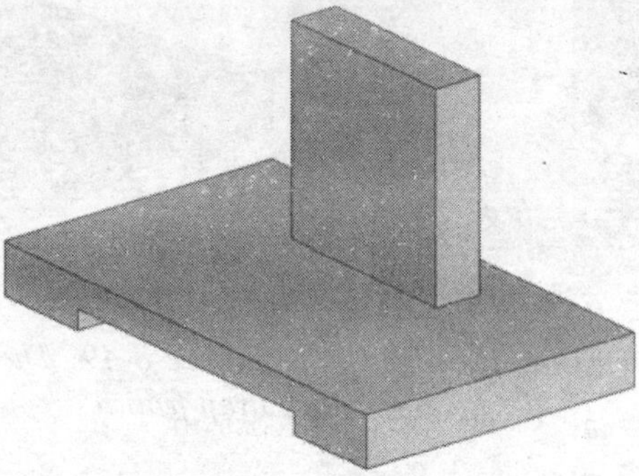

Figure 8-47 The model after creating the rectangular pad feature

Creating the Edge Blend Feature

1. Choose the **Edge Blend** button from the **Feature Operation** toolbar; the **Edge Blend** dialog box is displayed.

2. From the top face of the pad feature, select the two edges that measure 10 mm. Enter **20** in the **Radius 1** edit box.

3. Choose the **OK** button from the **Edge Blend** dialog box. The rectangular pad after creating the edge blend feature is shown in Figure 8-48.

Creating the Draft Feature

Next, you need to create the draft feature on the side faces of the pad feature. To do so, you need to follow the steps given next.

1. Choose the **Draft** button from the **Feature Operation** toolbar; the **Draft** dialog box is displayed.

2. Select the **Tangent to Faces** option from the drop-down list in the **Type** rollout; you are prompted to specify the draw direction. Select the **ZC Axis** option from the **Inferred Vector** drop-down list in the **Draw Direction** rollout; you are prompted to select the tangent faces.

3. Select the blended face from the rectangular pad feature. The two side faces that are tangent to the blended face are also selected automatically.

4. Enter **20** in the **Angle 1** edit box of the **Tangent Faces** rollout in the dialog box. Next, choose the **Apply** button and then the **Cancel** button. The resulting model is shown in Figure 8-49.

Figure 8-48 The model after creating the edge blend feature

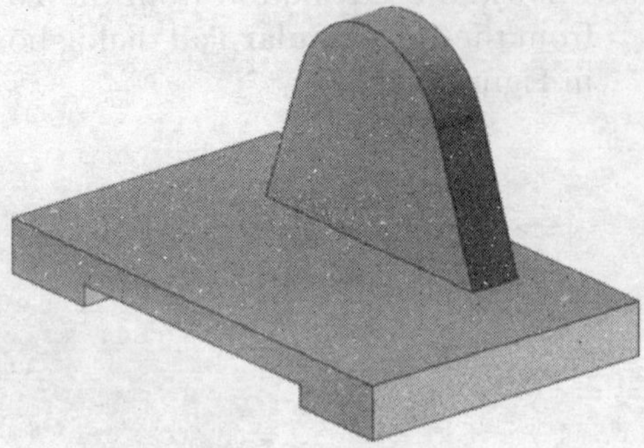

Figure 8-49 The model after creating the draft feature

Creating the Cylindrical Pocket Feature

You need to create the hole in the pad feature by using the cylindrical pocket feature.

1. Choose the **Pocket** button from the **Feature** toolbar; the **Pocket** dialog box is displayed and you are prompted to select the pocket type.

2. Choose the **Cylindrical** button from this dialog box; the **Cylindrical Pocket** dialog box is displayed and you are prompted to select the planar placement face.

3. Select the front face of the rectangular pad feature; the **Cylindrical Pocket** dialog box is displayed and you are prompted to enter the pocket parameters.

4. Enter **15** for the pocket diameter and **10** for the depth in the respective edit boxes. Make sure that the value in the **Floor Radius** and **Taper Angle** edit boxes in the dialog box is set to 0. Next, choose the **OK** button from the dialog box; the **Positioning** dialog box, along with the preview of the pocket is displayed.

5. Choose the **Point onto Point** button from the **Positioning** dialog box; the **Point onto Point** dialog box is displayed. Next, select the curved edge that is created by using the **Edge Blend** tool; the **Set Arc Position** dialog box is displayed. Next, choose the **Arc Center** button from this dialog box.

6. Next, select the cylindrical pocket edge from the preview of the pocket and choose the **Arc Center** button from the **Set Arc Position** dialog box. The cylindrical pocket is created, as shown in Figure 8-50. Close the dialog box by choosing the **Cancel** button.

Mirroring Features

1. Choose the **Mirror Feature** button from the **Feature Operation** toolbar; the **Mirror Feature** dialog box is displayed and you are prompted to select the features to be mirrored.

2. Expand the **Related Features** sub-rollout, if is not expanded. Next, select the Rectangular

Pad feature and all features below it from the list in this sub-rollout. The selected features are highlighted in the drawing window.

3. Select the **Existing Plane** option from the **Plane** drop-down list in the **Mirror Plane** rollout, if it is not selected by default. Next, choose the **Plane** button from the **Mirror Plane** rollout of the dialog box; you are prompted to select the plane to mirror about.

4. Select the XC-ZC plane as the mirror plane. Note that you may need to zoom out the drawing view to select the XC-ZC plane. Next, choose the **Apply** button and then the **Cancel** button. The resulting model is shown in Figure 8-51.

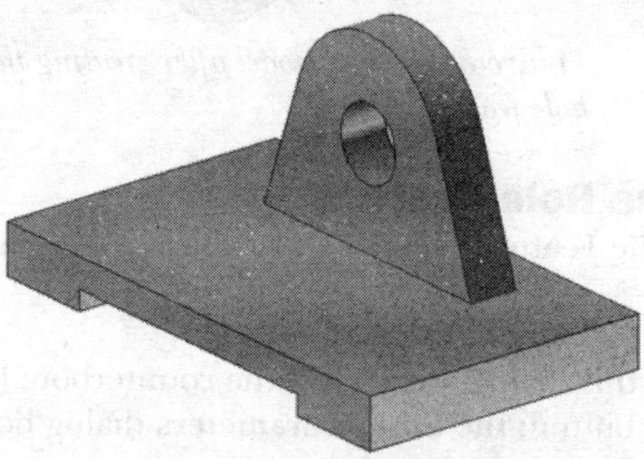

Figure 8-50 *The model after creating the cylindrical pocket feature*

Figure 8-51 *The model after creating the mirror feature*

Creating the Counterbore Hole Feature on the Base Feature

1. Choose the **Hole** button from the **Feature** toolbar; the **Hole** dialog box is displayed and you are prompted to select the placement face.

2. Select the **General Hole** option from the drop-down list in the **Type** rollout, if it is not selected by default. Next, select the **Counterbored** option from the **Form** drop-down list in the **Form and Dimensions** rollout of the dialog box.

3. Select the top face of the base feature as the placement face; the Sketcher environment is invoked. Also, the **Point** dialog box is displayed in the drawing area.

4. Place the point and apply dimensions to it, refer to Figure 8-52.

5. Exit the Sketcher environment; the preview of the hole is displayed with the default dimensions.

6. Enter **12** in the **C-Bore Diameter** edit box, **3** in the **C-Bore Depth** edit box, **8** in the **Diameter** edit box, and **10** in the **Depth** edit box of the **Dimensions** sub-rollout. Note that the **Depth** edit box is displayed in this sub-rollout only when the **Value** option is selected in the **Depth Limit** drop-down list. Make sure that the value in the **Tip Angle** edit box is set to 0.

7. Accept the other default settings and choose the **OK** button; the counterbore hole is created, as shown in Figure 8-53.

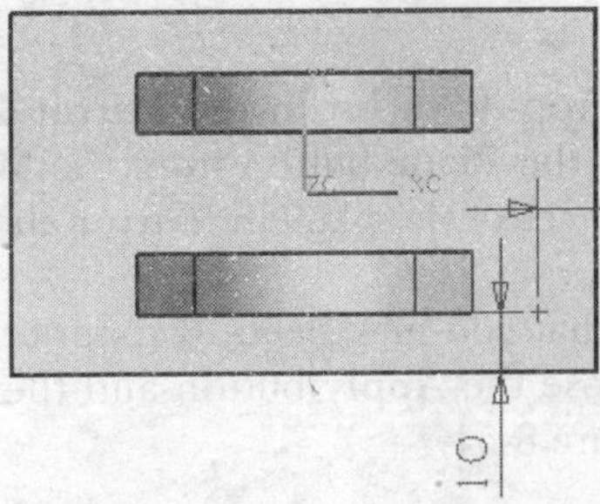

Figure 8-52 Dimensions applied to the point

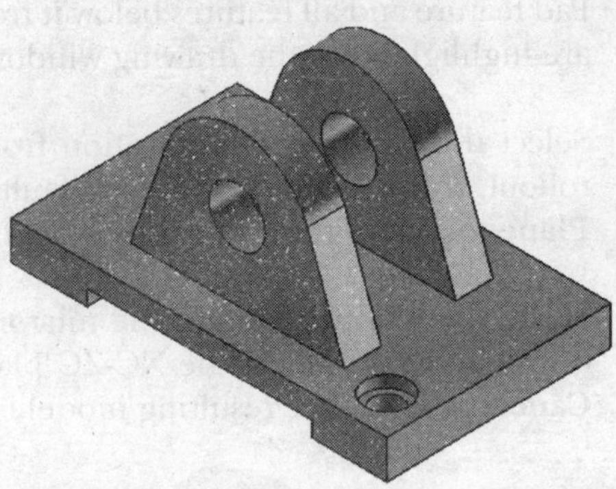

Figure 8-53 The model after creating the hole feature

Creating the Rectangular Array of the Hole Feature

1. Choose the **Instance Feature** button from the **Feature Operation** toolbar; the **Instance** dialog box is displayed.

2. Choose the **Rectangular Array** button from this dialog box. Select the counterbore hole from the **Filter** list and then choose the **OK** button; the **Enter Parameters** dialog box is displayed.

3. Enter **2** in the **Number Along XC** and **Number Along YC** edit boxes. Enter **-80** in the **XC Offset** edit box and **40** in the **YC Offset** edit box.

4. Choose the **OK** button from the **Enter parameters** dialog box, and then choose the **Yes** button from the **Create instances** dialog box. Exit the **Instance** dialog box. The final model is shown in Figure 8-54.

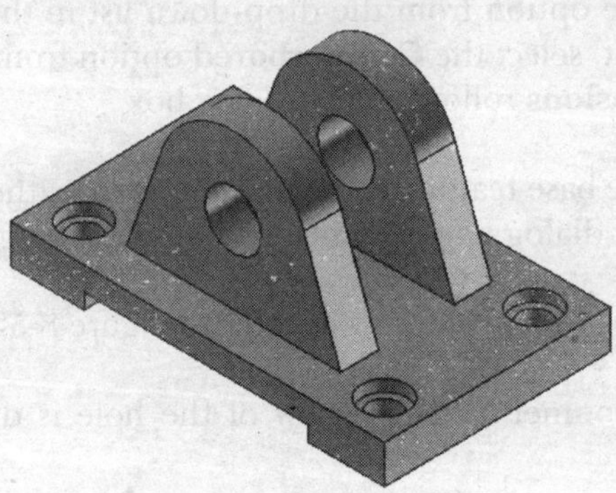

Figure 8-54 The final model

5. Choose **File > Close > Save and Close** from the menu bar to save and close the part file.

Tutorial 3

In this tutorial, you will create the model shown in Figure 8-55. The dimensions of this model are shown in Figure 8-56. After creating the solid model, save it with the name *c08tut3.prt* at the location *\NX 7\c08.* **(Expected time: 30 min)**

Figure 8-55 *The solid model for Tutorial 3*

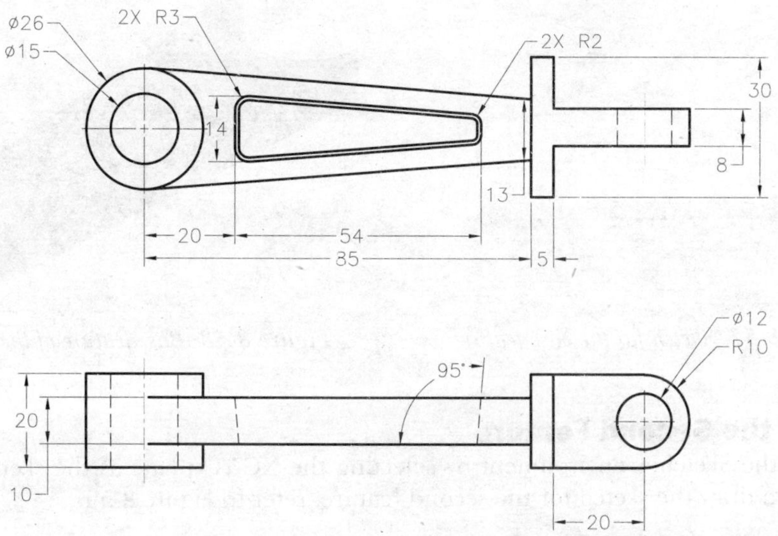

Figure 8-56 *Views and dimensions of the model for Tutorial 3*

The following steps are required to complete this tutorial:

a. Draw the sketch for the base feature and extrude it.
b. Draw the sketch for the second feature and extrude it.
c. Create the cylindrical pocket in the second feature by using the **Pocket** tool.
d. Create the cut extrude feature.
e. Create the rectangular pad feature by using the **Pad** tool.

f. Create the second rectangular pad feature by using the **Pad** tool.
g. Create the edge blend feature by using the **Edge blend** tool.
h. Create the cylindrical pocket in the rectangular pad by using the **Pocket** tool.
i. Save the file.

Creating the Base Feature of the Model

1. Start a new file with the name *c08tut3.prt* using the **Model** template and specify its location as *C:\NX 7\c08*.

2. Invoke the Sketcher environment by selecting the XC-YC plane as the sketching plane and then create the sketch for the base feature, as shown in Figure 8-57.

3. Exit the Sketcher environment and extrude the sketch to a depth of 5 mm by using the **Symmetric Value** option.

4. Turn off the display of all entities except the base feature. The resulting base feature is shown in Figure 8-58.

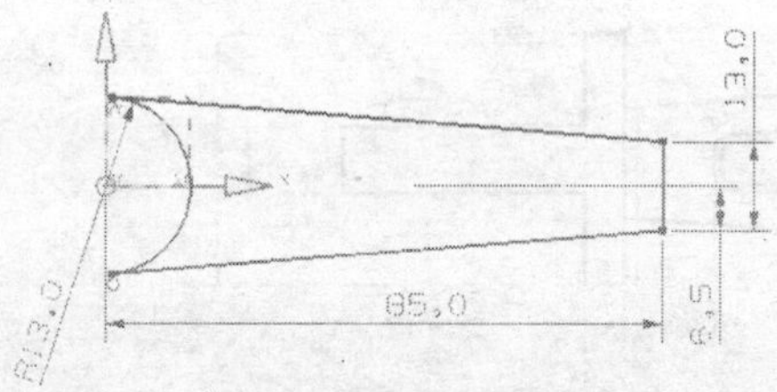

Figure 8-57 *Sketch for the base feature*

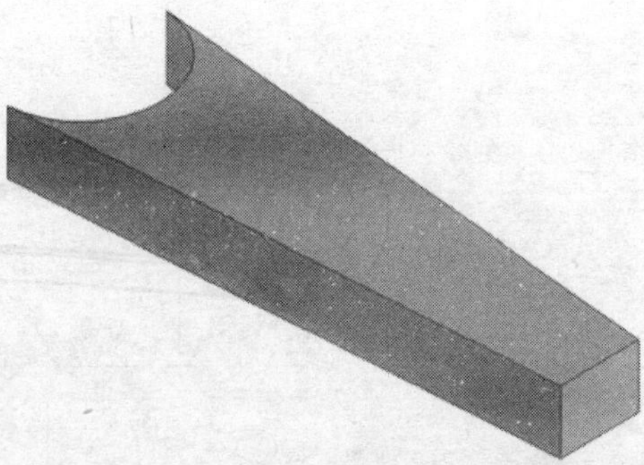

Figure 8-58 *Base feature of the model*

Creating the Second Feature

1. Invoke the Sketcher environment by selecting the XC-YC plane as the sketching plane and then draw the sketch for the second feature, refer to Figure 8-59.

2. Exit the Sketcher environment and invoke the **Extrude** dialog box. Select the sketch created for the second feature from the drawing window.

3. Select the **Symmetric Value** option from the **Start** drop-down list in the **Limits** rollout. Enter **10** in the **Distance** edit box. Next, select the **Unite** option from the **Boolean** drop-down list.

4. Choose the **OK** button to create the second feature. The resulting model is shown in Figure 8-60.

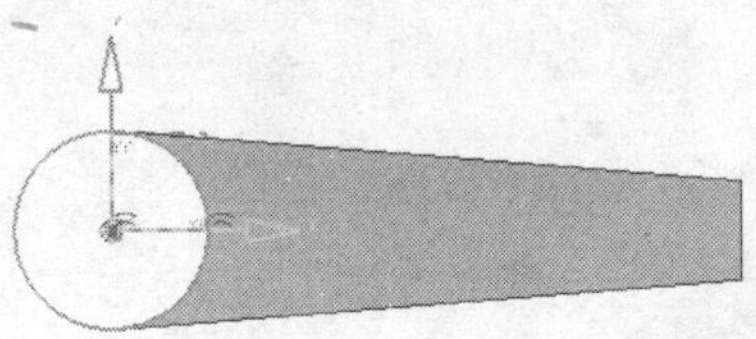

Figure 8-59 Sketch for the second feature

Figure 8-60 The model after creating the second feature

Creating the Cylindrical Pocket Feature

Now, you need to create the cylindrical pocket feature by using the following steps:

1. Choose the **Pocket** button from the **Feature** toolbar; the **Pocket** dialog box is displayed and you are prompted to select the pocket type.

2. Choose the **Cylindrical** button from this dialog box; the **Cylindrical Pocket** dialog box is displayed and you are prompted to select the planar placement face.

3. Select the top face of the second feature; the **Cylindrical Pocket** dialog box is modified and you are prompted to enter the pocket parameters.

4. Enter **15** as the pocket diameter value and **20** as the depth value in the respective edit boxes. Make sure that the values in the **Floor Radius** and **Taper Angle** edit boxes are set to 0. Next, choose the **OK** button from the dialog box; the **Positioning** dialog box is displayed. Also, the preview of the cylindrical pocket feature is displayed in the drawing window.

   Next, you need to position the pocket on the face of the second feature.

5. Choose the **Point onto Point** button from the **Positioning** dialog box and select the circular edge of the second feature; the **Set Arc Position** dialog box is displayed. Choose the **Arc Center** button from this dialog box.

6. Next, select the circular edge of the cylindrical pocket feature from its preview and choose the **Arc Center** button from the **Set Arc Position** dialog box; the cylindrical pocket feature is created, as shown in Figure 8-61. Now, exit from the dialog box by choosing the **Cancel** button.

Creating the Cut Extrude Feature

Next, you need to create the cut extrude feature. You will create the sketch for this feature on the top face of the base feature. Also, you may need to define the XC-axis as the horizontal reference in the **Create Sketch** dialog box, while invoking the Sketcher environment.

Figure 8-61 Model after creating the pocket feature

1. Invoke the Sketcher environment by selecting the top planar face of the base feature as the sketching plane and then create the sketch for the cut extrude feature, refer to Figure 8-62.

2. Exit the Sketcher environment and then subtract the material from the base feature with 5-degree as the draft angle by using the sketch created.

3. Turn off the display of all entities except the model. The model after creating the cut extrude feature is shown in Figure 8-63.

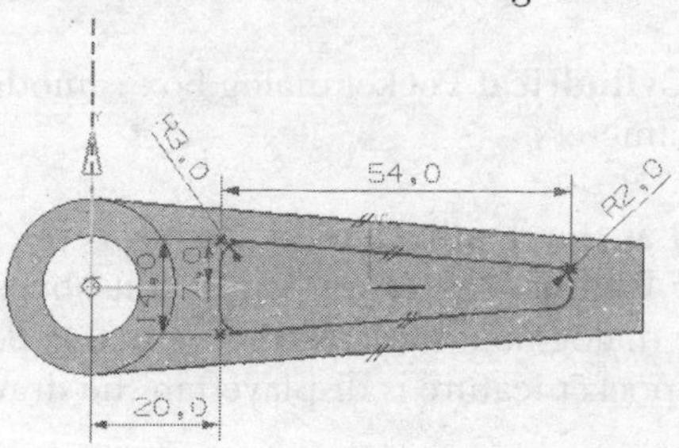

Figure 8-62 Sketch for the cut extrude feature

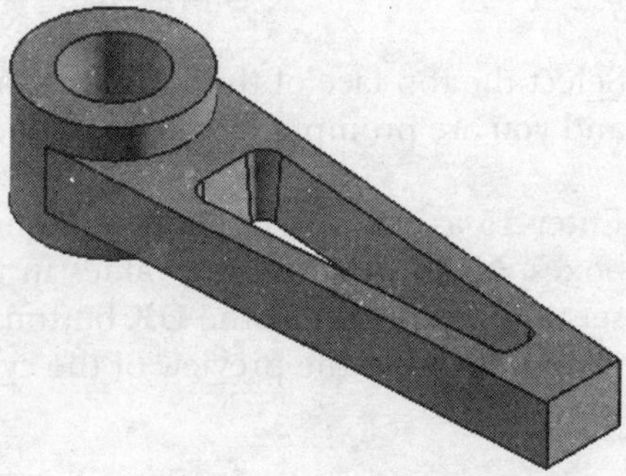

Figure 8-63 The model after creating the cut extrude feature

Creating the Rectangular Pad Feature

Next, you need to create the rectangular pad feature on the right face of the base feature.

1. Choose the **Pad** button from the **Feature** toolbar; the **Pad** dialog box is displayed and you are prompted to select the pad type.

2. Choose the **Rectangular** button from this dialog box; the **Rectangular Pad** dialog box is displayed and you are prompted to select the planar placement face.

3. Select the right face of the base feature as the placement face; the **Horizontal Reference** dialog box is displayed and you are prompted to select the horizontal reference.

4. Select the top edge of the right face of the base feature that measures 13 mm; the **Rectangular Pad** dialog box is displayed. Enter **30** as length, **20** as width, and **5** as height in their respective edit boxes. Make sure that the value in the **Corner Radius** and **Taper Angle** edit boxes is set to 0.

5. Choose the **OK** button from the dialog box; the **Positioning** dialog box along with the preview of the pad, is displayed.

6. Choose the **Perpendicular** button from the **Positioning** dialog box; the **Perpendicular** dialog box is displayed. Select any one of the edges of the right face of the base feature that measures 13 mm, and then the center line parallel to the selected edge from the preview of the rectangular pad; the **Create Expression** dialog box is displayed.

7. Enter **5** in the edit box of the **Create Expression** dialog box and choose the **OK** button; the **Positioning** dialog box is displayed.

8. Choose the **Perpendicular** button from the **Positioning** dialog box, and then select any of the edges that measures 10 mm from the right face of the base feature. Also, select the center line parallel to this edge from the preview of the rectangular pad; the **Create Expression** dialog box is displayed.

9. Enter **6.5** in the edit box of the **Create Expression** dialog box.

10. Choose the **OK** button twice and then the **Cancel** button once. The rectangular pad feature is created, as shown in Figure 8-64.

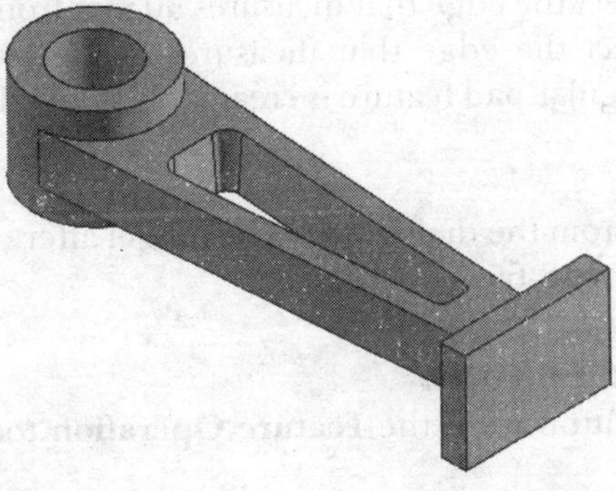

Figure 8-64 *The model after creating the pad feature*

Creating the Second Rectangular Pad Feature

The next feature is also a rectangular pad feature, and will be created on the right face of the previously created rectangular pad feature.

1. Choose the **Pad** button from the **Feature** toolbar; the **Pad** dialog box is displayed and you are prompted to select the pad type.

2. Choose the **Rectangular** button from the **Pad** dialog box; the **Rectangular Pad** dialog box is displayed and you are prompted to select the planar placement face.

3. Select the right face of the previous rectangular pad feature; the **Horizontal Reference** dialog box is displayed and you are prompted to select the horizontal reference.

4. Select the edge of the rectangular pad feature that measures 20 mm; the **Rectangular Pad** dialog box is displayed. Enter **20** as the value for length, **8** for width, and **30** for height in their respective edit boxes.

5. Choose the **OK** button from the dialog box; the **Positioning** dialog box along with the preview of the pad is displayed.

6. Choose the **Perpendicular** button from the **Positioning** dialog box; the **Perpendicular** dialog box is displayed. Select the edge that measures 20 mm from the previously created rectangular pad feature and then select the center line parallel to this edge from the preview of the rectangular pad; the **Create Expression** dialog box is displayed.

Note

*To select center lines from the preview of the rectangular pad, you may need to change the current display of the model to static wireframe. To do so, click on the down-arrow left to the **Shaded With Edges** button in the **View** toolbar; a flyout is displayed. Choose the **Static Wireframe** option from the flyout; the display of the model is changed.*

7. Enter **15** in the edit box of the **Create Expression** dialog box and choose the **OK** button; the **Positioning** dialog box is displayed.

8. Choose the **Line onto Line** button from the **Positioning** dialog box; the **Line onto Line** dialog box is displayed. Select the edge that measures 30 mm from the previously created pad feature and then select the edge that measures 8 mm from the preview of the rectangular pad; the rectangular pad feature is created. Also, the **Rectangular Pad** dialog box is displayed.

9. Choose the **Cancel** button from the dialog box. The model after creating the rectangular pad feature is shown in Figure 8-65.

Creating the Edge Blend Feature

1. Choose the **Edge Blend** button from the **Feature Operation** toolbar; the **Edge Blend** dialog box is displayed.

2. Select the upper and lower edges of the right face of the second pad feature. Both these edges measure 8 mm. Next, enter **10** in the **Radius 1** edit box of the **Edge to Blend** rollout in the dialog box.

3. Choose the **OK** button from the **Edge Blend** dialog box. The rectangular pad after creating the edge blend feature is shown in Figure 8-66.

Creating the Cylindrical Pocket Feature

To complete this model, you need to add a cylindrical pocket feature to the second rectangular pad feature.

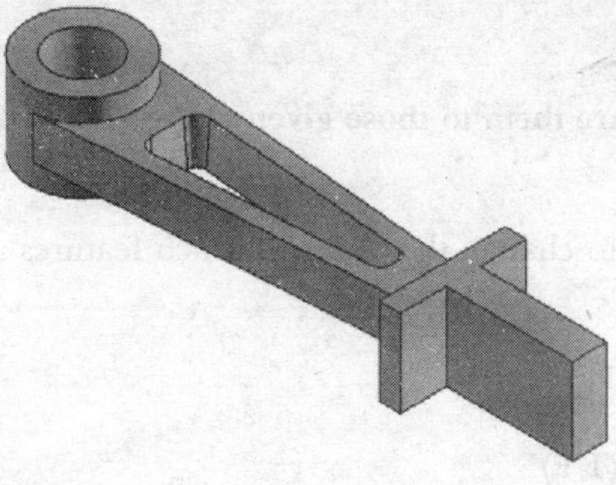

Figure 8-65 Model after creating the pad feature

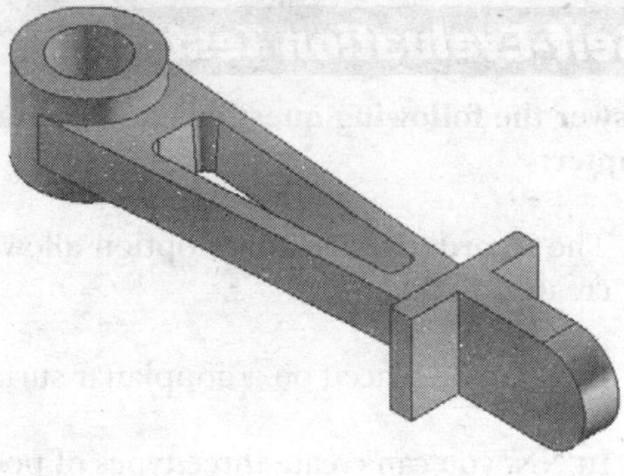

Figure 8-66 Model after creating the edge blend feature

1. Choose the **Pocket** button from the **Feature** toolbar; the **Pocket** dialog box is displayed and you are prompted to select the pocket type.

2. Choose the **Cylindrical** button from this dialog box; the **Cylindrical Pocket** dialog box is displayed and you are prompted to select the planar placement face.

3. Select the front face of the previously created rectangular pad feature; the **Cylindrical Pocket** dialog box is modified and you are prompted to enter the pocket parameters. Enter **12** as the diameter value and **10** as the depth value in their respective edit boxes. Also, make sure that the value in the **Floor Radius** and **Taper Angle** edit boxes is set to 0.

4. Choose the **OK** button from the dialog box; the **Positioning** dialog box along with the preview of the pocket is displayed.

5. Choose the **Point onto Point** button from the **Positioning** dialog box; the **Point onto Point** dialog box is displayed. Now, select the curve edge of the blend feature; the **Set Arc Position** dialog box is displayed. Choose the **Arc Center** button from the dialog box; the **Point onto Point** dialog box is displayed again.

6. Select the cylindrical pocket edge from the preview of the pocket; the **Set Arc Position** dialog box is displayed. Now, choose the **Arc Center** button from this dialog box; the cylindrical pocket is placed on the rectangular pad feature. The final model is shown in Figure 8-67. Next, choose the **Cancel** button to exit from the dialog box.

7. Choose **File > Close > Save and Close** from the menu bar to save and close the part file.

Figure 8-67 The final model for Tutorial 3

Self-Evaluation Test

Answer the following questions and then compare them to those given at the end of this chapter:

1. The **Reordering Features** option allows you to change the order in which features are created. (T/F)

2. Boss can be placed on a nonplanar surface. (T/F)

3. In NX, you can create three types of pockets. (T/F)

4. The pad feature is defined as the process of adding material to a model. (T/F)

5. In the **Tangent to Faces** draft type, there is no need to select a stationary plane. (T/F)

6. General pockets can be created on both ________ and ________ faces.

7. In NX, you can create ________ types of drafts.

8. In the **Draft** dialog box, the ________ check box allows you to select whether to taper only the specified instance or all instances in array features.

9. The **Tangent to Faces** type is used to create a draft, which is ________ to the selected faces.

10. The length of a rectangular pad is ________ to a horizontal reference.

Review Questions

Answer the following questions:

1. Which of the following cross-sections does have the boss feature?

   (a) **Circular** (b) **Rectangle**
   (c) **Square** (d) None of these

2. Which tool is used to create the cutout feature?

   (a) **Pad** (b) **Pocket**
   (c) **Boss** (d) None of these

3. Which of the following pocket types needs a sketch?

   (a) **Cylindrical pocket** (b) **General pocket**
   (c) **Rectangular pocket** (d) None of these

4. Which draft type is used to create a draft on nonuniform edges?

   (a) **From Plane** (b) **From Edges**
   (c) **Tangent to Faces** (d) None of these

5. Which one of the following is the radius between the placement face and the side faces of the pocket?

   (a) Placement radius (b) Corner radius
   (c) Floor radius (d) None of these

6. Which tool is used to create the cylindrical extrusion feature?

   (a) **Boss** (b) **Pad**
   (c) **Pocket** (d) None of these

7. The **Inferred Vector** drop-down list in the **Draft** dialog box is used to specify the draw direction of taper. (T/F)

8. A datum plane can be selected as the placement face for the boss feature. (T/F)

9. A boss is a feature that has a uniform diameter throughout its length. (T/F)

10. A draft feature can be placed on the surface body. (T/F)

Exercises

Exercise 1

Create the model shown in Figure 8-68. The drawing views and dimensions of the model are shown in Figure 8-69. After creating the model, save it with the name *c08exr1.prt* at the location *\NX 7\c08.* **(Expected time: 30 min)**

Figure 8-68 *The solid model for Exercise 1*

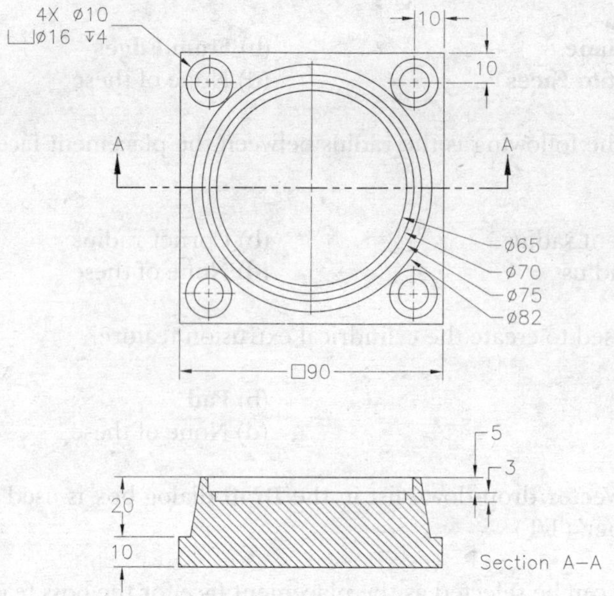

Figure 8-69 Views and dimensions for Exercise 1

Exercise 2

Create the model shown in Figure 8-70. The drawing views and dimensions of the model are shown in Figure 8-71. After creating the model, save it with the name *c08exr2.prt* at the location *\NX 7\c08.* **(Expected time: 30 min)**

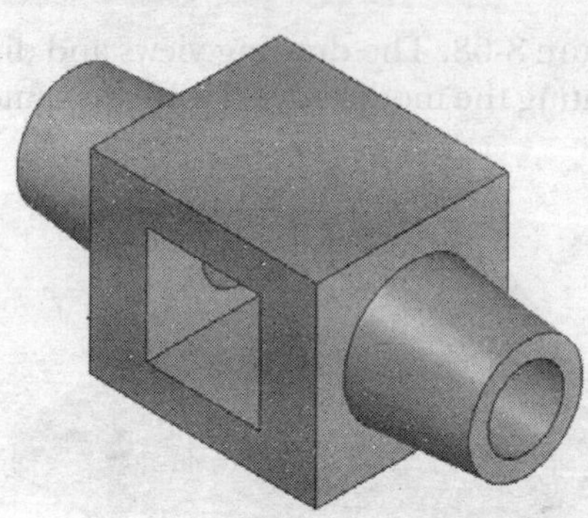

Figure 8-70 The solid model for Exercise 2

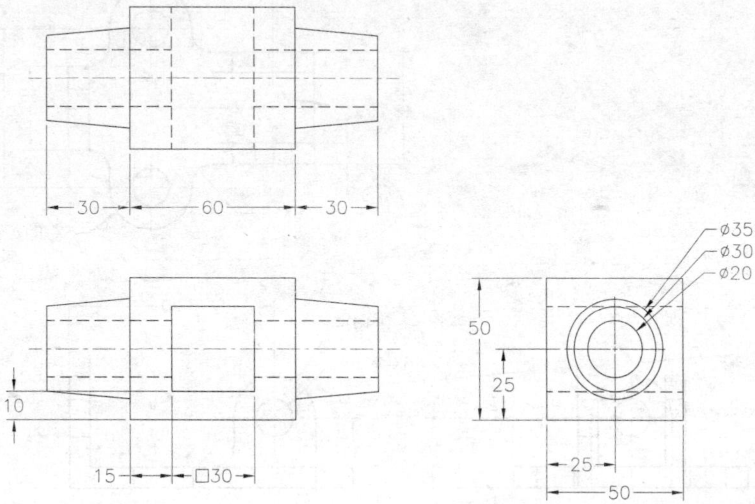

Figure 8-71 Views and dimensions for Exercise 2

Exercise 3

Create the model shown in Figure 8-72. The drawing views and dimensions of the model are shown in Figure 8-73. After creating the model, save it with the name *c08exr3.prt* at the location *\NX 7\c08.* **(Expected time: 30 min)**

Figure 8-72 The solid model for Exercise 3

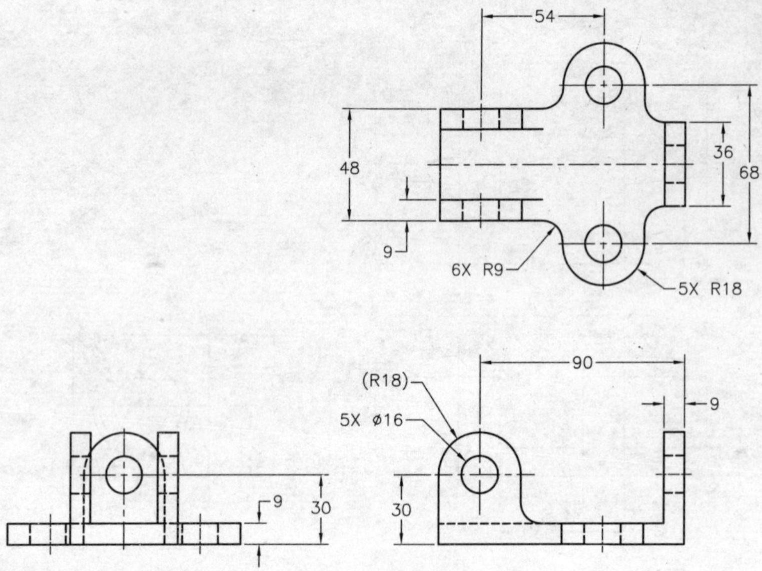

Figure 8-73 Views and dimensions for Exercise 3

Answers to Self-Evaluation Test

1.T, **2.** F, **3.** T, **4.** T, **5.** T, **6.** planar, nonplanar, **7.** four, **8. Draft All Instances**, **9.** tangent, **10.** parallel.

Chapter 9

Assembly Modeling-I

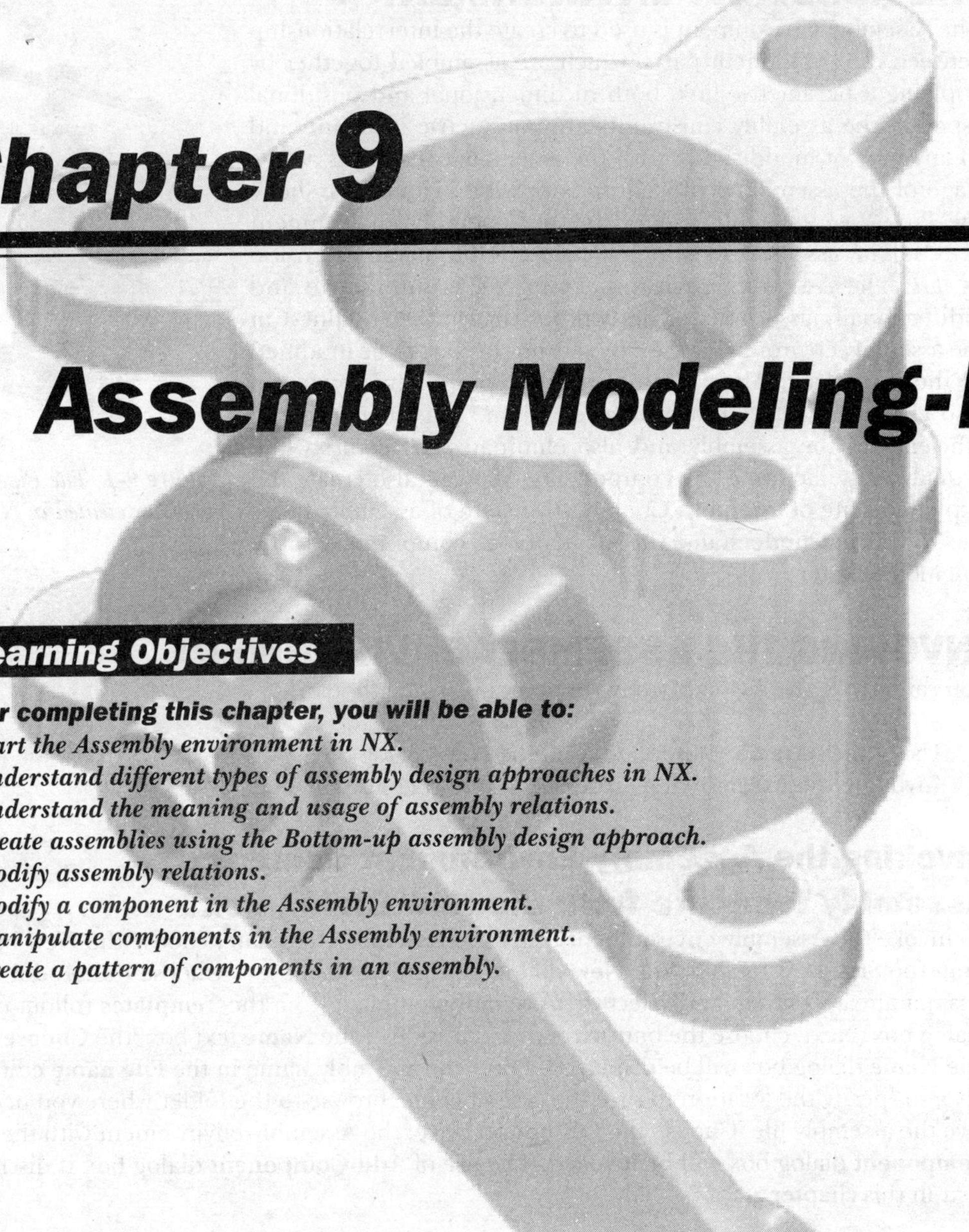

Learning Objectives

After completing this chapter, you will be able to:

- ***Start the Assembly environment in NX.***
- ***Understand different types of assembly design approaches in NX.***
- ***Understand the meaning and usage of assembly relations.***
- ***Create assemblies using the Bottom-up assembly design approach.***
- ***Modify assembly relations.***
- ***Modify a component in the Assembly environment.***
- ***Manipulate components in the Assembly environment.***
- ***Create a pattern of components in an assembly.***

THE ASSEMBLY ENVIRONMENT

The Assembly environment is used to create the interrelationship between the component parts, which are assembled together by applying a parametric link, both in dimensional and positional aspects. The assembly constraints are parametric in nature and so any type of modification with the assembly constraints at any stage of the assembling procedure is possible. Figure 9-1 shows the Pipe Vice assembly created in the Assembly environment of NX. The assembly files in NX have the file name extension as *.prt*. The Assembly environment in NX is interactive and bidirectionally associative. The component can be modified in the assembly environment itself by setting the part to be modified as the work part. After assembling the components, you can also check the interference between them. This increases the efficiency of the assembly and also eliminates the errors while actually manufacturing the components. You can also create the exploded state of assembly. Creating this state of assembly helps the technician understand the sequence of components to be assembled better.

***Figure 9-1** The Pipe Vice assembly created in NX*

INVOKING THE ASSEMBLY ENVIRONMENT

You can invoke the **Assembly** environment by two methods:

1. Using the **Assembly** template from the **New** dialog box.
2. Invoking the **Assembly** environment in the current part file.

Invoking the Assembly Environment Using the Assembly Template from the New Dialog Box

To invoke the Assembly environment using the **Assembly** template, choose the **New** button from the **Standard** toolbar; the **New** dialog box will be displayed. Choose the **Model** tab if it is not already chosen and select the **Assembly** template from the **Templates** rollout of the dialog box. Next, choose the button on the right side of the **Name** text box; the **Choose New File Name** dialog box will be displayed. Enter the assembly name in the **File name** edit box. Also, to specify the location to save the assembly file, browse to the folder where you need to save the assembly file. Choose the **OK** button twice; the Assembly environment with the **Add Component** dialog box will be invoked. The use of **Add Component** dialog box is discussed next in this chapter.

Invoking the Assembly Environment in the Current Part File

Toolbar: Standard > Start > Assemblies

As mentioned earlier, the Assembly environment is also invoked in the *.prt* file. Therefore, you need to start a new *.prt* file. Before invoking the Assembly environment, it is recommended that you invoke the Modeling environment. Then, choose **Start > Assemblies** from the **Standard** toolbar to invoke the Assembly environment; the NX 7 window, with the Assembly environment will be displayed, refer to Figure 9-2.

Figure 9-2 The NX 7 window in the Assembly environment

Note

*If the **Assemblies** toolbar is not displayed by default at the bottom, as shown in the Figure 9-2, you need to customize to add it in the Assembly environment of NX 7. To do so, right-click on the toolbar area and choose the **Assemblies** option from the shortcut menu displayed.*

Types of Assembly Design Approaches

In NX, the assemblies can be created using two types of design approaches, the bottom-up assembly design approach and the top-down assembly design approach. In this chapter, you will learn about the bottom-up assembly design approach. The top-down approach is discussed in the next chapter.

Bottom-up Assembly Design Approach

The Bottom-up assembly design approach is the most widely preferred traditional approach of assembly design. In this approach, all components are created as separate part files and placed in the assembly as external components. In this approach, you need to create components separately in the Modeling environment and save them as *.prt* files. After creating all components, you need to start a new file in the Assembly environment and place them in the assembly environment using the tools in the **Assemblies** toolbar. Next, you need to assemble the components using assembly constraints.

The main advantage of this approach is that you can pay more attention to the complexity of the component design as you create them before assembling. You can also capture the design intent easily. This approach is preferred while handling large assemblies or assemblies with complex components.

CREATING BOTTOM-UP ASSEMBLIES

As mentioned earlier, in the bottom-up assemblies, components are created as separate parts in the Modeling environment, and then they are placed in a new file that is started in the Assembly environment. In the assembly file, the parts are assembled using the assembly constraints. As discussed earlier, it is recommended that you first invoke the Modeling environment and then choose **Start > Assemblies** from the **Standard** toolbar to invoke the Assembly environment.

Placing Components in the Assembly Environment

Menu:	Assemblies > Components > Add Component
Toolbar:	Assemblies > Add Component

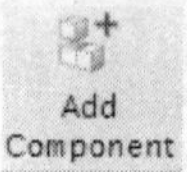

In NX, the components are placed in the Assembly environment using the **Add Component** tool available in the **Assemblies** toolbar. To place the component, choose the **Add Component** button from the **Assemblies** toolbar; the **Add Component** dialog box will be displayed. Choose the **Open** button from the dialog box; the **Part Name** dialog box will be displayed. Browse and select the component to be placed and choose the **OK** button from the **Part Name** dialog box; the **Component Preview** window will be displayed. In this window, you can preview the selected component. The component that is displayed in the **Component Preview** window is known as the displayed part. The Assembly environment window with the **Add Component** dialog box and the **Component Preview** window is shown in Figure 9-3.

The name of the component is displayed in the **Loaded Parts** list of the **Add Component** dialog box. The **Recent Parts** list displays the list of recently added parts in the Assembly environment. You can select the part files from this list also.

Note

*If the component to be assembled is already placed in the assembly, then for subsequent placements, you can directly retrieve it from the **Recent Parts** list of the dialog box.*

You can add multiple instances of the same component to the assembly file. To do so, expand the **Duplicates** sub-rollout of the **Part** rollout and then enter the number of instances in the **Count** edit box. The remaining options in the **Add Component** dialog box are discussed next.

Placement Rollout

The options in this rollout of the **Add Component** dialog box are discussed next.

Positioning

The options in the **Positioning** drop-down list are used to define the type of positioning required for placing the component in the assembly file. Select the **By Constraints** option from this drop-down list to create the assembly by applying assembly constraints between the components and the datum planes in the assembly file. The method of applying the constraints is discussed later in this chapter. If you select the **Absolute Origin** option from the **Positioning** drop-down list, the selected component will

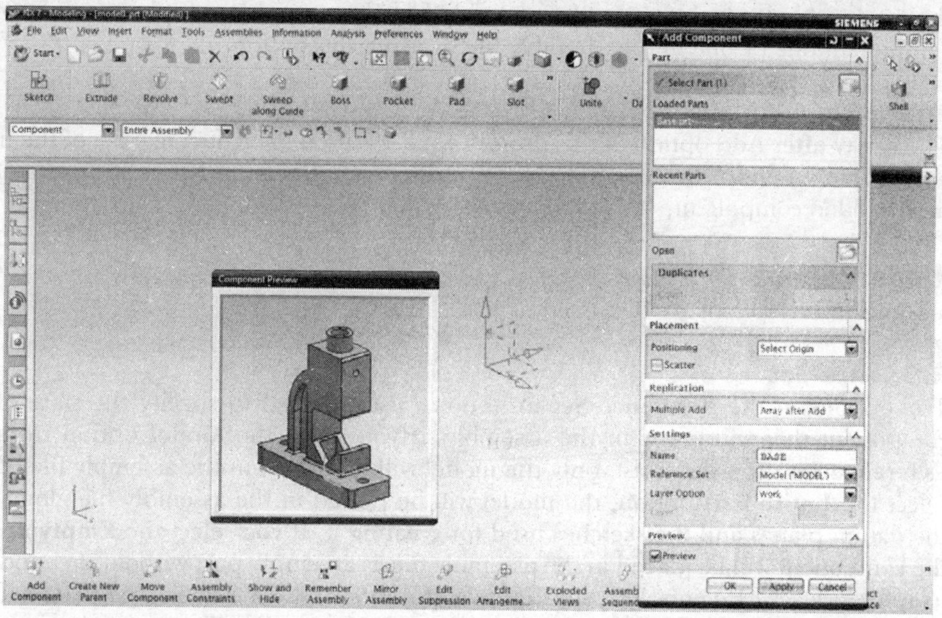

Figure 9-3 The Assembly environment window with the ***Add Component*** *dialog box and the* ***Component Preview*** *window*

be assembled by aligning the datum planes of the component with the datum planes of the assembly environment. In this case, you cannot use assembly constraints to make the component fully-constrained. However, you can position the component in the assembly file at absolute origin. By selecting the **Move** option from the **Positioning** drop-down list, you can place the component anywhere in the 3D space by using the options in the **Move Component** dialog box. The tools of the **Move Component** dialog box are discussed later in this chapter. The **Select Origin** option of the **Positioning** drop-down list is used to position the component at the selected point. In this case, the coordinate system of the component coincides with the selected point.

Scatter

You can select this check box to prevent the multiple instances to appear at the same position.

Replication Rollout

The **Multiple Add** drop-down list in this rollout allows you to add the multiple instances of the component to the assembly file. The options in this drop-down list are discussed next.

None

This option is selected by default in the **Multiple Add** drop-down list. This option allows you to add only one instance of the selected component in the assembly file.

Repeat after Add

The **Repeat after Add** option of this drop-down list is used to add another instance of the newly added component in the assembly file. You can add multiple instances of the component one by one in the assembly file by using this option.

Array after Add

The **Array after Add** option of this drop-down list is used to create an array of the newly added component in the assembly file. You can create linear and circular arrays of the newly added component.

Settings Rollout

The options in this rollout are discussed next.

Reference Set

The options in the **Reference Set** drop-down list are used to specify the state of the component that will occur in the assembly. If you select the **Model** option from the **Reference Set** drop-down list, only the model will be placed in the assembly file. If you select the **Entire Part** option, the model will be placed in the assembly file along with the datum planes and the sketches used for creating it. If you select the **Empty** option, the component will be placed in the assembly file as an empty part without the model or its reference sets. If you select the **Lightweight** option, the model will be placed in the assembly file along with the datum planes and sketches. But, it will consume less memory of the system, so the file size of the assembly will be less than the actual.

Name

This edit box is used to display the name of the currently selected component in the **Add component** dialog box.

Layer Option

The options in this drop-down list are used to specify different layers in the assembly file.

Tip: *It is recommended to assemble the base component by selecting the* ***Entire Part*** *option from the* ***Reference Set*** *drop-down list.*

Preview Rollout

On selecting the **Preview** check box in this rollout, the preview of the component to be added in the assembly will be displayed in the **Component Preview** window.

Changing the Reference Set of a Component

Toolbar:	Assemblies > Replace Reference Set *(Customize to add)*

As mentioned earlier, when you place a component using the **Entire Part** option from the **Reference Set** drop-down list of the **Add Component** dialog box, datum planes and sketches used to create that component are also displayed in the assembly file. However, after assembling the component, you do not need these datum planes and sketches as they cause confusion in the assembly file and restrict the display of other components as well.

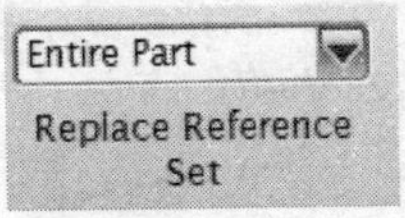

To change the reference set of a component, right-click on the component in the drawing window and choose **Replace Reference Set > MODEL**; the datum planes and sketches of the component will disappear. You can also select the model from the graphics window, and then select the **MODEL** option from the drop-down list available in the **Replace Reference Set** button in the **Assemblies** toolbar.

Alternatively, you can change the reference set of a component by using the **Replace Reference** button. To do so, choose the **Replace Reference** button from the **Assemblies** toolbar; the **Class Selection** dialog box will be displayed. Select a component from the graphics window and then choose the **OK** button from the dialog box; the **Replace Reference Set** dialog box will be displayed with a list of all reference sets. Select the required reference set for the selected component and then choose the **OK** button to apply it.

Note

*If the **Replace Reference** button is not displayed by default in the **Assemblies** toolbar, then you can customize to add it in this toolbar.*

Applying Assembly Constraints to Components

In NX, assembly constraints can be applied to components by using the **Assembly Constraints** dialog box. To invoke this dialog box, select the **By Constraints** option from the **Positioning** drop-down list of the **Add Component** dialog box. Next, choose the **OK** button from the dialog box; the **Assembly Constraints** dialog box will be displayed, as shown in Figure 9-4.

Note

*You can also invoke the **Assembly Constraints** dialog box by choosing the **Assembly Constraints** button from **Assemblies** toolbar.*

Assembly constraints are used to constrain the degree of freedom of a component in an assembly. By constraining the degrees of freedom of a component, you can restrict or determine the movement of the component. There are ten types of assembly constraints available in NX. All these constraints are available in the **Type** drop-down list of the **Assembly Constraints** dialog box, as shown in Figure 9-5. All these assembly constraints are discussed next.

Touch Align

The **Touch Align** constraint is used to constrain the motion of two selected reference faces or reference planes of different components such that they touch or align with each other. This constraint is also used to make edges or axis of components collinear, or to make points of components coincident to each other. To apply this constraint, select the **Touch Align** option from the **Type** drop-down list in the **Assembly Constraints** dialog box; you will be prompted to select the first reference object from the component to be mated. Select a planar face, curved face, edge, datum axis, or point as the reference object from the component to be mated; the selected reference object will be highlighted and you will be prompted to select the second reference object from the component to mate to.

Note

You can apply the ***Touch Align*** *constraint to constrain the components tangentially.*

Figure 9-4 The ***Assembly Constraints*** *dialog box*

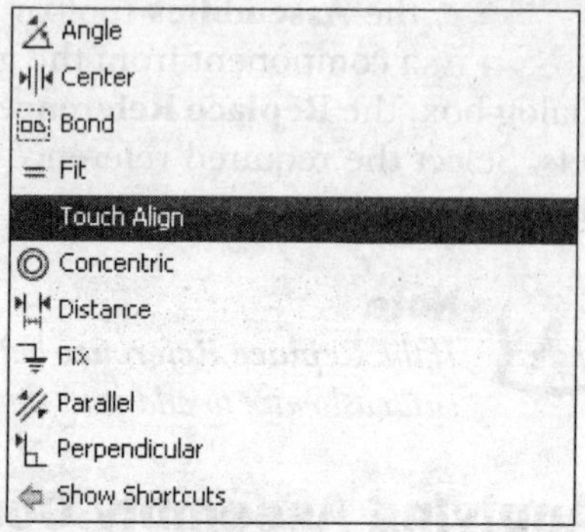

Figure 9-5 The ***Type*** *drop-down list*

Select a datum plane or any other reference object from the component displayed in the **Component Preview** window as the second reference object; the component will shift its position according to the constraint applied and a symbol of the constraint will be displayed on the component. Figure 9-6 shows the faces to be selected for applying the **Touch Align** constraint and Figure 9-7 shows components after applying the **Touch Align** constraint to them.

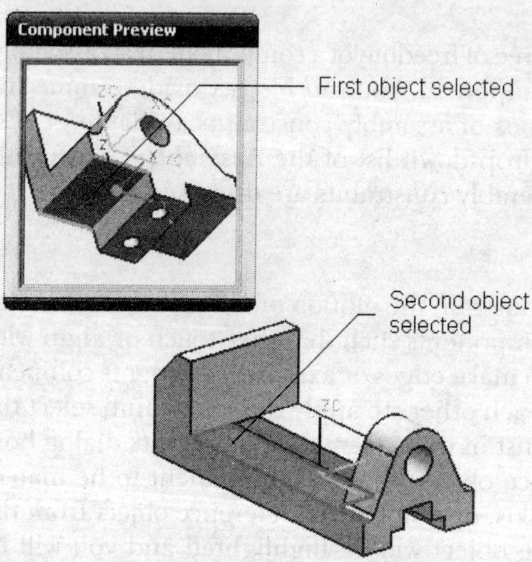

Figure 9-6 Faces selected as reference objects for applying the ***Touch Align*** *constraint*

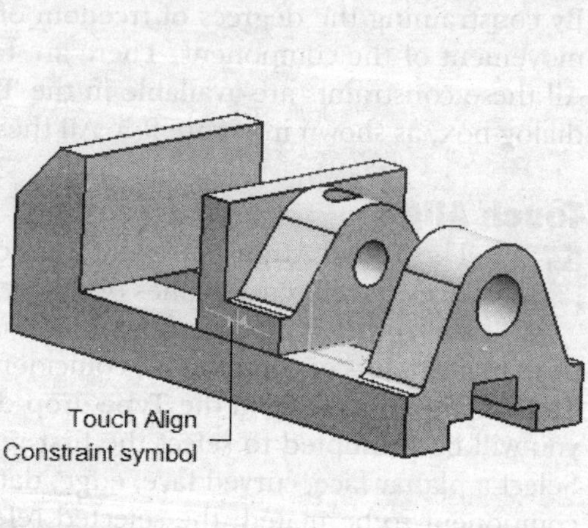

Figure 9-7 Components after applying the ***Touch Align*** *constraint*

Note that the options in the different rollouts of the dialog box will change, depending upon the options selected from the **Type** drop-down list. These options are discussed next.

Geometry to Constrain Rollout

The options in this rollout are used to select geometries and set priorities for alternative solution of constraints among the selected geometries. Some of the options in this rollout have been discussed in the earlier chapter and the other options are discussed next.

Orientation

This drop-down list will be available only when the **Touch Align** option is selected in the drop-down list of the **Type** rollout. If you select the **Touch** option from the **Orientation** drop-down list, then the selected surfaces will face each other in the opposite direction. Also, both surfaces will become coplanar. Similarly, if you select the **Align** option from the **Orientation** drop-down list, then the selected surfaces will turn in the same direction. Also, both the surfaces will become coplanar. By default, the **Prefer Touch** option is selected in the **Orientation** drop-down list. As a result, the **Touch** option is preferred over the **Align** option when both the touch and align solutions are possible. If the touch solution over-constrains the selected surfaces, then the **Align** option get the preference. You can make the axes of a selected cylindrical, conical, spherical face, or an edge coaxial using the **Infer Center/Axis** option from the **Orientation** drop-down list.

Settings Rollout

The options of this rollout are available for all types of constraints. The options of this rollout are discussed next.

Arrangements

In the assembly environment, you can create different arrangements for assembly using the **Edit Arrangements** tool. In the **Arrangements** drop-down list, the **Use Component Properties** option is selected by default. As a result, the constraint specified in the **Type** drop-down list is applied to all arrangements. If you select the **Apply to Used** option from this drop-down list, the constraint will be applied only to the currently active arrangement.

Dynamic Positioning

This check box is selected by default. As a result, constraints will be applied dynamically as soon as they are created. If you clear this check box, the constraint created will not be applied unless you choose the **OK** or **Apply** button.

Associative

This check box is selected by default. As a result, constraints will be applied only on choosing the **Apply** or **OK** button. If you clear this check box, constraints will be applied temporarily and will get deleted after choosing the **Apply** or **OK** button.

Move Curves and Routing Objects

If this check box is selected, the routing objects and the related curves will move when the constrains are applied to them.

Dynamic Update of Routing Solids

This check box is useful for the Routing Mechanical and Routing Electrical type of environments.

Preview Rollout

In the **Preview** rollout, the **Preview Window** check box is selected by default. As a result, you can preview the component in the **Component Preview** window. Select the **Preview Component in Main Window** check box, if you want to preview the component in the main window. Note that the **Preview** rollout will not be available when the **Assembly Constraints** dialog box is invoked by using the **Assembly Constraints** tool.

Angle

The **Angle** constraint is applied to specify an angle between two selected reference objects of components. To apply this constraint, select the **Angle** constraint from the **Type** drop-down list in the **Assembly Constraints** dialog box; the **Geometry to Constrain** rollout will be modified. By default, the **3D Angle** option will be selected from the **Subtype** drop-down list in this rollout. Also, you will be prompted to select the first object to apply the angle constraint. Select a face; you will be prompted to select the second object to apply constraint. Select the second face; two angular handles and a dynamic input box will be displayed in the graphics window. Also, the **Angle** rollout will be displayed in the **Assembly Constraints** dialog box. Next, enter the required angle either in the dynamic input box or in the **Angle** edit box of the **Angle** rollout. Figure 9-8 shows the faces selected as reference objects for applying the angle constraint and Figure 9-9 shows the preview of the component after the constraint has been applied.

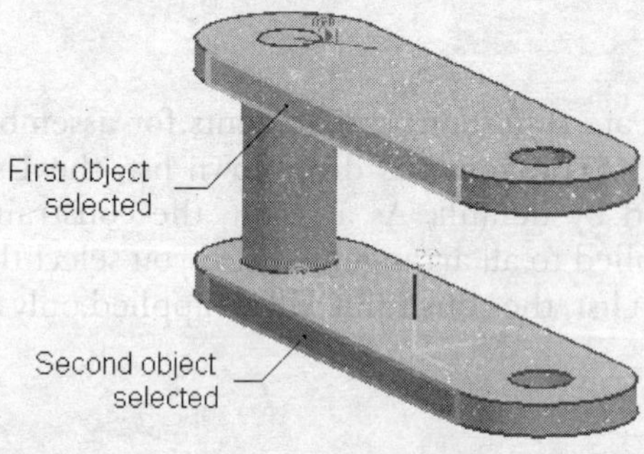

*Figure 9-8 Faces selected as reference objects for applying the **Angle** constraint*

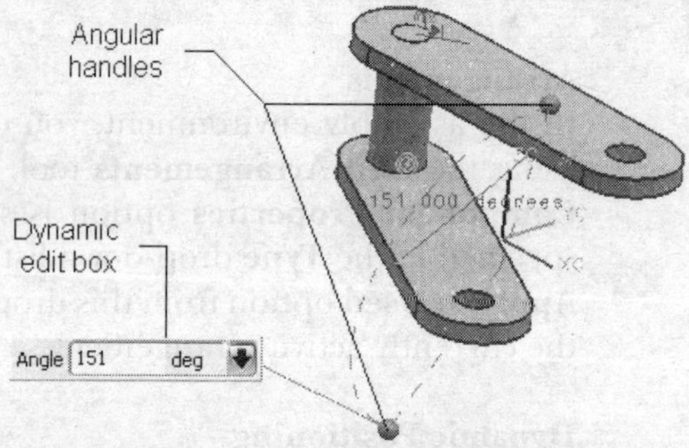

*Figure 9-9 Preview of the components after applying the **Angle** constraint*

If you select the **Orient Angle** option from the **Subtype** drop-down list, you will be prompted to select an axis for specifying the angle. Select an axis or an edge; you will be prompted to select the first object for applying the **Angle** constraint. Select the first face; you will be prompted to select the second object for applying **Angle** constraint. Select the second face of the object, as shown in Figure 9-10; two angular handles and a dynamic input box will be displayed in the graphics window. You can use these angular handles to dynamically orient the component with respect to the selected axis (the distance between the selected axis and the selected face remains the same throughout the process). While dragging the handle, the angle value will be displayed in the **Angle** edit box. Alternatively, you can enter the angle value manually in the **Angle** edit box. Figure 9-10 shows the edge and faces selected for applying the **Angle** constraint using the **Orient Angle** option. Figure 9-11 shows the preview of components after applying the **Angle** constraint using the **Orient Angle** option.

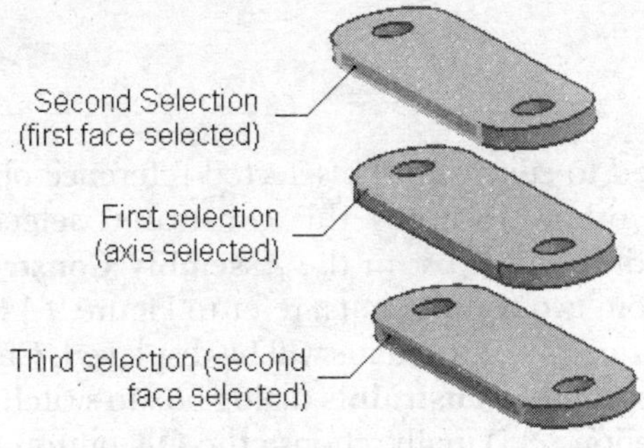

***Figure 9-10** Edge and faces selected for applying the **Angle** constraint*

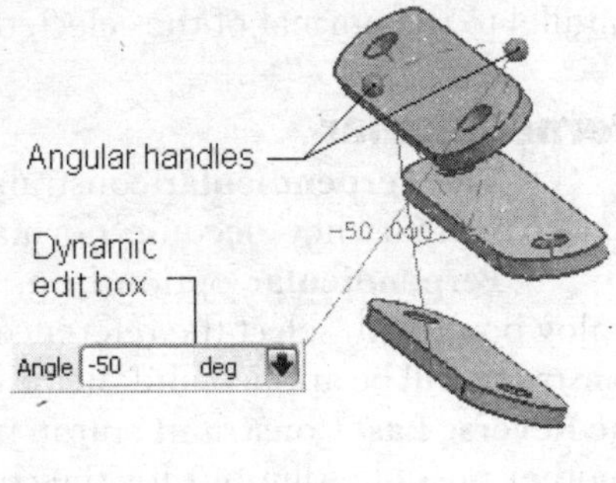

***Figure 9-11** Preview of the components after applying the **Angle** constraint*

Note

*The number of handles displayed in the graphics window depend upon the objects selected for applying the constraint. For example, if the objects selected for applying the **Angle** constraint are free to move in the angular direction, then two angular handles will be displayed in the graphics window. However, in case one of the selected objects is fixed, then only one angular handle will be displayed in the graphics window.*

Parallel

The **Parallel** constraint is applied to constrain the selected reference objects so that they become parallel to each other. To apply the **Parallel** constraint to objects, select the **Parallel** option from the **Type** drop-down list in the **Assembly Constraints** dialog box. Next, select the reference objects from two components, refer to Figure 9-12; the constraint will be applied and the resulting position of components will be displayed in the graphics window. Next, choose the **Reverse Last Constraint** button from the **Assembly Constraints** dialog box, if you want to switch over to other possible solutions for applying constraint. Next, choose the **OK** button from the **Assembly Constraints** dialog box; the **Parallel** constraint will be applied to components, refer to Figure 9-13.

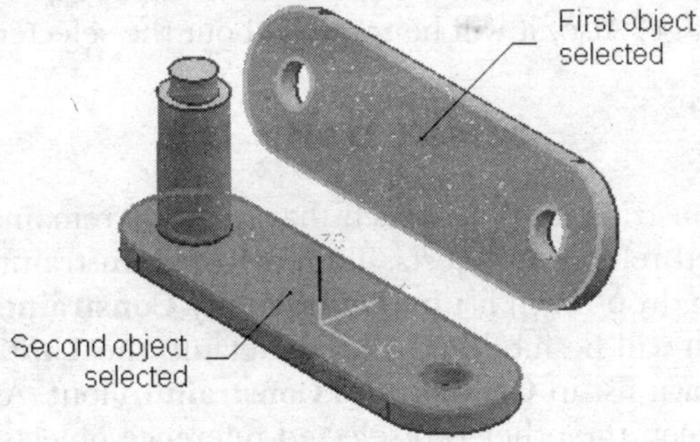

***Figure 9-12** Faces selected as reference objects for applying the **Parallel** constraint*

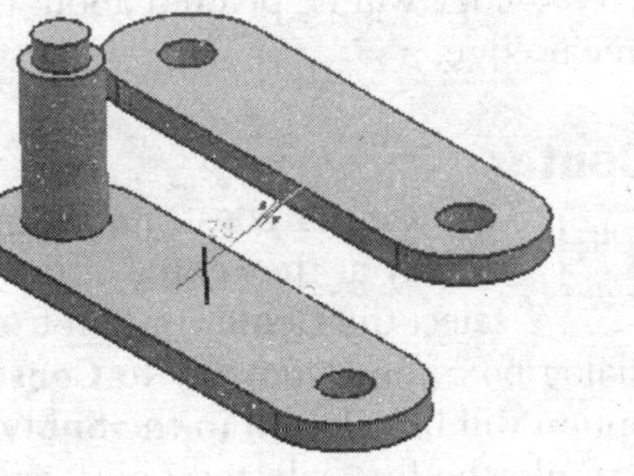

***Figure 9-13** Components after applying the **Parallel** constraint*

When you apply the **Parallel** constraint between the two cylindrical faces, the axes of the selected cylindrical faces become parallel to each other. However, if this constraint is applied between a cylindrical face and a planar face, the axis of the cylindrical face becomes parallel to the normal of the selected planar face.

Perpendicular

The **Perpendicular** constraint is applied to constrain the selected reference objects so that they become normal to each other. To apply this constraint, select the **Perpendicular** option from the **Type** drop-down list in the **Assembly Constraints** dialog box. Next, select the reference objects from two components, refer to Figure 9-14; the constraint will be applied and the resulting position of components will be displayed. Choose the **Reverse Last Constraint** button from the **Assembly Constraints** dialog box to switch over to other possible solutions for the current selection set. Finally, choose the **OK** button from the **Assembly Constraints** dialog box. Figure 9-15 shows the final view of components after applying the **Perpendicular** constraint to them.

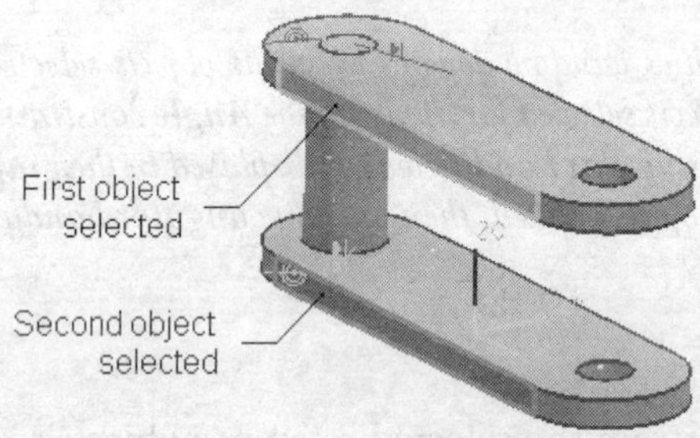

*Figure 9-14 Faces selected as reference objects for applying the **Perpendicular** constraint*

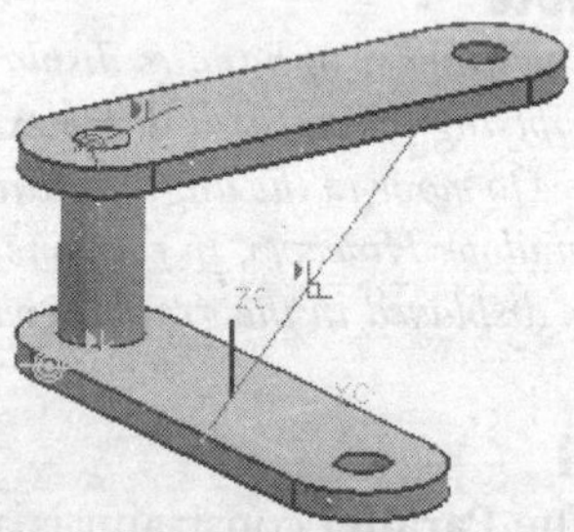

*Figure 9-15 Components after applying the **Perpendicular** constraint*

You can also apply the **Perpendicular** constraint between two cylindrical faces. In this case, the axes of the selected cylindrical faces become normal to each other. If you apply the **Perpendicular** constraint between a cylindrical face and a planar face, the axis of the cylindrical face will become normal to the selected planar face. If you apply this constraint between two selected curved edges, the selected curved edges will be placed normal to each other. If you apply the **Perpendicular** constraint between a linear edge and a curved edge, the curved edge will be pivoted about the linear edge. Also, it will be rotated about the selected linear edge.

Center

The **Center** constraint is applied to constrain an object such that it always remains exactly at the center of the two selected reference objects. To apply this constraint, select the **Center** option from the **Type** drop-down list in the **Assembly Constraints** dialog box; the **Geometry to Constrain** rollout will be modified and by default, the **1 to 2** option will be selected in the **Subtype** drop-down list in **Geometry to Constrain** rollout. As a result, the first selected object will shift between the other two selected reference objects. When you select the **Center** option from the **Type** drop-down list, you will be prompted to select the first object that will be at the center of the other two selected objects. After selecting the first object, you will be prompted to select the first reference object. Select any face, edge, or axis of the object as the first reference object; you will be prompted to select the second reference object. Select the second reference object; the first selected object will shift between the two selected reference objects. Figure 9-16 shows the object and reference objects and Figure 9-17 shows the components after the **Center** constraint is applied to them.

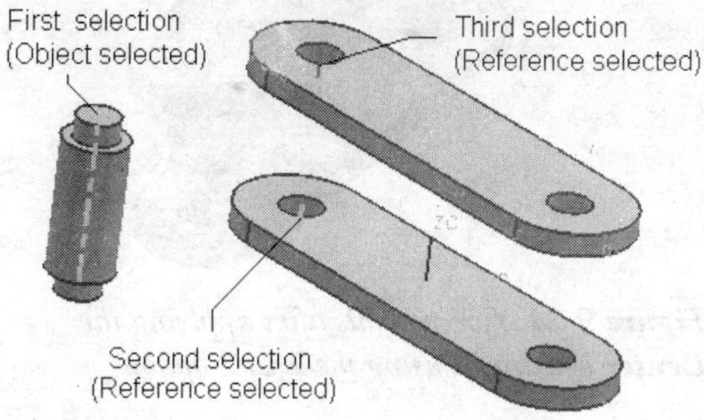

Figure 9-16 *Object and reference selection for applying the **Center** constraint using the **1 to 2** option*

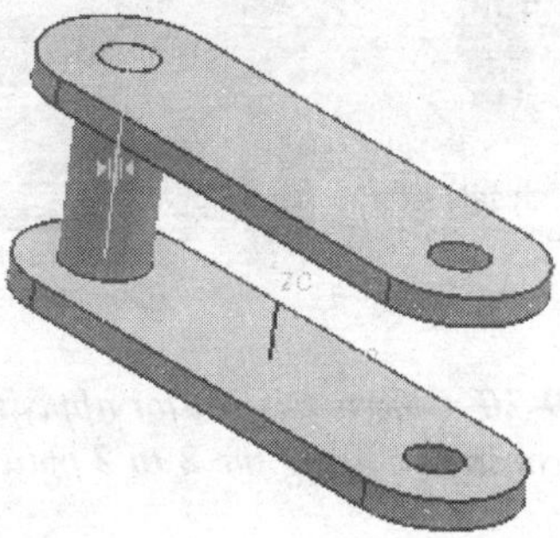

Figure 9-17 *Components after applying the **Center** constraint using the **1 to 2** option*

The **Subtype** drop-down list has two other options, **2 to 1** and **2 to 2**. You can use the **2 to 1** option from this drop-down list to shift the third selected object between the first two selected objects. Similarly, you can use the **2 to 2** option to bring the first two selected objects between the next two selected reference objects. Figures 9-18 and 9-19 show the first, second, and third selections for applying the **Center** constraint using the **2 to 1** option, and the objects after applying the required constraints, respectively.

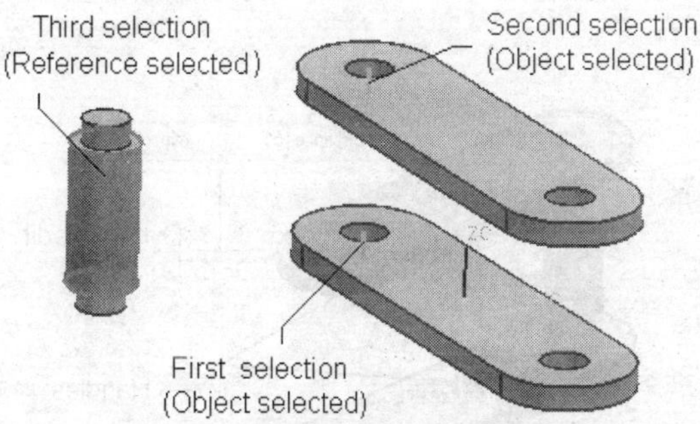

Figure 9-18 *Object and reference selection for applying the **Center** constraint using the **2 to 1** option*

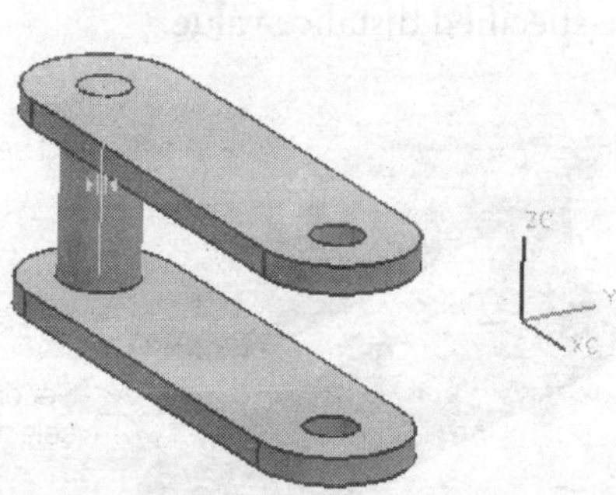

Figure 9-19 *Components after applying the **Center** constraint using the **2 to 1** option*

Figure 9-20 shows the first, second, third, and fourth selections of objects for applying the **Center** constraint using the **2 to 2** option and Figure 9-21 shows the objects after applying the **Center** constraint to them. When the **1 to 2** or **2 to 1** option is selected from the **Subtype** drop-down list, the **Axial Geometry** drop-down list is displayed in the **Geometry to Constrain** rollout. If you select the **Use Geometry** option from the **Axial Geometry** drop-down list, the selected cylindrical faces will be used for applying the **Center** constraint. If you select the

Infer Center/Axis option from the **Axial Geometry** drop-down list, the center or axis of the selected cylindrical faces will be used for applying the constraint.

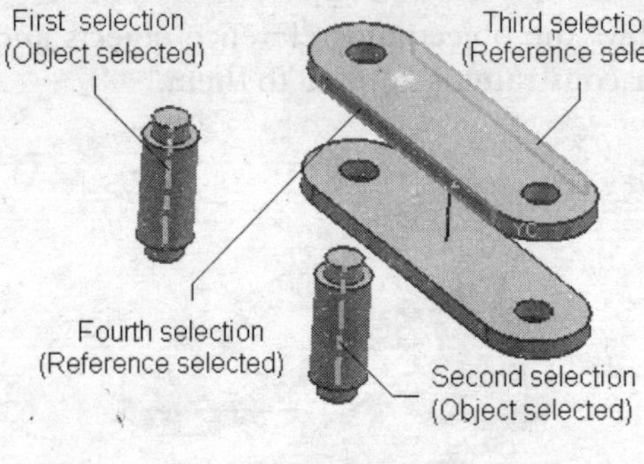

Figure 9-20 Objects selected for applying the ***Center*** *constraint using the* ***2 to 2*** *option*

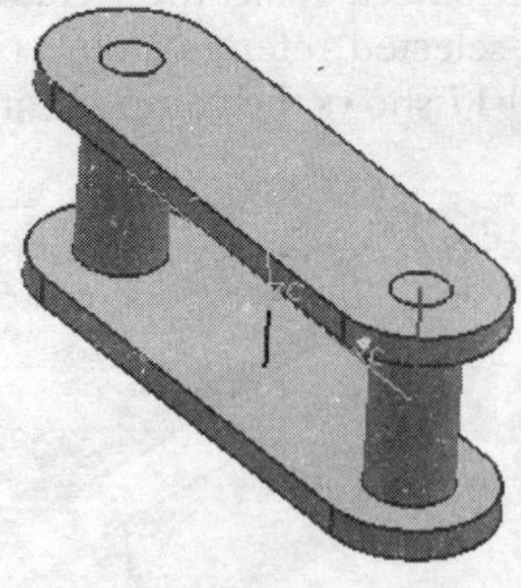

Figure 9-21 Components after applying the ***Center*** *constraint using the* ***2 to 2*** *option*

Distance

The **Distance** constraint is applied to maintain the required offset distance between the two selected reference objects. To apply this constraint, select the **Distance** option from the **Type** drop-down list in the **Assembly Constraints** dialog box; you will be prompted to select the first object. Select the first reference object, refer to Figure 9-22; you will be prompted to select the second object. Select the second object; the **Distance** edit box will be displayed in the **Distance** rollout and two handles with the dynamic input box will be displayed. Next, enter the required offset value in the **Distance** edit box and press ENTER; the preview of the resulting position of components will be displayed, refer to Figure 9-23. If the resulting position of the components is not satisfactory, choose the **Cycle Last Constraint** button from the **Assembly Constraints** dialog box to flip between the possible solutions for the specified distance value.

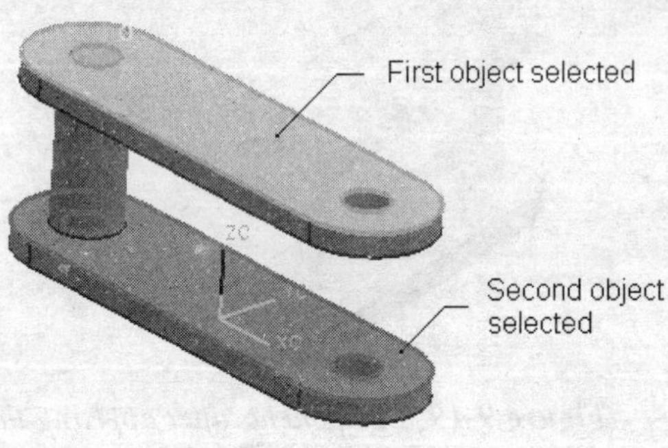

Figure 9-22 Faces selected as reference objects for applying the ***Distance*** *constraint*

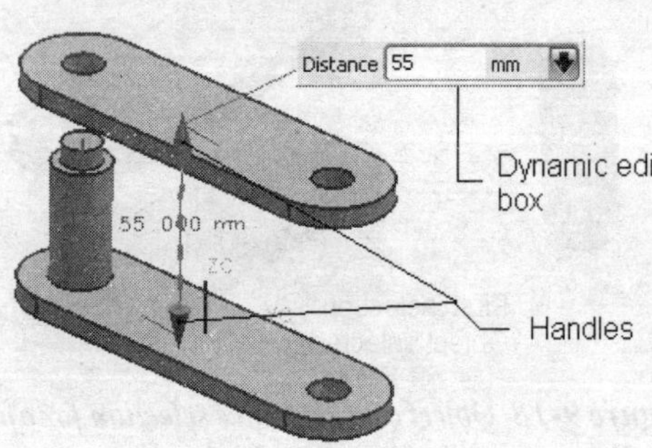

Figure 9-23 Components after applying the ***Distance*** *constraint*

You can also apply the **Distance** constraint between two cylindrical faces or circular edges. To do so, select the reference objects from both components and enter the required offset value in the **Distance** edit box; the constraint will be applied. Note that, in this case, the distance specified will be the distance between the axes of the selected objects.

Concentric

The **Concentric** constraint is applied to constrain the circular or elliptical edges of the components to coincide their centers as well as to make the selected edges coplanar. To apply this constraint, select the **Concentric** option from the **Type** drop-down list in the **Assembly Constraints** dialog box; you will be prompted to select the first circular object. Select the first circular object; you will be prompted to select the second circular object. Select the second circular object, refer to Figure 9-24; the centers of both circular edges will coincide and the selected edges will become coplanar, refer to Figure 9-25.

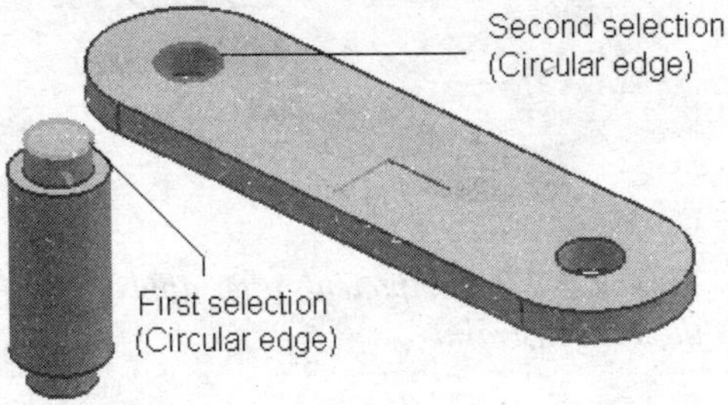

***Figure 9-24** Selecting circular edges for applying the **Concentric** constraint*

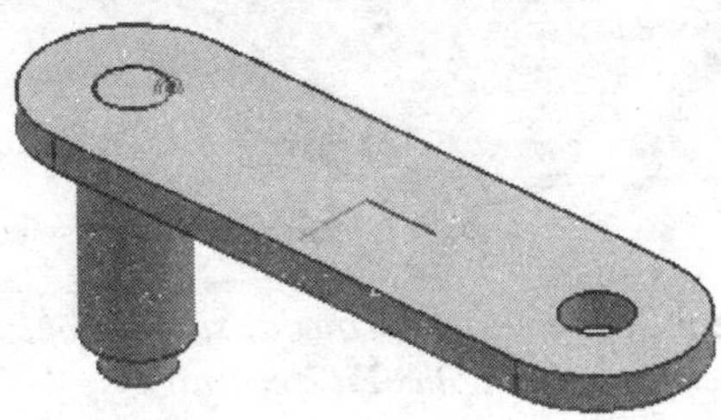

***Figure 9-25** Components after applying the **Concentric** constraint*

Fix

The **Fix** constraint is applied to fix the selected component at its current position in the 3D space. Once the component has been fixed, it cannot be changed and you can constrain other components with respect to the fixed component. To apply this constraint, select the **Fix** option from the **Type** drop-down list in the **Assembly Constraints** dialog box; you will be prompted to select the object to fix. Select the component; the selected component will be fixed at its current location and a small symbol will be displayed on it.

Bond

The **Bond** constraint is applied to fix the position of the selected components with respect to each other. Once the selected components are fixed using this constraint, they can be moved as a single component in such a way the position of one component will remain the same with respect to the other component. To apply this constraint, select the **Bond** option from the **Type** drop-down list in the **Assembly Constraints** dialog box; you will be prompted to select the objects that you want to bond. Select two or more components; the **Create Constraint** button will be displayed in the **Geometry to Constrain** rollout. Choose this button to apply the **Bond** constraint to the selected components.

Fit

The **Fit** constraint is applied to bring together two cylindrical faces of the same diameter. This constraint is useful for assembling nuts and bolts. To apply this constraint, select the **Fit** option from the **Type** drop-down list in the **Assembly Constraints** dialog box; you will be prompted to select the first object to fit. Select the first circular surface; you will be prompted to select the second object. Select the second circular surface of the same diameter; the axes of both components will coincide and they will become coaxial. Figure 9-26 shows components to apply the **Fit** constraint, and Figure 9-27 shows components after applying the **Fit** constraint. If the diameters of the selected surfaces (components) are not equal, the **Fit** constraint will become invalid.

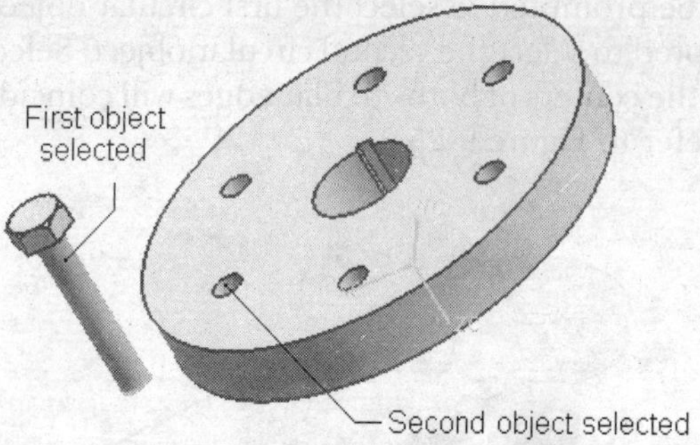

*Figure 9-26 Selection of circular surfaces of equal diameter for applying the **Fit** constraint*

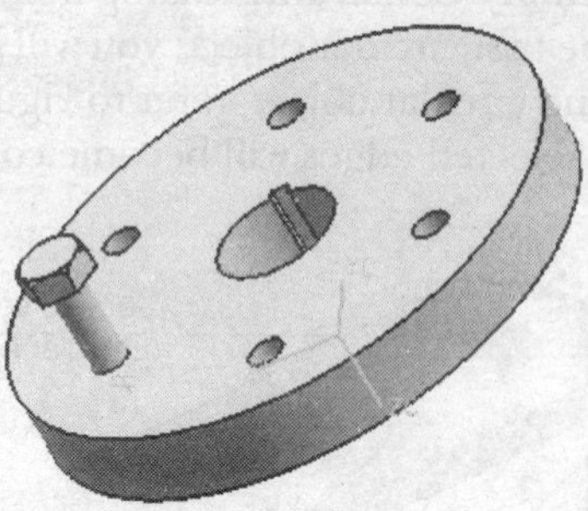

*Figure 9-27 Components after applying the **Fit** constraint*

Points to Remember while Assembling Components

The following points should be kept in mind to work efficiently in the Assembly environment of NX:

1. The first component should be assembled in the assembly file using the datum planes.
2. It is important to make the components fully constrained using the assembly constraints before placing the next component. The component that is partially constrained will be disturbed from its location while using it to assemble the other components.
3. If you have to place the same component at various positions in the same assembly, the second time onward, you can directly select the component from the **Recent Parts** list. There is no need of going to the **Part Name** dialog box again.
4. While making the component fully constrained, you can locate the temporary placement of the target component in the assembly using the **Preview Component in Main Window** check box that is available in the **Preview** rollout of the **Assembly Constraints** dialog box. At least, three assembly constraints will be needed to make the component fully constrained.

Creating a Component Array in an Assembly

Menu:	Assemblies > Components > Create Array
Toolbar:	Assemblies > Create Component Array *(Customize to add)*

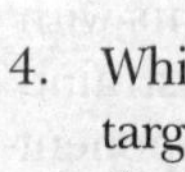

The **Create Component Array** tool is used to pattern a component in an assembly. It is similar to the method of patterning a feature in a component. For example, if in an assembly, there are ten bolts to be assembled, you don't have to assemble them ten times. Instead, assemble one of the bolts in any one of the holes and pattern it using the **Create Component Array** tool. To do so, choose the **Create Component**

Array button from the **Assemblies** toolbar; the **Class Selection** dialog box will be displayed and you will be prompted to select components. Select the component to array and press the middle mouse button; the **Create Component Array** dialog box will be displayed, as shown in Figure 9-28.

The procedure for creating the component array in an assembly is discussed next.

1. In the **Component Array Name** edit box, enter the name of the component array that is to be defined; this name will identify the array in the assembly.

2. To create a circular array, select the **Circular** radio button, and then choose the **OK** button from the **Create Component Array** dialog box; the **Create Circular Array** dialog box will be displayed, as shown in Figure 9-29, and you will be prompted to define an object as an array axis. You can select a cylindrical face, a datum axis, or an edge of the component to define the array axis. After selecting the array axis, the **Total Number** and **Angle** edit boxes will be activated in the dialog box. Specify the number of instances in the **Total Number** edit box, and then the angle of rotation in the **Angle** edit box of the **Create Circular Array** dialog box. Next, choose the **OK** button from the dialog box.

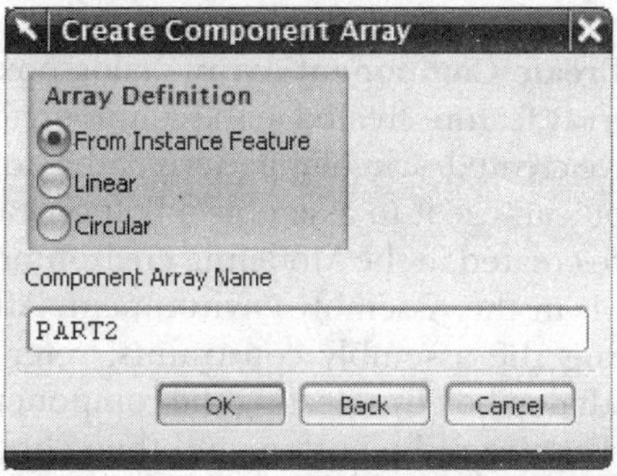

*Figure 9-28 The **Create Component Array** dialog box*

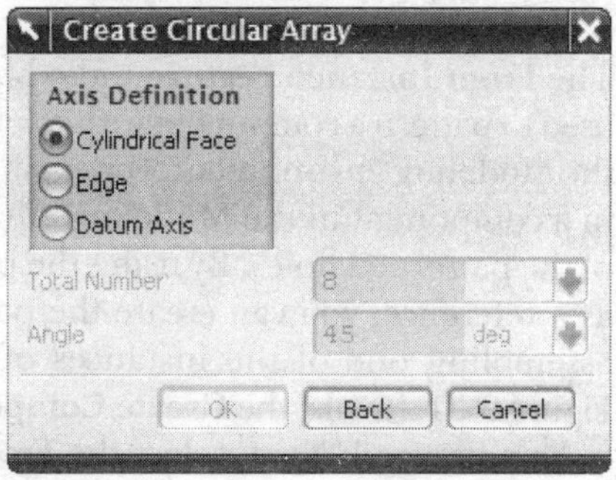

*Figure 9-29 The **Create Circular Array** dialog box*

Note

*The angle value specified in the **Angle** edit box of the **Create Circular Array** dialog box is used to measure the angle between two instances.*

3. In case of a linear pattern, select the **Linear** radio button from the **Create Component Array** dialog box and then choose **OK**; the **Create Linear Array** dialog box will be displayed, as shown in Figure 9-30, and you will be prompted to select the object to define the X direction. After you define the X direction, you will be prompted to select the object to define the Y direction. You can select a datum plane, edge, datum axis, or a face normal to the object for defining the X and Y directions. Enter the number of instances required along the X direction in the **Total Number - XC** edit box and enter the offset distance to be maintained between the components along the same direction in the **Offset - XC** edit box. Similarly, enter the number of instances required along the Y direction in the **Total Number - YC** edit box and enter the offset distance to be maintained between the components along the same direction in the **Offset - YC** edit box in the **Create Linear Array** dialog box. Next, choose the **OK** button from the dialog box.

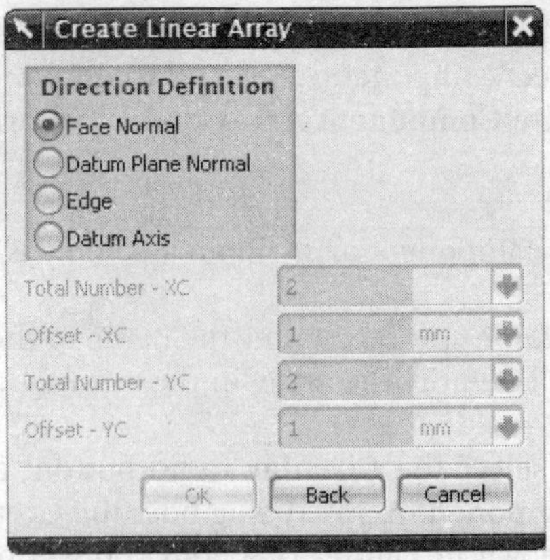

Figure 9-30 *The* ***Create Linear Array*** *dialog box*

Note

The radio buttons available in the ***Direction Definition*** *area of the* ***Create Linear Array*** *dialog box are used to specify the X and Y directions for the component to be arrayed.*

4. The **From Instance Feature** radio button in the **Create Component Array** dialog box is used to pattern a component with reference to the array feature created in the component in the Modeling environment. For example, if you have created a circular pattern of the holes in a component in the Modeling environment, you can use it to assemble a bolt on each of the patterned holes. By using the pattern feature created in the Modeling environment as a reference, you can create the pattern of a bolt in the Assembly environment. After assembling one of the instances of the bolt using the assembly constraints, refer to Figure 9-31, invoke the **Create Component Array** dialog box by selecting the components to be patterned. Next, select the **From Instance Feature** radio button, and then choose the **OK** button from the **Create Component Array** dialog box to automatically pattern the selected component in the assembly with reference to the pattern created in the Modeling environment, refer to Figure 9-32.

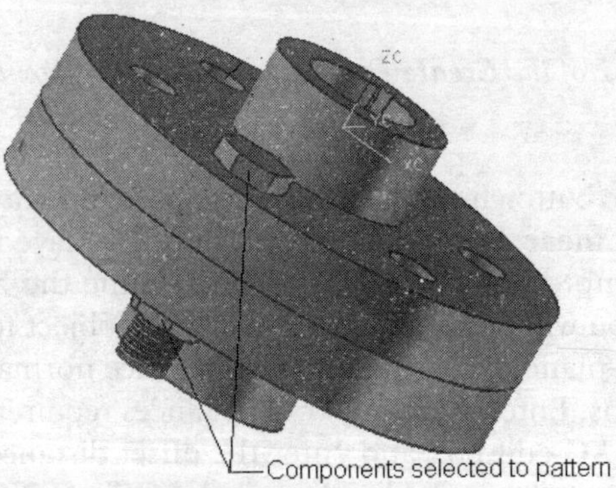

Figure 9-31 *Components and the instance of the pattern feature to be selected*

Figure 9-32 *Assembly after creating the derived component pattern*

Replacing a Component in an Assembly

Menu: Assemblies > Component > Replace Component
Toolbar: Assemblies > Replace Component *(Customize to add)*

The **Replace Component** tool is used to replace the component that is already placed in an assembly with the new component. If the new component has the same basic geometry as that of the original component, the new component will be placed exactly at the location where the original component was placed. To replace an existing component from an assembly, choose the **Replace Component** button from the **Assemblies** toolbar; the **Replace Component** dialog box will be displayed, as shown in Figure 9-33. The options in this dialog box are discussed next.

Note

*The geometry of the new component should be same in order to use the **Replace Component** tool; otherwise, the replaced component will be placed arbitrarily in the space without any association with the location where the component was present earlier.*

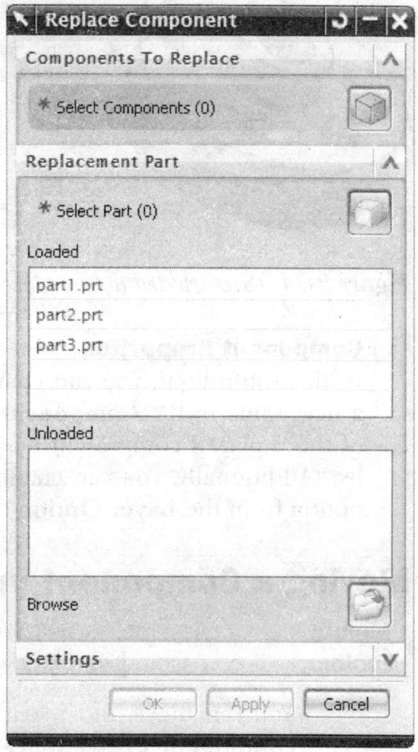

*Figure 9-33 The **Replace Component** dialog box*

Components To Replace Rollout

In this rollout, the **Select Components** area is activated by default. As a result, you will be prompted to select the components to be replaced. Select the components to be replaced, refer to Figure 9-34.

Replacement Part Rollout

In this rollout, you can select the required replacement component to replace the existing component of the assembly. To do so, click on the **Select Part** area of this rollout; you will be prompted to select the replacement part. You can select the replacement part either from the **Loaded** list or by choosing the **Browse** button from this rollout. If you choose the **Browse** button to select the component, the **Part Name** dialog box will be displayed. Next, browse to the required location, select the required part, and then choose **OK** from the dialog box; the name of the selected part will be displayed in the **Unloaded** list of the **Replace Component** dialog box. After selecting the required part, choose the **OK** button from the **Replace Component** dialog box; the selected component in the assembly will be replaced by the replacement component. Figure 9-34 shows the parts to be replaced and Figure 9-35 shows the assembly after replacing parts.

Settings Rollout

In this rollout, the **Maintain Relationships** check box is selected by default. As a result, all applied constraints are maintained even after replacing a component. If you select the **Replace All Occurrences in Assembly** check box, all instances in the assembly will be replaced by the replacement component. This rollout has a sub-rollout, called **Component Properties**, which is discussed next.

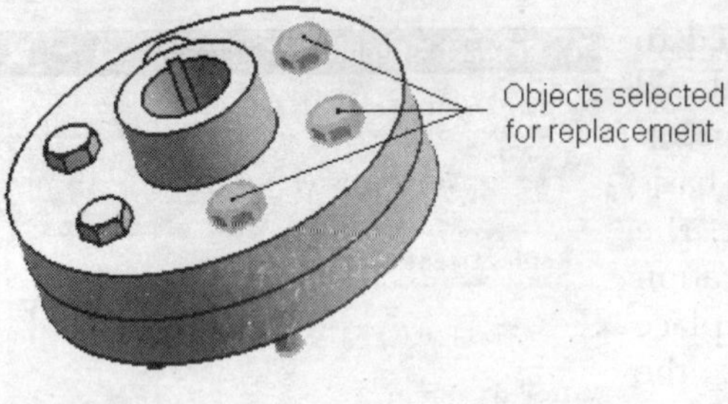

Figure 9-34 Parts selected to be replaced

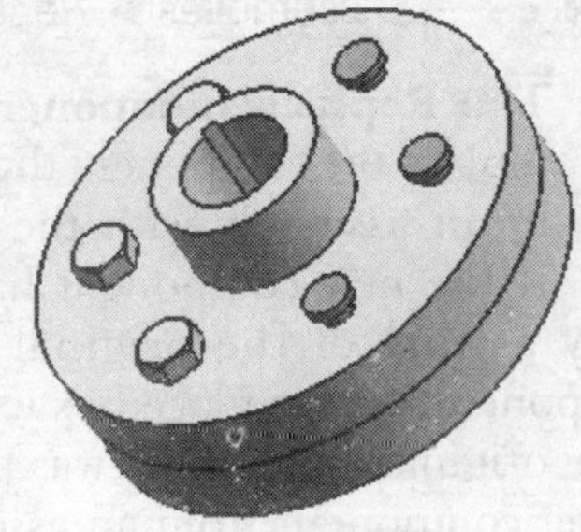

Figure 9-35 Resultant model after replacement

Component Properties

In this sub-rollout, you can change the name of the replaced component by specifying a new name in the **Component Name** edit box. You can also change the reference set of the replaced component by selecting an option from the **Reference Set** drop-down list. Additionally, you can change the layer of the replaced component by selecting an option from the **Layer Option** drop-down list in this rollout.

Moving a Component in an Assembly

Menu:	Assemblies > Components > Move Component
Toolbar:	Assemblies > Move Component

You can move and reorient an assembled component in 3D space using available degrees of freedom. Note that a component cannot be reoriented along the constrained degree of freedom. To move a component, you need to invoke the **Move Component** tool. To do so, choose the **Move Component** button from the **Assemblies** toolbar; the **Move Component** dialog box will be displayed, refer to Figure 9-36. Also, you will be prompted to select the components to be moved. Select the component that you want to move. Now, you can move the selected component by using different options available in the **Move Component** dialog box. The options in this dialog box are discussed next.

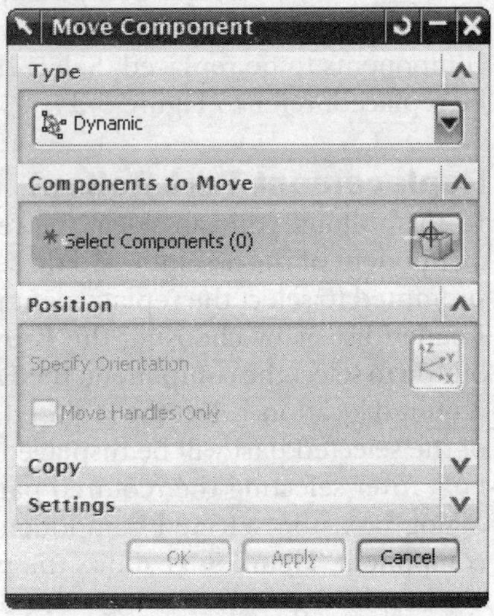

Figure 9-36 The Move Component dialog box

Type Rollout

The options in the **Type** rollout are used to specify the method to move components. These methods are discussed next.

Dynamic

This option is selected by default in the **Type** drop-down list. To move the selected component using this option, select the **Position** button from the **Position** rollout; a dynamic triad will be displayed on the component. The handles and angular handles of the triad can be used to move the component at the available degrees of freedom.

By Constraints

You can also move components by using the **By Constraints** option. If you select this option from the **Type** drop-down list, the **Move Component** dialog will be modified and the **Constraints** rollout will be displayed in it. The drop-down list available in this rollout is used to select the type of constraints. Select the required constraint from this drop-down list; the **Constraints** rollout will be modified based on the selected option. For example, if you select the **Touch Align** option from the drop-down list, the **Select Two Objects** area will be displayed in the **Geometry to Constrain** sub-rollout of the dialog box and it will be activated by default. As a result, you will be prompted to select the first object. Select a face; you will be prompted to select the second object to touch to. Select a face of another component; the selected faces will move based on the specified option.

Point to Point

This option is used to move component from one point to another point. If you select this option from the **Type** drop-down list, you will be prompted to select the component to move. Select the component that you want to move and choose the **Inferred Point** button from the **From Point** rollout; you will be prompted to select the object to infer point. Select the point with respect to which you want to move the selected component. Next, select the destination point; the selected component will be moved from its original location to the newly specified location.

Translate

This option is used to move the selected component from its position to the specified location with respect to the **WCS** or **Absolute** coordinate system. If you select this option from the **Type** drop-down list, you will be prompted to select the component to move. Select the component that you want to move; the **Translation** rollout will be activated. Select the **WCS** or **Absolute** radio button from the **Translation** rollout to move the component with respect to the **WCS** or **Absolute** coordinate system, respectively. Next, enter the X, Y and Z-coordinates in the **Delta X**, **Delta Y**, and **Delta Z** edit boxes, respectively; the selected component will move according to the specified values.

Along Vector

This option is used to move the selected component along the specified vector. If you select this option from the **Type** drop-down list, you will be prompted to select the component to move. Select the component that you want to move; the **Vector** rollout will be activated. Next, choose the **Inferred Vector** button from this rollout and specify the vector along which you want to move the selected component. Next, enter the required distance in the **Distance** edit box of the **Distance Along Vector** rollout and press ENTER; the selected component will shift its position to the specified position along the specified vector.

Rotate about Axis

This option is used to rotate the selected component about a specified axis and by a specified angle. If you select this option from the **Type** drop-down list, you will be prompted to select the component to move. Select the component that you want to move; the **Rotation Axis** rollout will be activated. Next, choose the **Inferred Vector** button from the **Rotation Axis** rollout and specify the direction vector about which the selected component will rotate. Next, click on the **Specify Point** area in the **Rotation Axis** rollout and specify the point through which the axis will pass. Next, enter the required angle value in the **Angle** edit box of the **Angle about Axis** rollout and press ENTER; the selected component will rotate about the specified axis and by the specified angle.

Between Two Axes

This option is used to rotate and move the selected components by specifying two direction vectors and an origin point. If you select this option from the **Type** drop-down list, you will be prompted to select the component to move. Select the component that you want to rotate and move. Next, choose the **Inferred Vector** button from the **From Vector** rollout and select the vector. This selected vector will align with the destination vector. Therefore, now you need to choose the **Inferred Vector** button from the **Destination Vector** rollout and select the destination vector. Next, choose the **Inferred Point** button from the **Origin** rollout and select a point; a displacement will occur with respect to the selected point. Figures 9-37 and 9-38 show components selected before using the **Between Two Axes** option and components after using the **Between Two Axes** option.

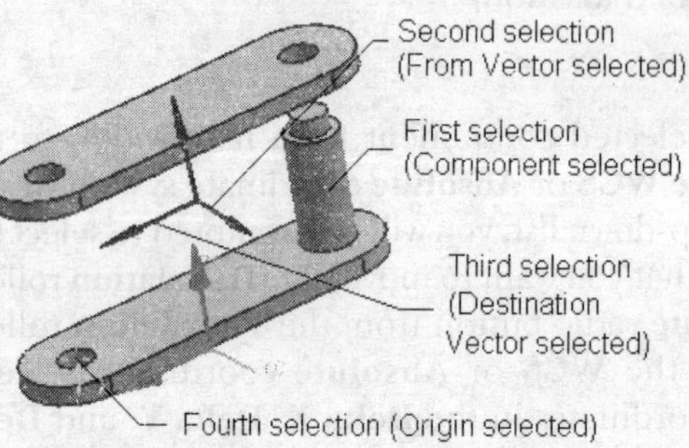

***Figure 9-37** Component and reference selection before using the **Between two Axes** option*

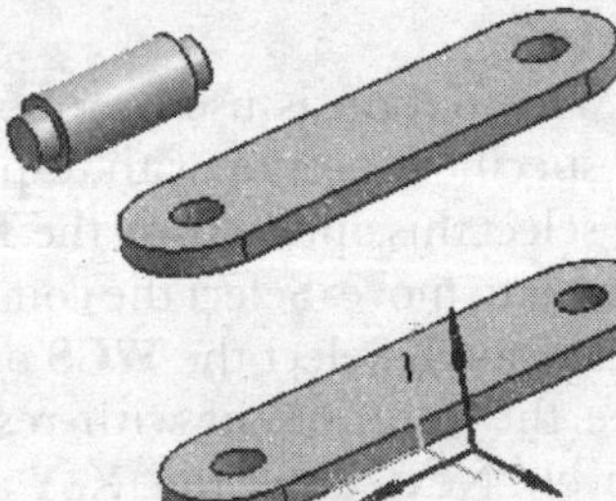

***Figure 9-38** Component after using the **Between two Axes** option*

Reposition

This option is used to reposition the selected components from one CSYS to another CSYS. If you select this option from the **Type** drop-down list, you will be prompted to select the components to reposition. Select the component that you want to reposition. Next, choose the **Inferred** button from the **From CSYS** rollout and then select two edges to define CSYS or any face. The selected CSYS will align with the destination CSYS. After specifying options in the **From CSYS** rollout, the **Specify CSYS** area will be activated in the **Destination CSYS** rollout. Next, specify the destination CSYS by specifying two edges or any face; the selected component will be repositioned as specified. Figure 9-39 shows the component before using the **Reposition** option and Figure 9-40 shows components after using the **Reposition** option.

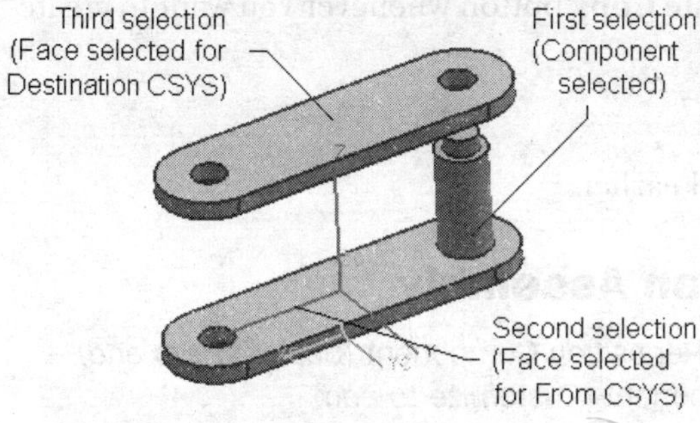

Figure 9-39 *Component and reference selection before using the* ***Reposition*** *option*

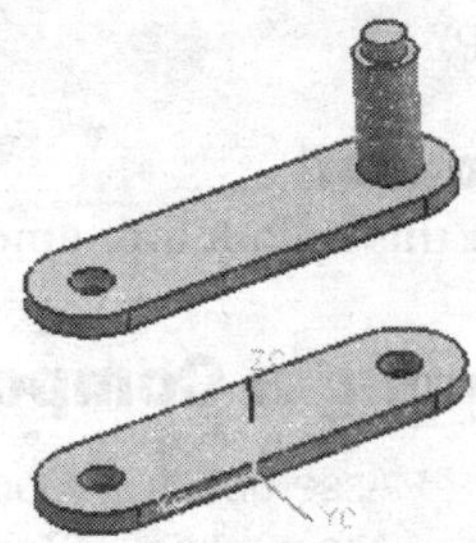

Figure 9-40 *Component after using the* ***Reposition*** *option*

Rotate Using Points

This option is similar to the **Rotate about Axis** option of the **Move Component** dialog box, with the only difference being that in this case you can just specify two points for rotation, instead of specifying the angle. If you select this option from the **Type** drop-down list, you will be prompted to select the components to rotate. Select the components that you want to rotate; the **Pivot Axis** rollout will be activated. Choose the **Inferred Vector** button from the **Pivot Axis** rollout and specify the axis of rotation. Also, choose the **Inferred Point** button from the **Pivot Axis** rollout and specify the point from which the rotation axis will pass. After specifying a point, the **Inferred Point** button in the **From Point** rollout will be chosen automatically. Specify the point with respect to which the component will be measured and then specify the point upto which you want to rotate components. Figure 9-41 shows the component before using the **Rotate Using Points** option and Figure 9-42 shows the component after rotating it using the **Rotate Using Points** option. Choose the **Apply** or **OK** button to accept the resultant position.

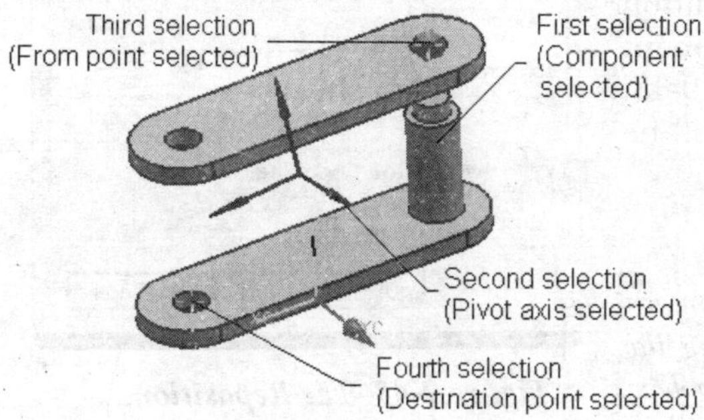

Figure 9-41 *Component and reference selection before using the* ***Rotate Using Points*** *option*

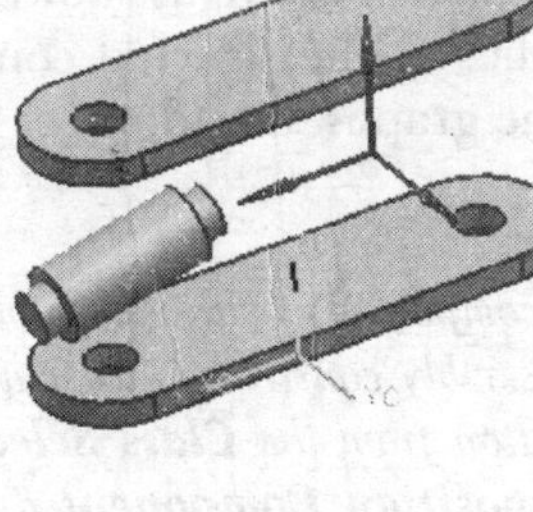

Figure 9-42 *Component after using the* ***Rotate Using Points*** *option*

Copy Rollout

In this rollout, the **No Copy** option is selected by default in the **Mode** drop-down list. As a result, a duplicate copy will not be created while moving the component. If you select the **Copy** option from this drop-down list, the original component will remain at its position and a duplicate copy of the component will be created at a new location. If you select the **Manual Copy** option from the **Mode** drop-down list, the **Create Copy** button will be displayed below the drop-down list. You need to choose the **Create Copy** button whenever you want to create a duplicate copy.

Settings Rollout

The options of this rollout are same as discussed earlier.

Repositioning a Component in an Assembly

Menu:	Assemblies > Components > Reposition Component *(Customize to add)*
Toolbar:	Assemblies > Reposition Component *(Customize to add)*

You can move and reorient an assembled component in 3D space, with respect to the available degrees of freedom by using the **Reposition Component** tool. This tool is not available by default in the **Assemblies** toolbar and the **Assemblies** menu. Therefore you need to customize it to make it available in this menu and toolbar. To do so, choose **Preferences > Assemblies** from the menu bar; the **Assembly Preferences** dialog box will be displayed. Next, select the **Mating Conditions** option from the **Interaction** drop-down list of the **Assembly Positioning** area, and then choose the **OK** button from the dialog box; the **Reposition Component** tool will be available in the **Assemblies** toolbar. Next, choose the **Reposition Component** button from the **Assemblies** toolbar; the **Class Selection** dialog box will be displayed and you will be prompted to select the component that is to be repositioned. Select the object to be moved and choose the **OK** button from the dialog box; the **Reposition Component** message box will be displayed. Choose the **OK** button from the message box; the **Reposition Component** dialog box will be displayed, as shown in Figure 9-43. Also, the handles of the selected component will be displayed in the graphics window.

***Figure 9-43** The **Reposition Component** dialog box*

> **Note**
>
> *If the components of the assembly do not contain any assembly constraint, then after choosing the **OK** button from the **Class Selection** dialog box, the **Reposition Component** dialog box will be displayed directly.*

The translation handles and rotational cubes of the handle are used to dynamically translate and rotate the selected component. After reorienting the component by using the handle, choose the **Apply** button from the dialog box; the component will be reoriented. Note that if you have reoriented the component along its constrained degrees of freedom, then after choosing the **Apply** button from the dialog box, the selected component will move back to its original position. You cannot reorient the component along the constrained degrees of freedom.

If you select the **Move Objects** radio button from the **Reposition Component** dialog box, the selected component will be repositioned along with the handles. If you select the **Move Handles Only** radio button from the dialog box, only the handles of the selected component will be repositioned. By default, when the **Reposition Component** dialog box is displayed, the **Move Objects** radio button is selected. In addition to the dynamic method of repositioning, you can also reposition the component using the methods in the **Reposition Component** dialog box. These methods are discussed next.

Point to Point

If you choose the **Point to Point** button from the **Reposition Component** dialog box, the **Point** dialog box will be displayed, and you will be prompted to select the first point for repositioning the component. Specify the first point; you will be prompted to specify the second point for repositioning the component. Specify the second point; the selected component will move and the **Reposition Component** dialog box will be displayed.

Translate

The **Translate** button in the **Reposition Component** dialog box is used to place the selected component in 3D space by specifying the X, Y, and Z coordinates. On choosing the **Translate** button from the **Reposition Component** dialog box, the **Transformations** dialog box will be displayed, as shown in Figure 9-44. The **Transformations** dialog box has separate edit boxes for entering the X, Y, and Z coordinates to position the selected component in 3D space with respect to the WCS of the assembly file. Enter the X, Y, and Z coordinate values in their respective edit boxes of the dialog box and choose the **OK** button; the selected component will move to the new location and the **Reposition Component** dialog box will be displayed.

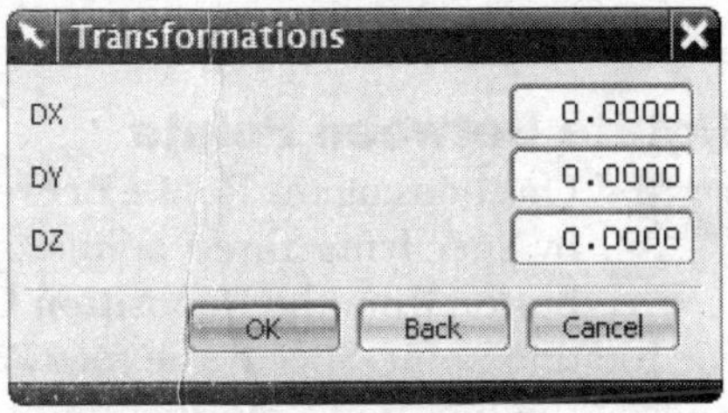

*Figure 9-44 The **Transformations** dialog box*

Rotate About a Point

On choosing the **Rotate About a Point** button from the **Reposition Component** dialog box, you can rotate a component about a specified point. To do so, choose this button; the **Point** dialog box will be displayed and you will be prompted to specify a rotation point. After specifying the rotation point, the handles of the selected component will move to the specified point. Now, by selecting the required angular handle, you can rotate the component about the specified point.

Rotate About a Line

On choosing the **Rotate About a Line** button from the **Reposition Component** dialog box, you can rotate the selected component about a line. To do so, choose this button; the **Point** dialog box will be displayed and you will be prompted to specify the start point of the line. Specify the start point; the **Vector** dialog box will be displayed and you will be prompted to specify the direction for creating the line from the specified start point. Specify the vector direction for constructing the line. Next, choose the **OK** button from the **Vector** dialog box; the handles of the selected component will move to the specified start point. Now, by selecting the required angular handle, you can rotate the selected component about the specified line.

Reposition

The **Reposition** button from the **Reposition Component** dialog box is used to move the component from one point to another by constructing new coordinate systems in 3D space. Choose the **Reposition** button from the **Reposition Component** dialog box; the **CSYS** dialog box will be displayed. Construct the new coordinate system by using the option available in this dialog box and then choose the **OK** button; the selected component will move to a new position.

Rotate Between Axes

The **Rotate Between Axes** button is used to rotate the selected component between two selected vectors. On choosing this button, the **Point** dialog box will be displayed and you will be prompted to specify the reference point. After you specify the reference point, the **Vector** dialog box will be displayed and you will be prompted to select the reference axis. Specify the reference axis and choose the **OK** button from the dialog box; the **Vector** dialog box will be displayed again and you will be prompted to select the destination axis. Select the destination axis and choose the **OK** button from the dialog box; a coordinate system will be formed and the **Reposition Component** dialog box will be displayed. Next, enter the rotational angle in the **Angle** edit box of the **Reposition Component** dialog box, and then choose the **Apply** button; the selected component will rotate accordingly. You can also drag the angular handles to rotate.

Rotate Between Points

On choosing the **Rotate Between Points** button, you can rotate the selected component by specifying three points on the same plane. Select the **Rotate Between Points** button from the **Reposition Component** dialog box; you will be prompted to specify the rotation point. Specify the rotation point; you will be prompted to specify the first point. Specify the first point representing the X axis; you will be prompted to specify the second point. Specify the second point representing the Y axis. Next, enter the angle of rotation in the **Angle** edit box and then choose the **OK** button from the dialog box; the component will be rotated.

Snap Handles to WCS

On choosing the **Snap Handles to WCS** button from the **Reposition Component** dialog box, you can make the handles of the selected component coincide with the WCS of the assembly file.

Motion Animation

The **Motion Animation** sliding bar of the **Reposition Component** dialog box is used to define the quality of motion which the component undergoes when it is being repositioned. The motion of the component can be controlled from fine to coarse using the sliding bar. If the sliding bar is closer to fine, the displacement of the component is visualized in a better way.

Collision Action

The **Collision Action** drop-down list is used to restrict the collision of one component with another component. If the **Highlight Collision** option is selected from the **Collision Action** drop-down list, the collision between the components will be highlighted in red during the process of repositioning. If the **Stop before Collision** option is selected, the movement of the component will be stopped when it will collide with the other component. No further movement is possible after collision in the latter case.

Note

It is recommended that after using the ***Reposition Component*** *tool, you change the setting to the default one.*

Mirroring a Component in an Assembly

Menu:	Assemblies > Components > Mirror Assembly
Toolbar:	Assemblies > Mirror Assembly

The **Mirror Assembly** tool is used for mirroring the assembly or any of the individual components in the assembly about a reference plane. Note that you cannot select a planar face of a component for this purpose. When you choose the **Mirror Assembly** button from the **Assemblies** toolbar, the **Mirror Assemblies Wizard** dialog box will be displayed with the **Welcome** page, as shown in Figure 9-45.

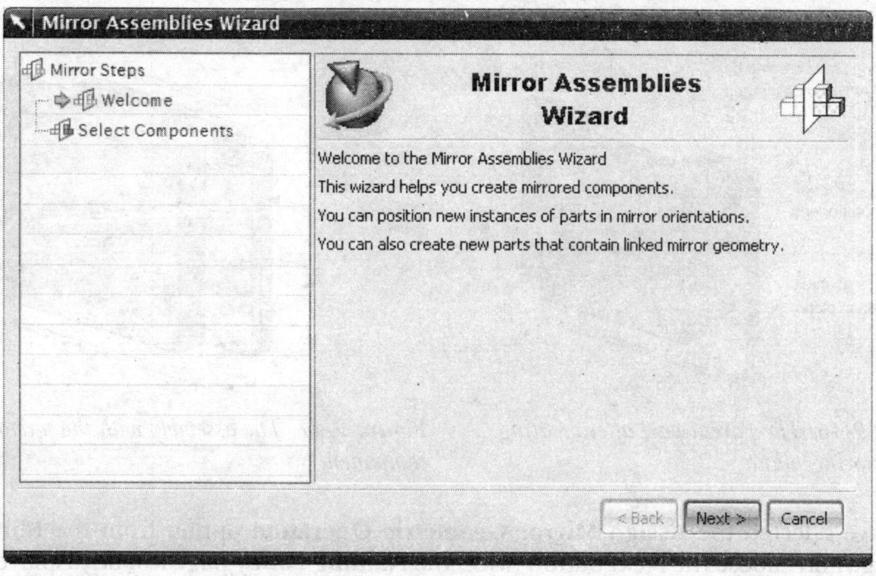

Figure 9-45 *The* ***Welcome*** *page of the* ***Mirror Assemblies Wizard*** *dialog box*

To select components or an assembly to mirror, choose the **Next** button; the **Select Components** page will be displayed and you will be prompted to select the components to be mirrored. Select the components that are to be mirrored and choose the **Next** button to proceed to the **Select Plane** page.

Select any of the reference planes as the mirroring plane. You can also create a mirroring plane, refer to Figure 9-46. To do so, choose the **Create Datum Plane** button from the **Select Plane** page; the **Datum Plane** dialog box will be displayed. Now, create a mirroring plane using the options available in this dialog box. After selecting the plane, choose the **Next** button to proceed to the **Mirror Setup** page. There are two types of mirroring operations available. By default, the **Assign Reposition Operation** type will be chosen. If the mirroring operation is performed by using this type, the mirrored component will be the same part file. This means an associative link will be maintained between the parent and the mirrored component. Also, the name of the mirrored component will be the same as that of the parent component.

If the mirroring operation is performed by using the **Assign Mirror Geometry Operation** option, the mirrored component will be a separate copy of the parent component and also an associative link will be maintained between the parent and the mirrored components. Note that the **Assign Mirror Geometry Operation** button will be available only after you select the components from the list box in this area.

After choosing the mirror type, choose the **Next** button; the **Mirror Review** page will be displayed. On this page, you can use the **Cycle Mirror Solutions** button to cycle through the possible solutions. You can also directly select the required solution from the **Cycle Mirror Solutions** drop-down list. After selecting the solution, choose the **Finish** button to view the mirrored component in the assembly, as shown in Figure 9-47.

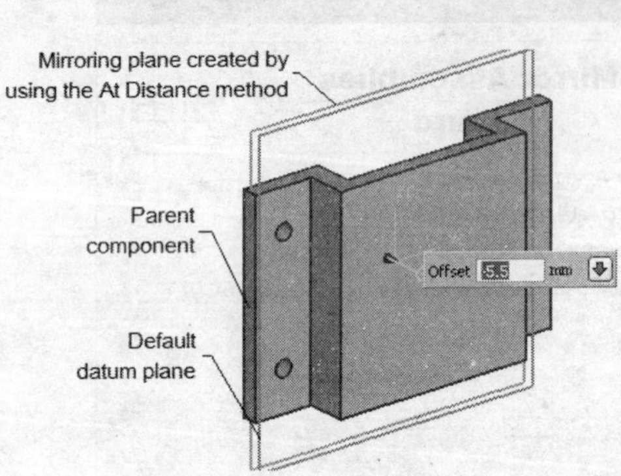

Figure 9-46 The parent part after creating the mirroring plane

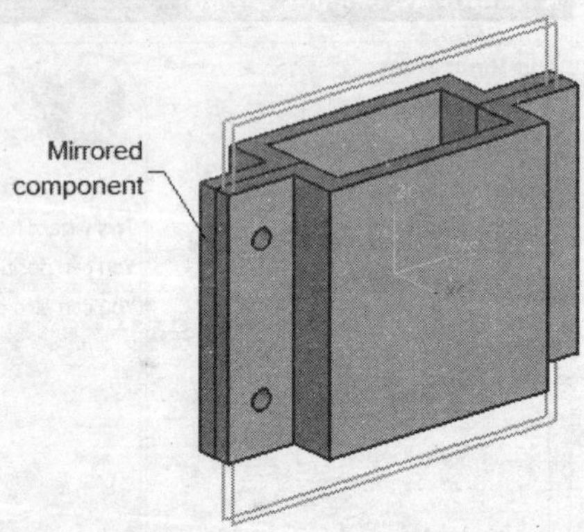

Figure 9-47 The assembly with the mirrored component

If you have selected the **Assign Mirror Geometric Operation** option from the **Mirroring Setup** page and choose the **Next** button twice, the **Naming Policy** page will be displayed. You can assign a new name for the mirrored component by adding a prefix or suffix to the parent component's name. To add a suffix, select the **Add this as suffix to the original name** radio button from the **Naming Rule** area and enter the suffix in the edit box provided in the same area. To add a prefix, select the **Add this as prefix to the original name** radio button from the **Naming Rule** area and enter the prefix in the edit box provided in the same area.

To save the mirrored component in a different folder, select the **Add new parts to the specified directory** radio button from the **Directory Rule** area of the **Naming Policy** page; the **Browse** button will be available. When you choose this button, the **Choose New Part Save Directory** dialog box will be displayed. You can browse to a new directory for saving the mirrored component.

Next, choose the **Finish** button to exit the **Mirror Assemblies Wizard** dialog box. To completely change the name of the mirrored component, choose the **Next** button from the **Naming Policy** page; the **Name New Part Files** page will be displayed. Double-click on the part name to be changed; the **Rename New Part File** dialog box will be displayed where you can specify a new name for the file. After changing the name, choose the **OK** button; the **Name New Part Files** page will be displayed with a new name, as shown in Figure 9-48.

Note

The mirrored components do not have assembly constraints. You need to manually add these constraints to the mirrored components.

*Figure 9-48 The **Name New Part Files** page of the **Mirror Assemblies Wizard** dialog box*

Modifying a Component in the Assembly File

Menu:	Assemblies > Context Control > Set Work Part
Toolbar:	Assemblies > Make Work Part

The **Make Work Part** tool is used to modify or add sketches and features to the component that are placed in the assembly file by bringing the component into the current **Work Part** category. The procedure to modify the component in the assembly file is discussed next.

Choose the **Make Work Part** button from the **Assemblies** toolbar; the **Set Work Part** dialog box will be displayed, as shown in Figure 9-49 and you will be prompted to choose the option or select from view. Select the component from the assembly and choose the **OK** button. The components other than the selected ones will become faded. After converting the component into **Work Part**, you can perform any type of feature or sketch-based operation. The changes made in the component in the assembly are also updated in the part file of the component. After making the required modification in the component, choose the **Assembly Navigator** tab from the **Resource Bar**; a cascading menu will be displayed. Select the assembly name from the assembly node tree and right-click on it. Next, choose the **Make Work Part** option from the shortcut menu. When you select the assembly as a work part, the whole assembly will be displayed in the same color.

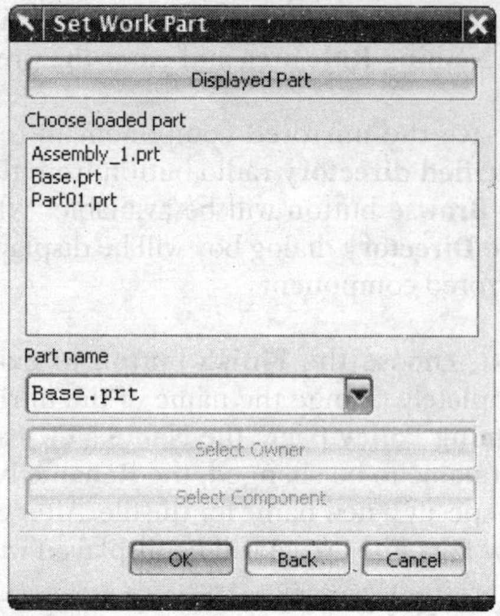

***Figure 9-49** The **Set Work Part** dialog box*

Note

*You can select only one component at a time in the **Work Part** category. After you make the changes in the component, you can directly save the changes in the component file by saving the assembly file.*

TUTORIALS

Tutorial 1

In this tutorial, you will create all components of the Pipe Vice assembly and then assemble them, as shown in Figure 9-50. The dimensions of the components are given in Figures 9-51 and 9-52. Save the file with the name *Pipe Vice.prt* at the location *NX 7\c09\Pipe Vice.*

(Expected time: 2.5 hrs)

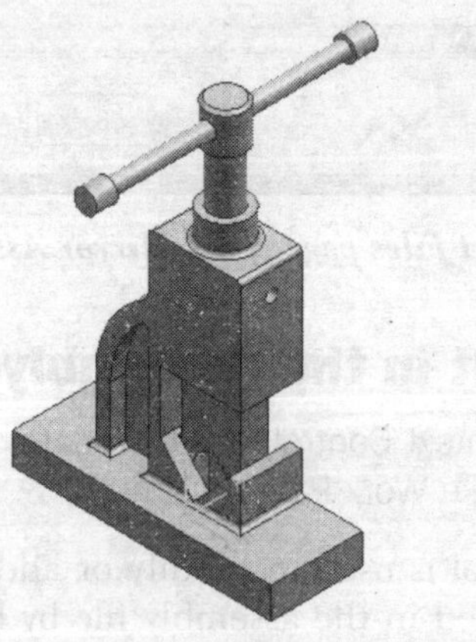

***Figure 9-50** The Pipe Vice assembly*

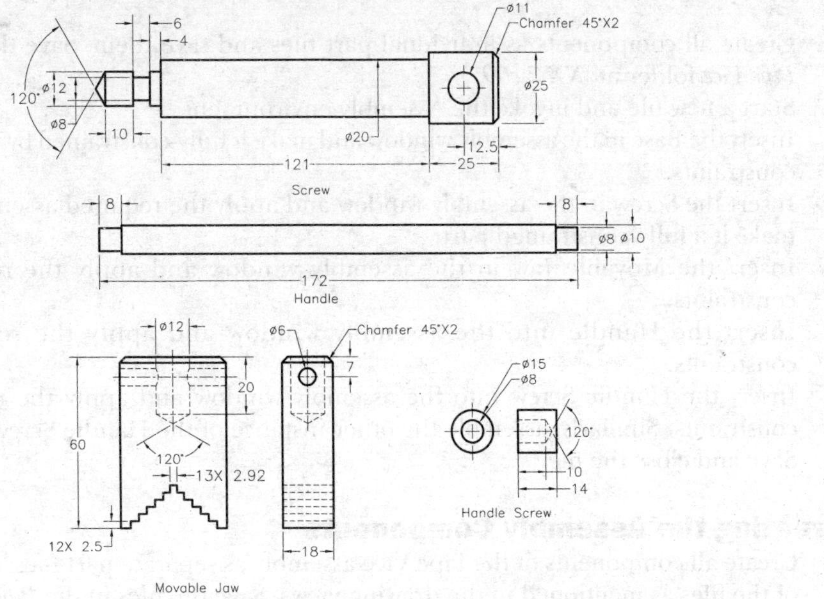

***Figure 9-51** Views and dimensions of the Screw, Handle, Movable Jaw, and Handle Screw*

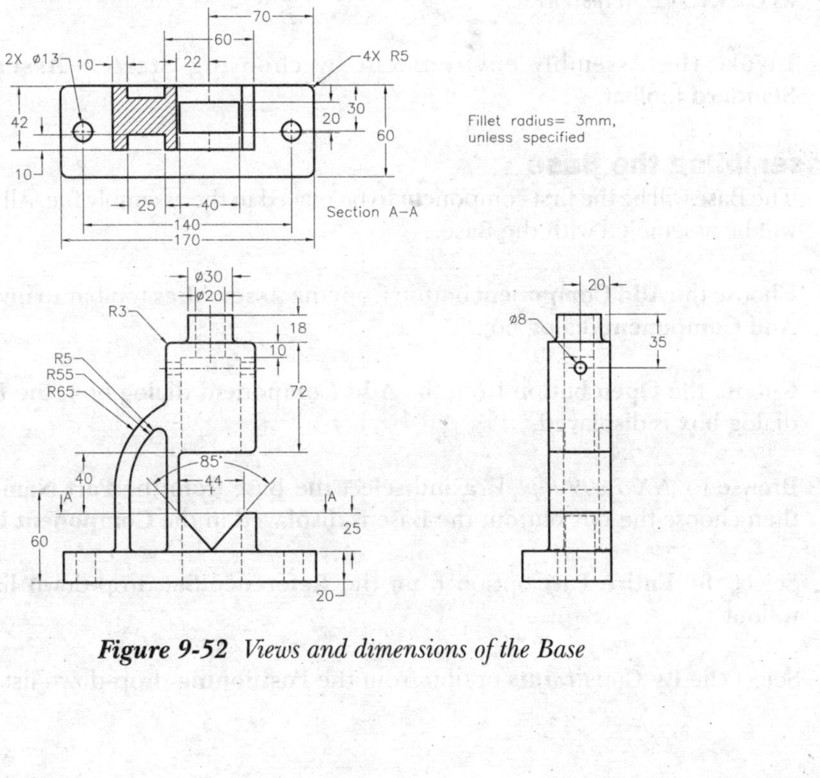

***Figure 9-52** Views and dimensions of the Base*

The following steps are required to complete this tutorial:

a. Create all components as individual part files and save them. Save the part files in the *Pipe Vice* folder at *\NX 7\c09*.
b. Start a new file and invoke the Assembly environment.
c. Insert the Base in the assembly window and make it fully-constrained by using the assembly constraints.
d. Insert the Screw in the assembly window and apply the required assembly constraints to make it a fully-constrained part.
e. Insert the Movable Jaw in the assembly window and apply the required assembly constraints.
f. Insert the Handle into the assembly window and apply the required assembly constraints.
g. Insert the Handle Screw into the assembly window and apply the required assembly constraints. Similarly, assemble the other instance of the Handle Screw to the assembly.
h. Save and close the file.

Creating the Assembly Components

1. Create all components of the Pipe Vice assembly as separate part files. Specify the names of the files as mentioned in the drawing views. Save the files in the *Pipe Vice* folder at the location *\NX 7\c09*.

Starting a New Assembly File

1. Start a new file with the name *Pipe Vice.prt* using the **Model** template and specify its location as *C:\NX 7\c09\Pipe Vice.*

2. Invoke the Assembly environment by choosing **Start > Assemblies** from the **Standard** toolbar.

Assembling the Base

The Base will be the first component to be placed in the assembly file. All other components will be assembled with the Base.

1. Choose the **Add Component** button from the **Assemblies** toolbar to invoke the **Add Component** dialog box.

2. Choose the **Open** button from the **Add Component** dialog box; the **Part Name** dialog box is displayed.

3. Browse to *\NX 7\c09\Pipe Vice* and select the Base from the **Part Name** dialog box, and then choose the **OK** button; the Base is displayed in the **Component Preview** window.

4. Select the **Entire Part** option from the **Reference Set** drop-down list in the **Settings** rollout.

5. Select the **By Constraints** option from the **Positioning** drop-down list in the **Placement**

rollout. Choose the **OK** button from the **Add Component** dialog box; the **Assembly Constraints** dialog box is displayed.

6. Select the **Touch Align** option from the **Type** drop-down list and the **Align** option from the **Orientation** drop-down list in the **Assembly Constraints** dialog box. 

7. Select the XC-YC plane of the Base from the **Component Preview** window and the XC-YC plane from the drawing window.

8. Select the ZC-YC plane of the Base from the **Component Preview** window and the ZC-YC plane from the drawing window.

9. Select the ZC-XC plane of the Base from the **Component Preview** window and the ZC-XC plane from the drawing window. Next, select the **Preview Component in Main Window** check box, if it is clear; the component is displayed in the main window.

Tip: *You can also restrict all the degrees of freedom of the Base component by selecting the* ***Fix*** *option from the* ***Type*** *drop-down list of the* ***Assembly Constraints*** *dialog box.*

10. Choose the **OK** button from the **Assembly Constraints** dialog box.

Next, you can change the reference set of the Base so that the datum planes and sketches used to create it are no more displayed.

11. Right-click on the Base and select the **Replace Reference Set > MODEL** from the shortcut menu. The assembly after assembling the Base is shown in Figure 9-53.

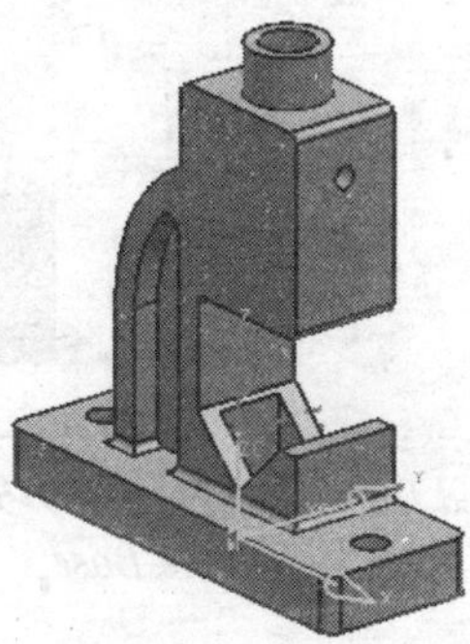

Figure 9-53 *The assembly after assembling the Base*

Note

It is recommended to use the selection bar in case of complex assemblies for precise selection of components, planes, or entities.

12. Turn off the display of the assembly datum planes by using the **Show and Hide** tool from the **Utility** toolbar.

Assembling the Second Component

The second component that you need to assemble is the Screw. This component will be assembled with the Base.

1. Choose the **Add Component** button from the **Assemblies** toolbar; the **Add Component** dialog box is displayed.

2. Choose the **Open** button; the **Part Name** dialog box is displayed. Select Screw from it and choose the **OK** button; the Screw is displayed in the **Component Preview** window. Select the **By Constraints** option from the **Positioning** drop-down list, if not selected by default.

3. Select the **Entire Part** option from the **Reference Set** drop-down list in the **Settings** rollout of the **Add Component** dialog box, and then choose the **OK** button; the **Assembly Constraints** dialog box is displayed.

4. Make sure the **Touch Align** option is selected in the **Type** drop-down list of the **Assembly Constraints** dialog box and then select the **Infer Center/Axis** option from the **Orientation** drop-down list.

5. Select the cylindrical face of the Screw, refer to Figure 9-54. Next, select the cylindrical face of the Base, refer to Figure 9-55. Next, choose the **Apply** button.

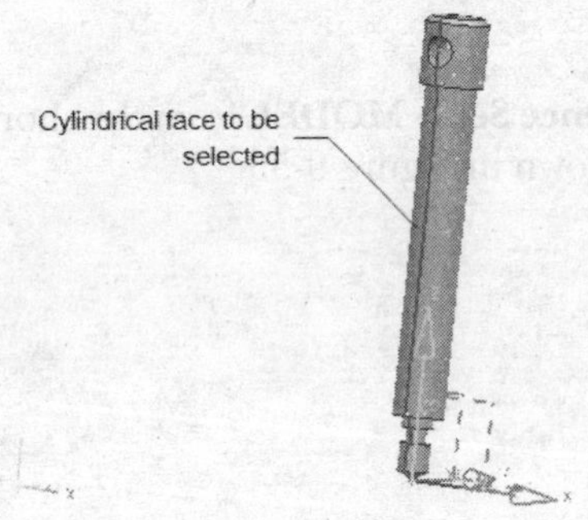

Figure 9-54 *Cylindrical face to be selected from the Screw*

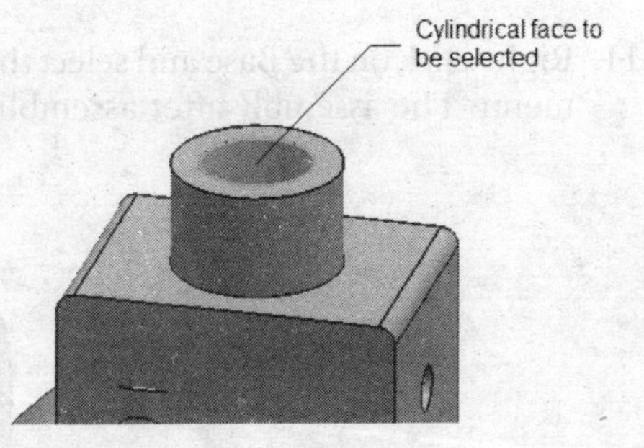

Figure 9-55 *Cylindrical face to be selected from the Base*

6. Now, select the **Distance** option from the drop-down list in the **Type** rollout.

7. Select the planar face of the Screw, refer to Figure 9-56. Next, select the planar face of the Base component, refer to Figure 9-57.

8. Enter the offset value **-35** in the **Distance** edit box of the **Distance** rollout and choose the **Apply** button in the **Assembly Constraints** dialog box.

9. Select the **Parallel** option from the drop-down list in the **Type** rollout.

10. Select the XC-ZC plane from the Screw and then select the front face of the Base, refer to Figure 9-58.

11. Choose the **OK** button from the **Assembly Constraints** dialog box. The assembly after assembling the Screw is shown in Figure 9-59.

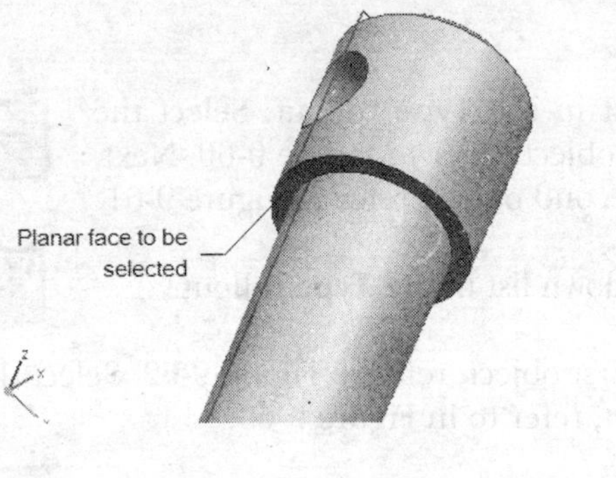

Figure 9-56 Planar face to be selected from the Screw

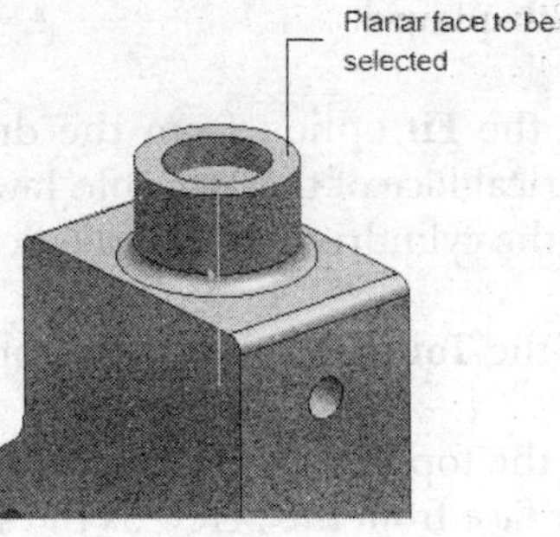

Figure 9-57 Planar face to be selected from the Base

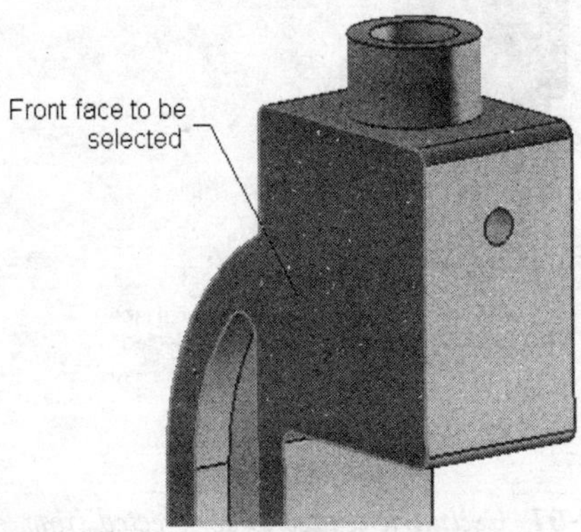

Figure 9-58 Front face of the Base to be selected

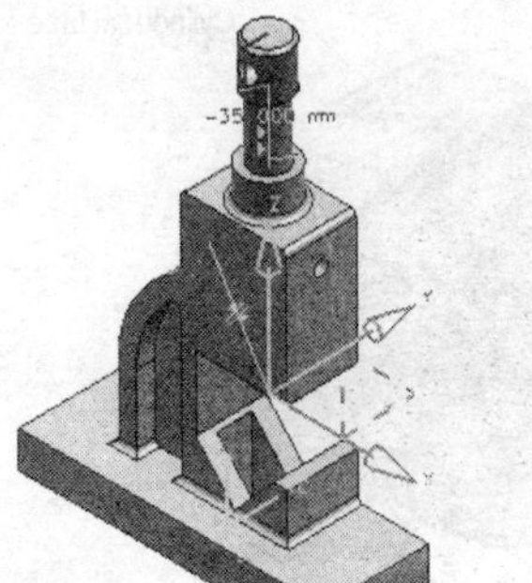

Figure 9-59 The assembly after assembling the Screw

Assembling the Third Component

Next, you need to assemble the Movable Jaw with the Screw. It is recommended that before assembling the Movable Jaw, you should hide the Base. This will provide a better display of the Screw.

1. Choose the **Assembly Navigator** tab from the **Resource Bar**; the **Assembly Navigator** cascading menu is displayed. Click on the check box on the left of the **Base**; the display of the Base is turned off.

2. Choose the **Add Component** button from the **Assemblies** toolbar; the **Add Component** dialog box is displayed. Choose the **Open** button; the **Part Name** dialog box is displayed.

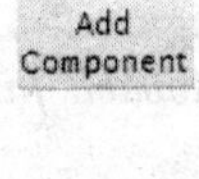

3. Select the Movable Jaw from the **Part Name** dialog box and choose the **OK** button; the Movable Jaw is displayed in the **Component Preview** window.

4. Select the **Model** option from the **Reference Set** drop-down list in the **Settings** rollout and make sure the **By Constraints** option is selected in the **Positioning** drop-down list of the **Placement** rollout. Next, choose the **OK** button; the **Assembly Constraints** dialog box is displayed.

5. Select the **Fit** option from the drop-down list in the **Type** rollout. Select the cylindrical face of the Movable Jaw as the first object, refer to Figure 9-60. Next, select the cylindrical face of the Screw as the second object, refer to Figure 9-61.

6. Select the **Touch Align** option from the drop-down list in the **Type** rollout.

7. Select the top face of the Movable Jaw as the first object, refer to Figure 9-62. Select the planar face from the Screw as the second object, refer to in Figure 9-63.

8. Select the **Parallel** option from the drop-down list in the **Type** rollout.

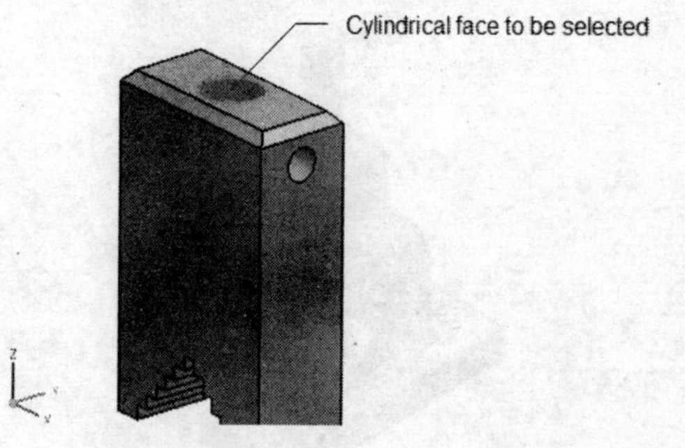

Figure 9-60 *Cylindrical face to be selected from the Movable Jaw*

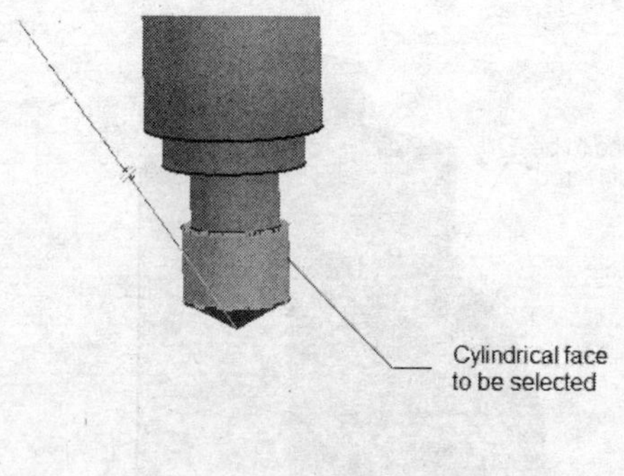

Figure 9-61 *Cylindrical face to be selected from the Screw*

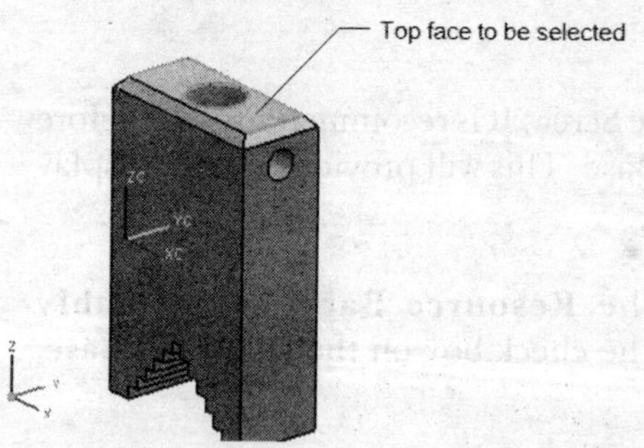

Figure 9-62 *Top face to be selected from the Movable Jaw*

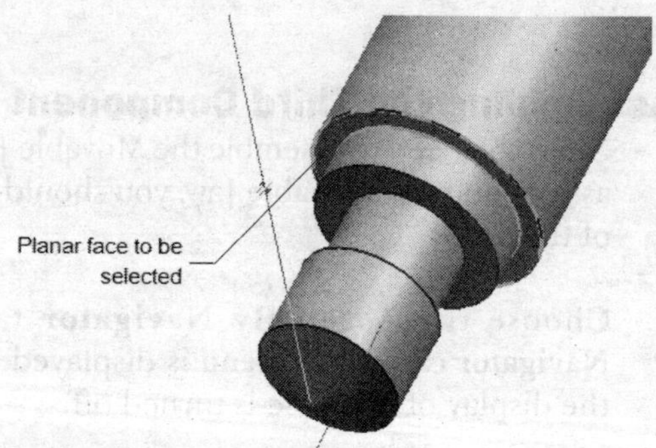

Figure 9-63 *Planar face to be selected from the Screw*

9. Select the front planar face of the Movable Jaw as the first object, refer to Figure 9-64. Next, select the XC-ZC plane of the Screw as the second object to apply the parallel constraint.

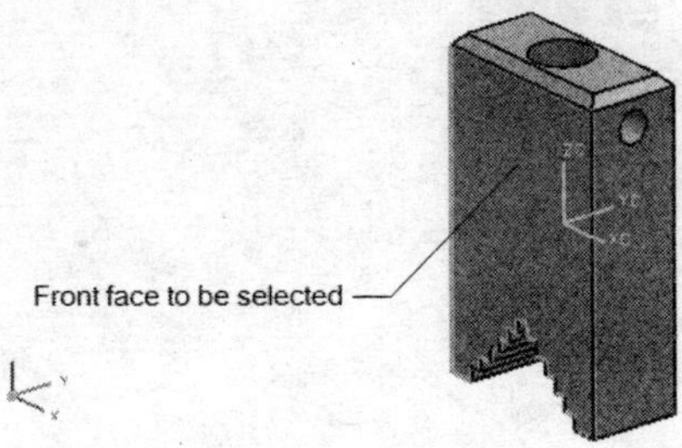

***Figure 9-64** Front face of the Movable Jaw to be selected*

10. Choose the **OK** button from the **Assembly Constraints** dialog box to exit this dialog box.

    After applying the three assembly constraints between the Movable Jaw and the Screw, you can cross check to ensure whether the component is fully-constrained or not using the **Move Component** tool from the **Assemblies** toolbar.

    Next, you need to turn on the display of the Base.

11. Invoke the **Assembly Navigator** cascading menu. Click on the check box on the left of the **Base**; the display of the Base is turned on.

    It is recommended that you change the texture of the Base component from solid to transparent. This is done to display the components that are assembled inside the Base such as the Movable Jaw and the Screw.

12. Choose **Edit > Object Display** from the menu bar; the **Class Selection** dialog box is displayed and you are prompted to select the objects to edit. Select the Base and choose the **OK** button; the **Edit Object Display** dialog box is displayed.

    By dragging the **Translucency** sliding bar, you can change the transparency property of the Base from 0 to 100.

13. Drag the **Translucency** sliding bar to a value of 75 and choose the **OK** button. If the **Translucency Performance Warning** window is displayed, choose the **OK** button. This window informs you that enabling the translucency will decrease the performance of the graphics.

    The assembly after modifying the display of the Base is shown in Figure 9-65.

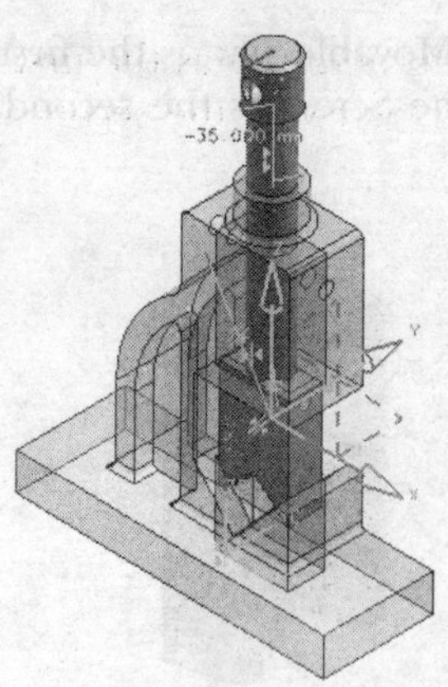

Figure 9-65 The assembly after making the Base translucent

Assembling the Handle

Next, you need to assemble the Handle with the Screw.

1. Choose the **Add Component** button from the **Assemblies** toolbar; the **Add Component** dialog box is displayed.

2. Choose the **Open** button and select the Handle from the **Part Name** dialog box. Next, choose the **OK** button from this dialog box.

3. Select the **Entire Part** option from the **Reference Set** drop-down list in the **Settings** rollout and make sure the **By Constraints** option is selected in the **Positioning** drop-down list. Next, choose the **OK** button; the **Assembly Constraints** dialog box is displayed.

4. Select the **Touch Align** option from the **Type** drop-down list and then select the **Infer Center/Axis** option from the **Orientation** drop-down list.

5. Select the cylindrical face of the Handle as the first object, refer to Figure 9-66. Next, select the cylindrical face of the Screw as the second object, refer to Figure 9-67.

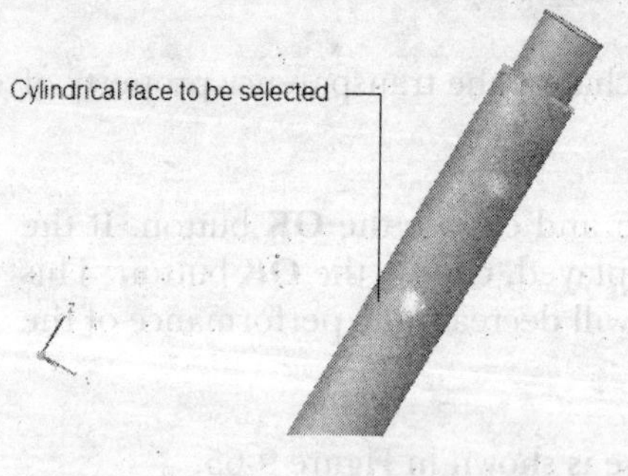

Figure 9-66 Cylindrical face to be selected from the Handle

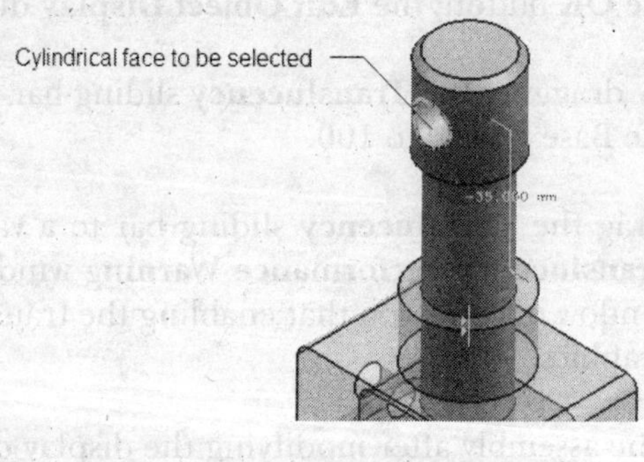

Figure 9-67 Cylindrical face to be selected from the Screw

6. Next, select the **Touch** option from the **Orientation** drop-down list in the **Assembly Constraints** dialog box.

7. Select the XC-YC plane of the Handle as the first object, refer to Figure 9-68, and then select the XC-ZC plane of the Screw as the second object. Next, choose the **Apply** button from the **Assembly Constraints** dialog box.

8. Select the **Parallel** option from the **Type** drop-down list in the dialog box.

9. Select the datum plane of the Handle as the first object, refer to Figure 9-69. Next, select the top planar face of the Screw as the second object, refer to Figure 9-70.

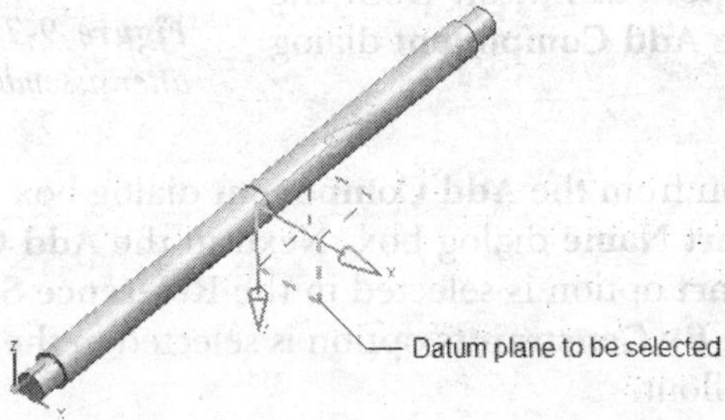

Figure 9-68 Datum plane to be selected from the Handle

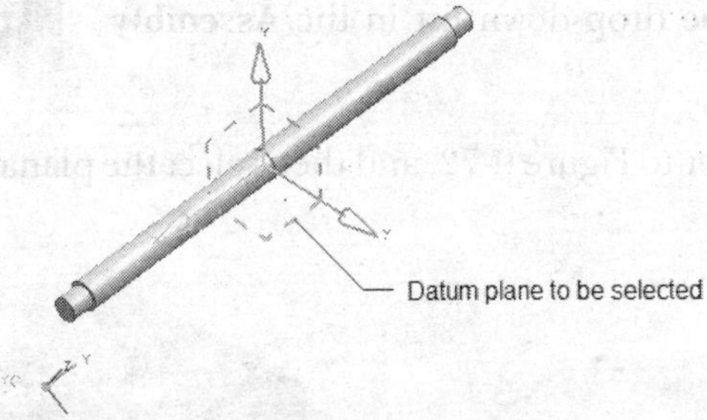

Figure 9-69 Datum plane to be selected from the Handle

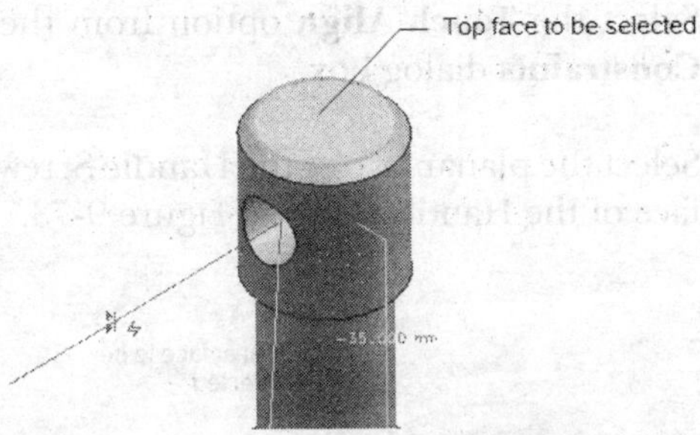

Figure 9-70 Top face to be selected from the Screw

10. Choose the **OK** button from the **Assembly Constraints** dialog box to exit the dialog box.

11. Choose the **Replace Reference Set** button from the **Assemblies** toolbar; the **Class Selection** dialog box is displayed. Select the Handle and the Screw from the assembly and choose the **OK** button from the **Class Selection** dialog box; the **Replace Reference Set** dialog box is displayed.

12. Select the **MODEL** option from the list box of the dialog box. Next, choose the **OK** button; the display of the reference sets of the Handle and the Screw is changed. The resulting assembly after assembling the Handle is shown in Figure 9-71.

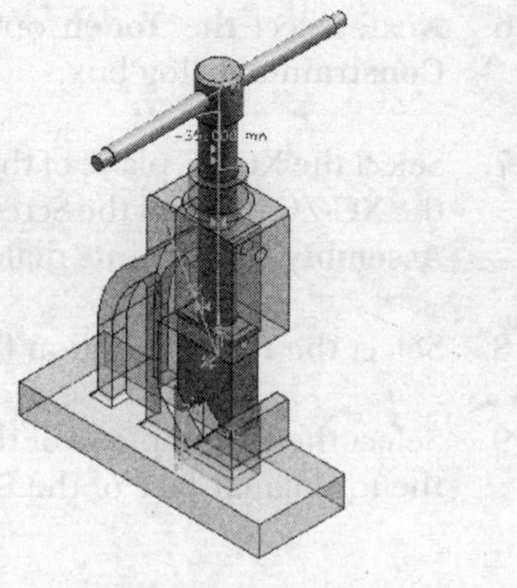

Figure 9-71 The resulting assembly after assembling the Handle

Assembling the Handle Screw

Next, you need to assemble the Handle Screw.

1. Change the reference set of the Handle back to **Entire Part**.

2. Choose the **Add Component** button from the **Assemblies** toolbar; the **Add Component** dialog box is displayed.

3. Choose the **Open** button from the **Add Component** dialog box and double-click on the Handle Screw in the **Part Name** dialog box. Next, in the **Add Component** dialog box, make sure the **Entire Part** option is selected in the **Reference Set** drop-down list of the **Settings** rollout and the **By Constraints** option is selected in the **Positioning** drop-down list of the **Placement** rollout.

4. Choose the **OK** button from the **Add Component** dialog box; the **Assembly Constraints** dialog box is displayed.

5. Select the **Touch Align** option from the **Type** drop-down list in the **Assembly Constraints** dialog box.

6. Select the planar face of the Handle Screw, refer to Figure 9-72, and then select the planar face of the Handle, refer to Figure 9-73.

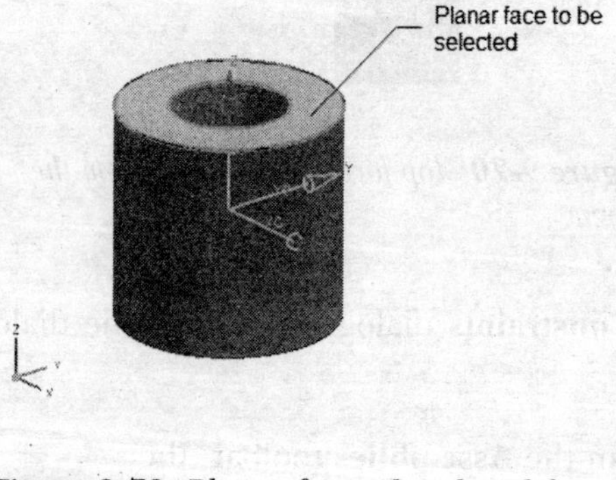

***Figure 9-72** Planar face to be selected from the Handle Screw*

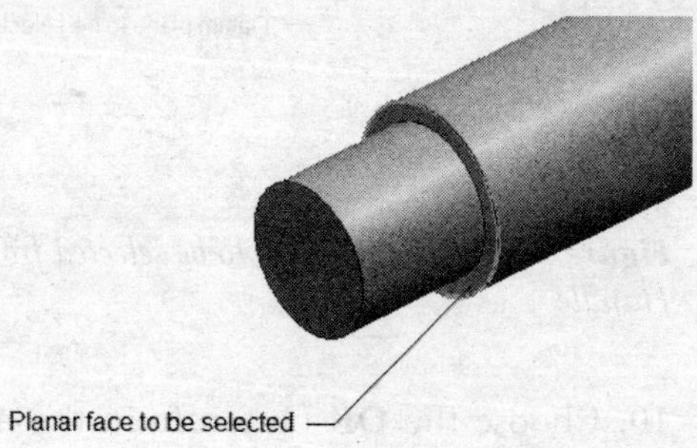

***Figure 9-73** Planar face to be selected from the Handle*

7. Next, select the **Infer Center/Axis** option from the **Orientation** drop-down list of the dialog box.

8. Select the cylindrical face of the Handle Screw, refer to Figure 9-74, and then select the cylindrical face of the Handle, refer to Figure 9-75.

9. Select the **Parallel** option from the **Type** drop-down list of the dialog box. 

10. Select the right datum plane of the Handle Screw, refer to Figure 9-76, and then select the right datum plane of the Handle, refer to Figure 9-77.

11. Choose the **OK** button from the **Assembly Constraints** dialog box to exit it.

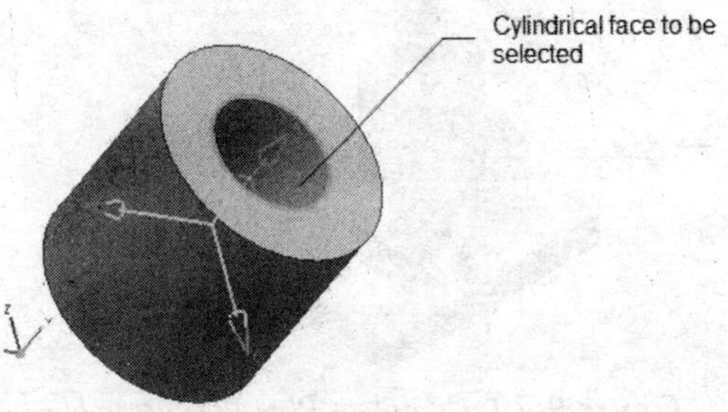

Figure 9-74 *Cylindrical face to be selected from the Handle Screw*

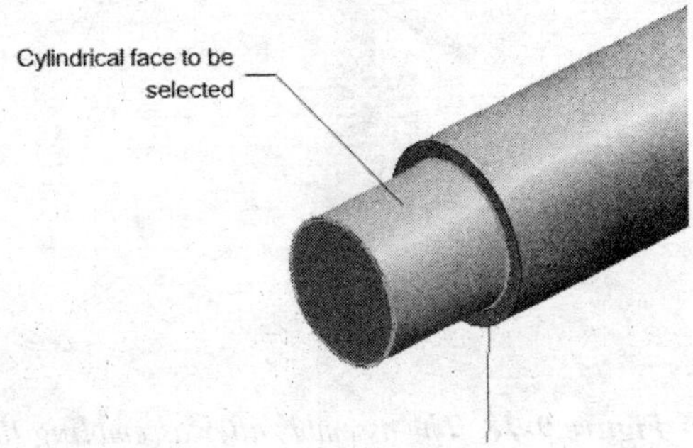

Figure 9-75 *Cylindrical face to be selected from the Handle*

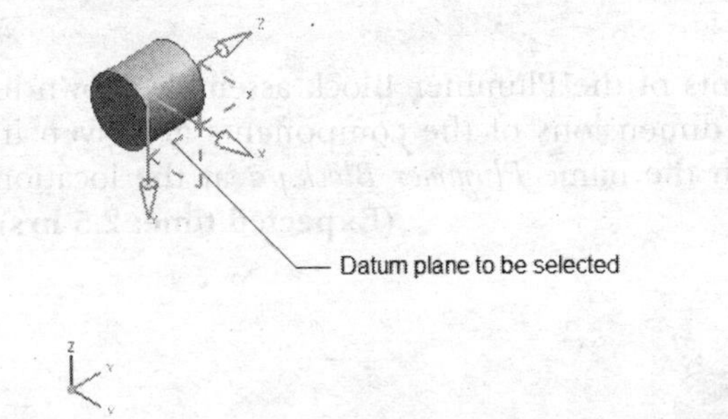

Figure 9-76 *Datum plane to be selected from the Handle Screw*

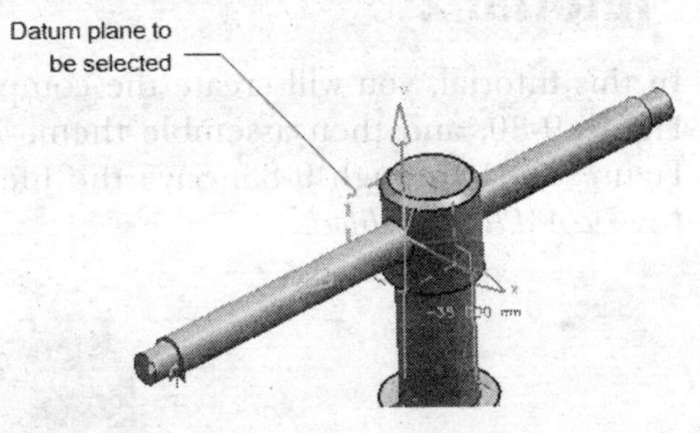

Figure 9-77 *Datum plane to be selected from the Handle*

12. Change the reference set of the Handle Screw and the Handle to **MODEL**. The assembly, after assembling one of the Handle Screws, is shown in Figure 9-78.

13. Similarly, assemble the other instance of the Handle Screw at the other end of the Handle.

14. Change the reference set of all components to **MODEL**. Also, change the texture of the Base component from transparent to solid. The final Pipe Vice assembly is shown in Figure 9-79.

Note

To turn off the display of the constraints as shown in Figure 9-79, click on the ***Assembly Navigator*** *tab from the* ***Resource Bar****; the* ***Assembly Navigator*** *cascading menu is displayed. Next, right-click on the* ***Constraints*** *node; a shortcut menu is displayed. Next, clear the check mark on the left of the* ***Display Constraints in Graphics Window*** *option by choosing it.*

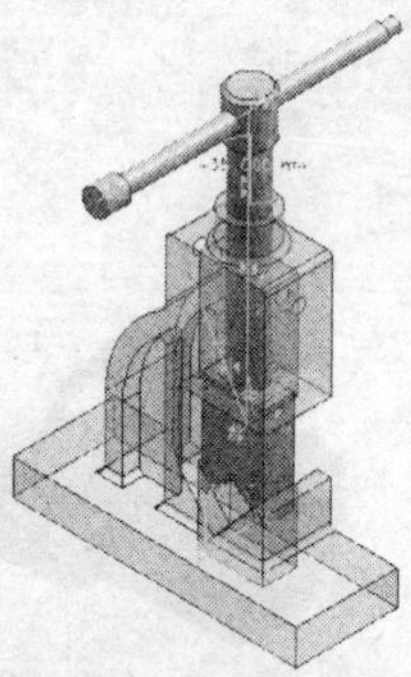

Figure 9-78 *The assembly after assembling the left side Handle Screw*

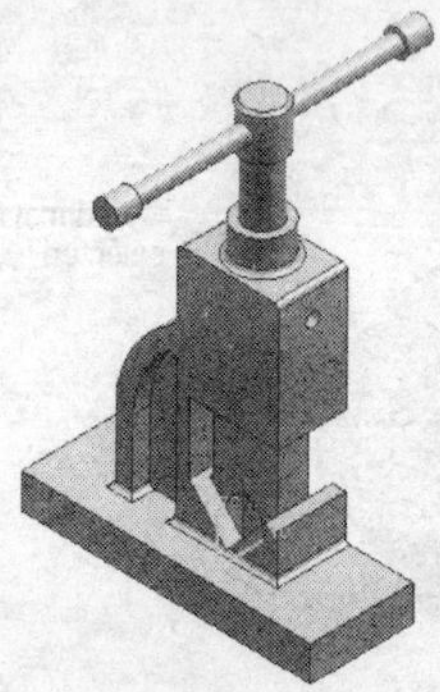

Figure 9-79 *Complete Pipe Vice assembly*

Saving and Closing the File

1. Choose **File > Close > Save and Close** from the menu bar to save and close the file.

Tutorial 2

In this tutorial, you will create the components of the Plummer Block assembly shown in Figure 9-80, and then assemble them. The dimensions of the components are given in Figures 9-81 through 9-83. Save the file with the name *Plummer Block.prt* at the location *NX 7\c09\Plummer Block.*

(Expected time: 2.5 hrs)

Figure 9-80 *The Plummer Block assembly*

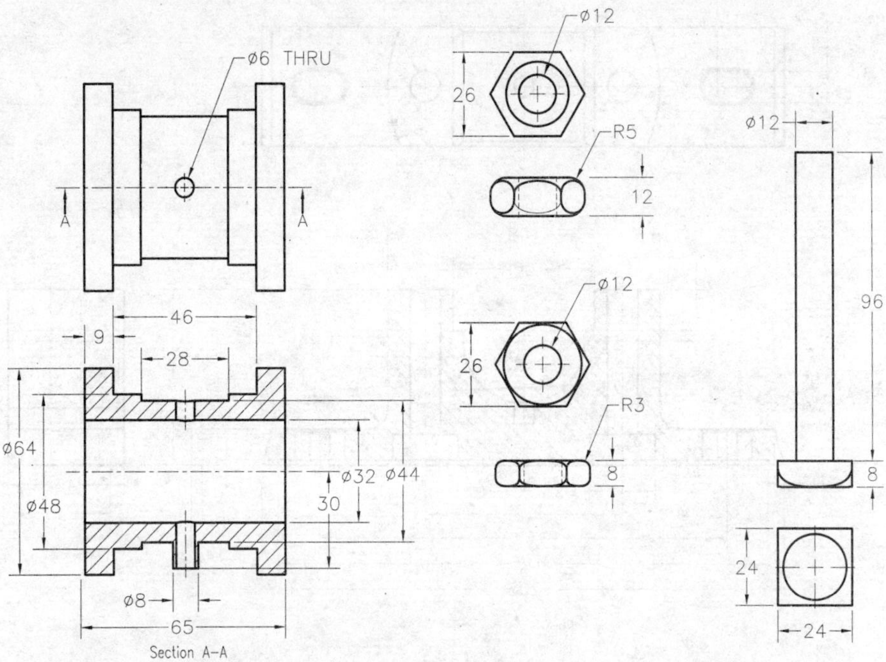

Figure 9-81 Views and dimensions of Brasses, Nut, Lock Nut, and Bolt

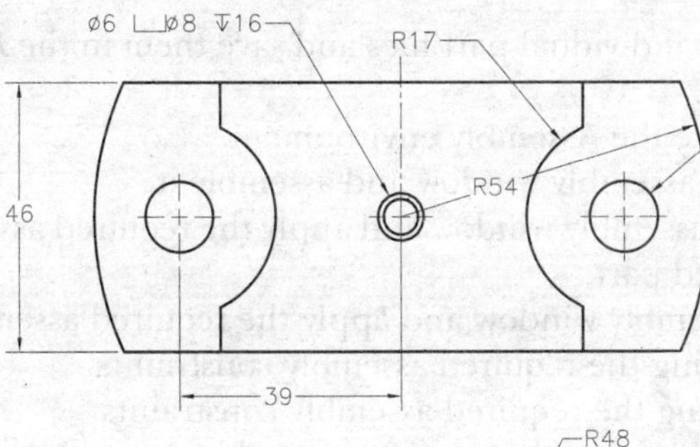

Figure 9-82 Views and dimensions of the Cap

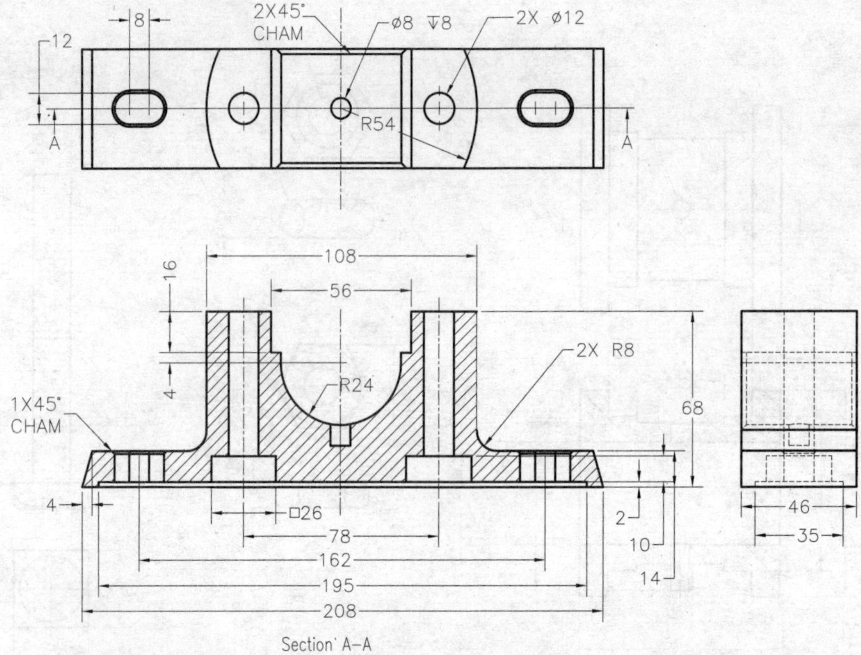

Figure 9-83 Views and dimensions of the Casting

The following steps are required to complete this tutorial:

a. Create all components as individual part files and save them in the *Plummer Block* folder at the location *\NX 7\c09*.
b. Start a new file and invoke the Assembly environment.
c. Insert the Casting in the assembly window and assemble it.
d. Insert the Brasses in the assembly window and apply the required assembly constraints to make it a fully-constrained part.
e. Insert the Cap in the assembly window and apply the required assembly constraints.
f. Assemble the Bolts by using the required assembly constraints.
g. Assemble the Nuts by using the required assembly constraints.
h. Assemble the Lock Nuts by using the required assembly constraints.

Creating Assembly Components

1. Create all components of the Plummer Block assembly as separate part files. Specify the names of the files as mentioned in the drawing views. Save the files at the location *\NX 7\c09\Plummer Block*.

Starting a New Assembly File

1. Start a new file with the name *Plummer Block.prt* using the **Model** template and specify its location as *C:\NX 7\c09\Plummer Block*.

2. Invoke the Assembly environment, if it is not already invoked, by choosing **Start > Assemblies** from the **Standard** toolbar.

Assembling the Casting with the Datum Planes

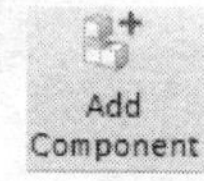

1. Choose the **Add Component** button from the **Assemblies** toolbar; the **Add Component** dialog box is displayed.

2. Choose the **Open** button from the **Add Component** dialog box; the **Part Name** dialog box is displayed.

3. Double-click on the Casting in the **Part Name** dialog box; the Casting is displayed in the **Component Preview** window.

4. Select the **Entire Part** option from the **Reference Set** drop-down list in the **Settings** rollout.

5. Select the **Absolute Origin** option from the **Positioning** drop-down list in the **Placement** rollout of the **Add Component** dialog box, and then choose the **OK** button from it.

6. Choose the **Assembly Constraints** button from the **Assemblies** toolbar; the **Assembly Constraints** dialog box is displayed.

7. To restrict all degrees of freedom of the casting, select the **Fix** option from the **Type** drop-down list in the **Assembly Constraints** dialog box and then select Casting from the drawing window.

8. Choose the **OK** button from the **Assembly Constraints** dialog box; the fix constraint is applied to the Casting.

9. Right-click on the Casting to display a shortcut menu. Next, choose **Replace Reference Set > MODEL** from the shortcut menu. The assembly after assembling the Casting is shown in Figure 9-84.

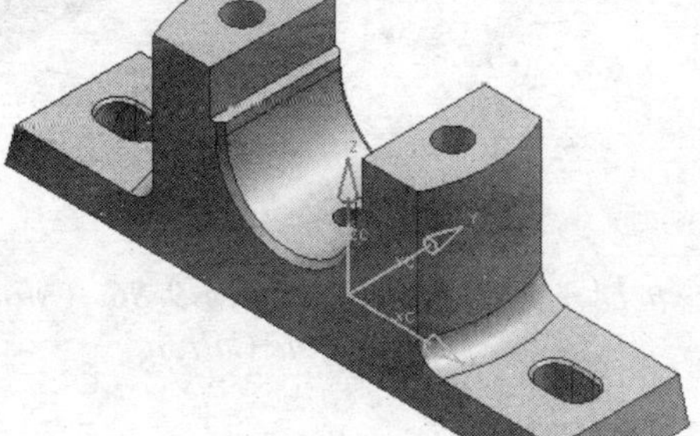

Figure 9-84 *Casting assembled with three default planes*

Note

*In this Tutorial, the display of constraints is turned off. To do so, click on the **Assembly Navigator** tab from the **Resource Bar**; the **Assembly Navigator** cascading menu is displayed. Right-click on the **Constraints** node; a shortcut menu is displayed. Next, clear the check mark on the left of the **Display Constraints in Graphics Window** option by choosing it.*

Assembling the Second Component

After inserting the Casting, you need to assemble Brasses as the second component.

1. Choose the **Add Component** button from the **Assemblies** toolbar; the **Add Component** dialog box is displayed.

2. Choose the **Open** button from the **Add Component** dialog box; the **Part Name** dialog box is displayed.

3. Double-click on the Brasses in the **Part Name** dialog box; the Brasses are displayed in the **Component Preview** window.

4. Select the **Model ("MODEL")** option from the **Reference Set** drop-down list and the **By Constraints** option from the **Positioning** drop-down list of the **Add Component** dialog box. Next, choose the **OK** button; the **Assembly Constraints** dialog box is displayed.

5. Select the **Touch Align** option from the drop-down list in the **Type** rollout and then select the **Infer Center/Axis** option from the **Orientation** drop-down list.

6. Select the cylindrical face of the Brasses, refer to Figure 9-85, and then select the cylindrical face of the Casting, refer to Figure 9-86.

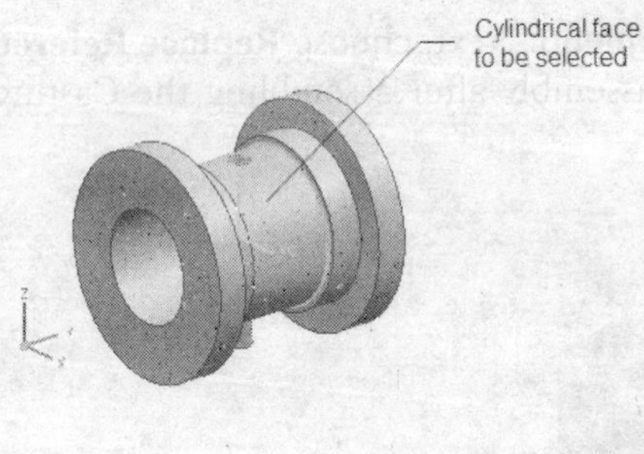

Figure 9-85 *Cylindrical face to be selected from the Brasses*

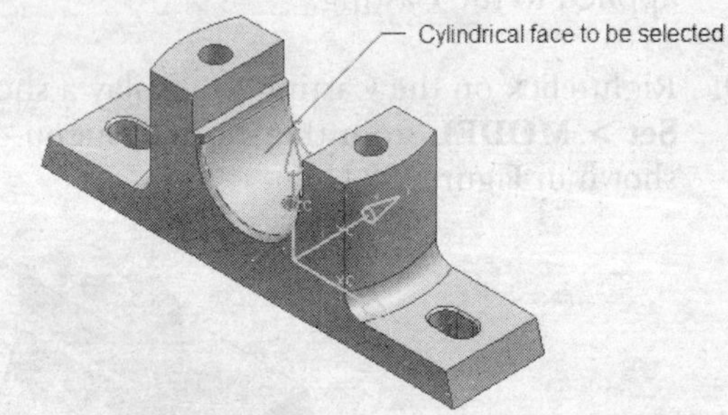

Figure 9-86 *Cylindrical face to be selected from the Casting*

7. Choose the **Apply** button from the **Assembly Constraints** dialog box. Next, clear the **Preview Component in Main Window** check box in the **Preview** rollout of the **Assembly Constraints** dialog box.

8. Next, select the **Fit** option from the **Type** drop-down list in the **Assembly Constraints** dialog box.

9. Select the cylindrical face of the Brasses, refer to Figure 9-87, and then select the cylindrical face of the Casting, refer to Figure 9-88.

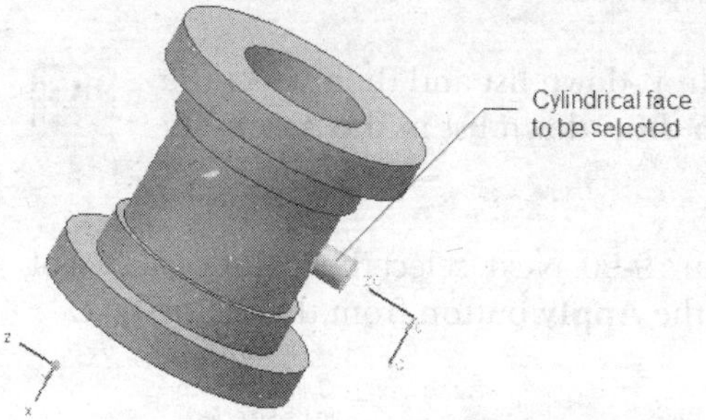

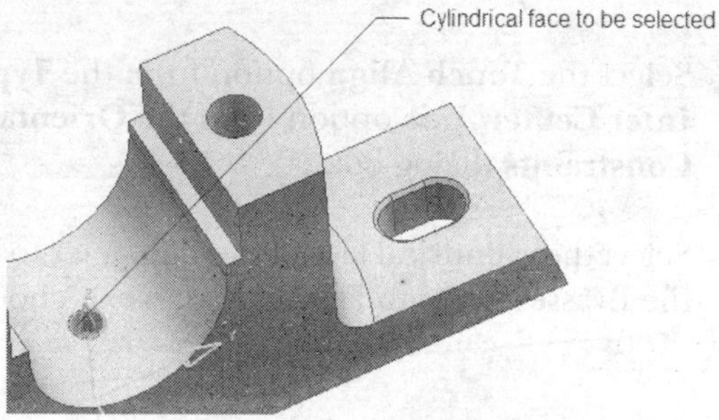

Figure 9-87 *Cylindrical face to be selected from the Brasses*

Figure 9-88 *Cylindrical face to be selected from the Casting*

10. Choose the **OK** button from the **Assembly Constraints** dialog box to exit it.

11. The assembly after assembling the Brasses is shown in Figure 9-89.

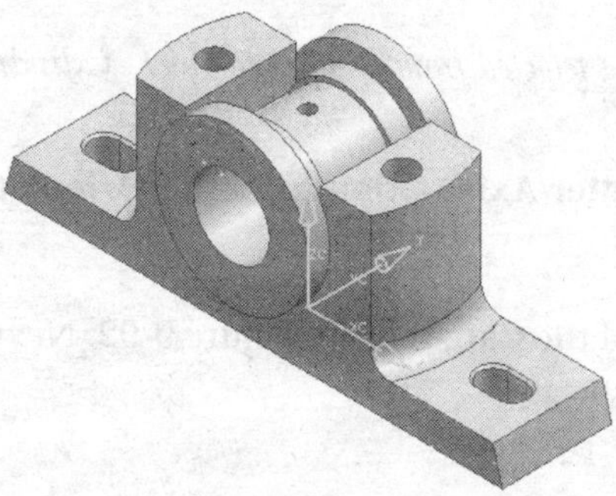

Figure 9-89 *Resulting assembly after assembling the Brasses*

Assembling the Third Component

Next, you need to assemble the Cap.

1. Choose the **Add Component** button from the **Assemblies** toolbar; the **Add Component** dialog box is displayed.

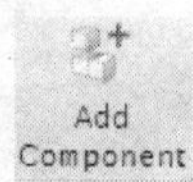

2. Choose the **Open** button from the **Add Component** dialog box; the **Part Name** dialog box is displayed.

3. Double-click on the Cap in the **Part Name** dialog box; the Cap is displayed in the **Component Preview** window.

4. Select the **Model ("MODEL")** option from the **Reference Set** drop-down list and the **By Constraints** option from the **Positioning** drop-down list. Next, choose **OK** from the dialog box; the **Assembly Constraints** dialog box is displayed.

5. Select the **Touch Align** option from the **Type** drop-down list and then select the **Infer Center/Axis** option from the **Orientation** drop-down list in the **Assembly Constraints** dialog box.

6. Select the cylindrical face of the Cap, refer to Figure 9-90. Next, select the cylindrical face of the Brasses, refer to Figure 9-91. Next, choose the **Apply** button from the dialog box.

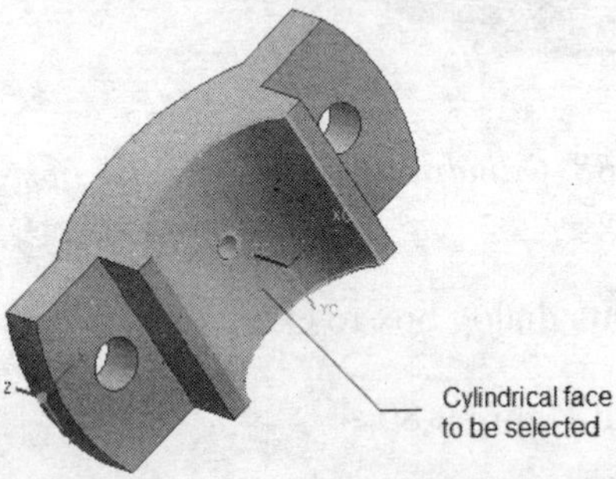

Figure 9-90 *Cylindrical face to be selected from the Cap*

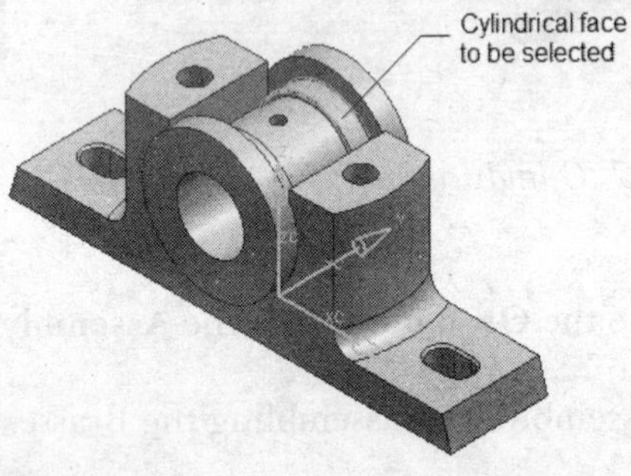

Figure 9-91 *Cylindrical face to be selected from the Brasses*

7. Again, select the **Infer Center/Axis** option from the **Orientation** drop-down list of the dialog box.

8. Select the cylindrical face of the Cap, refer to Figure 9-92. Next, select the cylindrical face of the Brasses, refer to Figure 9-93.

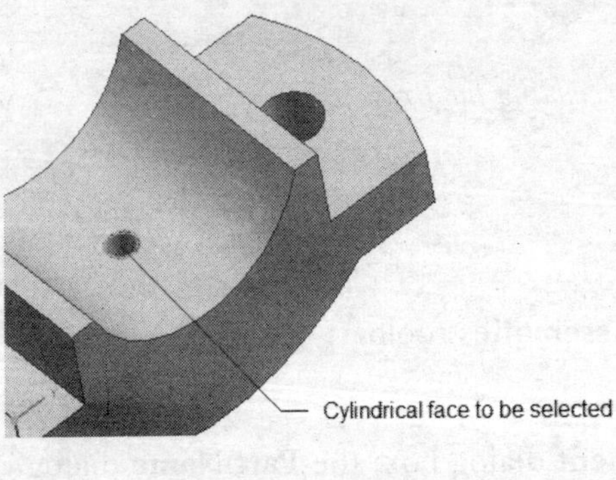

Figure 9-92 *Cylindrical face to be selected from the Cap*

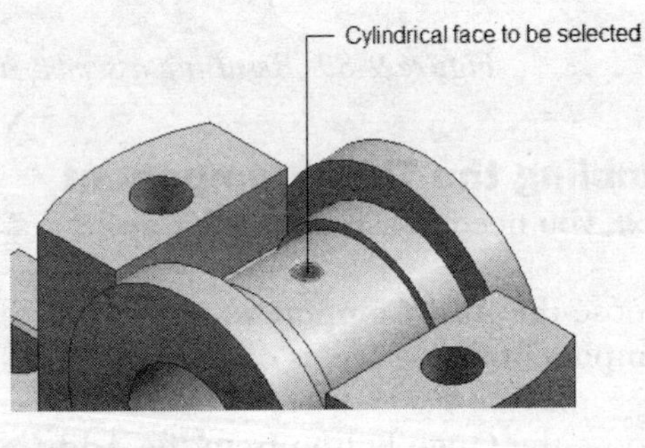

Figure 9-93 *Cylindrical face to be selected from the Brasses*

9. Choose the **OK** button from the **Assembly Constraints** dialog box to exit it. The resulting assembly after assembling the Cap is shown in Figure 9-94.

Figure 9-94 *The assembly after assembling the Cap*

Assembling the Bolts

Next, you need to assemble the Bolt as the fourth component.

1. Choose the **Add Component** button from the **Assemblies** toolbar; the **Add Component** dialog box is displayed.
2. Choose the **Open** button from the **Add Component** dialog box; the **Part Name** dialog box is displayed.
3. Double-click on the Bolt in the **Part Name** dialog box; the Bolt is displayed in the **Component Preview** window.
4. Select the **Model ("MODEL")** option from the **Reference Set** drop-down list and the **By Constraints** option from the **Positioning** drop-down list. Next, choose the **OK** button from the **Add Component** dialog box; the **Assembly Constraints** dialog box is displayed.

5. In the **Assembly Constraints** dialog box, select the **Touch Align** option from the **Type** drop-down list and the **Infer Center/Axis** option from the **Orientation** drop-down list.
6. Select the cylindrical face of the Bolt, refer to Figure 9-95. Next, select the cylindrical face from the Casting, refer to Figure 9-96. Next, choose the **Apply** button from the dialog box.
7. Select the **Touch** option from the **Orientation** drop-down list of the **Assembly Constraints** dialog box.
8. Select a planar face of the Bolt, refer to Figure 9-97. Next, select a planar face of the Casting, refer to Figure 9-98.

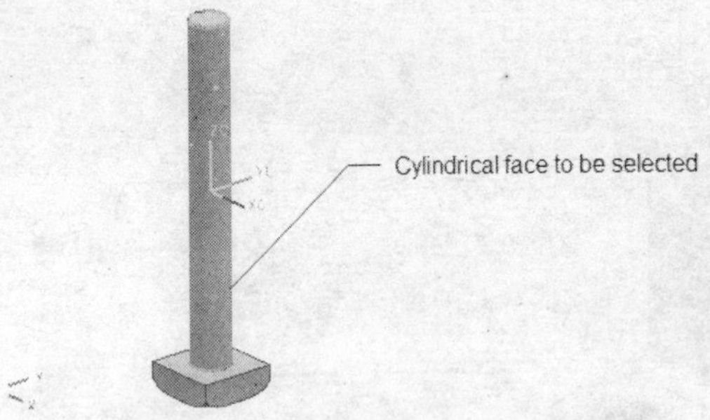

Figure 9-95 *Cylindrical face to be selected from the Bolt*

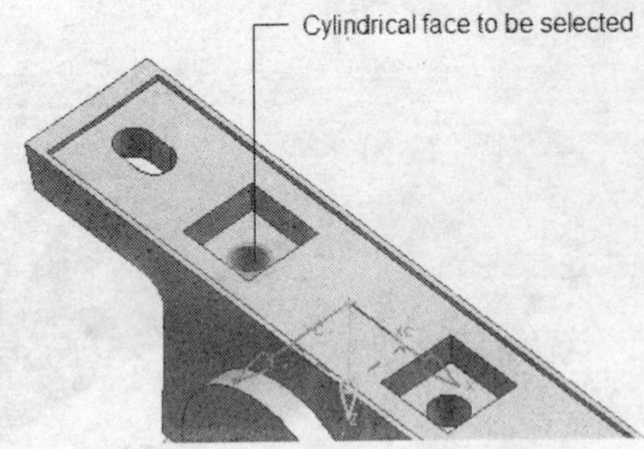

Figure 9-96 *Cylindrical face to be selected from the Casting*

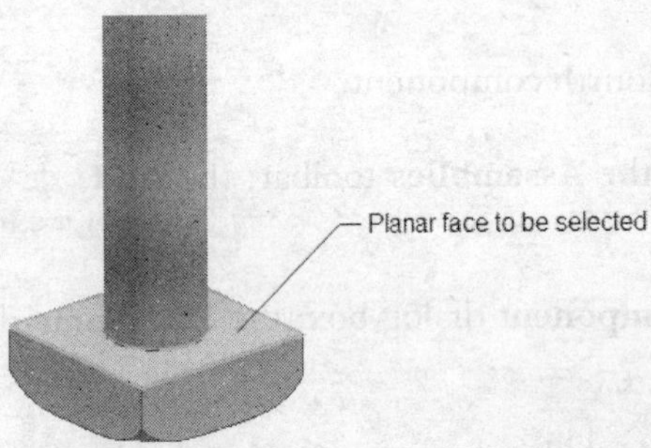

Figure 9-97 *Planar face to be selected from the Bolt*

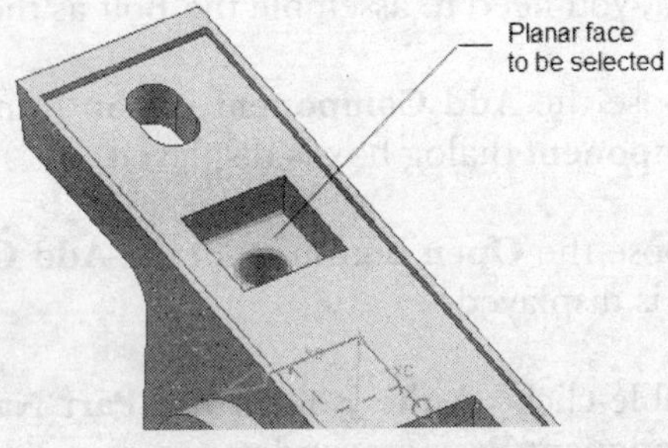

Figure 9-98 *Planar face to be selected from the Casting*

9. Select the **Parallel** option from the **Type** drop-down list in the **Assembly Constraints** dialog box.

10. Select a planar face of the Bolt, refer to Figure 9-99. Next, select a planar face of the Casting, refer to Figure 9-100.

11. Choose the **OK** button from the **Assembly Constraints** dialog box to exit.

12. Similarly, assemble the second instance of the Bolt on the other side. Next, apply the same three assembly constraints. The assembly after assembling the bolts is shown in Figure 9-101.

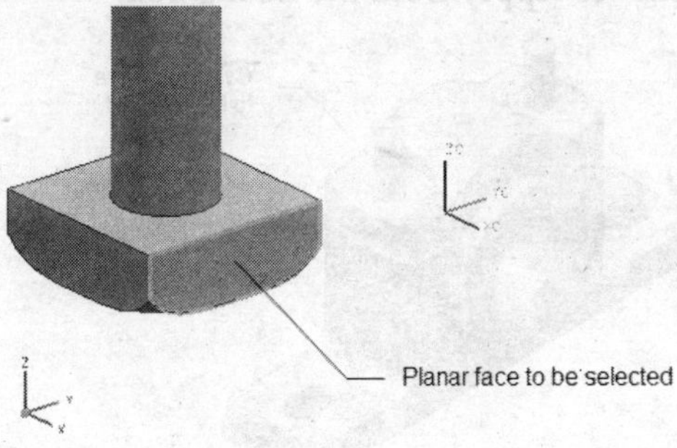

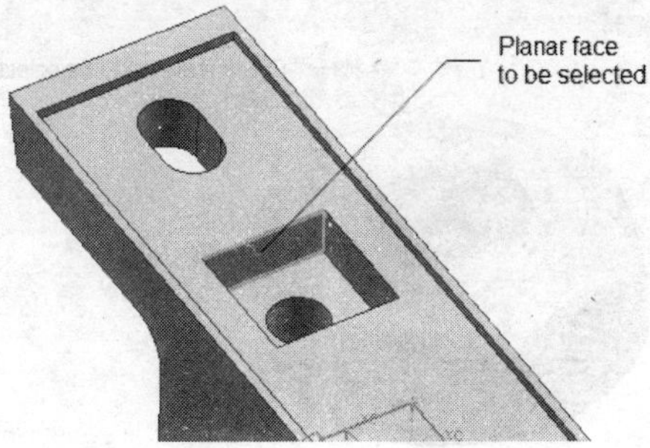

Figure 9-99 *Planar face to be selected from the Bolt*

Figure 9-100 *Planar face to be selected from the Casting*

Figure 9-101 *The resulting assembly after assembling the Bolts*

Assembling the Nuts

Next, you need to assemble the Nut as the fifth component.

1. Choose the **Add Component** button from the **Assemblies** toolbar; the **Add Component** dialog box is displayed.

2. Choose the **Open** button from the **Add Component** dialog box; the **Part Name** dialog box is displayed.

3. Double-click on the Nut in the **Part Name** dialog box; the Nut is displayed in the **Component Preview** window.

4. In the **Add Component** dialog box, select the **Model ("MODEL")** option from the **Reference Set** drop-down list and the **By Constraints** option from the **Positioning** drop-down list. Next, choose the **OK** button; the **Assembly Constraints** dialog box is displayed.

5. Select the **Touch Align** option from the **Type** rollout and then select the **Infer Center/Axis** option from the **Orientation** drop-down list.

6. Select the cylindrical face of the Nut, refer to Figure 9-102. Next, select the cylindrical face of the Bolt, refer to Figure 9-103. Next, choose **Apply** from the dialog box.

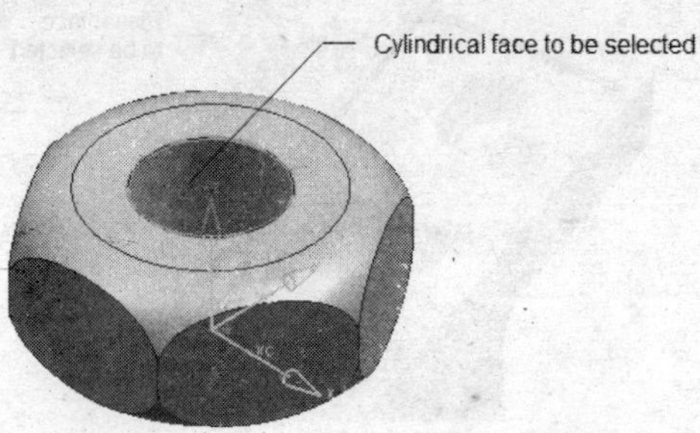

Figure 9-102 Cylindrical face to be selected from the Nut

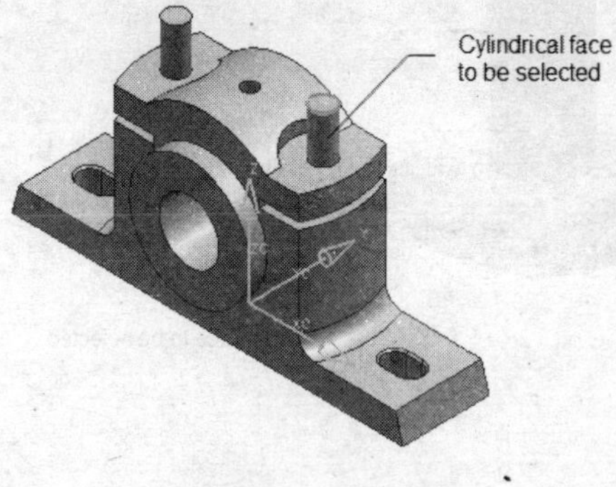

Figure 9-103 Cylindrical face to be selected from Bolt

7. Next, select the **Touch** option from the **Orientation** drop-down list in the **Assembly Constraints** dialog box.

8. Rotate the view of the Nut and select its bottom planar face, refer to Figure 9-104. Next, select the planar face from the Cap, refer to Figure 9-105.

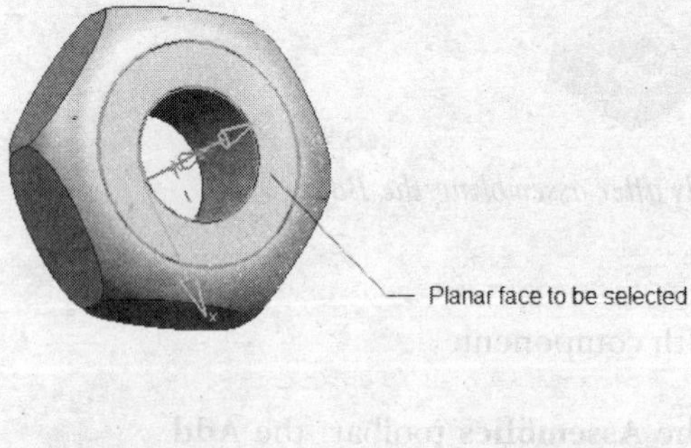

Figure 9-104 Bottom planar face to be selected from the Nut

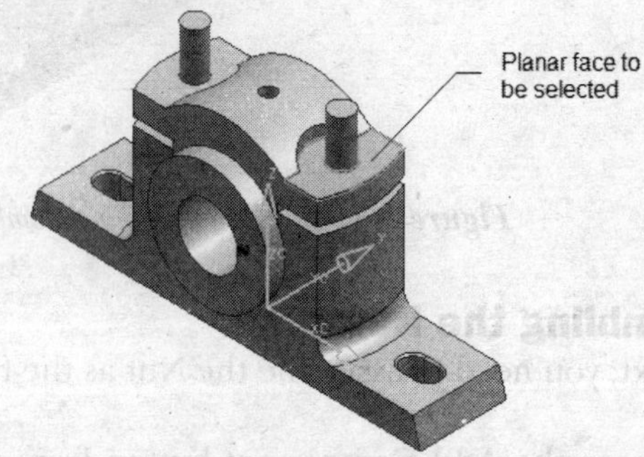

Figure 9-105 Planar face to be selected from the Cap

9. Choose the **OK** button in the **Assembly Constraints** dialog box to exit it.

10. Similarly, assemble the second instance of the Nut on the other side. The assembly, after assembling the Nuts, is shown in Figure 9-106.

Assembling the Lock Nut

Next, you need to assemble the Lock Nut as the sixth component.

1. Choose the **Add Component** button from the **Assemblies** toolbar; the **Add Component** dialog box is displayed.

Figure 9-106 The resulting assembly after assembling the Nuts

Tip: *During assembling the Nut in the assembly, you should not constrain its rotational degree of freedom because on doing so, it will not be able to pass through the bolt threads to lock the Cap and Brasses with the Casting.*

2. Choose the **Open** button from the **Add Component** dialog box; the **Part Name** dialog box is displayed.

3. Double-click on the Lock Nut in the **Part Name** dialog box; the Lock Nut is displayed in the **Component Preview** window.

4. In the **Add Component** dialog box, make sure that the **Model ("MODEL")** option is selected in the **Reference Set** drop-down list and the **By Constraints** option is selected in the **Positioning** drop-down list. Next, choose the **OK** button; the **Assembly Constraints** dialog box is displayed.

5. In the **Assembly Constraints** dialog box, select the **Touch Align** option from the **Type** rollout and then the **Touch** option from the **Orientation** drop-down list.

6. Select a planar face of the Lock Nut, refer to Figure 9-107. Next, select a planar face of the Nut, refer to Figure 9-108. Next, choose **Apply** from the dialog box.

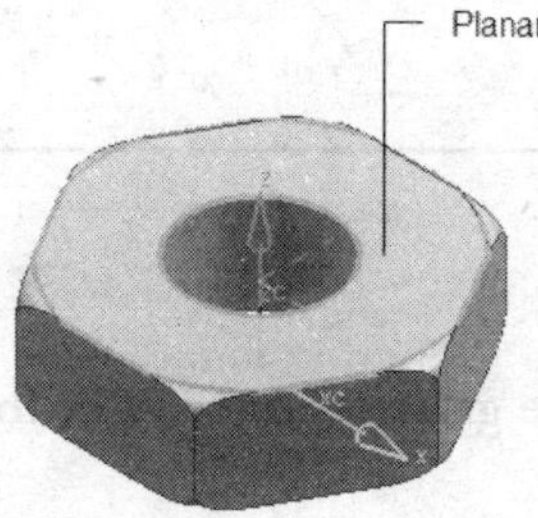

Figure 9-107 *Planar face to be selected from the Lock Nut*

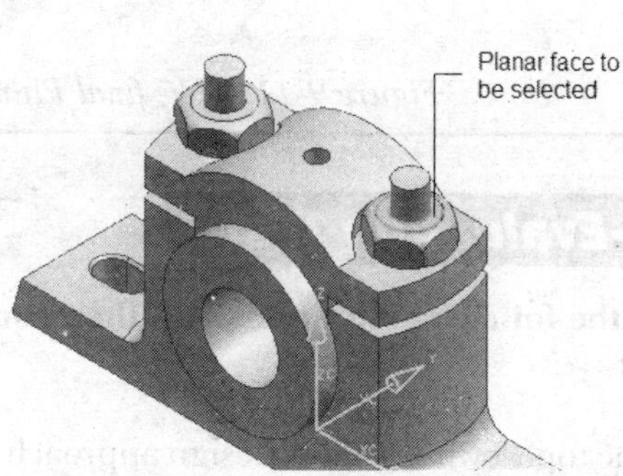

Figure 9-108 *Planar face to be selected from the Nut*

7. Select the **Infer Center/Axis** option from the **Orientation** drop-down list.

8. Select the cylindrical face of the Lock Nut, as shown in Figure 9-109. Next, select the cylindrical face of the Bolt, as shown in Figure 9-110.

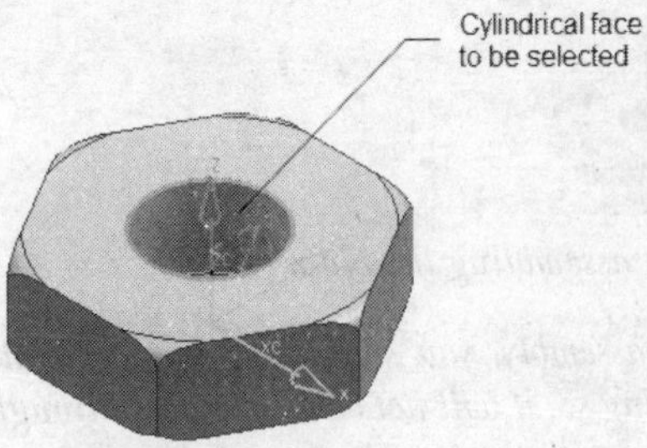

Figure 9-109 *Cylindrical face to be selected from the Lock Nut*

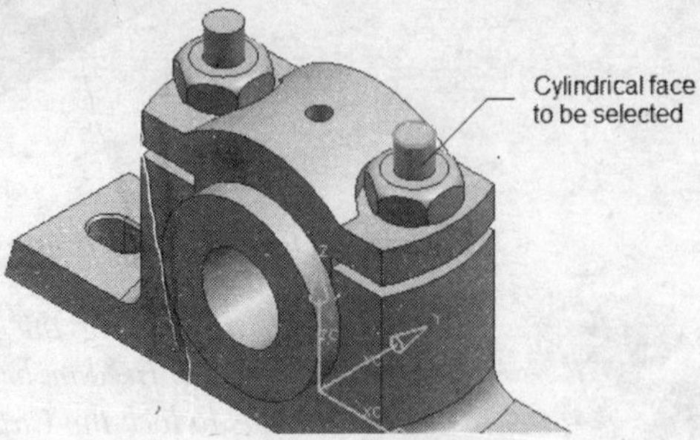

Figure 9-110 *Cylindrical face to be selected from the Bolt*

9. Choose the **OK** button to exit the dialog box.

10. Similarly, assemble the second instance of the Lock Nut on the other side. The completed Plummer Block assembly is shown in Figure 9-111.

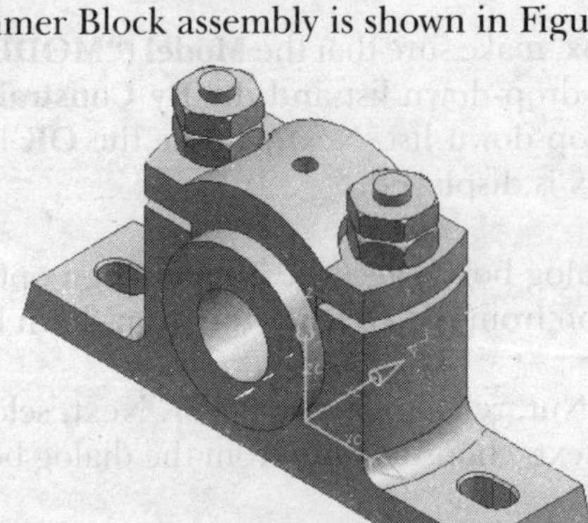

Figure 9-111 *The final Plummer Block assembly*

Self-Evaluation Test

Answer the following questions and then compare them to those given at the end of this chapter:

1. In the top-down assembly design approach, all components are created within the same assembly file. (T/F)

2. You can maintain an offset value between two faces by using the **Parallel** constraint. (T/F)

3. You cannot create a component in the **Assembly** environment. (T/F)

4. You can invoke the **Assembly Constraints** dialog box by choosing the **Assembly Constraints** button from the **Assemblies** toolbar. (T/F)

5. The **Replace Reference Set** tool is used to change the reference set of the component assembled. (T/F)

6. For assembling the base component, it is mandatory to select the **Absolute Origin** option from the **Positioning** drop-down list in the **Add Component** dialog box. (T/F)

7. The __________ is the file name extension for the assembly files.

8. The __________ assembly constraint is used to maintain an offset value between the reference faces.

9. You can move and reorient an assembled component in 3D space along available degrees of freedom using the __________ tool.

10. The __________ constraint is used to constrain two circular or elliptical edges of the components to coincide their centers as well as to make the selected edges coplanar.

Review Questions

Answer the following questions:

1. Which of the following buttons is used to invoke the **Mirror Assemblies Wizard** dialog box?

   (a) **Mirror Assembly** (b) **Create Component Array**
   (c) **Replace Reference Set** (d) None of these

2. Which of the following options is used to make two faces of a component coplanar?

   (a) **Touch Align** (b) **Parallel**
   (c) **Angle** (d) None of these

3. Which of the following options is used to align the center axis of two cylindrical components?

   (a) **Infer Center/Axis** (b) **Perpendicular**
   (c) **Center** (d) None of these

4. The **Angle** constraint is used to specify an angle between the two selected reference objects of the components. (T/F)

5. You cannot edit Assembly constraints. (T/F)

6. In the assembly environment, the modification of the components is not possible. (T/F)

7. The **Fit** constraint is used to bring together two cylindrical faces of different diameters. (T/F)

8. You can apply the **Touch Align** constraint to constrain the components tangentially. (T/F)

9. If you clear the **Associative** check box in the **Settings** rollout of the **Assembly Constraint** dialog box, the constraint will not be applied after choosing the **OK** button. (T/F)

10. The **Bond** constraint is used to fix the position of the selected components with respect to each other. (T/F)

Exercises

Exercise 1

Create the components of the Butterfly Valve assembly and then assemble them, as shown in Figure 9-112. The dimensions of the components are shown in Figures 9-113 through 9-117. Create a folder with the name \c09\Butterfly Valve Assembly and save all component files and assembly file in it. Assume the missing dimensions. **(Expected time: 4 hrs)**

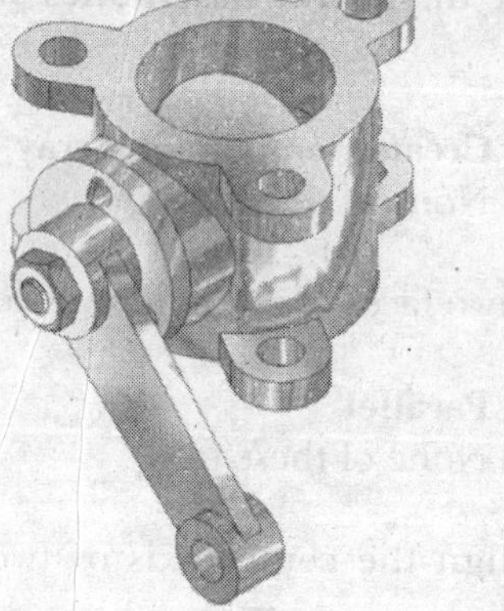

Figure 9-112 The Butterfly Valve assembly

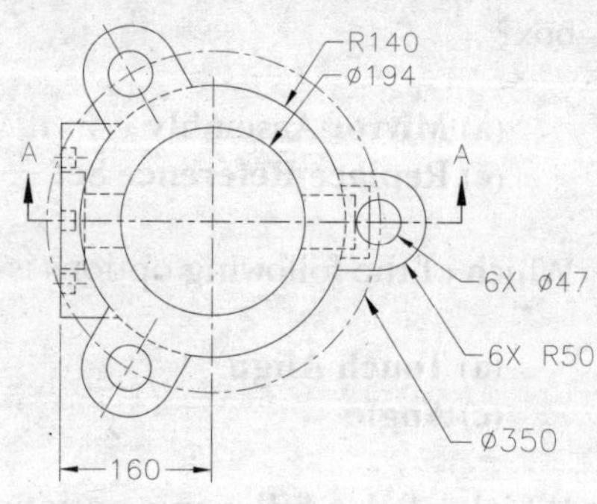

Figure 9-113a Top View of the Body

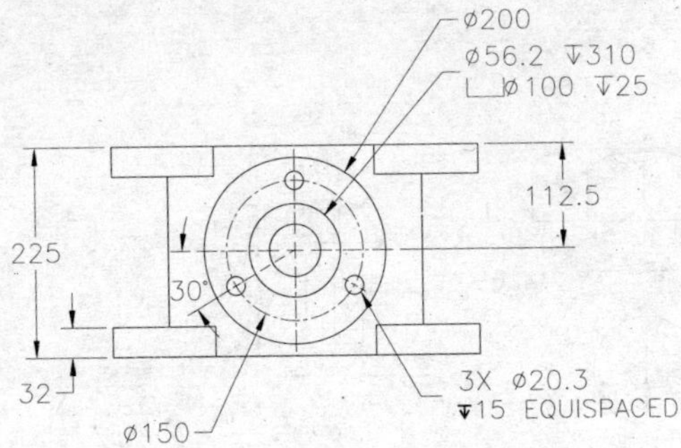

Figure 9-113b Left side view of the Body

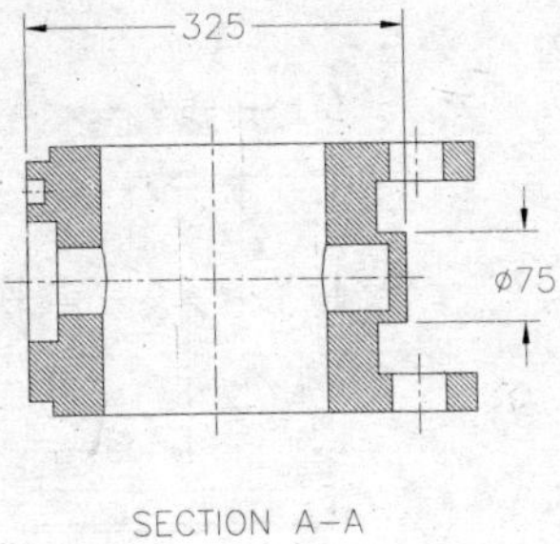

Figure 9-113c Sectional front view of the Body

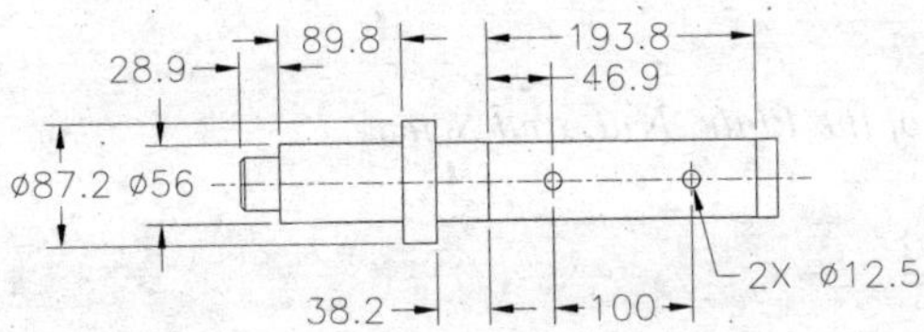

Figure 9-114 Dimensions of the Shaft

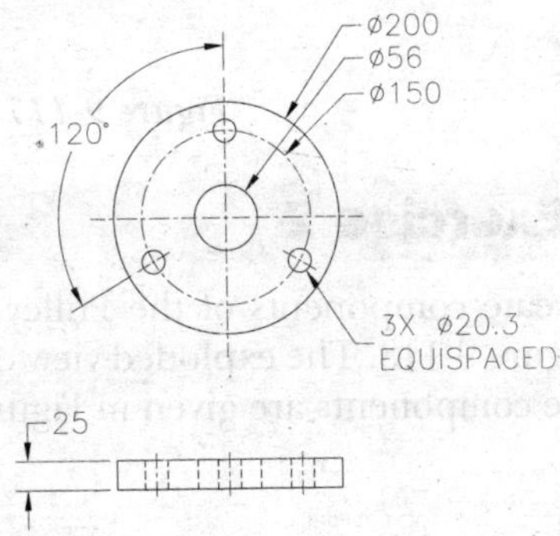

Figure 9-115 Dimensions of the Retainer

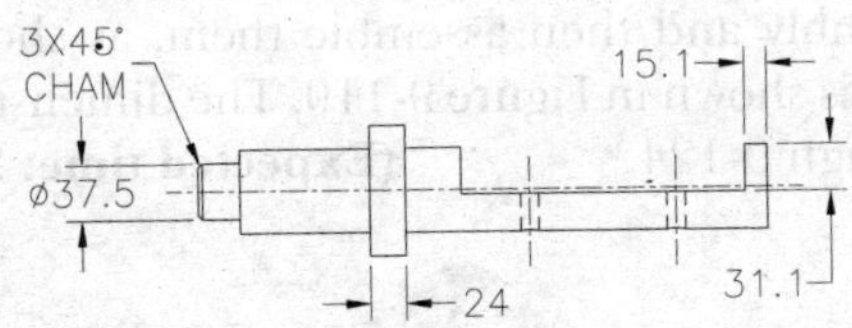

Figure 9-116a Top view of the Arm

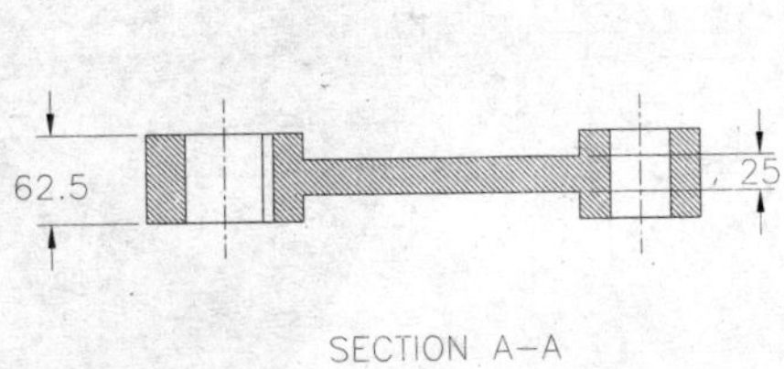

Figure 9-116b Sectional front view of the Arm

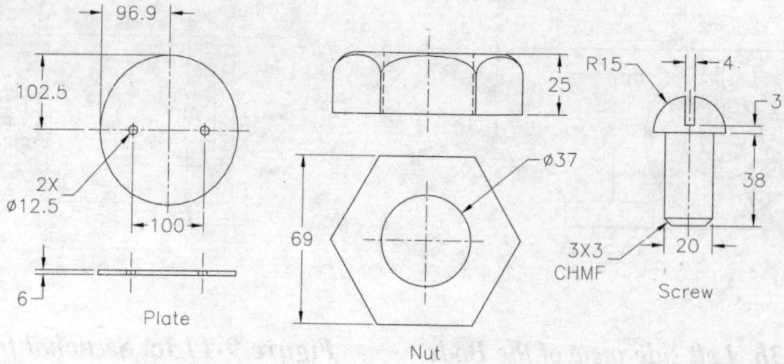

Figure 9-117 Dimensions of the Plate, Nut, and Screw

Exercise 2

Create components of the Pulley Support assembly and then assemble them, as shown in Figure 9-118. The exploded view of the assembly is shown in Figure 9-119. The dimensions of the components are given in Figures 9-120 through 9-124. **(Expected time: 3 hrs)**

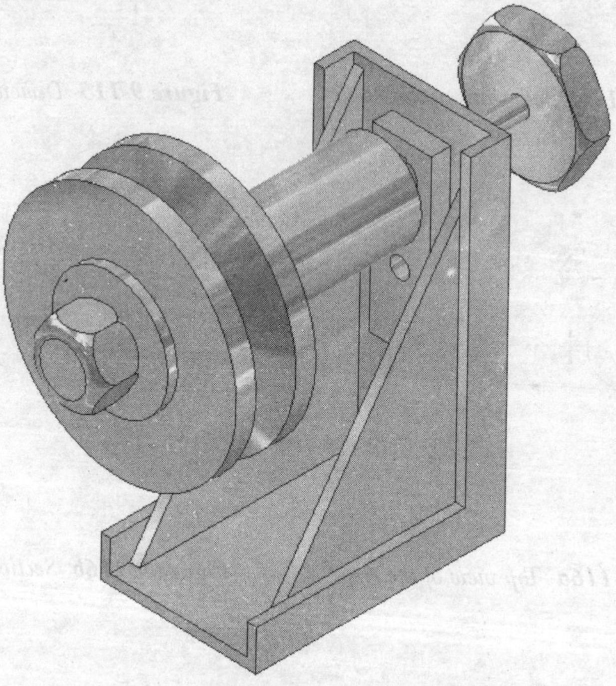

Figure 9-118 The Pulley Support assembly

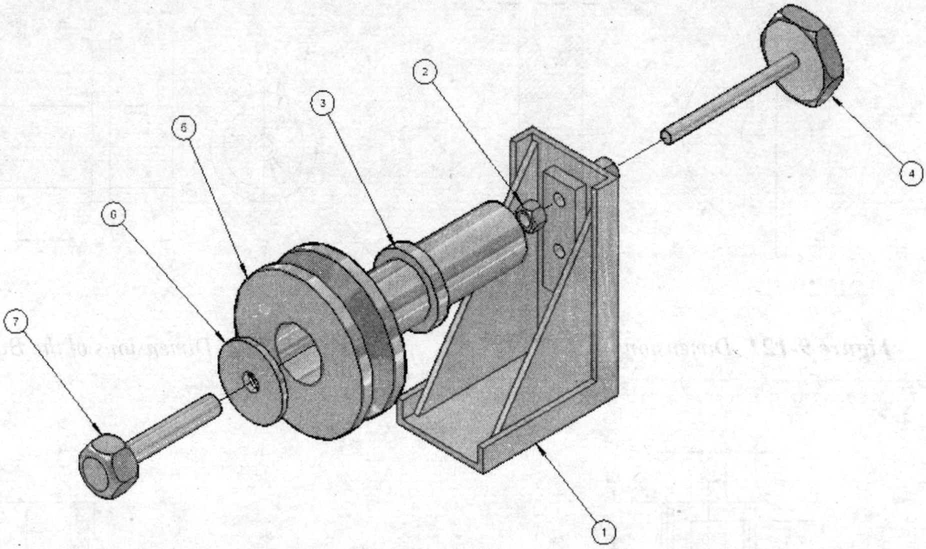

Figure 9-119 *Exploded view of the Pulley Support assembly*

PARTS LIST			
ITEM	QTY	NAME	MATERIAL
1	1	Bracket	Steel
2	2	Nut	Steel
3	1	Bushing	Steel
4	1	Turn Screw	Steel
5	1	Pulley	Steel
6	1	Washer	Steel
7	1	Cap Screw	Steel

Figure 9-120 *Parts list for the Pulley Support assembly*

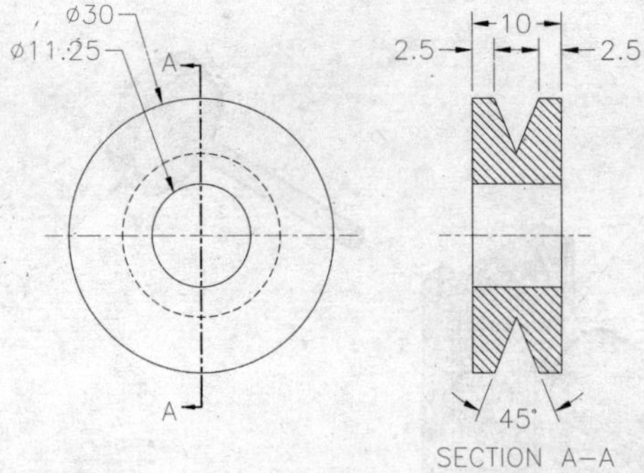

Figure 9-121 Dimensions of the Pulley

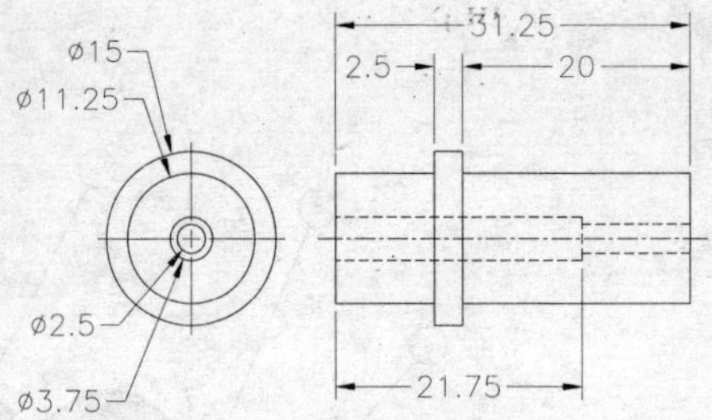

Figure 9-122 Dimensions of the Bushing

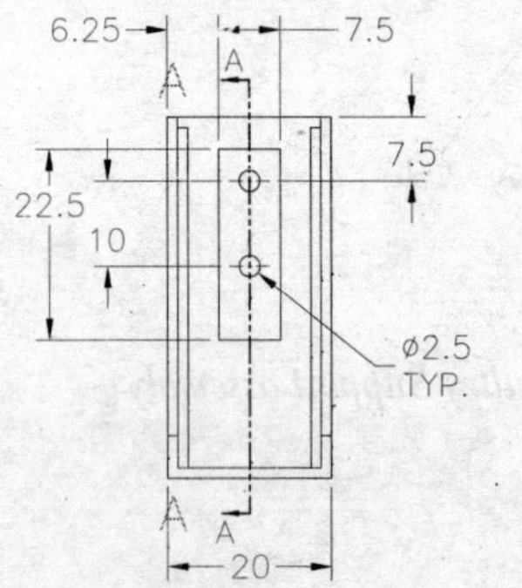

Figure 9-123a Left-side view of the Bracket

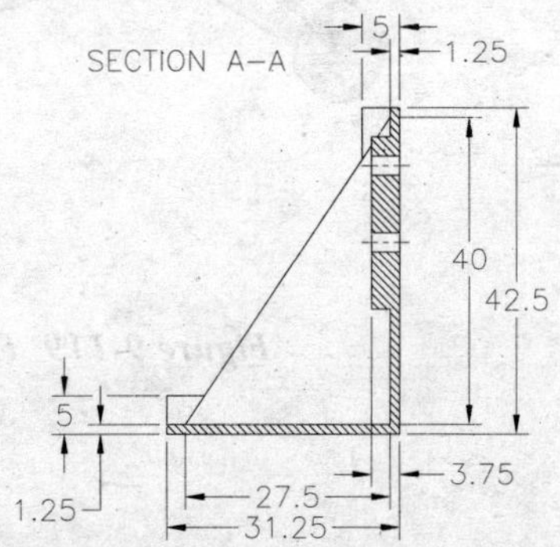

Figure 9-123b Sectioned front view of the Bracket

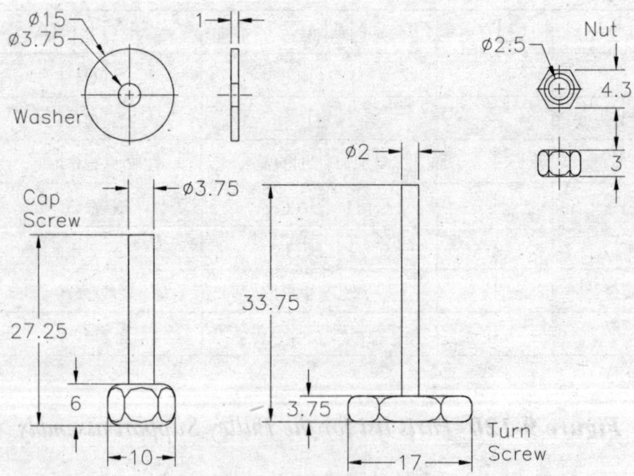

Figure 9-124 Dimensions of the Washer, Cap Screw, Turn Screw, and Nut

Exercise 3

Create the Stock Bracket assembly shown in Figure 9-125. The dimensions of the components of the assembly are given in Figures 9-126 through 9-132. **(Expected time: 4 hrs)**

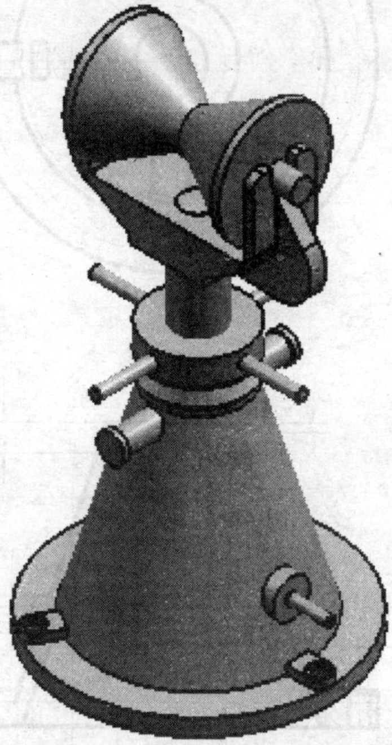

Figure 9-125 *The Stock Bracket assembly*

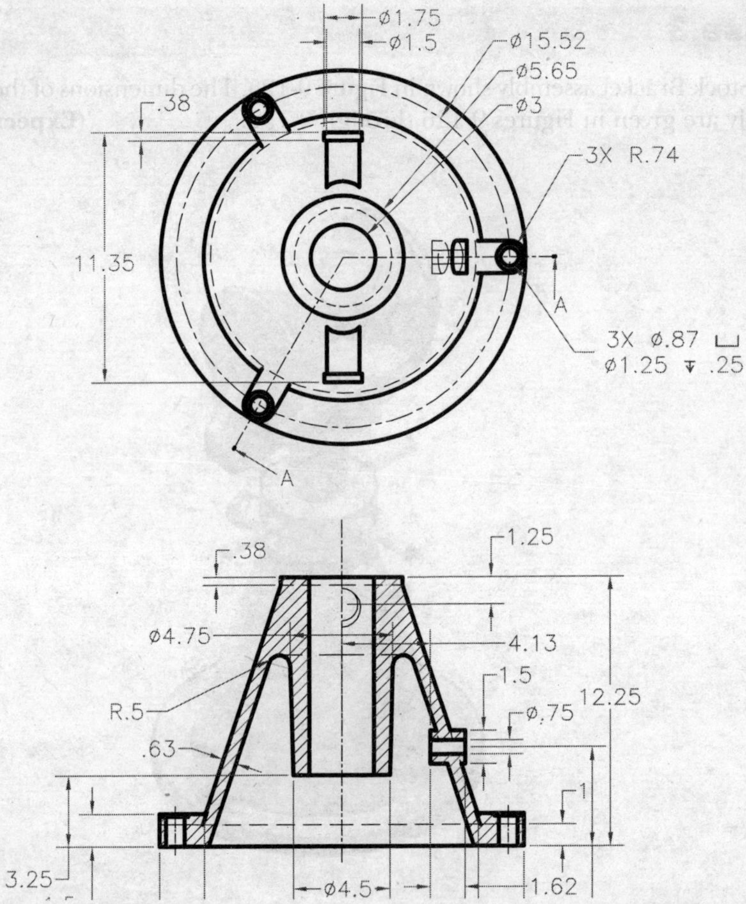

Figure 9-126 Top and front views of the Stock Support Base

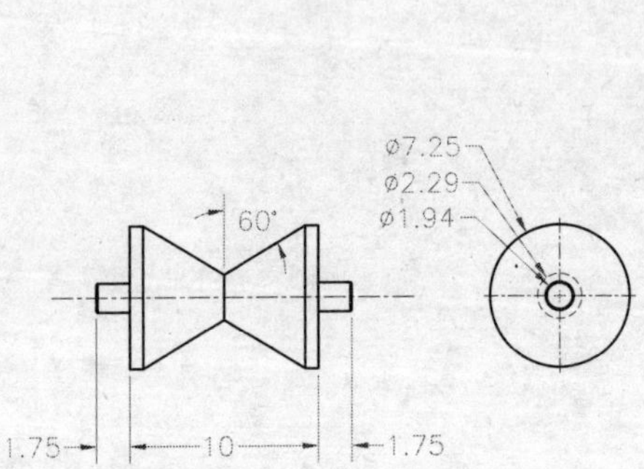

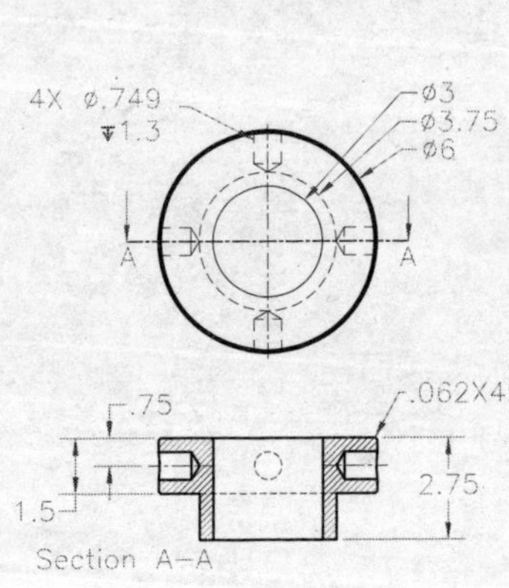

Figure 9-127 *Front and right-side views of the Stock Support Roller*

Figure 9-128 *Top and front views of the Adjusting Screw Nut*

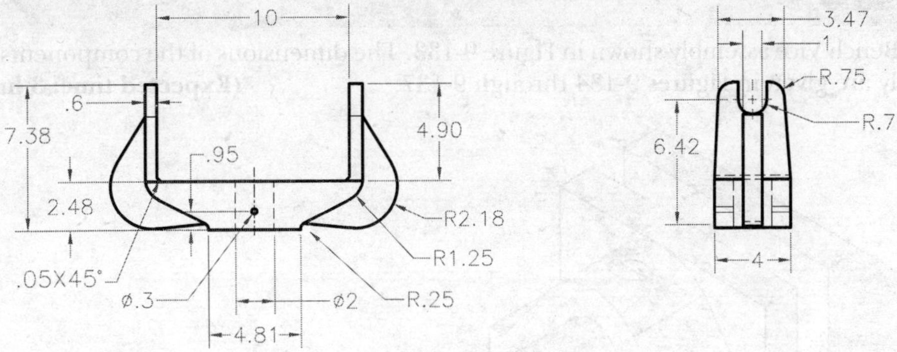

Figure 9-129 *Front and right-side views of the Support Roller Bracket*

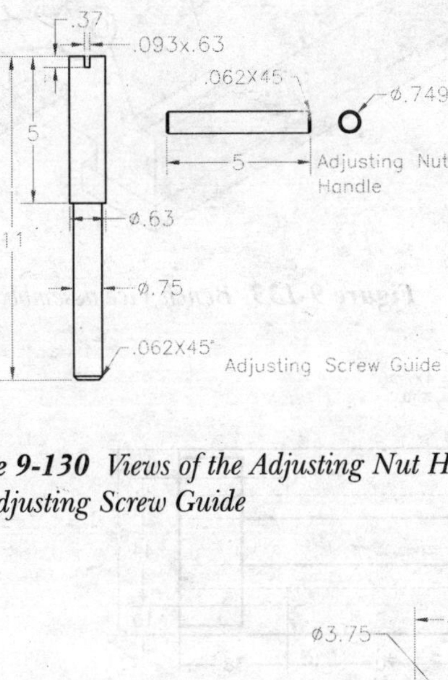

Figure 9-130 *Views of the Adjusting Nut Handle and Adjusting Screw Guide*

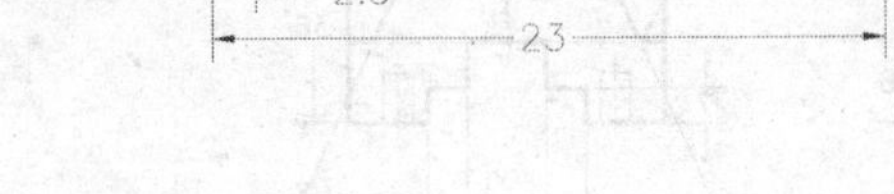

Figure 9-131 *Views of the Support Adjusting Screw*

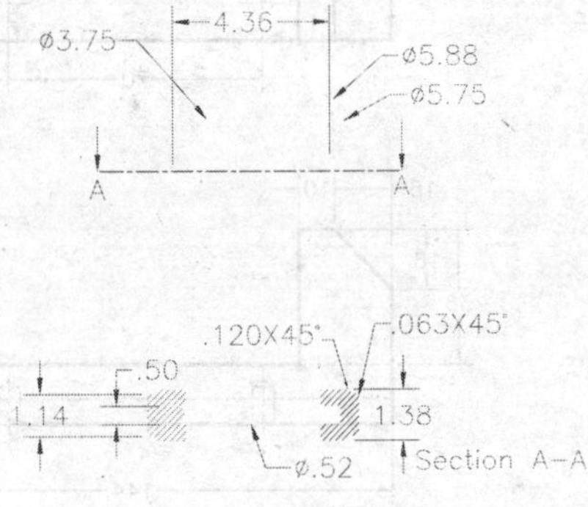

Figure 9-132 *Top and front views of the Thrust Bearing*

Exercise 4

Create the Bench Vice assembly shown in Figure 9-133. The dimensions of the components of the assembly are given in Figures 9-134 through 9-137. **(Expected time: 3 hrs)**

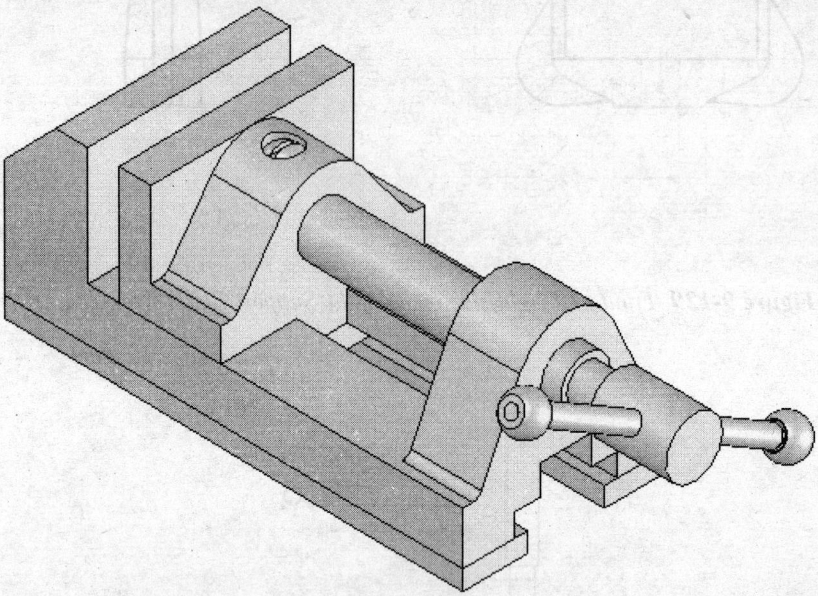

Figure 9-133 *Bench Vice assembly*

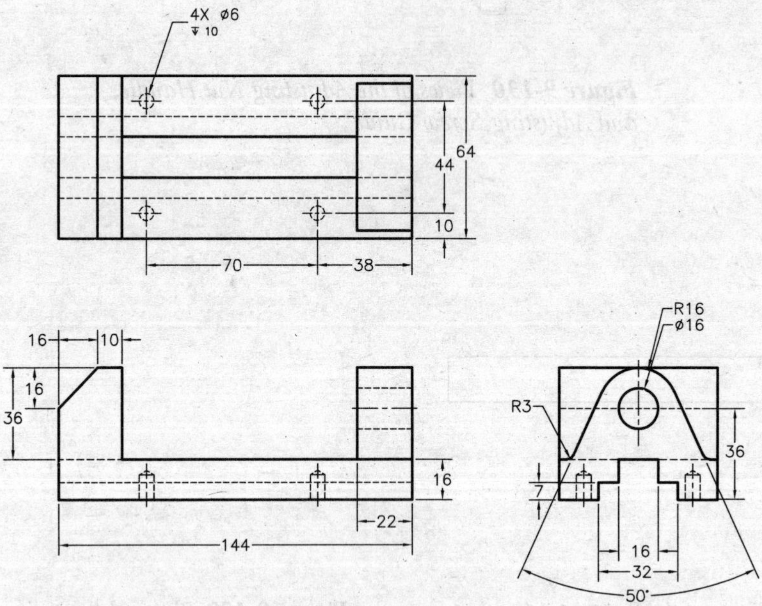

Figure 9-134 *Views and dimensions of the Vice Body*

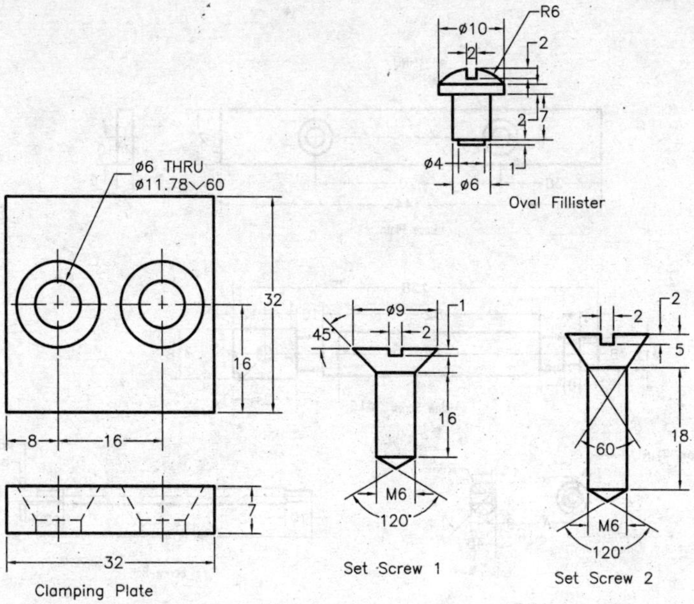

***Figure 9-135** Views and dimensions of the Clamping Plate, Oval Fillister, Set Screw 1, and Set Screw 2*

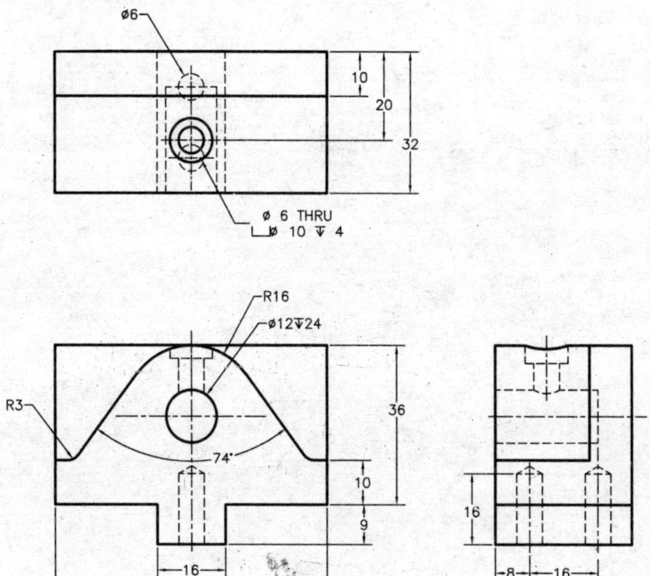

***Figure 9-136** Views and dimensions of the Vice Jaw*

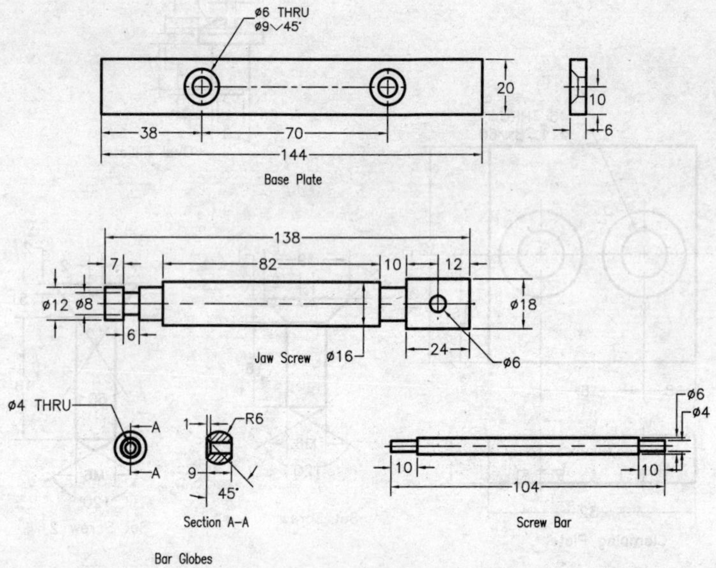

Figure 9-137 *Views and dimensions of Base Plate, Jaw Screw, Screw Bar, and Bar Globes*

Answers to Self-Evaluation Test

1. T, **2.** F, **3.** F, **4.** T, **5.** T, **6.** F, **7.** **.prt*, **8. Distance**, **9. Move Component**, **10. Concentric**

Chapter 10

Assembly Modeling-II

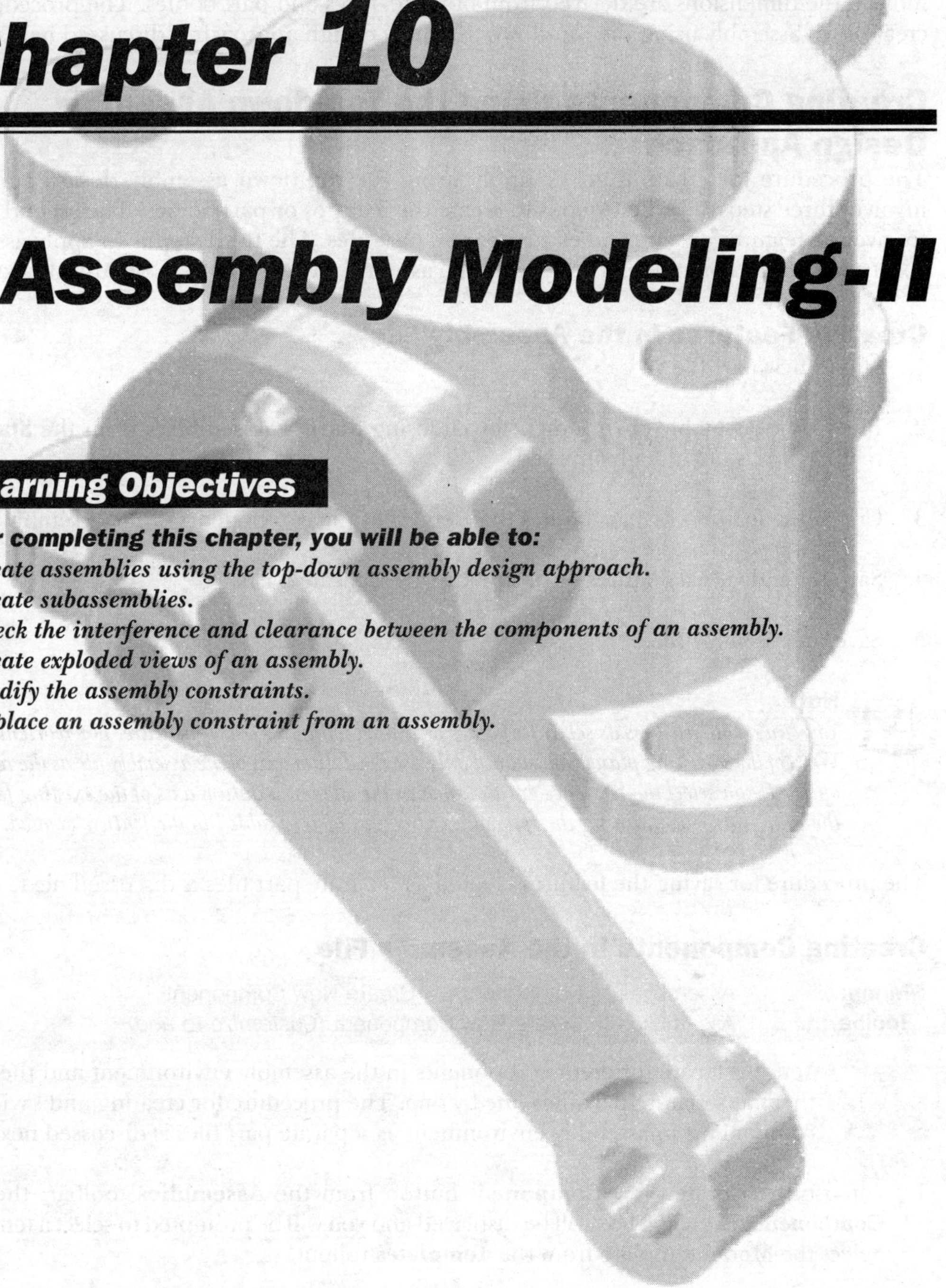

Learning Objectives

After completing this chapter, you will be able to:

- *Create assemblies using the top-down assembly design approach.*
- *Create subassemblies.*
- *Check the interference and clearance between the components of an assembly.*
- *Create exploded views of an assembly.*
- *Modify the assembly constraints.*
- *Replace an assembly constraint from an assembly.*

THE TOP-DOWN ASSEMBLY DESIGN APPROACH

As discussed in the previous chapter, you can also create all the components of the assembly in the same file as separate bodies or features and then save them as separate parts. This approach of creating an assembly is known as the top-down assembly design approach. In this approach, most of the dimensions are derived from other features and part bodies. The procedure for creating an assembly using the top-down assembly design approach is discussed next.

Creating Components Using the Top-down Assembly Design Approach

The procedure for creating an assembly using the top-down assembly design approach involves three steps. The first step is to create the features or part bodies. The second step is to save the features or part bodies as separate part files. The third step is to apply assembly constraints to the components and create the assembly. These steps are discussed next.

Creating Features in the Assembly File

1. Start a new part file.
2. Invoke the Assembly environment by choosing **Start > Assemblies** from the **Standard** toolbar, if it is not already invoked.
3. Create the features or part bodies that represent the components of the assembly.
4. Save the individual features or part bodies as separate parts.
5. Save the assembly file.

Note

You can create features as separate bodies or united with an existing feature. For reorienting the WCS of the sketching plane, you should only use the datum axis of the assembly file as the reference entity. If you select the reference entities such as the edge or a datum axis of the existing features, then the feature containing the reference entity will also be added to the feature created.

The procedure for saving the features created as separate part files is discussed next.

Creating Components in the Assembly File

Menu:	Assemblies > Components > Create New Component
Toolbar:	Assemblies > Create New Component *(Customize to add)*

You can create different components in the assembly environment and then save them as separate part files one by one. The procedure for creating and saving the components in assembly environment as separate part files is discussed next.

1. Choose the **Create New Component** button from the **Assemblies** toolbar; the **New Component File** dialog box will be displayed and you will be prompted to select a template. Select the **Model** template from the **Templates** rollout.

2. Specify the name and location of the file in the **New File Name** rollout of the **New Component File** dialog box.

3. Choose the **OK** button from the dialog box; the **Create New Component** dialog box will be displayed, as shown in Figure 10-1.

   By default, the file name that is specified in step 2 in the **New Component File** dialog box will be displayed in the **Component Name** text box of the **Settings** rollout.

***Figure 10-1** The **Create New Component** dialog box*

4. By default, the **Select Object** button is chosen in the **Create New Component** dialog box and you will be prompted to select objects for the new component. If you have created any object, you can select it to include in the new part file. Else, you can create an empty part file.

   Also, the **Add Defining Objects** check box is selected by default in the **Create New Component** dialog box. As a result, the defined objects such as datum planes, axes, or points of the selected object will be included in the new part file. To exclude the defined objects from the new part file, clear the **Add Defining Objects** check box.

5. Now, you need to specify the required settings in the **Settings** rollout. Select the required reference set from the **Reference Set** drop-down list in the **Settings** rollout.

   Next, in the **Component Origin** drop-down list, the **WCS** option is selected by default. As a result, the absolute coordinate system will be oriented exactly as the coordinate system of the displayed part. If you select the **Absolute** option from the **Component Origin** drop-down list, the absolute coordinate system will be oriented exactly as the coordinate system of the work part.

   In the **Settings** rollout, the **Delete Original Objects** check box is selected by default. As a result, the selected body will be saved as a new part file at the specified location, but it will be deleted from its original location. If you clear this check box, the selected body will be saved as a new part file at the specified location without being deleted from the original location in the part assembly.

6. After setting the required options in the **Create New Component** dialog box, choose the **OK** button; the name and node of the newly created part file will be displayed in the **Assembly Navigator** cascading menu below the parent assembly file node.

7. If you double-click on the name of the newly created part file in the **Assembly Navigator** cascading menu, the part will get activated, and the other parts as well as the parent assembly will get deactivated. You can modify the created part as per your requirement.

8. To activate the parent assembly, double-click on the name of the parent assembly in the **Assembly Navigator** cascading menu.

To create the remaining parts of the parent assembly, you need to follow the same procedure as mentioned above.

9. After creating all the parts of the assembly in the assembly file, choose the **Save** button; all parts will be saved as separate part files at the specified location.

Applying Assembly Constraints

After creating different parts in the Assembly file using the Top-down Assembly design approach and then saving them as separate part files, you need to apply the assembly constraints to the components by using the **Assembly Constraints** tool for making fully constrained assembly.

CREATING SUBASSEMBLIES

In the previous chapter, you learned to place components in the assembly file and apply assembly constraints to components. In this chapter, you will learn to create subassemblies and insert them in the main assembly.

Subassemblies are created in the assembly file of the Assembly environment of NX. After placing and assembling the components to be included in the subassembly, you need to save it. Open the master assembly file to place the instances of the subassembly and choose the **Add Component** button from the **Assemblies** toolbar; the **Add Component** dialog box will be displayed. Choose the **Open** button from this dialog box. Double-click on the subassembly file that is displayed in the **Part Name** dialog box. Place the instance of the subassembly and apply the assembly constraints using the **Assembly Constraints** dialog box. Figure 10-2 shows the subassembly of the Articulated Rod and Piston. Figure 10-3 shows the subassembly of the Master Rod and Piston. Figure 10-4 shows the main assembly that is created using the subassembly concept.

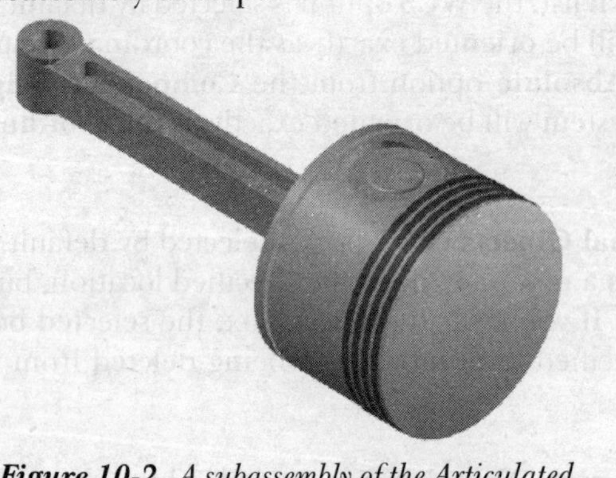

***Figure 10-2** A subassembly of the Articulated Rod and Piston*

***Figure 10-3** A subassembly of the Master Rod and Piston*

EDITING ASSEMBLY CONSTRAINTS

Generally, after creating the assembly or during the process of assembling the components, you need to edit the assembly constraints. The editing operations that can be performed on an assembly are:

Figure 10-4 Main assembly created

1. Modifying the angle and distance offset values.
2. Adding constraints to a partially constrained component.
3. Replacing an assembly constraint.

These editing operations are discussed next.

Modifying the Assembly Constraints

Whenever a constraint is applied to a component, the symbol of the applied constraint is displayed in blue color on the component in the graphics window. If you double-click on this symbol, the parameters of the constraint will be displayed in the **Assembly Constraints** dialog box. You can use this dialog box to redefine the parameters and modify the values of assembly constraints as well as to replace the applied constraint using the **Type** drop-down list. Alternatively, click on the plus (+) sign left to the **Constraints** node in the **Assembly Navigator** cascading menu; names of all constraints applied to the component will be displayed under the **Constraints** node. If you right-click on any of the applied constraints, a shortcut menu will be displayed. Choose the **Redefine** option from the shortcut menu; the parameters of the respective constraint will be displayed in the **Assembly Constraints** dialog box. Now, you can modify the parameters or replace the constraint as per your requirement.

Tip. *If you have an assembly created in NX5 or version earlier to it, then to modify the assembly constraints applied to that assembly using the* ***Assembly Constraints*** *tool, you need to convert the constraints from mating conditions to assembly constraints. To do so, invoke the* ***Assembly Constraints*** *tool from the* ***Assemblies*** *toolbar; the* ***Assembly Constraints*** *message box will be displayed. Choose the* ***Convert Mating Conditions*** *button from the message box; the* ***Convert Mating Conditions*** *dialog box will be displayed. Select the* ***Work Part and All Children*** *radio button from this dialog box and also make sure that all check boxes in the* ***Settings*** *rollout are selected. Next, choose* ***OK*** *from the* ***Convert Mating Conditions*** *dialog box; the* ***Constraint Conversion*** *message box along with the* ***Information*** *window will be displayed. Now, choose* ***OK*** *from the* ***Constraint Conversion*** *message box and close the* ***Information*** *window; all applied constraints will be updated and the* ***Assembly Constraints*** *dialog box will be displayed. You can now modify the constraints according to your requirements in this dialog box.*

CHECKING THE INTERFERENCE BETWEEN THE COMPONENTS OF AN ASSEMBLY

During the process of creating an assembly, the assembly constraints are applied between the components by selecting the corresponding reference object. In any assembly, the surface contact made between the mating components are equally important. In NX, you have the provision for checking the interferences between the components in an assembly. Checking for interference between the components is essential before sending the components for manufacturing. The interference can be checked using the **Check Clearances** tool. In NX, there are three methods to check interference: the check clearance analysis, the assembly clearance method and the view section.

Checking Interference and Clearance Using the Check Clearance Analysis

Menu:	Assemblies > Components > Check Clearances
Toolbar:	Assemblies > Check Clearances

In this method, instead of checking clearances for the whole assembly, you can just check clearances for the selected components of the assembly. It is recommended to use this method to check clearances of only the crucial components of a large assembly, so that you can save time and concentrate more on the crucial components. To perform the check clearance analysis, choose the **Check Clearances** button from the **Assemblies** toolbar; the **Class Selection** dialog box will be displayed and you will be prompted to select components. Select the components one by one or the whole assembly by the rectangle selection method and then choose the **OK** button. If there is clearance fit between the components, you will be informed in the **Clearance Analysis Information** window that no interferences were found, as shown in Figure 10-5.

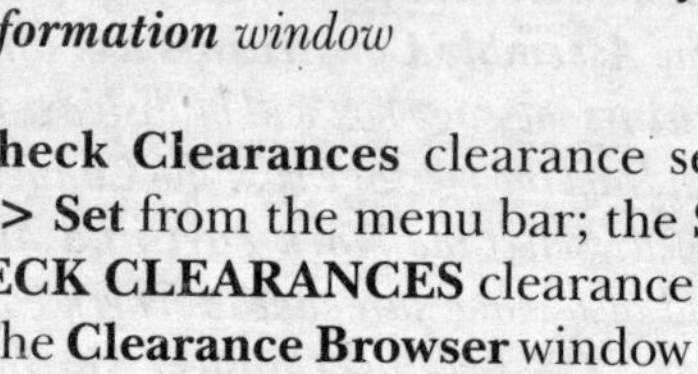

***Figure 10-5** The **Clearance Analysis Information** window*

To make changes in the **Check Clearances** clearance set, select **Analysis > Assembly Clearance > Clearance Set > Set** from the menu bar; the **Set Clearance Set** dialog box will be displayed. Select the **CHECK CLEARANCES** clearance set name listed in the dialog box and choose the **OK** button. The **Clearance Browser** window will be displayed. Double-click on the **Clearance Set** node of the **Clearance Browser** window; the **Clearance Properties** dialog box will be displayed. The procedure for setting the parameters in the **Clearance Properties** dialog box will be discussed later in this chapter.

If the selected components interfere with the other components in the assembly, the **Interference Check** report window will be generated and displayed, as shown in Figure 10-6. The columns displayed in the **Interference Check** report window are discussed next.

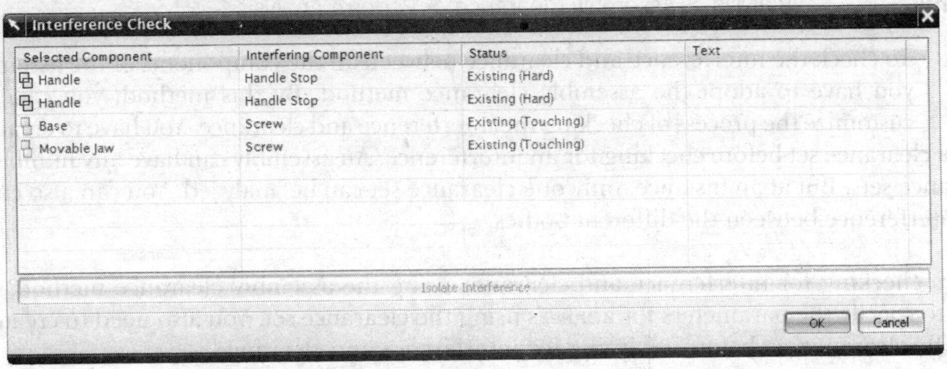

Figure 10-6 The ***Interference Check*** *report window*

Selected Component

The components selected for an interference check from the assembly are listed in the **Selected Component** column of the **Interference Check** report window.

Interfering Component

The components that interfere with the selected components are listed in the **Interfering Component** column of the **Interference Check** report window.

Status

The status column shows the type of interference between the interfering components. A hard result means that the interfering component is intersecting and occupying some of the space of the selected component. A touching result means that the interfering component does not intersect the selected component but both the components touch each other. A soft result means that the minimum distance between the interfering component and the selected component is less than or equal to the default clearance value in the **Default Clearance Zone** edit box of the **Clearance Properties** dialog box.

The interference detected after the last check is defined as **New** and the previously detected interferences are defined as **Existing**.

Note

You can also highlight a particular interference set. To do so, select the interference object from the ***Interference Check*** *report window and then choose the* ***Isolate Interference*** *button; the selected interference object will be displayed in the assembly and the rest of components will be hidden. To display the hidden components again in the drawing window, you need to select the hidden components from the* ***Assembly Navigator*** *and then right-click to display the shortcut menu. Next, choose the* ***Show*** *option from the shortcut menu.*

Checking Interference Using the Assembly Clearance Method

Menu: Analysis > Assembly Clearance > Perform Analysis

To check the interference and clearance between all the components of the assembly, you have to adopt the assembly clearance method. By this method, you can also customize the process of checking the interference and clearance. You have to create or load a clearance set before checking for an interference. An assembly can have any number of clearance sets. But at an instance, only one clearance set can be analyzed. You can also check the interference between the different bodies.

Before checking for interference and clearance using the assembly clearance method, you need to specify the parameters for analysis using the clearance set. You also need to create or load the clearance set before analyzing for interference and clearance.

Checking Interference by Loading the Clearance Set

After creating the assembly, you have to load the clearance set before proceeding to the analysis part. Choose **Analysis > Assembly Clearance > Clearance Set > Set** from the menu bar; the **Set Clearance Set** dialog box will be displayed, refer to Figure 10-7.

All the previously created clearance sets are listed in the list box. Select the clearance set name to be loaded and choose the **OK** button; the **Clearance Browser** window will be displayed with results, as shown in Figure 10-8. The results are based on the parameters defined in the clearance set.

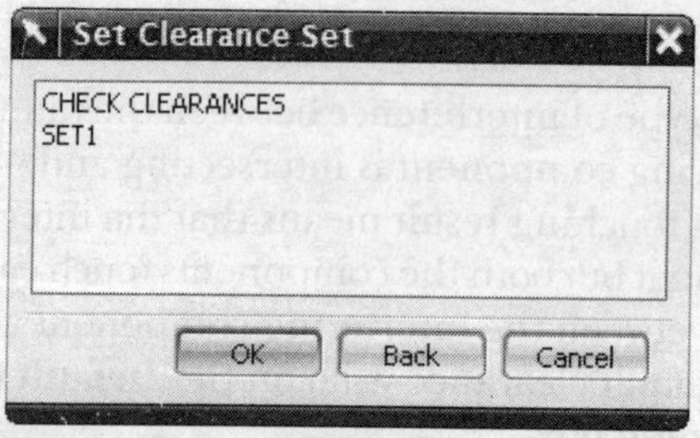

*Figure 10-7 The **Set Clearance Set** dialog box*

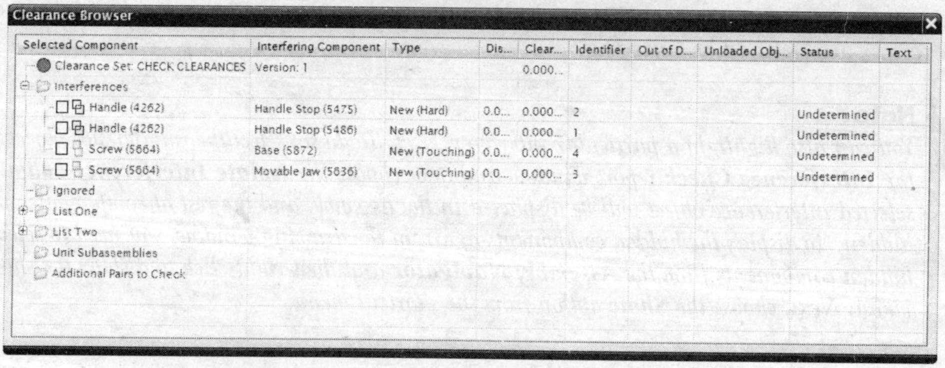

*Figure 10-8 The **Clearance Browser** window*

Note

You can reorder the components listed in the columns by their names in an alphabetical or reverse alphabetical order by clicking on the respective column.

Selected Component

The **Selected Component** column of the **Clearance Browser** window consists of the names of the components that are treated as the first object in the pair used for checking the interference or clearance.

Interfering Component

The **Interfering Component** column consists of the names of the components that are treated as the second object in the pair used for checking the interference or clearance.

Type

The **Type** column lists the result and the type of interference between the components.

Distance

In the **Distance** column, the distance between two object pairs is given in millimeters. The **Clearance** column displays the clearance value given in the **Default Clearance Zone** edit box of the **Clearance Properties** dialog box.

Note

The name of the clearance set loaded for analysis is displayed in the ***Clearance Set*** *node of the* ***Clearance Browser*** *window. To make any changes in the parameters defined in the* ***Clearance Set****, double-click on the* ***Clearance Set*** *node from the* ***Clearance Browser*** *window; the* ***Clearance Properties*** *dialog box will be displayed. Make the required changes and choose the* ***Apply*** *button and then the* ***OK*** *button to reflect the changes. After updating the parameters in the* ***Clearance Properties*** *dialog box, run the analysis once more to update the result. For updating the result, right-click on the* ***Clearance Set*** *node in the* ***Clearance Browser*** *window and choose the* ***Perform Analysis*** *option from the shortcut menu. The result will be updated for the modified clearance set.*

To isolate an interference detected in the analysis, double-click on the interference result in the ***Type*** *column; the interference will be isolated in the graphics window and the interference area will be marked with the interference color specified in the clearance set. Again, to retain whole assembly, right-click on the isolated interference result in the* ***Clearance Browser*** *window and then choose the* ***Restore Component Visibility*** *option from the shortcut menu.*

Ignored Folder

The interference result in the **Ignored** folder is ignored for the consecutive analysis. You can dynamically move the interference result by selecting and dragging it to the **Ignored** folder. To include the ignored interference result in the consecutive analysis, select the ignored interference result from the **Ignored** folder of the **Clearance Browser** window and right-click on it. Choose the **Reanalyze** option from the shortcut menu; the interference result will be added for the analysis.

Saving the Report Generated

The generated interference report can be saved as a *.txt* file. To save it, right-click on the **Clearance Set** node from the **Clearance Browser** window and choose the **Save Report** option from the shortcut menu. The **Report File** dialog box will be displayed and you will be prompted to specify the report file for the clearance analysis. Specify the directory and enter the file name in the **File Name** edit box to save the report. Choose the **OK** button; the report will be saved in the specified directory as a *.txt* file.

Deleting a Clearance Set

To delete a clearance set, right-click on the **Clearance Set** node from the **Clearance Browser** window. Choose **Clearance Set > Delete** from the shortcut menu; the **Delete Clearance Set** window will be displayed, as shown in Figure 10-9, and you will be informed that this result will delete the clearance set and you will be prompted to specify if you want to continue. Choose the **Yes** button to delete the current clearance set.

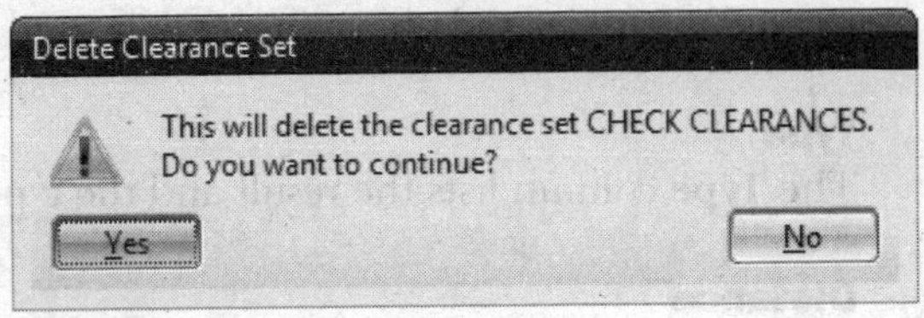

***Figure 10-9** The **Delete Clearance Set** window*

Checking for Interference by Creating a New Clearance Set

After creating the assembly, choose **Analysis > Assembly Clearance > Clearance Set > New** from the menu bar; the **Clearance Properties** dialog box will be displayed, as shown in Figure 10-10. The options in this dialog box are discussed next.

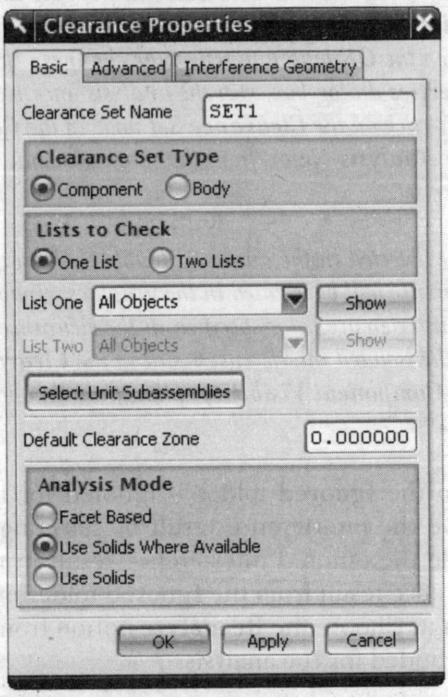

***Figure 10-10** The **Clearance Properties** dialog box*

Basic Tab

This tab is chosen by default. In this tab, you can enter the name for the clearance set in the **Clearance Set Name** edit box. If you select the **Component** radio button from the **Clearance Set Type** area, the components will be included for the interference check. If you select the **Body** radio button from this area, the separate bodies of the components will be selected for the clearance check.

To check the interference between the components in the same assembly, select the **One List** radio button from the **Lists to Check** area. For an interference check between a user-defined set of components within the assembly, select the **Two Lists** radio button from the **Lists to Check** area.

Note

*If you select the **One List** radio button from the **Lists to Check** area, only the **List One** drop-down list and the corresponding **Show** button will be enabled. On selecting the **Two Lists** radio button from this area, both the **List One** and **List Two** drop-down lists and their corresponding **Show** buttons will be enabled. After selecting the required option from the **List One** and **List Two** drop-down lists, you can add the components of the assembly in the aforesaid lists using the **Edit** button. The **Edit** button will be enabled if you select the **All But Selected Objects** or **Class Selection** option from the **List One** and **List Two** drop-down lists. The **Show** button will be available for verifying the selected components.*

You can also check for the existence of the clearance value between the mating components using this dialog box. To do so, enter the reference clearance value to be maintained in the **Default Clearance Zone** edit box. If the clearance value detected is less than or equal to the reference clearance value given in the **Default Clearance Zone** edit box, **Soft** will be displayed in the **Type** column of the **Clearance Browser** window.

Advanced Tab

While analyzing some assemblies, you may need to ignore certain component pairs. In NX, options are available to categorize the component pairs that have to be ignored. These options are available in the **Explicitly Ignored** area of the **Advanced** tab in the **Clearance Properties** dialog box. By selecting the respective check boxes, you can ignore the component pairs under a specified category. For example, if you select the **Mated Pairs** check box from the **Explicitly Ignored** area, the components assembled using the mating conditions will be ignored during analysis.

To add some of the components manually from the assembly under the **Ignored** category, choose the **Ignored Pairs** button from the **Ignored** area of the **Advanced** tab; the **Select Objects** dialog box will be displayed and you will be prompted to select the clearance analysis objects. Select the pairs to be ignored and choose the **OK** button; the **Ignored Pairs** dialog box will be displayed and you will be prompted to enter the reason for exclusion of the pairs. Enter the reason in the **Reason** edit box of **Ignored Pairs** dialog box and choose **OK**; the **Clearance Properties** dialog box will be displayed again.

Note

*You need to select at least two components to ignore them. Otherwise, the **Bad Selection** error message window will be displayed, informing you that you must select more than one object.*

If you have selected the **Mated Pairs** check box from the **Explicitly Ignored** area of the **Advanced** tab, all component pairs in the assembly will be ignored. To add the additional pairs to the analysis, choose the **Additional Pairs** button from the **Additional** area of the **Advanced** tab; the **Select Objects** dialog box will be displayed and you will be prompted to select the clearance analysis objects. Select the components to be added and choose the **OK** button; the **Additional Pairs** dialog box will be displayed and you will be prompted to enter the reason for inclusion of components. Enter the reason in the **Reason** edit box of the **Additional Pairs** dialog box and choose **OK**; the **Clearance Properties** dialog box will be displayed again.

You can assign any clearance value other than the specified general clearance value to a component pair in the **Default Clearance Zone** edit box of the **Clearance Properties** dialog box. To do so, choose the **Pair Zones** button from the **Clearance Zones** area; the **Pair Clearance Zones** dialog box will be displayed, as shown in Figure 10-11. Also, you will be prompted to select a pair clearance zone operation. Enter the new clearance value in the **Current Zone** edit box and choose the **Assign To Pairs** button from the **Pair Clearance Zones** dialog box; the **Select Objects** dialog box will be displayed and you will be prompted to select the clearance analysis objects. Select the component pairs from the assembly and choose the **OK** button twice.

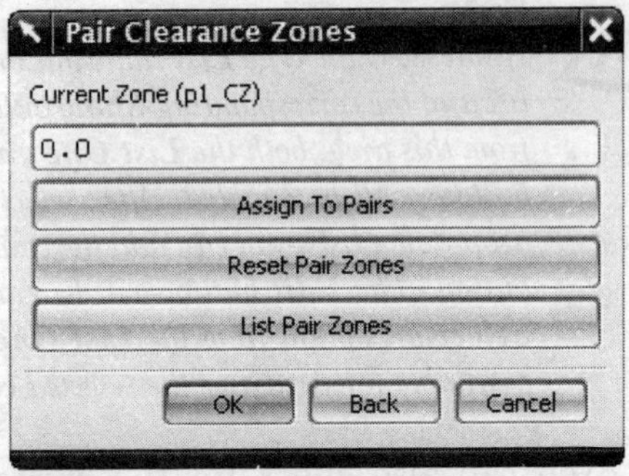

*Figure 10-11 The **Pair Clearance Zones** dialog box*

Note

*To list information about the clearance value defined between the components, choose the **List Pair Zones** button from the **Pair Clearance Zones** dialog box. The details of the clearance value defined between the components in the assembly will be displayed in the **Information** window.*

To define the clearance value for one or more objects, choose the **Object Zones** button from the **Clearance Zones** area; the **Object Clearance Zones** dialog box will be displayed. Enter the clearance value in the **Current Zone** edit box and then choose the **Assign To Objects** button from this dialog box; the **Select Objects** dialog box will be displayed and you will be prompted to select the clearance analysis objects. Select the objects from the assembly and choose the **OK** button; the **Object Clearance Zones** dialog box will be displayed again.

Note

*You can select one or more objects using the **Object Zones** button, whereas while using the **Pair Zones** button, it is mandatory to select a pair of objects from the assembly.*

Interference Geometry Tab

You can change the color used to highlight the interference between the selected components in an assembly by choosing the **Interference Color** swatch from the **Interference Geometry** tab of the **Clearance Properties** dialog box.

Now you need to run the analysis for the parameters defined in the clearance set. After defining the parameters for the clearance set, choose the **OK** button from the **Clearance Properties** dialog box; the **Clearance Browser** window will be displayed without the analysis data, as shown in Figure 10-12. Right-click on the **Clearance Set** node and choose the **Perform Analysis** option from the shortcut menu displayed; the results will be generated in the **Clearance Browser** window, as shown in Figure 10-13.

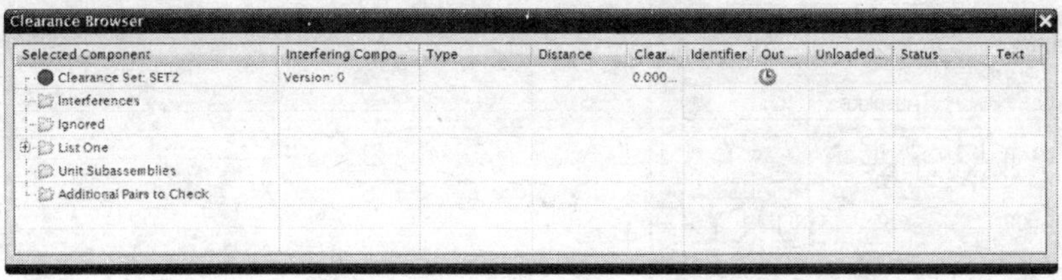

***Figure 10-12** The empty **Clearance Browser** window*

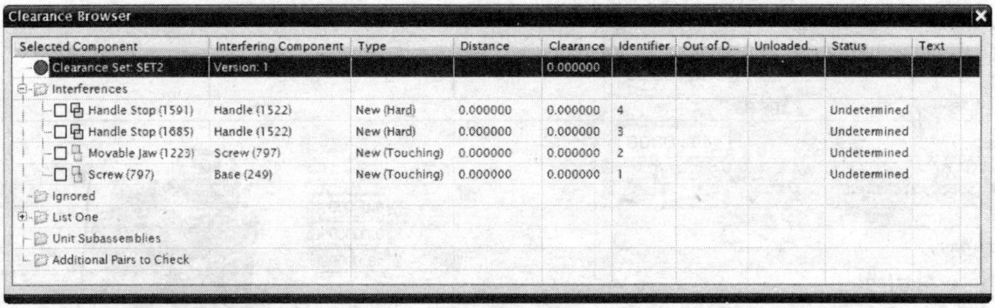

***Figure 10-13** The **Clearance Browser** window after performing analysis*

Checking Interference and Clearance, and Analyzing Cross-sections of Components Using the View Section Tool

Menu: View > Operation > Edit Work Section
Toolbar: View > Edit Work Section

You can check the interference and clearance between the components using the **View Section** dialog box. Using the options in this dialog box, you can dynamically view the cross-sections, interferences, and clearances as well as create section views of components. Moreover, you can use this dialog box to create datum planes. To invoke this dialog box, choose the **Edit Work Section** button from the **View** toolbar; the **View Section** dialog box will be displayed, refer to Figure 10-14. Note that as soon as you choose the **Edit Work Section** button from the **View** toolbar, the **Clip Work Section** button in the **View** toolbar will be activated and a cross-section of the model will be displayed in the graphics window, refer to Figure 10-15. If you choose the **Clip Work Section** button, the cross-section will be turned off and the complete model will become visible. Various options in the **View Section** dialog box are discussed next.

Type Rollout

In this rollout, the **One Plane** option is selected by default. As a result, a single plane along

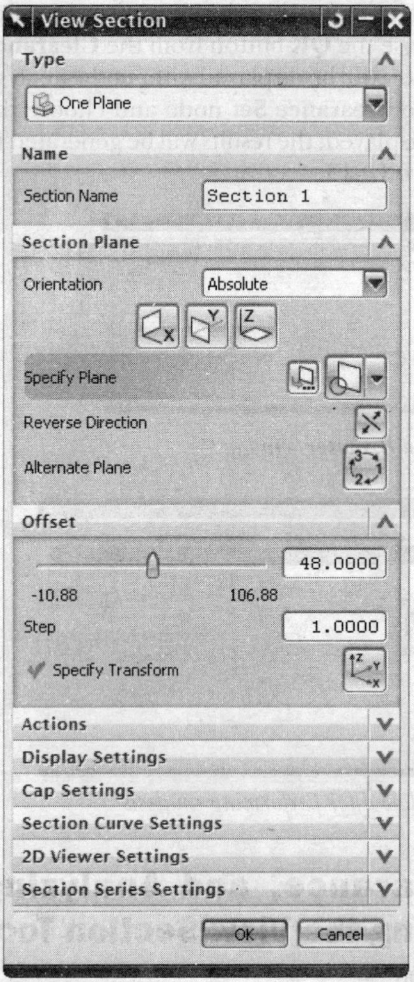

*Figure 10-14 The **View Section** dialog box*

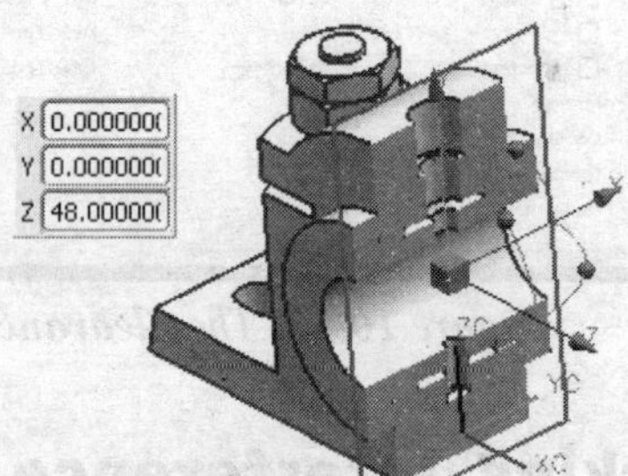

Figure 10-15 The cross-section of the assembly

with the triad of dynamic handles will be displayed in the graphics window that enables you to analyze the cross-section of the component. If you drag any of these handles, the plane of cross-section moves accordingly. If you drag any of the angular handles, the plane of cross-section will orient along with the movement of cursor.

If you select the **Two Parallel Planes** option from the **Type** rollout, two parallel planes will be displayed in the graphics window to analyze the cross-section of the component. Also, a triad of dynamic handles will be displayed only on the activated plane. Note that out of the two planes, only one plane will be activated at a time. To activate the other plane, select the plane from the graphics window; the selected plane will be activated. Now, you can move this plane to view the cross-sections of various parts at different locations.

If you select the **Box** option from the **Type** rollout, a box of planes will be displayed in the graphics window to analyze the cross-section of the component, and a triad of dynamic handles will be displayed only on the activated plane. Out of all the planes, only one plane will be active at a time. To activate the other plane, move the cursor over an edge of the box; the respective plane will be highlighted. Select the highlighted plane from the graphics window; the selected plane will be activated. Now, you can move this plane to view the cross-sections of various parts at different locations.

Name Rollout

In this rollout, **Section 1** is displayed by default in the **Section Name** edit box. You can use this edit box to specify a user-defined name for the section to be created. Choose **OK** from the **View Section** dialog box or choose the **New Section** button from the **View** toolbar; the user-defined section view will be created under the **Sections** node in the **Assembly Navigator** cascading menu. You can double-click on this section view in the **Sections** node to display it in the graphics window.

Section Plane Rollout

This rollout is used to set the location and orientation of the selected plane. You can specify the orientation reference of the section plane by selecting the desired option from the **Orientation** drop-down list. After selecting the orientation reference, you can orient the section plane along the X, Y, or Z direction by choosing the **Set Plane To X**, **Set Plane To Y**, or **Set Plane To Z** button, respectively. These buttons are available below the **Orientation** drop-down list in the **Section Plane** rollout. Using the options in the **Specify Plane** area of this rollout, you can specify the user-defined section plane.

You can flip the direction of the active plane by using the **Reverse Direction** button. You can also cycle through the X, Y, or Z standard section planes by choosing the **Alternate Plane** button.

Offset Rollout

In this rollout, you can specify the offset distance of the active plane from its initial position using the slider bar or the edit box given on the right of the slider bar. The **Step** edit box in this rollout is used to specify the increment value by which the section plane will move while dragging it using handles. You can also specify the position of the dynamic triad by choosing the **Point Dialog** button from the **Offset** rollout.

Actions Rollout

You can create a datum plane at the current location of the section plane by choosing the **Create Datum Plane** button from the **Actions** rollout.

Display Settings Rollout

In this rollout, the **Type** drop-down list will be available only when the **One Plane** option is selected from the **Type** rollout. By default, the **Section** option is selected in the **Type** drop-down list. As a result, the cross-section of the selected part will be displayed in the graphics window, refer to Figure 10-15. If you select the **Slice** option from the **Type** drop-down list, only the cross-section of the part will be displayed, as shown in Figure 10-16.

The **Show Manipulator** check box in this rollout is selected by default. As a result, the triad of dynamic handles is displayed in the graphics window. If you clear this check box, the triad of dynamic handles will not be visible. If the triad of dynamic handles is out of the drawing window, you can bring the triad in the graphics window by choosing the **Move Manipulator in View** button from this rollout. This option is very useful while handling large assemblies.

If you choose the **Orient View to Plane** button, the section view will be oriented parallel to the screen. By default, the **Show Grid** check box in this rollout is cleared. As a result, the grid lines will not be displayed in the section plane. Select this check box, if you want the grid lines to be displayed in the section plane, as shown in Figure 10-17. The **Edit Grid Setting** button from this rollout is used to specify the grid setting. On choosing this button, the **Plain Grid** dialog box will be displayed. You can use this dialog box to change the grid settings.

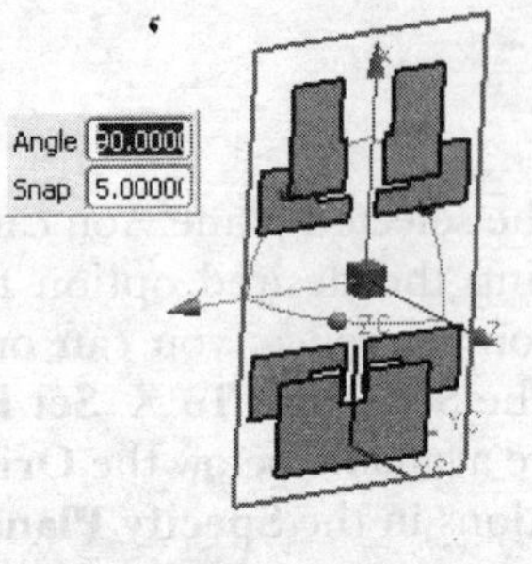

Figure 10-16 Cross-section of a part

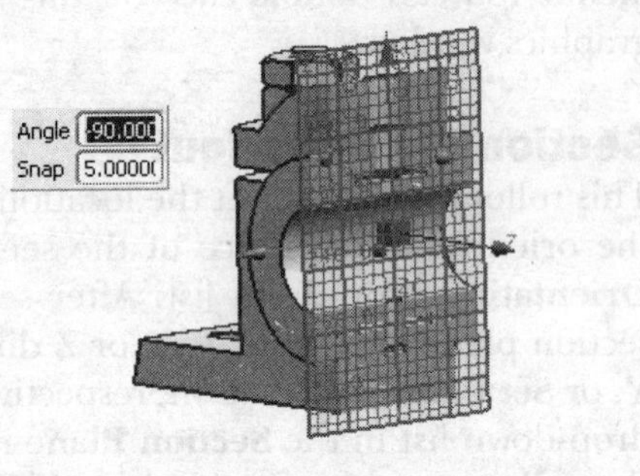

Figure 10-17 Cross-section with grid lines

Cap Settings Rollout

In this rollout, the **Show Cap** check box is selected by default. As a result, you can view the cross-section of a component in different colors. If you clear this check box, the remaining options in this rollout will not be available and the cross-sectional surface will become transparent, as shown in Figure 10-18. The **Color Option** drop-down list in this rollout is used to specify the color of the cross-section of the component. By default, the **Specify Color** option is selected in this drop-down list. As a result, the color of the cross-section of the component will be displayed in light green. You can also apply the user-defined colors to the cross-section. To do so, click on the **Cap Color** swatch from the **Cap Settings** rollout; the **Color** dialog box will be displayed. Select the required color from this dialog box and then choose **OK**; the selected color will be applied to the cross-section. If you select the **Body Color** option from the **Color Option** drop-down list, the cross-section of the component will be displayed in the same color as the color of the component. If you select the **Show Interference** check box, the interference of components in the assembly at the currently active cross-section will be highlighted in the default color specified in the **Interference Color** swatch in this rollout, as shown in Figure 10-19. You can change this default color to any user-defined color by selecting the desired color from the **Color** dialog box that will be displayed after clicking on the **Interference Color** swatch.

Section Curve Settings Rollout

If you select the **Show Section Curves Preview** check box from this rollout, the section curves of components will be highlighted in dark blue. You can also save the section curves that are highlighted in the graphics window. To do so, choose the **Save Copy of Section Curves** button from this rollout; the highlighted section curves will be saved at their respective places.

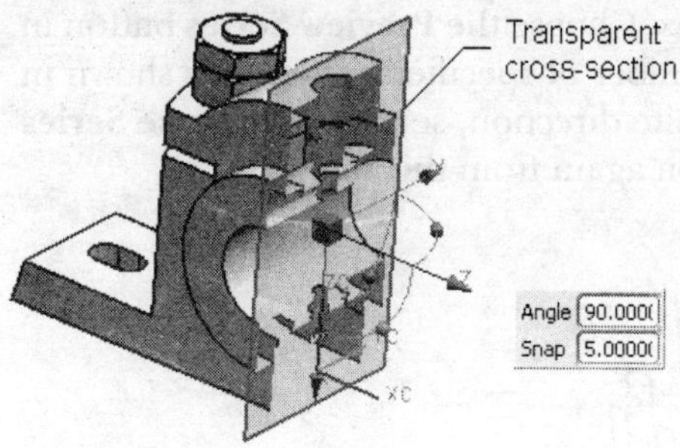

Figure 10-18 *Transparent cross-section*

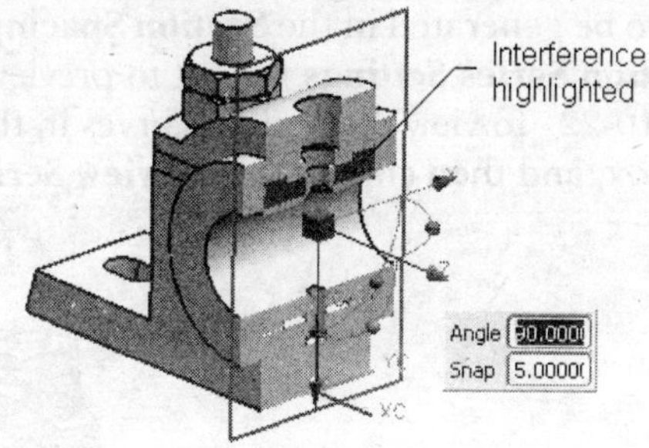

Figure 10-19 *Interference highlighted at the active cross-section in the assembly*

2D Viewer Settings Rollout

In this rollout, the **Show 2D Viewer** check box is clear by default. If you select this check box, the **2D Section Viewer** window will be displayed, as shown in Figure 10-20, and the **2D Viewer Settings** rollout will be modified, refer to Figure 10-21. In the **2D Section Viewer** window, you can see that the section curves of the active cross-section are displayed in 2D view. If you select the **Shaded Cap Preview in 2D View** check box from the **2D Viewer Settings** rollout, the cross-section as well as its color will be displayed in the window. You can rotate the cross-section in the **2D Section Viewer** window according to your requirement using the **Rotate Right**, **Rotate Left**, **Reflect X-Axis**, or **Reflect Y-Axis** button in the **2D Viewer Settings** rollout.

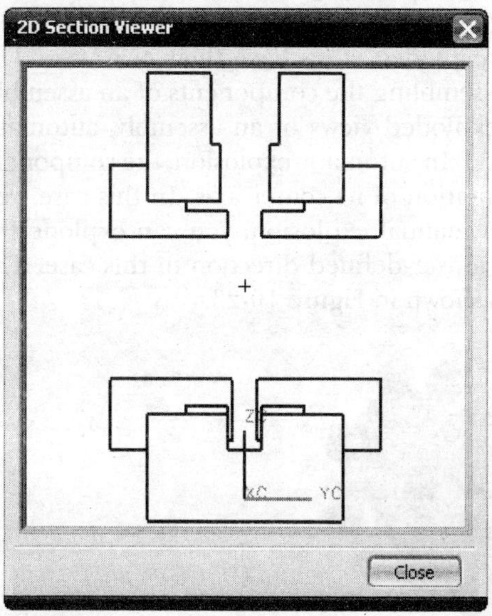

Figure 10-20 *The* **2D Section Viewer** *window*

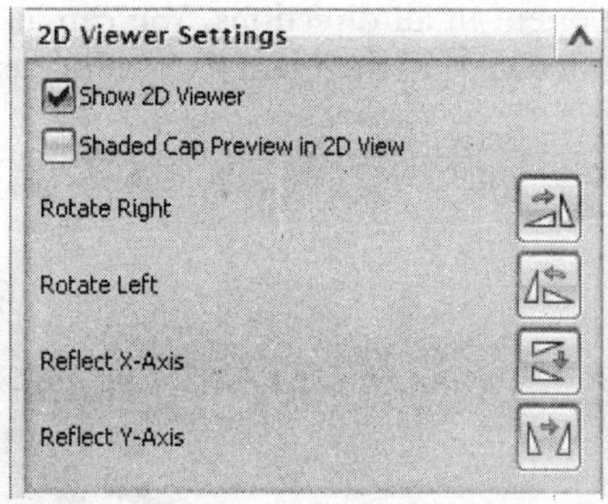

Figure 10-21 *The modified* **2D Viewer Settings** *rollout*

Section Series Settings Rollout

This rollout is used to view the number of section curves at different cross-sections. To view the section curves at different cross-sections, you can specify the number of sections in the

Number of Sections edit box. Additionally, you can specify the distance between the section planes to be generated in the **Section Spacing** edit box. Choose the **Preview Series** button in the **Section Series Settings** rollout to preview the number of specified sections, as shown in Figure 10-22. To view the section curves in the opposite direction, select the **Reverse Series** check box, and then choose the **Preview Series** button again from this rollout.

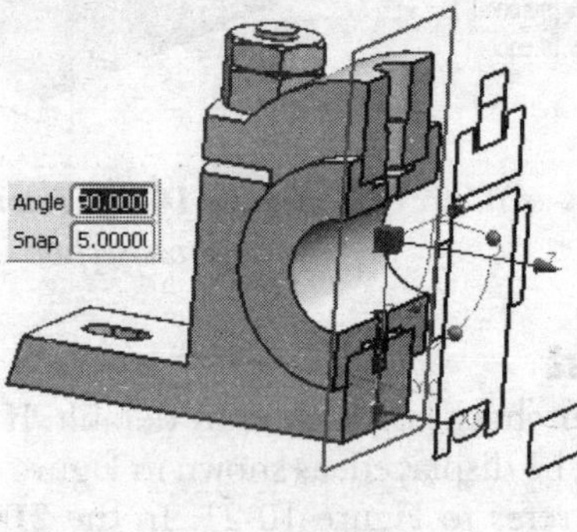

Figure 10-22 Multiple section curves displayed at different cross-sections

CREATING EXPLODED VIEWS OF AN ASSEMBLY

The exploded views of an assembly are created to expose the internal components of a complex assembly. The exploded views also provide a clear idea about the orientation of the components in an assembly. In a shop floor, the exploded views have their own uses. The assembly technicians use the exploded views for assembling the components of an assembly. In NX, you have two methods for creating the exploded views of an assembly, automatic explosion method and the manual explosion method. In automatic explosion, the component can only be exploded in the direction of the orientation of its center axis. In this case, you cannot specify the direction for the explosion. In manual explosion, you can explode the component in all directions. You can also specify a user-defined direction in this case. The exploded view of the Flange Coupling assembly is shown in Figure 10-23.

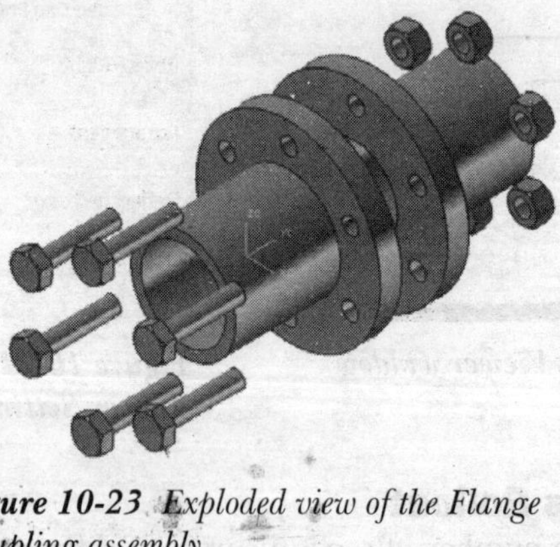

Figure 10-23 Exploded view of the Flange Coupling assembly

The **Exploded Views** toolbar provides the tools for creating and editing various types of exploded views. Before creating the exploded views, you need to invoke the **Exploded Views** toolbar. There are three methods for invoking the **Exploded Views** toolbar. The first method is to choose **Assemblies > Exploded Views > Show Toolbar** from the menu bar. Alternatively, you need to right-click on the toolbar area of the main window and choose the **Exploded Views** option from the shortcut menu. The third method is to choose the **Exploded Views** button from the **Assemblies** toolbar.

Exploding Views Automatically

In NX, you have to adopt two steps for creating the automatic exploded view. The first step comprises of creating the name for the exploded views. The second step is to explode the component automatically. The components selected for explosion are always exploded in the direction of the orientation of their own center axis.

Creating Names for Exploded Views

Menu:	Assemblies > Exploded Views > New Explosion
Toolbar:	Exploded Views > Create Explosion

The explosion name is created to identify the exploded state in the assembly. All explosion names are listed in the **Work View Explosion** drop-down list of the **Exploded Views** toolbar. The names created for exploded views are used to select the exploded view while editing. For creating the explosion name, choose the **Create Explosion** button from the **Exploded Views** toolbar; the **Create Explosion** dialog box will be displayed, as shown in Figure 10-24. By default, the name of the explosions will be displayed as **Explosion 1**, **Explosion 2**, **Explosion 3**, and so on. To change the name of the explosion state, enter a user-defined name for the explosion state in the **Name** edit box of the **Create Explosion** dialog box and then choose the **OK** button. The **Auto-explode Components** tool will be available in the **Exploded Views** toolbar. Now, you can create the automatic exploded view for the components by using this tool.

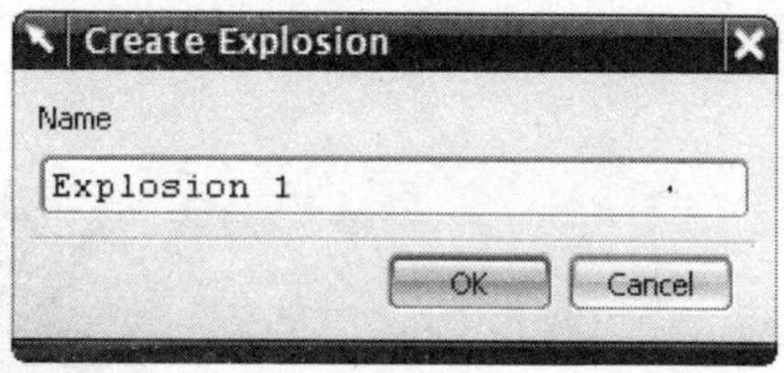

*Figure 10-24 The **Create Explosion** dialog box*

Creating Automatic Exploded Views

Menu:	Assemblies > Exploded Views > Auto-explode Components
Toolbar:	Exploded Views > Auto-explode Components

The **Auto-explode Components** tool is used to create the automatic exploded view for the components. Choose the **Auto-explode Components** button from the **Exploded Views** toolbar; the **Class Selection** dialog box will be displayed and you will be prompted to select the components. You can select components individually or a group of components from the assembly, as shown in Figure 10-25.

After selecting the components for exploding, choose the **OK** button from the **Class Selection** dialog box; the **Explosion Distance** dialog box will be displayed, as shown in Figure 10-26.

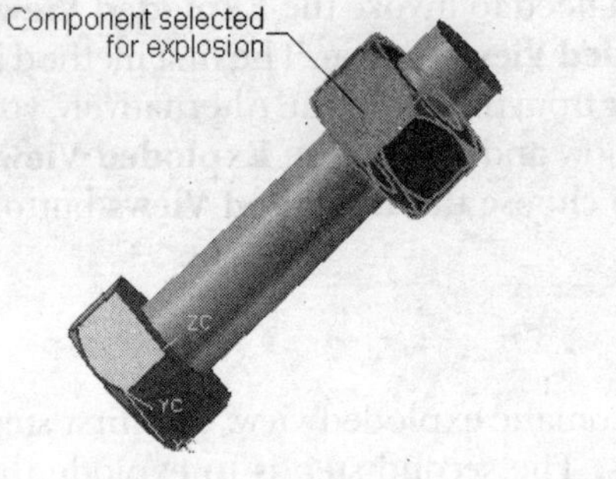

Figure 10-25 Component selected from an assembly for automatic explosion

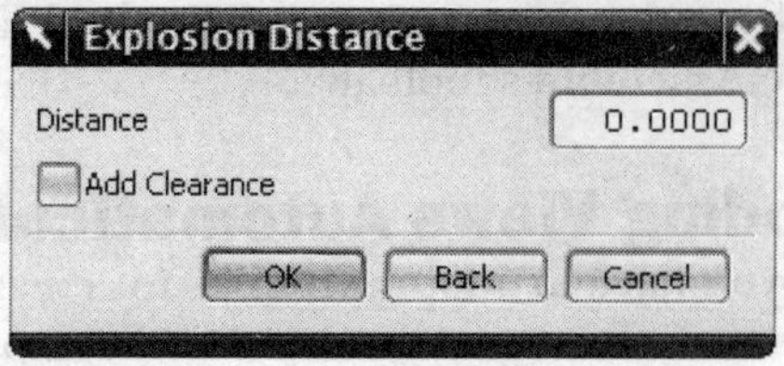

Figure 10-26 *The **Explosion Distance** dialog box*

Enter the explosion distance value in the **Distance** edit box. If you select the **Add Clearance** check box, a predefined clearance value will be added to the explosion distance. Choose the **OK** button from the same dialog box to create the automatic explosion of the selected component, as shown in Figure 10-27.

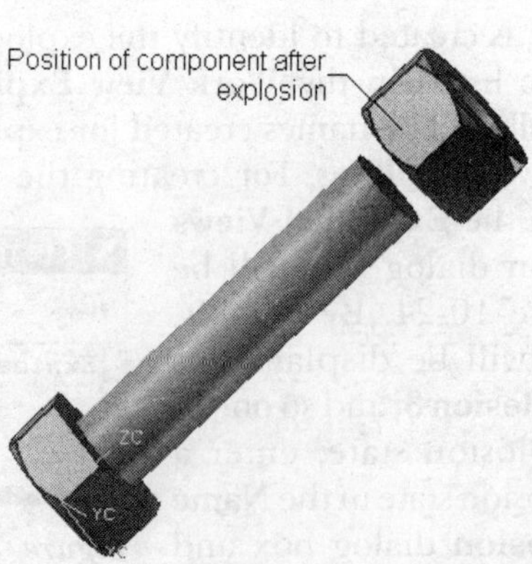

Figure 10-27 *Position of the component after explosion*

Note

*To edit the explosion distance after creating the automatic explosion, select the component and choose the **Auto-explode Components** button from the **Assemblies** toolbar; the **Explosion Distance** dialog box will be displayed with the previous explosion distance given in the **Distance** edit box. Enter the new explosion distance value in the **Distance** edit box and choose the **OK** button. You can enter both positive and negative values for the explosion distance. The component will be exploded in the positive or negative direction with respect to the assembly WCS.*

Exploding Views Manually

After creating the automatic exploded views using the **Auto-explode Components** tool, you may need to explode the component manually to get the desired results. The components can be manually exploded even when the assembly constraints are applied to them. In NX, you have to adopt two steps to create the exploded views manually. The procedure for creating the exploded views manually is discussed next.

Creating Exploded Views Manually

Menu:	Assemblies > Exploded Views > Edit Explosion
Toolbar:	Exploded Views > Edit Explosion

The **Edit Explosion** tool is used to create exploded views manually. You can explode the component in any direction. You can also explode only the handles of the component. Choose the **Edit Explosion** button from the **Exploded Views** toolbar; the **Edit Explosion** dialog box will be displayed, as shown in Figure 10-28.

By default, the **Select Objects** radio button will be selected from the **Edit Explosion** dialog box and you will be prompted to select the components. Select the components to be included in the exploded view and then select the **Move Objects** radio button; the selected component will be displayed, as shown in Figure 10-29. Select the direction of explosion for the selected component by clicking on the appropriate translation handle.

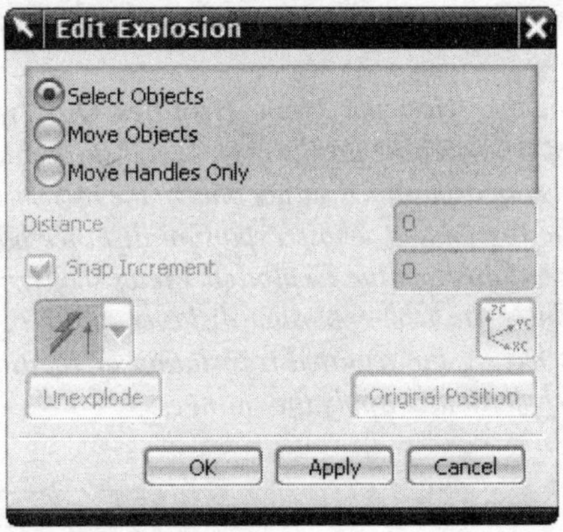

*Figure 10-28 The **Edit Explosion** dialog box*

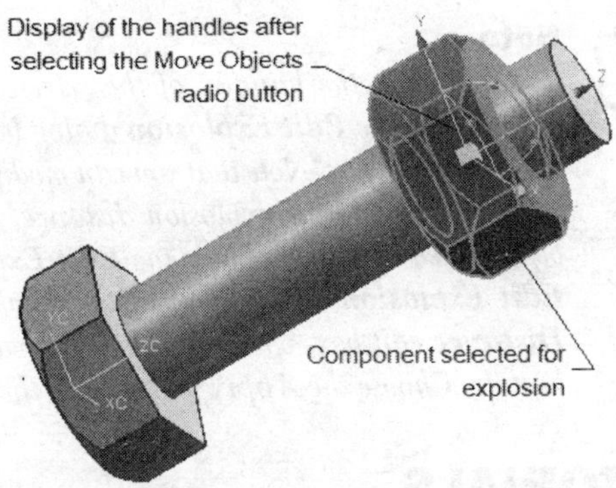

Figure 10-29 Component selected from the assembly for manual explosion

Note

*If you select the translation handle, the **Distance** edit box and the **Vector tool** drop-down list will be available in the **Edit Explosion** dialog box. If you select the angular handle, the **Angle** edit box will be available in the dialog box.*

The **Snap Handles to WCS** button from the **Edit Explosion** dialog box will be used for coinciding the handles of the selected component with the WCS of the assembly file. If you select the **Snap Increment** check box, then **Snap Increment** edit box will be available in the **Edit Explosion** dialog box. The value entered in this edit box will be treated as a step increment value and considered whenever the selected objects are exploded dynamically by dragging the handles. After selecting the required options from the **Edit Explosion** dialog box, choose **Apply** and then the **OK** button to create the exploded view, as shown in Figure 10-30.

If you choose the **Unexplode** button from the **Edit Explosion** dialog box, which is enabled after exploding a selected component, the component will be unexploded. Also, the component will be retained to its original position in the assembly.

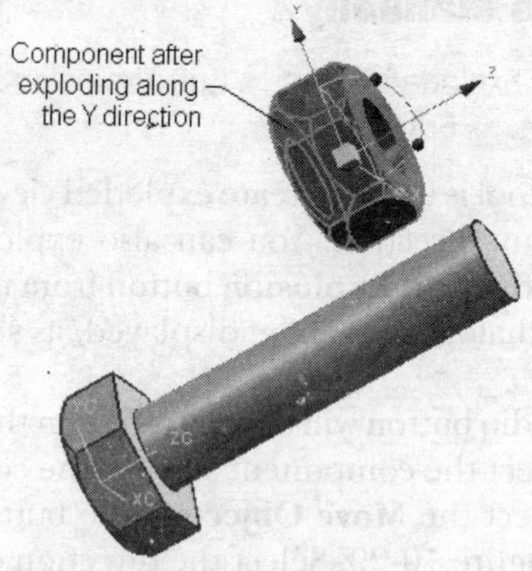

Figure 10-30 Position of the component after exploding along the Y direction

Note

*To move only the handles of the selected component, select the **Move Handles Only** radio button from the **Edit Explosion** dialog box and specify a value for the explosion distance in the **Distance** edit box. Note that you can modify an existing explosion distance only in the incremental mode. To modify the explosion distance, select the component whose explosion distance has to be modified and then choose the **Edit Explosion** button from the **Exploded Views** toolbar; the **Edit Explosion** dialog box will be displayed. Enter the new explosion distance value in the **Distance** edit box, which will be enabled after selecting the required translation or rotational handle. Choose the **Apply** button and then the **OK** button to apply the changes.*

TUTORIALS

Tutorial 1

In this tutorial, you will create the exploded views of the Flange Coupling assembly. The exploded state of the Flange Coupling assembly is shown in Figure 10-31. The dimensions of the components are given in Figures 10-32 through 10-34. You will use the automatic explosion method for completing this tutorial. Save the configuration with the name *Flange Coupling.prt* at the location *\NX 7\c10\Flange Coupling*. Assume the missing dimensions.

(Expected time: 1.5 hrs)

The following steps are required to complete this tutorial:

a. Create all components of the Flange Coupling assembly by using the dimensions given in Figures 10-32 through 10-34. Save the components in the specified folder.
b. Create a new assembly file and assemble all the components of the Flange Coupling by using the assembly constraints.
c. Invoke the **Exploded Views** toolbar in the **Assembly** application and create the exploded views of the Flange Coupling assembly.
d. Save the exploded view of the Flange Coupling assembly in the configuration file.

Figure 10-31 The exploded view of the Flange Coupling assembly

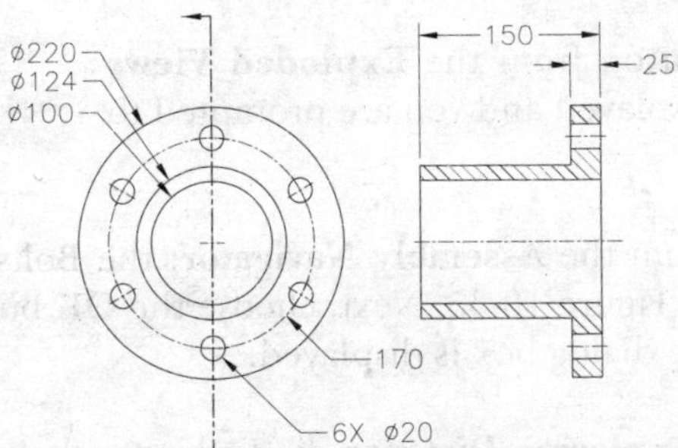

Figure 10-32 Dimensions and views of the flange

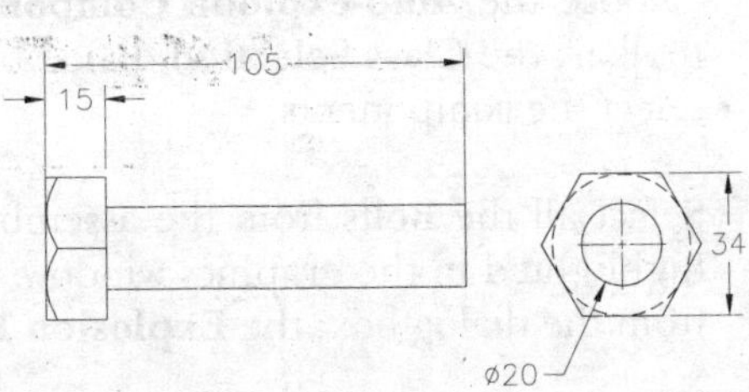

Figure 10-33 Dimensions and views of the Bolt

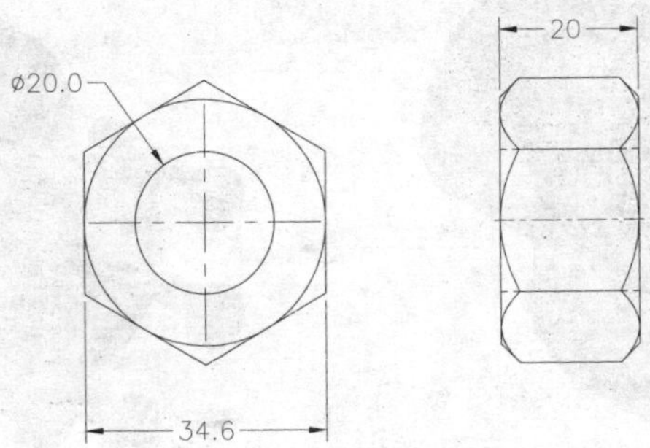

Figure 10-34 Dimensions and the views of the nut

Creating the Components of the Flange Coupling Assembly

1. Create all components of the Flange Coupling assembly as separate part files and save them at the location *\NX 7\c10\Flange Coupling*. The views and dimensions of the components are given in Figures 10-31 through 10-34.

2. Start a new file and assemble all the components, refer to Figure 10-31. Save the assembly file in the same folder where the component files were saved.

Invoking the Exploded Views Toolbar

1. Choose the **Exploded Views** button from the **Assemblies** toolbar, or choose **Assemblies > Exploded Views > Show Toolbar** from the menu bar; the **Exploded Views** toolbar is displayed in the drawing window.

Creating the Exploded View of the Assembly

After invoking the **Exploded Views** toolbar, you can explode the Flange Coupling assembly by following the procedure given next.

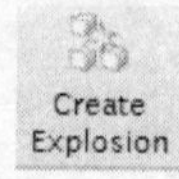

1. Choose the **Create Explosion** button from the **Exploded Views** toolbar; the **Create Explosion** dialog box is displayed with the default name of the explosion scheme in the **Name** edit box. Enter **Explosion Tut-01** in the **Name** edit box of the **Create Explosion** dialog box and choose the **OK** button.

2. Choose the **Auto-explode Components** button from the **Exploded Views** toolbar; the **Class Selection** dialog box is displayed and you are prompted to select the components.

3. Select all the Bolts from the assembly or from the **Assembly Navigator**; the Bolts are highlighted in the graphics window, refer to Figure 10-35. Next, choose the **OK** button from the dialog box; the **Explosion Distance** dialog box is displayed.

4. Enter **150** in the **Distance** edit box of the **Explosion Distance** dialog box and choose the **OK** button. The exploded view of the assembly after exploding all the Bolts from the assembly is shown in Figure 10-36.

Figure 10-35 Bolts selected from the assembly for explosion

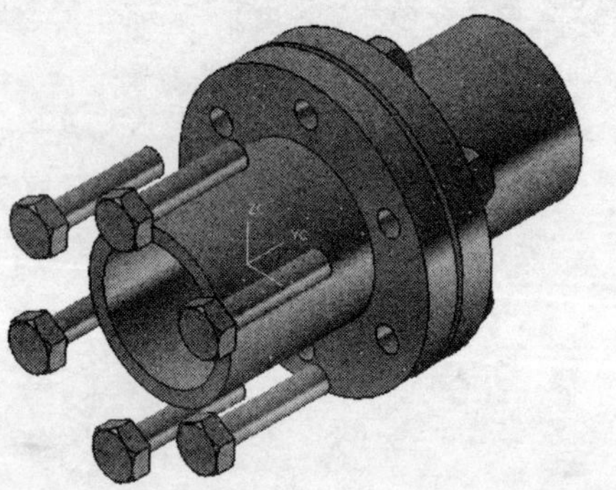

Figure 10-36 The assembly after exploding the Bolts

Note

In this Tutorial, the display of the Datum Coordinate System is turned off.

5. Again, choose the **Auto-explode Components** button from the **Exploded Views** toolbar; the **Class Selection** dialog box is displayed and you are prompted to select the components.

6. Select all Nuts from the assembly; the Nuts are highlighted in the graphics window, refer to Figure 10-37. Next, choose the **OK** button from the dialog box; the **Explosion Distance** dialog box is displayed.

7. Enter **150** in the **Distance** edit box of the **Explosion Distance** dialog box and choose the **OK** button; the Nuts are exploded. The assembly after exploding all nuts is shown in Figure 10-38.

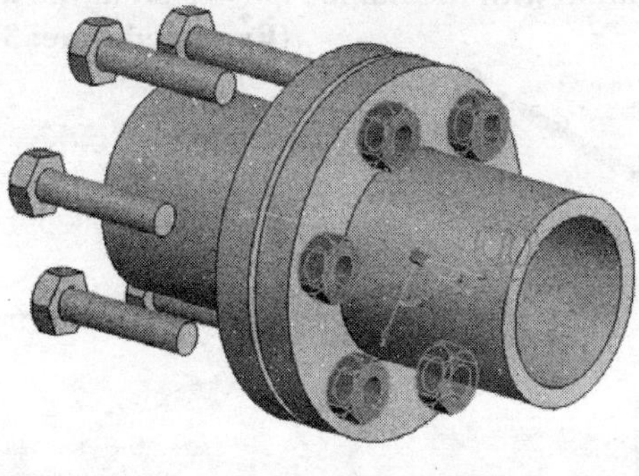

Figure 10-37 *Nuts selected from the assembly for explosion*

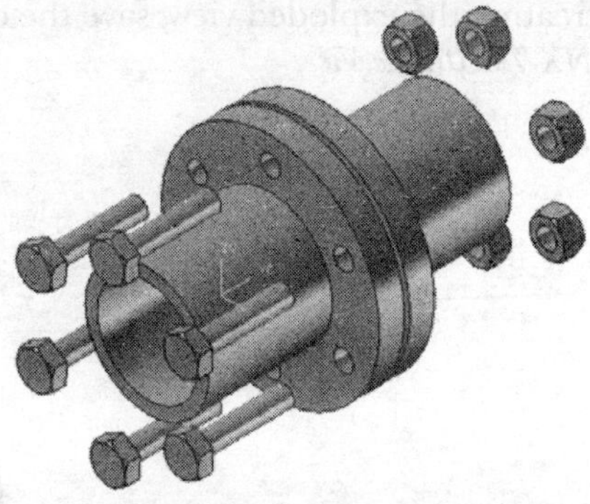

Figure 10-38 *The assembly after exploding all Nuts*

8. Choose the **Auto-explode Components** button from the **Exploded Views** toolbar; the **Class Selection** dialog box is displayed and you are prompted to select the components.

9. Select the back Flange from the assembly, refer to Figure 10-39. Next, choose the **OK** button from the dialog box; the **Explosion Distance** dialog box is displayed.

10. Enter **-50** in the **Distance** edit box of the **Explosion Distance** dialog box and choose the **OK** button; the Flange is exploded. The final exploded view of the Flange Coupling assembly is shown in Figure 10-40.

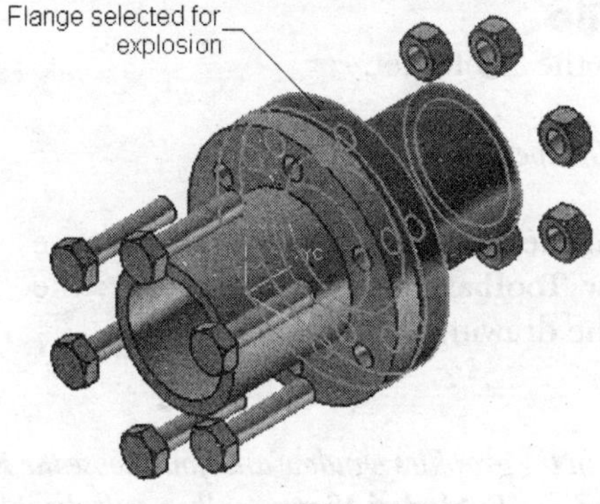

Figure 10-39 *The Flange selected from the assembly for explosion*

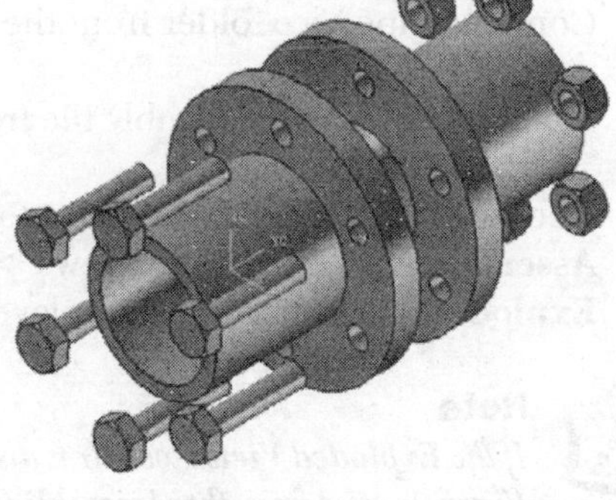

Figure 10-40 *The final exploded view of the Flange Coupling assembly*

Saving the Exploded View

1. Choose **File > Close > Save and Close** from the menu bar to save and close the file.

Tutorial 2

In this tutorial, you will create the manually exploded view of the Pipe Vice assembly created in Chapter 9. The exploded view of the Pipe Vice assembly is shown in Figure 10-41. After creating the exploded view, save the configuration with the name *Pipe Vice.prt* at the location *\NX 7\c10\Pipe Vice.* **(Expected time: 30 min)**

Figure 10-41 The exploded view of the Pipe Vice assembly

The following steps are required to complete this tutorial:

a. Copy the Pipe Vice folder from the *c09* to the *c10* folder.
b. Open the Pipe Vice assembly file.
c. Invoke the **Exploded Views** toolbar in the Assembly environment.
d. Create the exploded view of the Pipe Vice assembly using the **Edit Explosion** tool.
e. Save the exploded view of the Pipe Vice assembly in the configuration file.

Opening the Pipe Vice Assembly File

1. Copy the Pipe Vice folder from the *c09* to the *c10* folder.

2. Open the Pipe Vice assembly file from *c10/Pipe Vice*.

3. Choose the **Exploded Views** button from the **Assemblies** toolbar, or choose **Assemblies > Exploded Views > Show Toolbar** from the menu bar; the **Exploded Views** toolbar is displayed in the drawing window.

Note

*If the **Exploded Views** toolbar is displayed in the graphics window and you choose the **Exploded Views** button from the **Assemblies** toolbar, the **Exploded Views** toolbar will disappear from the graphics window. To display it again, you need to again choose the **Exploded Views** button from the **Assemblies** toolbar.*

Assigning a Name to the Exploded View

1. Choose the **Create Explosion** button from the **Exploded Views** toolbar; the **Create Explosion** dialog box is displayed with the default name of the explosion in the **Name** edit box.

2. Enter **Explosion Tut-02** as the name of the explosion in the **Name** edit box of the **Create Explosion** dialog box and choose the **OK** button; the **Edit Explosion** button is enabled in the **Exploded Views** toolbar.

Exploding the Screw, Handle Screw, and Handle Along the Z Direction

Next, you need to explode the Screw, Handle Screw, and Handle along the Z direction.

1. Choose the **Edit Explosion** button from the **Exploded Views** toolbar; the **Edit Explosion** dialog box is displayed. By default, the **Select Objects** radio button is selected in this dialog box and you are prompted to select the components to explode.

2. Select the Screw, Handle Screw, and Handle from the assembly and then select the **Move Objects** radio button from the dialog box; a coordinate system is displayed, refer to Figure 10-42.

3. Click on the arrowhead of the Z handle of the coordinate system; the **Distance** edit box is enabled in the **Edit Explosion** dialog box.

4. Enter **120** as the explosion distance in the **Distance** edit box.

5. Choose the **OK** button from the **Edit Explosion** dialog box; the selected components are exploded, as shown in Figure 10-43.

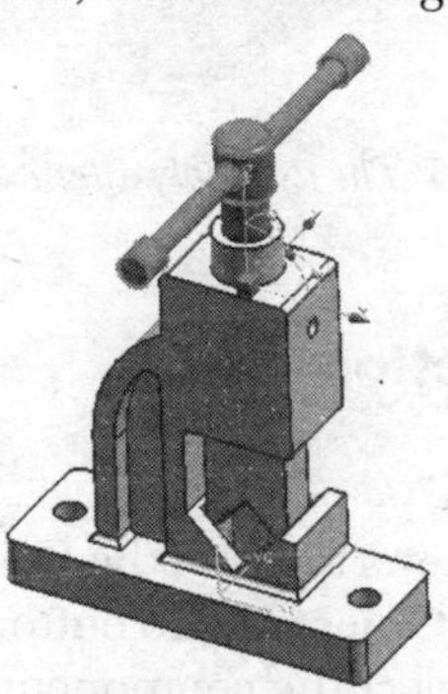

Figure 10-42 *The components selected for explosion*

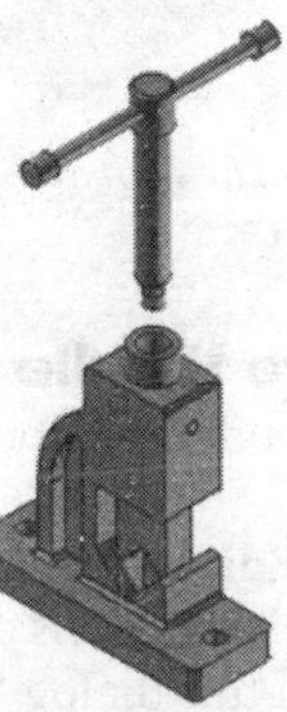

Figure 10-43 *The assembly after exploding the selected components*

Note

In this Tutorial, the display of the Datum Coordinate System is turned off.

Exploding the Movable Jaw

Now, you need to explode the Movable Jaw using the following steps:

1. Choose the **Edit Explosion** button from the **Exploded Views** toolbar; the **Edit Explosion** dialog box is displayed. By default, the **Select Objects** radio button is selected in this dialog box and you are prompted to select the components to explode.

2. Select the Movable Jaw from the assembly and then select the **Move Objects** radio button from the **Edit Explosion** dialog box; the coordinate system of the Movable Jaw is displayed, as shown in Figure 10-44.

3. Click on the arrowhead of the Z Handle of the coordinate system; the **Distance** edit box is enabled in the **Edit Explosion** dialog box.

4. Enter **-30** as the explosion distance in the **Distance** edit box.

5. Choose the **OK** button from the **Edit Explosion** dialog box; the Movable Jaw is exploded. The resulting exploded view of the assembly is shown in Figure 10-45.

Figure 10-44 The Movable Jaw selected for explosion

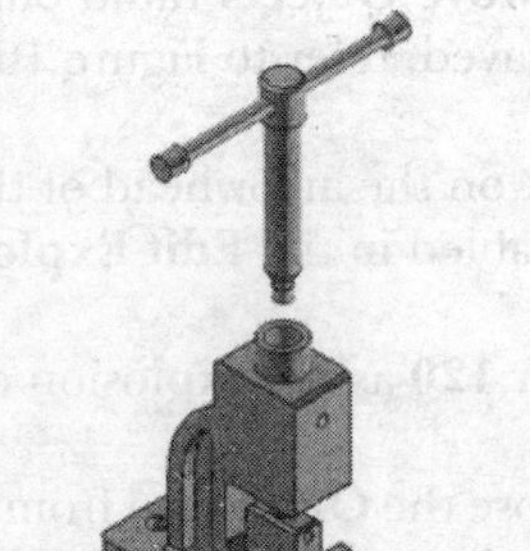

Figure 10-45 The assembly after exploding the Movable Jaw

Exploding the Handle Screw Along the Y Direction

Next, you need to explode the Handle screw.

1. Choose the **Edit Explosion** button from the **Exploded Views** toolbar; the **Edit Explosion** dialog box is displayed. By default, the **Select Objects** radio button is selected in this dialog box and you are prompted to select the components to explode.

2. Select the right Handle Screw from the assembly and then select the **Move Objects** radio button from the **Edit Explosion** dialog box; the coordinate system of the Handle Screw is displayed, refer to Figure 10-46.

3. Click on the arrowhead of the Y Handle of the coordinate system; the **Distance** edit box is enabled in the **Edit Explosion** dialog box.

4. Enter **140** as the explosion distance in the **Distance** edit box of the dialog box.

5. Choose the **OK** button from the **Edit Explosion** dialog box to exit it. The resulting exploded view of the assembly is shown in Figure 10-47.

Figure 10-46 *The Handle Screw selected from the assembly for explosion*

Figure 10-47 *The assembly after exploding the Handle Screw*

Exploding the Handle Along the Y Direction

Next, you need to explode the Handle.

1. Choose the **Edit Explosion** button from the **Exploded Views** toolbar; the **Edit Explosion** dialog box is displayed. By default, the **Select Objects** radio button is selected in this dialog box and you are prompted to select the components to explode.

2. Select the Handle from the assembly and then select the **Move Objects** radio button from the **Edit Explosion** dialog box; the coordinate system of the Handle is displayed, refer to Figure 10-48.

3. Click on the arrowhead of the Y Handle of the coordinate system; the **Distance** edit box is enabled in the **Edit Explosion** dialog box.

4. Enter **115** as the explosion distance in the **Distance** edit box of the dialog box.

5. Choose the **OK** button from the **Edit Explosion** dialog box to exit it. The resulting exploded view of the assembly is shown in Figure 10-49.

Saving the Exploded Views

1. Choose **File > Save** from the menu bar to save the exploded view. The final exploded view of the Pipe Vice assembly is shown in Figure 10-50. Next, close the file.

Figure 10-48 *The Handle selected from the assembly for explosion*

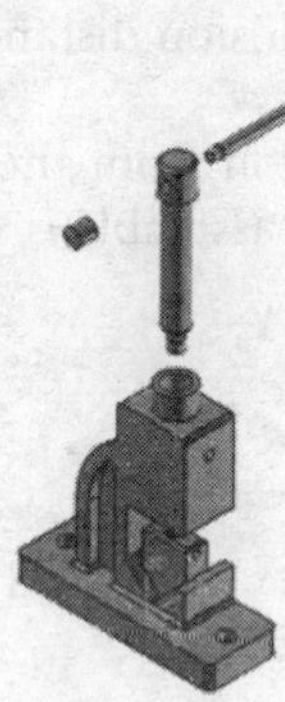

Figure 10-49 *The assembly after exploding the Handle*

Figure 10-50 *The final exploded view of the Pipe Vice assembly*

Tutorial 3

In this tutorial, you will create the Radial Engine assembly shown in Figures 10-51 and 10-52. The Radial Engine assembly will be created in two parts, one will be the subassembly and the other will be the main assembly. The dimensions of the components of the Radial Engine assembly are shown in Figures 10-53 through 10-56. Save the assembly file with the name *Radial Engine.prt* at the location *\NX 7\c10\Radial Engine.* **(Expected time: 4 hrs)**

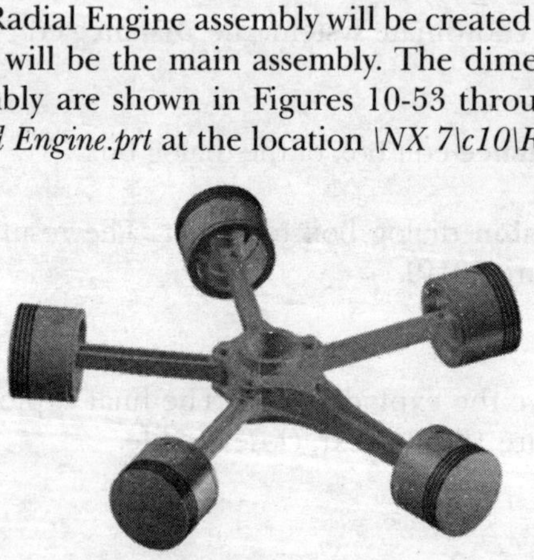

Figure 10-51 *The Radial Engine assembly*

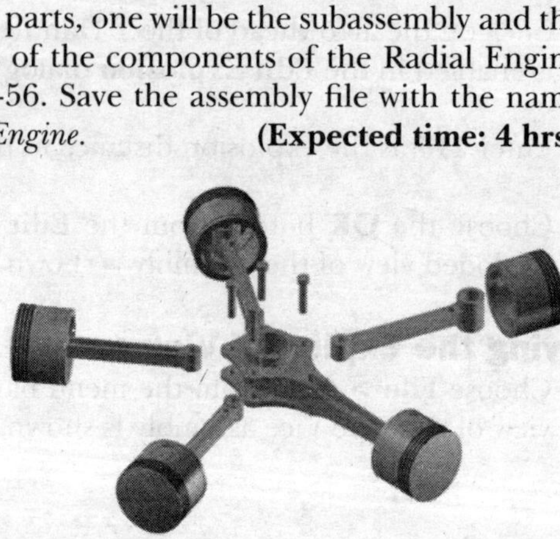

Figure 10-52 *The exploded view of the assembly*

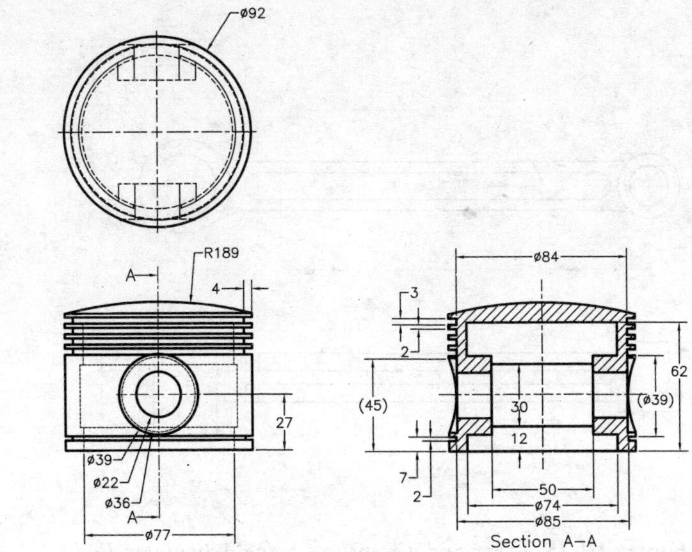

Figure 10-53 *Views and dimensions of the Piston*

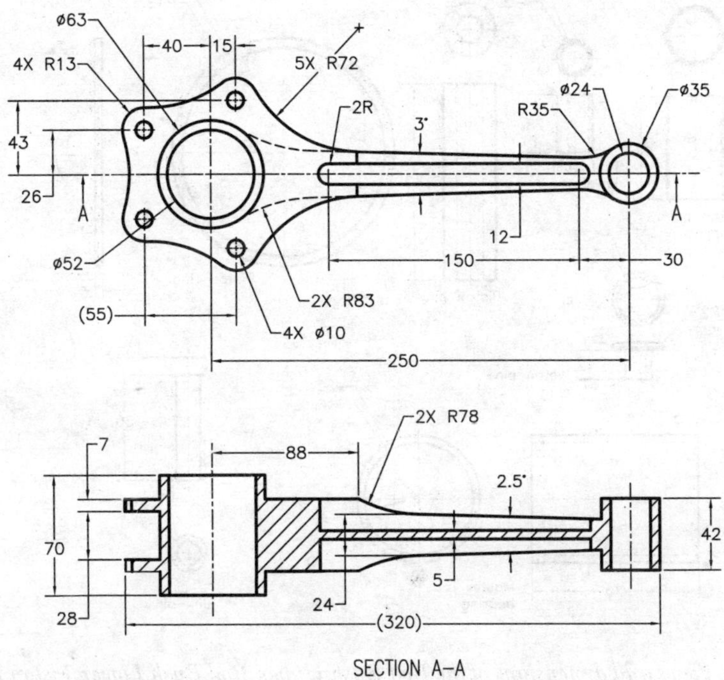

Figure 10-54 *Views and dimensions of the Master Rod*

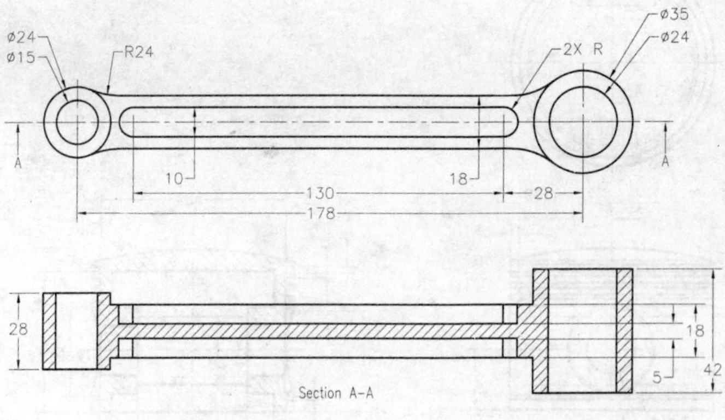

Figure 10-55 *Views and dimensions of the Articulated Rod*

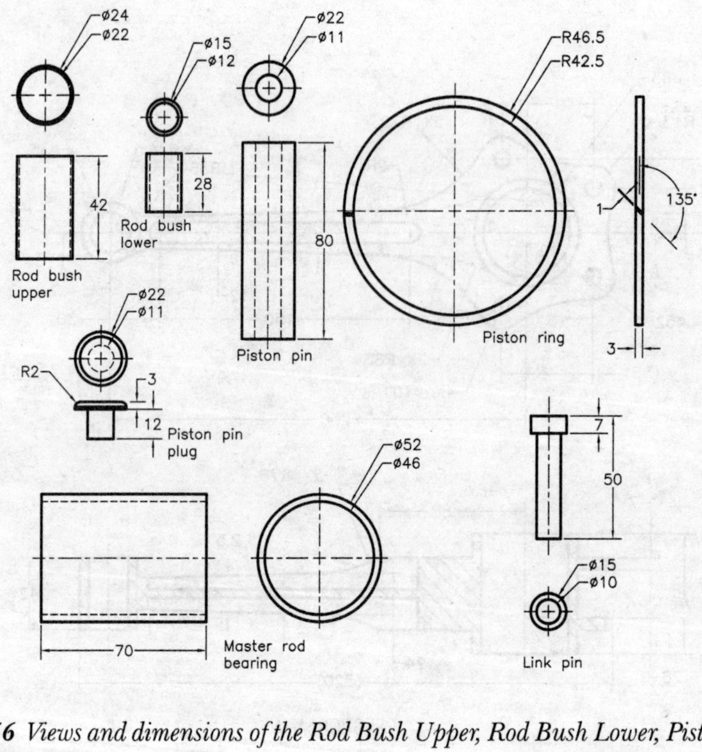

Figure 10-56 *Views and dimensions of the Rod Bush Upper, Rod Bush Lower, Piston Pin Plug, Piston Pin, Piston Rings, and Master Rod Bearing*

Since this is a large assembly, you need to create it in two steps. First, you need to create the subassembly, consisting of the Articulated Rod, Piston, Rings, Piston Pin, Rod Bush Upper, Rod Bush Lower, and Piston Pin Plug. Next, you will create the main assembly by assembling the Master Rod with the Piston, Piston Rings, Piston pin, Master Rod Bearing and piston pin Plug and the instances of the subassembly.

The following steps are required to complete this tutorial:

a. Create all components of the Radial Engine assembly and save them in the *Radial Engine* folder.
b. Start a new file and create the subassembly.
c. Start a new assembly and assemble the subassembly and the individual components to create the main assembly.
d. Save the file.

Creating the Components

1. Create a folder with the name *Radial Engine* at */NX 7/c10*. Create all the components of the Radial Engine as individual part files and save them in this folder. The views and dimensions of the components are given in Figures 10-53 through 10-56.

Creating the Subassembly

1. Start a new file with the name *Articulated Rod_Piston* and specify its location in the same folder where the parts were saved. Next, invoke the Assembly environment.

2. Assemble the components in the sequence as illustrated in Figure 10-57. The assembly after assembling the Rod Bush Upper, Rod Bush Lower, Piston Pin, Piston, and Piston Pin Plug is shown in Figure 10-58.

3. Assemble the Piston Ring to the Piston by using the assembly constraints. The completed Articulated Rod_Piston subassembly is shown in Figure 10-59. Next, choose the **Save** button.

Note

*You can change the color of the Piston Rings for a better display. To do so, choose **Edit > Object Display** from the menu bar; the **Class Selection** dialog box is displayed and you are prompted to select the objects to edit. Select the Piston Rings from the subassembly and choose the **OK** button; the **Edit Object Display** dialog box is displayed. Choose the **Color** swatch; the **Color** dialog box is displayed. Select the required color and then choose the **OK** button from the **Color** dialog box; the **Edit Object Display** dialog box is displayed again. Next, choose the **OK** button from it.*

*In Figure 10-58, the solid texture of the Piston has been changed to the transparent texture. This is done to view the components that are assembled inside the Piston. To change the solid texture of the Piston to the transparent texture, select the Piston from the graphics window and then invoke the **Edit Object Display** dialog box. Next, move the **Translucency** sliding bar to the value of 75 and then choose the **OK** button from the **Edit Object Display** dialog box. Note that you can vary the transparency value of the Piston from 0 to 100.*

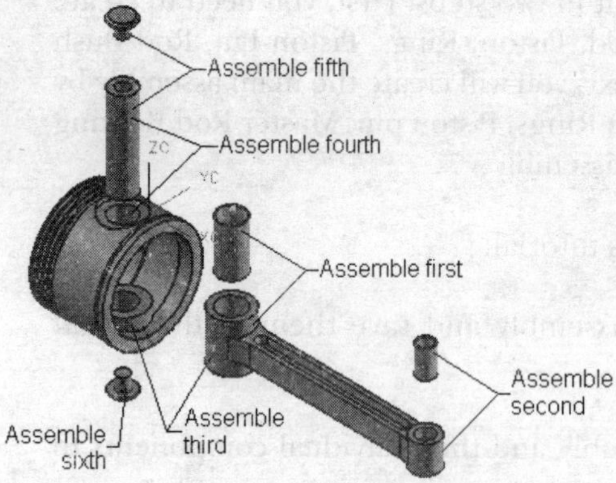

Figure 10-57 Sequence for assembling the components to create the subassembly

Figure 10-58 The subassembly after assembling the Rod Bush Lower, Rod Bush Upper, Articulated Rod, Piston, Piston Pin, and Piston Pin Plug

Figure 10-59 The subassembly after assembling all instances of the Piston Rings

Creating the Main Assembly

Create the main assembly by assembling the subassembly and the individual components.

1. Start a new file with the name *Radial Engine* and specify its location in the same folder where the components and the subassembly are saved. Next, invoke the Assembly environment.

2. Assemble the Master Rod, Rod Bush Upper, and Master Rod Bearing using the assembly constraints, refer to Figure 10-60.

3. Next, assemble the Piston, Piston Pin, and Piston Pin Plug using the assembly constraints, refer to Figure 10-60.

4. Assemble the Piston Rings with the Piston. Change the color of the Piston Rings. The assembly after assembling the above-mentioned components is shown in Figure 10-60.

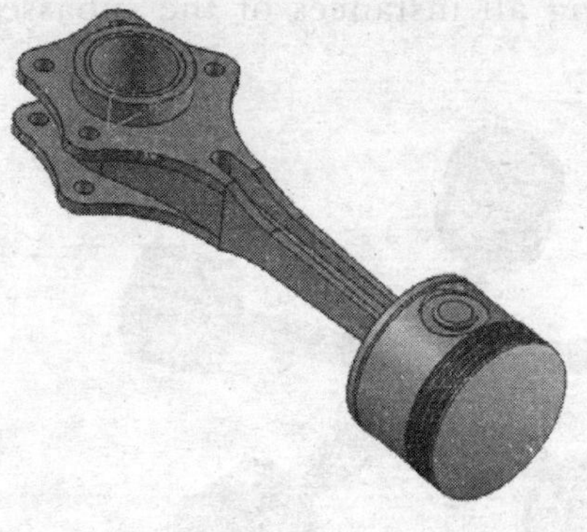

Figure 10-60 *Components assembled in the main assembly*

Assembling the Subassembly with the Main Assembly

Next, you need to assemble the instances of the Articulated Rod_Piston subassembly with the main assembly by using the assembly constraints.

1. Choose the **Add Component** button from the **Assemblies** toolbar; the **Add Component** dialog box is displayed.

2. Choose the **Open** button from the **Add Component** dialog box; the **Part Name** dialog box is displayed. Select the Articulated Rod_Piston subassembly from the dialog box and choose the **OK** button; the subassembly is displayed in the **Component Preview** window.

3. Assemble the first instance of the Articulated Rod_Piston subassembly with the main assembly by using the assembly constraints. The assembly after assembling the first instance of the subassembly is shown in Figure 10-61.

4. Similarly, assemble the other instances of the subassembly with the main assembly by using the assembly constraints. The assembly structure to be followed while assembling the subassemblies with the main assembly is shown in Figure 10-62.

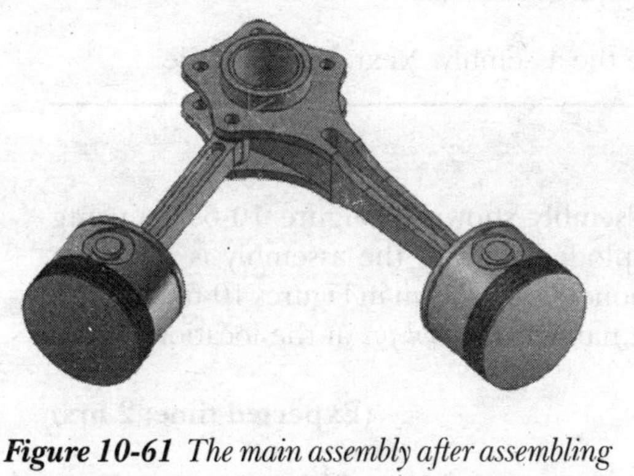

Figure 10-61 The main assembly after assembling the first instance of the subassembly

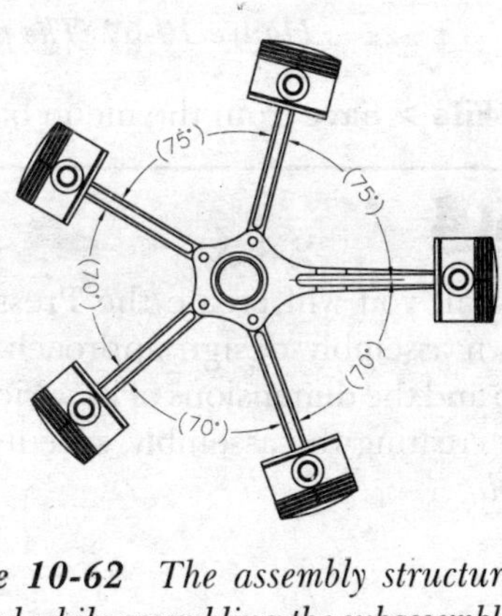

Figure 10-62 The assembly structure to be followed while assembling the subassemblies with the Master Rod

The assembly after assembling all instances of the subassembly is shown in Figure 10-63.

Figure 10-63 The assembly after assembling all instances of the subassembly with the main assembly

Assembling the Link Pin

1. Assemble four instances of the Link Pin with the Master Rod by using the assembly constraints. Modify the color of the Link Pin. The resulting assembly after assembling the Link Pins is shown in Figure 10-64.

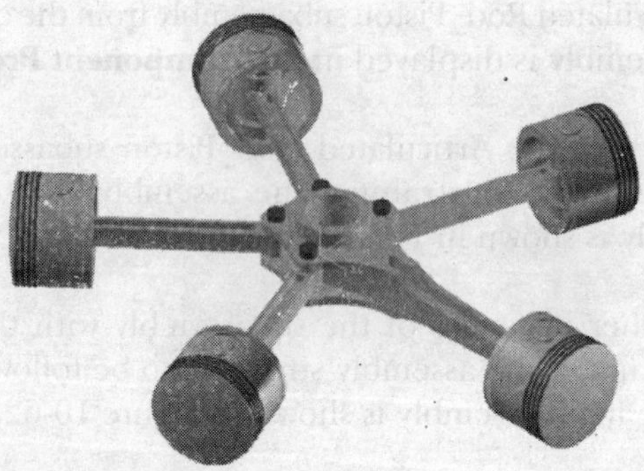

Figure 10-64 The final Radial Engine assembly

2. Choose **File > Save** from the menu bar to save the assembly. Next, close the file.

Tutorial 4

In this tutorial, you will create the Press Tool assembly shown in Figure 10-65 by using the Top-down assembly design approach. The exploded state of the assembly is shown in Figure 10-66 and the dimensions of its various components are shown in Figures 10-67 through 10-69. After creating the assembly, save it with the name *Press Tool.prt* at the location *\NX 7\c10\Press Tool.*

(Expected time: 2 hrs)

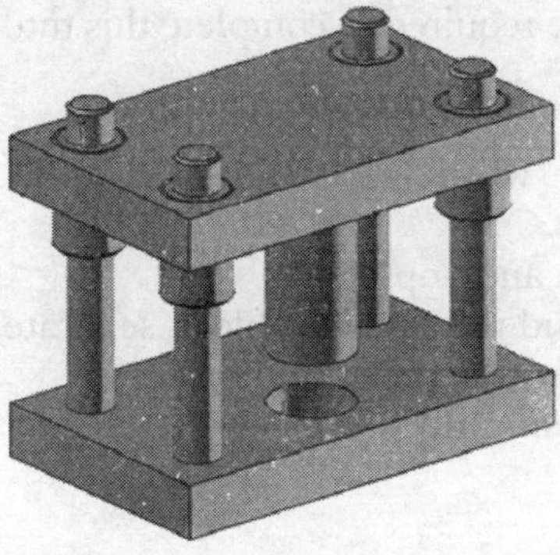

Figure 10-65 The completed Press Tool assembly after assembling the Top Plate with the assembly

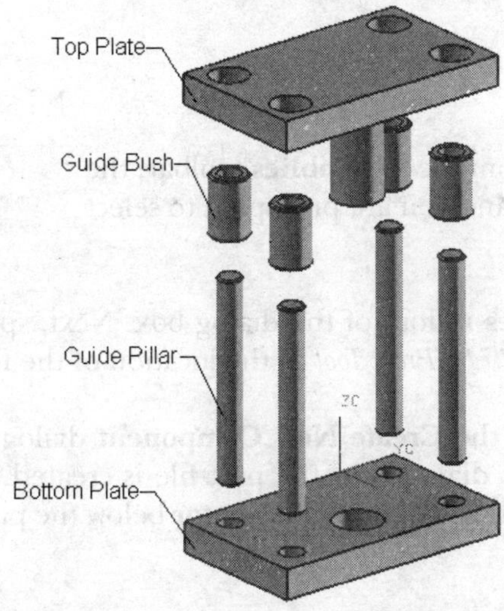

Figure 10-66 The exploded view of the Press Tool assembly

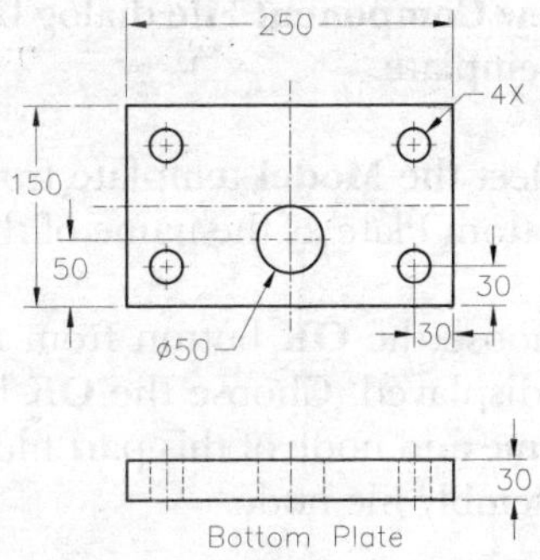

Figure 10-67 Dimensions and views of the Bottom Plate

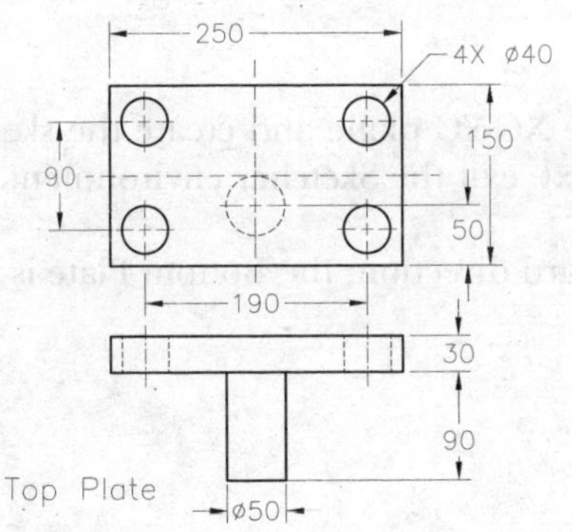

Figure 10-68 Dimensions and views of the Top Plate

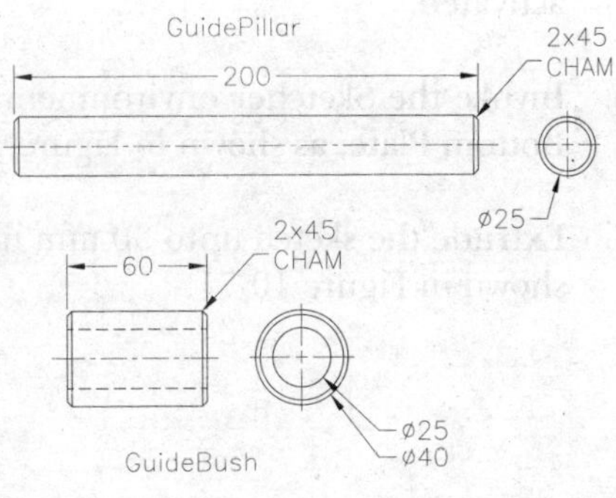

Figure 10-69 Dimensions and views of the Guide Pillar and Guide Bush

The following steps are required to complete this tutorial:

a. Start a new file.
b. Create the base feature, which is the Bottom Plate.
c. Create the Guide Pillar.
d. Create the Guide Bush and Top Plate.
e. Save all components and the assembly file as separate files.
f. Assemble the components in the assembly file.
g. Save and close the assembly file.

Starting a New File

1. Start a new file with the name *Press Tool* using the **Model** template and specify its location as *\NX 7\c10\Press Tool*. Next, invoke the Assembly environment by choosing **Start > Assemblies** from the **Standard** toolbar.

Creating the Bottom Plate

Next, you need to create the Bottom Plate.

1. Choose the **Create New Component** button from the **Assemblies** toolbar; the **New Component File** dialog box is displayed and you are prompted to select a template.

2. Select the **Model** template from the **Templates** rollout of the dialog box. Next, specify Bottom Plate as the name of the file and *\NX 7\c10\Press Tool* as the location of the file.

3. Choose the **OK** button from the dialog box; the **Create New Component** dialog box is displayed. Choose the **OK** button from this dialog box; the part file is created. The name and node of this part file is displayed in the **Assembly Navigator** below the parent assembly file node.

4. Choose the **Assembly Navigator** tab from the **Resource Bar**; the **Assembly Navigator** is displayed.

5. Double-click on the name **Bottom Plate** in the **Assembly Navigator**; the part gets activated.

6. Invoke the Sketcher environment using the XC-YC plane and create the sketch for the Bottom Plate, as shown in Figure 10-70. Next, exit the Sketcher environment.

7. Extrude the sketch upto 30 mm in the upward direction; the Bottom Plate is created, as shown in Figure 10-71.

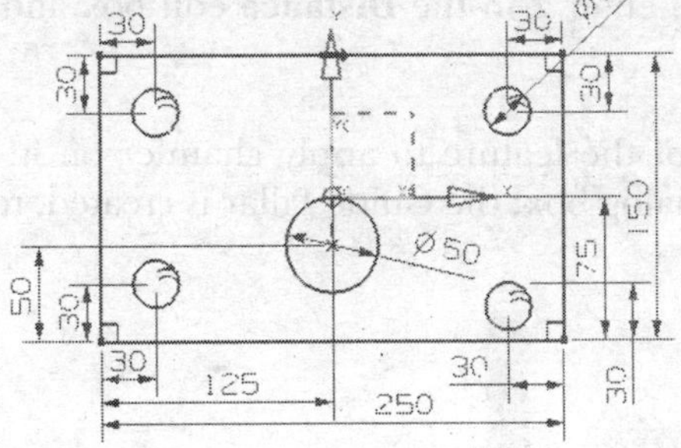

Figure 10-70 The sketch of the base feature

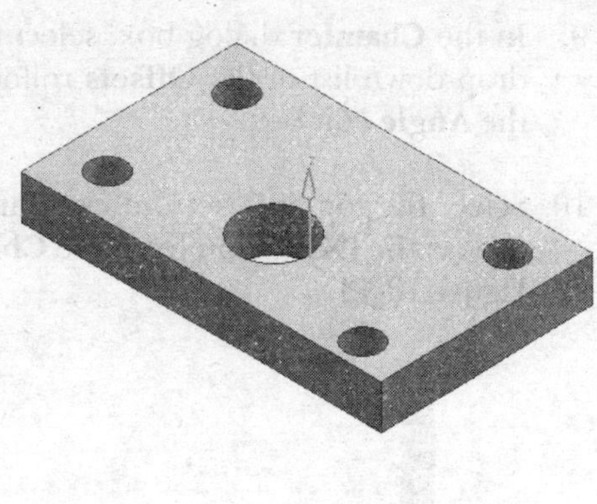

Figure 10-71 The base feature created

8. Double-click on the **Press Tool** (parent assembly) in the **Assembly Navigator** to activate it.

Creating the Guide Pillar

Next, you need to create the Guide Pillar.

1. Choose the **Create New Component** button from the **Assemblies** toolbar; the **New Component File** dialog box is displayed and you are prompted to select a template.

2. Select the **Model** template from the **Templates** rollout of the dialog box. Next, specify Guide Pillar as the name of the file and *\NX 7\c10\Press Tool* as the location of the file.

3. Choose the **OK** button from the dialog box; the **Create New Component** dialog box is displayed. In this dialog box, select the **Model** option from the **Reference Set** drop-down list in the **Settings** rollout and then choose the **OK** button; the new part file is created.

4. Choose the **Assembly Navigator** tab from the **Resource Bar**; the **Assembly Navigator** is displayed.

5. Double-click on the name **Guide Pillar** in the **Assembly Navigator**; the part gets activated, and the Bottom Plate as well as the parent assembly get deactivated.

6. Invoke the Sketcher environment by selecting the XC-YC plane as the sketching plane. Next, create a circle of diameter 25 mm anywhere in the drawing window and then exit the Sketcher environment.

7. Extrude the sketch upto 200 mm in the upward direction, refer to Figure 10-72.

8. Choose the **Chamfer** button from the **Feature Operation** toolbar; the **Chamfer** dialog box is displayed.

9. In the **Chamfer** dialog box, select the **Offset and Angle** option from the **Cross Section** drop-down list of the **Offsets** rollout. Next, enter **2** in the **Distance** edit box and **45** in the **Angle** edit box.

10. Select the top and bottom circular edges of the feature to apply chamfer on it. Next, choose the **OK** button from the **Chamfer** dialog box; the Guide Pillar is created, refer to Figure 10-73.

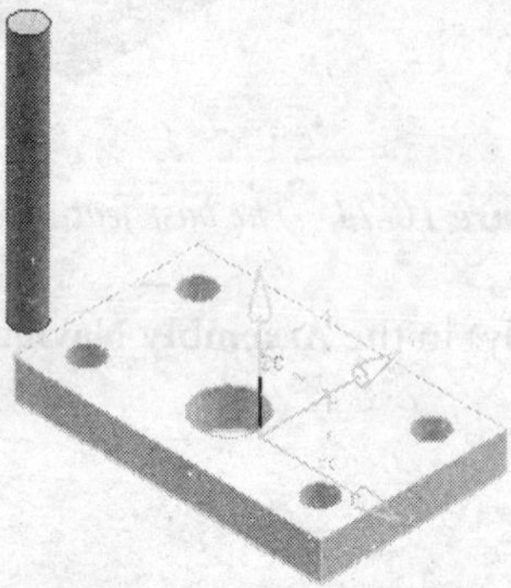

Figure 10-72 Guide Pillar before creating the chamfer feature

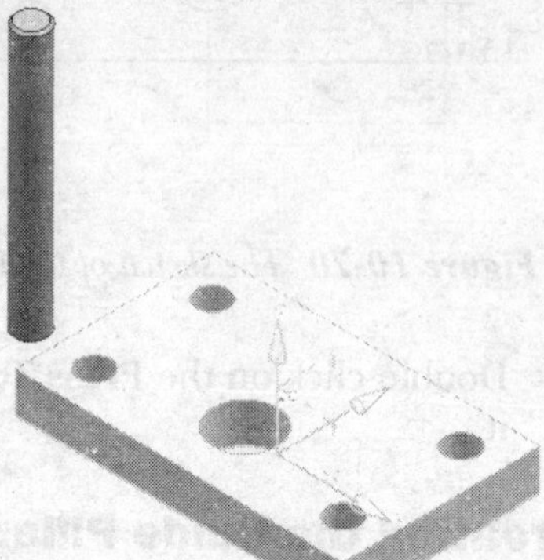

Figure 10-73 Guide Pillar after creating the chamfer feature

11. Double-click on the **Press Tool** (parent assembly) in the **Assembly Navigator** to activate it.

12. Create the Guide Bush and the Top Plate as you created the Guide Pillar, refer to Figure 10-74. For dimensions, refer to Figures 10-68 and 10-69.

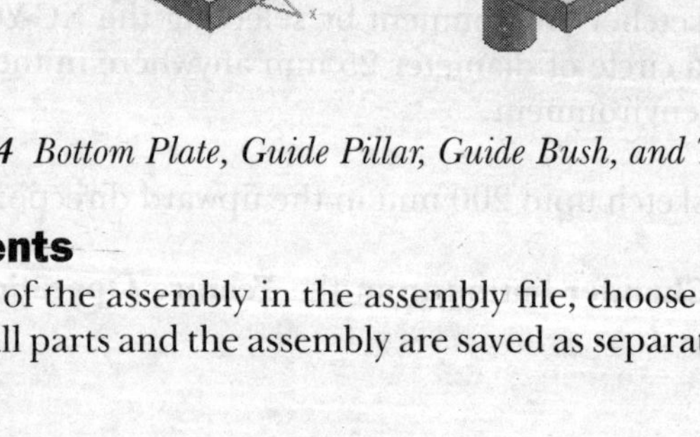

Figure 10-74 Bottom Plate, Guide Pillar, Guide Bush, and Top Plate

Saving the Components

1. After creating all parts of the assembly in the assembly file, choose the **Save** button from the **Standard** toolbar; all parts and the assembly are saved as separate files at the specified location.

2. After saving all components and the assembly file, close the assembly file.

Assembling the Individual Components

1. Open the Press Tool assembly file.

2. Insert three instances of Guide Bush and Guide Pillar in the graphics window by using the **Add Component** tool.

3. Choose the **Assembly Constraints** button from the **Assemblies** toolbar and apply the required assembly constraints to all components. The final Press Tool assembly is shown in Figure 10-75.

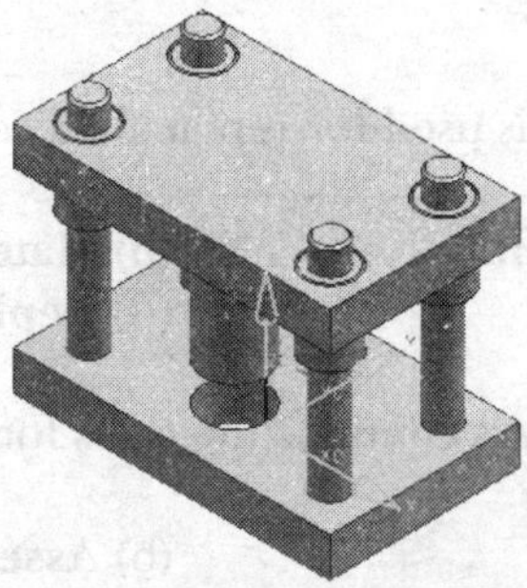

Figure 10-75 *The final Press Tool assembly*

4. Save the assembly file and then close it.

Self-Evaluation Test

Answer the following questions and then compare them to those given at the end of this chapter:

1. In NX, you have a separate tool for creating subassemblies. (T/F)

2. The subassembly files have the same file name extension as the assembly files. (T/F)

3. You can create datum planes using the **View Section** dialog box. (T/F)

4. Exploded views, once created, can be modified in the assembly application of NX. (T/F)

5. There is a separate tool for manually exploding the components in the **Assembly** application. (T/F)

6. Clearance between the components can be checked by using the **Analysis > Assembly Clearance > Perform Analysis** option from the menu bar. (T/F)

7. The ________________ toolbar contains a set of tools for creating the exploded views.

8. The ________________ tool is used to save the solid bodies created as separate part files in the top-down assembly design approach.

9. The ________________ tool is used for editing an exploded view.

10. The ________________ tool is used for exploding the components automatically.

Review Questions

Answer the following questions:

1. Which of the following tools is used for replacing a component in an assembly?

   (a) **Substitute Component** (b) **Mate Component**
   (c) **Edit Explosion** (d) **Replace Component**

2. Which of the following toolbars contains the tools for creating the exploded views?

   (a) **Exploded Views** (b) **Assemblies**
   (c) **Assembly Sequencing Playback** (d) None of these

3. Which of the following tools is used for performing an interference check in an assembly?

   (a) **Exploded Views** (b) **Standard**
   (c) **Check Clearances** (d) None of these

4. Which of the following tools is used to create the automatic exploded view of the components?

   (a) **Exploded Views** (b) **Assemble**
   (c) **Auto-explode Components** (d) None of these

5. One assembly can have only one exploded view. (T/F)

6. The **Delete Explosion** tool is used to delete an exploded view. (T/F)

7. You can modify the dimensions of a component in the Assembly environment. (T/F)

8. The **Check Clearance** tool is used to check the interference between the components in the assembly. (T/F)

9. You can set the transparency of a component in the assembly application for simplifying the assembly. (T/F)

10. Assembly constraints have no relation with the exploded views (T/F)

Exercise

Exercise 1

Create the Shaper Tool Head assembly shown in Figure 10-76. After creating the assembly, create its exploded view, as shown in Figure 10-77. The dimensions of the components are given in Figures 10-78 through 10-82. Save the assembly file with the name *Shaper.prt* at the location *\NX 7\c10\Shaper Tool head.* **(Expected time: 4 hrs)**

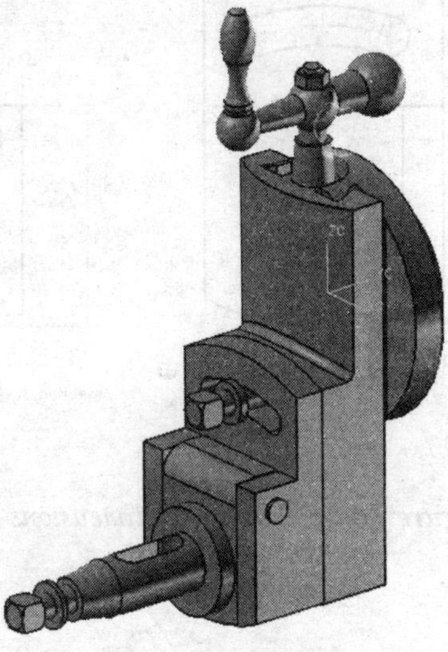

Figure 10-76 *The Shaper Tool Head assembly*

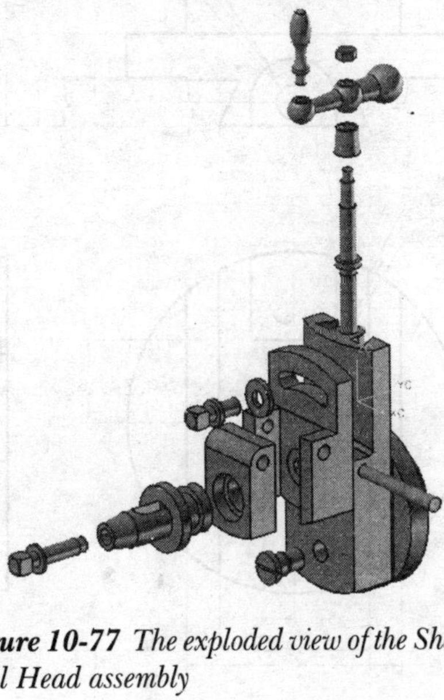

Figure 10-77 *The exploded view of the Shaper Tool Head assembly*

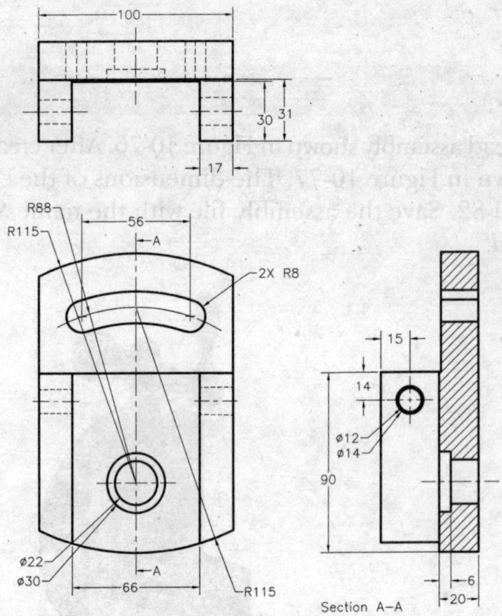

Figure 10-78 *Views and dimensions of the Swivel Plate*

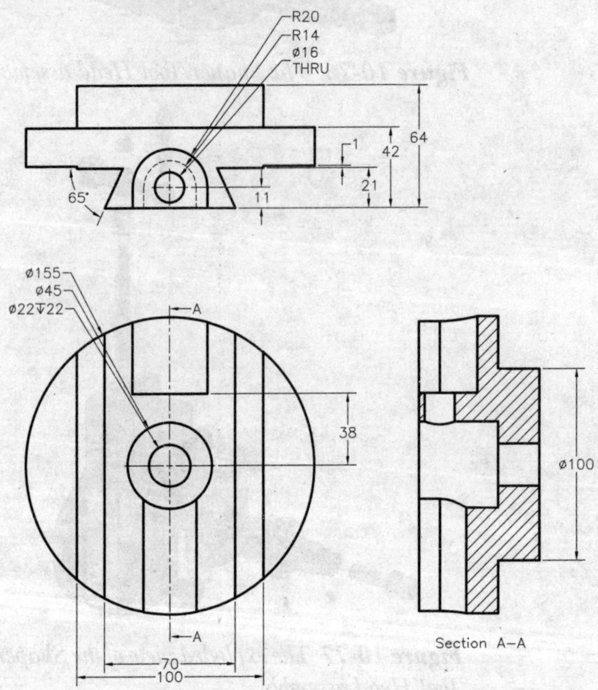

Figure 10-79 *Views and dimensions of the Back Plate*

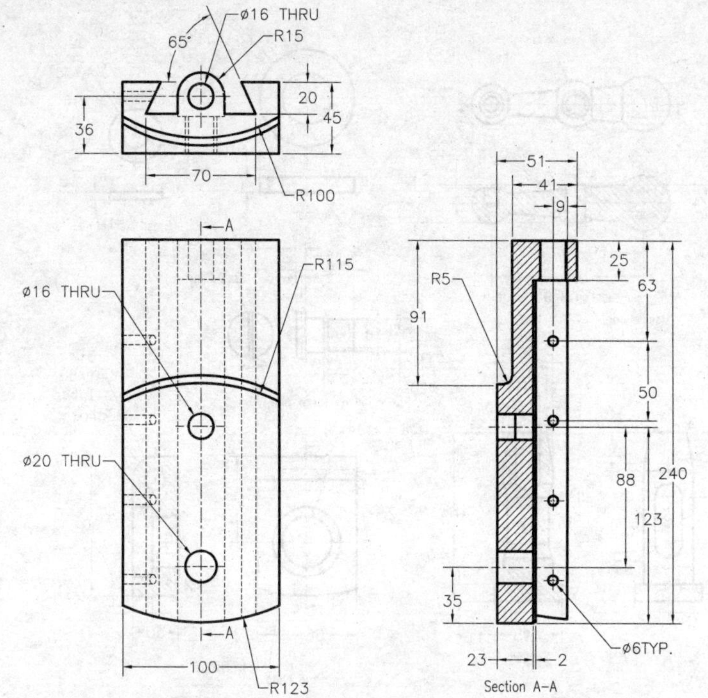

Figure 10-80 *Views and dimensions of the Vertical Slide*

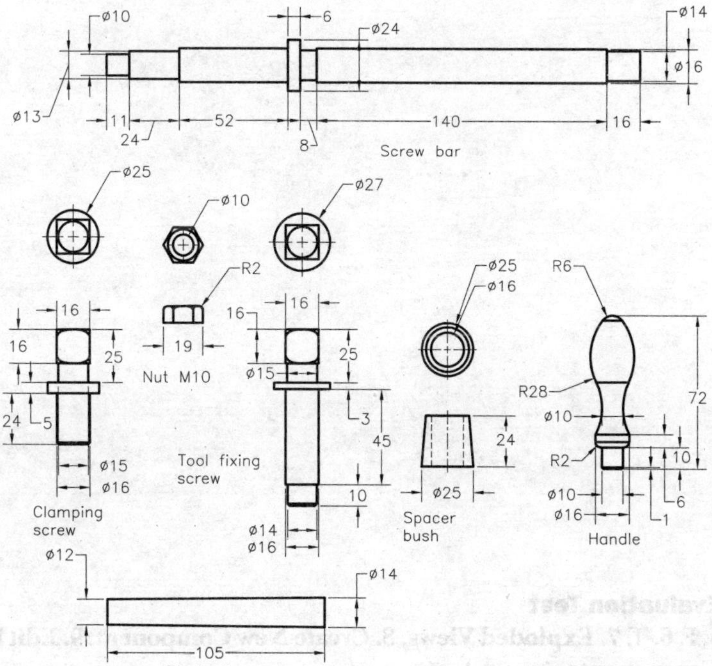

Figure 10-81 *Views and dimensions of various components*

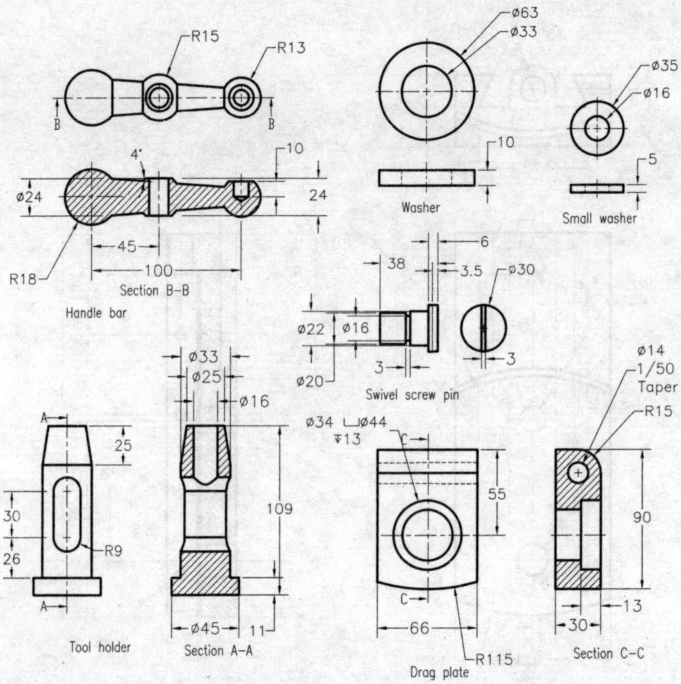

Figure 10-82 Views and dimensions of various components

Answers to Self-Evaluation Test

1. F, **2.** T, **3.** T, **4.** T, **5.** F, **6.** T, **7. Exploded Views**, **8. Create New Component**, **9. Edit Explosion**, **10. Auto-explode Components**

Chapter 11

Surface Modeling

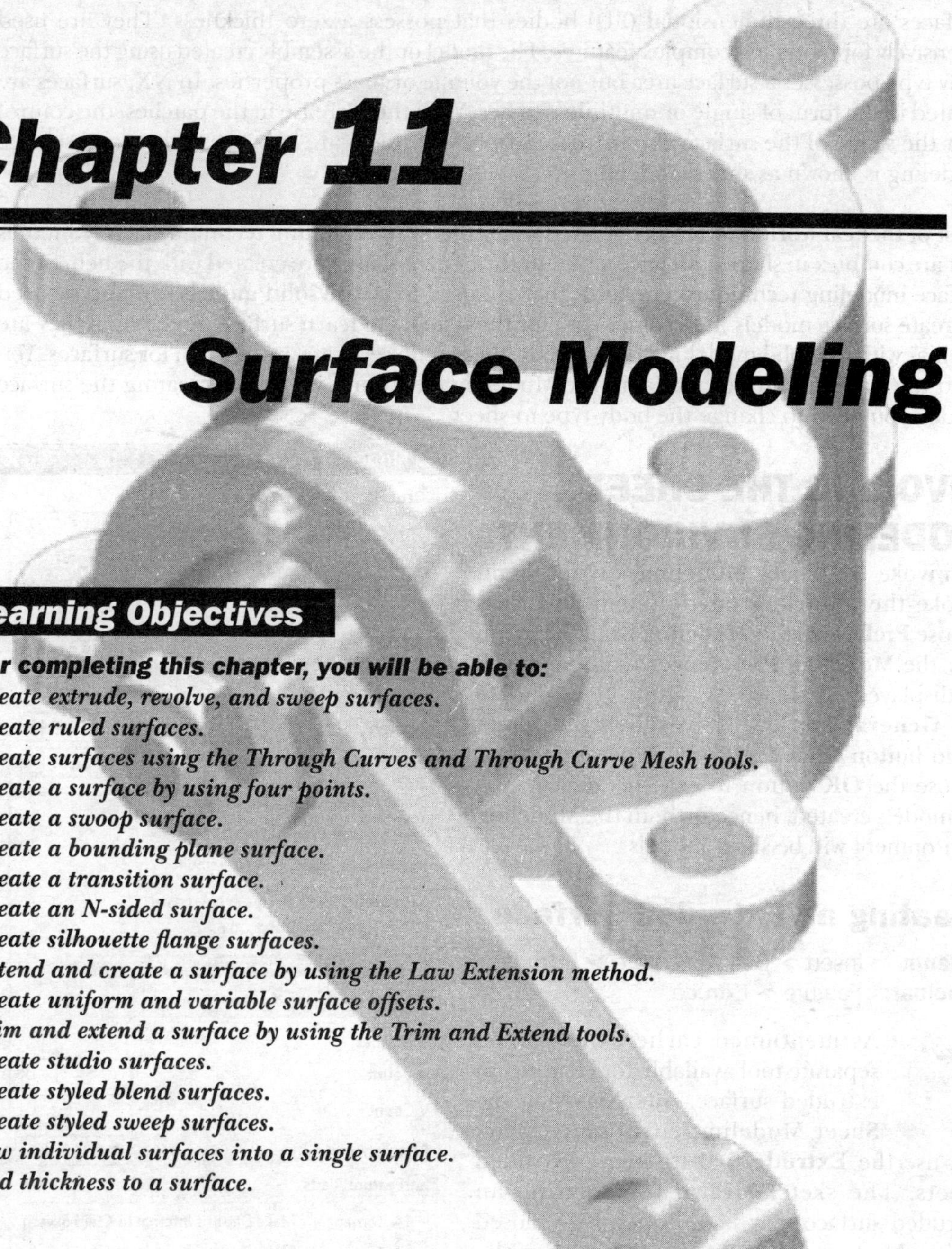

Learning Objectives

After completing this chapter, you will be able to:

- *Create extrude, revolve, and sweep surfaces.*
- *Create ruled surfaces.*
- *Create surfaces using the Through Curves and Through Curve Mesh tools.*
- *Create a surface by using four points.*
- *Create a swoop surface.*
- *Create a bounding plane surface.*
- *Create a transition surface.*
- *Create an N-sided surface.*
- *Create silhouette flange surfaces.*
- *Extend and create a surface by using the Law Extension method.*
- *Create uniform and variable surface offsets.*
- *Trim and extend a surface by using the Trim and Extend tools.*
- *Create studio surfaces.*
- *Create styled blend surfaces.*
- *Create styled sweep surfaces.*
- *Sew individual surfaces into a single surface.*
- *Add thickness to a surface.*

INTRODUCTION TO SURFACE MODELING

Surfaces are three dimensional (3D) bodies that possess a zero thickness. They are used extensively for modeling complex features. The model or the assembly created using the surface body type possesses a surface area but not the volume or mass properties. In NX, surfaces are created in the form of single or multiple patches. With the increase in the patches, the control over the shape of the surface also increases. In NX, surfaces are known as sheets and surface modeling is known as sheet modeling.

Most of the real world models are created using the solid modeling techniques. Only models that are complex in shape and have a nonuniform surface area are created with the help of the surface modeling technique. The tools that are used to create solid models can also be used to create surface models. It becomes easy for the readers to learn surface modeling if they are familiar with the solid modeling tools. In NX, there is no separate application for surfaces. You need to create the surface model in the Modeling environment. Before creating the surface model, you need to change the body type to sheet.

INVOKING THE SHEET MODELING ENVIRONMENT

To invoke the Sheet Modeling environment, invoke the Modeling environment and then choose **Preferences > Modeling** from the menu bar; the **Modeling Preferences** dialog box will be displayed, as shown in Figure 11-1. Choose the **General** tab and then select the **Sheet** radio button from the **Body Type** area. Next, choose the **OK** button to exit this dialog box. All models created, henceforth, in the Modeling environment will be sheet models.

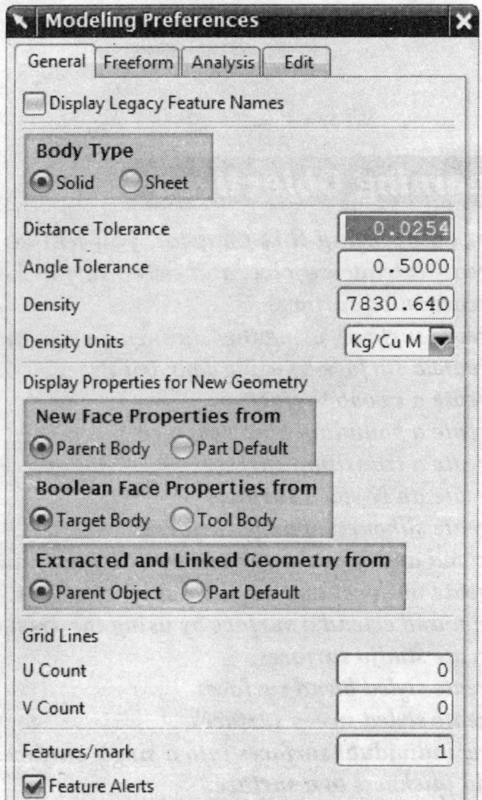

*Figure 11-1 The **Modeling Preferences** dialog box*

Creating an Extruded Surface

Menu: Insert > Design Feature > Extrude
Toolbar: Feature > Extrude

As mentioned earlier, there is no separate tool available for creating an extruded surface. After invoking the Sheet Modeling environment, you can use the **Extrude** tool to create extruded sheets. The sketch drawn for creating an extruded surface may be an open or a closed entity. After creating the sketch, choose the **Extrude** button from the **Feature** toolbar; the **Extrude** dialog box will be displayed and you will be prompted to select the section geometry to extrude. Select the sketch and enter the start and end extrusion values in their respective

Distance edit boxes, which are available below the **Start** and **End** drop-down lists of the **Limits** rollout in the dialog box. Next, choose the **OK** button from the **Extrude** dialog box; a sheet will be created. The options in the **Extrude** dialog box are the same as those discussed in Chapter 4. Figures 11-2 and 11-3 show the extruded surfaces created by using the open and closed sketches.

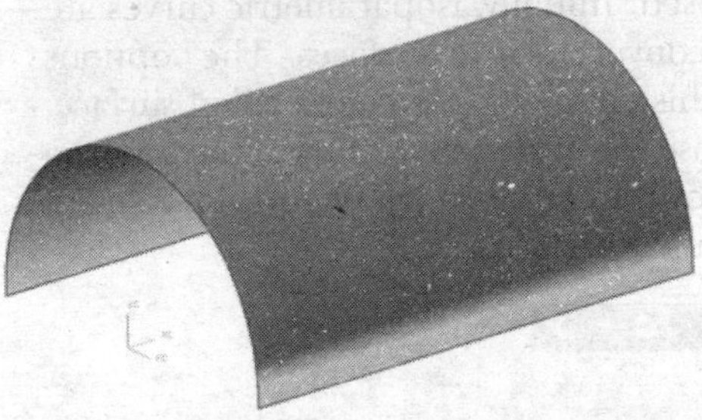

Figure 11-2 Extruded surface created on an open sketch

Figure 11-3 Extruded surface created on a closed sketch

Note

*You can use only the **None** option from the **Boolean** drop-down list in the **Sheet Modeling** environment. The other options of this drop-down list are not available in this environment.*

Creating a Revolved Surface

Menu:	Insert > Design Feature > Revolve
Toolbar:	Feature > Revolve

The **Revolve** tool is used to create a revolved surface. To create a revolved surface, first create a sketch, and then choose the **Revolve** button from the **Feature** toolbar; the **Revolve** dialog box will be displayed. Also, you will be prompted to select the section geometry. Select the sketch drawn for the revolved surface. Next, click on the **Specify Vector** area in the **Axis** rollout of the dialog box and specify the axis of revolution. Specify the start and end angles in the **Angle** edit boxes, respectively. Next, choose the **OK** button; a revolved surface will be created. The revolved surface models created by using an open sketch and a closed sketch are shown in Figures 11-4 and 11-5, respectively.

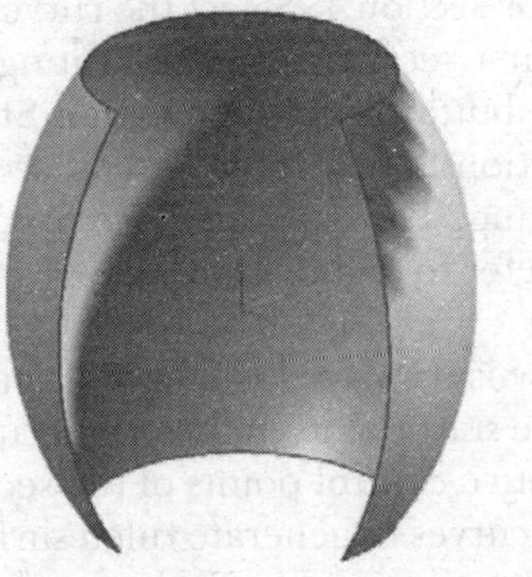

Figure 11-4 Revolved surface created using an open sketch

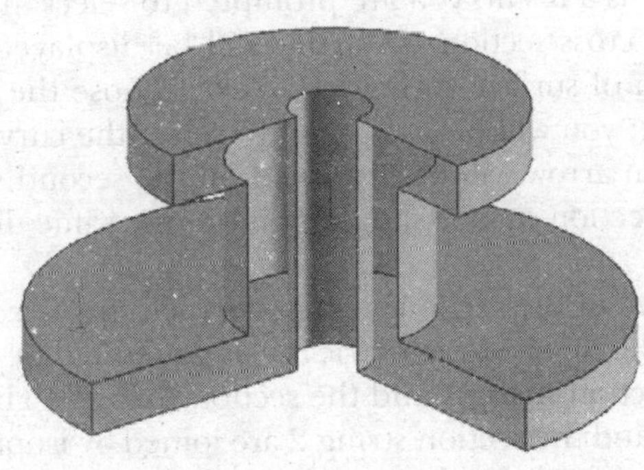

Figure 11-5 Revolved surface created using a closed sketch

Creating a Ruled Surface

Toolbar: Surface > Ruled *(Customize to add)*

The **Ruled** tool is used to create ruled surfaces. These surfaces are always created between two similar or dissimilar cross-sections lying on different planes. The sketches for this feature may be open or closed. Initially, isoparametric curves are formed to create patches, which are then converted into surfaces. The options to create isoparametric curves are discussed later in this chapter. To create a ruled surface, create two cross-sections on two different planes. Choose the **Ruled** button from the **Surface** toolbar; the **Ruled** dialog box will be displayed, as shown in Figure 11-6. Figure 11-7 shows two cross-sections on two different planes to create a ruled surface.

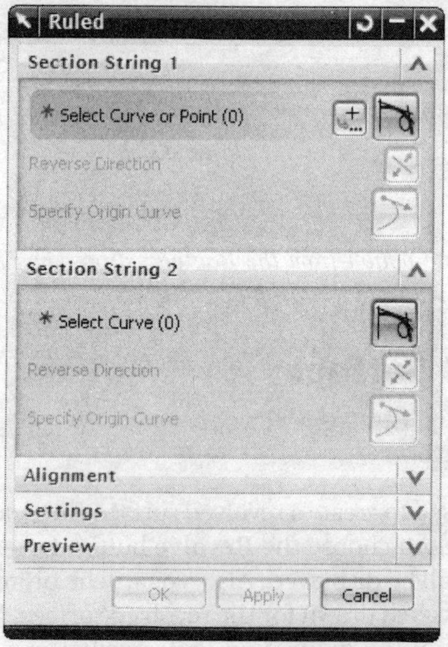

*Figure 11-6 The **Ruled** dialog box*

In the **Section String 1** rollout of the **Ruled** dialog box, the **Section 1** button is chosen by default. As a result, you are prompted to select the curves for section 1. Select the curves for the first cross-section; an arrow will be displayed on the first section string indicating the direction of surface formation. Next, choose the **Section 2** button from the **Section String 2** rollout; you will be prompted to select the curves for Section 2. Select the second section string; an arrow will be displayed on the second section string. The arrows on the first and second section strings should point in the same direction, refer to Figure 11-8.

The curve of the section string on which the direction arrow is displayed is known as origin curve. The first isoparametric line is generated by joining the start points of the origin curves of the section string 1 and the section string 2. The consecutive control points of the section string 1 and the section string 2 are joined by isoparametric curves to generate ruled surface. You can control the shape of a ruled surface by changing its origin curve. To do so, choose the **Specify Origin Curve** button from the respective rollouts in the **Ruled** dialog box and select the curve that you want to make as origin curve from the section string. Note that the **Specify Origin Curve** button will be available only if you select the closed sections as section strings. Note that you can use different rollouts in the **Ruled** dialog box to modify a surface. These rollouts are discussed next.

Alignment Rollout

The **Alignment** drop-down list in the **Alignment** rollout is used to specify different methods to distribute control points on section strings for creating isoparametric lines that form patches. If you select the **Parameter** option, the control points will be distributed such that the isoparametric lines are formed at uniform intervals. If you select the **By Points** option from the **Alignment** drop-down list, then isoparametric lines and control points will be displayed along the section string and the **Alignment** rollout will be modified. If you select the control point, the dynamic edit box will be displayed, as shown in Figure 11-8. You can drag the selected control point to change its position. Alternatively, you can directly enter the arc percentage in the dynamic edit box. To add a new control point in the section, click on the required curve; a control point will be created at that curve. To reset control points, choose the **Reset** button from the **Alignment** rollout. If you clear the **Preserve Shape** check box from the **Settings** rollout, some options will be displayed in the **Alignment** drop-down list, which are discussed next. If you select the **Arc length** option from the **Alignment** drop-down list, the entire curve will be divided into two equal segments with respect to arc length. Also, the isoparametric curve will pass through the dividing points.

Settings Rollout

By default, the **Preserve Shape** check box is selected in this rollout. As a result, sharp corners will be created while modifying control points. If you clear this check box, a smooth curvature will be formed while modifying the position of control points. You can use the **GO (position)** edit box only when the **Preserve Shape** check box is clear. In this edit box, you can enter maximum distance value upto which the shape of a ruled surface can be modified at sharp corners.

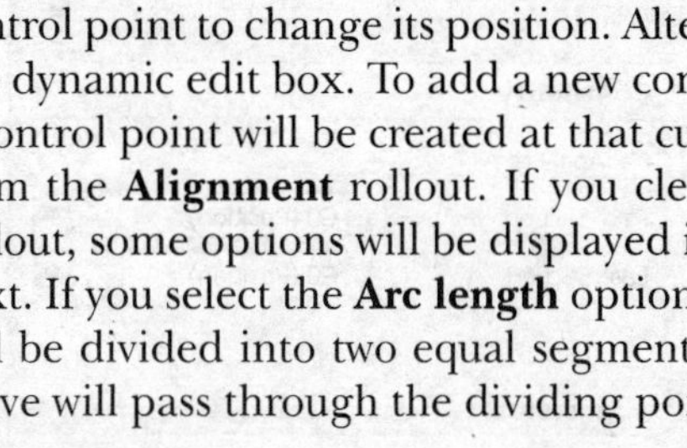

Figure 11-7 The section strings selected for creating the ruled surface

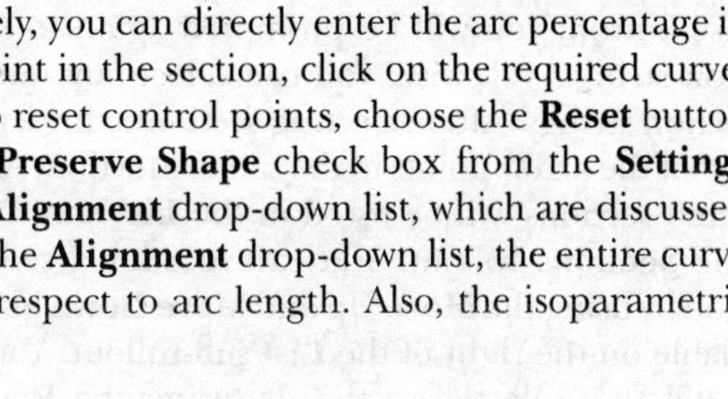

Figure 11-8 The ruled surface created from the selected section strings

Note

The maximum allowed and the minimum required numbers of cross-sections for creating a ruled surface are two.

Creating a Surface Using the Through Curves Tool

Menu: Insert > Mesh Surface > Through Curves
Toolbar: Surface > Through Curves

You can create surfaces with multiple section strings by using the **Through Curves** tool. This method allows you to select any number of section strings. To create surfaces by using the **Through Curves** tool, choose the **Through Curves** button from the **Surface** toolbar; the **Through Curves** dialog box will be displayed, as shown in Figure 11-9, and you will be prompted to select the section. Select the strings for first section and press the middle mouse button; you will be prompted again to select section strings. Likewise, you can select any number of section strings. After selecting section strings, make sure that the arrow points in the same direction. All the selected sections will be listed in the **List** sub-rollout of the **Sections** rollout. You can reorder a selected section by using the **Move Up** and **Move Down** buttons available on the right of the **List** sub-rollout. You can also delete a selected section by using the **Remove** button.

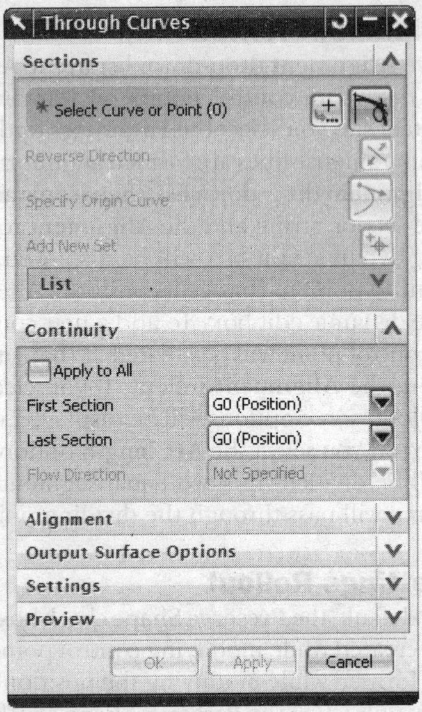

Figure 11-9 The Through Curves dialog box

In the **Patch Type** drop-down list of the **Output Surface Options** rollout, there are three options, **Single**, **Multiple**, and **Match String**. If you select the **Single** option, a surface will be created with a single patch. If you select the **Multiple** option, the surface will be created with multiple patches. The number of patches formed depends upon the **Alignment** option selected from the **Alignment** rollout.

When you select the **Multiple** option from the **Patch Type** drop-down list of the **Output Surface Options** rollout, the **Closed in V** and **Normal to End Sections** check boxes will be enabled. If you select the **Closed in V** check box, the surface body will be closed in the V direction and the **Normal to End Sections** check box will be deactivated. If you select the **Normal to End Sections** check box, the resultant surface will be normal to the two end sections and the options in the **Continuity** rollout will be deactivated. Figure 11-10 shows the section strings selected for creating surfaces through curves and Figure 11-11 shows the resulting surface.

Creating a Surface Using the Through Curve Mesh Tool

Menu: Insert > Mesh Surface > Through Curve Mesh
Toolbar: Surface > Through Curve Mesh

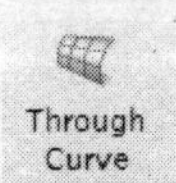

You can create surfaces by specifying section strings and guide strings using the **Through Curve Mesh** tool. You can specify any number of section strings and guide

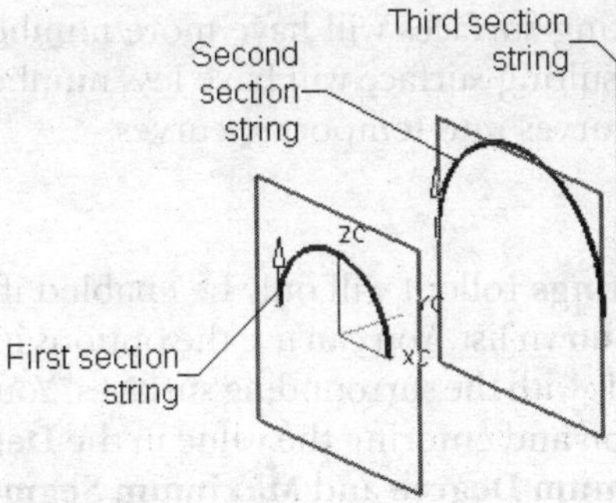

*Figure 11-10 Section strings selected for creating the **Through Curves** surface*

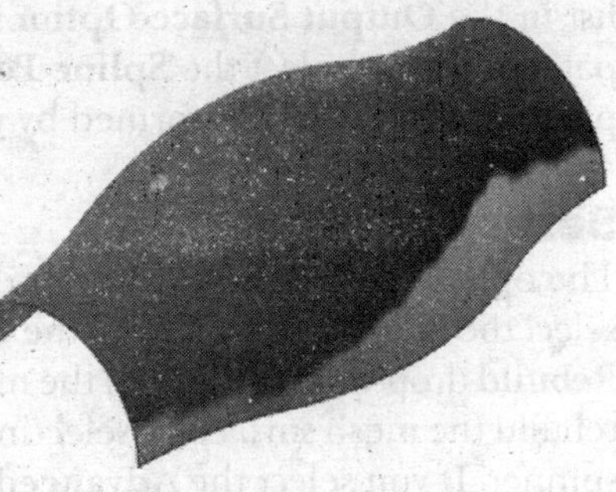

Figure 11-11 The resulting surface

strings. If you want to select multiple guide strings, they should be connected end-to-end with each other. To create a surface by using the **Through Curve Mesh** method, invoke the **Through Curve Mesh** tool from the **Surface** toolbar; the **Through Curve Mesh** dialog box will be displayed, as shown in Figure 11-12, and you will be prompted to select primary curve. You need to select a collection of control curves. Select the first primary curves and press the middle mouse button to select the next primary curve. Similarly, you can select any number of primary curves. Next, choose the **Cross Curves** button from the **Cross Curves** rollout; you will be prompted to select cross curves. Select the first cross curve and press the middle mouse button to select the next cross curve. Similarly, you can select any number of cross curves.

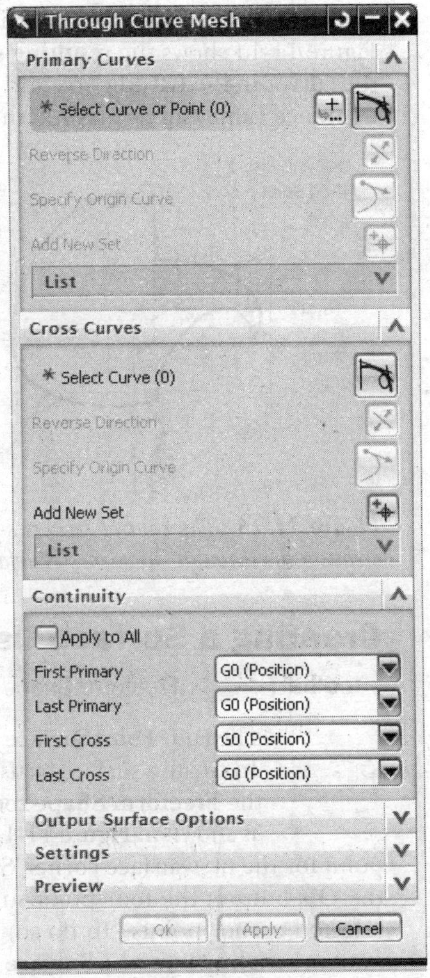

*Figure 11-12 The **Through Curve Mesh** dialog box*

Note that after selecting two primary curves, the **Spine** rollout will be added to the **Through Curve Mesh** dialog box. The **Spline** button in this rollout allows you to select the spine string. This spine string improves the smoothness of the surface and it must be normal to all primary strings. However, the selection of the spine string is optional. If you want to skip this step, do not choose this button.

Output Surface Options Rollout

The options from the **Emphasis** drop-down list in the **Output Surface Options** rollout are used to define the set of curves that affect the shape of the surface to be created. Select the **Both** option from the **Emphasis** drop-down list, the primary curves and cross curves will have an equal effect. If you select the **Normal** option from the **Construction** drop-down list in the **Output Surface Options** rollout, the resulting surfaces will have more number of patches. If you select the **Spline Points** option, the resulting surface will have less number of patches. The surface is formed by reparameterizing curves into temporary curves.

Settings Rollout

The options in the **Rebuild** drop-down list of the **Settings** rollout will only be enabled if you select the **Normal** option from the **Construction** drop-down list. You can use the options in the **Rebuild** drop-down list to join the mesh surface smoothly with the surrounding surfaces. You can rebuild the mesh surface by selecting the **Manual** option and entering the value in the **Degree** spinner. If you select the **Advanced** option, the **Maximum Degree** and **Maximum Segments** spinners will be enabled. You can set the values in these spinners to rebuild the mesh surface automatically.

Figure 11-13 shows the control strings selected for creating the through curve mesh surface and Figure 11-14 shows the resulting surface. You can enter the distance tolerance value between the curves in the **G0** edit box and the angle tolerance value in the **G1** edit box. The curvature tolerance value can be entered in the **G2** edit box.

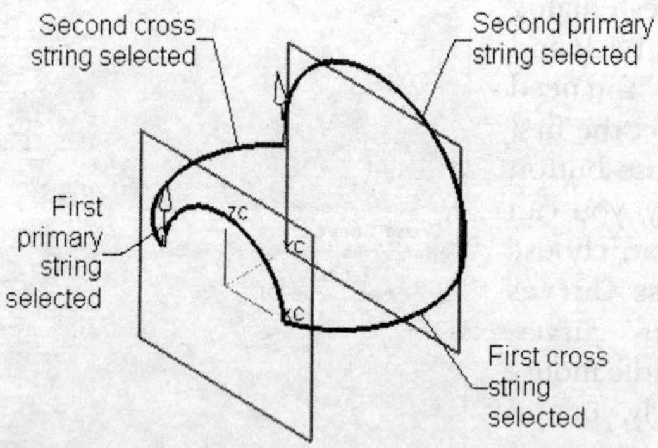

Figure 11-13 The control strings selected for creating the through curve mesh surface

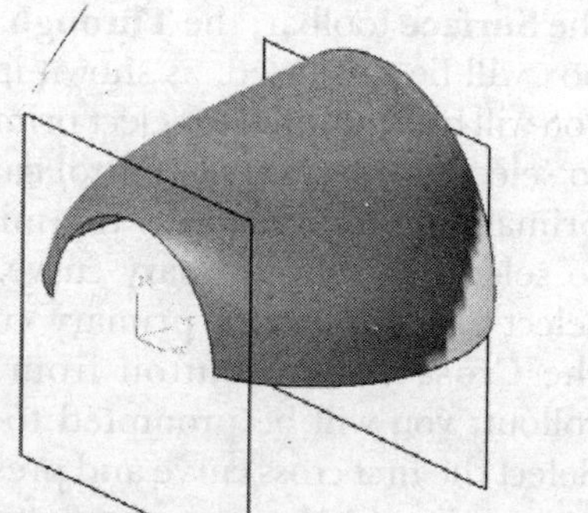

Figure 11-14 The resulting through curve mesh surface

Creating a Surface Using the Four Point Surface Tool

Toolbar: Freeform Shape > Four Point Surface

The **Four Point Surface** tool is used to create a planar (2D) or non-planar (3D) surface. To create a surface by using this method, choose the **Four Point Surface** button from the **Freeform Shape** toolbar; the **Four Point Surface** dialog box will be displayed, as shown in Figure 11-15, and you will be prompted to specify the point. Specify the point for the first surface corner. Similarly, specify the other three surface corners and choose the **OK** button; the four point surface will be created. You can also redefine the previously selected corner points. To do so, choose the button corresponding to the point, which you want to redefine from the **Surface Corners** rollout; the respective point will be highlighted in the graphics window. Again, specify the point for the corner. Figure 11-16 shows the corner points to be selected for creating a surface. Figure 11-17 shows the resulting surface formed by enclosing the specified corner points.

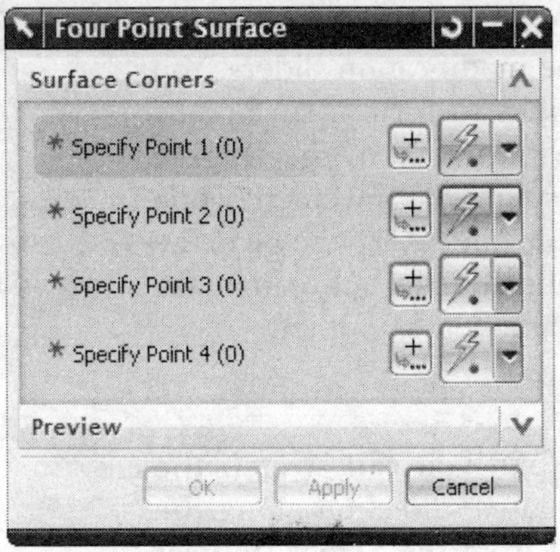

*Figure 11-15 The **Four Point Surface** dialog box*

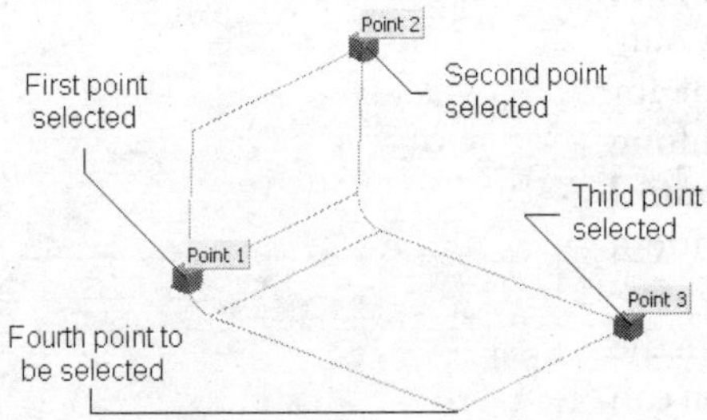

Figure 11-16 The four corner points to be selected for creating a surface

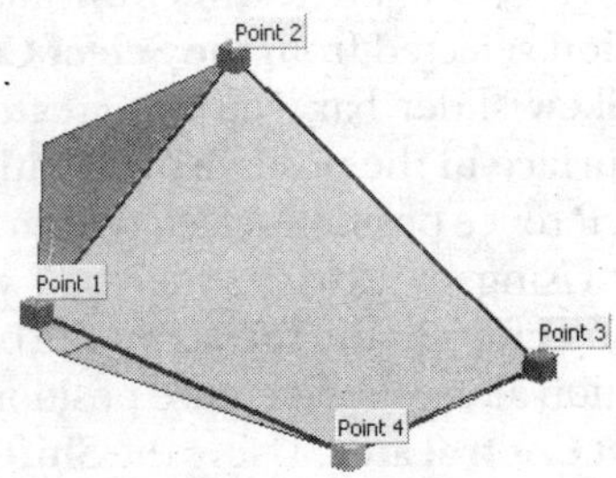

Figure 11-17 The resulting surface

Creating a Swoop Surface

Toolbar:	Freeform Shape > Swoop

Swoop surfaces are created as rectangular or square shaped planar (2D) surfaces, and later modified into 3D surfaces by using the options in the **Swoop** tool. To create a swoop surface, choose the **Swoop** button from the **Freeform Shape** toolbar; the **Point** dialog box will be displayed and you will be prompted to select a point. Specify the point for the first corner of the rectangle; you will be prompted to select the second corner point of the rectangle. Also, an imaginary rectangle will be displayed with one corner attached to the first specified corner point and the second corner point to the cursor. Specify the second corner of the rectangle; the planar surface will be created. The vertical and horizontal axes will be displayed over the planar surface. Also, the **Swoop Shape Control** dialog box will be displayed, as shown in Figure 11-18. The **Swoop Shape Control** dialog box is used to modify the shape of the default surface formed. In the **Select Control** area, you have all the possible reference positions of the surface. At a time, the shape of the surface can be modified only at one reference position. You can select any one option and the shape of the surface will be altered in the selected reference position by using the shape modification sliders. You can use the 3 degree splines to form a surface by selecting the **Cubic** radio button from the **Degree** area. The use of 3 degree splines is convenient while transferring surface data from one CAD package to the other. You can select the **Quintic** radio button to make the resulting surface comparatively smoother.

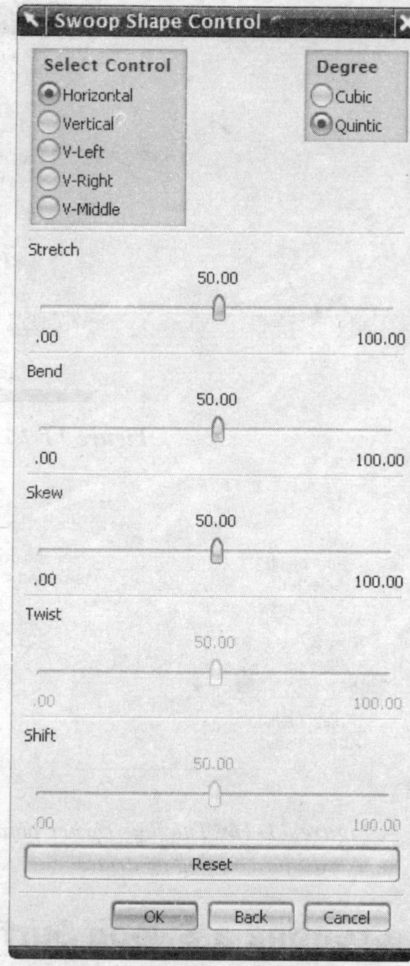

Figure 11-18 *The* ***Swoop Shape Control*** *dialog box*

Sliding Bars

Using the **Stretch** slider bar, you can stretch the surface in a positive or negative direction along the reference position selected from the **Select Control** area. The neutral value is 50 for all sliders. Using the **Bend** slider bar, you can bend the surface in a positive or negative direction along the reference position selected from the **Select Control** area. Using the **Skew** slider bar, you can create a skew factor for the surface in the positive or negative direction along the reference position selected from the **Select Control** area. Using the **Twist** slider bar, you can provide a twisting effect to the surface in the positive or negative direction along the reference position selected from the **Select Control** area. Using the **Shift** slider bar, you can shift the other edge of the surface in the positive or negative direction along the reference position selected from the **Select Control** area. Figure 11-19 shows the planar surface created after specifying two corners of the rectangle. Figure 11-20 shows the 3D surface created on modifying the planar surface by using the shape modification sliding bars.

Figure 11-19 *The planar surface created after specifying two corners of the rectangle*

Figure 11-20 *The 3D surface created on modifying the planar surface*

Creating Planar Surfaces from 2D Sketches and Edges of Solid or Surface

Toolbar: Feature > Bounded Plane *(Customize to add)*

The **Bounded Plane** tool is used to create a surface from 2D sketches or closed coplanar edges. If you need to enclose a 2D sketch or a closed coplanar edges with a surface, choose the **Bounded Plane** button from the **Feature** toolbar; the **Bounded Plane** dialog box will be displayed, as shown in Figure 11-21, and you will be prompted to select curves for the bounded plane. Select the closed coplanar edges of the object or the closed coplanar sketch and then choose the **OK** button; the bounded plane surface will be created. Figure 11-22 shows a bounded plane surface enclosing a 2D sketch and Figure 11-23 shows a bounded plane surface created from a circular edge. You can create a bounded plane surface by selecting the closed coplanar edges of the solid and surface bodies.

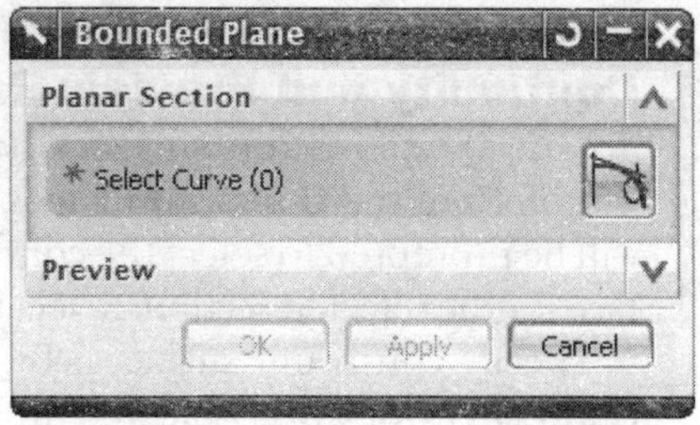

***Figure 11-21** The **Bounded Plane** dialog box*

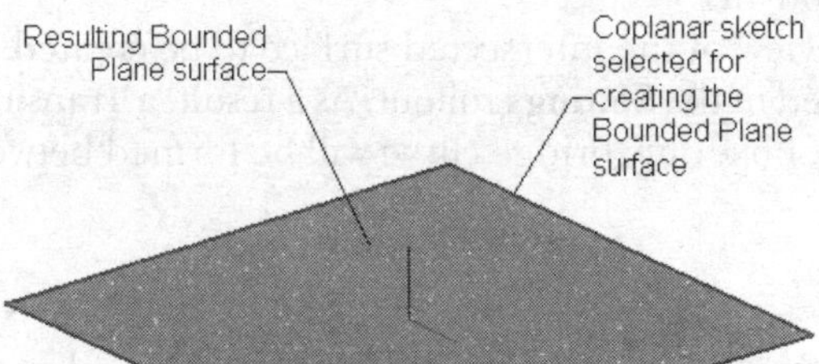

***Figure 11-22** The bounded plane surface formed from a 2D sketch*

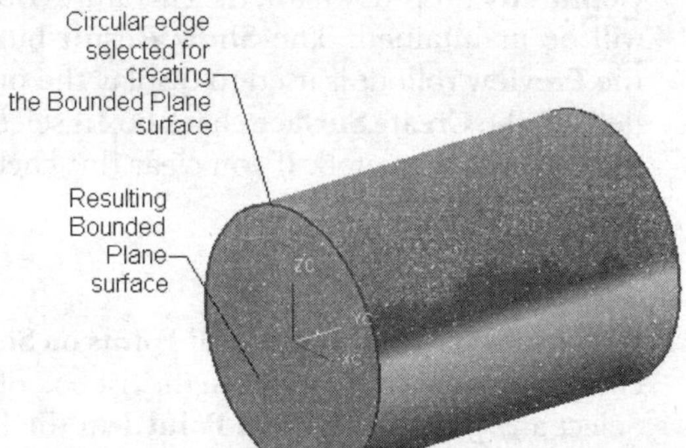

***Figure 11-23** The bounded plane surface formed from a circular edge*

Creating a Transition Surface Using the Transition Tool

Toolbar: Surface > Transition

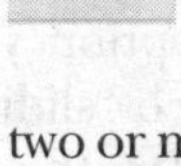

Generally, creation of a transition surface involves with the selection of required cross-sections and mapping the intersected surface formed between the selected cross-sections automatically. You can define the shape constraint for a connecting (intersecting) surface. To create a transition surface, you need to create two or more than two cross-sections. After creating cross-sections, choose the **Transition** button from the **Surface** toolbar; the **Transition** dialog box will be displayed, as shown in Figure 11-24 and you will be prompted to select curves/edges to section because the **Sections** button in the **Sections** rollout is chosen by default. Select sections and choose the **OK** button. Note that you need to press the middle mouse button after selecting every section. After selecting sections, the wireframe preview of the resultant model will be displayed. Figure 11-25 shows the wireframe view of the resultant model and Figure 11-26 shows the resulting surface.

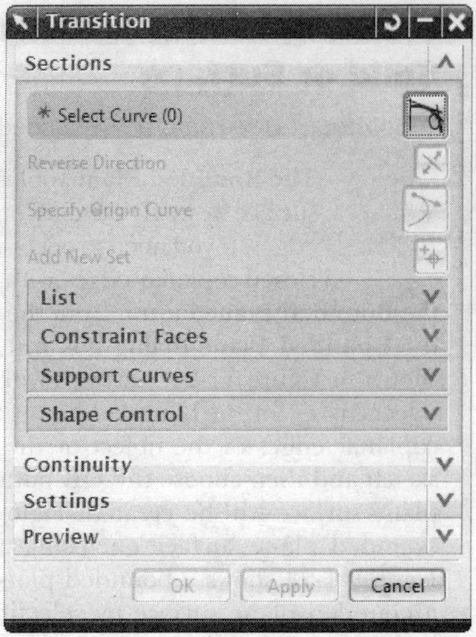

*Figure 11-24 The **Transition** dialog box*

Constraint Faces Sub-rollout, and Continuity and Preview Rollouts

To specify constraint surfaces, choose the **Face** button from the **Constraint Faces** sub-rollout; you will be prompted to select the continuity constraint face for the selected section. Select the required face to specify constraint surfaces. By default, the **G1 (Tangent)** option is selected in the **Continuity** drop-down list of the **Continuity** rollout. As a result, there is tangential continuity constraint with the intersected surface. If you select the **G0 (Position)** option from the **Continuity** drop-down list, the positioned continuity will be maintained. If you select the **G2 (Curvature)** option from the **Continuity** drop-down list, the curvature continuity will be maintained. The **Show Result** button in the **Preview** rollout is used to display the preview of the intersected surface to be created. By default, the **Create Surface** check box is selected in the **Settings** rollout. As a result, a Transition surface will be created. If you clear this check box, only bridge curve will be formed between cross-sections.

Support Curves

In this sub-rollout, the **Show All Points on Section** check box is clear by default. If you select this check box, all section points in the list box of the **Support Curves** sub-rollout will be displayed. Select any point other than **Point 1** in the list box; the **Add** button will be activated. Choose this button; a new section point will be added in the list box as well as on the selected section. You can move this new section point by dragging it. To remove the created section point, select it and choose the **Remove** button from this sub-rollout.

Shape Control

The bridge curves formed after selecting the cross-sections of the surfaces are listed as individual curves and separate groups in the **Bridge Curves** drop-down list of this sub-rollout. You can select the required bridge curve from the **Bridge Curves** drop-down list. By selecting the required curve from the **Bridge Curves** drop-down list, you can control the shape of the selected bridge curve in two ways: using the **Tangent Magnitude** and the **Depth And Skew** options available in the **Type** drop-down list. If you select the **Tangent Magnitude** option, you can control the shape of the selected curve from the start point or the end point by sliding the **Start** or **End** slider bars. If you select the **Depth And Skew** option, then the **Depth** and **Skew** slider bars will be available in this sub-rollout to control the depth and the skew angle of the selected bridge curve.

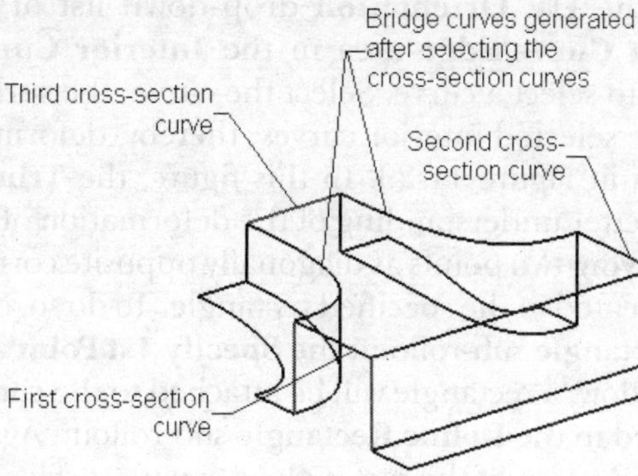

Figure 11-25 The wireframe view of the resulting transition surface created from cross-sections

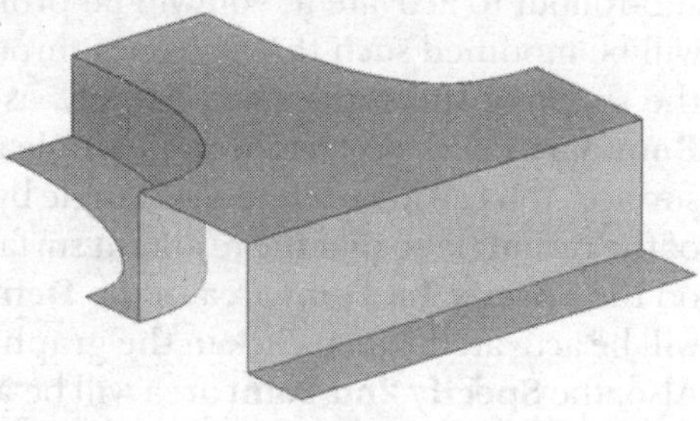

Figure 11-26 The resulting transition surface created from cross-sections

Creating an N-sided Surface

Toolbar:	Surface > N-sided Surface

The **N-sided Surface** tool is used to create a single patch surface or multi-patches triangular surfaces that enclose a closed 2D sketch or a closed 3D curve. While doing so, an existing surface can optionally be selected as a reference for maintaining the shape of the surface to be created. To create an N-sided surface, choose the **N-sided Surface** button from the **Surface** toolbar; the **N-sided Surface** dialog box will be displayed, as shown in Figure 11-27, and you will be prompted to select a closed loop of curves or edges. By default, the **Trimmed** option is selected in the **Type** drop-down list. As a result, a surface with a single patch will be created. To create a surface with multiple triangular patches, you need to select the **Triangular** option from the **Type** drop-down list. Both the options used for creating the N-sided surface are discussed next.

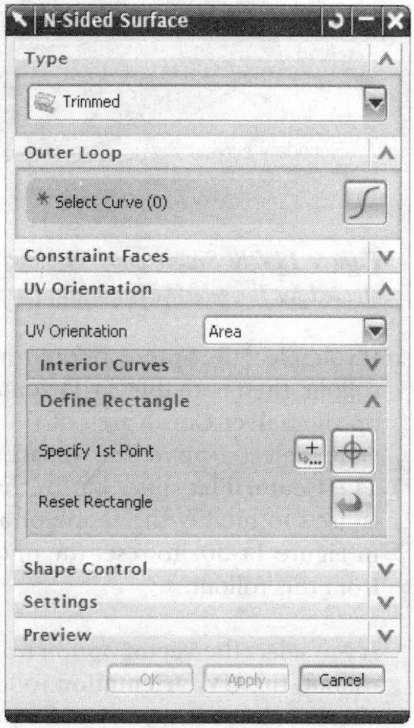

Figure 11-27 The N-Sided Surface dialog box

Trimmed

By default, the **Curve** button is chosen in the **Outer Loop** rollout. As a result, you will be prompted to select a closed loop. Select a closed boundary of a 2D sketch, edges, or a 3D curve; the preview of the new surface will be displayed. Next, select the **Trim to Boundary** check box from the **Settings** rollout; the surface created will automatically be trimmed with respect to the closed loop of the curve, as shown in Figure 11-28.

By default, the **Area** option is selected in the **UV Orientation** drop-down list of the **UV Orientation** rollout. Click on the **Select Curve/Edge** area in the **Interior Curves** sub-rollout to activate it; you will be prompted to select a curve. Select the curve; the surface will be modified such that it passes through the selected interior curves; thereby, deforming the shape of the surface accordingly, as shown in Figure 11-29. In this figure, the **Trim to Boundary** check box has been made clear for better understanding of the deformation of the surface. You can also define a rectangle by specifying two points as diagonally opposite corners of the rectangle so that the resultant surface is created in the specified rectangle. To do so, click on the **Specify 1st Point** area in the **Define Rectangle** sub-rollout; the **Specify 1st Point** area will be activated. Next, click in the graphics window; a rectangle will be attached to the cursor. Also, the **Specify 2nd Point** area will be activated in the **Define Rectangle** sub-rollout. Again, click in the graphic window to specify the second point of the rectangle; a square surface will be created in the graphic window. To reset the rectangle created, choose the **Reset Rectangle** button from the **Define Rectangle** sub-rollout.

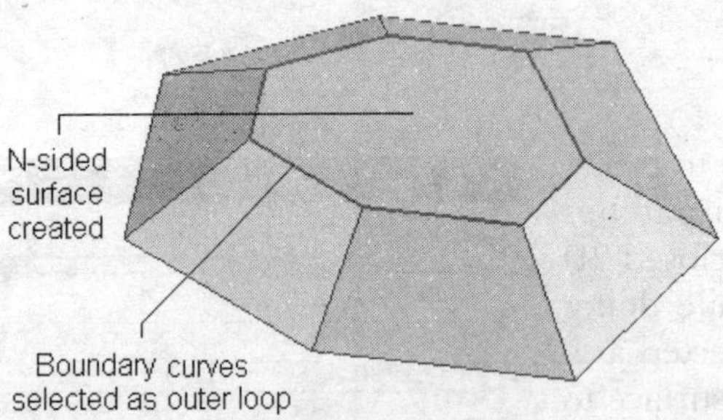

Figure 11-28 Single patch N-sided surface created for the selected boundary curve

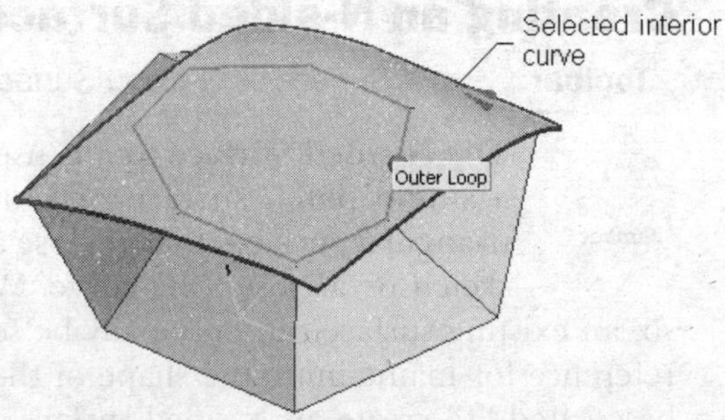

Figure 11-29 Modified part with interior curve selected

If you select the **Spine** option from the **UV Orientation** drop-down list in the **UV Orientation** rollout, then both the **UV Orientation** and the **Shape Control** rollouts will be modified. Click on the **Select Curve** area of the **Spine** sub-rollout; you will be prompted to select a curve/ edge. Select a curve; the surface will be oriented perpendicular to the selected spine curve. The **Center Flat** slider bar in the **Central Control** sub-rollout of the **Shape Control** rollout is used to modify the shape of a surface created with respect to a selected curve, as shown in Figure 11-30. To reset the options in the **Shape Control** rollout, choose the **Reset** button from this rollout.

If you select the **Vector** option from the **UV Orientation** drop-down list in the **UV Orientation** rollout, the **UV Orientation** rollout will be modified. Click on the **Specify Vector** area of the **Vector** sub-rollout; you will be prompted to select the object to infer vector. Select a vector; the surface will follow the selected vector direction. The **Center Flat** slider bar in the **Central Control** sub-rollout of the **Shape Control** rollout is used to modify the shape of a surface created with respect to a specified vector, as shown in Figure 11-31. To reset the options in the **Shape Control** rollout, choose the **Reset** button from the **Shape Control** rollout.

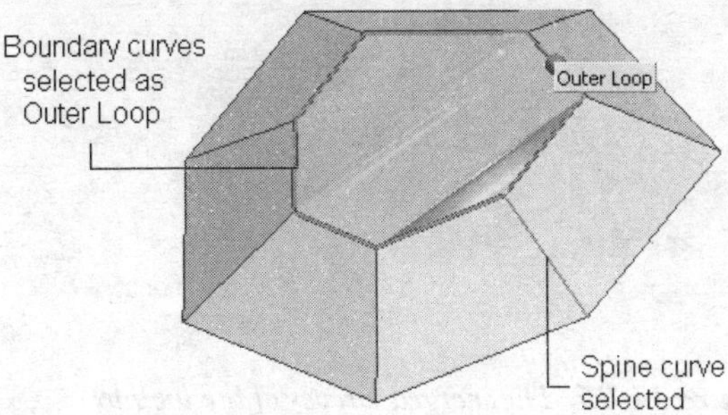

Figure 11-30 *Modified part with the spine curve selected*

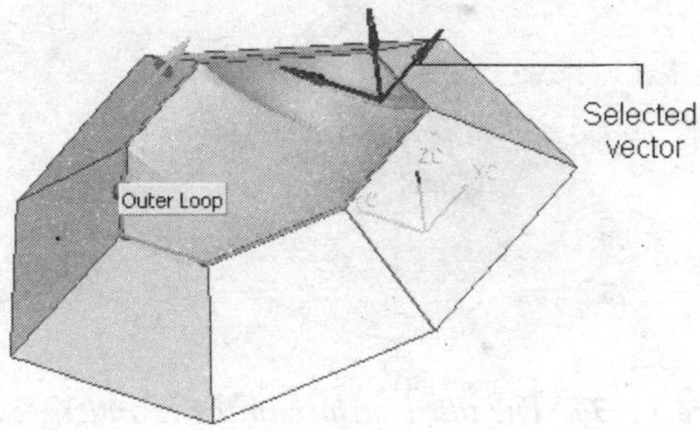

Figure 11-31 *Modified part with the selected vector*

Triangular

To create a triangular patch surface, select the **Triangular** option from the **Type** drop-down list in the **Type** rollout; you will be prompted to select a curve/edge. Select the closed entity; the preview of the selected surface will be displayed in the graphics window, as shown in Figure 11-32 and the **Shape Control** and **Settings** rollouts will be modified.

By default, the **Position** option is selected in the **Control** drop-down list of the **Center Control** sub-rollout in the **Shape Control** rollout. You can move the center point of the new surface in the X, Y, and Z directions by using the **X**, **Y**, and **Z** slider bars, respectively, as shown in Figure 11-33. You can specify the flow direction of the new surface as per your requirement by selecting any one of the following options from the **Flow Direction** drop-down list: **Not Specified**, **Perpendicular**, **Iso U/V Line**, or **Adjacent Edge**.

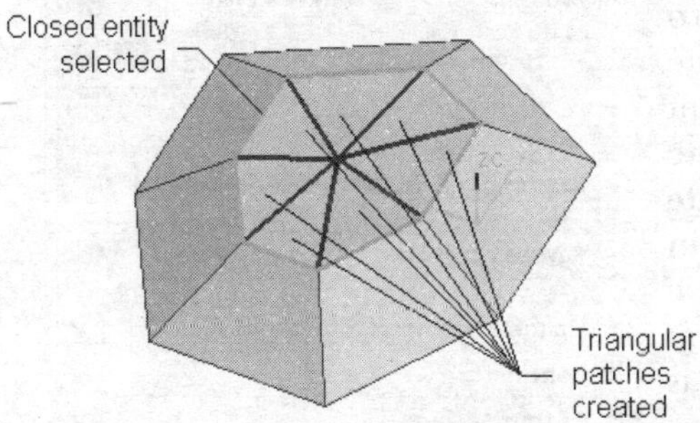

Figure 11-32 *Triangular patches created using the **Triangular** option*

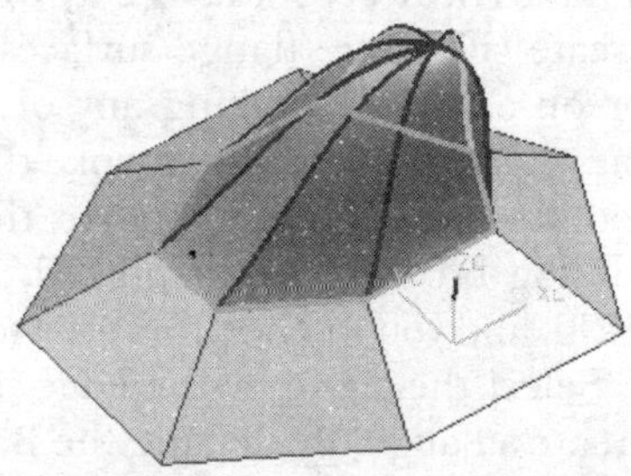

Figure 11-33 *Modified surface in the X, Y, and Z directions*

Select the **Tilting** option from the **Control** drop-down list and then use the **X** and **Y** slider bars to tilt the created surface in the X and Y directions, respectively, as shown in Figure 11-34. By default, the **Merge Faces if Possible** check box in the **Settings** rollout is clear. As a result, patches are created for each edge of the loop. If you select this check box, the patches of the loop will be removed by treating the tangent continuous edges as a single loop, as shown in Figure 11-35.

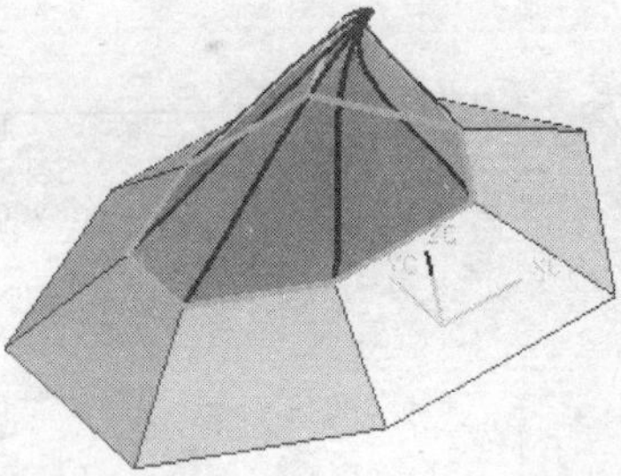

Figure 11-34 The tilted surface in the X and Y directions

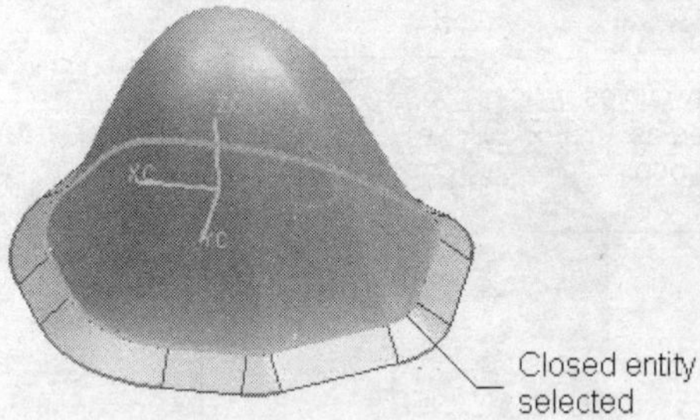

*Figure 11-35 The merged curves of the loop by selecting the **Merge Faces if Possible** check box*

Creating a Silhouette Flange Surface

Toolbar: Surface > Silhouette Flange

The silhouette flange surfaces are created with respect to an existing surface such that the aesthetic shape, quality, and the slope continuity of the existing surface are maintained. The flange surface is created with a full round surface or a fillet at the start point. The flange created can be dynamically modified in shape and size. The silhouette flange surface can be created by using any of the three methods discussed next.

Creating a Silhouette Flange Surface Using the Basic Method

The **Silhouette Flange** tool is used to create silhouette flange surfaces on an edge or on a curve by taking any of the adjacent surfaces as reference. To do so, invoke the **Silhouette Flange** tool from the **Surface** toolbar; the **Silhouette Flange** dialog box will be displayed, as shown in Figure 11-36, and you will be prompted to select curve or edges. Select the curve or the edge on which you want to create a flange. By default, the **Basic** option is selected in the **Type** drop-down list and the **Curve** button is chosen in the **Base Curve** rollout. Selecting the **Basic** option enables you to create a flange without the help of any other existing flange surfaces. Select an edge or a curve for creating the silhouette flange surface and choose the **Face** button from the **Base Face** rollout; you will be prompted to select the face that will act as base face. Select the desired face. The other options in this dialog box are discussed next.

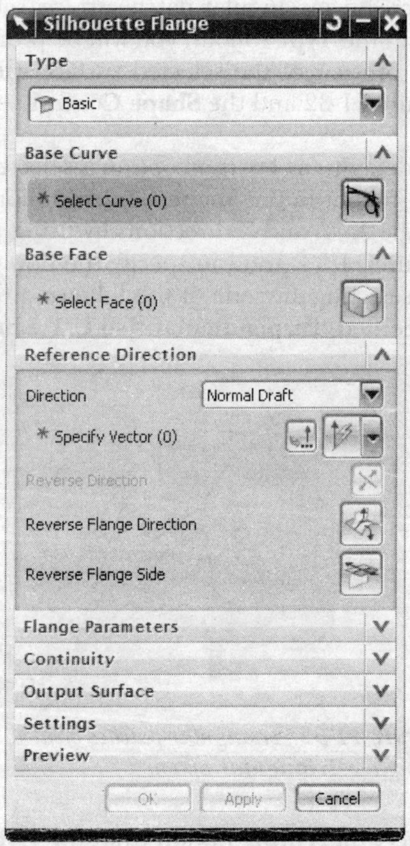

*Figure 11-36 The **Silhouette Flange** dialog box*

Reference Direction Rollout

In this rollout, you can specify the direction of a flange by selecting any one of the options from the **Direction** drop-down list. These options are **Face Normal**, **Vector**, **Normal Draft**, and **Vector Draft**. By default, the **Normal draft** option is selected in the **Direction** drop-down list. Clink on the **Specify Vecto**r area of this rollout to activate it, and then select the vector; the preview of the flange surface will be displayed, as shown in Figure 11-37. To change the direction of the flange to opposite direction, choose the **Reverse Flange Direction** button from this rollout; the direction of the flange will be reversed. To switch the flange extension to the opposite side of the bend, select the **Reverse Flange Side** button from this rollout. If you do not get the desired result after choosing this button, choose the **Reverse Direction** button from this rollout.

Flange Parameters Rollout

You can use the options in this rollout to control the parameters of a flange. Alternatively, you can control the parameters of the flange by using the handle and angular handles in the graphic window. If you select a handle from the graphic window, then the respective dynamic edit box will be displayed. You can enter value in the edit box or drag the handle to modify the respective parameters of the flange.

By default, the **Specify New Location** area is activated in the **Length** sub-rollout. As a result, you will be prompted to select the object to infer point. Select the point on the base curve; a control point and a dynamic edit box will be displayed. Enter the desired value in this edit box to specify the location of the point on curve. To change the radius at this point, drag the handle pointing normal to the flange; the radius at that point will be changed. To change the length of the flange at the selected point, drag the handle pointing parallel to the flange. To change the bend angle of the flange, drag the angular handle; the bend angle of the flange will be changed.

You can change the transition type of the bend radius of the flange to modify the bend radius by selecting the options **(Constant**, **Linear**, **Blend**, and **Minimum/Maximum)** from in the **Values Along Spine** sub-rollout of the **Flange Parameters** rollout. You can change the transition type of the length of the flange to modify the length by selecting the options **(Constant**, **Linear**, **Bend**, and **Minimum/Maximum)** from the **Length** sub-rollout, refer to Figure 11-38.

Continuity Rollout

You can control the continuity between the base and the bent portion using the options in the **Base and Pipe** sub-rollout of the **Continuity** rollout. To do so, select the required G1, G2, and G3 continuities in the **Continuity** drop-down list of the **Base and Pipe** sub-rollout. To control the amount of edge shift, you can use the **Lead-in** slider bar. Alternatively, you can use the **Lead-in** edit box to control the edge shift. Similarly, you can control the continuity between the flange and the bent portion in the **Flange and Pipe** sub-rollout of this rollout, refer to Figure 11- 38.

Output Surface Rollout

In this rollout, the **Bend and Flange** option is selected by default in the **Output Options** drop-down list. If you select the **Pipe Only** option from this drop-down list, then only a pipe will be created. If you select the **Flange Only** option from the **Output Options**

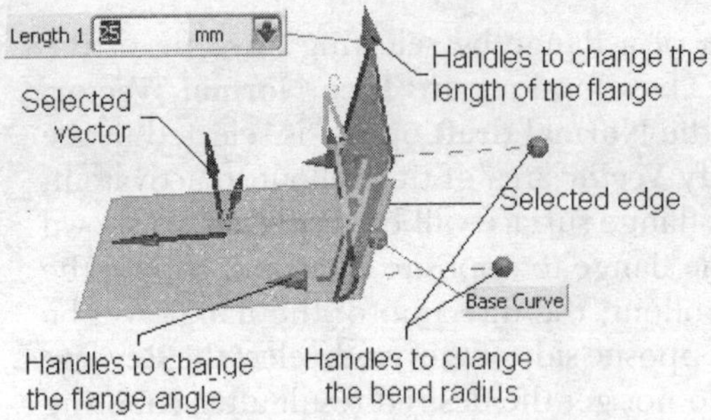

Figure 11-37 Preview of the component

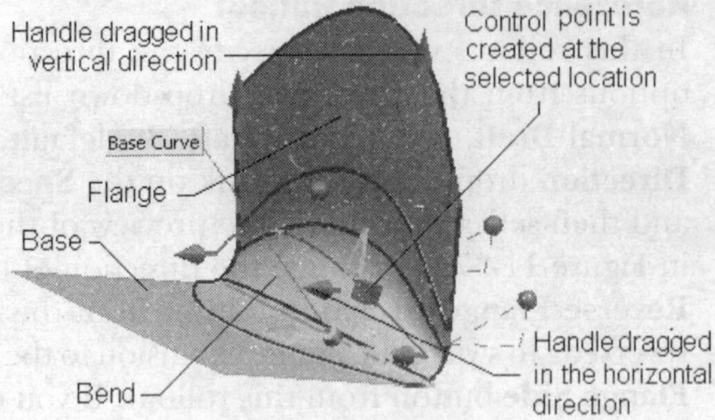

Figure 11-38 Part modified using the ***Flange Parameters*** *and* ***Continuity*** *rollouts*

drop-down list, then only a flange will be created. By default, the **Trim Base Faces** check box is clear in this rollout. As a result, the portion extended beyond the flange will be retained, as shown in Figure 11-39. If you want to remove the unwanted portion of the flange, select the **Trim Base Faces** check box. The **Extend Flange** check box will be available only when the **Trim Base Faces** check box is clear. If you select this check box, the flange will be extended to cover the entire span of the base surface.

Settings Rollout

By default, the **Create Curves** check box is clear in this rollout. If you select this check box, two curves will be created along the center of the bend radius and at the intersection of the bend and the flange. If you select the **Show Pipe** check box in this rollout; the pipe of the bend radius will be displayed in the preview, as shown in Figure 11-40.

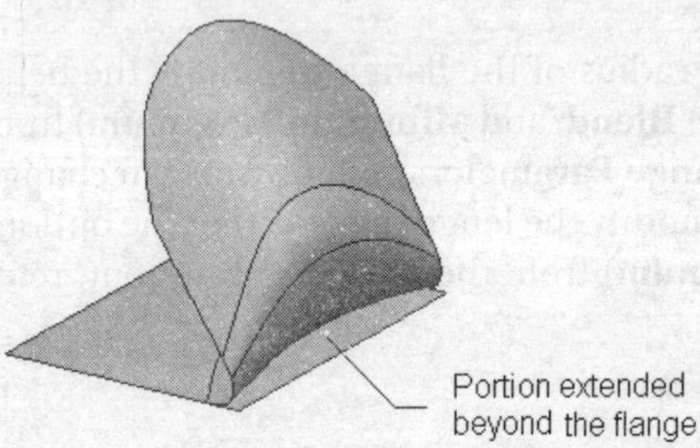

Figure 11-39 Unwanted extended surface

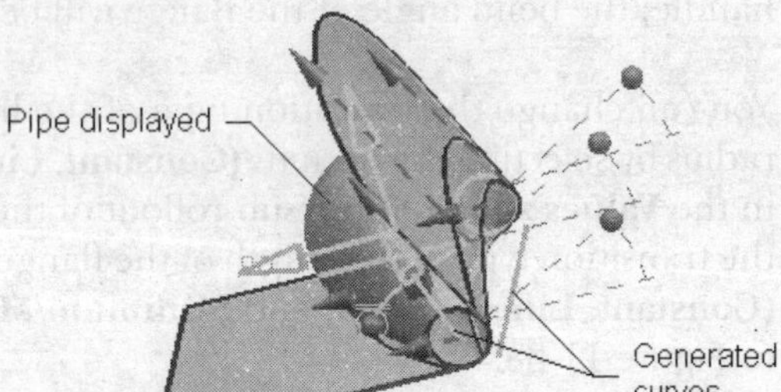

Figure 11-40 Pipe of the bend radius displayed in the preview

Creating a Silhouette Flange Surface Using the Absolute Gap Method

By selecting the **Absolute Gap** option from the **Type** drop-down list in the **Type** rollout, you can create a silhouette flange surface relative to an existing silhouette flange surface by maintaining a predefined gap. The minimum gap is calculated by taking the center line of the bend radius of the two pipes and the nearest tangential distance between them. You can also maintain the predefined gap between two silhouette flange surfaces by entering a gap value in the **Gap** edit box.

If you select the **Absolute Gap** option from the **Type** drop-down list in the **Type** rollout, the **Base Feature** rollout will be displayed. By default, the **Base Feature** button is chosen in the **Base Face** rollout. As a result, you will be prompted to select the silhouette flange to define the base flange. Select the existing flange, and then click on the **Select Face** area of the **Base Face** rollout; you will be prompted to select the faces to define the base face. Select the reference face. Next, specify the reference direction in the **Reference Direction** rollout. To do so, choose the **Reverse Flange Side** button in the **Reference Direction** rollout; the preview of the resultant component will be displayed, as shown in Figure 11-41. To change the gap between the created flange and the existing selected flange, you can enter the required value in the **Gap** edit box, which is available at the bottom of the **Flange Parameters** rollout.

Creating a Silhouette Flange Surface Using the Visual Gap Method

The **Visual Gap** option from the **Type** drop-down list in the **Type** rollout is used to create a flange surface in accordance with an existing flange surface by specifying a visual gap attribute between the two flange surfaces. To create the silhouette flange surface using the visual gap method, select the **Visual Gap** option from the **Type** drop-down list in the **Type** rollout of the **Silhouette Flange** dialog box. The selection procedure for reference objects is the same as discussed in the previous two methods. Enter the gap value in the **Gap** edit box and choose the **OK** button to create the surface. Figure 11-42 shows the silhouette flange created by using the **Visual Gap** method.

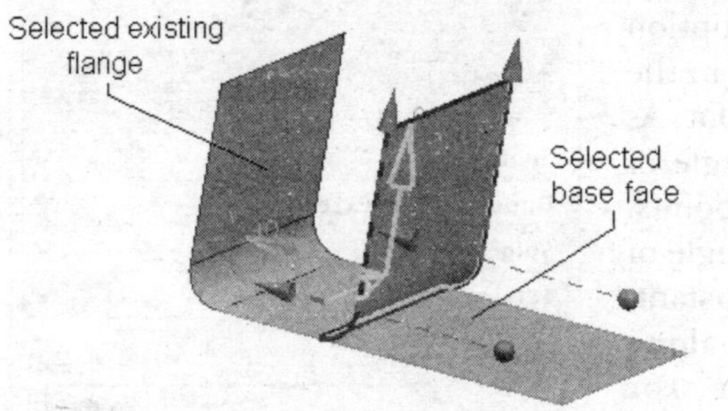

Figure 11-41 The newly created silhouette flange surface displayed along with handles and pipe

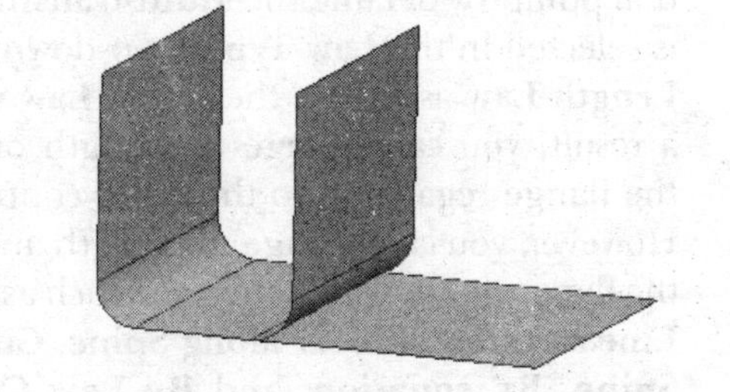

*Figure 11-42 The resultant silhouette flange surface created using the **Visual Gap** method*

Extending a Surface Using the Law Extension Tool

Toolbar: Surface > Law Extension

The **Law Extension** tool is used to extend a surface either dynamically or by defining different type of laws for an extension. The extension of the surface can be carried out in both the directions of the edge or the curve selected. The process of extending the surface by using each of these methods is discussed next.

Extending a Surface Dynamically Using the Faces Option

As discussed earlier, you can extend a surface dynamically by using the **Law Extension** tool. To do so, choose the **Law Extension** button from the **Surface** toolbar; the

Law Extension dialog box will be displayed, refer to Figure 11-43 and you will be prompted to select the base curve profile. By default, the **Faces** option is selected from the **Type** drop-down list in the **Type** rollout. Using this method, you can extend the surface by taking an existing face as reference. Select the curve string that you want to extend from the surface and choose the **Face** button from the **Reference Faces** rollout; you will be prompted to select reference faces. Select the required face as the reference face and then click on the **Specify New Location** area in the **Length Law** rollout; the preview of the surface will be displayed, as shown in Figure 11-44.

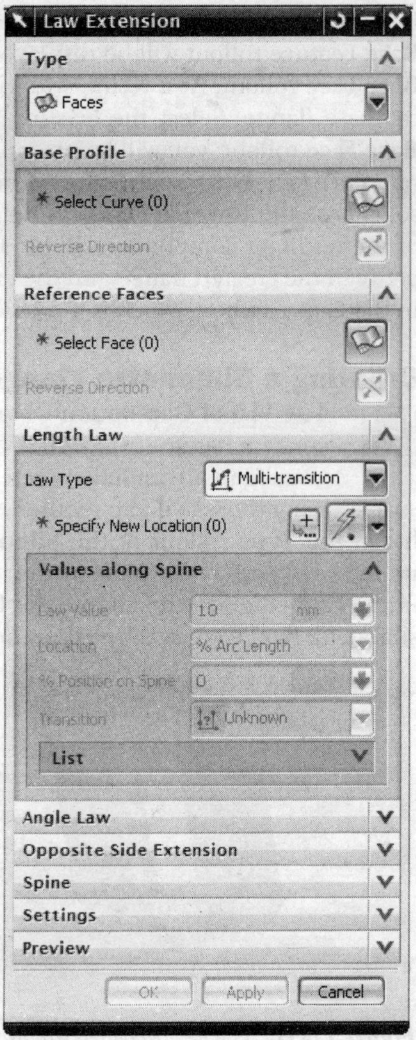

Figure 11-43 The Law Extension dialog box

Length Law and Angle Law Rollouts

The options in the **Length Law** and **Angle Law** rollouts are the same with the only difference that the length law is applicable for the length of the flange, where as the angle law is applicable for the angle of the flange. If you select the point on the selected curve for the **Specify New Location** option, then a new control point will be displayed at that point. By default, the **Multi-transition** option is selected in the **Law Type** drop-down list in the **Length Law** as well as the **Angle Law** rollout. As a result, you can change the length or angle of the flange regardless to the other control points. However, you can change the length and angle of the flange by applying other laws such as **Constant**, **Linear**, **Cubic**, **Linear along Spine**, **Cubic along Spine**, **By equation**, and **By Law Curve**. For example, select the **Linear** option from the **Law Type** drop-down list; the **Start** and **End** edit boxes will be displayed in this rollout. Enter the start and end values in the **Start** and **End** edit boxes, respectively, and then choose the **OK** button; the modified extended surface will be displayed.

Opposite Side Extension Rollout

By default, the **None** option is selected in the **Extension Type** drop-down list. If you select the **Symmetric** option from the **Extension Type** drop-down list; a symmetric flange will be created on the opposite side of the created flange. If you select the **Asymmetric** option from the **Extension Type** drop-down list; the **Length Law** and **Values along Spine** sub-rollouts will be displayed in this rollout. Also, the new flange will be created on the opposite side of the created flange. You can modify this new flange by using the **Length Law** and **Values along Spine** sub-rollouts.

Spine Rollout

This rollout is used to select a curve by using the **Curve** button. Choose the **Curve** button from this rollout and then select the curve, refer to Figure 11-45. The imaginary plane will be placed perpendicular to the selected curve, with respect to which the angle of the flange will be measured, refer to Figure 11-45.

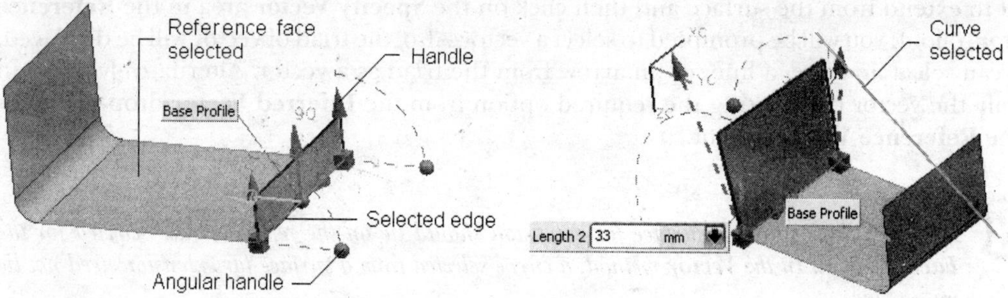

Figure 11-44 Preview of the component

*Figure 11-45 Curve selected using the **Curve** button in the **Spline** rollout*

Settings Rollout

In this rollout, the **Lock End Length/Angle Handles** check box is clear, by default. As a result, you can move handles and angular handles regardless to each other, refer to Figure 11-46. If you select this check box, the end handles of the profile will be locked. As a result, if you drag the handles at the start point, the handle at the end point will be modified simultaneously.

In the **Base Profile** area of the **Settings** rollout, you can redefine the degree and knot points of the curve already selected from **Base Profile** rollout. This helps in rebuilding the flange of desired shape and to maintain continuity between the reference faces and the law extension surfaces.

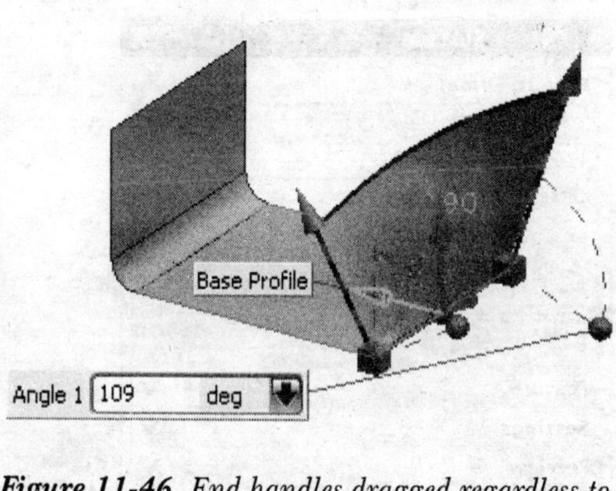

Figure 11-46 End handles dragged regardless to each other

Extending a Surface Dynamically Using the Vector Option

To extend a surface dynamically by using the **Vector** option, select the **Vector** option from the **Type** drop-down list of the **Type** rollout; the **Reference Faces** rollout will be replaced by the **Reference Vector** rollout and the rest of the options will remain the same. In this method, instead of selecting reference faces, you can select reference vector so that the extended surface is created along the normal of the selected vector. To do so, select the curve string that you want to extend from the surface and then click on the **Specify Vector** area in the **Reference Vector** rollout; you will be prompted to select a vector. Also, the triad of vector will be displayed. You can select an edge, a line, or an arrow from the triad as a vector. Alternatively, you can specify the vector by selecting the required option from the **Inferred Vector** drop-down list in the **Reference Vector** rollout.

Note

*A curve selected from a surface for extension should lie on the reference face selected for the **Faces** method. In the **Vector** method, a curve selected from a surface for extension need not lie on any face.*

Creating a Surface Offset Using the Offset Surface Tool

Menu:	Insert > Offset /Scale > Offset Surface
Toolbar:	Surface > Offset Surface

The **Offset Surface** tool is used to offset a surface in the direction normal to a selected surface. To offset a surface, choose the **Offset Surface** button from the **Surface** toolbar; the **Offset Surface** dialog box will be displayed, as shown in Figure 11-47. By default, the **Face** button is chosen in the **Face to Offset** rollout. As a result, you will be prompted to select the faces for the new set. Select the face, refer to Figure 11-48. Next, enter the offset value in the **Offset 1** edit box. If you want to create a new set, choose the **Add New Set** button from the **Face to Offset** rollout and select the faces for the second set. To flip the offset direction, choose the **Reverse Direction** button. Next, choose the **OK** button; the resulting offset surface will be created, as shown in Figure 11-48.

*Figure 11-47 The **Offset Surface** dialog box*

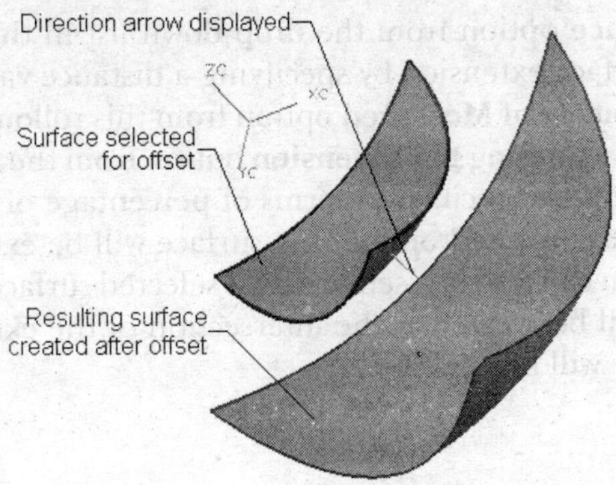

Figure 11-48 Offset surface created

Trimming and Extending a Surface Using the Trim and Extend Tool

Toolbar:	Surface > Trim and Extend

The **Trim and Extend** tool is used to trim or extend an open or a closed surface. To trim or extend a surface, choose the **Trim and Extend** button from the **Surface** toolbar; the **Trim and Extend** dialog box will be displayed, as shown in Figure 11-49, and you will be prompted to select the target edge to extend. Select a single edge or multiple edges from the surface to be extended. When you select multiple edges for extending them, ensure that the selected edges are in continuity. If the **Preview** check box is selected in the **Preview** rollout, the preview of the extended surface will be displayed. The different rollouts in the **Trim and Extend** dialog box are discussed next.

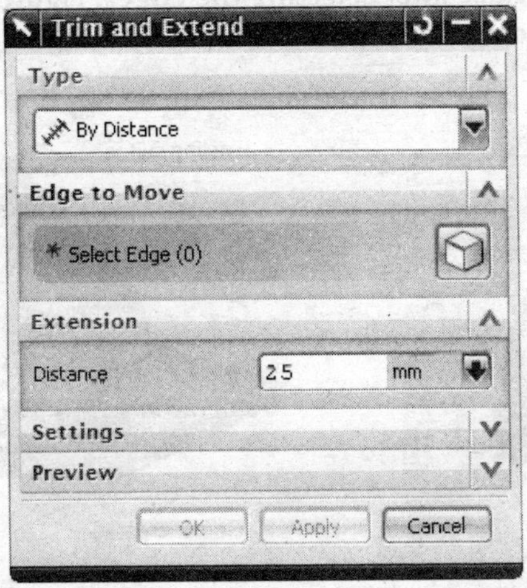

*Figure 11-49 The **Trim and Extend** dialog box*

Type Rollout

On selecting the **By Distance** option from the drop-down list in the **Type** rollout, you can define the length of the surface extension by specifying a distance value in the **Distance** edit box. If you select the **Percentage of Measured** option from this rollout, you need to select the edge to measure distance by choosing the **Extension** button from the **Extension** rollout. Note that the extension length will be specified in terms of percentage of the selected measuring edge. On selecting the **Until Selected** option, the surface will be extended up to a selected reference object. This option can also be used to trim a selected surface. If you select the **Make Corner** option, a corner will be created at the intersection of the extended surface with the tool body and the tool body will be trimmed.

Settings Rollout

The options in the **Extension Method** drop-down list of the **Settings** rollout are used to define the continuity of the extended surface with the existing surface. If you select the **Natural Curvature** option, the surface will be extended normally to the selected edge. If you select the **Natural Tangent** option, the surface will be extended by maintaining an angular curvature of 3 degree at the start point of the selected edge. If you select the **Mirrored** option, the surface will be extended along the curvature of the existing surface.

Note that if you select the **Until Selected** option from the drop-down list in the **Type** rollout, you need to select the tool body that serves as the boundary object after selecting the edge for extension. Choose the **Tool** button from the **Tool** rollout and select the boundary object. Next, choose the **OK** button to extend the surface up to the selected boundary object. The options in the **Arrow Side** drop-down list of the **Desired Results** rollout are used to retain or discard a selected tool body. If you select the **Retain** option, the selected tool body will be retained after trimming. If you select the **Delete** option, the material from the tool body will be removed in the direction of the arrow displayed on selecting the tool body. Figure 11-50 shows the preview of the extended surface after selecting the edges. Figure 11-51 shows the surface extended by using the **Make Corner** option.

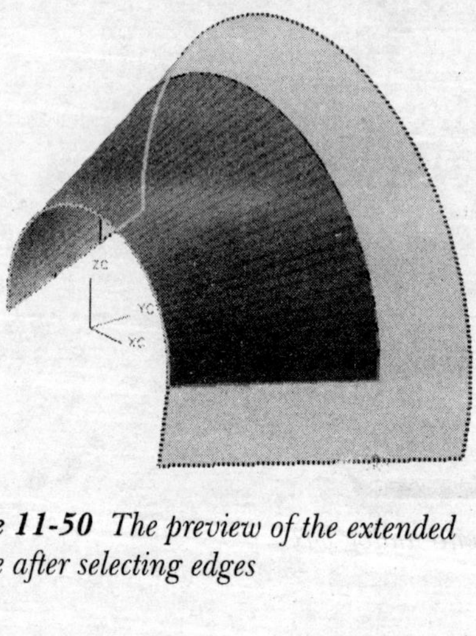

***Figure 11-50** The preview of the extended surface after selecting edges*

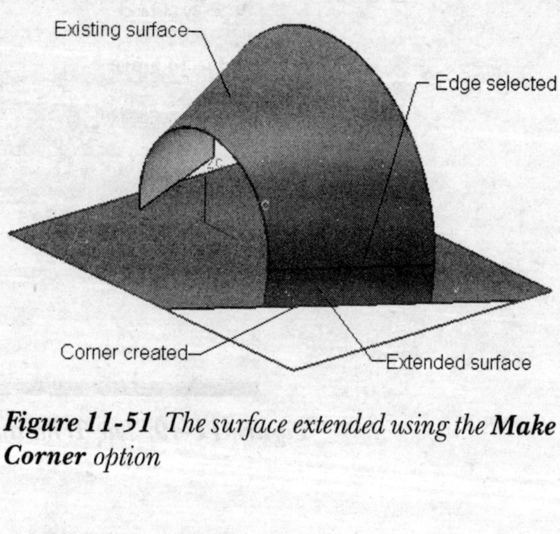

***Figure 11-51** The surface extended using the **Make Corner** option*

Trimming a Sheet by Using the Trimmed Sheet Tool

Menu:	Insert > Trim > Trimmed Sheet
Toolbar:	Surface > Trimmed Sheet

The **Trimmed Sheet** tool is used to trim a sheet by defining the trim boundary. You can also trim a sheet by projecting a curve and then defining it as trim boundary. If the trim boundary is a surface, then the surface to be trimmed must be intersected completely with the trimming surface. Choose the **Trimmed Sheet** button from the **Surface** toolbar; the **Trimmed Sheet** dialog box will be displayed, as shown in Figure 11-52, and you will be prompted to select a target sheet body. By default, the **Sheet Body** button is chosen in the **Target** rollout. Select the sheet to be trimmed and then press the middle mouse button. Next, you will be prompted to select the boundary objects. Select boundary objects. Next, choose the **Region** button from the **Region** rollout; the surface will be highlighted. The highlighted surface indicates whether this region is to be kept or discarded. You need to select the **Keep** or **Discard** radio button in the **Region** rollout to specify whether the area highlighted has to be kept or discarded. If you select the **Keep** radio button from this rollout, the highlighted region will be retained, and the other region will be removed. If you select the **Discard** radio button, the highlighted region will be removed (trimmed) and the other region will be retained.

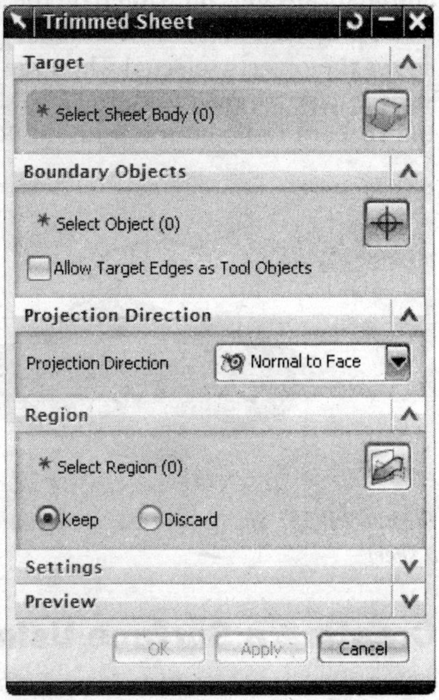

*Figure 11-52 The **Trimmed Sheet** dialog box*

Figure 11-53 shows the entities selected for trimming a surface. Figure 11-54 shows the resulting trimmed surface created after selecting the **Discard** radio button from the **Region** rollout.

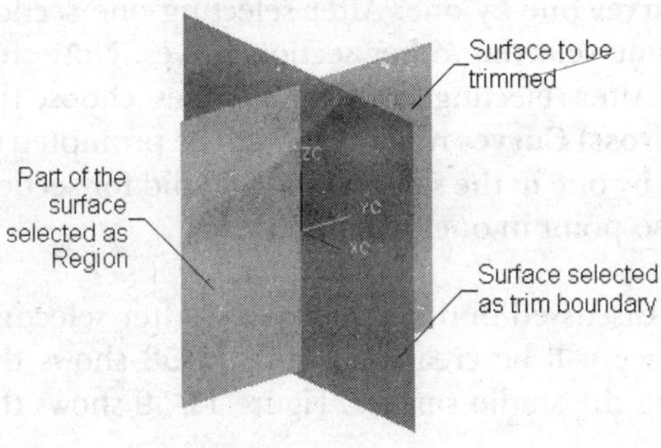

Figure 11-53 Entities selected for trimming a sheet

*Figure 11-54 The resulting trimmed sheet created after selecting the **Discard** radio button*

The **Projection Direction** drop-down list contains the options for projecting (imprinting) a curve or a sketch on the surface to be trimmed. The projection curve or sketch can be defined as the trimming boundary. Select the surface to be trimmed and press the middle mouse button. Next, select the curve or the sketch as the trim boundary. The selected curve or the sketch automatically gets imprinted on the surface to be trimmed and forms the trim boundary. The curve projected as the trim boundary should intersect the surface to be trimmed. Figure 11-55 shows the objects selected when the trim boundary is created by imprinting a curve on the surface to be trimmed. Figure 11-56 shows the resulting trimmed surface created after selecting the **Discard** radio button from the **Region** rollout.

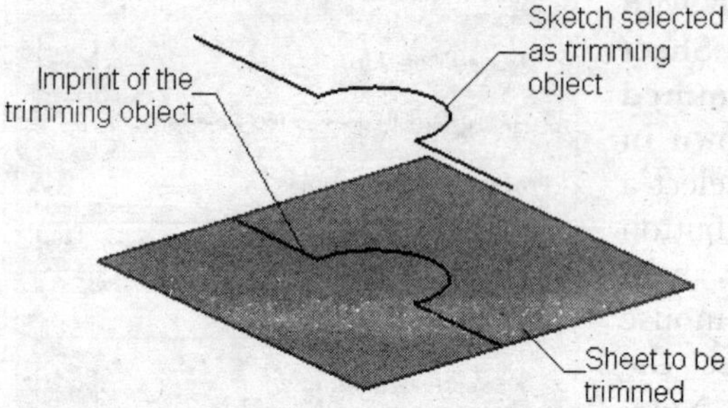

***Figure 11-55** Sketch selected for trimming a sheet*

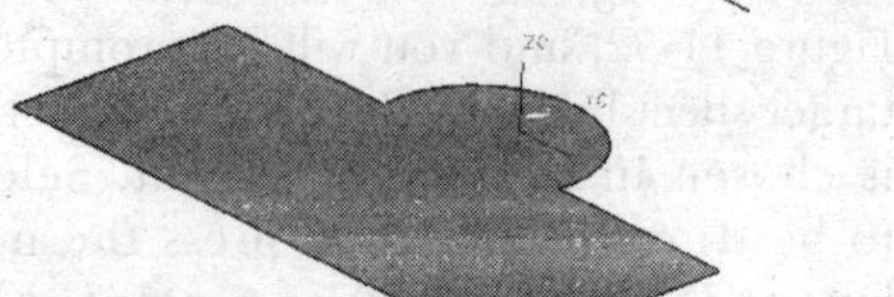

***Figure 11-56** The resulting trimmed sheet created after selecting the **Discard** radio button*

Creating a Surface Using the Studio Surface Tool

Menu: Insert > Mesh Surface > Studio Surface
Toolbar: Freeform Shape > Studio Surface

The **Studio Surface** tool is used to create a surface by sweeping a single section or multiple sections along single or multiple guide curves. The selected guide and section curves can be open or closed.

Choose the **Studio Surface** button from the **Freeform Shape** toolbar; the **Studio Surface** dialog box will be displayed, as shown in Figure 11-57, and you will be prompted to select a section. By default, the **Section (Primary) Curves** button will be chosen from the **Section (Primary) Curves** rollout. Select the section curves one by one. After selecting one section curve, press the middle mouse button to continue selecting other section curves. Note that all section curves should point in one direction. After selecting the section curves, choose the **Guide (Cross) Curves** button from the **Guide (Cross) Curves** rollout; you will be prompted to select a guide curve. Select the guide curves one by one in the same way as you did for section curves. Note that all the guide curves should also point in one direction.

The other options in the dialog box have been discussed in the earlier tools. After selecting all parameters, choose the **OK** button; a surface will be created. Figure 11-58 shows the section and the guide curve selected for creating the studio surface. Figure 11-59 shows the preview of the resulting studio surface.

Figure 11-60 shows a single section and two guide curves selected for creating a studio surface and Figure 11-61 shows the resulting studio surface.

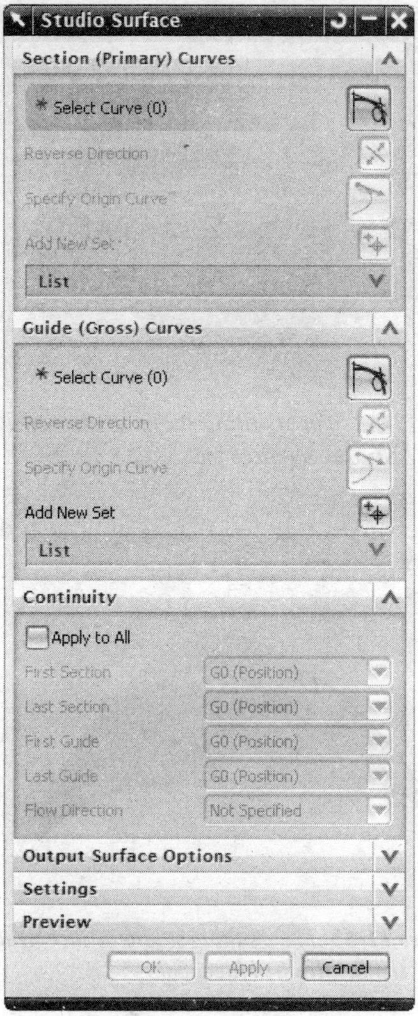

Figure 11-57 *The* ***Studio Surface*** *dialog box*

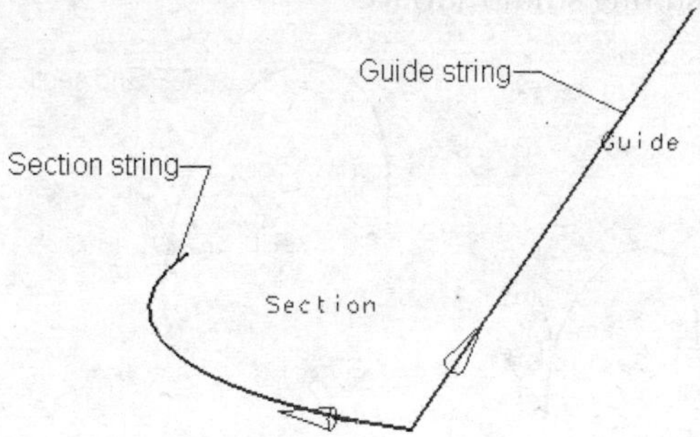

Figure 11-58 *The section string and the guide string selected for creating a studio surface*

Figure 11-59 *The preview of the studio surface created using the* ***Studio Surface*** *tool*

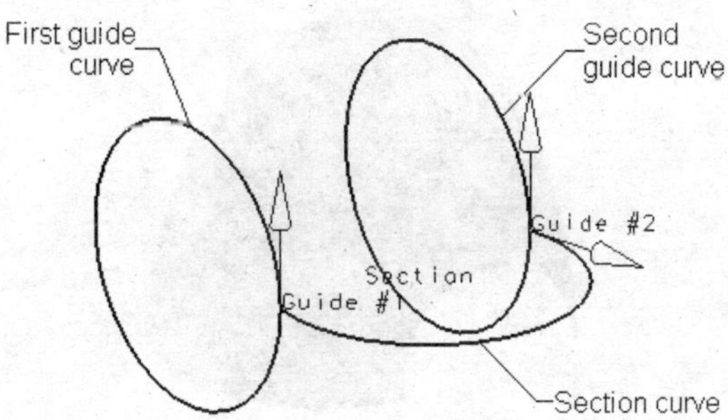

Figure 11-60 *The section curve and the guide curves selected for creating the studio surface*

Figure 11-61 *The resulting studio surface*

Figure 11-62 shows the selected start and end section curves and Figure 11-63 shows the resulting studio surface.

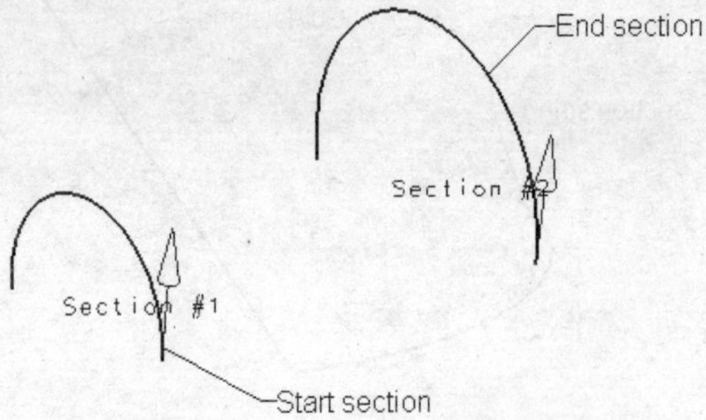

Figure 11-62 *The section curves selected for creating a studio surface*

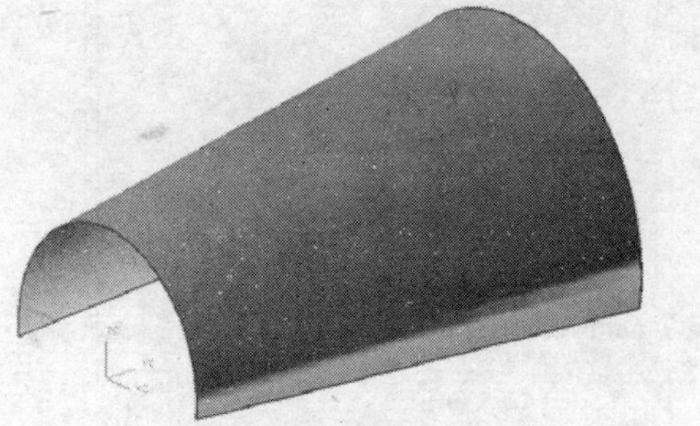

Figure 11-63 *The resulting studio surface created using the* ***Studio Surface*** *tool*

Figure 11-64 shows two section curves and two guide curves selected for creating a studio surface. Figure 11-65 shows the resulting studio surface.

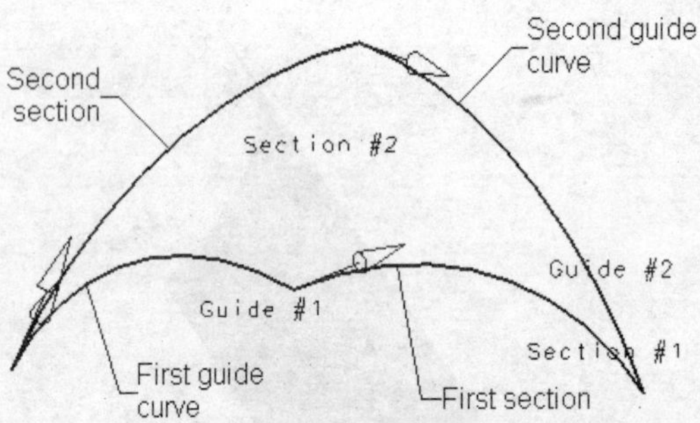

Figure 11-64 *The section and guide curves selected for creating a studio surface*

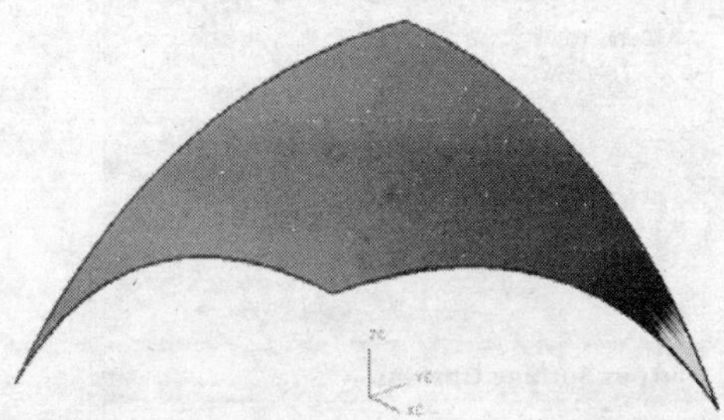

Figure 11-65 *The resulting studio surface created using the* ***Studio Surface*** *tool*

Figure 11-66 shows the selected section curves and guide curves. Figure 11-67 shows the resulting studio surface.

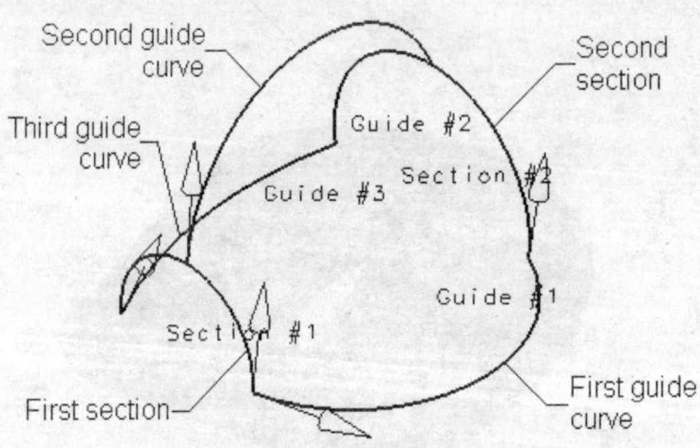

Figure 11-66 *The section curves and the guide curves selected to create a studio surface*

Figure 11-67 *The resulting studio surface created using the* ***Studio Surface*** *tool*

Creating a Surface between Two Walls Using the Styled Blend Tool

Menu: Insert > Detail Feature > Styled Blend
Toolbar: Freeform Shape > Styled Blend

The **Styled Blend** tool is used to create a fillet surface between two intersecting walls. While creating fillet surfaces, you can maintain a tangent or curvature continuity among walls. You can also create variable fillets using this tool. To create a fillet surface using this tool, choose the **Styled Blend** button from the **Freeform Shape** toolbar; the **Styled Blend** dialog box will be displayed, as shown in Figure 11-68, and you will be prompted to select the faces for wall 1.

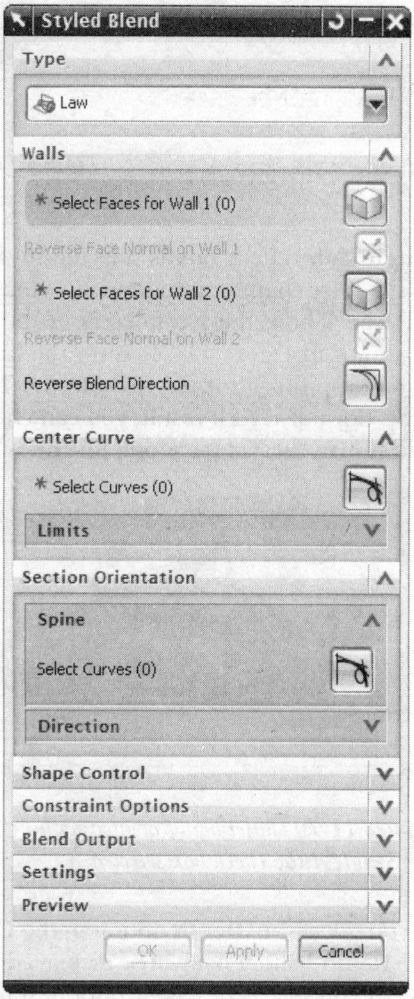

*Figure 11-68 The **Styled Blend** dialog box*

The method of formation of the blend surface is defined by the type of option you select from the **Type** drop-down list in the **Type** rollout. If you select the **Law** option, the lines holding the tangent will automatically be created with respect to the pipe radius specified for the fillet. In case of selecting the **Curve** option you need to select the tangent holding curves for creating the fillet. If you select the **Profile** option, the tangent holding lines will be created by imprinting a curve or a sketch on both the surfaces between which the surface is to be created.

Creating a Styled Blend Surface Using the Law Option

By default, the **Law** option is selected in the **Type** drop-down list of the **Type** rollout and the **Select Faces for Wall 1** area is activated in the **Walls** rollout. Select the first wall and then click on the **Select Faces for Wall 2** area in the **Walls** rollout. While selecting both the walls, you need to ensure that the arrow displayed on the walls are facing inward where the surface is to be created. You can use the **Reverse Direction** button in the **Walls** rollout to flip the direction of the arrow. Select the second wall and press the middle mouse button; the preview of the fillet along with the handles and dynamic edit box will be displayed, as shown in Figure 11-69. Also, the **Specify New Location** area in the **Shape Control** rollout will be activated. You can view the alternate solutions of the displayed fillet by clicking on the **Reverse Blend Direction** button in the **Walls** rollout. If you click on the intersection of two walls, a new control point will be added to that location. You can change the radius of the fillet by dragging handles. By default, the

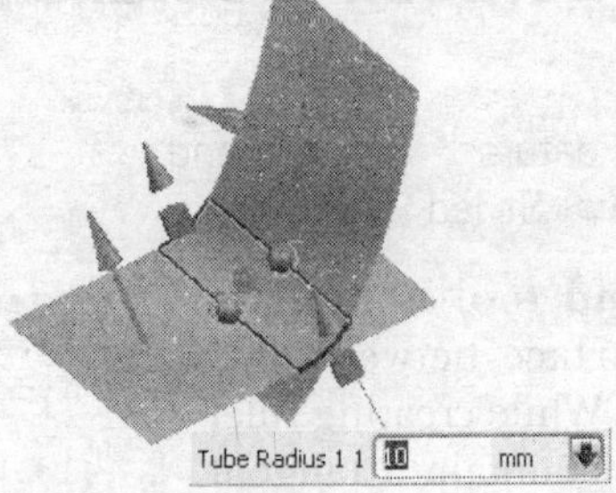

Figure 11-69 Preview of the fillet created between two walls

Single Tube check box is selected in the **Shape Control** rollout, As a result, the parameters of the fillet change simultaneously for both the walls, as shown in Figure 11-70. If you clear this check box, the parameters of the fillet will change simultaneously only for the wall 1, as shown in Figure 11-71. Also, the **Tube Radius 2** option will be activated in the **Control Type** drop-down list. By default, the **Tube Radius 1** option is selected in the **Control Type** drop-down list. As a result, you can change the radius of the fillet by using the **Tube Radius** edit box in the **Values along Spline** sub-rollout.

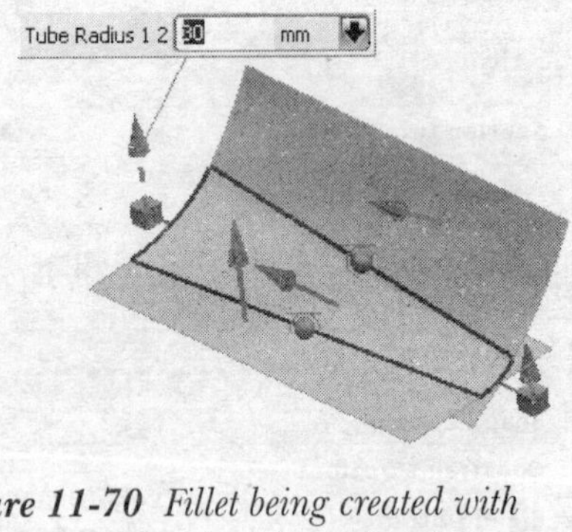

*Figure 11-70 Fillet being created with the **Single Tube** check box selected*

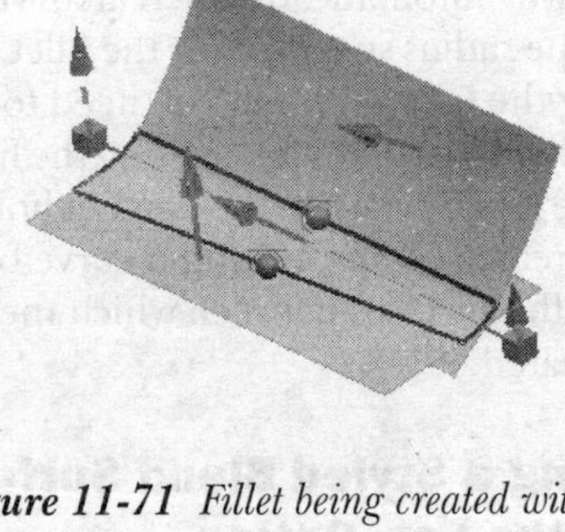

*Figure 11-71 Fillet being created with the **Single Tube** check box clear*

If you select the **Depth** option in the **Control Type** drop-down list; the **Depth 1** edit box and the **Depth 1** slider bar will be displayed. You can change the depth of the blend using this slider bar. If you select the **Skew** option in the **Control Type** drop-down list, then the **Skew 1** edit box and the **Skew 1** slider bar will be displayed. You can change the skew of the blend using this slider bar. If you select the **Tangent Magnitude** option in the **Control Type** drop-down list; the **Tangent Magnitude 11** edit box and the **Tangent Magnitude 11** slider bar will be displayed. You can change the tangent magnitude of the blend using this slider bar.

If you have already created a curve, as shown in Figure 11-72, then you can use that curve as the center of the blend. To do so, choose the **Curve** button from the **Center Curve** rollout and select the curve; the preview of the blend will be displayed by using the selected curve as the center, as shown in Figure 11-73. By default, line curve will be extended by 10 % of its original length at the start point and end point. You can edit this value in the **Limits** sub-rollout.

Figure 11-72 Existing curve to be selected as the center of the bend

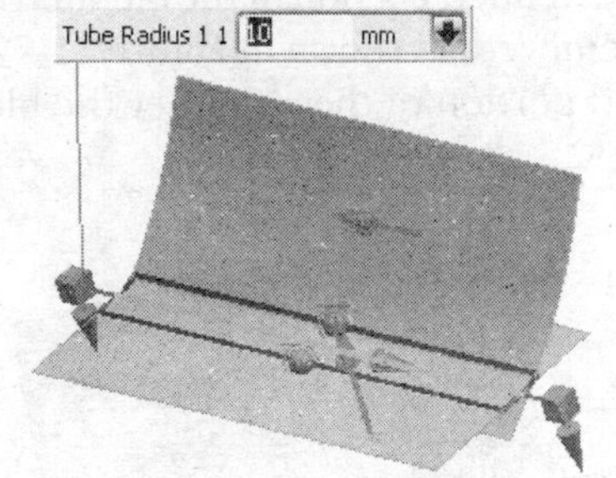

Figure 11-73 Preview of the resultant model

You can restrict the length of the blend by using the **Section Orientation** rollout. To do so, select the **Curve** button from the **Spine** sub-rollout; you will be prompted to select the curves for spline. Select a curve, as shown in Figure 11-74; the preview of the resultant model will be displayed, as shown in Figure 11-75. By default, the **Use Center Curve As Spine** check box is clear. If you select this check box, the center curve will be used as spine curve.

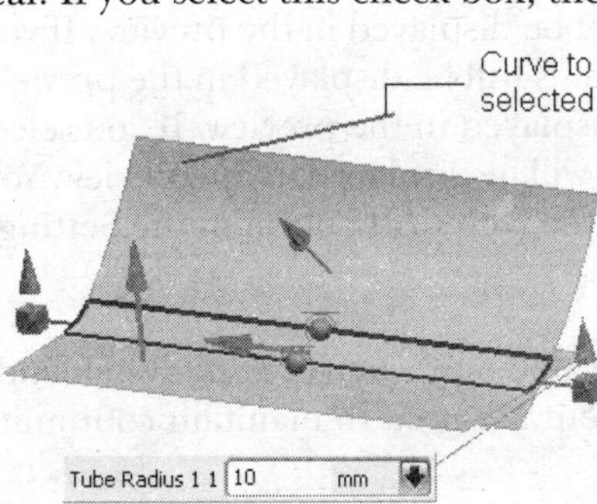

Figure 11-74 The curve to be selected to restrict fillet

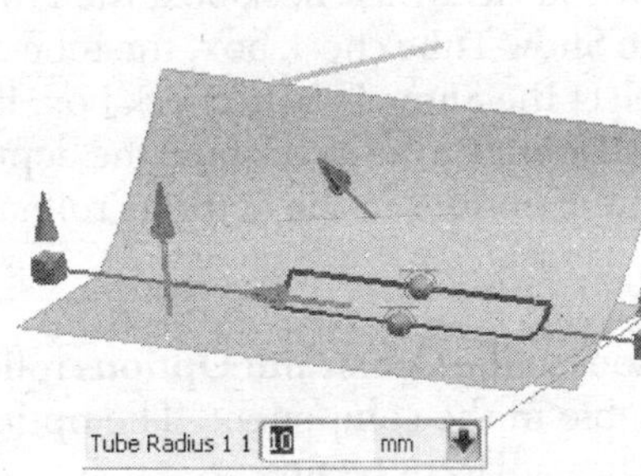

Figure 11-75 Preview of the resultant model

To enable the **Extend Blend** check box in the **Blend Output** rollout, select the **Use Center Curve As Spine** check box from the **Spine** sub-rollout in the **Section Orientation** rollout. If you select the **Extend Blend** check box, the fillet will extend throughout the center line, as shown in Figure 11-76. By default, the **No Trim** option is selected in the **Trimming Method** drop-down list of the **Blend Output** rollout, As a result, it keeps the extended portion after the blend in the resultant model. If you select the **Trim & Attach** option from this drop-down list, the extended portion of the wall after the blend

*Figure 11-76 Preview of the fillet with the **Extended Blend** check box selected*

and the extended portion of the blended curve after the boundary edges in the resultant model will be removed, as shown in Figure 11-77. If you select the **Trim Input Walls** option, only the extended portion of the wall after the blend will be removed, as shown in Figure 11- 78.

Figure 11-77 *The styled blend created using the* ***Trim & Attach*** *option*

Figure 11-78 *The styled blend created using the* ***Trim Input Walls*** *option*

By default, the **Show Blend** check box is selected in the **Show** sub-rollout of the **Settings** rollout. If you clear this check box, then the blend will not be displayed in the preview. If you select the **Show Tube** check box, the tube of specified radius will be displayed in the preview. If you select the **Show Labels** check box, labels will be displayed in the preview. If you select the **Show Depth Curve** check box, the depth of curvature will be displayed in the preview. You can reset the options in the **Settings** rollout by choosing the **Reset All** button in the **Settings** rollout.

The options in the **Constraint Options** rollout will be activated only when two adjacent blends are available in the component. The options in this rollout are used to maintain continuity between two adjacent blends

Creating a Styled Blend Surface Using the Curve Option

To create a styled blend surface by using the **Curve** option, select the **Curve** option from the **Type** drop-down list in the **Type** rollout; you will be prompted to select the faces for wall 1. Select the first wall and then click on the **Select Faces for Wall 2** area in the **Walls** rollout; you will be prompted to select the faces for wall 2. Select the second wall and press the middle mouse button; the **Select Curves For Curve Set 1** area in the **Tangent Curves** rollout will be activated and you will be prompted to select the curves for curve set 1. Select the first tangential curve from the first wall selected and then click on the **Select Curves For Curve Set 2** area; you will be prompted to select the curves for curve set 2. Select the second tangential curve from the selected second wall, refer to Figure 11-79 for selection; the preview of the fillet will be displayed, as shown in Figure 11- 80. Note that you may need to choose the **Reverse Direction** button to reverse the direction of surface creation.

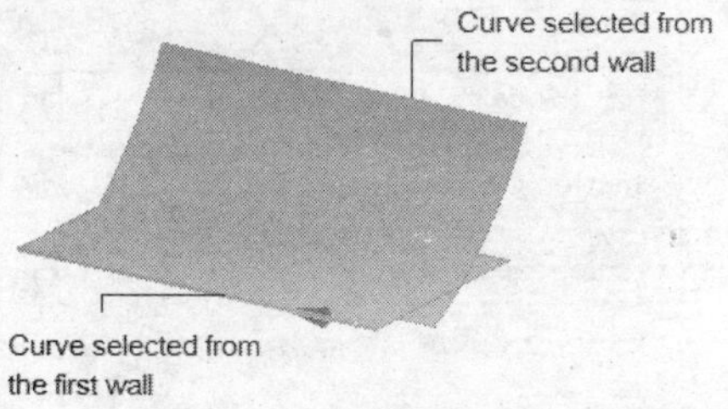

*Figure 11-79 Reference selection for the **Curve** option*

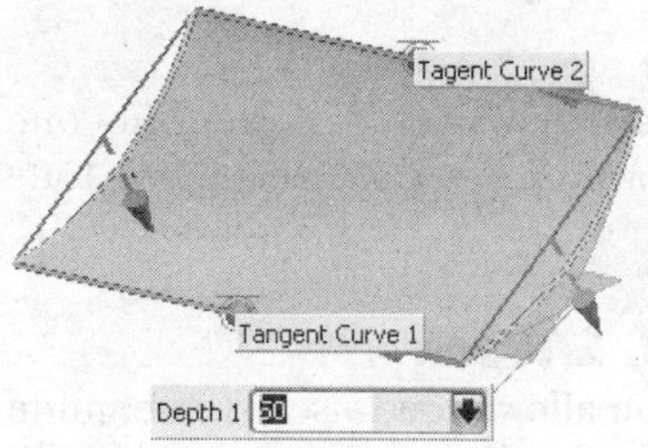

Figure 11-80 Preview of the fillet

Creating a Styled Blend Surface Using the Profile Option

To create a styled blend surface by using the **Profile** option, select the **Profile** option from the **Type** drop-down list in the **Type** rollout; you will be prompted to select the faces for wall 1. Select the first wall and press the middle mouse button. Next, select the second wall and press the middle mouse button; the **Select Curves** area in the **Profile** rollout will be activated. Also, you will be prompted to select the curves for profile curve. Select the curve, refer to Figure 11-81; the preview of the fillet will be displayed, as shown in Figure 11-82. Remaining options are the same as discussed earlier.

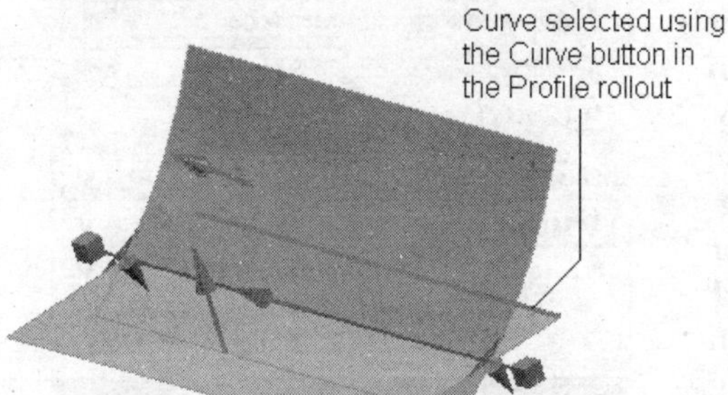

*Figure 11-81 The curve selected for creating the Styled Blend surface using the **Profile** option*

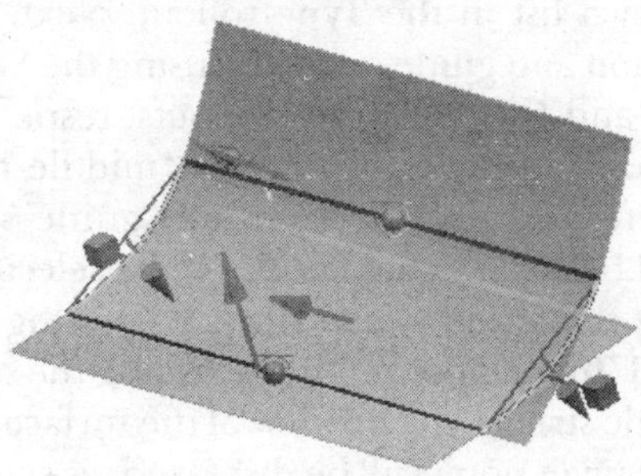

*Figure 11-82 The preview of the Styled Blend surface using the **Profile** option*

Creating Surfaces Using the Styled Sweep Tool

Toolbar:	Freeform Shape > Styled Sweep

Styled Sweep

The **Styled Sweep** tool is used to create surfaces by sweeping cross-sections along one or two guide curves. A surface created by using this tool can be modified dynamically by dragging the pivot point displayed along with the surface. To create a styled sweep surface, choose the **Styled Sweep** button from the **Freeform Shape** toolbar; the **Styled Sweep** dialog box will be displayed, as shown in Figure 11-83.

The options in the **Type** drop-down list of the **Type** rollout are used to specify the number of guide, touch, and orientation strings. These options are discussed next.

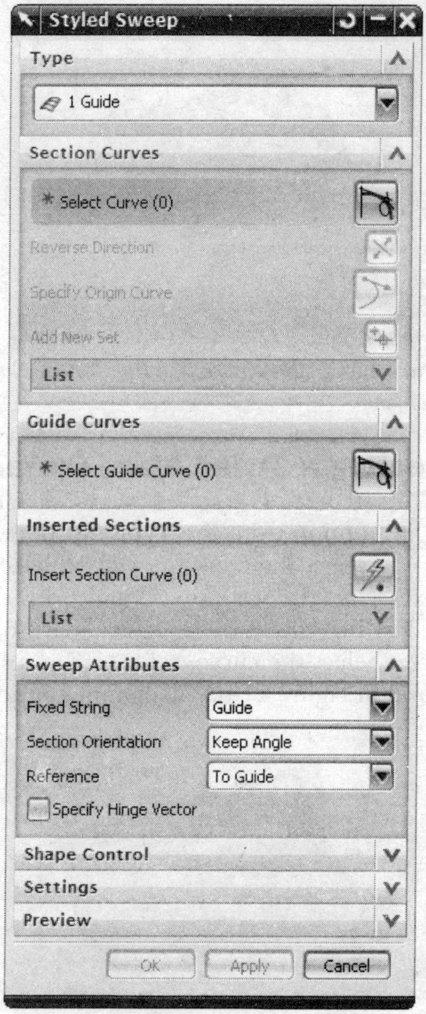

*Figure 11-83 The **Styled Sweep** dialog box*

1 Guide
This option allows you to select only one guide string. However, you can select up to 150 section strings.

1 Guide, 1 Touch
This option allows you to select one guide string and one touch string and one section string.

1 Guide, 1 Orientation
This option allows you to select one guide string and one orientation string.

2 Guides
This option allows you to select two guide strings only. However, you can select up to 150 section strings.

Select the required option from the **Type** drop-down list in the **Type** rollout. Next, select the section and guide curves by using the **Section Curves** and **Guide Curves** rollouts, respectively. Note that you need to press the middle mouse button to add each section and guide string. Figure 11-84 shows the entities to be selected for creating the styled sweep surface by using the **1 Guide, 1 Touch** option. After selecting the section and guide strings, the preview of the surface along with the pivot point will be displayed, as shown in Figure 11- 85.

You can modify the shape and size of the surface by dragging the pivot point. Alternatively, you can use the slider bar in the **Shape Control** rollout to modify the shape and size of the surface. The options in the **Shape Control** rollout are used to display different types of handles for the surface created, which can be used to modify the surface dynamically.

Sewing Individual Surfaces into a Single Surface

Menu:	Insert > Combine Bodies > Sew
Toolbar:	Feature Operation > Sew *(Customize to add)*

The **Sew** tool is used to stitch individual surfaces into a single surface with a common edge. When a selected individual surfaces encloses a volume, it creates a solid body. A

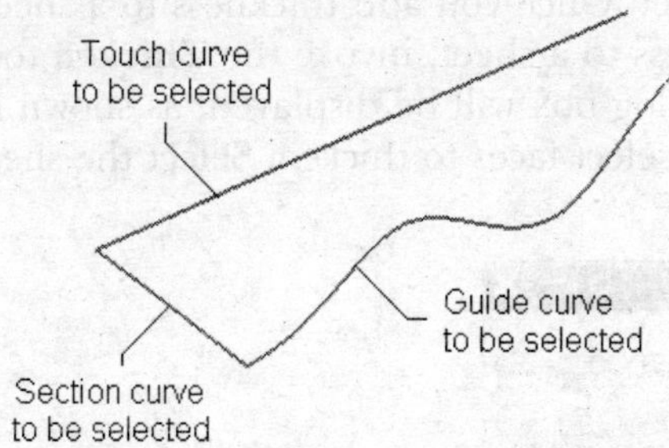

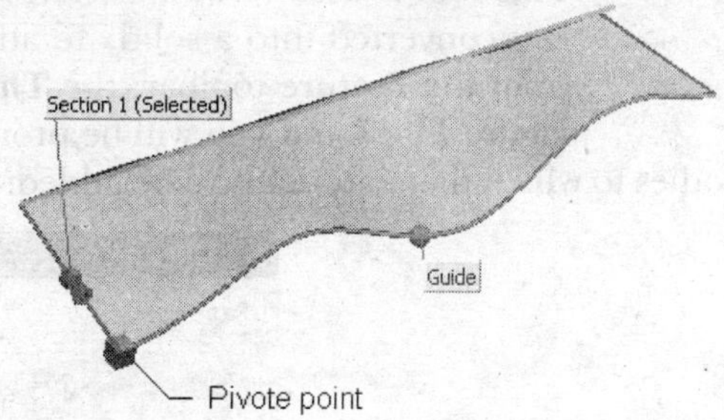

***Figure 11-84** Entities to be selected for creating the styled sweep surface*

***Figure 11-85** Preview of the resulting styled sweep surface*

sheet to which all other individual sheets to be stitched is known as target sheet, and the individual sheets to be stitched are known as the tool sheets. You cannot stitch the tool sheets that intersect a target sheet and extend from it.

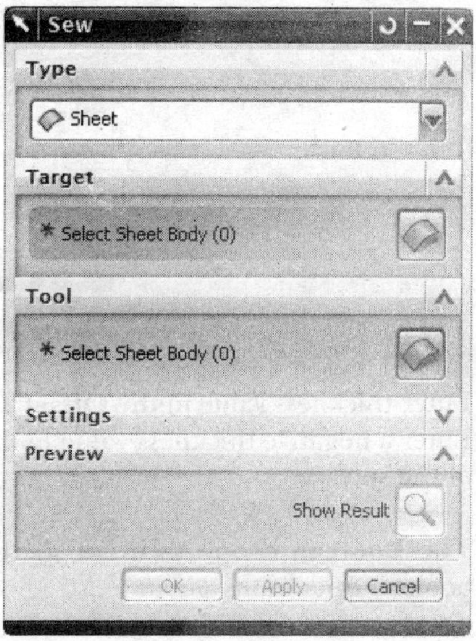

***Figure 11-86** The Sew dialog box*

To stitch individual surfaces to a single surface, choose the **Sew** button from the **Feature Operation** toolbar; the **Sew** dialog box will be displayed, as shown in Figure 11-86. By default, the **Sheet** option is selected from the drop-down list in the **Type** rollout and you are prompted to select the target sheet body. Select the target sheet body; you will be prompted to select the tool sheet bodies to sew. The border of the selected tool sheets should lie within the target sheet boundary. Otherwise, the selected tool sheet will not get stitched to the target sheet. Select the tool sheet bodies and choose the **OK** button; the sheet bodies will be stitched.

Similarly, to combine solid bodies, select the **Solid** option from the drop-down list in the **Type** rollout. Note that you can sew two solid bodies together only if they share one or more common (coincident) faces. You can also enter sew tolerance value in the **Tolerance** edit box of the **Settings** rollout. If the selected object is an instance of an array and the **Sew All Instances** check box is selected, all instances of the array will be stitched together. Note that this check box will be enabled only after selecting the **Solid** option from the drop-down list in the **Type** rollout.

Adding Thickness to a Surface

Menu:	Insert > Offset/Scale > Thicken
Toolbar:	Feature > Thicken *(Customize to add)*

This tool is used to add thickness to a sheet. Once you add thickness to a sheet, it is converted into a solid. To add thickness to a sheet, invoke the **Thicken** tool from the **Feature** toolbar; the **Thicken** dialog box will be displayed, as shown in Figure 11-87 and you will be prompted to select faces to thicken. Select the sheet bodies to which the material is to be added.

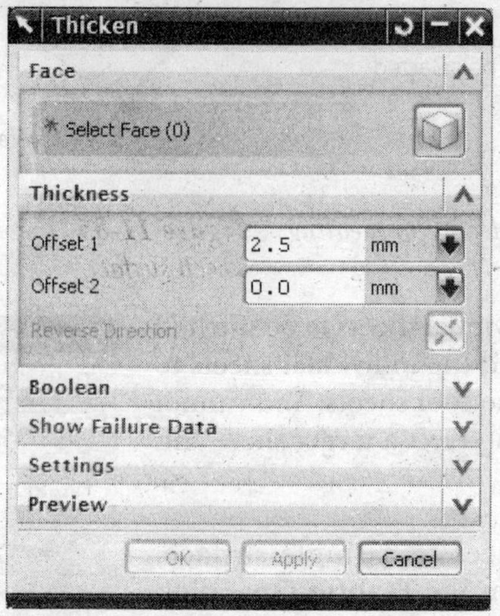

Figure 11-87 *The* ***Thicken*** *dialog box*

Enter thickness value in the **Offset 2** edit box to add thickness along the direction of handle. Enter a negative thickness value in the **Offset 1** edit box to assign thickness on the other side of the surface.

The **Boolean** drop-down list in the **Boolean** rollout provides options to perform the boolean operations on an existing solid body. Select the required option from the **Boolean** drop-down list and choose the **Body** button from the **Boolean** rollout. Next, select the target solid body; the boolean operation will be performed.

Figure 11-88 shows the sheet to add thickness and Figure 11-89 shows the resulting solid body.

Figure 11-88 *The sheet selected for adding material*

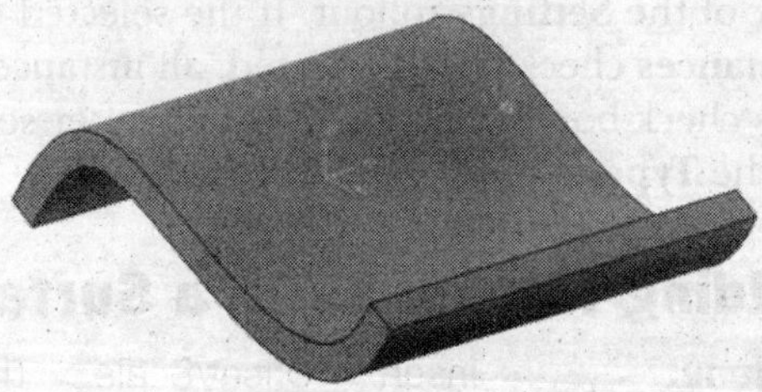

Figure 11-89 *The sheet after adding thickness to it*

TUTORIALS

Tutorial 1

In this tutorial, you will create the surface model shown in Figure 11-90. The dimensions and orthographic views of the model are shown in Figure 11-91. After creating the surface, save it with the name *c11tut1.prt* at the location *\NX 7\c11*. **(Expected time: 30 min)**

Figure 11-90 *The isometric view of the surface model*

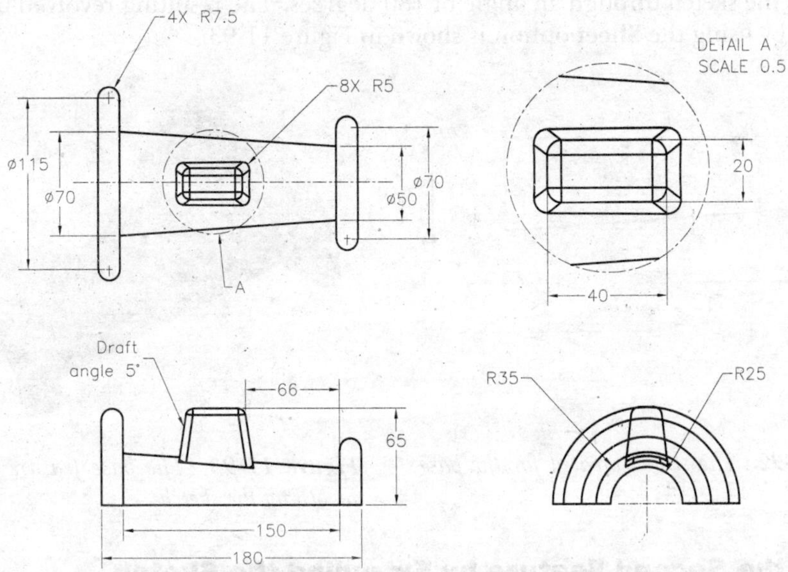

Figure 11-91 *Dimensions and drawing views of the surface model*

The following steps are required to complete this tutorial:

a. Start a new file and then set the sheet environment.
b. Create the sketch for the base surface and then revolve it.
c. Create the second feature, which is an extruded surface.
d. Trim the base surface.

e. Trim the extended part of the third feature.
f. Create the bounded plane surface.
g. Stitch the bounded plane and extruded surfaces with the revolved surface.
h. Fillet the stitched surface.
i. Save and close the file.

Starting a New File and Setting the Sheet Environment

1. Start a new file with the name *c11tut1.prt* using the **Model** template and specify its location as *C:\NX 7\c11*.

2. Choose **Preferences > Modeling** from the menu bar; the **Modeling Preferences** dialog box is displayed.

3. In this dialog box, select the **Sheet** radio button from the **Body Type** area and choose the **OK** button.

Creating the Base Feature by Revolving the Sketch

1. Create the sketch for the base surface on the XC-YC plane, as shown in Figure 11-92.

2. Revolve the sketch through an angle of 180 degrees. The resulting revolved base feature created by using the **Sheet** option is shown in Figure 11-93.

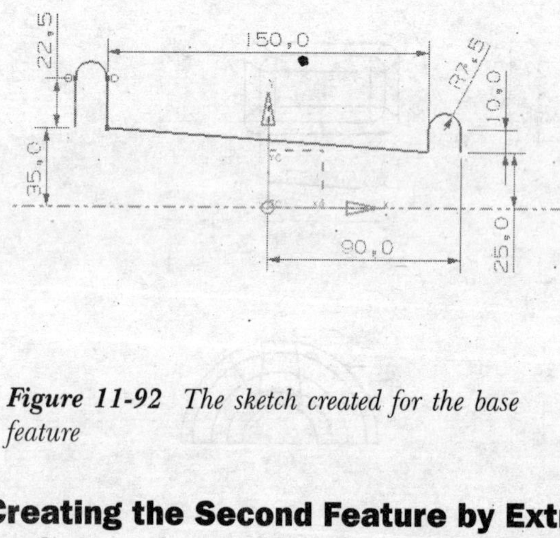

Figure 11-92 The sketch created for the base feature

Figure 11-93 The base feature created by revolving the sketch

Creating the Second Feature by Extruding the Sketch

1. Create a datum plane at an offset of 65 mm from the XC-YC plane in the upward direction.

2. Create the sketch for the second feature by selecting the offset plane as the sketching plane, as shown in Figure 11-94.

3. Extrude the sketch through a distance of 50 mm in the downward direction and at the draft angle of -5 degrees by selecting the **From Start Limit** option from the **Draft** drop-down list. The resulting extruded surface model is shown in Figure 11-95.

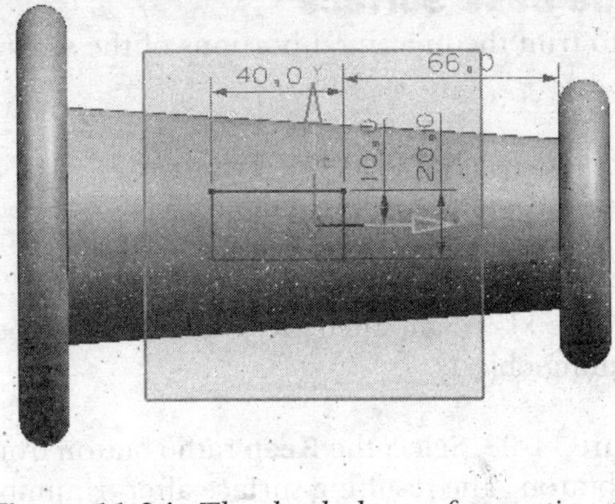

Figure 11-94 The sketch drawn for creating the extruded feature

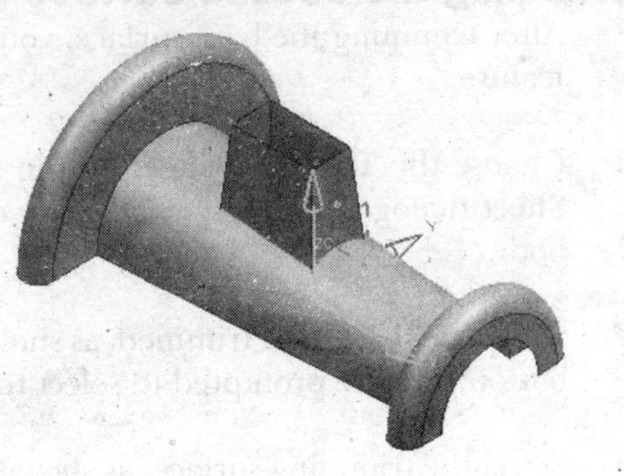

Figure 11-95 The resulting extruded surface

Trimming the Base Surface with respect to the Second Surface

Next, you need to trim the base surface with respect to the second feature.

1. Choose the **Trimmed Sheet** button from the **Surface** toolbar; the **Trimmed Sheet** dialog box is displayed and you are prompted to select the target sheet body.

2. Select the sheet to be trimmed, as shown in Figure 11-96. Make sure that you select the sheet by using the selection points shown in this figure. After selecting the target sheet body, press the middle mouse button; you are prompted to select the trimming objects.

3. Select the trimming surfaces, as shown in Figure 11-96. Make sure that you select the surfaces by using the points shown in this figure.

4. Select the **Keep** radio button from the **Region** rollout and then choose the **OK** button. The trimmed surface model is shown in Figure 11-97.

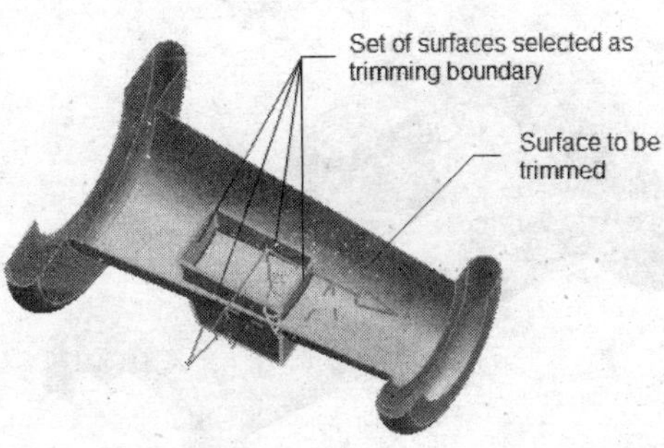

Figure 11-96 The surface to be trimmed and the trimming surfaces selected from the model

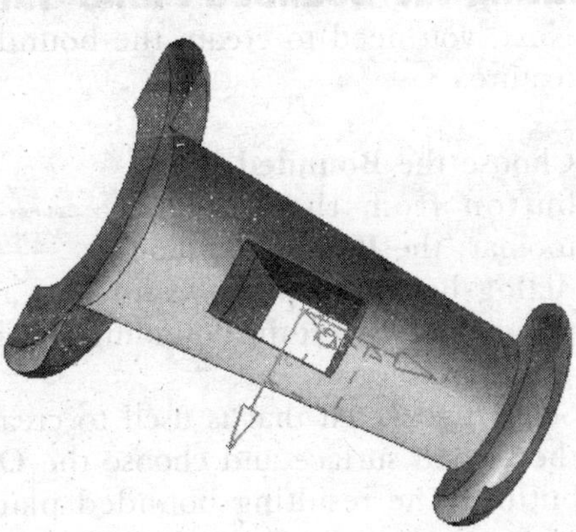

Figure 11-97 The surface model after trimming the base surface with respect to the extruded surface

Trimming the Second Surface with the Base Surface

After trimming the base surface, you need to trim the unwanted portions of the second feature.

1. Choose the **Trimmed Sheet** button from the **Surface** toolbar; the **Trimmed Sheet** dialog box is displayed and you are prompted to select a target sheet body.

2. Select the sheet to be trimmed, as shown in Figure 11-98, and then press the middle mouse button; you are prompted to select the trimming objects.

3. Select the trimming surface, as shown in Figure 11-98. Select the **Keep** radio button from the **Region** rollout and then choose the **OK** button. The resulting surface after trimming the extended portion of the extruded surface is shown in Figure 11-99.

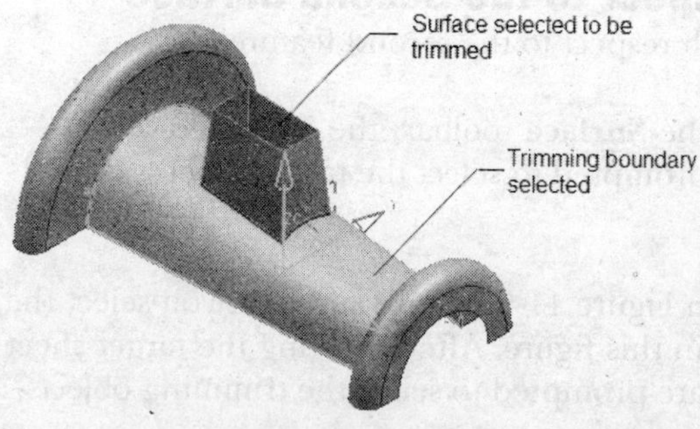

Figure 11-98 The surface to be trimmed and the trimming surface selected from the model

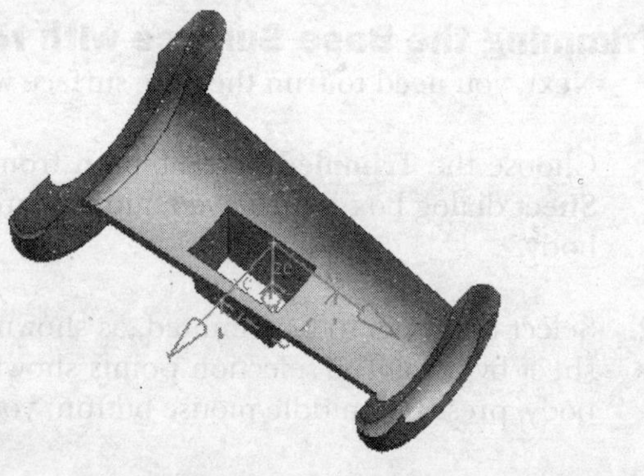

Figure 11-99 The resulting surface after trimming the extended portion of the extruded surface

Creating the Bounded Plane Surface

Next, you need to create the bounded surface to close the top face of the second feature.

1. Choose the **Bounded Plane** button from the **Feature** toolbar; the **Bounded Plane** dialog box is displayed and you are prompted to select the bounding string.

2. Select the sketch that is used to create the second surface and choose the **OK** button. The resulting bounded plane surface is shown in Figure 11-100.

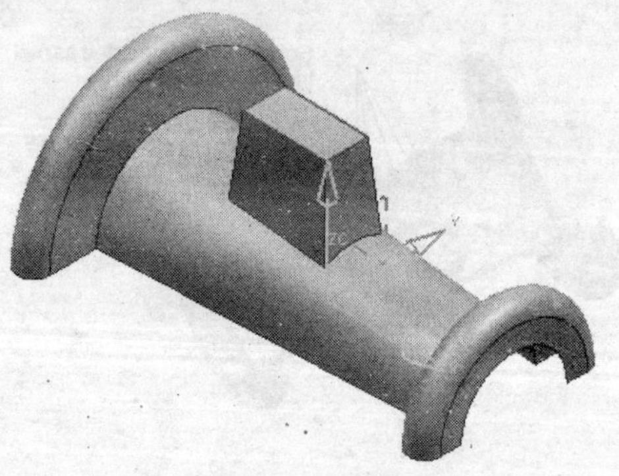

Figure 11-100 The resulting bounded plane surface

Stitching the Bounded Plane Surface and the Extruded Surface with the Revolved Surface

After creating all surfaces, you need to stitch them together by using the **Sew** tool.

1. Choose the **Sew** button from the **Feature Operation** toolbar; the **Sew** dialog box is displayed and you are prompted to select a target sheet to sew.

2. Select the revolved surface; you are prompted to select the tool sheets to sew.

3. Select the bounded plane and the extruded surface.

4. Choose the **OK** button; all surfaces are stitched together.

Note
*After stitching individual surfaces together into a single surface, you can hide the sketch created for revolving the base feature, the sketch created for extruding the second feature, and the datum plane. To hide these entities, press Ctrl+B; the **Class Selection** dialog box is displayed. Select the entities and choose the **OK** button.*

Creating Fillets on Edges Using the Edge Blend Tool

Next, you need to fillet edges.

1. Choose the **Edge Blend** button from the **Feature Operation** toolbar; the **Edge Blend** dialog box is displayed and you are prompted to select the edges for a new set.

2. Select the edges of the surface, refer to Figure 11-101. Enter **5** as the fillet radius value in the **Radius 1** edit box.

3. Choose the **OK** button from the **Edge Blend** dialog box. The completed surface model after adding fillets to edges is shown in Figure 11-102.

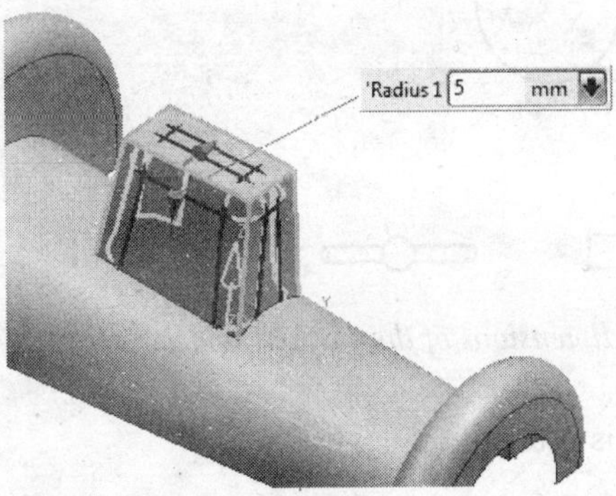

***Figure 11-101** The preview of the fillets displayed after selecting the edges*

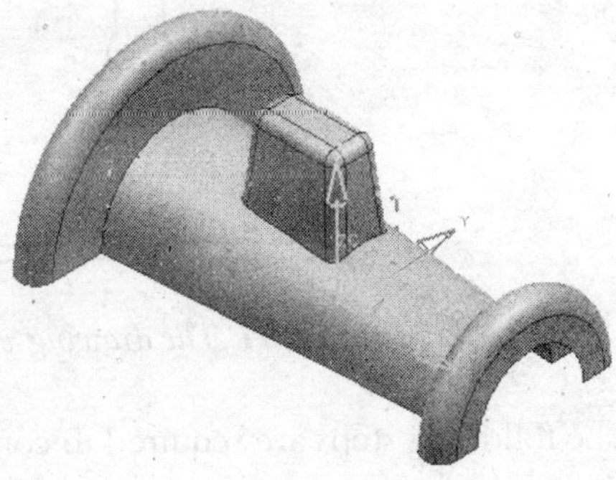

***Figure 11-102** The final surface model*

Saving and Closing the File

1. Choose **File > Close > Save and Close** from the menu bar to save and close the file.

Tutorial 2

In this tutorial, you will create the surface model shown in Figure 11-103. The drawing views and dimensions of the surface model are shown in Figure 11-104. After creating the model, save it with the name *c11tut2.prt* at the location *\NX 7\c11.* **(Expected time: 45 min)**

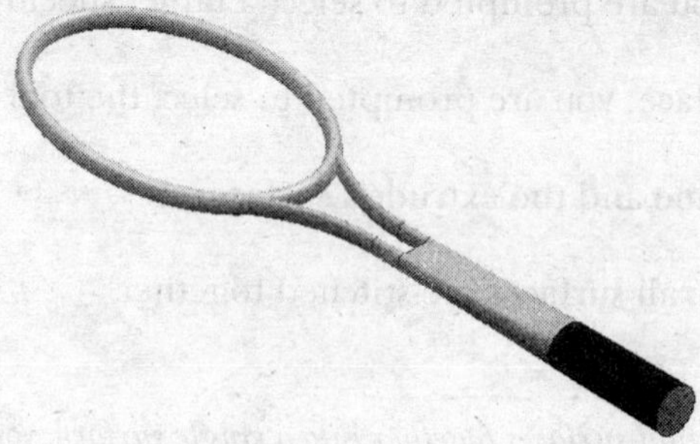

***Figure 11-103** The isometric view of the surface model*

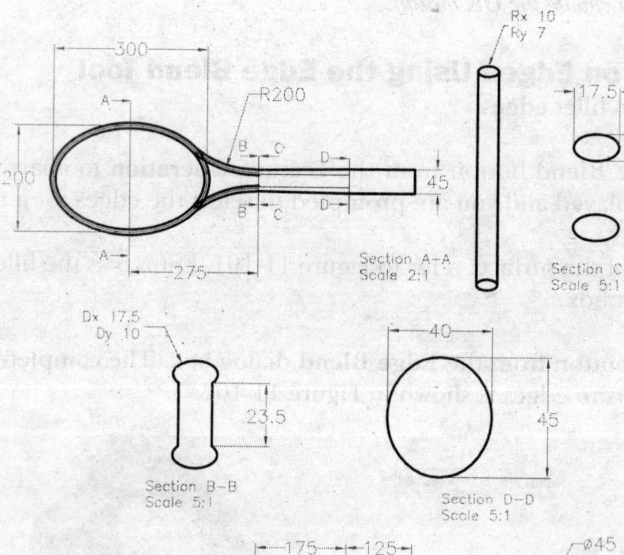

***Figure 11-104** The drawing views and dimensions of the surface model*

The following steps are required to complete this tutorial:

a. Start a new file and set the sheet environment.
b. Create the styled sweep surface as the base feature.
c. Create the sweep surface as the second feature and mirror the surface.
d Create the studio surface as the third feature.

e. Create the ruled surface as the fourth feature.
f. Create the bounded plane surface as the fifth feature.
g. Create another bounded plane surface as the sixth feature.
h. Save and close the file.

Starting the New File and Setting the Sheet Environment

1. Start a new file with the name *c11tut2.prt* using the **Model** template and specify its location as *C:\NX 7\c11*.

2. Choose **Preferences > Modeling** from the menu bar; the **Modeling Preferences** dialog box is displayed.

3. Select the **Sheet** radio button from the **Body Type** area and choose the **OK** button.

Creating the Styled Sweep Surface as the Base Feature

As mentioned earlier, the styled sweep surface will be the base feature.

1. Draw an ellipse on the XC-YC plane, as shown in Figure 11-105, and exit the Sketcher environment.

2. Draw another ellipse on the XC-ZC plane, as shown in Figure 11-106, and exit the Sketcher environment.

3. Choose the **Styled Sweep** button from the **Freeform Shape** toolbar; the **Styled Sweep** dialog box is displayed and you are prompted to select the section string.

4. Select the **1 Guide** option from the **Type** drop-down list of the **Type** rollout in the dialog box, if it is not selected by default.

5. Select the section curve drawn on the XC-ZC plane and press the middle mouse button.

6. Choose the **Guide** button from the **Guide Curves** rollout and then select the guide curve drawn on the XC-YC plane; the preview of the styled sweep surface is displayed in the graphics window. Next, press the middle mouse button.

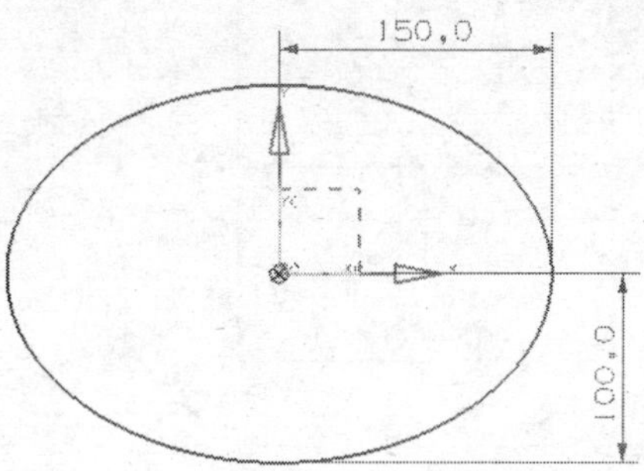

Figure 11-105 The sketch for the guide string

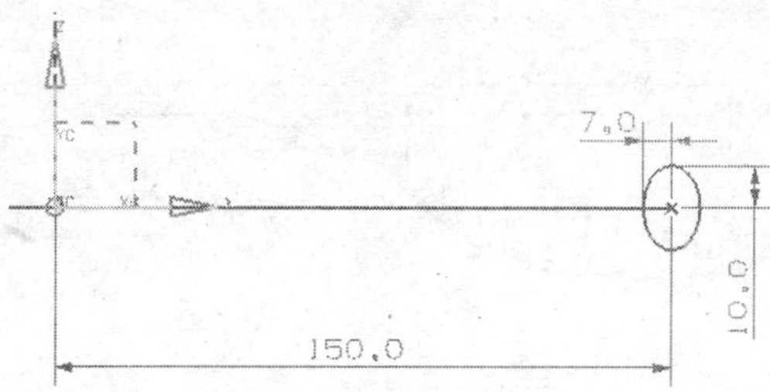

Figure 11-106 The sketch for the section string

7. Select the **Guide and Section** option from the **Fixed String** drop-down list of the **Sweep Attributes** rollout in the dialog box.

8. Choose the **OK** button to create the styled sweep surface. Hide the sketch that is used to create the styled surface. The resulting styled sweep surface is shown in Figure 11-107.

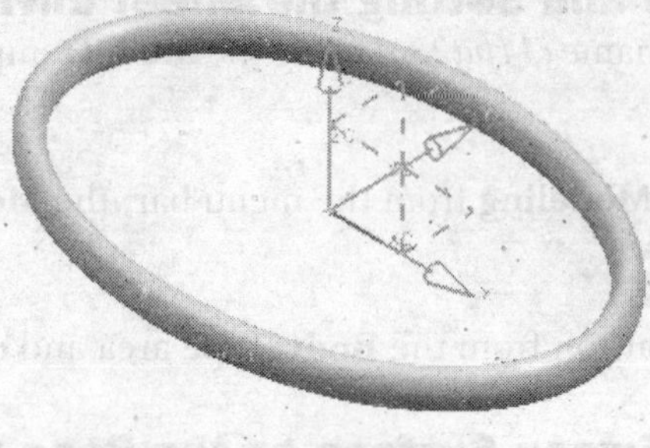

Figure 11-107 The base feature of the surface model

Creating the Sweep Surface

The second feature is a sweep surface.

1. Select the XC-YC plane as the sketching plane and draw the guide curve, as shown in Figure 11-108. Next, exit the sketcher environment.

2. Create a new datum plane perpendicular to the guide curve by entering 0 as the arclength value.

Note

In this tutorial, the datum plane perpendicular to the guide curve is created by selecting the entity of the guide curve that measures 30 mm.

3. Invoke the Sketcher environment by selecting the newly created plane as a sketching plane. Note that you may need to specify horizontal or vertical reference for the sketch in the **Create Sketch** dialog box to invoke the Sketcher environment. Next, draw the ellipse (section curve), refer to Figure 11-109, and then exit the Sketcher environment.

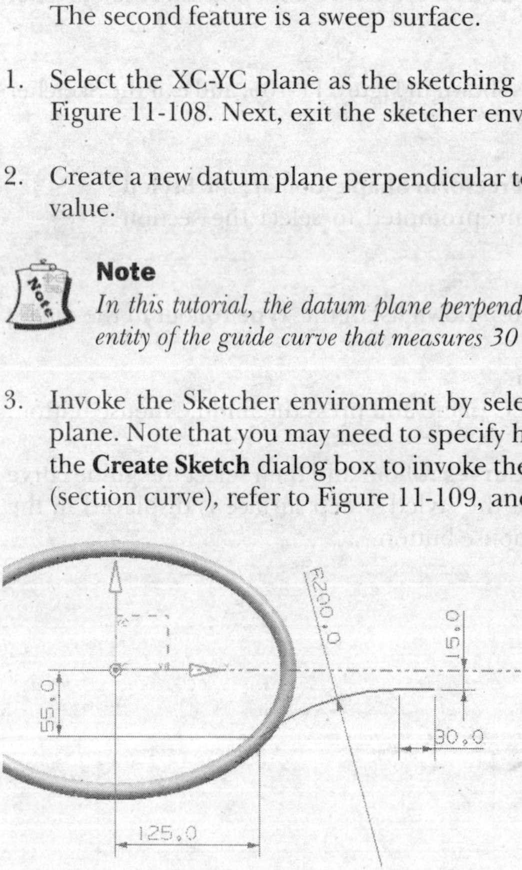

***Figure 11-108** The guide curve for creating the sweep surface*

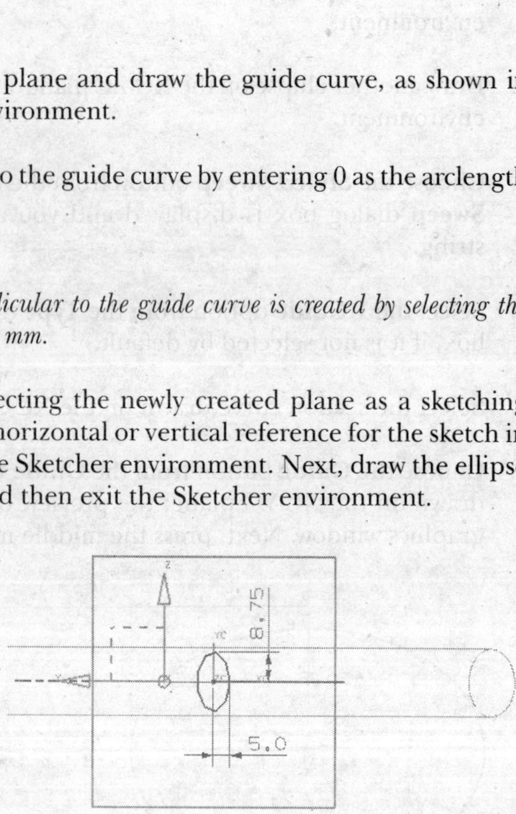

***Figure 11-109** The section curve drawn for creating the sweep surface*

4. Choose the **Sweep along Guide** button from the **Feature** toolbar; the **Sweep along Guide** dialog box is displayed and you are prompted to select the section strings.

5. Select the section curve and then press the middle mouse button; you are prompted to select the guide curve.

6. Select the guide curve and then choose the **OK** button; the sweep surface is created. Hide the sketches that are used to create the sweep surface. The resulting surface model is shown in Figure 11-110.

Mirroring the Sweep Surface

1. Mirror the last created surface by using the XC-ZC plane as the mirror plane. The surface model after mirroring the sweep surface is shown in Figure 11-111.

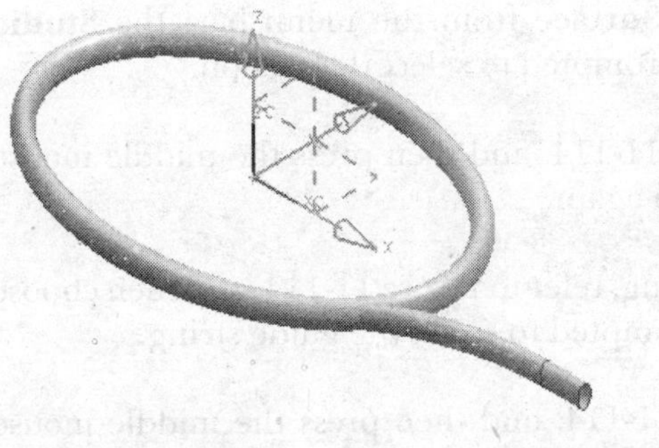

Figure 11-110 *The surface model after creating the sweep surface*

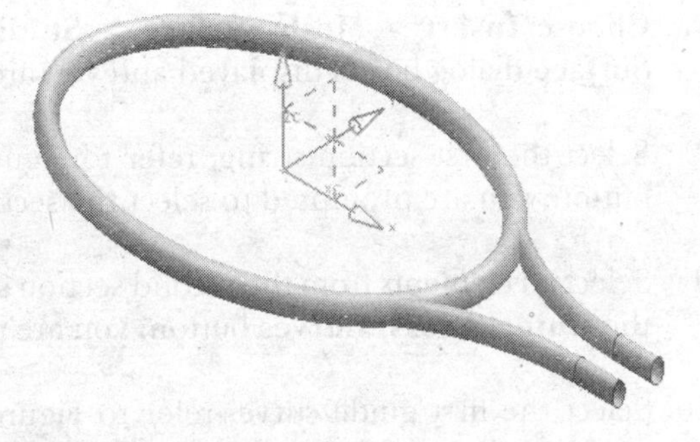

Figure 11-111 *The surface model after mirroring the sweep surface*

Creating the Studio Surface

The third feature is a surface, which will be created by using the **Studio Surface** tool.

1. Invoke the Sketcher environment by using the last datum plane created to draw the section of the sweep surface.

2. Choose **Insert > Recipe Curve > Project Curve** from the menu bar; the **Project Curve** dialog box is displayed and you are prompted to select the geometry to project. Make sure the **Single Spline** option is selected in the **Output Curve Type** drop-down list of the **Settings** rollout.

3. Select the edges of the sweep surfaces and create a profile, as shown in Figure 11-112. Exit the Sketcher environment.

4. Create a datum plane parallel to the YC-ZC plane at a distance of 450 mm.

5. Select the newly created datum plane as the sketching plane and create the second section curve, as shown in Figure 11-113. For dimensions, refer to Figure 11-104.

6. Create the guide strings, refer to Figure 11-113.

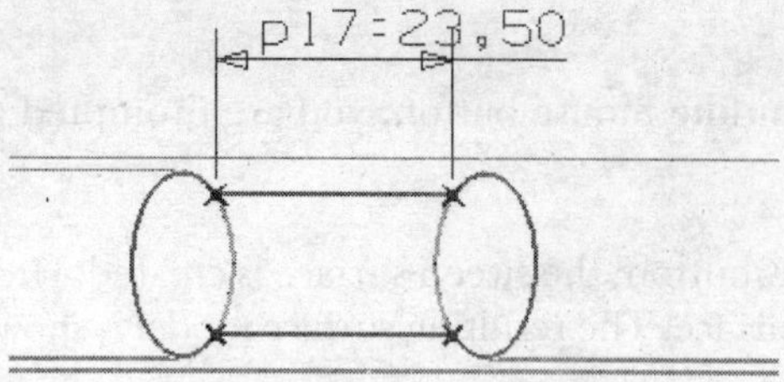

Figure 11-112 The first section curve drawn to create the through curve mesh surface

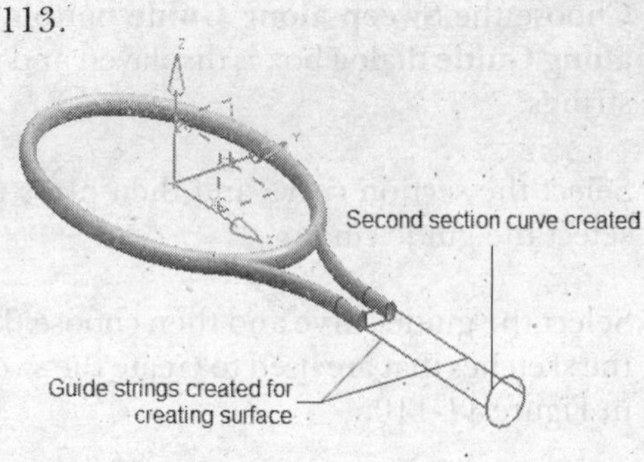

Figure 11-113 The second section curve and the guide strings to create a surface

7. Choose **Insert > Mesh Surface > Studio Surface** from the menu bar; the **Studio Surface** dialog box is displayed and you are prompted to select the section.

8. Select the first section string, refer to Figure 11-114, and then press the middle mouse button; you are prompted to select the section again.

9. Select all elements from the second section string, refer to Figure 11-114, and then choose the **Guide (Cross) Curves** button; you are prompted to select the guide string.

10. Select the first guide curve, refer to Figure 11-114, and then press the middle mouse button; you are prompted to select the guide string again.

11. Select the second guide curve, refer to Figure 11-114. The preview of the studio surface after selecting the sections and the guide curves is shown in Figure 11-114. Next, choose the **Apply** button and then the **Cancel** button to create the studio surface.

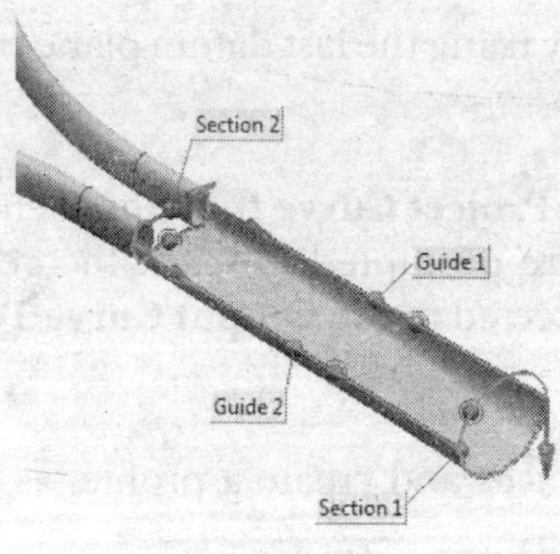

Figure 11-114 Entities to be selected for creating the studio surface

Mirroring the Studio Surface

1. Mirror the studio surface using the XC-YC plane as the mirror plane. The surface model after mirroring the studio surface is shown in Figure 11-115.

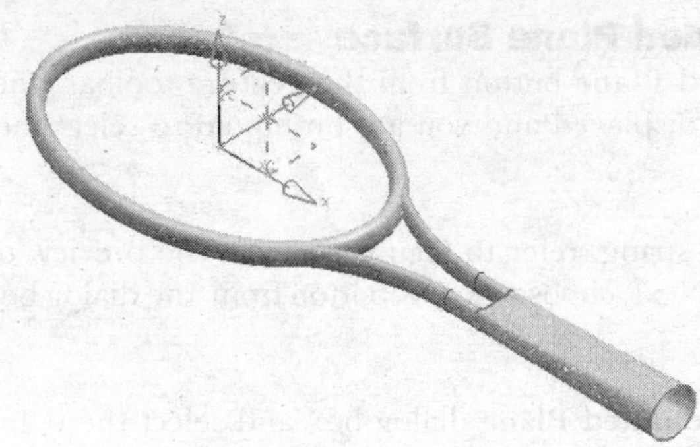

Figure 11-115 The surface model after mirroring the studio surface

Creating the Ruled Surface

Next, you need to create the ruled surface.

1. Create a plane parallel to the YC-ZC plane at a distance of 575 mm.

2. Select the newly created plane as the sketching plane and draw the sketch, as shown in Figure 11-116.

3. Exit the Sketcher environment and choose the **Ruled** button from the **Surface** toolbar; the **Ruled** dialog box is displayed and you are prompted to select the first section string.

4. Select the first section string, as shown in Figure 11-117. Next, press the middle mouse button; you are prompted to select the second section string.

5. Select the second section string, which is the edge of the surface created earlier, as shown in Figure 11-117. Note that the arrows should point in the same direction. Next, choose the **OK** button; the ruled surface is created.

6. Change the color of the ruled surface to black.

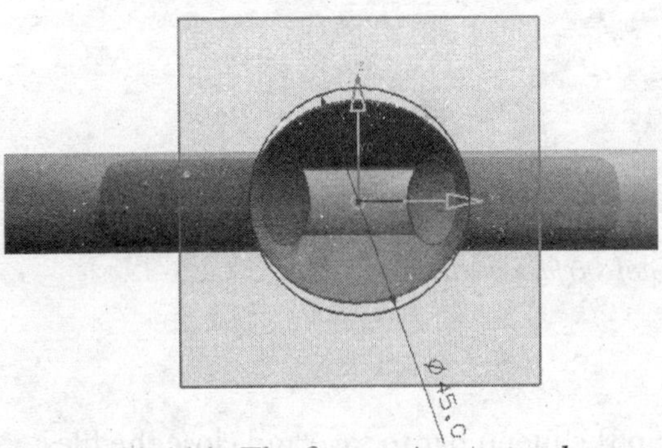

Figure 11-116 *The first section curve drawn to create the ruled surface*

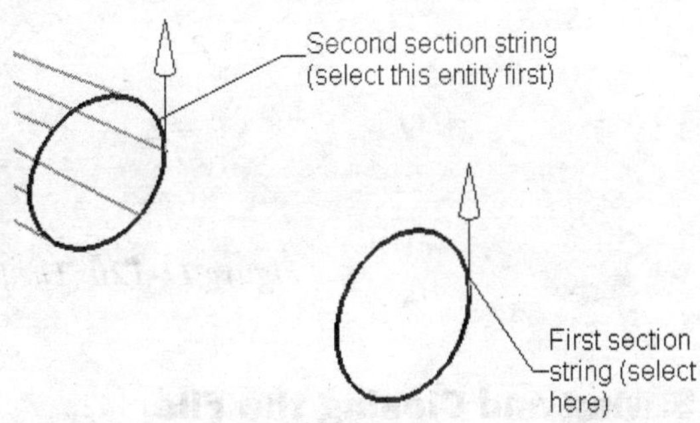

Figure 11-117 *The ruled surface created after selecting both cross-sections*

Creating the Bounded Plane Surface

1. Choose the **Bounded Plane** button from the **Feature** toolbar; the **Bounded Plane** dialog box is displayed and you are prompted to select the bounding string.

2. Select the bounding string, refer to Figure 11-118. The preview of the bounded plane surface is displayed. Next, choose the **OK** button from the dialog box; the bounded plane surface is created.

3. Again, invoke the **Bounded Plane** dialog box and select the bounding string, refer to Figure 11-119. Next, choose the **OK** button from this dialog box. The bounded plane surface is created. The final surface model after hiding all sketches and datum planes is shown in Figure 11-120.

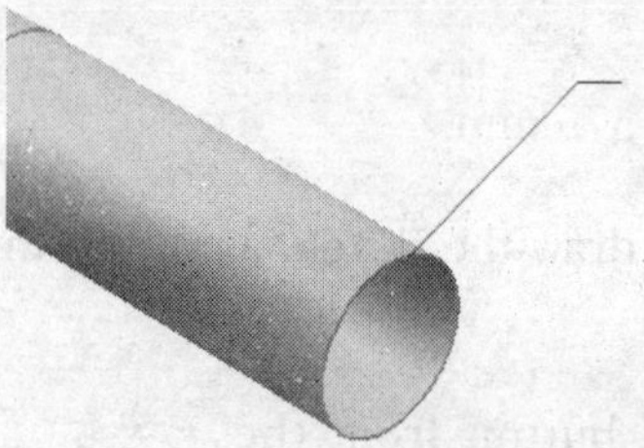

Figure 11-118 The bounding string to be selected

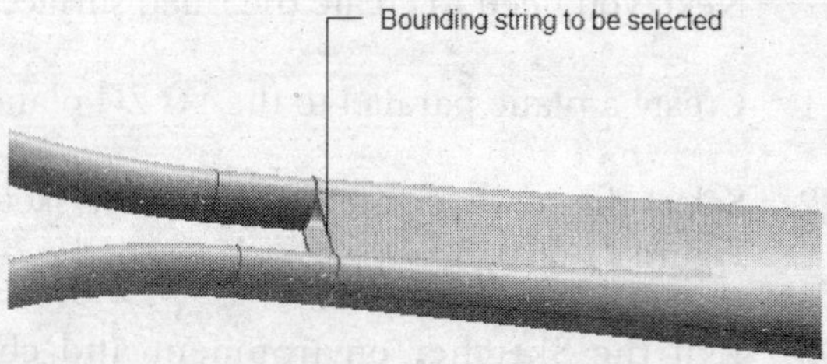

Figure 11-119 The bounding string to be selected

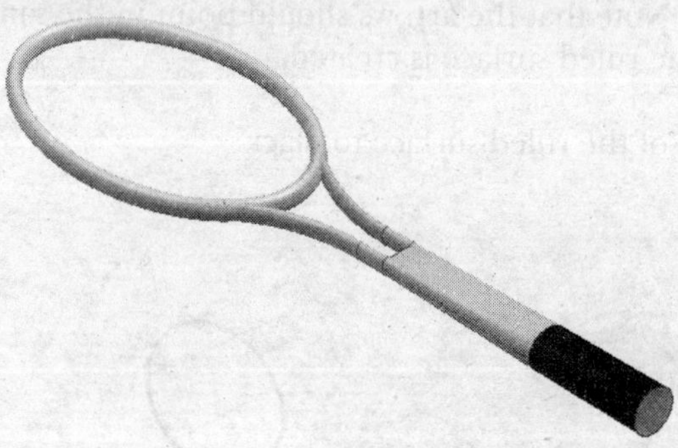

Figure 11-120 The final surface model

Saving and Closing the File

1. Choose **File > Close > Save and Close** from the menu bar to save and close the file.

Self-Evaluation Test

Answer the following questions and then compare them to those given at the end of this chapter:

1. In NX, surfaces are termed as sheets. (T/F)

2. The **Trim and Extend** tool is used to trim or extend an open or a closed surface. (T/F)

3. You can use the **Until Selected** and **Until Next** options from the **End** drop-down list of the **Extrude** dialog box to create a base sheet. (T/F)

4. The default tolerance value for creating a sheet is 0.0254. (T/F)

5. The maximum number of sections that can be used to create a sheet by using the **Ruled** tool in the **Surface** toolbar is __________.

6. The __________ tool is used to create a sheet from n number of guide curves and n number of section curves.

7. The __________ tool is used to stitch individual surfaces into a single surface.

8. The __________ tool is used to trim and extend a surface.

9. The __________ tool is used to create a planar surface.

10. The __________ tool is used to create an offset surface.

Review Questions

Answer the following questions:

1. How many points are required to create a surface by using the **Four Point Surface** tool?

   (a) Three (b) Four
   (c) Five (d) None of these

2. Which of the following tools is used to create a single patch surface or a multi-patches triangular surfaces that encloses a closed 2D sketch or a closed 3D curve?

   (a) **N-Sided Surface** (b) **Silhouette Flange**
   (b) **Law Extension** (d) None of these

3. Which of the following options is available in the **Type** rollout of the **Law Extension** rollout?

   (a) **Faces, Vector** (b) **Visual Gap, Absolute Gap**
   (c) **Basic, Absolute Gap** (d) None of these

4. Before adding a fillet at the intersection of two surfaces, the surfaces have to be

   (a) Stitched using the **Sew** tool   (b) Merged
   (c) Trimmed   (d) None of these

5. You can invoke the **Bounded Plane** tool by choosing **Surface > Bounded Plane** from the menu bar. (T/F)

6. You can select an open sketch to create a bounded plane surface. (T/F)

7. Surface models do not have mass properties. (T/F)

8. You can create a surface from a closed or an open sketch. (T/F)

9. Once thickness has been added to a sheet, it is converted into a solid. (T/F)

10. You can create a hole feature on a planar surface by using the **Hole** tool. (T/F)

Exercises

Exercise 1

Create the surface model shown in Figure 11-121. The drawing views and dimensions of the surface model are shown in the Figure 11-122. Save the model with the name *c11exr1.prt* at the location *\NX 7\c11.* **(Expected time: 30 min)**

Figure 11-121 *Surface model for Exercise 1*

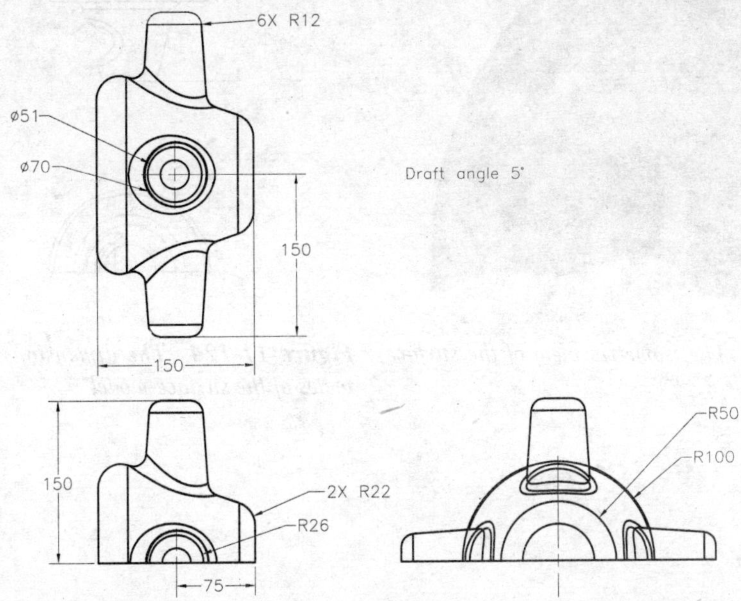

Figure 11-122 Drawing views and dimensions of the surface model for Exercise 1

Exercise 2

Create the surface model shown in Figure 11-123. The drawing views and dimensions of the surface model are shown in Figure 11-124. Save the model with the name *c11exr2.prt* at the location *\NX 7\c11.* **(Expected time: 30 min)**

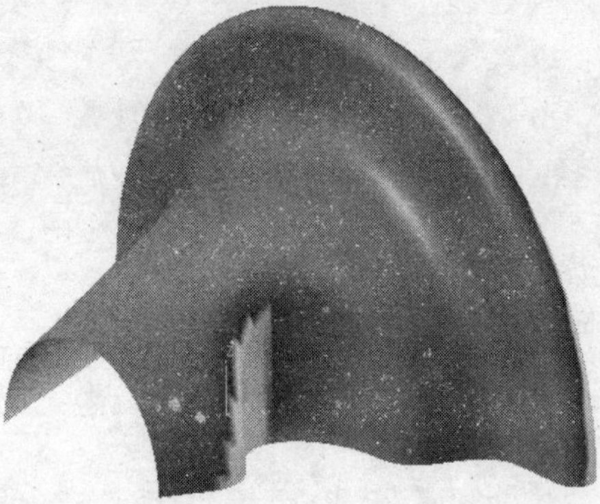

Figure 11-123 *The isometric view of the surface model for Exercise 2*

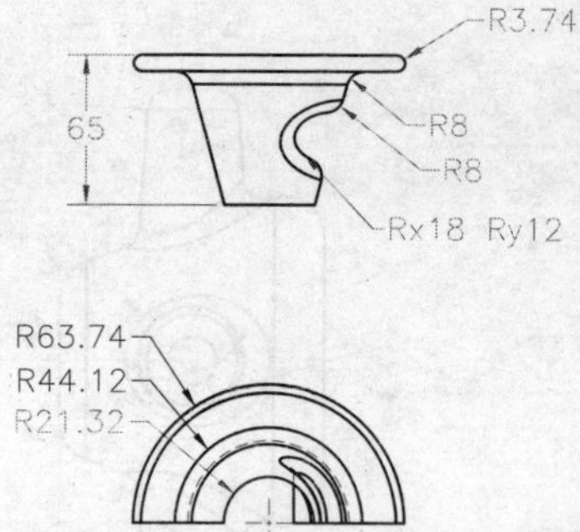

Figure 11-124 *The dimensions and drawing views of the surface model*

Answers to Self-Evaluation Test

1. T, **2.** T, **3.** F, **4.** T, **5.** Two, **6. Studio Surface**, **7. Sew**, **8. Trim and Extend**, **9. Bounded Plane**, **10. Offset Surface**

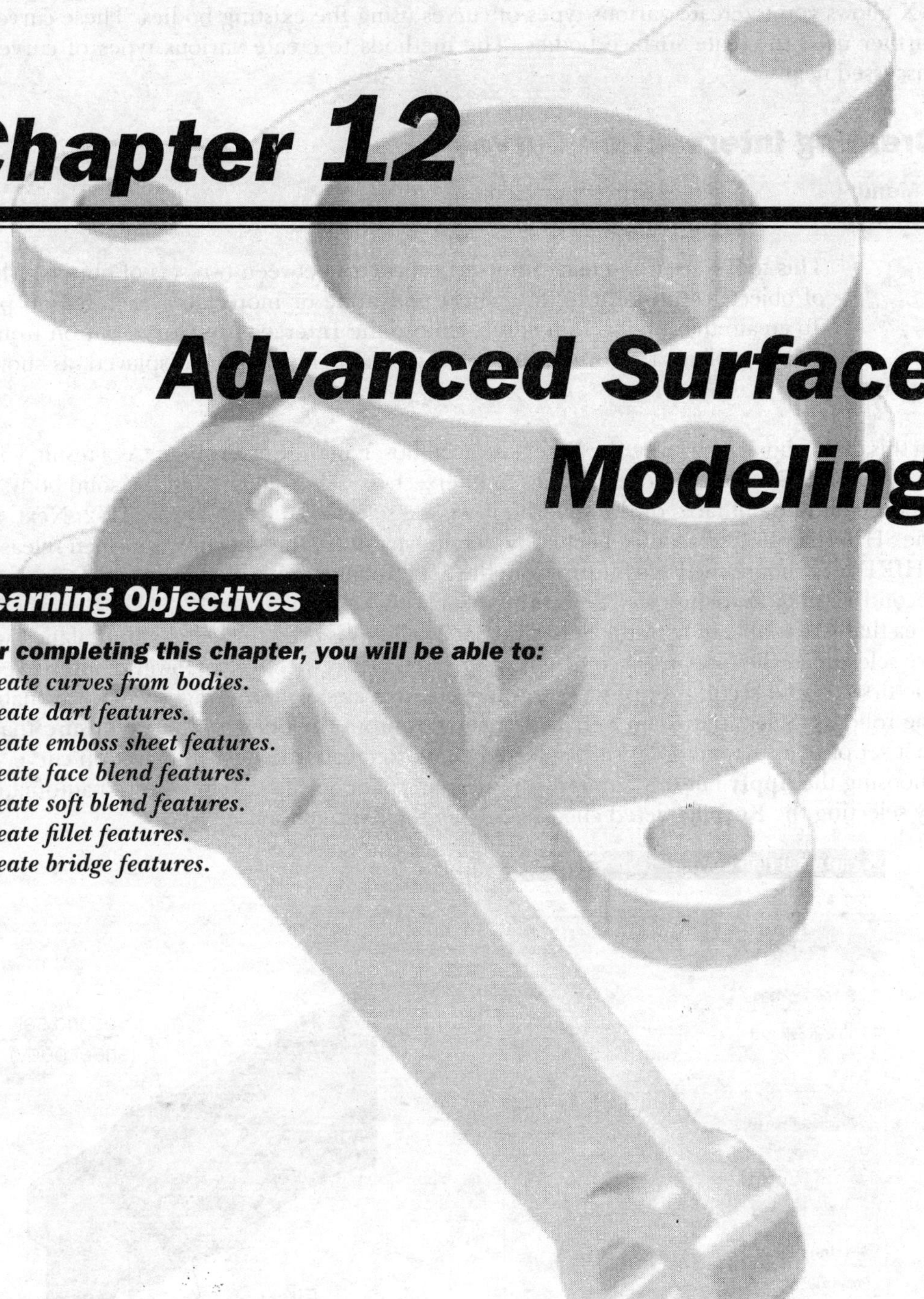

Chapter 12

Advanced Surface Modeling

Learning Objectives

After completing this chapter, you will be able to:

- *Create curves from bodies.*
- *Create dart features.*
- *Create emboss sheet features.*
- *Create face blend features.*
- *Create soft blend features.*
- *Create fillet features.*
- *Create bridge features.*

CREATING CURVES FROM BODIES

NX allows you to create various types of curves using the existing bodies. These curves are further used to create surface bodies. The methods to create various types of curves are discussed next.

Creating Intersection Curves

Menu:	Insert > Curve from Bodies > Intersect
Toolbar:	Curve > Project Curve > Intersection Curve

This tool is used to create intersection curves between two sets of objects. The set of objects could be a solid, a sheet body, one or more faces, or a datum plane. To create the intersection curve, choose the **Intersection Curve** button from the **Curve** toolbar; the **Intersection Curve** dialog box will be displayed, as shown in Figure 12-1.

In this dialog box, by default, the **Face** button is chosen in the **Set 1** rollout. As a result, you are prompted to select the first set of faces to intersect. To select all faces of the solid body, drag a box around it; all faces of the solid body will be selected, refer to Figure 12-2. Next, press the SHIFT key and select the sheet body to remove it from the selection and then release the SHIFT key. Choose the **Face** button from the **Set 2** rollout; you will be prompted to select the second set of faces to intersect. Select the sheet body, refer to Figure 12-2. The **Specify Plane** area that is available in both the **Set 1** and **Set 2** rollouts is used to create datum planes, which are selected as the first and second sets of intersection, respectively. However, after selecting the first set and second set of faces to intersect, this area will no longer will be available in the rollouts. Select the **Keep Selected** check box from the **Set 1** rollout to ensure that the first set of objects is automatically selected again to create the next intersection curve, after choosing the **Apply** button. Similarly, the second set of objects can be selected automatically by selecting the **Keep Selected** check box from the **Set 2** rollout.

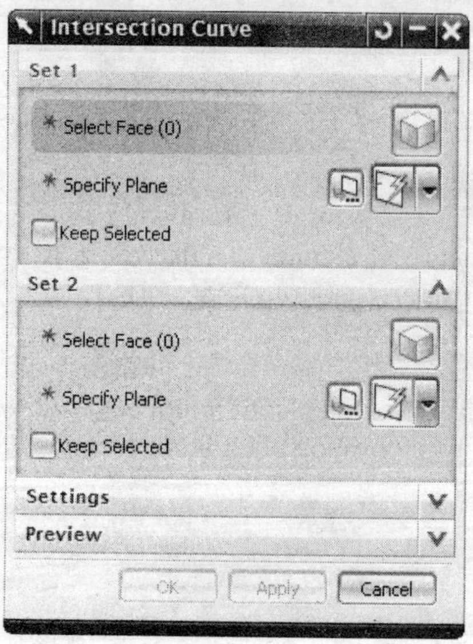

Figure 12-1 *The* ***Intersection Curve*** *dialog box*

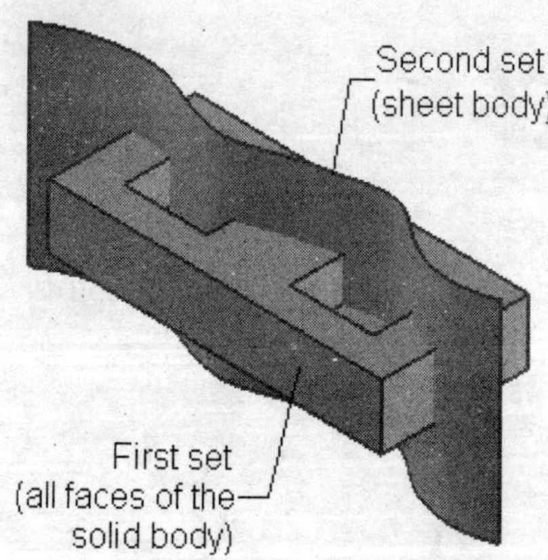

Figure 12-2 *Objects to be selected*

You need to expand the **Settings** rollout for some additional options. The **Associative** check box in this rollout allows you to specify whether the intersection curve is associative or not. An associative intersection curve will update automatically when changes are made to its source objects. If you need the curves to be approximated by spine, then use the options in the **Curve Fit** drop-down list to control the fitting method. The options in this drop-down list are discussed next.

Cubic

Curves created with the **Cubic** option selected are degree 3 splines. Use this option when you want to transfer your spline to another CAD system that supports only degree 3 splines.

Quintic

Curves created with the **Quintic** option are degree 5 splines with smoother curvature.

Advanced

The **Advanced** option allows you to create splines by specifying the number of degrees.

An intersection curve resulting from the selections made in Figure 12-2 is shown in Figure 12-3.

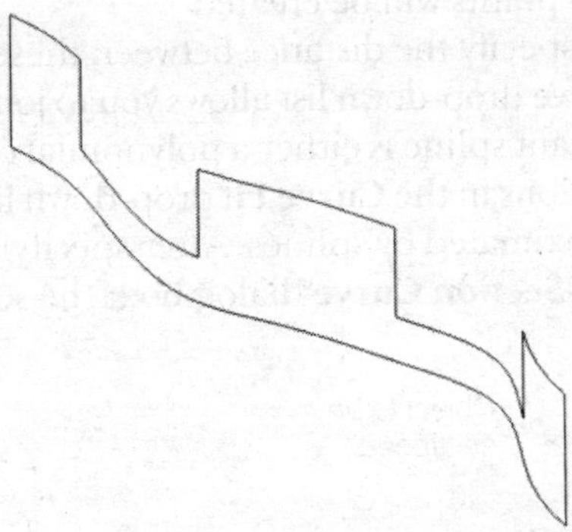

Figure 12-3 *Resulting intersection curve*

Creating Section Curves

Menu:	Insert > Curve from Bodies > Section
Toolbar:	Curve > Section Curve *(Customize to add)*

This tool is used to create the section curves between specified planes and solid bodies, surfaces, or curves. The output curve can be associative. The section curves can be created by four methods: Selected Planes, Parallel Planes, Radial Planes, and Planes Perpendicular to Curve. The selection steps for each method are different. The methods for creating section curves are discussed next.

Creating Section Curves by Using the Selected Planes Method

This method is used to create section curves by specifying solid or sheet bodies and one or more section planes. To create section curve by selecting planes, choose the **Section Curve** button from the **Curve** toolbar; the **Section Curve** dialog box will be displayed, as shown in

Figure 12-4. By default, the **Selected Planes** option is selected in the drop-down list in the **Type** rollout, and the **Object** button is chosen in the **Object to Section** rollout. As a result, you will be prompted to select the object to be sectioned. Select the face of the solid body from the graphics window, refer to Figure 12-5. Choose the **Plane** button from the **Section Plane** rollout; you will be prompted to select the plane to section. Select the plane, refer to Figure 12-5. Expand the **Settings** rollout to use some additional options. By default, the **Associative** check box is selected in the **Settings** rollout. As a result, the intersection curve will be associative to the source object. Clear the check box; the **Non-associative Settings** sub-rollout will be displayed. In this sub-rollout, the **Group Objects** check box allows you to automatically group the output curves and the points that are created for each plane. In the **Non-associative Settings** sub-rollout, the **Output Sampled Points** check box is clear. If you select this check box, instead of curve, the points will be created in the resultant model. You can specify the distance between these points by using the **Sample Distance** edit box. The **Join Curve** drop-down list allows you to join a chain of curves to create a single B-spline curve. The resultant spline is either a polynomial cubic spline, a general spline, or a polynomial quintic. The options in the **Curve Fit** drop-down list control the fitting method used when curves must be approximated by splines. After specifying the required parameters, choose the **OK** button from the **Section Curve** dialog box; the section curves will be created, refer to Figure 12-6.

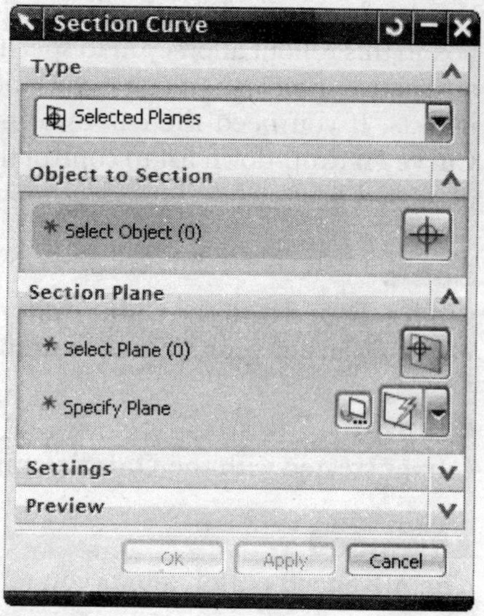

Figure 12-4 The Section Curve dialog box

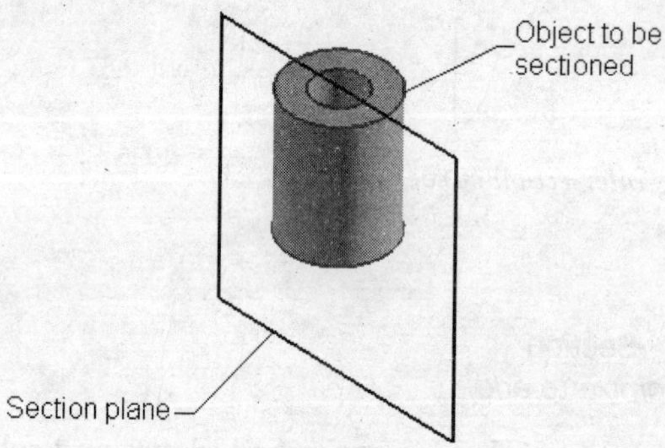

Figure 12-5 Objects to be selected

Figure 12-6 Section curves created

Creating Section Curves by Using the Parallel Planes Method

This method is used to create the section curves by specifying the base plane, step distance, start distance, and end distance. A series of parallel planes are spaced at the equal distances and are further used to create the section of the selected object. To create the section curves using this method, choose the **Section Curve** button from the **Curve** toolbar; the **Section Curve** dialog box will be displayed. Select the **Parallel Planes** option from the drop-down list in the **Type** rollout; you will be prompted to select the objects to be sectioned. Select the solid body, refer to Figure 12-7.

Now, choose the **Inferred** button from the **Base Plane** rollout; you will be prompted to select the objects to define a plane. Select the plane, refer to Figure 12-7. Next, enter the step, start, and end distance values in their corresponding edit boxes. The step distance is the distance between two parallel planes. The start and the end distances are measured from the base plane. The software generates as many planes as possible between the start and end distances by maintaining a step distance between the consecutive planes.

Next, choose the **OK** button to create curves. The section curves created using the selections made in Figure 12-7 are shown in Figure 12-8.

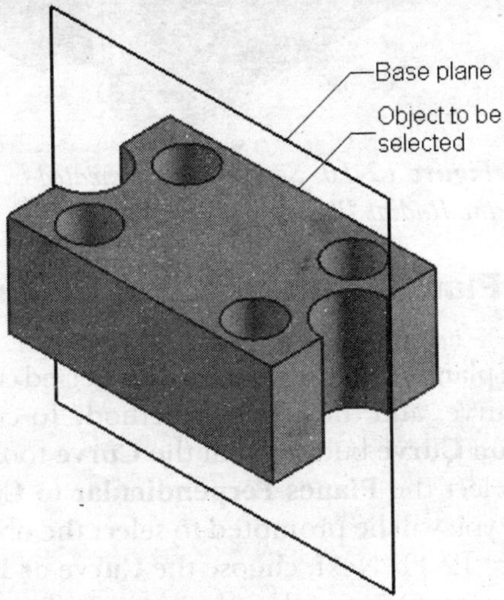

Figure 12-7 Objects to be selected

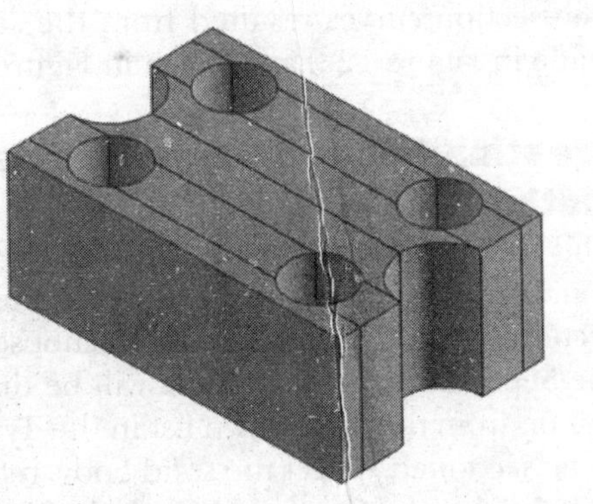

Figure 12-8 Section curves created by using the Parallel Planes method

Creating Section Curves by Using the Radial Planes Method

This method is used to specify the planes spaced at equal angles, which are further used to section the selected bodies. The planes are pivoted around a common axis. To create the section curves using this method, choose the **Section Curve** button from the **Curve** toolbar; the **Section Curve** dialog box will be displayed. Select the **Radial Planes** option from the drop-down list in the **Type** rollout; you will be prompted to select the objects to be sectioned. Select the solid body, refer to Figure 12-9. Next, choose the **Inferred Vector** button from the **Radial Axis** rollout; you will be prompted to select objects to infer vector. Select the edge of the object, refer to Figure 12-9. Alternatively, you can use the **Vector Constructor** button to create a vector.

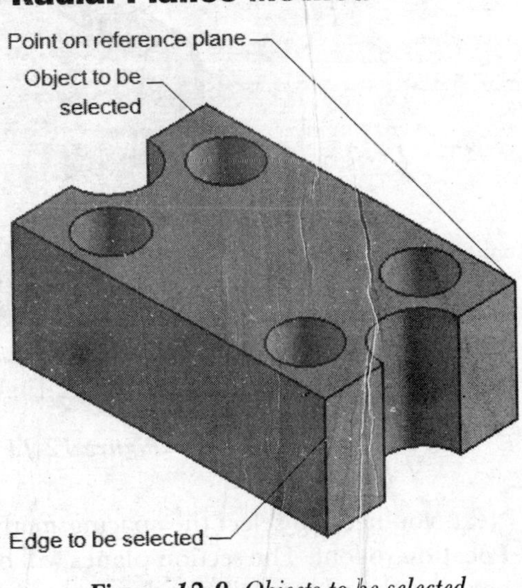

Figure 12-9 Objects to be selected

Choose the **Inferred Point** button from the **Point on Reference Plane** rollout; you will be prompted to select the object to infer point. Select the radial reference point, refer to Figure 12-9. Next, enter the values for the step, start, and end angles in their corresponding edit boxes. The step angle is the angle between two radial planes. The start and end angles are measured from the base plane. The base plane passes through the radial axis and the point on the reference plane. The software generates as many planes as possible between the start and end angles by maintaining the step distance between the consecutive planes.

The section curves resulted from the selections made in Figure 12-9 are shown in Figure 12-10.

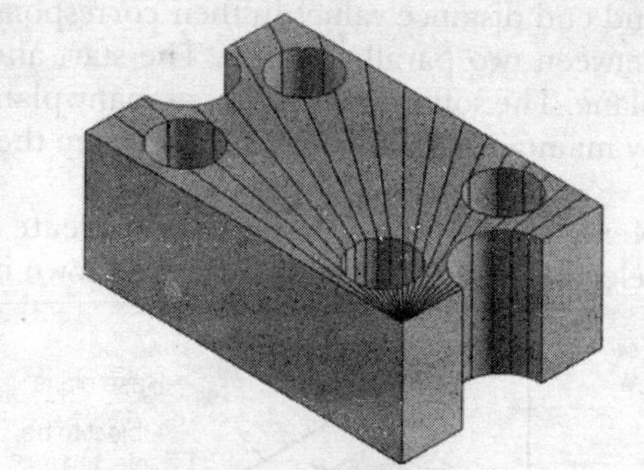

Figure 12-10 Section curves created by the Radial Planes method

Creating Section Curves by Using the Planes Perpendicular to Curve Method

This method is used to create section curves along the planes perpendicular to the selected curve. You need to specify the solid or the sheet body, curve, and the spacing method. To create section curves using this method, choose the **Section Curve** button from the **Curve** toolbar; the **Section Curve** dialog box will be displayed. Select the **Planes Perpendicular to Curve** option from the drop-down list in the **Type** rollout; you will be prompted to select the objects to be sectioned. Select the solid body, refer to Figure 12-11. Next, choose the **Curve or Edge** button from the **Curve or Edge** rollout; you will be prompted to select the curve or the edge. Select the curve along which the perpendicular planes will be created, refer to Figure 12-11.

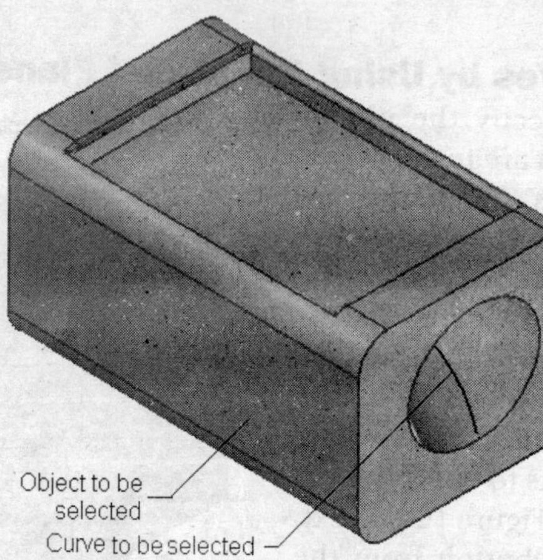

Figure 12-11 Objects to be selected

Next, you need to select the spacing method from the **Spacing** drop-down list in the **Plane Location** rollout. The section planes will be placed perpendicular to the curve. The distance between the planes will be determined by the spacing method. You can use one of the following spacing methods:

Equal Arc Length
This option allows you to create sections using the planes at equal arc lengths along the curve. You need to enter the values for the number of section planes on the curve. Similarly, enter the start and end percentage values relative to the arc length of the curve.

Equal Parameters
This option allows you to create sections using the planes based on the parameterization of the curve. You need to enter the values for the number of section planes on the curve. Similarly, enter the start and the end percentage values relative to the arc length of the curve.

Geometric Progression
This option allows you to create sections using the planes based on a geometric ratio. You need to enter the values for the number of section planes on the curve as well as the start and the end percentage values relative to the arc length of the curve. Similarly, enter a value in the **Ratio** edit box to determine the mathematical ratio for spacing the planes between the start and end percentage points.

Chordal Tolerance
This option allows you to create sections using the planes based on a chordal tolerance. In this case, you need to enter the value for the chordal tolerance.

Incremental Arc Length
This option allows you to create sections using the planes placed at increments along the curve. In this case, you need to enter the value for the arc length.

Select the **Equal Arc Length** method from the **Spacing** drop-down list of the **Plane Location** rollout. Next, enter the values for the number of copies, start percentage, and end percentage in their corresponding edit boxes. Choose the **OK** button from the dialog box. The section curves are created, as shown in Figure 12-12.

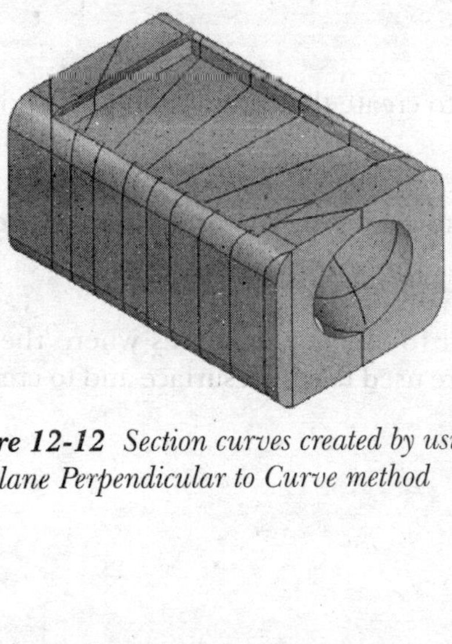

***Figure 12-12** Section curves created by using the Plane Perpendicular to Curve method*

Creating Extract Curves

Toolbar: Curve > Extract Curve *(Customize to add)*

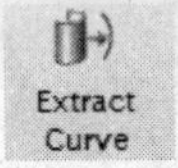

This tool is used to create the curves using the edges or faces of the solid or sheet bodies. To create the extract curves, choose the **Extract Curve** button from the **Curve** toolbar; the **Extract Curve** dialog box will be displayed, as shown in Figure 12-13. Different extract curve methods are discussed next.

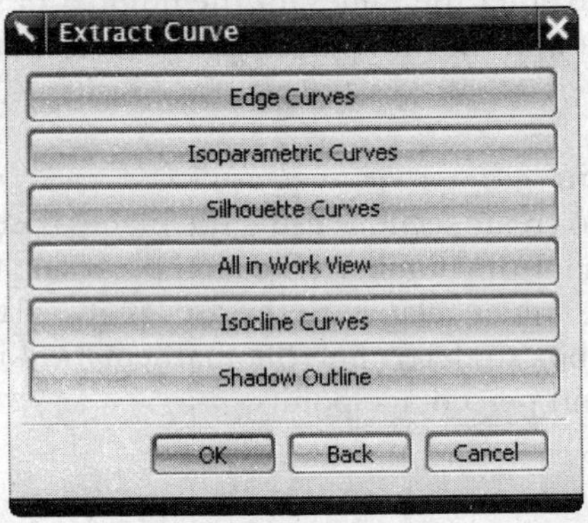

***Figure 12-13** The **Extract Curve** dialog box*

Edge Curves

This method allows you to extract the curves from the selected edges, faces, or bodies. When you choose the **Extract Curves** button, the **Single Edge Curve** dialog box will be displayed and you will be prompted to select edge 1. Select the edges that you want to extract. Alternatively, you can use the other options from the **Single Edge Curve** dialog box to extract the curves.

Isoparametric Curves

This method allows you to create the isoparametric curves on a selected face. It is used to generate the curves along the U/V parameters on a face.

Silhouette Curves

This method allows you to create the curves from the silhouette edges.

All in Work View

This method allows you to create the curves from all the edges of all bodies in the part file.

Isocline Curves

This method allows you to create the curves where the draft angle on a set of faces is constant. These curves are used to split a surface and to create the parting surfaces on a mold or casting.

Shadow Outline
This method allows you to create the curves that show only the outline of bodies in part file. To use this option, first you need to set up the work view to **Static Wireframe**.

The use of some of these extract options is discussed next.

Creating Edge Curves
To create the edge curves, choose the **Edge Curves** button from the **Extract Curve** dialog box; the **Single Edge Curve** dialog box will be displayed, as shown in Figure 12-14, and you will be prompted to select edge 1. Select the edges that you want to extract. Alternatively, you can use the other options from the **Single Edge Curve** dialog box to extract the curves. These options are discussed next.

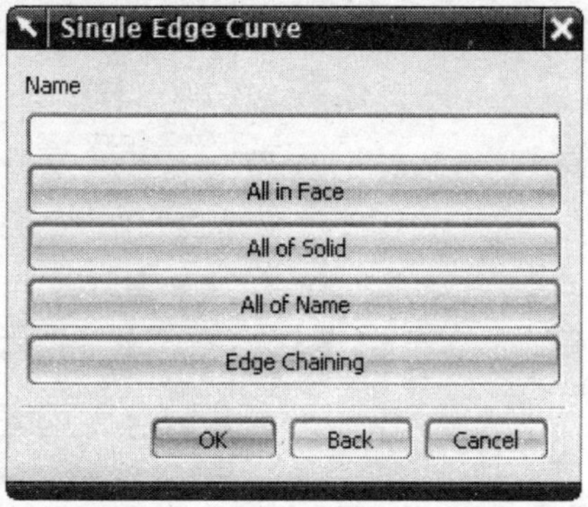

*Figure 12-14 The **Single Edge Curve** dialog box*

All in Face
This option allows you to extract the curves from all edges of the selected face.

All of Solid
This option allows you to extract the curves from all edges of the selected solid.

All of Name
This option allows you to enter the name of edges to be extracted.

Edge Chaining
This option allows you to extract the connected curves. Figure 12-15 shows curves extracted by using the **All of Solid** option.

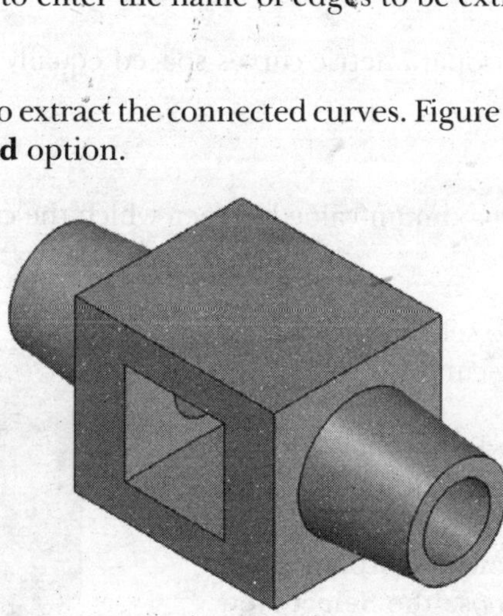

*Figure 12-15 Curves extracted using the **All of Solid** option*

Creating Isoparametric Curves

To create the isoparametric curves, choose the **Isoparametric Curves** button from the **Extract Curves** dialog box; the **Isoparametric Curves** dialog box will be displayed, as shown in Figure 12-16.

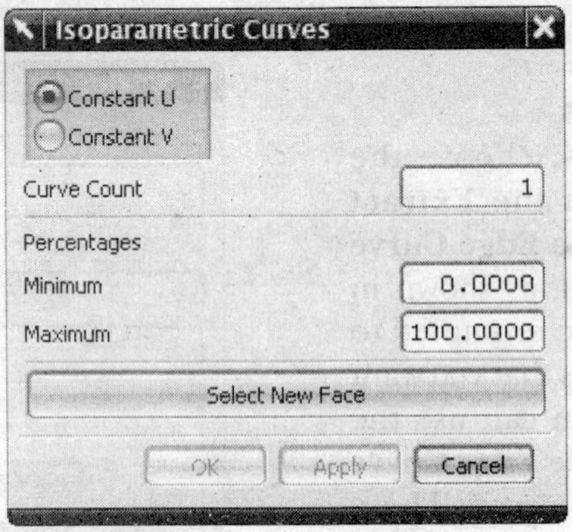

*Figure 12-16 The **Isoparametric Curves** dialog box*

Also, you will be prompted to select the face of the model. Select the side face of the model; you will be prompted to enter the parameters for creating the curve. These parameters are discussed next.

Constant U & Constant V

These are the directions in which the curves will be created.

Curve Count

It is the number of the isoparametric curves spaced equally between the minimum and maximum percentages.

Percentages

It is the minimum and maximum value between which the curves will be created.

Select New Face

This button allows you to select a new face to create the isoparametric curves.

By default, the **Constant U** radio button is selected in the **Isoparametric Curves** dialog box. Enter **10** in the **Curve Count** edit box and choose the **Apply** button. Choose the **Constant V** button and then the **Apply** button. Choose the **Select New Face** button from the dialog box and select the top face of the model. Repeat the same procedure to create the curves in the U and V directions. The resultant curves are shown in Figure 12-17.

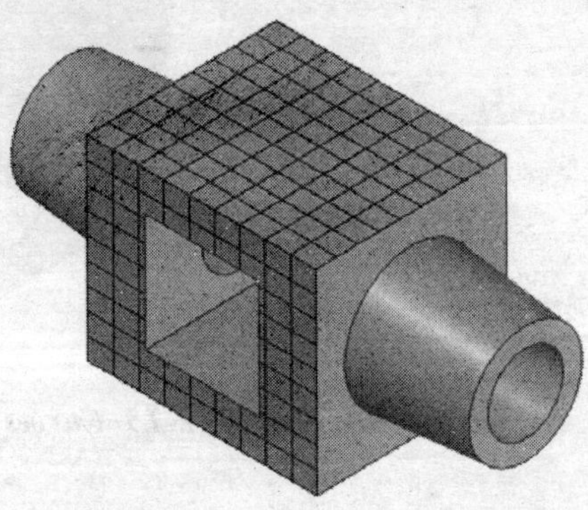

***Figure 12-17** Curves created by using the Isoparametric method*

ADVANCED SURFACE MODELING TOOLS

These tools are used to create the basic and advanced surfaces and are discussed next.

Creating Dart Features

Toolbar: Feature > Dart *(Customize to add)*

The **Dart** tool is used to add a rib along the intersection curve of two faces. The dart feature can be added to the solid body or sheet body. To create the dart feature, you need to select two intersecting faces. The dart will be placed on a plane that is perpendicular to the intersection curve of the two faces. You can define the orientation manually. You need to enter the dimensional values of the dart for angle, depth, and radius. To create the dart feature, choose the **Dart** button from the **Feature** toolbar; the **Dart** dialog box will be displayed, as shown in Figure 12-18. By default, the **First Set** button is chosen, and therefore you will be prompted to select faces for the first set. Select the surface, refer to Figure 12-19. Next, choose the **Second Set** button; you will be prompted to select faces for the second set. Select the surface, refer to Figure 12-19. The preview of the dart will be displayed on the intersection curve of two faces. Choose the **Location Plane** button, if you want to position the dart feature relative to a plane. Note that this option will be activated only when the **Position** option is selected in the **Method** drop-down list. Next, choose the **Orientation Plane** button to select a plane for orienting the dart feature, if needed. To trim the surfaces enclosed within the **Dart** feature created, select the **Trim All** option from the **Trim Option** drop-down list. Else, select the **No Trim** option. To trim the surfaces enclosed within the **Dart** feature created and form a single surface with a common edge, select the **Trim and Sew** option from the drop-down list. Note that the **Trim All** and **Trim and Sew** options will be available in the **Trim Options** drop-down list only if the faces selected to create the draft are stitched together by using the **Sew** tool. To position the dart manually, there are two options in the **Method** drop down list. These options are discussed next.

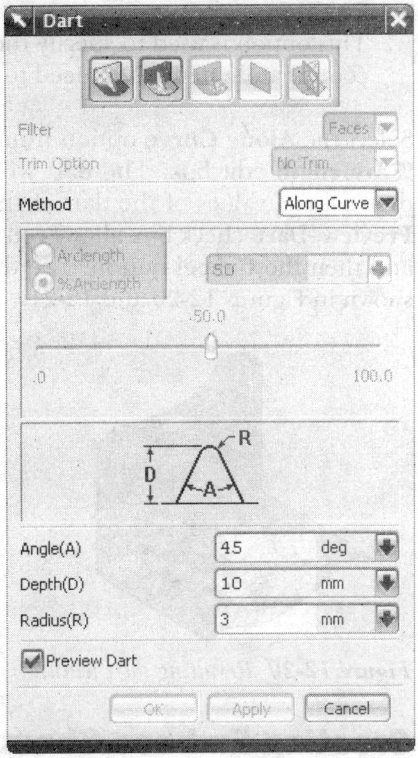

*Figure 12-18 The **Dart** dialog box*

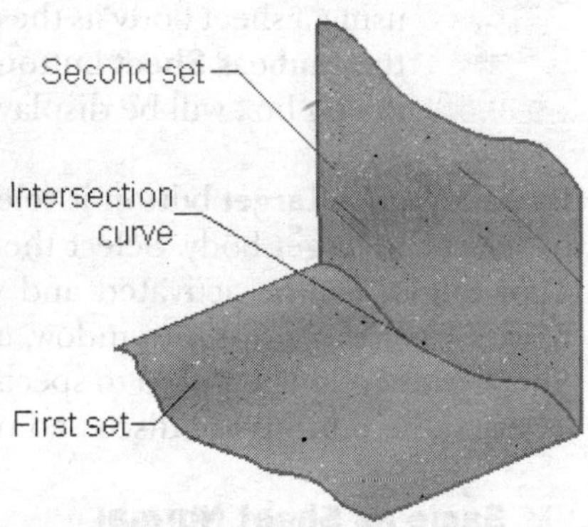

Figure 12-19 Objects to be selected

Along Curve

This option is used to define a base point for the dart anywhere on the intersection curve. You can enter the value for the arc length in the **Arclength** edit box. Alternatively, you can enter the value for the percentage arclength in the **%Arclength** edit box. You need to select the respective radio button to display these edit boxes. You can also use the respective slider to drag the base point in terms of arc length and % arc length along the curve.

Position

This option is used to specify the location for the dart by using the WCS or the absolute coordinate systems. You need to enter the values for the X, Y, Z positions.

Select the **Along Curve** option from the **Method** drop-down list and enter the value in the **%Arclength** edit box. The dart will be placed on the intersection curve. Next, enter the dimensional values of the dart in the **Angle(A)**, **Depth(D)**, and **Radius(R)** edit boxes. The **Preview Dart** check box allows you to see the preview of the dart. Choose the **Apply** button and then the **Cancel** button. The dart feature created between the two selected surfaces is shown in Figures 12-20 and 12-21.

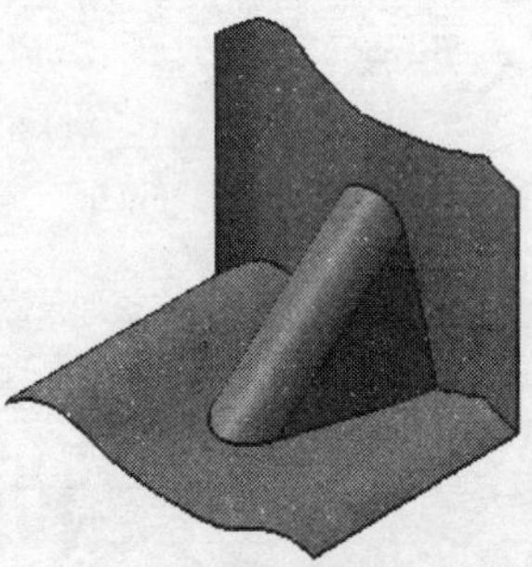

Figure 12-20 *Resulting dart feature*

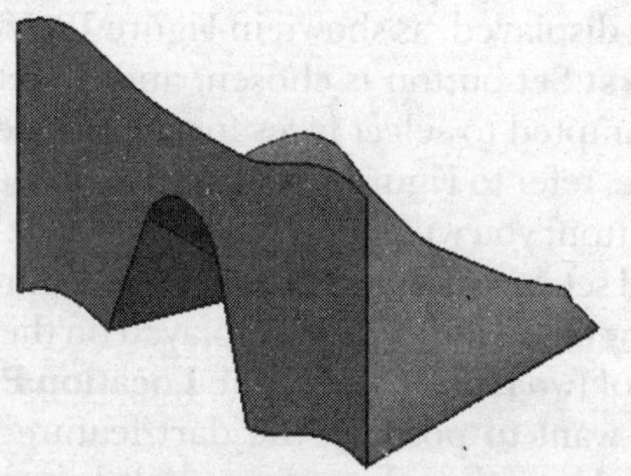

Figure 12-21 *Rotated view of the resulting dart feature*

Creating Emboss Sheet Features

Toolbar: Feature Operation > Emboss Sheet *(Customize to add)*

The **Emboss Sheet** tool is used to convert the shapes of solid bodies into a sheet, using a sheet body as the cutting object. To create the emboss sheet feature, choose the **Emboss Sheet** button from the **Feature Operation** toolbar; the **Emboss Sheet** dialog box will be displayed, as shown in Figure 12-22.

By default, the **Target** button is selected in the **Target** rollout. As a result, you are prompted to select the target body. Select the sheet, as shown in Figure 12-23; the **Tool** button in the **Tool** rollout will be activated and you will be prompted to select tool bodies. Select solid bodies from the graphics window, as shown in Figure 12-23. The radio buttons in the **Tool Shape Side** rollout are used to specify which part of tool bodies need to be added to the sheet. These radio buttons are discussed next.

Same as Sheet Normal

The portions of the tool bodies above the sheet body and in the direction of the sheet normal vector are added to the shape of the sheet. The other portions are discarded.

Opposite of Sheet Normal
The portions of the tool bodies below the sheet body and in the direction opposite to the sheet normal vector are added to the shape of the sheet. The other portions are discarded.

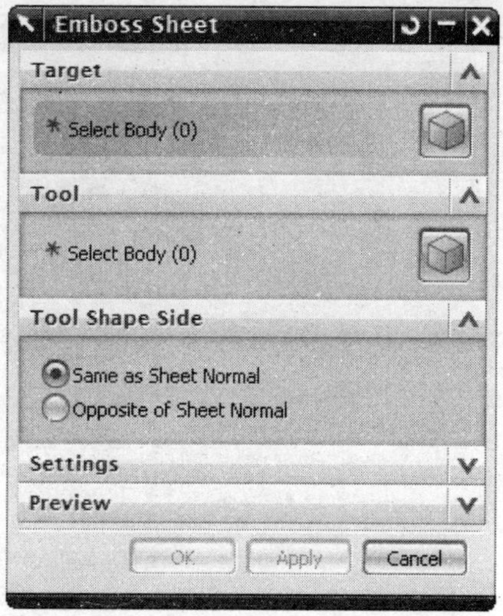

*Figure 12-22 The **Emboss Sheet** dialog box*

By default, the **Keep Target** and **Keep Tool** check boxes are clear in the **Settings** rollout. If you select the **Keep Target** check box, the target body will not be discarded from the resultant model. If you select the **Keep Tool** check box, the tool body will not be discarded from the resultant model.

Choose the **Show Results** button from the **Preview** rollout to view the preview of the resultant model. Next, choose the **OK** button from the **Emboss Sheet** dialog box; the emboss sheet feature will be created, as shown in Figure 12-24.

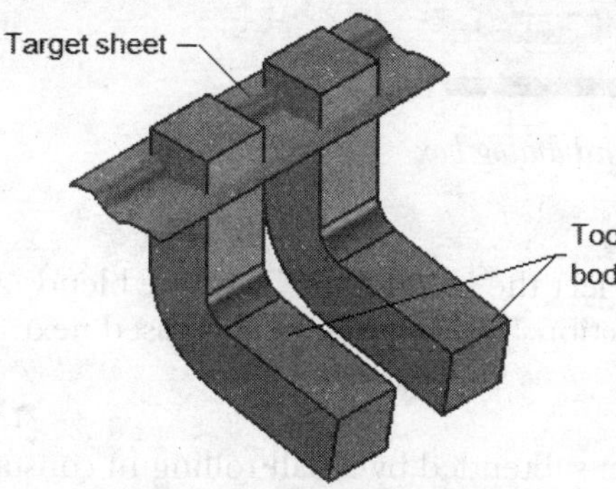

Figure 12-23 Objects to be selected

Figure 12-24 Resulting emboss sheet feature

Creating Face Blend Features

Menu:	Insert > Detail Feature > Face Blend
Toolbar:	Feature Operation > Face Blend *(Customize to add)*

This tool is used to create complicated blends tangent to a specified set of faces. A face blend can be created between the faces of the solid or sheet bodies. The wall faces of the blend can be trimmed automatically. To create the face blend feature, choose the **Face Blend** button from the **Feature Operation** toolbar; the **Face Blend** dialog box will be displayed, as shown in Figure 12-25. The options in various rollouts of this dialog box are discussed next.

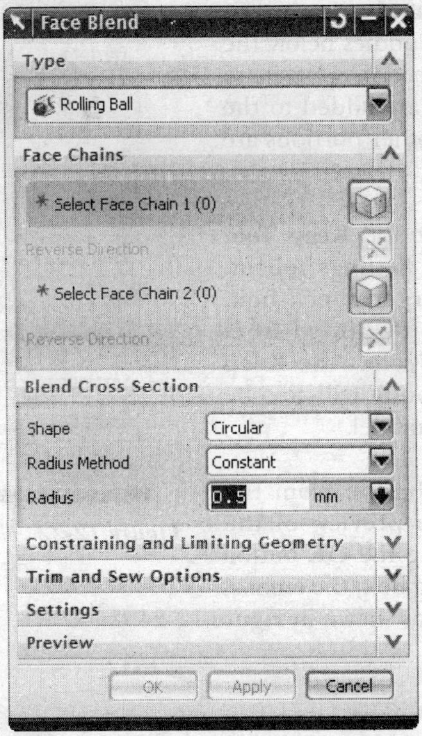

*Figure 12-25 The **Face Blend** dialog box*

Type Rollout

The drop-down list in the **Type** rollout is used to select the blend type. The face blends are classified into two types based on the blend cross-section. These types are discussed next.

Rolling Ball

This blend type creates a face blend as if it were subtended by a ball rolling in constant contact with two sets of input faces.

Swept Section

This blend type creates a face blend whose surface is controlled by a tangent curve. This tangent curve will sweep along a spine curve.

Face Chains Rollout

This rollout is used to select the first and the second set of faces for blending. There are two **Face** buttons in this rollout. The first **Face** button allows you to select the first set of faces for blending. You can also select edges, instead of faces. After selecting the faces, a vector will be displayed. This vector should point toward the center of the blend. Choose the **Reverse Direction** button to reverse the direction of the vector. The second **Face** button allows you to choose the second set of faces for blending. As mentioned earlier, after selecting the face, a vector will be displayed. This vector should point toward the center of the blend.

Blend Cross Section Rollout

This rollout allows you to specify the cross-section radius of bend using different methods, which are discussed next. On selecting the **Circular** option from the **Shape** drop-down list, the following options will be available in the **Radius Method** drop-down list to control the cross-section:

Constant

This option allows you to enter the positive values for the constant radius blends.

Law Controlled

This option allows you to define variable radii at two or more individual points along the spine curve, based on the law type selected in the **Law Type** drop-down list and the value entered in the **Value** edit box in the **Blend Cross Section** rollout.

Tangency Constraint

This option is used to set the blend radius based on the curves or edges selected for creating the face blend. On selecting this option from the **Radius Method** drop-down list, the **Select Tangent Curve** area will be displayed in the **Constraining and Limiting Geometry** rollout and you will be prompted to select the curve. Note that the curve must lie on one of the faces selected.

On selecting the **Conic** option from the **Shape** drop-down list, the following options will be available to control the cross-section:

Offset 1 Method

By default, the **Constant** option is selected in the **Offset 1 Method** drop-down list. As a result, you can define a constant offset value for the first face selected. Alternatively, you can select the **Law controlled** option from this drop-down list to define the law.

Offset 1 Distance

This edit box is used to set the distance of the conic offset from the first face.

Offset 2 Method

By default, the **Constant** option is selected in the **Offset 2 Method** drop-down list. As a result, you can define a constant offset value for the second face selected. Alternatively, you can select the **Law controlled** option from this drop-down list to define the law.

Offset 2 Distance

This edit box is used to set the distance of the conic offset from the second face.

Rho Method

The options available in this **Rho Method** drop-down list are used to specify the rho method for the conic cross-sections.

Constraining and Limiting Geometry Rollout

This rollout is used to select the coincident edges and tangency control objects for the blend.

Edge

This button allows you to apply a constant-radius blend at the coincident edges along the first and the second blend faces.

Curve

This button allows you to control the radius of the sphere, or an offset of the conic by maintaining a tangency between the blend surface and an underlying face set along a specified curve or edge.

Tangent Curves

The options available in the **Tangent Curves** drop-down list are used to specify whether the constraining curve is on the first face chain or the second face chain.

Trim and Sew Options Rollout

The options in this rollout are used to specify the trim and sew conditions for the blend. By default, the **Trim to All Input Faces** option is selected in the **Blend Faces** drop-down list.

The following steps explain the procedure to create a rolling ball face blend:

1. Choose the **Face Blend** button from the **Feature Operation** toolbar; the **Face Blend** dialog box will be displayed. By default, the **Rolling Ball** option is selected from the drop-down list in the **Type** rollout and the **Face** button is chosen from the **Face Chains** rollout. Therefore, you will be prompted to select the face for the first chain.

2. Select the first chain face, refer to Figure 12-26 and make sure that the normal vector points in the upward direction.

3. Choose the second **Face** button from the **Face Chains** rollout; you will be prompted to select the face for the second chain. Select the second chain face, refer to Figure 12-26.

4. Choose the **Edge** button from the **Constraining and Limiting Geometry** rollout; you will be prompted to select the coincident edges. Select the coincident edges, refer to Figure 12-26.

5. Enter the value of the radius in the **Radius** edit box.

6. Select the **Trim to All Input Faces** option from the **Trim and Sew Options** rollout and choose the **OK** button. The resulting face blend feature is shown in Figure 12-27.

Creating Soft Blend Features

Toolbar: Feature Operation > Soft Blend *(Customize to add)*

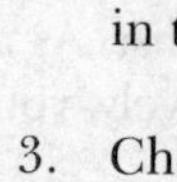

This tool is used to create the blended cross-section other than the circular blend and will give you more control over the cross-sectional shape. You will have more control on the edges of the blend. It allows you to create the designs that are more aesthetically pleasing than the other types of blends. Some of the options in the **Soft**

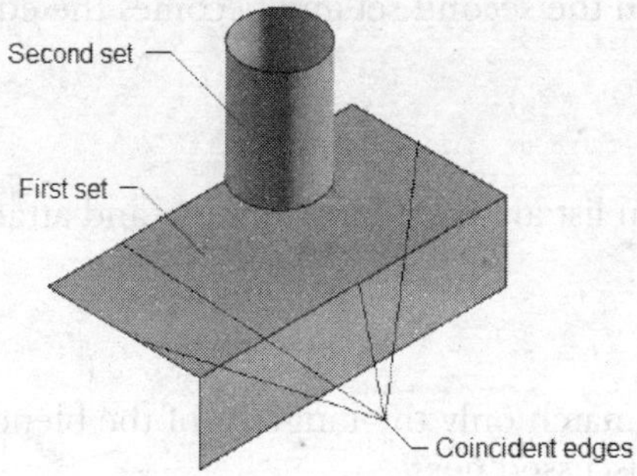

Figure 12-26 Objects to be selected

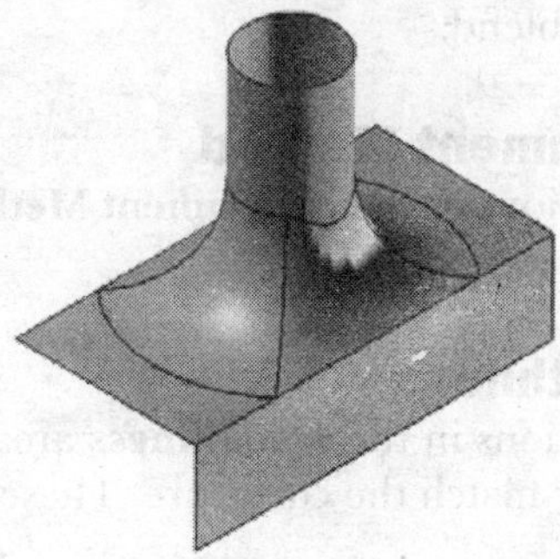

Figure 12-27 Resulting face blend feature

Blend dialog box are the same as in the **Face Blend** dialog box. To create the soft blend feature, choose the **Soft Blend** button from the **Feature Operation** toolbar; the **Soft Blend** dialog box will be displayed, as shown in Figure 12-28.

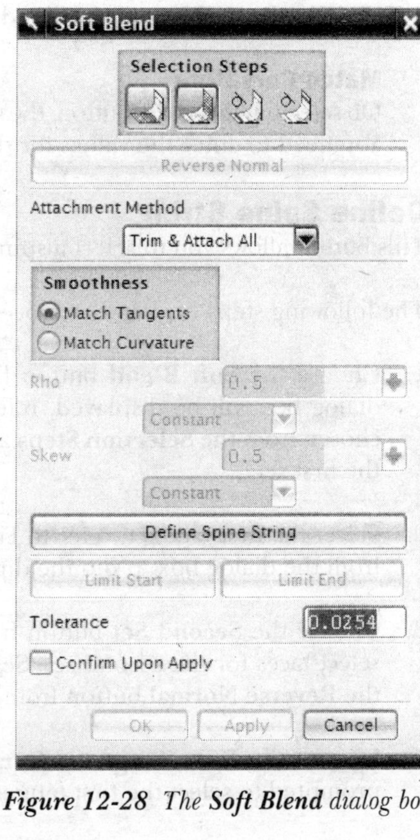

*Figure 12-28 The **Soft Blend** dialog box*

The options in the **Soft Blend** dialog box are discussed next.

Selection Steps Area

The buttons in the **Selection Steps** area are used to select the faces and tangency curves for the blend. These buttons are discussed next.

First Set

This button allows you to select the first set of faces for blending. After selecting a face, a vector will be displayed. This vector should point toward the center of the blend. Choose the **Reverse Normal** button to reverse the direction of the vector.

Second Set

This button allows you to select the second set of faces for blending. After selecting a face, a vector will be displayed. This vector should point toward the center of the blend. Choose the **Reverse Normal** button to reverse the direction of the vector.

First Tangency Curve

This button allows you to select a curve that lies on the first set and becomes the edge of the blend.

Second Tangency Curve

This button is used to select a curve that lies on the second set and becomes the edge of the blend.

Attachment Method

The options in the **Attachment Method** drop-down list are used for trimming and attaching the soft blend.

Smoothness

The options in the **Smoothness** area allow you to match only the tangents of the blend and faces, or match the curvature. These options are discussed next.

Match Tangents

On selecting this radio button, the selected faces will match with a tangency. The cross-sectional shape of the blend is an ellipse.

Match Curvature

On selecting this radio button, the selected faces will match with a tangency and a curvature. You need to enter the values for the two shape control parameters: rho and skew.

Define Spine String

This button allows you to select a spine string for the soft blend.

The following steps explain the procedure of creating a soft blend:

1. Choose the **Soft Blend** button from the **Feature Operation** toolbar; the **Soft Blend** dialog box will be displayed, refer to Figure 12-28. By default, the **First Set** button is chosen from the **Selection Steps** area. As a result, you will be prompted to select faces for the first set.

2. Select the first face set, refer to Figure 12-29. Next, choose the **Reverse Normal** button from the dialog box to flip the direction, if required.

3. Choose the **Second Set** button from the **Selection Step** area; you will be prompted to select faces for the second set. Select the second face set, refer to Figure 12-29. Choose the **Reverse Normal** button from the dialog box, if required.

4. Choose the **First Tangency Curve** button from the **Selection Step** area; you will be prompted to select the first tangency curve. Select the curve, refer to Figure 12-29.

5. Choose the **Second Tangency Curve** button from the **Selection Step** area; you will be prompted to select the second tangency curve. Select the curve, refer to Figure 12-29.

6. Choose the **Define Spline String** button; you will be prompted to select the spine string. Select the spine string, refer to Figure 12-29. Choose the **OK** button twice. The resultant soft blend feature is shown in Figure 12-30.

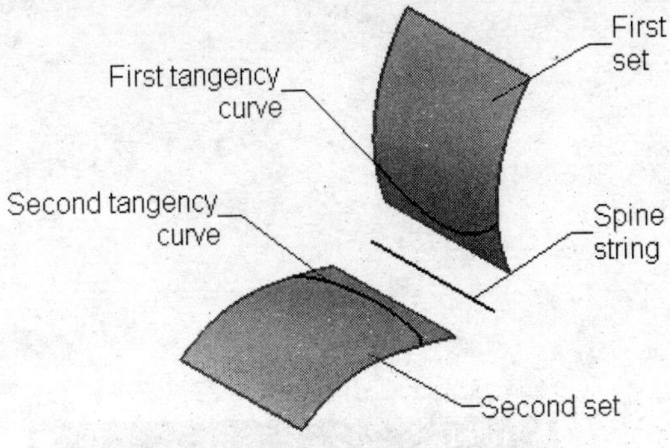

Figure 12-29 Objects to be selected

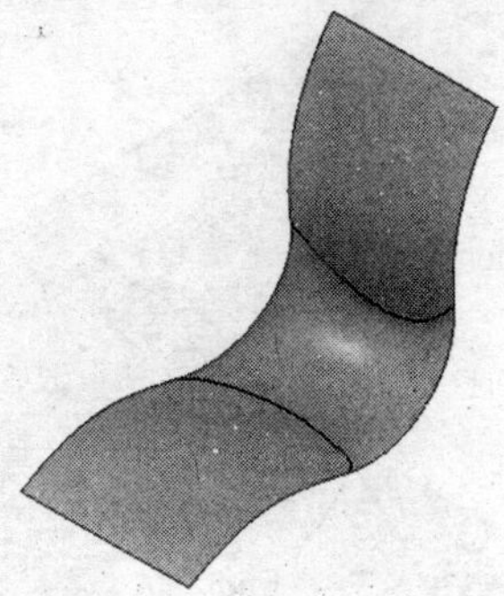

Figure 12-30 Resulting soft blend feature

Creating Fillet Features

Toolbar: Surface > Fillet Surface *(Customize to add)*

This tool is used to create fillets of a constant or variable radius between two faces of the solid or sheet bodies. The fillet created will be tangent to the two faces. The faces need to intersect or be close enough so that the fillet touches both the faces. You can create four types of fillets, constant, linear, S-shaped, and general. This feature is not parametric, which means that you cannot edit the parameters after creation of the feature. The procedure for creating the fillets is discussed next.

Creating Constant Radius Fillet

To create the constant radius fillet, you need to enter a radius, start point, and end point.

The following steps are required to create the constant fillet:

1. Choose the **Fillet Surface** button from the **Surface** toolbar; the **Fillet** dialog box will be displayed and you will be prompted to select the first face to fillet. Select the first face, refer to Figure 12-31; the selected face will be highlighted with the normal direction vector and you will be prompted to decide if the normal direction is right. This vector should point toward the center of the blend. Choose the **No** button to flip the direction, if required. You will be prompted to select the second face.

2. Select the second face, refer to Figure 12-31. Flip the direction by choosing the **No** button, if required.

3. On selecting the second face, you will be prompted to select the spine curve. This is optional for the constant fillet. You need to select the spline curve only for the general fillet type. Choose **OK**. You will be prompted to choose the creation options from the **Fillet** dialog box, as shown in Figure 12-32. These options are discussed next.

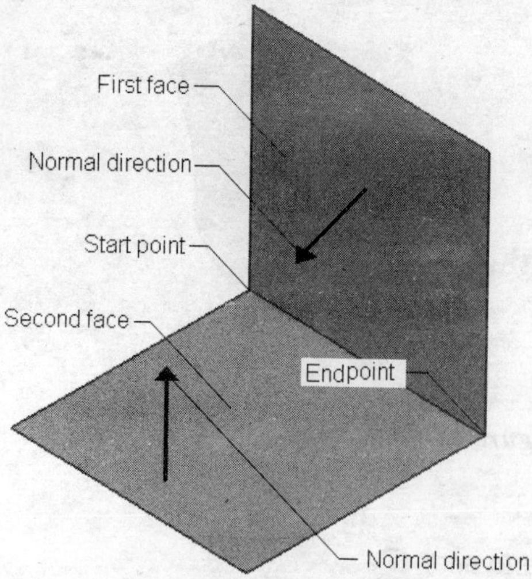

Figure 12-31 Objects to be selected

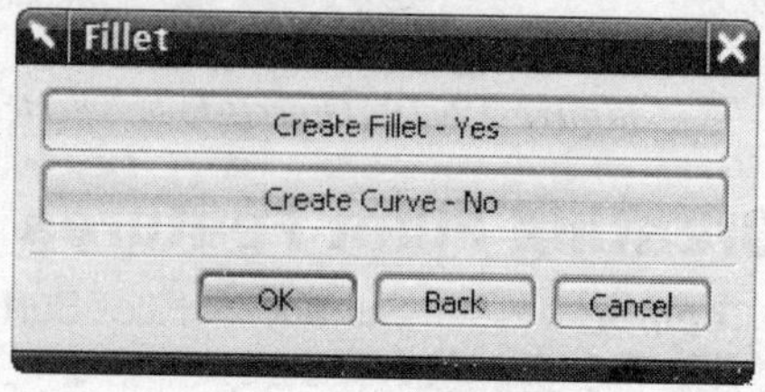

***Figure 12-32** The **Fillet** dialog box*

Create Fillet

This button enables you to specify whether or not you want to create a fillet. By default, the **Yes** option is chosen.

Create Curve

This button allows you to create the offset intersection curve between the two faces. By default, the **No** option is chosen.

4. Choose the **OK** button to accept the default options. The options in the **Fillet** dialog box will be modified, as shown in Figure 12-33, and you will be prompted to choose the cross-section type.

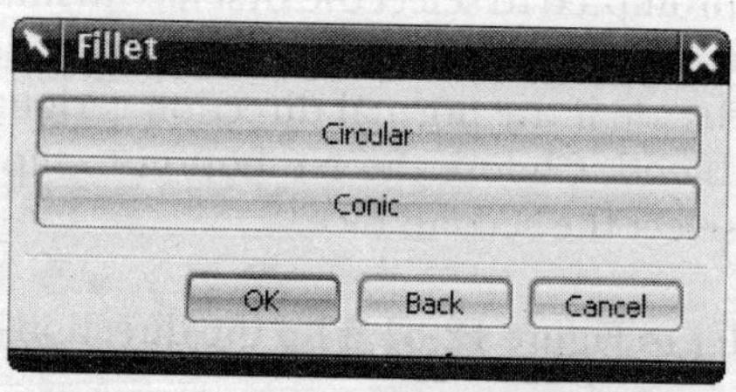

***Figure 12-33** The modified **Fillet** dialog box*

Circular

On choosing this button, the cross-section will be circular in shape and will have a specified radius value.

Conic

On choosing this button, the cross-section will be conic in shape and will have specified radius, ratio, and rho values.

5. Choose the **Circular** button from the dialog box. The options in the **Fillet** dialog box will be modified, as shown in Figure 12-34, and you will be prompted to select the fillet type.

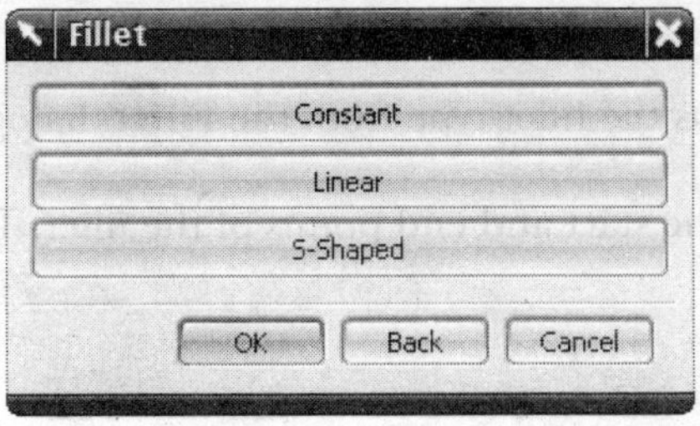

***Figure 12-34** The **Fillet** dialog box*

6. Choose the **Constant** button from the dialog box; you will be prompted to select the fillet start point in the **Fillet** dialog box, refer to Figure 12-35.

7. Choose the **Limit Point** button; the **Point** dialog box will be displayed and you will be prompted to select the inferred point.

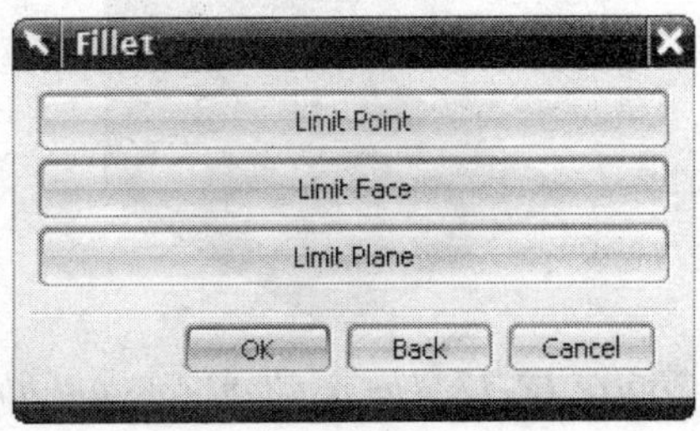

***Figure 12-35** The **Fillet** dialog box*

8. Select the endpoints of one of the faces as the start point of the fillet, refer to Figure 12-31. The options in the **Fillet** dialog box will be modified and you will be prompted to enter the radius.

9. Enter the radius value in the **Radius** edit box, refer to Figure 12-36. Next, choose the **OK** button; you will be prompted to check the direction.

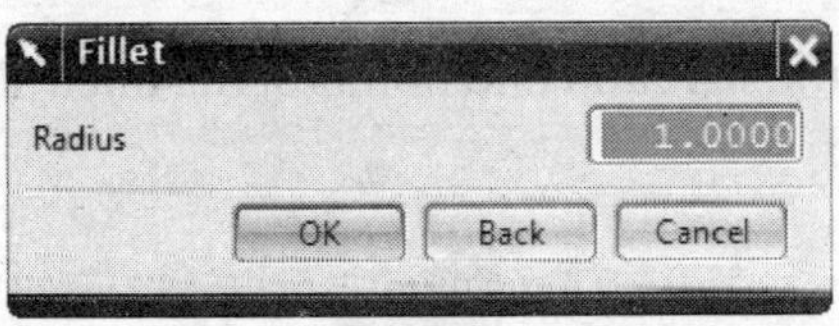

***Figure 12-36** The modified **Fillet** dialog box*

10. Choose the **Yes** button to accept the default direction or choose the **No** button to flip the direction. On doing so, you will be prompted to select the endpoint. Choose the **Limit Point** button from the **Fillet** dialog box; the **Point** dialog box will be displayed and you will be prompted to select the inferred point. Select the endpoint, refer to Figure 12-31; you will be prompted to check the direction. Choose the **Yes** button to accept the default direction or choose the **No** button to flip the direction. The resultant constant fillet is shown in Figure 12-37. Next, choose the **Cancel** button to exit from the dialog box.

Creating Linear Fillet Features

This type of fillet has two radius values. The radius will be linear throughout the fillet. The procedure to create the linear fillet is the same as the constant fillet, with a few exceptions that are discussed next.

1. Choose the **Linear** button as the fillet type from the **Fillet** dialog box.

2. Enter the radius values at the start and end points of the fillet. The resulting linear fillet is shown in Figure 12-38.

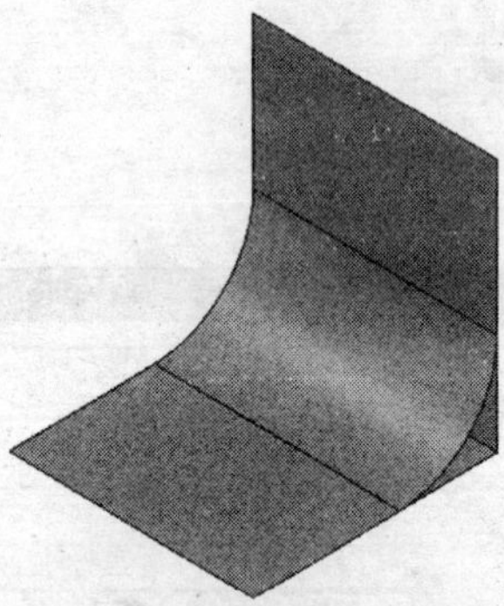

Figure 12-37 *The resultant constant fillet*

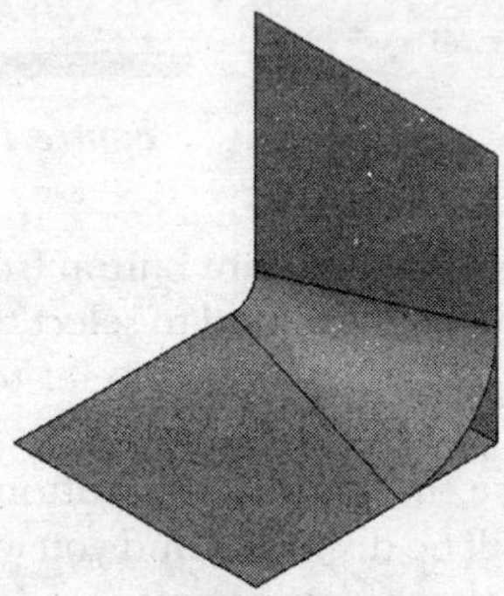

Figure 12-38 *The resultant linear fillet*

Creating S-Shaped Fillet Features

This type of fillet is used to create a variable radii fillet of an S-shaped curvature. In this type of fillet, the radius will vary throughout the fillet. The procedure to create the S-shaped fillet is the same as the constant fillet, with a few exceptions that are discussed next.

1. Choose the **S-Shaped** button as a fillet type from the **Fillet** dialog box.

2. Enter the radius values at the start and end points of the fillet. The resultant S-shaped fillet is shown in Figure 12-39.

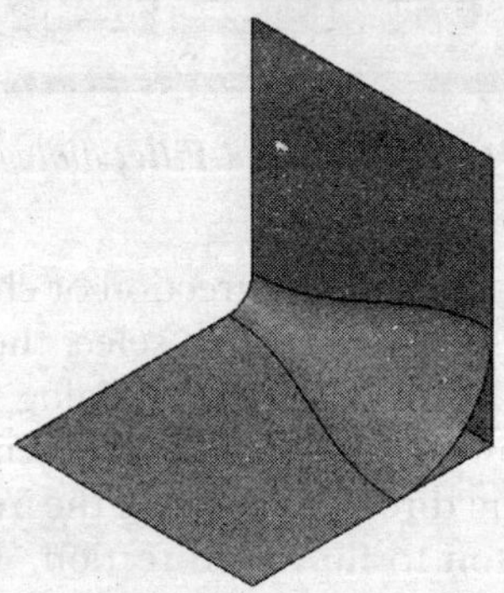

Figure 12-39 *Resultant S-shaped fillet*

Creating General Fillet Features

This type of fillet is used to create a variable radius fillet by specifying the multiple points on the spline curve. The procedure to create the general fillet is the same as the constant fillet, with a few exceptions that are discussed next.

1. Select the spline curve when you are prompted to do so, refer to Figure 12-40. Note that you need to create a curve at the intersection edge of the two surfaces.

2. Choose the **General** button as a fillet type from the **Fillet** dialog box. With the help of the **Point** dialog box, you need to select multiple points on the spline curve, refer to Figure 12-40, and enter the radius values at these points. The resulting general fillet is shown in Figure 12-41.

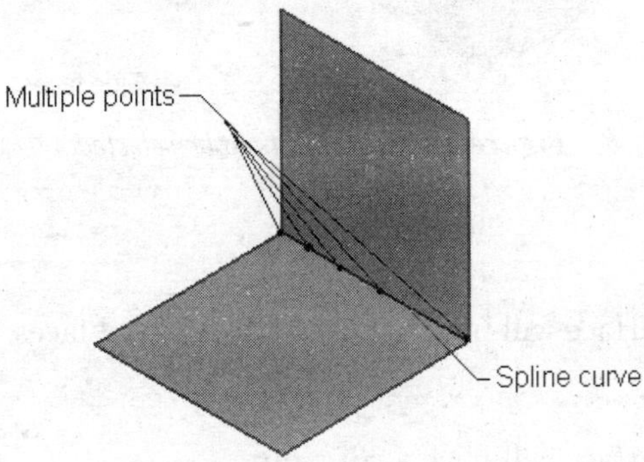

***Figure 12-40** Objects to be selected*

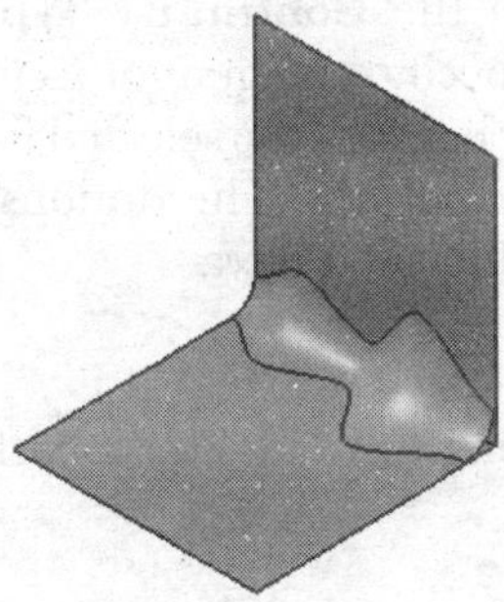

***Figure 12-41** Resulting general fillet*

Creating Bridge Features

Toolbar:	Surface > Bridge *(Customize to add)*

This tool is used to create the bridge surface that joins the edges of the surfaces. You can specify a tangent or a curvature continuity between the bridge surface and the defining faces. You can control the bridge surface by side faces, side strings, or by dragging. These methods are discussed next.

Creating Bridge Features by Specifying Side Faces

The following steps are required to create the bridge feature by side faces:

1. Choose the **Bridge** button from the **Surface** toolbar; the **Bridge** dialog box will be displayed, as shown in Figure 12-42.

2. By default, the **Primary faces** button is chosen from the **Selection Steps** area and you will be prompted to select the primary faces. Select the primary faces, refer to Figure 12-43.

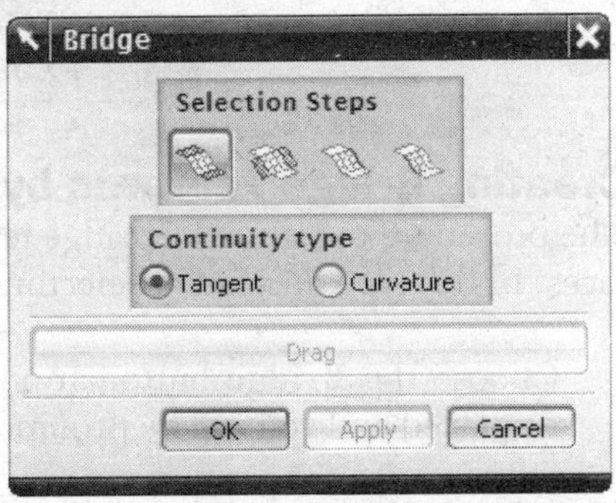

***Figure 12-42** The **Bridge** dialog box*

Note that you need to select the faces by specifying a point close to the edge, along which you want to create the bridge surface. Also, the arrowheads of the selected edges must be in the same direction.

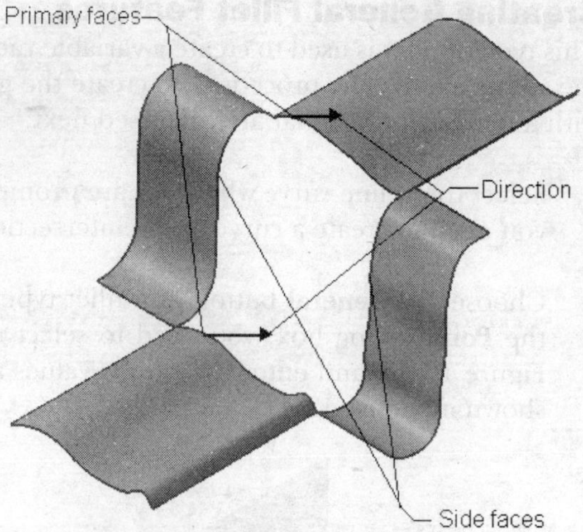

Figure 12-43 Objects to be selected

3. Choose the **Side faces** button from the **Selection Steps** area; you will be prompted to select the side faces. Select the side faces, refer to Figure 12-43.

4. Next, you need to choose the continuity type from the **Continuity Type** area. You can specify a tangent or a curvature continuity between the selected faces and the bridge surface. The options in this area are discussed next.

Tangent

On selecting this radio button, the bridge surface will be tangent to the selected faces.

Curvature

On selecting this radio button, the bridge surface will have a curvature.

5. Select the **Tangent** radio button and then the **Apply** button. The resulting bridge surface is shown in Figure 12-44.

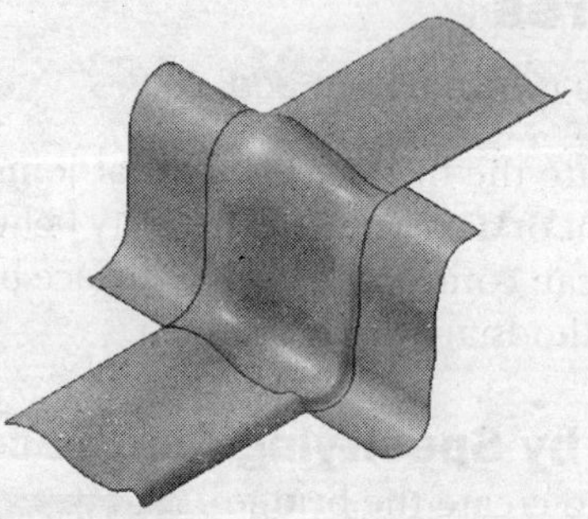

Figure 12-44 Resulting bridge surface

Creating Bridge Features by Specifying Side Strings

The procedure to create the bridge feature by side strings is the same as for creating the side faces. In this type, instead of selecting the side faces, you have to select the side strings.

1. Choose the **Bridge** button from the **Surface** toolbar; the **Bridge** dialog box will be displayed and you will be prompted to select the primary faces. Select the primary faces,

refer to Figure 12-45. You need to select each face close to the edge along which you want to create the bridge surface. Also, the arrowheads of the selected edges must be in the same direction.

2. Choose the **First side string** button from the **Selection Steps** area; you will be prompted to select the first side string. Select the curve, refer to Figure 12-45.

3. Choose the **Second side string** button from the **Selection Steps** area; you will be prompted to select the second side string. Select the curve, refer to Figure 12-45.

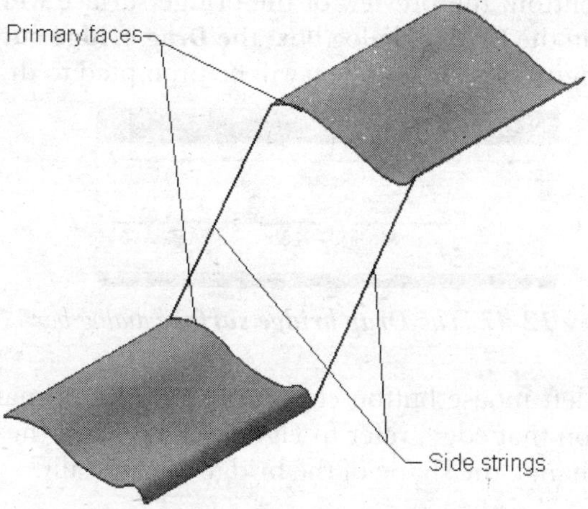

***Figure 12-45** Objects to be selected*

4. Next, you need to select the continuity type from the **Continuity Type** area. Select the **Tangent** radio button. Choose the **OK** button. The resultant bridge surface is shown in Figure 12-46.

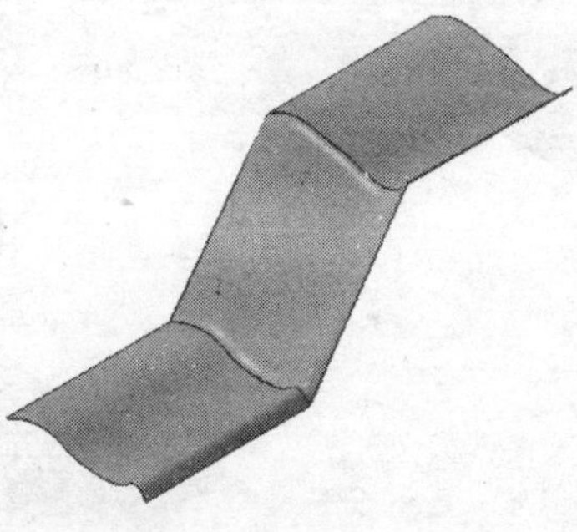

***Figure 12-46** Resultant bridge surface*

Creating Bridge Features by Dragging

The following steps are required to create the bridge feature by dragging:

1. Choose the **Bridge** button from the **Surface** toolbar; the **Bridge** dialog box will be

displayed. By default, the **Primary faces** button is chosen from the **Selection Steps** area and you will be prompted to select the primary faces. Select the primary faces, refer to Figure 12-43.

As mentioned earlier, you need to select each face close to the edge along which you want to create the bridge surface. Also, the arrowheads of the selected edges must be in the same direction.

2. Select the **Tangent** radio button, if it is not already selected.

3. Choose the **Apply** button; the preview of the bridge surface will be displayed. Choose the **Drag** button from the **Bridge** dialog box; the **Drag bridge surface** dialog box will be displayed, refer to Figure 12-47. Also, you will be prompted to drag the bridge surface.

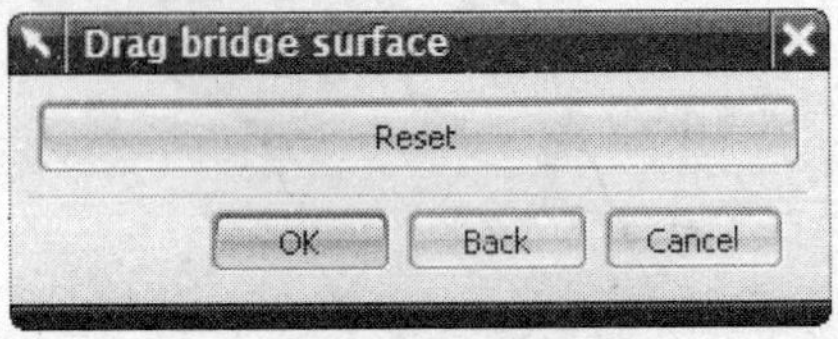

*Figure 12-47 The **Drag bridge surface** dialog box*

4. Press and hold the left mouse button close to one of the primary surfaces; a series of vectors will appear on that edge, refer to Figure 12-48. Hold the left mouse button and drag the cursor to change the shape of the bridge dynamically.

5. Similarly, press and hold the left mouse button close to the other edge of the bridge and modify it. After making the required modifications, choose the **OK** button. The **Reset** button from the **Drag bridge feature** dialog box is used to retain the bridge surface prior to the dragging. Next, choose the **OK** button from the **Bridge** dialog box. The bridge surface created by dragging is shown in Figure 12-49.

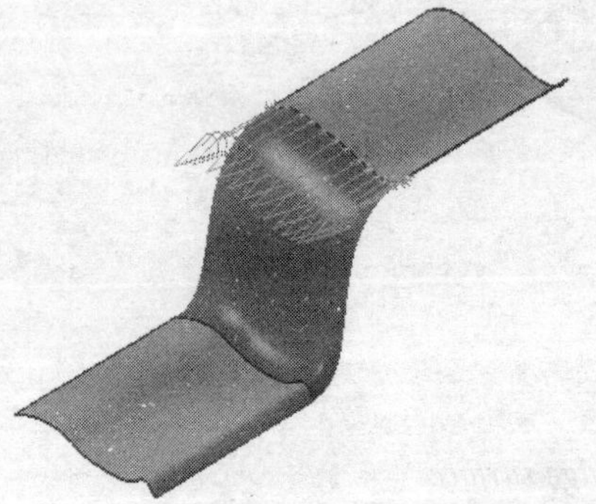

Figure 12-48 *Series of vectors on the edge*

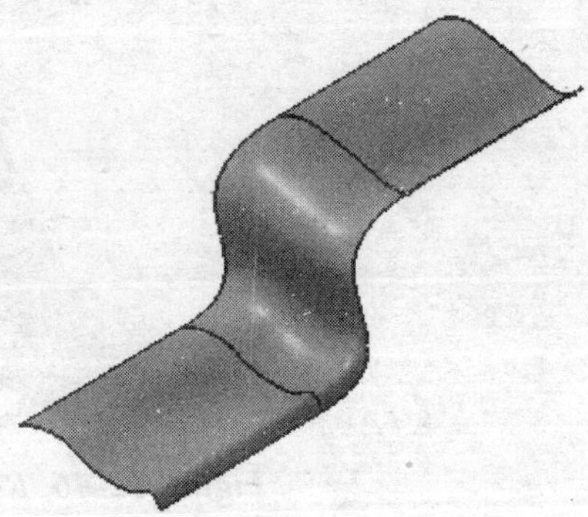

Figure 12-49 *Resulting bridge surface*

TUTORIALS

Tutorial 1

In this tutorial, you will create the model shown in Figure 12-50. First, you need to create the surface model using the dimensions and orthographic views shown in Figure 12-51. After creating the surface model, you need to apply thickness of 1 mm in the outward direction. Assume the missing dimensions. Save the model with the name *c12tut1.prt* at the location *\NX 7\c12*. **(Expected time: 45 min)**

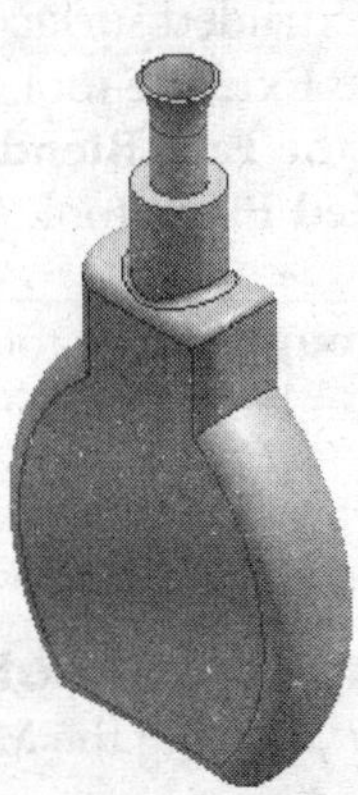

Figure 12-50 Model for Tutorial 1

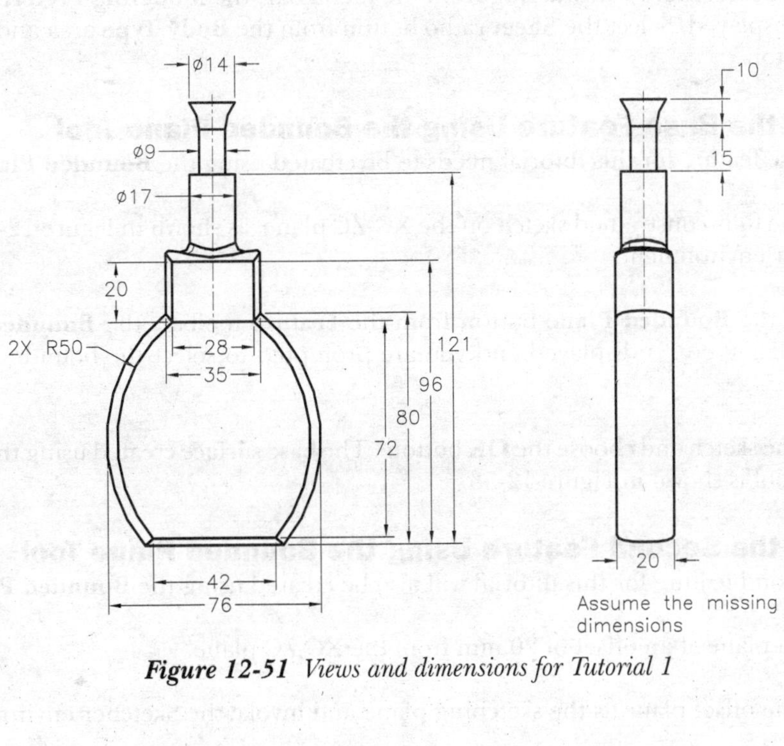

Figure 12-51 Views and dimensions for Tutorial 1

The following steps are required to complete this tutorial:

a. Start a new file and set the sheet environment.
b. Create the base feature using the **Bounded Plane** tool.
c. Create the second feature using the **Bounded Plane** tool.
d. Create the third feature using the **Bridge** tool that will join the two bounded surfaces.
e. Mirror the bridge surface about the YC-ZC plane.
f. Create the bottom surface of the model using the **Bridge** tool.
g. Extrude edges of the model.
h. Create the bridge surface over the extruded surface using the **Bridge** tool.
i. Create the extrude feature using the **Extrude** tool.
j. Create the face blend feature using the **Face Blend** tool.
k. Create the surface using the **Bounded Plane** tool.
l. Extrude the sketch.
m. Create the surface by using the **Through Curve** tool.
n. Sew the individual surfaces into a single surface.
o. Add thickness to the surface model.
p. Save and close the file.

Starting a New File and Setting the Sheet Environment

1. Start a new file with the name *c12tut1.prt* using the **Model** template and specify its location as *C:\NX 7\c12*.

2. Choose **Preferences > Modeling** from the menu bar; the **Modeling Preferences** dialog box is displayed. Select the **Sheet** radio button from the **Body Type** area and choose the **OK** button.

Creating the Base Feature Using the Bounded Plane Tool

The base feature for this tutorial needs to be created using the **Bounded Plane** tool.

1. Draw the fully constrained sketch on the XC-ZC plane, as shown in Figure 12-52. Exit the Sketcher environment.

2. Choose the **Bounded Plane** button from the **Feature** toolbar; the **Bounded Plane** dialog box is displayed and you are prompted to select the bounding string.

3. Select the sketch and choose the **OK** button. The base surface created using the **Bounded Plane** tool is shown in Figure 12-53.

Creating the Second Feature Using the Bounded Plane Tool

The second feature for this tutorial will also be created using the **Bounded Plane** tool.

1. Create a plane at an offset of 20 mm from the XC-ZC plane.

2. Select the offset plane as the sketching plane and invoke the Sketcher environment.

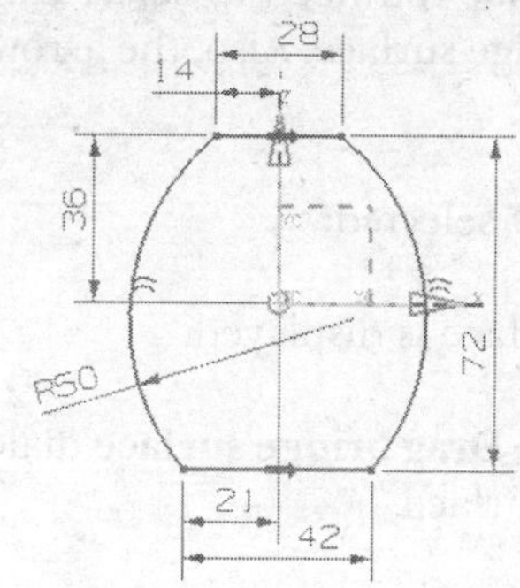

Figure 12-52 Sketch for the base feature

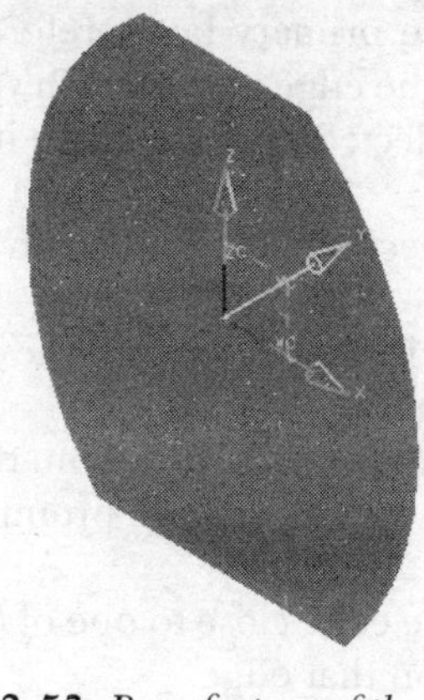

Figure 12-53 Base feature of the surface model

3. Choose the **Insert > Recipe Curve > Project Curve** from the menu bar; the **Project Curve** dialog box is displayed and you are prompted to select the curve to project. Select the base feature and choose the **OK** button.

4. Exit the Sketcher environment; the curves are projected, refer to Figure 12-54.

5. Choose the **Bounded Plane** button from the **Feature** toolbar; the **Bounded Plane** dialog box is displayed and you are prompted to select the bounding string.

6. Select the projected curves, as shown in Figure 12-54, and choose the **OK** button. The second feature is created, as shown in Figure 12-55.

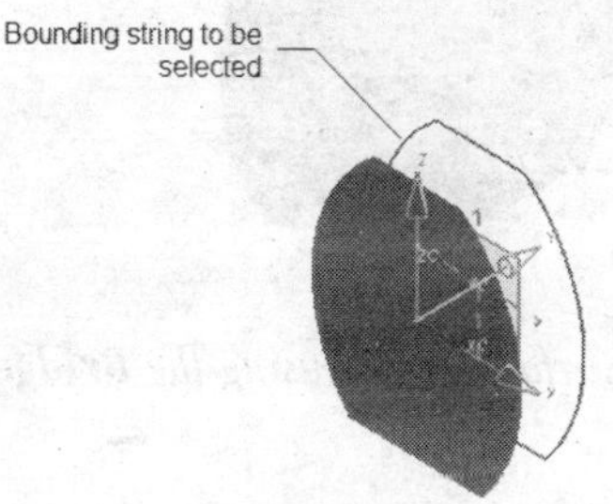

Figure 12-54 Projected curves

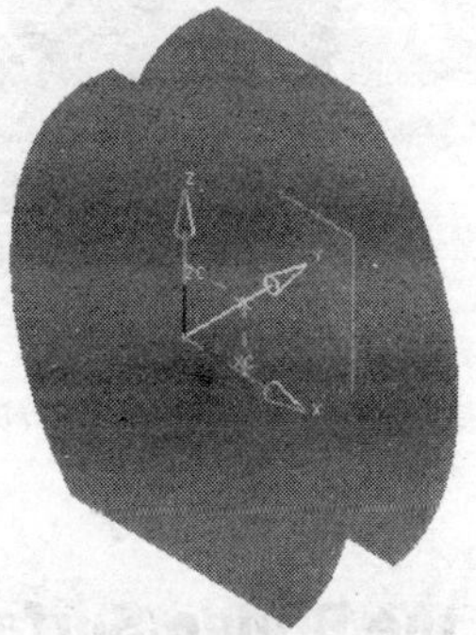

Figure 12-55 Second feature of the surface model

Creating the Bridge Surface Using the Bridge Tool

The third feature for this tutorial is a bridge surface.

1. Choose the **Bridge** button from the **Surface** toolbar; the **Bridge** dialog box is displayed. By default, the **Primary faces** button is chosen from the **Selection Steps** area and you are prompted to select the primary faces.

2. Select the primary faces, refer to Figure 12-56. Note that you need to select each face close to the edge along which you want to create the bridge surface. Also, the arrowheads of the selected edges must be in the same direction.

3. Next, select the **Tangent** radio button, if it is not already selected.

4. Choose the **Apply** button; the preview of the bridge surface is displayed.

5. Choose the **Drag** button from the **Bridge** dialog box; the **Drag bridge surface** dialog box is displayed and you are prompted to drag the bridge surface.

6. Select the edge close to one of the primary faces, refer to Figure 12-56; a series of vectors appear on that edge.

7. Hold the left mouse button and drag the cursor to change the shape of the bridge dynamically.

8. Similarly, modify the bridge at the other surface. Next, choose the **OK** button from the **Drag bridge surface** dialog box; the **Bridge** dialog box is displayed. Choose the **Cancel** button from the dialog box. The surface created using the **Bridge** tool is shown in Figure 12-57.

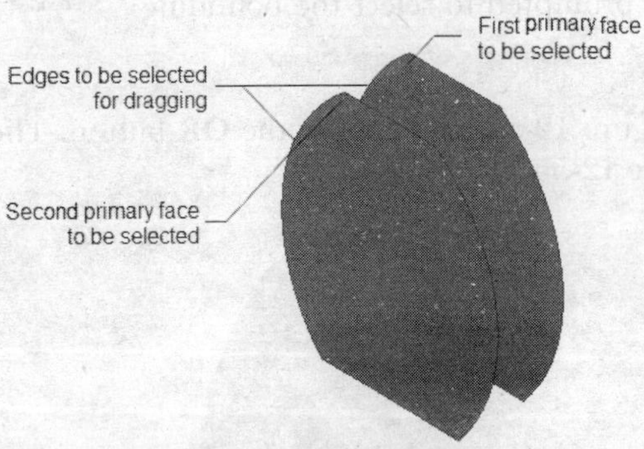

***Figure 12-56** Objects to be selected*

***Figure 12-57** Surface created using the **Bridge** tool*

Mirroring the Bridge Surface

1. After creating the bridge surface, mirror it about the YC-ZC plane. Turn off the display of the plane. The model after creating the mirror feature is shown in Figure 12-58.

Creating the Bottom Face of the Model Using the Bridge Tool

The fifth feature for this tutorial is the bottom surface of the model.

1. Choose the **Bridge** button from the **Surface** toolbar; the **Bridge** dialog box is displayed. Select the primary faces, refer to Figure 12-59.

Figure 12-58 The model after mirroring the bridge surface

2. Choose the **First side string** button; you are prompted to select the first side string. Select the edge of the model as the first side string, refer to Figure 12-59.

3. Similarly, choose the **Second side string** button and select the second edge of the model as the second side string, refer to Figure 12-59.

4. Choose the **OK** button; the surface created using the **Bridge** tool is shown in Figure 12-60.

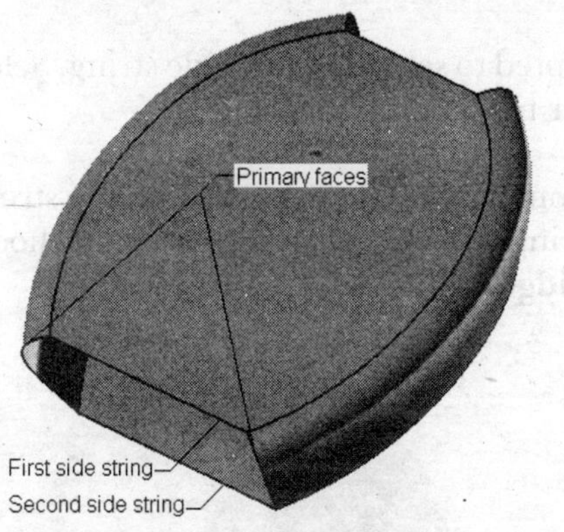

Figure 12-59 Objects to be selected

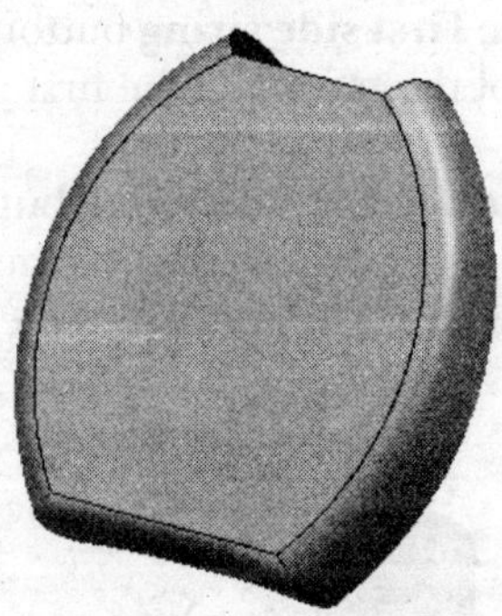

Figure 12-60 Resulting bridge surface

Creating the Sixth Feature by Extruding the Edges

The sixth feature needs to be created by extruding the edges of the model.

1. Choose the **Extrude** button from the **Feature** toolbar and select the edges of the model, refer to Figure 12-61.

2. Enter the value **20** in the **Distance** edit box available below the **End** drop-down list and choose the **OK** button. The resulting surface model is shown in Figure 12-62.

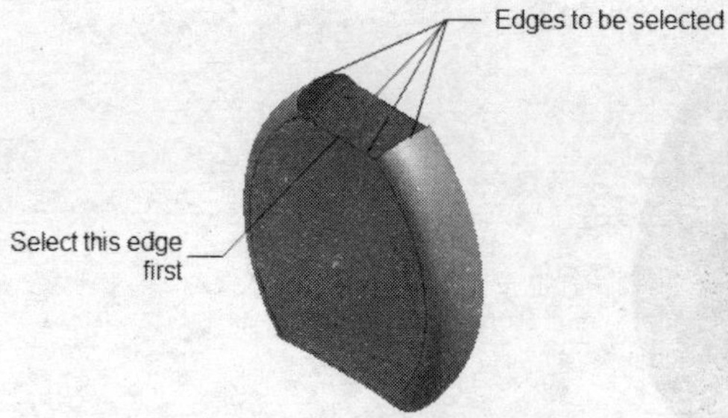

Figure 12-61 Edges to be selected

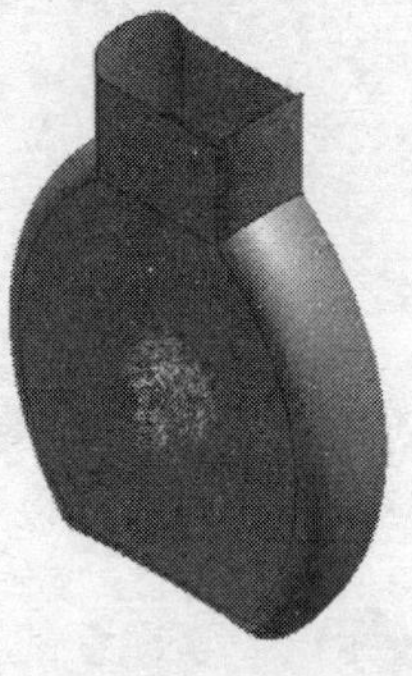

Figure 12-62 The surface model after creating the extrude feature

Creating the Surface Using the Bridge Tool

The seventh feature for this tutorial also needs to be created using the bridge surface.

1. Choose the **Bridge** button from the **Surface** toolbar; the **Bridge** dialog box is displayed. By default, the **Primary faces** button is chosen in the **Selection Steps** area and you are prompted to select the primary faces.

2. Select the primary faces, refer to Figure 12-63.

3. Choose the **First side string** button; you are prompted to select the first side string. Select the edge of the model as the first side string, refer to Figure 12-63.

4. Choose the **Second side string** button; you are prompted to select the second side string. Select the edge of the model, as the second side string, refer to Figure 12-63. Next, choose the **OK** button. The surface created using the **Bridge** tool is shown in Figure 12-64.

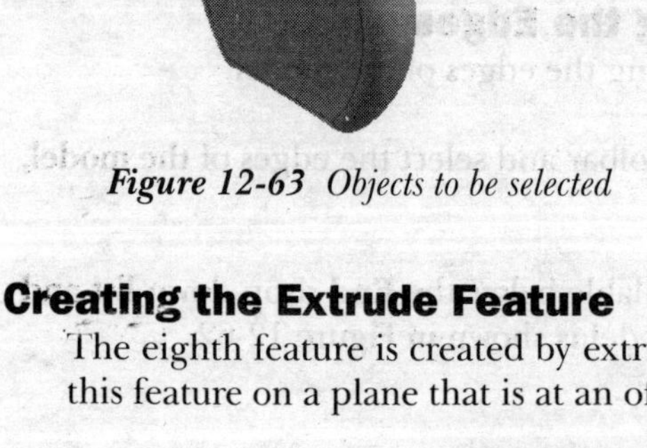

Figure 12-63 Objects to be selected

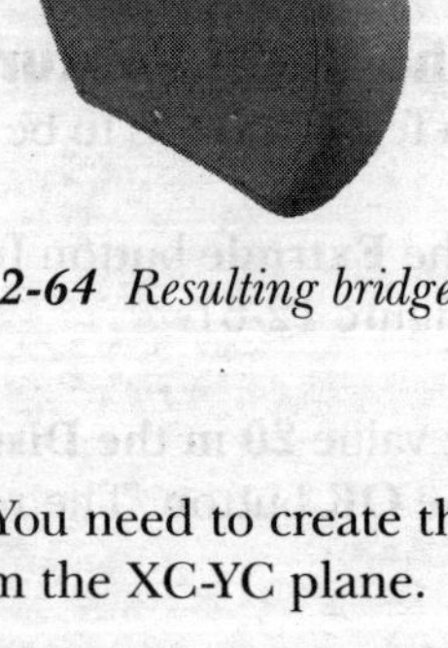

Figure 12-64 Resulting bridge surface

Creating the Extrude Feature

The eighth feature is created by extruding the sketch. You need to create the sketch for this feature on a plane that is at an offset of 81 mm from the XC-YC plane.

1. Create the datum plane at an offset of 81 mm from the XC-YC plane and create the sketch for the eighth feature by selecting the offset plane as the sketching plane, as shown in Figure 12-65.

2. Extrude this sketch through a distance of 25 mm in the downward direction. The resulting surface model is shown in Figure 12-66.

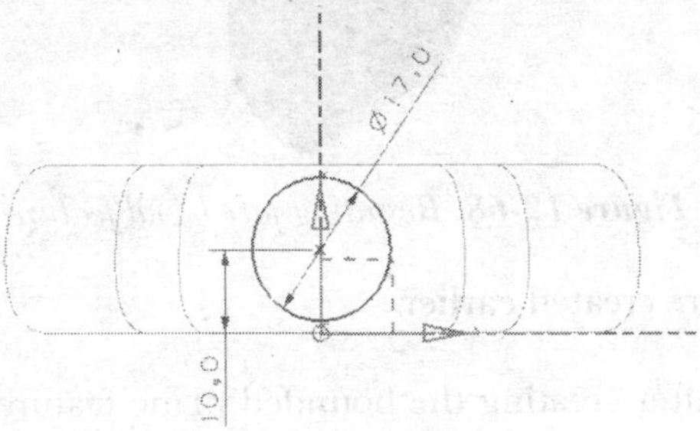

Figure 12-65 *Sketch drawn for the extrude feature*

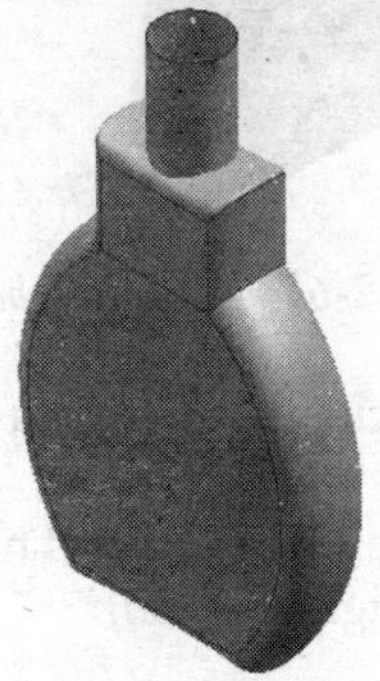

Figure 12-66 *Resulting extruded surface*

Creating the Face Blend Feature

Next, you need to create a face blend feature to blend the extruded surface created in the previous section with the bridge surface. The blending will also ensure that the portion of the extruded surface that extends below the bridge surface is removed.

1. Choose the **Face Blend** button from the **Feature Operation** toolbar; the **Face Blend** dialog box is displayed.

2. By default, the **Rolling Ball** option is selected from drop-down list in the **Type** rollout and the **Face** button is chosen from the **Free Chains** rollout. As a result, you are prompted to select the faces for the first chain. Select the face, refer to Figure 12-67. An arrow is displayed on selecting the face. Make sure the arrow points outward. If not, choose the **Reverse Direction** button to flip the direction.

3. Choose the second **Face** button from the **Free Chains** rollout and select the second face, refer to Figure 12-67. An arrow is displayed on selecting the face. If this arrow does not point upward, reverse the direction.

4. Enter the value **3** in the **Radius** edit box and choose the **OK** button. The resulting face blend feature is shown in Figure 12-68.

Creating the Tenth Feature Using the Bounded Plane Tool

The tenth feature will be created using the **Bounded Plane** tool.

1. Choose the **Bounded Plane** button from the **Feature** toolbar; the **Bounded Plane** dialog box is displayed and you are prompted to select the bounding string.

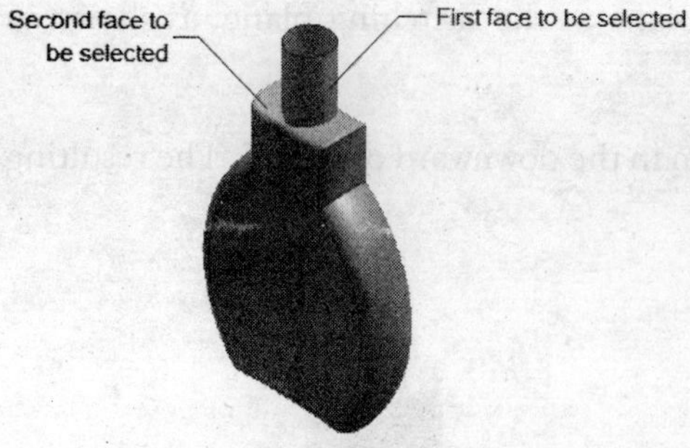

Figure 12-67 Entities to be selected

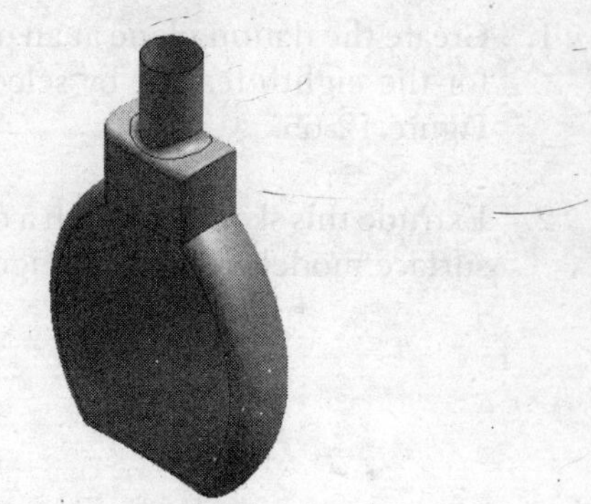

Figure 12-68 Resulting face blend feature

2. Select the circular edge of the extruded feature created earlier.

3. Choose the **OK** button. The surface model after creating the bounded plane feature is shown in Figure 12-69.

Figure 12-69 The model after creating the bounded plane feature

Creating the Extrude Feature

The eleventh feature will be created by extruding the sketch. You need to create the sketch for this feature on the bounded surface created earlier.

1. Create the sketch for the eleventh feature by selecting the bounded surface created earlier as the sketching plane, refer to Figure 12-70.

2. Choose the **Extrude** button from the **Feature** toolbar; the **Extrude** dialog box is displayed and you are prompted to select the section geometry to be extruded.

3. Select the sketch and enter the value **15** in the **Distance** edit box available below the **End** drop-down list . Next, choose the **OK** button from the **Extrude** dialog box. The resulting surface model is shown in Figure 12-71.

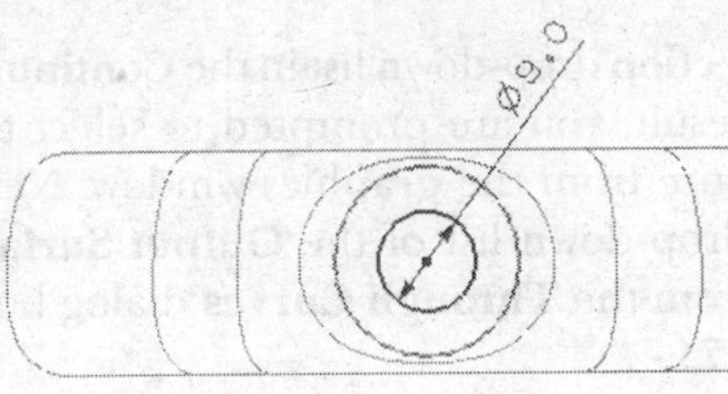

Figure 12-70 *Sketch drawn for the eleventh feature*

Figure 12-71 *The surface model after creating the extrude feature*

Trimming the Sheet

Next, you need to trim the unwanted portion of the surface model using the **Trimmed Sheet** tool.

1. Choose the **Trimmed Sheet** button from the **Surface** toolbar; the **Trimmed Sheet** dialog box is displayed.

2. Select the tenth feature created using the **Boundary Plane** tool and then press the middle mouse button.

3. Select the extruded sheet feature created in the previous step and then select the **Keep** radio button from the **Region** rollout of the dialog box. Next, choose the **OK** button. The portion of the boundary plane surface that is enclosed inside the extruded surface is trimmed.

Creating the Through Curves Surface

This feature will be created using the **Through Curves** tool. You need to create the sketch for this feature on a plane at an offset of 106 from the XC-YC plane. The following steps are required to create the twelfth feature:

1. Create a datum plane at an offset of 106 mm from the XC-YC plane in the upward direction.

2. Create the sketch of the twelfth feature by selecting the offset plane as the sketching plane, refer to Figure 12-72.

3. Choose the **Through Curves** button from the **Surface** toolbar; the **Through Curves** dialog box is displayed and you are prompted to select the section.

4. Select the edge as the first section string from the previous extruded feature, refer to Figure 12-73, and press the middle mouse button; you are again prompted to select the section.

5. Select the sketch as the second section string, refer to Figure 12-73 and press the middle mouse button. Make sure the arrows in both sections point in the same direction.

6. Next, select the **G1(Tangent)** option from the **First Section** drop-down list in the **Continuity** rollout; the **Select Face** option is activated. As a result, you are prompted to select the continuity constraint face. Select the eleventh feature from the graphics window. Next, select the **Multiple** option from the **Patch Type** drop-down list of the **Output Surface Options** rollout, and then choose the **OK** button from the **Through Curves** dialog box. The resulting surface model is shown in Figure 12-74.

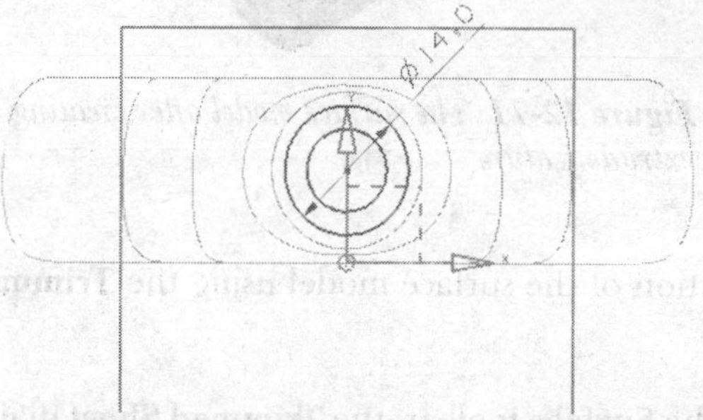

Figure 12-72 Sketch for the through curve surface

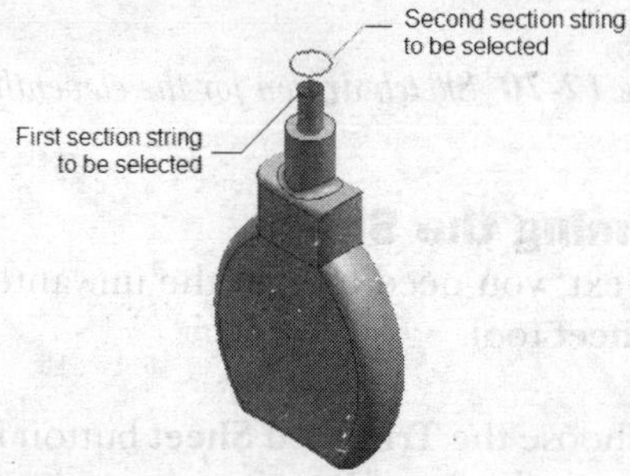

Figure 12-73 Objects to be selected

Figure 12-74 The resulting through curves surface feature

Sewing Individual Surfaces into a Single Surface

After creating the surface model, you need to sew the individual surfaces into a single surface using the **Sew** tool.

1. Invoke the **Sew** tool by choosing **Insert > Combine Bodies > Sew** from the menu bar; the **Sew** dialog box is displayed.

2. Select the **Sheet** option from drop-down list in the **Type** rollout, if it is not selected.

3. Select the base feature that is created using the **Bounded Plane** tool as the target body and then select all the remaining surfaces as the tool sheet bodies.

4. Choose the **OK** button. The resultant model after sewing individual surfaces into a single surface with a common edge is shown in Figure 12-75.

Adding Thickness to the Surface Model

Now, you need to add thickness to the surface model.

1. Choose **Insert > Offset/Scale > Thicken** from the menu bar; the **Thicken** dialog box is displayed. Also, you are prompted to select the faces to thicken.

2. Select the surface model from the graphics window. Next, enter the thickness value as **0** and **1** in the **Offset 1** and **Offset 2** edit boxes, respectively.

3. Choose the **OK** button from the dialog box. The final model after applying the thickness is shown in Figure 12-76.

Figure 12-75 *The surface model after sewing the surfaces*

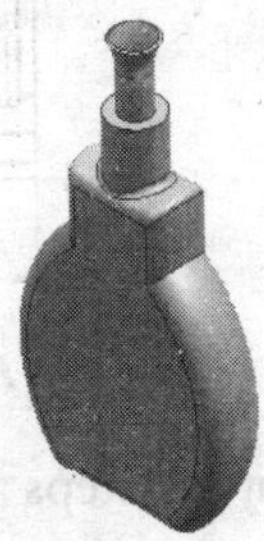

Figure 12-76 *The final model after applying the thickness*

Saving and Closing the File

1. Choose **File > Close > Save and Close** from the menu bar to save and close the file.

Tutorial 2

In this tutorial, you will create the model shown in Figure 12-77. First, you need to create the surface model using the dimensions and orthographic views shown in Figure 12-78. After creating the surface model, you need to apply thickness of 1 mm in the outward direction. Assume the missing dimensions. Save the model with the name *c12tut2.prt* at the location *\NX 7\c12*. **(Expected time: 30 min)**

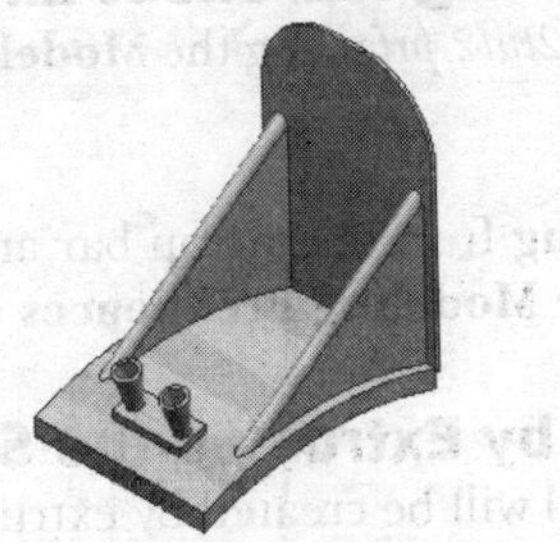

Figure 12-77 *Surface model for Tutorial 2*

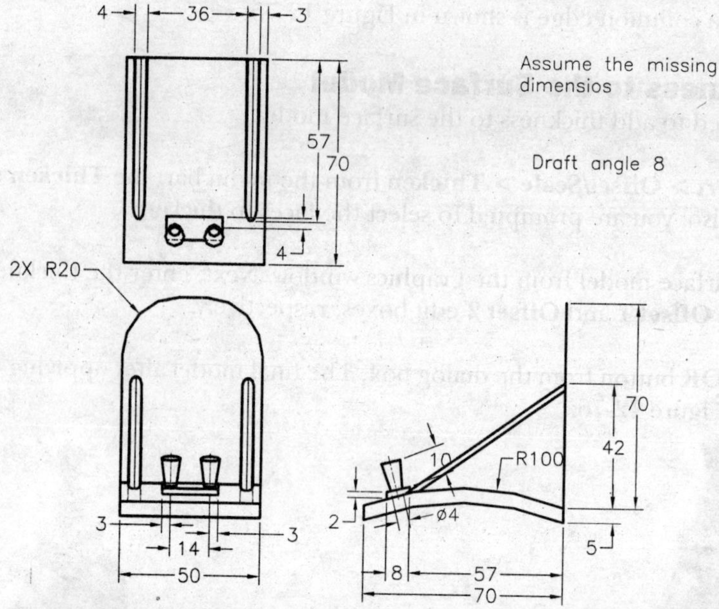

Figure 12-78 *Views and dimensions for Tutorial 2*

The following steps are required to complete this tutorial:

a. Start a new file and set the sheet environment.
b. Create the base feature by extruding the base sketch.
c. Create the second feature by extruding the edges of the base feature.
d. Create the third feature by extruding the sketch.
e. Create the fourth feature by extruding the sketch.
f. Create the fifth feature by extruding the edge from the base feature.
g. Trim the fifth feature using the **Trimmed Sheet** tool.
h. Create the dart feature.
i. Mirror the dart feature and the fourth extruded feature using the YC-ZC plane.
j. Sew the individual surfaces into a single surface.
k. Add thickness to the surface model.
l. Save and close the file.

Starting a New File and Setting the Sheet Environment

1. Start a new file with the name *c12tut2.prt* using the **Model** template and specify its location as *C:\NX 7\c12*.

2. Choose **Preferences > Modeling** from the menu bar and select the **Sheet** radio button from the **Body Type** area of the **Modeling Preferences** dialog box. Next, choose **OK**.

Creating the Base Feature by Extruding the Sketch

The base feature for this tutorial will be created by extruding the sketch.

1. Create the sketch of the base feature on the YC-ZC plane, as shown in Figure 12-79.

2. Extrude the sketch symmetrically on both sides of the sketching plane through a symmetric distance of 25 mm. The base feature of the surface model is shown in Figure 12-80.

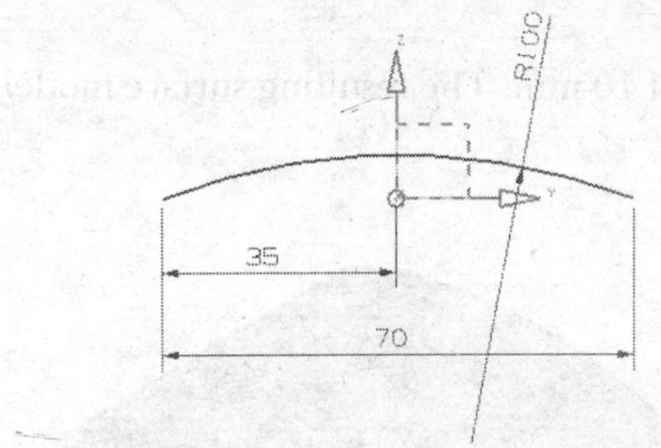

Figure 12-79 *Sketch of the base feature*

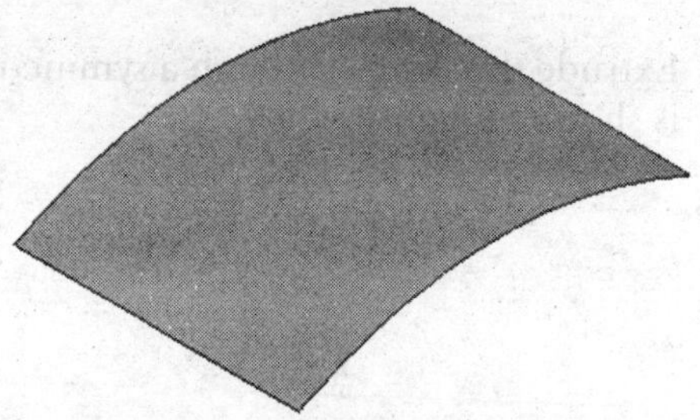

Figure 12-80 *Base feature of the surface model*

Creating the Second Feature by Extruding the Edges

The second feature will be created by extruding the edges of the base feature. The following steps are required to create the second feature:

1. Invoke the **Extrude** tool, and then select the edges of the base surface, refer to Figure 12-81.

2. Define the -ZC-axis direction as the direction of extrusion using the **Inferred Vector** drop-down list. Enter **5** in the **Distance** edit box available below the **End** drop-down list.

3. Choose the **OK** button. The resulting surface model is shown in Figure 12-82.

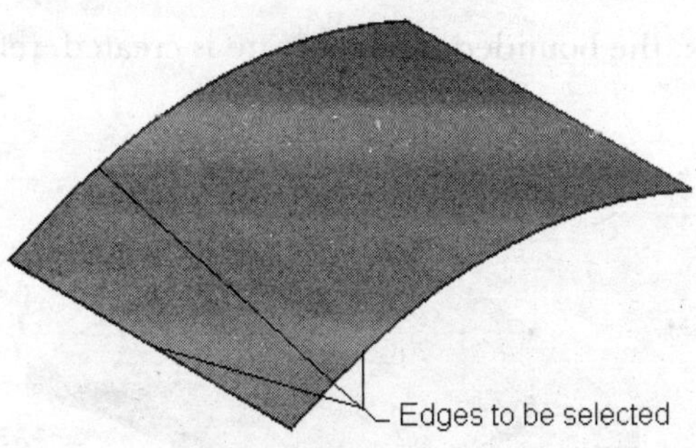

Figure 12-81 *Edges to be selected*

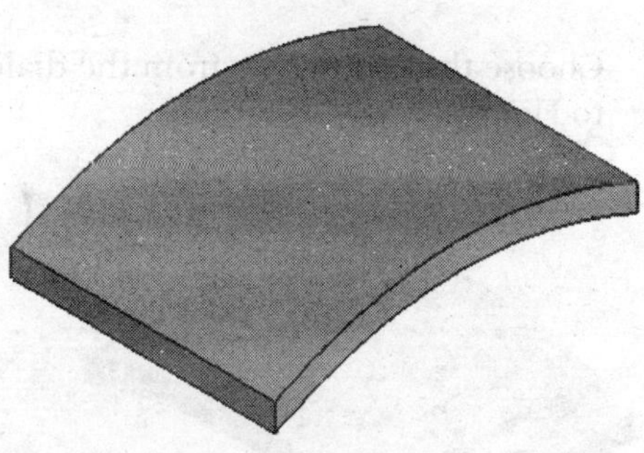

Figure 12-82 *The second feature created by the **Extrude** tool*

Creating the Third Feature by Extruding the Sketch

The third feature will be created by extruding a sketch. You need to create the sketch for the third feature on the YC-ZC plane.

1. Create the sketch for the third feature by selecting the YC-ZC plane as the sketching plane, as shown in Figure 12-83.

2. Extrude the sketch through a symmetric distance of 10 mm. The resulting surface model is shown in Figure 12-84.

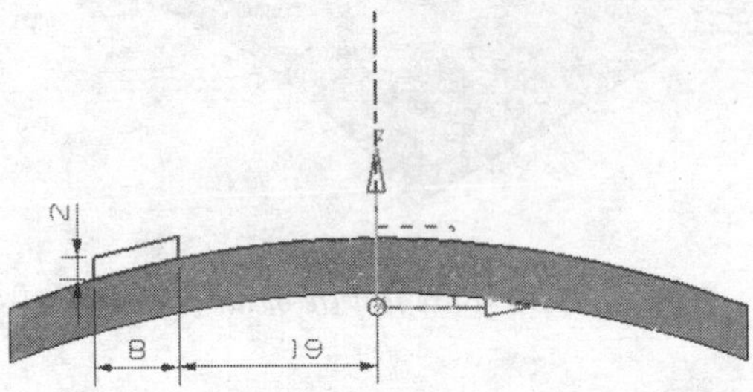

Figure 12-83 *Sketch drawn for the extrusion*

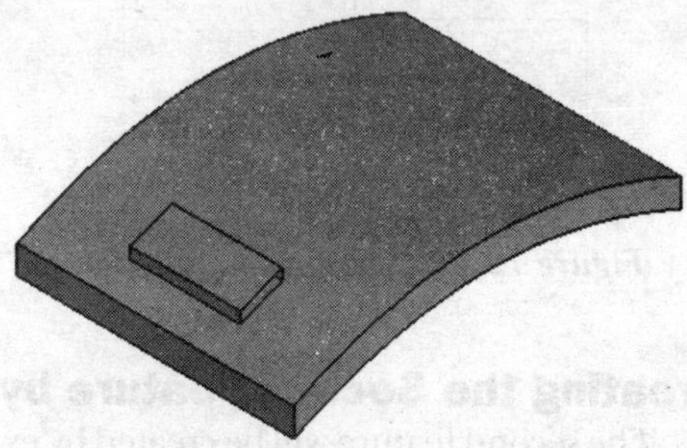

Figure 12-84 *Resulting extruded feature*

Creating the Bounded Plane Features

Now, you need to create bounded plane features by using the **Bounded Plane** tool.

1. Choose the **Bounded Plane** button from the **Feature** toolbar; the **Bounded Plane** dialog box is displayed and you are prompted to select the bounding string.

2. Select the edges of the third feature to create a bounded plane, refer to Figure 12-85.

3. Choose the **OK** button from the dialog box; the bounded plane feature is created, refer to Figure 12-86.

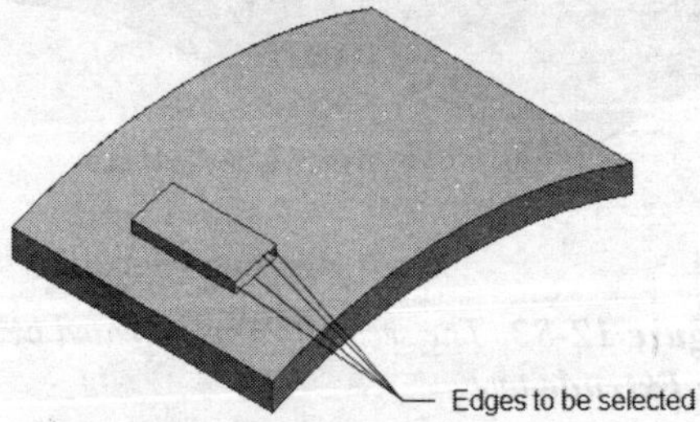

Figure 12-85 *Edges to be selected*

Figure 12-86 *Resulting bounded plane feature*

4. Similarly, create the bounded plane feature on the other side of the third extruded feature.

Trimming the Surfaces Using the Trimmed Sheet Tool

The unwanted surfaces will be trimmed using the **Trimmed Sheet** tool. The following steps are required to trim the unwanted surfaces.

1. Choose the **Trimmed Sheet** button from the **Surface** toolbar; the **Trimmed Sheet** dialog box is displayed and you are prompted to select the target sheet body.

2. Select the third surface feature created and press the middle mouse button; you are prompted to select the trimming objects.

3. Select the base surface created, and then choose the **Apply** button; the third feature is trimmed. You are again prompted to select the sheet body to trim.

4. Select the base surface created as the sheet body to be trimmed, and then press the middle mouse button. You are prompted to select the trimming objects.

5. Select the surfaces as the trimming objects, refer to Figure 12-87. Next, choose the **OK** button from the **Trimmed Sheet** dialog box. The rotated view of the resultant surface model is shown in Figure 12-88.

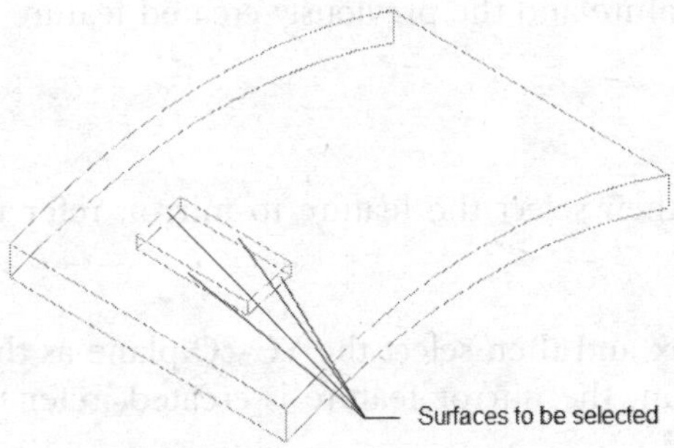

Figure 12-87 *Surfaces to be selected*

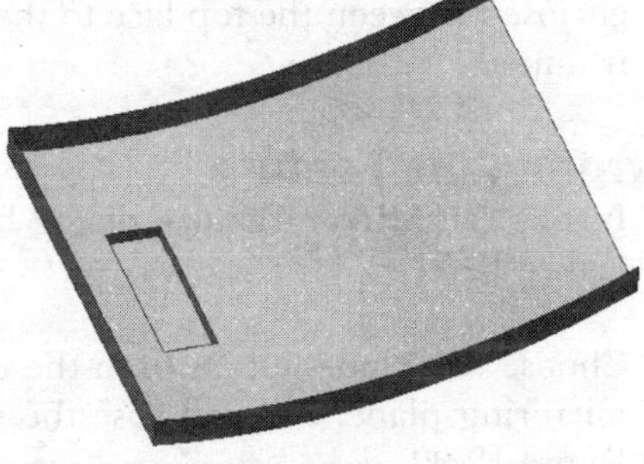

Figure 12-88 *Resultant surface model*

Creating the Next Feature by Extruding the Sketch

The next feature will be created by extruding the sketch. You need to create the sketch for this feature on the top face of the third feature.

1. Create the sketch for this feature by selecting the top face of the third feature as the sketching plane, as shown in Figure 12-89.

2. Extrude this sketch through a distance of 10 mm with -8 degrees as the draft angle by using the **From Start Limit** option. The resulting surface model is shown in Figure 12-90.

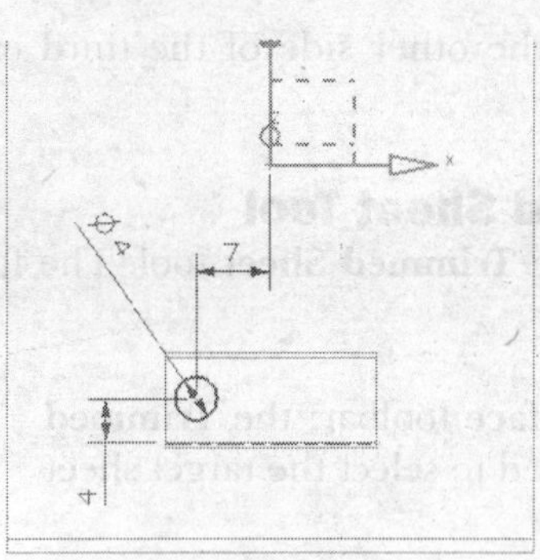

Figure 12-89 Sketch created

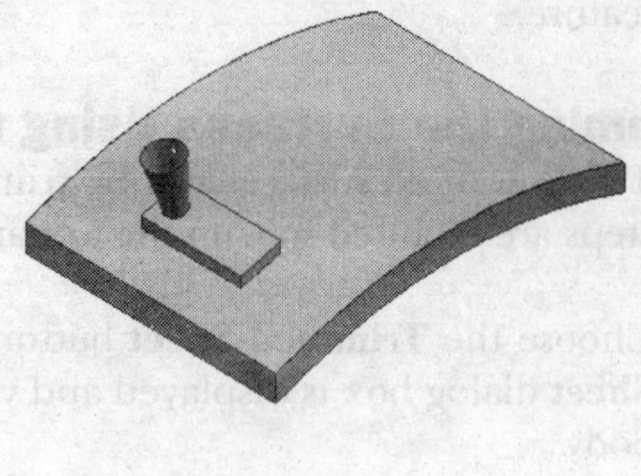

Figure 12-90 Resultant fourth feature

Trimming the Surface Using the Trimmed Sheet Tool

Now, the surface that is enclosed between the top face of the third feature and the previously created feature will be trimmed using the **Trimmed Sheet** tool.

1. Choose the **Trimmed Sheet** button from the **Surface** toolbar; the **Trimmed Sheet** dialog box is displayed and you are prompted to select the target sheet body.

2. Select the third surface feature created and press the middle mouse button; you are prompted to select the trimming objects.

3. Select the previously created extruded surface and then choose the **OK** button; the surface enclosed between the top face to the third feature and the previously created feature is trimmed.

Mirroring the Feature

1. Invoke the **Mirror Feature** dialog box and then select the feature to mirror, refer to Figure 12-91.

2. Choose the **Plane** button from the dialog box and then select the YC-ZC plane as the mirroring plane. Next, choose the **OK** button; the mirror feature is created, refer to Figure 12-92.

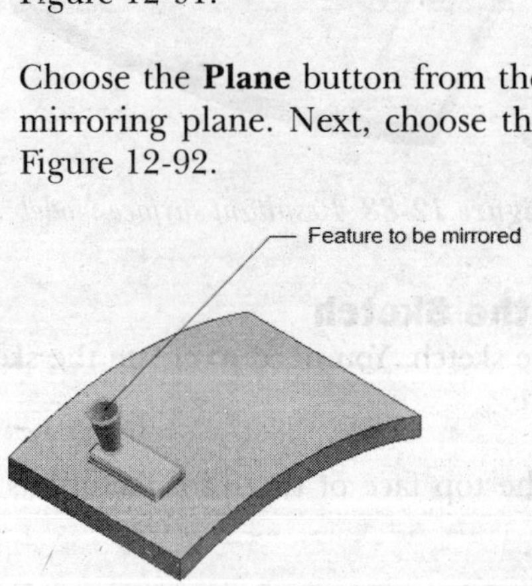

Figure 12-91 Feature to be mirrored

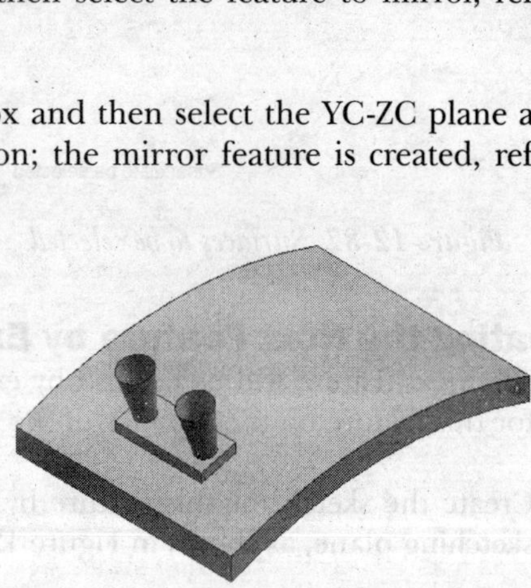

Figure 12-92 Resultant surface model with the mirrored feature

Creating the Next Feature by Extruding the Edge

The next feature will be created by extruding the edge of the base feature

1. Invoke the **Extrude** dialog box and then select the edge, refer to Figure 12-93. Next, extrude it through a distance of 70 mm in the upward direction. The resulting surface model is shown in Figure 12-94.

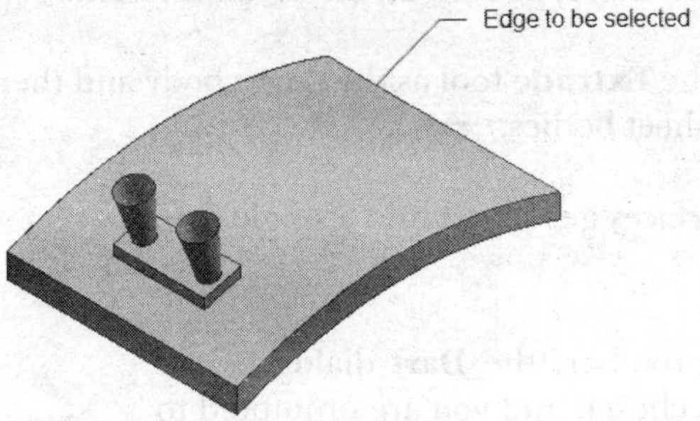

Figure 12-93 The edge to be selected

Figure 12-94 Resultant surface model

Trimming the Previously Created Extruded Surface

Now, the previously created extruded surface will be trimmed using the **Trimmed Sheet** tool.

1. Select the previously created surface as the sketching plane and draw the sketch, as shown in Figure 12-95.

2. Choose the **Trimmed Sheet** button from the **Surface** toolbar; the **Trimmed Sheet** dialog box is displayed and you are prompted to select the target sheet body.

3. Select the previously created extruded surface and press the middle mouse button; you are prompted to select the trimming objects. Select the sketch created and then choose the **OK** button. The resulting surface model is shown in Figure 12-96.

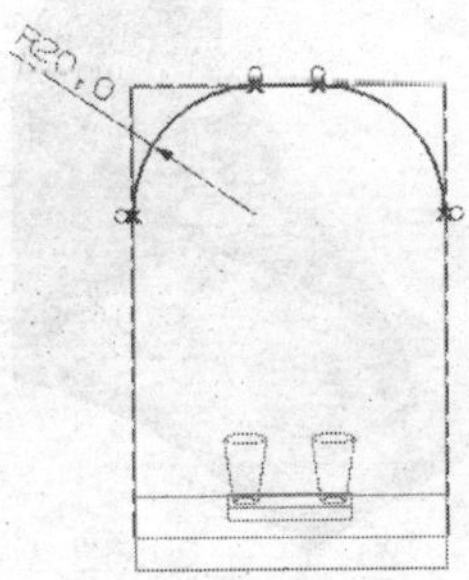

Figure 12-95 Sketch drawn for trimming

Figure 12-96 The resulting surface model after trimming the fifth feature

Sewing the Individual Surfaces into a Single Surface

Now, you need to sew the individual surfaces of the surface model into a single surface by using the **Sew** tool.

1. Invoke the **Sew** tool by choosing **Insert > Combine Bodies > Sew** from the menu bar; the **Sew** dialog box is displayed.

2. Select the **Sheet** option from drop-down list in the **Type** rollout, if it is not selected.

3. Select the base feature that is created using the **Extrude** tool as the target body and then select all the remaining surfaces as the tool sheet bodies.

4. Choose the **OK** button; all the individual surfaces get sewed into a single surface.

Creating the Dart Feature

1. Choose the **Dart** button from the **Feature** toolbar; the **Dart** dialog box is displayed. By default, the **First Set** button is chosen and you are prompted to select the faces for the first set. Select the surface, refer to Figure 12-97.

2. Choose the **Second Set** button; you are prompted to select the faces for the second set. Select the base feature surface, refer to Figure 12-97; the preview of the dart is displayed along the intersection curve of the two faces.

3. Select the **Along Curve** option from the **Method** drop-down list, if it is not selected by default. Enter **10** as the value in the **%Arclength** edit box.

4. Select the **Trim All** option from the **Trim Option** drop-down list. Next, enter the dimensional values of the dart as **1**, **35**, and **2** in the **Angle(A)**, **Depth(D)**, and **Radius(R)** edit boxes, respectively.

5. Choose the **OK** button. The dart feature created between the two selected surfaces is shown in Figure 12-98.

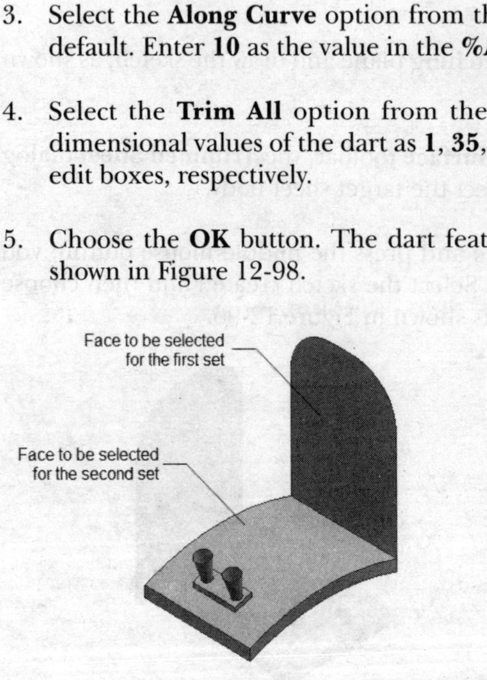

***Figure 12-97** Faces to be selected for the first and second sets*

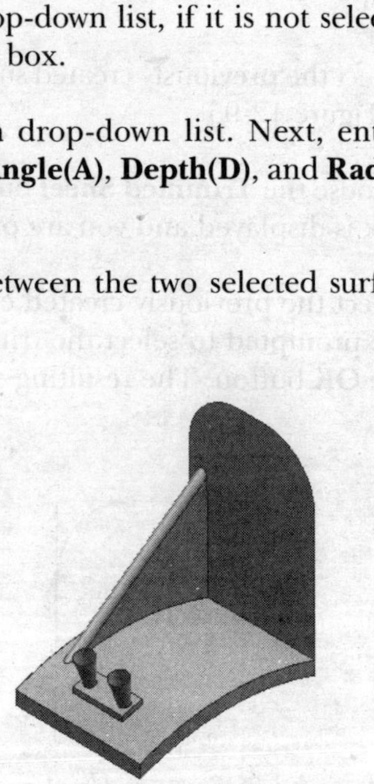

***Figure 12-98** Resultant surface model after creating the draft feature*

Mirroring the Dart Feature

After creating the dart feature, you need to mirror it about the YC-ZC plane. The following steps are required to create the mirror feature.

1. Invoke the **Mirror Feature** dialog box.

2. Select the dart feature and then mirror it about the YC-ZC plane. The resultant model is shown in Figure 12-99.

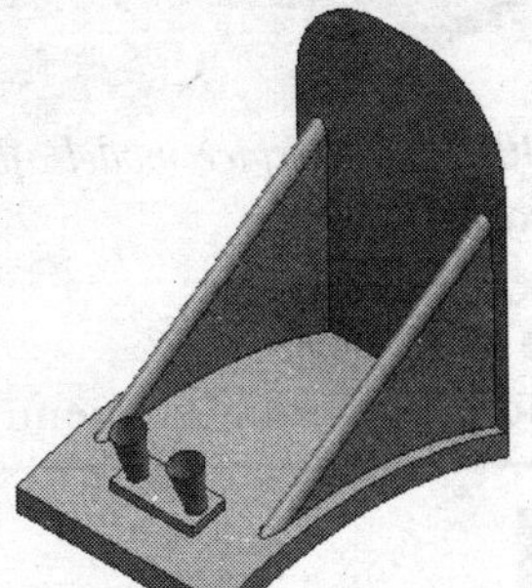

Figure 12-99 The surface model after mirroring the dart feature

Sewing the Dart Features

1. Invoke the **Sew** tool by choosing **Insert > Combine Bodies > Sew** from the menu bar; the **Sew** dialog box is displayed.

2. Select the **Sheet** option from drop-down list in the **Type** rollout, if it is not selected.

3. Select the surface model as the target body and then select the dart features as the tool sheet bodies.

4. Choose the **OK** button; all selected surfaces are sewed into a single surface.

Adding Thickness to the Surface Model

Now, you need to add thickness to the surface model.

1. Choose **Insert > Offset/Scale > Thicken** from the menu bar; the **Thicken** dialog box is displayed. Also, you are prompted to select the faces to thicken.

2. Select the surface model from the graphics window. Next, enter the thickness value as **0** and **1** in the **Offset 1** and **Offset 2** edit boxes, respectively.

3. Choose the **OK** button from the dialog box. The final model after adding the thickness is shown in Figure 12-100.

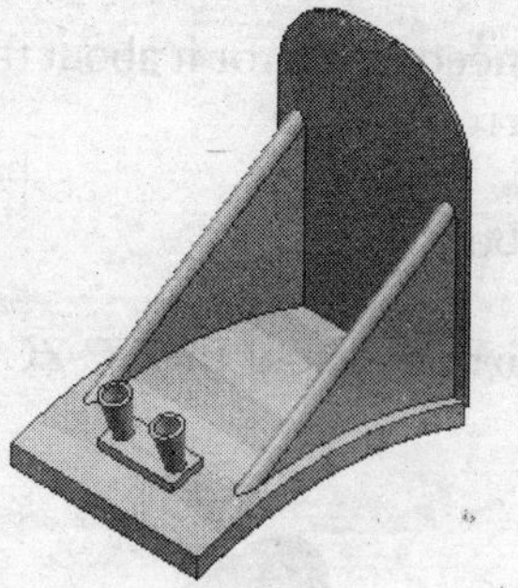

Figure 12-100 Final surface model after adding the thickness

Saving and Closing the File

1. Choose **File > Close > Save and Close** from the menu bar to save and close the file.

Self-Evaluation Test

Answer the following questions and then compare them to those given at the end of this chapter:

1. The **Emboss Sheet** tool is used to convert the shapes of solid bodies into a sheet. (T/F)
2. The **Fillet Surface** tool is used to create fillets of a constant or variable radius between two faces of the solid or sheet bodies. (T/F)
3. In a linear fillet, the radius is linear throughout the fillet. (T/F)
4. A dart feature can be created on solids. (T/F)
5. The maximum number of primary faces that can be used to create the bridge surface is __________.
6. The ____________ fillet type is used to create a fillet that has multiple radii.
7. The ____________ tool is used to extract edges from a solid body.
8. In the **Bridge** tool, the __________ button is used to retain the bridge surface prior to the dragging operation.
9. The ____________ tool is used to create section curves.
10. The ____________ tool is used to create complicated blends tangent to the specified sets of faces.

Review Questions

Answer the following questions:

1. How many types of fillets can be created in NX?

   (a)Three (b) Four
   (c) Five (d) None of these

2. Which of the following toolbar is used to create curves from bodies?

   (a) **Intersection Curve** (b) **Extract Curves**
   (c) **Curve** (d) **Section Curves**

3. Which of the following tools is used to create intersection curves between two sets of objects?

   (a) **Curve Intersection** (b) **Intersection Curve**
   (b) **Extract Curves** (d) **Section Curve**

4. Which of the following tools is used to create the sheet body that joins the two edges of faces?

   (a) **Bridge** (b) **Fillet**
   (c) **Soft Blend** (d) None of these

5. To create a dart feature, you need to choose the **Dart** button from the **Feature Operation** toolbar. (T/F)

6. The shape of the bridge can be controlled by specifying side faces or strings. (T/F)

7. The isoparametric blend is used for turbine blades. (T/F)

8. You can create a surface body from a closed sketch. (T/F)

9. The **Emboss Sheet** tool is used to convert shapes of solid bodies into a sheet. (T/F)

10. The **Dart** tool is used to add a rib along the intersection curve of two faces. (T/F)

Exercises

Exercise 1

Create the surface model shown in Figure 12-101. The drawing views and dimensions of the surface model are shown in Figure 12-102. Assume the missing dimensions. After creating the surface model, save it with the name *c12exr1.prt* at the location *\NX 7\c12.*

(Expected time: 45 min)

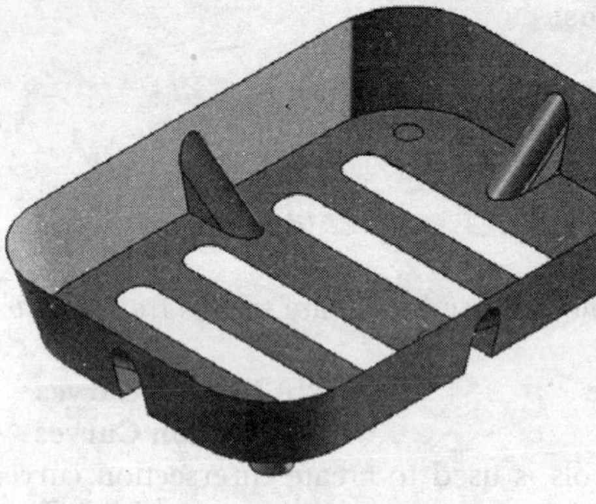

Figure 12-101 Surface model for Exercise 1

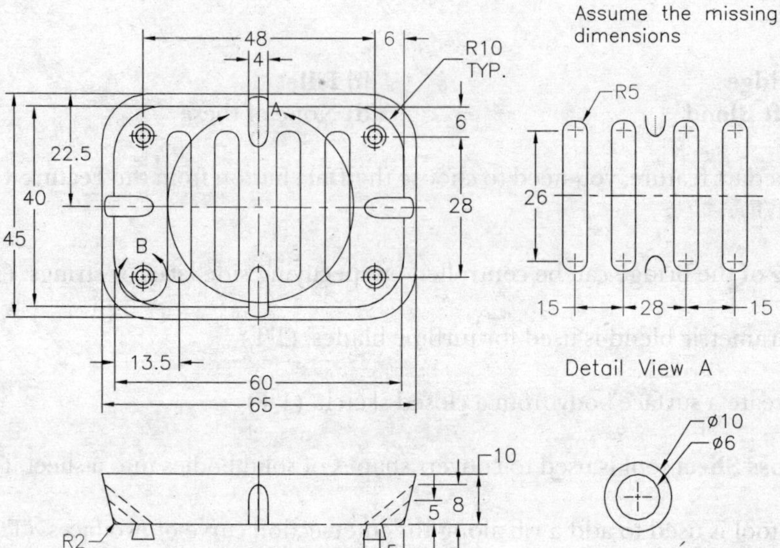

Figure 12-102 Views and dimensions for Exercise 1

Exercise 2

Create the surface model shown in Figure 12-103. The drawing views and dimensions of the surface model are shown in Figure 12-104. Assume the missing dimensions. After creating the surface model, save it with the name *c12exr2.prt* at the location *\NX 7\c12*.

(Expected time: 45 min)

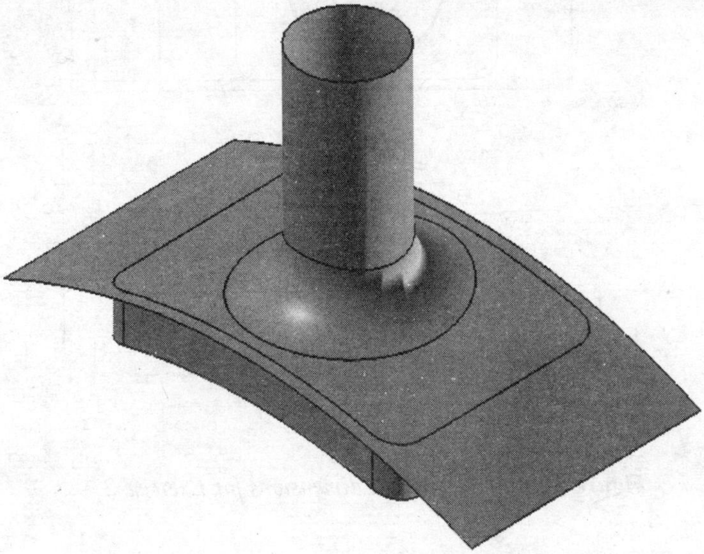

Figure 12-103 *Surface model for Exercise 2*

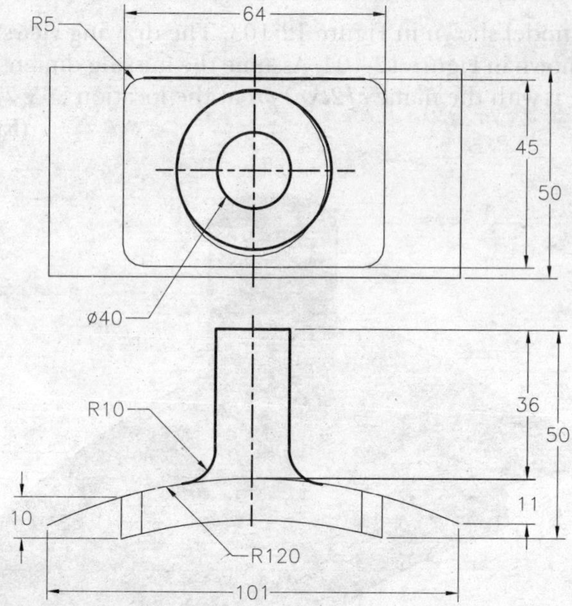

Figure 12-104 Views and dimensions for Exercise 2

Answers to Self-Evaluation Test

1. T, **2.** T, **3.** T, **4.** T, **5.** two, **6.** General, **7. Extract Curve**, **8. Reset**, **9. Section Curve**, **10. Face Blend**

Chapter 13

Generating, Editing, and Dimensioning the Drawing Views

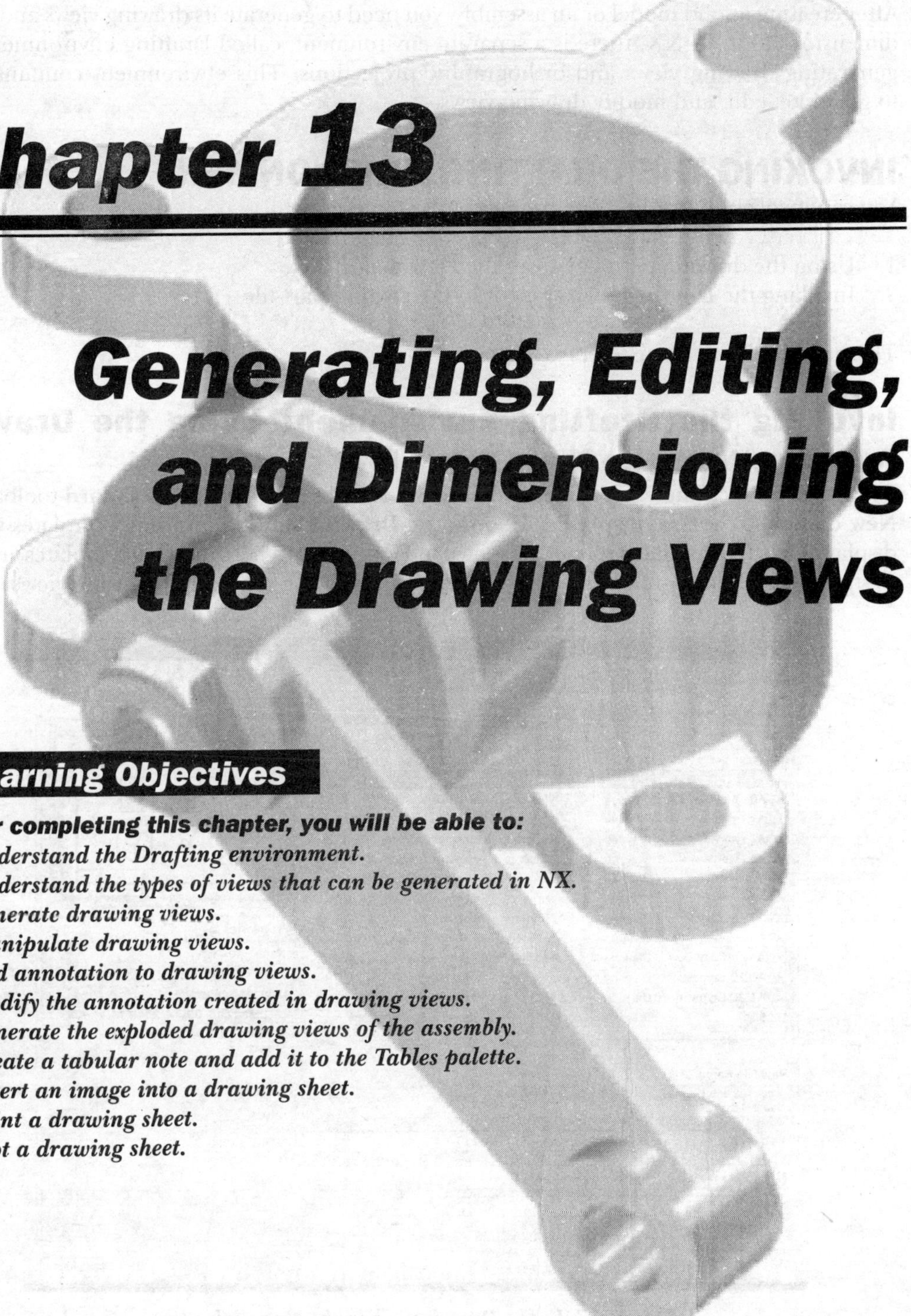

Learning Objectives

After completing this chapter, you will be able to:

- *Understand the Drafting environment.*
- *Understand the types of views that can be generated in NX.*
- *Generate drawing views.*
- *Manipulate drawing views.*
- *Add annotation to drawing views.*
- *Modify the annotation created in drawing views.*
- *Generate the exploded drawing views of the assembly.*
- *Create a tabular note and add it to the Tables palette.*
- *Insert an image into a drawing sheet.*
- *Print a drawing sheet.*
- *Plot a drawing sheet.*

THE DRAFTING ENVIRONMENT

After creating a solid model or an assembly, you need to generate its drawing views and apply dimensions to it. In NX, there is a separate environment, called Drafting environment, for generating drawing views and orthographic projections. This environment contains tools to generate, edit, and modify drawing views.

INVOKING THE DRAFTING ENVIRONMENT

You can invoke the Drafting environment by two methods:

1. Using the drawing template from the **New** dialog box.
2. Invoking the Drafting environment in the current part file.

These methods are discussed next.

Invoking the Drafting Environment Using the Drawing Template from the New Dialog Box

To invoke the Drafting environment, choose the **New** button from the **Standard** toolbar; the **New** dialog box will be displayed. Choose the **Drawing** tab; the drawing templates will be displayed in the **Templates** rollout, as shown in Figure 13-1. These drawing templates are used to start a new drawing file in the Drafting environment for generating drawing views.

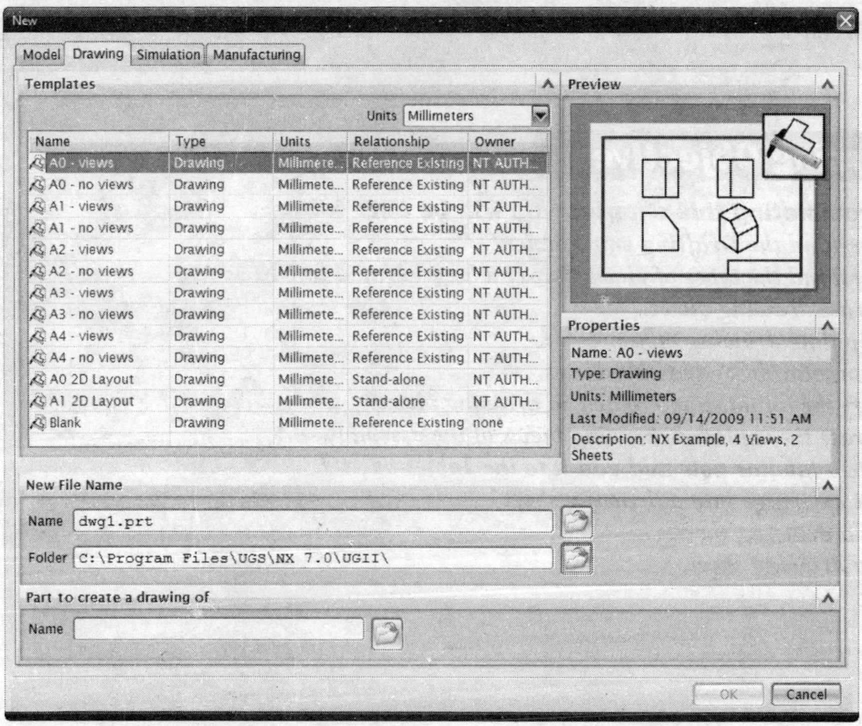

*Figure 13-1 The **Drawing** tab in the **New** dialog box*

These drawing templates are arranged according to the sheet size (A0, A1, A2, A3, and A4) in the **Drawing** tab. There are two types of templates for each sheet size, views and no views. If you select the views template, then the drawing views will be generated automatically in the drawing sheet. If you select the no views template, then a blank drawing sheet will open, and you need to generate drawing views manually on it.

Select the required drawing template. Now, you need to specify the part file for which you want to generate the drawing views. To do so, choose the button on the right of the **Name** edit box in the **Part to create a drawing of** rollout; the **Select master part** dialog box will be displayed. Choose the **Open** button; the **Part Name** dialog box will be displayed. Next, browse to the folder where you have saved the part file and select it. Choose the **OK** button; the selected part file will be added to the **Loaded Parts** list area of the **Select master part** dialog box. Next, choose the **OK** button from this dialog box; the **New** dialog box will be displayed. Also, the name of the part file and its location will be displayed in the **New File Name** rollout. Choose the **OK** button from the dialog box; the Drafting environment will be invoked.

If you have selected the views template, four drawing views will be generated and placed automatically in the drawing sheet, as shown in Figure 13-2. By default, the third angle projection method is used to create the drawing views. If you have selected the no views template, the **Base View** dialog box will be displayed with the **View** button chosen in it. Also, the floating drawing view (Top view) will be attached to the cursor, refer to Figure 13-3, and you will be prompted to specify the center of the base view on the sheet. The details about the generation of the drawing views are discussed next.

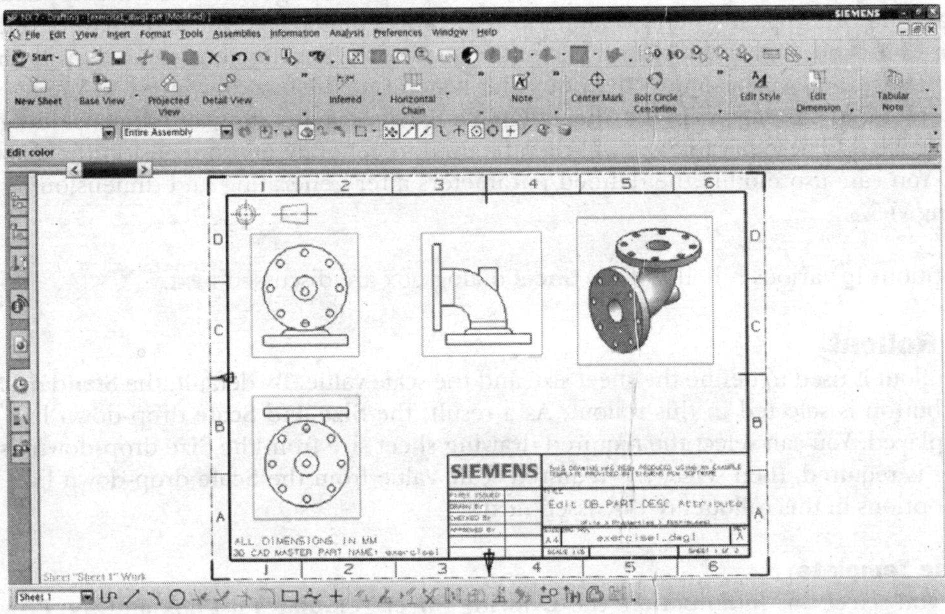

Figure 13-2 The four drawing views created and placed automatically

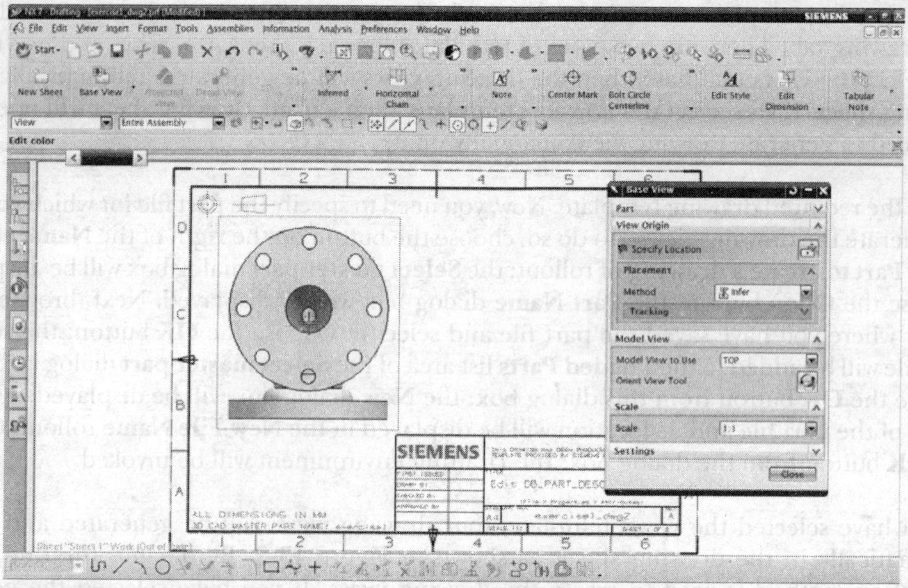

Figure 13-3 The Drafting environment invoked using the no views template

Invoking the Drafting Environment in the Current Part File

To invoke the Drafting environment in the current part file, open the part file and choose **Start > Drafting** from the **Standard** toolbar or choose the **Drafting** button from the **Application** toolbar. The Drafting environment along with the **Sheet** dialog box will be displayed, refer to Figure 13-4. Note that at this stage some of the tools of the Drafting environment will not be active. These tools will become active only after generating the first drawing view. You need to set the required parameters in the **Sheet** dialog box before generating and dimensioning the drawing views. These parameters will then be used to generate and dimension the drawing views. You can also modify the defined parameters after generating and dimensioning the drawing views.

The options in various rollouts of the **Sheet** dialog box are discussed next.

Size Rollout

This rollout is used to define the sheet size and the scale value. By default, the **Standard Size** radio button is selected in this rollout. As a result, the **Size** and **Scale** drop-down lists will be displayed. You can select the required drawing sheet size from the **Size** drop-down list. If scaling is required, then select the required scale value from the **Scale** drop-down list. The other options in this rollout are discussed next.

Use Template

If you select this radio button, the **Drawing Sheet Templates** list box and the **Preview** rollout will be displayed in the dialog box. You can select the required drawing template from this list box. On doing so, the preview of the selected drawing template will be displayed in the **Preview** rollout.

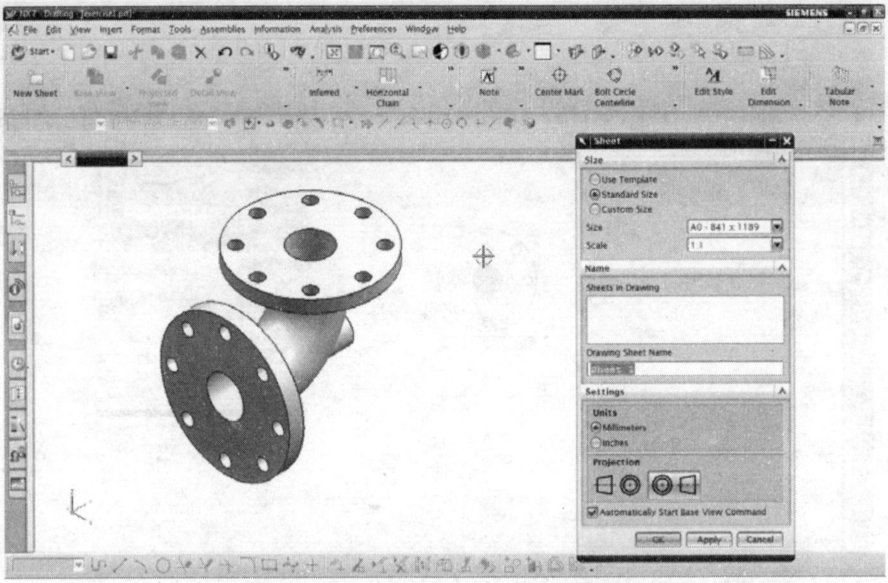

Figure 13-4 The Drafting environment window of NX

Custom Size

This radio button is used to define the user-define drawing sheet size. If you select this radio button, the **Height** and **Length** edit boxes will be displayed. You can enter the height and length values for a drawing sheet in the respective edit boxes. Also, if scaling is required, then select the required scale value from the **Scale** drop-down list.

Name Rollout

You can enter the name of a drawing sheet in the **Drawing Sheet Name** edit box of the **Sheet** dialog box. You can enter up to 30 characters for a name in this edit box.

Settings Rollout

This rollout is used to set units and projection method for generating drawing views. The dimensions of these views can be set in millimeters or inches by selecting the **Millimeters** or **Inches** radio button. Similarly, you can set the first angle or third angle projection method for generating the drawing views by choosing the **1st Angle Projection** or **3rd Angle Projection** button. If you select the **Automatically Start Base View Command** check box in this rollout, then the floating drawing view (Top view) will be attached to the cursor after choosing the **OK** button.

After setting the required parameters in the **Sheet** dialog box, choose the **OK** button; the Drafting environment will be invoked and the **Base View** dialog box will be displayed in it, as shown in Figure 13-5. Also, you will be prompted to specify the location to place the view. Specify the location to place the drawing view on the sheet; the drawing view (Top view) will be placed on the specified location and the **Projected View** dialog box will be displayed. Also, the projected view of the model will be attached to the cursor, depending upon the movement of the cursor. Specify the location to place the first projected view. Similarly, place all the required projected views on the sheet and then exit the dialog box.

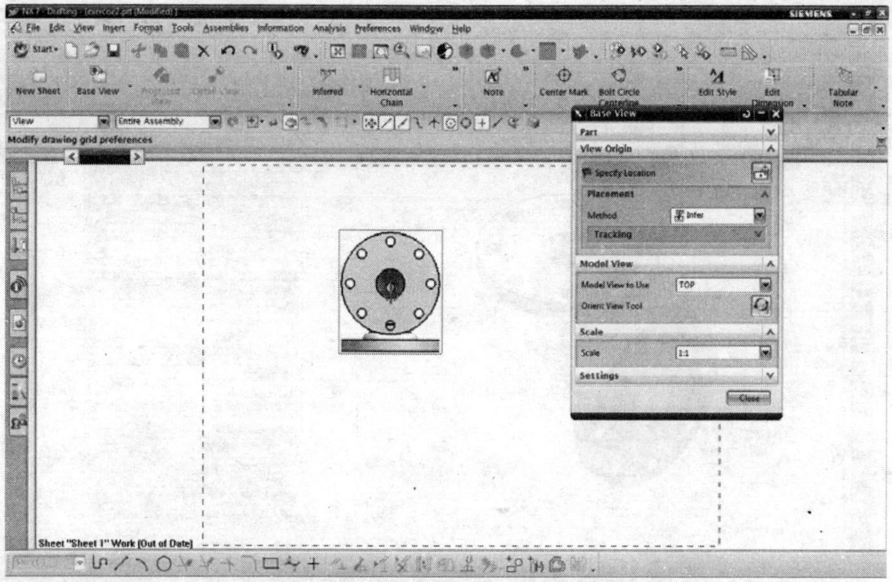

Figure 13-5 The Drafting environment of NX

Note

*If the display of the grid is turned on, choose **Preferences > Grid and Work Plane** from the menu bar; the **Grid and Work Plane** dialog box will be displayed. Clear the **Show** check box from the **Grid Settings** rollout and choose the **OK** button to exit the dialog box; the display of the grid will be turned off.*

*To change the background to white, choose **Preferences > Visualization** from the menu bar; the **Visualization Preferences** dialog box will be displayed. In this dialog box, choose the **Color Settings** tab, select the **Monochrome Display** check box, and then select the **Background** swatch from the **Drawing Part Settings** rollout; the **Color** dialog box will be displayed. Select the white swatch from this dialog box, and then choose the **OK** button twice.*

EDITING THE DRAWING SHEET PARAMETERS IN THE DRAFTING ENVIRONMENT

After invoking the Drafting environment, you can edit the parameters of the drawing sheet in the **Sheet** dialog box by following the steps discussed next. Right-click on the drawing limits border represented by the dashed lines and select the **Edit Sheet** option from the shortcut menu; the **Sheet** dialog box will be displayed. Next, change the parameters in the **Sheet** dialog box and choose the **OK** button to reflect the changes.

INVOKING THE DRAFTING TOOLS

After invoking the Drafting environment, you need to invoke the drafting toolbars. By default, the **Drawing** and **Dimension** toolbars are displayed. If they are not displayed by default, you need to right-clicking on the main menu bar and then choose the **Drawing** and

Dimension options from the toolbars shortcut menu to invoke these toolbars. Using the tools in the **Drawing** toolbar, you can generate the drawing views. Using the tools in the **Drawing** and **Dimension** toolbars, you can generate the drawing views and add dimensions to them.

TYPES OF DRAWING VIEWS IN NX

In the Drafting environment of NX, you can generate different types of drawing views for a component or an assembly. The drawing views that can be generated in the Drafting environment of NX are discussed next.

Base View

The **Base View** is the parent drawing view generated from model or an assembly, which is currently opened in the Modeling environment. This view is an independent view and is not affected by the changes made in any other view in the drawing sheet. Most of the other views are generated by using the Base view as the parent drawing view. If the dimensional aspects of the parent model are modified, all the views need to be updated manually by right-clicking on the view boundary and selecting the **Update** option from the shortcut menu.

In NX, you can also create a drawing view from a model or an assembly, which is not currently opened in the Modeling environment. This enables you to have drawing views of different models without opening the corresponding models in the Modeling environment.

Projected View

The projected views are the orthographic projections generated from the base view. These views are used to understand the model from the drawing views in terms of shape and size.

Detail View

The detail view is used to magnify the congested area of the drawing view. The congested area is scaled to a greater value and elaborately defined at the side of the same drawing view. The scale value of the detail view will be higher than the one specified for the drawing view.

Section View

The section view is generated by chopping an existing view using a section line at any cross-section and viewing the parent view normal to it. The section views are used to display the internal features of the model at any cross-section.

Auxiliary View

The auxiliary view is generated by projecting the section exactly normal to the cutting member. An auxiliary view is used to show the true dimensions of the features that are created on an inclined face. For example, an inclined circular hole feature will be displayed as an elliptical cross-section when viewed from the side. This error in viewing can be eliminated by viewing the same hole feature normal to its center axis. In NX, there is no separate tool for generating an auxiliary view. Instead, the **Projected View** tool can be used to generate the auxiliary view.

Half-Section View

The half-section view is generated by chopping a section of the drawing view and viewing the model normal to the cross-section. In NX, using the **Half Section View** tool, you can generate a section of a required length along the cutting plane. This section can be trimmed to a user-defined value when it is formed.

Revolved Section View

The revolved section view is generated for drawing views that can be revolved about an axis. Here, the first cutting plane is placed stationary at the base point and the second cutting plane is rotated at an angle around it.

Break-Out Section View

The break-out section view is used to remove the part of the existing view and display the area of the model or an assembly that lies behind the removed portion.

Broken View

The broken view is one, in which a user-defined portion of the drawing view is removed, keeping the ends of the drawing view intact. The broken view is used for displaying the drawing view, which has a high length to width ratio. By generating the broken view, you can shorten the length or width of the drawing view and accommodate it in the drawing sheet as a drawing view of normal size.

GENERATING DRAWING VIEWS

In NX, the base view is generated as the parent view from the model or an assembly. The other views are generated and projected directly from the base view. The steps for generating all the ten types of drawing views are discussed next.

Generating the Base View

Menu:	Insert > View > Base View
Toolbar:	Drawing > Base View

As mentioned earlier, the base view is created as the parent drawing view from a model or an assembly. To generate the base view of a model or an assembly, choose the **Base View** button from the **Drawing** toolbar; the **Base View** dialog box will be displayed, as shown in Figure 13-6. As discussed earlier, if you have selected the no views template, then the **Base View** dialog box will be displayed by default in the drawing window. The options in this dialog box are discussed next.

Part Rollout

This rollout is used to select components for drafting. In this rollout, the **Loaded Parts** area lists the components that were opened in the current NX 7 session before opening the new drawing sheet. You can select these components to create a base view. Alternatively, choose the **Open** button in the **Part** rollout and select a new component to create a base view.

View Origin Rollout

By default, the **Specify Location** area remains active in the **View Origin** rollout. Also, the **Infer** option is selected in the **Method** drop-down list. As a result, you can place the drawing view anywhere in the drawing sheet by clicking in the drawing sheet.

You can specify the method of placement and the alignment of the new base view by selecting an option from the **Method** and **Alignment** drop-down lists, respectively. Note, that the **Alignment** drop-down list will be displayed when you select an option other than the **Infer** option from the **Method** drop-down list. To place and align a base view horizontally to another view, select the **Horizontal** option from the **Method** drop-down list. Next, you need to specify the alignment of the resulting view. To do so, select an option from the **Alignment** drop-down list. By default, the **To View** option is selected in this drop-down list, as a result, you will be prompted to select a view to which the resulting view has to be aligned. Select a view and place the new base view; the resulting view will be placed and aligned horizontally to the selected view.

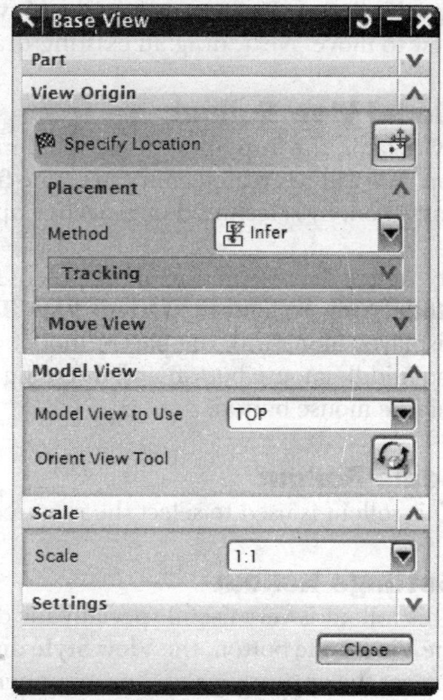

*Figure 13-6 The **Base View** dialog box*

To place a view horizontally and align it with respect to the specified point from the model, select the **Horizontal** option from the **Method** drop-down list and then select the **Model Point** option from the **Alignment** drop-down list; the **Specify Stationary View Point** area will be highlighted and you will be prompted to specify the point to which the resulting view has to be aligned. Specify the point from the view and place the new base view; the resulting view will be placed horizontally and aligned with respect to the selected point.

To place a view horizontally and align it with respect to two points, select the **Horizontal** option from the **Method** drop-down list. Next, select the **Point to Point** option from the **Alignment** drop-down list; the **Specify Stationary View Point** area will be highlighted and you will be prompted to specify the stationary point. Specify a point from the view; the **Specify Current View Point** area will be highlighted and you will be prompted to specify a point to which the resulting view has to be aligned. Specify a point from the view and place the new base view; the resulting view will be placed horizontally and will be aligned with respect to the two points.

Similarly, you can select other options from the **Method** drop-down list and specify its alignment by selecting an option from the **Alignment** drop-down list.

By default, the **Cursor Tracking** check box is clear in the **Tracking** sub-rollout. If you select this check box, the **Offset**, **X**, and **Y** edit boxes will be displayed in this sub-rollout. You can specify the location of the current drawing view by specifying the values in these edit boxes.

You can also change the location of an existing created drawing view. To do so, click on the **Specify Screen Position** area in the **Move View** sub-rollout; you will be prompted to drag the view to move. Next, drag an existing drawing view and place it at the required location.

Model View Rollout

By default, the **Top** option is selected in the **Model View to Use** drop-down list. As a result, top view will be created. You can create front view, right hand side view, or left hand side view, and so on, by selecting the respective option from the **Model View to Use** drop-down list.

To change the orientation of the parent model, choose the **Orient View Tool** button from the **Model View** rollout; the **Orient View Tool** dialog box and the **Orient View** window will be displayed along with the parent model. You can dynamically reorient the model by pressing the middle mouse button and dragging the mouse. To accept the new orientation, press the middle mouse button.

Scale Rollout

This rollout is used to select the required scale ratio value from the **Scale** drop-down list.

Settings Rollout

This rollout is very useful specially for drafting the assembly with the desired effect. Choose the **View Style** button; the **View Style** dialog box will be displayed. Using this dialog box, you can set the appearance of the component, edges, threads and so on.

The **Hidden Components** sub-rollout will be displayed while generating a drawing view of an assembly. You can hide the selected components of the assembly using the **Hidden Components** sub-rollout. To do so, click on the **Select Object** area in the **Hidden Components** sub-rollout; you will be prompted to select the components to hide. Select the components from the view; the selected components will not be displayed in the resultant view and the name of those components will be displayed in the list of the **Hidden Components** sub-rollout. To redisplay the component, select the name of that component from the list of the **Hidden Components** sub-rollout; the **Remove** button will be activated. Next, choose this button; the component will be redisplayed.

Standard parts such as nuts, bolts, washers, pins, and so on should be excluded from sectioning in the drawing. To exclude the selected part from sectioning, click on the **Select Object** area in the **Non-Sectioned** sub-rollout; you will be prompted to select components. Select the components from the resultant view; the selected components will not be considered for sectioning in the section view and the name of the selected components will be displayed in the list of the **Non-Sectioned** sub-rollout. To redisplay the component, select the name of that component from the list of the **Non-Sectioned** sub-rollout; the **Remove** button will be activated. Choose the **Remove** button; the component will be redisplayed. The **Section View** tool is discussed later in this chapter.

Note

*If the borders are generated along with the drawing views and you do not want them to displayed, choose **Preferences > Drafting** from the menu bar. The **Drafting Preferences** dialog box will* *be displayed. Choose the **View** tab and clear the **Display Borders** check box from the **Borders** area. Choose the **OK** button; the borders will be cleared from the generated drawing views.*

Generating the Orthographic Drawing Views Using the Projected View Tool

Menu:	Insert > View > Projected View
Toolbar:	Drawing > Projected View

The **Projected View** tool is used to generate the projection views of a model from the base view. After positioning the base view in the drawing sheet by using the **Base View** tool, the **Projected View** dialog box is displayed automatically and the projected view of the model attached to the cursor is displayed in the drawing window. The display of hinge line from the base view confirms that the **Projected View** tool has been invoked. Apart from the Base View, you can also generate the projection views from an existing drawing view. In the aforesaid case, you need to select the parent view and invoke the **Projected View** tool by choosing the **Projected View** button from the **Drawing** toolbar. On doing so, the preview of the projected view will be displayed in the graphics window. Also, the **Projected View** dialog box will be displayed, refer to Figure 13-7. You will notice that the hinge line is attached to the parent view and the appearance of the projection view changes as you move the cursor around the parent view. To place the projection view in the drawing sheet, click the left mouse button at the required location.

***Figure 13-7** The **Projected View** dialog box*

Hinge Line Rollout

By default, the **Inferred** option is selected in the **Vector Option** drop-down list. As a result, the hinge line rotates as you move the cursor around the parent view. Also, the appearance of the projection view changes according to the movement of the cursor. If you select the **Reverse Projected Direction** check box in this rollout, then the projected direction of the view will be reversed. You can generate any number of projection views at a time using the **Projected View** tool. For placing the generated projection view, click the left mouse button. Next, exit the **Projected View** tool by pressing the ESC key or the middle mouse button. Figure 13-8 shows the projected drawing views, hinge line, unpositioned drawing view, and drawing limits.

To create an auxiliary view with respect to the defined hinge line by using the **Projected View** tool, select the **Defined** option from the **Vector Option** drop-down list in the **Hinge Line** rollout; the **Specify Vector** area in the **Hinge Line** rollout will be active. Also, you will be prompted to select objects to infer vector. Specify the direction vector in the drawing sheet;

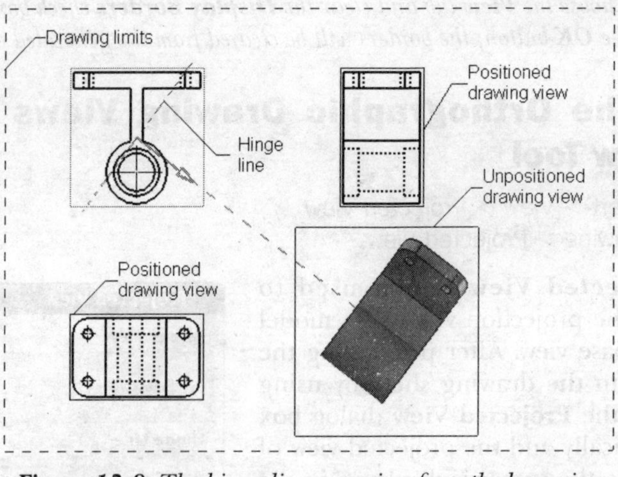

Figure 13-8 The hinge line emerging from the base view

the auxiliary view with respect to the direction vector specified will be displayed. Click at the required location in the drawing sheet to place the drawing view.

The remaining options of this dialog box are the same as those of the **Base View** tool, as discussed earlier.

Generating the Detail View Using the Detail View Tool

Menu:	Insert > View > Detail View
Toolbar:	Drawing > Detail View

The **Detail View** tool is used to generate the detail views for a drawing view. To generate the detail view for a drawing view, choose the **Detail View** button from the **Drawing** toolbar; the **Detail View** dialog box will be displayed, as shown in Figure 13-9.

In the **Detail View** dialog box, select the **Circular** option from the **Type** rollout; you will be prompted to select object to infer point. Specify the center point for drawing the detail view boundary; you will be prompted to select object to infer point. Specify the radius point. After you specify the radius for the circular boundary, the detail view will be generated and you will be prompted to specify location to place view. You can also define the scale value for the detail view from the **Scale** drop-down list in the **Scale** rollout. Next, position it in the

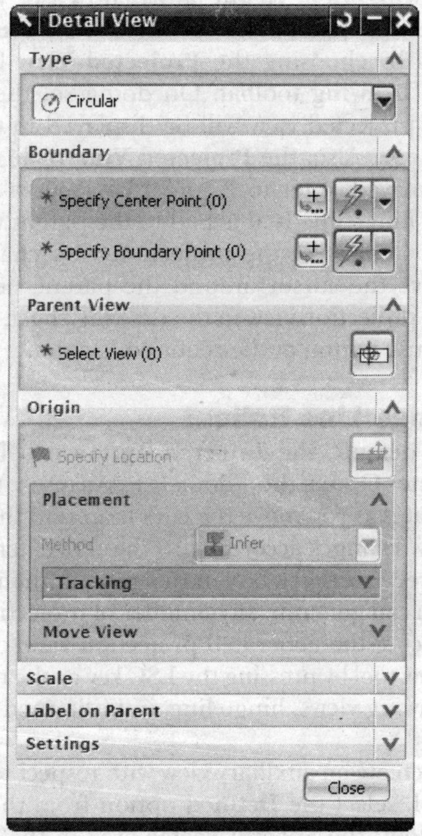

*Figure 13-9 The **Detail View** dialog box*

drawing sheet by pressing the left mouse button. The detail view representing the cooling fins of the piston is generated and placed in the drawing sheet, along with the label, as shown in Figure 13-10.

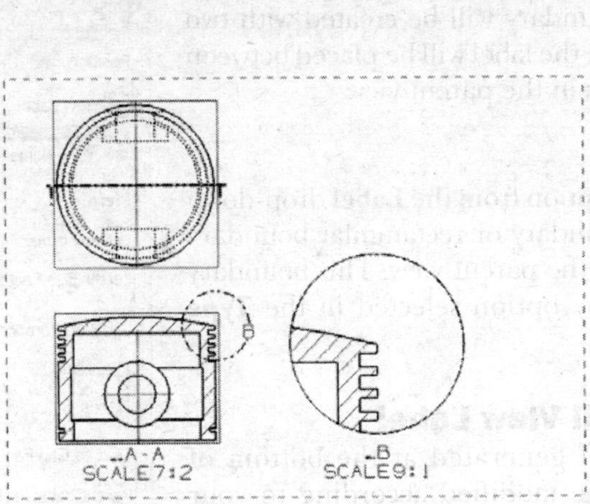

Figure 13-10 *The detail view generated for the piston to show the fins*

Instead of a circular boundary, you can define a rectangular boundary by using the **Rectangle by Corners** or **Rectangle by Center and Corner** option from the drop-down list in the **Type** rollout. The process for generating the detail view using the rectangular boundary is the same as that of the circular boundary.

Label on Parent Rollout

There are different types of options for specifying the label style of the detail view in the **Label** drop-down list of the **Label on Parent** rollout. You can use any of these label styles to label the parent view. These label styles are discussed next.

None

If you select this option from the **Label** drop-down list, no boundary will be created in the parent view.

Circle

If you select this option from the **Label** drop-down list, a circular boundary will be created in the parent view.

Note

If you select this option from the **Label** drop-down list, a circular boundary with label, but without any leader, will be created in the parent view.

Label

If you select this option from the **Label** drop-down list, a circular boundary with label, and along with the leader, will be created in the parent view.

Embedded

If you select this option from the **Label** drop-down list, a circular boundary will be created with two arrow heads. Also, the label will be placed between these arrow heads in the parent view.

Boundary

If you select this option from the **Label** drop-down list, a circular boundary or rectangular boundary will be created in the parent view. This boundary depends upon the option selected in the **Type** rollout.

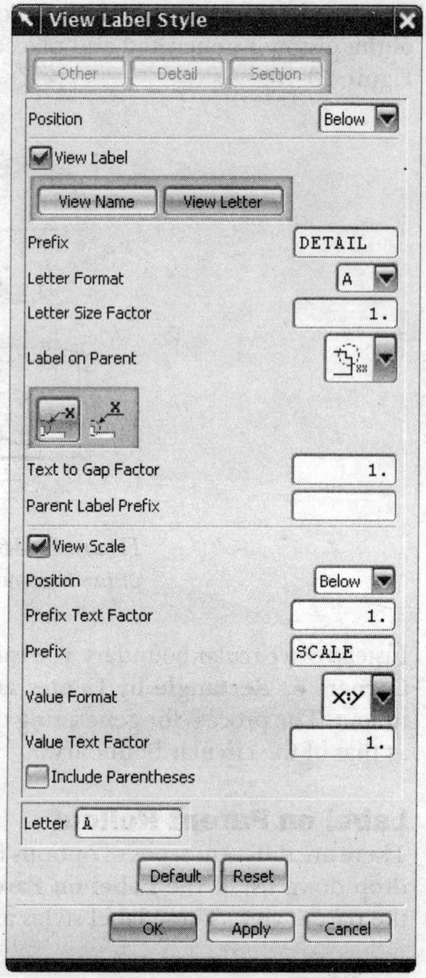

Figure 13-11 The View Label Style dialog box

Editing the Detail View Label

The detail view label generated at the bottom of the detail view can be modified according to your requirement. To do so, right-click on the detail view label, and then select the **Edit View Label** option from the shortcut menu; the **View Label Style** dialog box will be displayed, refer to Figure 13-11. To change the label name of the detail view, select the **View Label** check box in the **View Label Style** dialog box, if it is not selected. Choose the **View Letter** button, if it is not chosen, the **Letter** text box in the **View Label Style** dialog box will be enabled. Enter a name in the **Letter** text box and choose the **Apply** button and then the **OK** button for reflecting the changes.

Adding a Prefix Text to the View Label

To define any prefix text, enter the text in the **Prefix** text box of the **View Label Style** dialog box. The prefix text may contain alphabets, numeric values, and also special characters. A combination of these three is also possible. The label letter size can be modified by entering the scale value in the **Letter Size Factor** edit box. The label created in the parent view is called the parent label. In the **Label on Parent** drop-down list, you have various styles for defining the parent label's letter style with respect to the detailing boundary specified.

If you require a prefix text for the parent label, enter text in the **Parent Label Prefix** text box. You can align the scale value above or below the label name by selecting the **Above** or **Below** option, respectively, from the **Position** drop-down list.

The text for the prefix of the scale value can be entered in the **Prefix** text box below the **Prefix Text Factor** edit box. To change the format of the scale value, you can select the required format option from the **Value Format** drop-down list. To change the size of the scale value, enter the required scale value in the **Value Text Factor** edit box.

Generating Section Views Using the Section View Tool

Menu: Insert > View > Section View
Toolbar: Drawing > Section View

As mentioned earlier, the section view is generated by chopping the existing view at any cross-section and viewing the parent view from a direction normal to the cross-section. The **Section View** tool is used to generate the section view of a model or an assembly. A section view is generated by defining the section line at any cross-section of the drawing view of a model or an assembly. In NX, section views can also be generated by defining a multisegment section line. The full section view generated by using the segmented and multisegmented section lines is shown in Figures 13-12 and 13-13, respectively.

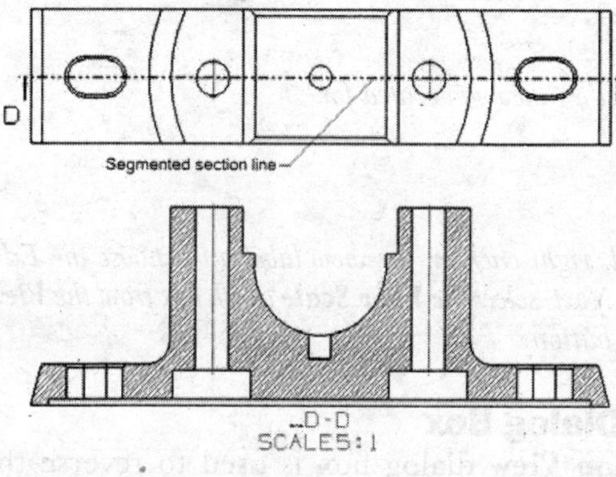

Figure 13-12 Section view generated using a segmented section line

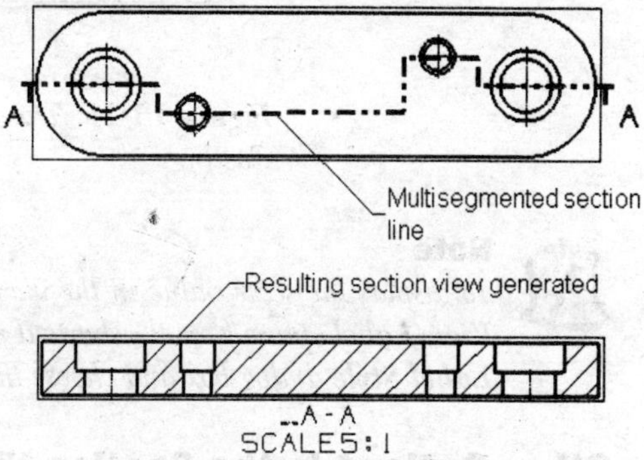

Figure 13-13 Section view generated using multisegmented section line

To generate the section view, choose the **Section View** button from the **Drawing** toolbar; the **Section View** dialog box will be displayed and you will be prompted to select the parent view. Select the parent view from the drawing window; the **Section View** dialog box will be modified, as shown in Figure 13-14.

*Figure 13-14 The modified **Section View** dialog box*

A floating horizontal section line attached with the cursor will also be displayed. You need to fix the section line by specifying a pivot point on the parent view. The pivot point should be specified by clicking on the parent view. After you specify the pivot point for the section line, the section line will become fixed. The section line can be rotated about the pivot point. Move the cursor where you want to place the section view and adjust the angle of the section line. Next, press the left mouse button to place the section view; the section view along with the section view label will be generated. Figure 13-15 shows the section view after modifying the character size of the view label. You will learn how to modify the character size and other properties of the view label later in this chapter.

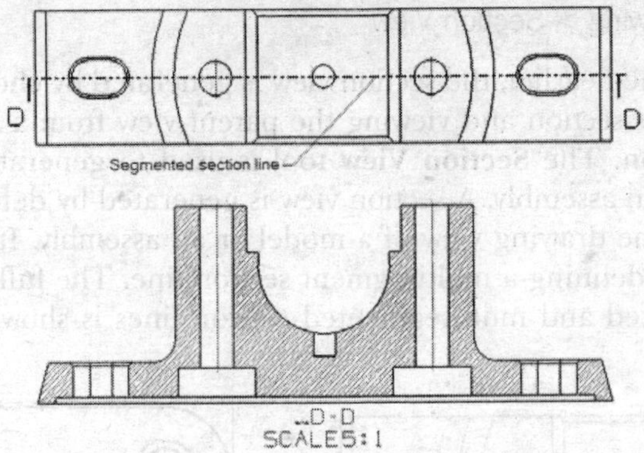

Figure 13-15 The full section view generated for Casting

Note

*To display the scale value in the view label, right-click on the view label and choose the **Edit View Label** option from the shortcut menu. Next, select the **View Scale** check box from the **View Label Style** dialog box and choose the **OK** button.*

Other Options in the Section View Dialog Box

The **Reverse Direction** button in the **Section View** dialog box is used to reverse the viewing direction. If you choose the **Define Hinge Line** toggle button from the **Hinge Line** area, then the display of the hinge line from the parent view will turn on and off. To modify the size and shape of the arrow head of the section line, choose the **Section Line Style** button from the **Settings** area; the **Section Line Style** dialog box will be displayed. Make necessary changes and choose **OK** button to reflect the changes. On choosing the **Style** button from the **Settings** area, the **View Style** dialog box will be displayed. This dialog box is used to create or modify the visual appearance of a view as well as to control the preference setting for the style options associated with all view types. The options in the **View Style** dialog box are discussed later in this chapter.

While generating section views for an assembly, you may need to avoid sectioning the assembled standard parts such as bolt, fasteners, nut, and so on. To avoid sectioning standard parts, choose the **Non-sectioned Component/Solid** button from the **Settings** area; the **Class Selection** dialog box will be displayed and you will be prompted to select components. Select the components that are not to be sectioned and choose the **OK** button. Note that you need to select the components that are not to be sectioned before placing the section view. You can also section a component that is selected as a non-sectioned component. For sectioning such components, choose the **Sectioned Component/Solid** button that will be enabled after using the **Non-sectioned Component/Solid** button; the **Select unsectioned component or solid bodies to section** dialog box will be displayed. In the list box of this dialog box, the name of the components selected in the category of the non-sectioned component will be displayed. Select the component to be sectioned from the list box or directly enter its name in the **Component Name** edit box and choose the **OK** button; the selected component will be sectioned again.

Note

If the hatching is not displayed on the sectioned component, select the section view and right-click on it and select the ***Style*** *option from the shortcut menu; the* ***View Style*** *dialog box will be displayed. Choose the* ***Section*** *tab and select the* ***Crosshatch*** *check box. Next, choose the* ***OK*** *button; the hatching pattern will be displayed.*

The sectional view previously generated can also be used as a parent view for generating the section view.

To move the views created earlier, choose the **Move View** button from the **Preview** area of the **Section View** dialog box; you will be prompted to move one or more views. Select the required view and drag it to the desired location. After specifying the new location, press the middle mouse button to exit the **Move View** tool.

Modifying the Properties of the Section View Label

Select the view label and right-click on it; a shortcut menu will be displayed. Choose the **Edit View Label** option from the shortcut menu; the **View Label Style** dialog box will be displayed. Select the **View Scale** check box. The options related to the scale value and the scale format will be enabled in the **View Scale** area. Now, you can modify the scale value and the scale format, as discussed earlier. The process to modify the properties is discussed briefly in the topics **Editing the Detail View Label** and **Adding a Prefix text to the View Label** in this chapter.

Editing the Section Line

The section line defined for a section view can be edited in order to attain perfect results in the section view. To edit the section line, right-click on the section line, and then choose the **Edit** option from the shortcut menu displayed; the **Section Line** dialog box will be displayed, as shown in Figure 13-16.

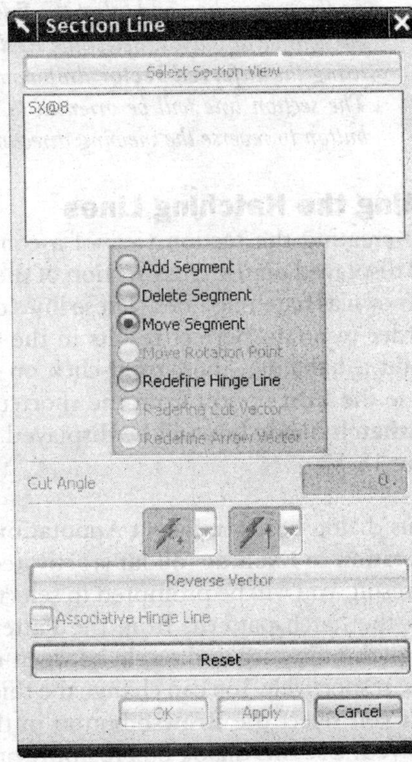

Figure 13-16 The ***Section Line*** *dialog box*

Adding a Segment in the Section Line

You can add any number of segments to a section line. To add a segment to the section line, select the **Add Segment** radio button from the **Section Line** dialog box. Specify the break points in the section line dynamically or by using the **Inferred Point** drop-down list; the break points are marked in orange. You can also delete the segments already created on the section line. For deleting a segment, select the **Delete Segment** radio button; you will be prompted to select the segments to be deleted. Select the segments; the selected segment will be merged with the nearby segment. Choose **Apply** and then the **Cancel** button to exit the dialog box. To update the section view, right-click on the old section view and select the **Update** option from the shortcut menu.

Moving a Segment

Select the **Move Segment** radio button from the **Section Line** dialog box and then select the individual members to be moved. After selecting the members, specify the destination point for positioning the selected members in the drawing limits. The **Inferred Point** drop-down list can be used to specify the new destination for the segments. Choose **Apply** and then the **Cancel** button to exit the dialog box. To update the section view, right-click on the old section view and select the **Update** option from the shortcut menu.

Note

After generating the section view, you can also change the direction and orientation of the section line about the pivot point. To change the direction and orientation of the section line, right-click on the section line and select the ***Edit*** *option from the shortcut menu; the* ***Section Line*** *dialog box will be displayed. Select the* ***Redefine Hinge Line*** *radio button from the dialog box. Next, using the* ***Inferred Vector*** *drop-down list, specify the new vector direction for the section line. The section line will be oriented to the newly specified direction. Choose the* ***Reverse Vector*** *button to reverse the viewing direction.*

Editing the Hatching Lines

After creating the section view of a component, the lines displayed on the cross-section of the component are known as hatching lines. These lines can be edited in order to attain perfect results in the section view. To edit a hatching lines, right-click on it, and then choose the **Edit** option from the shortcut menu; the **Crosshatch** dialog box will be displayed, as shown in Figure 13-17.

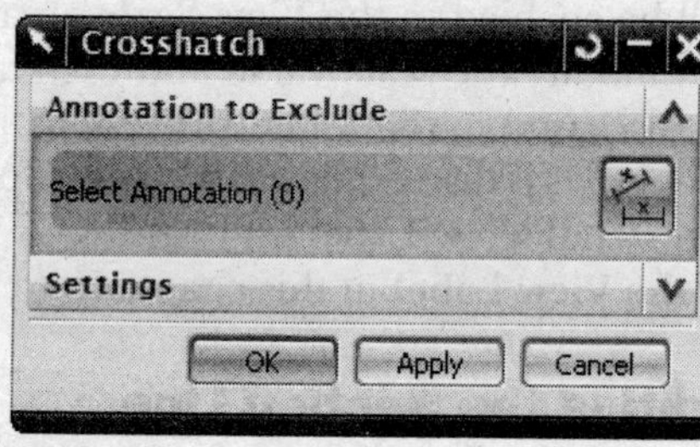

Figure 13-17 The ***Crosshatch*** *dialog box*

In this dialog box, the **Select Annotation** area in the **Annotation to Exclude** rollout is activated by default. As a result, you will be prompted to select annotation. Select annotations to exclude. You can select the hatch patterns from the **Pattern** drop-down list in the **Settings** rollout. You can change the distance and angle between two hatch lines using the **Distance** and **Angle** edit boxes, respectively. You can change the thickness of the hatch lines using the **Width** drop-down list. If you select the **Browse** button in this rollout, the **Crosshatch File** dialog box will be displayed. Use this dialog box to apply predefined hatch patterns. The *.*chx* files are used to save the predefined hatch patterns.

Generating the Half Section View Using the Half Section View Tool

Menu:	Insert > View > Half Section View
Toolbar:	Drawing > Section View > Half Section View

The **Half Section View** tool is used for generating the half section view of a drawing view. The **Half Section View** tool also helps you to generate section views of a required length from the parent drawing view. To generate the half section view, choose the **Half Section View** button from the **Drawing** toolbar. The **Half Section View** dialog box will be displayed and you will be prompted to select the parent view. On selecting the parent view, the section line attached with the cursor will be displayed and you will be prompted to specify the cut position by inferred point. Specify the pivot point to fix the section line; you will be prompted to specify the bend position by inferred point. Move the cursor around the pivot point and specify the bending position for the section line, as shown in Figure 13-18. On specifying the bend position, you will be prompted to indicate the center of the section view on the sheet. Specify the center point to place the generated half section view; the half section view will be placed at the center point specified on the sheet, as shown in Figure 13-19. Press the **Esc** key to exit the tool.

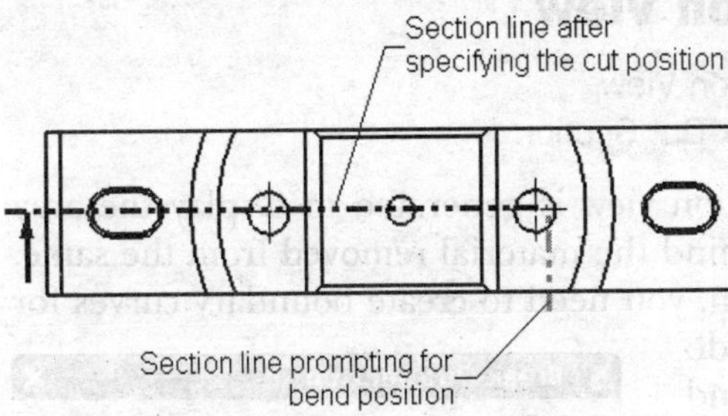

Figure 13-18 Section line prompting for the bend position

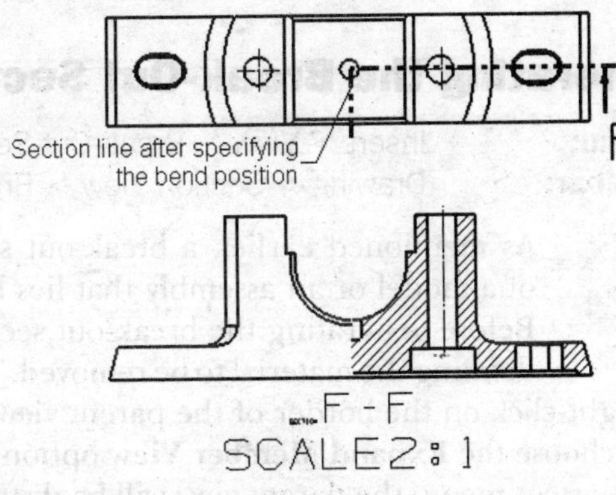

Figure 13-19 Half section view generated

Generating the Revolved Section View

Menu:	Insert > View > Revolved Section View
Toolbar:	Drawing > Section View > Revolved Section View

As mentioned earlier, a revolved section view is generated for the drawing views that are revolved about an axis. To create a revolved section view for an existing drawing view, choose the **Revolved Section View** button from the **Drawing** toolbar; you will be prompted to select the parent view. Select the parent view for generating the revolved section view; the section line attached with the cursor will be displayed and you will be prompted to specify the revolution point. Specify the revolution point on the parent view to fix the center of revolution for the section line, refer to Figure 13-20. After specifying the revolution point for the section line, you need to fix the angle of the first and second legs of the section line by moving the cursor dynamically. After positioning the section line, you need to specify the location for placing the revolved section view. Click the left mouse button to place the view at the required position; the revolved section view will be generated, refer to Figure 13-21.

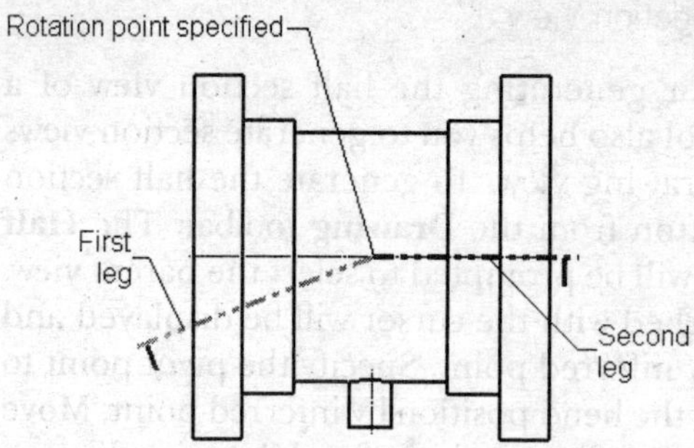

Figure 13-20 Section line after specifying the rotation point

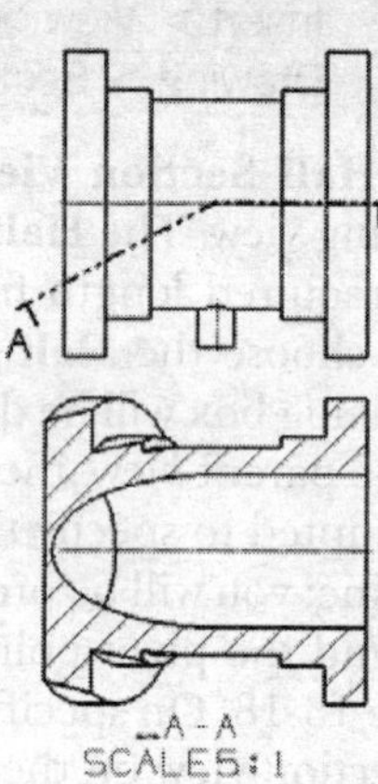

Figure 13-21 The revolved section view

Generating the Break-Out Section View

Menu:	Insert > View > Break-Out Section View
Toolbar:	Drawing > Section View > Break-Out Section

As mentioned earlier, a break-out section view is generated to display the area of a model or an assembly that lies behind the material removed from the same. Before generating the break-out section, you need to create boundary curves for defining the material to be removed. To do so, right-click on the border of the parent view, and then choose the **Expand Member View** option from the shortcut menu; the parent view will be displayed in the **WORK In Member View** window. Next, you need to draw boundary curves by using the **Curve** toolbar. The boundary curve must be closed if it is a single curve. If there are more than two or equal to two curves, the separate curves will close automatically. After drawing the boundary curve, exit the drafting environment by right-clicking on the border of the parent view and then choose the **Expand Member View** option from the shortcut menu. Next, choose the **Break-Out Section** button from the **Drawing** toolbar; the **Break-Out Section** dialog box will be displayed, as shown in Figure 13-22.

Figure 13-22 The Break-Out Section dialog box

To generate a new break-out section, you need to select the **Create** radio button. To edit an already generated break-out section, select the **Edit** radio button. To delete an already defined break-out section, select the **Delete** radio button. By default, the **Create** radio button is selected from the **Break-Out Section** dialog box. Also, the **Select View** button will be enabled and you will be prompted to select a view for the break-out section. Select the parent view. After you select the parent view, all the other buttons except the **Modify Boundary Curves** button will be enabled and you will be prompted to specify the inferred point. Specify the base point by using the curves in the drawing view. The base point is the reference point from which the boundary curve is swept through the model along the extrusion vector direction. Next, you will be prompted to define the extrusion vector. By default, the Z axis is selected for specifying the vector direction. To define the direction, define the vector by selecting the curves from the drawing view or by using the **Inferred Vector** drop-down list. The **Reverse Vector** button is used to reverse the direction of the extrusion vector. If the **Cut Through Model** check box is selected, then the boundary curve will be swept through the model in both directions. Choose the **Select Curves** button; you will be prompted to select a break line near the start of the line. Select the boundary curve created, as shown in Figure 13-23, and choose the **Apply** button. The break-out section is generated, as shown in Figure 13-24.

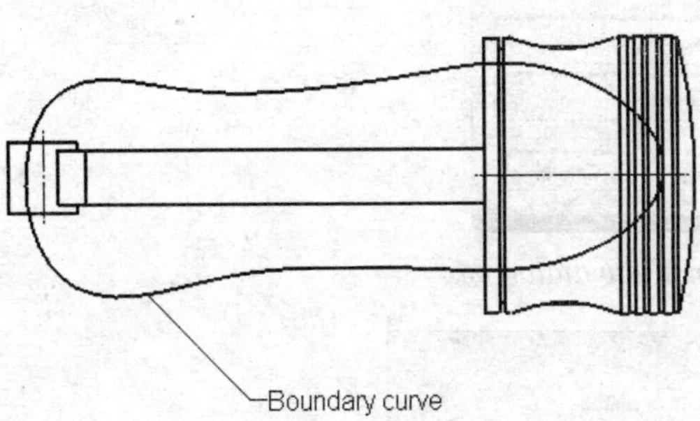

***Figure 13-23** The boundary curve defined for generating the break-out section view*

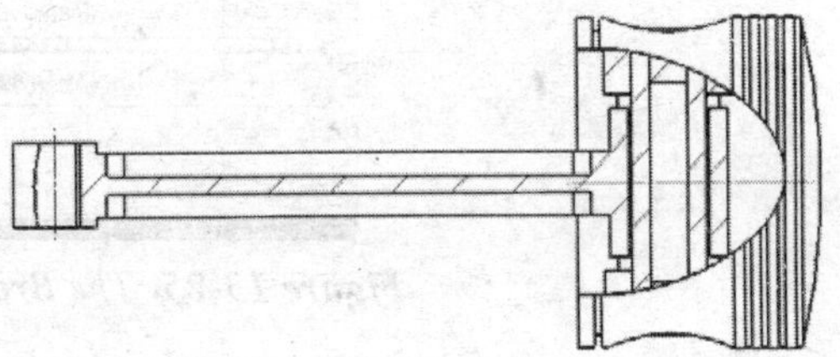

***Figure 13-24** The resulting break-out section view*

Generating the Broken View

Menu:	Insert > View > Broken View
Toolbar:	Drawing > Base View > Broken View

The **Broken View** tool is used to generate a broken view for an existing drawing view that has a high length to width aspect ratio. In such cases, the view is broken at an intermediate distance to fit into the drawing sheet as a normal drawing view. Note that this tool does not create a separate drawing view.

In NX, you need to define a closed boundary for removing the unwanted portion of the view. The part of the drawing view enclosed in the closed boundary will exist and the portion outside the closed boundary will be eliminated from the view. You can draw any number of closed boundaries to include the portion of the view to be displayed. To generate the broken view for a drawing view, select the parent view and choose the **Broken View** button from the **Drawing** toolbar; the **Broken View** dialog box will be displayed, as shown in Figure 13-25. Also, the **Tracking Bar** dialog box will be displayed, as shown in Figure 13-26.

*Figure 13-25 The **Broken View** dialog box*

*Figure 13-26 The **Tracking Bar** dialog box*

If there is only one drawing view on the sheet, you can choose the **Broken View** button directly without selecting the parent drawing view. The parent view will be displayed in the **WORK In Member View** window and you will be prompted to define the start point for the closed boundary. Select the required curve option for defining the boundary from the **Curve Type** drop-down list and start creating the boundary.

Curve Type Drop-down List

By default, the **Simple Break** curve type is selected from the **Curve Type** drop-down list. After you create a type of curve by selecting it, the curve type changes to a construction line type. After you specify the start point for the closed boundary, the **Mirror Spline** button is enabled in the **Broken View** dialog box. Also, the **Spline Amplitude** edit box is enabled in the **Tracking Bar** dialog box.

You can control the amplitude of a spline by entering the amplitude value in the **Spline Amplitude** edit box of the **Tracking Bar** dialog box. You can reverse a spline about 180 degrees with respect to the axis of the defined spline. After creating a separate closed boundary, you are prompted to define an anchor point. You can specify the anchor point in or outside the closed boundary. The anchor point is specified to fix a model with respect to a drawing view and to associate the closed boundary created to the model. At any phase of generating the broken view, you can return to the drawing sheet by choosing the **Display Drawing Sheet** button. To create a new closed boundary, choose the **Apply** button from the **Broken View** dialog box. Note that the **Apply** button is enabled only after specifying the anchor point. After creating all the required closed boundaries, choose the **OK** button from the same dialog box to create the broken view of the defined closed boundaries. Figure 13-27 shows the closed boundaries selected and Figure 13-28 shows the resulting broken view.

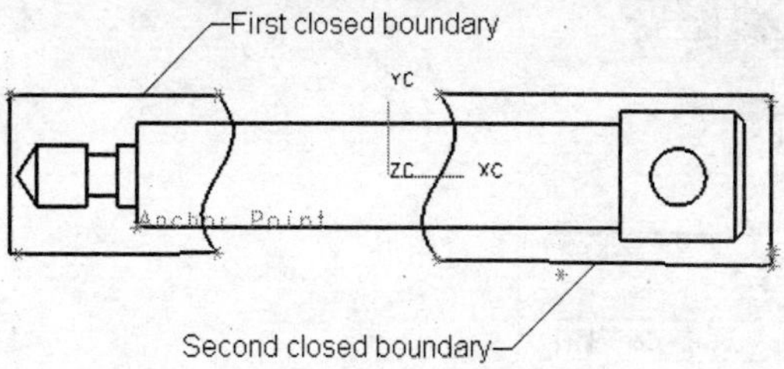

Figure 13-27 *The closed boundaries created to define the broken view*

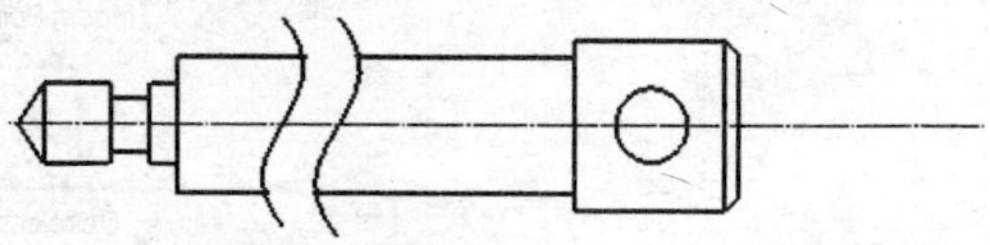

Figure 13-28 *Resulting broken view*

You can snap the endpoints of the construction line to the endpoints of the vertical, horizontal, and 45 degrees inclined lines by selecting the **Snap Construction Lines** check box. After generating the broken view, you can also dynamically change the distance between the break region by using the **Position Break Region** button from the **Broken View** dialog box. To modify the distance between the break region, choose the **Position Break Region** button from the **Broken View** dialog box, and then select the **Preview and Position** check box; the drawing view will be displayed in the drawing sheet and you will be prompted to select a break region to be positioned. Select the break region. After selecting the break region, the **XC** and **YC** edit boxes of the **Tracking Bar** dialog box will be enabled and you will be prompted to specify the new position. You can specify the new position for the break region by entering the coordinates value in the **XC** and **YC** edit boxes in the **Tracking Bar** dialog box or by dynamically moving the break region and specifying the destination point by pressing the left mouse button.

MANIPULATING THE DRAWING VIEWS

After the drawing views are created, it is important to learn how they can be modified or edited. The following editing operations can be performed on the existing drawing views.

Aligning the Drawing Views Using the Align View Tool

Menu: Edit > View > Align View
Toolbar: Drawing > Align View *(Customize to add)*

The **Align View** tool is used to align the generated drawing views as per requirement. To align the generated drawing views, choose the **Align View** button from the **Drawing** toolbar; the **Align View** dialog box will be displayed, refer to Figure 13-29. In the list box of the **Align View** dialog box, all names of the drawing views in the drawing sheet are listed. The options in the **Align View** dialog box are discussed next.

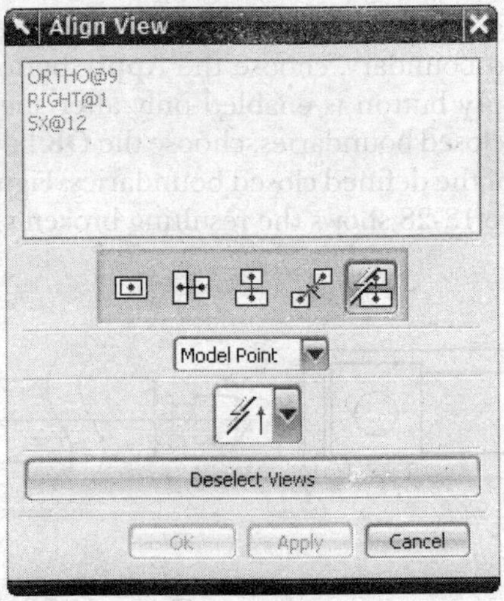

Figure 13-29 The ***Align View*** *dialog box*

Alignment Options Drop-down List

The **Alignment Options** drop-down list consists of various types of aligning methods. It contains the reference point selection method. The selected drawing views are aligned in accordance to the reference point specified. If the **View Centers** option is selected from the **Alignment Options** drop-down list, the center points of the drawing views will coincide with each other at the time of aligning. If the **Point to Point** option is selected, you can specify the reference point both from the stationary view and all the other views meant for aligning. If the **Model Point** option is selected, then the reference point selected in the stationary view is considered as the reference point for all the views meant for aligning.

Methods for Aligning Drawing Views

After selecting the required alignment option from the **Alignment Options** drop-down list, the stationary drawing view, and the drawing views to align, you need to define the method of alignment.

Overlay

The **Overlay** button from the **Align View** dialog box is used to superimpose the drawing views one over the other. After selecting the required alignment option from the **Alignment Options** drop-down list, the stationary drawing view, and the drawing views to align. Choose the **Overlay** button from the **Align View** dialog box. The selected drawing views will be overlaid on the stationary view as per the alignment points.

Horizontally

The **Horizontally** button is used to align the drawing views horizontal to each other. After selecting the required alignment option from the **Alignment Options** drop-down list, the stationary drawing view, and the drawing views to align. Choose the **Horizontally** button from the **Align View** dialog box. The drawing views will be aligned horizontally with respect to the stationary view as per the alignment points.

Vertically

The **Vertically** button is used to align the drawing views vertical to each other. After selecting the required alignment option from the **Alignment Options** drop-down list, the stationary drawing view, and the drawing views to align. Choose the **Vertically** button from the **Align View** dialog box. The selected drawing views will be aligned vertically with the stationary view as per the alignment points.

Perpendicular to a Line

The **Perpendicular to a Line** button is used to align the drawing views normal to each other with respect to a reference line. First, you need to create a reference line in the drawing view, which is selected as the stationary view. To create a reference line, select the stationary view, right-click on it, and then choose the **Expand Member View** option from the shortcut menu. In the **WORK in Member View** window, you can create a reference line by choosing the **Line** button from the **Curve** toolbar. After creating a reference line, exit the **WORK In Member View** window by right-clicking in the same window and then choosing the **Expand Member View** option from the shortcut menu. Select the required alignment option from the **Alignment Options** drop-down list and the drawing views to align. Next, choose the **Perpendicular to a Line** button from the **Align View** dialog box; you will be prompted to define a reference line. Select the reference line created in the **WORK In Member View** window and press the middle mouse button; the selected views will be aligned normal to each other.

Infer

The **Infer** button is chosen from the **Align View** dialog box to align the drawing views among the four available methods of aligning. The aligning will be done according to the selection procedure. For example, if you select two drawing views and a reference line, then the drawing views will be aligned normal to each other.

View Boundary

Menu:	Edit > View > View Boundary
Toolbar:	Drawing > View Boundary *(Customize to add)*

The **View Boundary** tool is used to create the outer boundary for enclosing the drawing views. To create the outer boundary, choose the **View Boundary** button from the **Drawing** toolbar; the **View Boundary** dialog box will be displayed, refer to Figure 13-30. Also, the names of the drawing views in the drawing sheet will be displayed in the list box of the **View Boundary** dialog box and you will be prompted to select a view to define the view boundary. Select the drawing view to define the view boundary; some of the buttons of the dialog box will be enabled. If you want to increase or decrease the diameter of the detail view boundary, select the **Break Line / Detail** option from the **View Boundary Type** drop-down list. Next, select the circle created using the **Detail View** tool; the circumference of the circle is attached with the cursor. Now, you can increase or decrease the diameter of the boundary of the detail view by move the cursor away or toward the center point. If you select the **Automatic Rectangle** option, then a rectangular boundary will be created and enclose the selected drawing view. If you want to enclose the drawing view by drawing a rectangle manually, then select the **Manual Rectangle** option. In the above said case, the rectangle drawn should not touch the other drawing views.

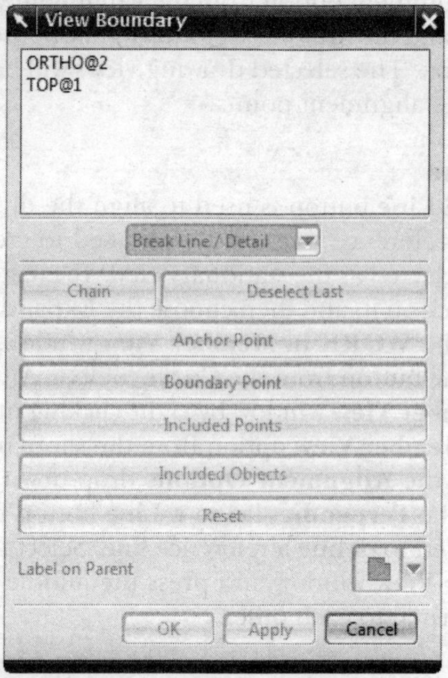

***Figure 13-30** The **View Boundary** dialog box*

Anchor Point

The **Anchor Point** button in the **View Boundary** dialog box is used to specify an anchor point for the drawing view. Generally, the anchor point is specified to fix the drawing view at a position. Any further changes made in the model will be updated in the drawing view with respect to the anchor point specified. To specify an anchor point, choose the **Anchor Point** button from the **View Boundary** dialog box. Next, specify the anchor point on the drawing view and choose the **Apply** button.

Displaying the Model Using the Display Sheet Tool

Menu:	View > Display Sheet
Toolbar:	Drawing > Display Sheet *(Customize to add)*

The **Display Sheet** button is used to toggle between the modeling view display and the drawing view display. To change the drawing view display of a model to the modeling view display, choose the **Display Sheet** button from the **Drawing** toolbar. To display the drawing view again, choose the **Display Sheet** button from the **Drawing** toolbar.

Inserting a Drawing Sheet Using the New Sheet Tool

Menu:	Insert > Sheet
Toolbar:	Drawing > New Sheet

In NX, you can add any number of drawing sheets to a drawing file. After generating the drawing views in the first drawing sheet, you may need to add a new drawing sheet. To add the new drawing sheet in the Drafting environment, choose the **New Sheet** button from the **Drawing** toolbar to display the **Sheet** dialog box. Enter the parameters for the new drawing sheet in their respective edit boxes and choose the **OK** button from the **Sheet** dialog box; the new sheet will be created and displayed in the Drafting environment.

MODIFYING THE PROPERTIES OF A GENERATED DRAWING VIEW

The properties of the generated drawing views can be edited by using the methods discussed next.

Modifying the Scale Value of the Drawing View

By default, the scale value of a generated drawing view is 1:1. If the scale value specified to the drawing view does not satisfy the requirement, you can modify the scale value To modify the scale value, select the view and right-click on it. Next, choose the **Style** option from the shortcut menu; the **View Style** dialog box will be displayed, as shown in Figure 13-31.

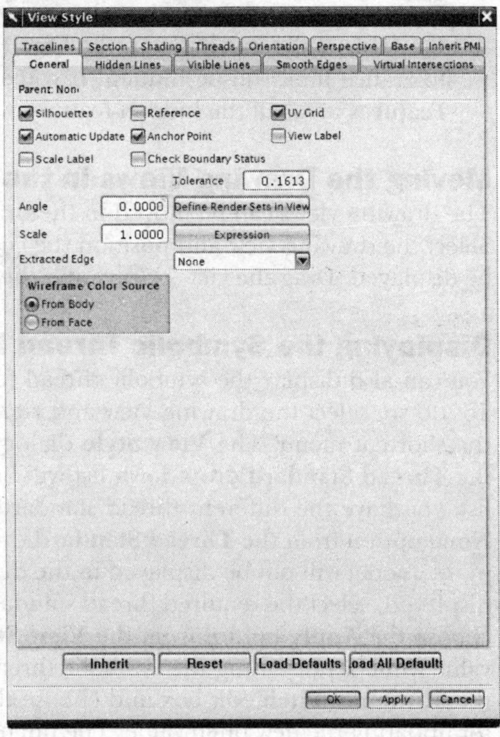

*Figure 13-31 The **View Style** dialog box*

Choose the **General** tab from the **View Style** dialog box. Enter the new scale value in the **Scale** edit box and choose the **Apply** button. You can also align the drawing view at an angle in the view boundary by specifying the angle value in the **Angle** edit box of the **General** tab. By selecting the **View Label** check box from the **General** tab, you can display the view label for the drawing view selected. By selecting the **Scale Label** check box from the **General** tab, you can display the scale label for the drawing view selected. By selecting the **Reference** check box from the **General** tab, you can display only the reference origin and not the drawing view.

Displaying Hidden Lines in a Drawing View

When the drawing views are generated from the model that has internal edges, then the internal edges will not be displayed in the view, unless it is a section view. To display the hidden lines as dashed lines or dotted lines, select the drawing view and right-click on it. Next, select the **Style** option from the shortcut menu; the **View Style** dialog box will be displayed. Choose the **Hidden Lines** tab, which contains the parameters for displaying the hidden lines in the drawing view. The **Hidden Line** check box will be selected by default in the **Hidden Lines** tab. In the **Hidden Lines** tab, you have the **Font** and **Width** drop-down lists for modifying the style of the hidden lines. The **Font** drop-down list consists of various line types used at various places in the drawing view and the **Width** drop-down list consists of lines with various predefined line widths, and these are used at various places in the drawing views. Select the **Dashed** option from the **Font** drop-down list and the **Normal** option from the **Width** drop-down list. The color of the hidden line can be changed using the **Color** swatch in the **Hidden Lines** tab. Choose the **Apply** button and then the **OK** button to exit the **View Style** dialog box.

Other Options in the Hidden Lines Tab

To display the hidden edges, select the **Edges Hidden by Edges** check box. If you have too many small features in the model, then you can filter their display by fixing a cutoff percentage regarding their size using the **Small Features** slider. You can restrict displaying the small features by selecting the **Simplify** radio button from the **Small Features** area and fixing the tolerance value using the **Small Features** slider. If you select the **Hide** radio button from the **Small Features** area, then the features in the selected tolerance limit will be hidden. If you select the **Show All** radio button from the **Small Features** area, all the hidden features will be displayed in the drawing view.

Moving the Drawing Views in the Drawing Sheet

The drawing views can be moved in the drawing limits area and be dynamically positioned. Select the drawing view and position the cursor over the view boundary; the drag cursor will be displayed. Drag the view by pressing the left mouse button and dynamically position it.

Displaying the Symbolic Thread Feature

You can also display the symbolic thread feature created in the model in the drawing view. To do so, select the drawing view and right- click on it. Next, select the **Style** option from the shortcut menu. The **View Style** dialog box will be displayed; choose the **Threads** tab; the **Thread Standard** drop-down list will be displayed. In the **Thread Standard** drop-down list, you have the different thread standards, along with the **None** option. If you select the **None** option from the **Thread Standard** drop-down list, the symbolic thread feature created in the model will not be displayed in the drawing view. If you want the symbolic thread to be displayed, select the required thread standard from the **Thread Standard** drop-down list and choose the **Apply** button from the **View Style** dialog box. You can also define a fake pitch value while representing the symbolic threads in the drawing view. Enter the pitch value in the **Minimum Pitch** edit box and choose the **Apply** button from the **View Style** dialog box for updating the new pitch value. The pitch value entered while generating the drawing view is not associated with the pitch specified in the model. The original pitch specified in the model remains unchanged. If the threads are still not displayed in the drawing view, choose the **Hidden Line** tab and clear the **Hidden Line** check box. Choose the **Apply** button; the threads will be displayed.

ADDING DIMENSIONS TO THE DRAWING VIEWS

After you generate the drawing views, you need to add dimensions to them. In NX, you can add dimensions by using two methods. One is the generative method of retrieving the dimensions and the other is the interactive method of creating them. These methods are discussed next.

Retrieving Dimensions from the Model

Menu:	Insert > Feature Parameters
Toolbar:	Annotation > Feature Parameters *(Customize to add)*

The process of retrieving a dimension applied to a model in the **Drafting** environment is known as generative dimensioning. To retrieve dimensions, choose the **Feature Parameters** button from the **Annotation** toolbar; the **Feature Parameters** dialog box will be displayed, as shown in Figure 13-32. The features created in the model will be listed in the list box of the **Feature Parameters** dialog box. Select the feature for which the dimensions are to be retrieved from the model. Next, choose the **Select Views** button from the **Feature Parameters** dialog box and select the views for which the dimensions are to be retrieved. To adopt a selective dimension standard for drafting, select the required dimension standard from the **Template** drop-down list of the **Feature Parameters** dialog box. Choose the **Apply** button from the **Feature Parameters** dialog box for displaying the retrieved dimensions.

Adding Dimensions to the Drawing View

Although generating the dimensions from the parent model is the most effective way of dimensioning, sometimes you may also have to dimension the drawing views manually. The tools for dimensioning the drawing view manually are available in the **Dimension** toolbar. These options are the same as those discussed in the Sketching environment.

In addition to the dimensioning method in the Sketching environment, you have four more methods of dimensioning in the Drafting environment. These methods are discussed next.

Chamfer Dimensioning

Menu:	Insert > Dimension > Chamfer
Toolbar:	Dimension > Inferred > Chamfer

The **Chamfer** tool in the **Dimension** toolbar is used to dimension the chamfer feature. The method adopted for creating a chamfer feature in the model can be shown in the drawing view. To create the chamfer dimension, choose the **Chamfer** button from the **Dimension** toolbar; you will be prompted to select a linear object for chamfer dimension. Select the linear edge (chamfer); the dimension of the chamfer gets attached to the cursor. Place the dimension at the required position. Note that if you want to change the orientation of the dimension, then you need to select the corresponding edge for orientation. To edit the chamfer dimension, right-click on it and select the **Style**

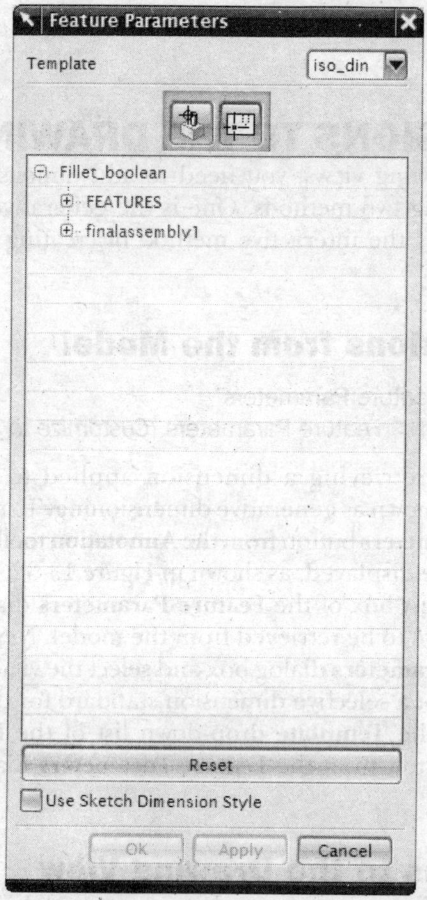

*Figure 13-32 The **Feature Parameters** dialog box*

option from the shortcut menu. The **Annotation Style** dialog box will be displayed. In the **Chamfer** area of the **Dimension** tab, you have various methods to denote a chamfer feature. After you select the required options from the drop-down list, choose the **Apply** button from the **Annotation Style** dialog box to reflect the changes.

Cylindrical Dimensioning

Menu: Insert > Dimension > Cylindrical
Toolbar: Dimension > Inferred > Cylindrical

The **Cylindrical** tool from the **Dimension** toolbar is used to generate the dimension for the front view of the cylindrical section. To create the **Cylindrical** dimension, choose the **Cylindrical** button from the **Dimension** toolbar; you will be prompted to select the first object for the cylindrical dimension. Select the first silhouette edge of the cylinder; you will be prompted to select the second object for cylindrical dimension. Select the second silhouette edge and press the left mouse button for placing the generated dimension.

Baseline Dimensioning

Menu:	Insert > Dimension > Horizontal Baseline / Vertical Baseline
Toolbar:	Dimension > Horizontal Baseline / Vertical Baseline *(Customize to add)*

The baseline dimensioning is defined as the method of creating dimensions by taking one dimension as a common reference. The **Dimension** toolbar contains two types of base line dimensioning tools. Generally, the baseline dimensions are given in the drawing view by taking a reference dimension in the horizontal or vertical direction.

Horizontal Baseline Dimensions

To create the horizontal baseline dimensions, choose the **Horizontal Baseline** button from the **Dimension** toolbar. You will be prompted to select the first object for the horizontal baseline dimension. Select any of the vertical objects from the drawing view; you will be prompted to select other objects for the baseline dimension. Select the other vertical object; again you will be prompted to select objects for the baseline dimension. Select the other vertical object to create the dimensions and press the left mouse button outside the drawing view to place it.

Vertical Baseline Dimensions

To create a vertical baseline dimensions, choose the **Vertical Baseline** button from the **Dimension** toolbar. You will be prompted to select the first object for the vertical baseline dimension. Select any of the horizontal objects from the drawing view. You will be prompted to select the other objects for the baseline dimensions. Select the other horizontal object; again you will be prompted to select objects for the baseline dimension. Select the other horizontal object to create the dimensions and the press left mouse button outside the drawing view to place the dimensions created.

Note

After you generate the dimensions, you can edit them individually. To modify a dimension, right-click on it and select the ***Style*** *option from the shortcut menu; the* ***Annotation Style*** *dialog box will be displayed. You can make the changes through the* ***Annotation Style*** *dialog box, as discussed earlier. The dimensions generated by the* ***Horizontal Baseline*** *and* ***Vertical Baseline*** *tools are in absolute mode with respect to the reference object selected.*

Chain Dimensioning

Menu:	Insert > Dimension > Horizontal Chain / Vertical Chain
Toolbar:	Dimension > Horizontal Chain / Vertical Chain

Chain dimensioning is defined as the method of applying dimensions to a set of horizontal objects or vertical objects, which are situated at a successive distance. The dimensions are created in the incremental mode.

Horizontal Chain Dimensions

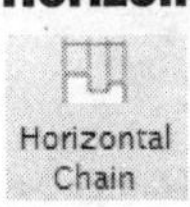

To create the horizontal chain dimensions, choose the **Horizontal Chain** button from the **Dimension** toolbar. On doing so, you will be prompted to select the first object for the horizontal chain dimension. Select any of the vertical object; the selected object will be treated as the reference and the incremental dimensions will be created in either direction. Also, you will be prompted to select other objects for the chain dimensions. Select the vertical object; again you will be prompted to select other objects for the chain dimension. Select the other vertical object for the chain dimension and press the left mouse button for placing the chain dimensions created.

Vertical Chain Dimensions

To create the vertical chain dimensions, choose the **Vertical Chain** button from the **Dimension** toolbar. You will be prompted to select the first object for the vertical chain dimension. Select any horizontal object; the selected object will be treated as the reference and the incremental dimensions will be created in either direction. You will be prompted to select the other objects for the chain dimension. Select the horizontal object; again you will be prompted to select other objects for the chain dimension. Select the other vertical object for chain dimension and press the left mouse button for placing the chain dimensions created.

Note

*The dimensions generated by the **Horizontal Chain** and the **Vertical Chain** tool are in the incremental mode with respect to the reference object selected.*

GENERATING EXPLODED VIEWS OF AN ASSEMBLY

Menu:	Insert > View > Base View
Toolbar:	Drawing > Base View

In NX, you can generate drawing view for the exploded state of an assembly. To generate drawing view, choose the **Base View** button from the **Drawing** toolbar; the **Base View** dialog box will be displayed. In this dialog box, select the **TFR-TRI** option from the **Model View to Use** drop-down list; the exploded view created in the Assembly environment will be generated as the drawing view. Next, place the exploded view in the drawing sheet, refer to Figure 13-33. Irrespective of the orientation of the assembly in the Assembly environment, the orientation of the drawing view generated for the exploded state of an assembly is always isometric. Note that before creating the base view, the assembly must be exploded in the Assembly environment.

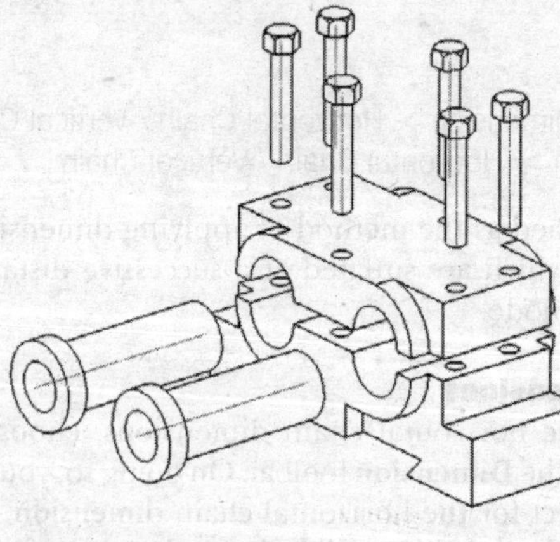

Figure 13-33 The drawing view generated for the exploded state of an assembly

CREATING PARTS LIST AND ASSOCIATIVE BALLOONS

For every assembly drawing, the details about the components such as the component name, number of the same components utilized in the assembly and material property of the component are listed in a tabular format known as the Bill of Materials. In NX, the Bill of Materials is called as the Parts List.

Creating a Parts List for an Assembly

Menu:	Insert > Parts List
Toolbar:	Tables > Tabular Note > Parts List

To create the parts list for an assembly, choose the **Parts List** button from the **Tables** toolbar; you will be prompted to indicate a position for the new parts list. Specify a point for placing the parts list. The generated parts list after increasing the cell size is shown in Figure 13-34. You can create the parts list for the assembly by using any drawing view of the assembly. You can dynamically modify the width and height of the cells of the parts list by dragging the cell borders with the left mouse button pressed. To edit the default text in the cells of the **Parts List**, double-click on cells; the **Attribute Cell Edit** message box will be displayed. Choose the **OK** button from this message box and enter the text in the text box. To change the text size, choose the cell or collection of cells and right-click. Next, select the **Cell Style** option from the shortcut menu. The **Annotation Style** dialog box will be displayed. Enter the new text size in the **Character Size** edit box and choose the **Apply** button and then the **OK** button. The parts list will be created for the assembly opened in the Modeling environment of NX.

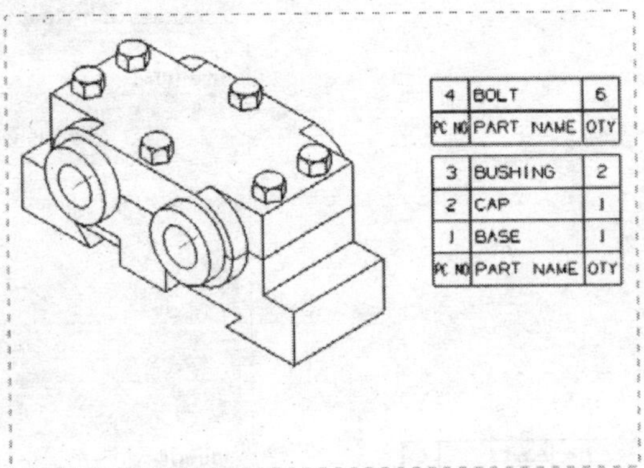

Figure 13-34 The resulting drawing sheet after generating the parts list

Creating Associative Balloons

Toolbar:	Tables > Tabular Note > Auto Balloon

Associative balloons are created to identify the components in an assembly, which are listed in the parts list. To create associative balloons, choose the **Auto balloon** button from the **Tables** toolbar; the **Parts List Auto Balloon** dialog box will be displayed and you will be prompted to select the parts list to autoballoon. Select the parts list and choose the **OK** button; the **Parts List Auto Balloon** dialog box will be modified and the list of drawing views will be displayed in it. Select the view to which you want to add the balloons from the list area and choose the **OK** button; autoballoons will be added to the specified drawing views. Note that if a single drawing view is available in the drawing sheet, the autoballoons will be added automatically to the drawing view on selecting the part list. Figure 13-35 shows the autoballoons created after modifying their positions. To modify the position of the balloon, double-click on a balloon; the **Identification Symbol** dialog box will be displayed, as shown in Figure 13- 36. You can specify the location of the balloon by using the **Origin** rollout of this dialog box. To do so, click on the **Specify Location** area in the **Origin** rollout; you will be prompted to specify the new origin location. Click in the drawing sheet; the balloon will be placed at the specified location. You can modify the leader of a balloon by using the **Leader** rollout. Similarly, to modify the size ID symbol, enter a new value in the **Size** edit box in the **Settings** rollout. Next, choose the **OK** button to reflect the changes made. You can also navigate to the part listed in the parts list from the corresponding autoballoon. To do so, select the autoballoon and right-click on it. Next, choose the **Navigate to Parts List Row** option from the shortcut menu. The part name, corresponding to the selected autoballoon, will be zoomed to fit and displayed.

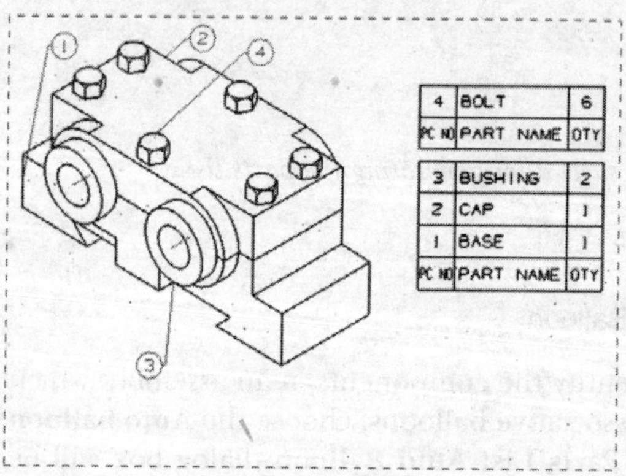

Figure 13-35 The drawing sheet with autoballoons created

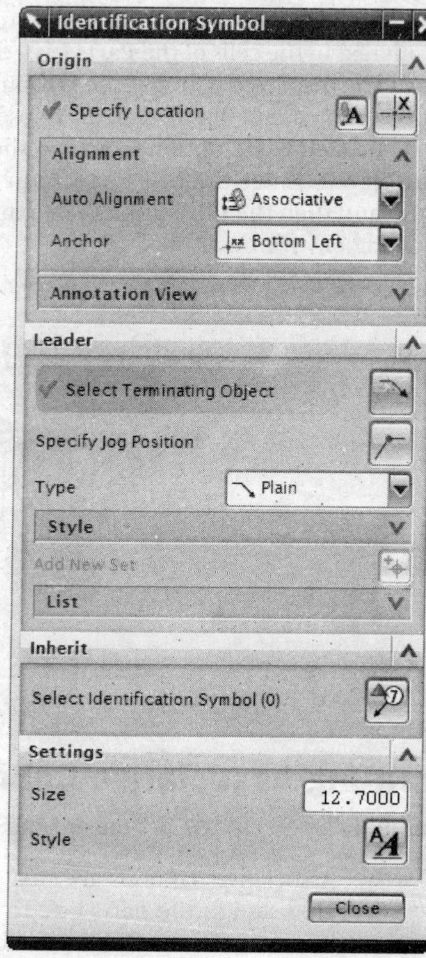

*Figure 13-36 The **Identification Symbol** dialog box*

Creating a Tabular Note (Title Block)

Menu:	Insert > Table > Tabular Note
Toolbar:	Tables > Tabular Note

The title block of a drawing sheet consists of details about a drafting work such as the name of the draftsman, date of drafting, name of the person who verified the drafting, the angle of projection method adopted, and so on. In NX, the title block is termed as the tabular note. The drawing sheet created for the shop floor also contains the name and logo of a company, and sheet number details. To create a user-defined tabular note, choose the **Tabular Note** button from the **Tables** toolbar; you will be prompted to indicate a position for the new tabular note. Specify a point for placing the tabular note; the default tabular note with five rows and columns will be placed. To enter text in the cells, double-click in the respective cell; a text box will be displayed. Enter the required text and press the ENTER key.

Resizing and Merging the Rows and Columns of the Tabular Note

You can dynamically resize the rows and columns by dragging the borders. If you want to merge two or more cells together, select the cells by dragging the cursor on them with the left mouse button pressed. The selected cells will be highlighted in red. Right-click in the selection area and select the **Merge Cells** option from the shortcut menu. To delete a row or column, select the row or column and right-click on it and select the **Delete** option from the shortcut menu. The selected row or column will be deleted. To modify the size of the text in the tabular note, select the cell and right-click. Choose the **Style** option from the shortcut menu; the **Annotation Style** dialog box will be displayed. Enter a new value for the text in the **Character Size** edit box, choose the **Apply** button and then the **OK** button to reflect the changes. Figure 13-37 shows a tabular note that is created and modified to be accommodated in the drawing sheet.

Adding a User-defined Tabular Note to the Tables Palette

After you create the required tabular note, you can add it to the library also. To add a user-defined tabular note in the library, select the tabular note from the left-upper corner and right-click on it. Next, select the **Save as Template** option from the shortcut menu; the **Save As Template** dialog box will be displayed and you will be prompted to specify a name for the template. Enter the name in the **File name** drop-down list and choose the **OK** button; the tabular note will be saved. By default, the user-defined tabular notes are saved in **Program Files > UGS > NX 7.0 >UG II > table_files.**

Inserting the Company Logo (Image) into the Tabular Note

Menu:	Insert > Image
Toolbar:	Annotation > Image *(Customize to add)*

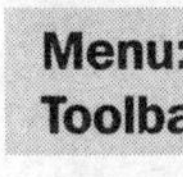

After entering the required data in the cells of the tabular note, you may need to insert the company logo also. You can insert an image into the drawing sheet, which has the file name extension as .JPG, .TIFF or .PNG. To insert the image, choose the **Image** button from the **Annotation** toolbar; the **Open Image** dialog box will be displayed. Browse to the image and choose the **OK** button; the image will be displayed in the drawing sheet, along with the handles and the **Image Display** options. By choosing the **Lock Aspect** button from the **Image Display** options, you can lock the aspect ratio for the scaling and further scaling will be uniform as per the locking made. Using the translational handles, you can position the image at any area in the drawing sheet. The drawing sheet after inserting the company logo is shown in Figure 13-38.

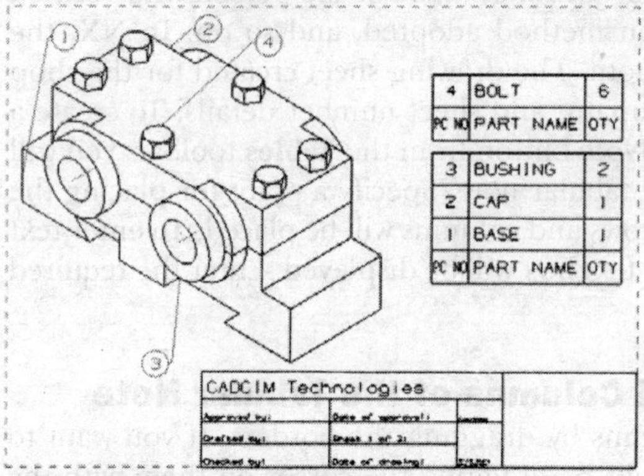

Figure 13-37 The drawing sheet with the tabular note (title block)

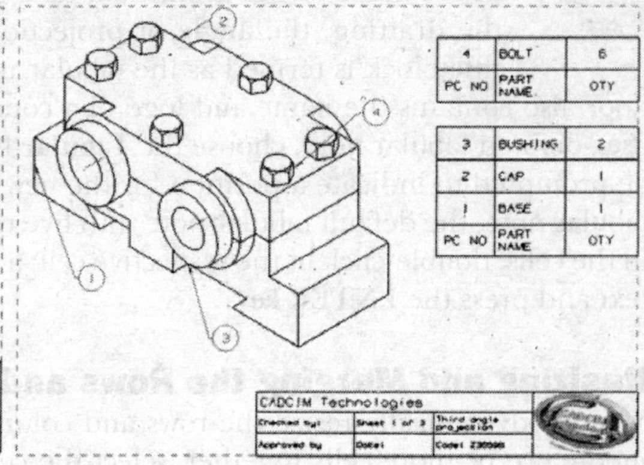

Figure 13-38 The drawing sheet after inserting the image

ADDING MULTILINE TEXT TO A DRAWING SHEET

Menu: Insert > Note
Toolbar: Annotation > Note *(Customize to add)*

To enter a multiline text in the drawing, choose the **Note** button from the **Annotation** toolbar; the **Note** dialog box will be displayed, as shown in Figure 13-39. Enter the text to be added in the drawing view in the text edit box in the **Text Input** rollout. After entering the text, you can place it by clicking in the drawing limits area. Press the middle mouse button to exit the tool.

You can specify the view and alignment of the text in the **Origin** rollout. You can edit and format the text written in the text edit box in the **Text Input** rollout using the **Edit Text** and **Formatting** sub-rollouts, respectively. You can add geometrical symbols to the multiline text using the **Symbols** sub-rollout. You can insert the text from the already saved *. *txt* files, using the **Insert Text From File** button. Similarly, you can save the created text in the *. *txt* file format using the **Save As** button in the **Import/Export** sub-rollout. To place the text vertically, choose the **Vertical Text** check box. You can modify the parameters of the text using the **Settings** rollout.

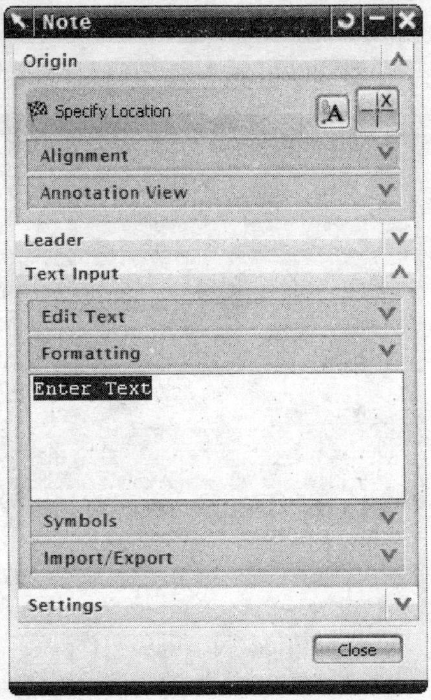

*Figure 13-39 The **Note** dialog box*

PRINTING TOOLS

After generating the required drawing views, you may need to print the drawing sheet to send it for manufacturing. Also, you need to create the quality print representations of your designs. This can be done using the following printing tools:

Print

Menu:	File > Print
Toolbar:	Standard > Print *(Customize to add)*

This tool is used to print the entities displayed in the drawing window. The entities to be printed may be solid model or drawing views of the solid model. To print the solid model, you need to invoke the Modeling environment. Similarly, to print the drawing sheet, you need to invoke the Drafting environment.

Invoke the Modeling or Drafting environment and choose **File > Print** from the menu bar; the **Print** dialog box will be displayed, refer to Figure 13-40.

Select the name of the printer connected to your computer from the **Printer** drop-down list in the **Printer** rollout. Choose the **Properties** button; the printer properties dialog box will be displayed. You can use this dialog box to set the printing properties. After specifying the required options, choose **OK** from the printer properties dialog box.

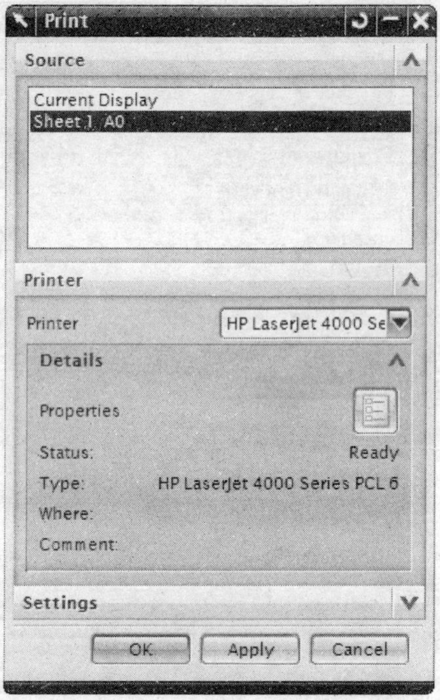

*Figure 13-40 The **Print** dialog box*

To change color settings of the printer, you can use the options in the **Output** drop-down list from the **Settings** rollout. Enter the number of copies to be printed in the **Number of copies** spinner and select the required check box from the **Settings** area. To set the printing quality, select the required option from the **Image Resolution** drop-down list. The various options in the **Print Options** area are discussed next.

After setting the required parameters, choose the **OK** button from the **Print** dialog box; the printer will start printing the file.

Plot

Menu: File > Plot

The **Plot** tool is used to create quality print representations of your designs. You can save the output of the file in the TIFF, JPEG, EMF, CGM, and PNG format. To plot the drawing sheet, choose **File > Plot** from the menu bar; the **Plot** dialog box will be displayed, as shown in Figure 13-41.

Select the required output format of the file from the **Printer** drop-down list of the **Plotter** rollout. The options available in this drop-down list include TIFF, JPEG, EMF, CGM, and PNG. Next, choose the **Browse** button from the **Plotter** rollout and specify the location to save the output file. If you want to set the advanced parameters, specify them in the **Banner**, **Actions**, **Color And Width**, and **Settings** rollouts. After setting the required parameters, choose the **OK** button; the file will be plotted at the specified location.

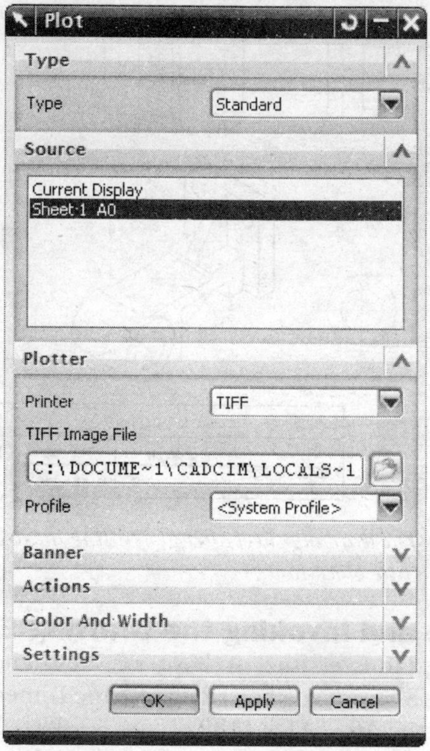

*Figure 13-41 The **Plot** dialog box*

TUTORIALS

Tutorial 1

In this tutorial, you will generate the top view, front view, right-side view, and isometric view of the model created in Exercise 2 of chapter 6. Use the standard A2 landscape sheet format for generating the drawing views. You will also create a tabular note for the drawing sheet and add an image to it and save it in the **Tables** palette. After generating the drawing views of the model and creating the tabular note, the drawing sheet will appear, as shown in Figure 13-42. **(Expected time: 1 hr)**

The following steps are required to complete this tutorial:

a. Open the model created in Exercise 2 of chapter 6 and then invoke the Drafting environment.
b. Generate the drawing views of the model.
c. Add a tabular note to the drawing sheet.
d. Insert the logo of company into the tabular note.
e. Add the tabular note to the **Tables** palette.
f. Print the drawing sheet.
g. Plot the drawing sheet.
h. Save the drawing file.

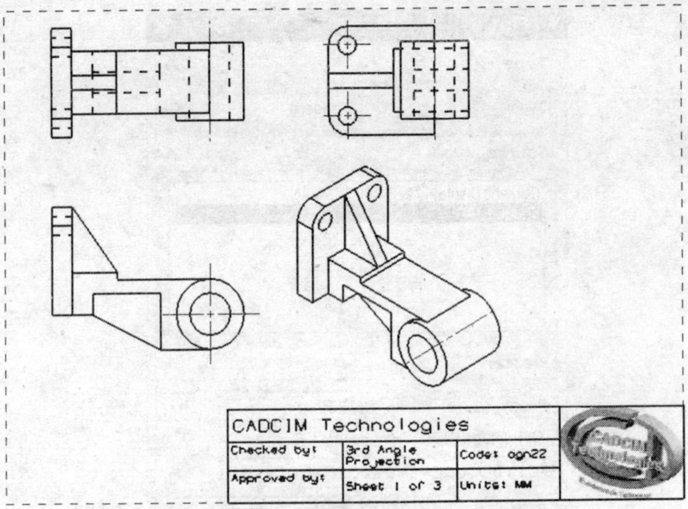

Figure 13-42 The drawing sheet after generating the drawing views and adding the title block to it

Opening the Part File and Invoking the Drafting Environment

1. Open the part file created in Exercise 2 of chapter 6. Next, choose **Start > Drafting** from the **Standard** toolbar; the **Sheet** dialog box along with the **Dimension** and **Drawing** toolbars is displayed. By default, the **A0 - 841 x 1189** option is selected in the **Size** drop-down list and the name of the drawing sheet is displayed as **Sheet 1** in the **Drawing Sheet Name** text box.

2. Select the sheet size **A2 - 420 x 594** from the **Size** drop-down list. By default, the **3rd Angle Projection** button is chosen and the **Millimeters** radio button is selected in the **Settings** rollout. The default scale value selected in the **Scale** drop-down list is **1:1**. Accept all the default parameters specified and choose the **OK** button to invoke the Drafting environment.

   Now, you are in the Drafting environment, and the empty drawing sheet along with the floating top view attached to the cursor is displayed. Also, the **Base View** dialog box is displayed, see Figure 13-43.

Note

*For the purpose of printing, you should turn off the display of grids. To do so, choose **Preferences > Grid and Work Plane** from the menu bar; the **Grid and Work Plane** dialog box is displayed. Clear the **Show** check box from the **Grid Settings** rollout and choose the **OK** button; the display of grids is turned off.*

Generating the Top, Front, and Right-Side Views of the Model

1. Choose **Preferences > Drafting** from the menu bar; the **Drafting Preferences** dialog box is displayed. Choose the **View** tab and clear the **Display Borders** check box, if it is

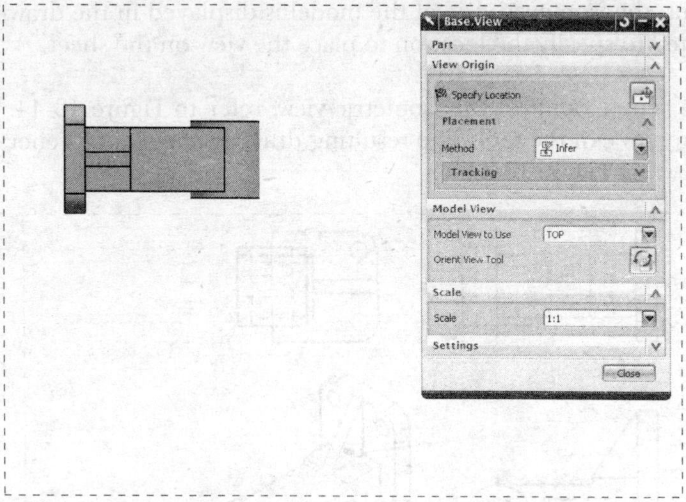

Figure 13-43 The empty drawing sheet displayed after invoking the Drafting environment

selected. Choose the **OK** button; the **Base View** dialog box is displayed again and you are prompted to specify the location to place the view on the sheet.

2. Specify the center point for the generated drawing view, refer to Figure 13-44. After generating the base view, the **Projected View** tool is automatically invoked from the **Drawing** toolbar and the **Projected View** dialog box is displayed.

3. Move the cursor and click the left mouse button on the right and then at the bottom of the base view to generate the right-side view and the front view, respectively. Press the middle mouse button to exit the tool.

4. If the hidden lines are not displayed, select the drawing views and right-click on a view. Choose the **Style** option from the shortcut menu; the **View Style** dialog box is displayed.

5. Choose the **Hidden Lines** tab; the **Hidden Line** check box is selected by default. Select the **Dashed** option from the **Font** drop-down list and the **Normal** option from the **Width** drop-down list.

6. Choose the **OK** button to exit the **View Style** dialog box; the hidden lines are displayed. The top view, the right-side view, and the front view of the model are shown in Figure 13-44.

Generating the Isometric View of the Model

1. Choose the **Base View** button from the **Drawing** toolbar; the **Base View** dialog box is displayed. Also, the floating top view of the model attached to the cursor is displayed in the drawing sheet.

2. Select the **TFR-ISO** option from the **Model View to Use** drop-down list of the **Model**

View rollout; the isometric view of the model is displayed in the drawing sheet and you are prompted to specify the location to place the view on the sheet.

3. Specify the center point of the isometric view, refer to Figure 13-44. Press the middle mouse button to exit the tool. The resulting drawing sheet after generating the drawing views is shown in Figure 13-44.

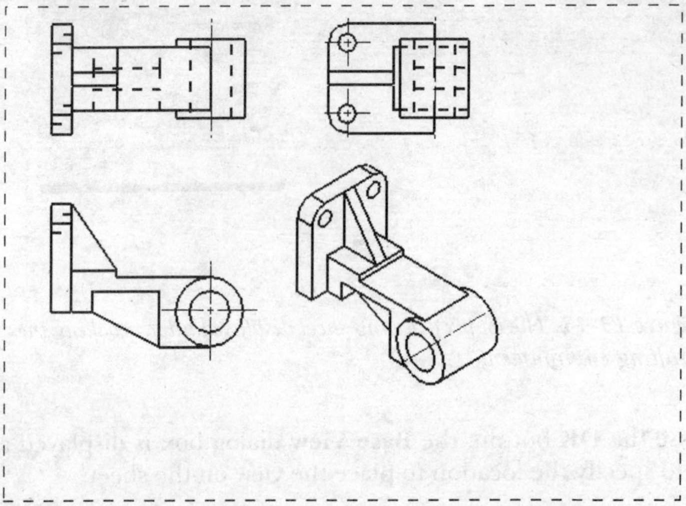

Figure 13-44 The drawing sheet after creating the drawing views

Creating the Tabular Note for the Drawing Sheet

1. Choose the **Tabular Note** button from the **Tables** toolbar; the floating tabular note is attached to the cursor. Position the tabular note on the drawing sheet, refer to Figure 13-45.

2. Select the last two columns of the tabular note by moving the cursor on the columns with the left mouse button pressed. The selected two columns are displayed in orange.

3. Right-click in the selection area, and then choose the **Merge Cells** option from the shortcut menu; the selected cells are merged together.

4. Drag the cells dynamically to modify their size with the left mouse button pressed. The width and height of the cells should be 50 and 14, respectively.

5. Merge the cells of the first three rows and modify its height to 16, refer to Figure 13-45. Next, you need to enter the text in the cells.

6. Enter the text in all cells as mentioned in Figure 13-45 by double-clicking on a cell and entering required text in the text box.

7. Select the cell from the first row in which the text is entered and then right-click on it. Next, choose the **Style** option from the shortcut menu; the **Annotation Style** dialog box is displayed.

8. Choose the **Lettering** tab and enter **5** in the **Character Size** edit box. Choose the **OK** button to reflect the changes. The resulting drawing sheet after creating the tabular note is displayed, as shown in Figure 13-45.

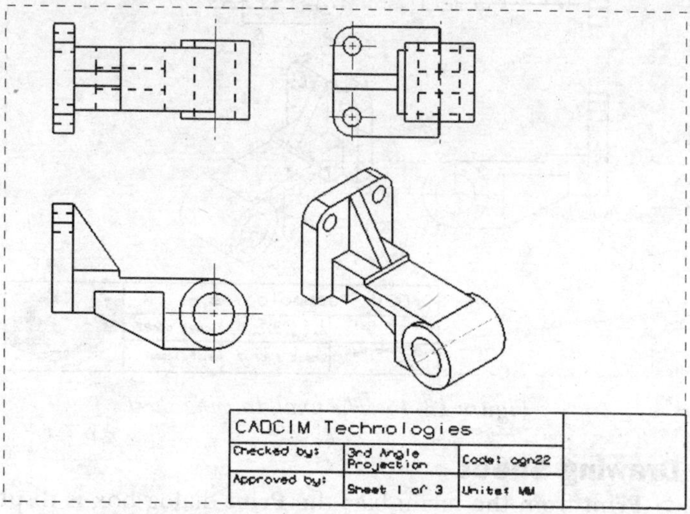

Figure 13-45 *The drawing sheet after creating the drawing views and the tabular note*

Inserting the Image into the Tabular Note

1. Choose the **Image** button from the **Annotation** toolbar; the **Open Image** dialog box is displayed. Browse the image by using the **Look in** drop-down list and select it. Next, choose the **OK** button. The image along with the handles and the Image Display input box is displayed in the drawing sheet.

2. Position the image in the tabular note by using the handles. If necessary, choose the **Lock Aspect** button from the Image Display input box to unlock the scaling factor. After positioning the image, press the ESC key to exit. The completed drawing sheet after inserting the image is shown in Figure 13-46.

Adding the Tabular Note to the Tables Palette

1. Move the cursor to the left-upper corner of the tabular note; the tabular note section is displayed. Select the tabular note section. The complete tabular note turns to the magenta color.

2. Right-click on the tabular note section, and then choose the **Save As Template** option from the shortcut menu; the **Save As Template** dialog box is displayed. Enter **Table-1** as the name of the tabular note in the **File name** text box and choose the **OK** button; the name of the tabular note is saved as **Table-1** and added as the tabular note at the specified location.

Note

To save a tabular note as a template, you may need to run NX as administrator.

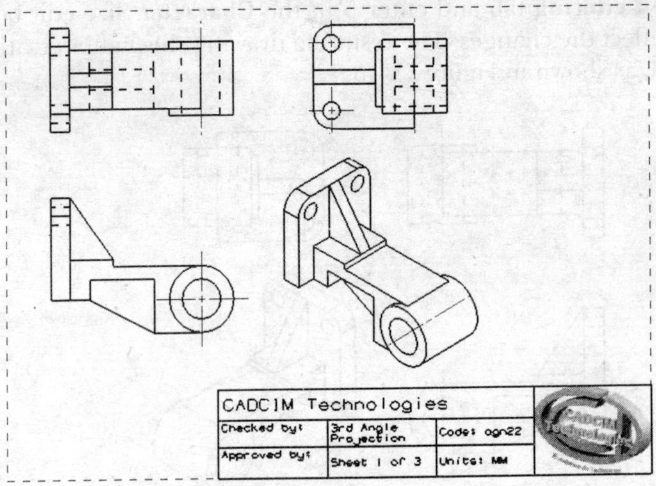

Figure 13-46 The final drawing sheet

Printing the Drawing Sheet

1. Choose **File > Print** from the menu bar; the **Print** dialog box is displayed. Select the printer connected to your computer from the **Printer** drop-down list.

2. Choose the **Properties** button and make the orientation of the paper to Landscape. Change the color settings, if required, and choose **OK**.

3. Set the value in the **Copies** spinner of the **Settings** rollout to **1** and choose the **OK** button; the drawing sheet is printed.

Plotting and Saving the Drawing Sheet

1. Choose **File > Plot** from the menu bar; the **Plot** dialog box is displayed. Select **JPEG** from the **Printer** drop-down list of the **Plotter** rollout.

2. Choose the **Browse** button from the **Plotter** rollout and specify the location to save the output file. Enter the name of the output file in the **File name** edit box. Next, choose the **OK** button twice; the file is plotted at the specified location.

3. Choose **File > Save** from the menu bar; the drawing file is saved. Next, close the file.

Tutorial 2

In this tutorial, you will create all parts of the Double Bearing assembly in the Modeling environment and save them in the specified folder. Next, you will assemble them in the Assembly environment. After creating the assembly, you will create its exploded view in the assembly file. Next, you will generate the drawing views of the Double Bearing assembly in the Drafting environment. Also, you will generate the Parts List and Autoballoons and insert the tabular note **Table-1** from the **Tables** palette, as shown in Figure 13-47. The dimensions and drawing views of various components in the assembly are shown in Figure 13-48 through Figure 13-52. **(Expected time: 2 hrs)**

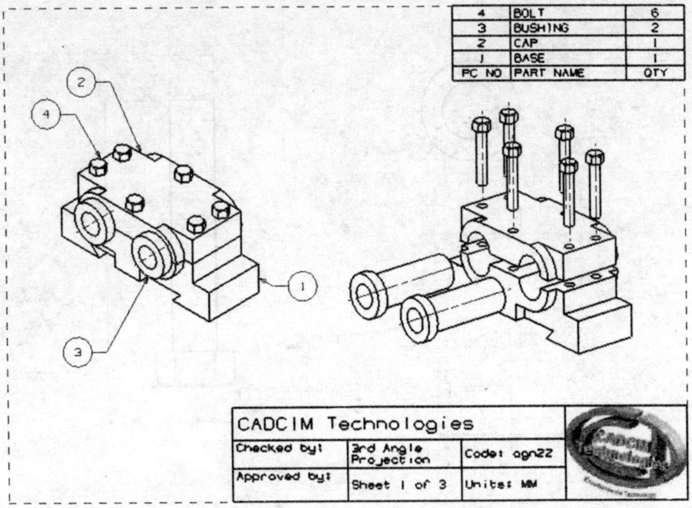

Figure 13-47 The drawing sheet after generating drawing views, parts list, autoballoons, and inserting the title block

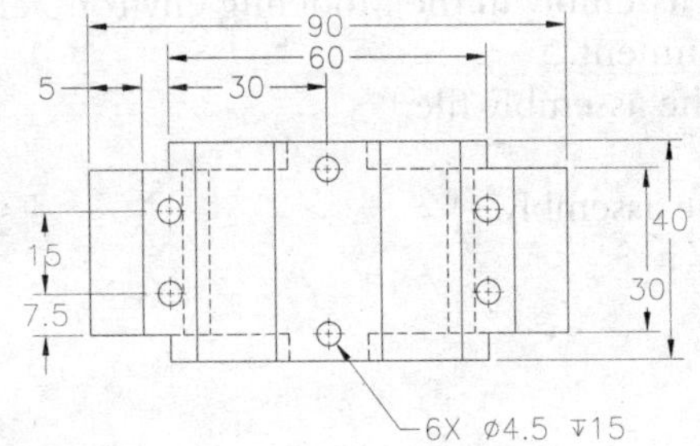

Figure 13-48 *Top view of the Base*

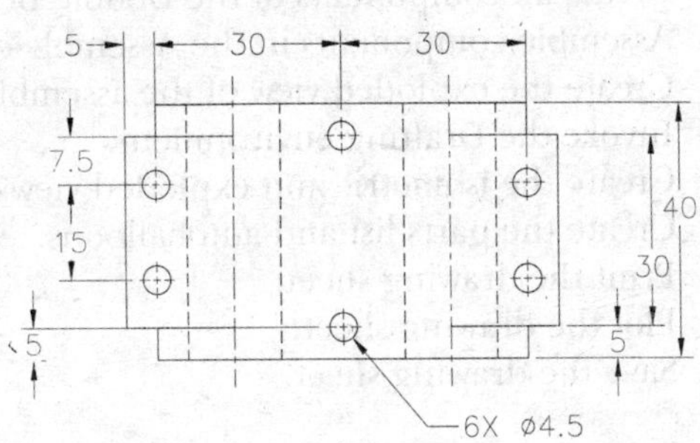

Figure 13-49 *Top view of the Cap*

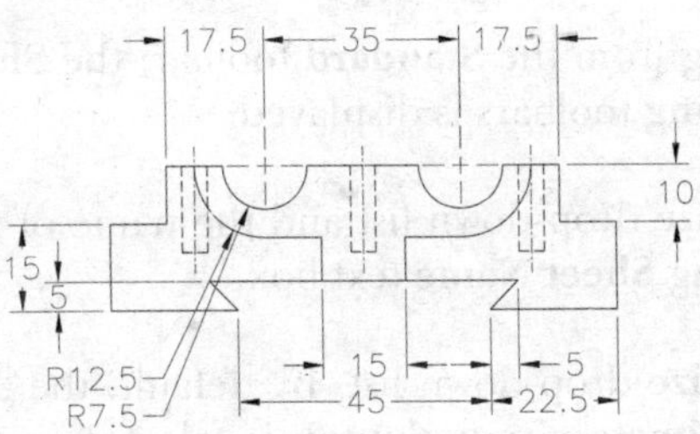

Figure 13-50 *Front view of the Base*

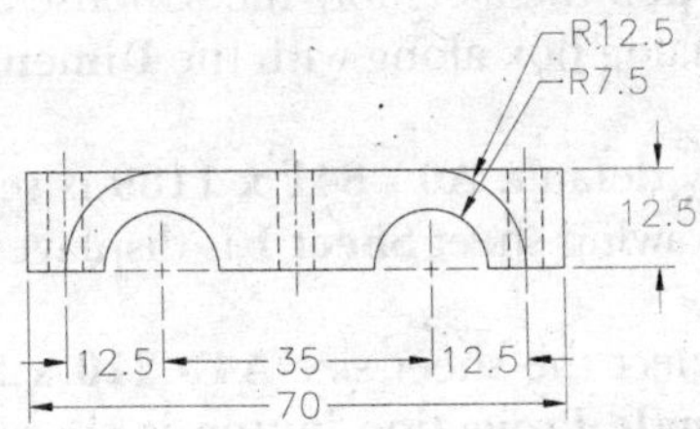

Figure 13-51 *Front view of the Cap*

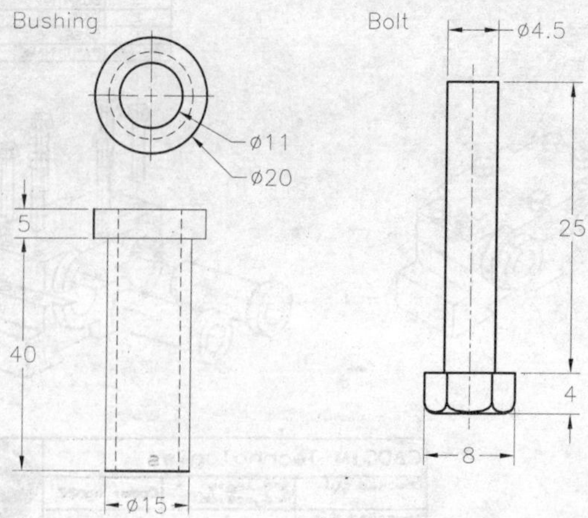

Figure 13-52 Dimensions and drawing views of the Bushing and the Bolt

The following steps are required to complete this tutorial:

a. Create all components of the Double Bearing assembly in the Modeling environment.
b. Assemble components in the Assembly environment.
c. Create the exploded view of the assembly in the assembly file.
d. Invoke the Drafting environment.
e. Create the isometric and exploded views of the assembly.
f. Create the parts list and autoballoons.
g. Print the drawing sheet.
h. Plot the drawing sheet.
i. Save the drawing sheet.

Creating and Assembling the Components of the Assembly

1. Create all components of the Double Bearing assembly and then assemble them in the Assembly environment. Next, generate the exploded view of the assembly, refer to Figure 13-47.

Invoking the Drafting Environment

1. Open the assembly file. Choose **Start > Drafting** from the **Standard** toolbar; the **Sheet** dialog box along with the **Dimension** and **Drawing** toolbars is displayed.

   By default, **A0 - 841 x 1189** is selected in the **Size** drop-down list and the name of the drawing sheet **Sheet 1** is displayed in the **Drawing Sheet Name** text box.

2. Select the sheet size **A4 - 210 x 297** from the **Size** drop-down list. By default, the **3rd Angle Projection** button is chosen and the **Millimeters** radio button is selected in the **Settings** rollout. The default scale value selected in the **Scale** drop-down list is **1:1**. Accept all default parameters and choose the **OK** button to invoke the Drafting environment.

Generating the Isometric Drawing View of the Assembly

By default, the **Drawing** and **Drafting Edit** toolbars are displayed in the **Drafting** environment. If they are not displayed, then invoke them by right-clicking in the toolbars area and choosing the **Drawing** option and then the **Drafting Edit** option from the shortcut menu.

1. By default, the **Base View** button is chosen in the **Drawing** toolbar and the **Base View** dialog box along with the floating top view of the model is displayed.

2. Select the **TFR-ISO** option from the **Model View to Use** drop-down list. The floating isometric view of the assembly is displayed on the drawing sheet and you are prompted to indicate the center of the base view on the sheet. Position the drawing view generated in the drawing sheet by pressing the left mouse button, refer to Figure 13-53. Next, press the middle mouse button to exit the tool. The isometric view of the model is displayed in the drawing sheet, refer to Figure 13-53.

Note

If the borders are generated along with the drawing views, choose ***Preferences > Drafting*** *from the menu bar; the* ***Drafting Preferences*** *dialog box is displayed. Choose the* ***View*** *tab and clear the* ***Display Borders*** *check box from the* ***Borders*** *area and choose the* ***OK*** *button. The borders are cleared from the drawing views.*

Generating the Exploded Drawing View of the Assembly

1. Before generating the exploded drawing view of the assembly, invoke the Modeling environment by choosing **Start > Modeling** from the **Standard** toolbar. The assembly is displayed in the Modeling environment.

2. Select the name of the explosion view that you have generated in the Assembly environment from the **Work View Explosion** drop-down list of the **Exploded Views** toolbar. The exploded view of the assembly is displayed. Next, choose **Start > Drafting** from the **Standard** toolbar to invoke the Drafting environment.

3. Choose the **Base View** button from the **Drawing** toolbar; the **Base View** dialog box along with the floating top view of the assembly is displayed.

4. Select the **TFR-TRI** option from the **Model View to Use** drop-down list of the **Model View** rollout. The floating exploded view of the assembly is attached to the cursor and you are prompted to indicate the center of the base view on the sheet.

5. Specify the center for the generated drawing view by pressing the left mouse button on the drawing sheet, refer to Figure 13-53. Press the middle mouse button to exit the tool. The exploded drawing view of the assembly is generated, as shown in Figure 13-53.

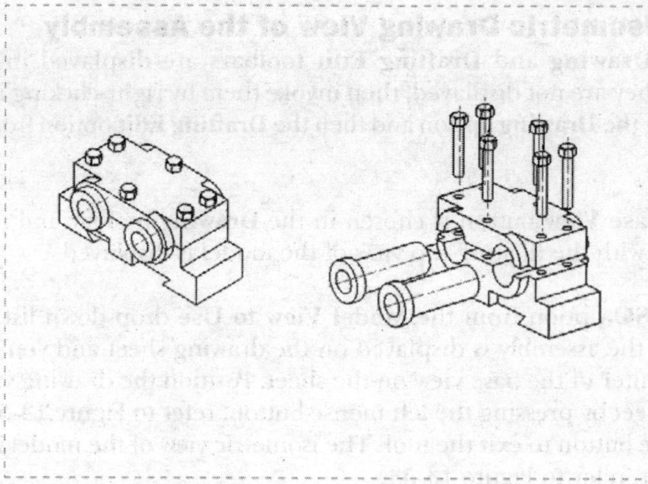

Figure 13-53 The drawing sheet after generating the isometric and exploded drawing views of the assembly

Generating the Parts List of the Assembly

1. Choose the **Parts List** button from the **Tables** toolbar; you are prompted to indicate a position for the new parts list. Also, the floating rectangle is displayed in the drawing sheet.

2. Position the parts list by pressing the left mouse button in the drawing sheet at the location shown in Figure 13-54.

Generating Associative Autoballoons for the Parts List

1. Choose the **Auto Balloon** button from the **Tables** toolbar; the **Parts List Auto Balloon** dialog box is displayed and you are prompted to select the parts list to autoballoon.

2. Select the parts list generated in the previous step and choose the **OK** button; the modified **Parts List Auto Balloon** dialog box is displayed and you are prompted to select views to autoballoon.

3. Select **TFR-ISO** from the list box of the same dialog box. The selected view is enclosed in an orange color border. Choose the **OK** button; the autoballoons are generated. The drawing sheet after generating the autoballoons along with the drawing views and the parts list is shown in Figure 13-54.

Inserting the Tabular Note (Table-1) from the Tables Palette

By default, the **Tables** palette is not present in the **Resource Bar**. You need to retrieve it from the palettes option.

1. Choose **Preferences > Palettes** from the menu bar; the **Palettes** dialog box is displayed.

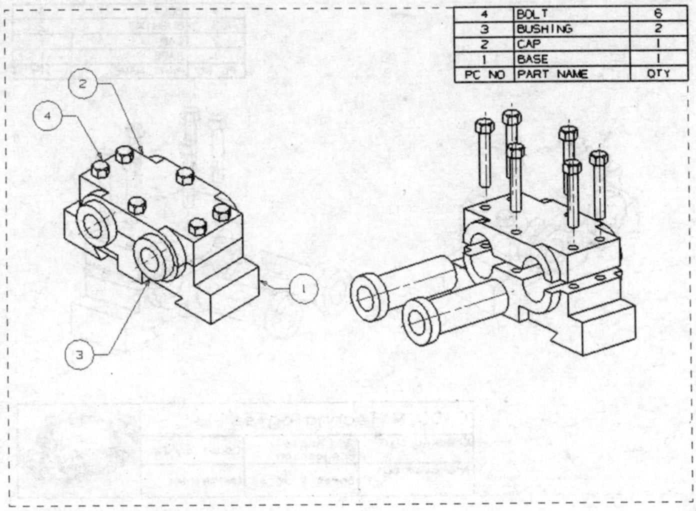

Figure 13-54 The drawing sheet after generating the drawing view, parts list, and autoballoons for the assembly

2. Choose the **Open Palette File** button from the **Palettes** dialog box; the **Open Palette** dialog box is displayed.

3. Choose the **Browse** button and browse to *C:\Program Files\UGS\NX 7.0\UGII\table_files*. Next, select the **tables.pax** file from the dialog box and choose the **OK** button twice; the **Tables** palette is added to the **Resource Bar**. Close the **Palettes** dialog box.

4. Next, choose the **Tables** tab from the **Resource Bar**; the **Tables** cascading menu is displayed.

5. Drag the tabular note named **Table-1** from the list of tables displayed and drop it in the drawing sheet. Position the tabular note in the drawing sheet, as shown in Figure 13-55. Add the company logo to the tabular note as discussed in the previous tutorial. The completed drawing sheet is displayed, as shown in Figure 13-55.

Printing the Drawing Sheet

1. Choose **File > Print** from the menu bar; the **Print** dialog box is displayed. Select the printer connected to your computer from the **Printer** drop-down list.

2. Choose the **Properties** button from the **Details** sub-rollout and make the orientation of the paper to Landscape. Change the color settings, if required and choose **OK**.

3. Set the value **1** in the **Copies** spinner of the **Settings** rollout and choose the **OK** button; the drawing sheet is printed.

Plotting the Drawing Sheet

1. Choose **File > Plot** from the menu bar; the **Plot** dialog box is displayed.

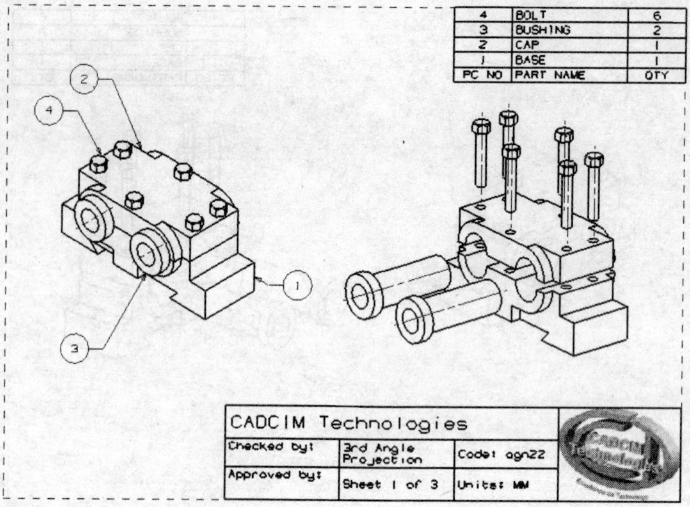

Figure 13-55 The completed drawing sheet after generating the drawing view, parts list, autoballoons, and inserting the title block

2. Select **TIFF** from the **Printer** drop-down list of the **Plotter** rollout.

3. Choose the **Browse** button from the **Plotter** rollout. Specify the location and name to save the output file.

4. Choose the **OK** button twice; the file is plotted at the specified location.

Saving the Drawing Sheet

1. Choose **File > Save** from the menu bar; the drawing sheet is saved. Next, close the file.

Tutorial 3

In this tutorial, you will generate the front view, left-side view, and top view of the model created in Tutorial 1 of Chapter 7. You need to retrieve the dimensions from the model and manually add the required dimensions to the drawing views shown in Figure 13-56.

(Expected time: 30 min)

The following steps are required to complete this tutorial:

a. Open the part file created in Chapter 7 and invoke the Drafting environment.
b. Generate the drawing views of the model.
c. Create dimensions for all views.
d. Save and close the drawing file.

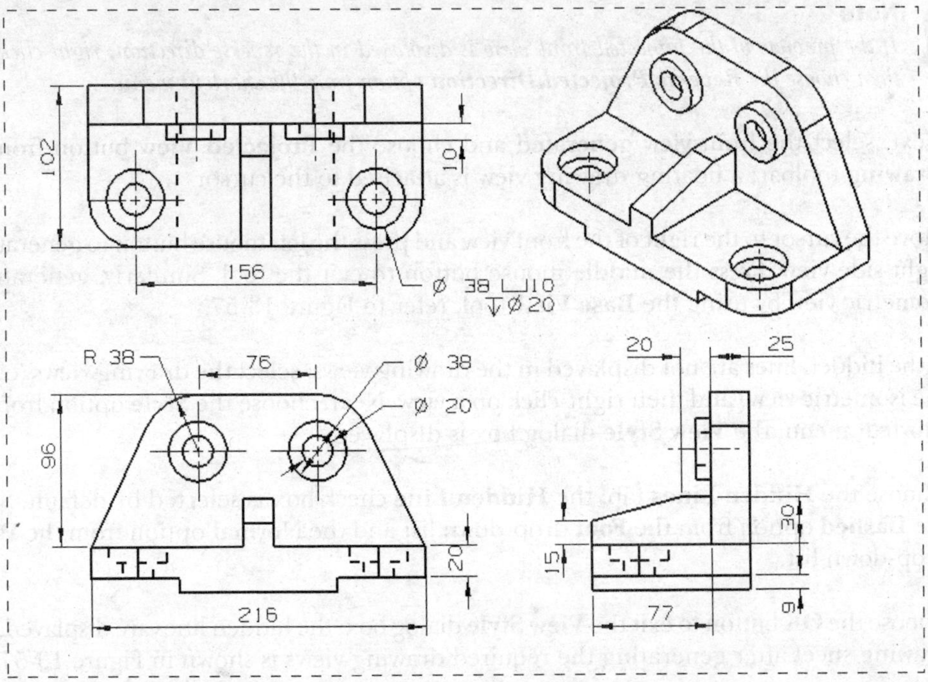

Figure 13-56 The drawing views of the model after retrieving and creating the dimensions

Opening the Part File and Invoking the Drafting Application

1. Open the part file created in Chapter 7 (Tutorial 1). Choose **Start > Drafting** from the **Standard** toolbar; the **Sheet** dialog box along with the **Dimension** and **Drawing** toolbars is displayed.

2. Select **A2 - 420 x 594** as the sheet size from the **Size** drop-down list. By default, the **3rd Angle Projection** button is chosen and the **Millimeters** radio button is selected in the **Settings** rollout. The default scale value selected in the **Scale** drop-down list is **1:1**. Accept all default parameters and choose the **OK** button to invoke the Drafting environment.

Generating the Drawing Views of the Model

1. By default, the **Base View** dialog box is invoked from the **Drawing** toolbar. The floating top view of the model along with the **Base View** dialog box is displayed in the drawing sheet. Also, you are prompted to indicate the center of the base view on the sheet.

2. Specify the center point of the drawing view, refer to Figure 13-57. After generating the base view, the **Projected View** tool is invoked automatically from the **Drawing** toolbar.

3. Move the cursor towards the bottom of the base view and press the left mouse button to generate the front view. Press the middle mouse button to exit the tool.

Note

If the preview of the projected front view is displayed in the reverse direction, right-click, and then choose the ***Reverse Projected Direction*** *option from the shortcut menu.*

4. Next, select the front view generated and choose the **Projected View** button from the **Drawing** toolbar; a floating drawing view is attached to the cursor.

5. Move the cursor to the right of the front view and press the left mouse button to generate the right-side view. Press the middle mouse button to exit the tool. Similarly, generate the isometric view by using the **Base View** tool, refer to Figure 13-57.

6. If the hidden lines are not displayed in the drawing views, select the drawing views (except the isometric view) and then right-click on a view. Next, choose the **Style** option from the shortcut menu; the **View Style** dialog box is displayed.

7. Choose the **Hidden Lines** tab; the **Hidden Line** check box is selected by default. Select the **Dashed** option from the **Font** drop-down list and the **Normal** option from the **Width** drop-down list.

8. Choose the **OK** button to exit the **View Style** dialog box; the hidden lines are displayed. The drawing sheet after generating the required drawing views is shown in Figure 13-57.

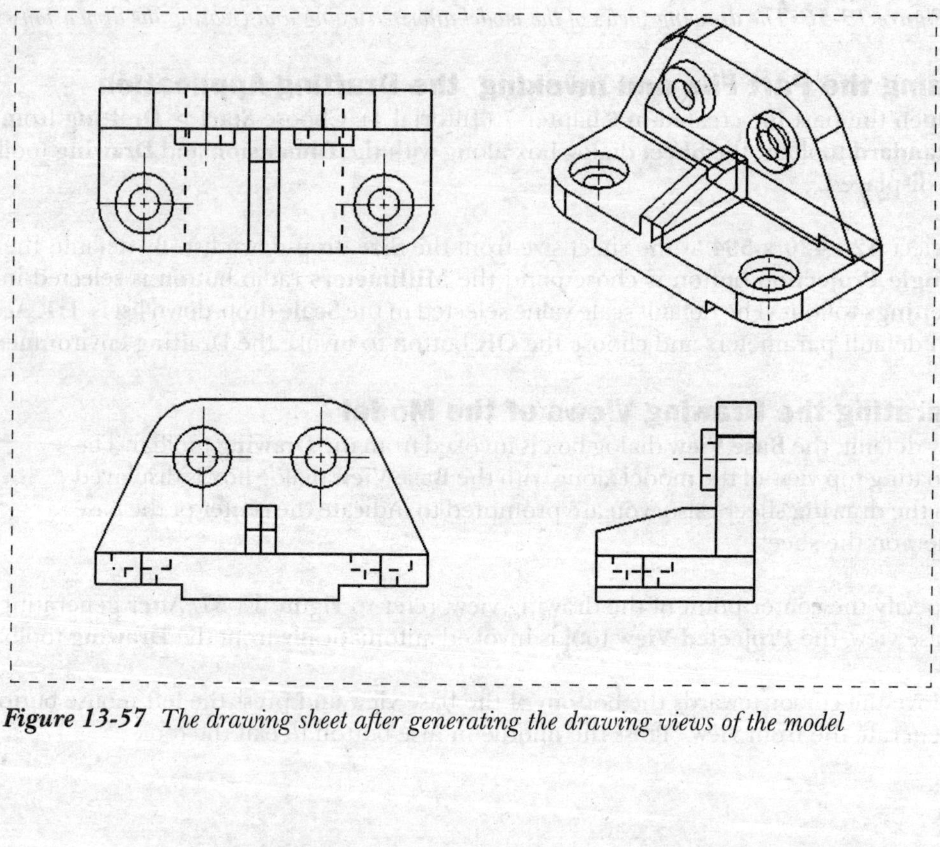

Figure 13-57 The drawing sheet after generating the drawing views of the model

Retrieving and Creating Dimensions for the Front View

Before retrieving dimensions, you need to set some dimension parameters.

1. Choose **Preferences > Annotation** from the menu bar; the **Annotation Preferences** dialog box is displayed.

2. Choose the **Dimensions** tab, if it has not already been chosen. Next, select the **No Leader** option from the **Leader** drop-down list in the **Narrow** area. Next, select the **Horizontal** option from the **Dimension Text Orientation** drop-down list, which is available above the **Precision and Tolerance** area.

3. Choose the **Line/Arrow** tab and enter **18.5** in the **B** edit box and **6** in the **A** edit box. Next, select the **Filled Arrow** option from the **Arrow Style** drop-down list available at the top left corner of the dialog box.

4. Choose the **Lettering** tab and enter **6** in the **Character Size** edit box. Choose the **OK** button. Now, you can retrieve the dimensions.

5. Choose the **Feature Parameters** button from the **Annotation** toolbar; the **Feature Parameters** dialog box is displayed and you are prompted to select the features. By default, the **Select features** button is chosen in the **Feature Parameters** dialog box.

6. Click on the plus sign (+) to expand the **FEATURES** node in the list box. Select the **ansi_mm** option from the **Template** drop-down list.

7. Select the first, second, fourth, fifth, and seventh features that are listed in the **FEATURES** node.

8. Next, choose the **Select views** button from the **Feature Parameters** dialog box; you are prompted to select the views. The name of the drawing views are displayed in the list box of the dialog box.

9. Select the front view from the list box and choose the **OK** button; the dimensions are retrieved for the front view of the model, refer to Figure 13-58.

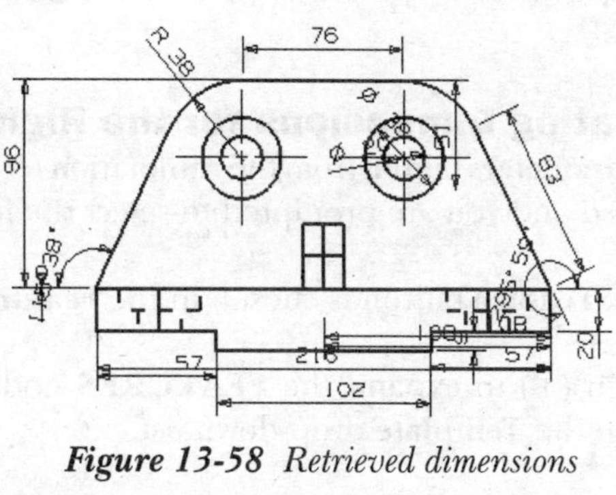

Figure 13-58 *Retrieved dimensions*

The dimensions that are retrieved may differ based on the sketch drawn to create the model. If the dimensions are different from the one given in Figure 13-58, you need to check the sketches drawn.

The dimensions retrieved are scattered on the drawing view and placed improperly. You need to delete the unwanted dimensions and place the required dimensions at the right position.

10. Select the unwanted dimensions and press the DELETE key; the selected dimensions are deleted.

11. Select the dimensions and position around the front view by dragging them. The drawing view with the retrieved dimensions is shown in Figure 13-59.

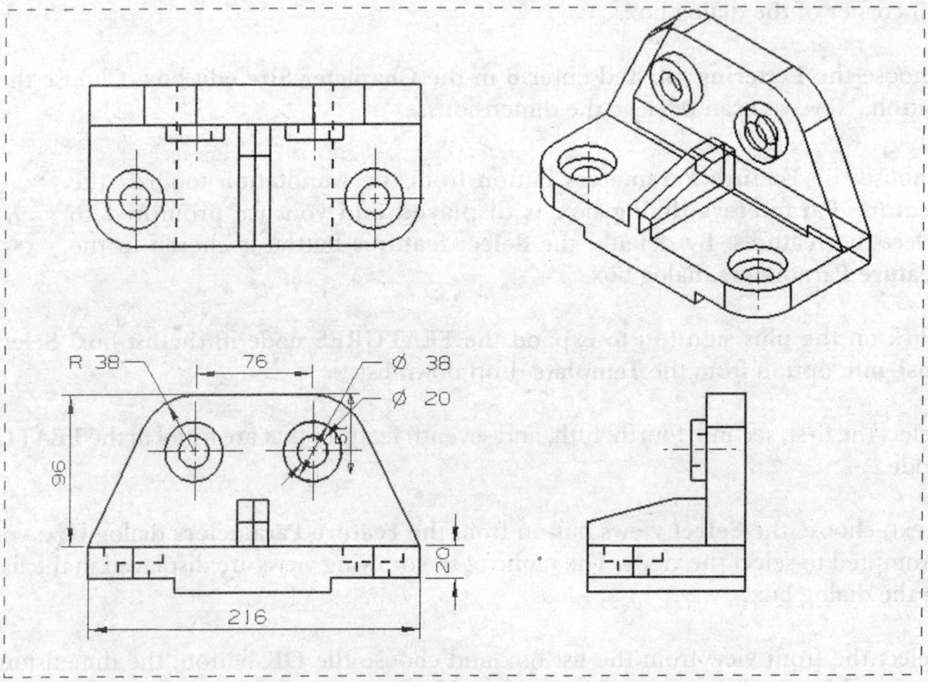

Figure 13-59 The drawing view after retrieving the dimensions and placing them in the proper position

Retrieving and Creating Dimensions for the Right-Side View

1. Choose the **Feature Parameters** button from the **Annotation** toolbar; the **Feature Parameters** dialog box is displayed and you are prompted to select the features.

   By default, the **Select Feature** button is chosen in the **Feature Parameters** dialog box.

2. Click on the plus sign (+) to expand the **FEATURES** node in the list box. Select the **ansi_mm** option from the **Template** drop-down list.

3. Select the fifth sketch that is listed in the **FEATURES** node. Choose the **Select Views** button from the **Feature Parameters** dialog box; you are prompted to select the views. The drawing views in the drawing sheet are displayed in the list box.

4. Select the right-side view from the list box and choose the **OK** button. All the required dimensions are not retrieved. You need to create the required dimensions.

5. Choose the **Inferred** button from the **Dimension** toolbar and add the missing dimensions. The retrieved and created dimensions for the drawing views are shown in Figure 13-60.

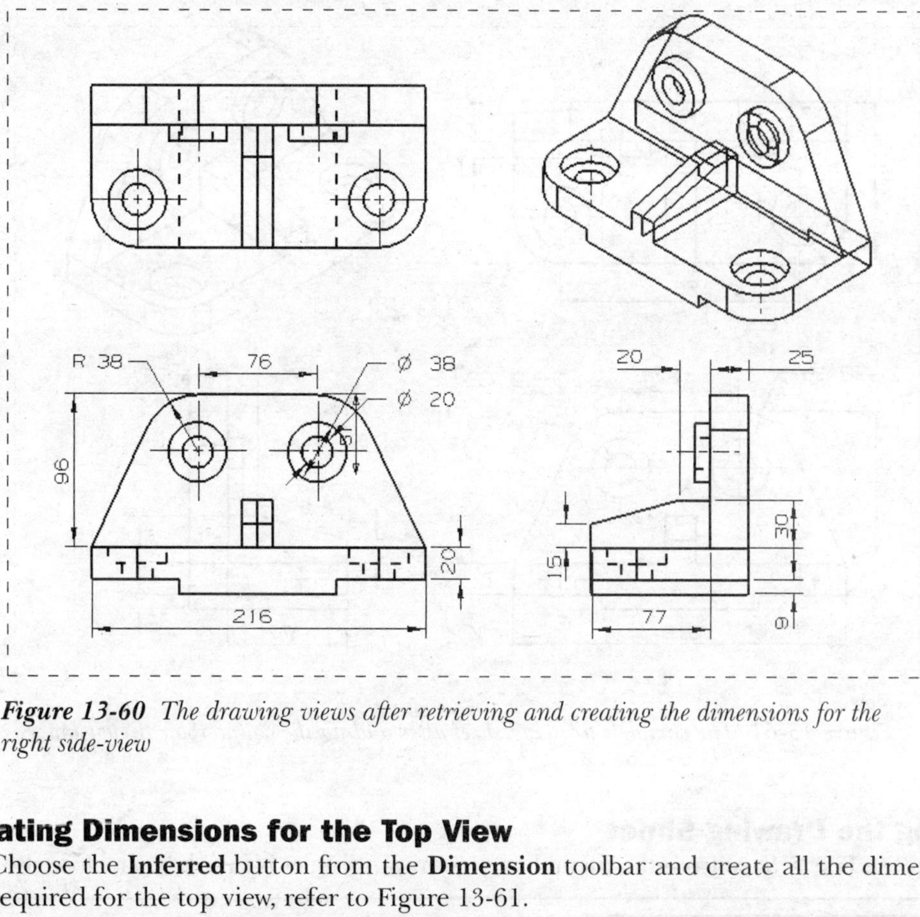

Figure 13-60 The drawing views after retrieving and creating the dimensions for the right side-view

Creating Dimensions for the Top View

1. Choose the **Inferred** button from the **Dimension** toolbar and create all the dimensions required for the top view, refer to Figure 13-61.

2. To add a counterbore note, choose the **Diameter** button from the **Dimension** toolbar; you are prompted to select an object for the diameter dimension. Select the 38 mm diameter circle from the top view and place the dimension. Next, press the ESC key.

3. Right-click on the dimension, and then choose the **Edit Appended Text** option from the shortcut menu; the **Text Editor** dialog box is displayed.

4. In this dialog box, choose the **After** button from the **Appended Text** area. Choose the **Counterbore** button from the **Drafting Symbols** tab. The code corresponding to the counterbore symbol is displayed in the text box. Type the text in the text box after the counterbore code, refer to Figure 13-61.

5. Choose the **Close** button from the **Text Editor** dialog box to exit it. The drawing sheet after creating the counterbore dimension is shown in Figure 13-61.

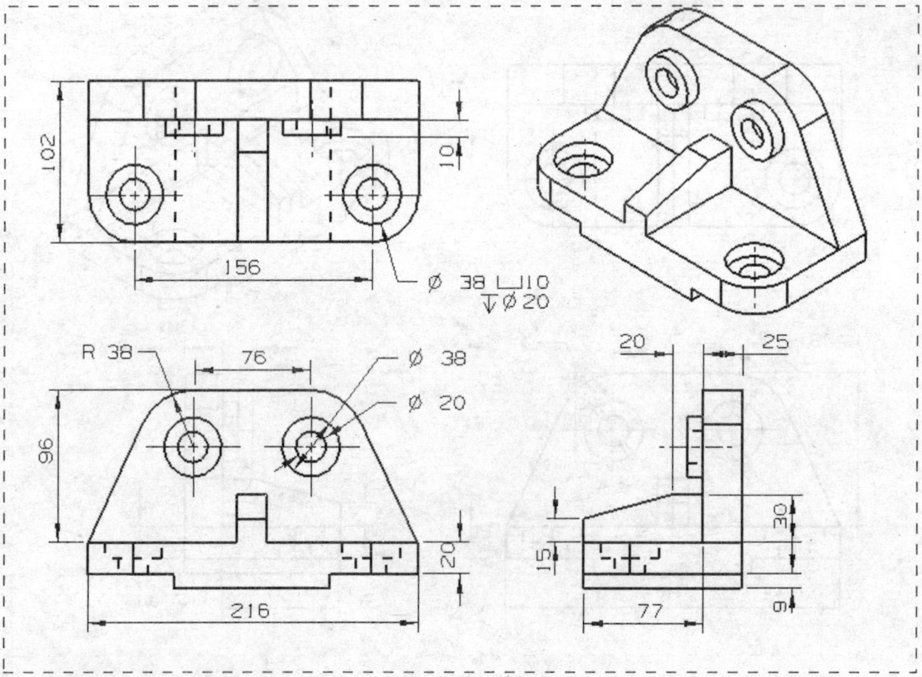

Figure 13-61 The complete drawing sheet after adding the counterbore dimension

Saving the Drawing Sheet

1. Choose **File > Save** from the menu bar; the drawing sheet is saved. Next, close the file.

Self-Evaluation Test

Answer the following questions and then compare them to those given at the end of this chapter:

1. When you enter the Drafting environment, the title block is readily available in the drawing sheet. (T/F)

2. By default, a grid exists in a drawing sheet. (T/F)

3. You cannot place the generated drawing views outside the drawing limits area of a drawing sheet. (T/F)

4. You can insert any number of drawing sheets into a drawing file. (T/F)

5. In the Drafting environment, you can change the orientation of a model while generating drawing views. (T/F)

6. After generating the base view, the **Projected View** tool is invoked automatically. (T/F)

7. The __________ is the file extension for the files created in the Drafting environment of NX.

8. While generating drawing views, the __________ tool is used to display a model in the Drafting environment.

9. The __________ tool is used to insert a new drawing sheet into a drawing file.

10. To generate a section drawing view, you need choose __________button.

Review Questions

Answer the following questions:

1. Which of the following tools is used to automatically retrieve the dimensions created in a model in the drawing view?

   (a) **Feature Parameters** (b) **Insert Sheet**
   (c) **Add Base View** (d) None of these

2. Which of the following options need to be selected from the **Model View to Use** drop-down list in the **Model View** area for generating an exploded drawing view?

   (a) **TFR - ISO** (b) **top**
   (c) **TFR - TRI** (d) None of these

3. Which of the following tools is used to create a title block in a drawing sheet?

   (a) **Tabular Note** (b) **Insert Parts List**
   (c) **Display Sheet** (d) None of these

4. Which of the following tools is used to insert an image into a drawing sheet?

   (a) **Image** (b) **ID Symbol**
   (c) **Custom Symbol** (d) None of these

5. Before creating part balloons, it is mandatory to create the Parts List of the assembly. (T/F)

6. A detail view can be generated directly from a model. (T/F)

7. After generating different drawing views, you can align them using the **Align View** tool. (T/F)

8. After invoking the Drafting environment, you can change the sheet specifications. (T/F)

9. The **Annotation Preferences** dialog box is used to set dimension parameters. (T/F)

10. Part balloons can be modified dynamically. (T/F)

Exercises

Exercise 1

Create the exploded view and the isometric view of the assembly created in Chapter 9, see Figure 13-62. Also, generate the parts list and autoballoons shown in the same figure. After completing the drawing sheet, print and plot it. **(Expected time: 30 min)**

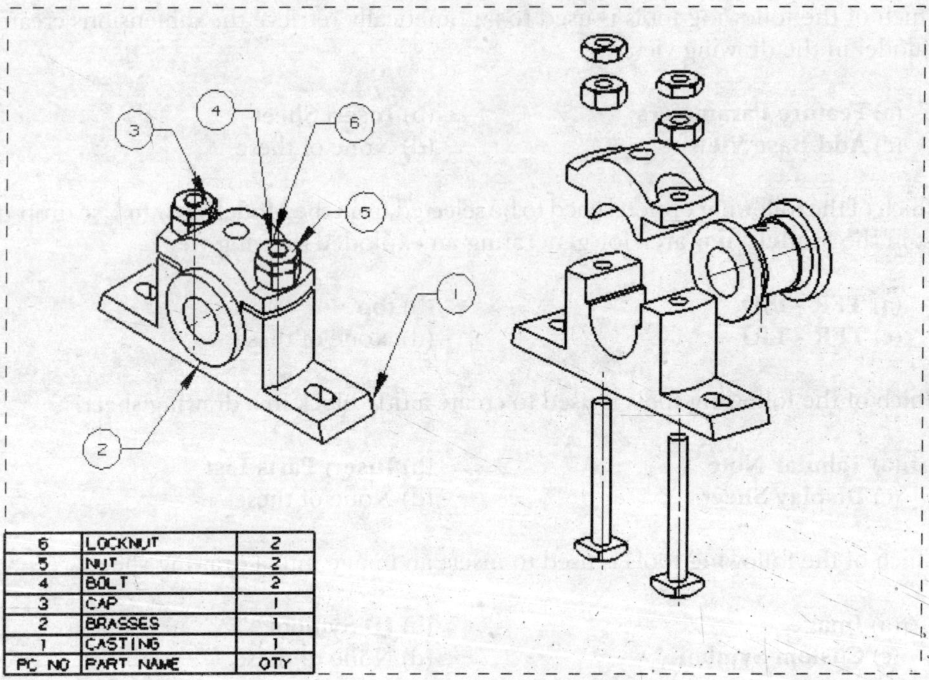

6	LOCKNUT	2
5	NUT	2
4	BOLT	2
3	CAP	1
2	BRASSES	1
1	CASTING	1
PC NO	PART NAME	QTY

***Figure 13-62** The drawing views of the assembly along with the parts list and autoballoons*

Exercise 2

Create the drawing views of the model created in Chapter 6. Generate the dimensions and add the required dimensions to the drawing views. Also, add the tabular note to the drawing sheet, as shown in Figure 13-63. After completing the drawing sheet, print and plot it.

(Expected time: 30 min)

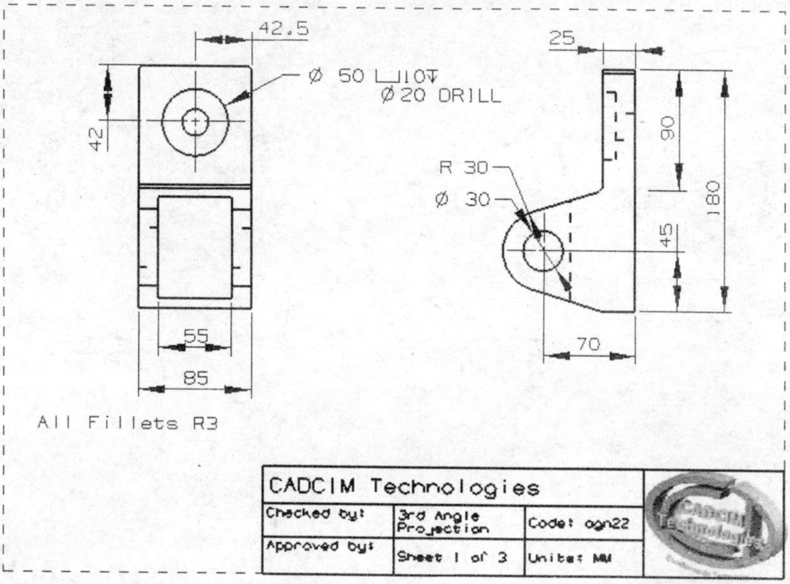

Figure 13-63 *The drawing sheet displaying the drawing views after retrieving and adding the dimensions along with the tabular note*

Answers to Self-Evaluation Test

1. F, **2.** T, **3.** T, **4.** T, **5.** T, **6.** T, **7.** *.prt,* **8. Display Sheet, 9. New Sheet, 10. Section View**

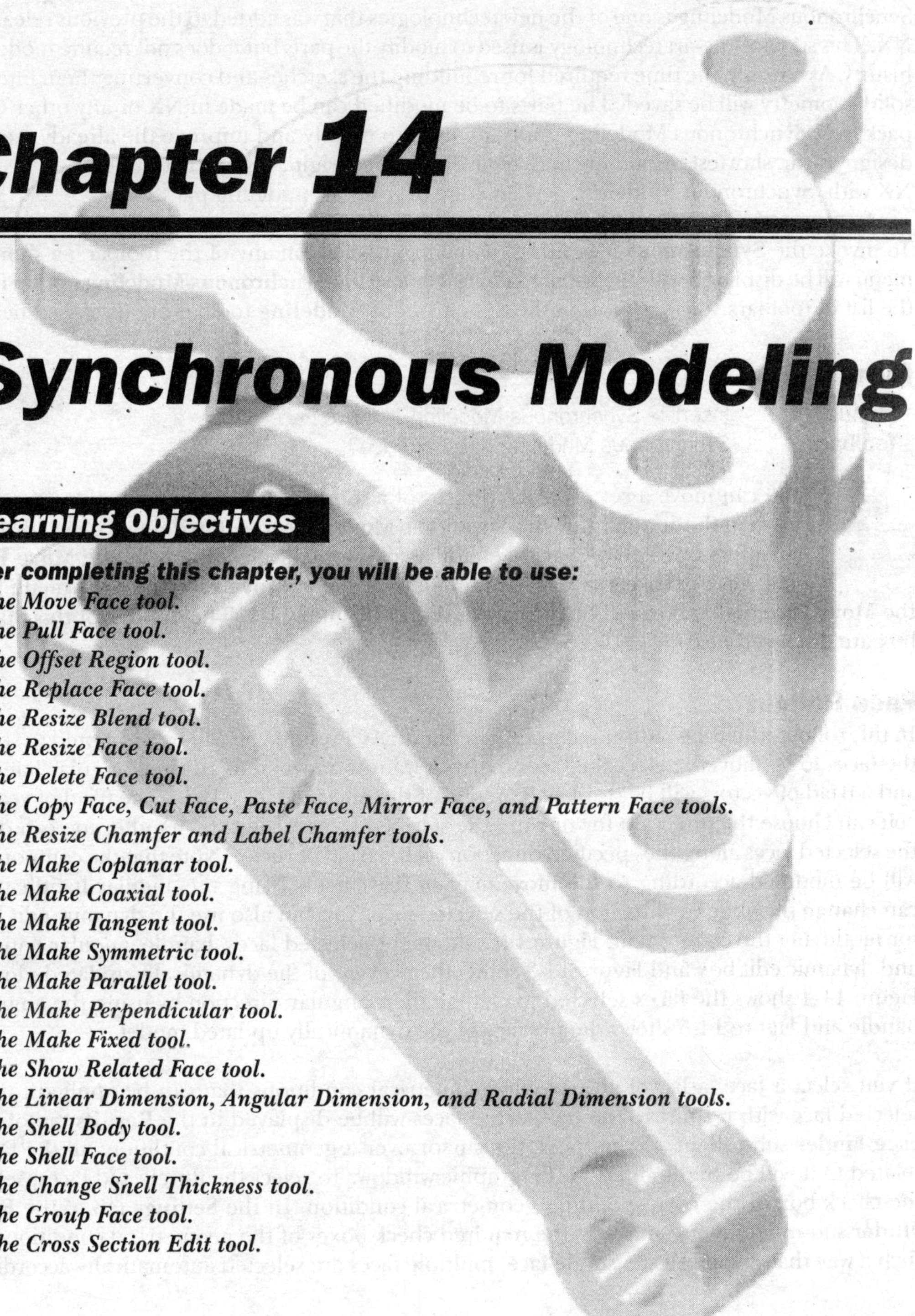

Chapter 14

Synchronous Modeling

Learning Objectives

After completing this chapter, you will be able to use:

- *The Move Face tool.*
- *The Pull Face tool.*
- *The Offset Region tool.*
- *The Replace Face tool.*
- *The Resize Blend tool.*
- *The Resize Face tool.*
- *The Delete Face tool.*
- *The Copy Face, Cut Face, Paste Face, Mirror Face, and Pattern Face tools.*
- *The Resize Chamfer and Label Chamfer tools.*
- *The Make Coplanar tool.*
- *The Make Coaxial tool.*
- *The Make Tangent tool.*
- *The Make Symmetric tool.*
- *The Make Parallel tool.*
- *The Make Perpendicular tool.*
- *The Make Fixed tool.*
- *The Show Related Face tool.*
- *The Linear Dimension, Angular Dimension, and Radial Dimension tools.*
- *The Shell Body tool.*
- *The Shell Face tool.*
- *The Change Shell Thickness tool.*
- *The Group Face tool.*
- *The Cross Section Edit tool.*

INTRODUCTION

Synchronous Modeling is one of the new technologies that was added to the previous release of NX. This state-of-the-art technology is used to modify the parts but it does not require modeling history. As a result, the time required for rebuilding the sketches and converting them into the solid geometry will be saved. The parts to be modified can be made in NX or any other CAD packages. Synchronous Modeling Tools are used to modify and improve the already created design in the shortest period of time, regardless of its origin, associativity, or feature history. NX with Synchronous Modeling gets an edge over other modeling packages.

To invoke the **Synchronous Modeling** toolbar, right-click on any of the toolbars; a shortcut menu will be displayed with the list of toolbars. Choose the **Synchronous Modeling** option from the list of toolbars. Various tools in the **Synchronous Modeling** toolbar are discussed next.

Move Face

Menu:	Insert > Synchronous Modeling > Move Face
Toolbar:	Synchronous Modeling > Move Face

You can move a set of selected faces of a model in the linear direction or orient them in the angular direction using the **Move Face** tool. On doing so, the adjacent chamfers or fillets will also get adjusted automatically. To invoke the **Move Face** tool, choose **Insert > Synchronous Modeling > Move Face** from the menu bar; the **Move Face** dialog box will be displayed, refer to Figure 14-1. The options of this dialog box are discussed next.

Face Rollout

In this rollout, the **Face** button is chosen by default. As a result, you will be prompted to select the faces to be moved. Select the faces that you want to move; a handle, an angular handle, and a triad of vectors will be displayed on one of the selected faces. Using the triad of vector, you can choose the direction for moving the selected faces. Using the handle, you can drag the selected faces along the specified direction on the triad of vector. Note that the component will be modified according to the movement of the cursor. Using the angular handle, you can change the angular direction of the selected face. You can also use the dynamic edit box for modifying the component. Figure 14-2 shows the selected faces, handle, angular handle, and dynamic edit box and Figure 14-3 shows the preview of the dynamically updated model. Figure 14-4 shows the faces selected to change their angular direction by using the angular handle and Figure 14-5 shows the preview of the dynamically updated model.

If you select a face, a list of all possible geometrical conditions that can be applied to the selected face with respect to the unselected faces will be displayed in the **Results** tab of the **Face Finder** sub-rollout. If you move the cursor over a geometrical condition, all the faces related to it will be highlighted in the graphic window. To select the unselected faces, select the check box of the corresponding geometrical condition. In the **Settings** tab of the **Face Finder** sub-rollout, you can select the required check boxes of the geometrical conditions in such a way that if you select a single face, multiple faces are selected automatically according

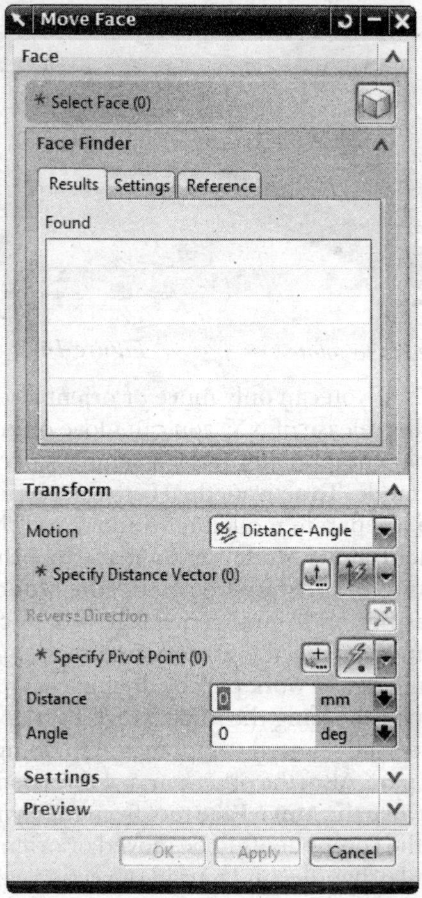

Figure 14-1 *The **Move Face** dialog box*

to the settings in the **Settings** tab. You can select the required coordinate system from the **Reference** drop-down list in the **Reference** tab, so that the faces move with reference to the selected coordinate system.

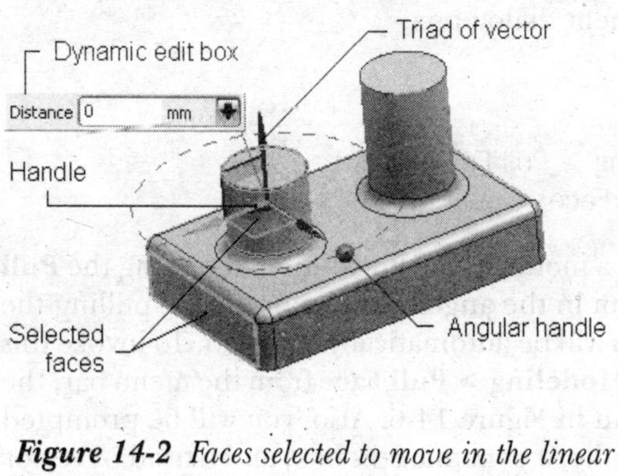

Figure 14-2 *Faces selected to move in the linear direction*

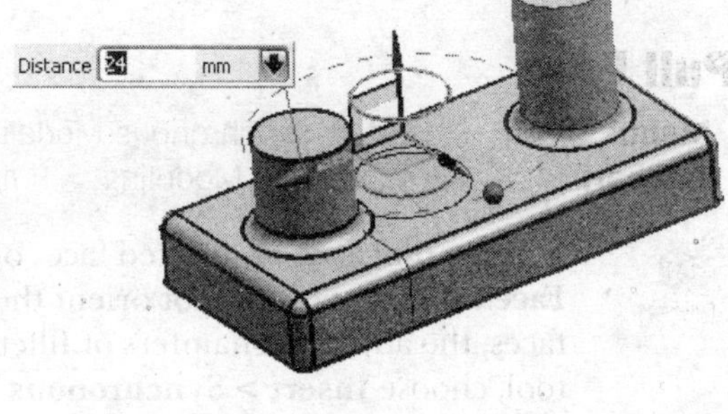

Figure 14-3 *Dynamically updated model*

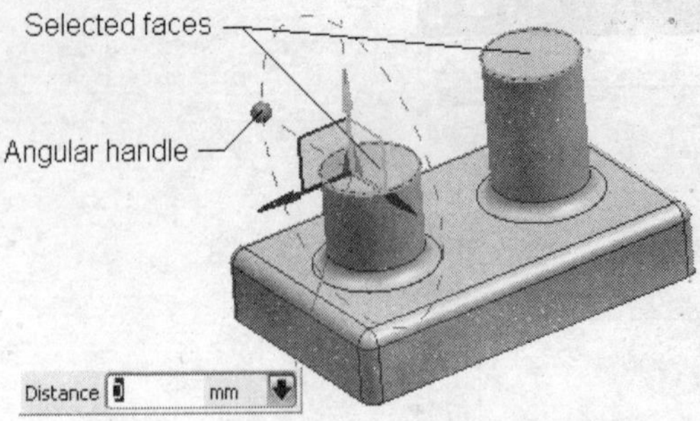

Figure 14-4 Faces selected to rotate

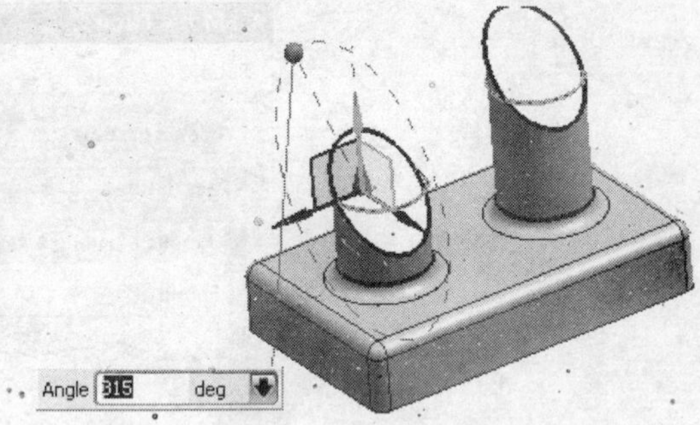

Figure 14-5 Dynamically updated model

In the previous releases of NX, you can only move or orient a set of faces of the work part in the assembly. However, in this release of NX, you can move or orient a set of faces not only of the work part but of the other components in the assembly as well. To do so, the components must be in the History-free mode. To activate the History-free mode, open the components of the assembly one by one in a separate modeling window, and then choose the **History-Free Mode** button from the **Synchronous Modeling** toolbar. Note that while changing the mode of the assembly components to the History-free mode, the **Modeling Mode** message box will be displayed. Chose the **Yes** button from this message box to continue. After changing the mode of the assembly components to the History-free mode, open the assembly and then activate the required component as a work part by double-clicking on it. You can also activate a component as a work part by choosing the **Make Work Part** option from the shortcut menu displayed by right-clicking on the selected component. On doing so, the selected component will be activated as the work part. Also, the other parts of the assembly and the parent assembly will be deactivated. Next, invoke the **Move Face** tool from the **Synchronous Modeling** toolbar and then select the faces of the components to be moved or oriented of the components in the assembly; a handle, an angular handle, and a triad of vectors will be displayed attached with the first selected face. Now, by using the handle and the angular handle, you can dynamically move or orient the selected faces of the components.

Transform Rollout

Instead of dragging the handle, angular handle, or using the dynamic input boxes to move the faces, you can use the **Transform** rollout to specify the values. The options in this rollout are similar to the options of the **Move Component** dialog box.

Pull Face

Menu:	Insert > Synchronous Modeling > Pull Face
Toolbar:	Synchronous Modeling > Pull Face

You can pull a set of selected faces of a model in the linear direction using the **Pull Face** tool, but you cannot orient them in the angular direction. While pulling the faces, the adjacent chamfers or fillets will be automatically adjusted. To invoke this tool, choose **Insert > Synchronous Modeling > Pull Face** from the menu bar; the **Pull Face** dialog box will be displayed, as shown in Figure 14-6. Also, you will be prompted to select the faces to pull. Select the faces; a handle, a dynamic edit box, and a triad of vector will be displayed on one of the selected faces, as shown in Figure 14-7. Drag the handle; the model will be dynamically updated, as shown in **Figure 14-8.**

Figure 14-6 *The **Pull Face** dialog box*

The options in the **Pull Face** dialog box are the same as those in the **Move Face** dialog box with the only difference that the **Move Face** tool is used to move the selected faces with respect to the adjacent geometry, whereas the **Pull Face** tool is used to pull the selected faces regardless of the adjacent geometry. For example, Figure 14-9 shows the face moved using the **Move Face** tool and Figure 14-10 shows the face moved using the **Pull Face** tool.

Figure 14-7 *Face selected to be pulled*

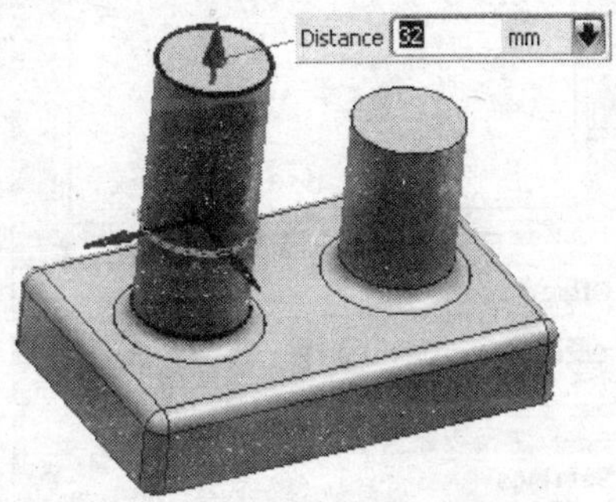

Figure 14-8 *Dynamically updated model*

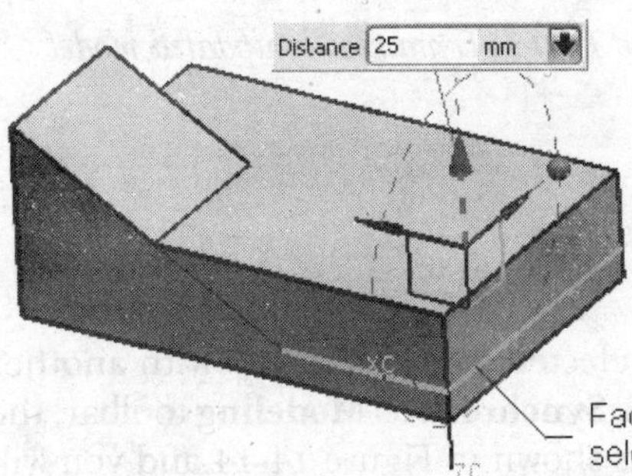

Figure 14-9 *Selected face moved using the **Move Face** tool*

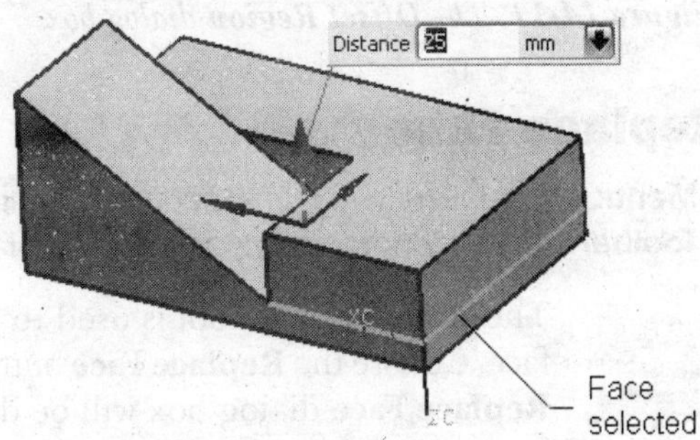

Figure 14-10 *Selected face moved using the **Pull Face** tool*

Offset Region

Menu:	Insert > Synchronous Modeling > Offset Region
Toolbar:	Synchronous Modeling > Offset Region

The **Offset Region** tool is used to offset a set of selected faces of a model along the normal of the selected faces. To do so, choose the **Offset Region** button from the **Synchronous Modeling** toolbar; the **Offset Region** dialog box will be displayed, refer to Figure 14-11 and you will be prompted to select the faces to offset. Select the faces; a handle and a dynamic edit box will be displayed on the first selected face, refer to Figure 14-12. Drag the handle; the model will be updated, refer to Figure 14-13. The options of the **Offset Region** dialog box are the same as those in the **Move Face** dialog box.

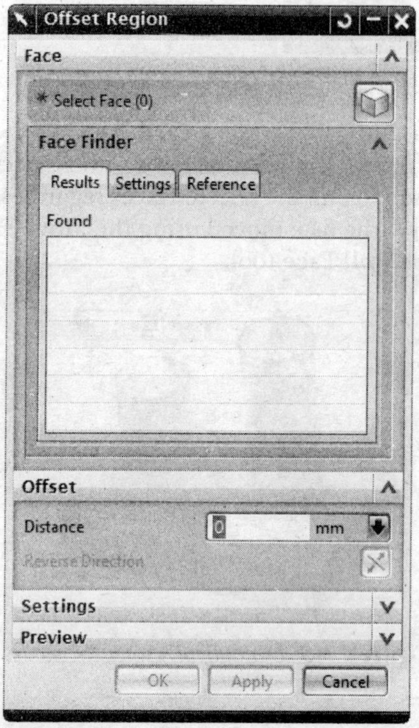

*Figure 14-11 The **Offset Region** dialog box*

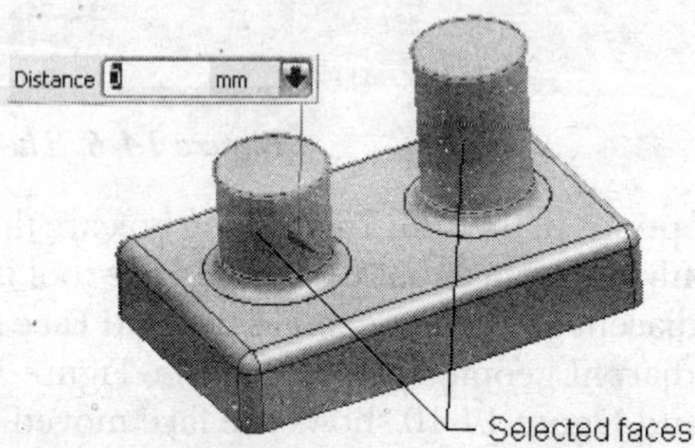

Figure 14-12 Faces selected to offset

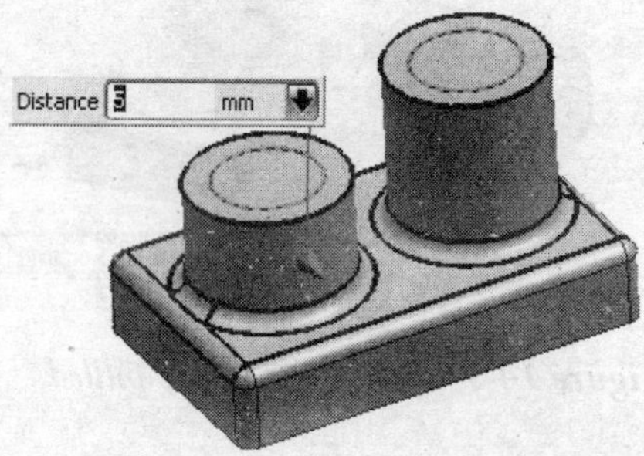

Figure 14-13 Dynamically updated model

Replace Face

Menu:	Insert > Synchronous Modeling > Replace Face
Toolbar:	Synchronous Modeling > Replace Face

The **Replace Face** tool is used to replace a selected face of a model with another face. Choose the **Replace Face** button from the **Synchronous Modeling** toolbar; the **Replace Face** dialog box will be displayed, as shown in Figure 14-14 and you will be prompted to select the faces to replace. Select the faces that you want to replace. Next, choose the **Face** button from the **Replacement Face** rollout; you will be prompted to

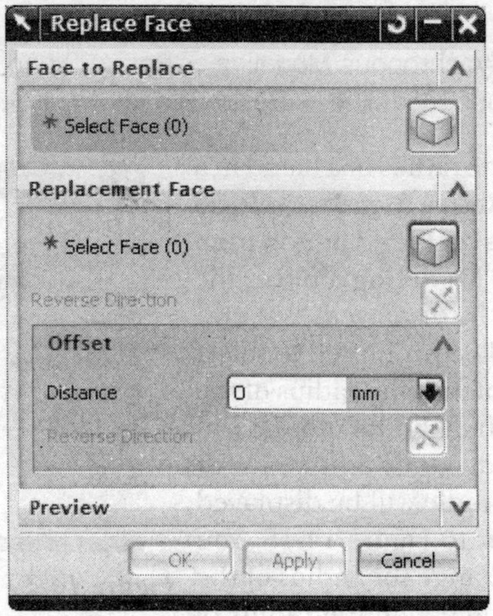

Figure 14-14 *The* ***Replace Face*** *dialog box*

select the replacement face. Select the replacement face; the face to be replaced will become coplanar with the replacement face. Also, a dynamic edit box, a handle, and a vector will be displayed on the replacement face. Figure 14-15 shows the faces selected and Figure 14-16 shows the preview of the resultant model along with the dynamic edit box, the handle, and the vector. You can further modify the selected face with respect to the replacement face by dragging the handle or by modifying the offset distance in the **Distance** edit box in the **Offset** sub-rollout. To change the direction of vector, use the **Reverse Direction** button from the **Replacement Face** rollout and to change the direction of the handle, use the **Reverse Direction** button from the **Offset** sub-rollout. To apply the changes and close the **Replace Face** dialog box, choose **OK**.

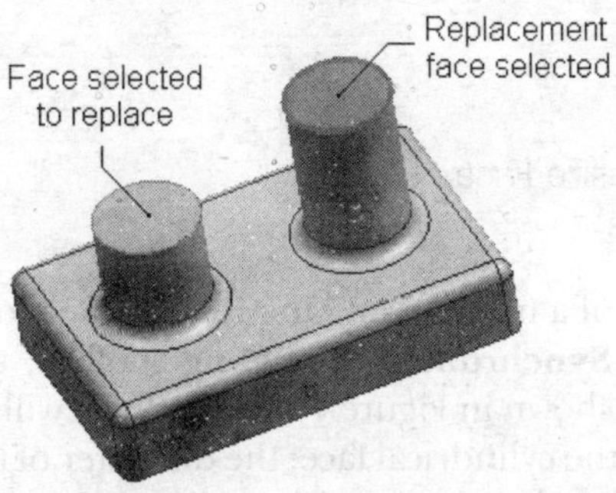

Figure 14-15 *Faces to be selected*

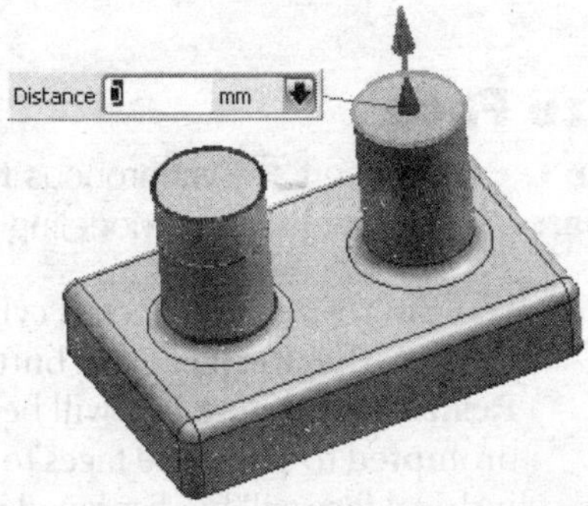

Figure 14-16 *Dynamically updated model after selecting the faces*

Resize Blend

Menu: Insert > Synchronous Modeling > Resize Blend
Toolbar: Synchronous Modeling > Resize Blend

You can change the radius of a blend in a model using the **Resize Blend** tool. To do so, choose the **Resize Blend** button from the **Synchronous Modeling** toolbar; the **Resize Blend** dialog box will be displayed, as shown in Figure 14-17, and you will be prompted to select the blend to resize. Select a blend; the radius of the blend will be displayed in the **Radius** edit box of the **Radius** rollout. Also, a dynamic edit box with the radius of blend, and a handle will be displayed in the graphics window, refer to Figure 14-18. You can use these edit boxes to change the radius of the blend. Alternatively, you can change the radius of the blend dynamically by dragging the handle, refer to Figure 14-19.

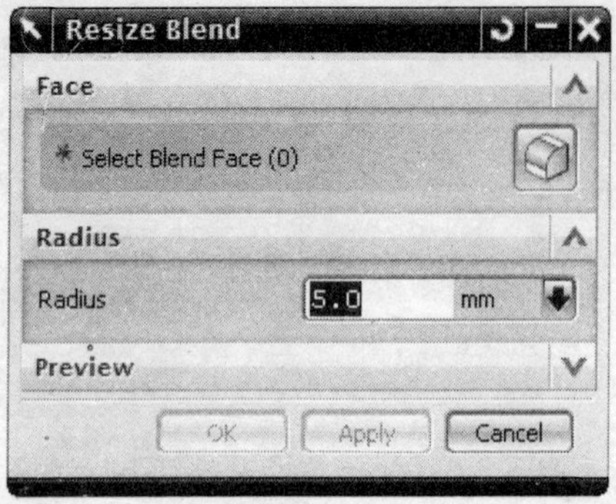

***Figure 14-17** The **Resize Blend** dialog box*

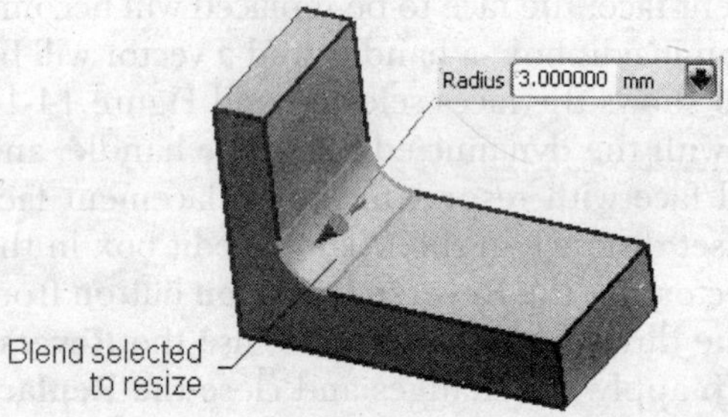

***Figure 14-18** Blend selected to resize*

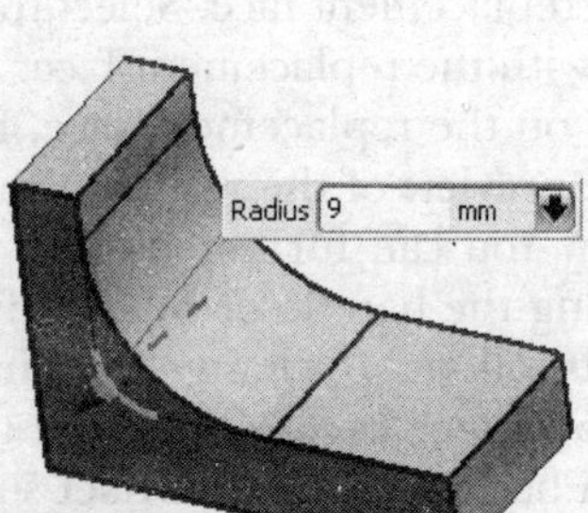

***Figure 14-19** Dynamically updated model*

Resize Face

Menu: Insert > Synchronous Modeling > Resize Face
Toolbar: Synchronous Modeling > Resize Face

You can resize the selected cylindrical faces of a model using the **Resize Face** tool. Choose the **Resize Face** button from the **Synchronous Modeling** toolbar; the **Resize Face** dialog box will be displayed, as shown in Figure 14-20, and you will be prompted to select the faces to resize. Select the cylindrical face; the diameter of the selected cylindrical face will be displayed in the **Diameter** edit box of the **Size** rollout. Now, you can use this edit box to change the diameter of the selected cylindrical face. Figure 14-21 shows the face selected to resize and Figure 14-22 show the model after resizing the selected face. The other options in this dialog box are the same as those discussed in the **Move Face** dialog box.

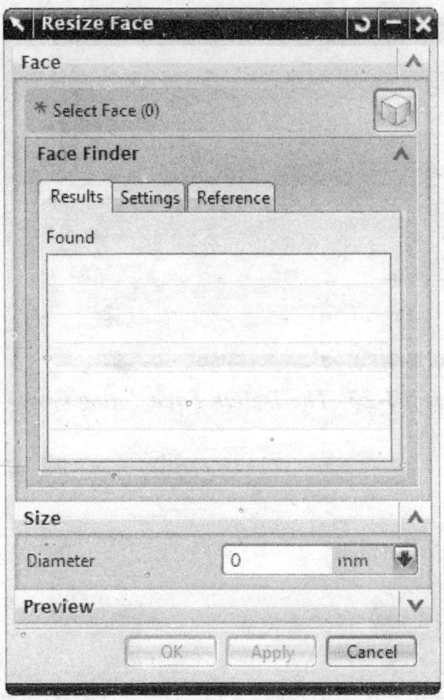

*Figure 14-20 The **Resize Face** dialog box*

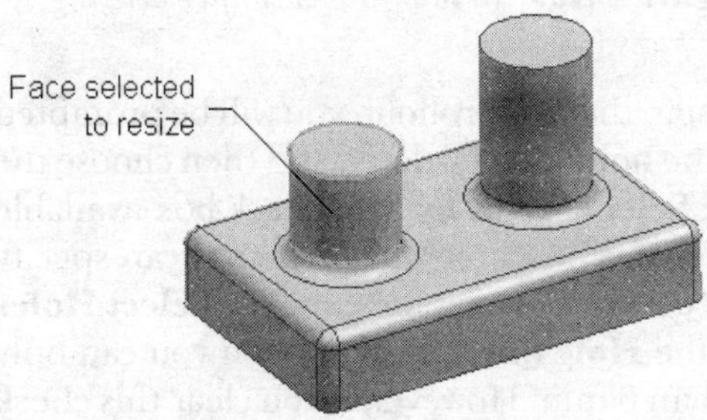

Figure 14-21 Face selected to resize

Figure 14-22 Dynamically updated model

Delete Face

Menu:	Insert > Synchronous Modeling > Delete Face
Toolbar:	Synchronous Modeling > Delete Face

The **Delete Face** tool is used for deleting the unwanted faces of a model by projecting its adjacent faces. Choose the **Delete Face** button from the **Synchronous Modeling** toolbar; the **Delete Face** dialog box will be displayed, as shown in Figure 14-23. In this dialog box, the **Face** option is selected by default in the drop-down list of the **Type** rollout. As a result, you will be prompted to select the faces to delete. Select the unwanted faces, refer to Figure 14-24. Next, choose the **OK** button; the selected faces will be deleted, refer to Figure 14-25.

Figure 14-23 *The* ***Delete Face*** *dialog box*

Figure 14-24 *Faces selected for deleting*

Figure 14-25 *Resultant model after deleting the faces*

If you select the **Hole** option from the drop-down list in the **Type** rollout, you will be prompted to select the faces of the holes to be deleted. Select the holes to be deleted and then choose the **OK** button; the selected holes will be deleted. The **Select Holes by Size** check box available in the **Face** rollout is used to select the holes of the specified hole diameter. You can specify the required diameter of the hole in the **Hole Size** edit box available below the **Select Holes by Size** check box. For example, if you enter **6** in the **Hole Size** edit box, then you can only select the holes whose diameter is equal to or less than 6 mm. However, if you clear this check box, you can select holes of any diameter.

Copy Face

Menu:	Insert > Synchronous Modeling > Reuse > Copy Face
Toolbar:	Synchronous Modeling > Copy Face

The **Copy Face** tool is used to copy and place the selected faces of a solid or surface body. You can place the selected faces as a surface or as a solid body. To place them as a solid body, the selected faces must be in the form of a closed entity. Choose the **Copy Face** button from the **Synchronous Modeling** toolbar; the **Copy Face** dialog box will be displayed, as shown in Figure 14-26 and you will be prompted to select the faces to copy. Select the faces; a handle, an angular handle, and an edit box will be displayed, refer to Figure 14-27. You can use these handles for moving the copied object, refer to Figure 14-28. Select the **Paste Copied Faces** check box from the **Paste** rollout and choose the **OK** button to generate a solid body. If you clear the **Paste Copied Faces** check box, the resulting surface generated will be a surface body. The remaining options in this dialog box are similar to those in the **Move Face** dialog box.

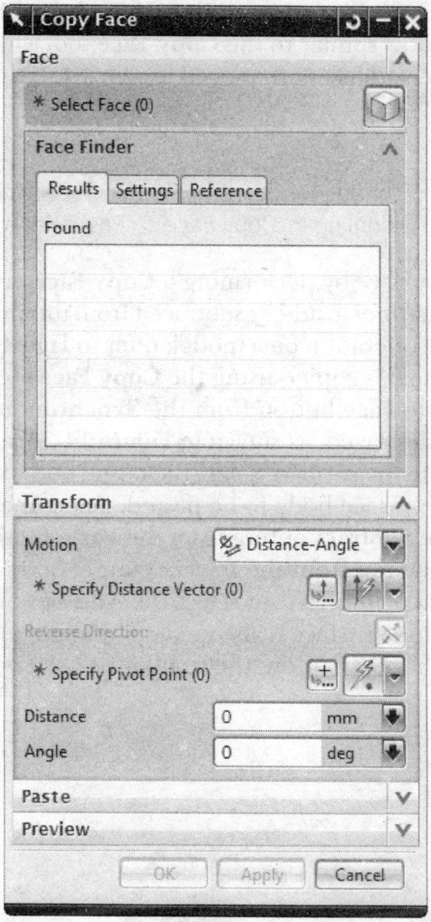

Figure 14-26 *The* ***Copy Face*** *dialog box*

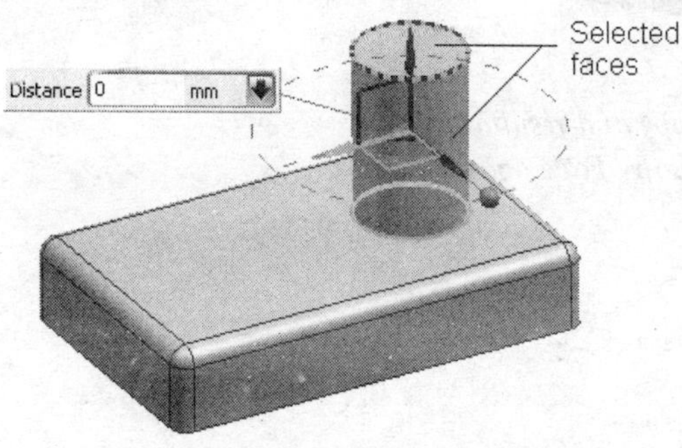

Figure 14-27 *Faces selected for copying*

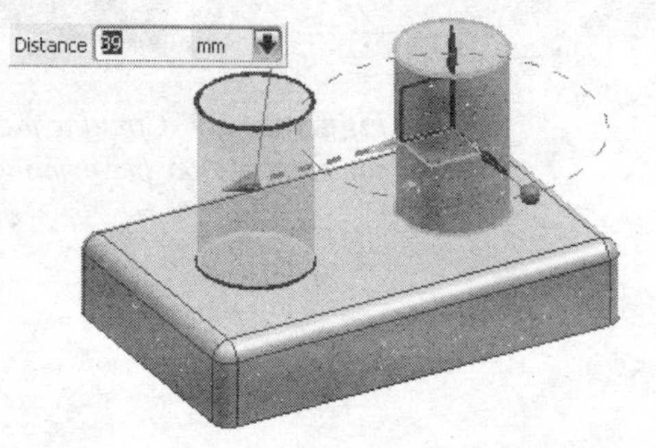

Figure 14-28 *Preview of the resultant model*

Cut Face

Menu:	Insert > Synchronous Modeling > Reuse > Cut Face
Toolbar:	Synchronous Modeling > Copy Face > Cut Face

The **Cut Face** tool is used to cut and place the selected faces of a solid or surface model. This tool works similar to the **Copy Face** tool with the only difference that in this case, the selected faces are moved to a new location.

Paste Face

Menu:	Insert > Synchronous Modeling > Reuse > Paste Face
Toolbar:	Synchronous Modeling > Copy Face > Paste Face

Once you create a surface by performing a **Copy Face** or **Cut Face** operation, you can use the **Paste Face** tool to add or subtract it from the attached body. For example, perform a copy face operation on a model, refer to Figure 14-29. In this figure, the circular surface of hole is copied using the **Copy Face** tool. Next, invoke the **Paste Face** tool by choosing the **Paste Face** button from the **Synchronous Modeling** toolbar; the **Paste Face** dialog box will be displayed, as shown in Figure 14-30, and you will be prompted to select the target body to paste the surface. Select the target body, refer to Figure 14-31; you will be prompted to select the surface body to be pasted. Select the surface created, refer to Figure 14-31. Next, choose the **Subtract** option from the **Paste Option** drop-down list in the **Tool** rollout to subtract the material from the selected target body. If the original feature is created by adding material, then you need to select the **Add** option from the **Paste Option** drop-down list so that the resulting surface is also created by adding material. After specifying the required options, choose the **OK** button; the resultant model will be displayed, as shown in Figure 14-32.

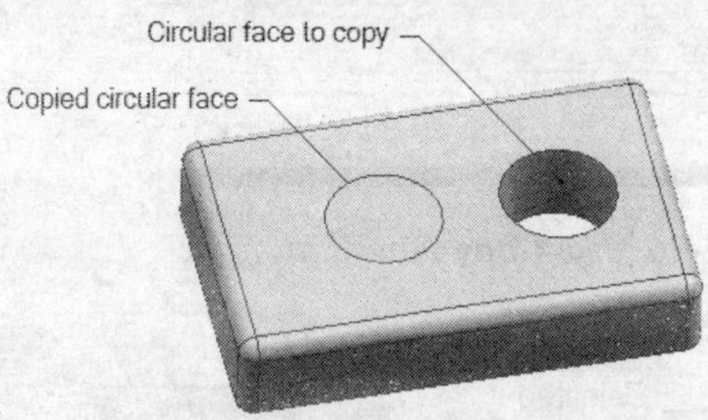

***Figure 14-29** Circular face to copy and resultant copied face after performing the **Copy Face** operation*

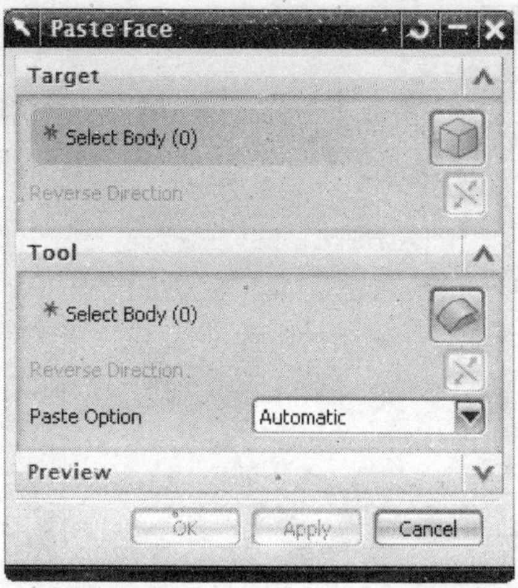

Figure 14-30 *The **Paste Face** dialog box*

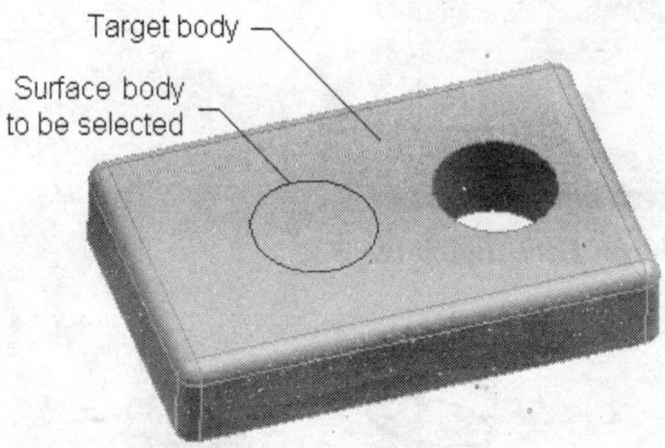

Figure 14-31 *Surface and target bodies to be selected*

Figure 14-32 *Resultant model*

Mirror Face

Menu:	Insert > Synchronous Modeling > Reuse > Mirror Face
Toolbar:	Synchronous Modeling > Copy Face > Mirror Face

The **Mirror Face** tool is used to mirror a set of faces in the same body about a selected plane. Choose the **Mirror Face** button from the **Synchronous Modeling** toolbar; the **Mirror Face** dialog box will be displayed, as shown in Figure 14-33 and you will be prompted to select the faces to mirror. Select the faces, refer to Figure 14-34. Next, choose the **Plane** button from the **Mirror Plane** rollout; you will be prompted to select a planar face or datum plane to mirror about. Select the required plane, as shown in Figure 14-34; the preview of the resultant model will be displayed, as shown in Figure 14-35. Choose the **OK** button; the selected set of faces will be mirrored about the selected plane.

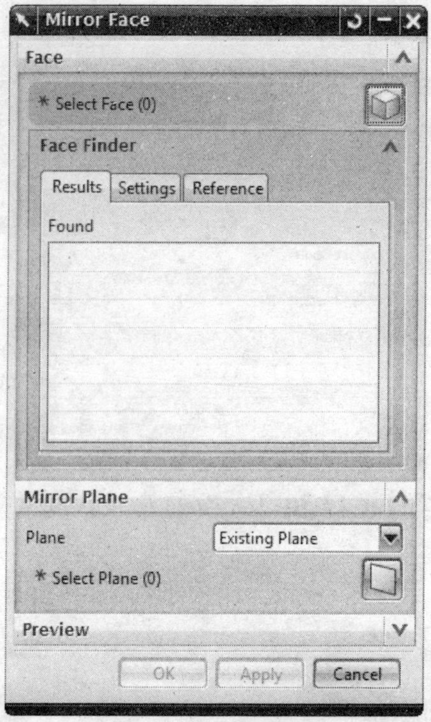

*Figure 14-33 The **Mirror Face** dialog box*

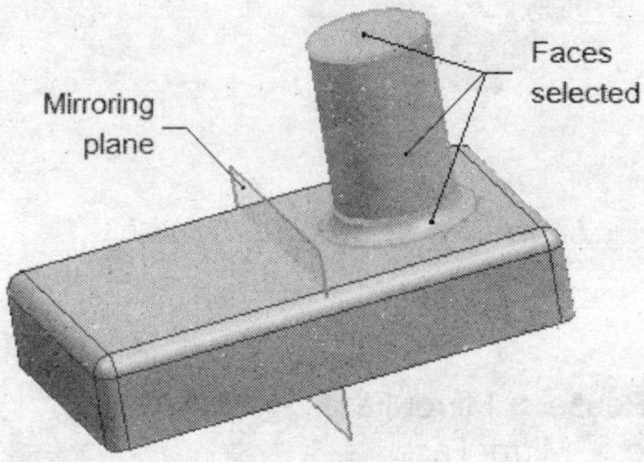

Figure 14-34 Faces and mirroring plane selected

Figure 14-35 Preview of the resultant model

Pattern Face

Menu: Insert > Synchronous Modeling > Reuse > Pattern Face
Toolbar: Synchronous Modeling > Copy Face > Pattern Face

You can pattern the selected faces of a component using the **Pattern Face** tool. Choose the **Pattern Face** button from the **Synchronous Modeling** toolbar; the **Pattern Face** dialog box will be displayed. The options in the **Pattern Face** dialog box are very much similar to the options in the **Instance Feature** tool discussed in

Chapter 7. In this release of NX, if you perform any operation such as moving a face, pulling a face, offsetting a region on any instance of the pattern, all instances of the pattern will be updated accordingly. But for updating all instances of the pattern accordingly, you need to create the pattern using the **Pattern Face** tool in the History-free mode.

Resize Chamfer

Menu: Insert > Synchronous Modeling > Chamfer > Resize Chamfer
Toolbar: Synchronous Modeling > Resize Chamfer

You can change the size of a chamfer in a model, regardless of its adjacent geometry, by using the **Resize Chamfer** tool. To do so, choose the **Resize Chamfer** button from the **Synchronous Modeling** toolbar; the **Resize Chamfer** dialog box will be displayed, as shown in Figure 14-36, and you will be prompted to select the chamfer to resize. Select the chamfer; the chamfer values will be displayed in their respective edit boxes in the **Offsets** rollout. Also, a dynamic edit box, a handle, and an angular handle will be displayed in the graphics window, refer to Figure 14-37. You can change the size of the chamfer using the edit boxes available in the **Offsets** rollout or by using the dynamic edit box. Alternatively, you can change the size of the chamfer using the handles, refer to Figure 14-38. Next, choose **OK**.

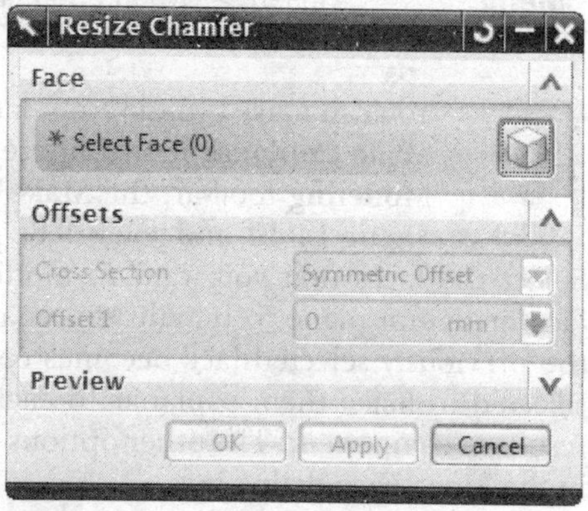

*Figure 14-36 The **Resize Chamfer** dialog box*

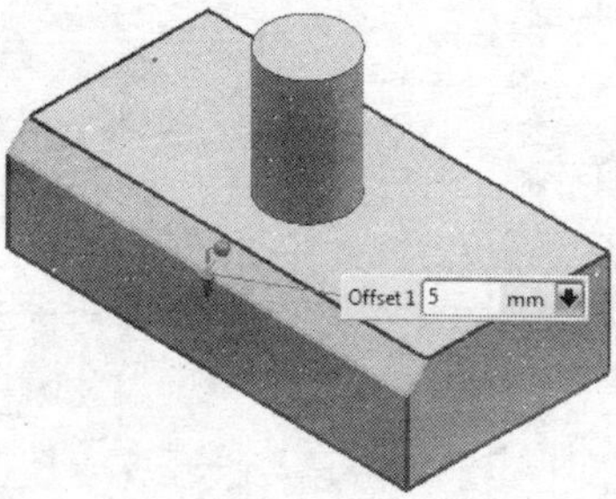

Figure 14-37 Model with a dynamic edit box, a handle, and an angular handle

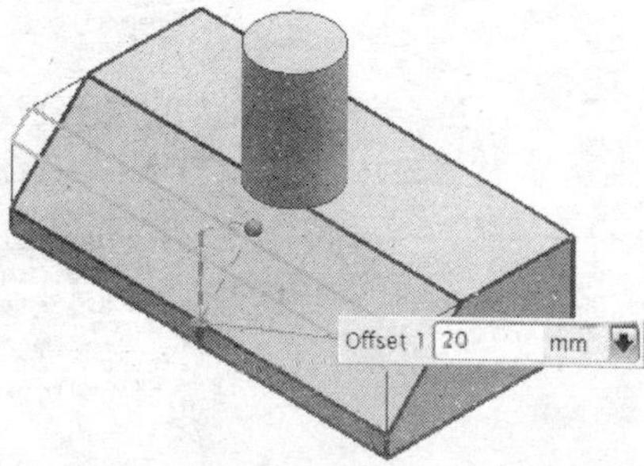

Figure 14-38 Preview of the resultant model

Label Chamfer

Menu: Insert > Synchronous Modeling > Chamfer > Label Chamfer
Toolbar: Synchronous Modeling > Label Chamfer

You can label an angular face, which is not created by the **Chamfer** tool, as a chamfer by using the **Label Chamfer** tool. To do so, invoke the **Label Chamfer**

tool and then select the angular face; the selected angular face will be labeled as a chamfer. After labeling the angular face as a chamfer, you can use the **Resize Chamfer** tool to resize it as a chamfer. Also, if you move its adjacent faces, it will move as a chamfer and its size will not change. However, if you move the faces adjacent to the angular face without labeling the angular face as a chamfer, the size of the angular face will change as you move the face using the **Move Face** tool.

Make Coplanar

Menu:	Insert > Synchronous Modeling > Relate > Make Coplanar
Toolbar:	Synchronous Modeling > Make Coplanar

You can make two different faces of a component coplanar to each other using the **Make Coplanar** tool. Choose the **Make Coplanar** button from the **Synchronous Modeling** toolbar; the **Make Coplanar** dialog box will be displayed, as shown in Figure 14-39, and you will be prompted to select a planar face to make it coplanar. Select the faces that you want to modify. Next, you will be prompted to select a planar face or datum plane to remain stationary. Select the required plane or planar face so that the previously selected face becomes coplanar with it. Figure 14-40 shows the planar faces selected to make them coplanar to each other and Figure 14-41 shows the preview of the resultant component. The other options of the **Make Coplanar** dialog box are similar to those in the **Move Face** dialog box.

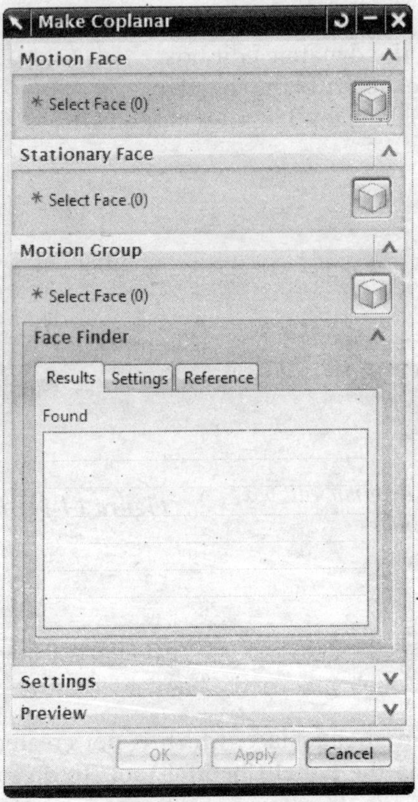

***Figure 14-39** The **Make Coplanar** dialog box*

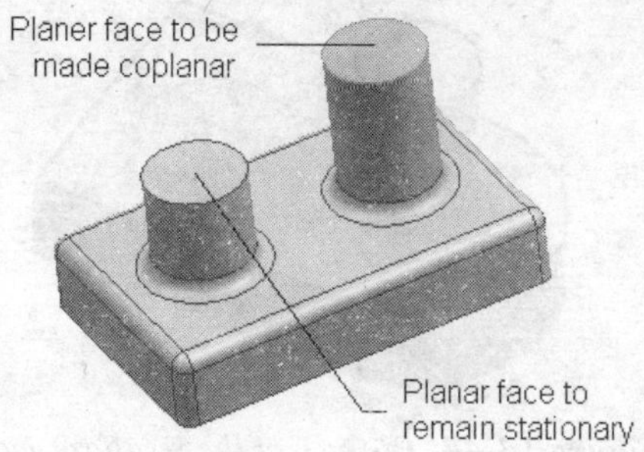

Figure 14-40 *Faces selected to make them coplanar*

Figure 14-41 *Preview of the resultant model*

Make Coaxial

Menu:	Insert > Synchronous Modeling > Relate > Make Coaxial
Toolbar:	Synchronous Modeling > Make Coplanar > Make Coaxial

You can make two different cylindrical faces of a component coaxial using the **Make Coaxial** tool. To do so, choose the **Make Coaxial** button from the **Synchronous Modeling** toolbar; the **Make Coaxial** dialog box will be displayed, as shown in Figure 14-42, and you will be prompted to select a cylinder, cone, or torus to be made coaxial. Select the required cylinder, cone, or torus; the **Face** button in the **Stationary Face** rollout will be chosen automatically and you will be prompted to select another cylinder, cone, or torus that has to be made coaxial with the previously selected entity. Select the required cylinder, cone, or torus, so that the entity selected earlier becomes coaxial to the entity selected later, refer to Figure 14-43, the preview of the resultant component will be displayed, as shown in Figure 14-44. The other options of the **Make Coplanar** dialog box are similar to those discussed in the **Move Face** dialog box.

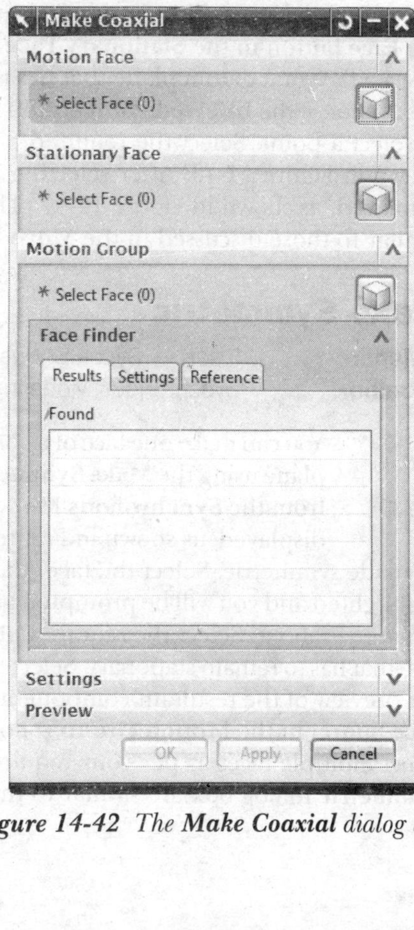

Figure 14-42 *The **Make Coaxial** dialog box*

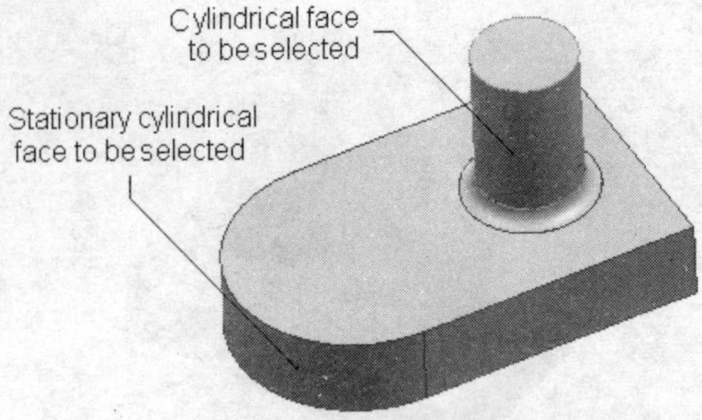

Figure 14-43 Faces selected to make them coaxial

Figure 14-44 Preview of the resultant model

Make Tangent

Menu: Insert > Synchronous Modeling > Relate > Make Tangent
Toolbar: Synchronous Modeling > Make Coplanar > Make Tangent

You can make one face of component tangent to another face using the **Make Tangent** tool. Choose the **Make Tangent** button from the **Synchronous Modeling** toolbar; the **Make Tangent** dialog box will be displayed, as shown in Figure 14-45 and you will be prompted to select the face to be made tangent. Select the face; the **Face** button in the **Stationary Face** rollout will be activated and you will be prompted to select a face or a datum plane that has to remain stationary. Select the required face or plane. Next, choose the **Inferred Point** button from the **Through Point** rollout; you will be prompted to select a point. Select the required point through which the resultant face should pass, as shown in Figure 14-46. After selecting the point and faces, the preview of the model will be displayed, as shown in Figure 14-47. The other options of the **Make Tangent** dialog box are similar to those discussed in the **Move Face** dialog box.

Make Symmetric

Menu: Insert > Synchronous Modeling > Relate > Make Symmetric
Toolbar: Synchronous Modeling > Make Coplanar > Make Symmetric

You can make one face of a component symmetric to another face about any specified plane using the **Make Symmetric** tool. To do so, choose the **Make Symmetric** button from the **Synchronous Modeling** toolbar; the **Make Symmetric** dialog box will be displayed, as shown in Figure 14-48, and you will be prompted to select the face to be made symmetric. Select the face; the **Plane** button in the **Symmetry Plane** rollout will be highlighted and you will be prompted to select a planar face or a datum plane to make the face symmetric about. Select the required planar face or plane; you will be prompted to select the face that has to remain stationary. Select the face to be remained stationary, refer to Figure 14-49, the preview of the resultant component will be displayed, as shown in Figure 14-50. Also, the **Face** button in the **Motion Group** rollout will be activated automatically. As a result, you can select multiple faces as per your requirement for modifying. The other options of the **Make Symmetric** dialog box are similar to the **Move Face** dialog box.

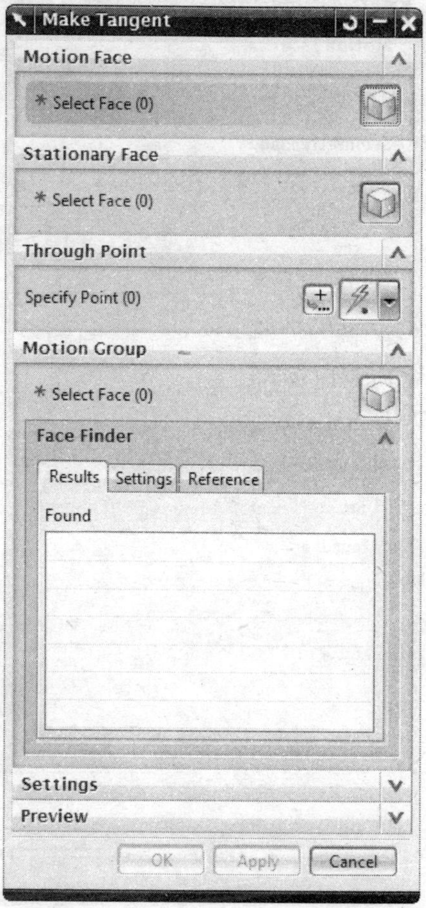

Figure 14-45 *The* ***Make Tangent*** *dialog box*

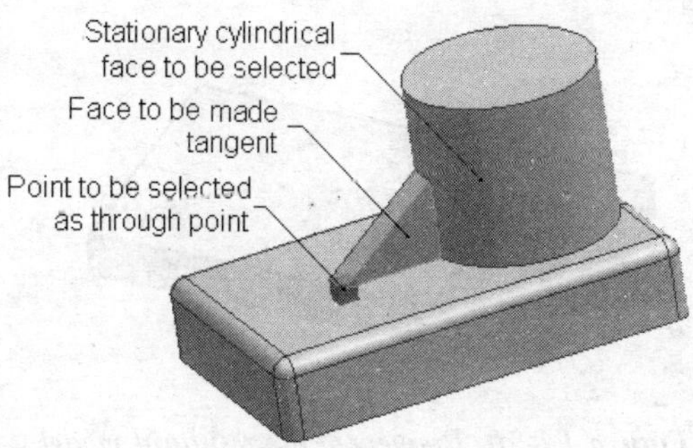

Figure 14-46 *Face selected to make tangent*

Figure 14-47 *Preview of the resultant model*

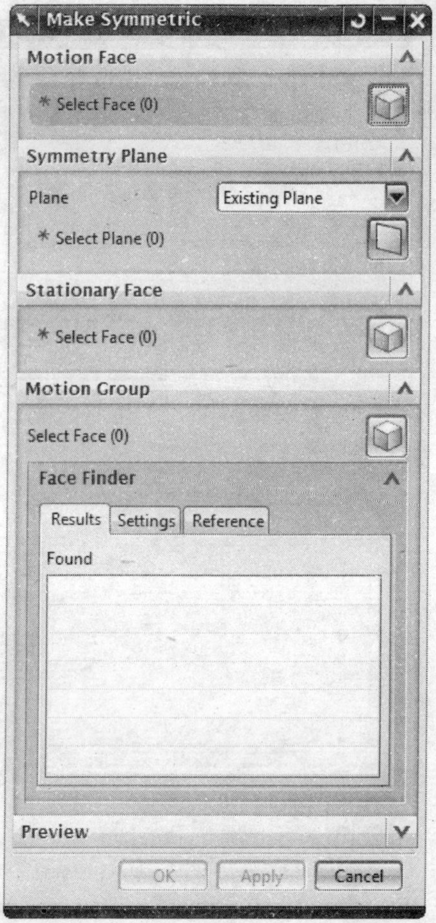

*Figure 14-48 The **Make Symmetric** dialog box*

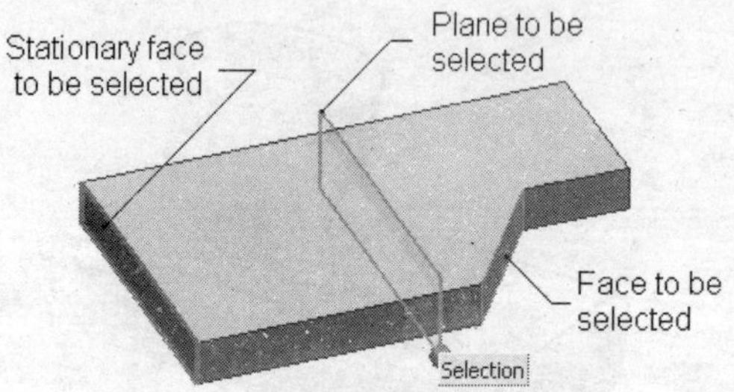

Figure 14-49 Faces and datum plane selected to make them symmetric

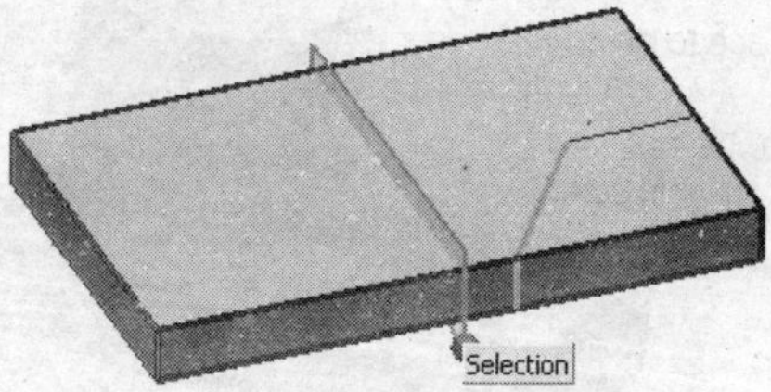

Figure 14-50 Preview of the resultant model

Make Parallel

Menu:	Insert > Synchronous Modeling > Relate > Make Parallel
Toolbar:	Synchronous Modeling > Make Coplanar > Make Parallel

You can make one planar face of a component parallel to another planar face using the **Make Parallel** tool. Choose the **Make Parallel** button from the **Synchronous Modeling** toolbar; the **Make Parallel** dialog box will be displayed, as shown in Figure 14-51, and you will be prompted to select the planar faces to be made parallel. Select the planar face that you want to modify; the **Face** button from the **Stationary face** rollout will be chosen automatically and you will be prompted to select the planar face or datum plane that has to remain stationary. Select the required planar face or plane. Next, choose the **Inferred Point** button from the **Through Point** rollout; you will be prompted to select a point. Select the point through which the face should pass, refer to Figure 14-52. On selecting the required point and faces, the preview of the resultant model will be displayed, as shown in Figure 14-53. The other options of the **Make Parallel** dialog box are similar to those discussed in the **Move Face** dialog box.

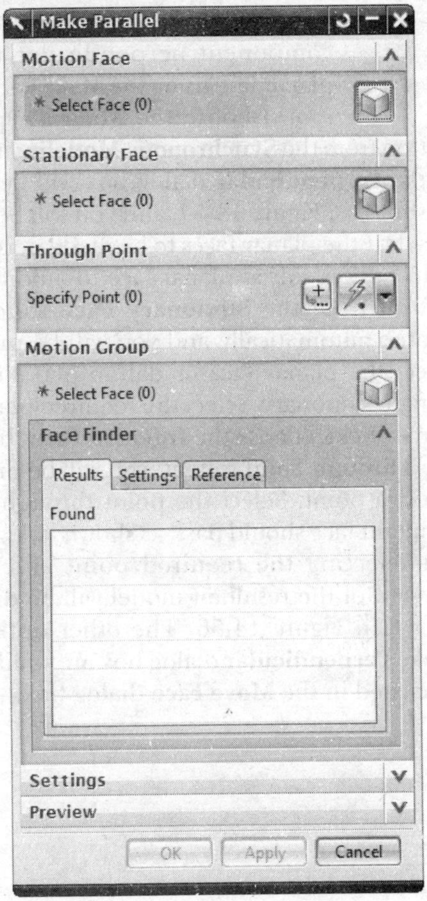

*Figure 14-51 The **Make Parallel** dialog box*

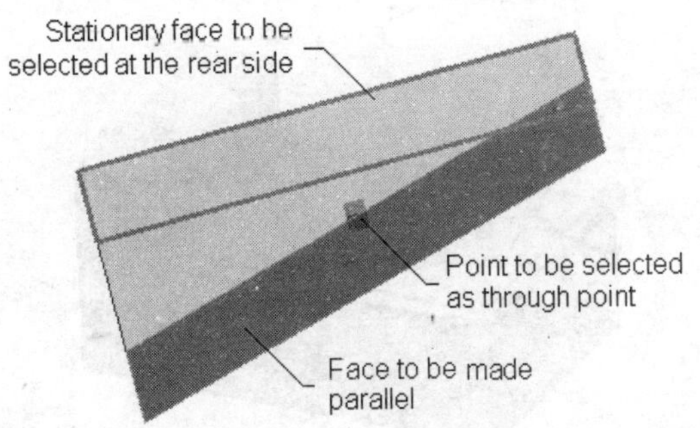

Figure 14-52 Faces selected to make them parallel

Figure 14-53 Preview of the resultant model

Make Perpendicular

Menu: Insert > Synchronous Modeling > Relate > Make Perpendicular
Toolbar: Synchronous Modeling > Make Coplanar > Make Perpendicular

You can make one planar face of a component perpendicular to another planar face using the **Make Perpendicular** tool. Choose the **Make Perpendicular** button from the **Synchronous Modeling** toolbar; the **Make Perpendicular** dialog box will be displayed, as shown in Figure 14-54, and you will be prompted to select the planar faces to be made perpendicular. Select the required planar face to modify; the **Face** button from the **Stationary Face** rollout will be chosen automatically and you will be prompted to select the planar face or datum plane that has to remain stationary. Select the required planar face or plane. Next, choose the **Inferred Point** button from the **Through Point** rollout; you will be prompted to select a point. Select the point through which the resultant face should pass, as shown in Figure 14-55. On selecting the required point and faces, the preview of the resultant model will be displayed as shown in Figure 14-56. The other options of the **Make Perpendicular** dialog box are similar to those discussed in the **Move Face** dialog box.

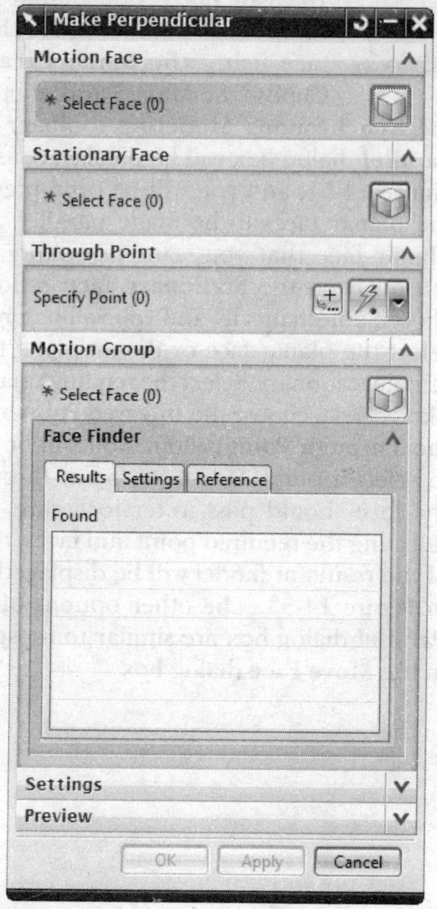

*Figure 14-54 The **Make Perpendicular** dialog box*

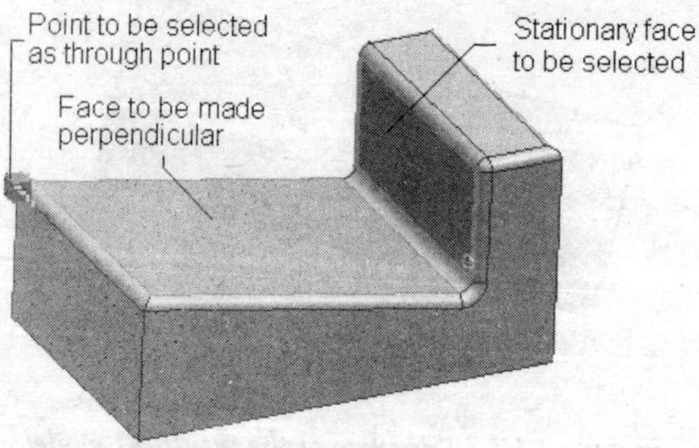

*Figure 14-55 Faces selected to apply the **Make Perpendicular** tool*

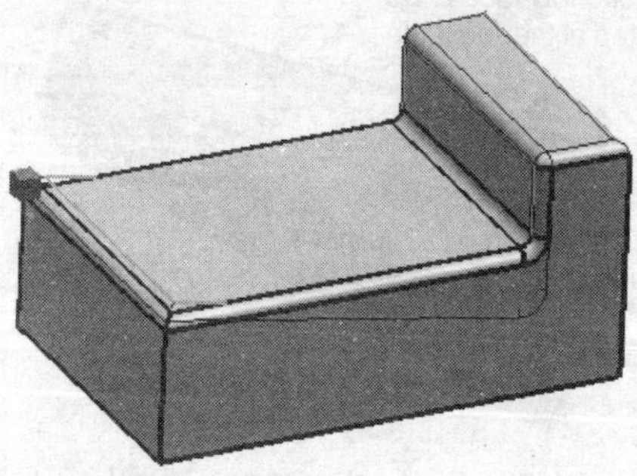

Figure 14-56 Preview of the resultant model

Make Fixed

Menu: Insert > Synchronous Modeling > Relate > Make Fixed
Toolbar: Synchronous Modeling > Make Coplanar > Make Fixed

The **Make Fixed** tool is used to make a face fixed by adding the fixed constraint to it. You can use this tool to prevent any change in the selected face. Note that this tool will be enabled only in the History-free mode. To make a face fixed, choose the **Make Fixed** button from the **Synchronous Modeling** toolbar; the **Make Fixed** dialog box will be displayed, as shown in Figure 14-57 and you will be prompted to select the faces to be made fixed. Select the required faces and choose the **OK** button; the selected faces will become fixed.

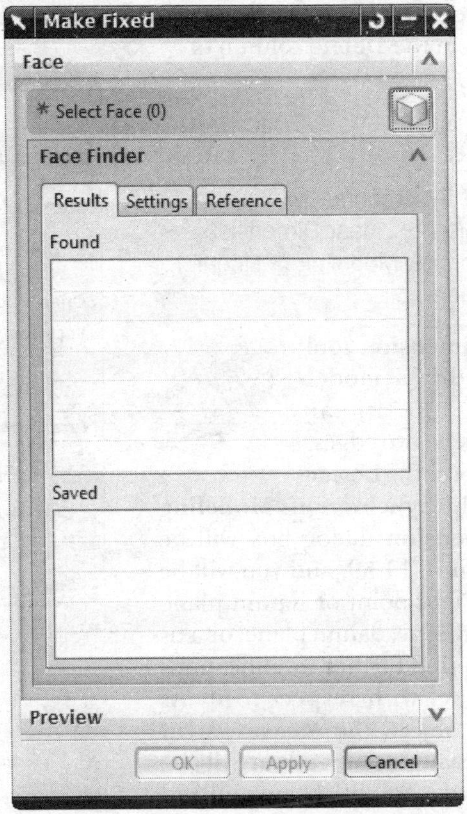

*Figure 14-57 The **Make Fixed** dialog box*

Show Related Face

Menu: Insert > Synchronous Modeling > Relate > Show Related Face
Toolbar: Synchronous Modeling > Make Coplanar > Show Related Face

The **Show Related Face** tool is used to highlight, review, and delete the relations that exist on the faces of a model. These relations can be fixed, linear dimension, angular dimension, radial dimension, and offset. Note that this tool will be enabled only in the History-free mode. To review and delete the relations existing on faces, choose the **Show Related Face** button from the **Synchronous Modeling** toolbar; the **Show Related Face** dialog box will be displayed, as shown in Figure 14-58, and you will be prompted to select the face to show relations. Also, all faces of the model will be displayed faded except the faces on which the relations exist. Select the required face; the **Relations** dialog box will be displayed, with all relations applied to the selected face listed in the **Relation** column. Now, you can delete relations of the selected face by clicking on the respective cross-mark in the **Delete** column of the dialog box.

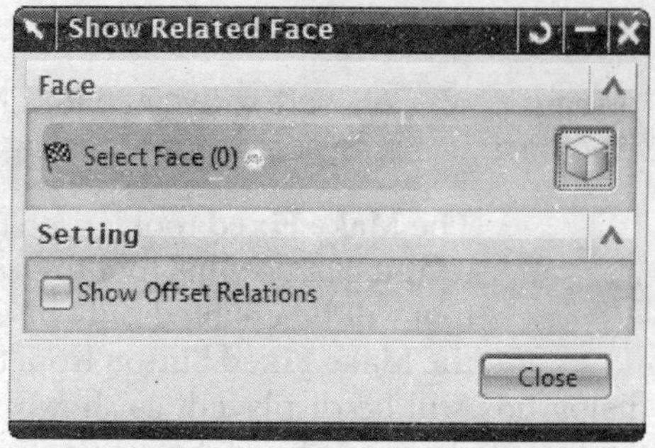

*Figure 14-58 The **Show Related Face** dialog box*

Linear Dimension

Menu:	Insert > Synchronous Modeling > Dimension > Linear Dimension
Toolbar:	Synchronous Modeling > Linear Dimension

The **Linear Dimension** tool is used to modify a model by modifying the linear dimension between two edges, axis, and faces. To do so, choose the **Linear Dimension** button from the **Synchronous Modeling** toolbar; the **Linear Dimension** dialog box will be displayed, as shown in Figure 14-59, and you will be prompted to select the origin point or datum plane for dimensioning. Select an edge, datum plane, or axis as the stationary object so that further modifications can be made in the model with respect to it. As you select the stationary object, the **Measurement Object** button in the **Measurement** rollout will be chosen automatically and you will be prompted to select a measurement point for dimensioning. Select the required edge; the distance between the origin and the selected edge will be displayed in the graphics window. Choose the **Specify Location** button from the **Location** rollout, if it is not chosen automatically. Now, you can locate the dimension by clicking in the graphics window. On doing so, the **Face** button from the **Face To Move** rollout will be chosen automatically and you will be prompted to select the faces to move. Select the faces that you want to move; a triad of vector and a dynamic edit box will

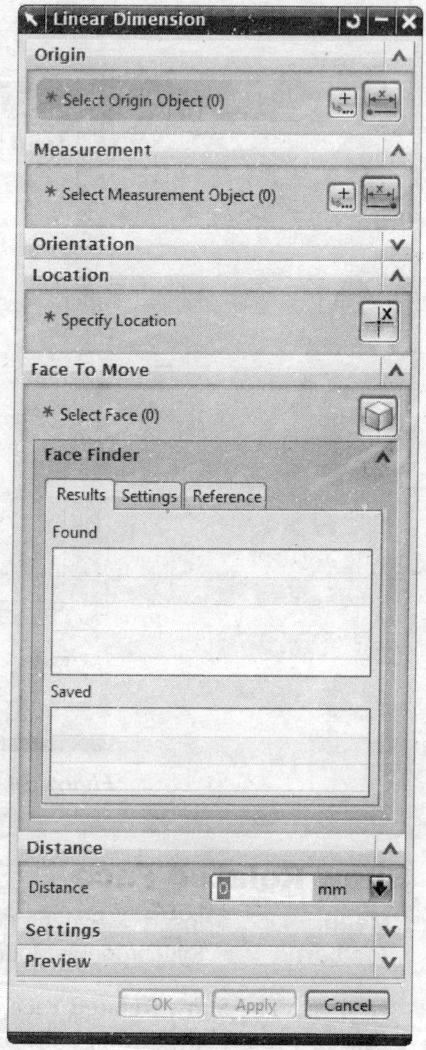

*Figure 14-59 The **Linear Dimension** dialog box*

be displayed, refer to Figure 14-60. You can move the selected faces by using the dynamic edit box or by specifying the required distance in the **Distance** rollout. On doing so, the preview of the resultant model will be displayed, as shown in Figure 14-61.

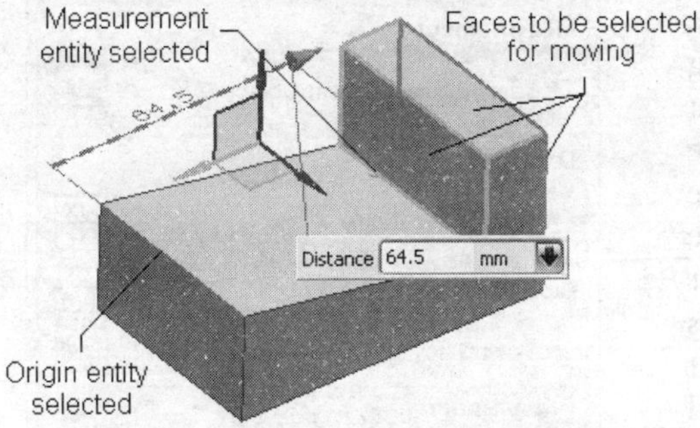

Figure 14-60 Edges selected for linear dimensioning

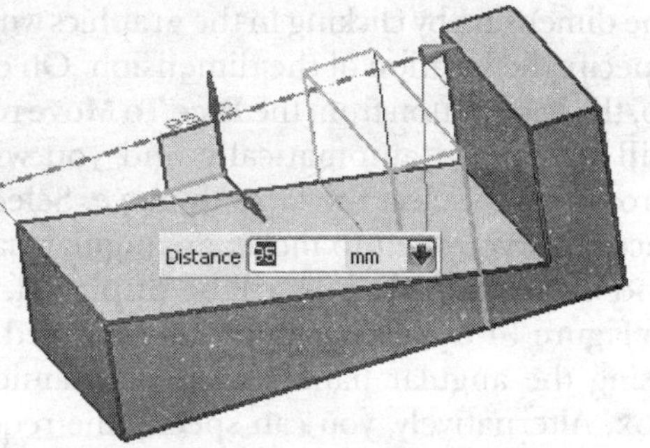

Figure 14-61 Preview of the resultant model

In the **Orientation** rollout of the **Linear Dimension** dialog box, you can either specify the axis or plane, or both for dimensioning, so that the modification can be made in the model with respect to them. By default, the **OrientXpress** option is selected in the **Direction** drop-down list, so that you can specify the required axis, plane, and coordinate system using the **Direction**, **Plane** and **Reference** drop-down lists in the **OrientXpress** sub-rollout, respectively. If you select the **Vector** option in the **Direction** drop-down list, the **Orientation** rollout will be modified and you will be prompted to select the object infer vector. Specify the required vector; the linear dimension will be displayed along the specified vector and the plane to modify.

In this release of NX, you can apply the static relationship between the selected edges and the faces of the model that are selected for applying the linear dimension. The static relationship will prevent the selected face from being changed. To apply the static relationship between edges and faces, select the **Lock Dimension** check box from the **Settings** rollout of the **Linear Dimension** dialog box. Note that this check box will be available only in the History-free mode.

Angular Dimension

Menu: Insert > Synchronous Modeling > Dimension > Angular Dimension
Toolbar: Synchronous Modeling > Linear Dimension > Angular Dimension

The **Angular Dimension** tool is used to move the selected face in the angular direction by modifying the angle between the two faces. Choose the **Angular Dimension** button from the **Synchronous Modeling** toolbar; the **Angular Dimension** dialog box will be displayed, refer to Figure 14-62 and you will be prompted to select the origin object for dimensioning. Select a face to remain stationary, refer to Figure 14-63. Now, the further modifications can be made with respect to this face. Also, the **Measurement Object** button from the **Measurement** rollout will be chosen automatically and you will be prompted to select the measurement object for dimensioning. Select the required face; the angle between two objects will be displayed in the graphics window, attached with the cursor and the **Specify Location** button will be chosen automatically in the **Location** rollout. As a result, you can locate the dimension by clicking in the graphics window. Specify the location of the dimension. On doing so, the **Face** button from the **Face To Move** rollout will be chosen automatically and you will be prompted to select the faces to move. Select the faces that you want to move; an angular handle and a dynamic edit box will be displayed, refer to Figure 14-63. You can move the selected faces using the angular handle or the dynamic edit box. Alternatively, you can specify the required angle in the **Angle** rollout. The preview of the resultant model will be displayed, as shown in Figure 14-64. Note that in the **Angle** rollout, the **Alternate Angle** check box is clear. If you select this check box, the value of alternate angle will be displayed in the graphics window.

In this release of NX, you can apply the static relationship between the selected edges and faces that are selected to apply the angular dimension. The static relationship will prevent the selected face from being changed. To apply the static relationship between edges and faces, select the **Lock Dimension** check box from the **Settings** rollout of the **Angular Dimension** dialog box. Note that this check box will be available only when you are in the History-free mode.

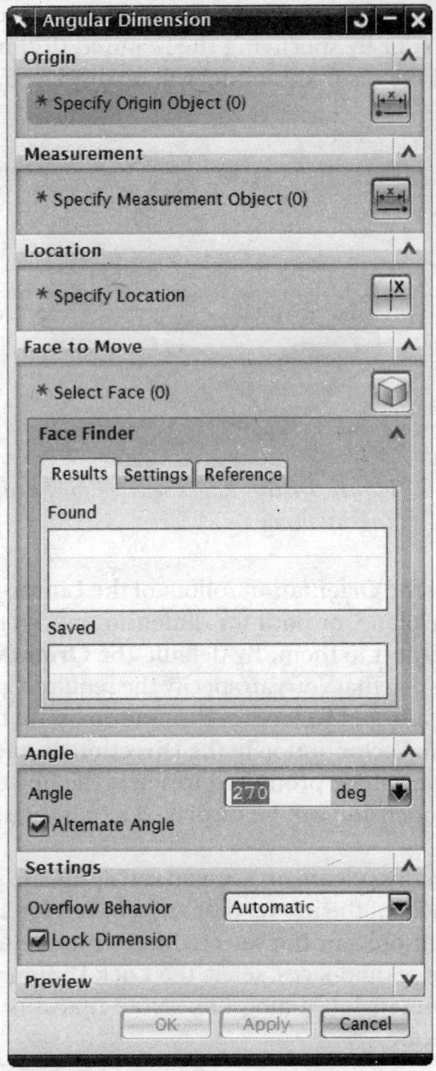

***Figure 14-62** The **Angular Dimension** dialog box*

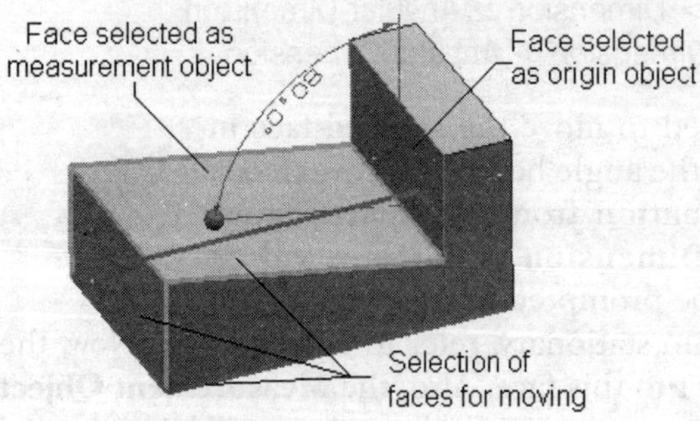

***Figure 14-63** Faces selected for angular dimensioning*

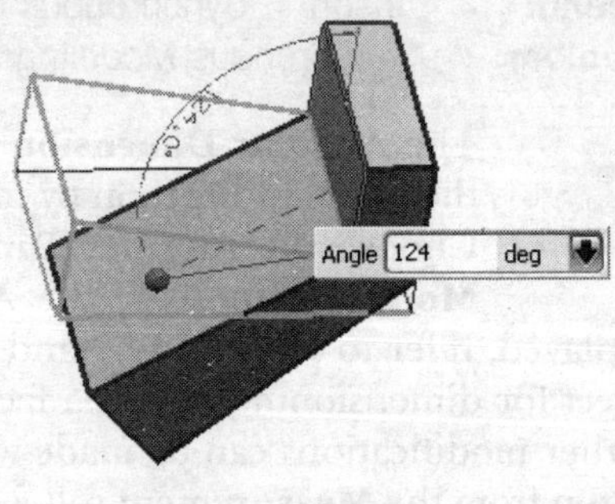

***Figure 14-64** Preview of the resultant model*

Radial Dimension

Menu: Insert > Synchronous Modeling > Dimension > Radial Dimension
Toolbar: Synchronous Modeling > Linear Dimension > Radial Dimension

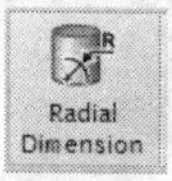

You can use the **Radial Dimension** tool to change the dimension of a cylindrical or spherical face of the model. Choose the **Radial Dimension** button from the **Synchronous Modeling** toolbar; the **Radial Dimension** dialog box will be displayed, as shown in Figure 14-65, and you will be prompted to select a face or edge to dimension. You can select a cylindrical or spherical face; a dynamic handle and a dynamic edit box will be displayed in the graphics window, refer to Figure 14-66. By default, the **Radius** radio button is selected in the **Size** rollout. As a result, the radius of the selected face is displayed in the dynamic edit box as well as in the **Radius** edit box of the dialog box. If you select the **Diameter** radio button in the **Size** rollout, the diameter of the selected face will be displayed in the dynamic edit box as well as in the **Radius** edit box. After selecting the required radio button from the **Size** rollout, drag the handle to change the radial dimension of the selected face. Alternatively, you can enter the radius or the diameter values in their respective edit boxes. The preview of the resultant model will be displayed, as shown in Figure 14-67.

In this release of NX, you can apply the static relationship between the selected cylindrical or spherical faces that are selected to apply the radial dimension. The static relationship will prevent the selected faces from being changed. To define the static relationship between cylindrical or spherical faces, select the **Lock Dimension** check box from the **Settings** rollout of the **Radial Dimension** dialog box. Note that this check box will be available only in the History free mode.

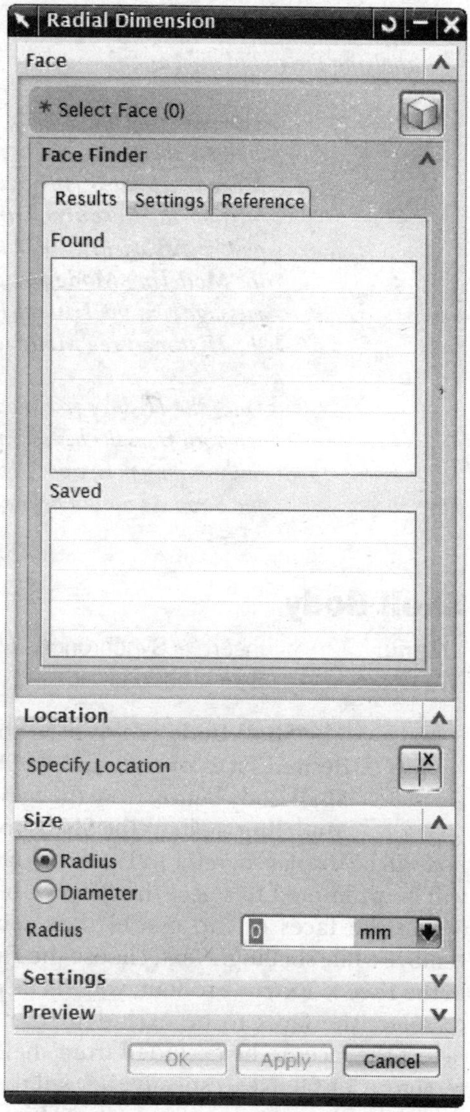

Figure 14-65 *The* ***Radial Dimension*** *dialog box*

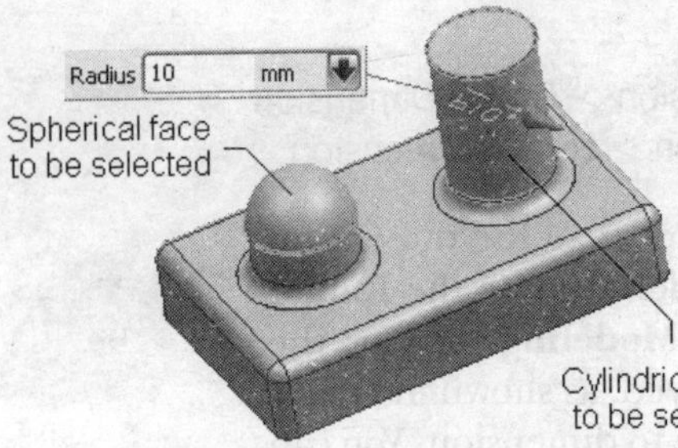

Figure 14-66 *Faces selected for applying the radial dimension*

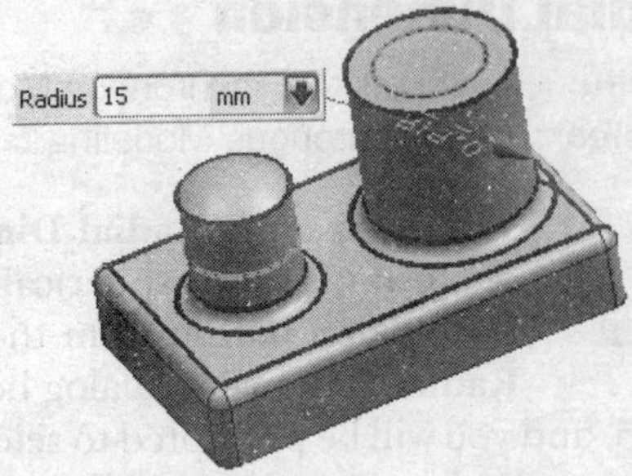

Figure 14-67 *Preview of the resultant model*

Tip. *Some of the tools of the **Synchronous Modeling** toolbar are inactive. To activate them, the History-free mode should be activated. By default, the History Mode is activated. To activate the History-free mode, click on the **Part Navigator** tab from the **Resource bar** and right-click on the **History Mode**; a shortcut menu will be displayed. Choose the **History-Free Mode** option from the shortcut menu; the **Modeling Mode** message box will be displayed. Choose the **Yes** button from the message box; the History-free mode will be activated. Alternatively, you can choose the **History-Free Mode** tool from the **Synchronous Modeling** toolbar.*

*Once the History-free mode is activated, the history of the created features will be removed from the history tree. As a result, the editing of the already created features will no longer be available. So, it is recommended that you save the model using the **Save As** option before activating the History-Free Mode.*

Shell Body

Menu:	Insert > Synchronous Modeling > Shell > Shell Body
Toolbar:	Synchronous Modeling > Shell Body

The **Shell Body** tool is used to shell the desired faces of the model. Choose the **Shell Body** button from the **Synchronous Modeling** toolbar; the **Shell Body** dialog box will be displayed, refer to Figure 14-68, and you will be prompted to select the faces to be pierced. Select the faces of the model that you want to remove while shelling. Next, choose the **Face** button in the **Face to Extrude** rollout; you will be prompted to select the faces to be excluded from shelling. Select the faces to be excluded from shelling, refer to Figure 14-69. Next, specify the wall thickness by using the dynamic handle or the **Thickness** edit box in the **Wall Thickness** rollout. Once you have

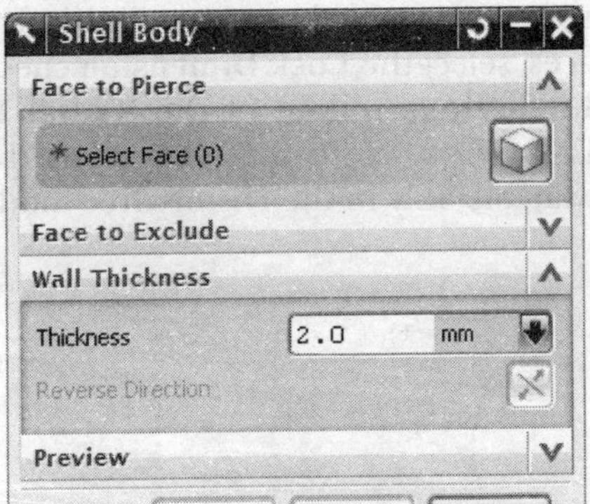

Figure 14-68 *The **Shell Body** dialog box*

made the required selections, the preview of the resultant model will be displayed, as shown in Figure 14-70.

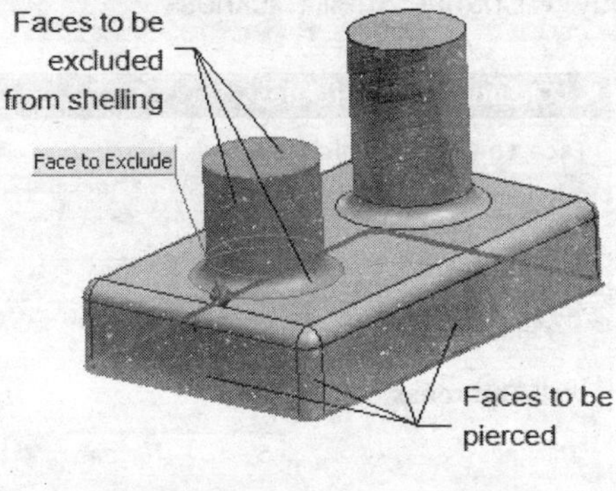

Figure 14-69 Faces selected for shelling

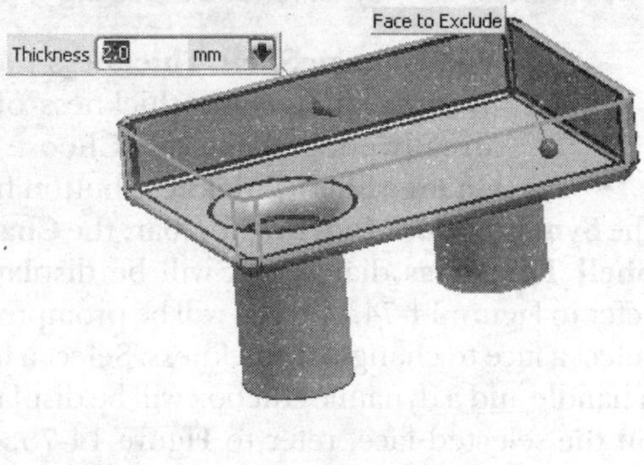

Figure 14-70 Preview of the resultant model

Shell Face

Menu:	Insert > Synchronous Modeling > Shell > Shell Face
Toolbar:	Synchronous Modeling > Shell Body > Shell Face

You can use the **Shell Face** tool to shell the required remaining faces of an already shelled model. Choose the **Shell Face** button from the **Synchronous Modeling** toolbar; the **Shell Face** dialog box will be displayed, refer to Figure 14-71, and you will be prompted to select the faces to be kept in the model. Select the faces that you want to keep. Next, choose the **Face** button in the **Face to Pierce** rollout; you will be prompted to select the faces to be pierced. Select the faces that you want to remove. Refer to Figure 14-72 for selections. You can use the dynamic handle or the **Thickness** edit box in the **Wall Thickness** rollout to define the wall thickness. Once you have made the required selections, the preview of the resultant model will be displayed, as shown in Figure 14-73.

*Figure 14-71 The **Shell Face** dialog box*

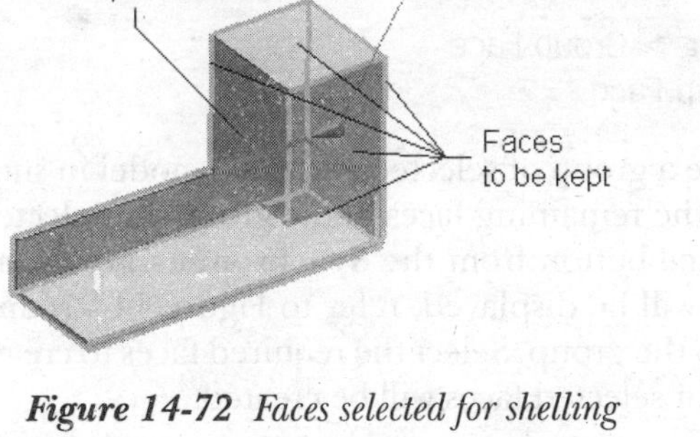

Figure 14-72 Faces selected for shelling

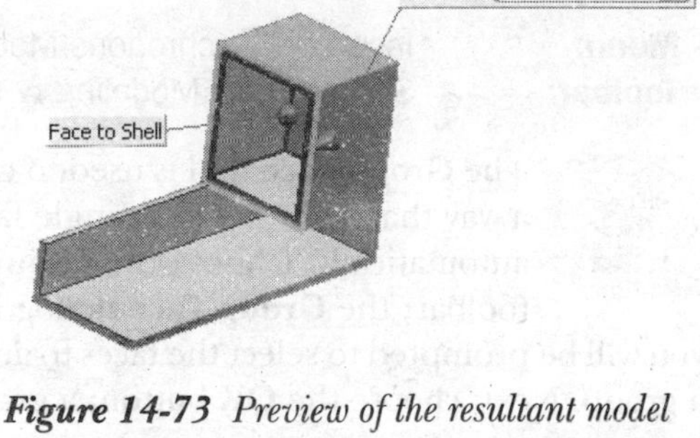

Figure 14-73 Preview of the resultant model

Change Shell Thickness

Menu:	Insert > Synchronous Modeling > Shell > Change Shell Thickness
Toolbar:	Synchronous Modeling > Shell Body > Change Shell Thickness

The **Change Shell Thickness** tool is used to change the thickness of an already shelled model. Choose the **Change Shell Thickness** button from the **Synchronous Modeling** toolbar; the **Change Shell Thickness** dialog box will be displayed, refer to Figure 14-74, and you will be prompted to select a face to change its thickness. Select a face; a handle and a dynamic edit box will be displayed on the selected face, refer to Figure 14-75. You can use the dynamic handle or the **Thickness** edit box in the **Wall Thickness** rollout of the dialog box to change the wall thickness. By default, the **Select Neighbors with Same Thickness** check box is selected in the **Face to Change Thickness** rollout so that all neighboring walls of the selected face having the same wall thickness are updated automatically, refer to Figure 14-76. If you clear this check box, only the selected face will be updated.

*Figure 14-74 The **Change Shell Thickness** dialog box*

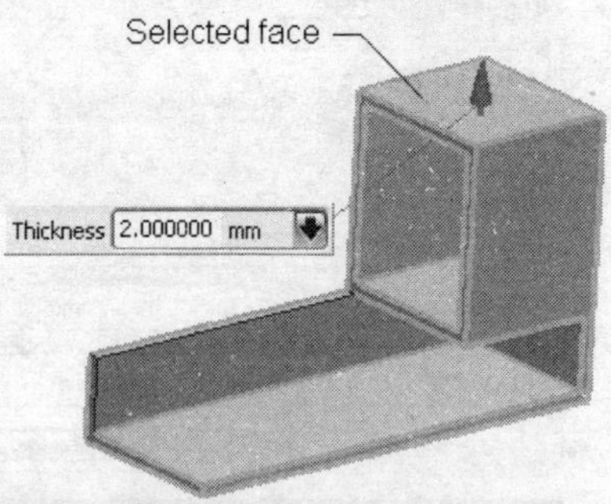

Figure 14-75 Face selected for changing its shell thickness

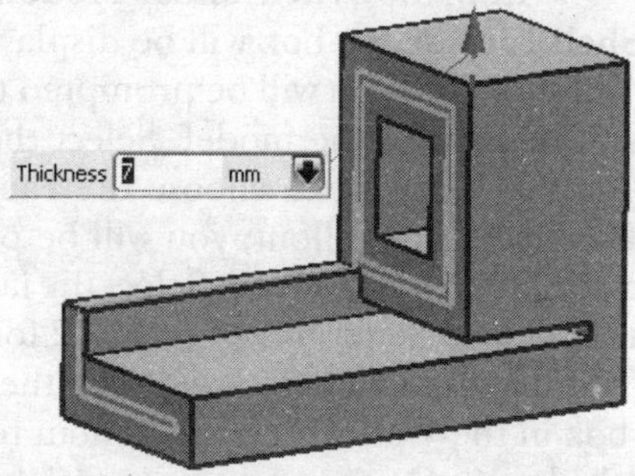

Figure 14-76 Preview of the resultant model

Group Face

Menu:	Insert > Synchronous Modeling > Group Face
Toolbar:	Synchronous Modeling > Group Face

The **Group Face** tool is used to create a group of selected faces of a model in such a way that if you select a single face, the remaining faces in the group are selected automatically. Choose the **Group Face** button from the **Synchronous Modeling** toolbar; the **Group Face** dialog box will be displayed, refer to Figure 14-77, and you will be prompted to select the faces to add to the group. Select the required faces to create a group. Next, choose the **OK** button; a group of selected faces will be created.

Cross Section

Menu:	Insert > Synchronous Modeling > Cross Section Edit
Toolbar:	Synchronous Modeling > Cross Section Edit

The **Cross Section Edit** tool is used to modify the cross-section of a model in the sketching environment. Choose the **Cross Section Edit** button from the **Synchronous Modeling** toolbar; the **SectionEdit** dialog box will be displayed, refer to Figure 14-78, and you will be prompted to select a face or a datum plane to define the sketching plane. Select any planar face or a datum plane, refer to Figure 14-79, and choose **OK**; the cross-section related to that plane will be invoked in the Sketching environment. You can change the cross-section of the model by dragging the entities or by dimensioning it. As you change the cross-section, the model will be updated accordingly, refer to Figure 14-80. After updating the sketch, exit from the Sketching environment. If you have multiple bodies, then on invoking the **Cross Section Edit** tool, the **Select Object** button will be chosen in the **Body to Section** rollout of the **SectionEdit** dialog box. Now, you can select the body to modify.

The options in the **Sketch Orientation** rollout of the **SectionEdit** dialog box are used to specify the orientation of model in the Sketching environment. To specify the orientation of the model, select the required option from the **Reference** drop-down list; you will be prompted

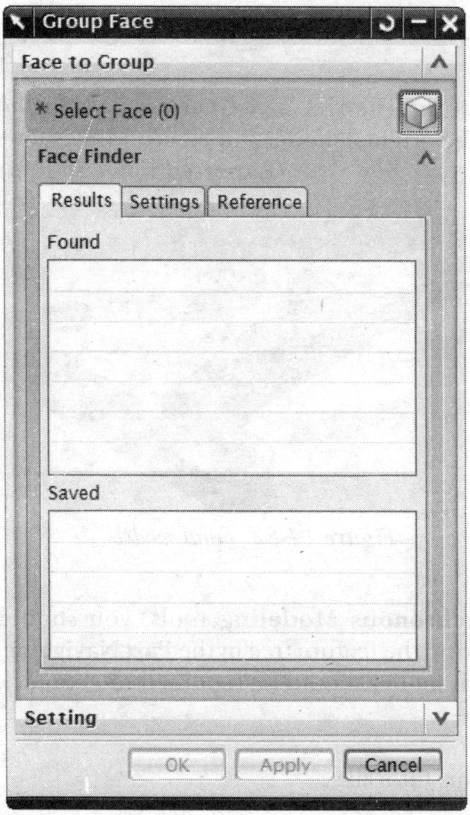

Figure 14-77 *The **Group Face** dialog box*

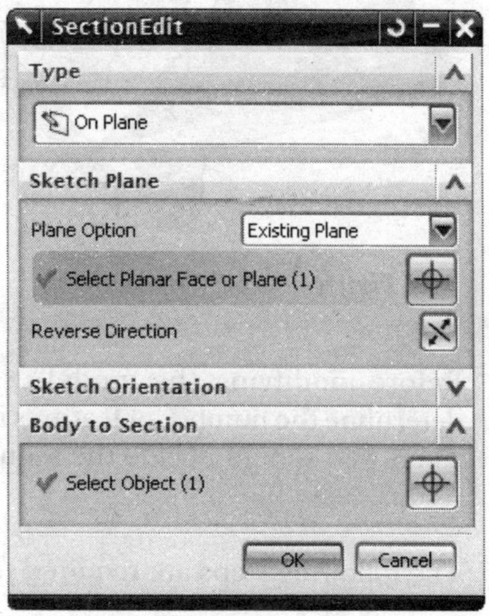

Figure 14-78 *The **SectionEdit** dialog box*

to select a reference object. Select the reference object from the graphics window and choose **OK** from the **SectionEdit** dialog box; the Sketching environment will be invoked. Next, choose the **Orient View to Sketch** button from the **Sketcher** toolbar; the selected reference object will be oriented according to the option selected from the **Reference** drop-down list. Also, the sketching plane will become parallel to the graphics window.

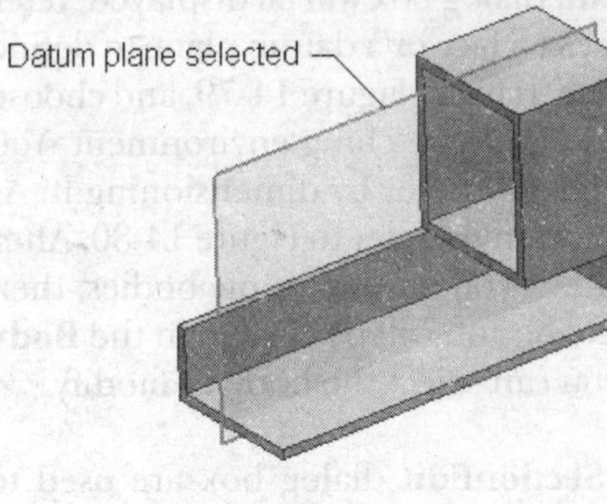

Figure 14-79 Datum plane selected

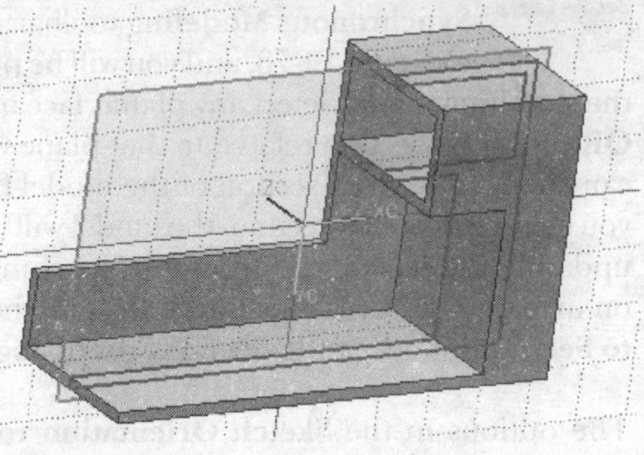

Figure 14-80 Preview of the resultant model

TUTORIALS

Tutorial 1

In this tutorial, you will modify the model created in Tutorial 3 of Chapter 5 using the **Synchronous Modeling** tools. Figure 14-81 shows the original model and Figure 14-82 shows the model after modification. **(Expected time: 30 min)**

Figure 14-81 Original model

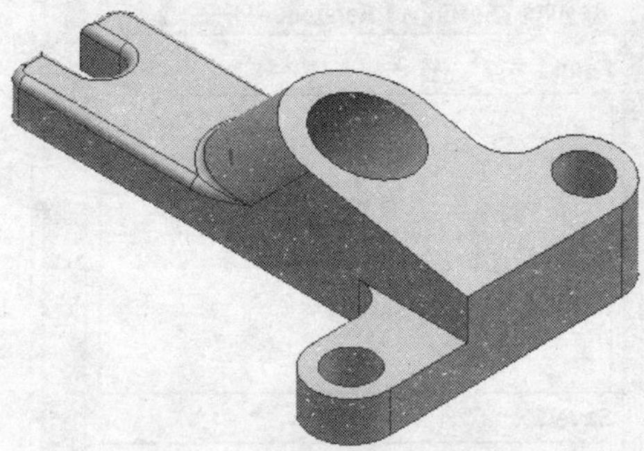

Figure 14-82 Final model

Before modifying the model using the **Synchronous Modeling** tools, you should determine the number of features in it by observing the feature tree in the **Part Navigator**. Then, you should decide the sequence in which model should be modified to get quick results.

The following steps are required to complete this tutorial:

a. Copy the file from Tutorial 3 of Chapter 5 then paste it at the location */NX 7/c14* and rename it as *c14tut1*.

b. Modify the angle between the inclined face and the vertical face using the **Move Face** or **Angular dimension** tool.
c. Increase the thickness of the base feature using the **Move Face** or **Pull Face** tool.
d. Increase the length of the base feature using the **Move Face** tool.
e. Align the inclined hole using the **Replace face** tool.
f. Decrease the thickness of the base feature using the **Move Face** tool.
g. Align the horizontal face to the inclined face using the **Replace face** tool.
h. Change the radius of the fillet using the **Resize Blend** tool.
i. Change the diameter of the vertical hole using the **Resize Face** or **Radial dimension** tool.
j. Change the diameter of the inclined hole using the **Resize Face** or **Radial dimension** tool.
k. Modify the distance between two vertical holes using the **Move Face** tool.
l. Apply fillets to the base plate, as shown in Figure 14-82, using the **Edge Blend** tool.

Copying the File

1. Copy the part file created in Tutorial 3 of Chapter 5 and paste it at the location */NX 7/c14* and then rename it as *c14tut1*.

2. Open the *c14tut1* file.

Modifying the Angle

1. Choose the **Move Face** button from the **Synchronous Modeling** toolbar; the **Move Face** dialog box is displayed and you are prompted to select the face to move.

2. Select the inclined face; an angular handle, a dynamic edit box, and a triad of vectors are displayed.

3. Select the **Angle** option from the **Motion** drop-down list of the **Transform** rollout; the **Inferred Vector** button is activated. Select the common edge between the angular face and the vertical face; an angular handle, a triad of vectors, and an arrow are displayed. Reverse the direction of the arrow, if required, refer to Figure 14-83. Click on the angular handle; the dynamic edit box is displayed.

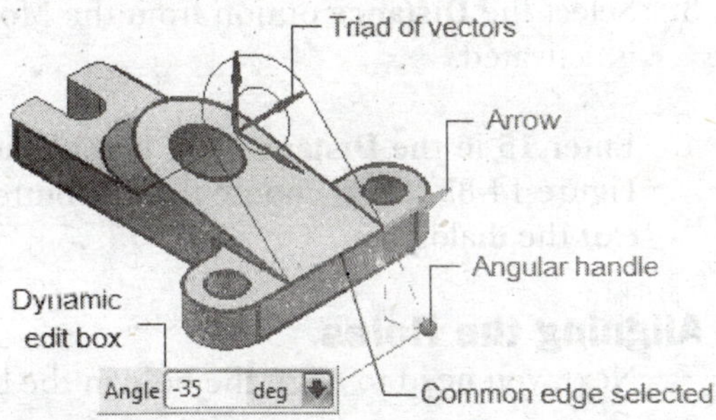

Figure 14-83 Common edge selected to move the inclined face

4. Enter **-35** in the dynamic edit box and press ENTER, refer to Figure 14-83. Next, choose **OK** from the **Move Face** dialog box.

Modifying the Thickness of the Base Plate

1. Choose the **Pull Face** button from the **Synchronous Modeling** toolbar; the **Pull Face** dialog box is displayed.

2. Select the **Point to Point** option from the **Motion** drop-down list of the **Transform** rollout; the **Specify From Point** area is highlighted in the **Transform** rollout. Note that if the **Point to Point** option is selected by default in the **Motion** drop-down list, then you need to click on the **Specify From Point** area of the **Transform** rollout to activate it. Select a point from the upper face of the base plate, refer to Figure 14-84; the **Specify To Point** area of the **Transform** rollout is activated. Select a point from the lower face of the base plate, refer to Figure 14-84; the **Face** button is activated in the **Face** rollout. Select the lower face of the base plate; the dynamic preview will be displayed, refer to Figure 14-84.

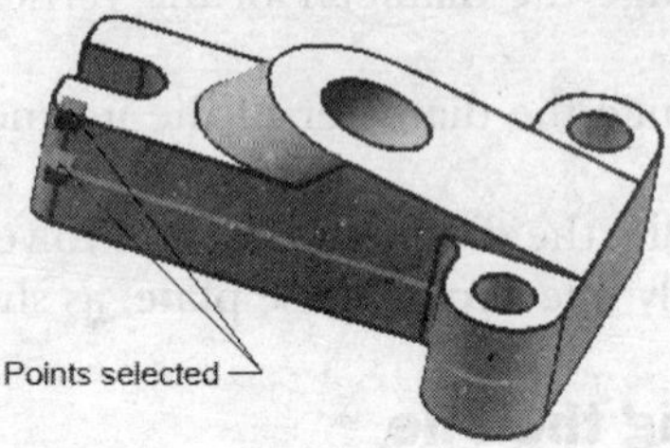

Figure 14-84 Entities selected to modify the thickness of the base feature

3. Choose the **OK** button from the dialog box to apply the changes and exit the dialog box.

Modifying the Length of the Base Plate

1. Choose the **Move Face** button from the **Synchronous Modeling** toolbar; the **Move Face** dialog box is displayed.

2. Select three faces of the base plate, refer to Figure 14-85.

3. Select the **Distance** option from the **Motion** drop-down list; the **Inferred Vector** button is activated.

4. Enter **15** in the **Distance** edit box of the **Transform** rollout and press ENTER, refer to Figure 14-85. Next, choose the **OK** button from the dialog box to apply the changes and exit the dialog box.

Aligning the Holes

Next, you need to align the hole in the base feature with the hole in the inclined face.

1. Choose the **Replace Face** button from the **Synchronous Modeling** toolbar; the **Replace Face** dialog box is displayed and you are prompted to select the faces to remove.

2. Select the hole from the base plate, refer to Figure 14-86.

3. Choose the **Face** button from the **Replacement Face** rollout and select the face of the inclined hole, refer to Figure 14-86. Next, choose the **OK** button from the dialog box.

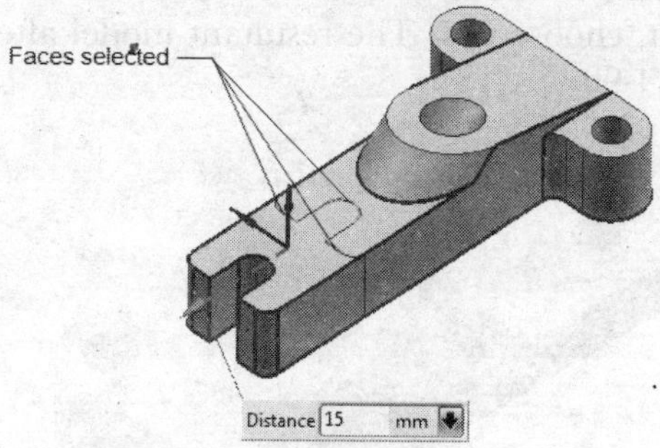

Figure 14-85 *Entities selected to modify the length of the base feature*

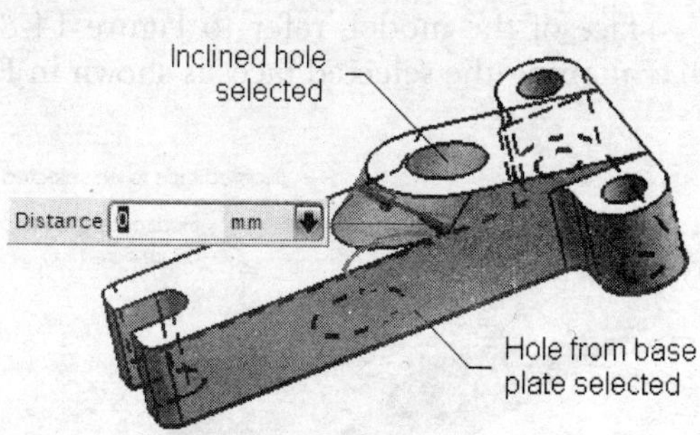

Figure 14-86 *Entities selected to modify the inclined hole*

Decreasing the Unwanted Thickness of the Base Plate

1. Choose the **Move Face** button from the **Synchronous Modeling** toolbar; the **Move Face** dialog box is displayed.

2. Select the two faces of the base plate, refer to Figure 14-87, and then choose the **Reverse Direction** button from the **Transform** rollout.

3. Enter **5** in the **Distance** edit box of the **Transform** rollout and choose the **OK** button from the dialog box to apply the changes. Next, exit the dialog box. The resultant model is shown in Figure 14-88.

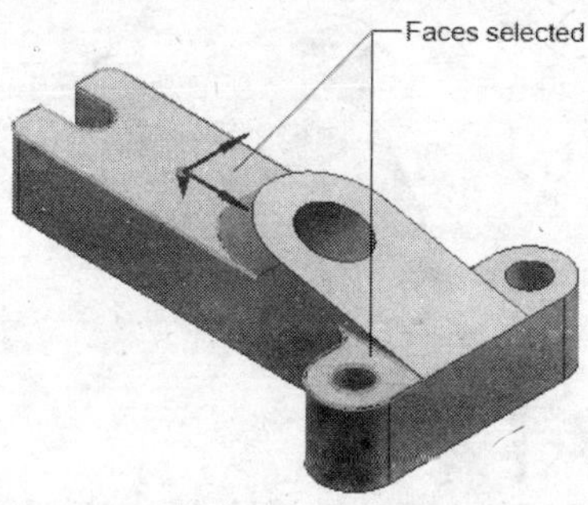

Figure 14-87 *Entities selected to modify the thickness of the base plate*

Figure 14-88 *The resultant model*

Aligning the Horizontal Face with the Inclined Face

1. Choose the **Replace Face** button from the **Synchronous Modeling** toolbar; the **Replace Face** dialog box is displayed.

2. Select the horizontal face of the base plate, refer to Figure 14-89.

3. Choose the **Face** button from the **Replacement Face** rollout, and then select the inclined face of the model, refer to Figure 14-89. Next, choose **OK**. The resultant model after aligning the selected faces is shown in Figure 14-90.

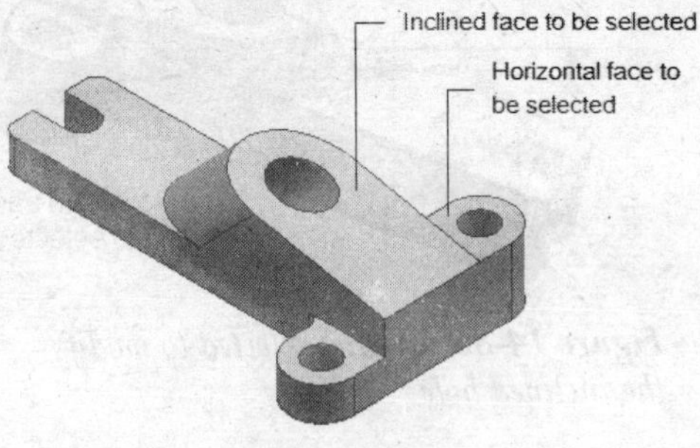

Figure 14-89 *Faces to be selected*

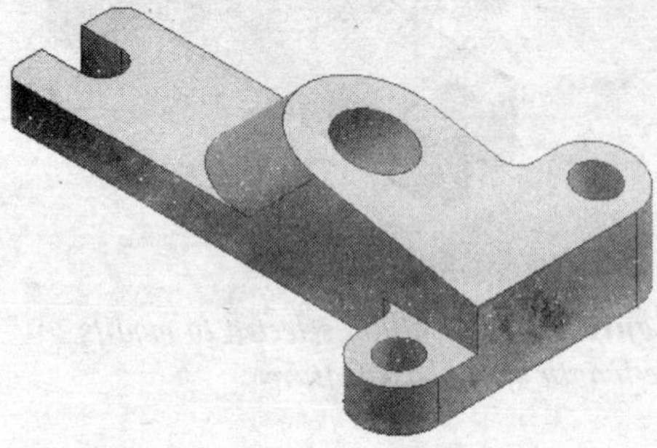

Figure 14-90 *The resultant model*

Changing the Radius of the Fillet

1. Choose the **Resize Blend** button from the **Synchronous Modeling** toolbar; the **Resize Blend** dialog box is displayed.
2. Select two blends of the base plate, refer to Figure 14-91.
3. Enter **4** in the **Radius** edit box of the **Radius** rollout and choose **OK**. Figure 14-92 shows the rotated view of the resultant model.

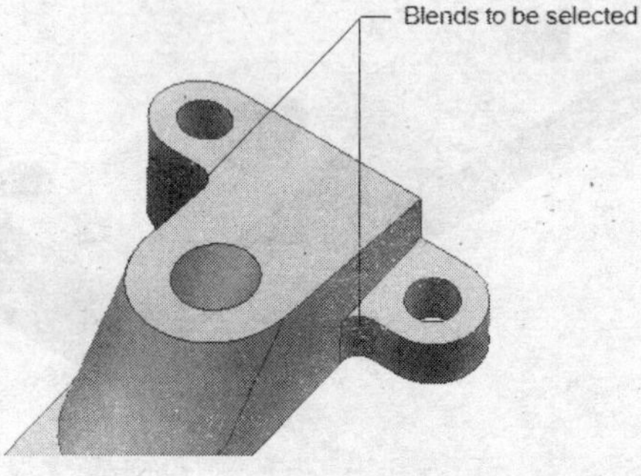

Figure 14-91 *Blends to be selected*

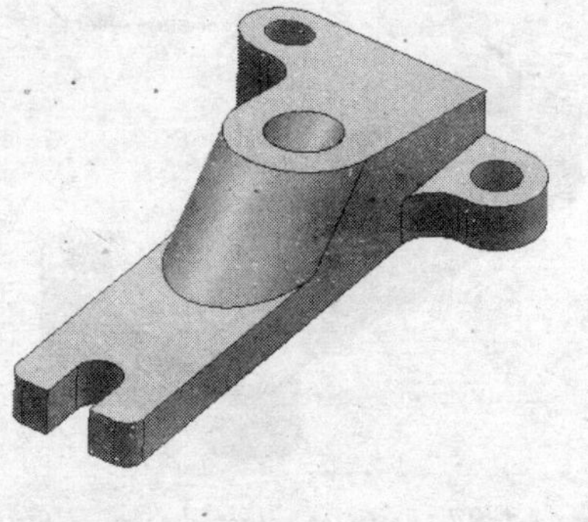

Figure 14-92 *The resultant model*

Changing the Diameter of the Vertical Holes

1. Choose the **Resize Face** button from the **Synchronous Modeling** toolbar; the **Resize Face** dialog box is displayed.
2. Select the vertical holes created on the base feature.
3. Enter **6** in the **Diameter** edit box of the **Size** rollout and choose **OK**; the diameter of the holes is updated.

Changing the Diameter of the Inclined Hole

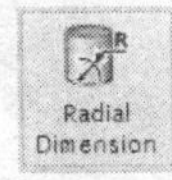

1. Choose the **Radial Dimension** button from the **Synchronous Modeling** toolbar; the **Radial Dimension** dialog box is displayed.

2. Select the inclined hole and then select the **Diameter** radio button from the **Size** rollout.

3. Enter **10** in the **Diameter** edit box of the **Size** rollout and choose **OK**; the diameter of the inclined hole is updated.

Modifying the Distance Between Two Vertical Holes

1. Choose the **Move Face** button from the **Synchronous Modeling** toolbar; the **Move Face** dialog box is displayed.

2. Select the circular face of the hole and the concentric semi-circular face of the base plate, refer to Figure 14-93.

3. Select the **Distance** option from the **Motion** drop-down list of the **Transform** rollout; you are prompted to select the object to infer vector.

4. Select the Y-axis of the triad of vector from the graphics window and then reverse the direction of handle by choosing the **Reverse Direction** button from the **Transform** rollout of the dialog box.

5. Enter **5** in the **Distance** edit box of the **Transform** rollout and choose **OK**. Figure 14-94 shows the model after modifying the distance.

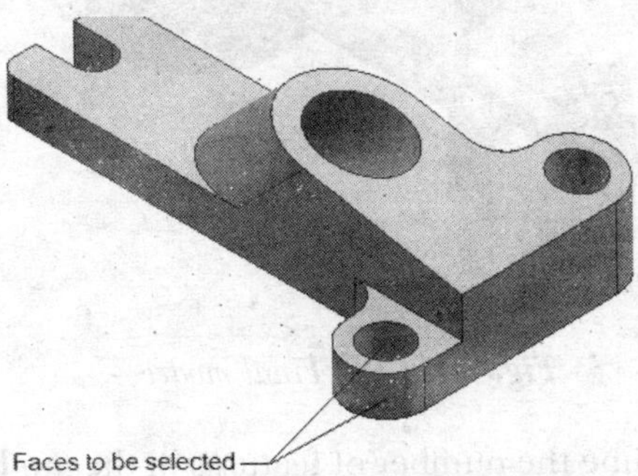

Figure 14-93 *Faces to be selected*

Figure 14-94 *The resultant model*

Applying Fillets to the Base Plate

1. Choose the **Edge Blend** button from the **Feature Operation** toolbar; the **Edge Blend** dialog box is displayed.

2. Select the edges of the base plate, refer to Figure 14-95.

3. Enter **1** in the **Radius 1** edit box of the **Edge to Blend** rollout and choose **OK**; the final model is displayed, as shown in Figure 14-96.

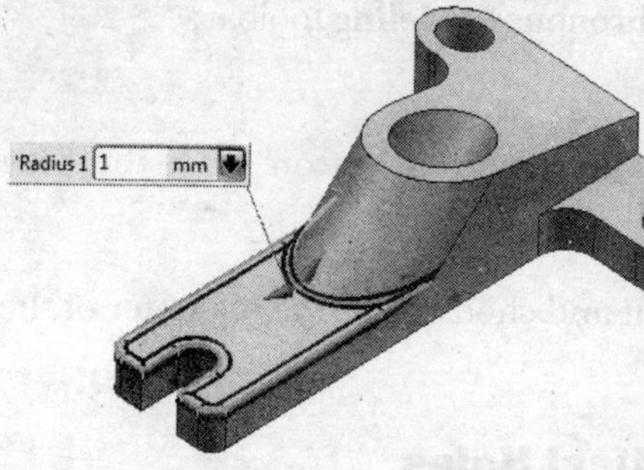

Figure 14-95 *Edges selected to apply fillet*

Figure 14-96 *The final model*

Saving and Closing the File

1. Choose **File > Close > Save and Close** from the menu bar to save and close the file.

Tutorial 2

In this tutorial, you will modify the model created in Exercise 3 of Chapter 6 using the **Synchronous Modeling** tools. Figure 14-97 shows the original model and Figure 14-98 shows the model after modification. **(Expected time: 30 min)**

Figure 14-97 *Original model*

Figure 14-98 *Final model*

Before modifying the model, you should determine the number of features in the model by observing the feature tree in the **Part Navigator** and then decide the sequence in which the model should be modified. This will help you in modifying the model quickly.

The following steps are required to complete this tutorial:

a. Copy the file from Exercise 3 of Chapter 6. Then, paste it at the location */NX 7/c14* and rename it as *c14tut2*.
b. Align the outer faces of the double flange using the **Offset Region** tool.
c. Increase the length of the circular rod using the **Move Face** tool.
d. Increase the length of the cylinder using the **Linear Dimension** tool.

e. Align the face of the single flange using the **Angular Dimension** tool.
f. Align the opposite face of the single flange using the **Make Symmetric** tool.
g. Decrease the internal diameter of the cylinder using the **Radial Dimension** tool.
h. Add two more holes to the cylinder using the **Copy Face** and then the **Paste Face** tool.
i. Add six more holes to the cylinder using the **Pattern face** tool.
j. Activate the **History-Free** Mode.
k. Edit the cross-section of the circular rod using the **Cross Section Edit** tool.
l. Shell the component using the **Shell Body** tool.
m. Modify the thickness of the cylinder using the **Change Shell Thickness** tool.

Copying the File

1. Copy the part file created in Exercise 3 of Chapter 6. Paste it at the location */NX 7/c14* and then rename it as *c14tut2*.

2. Open the *c14tut2* file.

Aligning the Outer Faces of the Double Flange

1. Choose the **Offset Region** button from the **Synchronous Modeling** toolbar; the **Offset Region** dialog box is displayed.

2. Select the outer faces of the double flange, refer to Figure 14-99 and enter **5** in the **Distance** edit box of the **Offset** rollout.

3. Choose the **OK** button from the dialog box to accept the changes. The resultant model is shown in Figure 14-100.

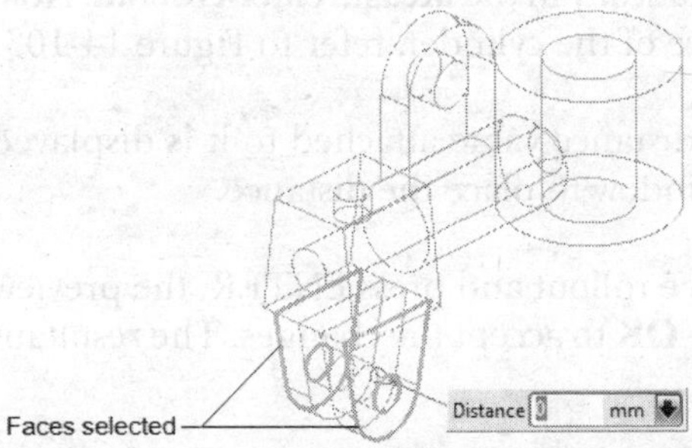

Figure 14-99 *Faces selected*

Figure 14-100 *Resultant model*

Increasing the Length of the Circular Rod

1. Choose the **Move Face** button from the **Synchronous Modeling** toolbar; the **Move Face** dialog box is displayed.

2. Select the outer face and the inner face of the cylinder, refer to Figure 14-101.

3. Select the **Distance** option from the **Motion** drop-down list in the **Transform** rollout; you are prompted to select the objects to infer vector. Note that if the **Distance** option is selected by default in the **Motion** drop-down list then you need to click on the **Specify Vector** area in the **Transform** rollout to activate it.

4. Select the Y-axis of the triad of vector from the graphics window. Next, enter **30** in the **Distance** edit box of the **Transform** rollout and choose the **OK** button from the dialog box. The resultant model is shown in Figure 14-102.

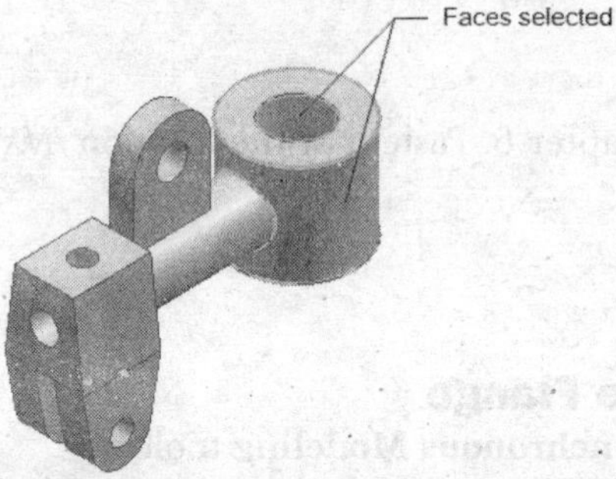

Figure 14-101 Faces selected

Figure 14-102 Resultant model

Increasing the Length of the Cylinder

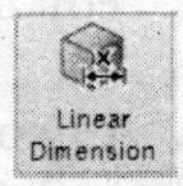

1. Choose the **Linear Dimension** button from the **Synchronous Modeling** toolbar; the **Linear Dimension** dialog box is displayed with the **Origin Object** button chosen by default in the **Origin** rollout.

2. Select the outer edge of the upper horizontal face of the cylinder, refer to Figure 14-103; the **Measurement Object** button is chosen automatically in the **Measurement** rollout. Now, select the outer edge of the lower horizontal face of the cylinder, refer to Figure 14-103.

3. Once the edges are selected, a cursor with the distance value attached to it is displayed in the graphics window. Click in the graphics window to place the distance.

4. Enter **60** in the **Distance** edit box of the **Distance** rollout and press ENTER; the preview of the resultant model is displayed. Next, choose **OK** to accept the changes. The resultant model is shown in Figure 14-104.

Aligning a Face of the Single Flange

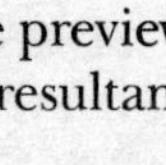

1. Choose **Linear Dimension > Angular Dimension** from the **Synchronous Modeling** toolbar; the **Angular Dimension** dialog box is displayed with the **Origin Object** button chosen by default in the **Origin** rollout.

2. Select a face of the block as the origin, refer to Figure 14-105; the **Measurement Object** button is chosen automatically in the **Measurement** rollout. Now, select a face of the single flange as the measurement object, refer to Figure 14-105; a cursor with the angle value attached to it is displayed in the graphics window.

3. Clear the **Alternate Angle** check box from the **Angle** rollout of the dialog box, if it is selected.

4. Move the cursor at the bottom of the double flange and place the angular dimension by clicking the left mouse button.

5. Enter **3** in the **Angle** edit box of the **Angle** rollout and press ENTER; the preview of the resultant model is displayed. Next, choose **OK** to accept the changes. The resultant model is shown in Figure 14-106.

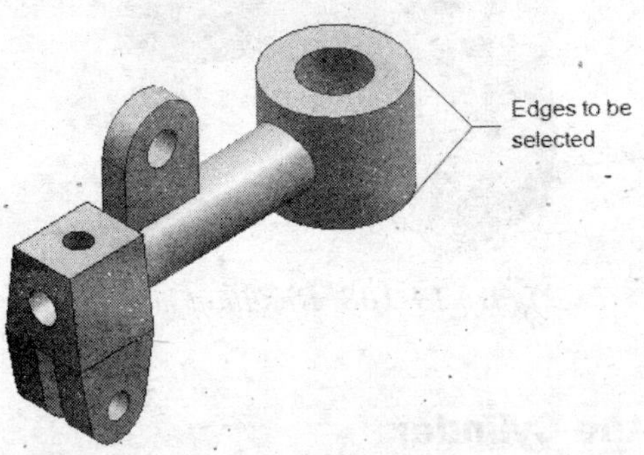

Figure 14-103 *Edges to be selected*

Figure 14-104 *Resultant model*

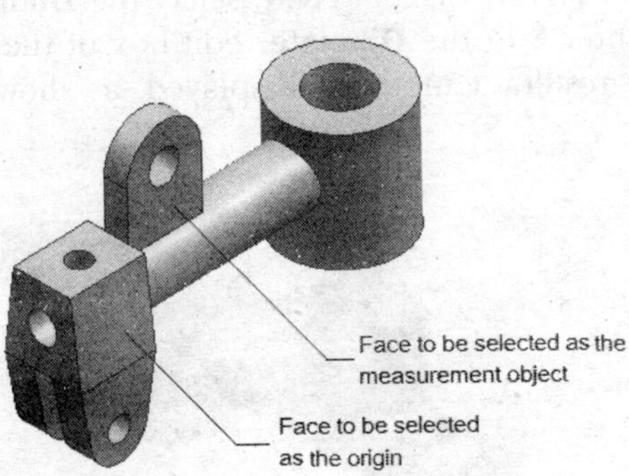

Figure 14-105 *Faces to be selected*

Figure 14-106 *Resultant model*

Aligning the Opposite Faces of the Single Flange

1. Choose **Make Coplanar > Make Symmetric** from the **Synchronous Modeling** toolbar; the **Make Symmetric** dialog box is displayed with the **Face** button chosen in the **Motion Face** rollout.

2. Select the opposite faces of the single flange as the motion face, refer to Figure 14-107. The **Plane** button is chosen automatically in the **Symmetry Plane** rollout. Select the middle plane of the component, refer to Figure 14-107; the **Face** button is chosen automatically

in the **Stationary Face** rollout. Select another face of the single flange as the stationary face, refer to Figure 14-107; the preview of the resultant model is displayed.

3. Choose the **OK** button to accept the changes. The resultant model is displayed, as shown in Figure 14-108.

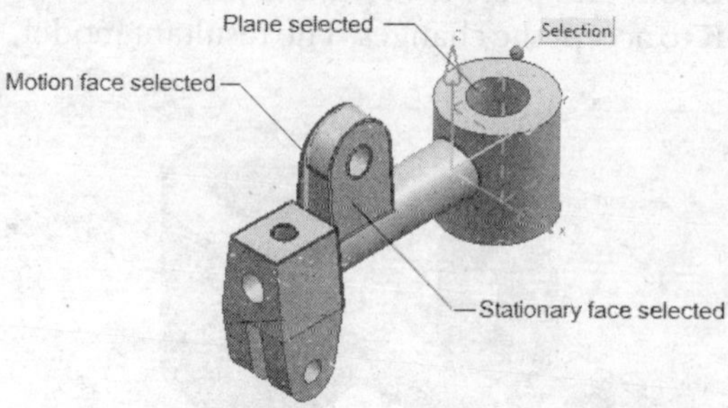

Figure 14-107 Entities selected to align the opposite face of the single flange

Figure 14-108 Resultant model

Decreasing the Internal Diameter of the Cylinder

1. Choose **Linear Dimension >Radial Dimension** from the **Synchronous Modeling** toolbar; the **Radial Dimension** dialog box is displayed.

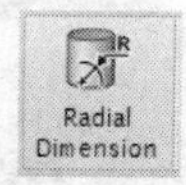

2. Select the inner face of the cylinder, refer to Figure 14-109. Next, select the **Diameter** radio button in the **Size** rollout and then enter **8** in the **Diameter** edit box of the **Size** rollout. Next, choose the **OK** button. The resultant model is displayed, as shown in Figure 14-110.

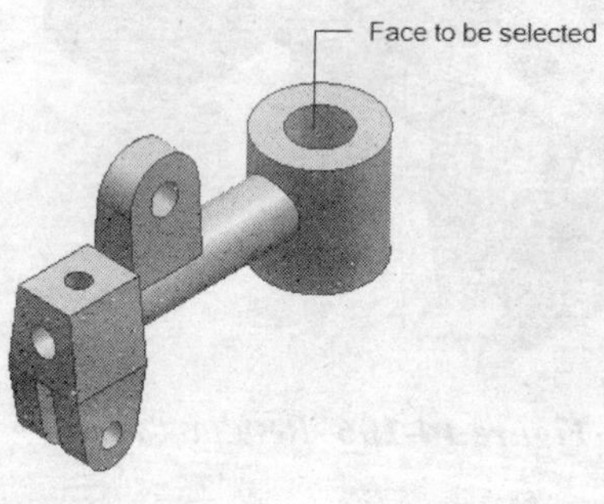

Figure 14-109 Inner Face to be selected

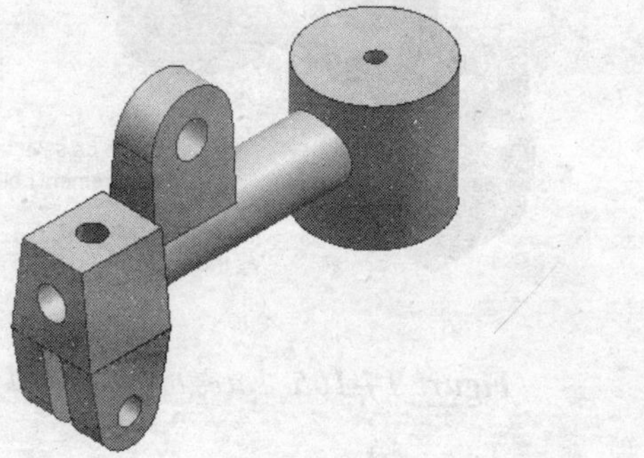

Figure 14-110 Resultant model

Adding Two More Holes to the Cylinder

1. Choose the **Copy Face** button from the **Synchronous Modeling** toolbar; the **Copy Face** dialog box is displayed.

2. Select the inner face of the cylinder, refer to Figure 14-111. The distance vector and pivot point are selected by default. Enter **15** in the **Distance** edit box of the **Transform** rollout and then press ENTER; the model is updated and the preview of the hole is displayed in the graphics window.

3. Choose the **Apply** button to accept the changes.

4. Select the inner face of the cylinder once again to create another hole, refer to Figure 14-111. Next, choose the **Reverse Direction** button to create the hole in the opposite direction of an already created hole. Enter **15** in the **Distance** edit box in the **Transform** rollout. Choose **OK** to copy the hole.

   You will observe that the material is still inside the circular hole because only the circular surfaces are copied by this tool. To remove the material from inside the circular face, you need to use the **Paste Face** tool. To do so, follow the steps given next.

5. Choose **Copy Face > Paste Face** from the **Synchronous Modeling** toolbar; the **Paste Face** dialog box is displayed with the **Target Body** button chosen by default in the **Target** rollout.

6. Select the model as the target body; the **Tool Body** button is chosen automatically in the **Tool** rollout. Select the faces created by using the **Copy Face** tool on the cylinder as the tool bodies; the preview of the resultant model is displayed.

7. Choose the **OK** button to accept the changes. The resultant model after creating the two holes on the cylinder is shown in Figure 14-112.

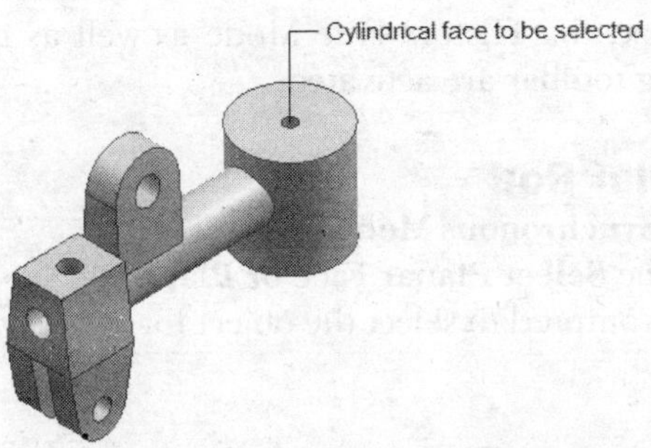

Figure 14-111 Cylindrical face to be selected

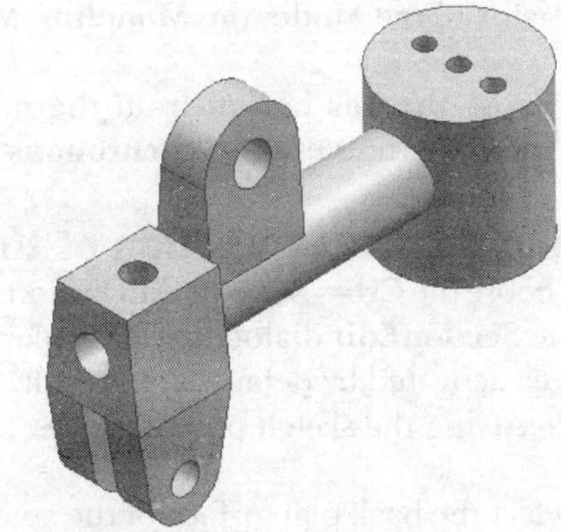

Figure 14-112 Model after adding holes

Adding Six More Holes to the Cylinder

1. Choose **Copy Face >Pattern Face** from the **Synchronous Modeling** toolbar; the **Pattern Face** dialog box is displayed.

2. Select the **Circular Pattern** option from the **Type** drop-down list; the **Face** button from the **Face** rollout is activated. Select the two outer holes created previously.

3. Click on the **Specify Vector** area in the **Axis** rollout; a triad of vector is displayed. Select the vertical axis from the triad; the **Specify Point** area is highlighted in the **Axis** rollout and you are prompted to select object to infer point.

4. Select the center point of the center hole.

5. Enter **45** in the **Angle** edit box and **4** in the **Circular Count** edit box in the **Pattern Properties** rollout. Press ENTER; the preview of the resultant model is displayed in the graphics window. Next, choose **OK** to accept the changes. The resultant model is shown in Figure 14-113.

***Figure 14-113** The resultant model*

For further modifications of the model using the **Synchronous Modeling** tools, you need to activate the History-free mode. Once you activate the History-free mode, the feature history will be removed. So it is recommended that you save the model with the name *c14tut2_history free mode* using the **Save As** option.

Activating the History-Free Mode

1. Click on the **Part Navigator** tab from the **Resource Bar**; the **Part Navigator** is displayed.

2. Right-click on the **History Mode** option; a shortcut menu is displayed. Select the **History-Free Mode**; the **Modeling Mode** message box is displayed.

3. Choose the **Yes** button from the message box; the History-Free Mode as well as the remaining tools of the **Synchronous Modeling** toolbar are activated.

Editing the Cross-section of the Circular Rod

1. Choose the **Cross Section Edit** button from the **Synchronous Modeling** toolbar; the **SectionEdit** dialog box is displayed with the **Select Planar Face or Plane** area activated by default. As a result, you are prompted to select the object for specifying the sketch plane.

2. Select the back planar face of the single flange, refer to Figure 14-114. Next, choose **OK**; the cross section of the circular rod is displayed in the Sketching environment, refer to Figure 14-115.

3. Choose **Inferred Dimensions > Diameter** from the **Sketch Tools** toolbar and select the inner circle of the cylindrical rod; a cursor with the internal diameter value attached to it is displayed in the graphics window. Next, click the left mouse button to place the diameter; the **Dimension** edit box is displayed.

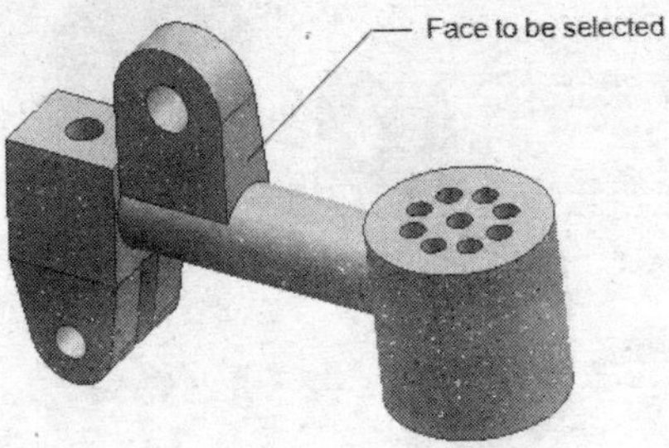

Figure 14-114 Face to be selected

Figure 14-115 Cross-section of the circular rod

4. Enter **10** in the **Dimension** edit box and press ENTER; the preview of the resultant model is displayed.

5. Choose the **Finish Sketch** button from the **Sketcher** toolbar to accept the changes. The resultant model after changing the internal diameter of the rod is shown in Figure 14-116.

Figure 14-116 The resultant model after changing the internal diameter of the rod

Shelling the Component

1. Choose the **Shell Body** button from the **Synchronous Modeling** toolbar; the **Shell Body** dialog box is displayed with the **Face** button activated in the **Face to Pierce** rollout.

2. Select the upper face of the cylinder, planar faces of the single flange, double flange, and block, refer to Figure 14-117.

3. Enter **1.5** in the **Thickness** edit box and press ENTER; the preview of the resultant model is displayed. Next, choose the **OK** button to accept the changes. The resultant model after shelling the component is shown in Figure 14-118.

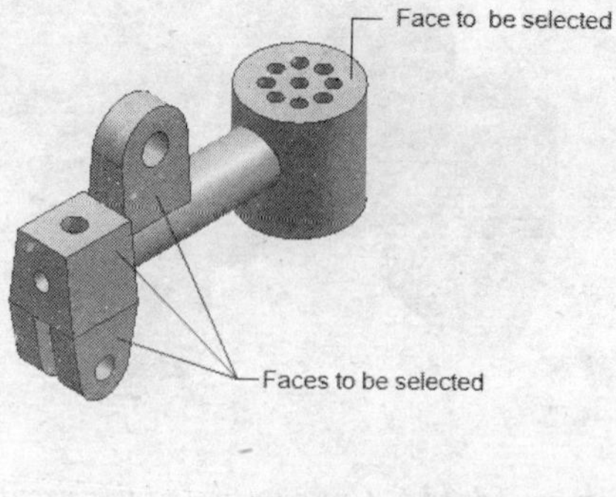

Figure 14-117 Faces to be selected

Figure 14-118 Model after shelling

Modifying the Thickness of the Cylinder

1. Choose **Shell Body > Change Shell Thickness** from the **Synchronous Modeling** toolbar; the **Change Shell Thickness** dialog box is displayed with the **Face** button chosen in the **Face to Change Thickness** rollout.

2. Clear the **Select Neighbors with Same Thickness** check box in the **Face to Change Thickness** rollout, and select the outer face of the cylinder.

3. Enter **5** in the **Thickness** edit box in the **Wall Thickness** rollout and press ENTER; the preview of the resultant model is displayed.

4. Choose the **OK** button from the dialog box to accept the changes; the final model is displayed, as shown in Figure 14-119.

Figure 14-119 The final model

Saving and Closing the File

1. Choose **File > Close > Save and Close** from the menu bar to save and close the file.

Self-Evaluation Test

Answer the following questions and then compare them to those given at the end of this chapter:

1. You can create new designs using the **Synchronous Modeling** tools. (T/F)
2. You can reorient a selected face using the **Move Face** tool. (T/F)
3. The **Transform** rollout in the **Move Face** dialog box cannot be used for moving a face. (T/F)
4. The **Pull Face** tool is used to pull the selected face regardless of the adjacent geometry. (T/F)
5. Using the **Offset Region** tool, you can offset a set of selected faces in the direction __________ to the selected faces.
6. Using the **Resize Blend** tool, you can change the __________ of existing blends.
7. Using the **Resize Face** tool, you can resize the selected __________ faces.
8. You can use the **Delete Face** tool to__________ the unwanted faces by projecting the adjacent faces.
9. You can move the selected face in the angular direction by modifying its value using the __________ tool.
10. The __________tool is used to copy the selected faces and place them in the same body or in a different body.

Review Questions

Answer the following questions:

1. The __________ tool is used to make two different faces of a component coplanar.
2. Which of the following tools is used to make two different cylindrical faces of a component coaxial?

   (a) **Make Coplanar** (b) **Make Tangent**
   (c) **Make Coaxial** (d) **Make Symmetric**

3. Which of the following tools is used to make one face of a component symmetric to another face.

   (a) **Make Symmetric** (b) **Make Coaxial**
   (c) **Make Tangent** (d) None of these

4. In which of the following environments can you modify the cross-section of the model using the **Cross Section** tool?

   (a) Sketching (b) Modeling
   (c) Assembly (d) Drafting

5. Which of the following modes should be invoked to activate the **Shell Body**, **Shell Face**, **Change Shell Thickness** and **Cross Section** tools?

   (a) **History** (b) **History-Free**
   (c) **Free** (d) **Free-History**

6. Which of the following tools is used to move a set of faces in angular direction by adding and then changing the dimension?

   (a) **Linear Dimension** (b) **Move Face**
   (c) **Cross Section Edit** (d) **Angular Dimension**

7. You can change the diameter of a spherical face of the model using the **Radial Dimension** tool. (T/F)

8. By clearing the **Select Neighbors With Same Thickness** check box in the **Change Shell Thickness** dialog box, you can select individual faces. (T/F)

9. The **Change Shell Thickness** tool is used to change the thickness of faces individually. (T/F)

10. The **Results** tab displays the list of all possible geometrical conditions for a selected face. (T/F)

Exercises

Exercise 1

In this exercise, you will modify the model created in Exercise 1 of Chapter 5 using the **Synchronous Modeling** tools. Figure 14-120 shows the original model and Figure 14-121 shows the model after modification. **(Expected time: 15 min)**

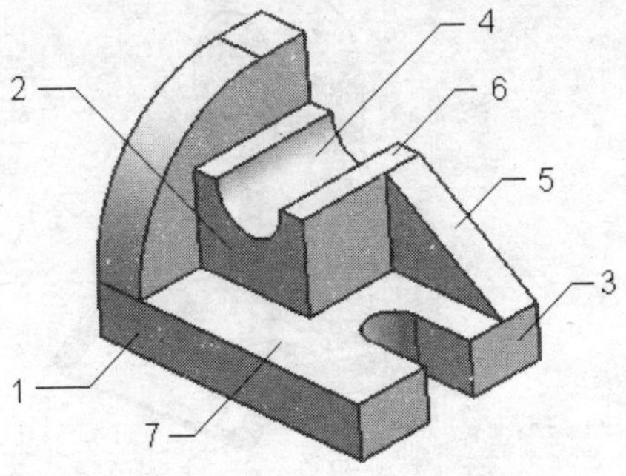

Figure 14-120 Model for Exercise 1

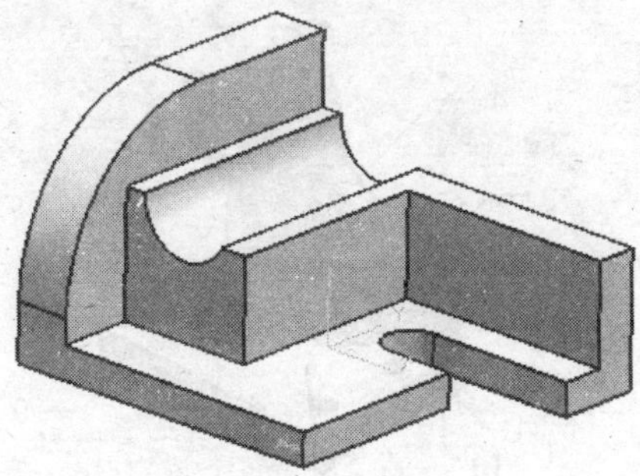

Figure 14-121 Final model

Hints

1. Increase the length of faces 1 and 2 by a distance of 30mm.
2. Pull face 3 by a distance of 25mm.
3. Increase the diameter of face 4 to 28mm.
4. Replace face 5 with face 3.
5. Offset face 6 and 7 by a distance of -7mm.

Exercise 2

In this exercise, you will modify the model created in Tutorial 1 of Chapter 6 using the **Synchronous Modeling** tools. Figure 14-122 shows the original model and Figure 14-123 shows the model after modification. **(Expected time: 30 min)**

Hint

1. Increase the length of faces 1 and 2 by a distance of 20mm.
2. Replace face 3 with face 4.
3. Increase the diameter of face 5 by 20mm.
4. Increase the diameter of face 6 with 50mm.
5. Add 4 more holes by an offset of 25mm.
6. Change the angle of face 2 to 45 degree.
7. Activate the **History-Free** Mode.
8. Shell the component by piercing faces 7, 8, 9, and 10. (4 mm Shell thickness)
9. Increase the shell thickness of face 11.

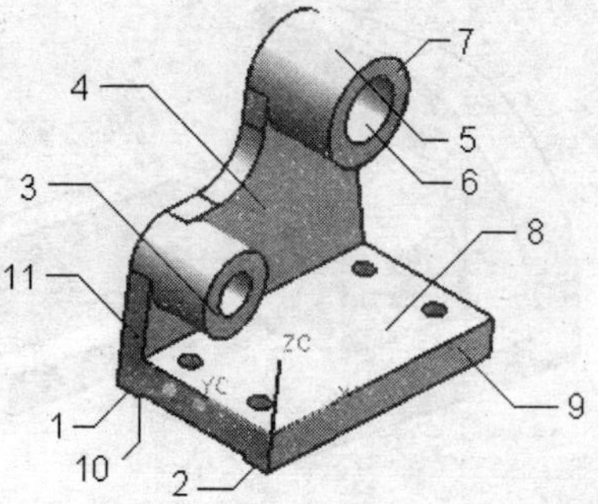

Figure 14-122 Model for Exercise 2

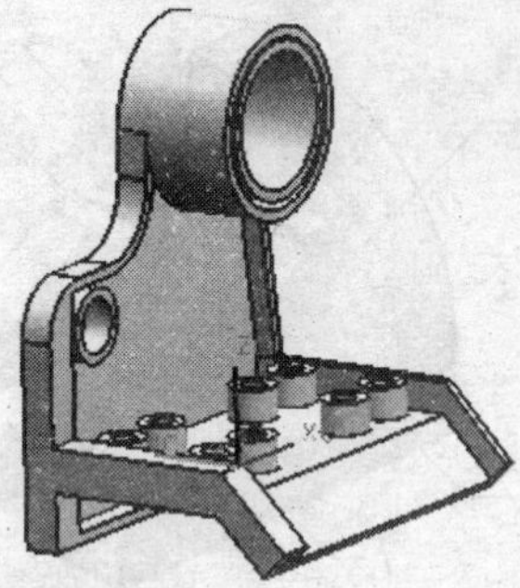

Figure 14-123 Final model

Answers to Self-Evaluation Test

1. F, **2.** T, **3.** F, **4.** T, **5.** normal, **6.** radius, **7.** cylindrical, **8.** Delete, **9. Angular Dimension**, **10. Copy Face**

Index

Symbols

A

B

C

D

M

N

O

P